36
30
30
35
7
35
30
27

Christian 1785

Century 21 SOUTH-WESTERN Accounting 9E
General Journal

NEW! Financial Literacy for the 21st Century Included!

Claudia Bienias Gilbertson, CPA, Ph.D
North Hennepin Community College
Brooklyn Park, Minnesota

Mark W. Lehman, CPA, Ph.D
Richard C. Adkerson School of Accountancy
Mississippi State University
Starkville, Mississippi

SOUTH-WESTERN CENGAGE Learning

Australia • Brazil • Japan • Korea • Mexico • Singapore • Spain • United Kingdom • United States

General Journal, Century 21 Accounting, 9E
Claudia Bienias Gilbertson, Mark W. Lehman

VP/Editorial Director: Jack W. Calhoun

VP/Editor-in-Chief: Karen Schmohe

VP Marketing: Cheryl Costantini

Sr. Acquisitions Editor: Michael Schenk

Developmental Editor: Lisa Loftus

Marketing Manager: Robin LeFevre

Marketing Coordinator: Julia Tucker

Marketing Communications Manager:
   Libby Shipp

Production Manager: Patricia Matthews Boies

Project Manager: Kim Kusnerak

Consulting Editor: Bill Lee

Special Consultants: Sara Wilson, Robert E. First

Manager of Technology, Editorial: Liz Wilkes

Technology Project Editor: Lysa Kosins

Website Project Manager: Ed Stubenrauch

Manufacturing Buyer: Kevin Kluck

Production House/Compositor:
   PreMedia Global

Content Project Manager: Joseph Malcolm

Sr. Art Director: Tippy McIntosh

Internal Designer: Nick & Diane Gliebe,
   Design Matters

Cover Designer: Nick & Diane Gliebe,
   Design Matters

Cover Images: Getty Images, Inc.

Photo Researcher: Darren Wright

© 2012, 2009, 2006 South-Western, Cengage Learning

ALL RIGHTS RESERVED. No part of this work covered by the copyright herein may be reproduced, transmitted, stored or used in any form or by any means graphic, electronic, or mechanical, including but not limited to photocopying, recording, scanning, digitizing, taping, Web distribution, information networks, or information storage and retrieval systems, except as permitted under Section 107 or 108 of the 1976 United States Copyright Act, without the prior written permission of the publisher.

> For product information and technology assistance, contact us at
> **Cengage Learning Customer & Sales Support, 1-800-354-9706**
> For permission to use material from this text or product,
> submit all requests online at **www.cengage.com/permissions**
> Further permissions questions can be emailed to
> **permissionrequest@cengage.com**

Exam*View*® is a registered trademark of eInstruction Corp. Windows is a registered trademark of the Microsoft Corporation used herein under license. Macintosh and Power Macintosh are registered trademarks of Apple Computer, Inc. used herein under license.

© 2008 Cengage Learning. All Rights Reserved.

ISBN-13: 978-1-111-98862-3

ISBN-10: 1-111-98862-5

South-Western
5191 Natorp Boulevard
Mason, OH 45040
USA

Cengage Learning products are represented in Canada by Nelson Education, Ltd.

For your course and learning solutions, visit **www.cengage.com/school**

Visit our company website at **www.cengage.com**

Printed in the United States of America
1 2 3 4 5 6 7 15 14 13 12 11

Century 21 SOUTH-WESTERN Accounting 9E

NEW! Financial Literacy for the 21st Century Included!

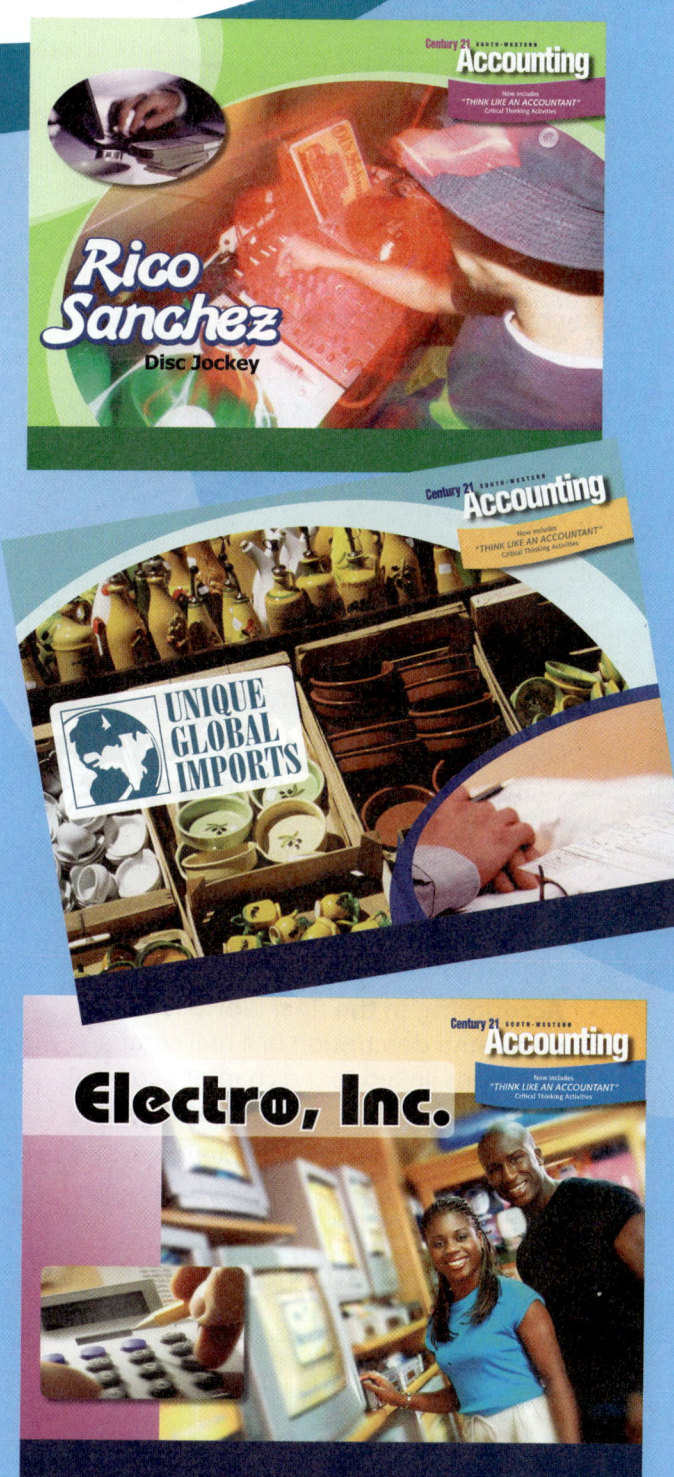

Give students real-life experience with Century 21 Accounting simulations and working papers!

SIMULATION 1: RICO SANCHEZ, DJ —
a service business organized as a proprietorship may be completed after Chapter 8

manual simulation: 0-538-44768-0
automated simulation: 0-538-44736-2

SIMULATION 2: UNIQUE GLOBAL IMPORTS —
a merchandising business organized as a corporation may be completed after Chapter 16

manual simulation: 0-538-44739-7
automated simulation: 0-538-44740-0

SIMULATION 3: ELECTRO, INC. —
a merchandising business organized as a corporation may be completed after Chapter 22

manual simulation: 0-538-44743-5
automated simulation: 0-538-44763-X

GENERAL JOURNAL WORKING PAPERS —

Student Edition Working Papers
Ch. 1–16: 0-538-44765-6

Teacher's Edition Working Papers
Ch. 1–16: 0-538-44772-9

Student Edition Working Papers
Ch. 17–24: 0-538-44766-4

Teacher's Edition Working Papers
Ch. 17–24: 0-538-44762-1

Join us on the Internet at www.C21accounting.com

How to Use This Book

PART OPENERS focus on a particular business that you'll learn about:

- **A listing of the chapters** covered in each Part helps you focus on what you'll be learning.
- **"The Business"** introduces you to the business you'll be studying throughout the Part.
- The **Chart of Accounts** used in the entire Part is provided for easy reference as you work through the chapters.

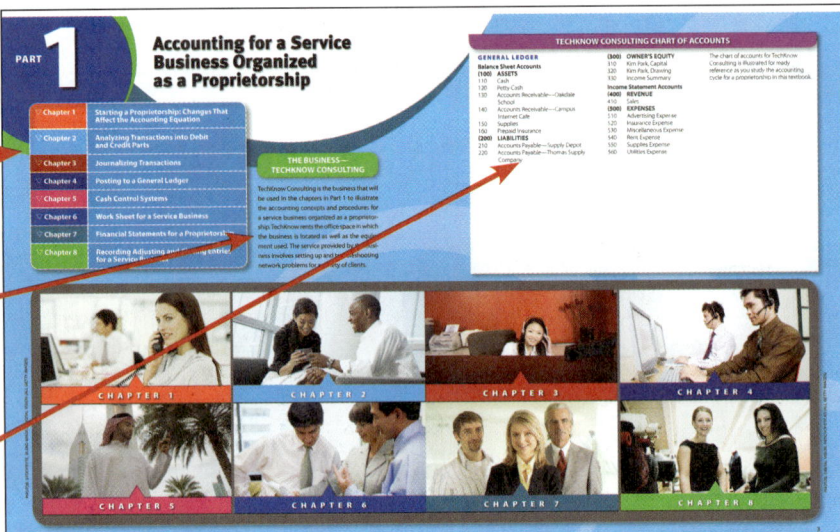

CHAPTER OPENERS introduce the subject matter you'll investigate:

- **Objectives** listed at the beginning of each chapter highlight lesson concepts and preview what you will learn.
- The **Key Terms** list displays all the key words introduced in the chapter. You can also find these terms and their definitions in the Glossary at the back of the text.
- **Accounting in the Real World** features a photo and description of a real company with questions linked to the chapter's content.
- **Internet Research Activity** sends you to the Internet to locate information to answer questions related to the chapter's subject matter.

LESSON OPENERS focus on one or two topics.

- Most **Illustrations** are placed above the text that discusses them. You can quickly find the illustrations when you're reviewing or working problems.
- **Steps and callouts** make it easy to understand and apply the procedures you learn. Clear instructions are directly linked to the part of the illustration where the work is recorded.

END-OF-LESSON REVIEW PAGES help you fully understand all concepts and procedures before moving on to the next lesson:

- **Terms Review** lists all the new words learned in the lesson.
- **Audit Your Understanding** asks two or more questions about the lesson material. You can check your answers in the Appendix.
- **Work Together** gives you guided practice through hands-on application of the lesson's procedures and concepts.
- **On Your Own** challenges you to complete problems by yourself.

v

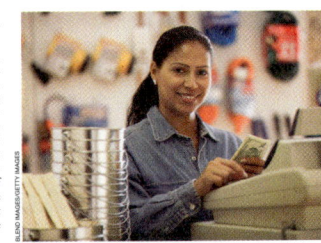

SPECIAL FEATURES provide information about real-life issues:

- **Careers in Accounting** introduces you to actual people working in accounting or in positions where accounting knowledge is useful. This feature includes entry-level job requirements, career tracks, and projected trends for the future.

- **Character Counts** helps you understand complicated issues in the business world, such as confidentiality and integrity.

- **Business Structures** provides information on characteristics of proprietorships, corporations, and partnerships.

SPECIAL FEATURES introduce key concepts in realistic settings:

- **Global Perspective** will expose you to some of the ways in which accounting and business differ in other countries.
- **Financial Literacy** teaches you about managing your personal finances.
- **Cultural Diversity** explains how different cultures have contributed to the field of accounting.

END-OF-CHAPTER PAGES give you opportunities to check your knowledge of the chapter content:

- **Chapter Summary** restates the chapter objectives for your reference.
- **Explore Accounting** includes opportunities for higher-level learning.

- Exercises contain at least one **Application Problem** for each lesson, plus one **Mastery Problem** and one **Challenge Problem** to test your understanding of the entire chapter. Many of these problems can also be worked using accounting software: **Automated Accounting, Peachtree®, QuickBooks®,** and **Microsoft® Excel!**

- Enrichment materials help you take a step further into understanding accounting. **Applied Communication** offers exercises for strengthening your communication skills—a must for future employment! **Cases for Critical Thinking** asks you to consider questions based on accounting scenarios. **SCANS Workplace Competency** helps you learn about skills you'll need in the business world.

- **Using Source Documents, Graphing Workshop,** and **Auditing for Errors** provide you with specific situations in which you can analyze and investigate accounting tools. **Analyzing Best Buy's Financial Statements** allows you to examine a real business's annual report and financial documents and put your knowledge to work.

Go Beyond the Book
For more information go to www.C21accounting.com

www.C21accounting.com offers a variety of resources and activities for you to explore. As you use this textbook, watch for the web site icons that will lead you to your online accounting connection!

TECHNOLOGY APPLICATIONS extend and enrich your learning:

- Instructions for completing Century 21 Accounting problems using **Peachtree, QuickBooks,** and **Microsoft Excel** are provided in each chapter.

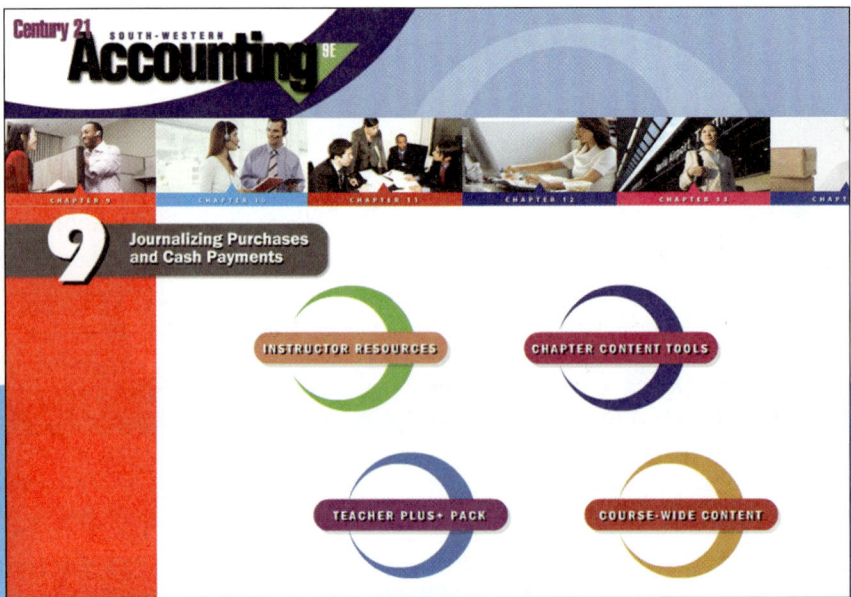

- Online learning is available at **www.C21accounting.com**. This dynamic web site extends your learning experience with interactive review, study tools, and engaging activities.

CONTENTS

PART 1
Accounting for a Service Business Organized as a Proprietorship

CHAPTER 1
Starting a Proprietorship: Changes That Affect the Accounting Equation 4

Accounting in the Real World: *Gold's Gym* 5
1-1 The Accounting Equation 6
1-2 How Business Activities Change the Accounting Equation 10
1-3 How Transactions Change Owner's Equity in an Accounting Equation 14
End of Chapter Problems 19

CHAPTER 2
Analyzing Transactions into Debit and Credit Parts 26

Accounting in the Real World: American Automobile Association (AAA) 27
2-1 Using T Accounts 28
2-2 Analyzing How Transactions Affect Accounts 32
2-3 Analyzing How Transactions Affect Owner's Equity Accounts 38
End of Chapter Problems 46

CHAPTER 3
Recording Transactions in a General Journal 54

Accounting in the Real World: *Travelocity* 55
3-1 Journals, Source Documents, and Recording Entries in a Journal 56
3-2 Journalizing Buying Insurance, Buying on Account, and Paying on Account 63
3-3 Journalizing Transactions That Affect Owner's Equity and Receiving Cash on Account 68
3-4 Starting a New Journal Page 74
End of Chapter Problems 79

CHAPTER 4
Posting from a General Journal to a General Ledger 88

Accounting in the Real World: *AMAZON.COM* 89

4-1 Preparing a Chart of Accounts 90
4-2 Posting from a General Journal to a General Ledger 96
4-3 Completed General Ledger, Proving Cash, and Making Correcting Entries 102
End of Chapter Problems 110

CHAPTER 5
Cash Control Systems 116

Accounting in the Real World: *Hard Rock Cafe* 117
5-1 Checking Accounts 118
5-2 Bank Reconciliation 124
5-3 Dishonored Checks and Electronic Banking 129
5-4 Petty Cash 134
End of Chapter Problems 140

REINFORCEMENT ACTIVITY 1—PART A
An Accounting Cycle for a Proprietorship: Journalizing and Posting Transactions 147

CHAPTER 6
Work Sheet for a Service Business 150

Accounting in the Real World: *The AICPA* 151
6-1 Creating a Work Sheet 152
6-2 Planning Adjusting Entries on a Work Sheet 157
6-3 Extending Financial Statement Information on a Work Sheet 162
6-4 Finding and Correcting Errors on the Work Sheet 167
End of Chapter Problems 172

CHAPTER 7
Financial Statements for a Proprietorship 178

Accounting in the Real World:
American Eagle Outfitters 179
7-1 Preparing an Income Statement 180
7-2 Balance Sheet Information on a Work Sheet 187
End of Chapter Problems 194

CHAPTER 8
Recording Adjusting and Closing Entries for a Service Business 200

Accounting in the Real World: *The Walt Disney Company* 201
8-1 Recording Adjusting Entries 202
8-2 Recording Closing Entries 206
8-3 Preparing a Post-Closing Trial Balance 213
End of Chapter Problems 221

REINFORCEMENT ACTIVITY 1—PART B
An Accounting Cycle for a Proprietorship: End-of-Fiscal-Period Work 228

PART 2
Accounting for a Merchandising Business Organized as a Corporation

CHAPTER 9
Journalizing Purchases and Cash Payments 232

Accounting in the Real World: *OfficeMax* 233
9-1 Journalizing Purchases Using a Purchases Journal 234
9-2 Journalizing Cash Payments Using a Cash Payments Journal 242
9-3 Performing Additional Cash Payments Journal Operations 248
9-4 Journalizing Other Transactions Using a General Journal 254
End of Chapter Problems 260

CHAPTER 10
Journalizing Sales and Cash Receipts Using Special Journals 268

Accounting in the Real World: *Best Buy* 269
10-1 Journalizing Sales on Account Using a Sales Journal 270
10-2 Journalizing Cash Receipts Using a Cash Receipts Journal 276
10-3 Recording Transactions Using a General Journal 285
End of Chapter Problems 289

CHAPTER 11
Posting to General and Subsidiary Ledgers 296

Accounting in the Real World: *palmONE, INC.* 297
11-1 Posting to an Accounts Payable Ledger 298
11-2 Posting to an Accounts Receivable Ledger ... 307
11-3 Posting from Journals to a General Ledger ... 315
11-4 Posting Special Journal Totals to a General Ledger 320
11-5 Correcting Errors in Subsidiary Ledger Accounts 327
End of Chapter Problems 331

CHAPTER 12
Preparing Payroll Records 338

Accounting in the Real World: *The Green Bay Packers* 339
12-1 Preparing Payroll Time Cards 340
12-2 Determining Payroll Tax Withholding 345
12-3 Preparing Payroll Records 351
12-4 Preparing Payroll Checks 356
End of Chapter Problems 360

CHAPTER 13
Payroll Accounting, Taxes, and Reports 366

Accounting in the Real World: *Intel* 367
13-1 Recording a Payroll 368
13-2 Recording Employer Payroll Taxes 373
13-3 Reporting Withholding and Payroll Taxes ... 378
13-4 Paying Withholding and Payroll Taxes 383
End of Chapter Problems 391

REINFORCEMENT ACTIVITY 2—PART A
An Accounting Cycle for a Corporation: Journalizing and Posting Transactions 398

CHAPTER 14
Distributing Dividends and Preparing a Work Sheet for a Merchandising Business 402

Accounting in the Real World: *Lowe's* 403
14-1 Distributing Corporate Earnings to Stockholders 404

14-2 Beginning an 8-Column Work Sheet for a Merchandising Business 409	15-4 Preparing a Balance Sheet 464
14-3 Planning and Recording a Merchandise Inventory Adjustment 415	End of Chapter Problems................................... 473

CHAPTER 16
Recording Adjusting and Closing Entries for a Corporation 478

14-4 Planning and Recording an Allowance for Uncollectible Accounts Adjustment 419	Accounting in the Real World: *Apple* 479
14-5 Planning and Recording Depreciation Adjustments... 423	16-1 Recording Adjusting Entries........................ 480
14-6 Calculating Federal Income Tax and Completing a Work Sheet 427	16-2 Recording Closing Entries for Income Statement Accounts................................ 487
End of Chapter Problems................................... 438	16-3 Preparing a Post-Closing Trial Balance 494
	End of Chapter Problems................................... 500

CHAPTER 15
Financial Statements for a Corporation 444

REINFORCEMENT ACTIVITY 2—PART B
An Accounting Cycle for a Corporation: End-of-Fiscal Period Work... 508

Accounting in the Real World: *Gap, Inc.*............. 445
15-1 Preparing an Income Statement................. 446
15-2 Analyzing an Income Statement 455
15-3 Preparing a Statement of Stockholders' Equity...... 461

PART 3
Accounting for a Merchandising Business Organized as a Corporation—Adjustments and Valuation

CHAPTER 17
Accounting for Uncollectible Accounts Receivable 512

CHAPTER 19
Accounting for Inventory.. 562

Accounting in the Real World: *Performance Food Group* 513	Accounting in the Real World: *Fender Guitars* 563
17-1 Uncollectible Accounts 514	19-1 Determining the Quantity of Merchandise Inventory.. 564
17-2 Writing Off and Collecting Uncollectible Accounts Receivable 519	19-2 Determining the Cost of Merchandise Inventory.. 569
End of Chapter Problems................................... 526	19-3 Estimating Inventory................................... 574
	End of Chapter Problems................................... 578

CHAPTER 18
Accounting for Plant Assets and Depreciation 532

CHAPTER 20
Accounting for Notes and Interest 586

Accounting in the Real World: *Carnival Cruise Lines*......... 533	Accounting in the Real World: *Bank of America*................ 587
18-1 Buying Plant Assets and Paying Property Tax 534	20-1 Promissory Notes 588
18-2 Calculating Depreciation Expense 538	20-2 Notes Payable 593
18-3 Journalizing Depreciation Expense 542	20-3 Notes Receivable 598
18-4 Disposing of Plant Assets 546	End of Chapter Problems................................... 604
18-5 Declining-Balance Method of Depreciation........... 551	
End of Chapter Problems................................... 556	

REINFORCEMENT ACTIVITY 3—PART A
An Accounting Cycle for a Corporation:
Journalizing and Posting Transactions.................... 610

CHAPTER 21
Accounting for Accrued Revenue and Expenses..... 614

Accounting in the Real World: *USA Today* 615
21-1 Accrued Revenue 616
21-2 Accrued Expenses 622
End of Chapter Problems 629

CHAPTER 22
End-of-Fiscal-Period Work for a Corporation 634

Accounting in the Real World: *Chico's* 635

22-1 Preparing a Work Sheet for a Corporation 636
22-2 Preparing an Income Statement 645
22-3 Preparing a Statement of Stockholders' Equity and Balance Sheet 649
22-4 Adjusting, Closing, and Reversing Entries for a Corporation 654
End of Chapter Problems 662

REINFORCEMENT ACTIVITY 3—PART B
An Accounting Cycle for a Corporation: End-of-Fiscal-Period Work 668

PART 4
Additional Accounting Procedures

CHAPTER 23
Accounting for Partnerships 672

Accounting in the Real World: *Cold Stone Creamery®* 673
23-1 Forming a Partnership 674
23-2 Distribution of Net Income and Owners' Equity Statements 680
23-3 Dissolving a Partnership 686
End of Chapter Problems 692

CHAPTER 24
Recording International and Internet Sales 700

Accounting in the Real World: *Honeywell* 701
24-1 Recording International Sales 702
24-2 Recording Internet Sales 710
End of Chapter Problems 714

APPENDIX A: STATEMENT OF CASH FLOWS A-1

APPENDIX B: BEST BUY'S FISCAL 2007 ANNUAL REPORT (SELECTED PAGES) B-1

APPENDIX C: USING A CALCULATOR AND COMPUTER KEYPAD C-1

APPENDIX D: RECYCLING PROBLEMS D-1

APPENDIX E: ANSWERS TO AUDIT YOUR UNDERSTANDING E-1

APPENDIX F: FINANCIAL LITERACY FOR THE 21st CENTURY F-1

GLOSSARY G-1

INDEX I-1

ADDITIONAL FEATURES IN THIS BOOK

FEATURES IN EVERY CHAPTER

ACCOUNTING IN THE REAL WORLD
5, 27, 55, 89, 117, 151, 179, 201, 233, 269, 297, 339, 367, 403, 445, 479, 513, 533, 563, 587, 615, 635, 673, 701

ACCOUNTING SOFTWARE
25, 52, 86, 114, 145, 176, 198, 226, 266, 294, 336, 364, 396, 442, 476, 506, 530, 560, 584, 608, 632, 666, 698, 717

BUSINESS STRUCTURES
7, 234, 271, 345, 470, 515, 553, 626, 688

CAREERS IN ACCOUNTING
43, 66, 137, 191, 218, 388, 431, 447, 601

CULTURAL DIVERSITY
75, 99, 323, 540, 596, 681

EXPLORE ACCOUNTING
18, 45, 78, 109, 139, 171, 193, 220, 259, 288, 330, 359, 390, 437, 472, 499, 525, 555, 577, 603, 628, 661, 691, 713

GLOBAL PERSPECTIVE
160, 251, 305, 646, 705

INTERNET ACTIVITY
5, 27, 55, 89, 117, 151, 179, 201, 233, 269, 297, 339, 367, 403, 445, 479, 513, 533, 563, 587, 615, 636, 674, 702

CHARACTER COUNTS
8, 28, 56, 90, 118, 153, 181, 203, 235, 270, 298, 340, 368, 404, 446, 481, 514, 534, 564, 588, 616, 636, 674, 702

SMALL BUSINESS SPOTLIGHT
74, 127, 318, 409, 490, 564

FINANCIAL LITERACY
30, 135, 281, 313, 369, 420, 575

LESSON REVIEW AND PRACTICE

TERMS REVIEW
9, 13, 17, 31, 37, 62, 95, 101, 108, 123, 128, 133, 138, 155, 161, 166, 186, 205, 212, 219, 241, 247, 253, 258, 275, 284, 287, 306, 314, 344, 350, 355, 377, 389, 408, 418, 422, 426, 454, 460, 463, 471, 524, 537, 545, 550, 554, 568, 573, 576, 592, 597, 602, 621, 627, 653, 679, 685, 690, 709

AUDIT YOUR UNDERSTANDING
9, 13, 17, 31, 37, 44, 62, 67, 73, 77, 95, 101, 108, 123, 128, 133, 138, 155, 161, 166, 170, 186, 192, 205, 212, 219, 241, 247, 253, 258, 275, 284, 287, 306, 314, 319, 326, 329, 344, 350, 355, 358, 372, 377, 382, 389, 408, 414, 418, 422, 426, 436, 454, 460, 463, 471, 486, 493, 498, 518, 524, 537, 541, 545, 550, 554, 568, 573, 576, 592, 597, 602, 621, 627, 644, 648, 653, 660, 679, 685, 690, 709, 712

WORK TOGETHER
9, 13, 17, 31, 37, 44, 62, 67, 73, 77, 95, 101, 108, 123, 128, 133, 138, 155, 161, 166, 170, 186, 192, 205, 212, 219, 241, 247, 253, 258, 275, 284, 287, 306, 314, 319, 326, 329, 344, 350, 355, 358, 372, 377, 382, 389, 408, 414, 418, 422, 426, 436, 454, 460, 463, 471, 486, 493, 498, 518, 524, 537, 541, 545, 550, 554, 568, 573, 576, 592, 597, 602, 621, 627, 644, 648, 653, 660, 679, 685, 690, 709, 712

ON YOUR OWN
9, 13, 17, 31, 37, 44, 62, 67, 73, 78, 95, 101, 108, 123, 128, 133, 138, 156, 161, 166, 170, 186, 192, 205, 212, 219, 241, 247, 253, 258, 275, 284, 287, 306, 314, 319, 326, 329, 344, 350, 355, 358, 372, 377, 382, 389, 408, 414, 418, 422, 426, 436, 454, 460, 463, 471, 486, 493, 498, 518, 524, 537, 541, 545, 550, 554, 568, 573, 576, 592, 597, 602, 621, 627, 644, 648, 653, 660, 679, 685, 690, 709, 712

CHAPTER REVIEW AND PRACTICE

CHAPTER SUMMARY
18, 45, 78, 109, 139, 171, 193, 220, 259, 288, 330, 359, 390, 437, 472, 499, 525, 555, 577, 603, 628, 661, 691, 713

APPLICATION PROBLEMS
19, 20, 46, 47, 79, 80, 81, 110, 140, 141, 172, 173, 194, 221, 222, 260, 261, 262, 289, 290, 331, 332, 360, 361, 391, 392, 438, 439, 473, 474, 500, 526, 556, 557, 578, 604, 605, 629, 662, 663, 692, 693, 714

MASTERY PROBLEMS
21, 48, 82, 111, 141, 173, 195, 222, 262, 290, 333, 361, 393, 439, 474, 501, 527, 557, 579, 606, 630, 663, 694, 715

CHALLENGE PROBLEMS
22, 49, 83, 112, 142, 174, 196, 223, 263, 291, 333, 362, 393, 440, 474, 504, 528, 558, 580, 606, 630, 664, 695, 715

APPLIED COMMUNICATION
22, 50, 84, 112, 143, 175, 197, 224, 264, 292, 334, 363, 395, 440, 475, 504, 528, 558, 581, 607, 631, 665, 696, 716

CASES FOR CRITICAL THINKING
23, 50, 84, 112, 143, 175, 197, 224, 264, 292, 334, 363, 395, 441, 475, 504, 528, 559, 581, 607, 631, 665, 696, 716

SCANS WORKPLACE COMPETENCY
23, 50, 84, 113, 143, 224, 264, 292, 505, 581, 696

GRAPHING WORKSHOP
23, 144, 197, 363, 475, 529, 582, 607, 665, 716

AUDITING FOR ERRORS
51, 175, 225, 335, 395, 441, 505, 559, 697

USING SOURCE DOCUMENTS
85, 113, 265, 293

ANALYZING BEST BUY'S FINANCIAL STATEMENTS
24, 51, 85, 113, 144, 175, 197, 225, 265, 293, 335, 363, 395, 441, 475, 505, 529, 559, 583, 607, 631, 665, 697, 716

Reviewers

Jon Abel, Salem, OR
*Marilyn Achelpohl, Orion, IL
Abe Aleman, Levelland, TX
*Cindy Anderson, Wyndmere, ND
Kathy Andreason, Salt Lake City, UT
Cynthia S. Aycock, Eagle Lake, FL
*Carolyn Balis, Northfield, OH
*Betty A. Banks-Burke, Hudson, OH
Tiffannie Barden, Phoenix, AZ
Jim Bauer, Cincinnati, OH
Reta Bell, Garden City, TX
Rose Berta, Redwood City, CA
Anne Berten, Portland, OR
Chad E. Bobb, Indianapolis, IN
*Debra L. Bushey, Derry, PA
*Monica Caillouet, Gonzales, LA
Ellen Clizbe, Moreno Valley, CA
Tony Composto, Brooklyn, NY
Becky Cornacchia, Naples, FL
Alicia E. Censi Corso, Los Angeles, CA
David Damme, Eureka, CA
*Debbie Darnell, Huntington, IN
Donna Davis, Charlotte, NC
Paula Davis, Atlanta, GA
Sylvia Davis, Lakewood, CA
Dana Dingell, Vienna, VA
Kathy Dixon, Richmond, VA
*Daniel Doseck, Albany, OH
Keith Downs, Dallastown, PA
Dr. Judith A. Drager-McCoy, Lititz, PA
Ann Droptini, Gladewater, TX
Kathy Dunaway, Erlanger, KY
Jean Eckert, Wexford, PA
Julie Eckhart, Salem, WI
*Fahryka Elliott, Richmond, VA
Carrie English, Woodbridge, VA
Barbara Erwin, Orlando, FL
*Jennie Ewert, Beaverton, MI
K. Skip Fabritius, Olympia, WA
*Erika Ferranti, Stoneham, MA
Debbie Fischer, St. Petersburg, FL
Matt Flanagan, Longmeadow, MA
Kathryn Focht, West Lawn, PA
Kathleen Ford, Rochester, MI
Lance B. Garvin, Indianapolis, IN
*Debbie Gentene, Mason, OH
Wendy Gentry, Garden Grove, CA
*Donna Gernert, Palm Coast, FL
Andy Gilley, Hendersonville, TN

*Sandy Giuliani, Grafton, WI
Kathy Goos, Moreno Valley, CA
Bonnie Graman, Hamilton, OH
Madge Gregg, Hoover, AL
Tracy Gutierrez, Garden Grove, CA
Stan Harder, Factoryville, PA
Kathy Harenka, Mukwonago, WI
Liz Hargis, Cincinnati, OH
*Jean Harms, Port Orange, FL
Cindy Hiester, Astoria, OR
Beth Hubbard, Virginia Beach, VA
Lisa Huddlestun, Kansas, IL
Steve Ingmire, Indianapolis, IN
Gladys Jackson, Woodbridge, NJ
Beverly Kaesar, Neenah, WI
Sheryl Kirby, Philadelphia, PA
*Trish Klinger, Steelton, PA
*Jane Knaub, York, PA
*Alvin Kroon, Mukilteo, WA
Jim Littenhoff, Cincinnati, OH
Darlene Londo, Appleton, WI
Fran Loos, Salt Lake City, UT
Ann M. Ludlow, St. Louis, MO
*Dennis Macy, Elkton, MD
Frances Mallard, Brentwood, TN
Diane Malley, Londonderry, NH
H. Jean Malonson, Hayward, CA
Lee C. Marcroux, Hartford, CT
Chris Marshall, Denver, CO
*Claire Martin, Onida, SD
Libby Martin, Chattanooga, TN
Sally M. Graham Martin, Nokesville, VA
Marge Marvell, Madison, IN
Barb Mason, Paris, MO
*Ronda Matthews, Gonzales, LA
Susan McClements, Nappanee, IN
Robin McCluggage, Cincinnati, OH
Kelvin Meeks, Memphis, TN
*Jane Melroy, Pratt, KS
Lori Meseke, CPA, Vandalia, IL
*Theresa Molitaris, Bridgeville, PA
*John Mondshein, Allentown, PA
Susan Moore, Meriden, CT
Heather Moraru, Suwanee, GA
Jennifer Mundy, O'Fallon, IL
Jospeh Nero, Red Hook, NY
Barb Nichols, Evansville, IN
*Julie Nguyen, West Chester, OH

*James O'Connell, Pittsburgh, PA
Carol Pearsall, Houston TX
Beverly Pettit, Willow Springs, MO
*Dick Pettit, Ovilla, TX
*Matt Pohlman, Latimer, IA
Katherine Prange, Breese, IL
Eleanor Rankin, Rio Rico, AZ
*Howard W. Rankin, MBA, Monticello, KY
Suzanne Rechenberg, Cincinnati, OH
Dr. Andrea B. Reiter, Dingman's Falls, PA
Nicole Reitz-Larson, Salt Lake City, UT
Dr. Harriet D. Rogers, Whitewater, WI
Tim Rohlinger, Kewaskum, WI
George Roth, Prairie du Sac, WI
Joyce Rowe, Lubbock, TX
Sam Sanchez, Laredo, TX
*Rob Schumacher, Middletown, DE
Peggy J. Scott, Chesapeake, VA
*Mark Sears, Winter Garden, FL
Christopher G. Shaffer, Cincinnati, OH
Janet Shaw, Bailey, NC
Mary Ann Shea, Amherst, MA
Jenny V. Shippy, Naples, FL
*Alice Sineath, Advance, NC
Sherri Small, Las Vegas, NV
H. Leland Smith, Racine, WI
Tommie Stanaland, Perry, FL
Dottie Starkey, Milford, DE
Laurel Stein, Wall, NJ
Jeynelle Strickland, Savannah, GA
*Diane Tanner, Jacksonville, FL
Susan Thie, Hamilton, OH
Claire Thoke, Glendale, CA
John Tingley, Bradley, IL
Linda Underwood, Gilcrest, CO
*Eileen Wascisin, Bellingham, WA
Jennifer Wegner, Mishicot, WI
Linda White, Fayetteville, PA
Parnell Wiggins, Memphis, TN
Lonnie Wilson, Evansville, IN
Vicki Winchester, Highland, KS
Vickie Wolfe, Glenns Ferry, ID
Kathy Woodard, Coventry, RI

* content verifier

PART 1: Accounting for a Service Business Organized as a Proprietorship

▽	Chapter 1	Starting a Proprietorship: Changes That Affect the Accounting Equation
▽	Chapter 2	Analyzing Transactions into Debit and Credit Parts
▽	Chapter 3	Recording Transactions in a General Journal
▽	Chapter 4	Posting from a General Journal to a General Ledger
▽	Chapter 5	Cash Control Systems
▽	Chapter 6	Work Sheet for a Service Business
▽	Chapter 7	Financial Statements for a Proprietorship
▽	Chapter 8	Recording Adjusting and Closing Entries for a Service Business

THE BUSINESS—TECHKNOW CONSULTING

TechKnow Consulting is the business that will be used in the chapters in Part 1 to illustrate the accounting concepts and procedures for a service business organized as a proprietorship. TechKnow rents the office space in which the business is located as well as the equipment used. The service provided by the business involves setting up and troubleshooting network problems for a variety of clients.

CHAPTER 1 | CHAPTER 2

CHAPTER 5 | CHAPTER 6

TECHKNOW CONSULTING CHART OF ACCOUNTS

GENERAL LEDGER

Balance Sheet Accounts

(100) ASSETS
- 110 Cash
- 120 Petty Cash
- 130 Accounts Receivable—Oakdale School
- 140 Accounts Receivable—Campus Internet Cafe
- 150 Supplies
- 160 Prepaid Insurance

(200) LIABILITIES
- 210 Accounts Payable—Supply Depot
- 220 Accounts Payable—Thomas Supply Company

(300) OWNER'S EQUITY
- 310 Kim Park, Capital
- 320 Kim Park, Drawing
- 330 Income Summary

Income Statement Accounts

(400) REVENUE
- 410 Sales

(500) EXPENSES
- 510 Advertising Expense
- 520 Insurance Expense
- 530 Miscellaneous Expense
- 540 Rent Expense
- 550 Supplies Expense
- 560 Utilities Expense

The chart of accounts for TechKnow Consulting is illustrated for ready reference as you study the accounting cycle for a proprietorship in this textbook.

CHAPTER 3

CHAPTER 4

CHAPTER 7

CHAPTER 8

CHAPTER 1
Starting a Proprietorship: Changes That Affect the Accounting Equation

OBJECTIVES

After studying Chapter 1, you will be able to:

1. Define accounting terms related to starting a service business organized as a proprietorship and to changes that affect the accounting equation.
2. Identify accounting concepts and practices related to starting a service business organized as a proprietorship and to changes that affect the accounting equation.
3. Classify accounts as assets, liabilities, or owner's equity and demonstrate their relationships in the accounting equation.
4. Analyze how transactions affect accounts in an accounting equation.

KEY TERMS

- accounting
- accounting system
- accounting records
- financial statements
- service business
- proprietorship
- asset
- equities
- liability
- owner's equity
- accounting equation
- ethics
- business ethics
- transaction
- account
- account title
- account balance
- capital
- revenue
- sale on account
- expense
- withdrawals

Point Your Browser
www.C21accounting.com

ACCOUNTING IN THE REAL WORLD

Gold's Gym

Gold's Gym and the Importance of Location

Are you ready for a good workout? With so many labor-saving devices available today, many people look to fitness facilities for their daily physical exercise. For a fee, a member can make use of a variety of cardiovascular machines, weightlifting/resistance equipment, free weights, and indoor tracks. Many facilities offer classes and personal trainers. You can even shop for specialty food and workout clothing.

Gold's Gym is a franchise operation, meaning that individuals or groups buy the right to open and operate a Gold's Gym. The first Gold's Gym opened in 1965 in Venice, California. Since then, more than 650 Gold's Gyms have opened in the United States and in 23 countries around the world.

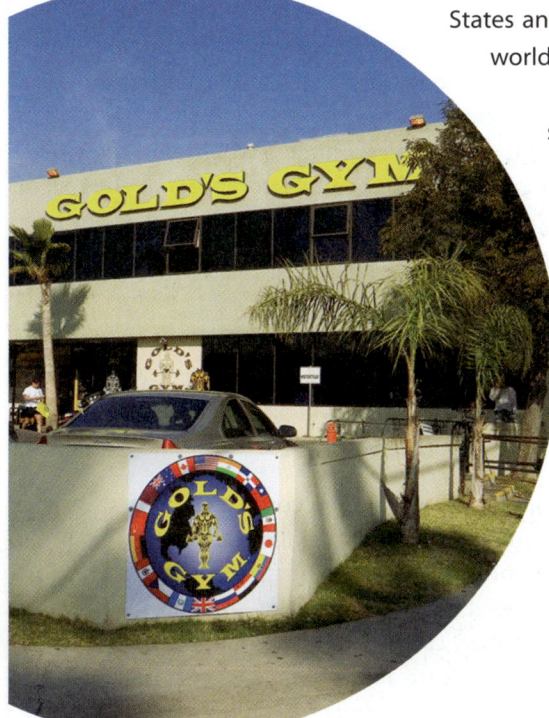

When considering the possibility of opening a new Gold's Gym, there are many decisions that have to be made. These decisions include where to locate the gym, how big the facility should be, what equipment to include, and how to let people know about the new facility.

Critical Thinking

1. Why is the location of a business important to the success of that business?
2. What things would you consider when deciding where to locate a business such as Gold's Gym?

Source: www.goldsgym.com

INTERNET ACTIVITY

Small Business Administration

Go to the homepage for the Small Business Administration, a government organization designed to help small businesses in the United States. Search the site for advice about starting a business. Use the link www.sba.gov, or do a search for the Small Business Administration if the link is no longer accurate.

Instructions

1. List at least five aids that the Small Business Administration site provides to help a person start a business.
2. Briefly explain which aid you feel is most helpful.

LESSON 1-1

The Accounting Equation

WHAT IS ACCOUNTING?

Planning, recording, analyzing, and interpreting financial information is called **accounting**. A planned process for providing financial information that will be useful to management is called an **accounting system**. Organized summaries of a business's financial activities are called **accounting records**.

Accounting is the language of business. Many individuals in a business complete accounting forms and prepare accounting reports. Owners, managers, and accounting personnel use their knowledge of accounting to understand the information provided in the accounting reports. Regardless of their responsibilities within an organization, individuals can perform their jobs more efficiently if they know the language of business—accounting.

Suppliers that are considering extending credit to a business and institutions that are considering extending loans to a business are also interested in a business's financial activities. Financial reports that summarize the financial condition and operations of a business are called **financial statements**. Business owners and managers also use financial statements to make business decisions.

Inaccurate accounting records often contribute to business failure and bankruptcy. Failure to understand accounting information can result in poor business decisions for both businesses and nonprofit organizations. Understanding accounting helps managers and owners make better business decisions.

In addition, nearly everyone in the United States earns money and must submit income tax reports to the federal and state governments. Everyone must plan ways to keep spending within available income in both their personal and business lives.

THE BUSINESS—TECHKNOW CONSULTING

A business that performs an activity for a fee is called a **service business**. Kim Park decided to start her own business, helping set up and troubleshoot computer networks. A business owned by one person is called a **proprietorship**. A proprietorship is also referred to as a *sole proprietorship*. Kim named her new proprietorship "TechKnow Consulting." TechKnow Consulting will rent office space and the equipment needed to troubleshoot network problems.

Since TechKnow Consulting is a new business, Kim must design the accounting system that will be used to keep TechKnow Consulting's accounting records. Kim must be careful to keep these accounting records separate from her own personal financial records. For example, Kim owns a house and a personal car. TechKnow Consulting's financial records must not include information about Kim's house, car, or other personal belongings. Kim must use one checking account for her personal expenses and another checking account for TechKnow Consulting. The accounting concept *Business Entity* is applied when a business's financial information is recorded and reported separately from the owner's personal financial information. [CONCEPT: Business Entity]

Accounting concepts are described throughout this textbook when an application of a concept first occurs. When additional applications occur, a concept reference, such as [CONCEPT: Business Entity], indicates an application of a specific accounting concept. A brief description of each accounting concept used in this text is also provided on the *Century 21 Accounting* web site at www.C21accounting.com.

After completing a computer networking program at a local community college, Kim decided to start her own business so she would have more control over her daily schedule. After only two months, she has made all the arrangements and is ready to begin.

Kim enjoys both helping schools, businesses, and individuals set up a computer network and troubleshooting a network that is not working properly. She also enjoys being her own boss. She gets satisfaction from keeping her own accounting records and seeing that she is making money every month.

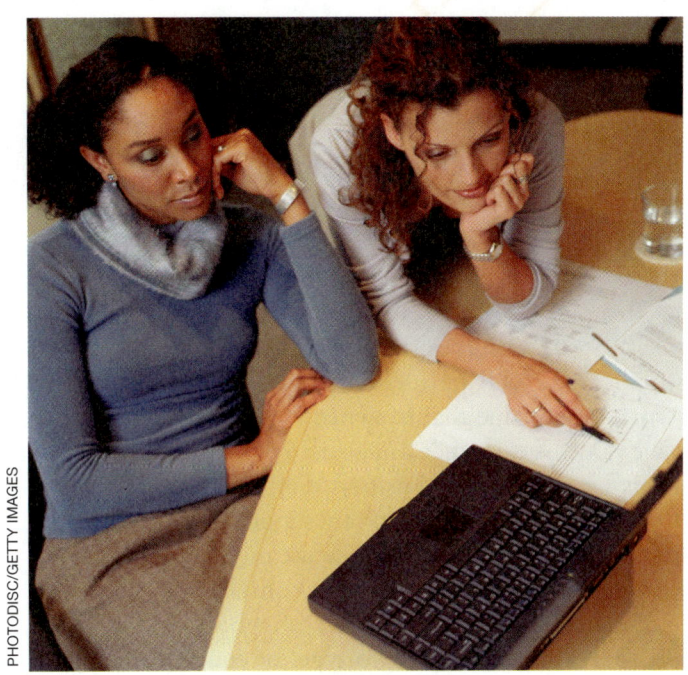

BUSINESS STRUCTURES

Forming and Dissolving a Proprietorship

A proprietorship is a business owned and controlled by one person. The advantages of a proprietorship include:

- *Ease of formation.*
- *Total control by the owner.*
- *Profits that are not shared.*

However, there are some disadvantages of organizing a proprietorship:

- *Limited resources.* The owner is the only person who can invest cash and other assets in the business.
- *Unlimited liability.* The owner is totally responsible for the liabilities of the business. Personal assets, such as a car, can be claimed by creditors to pay the business's liabilities.
- *Limited expertise.* Limited time, energy, and experience can be put into the business by the owner.
- *Limited life.* A proprietorship must be dissolved when the owner dies or decides to stop doing business.
- *Obligation to follow the laws of both the federal government and the state and city in which the business is formed.* Most cities and states have few, if any, legal procedures to follow. Once any legal requirements are met, the proprietorship can begin business. Should the owner decide to dissolve the proprietorship, he or she merely needs to stop doing business. Noncash assets can be sold, with the cash used to pay any outstanding liabilities.

Critical Thinking

1. Why do you think more businesses are organized as proprietorships than any other form of business organization?
2. What kinds of people do you think would be most successful as owners of a proprietorship?

The Accounting Equation

THE ACCOUNTING EQUATION

$$\text{Assets} = \text{Liabilities} + \text{Owner's Equity}$$

Left side amount		Right side amounts	
$0	=	$0 +	$0

TechKnow Consulting will own items such as cash and supplies that will be used to conduct daily operations. Anything of value that is owned is called an **asset**. Assets have value because they can be used either to acquire other assets or to operate a business. For example, TechKnow Consulting will use cash to buy supplies for the business. TechKnow Consulting will then use the asset—supplies—in the operation of the computer consulting business.

Financial rights to the assets of a business are called **equities**. A business has two types of equities: (1) *Equity of those to whom money is owed*. For example, TechKnow Consulting may buy some supplies and agree to pay for the supplies at a later date. The business from whom supplies are bought will have a right to some of TechKnow's assets until TechKnow pays for the supplies. An amount owed by a business is called a **liability**. (2) *Equity of the owner*. Kim will own TechKnow Consulting and invest in the assets of the business. Therefore, she will have a right to decide how the assets will be used. The amount remaining after the value of all liabilities is subtracted from the value of all assets is called **owner's equity**.

The relationship among assets, liabilities, and owner's equity can be written as an equation. An equation showing the relationship among assets, liabilities, and owner's equity is called the **accounting equation**. The accounting equation is most often stated as:

$$\text{Assets} = \text{Liabilities} + \text{Owner's Equity}$$

The accounting equation must be in balance. The total of the amounts on the left side must always equal the total of the amounts on the right side. Before a business starts, its accounting equation would show all zeros.

CHARACTER COUNTS

Accounting Scandals Rock the Financial World

Entering the 21st century, Enron, WorldCom, and Andersen were three of the most celebrated names in corporate America. But the actions of a few individuals forced financial mammoths Enron and WorldCom into bankruptcy. Andersen, once one of the prestigious "Big 5" accounting firms, was forced out of business. These accounting scandals caused hundreds of thousands of employees to lose their jobs and millions of individuals to lose billions of dollars in investment and retirement accounts. The scandals rocked the public's confidence in the accounting profession and the stock markets.

The principles of right and wrong that guide an individual in making decisions are called **ethics**. The use of ethics in making business decisions is called **business ethics**.

Making ethical business decisions is a skill you can learn. Each chapter of this textbook contains a feature on business ethics. In Part 1, you will explore a model that guides your evaluation of business decisions. In later chapters, you will apply that model to make ethical business decisions. You will also be exposed to sources that will enable you to continue learning about business ethics long after you have completed this accounting course.

Instructions
Obtain an article that describes an accounting scandal such as Enron, WorldCom, Adelphia, Healthcorp South, or Parmalat. Write a one-paragraph summary that describes what happened and the individuals involved.

TERMS REVIEW

- accounting
- accounting system
- accounting records
- financial statements
- service business
- proprietorship
- asset
- equities
- liability
- owner's equity
- accounting equation
- ethics
- business ethics

End of Lesson REVIEW

AUDIT YOUR UNDERSTANDING

1. What is accounting?
2. Give two examples of service businesses.
3. What is a proprietorship?
4. State the accounting equation.

WORK TOGETHER 1-1

Completing the accounting equation

Write the answers to the following problem in the *Working Papers*. Your instructor will guide you through the following example.

1. For each line, fill in the missing amount to complete the accounting equation.

Assets	=	Liabilities	+	Owner's Equity
?		3,000		8,000
10,000		?		6,000
63,000		35,000		?

ON YOUR OWN 1-1

Completing the accounting equation

Write the answers to the following problem in the *Working Papers*. Work this problem independently.

1. For each line, fill in the missing amount to complete the accounting equation.

Assets	=	Liabilities	+	Owner's Equity
30,000		?		13,000
?		60,000		20,000
51,000		25,000		?

The Accounting Equation

LESSON 1-2: How Business Activities Change the Accounting Equation

RECEIVING CASH

	Assets	=	Liabilities	+	Owner's Equity
	Cash	=			Kim Park, Capital
Beginning Balances	$0		$0		$0
Received cash from owner as an investment	+5,000				+5,000
New Balances	$5,000		$0		$5,000

Business activities change the amounts in the accounting equation. A business activity that changes assets, liabilities, or owner's equity is called a **transaction**. For example, a business that pays cash for supplies is engaging in a transaction. After each transaction, the accounting equation must remain in balance.

The accounting concept *Unit of Measurement* is applied when business transactions are stated in numbers that have common values—that is, using a common unit of measurement. [CONCEPT: Unit of Measurement] For example, in the United States, business transactions are recorded in dollars. The unit of measurement concept is followed so that the financial reports of businesses can be clearly stated and understood in numbers that have comparable values.

Received Cash Investment from Owner

Ms. Park uses $5,000.00 of her own money to invest in TechKnow Consulting. TechKnow Consulting should be concerned only with the effect of this transaction on TechKnow Consulting's records. The business should not be concerned about Ms. Park's personal records. [CONCEPT: Business Entity]

Transaction 1 August 1. Received cash from owner as an investment, $5,000.00.

A record summarizing all the information pertaining to a single item in the accounting equation is called an **account**. The name given to an account is called an **account title**. Each part of the accounting equation consists of one or more accounts.

In the accounting equation shown above, the asset account, Cash, is increased by $5,000.00, the amount of cash received by the business. This increase is on the left side of the accounting equation. The amount in an account is called the **account balance**. Before the owner's investment, the account balance of Cash was zero. After the owner's investment, the account balance of Cash is $5,000.00.

The account used to summarize the owner's equity in a business is called **capital**. The capital account is an owner's equity account. In the accounting equation shown above, the owner's equity account, Kim Park, Capital, is increased by $5,000.00. This increase is on the right side of the accounting equation. Before the owner's investment, the account balance of Kim Park, Capital was zero. After the owner's investment, the account balance of Kim Park, Capital is $5,000.00.

The accounting equation has changed as a result of the receipt of cash. However, both sides of the equation are changed by the same amount. The $5,000.00 increase on the left side of the equation equals the $5,000.00 increase on the right side of the equation. Therefore, the accounting equation is still in balance.

PAYING CASH

	Assets			=	Liabilities +	Owner's Equity
	Cash	+ Supplies +	Prepaid Insurance	=		Kim Park, Capital
Balances	$5,000	$0	$0		$0	$5,000
Paid cash for supplies	−275	+275				
Balances	$4,725	$275	$0		$0	$5,000
Paid cash for insurance	−1,200		+1,200			
New Balances	$3,525	$275	$1,200		$0	$5,000

TechKnow Consulting pays cash for supplies and insurance.

Paid Cash for Supplies
TechKnow Consulting needs supplies to operate the business. Kim Park uses some of TechKnow Consulting's cash to buy supplies.

> **Transaction 2** August 3. Paid cash for supplies, $275.00.

In this transaction, two asset accounts are changed. One asset, cash, has been exchanged for another asset, supplies. The asset account, Cash, is decreased by $275.00, the amount of cash paid out. This decrease is on the left side of the accounting equation. The asset account, Supplies, is increased by $275.00, the amount of supplies bought. This increase is also on the left side of the accounting equation.

For this transaction, two assets are changed. Therefore, the two changes are both on the left side of the accounting equation. When changes are made on only one side of the accounting equation, the equation must still be in balance. Therefore, if one account is increased, another account on the same side of the equation must be decreased. After this transaction, the new account balance of Cash is $4,725.00. The new account balance of Supplies is $275.00. The sum of the amounts on the left side is $5,000.00 (Cash, $4,725.00 + Supplies, $275.00). The amount on the right side is also $5,000.00. Therefore, the accounting equation is still in balance.

Paid Cash for Insurance
Insurance premiums must be paid in advance. For example, TechKnow Consulting pays a $1,200.00 insurance premium for future insurance coverage.

> **Transaction 3** August 4. Paid cash for insurance, $1,200.00.

In return for this payment, TechKnow Consulting is entitled to insurance coverage for the length of the policy. The insurance coverage is something of value owned by TechKnow Consulting. Therefore, the insurance coverage is an asset. Because insurance premiums are paid in advance, or prepaid, the premiums are recorded in an asset account titled Prepaid Insurance.

In this transaction, two assets are changed. One asset, cash, has been exchanged for another asset, prepaid insurance. The asset account, Cash, is decreased by $1,200.00, the amount of cash paid out. The asset account, Prepaid Insurance, is increased by $1,200.00, the amount of insurance bought.

After this transaction, the new account balance of Cash is $3,525.00. The new account balance of Prepaid Insurance is $1,200.00. The sum of the amounts on the left side is $5,000.00 (Cash, $3,525.00 + Supplies, $275.00 + Prepaid Insurance, $1,200.00). The amount on the right side is also $5,000.00. Therefore, the accounting equation is still in balance.

TRANSACTIONS ON ACCOUNT

	Assets			=	Liabilities	+	Owner's Equity
	Cash	+ Supplies	+ Prepaid Insurance	=	Accts. Pay.—Supply Depot	+	Kim Park, Capital
Balances	$3,525	$275	$1,200		$0		$5,000
Bought supplies on account		+500			+500		
New Balances	$3,525	$775	$1,200		$500		$5,000
Paid cash on account	−300				−300		
New Balances	$3,225	$775	$1,200		$200		$5,000

Bought Supplies on Account

TechKnow Consulting needs to buy additional supplies. The supplies are obtained from Supply Depot, and TechKnow arranges to pay for them at the end of the month. It is a common business practice to buy items and pay for them at a future date. Another way to state this activity is to say that these items are bought *on account*.

Transaction 4 *August 7. Bought supplies on account from Supply Depot, $500.00.*

In this transaction, one asset and one liability are changed. The asset account, Supplies, is increased by $500.00, the amount of supplies bought. Supply Depot will have a claim against some of TechKnow Consulting's assets until TechKnow Consulting pays for the supplies bought. Therefore, Accounts Payable—Supply Depot is a liability account. The liability account, Accounts Payable—Supply Depot, is increased by $500.00, the amount owed for the supplies.

After this transaction, the new account balance of Supplies is $775.00. The new account balance of Accounts Payable—Supply Depot is $500.00. The sum of the amounts on the left side is $5,500.00 (Cash, $3,525.00 + Supplies, $775.00 + Prepaid Insurance, $1,200.00). The sum of the amounts on the right side is also $5,500.00 (Accounts Payable—Supply Depot, $500.00 + Kim Park, Capital, $5,000.00). Therefore, the accounting equation is still in balance.

Paid Cash on Account

Since TechKnow Consulting is a new business, Supply Depot has not done business with TechKnow Consulting before. Supply Depot allows TechKnow Consulting to buy supplies on account but requires TechKnow Consulting to send a check for $300.00 immediately. TechKnow Consulting will pay the remaining portion of this liability at a later date.

Transaction 5 *August 11. Paid cash on account to Supply Depot, $300.00.*

In this transaction, one asset and one liability are changed. The asset account, Cash, is decreased by $300.00, the amount of cash paid out. After this payment, TechKnow Consulting owes less money to Supply Depot. Therefore, the liability account, Accounts Payable—Supply Depot, is decreased by $300.00, the amount paid on account.

After this transaction, the new account balance of Cash is $3,225.00. The new account balance of Accounts Payable—Supply Depot is $200.00. The sum of the amounts on the left side is $5,200.00 (Cash, $3,225.00 + Supplies, $775.00 + Prepaid Insurance, $1,200.00). The sum of the amounts on the right side is also $5,200.00 (Accounts Payable—Supply Depot, $200.00 + Kim Park, Capital, $5,000.00). Therefore, the accounting equation is still in balance.

REMEMBER

The left side of the accounting equation (assets) must always equal the right side (liabilities plus owner's equity).

End of Lesson REVIEW

TERMS REVIEW

transaction
account
account title
account balance
capital

AUDIT YOUR UNDERSTANDING

1. What must be done if a transaction increases the left side of the accounting equation?
2. How can a transaction affect only one side of the accounting equation?
3. To what does the phrase *on account* refer?

WORK TOGETHER 1-2

Determining how transactions change an accounting equation

Write the answers to the following problem in the *Working Papers*. Your instructor will guide you through the following example.

Trans. No.	Assets	=	Liabilities	+	Owner's Equity
1.					

1. For each transaction, place a plus (+) in the appropriate column if the classification is increased. Place a minus (−) in the appropriate column if the classification is decreased.

Transactions:
1. Bought supplies on account.
2. Received cash from owner as an investment.
3. Paid cash for insurance.
4. Paid cash on account.

ON YOUR OWN 1-2

Determining how transactions change an accounting equation

Write the answers to the following problem in the *Working Papers*. Work this problem independently.

Trans. No.	Assets	=	Liabilities	+	Owner's Equity
1.					

1. For each transaction, place a plus (+) in the appropriate column if the classification is increased. Place a minus (−) in the appropriate column if the classification is decreased.

Transactions:
1. Received cash from owner as an investment.
2. Bought supplies on account.
3. Paid cash for supplies.
4. Paid cash for insurance.
5. Paid cash on account.

LESSON 1-3

How Transactions Change Owner's Equity in an Accounting Equation

REVENUE TRANSACTIONS

	Assets				=	Liabilities	+	Owner's Equity
	Cash +	Accts. Rec.—Oakdale School +	Supplies +	Prepaid Insurance	=	Accts. Pay.—Supply Depot	+	Kim Park, Capital
Balances	$3,225	$0	$775	$1,200		$200		$5,000
Received cash from sales	+295							+295 (revenue)
New Balances	$3,520	$0	$775	$1,200		$200		$5,295
Sold services on account		+350						+350 (revenue)
New Balances	$3,520	$350	$775	$1,200		$200		$5,645

Total of left side:
$3,520 + $350 + $775 + $1,200 = $5,845

Total of right side:
$200 + $5,645 = $5,845

Received Cash from Sales

A transaction for the sale of goods or services results in an increase in owner's equity. An increase in owner's equity resulting from the operation of a business is called **revenue**. When cash is received from a sale, the total amount of both assets and owner's equity is increased.

> **Transaction 6** August 12. Received cash from sales, $295.00.

When TechKnow Consulting receives cash for services performed, the asset account, Cash, is increased by the amount of cash received, $295.00. This increase is on the left side of the equation. The owner's equity account, Kim Park, Capital, is also increased by $295.00. This increase is on the right side of the equation. After this transaction is recorded, the equation is still in balance.

In this chapter, three different kinds of transactions that affect owner's equity are described. Therefore, a description of the transaction is shown in parentheses to the right of the amount in the accounting equation.

Sold Services on Account

A sale for which cash will be received at a later date is called a **sale on account**, or a *charge sale*. TechKnow Consulting contracts with a school and an Internet cafe to provide consulting services for payment at a later date. All other customers must pay cash at the time of the service. Regardless of when payment is made, the revenue should be recorded at the time of a sale. The accounting concept *Realization of Revenue* is applied when revenue is recorded at the time goods or services are sold. [CONCEPT: Realization of Revenue]

> **Transaction 7** August 12. Sold services on account to Oakdale School, $350.00.

When TechKnow Consulting sells services on account, the asset account, Accounts Receivable—Oakdale School, is increased by $350.00, the amount of cash that will be received.

This increase is on the left side of the equation. The owner's equity account, Kim Park, Capital, is also increased by $350.00 on the right side of the equation. The equation is still in balance.

EXPENSE TRANSACTIONS

		Assets			=	Liabilities	+	Owner's Equity
	Cash +	Accts. Rec.— Oakdale School	+ Supplies +	Prepaid Insurance	=	Accts. Pay.— Supply Depot	+	Kim Park, Capital
Balances	$3,520	$350	$775	$1,200		$200		$5,645
Paid cash for rent	−300							−300 (expense)
New Balances	$3,220	$350	$775	$1,200		$200		$5,345
Paid cash for telephone bill	−40							−40 (expense)
New Balances	$3,180	$350	$775	$1,200		$200		$5,305

Total of left side:
$3,180 + $350 + $775 + $1,200 = $5,505

Total of right side:
$200 + $5,305 = $5,505

A transaction to pay for goods or services needed to operate a business results in a decrease in owner's equity. A decrease in owner's equity resulting from the operation of a business is called an **expense**. When cash is paid for expenses, the business has less cash. Therefore, the asset account, Cash, is decreased. The owner's equity account, Kim Park, Capital, is also decreased by the same amount.

Paid Cash for Rent

> **Transaction 8** August 12. Paid cash for rent, $300.00.

The asset account, Cash, is decreased by $300.00, the amount of cash paid out. This decrease is on the left side of the equation. The owner's equity account, Kim Park, Capital, is also decreased by $300.00. This decrease is on the right side of the equation. After this transaction is recorded, the equation is still in balance.

Paid Cash for Telephone Bill

> **Transaction 9** August 12. Paid cash for telephone bill, $40.00.

The asset account, Cash, is decreased by $40.00, the amount of cash paid out. This decrease is on the left side of the equation. The owner's equity account, Kim Park, Capital, is also decreased by $40.00. This decrease is on the right side of the equation. After this transaction is recorded, the equation is still in balance.

Other expense transactions might be for advertising, equipment rental or repairs, charitable contributions, and other miscellaneous items. All expense transactions affect the accounting equation in the same way as in Transactions 8 and 9.

How Transactions Change Owner's Equity in an Accounting Equation

OTHER CASH TRANSACTIONS

	Assets				=	Liabilities	+ Owner's Equity
	Cash +	Accts. Rec.—Oakdale School	+ Supplies +	Prepaid Insurance	=	Accts. Pay.—Supply Depot	+ Kim Park, Capital
Balances	$3,180	$350	$775	$1,200		$200	$5,305
Received cash on account	+200	−200					
New Balances	$3,380	$150	$775	$1,200		$200	$5,305
Paid cash to owner for personal use	−125						−125 (withdrawal)
New Balances	$3,255	$150	$775	$1,200		$200	$5,180

Total of left side: $3,255 + $150 + $775 + $1,200 = $5,380

Total of right side: $200 + $5,180 = $5,380

Received Cash on Account

When a business receives cash from a customer for a prior sale, the transaction increases the cash account balance and decreases the accounts receivable balance.

Transaction 10 August 18. Received cash on account from Oakdale School, $200.00.

The asset account, Cash, is increased by $200.00. This increase is on the left side of the equation. The asset account, Accounts Receivable—Oakdale School, is decreased by $200.00. This decrease is also on the left side of the equation. After this transaction is recorded, the equation is still in balance.

Paid Cash to Owner for Personal Use

Assets taken out of a business for the owner's personal use are called **withdrawals**. A withdrawal decreases owner's equity. Although an owner may withdraw any kind of asset, usually an owner withdraws cash. The withdrawal decreases the account balance of the withdrawn asset, such as Cash.

Transaction 11 August 18. Paid cash to owner for personal use, $125.00.

The asset account, Cash, is decreased by $125.00. This decrease is on the left side of the accounting equation. The owner's equity account, Kim Park, Capital, is also decreased by $125.00. This decrease is on the right side of the equation. After this transaction is recorded, the equation is still in balance.

A decrease in owner's equity because of a withdrawal is not a result of the normal operations of a business. Therefore, a withdrawal is not considered an expense.

Summary of Changes in Owner's Equity

Immediately after recording the beginning investment used to start TechKnow Consulting, the total owner's equity was $5,000.00, which represented the investment by the owner, Kim Park. Since that initial investment, five additional transactions that changed owner's equity were recorded in the accounting equation.

These transactions increased owner's equity by $180.00, from $5,000.00 to $5,180.00. Transaction 10, cash received on account, is not listed because it affects two accounts that are both on the left side of the accounting equation.

Transaction Number	Kind of Transaction	Change in Owner's Equity
6	Revenue (cash)	+295.00
7	Revenue (on account)	+350.00
8	Expense (rent)	−300.00
9	Expense (telephone)	− 40.00
11	Withdrawal	−125.00
Net change in owner's equity		+180.00

SUMMARY

After completing this chapter, you can:

1. Define accounting terms related to starting a service business organized as a proprietorship and to changes that affect the accounting equation.
2. Identify accounting concepts and practices related to starting a service business organized as a proprietorship and to changes that affect the accounting equation.
3. Classify accounts as assets, liabilities, or owner's equity and demonstrate their relationships in the accounting equation.
4. Analyze how transactions affect accounts in an accounting equation.

EXPLORE ACCOUNTING

What Is GAAP?

The standards and rules that accountants follow while recording and reporting financial activities are commonly referred to as *generally accepted accounting principles*, or *GAAP*. These rules have not been developed by any one group of rule makers but have instead evolved over time and from many sources.

By law, the Securities and Exchange Commission (SEC) has the authority to establish GAAP. The SEC, however, has allowed a series of private organizations to determine GAAP. Currently, the organization that has the authority to set accounting standards is the Financial Accounting Standards Board (FASB), which was established in 1973.

The standard-setting process includes getting input and feedback from many sources. FASB listens to this feedback and considers all sides of each issue.

Why Is GAAP Necessary?

Users of financial statements rely on the information those statements contain. If the preparers of financial statements were allowed to follow any measurement, recording, and reporting rules, the users of the statements would have no way to determine if the financial statements present fairly the financial position of the business.

By requiring the financial statement preparers to consistently follow certain standards and rules—such as GAAP—the users are able to compare the financial statements of several companies and to track the results of one company over several time periods.

Discussion: Why would a group of people disagree with a proposed accounting standard?

Research: Using your local library or the Internet, find additional information about the FASB. Write a one-page report on your findings.

End of Lesson REVIEW

TERMS REVIEW

- revenue
- sale on account
- expense
- withdrawals

AUDIT YOUR UNDERSTANDING

1. How is owner's equity affected when cash is received from sales?
2. How is owner's equity affected when services are sold on account?
3. How is owner's equity affected when cash is paid for expenses?

WORK TOGETHER 1-3

Determining how transactions change an accounting equation

Write the answers to the following problem in the *Working Papers*. Your instructor will guide you through the following example.

1. Place a plus (+) in the appropriate column if the account is increased. Place a minus (−) in the appropriate column if the account is decreased.

	Assets			=	Liabilities	+	Owner's Equity
Trans. No.	Cash +	Accts. Rec.—Bowman Co. +	Supplies + Prepaid Insurance	=	Accts. Pay.—Maxwell Co.	+	Susan Sanders, Capital
1.							

Transactions:

1. Received cash from sales.
2. Sold services on account to Bowman Company.
3. Paid cash for telephone bill.
4. Received cash on account from Bowman Company.
5. Paid cash to owner for personal use.

ON YOUR OWN 1-3

Determining how transactions change an accounting equation

Write the answers to the following problem in the *Working Papers*. Work this problem independently.

1. Place a plus (+) in the appropriate column if the account is increased. Place a minus (−) in the appropriate column if the account is decreased.

	Assets			=	Liabilities	+	Owner's Equity
Trans. No.	Cash +	Accts. Rec.—Navarro Co. +	Supplies + Prepaid Insurance	=	Accts. Pay.—Barrett Co.	+	Vincent Orr, Capital
1.							

Transactions:

1. Sold services on account to Navarro Company.
2. Received cash from sales.
3. Received cash on account from Navarro Company.
4. Paid cash to owner for personal use.
5. Paid cash for rent.

1-1 APPLICATION PROBLEM

Completing the accounting equation

Instructions:
For each line, fill in the missing amount to complete the accounting equation. Use the form in your *Working Papers* to complete this problem.

Assets	=	Liabilities	+	Owner's Equity
95,000		51,000		?
?		44,000		20,000
4,000		?		2,500
138,000		70,000		?
19,000		?		11,000
?		4,000		12,000
35,000		13,000		?
?		120,000		49,000
8,000		?		3,200
86,000		48,000		?
12,000		?		7,000
?		8,000		22,000
47,000		24,000		?
?		29,000		13,000
57,000		?		36,000
125,000		69,000		?
11,000		?		6,000
?		2,000		3,300

1-2 APPLICATION PROBLEM

Determining how transactions change an accounting equation

Calvin Parish is starting Parish Repair Shop, a small service business. Parish Repair Shop uses the accounts shown in the following accounting equation. Use the form in your *Working Papers* to complete this problem.

Trans. No.	Assets			=	Liabilities			+	Owner's Equity
	Cash	+ Supplies	+ Prepaid Insurance	=	Accts. Pay.—Five Star Supply	+	Accts. Pay.—Riverland Company	+	Calvin Parish, Capital
Beg. Bal.	0	0	0		0		0		0
1.	+3,000								+3,000
New Bal. 2.	3,000	0	0		0		0		3,000

Starting a Proprietorship: Changes That Affect the Accounting Equation

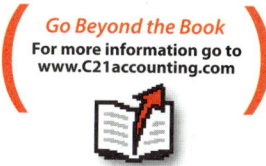

Transactions:

1. Received cash from owner as an investment, $3,000.00.
2. Paid cash for insurance, $1,600.00.
3. Bought supplies on account from Five Star Supply, $700.00.
4. Bought supplies on account from Riverland Company, $300.00.
5. Paid cash on account to Five Star Supply, $700.00.
6. Paid cash on account to Riverland Company, $200.00.
7. Paid cash for supplies, $100.00.
8. Received cash from owner as an investment, $1,500.00.

Instructions:

For each transaction, complete the following. Transaction 1 is given as an example.

a. Analyze the transaction to determine which accounts in the accounting equation are affected.
b. Write the amount in the appropriate columns using a plus (+) if the account increases or a minus (−) if the account decreases.
c. Calculate the new balance for each account in the accounting equation.
d. Before going on to the next transaction, determine that the accounting equation is still in balance.

1-3 APPLICATION PROBLEM

Determining how revenue, expense, and withdrawal transactions change an accounting equation

Peter Smith operates a service business called Peter's Service Company. Peter's Service Company uses the accounts shown in the following accounting equation. Use the form in your *Working Papers* to complete this problem.

Trans. No.	Assets				=	Liabilities	+	Owner's Equity
	Cash	+ Accts. Rec.— Lisa Lee	+ Supplies	+ Prepaid Insurance	=	Accts. Pay.— Kline Co.	+	Peter Smith, Capital
Beg. Bal.	625	0	375	300		200		1,100
1.	−300							−300 (expense)
New Bal.	325	0	375	300		200		800
2.								

Transactions:

1. Paid cash for rent, $300.00.
2. Paid cash to owner for personal use, $150.00.
3. Received cash from sales, $800.00.
4. Paid cash for equipment repairs, $100.00.
5. Sold services on account to Lisa Lee, $400.00.
6. Received cash from sales, $650.00.
7. Paid cash for charitable contributions, $35.00.
8. Received cash on account from Lisa Lee, $300.00.

Instructions:

For each transaction, complete the following. Transaction 1 is given as an example.

a. Analyze the transaction to determine which accounts in the accounting equation are affected.
b. Write the amount in the appropriate columns, using a plus (+) if the account increases or a minus (−) if the account decreases.
c. For transactions that change owner's equity, write in parentheses a description of the transaction to the right of the amount.
d. Calculate the new balance for each account in the accounting equation.
e. Before going on to the next transaction, determine that the accounting equation is still in balance.

1-4 MASTERY PROBLEM

Determining how transactions change an accounting equation

Marion Cassidy operates a service business called Cassidy Company. Cassidy Company uses the accounts shown in the following accounting equation. Use the form in your *Working Papers* to complete this problem.

Trans. No.	Cash	+	Accts. Rec.— Ana Santiago	+ Supplies +	Prepaid Insurance	=	Accts. Pay.— Delta Co.	+	Marion Cassidy, Capital
Beg. Bal.	2,300		0	200	100		1,800		800
1.	−400								−400 (expense)
New Bal.	1,900		0	200	100		1,800		400
2.									

Transactions:

1. Paid cash for rent, $400.00.
2. Received cash from owner as an investment, $500.00.
3. Paid cash for telephone bill, $50.00.
4. Received cash from sales, $1,025.00.
5. Bought supplies on account from Delta Company, $450.00.
6. Sold services on account to Ana Santiago, $730.00.
7. Paid cash for advertising, $660.00.
8. Paid cash for supplies, $150.00.
9. Received cash on account from Ana Santiago, $400.00.
10. Paid cash on account to Delta Company, $1,500.00.
11. Paid cash for one month of insurance, $100.00.
12. Received cash from sales, $1,230.00.
13. Paid cash to owner for personal use, $1,200.00.

Instructions:

For each transaction, complete the following. Transaction 1 is given as an example.

a. Analyze the transaction to determine which accounts in the accounting equation are affected.
b. Write the amount in the appropriate columns, using a plus (+) if the account increases or a minus (−) if the account decreases.
c. For transactions that change owner's equity, write in parentheses a description of the transaction to the right of the amount.
d. Calculate the new balance for each account in the accounting equation.
e. Before going on to the next transaction, determine that the accounting equation is still in balance.

1-5 CHALLENGE PROBLEM

Determining how transactions change an accounting equation

Zachary Martin owns Zachary's Repair Shop. On February 1, Zachary's Repair Shop's accounting equation indicated the following account balances. Use the form in your *Working Papers* to complete this problem.

Trans. No.	Assets				=	Liabilities	+	Owner's Equity
	Cash +	Accts. Rec.—Mary Lou Pier +	Supplies +	Prepaid Insurance	=	Accts. Pay.—Kollasch Co.	+	Zachary Martin, Capital
Beg. Bal.	8,552	1,748	1,485	615		3,145		9,255
1.								

Transactions:

1. Took $400.00 of supplies for personal use.
2. Had equipment repaired at Kollasch Company and agreed to pay Kollasch Company at a later date, $250.00.
3. Mr. Martin had some personal property, which he sold for $500.00 cash.
4. Paid Kollasch Company $120.00 on account.

Instructions:

1. For each transaction, complete the following.
    a. Analyze the transaction to determine which accounts in the accounting equation are affected.
    b. Write the amount in the appropriate columns, using a plus (+) if the account increases or a minus (−) if the account decreases.
    c. For transactions that change owner's equity, write in parentheses a description of the transaction to the right of the amount.
    d. Calculate the new balance for each account in the accounting equation.
    e. Before going on to the next transaction, determine that the accounting equation is still in balance.
2. Answer the following questions.
    a. Why can the owner of a business withdraw assets from that business for personal use?
    b. Why would the owner withdraw assets other than cash?

APPLIED COMMUNICATION

A resume provides a statement of your education, experience, and qualifications for a prospective employer. Your resume should be accurate, honest, and perfect in every respect. It should include all work experience along with the companies and dates of employment. Education, activities, and interests are all important items that should be covered.

Instructions:

Research how to prepare an appropriate resume using the library or the Internet. Then prepare a resume that you could send to a prospective employer.

CASES FOR CRITICAL THINKING

Case 1

Akira Shinoda starts a new business. Mr. Shinoda uses his personal car in the business with the expectation that later the business can buy a car. All expenses for operating the car, including license plates, gasoline, oil, tune-ups, and new tires, are paid for out of business funds. Is this an acceptable procedure? Explain.

Case 2

At the end of the first day of business, Quick Clean Laundry has the assets and liabilities shown below.

The owner, Anh Vu, wants to know the amount of her equity in Quick Clean Laundry. Determine this amount and explain what this amount represents.

Assets		Liabilities	
Cash	$3,500.00	A/P—Smith Office Supplies	$ 750.00
Supplies	950.00	A/P—Super Supplies Company	1,500.00
Prepaid Insurance	1,200.00		

GRAPHING WORKSHOP

The assets, liabilities, and owner's equity for three different companies are given in the graph at right.

Analyze the graph to answer the following questions.

1. Which category is largest?
2. Why will assets always be 50% of the total?

ANALYZING BEST BUY'S FINANCIAL STATEMENTS

Selected published financial information for Best Buy Co., Inc., is reproduced in Appendix B. Look at pages B-5 through B-8, where you will find Best Buy's financial statements. Under the heading on each page, you will see the phrase "$ in millions." This means that all dollar amounts are rounded to the nearest million. Therefore, an amount such as $174 actually means $174,000,000. Another way to think of this is that you can calculate the actual amount by multiplying the rounded amount by 1,000,000 ($174 × 1,000,000 = $174,000,000).

Not all companies round the amounts in their financial statements to the nearest million. Many companies round to the nearest thousand.

Instructions

1. List the actual amount of Accounts Payable and Revenue for Best Buy for 2007.
2. The financial statements for Barnes & Noble include the phrase "thousands of dollars." In 2005, the financial statements included Accounts Payable, $828,852, and Sales, $5,103,004. List the actual amount of Accounts Payable and Sales.

Accounting SOFTWARE

ACCOUNTING SOFTWARE

As you begin your journey into the exciting world of accounting, it is important that you also experience how today's businesses use personal computers to record their transactions and prepare financial statements. How are transactions entered onto computer screens? How does the computer keep track of the total of the Cash account? How is the information that is collected reported on financial statements?

At the end of every chapter, this feature will introduce you to Peachtree, one of the most widely recognized brands of computer accounting systems. Your teacher may also have you complete selected end-of-chapter problems using Peachtree. You will discover that the knowledge of accounting you learn in this textbook will enable you to understand how Peachtree operates and provides management with the information it needs to make good business decisions.

The Peachtree brand was first introduced in 1976, a time when personal computers were just beginning to become available to individuals and businesses. Since then, Peachtree Software has merged with many other software companies to form Sage Software. With millions of customers in the United States and Canada, Sage Software provides a wide variety of accounting and management software to small and medium-sized businesses.

PEACHTREE ACTIVITY*

1. Access the Sage Software web site at www.sagesoftware.com.
2. Identify the most current versions of Peachtree that are available.
3. Identify what version of Peachtree is available at your school.

ACCOUNTING SOFTWARE

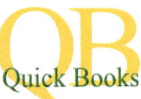

During your study of accounting, your instructor may introduce you to an accounting software program called QuickBooks. Accounting software programs are more efficient and can be much more accurate than completing tasks manually. Many companies require new employees to have some knowledge of accounting software programs. Therefore, learning how to use QuickBooks can make you more employable.

QuickBooks accounting software was developed by the Intuit Company, which was founded in 1983. The software is available in many versions. The version used by a company depends on the tasks that the company wishes to complete electronically. However, all versions of QuickBooks have general items in common. During your study of accounting, you will learn how to manually complete an accounting task. You may then be asked to complete the same task using QuickBooks. It is important to understand the manual tasks before using accounting software so that you can understand what the software is doing. An understanding of accounting also allows you to review the information that is produced electronically and check it for accuracy.

QUICKBOOKS ACTIVITY*

1. Access the Intuit web site at www.quickbooks.intuit.com.
2. Identify the most current versions of QuickBooks that are available.
3. Identify what version of QuickBooks is available at your school.

ACCOUNTING SOFTWARE

Electronic spreadsheets are one of the most popular software programs used by accountants. The reason is simple—the row and column structure of an electronic spreadsheet resembles the journal paper used by accountants for decades, some say even centuries.

It is not surprising, then, that publications read by accountants frequently contain articles about electronic spreadsheets. The *Journal of Accountancy*, published by the American Institute of Certified Public Accountants, is sent to over 300,000 accountants. The *Journal* regularly publishes articles that provide detailed instructions for using electronic spreadsheet features. More importantly, the articles provide examples of accounting applications of the features.

As you study accounting in this course, you will have the opportunity to complete several problems on an electronic spreadsheet. Along the way, you will learn a variety of helpful features. In some cases, you will be able to try out these features in your exercises.

EXCEL ACTIVITY*

1. Identify what electronic spreadsheet version is available at your school.
2. Access the *Journal of Accountancy* online at www.aicpa.org/pubs/jofa/joahome.htm. Perform a search for the name of your electronic spreadsheet.
3. Select one of the articles in the search results. Write a short summary of the feature described in the article.

ACCOUNTING SOFTWARE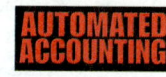

Automated Accounting was developed by Warren Allen and Dale Klooster in the late 1970s for use in their accounting classrooms. They were pioneers in the use of computer technology in the classroom. The software includes a complete accounting system, with modules for specialized activities such as bank statement reconciliation, plant assets, inventory, and payroll. The software was so comprehensive and easy to use that some small businesses also used the software for their business needs. South-Western acquired the software in the early 1980s as a companion to its *Century 21 Accounting* textbooks. Automated Accounting has been revised and updated continuously since then.

AUTOMATED ACCOUNTING ACTIVITY*

1. Consider the problems you have worked in Chapter 1. If you used a computerized accounting system to work the problems, what kinds of errors would the computerized accounting system prevent?
2. For the problems in Chapter 1, what kinds of errors would not be prevented by using a computerized accounting system?

*COMPUTER SAFETY AND HEALTH BASICS

There are some basic safety and health precautions for using computer equipment. Read the safety and health tips on the *Century 21 Accounting* web site.

Starting a Proprietorship: Changes That Affect the Accounting Equation

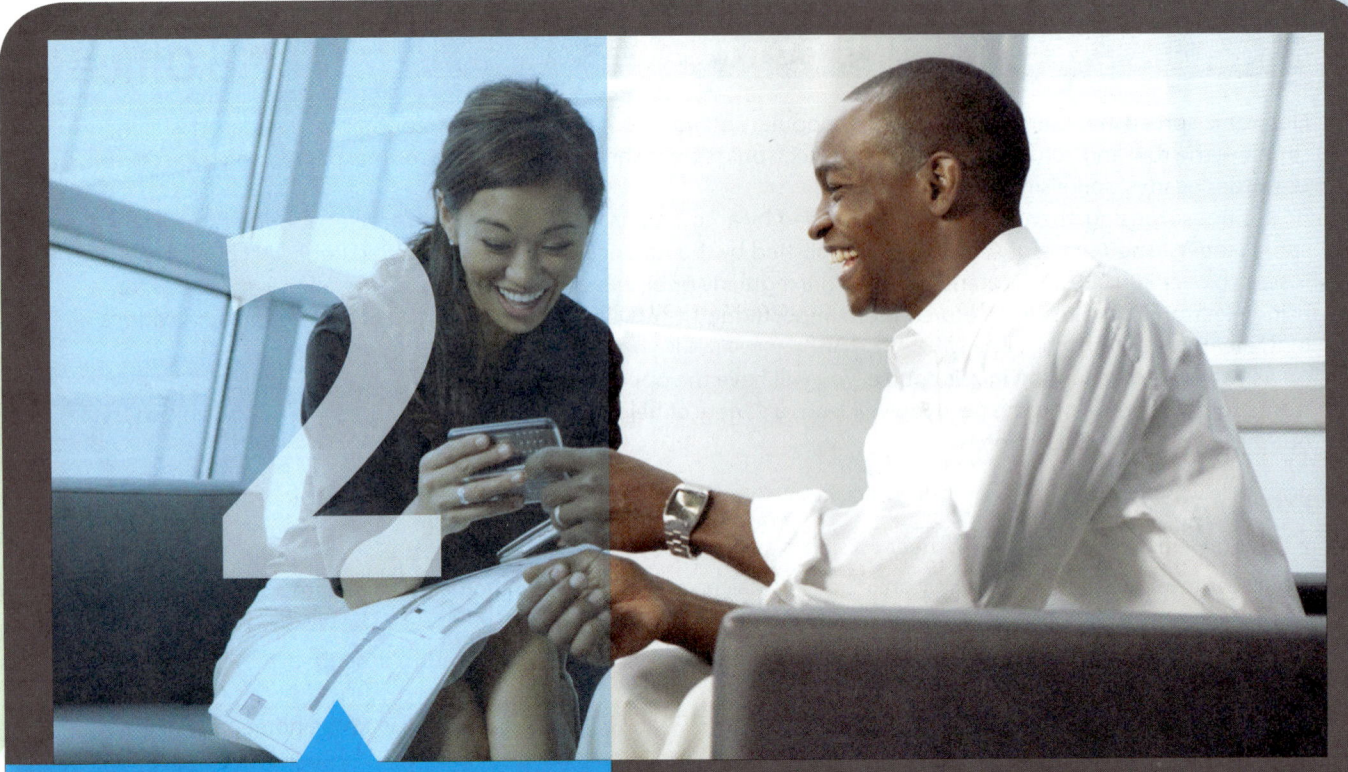

CHAPTER 2

Analyzing Transactions into Debit and Credit Parts

OBJECTIVES

After studying Chapter 2, you will be able to:

1. Define accounting terms related to analyzing transactions into debit and credit parts.
2. Identify accounting practices related to analyzing transactions into debit and credit parts.
3. Use T accounts to analyze transactions showing which accounts are debited or credited for each transaction.
4. Analyze how transactions to set up a business affect accounts.
5. Analyze how transactions affect owner's equity accounts.

KEY TERMS

- T account
- debit
- credit
- normal balance
- chart of accounts

Point Your Browser
www.C21accounting.com

ACCOUNTING IN THE REAL WORLD

American Automobile Association (AAA)

Traveling with the American Automobile Association (AAA)

Picture yourself driving on a dark, deserted road. Suddenly your car stalls. You pull over to the side of the road. What do you do next? If you are a member of the American Automobile Association (AAA), you can pick up your cell phone and call for emergency roadside assistance.

Many people realize the benefits of a membership with the AAA. However, not many people know that the AAA was instrumental in starting the nationwide School Safety Patrol program back in 1920. In 1930, the AAA pioneered the driver education program still in existence in many high schools. As early as 1916, the AAA was fighting for federal dollars to be used to construct a national highway system.

The AAA sells memberships to individuals and families. In exchange for the membership fee, the AAA provides an array of benefits including emergency roadside assistance, travel services, insurance services, driver protection services, and even emergency check cashing services.

Critical Thinking

1. What asset and liability accounts might the AAA use to record its transactions?
2. List at least two transactions that the AAA might record.

Source: www.aaa.com

INTERNET ACTIVITY

Company Headquarters
Go to the homepage of a company of your choice.

Instructions
Search the site to find when the company was started and where its headquarters (or home office) is located. This information is typically found under one of the following headings: "About Us," "Investor Relations," "History," or "Contact Us."

LESSON 2-1

Using T Accounts

ANALYZING THE ACCOUNTING EQUATION

Even though the effects of transactions can be recorded in an accounting equation, the procedure is not practical in an actual accounting system. The number of accounts used by most businesses would make the accounting equation cumbersome to use as a major financial record. Therefore, a separate record is commonly used for each account. The accounting equation can be represented as a T, as shown below.

Assets	=	Liabilities	+	Owner's Equity
Left side		Right side		

The values of all things owned (assets) are on the left side of the accounting equation. The values of all equities or claims against the assets (liabilities and owner's equity) are on the right side of the accounting equation. The total of amounts on the left side of the accounting equation must always equal the total of amounts on the right side. Therefore, the total of all assets on the left side of the accounting equation must always equal the total of all liabilities and owner's equity on the right side.

CHARACTER COUNTS

Ethics Versus Morality

Ethics and morality—these words are often used to refer to an individual's ability to "do what is right." These synonymous English words were derived from different languages. "Ethics" is derived from Greek, and "morality" is derived from Latin. Over time, our society has given a slightly different meaning to each word.

Over 100 years ago, C. C. Everett wrote, "Ethics is the science of morality." Morality is the standard of conduct that is acceptable in a society. Ethics is an organized method that relies on our morality to make moral decisions. Science students learn the scientific method—a model that guides how a proper experiment should be conducted. In the same manner, many ethical models have been proposed to guide individuals in applying their morality to business decisions.

The following ethical model will be used in this textbook:
1. Recognize you are facing an ethical dilemma.
2. Identify the action taken or the proposed action.
3. Analyze the action.
    a. Is the action illegal?
    b. Does the action violate company or professional standards?
    c. Who is affected, and how, by the action?
4. Determine if the action is ethical.

Instructions
Prepare a short report that contrasts the ethical model with the scientific method. How are the models similar? How are they different?

ACCOUNTS

A record summarizing all the information pertaining to a single item in the accounting equation is known as an *account*. Transactions change the balances of accounts in the accounting equation. Accounting transactions must be analyzed to determine how account balances are changed. An accounting device used to analyze transactions is called a **T account**.

There are special names for amounts recorded on the left and right sides of a T account. An amount recorded on the left side is called a **debit**. An amount recorded on the right side is called a **credit**. The words debit and credit come from the Latin and Italian words *debere* and *credere*. Common abbreviations are *dr.* for debit and *cr.* for credit.

ACCOUNT BALANCES

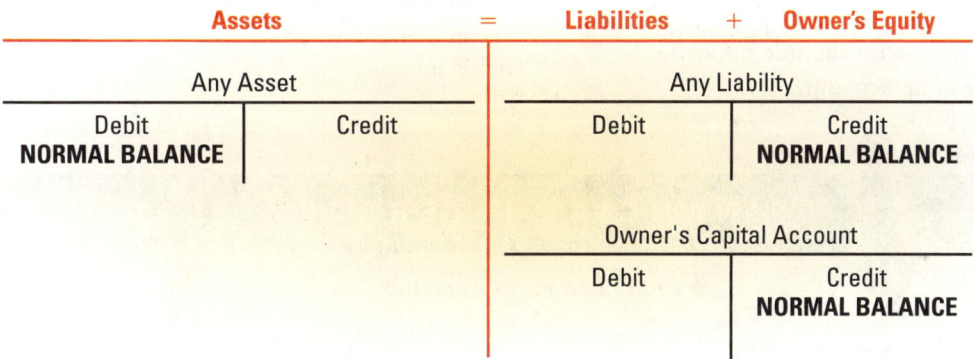

The side of the account that is increased is called the **normal balance**. The process of increasing or decreasing account balances is discussed on the next page. Assets are on the left side of the accounting equation and have normal debit balances (left side). Liabilities are on the right side of the accounting equation and have normal credit balances (right side). The owner's capital account is on the right side of the accounting equation and has a normal credit balance (right side).

Using T Accounts   Lesson 2-1

INCREASES AND DECREASES IN ACCOUNTS

Assets = Liabilities + Owner's Equity

Any Asset
- Debit: **NORMAL BALANCE** / Increase
- Credit: Decrease

Any Liability
- Debit: Decrease
- Credit: **NORMAL BALANCE** / Increase

Owner's Capital Account
- Debit: Decrease
- Credit: **NORMAL BALANCE** / Increase

The sides of a T account are used to show increases and decreases in account balances.

Two basic accounting rules regulate increases and decreases of account balances.

1. Account balances increase on the normal balance side of an account.
2. Account balances decrease on the side opposite the normal balance side of an account.

Asset accounts have normal debit balances; therefore, asset accounts increase on the debit side and decrease on the credit side. Liability accounts have normal credit balances; therefore, liability accounts increase on the credit side and decrease on the debit side. The owner's capital account has a normal credit balance; therefore, the capital account increases on the credit side and decreases on the debit side.

FINANCIAL LITERACY

First Day at Work

It is your first day at a new job. You feel you are totally prepared. But when you arrive, you are directed to the Human Resources Department, where you are asked many questions for which you do not know the answer. Which health plan do you want? How many dependents will you claim? Do you want to participate in the 401(k) plan? Do you want to buy additional life and/or disability insurance? These are just a few of the questions you could be asked as you begin a new job.

Many companies offer some form of health insurance. You may need to decide your level of coverage and who is to be covered by the insurance. Life insurance and disability insurance are sometimes provided by an employer, but additional levels of coverage may be available for purchase. Your employer may match your contributions into a retirement plan such as a 401(k), but you need to decide how much you can afford to contribute into the plan.

There may also be numerous forms to complete. For tax purposes, you need to know how many dependents you claim. You may need to fill out medical information, provide picture identification and a social security number, and compile a list of emergency contacts and phone numbers.

Activities

1. Set up an appointment with someone in the Human Resources Department at a local company. Ask what decisions must be made by a new employee. Summarize your findings in a written report.
2. Give a list of typical benefits to 10 people. Have each person identify the three benefits most important to him/her. Summarize your findings in a chart or table.

End of Lesson REVIEW

TERMS REVIEW

T account
debit
credit
normal balance

AUDIT YOUR UNDERSTANDING

1. Draw the accounting equation on a T account.
2. What are the two accounting rules that regulate increases and decreases of account balances?

WORK TOGETHER 2-1

Determining the normal balance and increase and decrease sides for accounts

Write the answers to the following problems in the *Working Papers*. Your instructor will guide you through the following examples.

Cash
Accounts Receivable—Christine Kelly
Supplies
Prepaid Insurance

Accounts Payable—Miller Supplies
Accounts Payable—Wayne Office Supplies
Jeff Dixon, Capital

For each of the accounts, complete the following:
1. Prepare a T account.
2. Label the debit and credit sides.
3. Label each side of the T account using the following labels:
   a. Normal Balance
   b. Increase
   c. Decrease

ON YOUR OWN 2-1

Determining the normal balance and increase and decrease sides for accounts

Write the answers to the following problems in the *Working Papers*. Work this problem independently.

Cash
Accounts Receivable—Lee McCann
Accounts Receivable—Sonya Lopez
Supplies

Prepaid Insurance
Accounts Payable—Topline Supplies
Vickie Monson, Capital

For each of the accounts, complete the following:
1. Prepare a T account.
2. Label the debit and credit sides.
3. Label each side of the T account using the following labels:
   a. Normal Balance
   b. Increase
   c. Decrease

Using T Accounts

LESSON 2-2

Analyzing How Transactions Affect Accounts

RECEIVED CASH FROM OWNER AS AN INVESTMENT

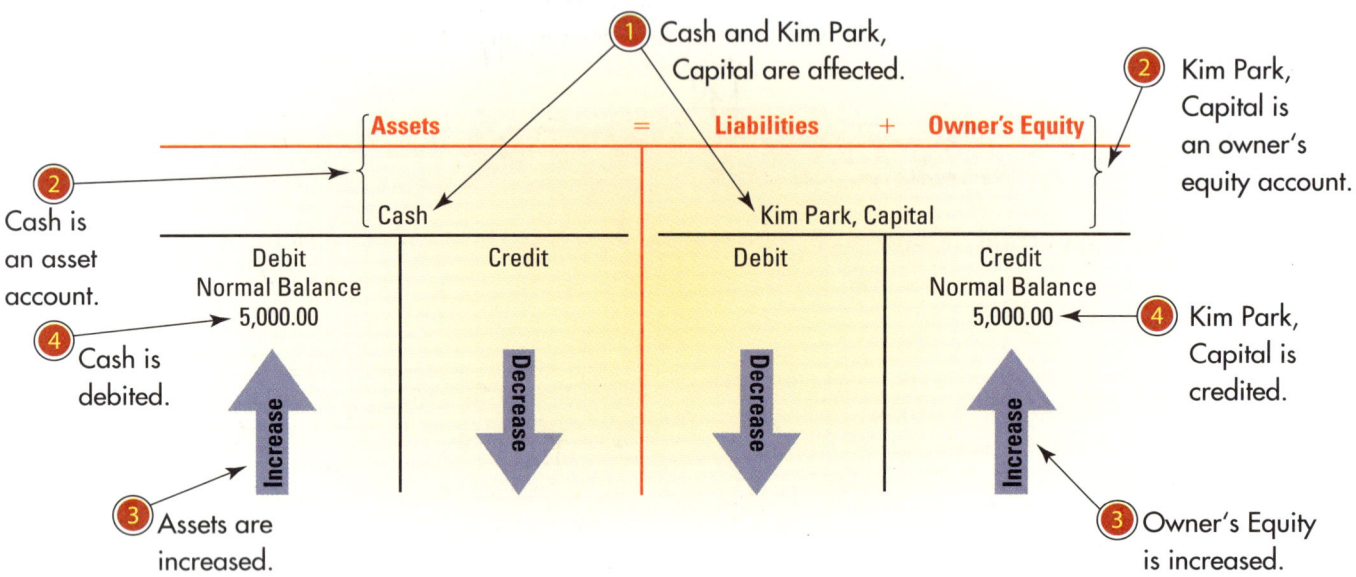

August 1. Received cash from owner as an investment, $5,000.00.

The effect of this transaction is shown in the illustration. Before a transaction is recorded in the records of a business, the information is analyzed to determine which accounts are changed and how. Each transaction changes the balances of at least two accounts. A list of accounts used by a business is called a **chart of accounts**. The chart of accounts for TechKnow Consulting is found on page 3.

When accounts are analyzed, debits must equal credits for each transaction. In addition, after a transaction is recorded, total debits must equal total credits.

The same four questions are used every time a transaction is analyzed into its debit and credit parts.

STEPS QUESTIONS FOR ANALYZING A TRANSACTION INTO ITS DEBIT AND CREDIT PARTS

1. Which accounts are affected?
   Cash and *Kim Park, Capital*

2. How is each account classified?
   Cash is an asset account. *Kim Park, Capital* is an owner's equity account.

3. How is each classification changed?
   Assets increase. Owner's equity increases.

4. How is each amount entered in the accounts?
   Assets increase on the debit side. Therefore, debit the asset account, *Cash*. Owner's equity accounts increase on the credit side. Therefore, credit the owner's equity account, *Kim Park, Capital*.

PAID CASH FOR SUPPLIES

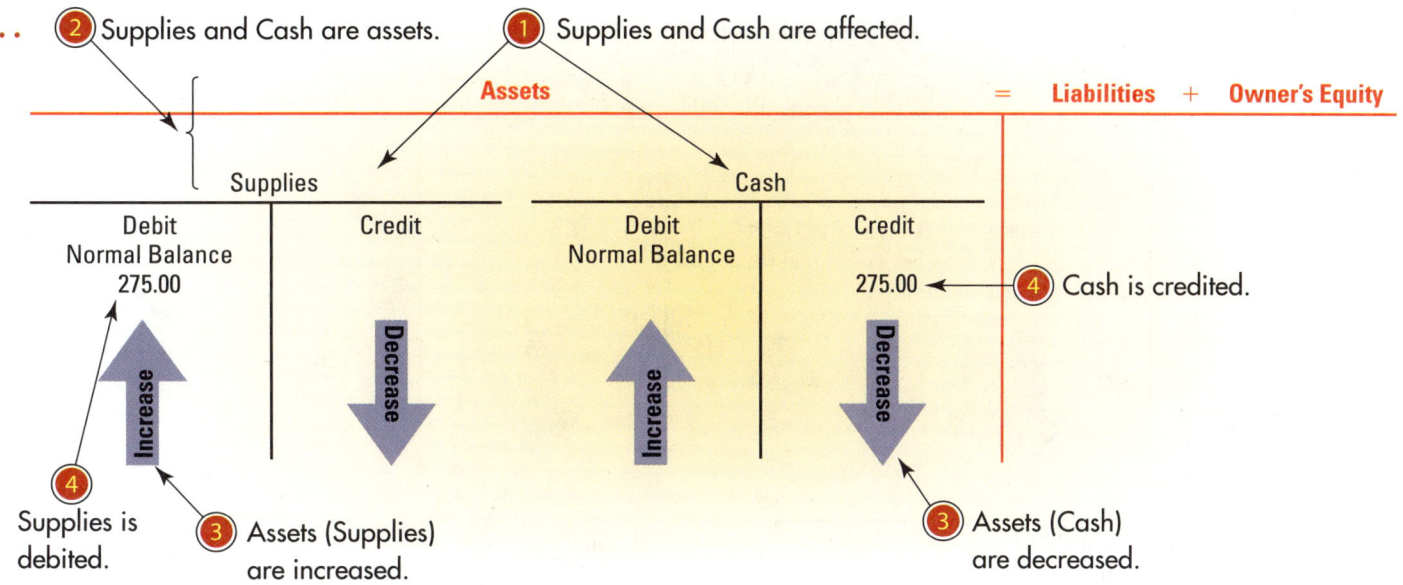

August 3. Paid cash for supplies, $275.00.

The effect of this transaction on the accounting equation is shown in the illustration. In this transaction, two asset accounts are changed. One asset, cash, has been exchanged for another asset, supplies. The asset account, Cash, decreases by $275.00, the amount of cash paid out. This decrease is on the left side of the accounting equation. The asset account, Supplies, increases by $275.00, the amount of supplies bought. This increase is also on the left side of the accounting equation.

The two changes are both on the left side of the accounting equation. When changes are made on only one side of the accounting equation, the equation must still be in balance. Therefore, if one account is increased, another account on the same side of the equation must be decreased.

As you have seen, transactions must be carefully analyzed. A transaction may affect accounts from both sides of the accounting equation. Or, a transaction may affect accounts that are on the same side of the accounting equation, as is true in this example. A common error is to assume that every transaction must affect accounts on both sides of the accounting equation.

STEPS: QUESTIONS FOR ANALYZING A TRANSACTION INTO ITS DEBIT AND CREDIT PARTS

1. Which accounts are affected?
   Supplies and *Cash*

2. How is each account classified?
   Supplies is an asset account. *Cash* is an asset account.

3. How is each classification changed?
   One asset (*Supplies*) increases and another asset (*Cash*) decreases.

4. How is each amount entered in the accounts?
   Assets increase on the debit side. Therefore, debit the asset account, *Supplies*. Assets decrease on the credit side. Therefore, credit the asset account, *Cash*.

Analyzing How Transactions Affect Accounts

PAID CASH FOR INSURANCE

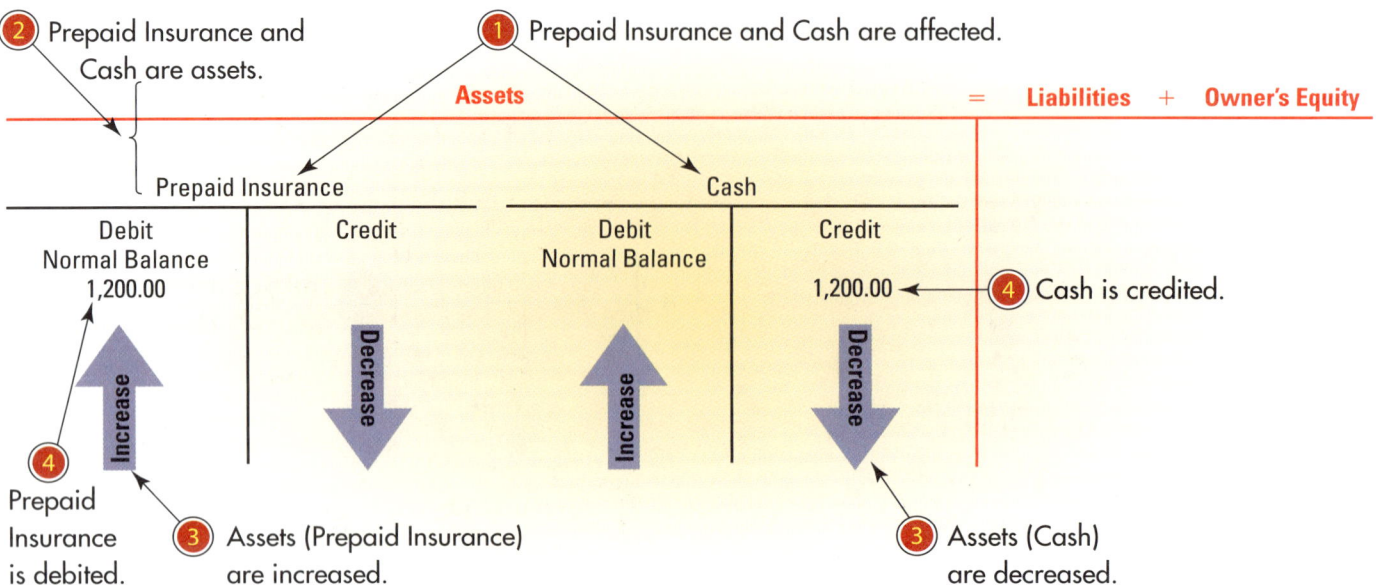

August 4. Paid cash for insurance, $1,200.00.

Paying cash for insurance is very similar to paying cash for supplies. One asset is increased and one asset is decreased.

The effect of this transaction on the accounting equation is shown in the illustration. In this transaction, two assets are changed. One asset, cash, has been exchanged for another asset, prepaid insurance. The asset account, Cash, decreases by $1,200.00, the amount of cash paid out. This decrease is on the left side of the accounting equation. The asset account, *Prepaid Insurance*, increases by $1,200.00, the amount of insurance bought. This increase is also on the left side of the accounting equation.

FOR YOUR INFORMATION

F Y I

T accounts get their name from the arrangement of the lines making up the account. The horizontal line on top of the centered vertical line looks like a capital "T."

FOR YOUR INFORMATION

F Y I

Paying cash for insurance and buying supplies for cash are examples of transactions that affect only one side of the accounting equation. All the accounts involved in these transactions are assets.

STEPS — QUESTIONS FOR ANALYZING A TRANSACTION INTO ITS DEBIT AND CREDIT PARTS

1. Which accounts are affected?
   Prepaid Insurance and *Cash*

2. How is each account classified?
   Prepaid Insurance is an asset account. *Cash* is an asset account.

3. How is each classification changed?
   One asset (*Prepaid Insurance*) increases and another asset (*Cash*) decreases.

4. How is each amount entered in the accounts?
   Assets increase on the debit side. Therefore, debit the asset account, *Prepaid Insurance*.
   Assets decrease on the credit side. Therefore, credit the asset account, *Cash*.

BOUGHT SUPPLIES ON ACCOUNT

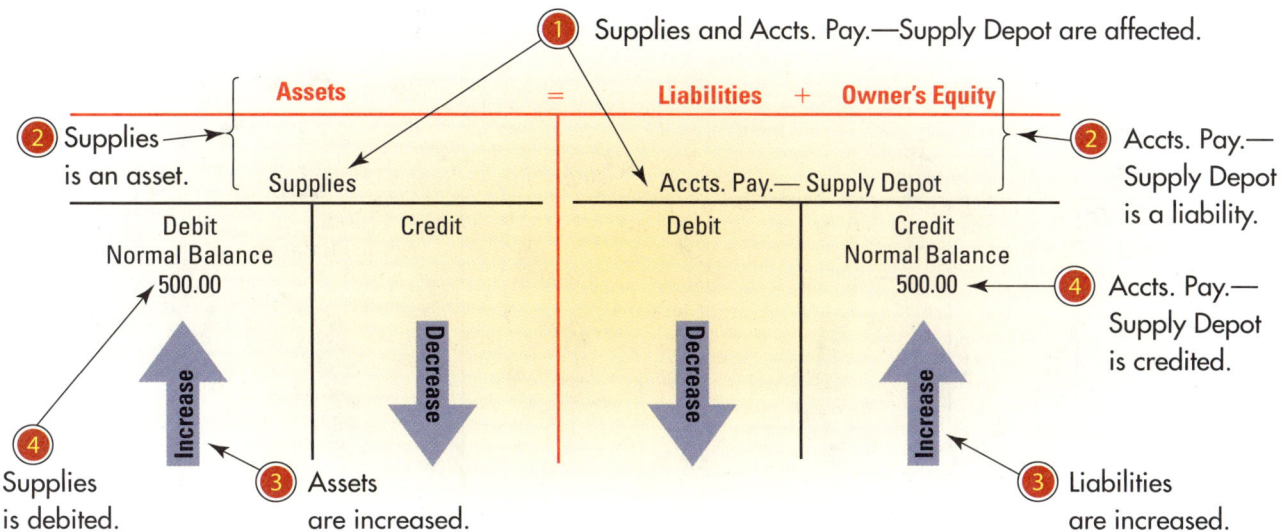

August 7. Bought supplies on account from Supply Depot, $500.00.

The effect of this transaction on the accounting equation is shown in the illustration. In this transaction, one asset and one liability are changed. The asset account, Supplies, increases by $500.00, the amount of supplies bought. This increase is on the left side of the accounting equation. Supply Depot will have a claim against some of TechKnow Consulting's assets until TechKnow Consulting pays for the supplies bought. Therefore, Accounts Payable—Supply Depot is a liability account. The liability account, Accounts Payable—Supply Depot, increases by $500.00, the amount owed for the supplies. This increase is on the right side of the accounting equation.

STEPS — QUESTIONS FOR ANALYZING A TRANSACTION INTO ITS DEBIT AND CREDIT PARTS

1. Which accounts are affected?
   Supplies and *Accounts Payable—Supply Depot*

2. How is each account classified?
   Supplies is an asset account. *Accounts Payable—Supply Depot* is a liability account.

3. How is each classification changed?
   Assets increase. Liabilities increase.

4. How is each amount entered in the accounts?
   Assets increase on the debit side. Therefore, debit the asset account, *Supplies*. Liabilities increase on the credit side. Therefore, credit the liability account, *Accounts Payable—Supply Depot*.

PAID CASH ON ACCOUNT

August 11. Paid cash on account to Supply Depot, $300.00.

The effect of this transaction on the accounting equation is shown in the illustration. In this transaction, one asset and one liability are changed. The asset account, Cash, is decreased by $300.00, the amount of cash paid out. This decrease is on the left side of the accounting equation. After this payment, TechKnow Consulting owes less money to Supply Depot. Therefore, the liability account, Accounts Payable—Supply Depot, is decreased by $300.00, the amount paid on account. The decrease is on the right side of the accounting equation.

STEPS QUESTIONS FOR ANALYZING A TRANSACTION INTO ITS DEBIT AND CREDIT PARTS

1. Which accounts are affected?
   Accounts Payable—Supply Depot and *Cash*

2. How is each account classified?
   Accounts Payable—Supply Depot is a liability account. *Cash* is an asset account.

3. How is each classification changed?
   Liabilities decrease. Assets decrease.

4. How is each amount entered in the accounts?
   Liabilities decrease on the debit side. Therefore, debit the liability account, *Accounts Payable—Supply Depot*. Assets decrease on the credit side. Therefore, credit the asset account, *Cash*.

REMEMBER

When you decrease an account balance, record the decrease on the side opposite the normal balance side of the account. The side opposite the normal balance side can be on the left or the right, depending on the type of account.

End of Lesson REVIEW

TERM REVIEW

chart of accounts

AUDIT YOUR UNDERSTANDING

1. State the four questions used to analyze a transaction.
2. What two accounts are affected when a business pays cash for supplies?

WORK TOGETHER 2-2

Analyzing transactions into debit and credit parts

T accounts are given in the *Working Papers*. Your instructor will guide you through the following examples. Kathy Bergum owns Bergum Services. Bergum Services uses the following accounts. Some of the accounts will be explained in Lesson 2-3.

Cash
Accts. Rec.—Sam Erickson
Supplies
Prepaid Insurance

Accts. Pay.—Bales Supplies
Kathy Bergum, Capital
Kathy Bergum, Drawing

Sales
Advertising Expense
Rent Expense

Transactions:
- Apr. 1. Received cash from owner as an investment, $5,000.00.
- 2. Paid cash for supplies, $50.00.
- 5. Paid cash for insurance, $75.00.
- 6. Bought supplies on account from Bales Supplies, $100.00.
- 9. Paid cash on account to Bales Supplies, $50.00.

1. Prepare two T accounts for each transaction. On each T account, write the account title of one of the accounts affected by the transaction.
2. Write the debit or credit amount in each T account to show the transaction's effect.

ON YOUR OWN 2-2

Analyzing transactions into debit and credit parts

T accounts are given in the *Working Papers*. Work this problem independently. Derrick Hoffman owns Hoffman Accounting Service. Hoffman Accounting Service uses the following accounts. Some of the accounts will be explained in Lesson 2-3.

Cash
Accts. Rec.—Jon Roe
Supplies
Prepaid Insurance

Accts. Pay.—Nash Supply
Derrick Hoffman, Capital
Derrick Hoffman, Drawing

Sales
Miscellaneous Expense
Utilities Expense

Transactions:
- Sept. 1. Received cash from owner as an investment, $2,000.00.
- 4. Paid cash for insurance, $300.00.
- 5. Paid cash for supplies, $100.00.
- 6. Bought supplies on account from Nash Supply, $230.00.
- 11. Paid cash on account to Nash Supply, $115.00.

1. Prepare two T accounts for each transaction. On each T account, write the account title of one of the accounts affected by the transaction.
2. Write the debit or credit amount in each T account to show the transaction's effect.

LESSON 2-3: Analyzing How Transactions Affect Owner's Equity Accounts

RECEIVED CASH FROM SALES

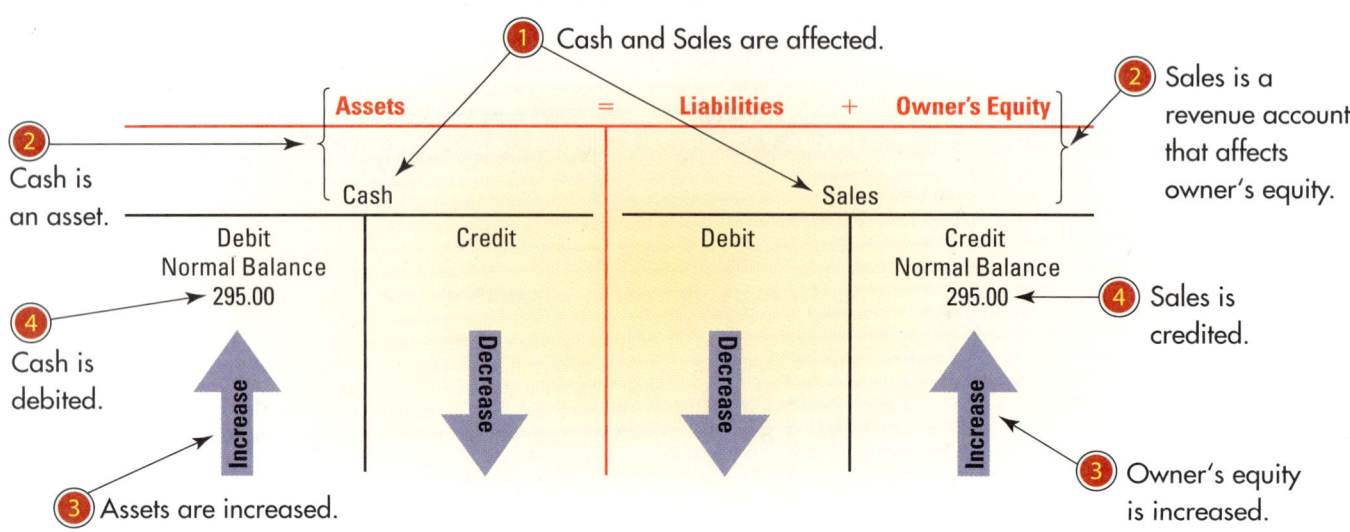

August 12. Received cash from sales, $295.00.

Revenue increases owner's equity. The increases from revenue could be recorded directly in the owner's capital account. However, to avoid a capital account with a large number of entries and to summarize revenue information separately from the other records, TechKnow Consulting uses a separate revenue account titled Sales.

The owner's capital account has a normal credit balance. Increases in the owner's capital account are shown as credits. Because revenue increases owner's equity, increases in revenue are also recorded as credits. Therefore, a revenue account has a normal credit balance.

STEPS — QUESTIONS FOR ANALYZING A TRANSACTION INTO ITS DEBIT AND CREDIT PARTS

1. Which accounts are affected?
   Cash and *Sales*

2. How is each account classified?
   Cash is an asset account. *Sales* is a revenue account that affects owner's equity.

3. How is each classification changed?
   Assets increase. Owner's equity increases.

4. How is each amount entered in the accounts?
   Assets increase on the debit side. Therefore, debit the asset account, *Cash*. Owner's equity accounts increase on the credit side. Revenue increases owner's equity. Therefore, credit the revenue account, *Sales*.

FOR YOUR INFORMATION — FYI

The Small Business Administration (SBA) offers two major types of loans to small businesses. One type of loan is made by private lending institutions. Another type of loan is made directly by the SBA.

SOLD SERVICES ON ACCOUNT

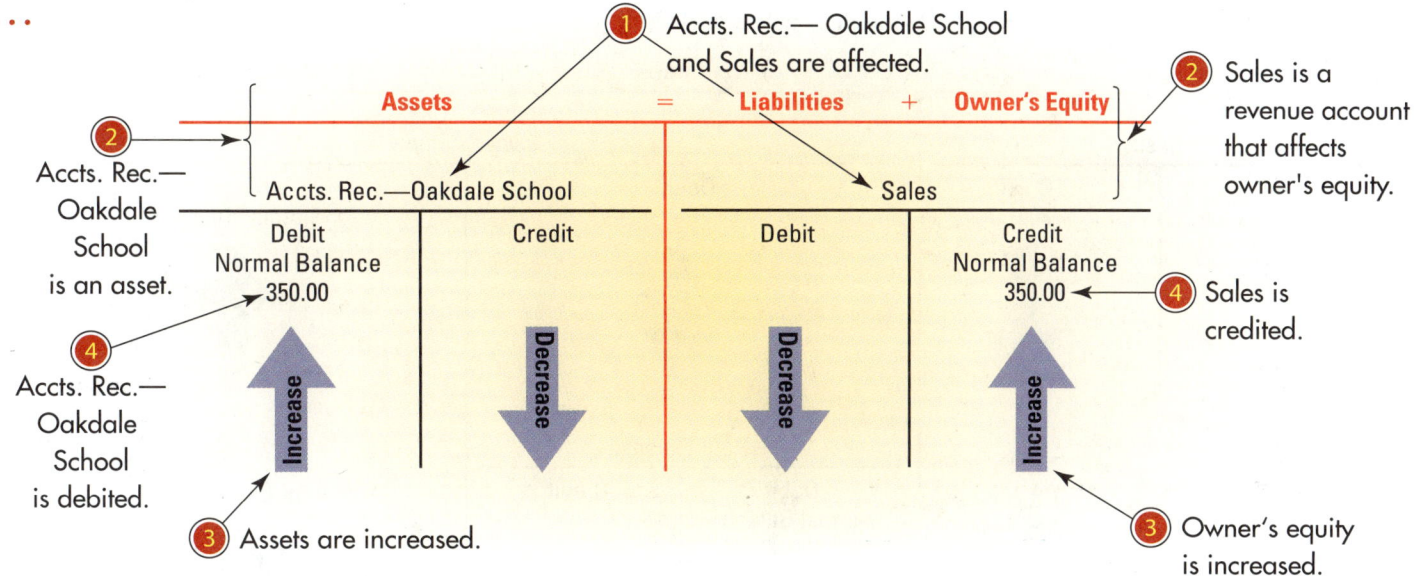

August 12. Sold services on account to Oakdale School, $350.00.

The analysis for selling services on account is similar to that for selling services for cash. The only difference is that cash is not received at this time; therefore, the cash account is not affected by the transaction. Instead, this transaction increases an accounts receivable account. The same four questions are used to analyze this transaction into its debit and credit parts.

STEPS — QUESTIONS FOR ANALYZING A TRANSACTION INTO ITS DEBIT AND CREDIT PARTS

1. Which accounts are affected?
   Accounts Receivable—Oakdale School and *Sales*

2. How is each account classified?
   Accounts Receivable—Oakdale School is an asset account. *Sales* is a revenue account that affects owner's equity.

3. How is each classification changed?
   Assets increase. Owner's equity increases.

4. How is each amount entered in the accounts?
   Assets increase on the debit side. Therefore, debit the asset account, *Accounts Receivable—Oakdale School*. Owner's equity accounts increase on the credit side. Revenue increases owner's equity. Therefore, credit the revenue account, *Sales*.

> **REMEMBER**
> Owner's equity is recorded on the right side of the accounting equation. The right side of a T account is the credit side. Therefore, owner's equity has a normal credit balance.

Analyzing How Transactions Affect Owner's Equity Accounts — Lesson 2-3

PAID CASH FOR AN EXPENSE

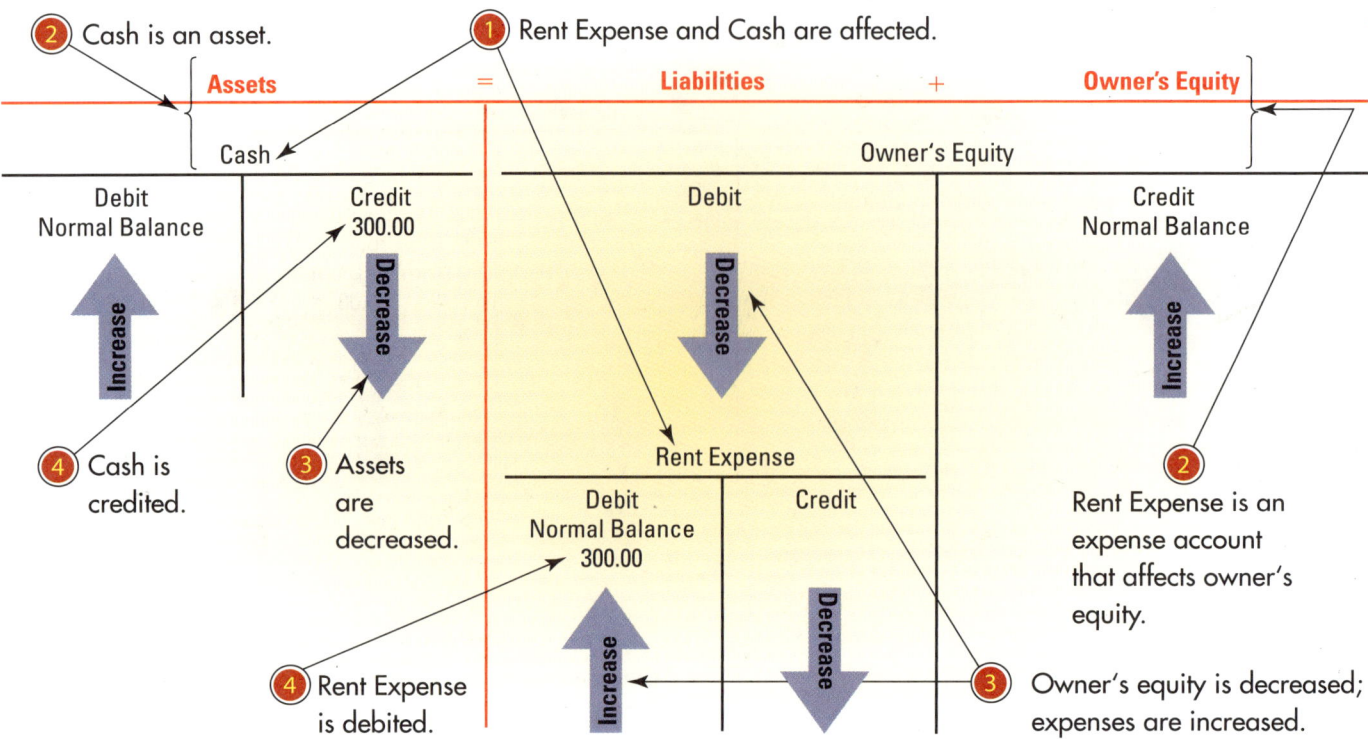

> *August 12. Paid cash for rent, $300.00.*

Expenses decrease owner's equity. The decreases from expenses could be recorded directly in the owner's capital account. However, to avoid a capital account with a large number of entries and to summarize expense information separately from the other records, TechKnow Consulting uses separate expense accounts.

The titles of TechKnow Consulting's expense accounts are shown on its chart of accounts. The expense account Rent Expense is used to record all payments for rent.

The owner's capital account has a normal credit balance. Decreases in the owner's capital account are shown as debits. Therefore, an expense account has a normal debit balance. Because expenses decrease owner's equity, increases in expenses are recorded as debits.

All expense transactions are recorded in a similar manner.

STEPS — QUESTIONS FOR ANALYZING A TRANSACTION INTO ITS DEBIT AND CREDIT PARTS

1. Which accounts are affected?
   Rent Expense and *Cash*

2. How is each account classified?
   Rent Expense is an expense account that affects owner's equity. *Cash* is an asset account.

3. How is each classification changed?
   Owner's equity decreases from an increase in expenses. Assets decrease.

4. How is each amount entered in the accounts?
   Owner's equity accounts decrease on the debit side. An increase in expenses decreases owner's equity. Expense accounts have normal debit balances. Therefore, debit the expense account, *Rent Expense*. Assets decrease on the credit side. Therefore, credit the asset account, *Cash*.

40 Chapter 2 Analyzing Transactions into Debit and Credit Parts

RECEIVED CASH ON ACCOUNT

August 18. Received cash on account from Oakdale School, $200.00.

STEPS — QUESTIONS FOR ANALYZING A TRANSACTION INTO ITS DEBIT AND CREDIT PARTS

1. Which accounts are affected?
   Cash and *Accounts Receivable—Oakdale School*

2. How is each account classified?
   Cash is an asset account. *Accounts Receivable—Oakdale School* is an asset account.

3. How is each classification changed?
   One asset (*Cash*) increases and another asset (*Accounts Receivable—Oakdale School*) decreases.

4. How is each amount entered in the accounts?
   Assets increase on the debit side. Therefore, debit the asset account, *Cash*. Assets decrease on the credit side. Therefore, credit the asset account, *Accounts Receivable—Oakdale School*.

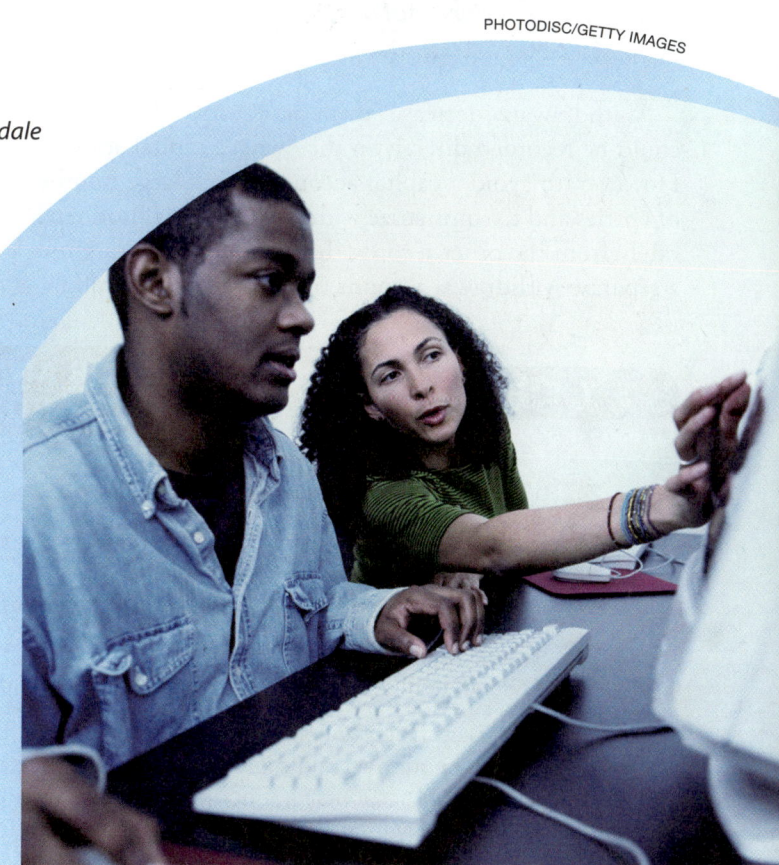

Analyzing How Transactions Affect Owner's Equity Accounts • Lesson 2-3 • 41

PAID CASH TO OWNER FOR PERSONAL USE

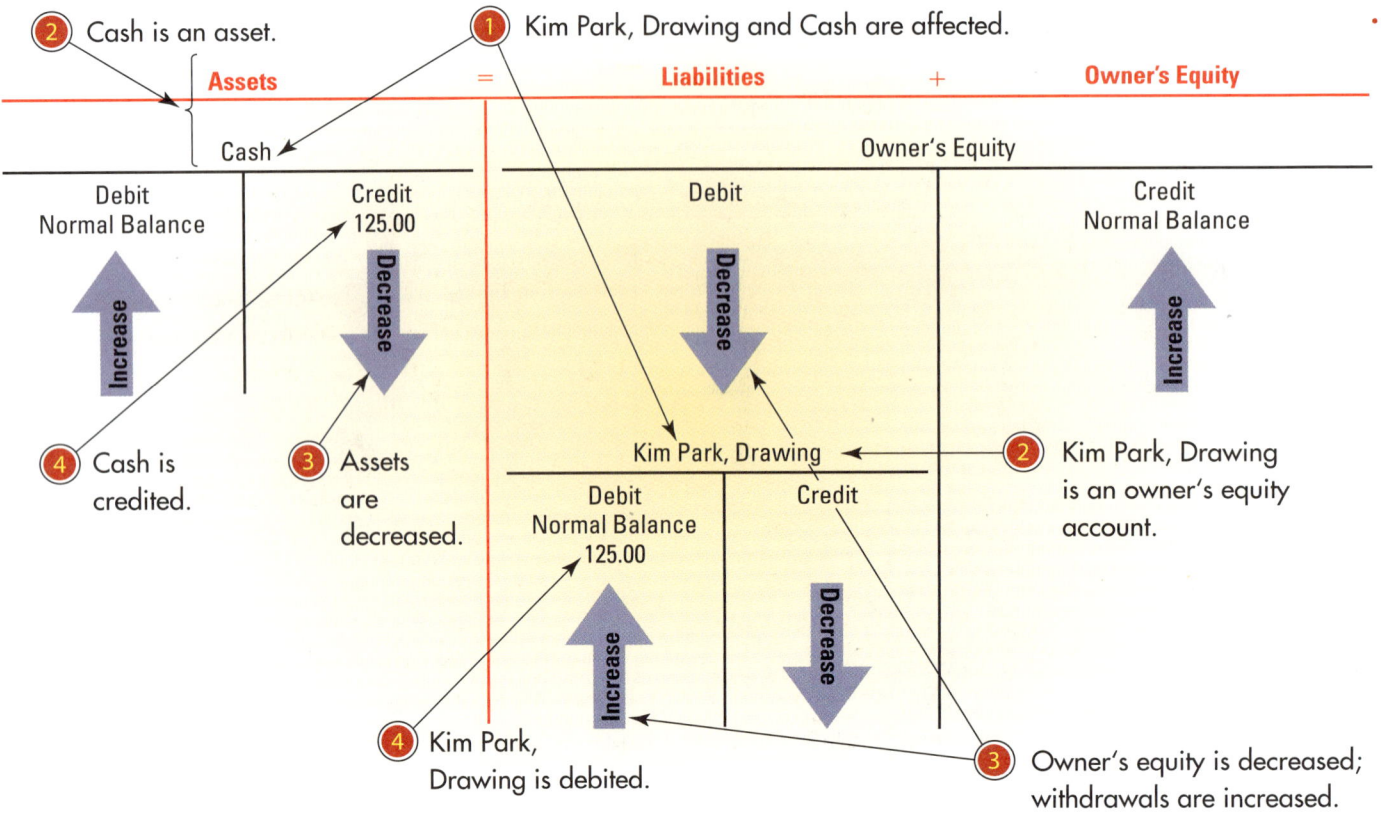

August 18. Paid cash to owner for personal use, $125.00.

Withdrawals decrease owner's equity. Withdrawals could be recorded directly in the owner's capital account. However, to avoid a capital account with a large number of entries and to summarize withdrawal information separately from the other records, TechKnow Consulting uses a separate withdrawal account titled Kim Park, Drawing.

FOR YOUR INFORMATION

F Y I

When drawing T accounts to analyze transactions, stack the accounts instead of writing them horizontally. Stacking the accounts will make it easier to recognize debits and credits.

STEPS QUESTIONS FOR ANALYZING A TRANSACTION INTO ITS DEBIT AND CREDIT PARTS

1. Which accounts are affected?
   Kim Park, Drawing and *Cash*

2. How is each account classified?
   Kim Park, Drawing is an owner's equity account. *Cash* is an asset account.

3. How is each classification changed?
   Owner's equity decreases from an increase in withdrawals. Assets decrease.

4. How is each amount entered in the accounts?
   Owner's equity accounts decrease on the debit side. An increase in withdrawals decreases owner's equity. Withdrawal accounts have normal debit balances. Therefore, debit the owner's equity account, *Kim Park, Drawing*. Assets decrease on the credit side. Therefore, credit the asset account, *Cash*.

42 Chapter 2   Analyzing Transactions into Debit and Credit Parts

CAREERS IN ACCOUNTING

Business, Management & Administration

Rita J. Cowans, Internal Auditor

COURTESY OF RITA J. COWANS

As a highly respected employee at FedEx Corporation, Rita J. Cowans is a Manager in the Internal Audit Department. During her tenure at FedEx, Rita has held various positions in financial, operational, international, and information systems audit. Presently she is responsible for the financial, information systems, and international audit activities for FedEx Worldwide operations.

Her audit team conducts business process reviews, integrated financial and information system reviews, international entity reviews, fraud examinations, and vendor audits. Rita has been a leader in developing and promoting best practices as an integral part of the Internal Audit Department. "It's my responsibility to ensure that the employees and management of FedEx are effectively safeguarding the assets of the corporation, complying with all laws and regulations, and accomplishing the corporate strategic objectives as established by senior management."

While in high school, Rita developed a love for mathematics and accounting. "I became a very critical and detail-oriented thinker and excelled at analyzing information and solving problems." With her parents' direction and strong support, she continued her education and graduated with a bachelor's degree in accounting. In addition, she successfully earned her Certified Internal Auditor (CIA) and Certified Information Systems Auditor (CISA) professional designations. "Being certified in the area of accounting in which you work is critical to your professional success. Certifications demonstrate that you are committed to your profession and communicate to others that you are an expert in your field."

Certifications also enable you to become active in organizations that provide educational opportunities for their members. Rita is a member of the Institute of Internal Auditors and Information Systems Audit and Control Association.

As a member of the FedEx Services Diversity Council, Rita works to ensure that individuals from every background have the opportunity to excel at FedEx. Ultimately, "having a passion for what you do and setting high standards will determine your level of success."

Salary Range: $30,000–$130,000 and up. Can lead to high-level careers at public accounting firms, private and public corporations, and government agencies, such as the Internal Revenue Service (IRS Auditor).

Qualifications: Bachelor's degree in accounting, finance, and information systems for entry-level position, plus normally five years of auditing experience for senior level or above. Professional Certifications preferred (CPA, CIA, CISA, CFE, etc). Familiarity with business, information technology, and legal concepts and procedures is beneficial.

Occupational Outlook: The Sarbanes-Oxley Act of 2002 requires public corporations to expand the documentation and testing of their accounting systems. Internal auditors are an integral part of corporations' compliance with this law. As a result, the demand for internal auditors will be strong for years to come.

End of Lesson REVIEW

AUDIT YOUR UNDERSTANDING

1. What two accounts are affected when a business receives cash from sales?
2. What two accounts are affected when services are sold on account?
3. What two accounts are affected when a business pays cash to the owner for personal use?
4. Are revenue accounts increased on the debit side or credit side? Explain why.
5. Are expense accounts increased on the debit side or credit side? Explain why.

WORK TOGETHER 2-3

Analyzing revenue, expense, and withdrawal transactions into debit and credit parts

T accounts are given in the *Working Papers*. Your instructor will guide you through the following examples.

Use the chart of accounts for Bergum Services in Work Together 2-2.

Transactions:
- Apr. 10. Received cash from sales, $600.00.
- 11. Sold services on account to Sam Erickson, $850.00.
- 14. Paid cash for rent, $250.00.
- 18. Received cash on account from Sam Erickson, $425.00.
- 20. Paid cash to owner for personal use, $300.00.

1. Prepare two T accounts for each transaction. In each T account, write the account title of one of the accounts affected by the transaction.
2. Write the debit or credit amount in each T account to show the transaction's effect.

ON YOUR OWN 2-3

Analyzing revenue, expense, and withdrawal transactions into debit and credit parts

T accounts are given in the *Working Papers*. Work this problem independently.

Use the chart of accounts for Hoffman Accounting Service in On Your Own 2-2.

Transactions:
- Sept. 13. Received cash from sales, $1,500.00.
- 15. Sold services on account to Jon Roe, $500.00.
- 16. Paid cash for utilities, $450.00.
- 18. Received cash on account from Jon Roe, $250.00.
- 21. Paid cash to owner for personal use, $700.00.

1. Prepare two T accounts for each transaction. On each T account, write the account title of one of the accounts affected by the transaction.
2. Write the debit or credit amount in each T account to show the transaction's effect.

SUMMARY

After completing this chapter, you can:

1. Define accounting terms related to analyzing transactions into debit and credit parts.
2. Identify accounting practices related to analyzing transactions into debit and credit parts.
3. Use T accounts to analyze transactions, showing which accounts are debited or credited for each transaction.
4. Analyze how transactions to set up a business affect accounts.
5. Analyze how transactions affect owner's equity accounts.

EXPLORE ACCOUNTING

Owner Withdrawals

Employee salaries are considered an expense that reduces the net income of a company. When the owner withdraws cash from the company, this withdrawal is not considered an expense. The income of a business is calculated by subtracting total expenses from total revenue. Since withdrawals are not considered to be an expense, they do not affect the business's income.

A business owned by one person is called a proprietorship. The Internal Revenue Service does not require the proprietorship, itself, to pay taxes. However, the owner of the proprietorship must include the net income of the proprietorship in his or her own taxable income.

Because the income of a proprietorship is not affected by owner withdrawals, the income tax paid by the owner is not affected by how much cash the owner withdraws from the business. If Wang Accounting Services has revenues of $2,500.00 and expenses of $1,100.00, its income is $1,400.00 ($2,500.00 − $1,100.00). Wang Accounting Services will have income of $1,400.00 regardless of whether the owner withdraws $100.00 or $1,000.00 from the business during that period.

Discussion

1. Hector Moya owns ESW Party Service. He is considering giving his employees a raise that would increase total salaries by $15,000.00 per year. What effect would this raise have on Mr. Moya's income tax?
2. Mr. Moya is also considering withdrawing $5,000.00 from ESW Party Service for his personal use. What effect would this withdrawal have on the income tax Mr. Moya must pay this year?

2-1 APPLICATION PROBLEM

Determining the normal balance and increase and decrease sides for accounts

Write the answers for the following problem in the *Working Papers*.

Cash
Accounts Receivable—Jens Olefson
Accounts Receivable—Toni Nolan
Supplies
Prepaid Insurance
Accounts Payable—United Company
Juan Reo, Capital

1	2	3	4	5	6	7	8
		Account's Normal Balance		Increase Side		Decrease Side	
Account	Account Classification	Debit	Credit	Debit	Credit	Debit	Credit
Cash	Asset	✓		✓			✓

Instructions:
Do the following for each account. The cash account is given as an example.
1. Write the account title in Column 1.
2. Write the account classification in Column 2.
3. Place a check mark in either Column 3 or 4 to indicate the normal balance of the account.
4. Place a check mark in either Column 5 or 6 to indicate the increase side of the account.
5. Place a check mark in either Column 7 or 8 to indicate the decrease side of the account.

2-2 APPLICATION PROBLEM

Analyzing transactions into debit and credit parts

Hal Rosen owns Hal's Marketing Services, which uses the following accounts.

Cash
Supplies
Prepaid Insurance
Accounts Receivable—Dominik Field
Accounts Payable—All Star Company
Hal Rosen, Capital
Hal Rosen, Drawing
Sales
Advertising Expense
Rent Expense

Transactions:
Mar. 1. Received cash from owner as an investment, $1,000.00.
    1. Paid cash for insurance, $400.00.
    3. Bought supplies on account from All Star Company, $600.00.
    5. Paid cash for supplies, $100.00.
    8. Paid cash on account to All Star Company, $400.00.

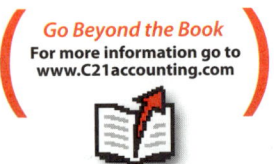

Go Beyond the Book
For more information go to www.C21accounting.com

Instructions:

1. Prepare two T accounts for each transaction. On each T account, write the account title of one of the accounts affected by the transaction. Use the forms in your *Working Papers*.
2. Write the debit or credit amount in each T account to show how the transaction affected that account. T accounts for the first transaction are given as an example.

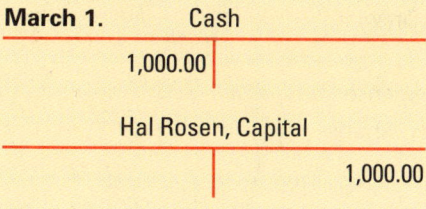

March 1.

Cash
1,000.00

Hal Rosen, Capital
　　　　1,000.00

2-3 APPLICATION PROBLEM

Analyzing revenue, expense, and withdrawal transactions into debit and credit parts

Use the chart of accounts for Hal's Marketing Services given in Application Problem 2-2.

Transactions:
- Mar. 11. Received cash from sales, $2,200.00.
- 12. Paid cash for advertising, $150.00.
- 14. Sold services on account to Dominik Field, $1,700.00.
- 18. Paid cash to owner for personal use, $500.00.
- 19. Received cash on account from Dominik Field, $1,000.00.

Instructions:

1. Prepare two T accounts for each transaction. On each T account, write the account title of one of the accounts affected by the transaction. Use the forms in your *Working Papers*.
2. Write the debit or credit amount in each T account to show how the transaction affected that account.

2-4 APPLICATION PROBLEM

Analyzing revenue, expense, and withdrawal transactions into debit and credit parts

Use the chart of accounts for Hal's Marketing Services given in Application Problem 2-2.

Transactions:
- Mar. 25. Sold services for cash, $1,100.00.
- 26. Performed $500.00 of services for Dominik Field on account.
- 27. Ran an ad in the local newspaper. Paid $125.00 cash.
- 28. Hal Rosen withdrew $450.00 for his personal use.
- 29. Received a $250.00 check from Dominik Field on account.

Instructions:

1. Prepare two T accounts for each transaction. On each T account, write the account title of one of the accounts affected by the transaction. Use the forms in your *Working Papers*.
2. Write the debit or credit amount in each T account to show how the transaction affected that account.

2-5 MASTERY PROBLEM

Analyzing transactions into debit and credit parts

Vickie Lands owns a business called LandScape. LandScape uses the following accounts.

Cash	Vickie Lands, Drawing
Accounts Receivable—Alston Goff	Sales
Accounts Receivable—Josie Leveson	Advertising Expense
Supplies	Miscellaneous Expense
Prepaid Insurance	Rent Expense
Accounts Payable—North End Supplies	Repair Expense
Accounts Payable—Bethany Supplies	Utilities Expense
Vickie Lands, Capital	

Instructions:

1. Prepare a T account for each account. Use the forms in your *Working Papers*.
2. Analyze each transaction into its debit and credit parts. Write the debit and credit amounts in the proper T accounts to show how each transaction changes account balances. Write the date of the transaction in parentheses before each amount.

Transactions:

June 1. Received cash from owner as an investment, $2,700.00.
2. Paid cash for rent, $500.00.
4. Paid cash for supplies, $300.00.
4. Received cash from sales, $850.00.
5. Paid cash for insurance, $275.00.
8. Sold services on account to Alston Goff, $700.00.
9. Bought supplies on account from Bethany Supplies, $200.00.
10. Paid cash for repairs, $75.00.
11. Received cash from owner as an investment, $1,900.00.
11. Received cash from sales, $900.00.
12. Bought supplies on account from North End Supplies, $130.00.
13. Received cash on account from Alston Goff, $500.00.
15. Paid cash for miscellaneous expense, $25.00.
16. Paid cash on account to Bethany Supplies, $50.00.
22. Paid cash for electric bill (utilities expense), $55.00.
23. Paid cash for advertising, $95.00.
25. Sold services on account to Josie Leveson, $450.00.
26. Paid cash to owner for personal use, $400.00.
30. Received cash on account from Josie Leveson, $200.00.

2-6 CHALLENGE PROBLEM

Analyzing transactions recorded in T accounts

Adriana Janek owns a business for which the following T accounts show the current financial situation. Write the answers for the following problem in the *Working Papers*.

```
          Cash                                    Sales
(1)  6,000.00 | (2)    100.00          | (5)    700.00
(5)    700.00 | (3)     65.00          | (8)    400.00
(8)    400.00 | (6)     75.00          | (9)    900.00
(9)    900.00 | (7)    900.00          | (13)   225.00
              | (10)   600.00
              | (11)   550.00
              | (12)   500.00

  Accts. Rec.—Ralph Dahl                 Advertising Expense
(13)   225.00                         (6)   75.00

        Supplies                         Miscellaneous Expense
(4)  1,100.00                         (3)   65.00
(10)   600.00

 Accts. Pay.—Tri City Supplies              Rent Expense
(11)   550.00 | (4) 1,100.00          (7)   900.00

     Adriana Janek, Capital              Utilities Expense
              | (1)  6,000.00          (2)   100.00

     Adriana Janek, Drawing
(12)   500.00
```

1	2	3	4	5	6
Trans. No.	Accounts Affected	Account Classification	Entered in Account as a Debit	Entered in Account as a Credit	Description of Transaction
1.	Cash Adriana Janek, Capital	Asset Owner's Equity	✓	✓	Received cash from owner as an investment

Instructions:

1. Analyze each numbered transaction in the T accounts. Write the titles of accounts affected in Column 2. For each account, write the classification of the account in Column 3.
2. For each account, place a check mark in either Column 4 or 5 to indicate if the account is affected by a debit or a credit.
3. For each transaction, write a brief statement in Column 6 describing the transaction. Information for Transaction 1 is given as an example.

APPLIED COMMUNICATION

An entrepreneur is a person who attempts to earn a profit by taking the risk of operating a business. You have expressed an interest in starting your own business after graduation. Your family has agreed to help finance your new business if you can convince them that you would be successful.

Instructions: Develop a formal plan outlining the details of the business you would operate. Describe the type of business, the equipment or resources needed, and financial information, such as start-up costs and expenses. Write clear and persuasive sentences.

CASES FOR CRITICAL THINKING

Case 1
Aruna Patel records all cash receipts as revenue and all cash payments as expenses. Is Ms. Patel recording her cash receipts and cash payments correctly? Explain your answer.

Case 2
Thomas Bueler records all investments, revenue, expenses, and withdrawals in his capital account. At the end of each month, Mr. Bueler sorts the information to prepare a summary of what has caused the changes in his capital account balance. To help Mr. Bueler prepare this summary in the future, what changes would you suggest he make in his records?

SCANS WORKPLACE COMPETENCY

Resource Competency: Ranking Activities

Concept: Employers need workers who can identify tasks to be completed and prioritize them so that time is spent on tasks that are the most productive. It is human nature to do the tasks that are enjoyable or easy to complete first; however, these tasks are not necessarily the ones that contribute most to the success of a business.

Application: Use the planning sheet on the website (www.C21accounting.com) or create your own form for prioritizing tasks. The form should have four narrow columns labeled A, B, C, and ✓ and a wider column for tasks that need to be completed. List all the tasks or activities you need to do tomorrow or this week in the wide column. Then place a check mark in one of the three columns for each item on the list to show whether it is of the highest priority (A), medium priority (B), or low priority (C). Place a check mark in the column labeled ✓ as each task is completed.

AUDITING FOR ERRORS

The bookkeeper for Lyons Company used T accounts to analyze three transactions as follows.

Transaction 1:

Cash		Ruth Lyons, Capital
200.00		200.00

Transaction 2:

Accounts Payable		Supplies
500.00		500.00

Transaction 3:

Accounts Receivable		Sales
100.00		100.00

Review the three sets of T accounts and answer the following questions.
1. Which T account analysis is incorrect? How did you determine it was incorrect?
2. What information would you need to determine the correct T account analysis for this transaction?

ANALYZING BEST BUY'S FINANCIAL STATEMENTS

The Best Buy financial statement on Appendix B page B-5 lists the assets, liabilities, and shareholder's equity of Best Buy. Shareholder's equity for a corporation is the same as capital for a proprietorship.

Instructions: Find the total assets, total liabilities, and total equity for Best Buy for 2006 and 2007. Put your answer in the form of an accounting equation. You will have to add the total current liabilities, long-term liabilities, and long-term debt to find the total liabilities. Minority interest, which is a special type of account, should be added to total liabilities and total equity in the accounting equation.

Accounting SOFTWARE

OPENING SOFTWARE AND PROBLEM FILES

Your first opportunity to enter transactions in Peachtree will be in Chapter 4. The first step in using Peachtree is to learn how to open the software and then open a problem data file. Problem data files have the chart of accounts and beginning account balances already set up. Therefore, once the data file is open, you are ready to begin entering transactions to solve a problem.

Each problem you will complete has an individual problem or data file. Detailed instructions for opening files and completing problems are provided on the *Century 21 Accounting* web site (www.C21accounting.com).

Peachtree uses unique terminology for opening data files. Rather than opening a file, the software will *restore* a file. The procedures for opening a problem data file depend on how your software is installed.

PEACHTREE ACTIVITY

1. Locate and open your Peachtree software. Depending on how the software was installed, you may be able to open Peachtree from your Start menu or you may have a Peachtree icon on your desktop.
2. Open the data file for Mastery Problem 4-5 (filename: 04-5MP.ptb).
3. Close the data file and exit the software.

OPENING SOFTWARE AND PROBLEM FILES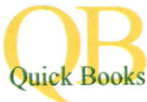

Your first opportunity to enter transactions in QuickBooks will be in Chapter 4. Learning some basic skills for using the software now will prepare you to complete these problems accurately and efficiently. Detailed instructions for opening files and completing problems are provided on the *Century 21 Accounting* web site (www.C21accounting.com).

Each problem you will complete has an individual problem or data file. The file is already set up for QuickBooks and includes company information and the chart of accounts and beginning balances at the point the problem begins.

QUICKBOOKS ACTIVITY

1. Locate and open your QuickBooks software. Depending on how the software was installed, you may be able to open QuickBooks from your Start menu or you may have a QuickBooks icon on your desktop.
2. Open the data file for Mastery Problem 4-5. QuickBooks uses the company name as the filename, so look for the file named O'Kalla Lawn and Garden.qbw.
3. Close the data file and exit the software.

OPENING SOFTWARE AND PROBLEM FILES

The birth of the electronic spreadsheet can be traced back to Dan Bricklin, a student at Harvard Business School, who was preparing a written worksheet analysis for a case study. Knowing that there must be a better alternative, Bricklin began programming an electronic version. His goal was to create a program in which the user could visualize the worksheet as it was created.

By 1979, Bricklin was marketing his program under the name *VisiCalc*, short for *visi*ble *calc*ulator. The program was an instant success and is credited with providing businesses a reason to finally purchase their first personal computer, an expensive purchase at that time.

This program had a dramatic impact in business. No longer were individuals required to create worksheets by hand, calculating each value with adding machines. Most important, if any number on the worksheet changed, other numbers calculated with formulas automatically changed. This power instantly transformed how businesses created budgets, analyzed financial statements, and performed "what if" analyses.

EXCEL ACTIVITY

1. Locate and open your Excel software. Depending on how the software was installed, you may be able to open Excel from your Start menu or you may have an Excel icon on your desktop.
2. Open the data file for Application Problem 5-2 (filename: F05-2.xls). Your instructor may have already copied the data files to your computer. They may also be downloaded from the *Century 21 Accounting* web site (www.C21accounting.com).
3. Close the data file and exit the software.

OPENING SOFTWARE AND PROBLEM FILES

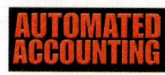

Using computer software to process accounting data can be an efficient and effective way to control the financial information of a business. In order to use the software, it is important to have a general understanding of computer and software terminology. Keyboarding skills are also essential for entering data. The more skilled you are and the greater your understanding, the better able you will be to accurately process financial information.

Automated Accounting software is used to teach students about computerized accounting principles. Accounting software is a set of instructions that operate the computer and enable the user to enter financial information and create reports, spreadsheets, graphs, and documents. Specifically, Automated Accounting can process transactions for:

- The purchase of assets, supplies, services, and the related payments.
- Investments in the business.
- Sales, cash receipts, and noncash transactions.

There are many other types of transactions that can be entered into an automated accounting system. Many of the various types of transactions will be studied in this course.

AUTOMATED ACCOUNTING ACTIVITY

1. Locate and open your Automated Accounting software. Depending on how the software was installed, you may be able to open Automated Accounting from your Start menu or you may have an Automated Accounting icon on your desktop. They may also be downloaded from the *Century 21 Accounting* web site (www.C21accounting.com).
2. Open the data file for Application Problem 3-5 (filename: F03-5.AA8). To open the data file, click the Open button on the toolbar. Then look in the C21 1st Year folder and double-click the appropriate filename.
3. Close the data file and exit the software.

CHAPTER 3

Recording Transactions in a General Journal

OBJECTIVES

After studying Chapter 3, you will be able to:

1. Define accounting terms related to journalizing transactions.
2. Identify accounting concepts and practices related to journalizing transactions.
3. Record in a general journal transactions to set up a business.
4. Record in a general journal transactions to buy insurance for cash and supplies on account.
5. Record in a general journal transactions that affect owner's equity and receiving cash on account.
6. Start a new journal page.

KEY TERMS

- journal
- journalizing
- entry
- general journal
- double-entry accounting
- source document
- check
- invoice
- sales invoice
- receipt
- memorandum

Point Your Browser
www.C21accounting.com

ACCOUNTING IN THE REAL WORLD

Travelocity

Taking Travel to a Better Place—Travelocity

Do you sometimes feel that you need a vacation but are unsure about how to coordinate airline, hotel, and ground transportation reservations? That's where a company like Travelocity can help. Travelocity can also help with cruises, rail travel, and mini travel guides.

Maybe you want to take an inexpensive vacation, and you don't have a specific destination in mind. By searching the Travelocity web site, you can quickly find the "top deals" in airfares, cruises, hotels, rental cars, and total vacation packages. You can even find suggestions about what to see and do at your destination.

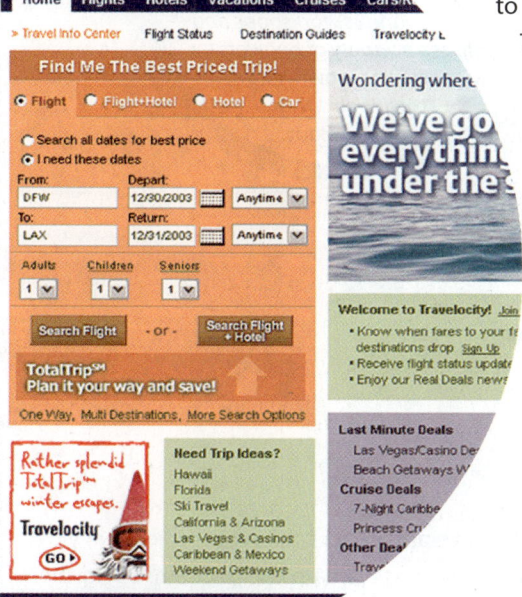

Want to travel throughout Europe? Travelocity will help you arrange rail travel across Europe, arrange for a place to stay, and help you get there. That's full service at its best.

All of this activity needs to be recorded in the accounting records of Travelocity.

Critical Thinking

1. What account would Travelocity credit when you make a reservation with them? What account would be debited?
2. Why do you think Travelocity might be able to get less expensive airline tickets than you, as an individual, could get?

Source: www.travelocity.com

INTERNET ACTIVITY

AICPA

Go to the homepage for the American Institute of Certified Public Accountants (AICPA) (www.aicpa.org). Search the site for information about the AICPA Mission Statement.

Instructions

1. Summarize the mission statement and the objectives of the AICPA.
2. Expand the search by looking at other pages. List three additional resources provided by the AICPA.

LESSON 3-1: Journals, Source Documents, and Recording Entries in a Journal

JOURNALS AND JOURNALIZING

As described in Chapter 2, transactions are analyzed into debit and credit parts before information is recorded. A form for recording transactions in chronological order is called a **journal**. Recording transactions in a journal is called **journalizing**.

Transactions could be recorded in the accounting equation. However, most companies wish to create a more permanent record by recording transactions in a journal.

Each business uses the kind of journal that best fits the needs of that business. The nature of a business and the number of transactions to be recorded determine the kind of journal to be used.

The word journal comes from the Latin *diurnalis*, meaning *daily*. Most businesses conduct transactions every day. To keep from getting overloaded, businesses usually record transactions in their journals every day.

> **FOR YOUR INFORMATION**
> **FYI**
>
> The Small Business Administration (SBA) has programs that offer free management and accounting advice to small business owners. The SBA sponsors various workshops and publishes a variety of booklets for small business owners. Visit their Web site at www.sba.gov.

CHARACTER COUNTS

Recognizing Ethical Dilemmas and Actions

How often have you said something you later regretted? Chances are you spoke before you thought about how your words might affect others. Had you taken the time to think how your words would hurt someone else, you might have said something different or simply kept quiet.

The first step of the ethical model is to recognize you are facing an ethical dilemma. Few business decisions will require you to act immediately. Take whatever time is required to determine whether your actions could harm someone else. If you have any doubts that your action will violate your morals, stop to evaluate the decision, using the ethical model.

The second step of the ethical model is to identify the action taken or the proposed action. Write down every possible action you think of, even if the idea might seem outrageous at first. Seek the advice of others who may have encountered similar dilemmas or whom you admire for their ethical behavior. Many companies assign a mentor to new employees to encourage them to seek advice.

Instructions

In private, write down the names of at least five individuals from whom you would feel comfortable seeking advice on ethical dilemmas.

A GENERAL JOURNAL

			GENERAL JOURNAL				PAGE
	DATE	ACCOUNT TITLE	DOC. NO.	POST. REF.	DEBIT	CREDIT	

Using a Journal

Information for each transaction recorded in a journal is called an **entry**. A journal with two amount columns in which all kinds of entries can be recorded is called a **general journal**. TechKnow Consulting uses a general journal.

The columns in TechKnow Consulting's general journal are Date, Account Title, Doc. No., Post. Ref., Debit, and Credit. The use of each column is described later in this chapter.

Accuracy

Information recorded in a journal includes the debit and credit parts of each transaction recorded in one place. The information can be verified by comparing the data in the journal with the transaction data.

Chronological Record

Transactions are recorded in a journal in order by date. All information for a transaction is recorded in one place, making the information for a specific transaction easy to locate.

Double-Entry Accounting

The recording of debit and credit parts of a transaction is called **double-entry accounting**. In double-entry accounting, each transaction affects at least two accounts. Both the debit and the credit parts are recorded, reflecting the dual effect of each transaction on the business's records. Double-entry accounting assures that debits equal credits.

Source Documents

A business paper from which information is obtained for a journal entry is called a **source document.** Each transaction is described by a source document that proves that the transaction did occur. For example, TechKnow Consulting prepares a check stub for each cash payment made. The check stub describes information about the cash payment transaction for which the check is prepared. The accounting concept *Objective Evidence* is applied when a source document is prepared for each transaction. [CONCEPT: Objective Evidence]

A transaction should be journalized only if it actually occurs. The amounts recorded must be accurate and true. Nearly all transactions result in the preparation of a source document. TechKnow Consulting uses five source documents: checks, sales invoices, receipts, calculator tapes, and memorandums.

CHECKS

A business form ordering a bank to pay cash from a bank account is called a **check**. The source document for cash payments is a check. TechKnow Consulting makes all cash payments by check. The checks are prenumbered to help TechKnow Consulting account for all checks. TechKnow Consulting's record of information on a check is the check stub prepared at the same time as the check.

Procedures for preparing checks and check stubs are described in Chapter 5.

SALES INVOICES

When services are sold on account, the seller prepares a form showing information about the sale. A form describing the goods or services sold, the quantity, and the price is called an **invoice**. An invoice used as a source document for recording a sale on account is called a **sales invoice**. A sales invoice is also referred to as a *sales ticket* or a *sales slip*.

A sales invoice is prepared in duplicate. The original is given to the customer. The copy is used as the source document for the sale on account transaction. [CONCEPT: Objective Evidence] Sales invoices are prenumbered in sequence to help account for all sales invoices.

OTHER SOURCE DOCUMENTS

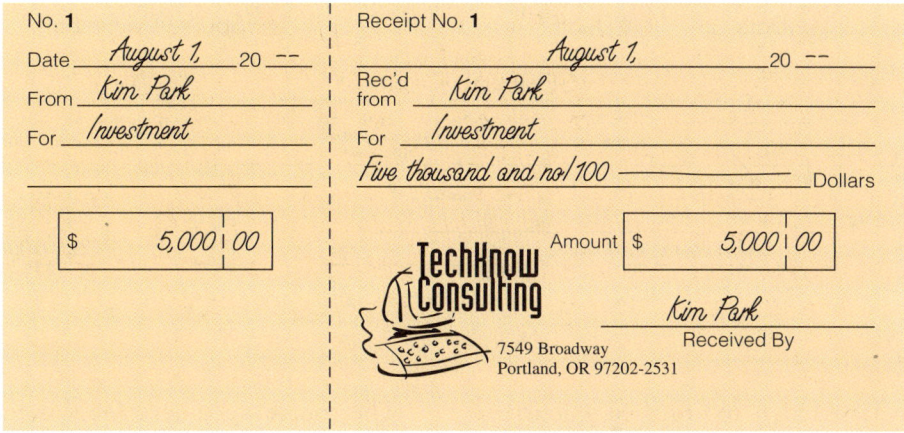

Receipts
A business form giving written acknowledgement for cash received is called a **receipt**. When cash is received from sources other than sales, TechKnow Consulting prepares a receipt. The receipts are prenumbered to help account for all of the receipts. A receipt is the source document for cash received from transactions other than sales. [CONCEPT: Objective Evidence]

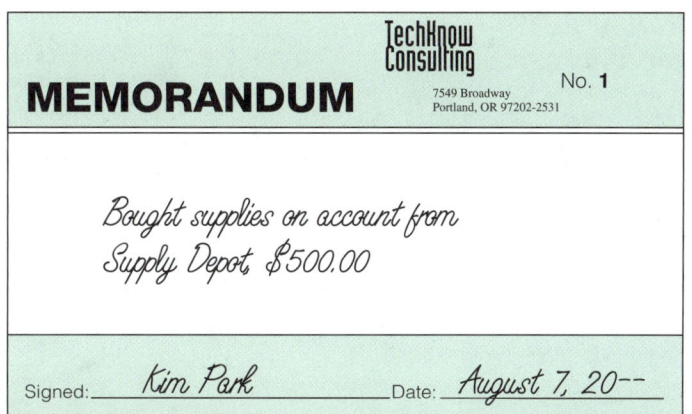

Memorandums
A form on which a brief message is written describing a transaction is called a **memorandum**. When no other source document is prepared for a transaction, or when an additional explanation is needed about a transaction, TechKnow Consulting prepares a memorandum. [CONCEPT: Objective Evidence] TechKnow Consulting's memorandums are prenumbered to help account for all memorandums. A brief note is written on the memorandum to describe the transaction.

Calculator Tapes
TechKnow Consulting collects cash at the time services are rendered to customers. At the end of each day, TechKnow Consulting uses a printing electronic calculator to total the amount of cash received from sales for that day. By totaling all the individual sales, a single source document is produced for the total sales of the day. Thus, time and space are saved by recording only one entry for all of a day's sales. The calculator tape is the source document for daily sales. [CONCEPT: Objective Evidence] A calculator tape used as a source document is shown here.

TechKnow Consulting dates and numbers each calculator tape. For example, in the illustration, the number *T12* indicates that the tape is for the twelfth day of the month.

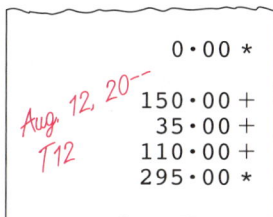

RECEIVED CASH FROM OWNER AS AN INVESTMENT

Information for each transaction recorded in a journal is known as an entry. An entry consists of four parts: (1) date, (2) debit, (3) credit, and (4) source document. Before a transaction is recorded in a journal, the transaction is analyzed into its debit and credit parts.

The source document for this transaction is Receipt No. 1. [CONCEPT: Objective Evidence] The analysis of this transaction is shown in the T accounts.

The asset account, Cash, increases by a debit, $5,000.00. The owner's capital account, Kim Park, Capital, increases by a credit, $5,000.00.

August 1. Received cash from owner as an investment, $5,000.00. Receipt No. 1.

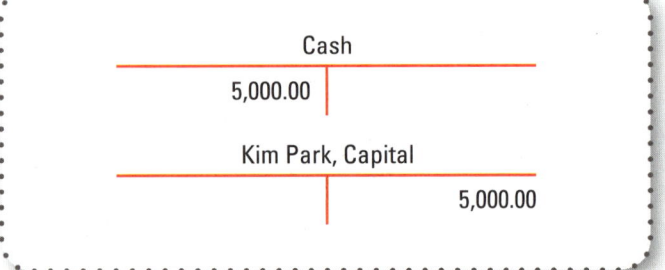

> **FOR YOUR INFORMATION**
>
> **FYI**
>
> *Dollars and cents signs and decimal points are not used when writing amounts on ruled accounting paper. Sometimes a color tint or a heavy vertical rule is used on printed accounting paper to separate the dollars and cents columns.*

STEPS — JOURNALIZING CASH RECEIVED FROM OWNER AS AN INVESTMENT

1. **Date.** Write the date, 20--, Aug. 1, in the Date column. This entry is the first one on this journal page. Therefore, the year and month are both written for this entry. Neither the year nor the month is written again on the same page.

2. **Debit.** Write the title of the account debited, *Cash*, in the Account Title column. Write the debit amount, *$5,000.00*, in the Debit column.

3. **Credit.** On the next line, indented about 1 centimeter, write the title of the account credited, *Kim Park, Capital*, in the Account Title column. This account title is indented to indicate that this account is credited. Write the credit amount, *$5,000.00*, in the Credit column.

4. **Source document.** On the first line of the entry, write the source document number, *R1*, in the Doc. No. column. The source document number, R1, indicates that this is Receipt No. 1. (The source document number is a cross reference from the journal to the source document. Receipt No. 1 is filed in case more details about this transaction are needed.)

   Debits must equal credits for each entry in a general journal. After the entry is journalized, the equality of debits and credits is verified. For this entry, the total debits, $5,000.00, equal the total credits, $5,000.00. The use of the Post. Ref. column is described in Chapter 4.

PAID CASH FOR SUPPLIES

August 3. Paid cash for supplies, $275.00. Check No. 1.

The source document for this transaction is Check No. 1. [CONCEPT: Objective Evidence] The analysis of this transaction is shown in the T accounts.

The asset account, Supplies, increases by a debit, $275.00. The asset account, Cash, decreases by a credit, $275.00.

FOR YOUR INFORMATION
FYI
Analyzing transactions with T accounts makes journaling easier.

STEPS JOURNALIZING CASH PAID FOR SUPPLIES

1. **Date.** Write the date, *3*, in the Date column. This is not the first entry on the journal page. Therefore, the year and month are not written for this entry.

2. **Debit.** Write the title of the account debited, *Supplies*, in the Account Title column. Write the debit amount, *$275.00*, in the Debit column.

3. **Credit.** On the next line, indented about 1 centimeter, write the title of the account credited, *Cash*, in the Account Title column. Write the credit amount, *$275.00*, in the Credit column.

4. **Source document.** On the first line on this entry, write the source document number, *C1*, in the Doc. No. Column. The source document number, *C1*, indicates that this is Check No. 1.

   For this entry, the total debits, $275.00, equal the total credits, $275.00.

REMEMBER
If you misspell words in your written communications, people may mistrust the quality of your accounting skills. Note that in the word receipt *the "e" comes before the "i" and there is a silent "p" before the "t" at the end of the word.*

Journals, Source Documents, and Recording Entries in a Journal — Lesson 3-1

End of Lesson REVIEW

TERMS REVIEW

journal
journalizing
entry
general journal
double-entry accounting
source document
check
invoice
sales invoice
receipt
memorandum

AUDIT YOUR UNDERSTANDING

1. In what order are transactions recorded in a journal?
2. Why are source documents important?
3. List the four parts of a journal entry.

WORK TOGETHER 3-1

Journalizing entries in a general journal

A journal is given in the *Working Papers*. Your instructor will guide you through the following example.

Norm Derner owns Derner Copy Center, which uses the following accounts.

Cash	Accts. Pay.—Palm Supply	Miscellaneous Expense
Accts. Rec.—L. Rohe	Norm Derner, Capital	Rent Expense
Supplies	Norm Derner, Drawing	Utilities Expense
Prepaid Insurance	Sales	

Transactions:
Apr. 1. Received cash from owner as an investment, $1,500.00. R1.
     2. Paid cash for supplies, $375.00. C1.

1. Journalize each transaction completed during April of the current year. Use page 1 of the general journal. Source documents are abbreviated as follows: check, C; receipt, R. Save your work to complete Work Together 3-2.

ON YOUR OWN 3-1

Journalizing entries in a general journal

A journal is given in the *Working Papers*. Work this problem independently.

Lou James owns Lou's Service Center, which uses the following accounts.

Cash	Accts. Pay.—OK Supplies	Advertising Expense
Accts. Rec.—C. Lord	Lou James, Capital	Miscellaneous Expense
Supplies	Lou James, Drawing	Rent Expense
Prepaid Insurance	Sales	

Transactions:
June 2. Received cash from owner as an investment, $3,000.00. R1.
     3. Paid cash for supplies, $950.00. C1.

1. Journalize each transaction completed during June of the current year. Use page 1 of the general journal. Source documents are abbreviated as follows: check, C; receipt, R. Save your work to complete On Your Own 3-2.

LESSON 3-2: Journalizing Buying Insurance, Buying on Account, and Paying on Account

PAID CASH FOR INSURANCE

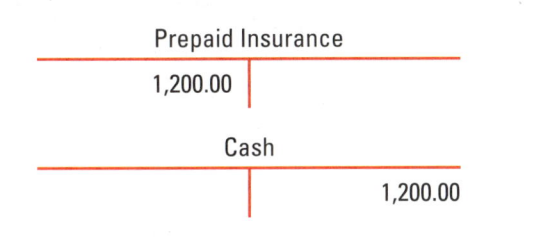

August 4. Paid cash for insurance, $1,200.00. Check No. 2.

The source document for this transaction is Check No. 2. [CONCEPT: Objective Evidence] The analysis of this transaction is shown in the T accounts.

The asset account, Prepaid Insurance, increases by a debit, $1,200.00. The asset account, Cash, decreases by a credit, $1,200.00.

STEPS JOURNALIZING CASH PAID FOR INSURANCE

1. **Date.** Write the date, *4*, in the Date column.

2. **Debit.** Write the title of the account debited, *Prepaid Insurance*, in the Account Title column. Write the debit amount, *$1,200.00*, in the Debit column.

3. **Credit.** On the next line, indented about 1 centimeter, write the title of the account credited, *Cash*, in the Account Title column. Write the credit amount, *$1,200.00*, in the Credit column.

4. **Source document.** On the first line of this entry, write the source document number, *C2*, in the Doc. No. column.
   For this entry, the total debits, $1,200.00, equal the total credits, $1,200.00.

> **REMEMBER**
>
> All amounts recorded in the general journal must have an account title written in the Account Title column.

BOUGHT SUPPLIES ON ACCOUNT

August 7. Bought supplies on account from Supply Depot, $500.00. Memorandum No. 1.

The source document for this transaction is Memorandum No. 1. [CONCEPT: Objective Evidence] The analysis of this transaction is shown in the T accounts.

The asset account, Supplies, increases by a debit, $500.00. The liability account, Accounts Payable—Supply Depot, increases by a credit, $500.00.

TechKnow Consulting ordered these supplies by telephone. TechKnow Consulting wishes to record this transaction immediately. Therefore, a memorandum is prepared that shows supplies bought on account.

FOR YOUR INFORMATION

F Y I

Account titles in accounting records should always be written so that there is no question about the meaning. The usual practice is to write the full account title. If a title is long, however, and the space is short, an account title may sometimes have to be abbreviated.

STEPS — JOURNALIZING SUPPLIES BOUGHT ON ACCOUNT

1. **Date.** Write the date, *7*, in the Date column.

2. **Debit.** Write the title of the account debited, *Supplies*, in the Account Title column. Write the debit amount, *$500.00*, in the Debit column.

3. **Credit.** On the next line, indented about 1 centimeter, write the title of the account credited, *Accounts Payable—Supply Depot*, in the Account Title column. Write the credit amount, *$500.00*, in the Credit column.

4. **Source document.** On the first line of this entry, write the source document number, *M1*, in the Doc. No. column.
   For this entry, the total debits, $500.00, equal the total credits, $500.00.

REMEMBER

When recording transactions in a general journal, the account title that is credited is normally indented.

64   Chapter 3   Recording Transactions in a General Journal

PAID CASH ON ACCOUNT

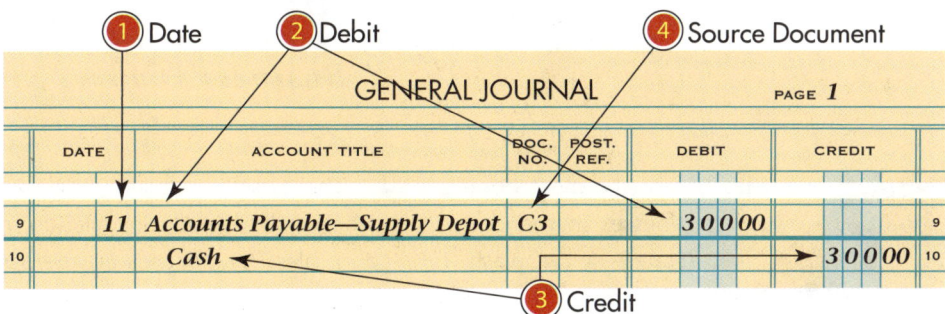

August 11. Paid cash on account to Supply Depot, $300.00. Check No. 3.

The source document for this transaction is Check No. 3. [CONCEPT: Objective Evidence] The analysis of this transaction is shown in the T accounts.

The liability account, Accounts Payable—Supply Depot, decreases by a debit, $300.00. The asset account, Cash, decreases by a credit, $300.00.

STEPS — JOURNALIZING CASH PAID ON ACCOUNT

1. **Date.** Write the date, 11, in the Date column.

2. **Debit.** Write the title of the account debited, *Accounts Payable—Supply Depot*, in the Account Title column. Write the debit amount, *$300.00*, in the Debit column.

3. **Credit.** On the next line, indented about 1 centimeter, write the title of the account credited, *Cash*, in the Account Title column. Write the credit amount, *$300.00*, in the Credit column.

4. **Source document.** On the first line of this entry, write the source document number, *C3*, in the Doc. No. column.

    For this entry, the total debits, $300.00, equal the total credits, $300.00.

PHOTODISC/GETTY IMAGES

Journalizing Buying Insurance, Buying on Account, and Paying on Account — Lesson 3-2

CAREERS IN ACCOUNTING

Business, Management & Administration

Ray and Monica Coselli, Business Owners

It's one of the most popular businesses in the United States—a car wash. If you are washing your car anywhere in east Texas, Louisiana, or northern Mexico, there is a chance you're washing your car with equipment installed by the business owned by Ray and Monica Coselli.

But the Cosellis don't own the car wash. Instead, the Cosellis help other people start their own businesses. The couple owns a small business that builds full-service, exterior, and self-service car washes. Once the car wash is operational, the Cosellis support the new owner by providing a one-stop source for service, parts, and chemicals.

The Cosellis explain, "We have seven employees whose jobs include installation, repairs, maintenance, and sales." Ray focuses on the operations of the business, from the purchase of equipment and supplies to customer sales. Monica manages the day-to-day operations of the office, including the accounting and payroll functions. Monica says, "I've had little formal training in accounting—a single accounting course in college. My true training has been on the job." When Monica started working with the business in 2002, she had to teach herself how to use QuickBooks to record the accounting transactions and prepare financial statements.

Monica is responsible for all incoming bills to the business and payments to those accounts. She also keeps track of large equipment deposits from businesses that are under construction. Monica disburses payments to the vendors when they are due. She says, "I enjoy keeping track of the cash flow for the business as well as maintaining our money market accounts."

Monica adds, "Ray and I both enjoy helping put people into their own businesses. With 25 years in this industry, we are committed to promoting high ethical standards and developing successful businesses!"

Salary Range: Although Monica's responsibilities are diverse, her primary job description is that of bookkeeper. According to the *Occupational Outlook Handbook*, the median annual earnings for a bookkeeper were $28,570 in 2004. (Source: Bureau of Labor Statistics, U.S. Department of Labor, *Occupational Outlook Handbook, 2006-07*, Bookkeeping, Accounting, and Auditing Clerks, www.bls.gov/oco/ocos144.htm [visited April 4, 2007].)

Qualifications: At a minimum, a bookkeeper should have a high school diploma. Having an associate's degree in accounting or business is becoming increasingly important in order to advance in a company. Like public accountants, bookkeepers can demonstrate their knowledge by earning the distinction of a "Certified Bookkeeper" as awarded by the American Institute of Professional Bookkeepers (see www.aipb.org). Individuals seeking this certification must have at least 2 years of bookkeeping experience, pass the exams, and follow a code of ethics.

Occupational Outlook: The *Occupational Outlook Handbook* reports that the growth of bookkeeping jobs will be less than overall job growth. However, many openings will occur as bookkeepers transfer to other occupations. Bookkeeping provides many opportunities for individuals seeking temporary or full-time work.

End of Lesson REVIEW

AUDIT YOUR UNDERSTANDING

1. When cash is paid for insurance, which account is listed on the first line of the entry?
2. When supplies are bought on account, which account is listed on the first line of the entry?
3. When supplies are bought on account, which account is listed on the second line of the entry?
4. When cash is paid on account, which account is listed on the second line of the entry?

WORK TOGETHER 3-2

Journalizing entries in a general journal

Use the general journal that you started for Work Together 3-1. Your instructor will guide you through the following example.

Norm Derner owns Derner Copy Center, which uses the following accounts.

Cash	Accts. Pay.—Palm Supply	Miscellaneous Expense
Accts. Rec.—L. Rohe	Norm Derner, Capital	Rent Expense
Supplies	Norm Derner, Drawing	Utilities Expense
Prepaid Insurance	Sales	

Transactions:
- Apr. 5. Bought supplies on account from Palm Supply, $500.00. M1.
- 7. Paid cash for insurance, $300.00. C2.
- 9. Paid cash on account to Palm Supply, $250.00. C3.

1. Journalize the transactions continuing on the next blank line of page 1 of the journal. Source documents are abbreviated as follows: check, C; memorandum, M. Save your work to complete Work Together 3-3.

ON YOUR OWN 3-2

Journalizing entries in a general journal

Use the general journal that you started for On Your Own 3-1. Work this problem independently.

Lou James owns Lou's Service Center, which uses the following accounts.

Cash	Accts. Pay.—OK Supplies	Advertising Expense
Accts. Rec.—C. Lord	Lou James, Capital	Miscellaneous Expense
Supplies	Lou James, Drawing	Rent Expense
Prepaid Insurance	Sales	

Transactions:
- June 5. Paid cash for insurance, $400.00. C2.
- 9. Bought supplies on account from OK Supplies, $300.00. M1.
- 10. Paid cash on account to OK Supplies, $300.00. C3.

1. Journalize the transactions continuing on the next blank line of page 1 of the journal. Source documents are abbreviated as follows: check, C; memorandum, M. Save your work to complete On Your Own 3-3.

LESSON 3-3

Journalizing Transactions That Affect Owner's Equity and Receiving Cash on Account

RECEIVED CASH FROM SALES

August 12. Received cash from sales, $295.00. Tape No. 12.

The source document for this transaction is Calculator Tape No. 12. [CONCEPT: Objective Evidence] The analysis of this transaction is shown in the T accounts.

The asset account, Cash, increases by a debit, $295.00. The revenue account, Sales, increases by a credit, $295.00.

The reason that Sales increases by a credit is discussed in the previous chapter. The owner's capital account has a normal credit balance. Increases in the owner's capital account are shown as credits. Because revenue increases owner's equity, increases in revenue are recorded as credits. A revenue account, therefore, has a normal credit balance.

STEPS JOURNALIZING CASH RECEIVED FROM SALES

① **Date.** Write the date, *12*, in the Date column.

② **Debit.** Write the title of the account debited, *Cash*, in the Account Title column. Write the debit amount, *$295.00*, in the Debit column.

③ **Credit.** On the next line, indented about 1 centimeter, write the title of the account credited, *Sales*, in the Account Title column. Write the credit amount, *$295.00*, in the Credit column.

④ **Source document.** On the first line of this entry, write the source document number, *T12*, in the Doc. No. column.
   For this entry, the total debits, $295.00, equal the total credits, $295.00.

> **REMEMBER**
>
> Don't forget to record the source document in the Doc. No. column of the general journal.

68 Chapter 3   Recording Transactions in a General Journal

SOLD SERVICES ON ACCOUNT

August 12. Sold services on account to Oakdale School, $350.00. Sales Invoice No. 1.

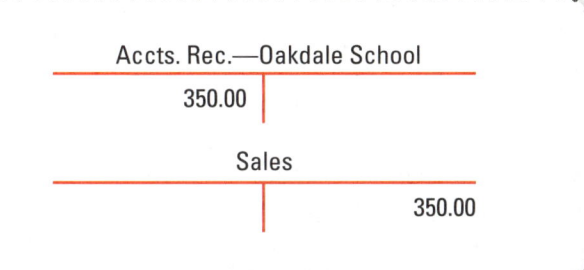

The source document for this transaction is Sales Invoice No. 1. [CONCEPT: Objective Evidence] The analysis of this transaction is shown in the T accounts.

The asset account, Accounts Receivable—Oakdale School, increases by a debit, $350.00. The revenue account, Sales, increases by a credit, $350.00.

STEPS — JOURNALIZING SERVICES SOLD ON ACCOUNT

1. **Date.** Write the date, *12*, in the Date column.

2. **Debit.** Write the title of the account debited, *Accounts Receivable—Oakdale School*, in the Account Title column. Write the debit amount, *$350.00*, in the Debit column.

3. **Credit.** On the next line, indented about 1 centimeter, write the title of the account credited, *Sales*, in the Account Title column. Write the credit amount, *$350.00*, in the Credit column.

4. **Source document.** Write the source document number, *S1*, in the Doc. No. column.

For this entry, the total debits, $350.00, equal the total credits, $350.00.

FOR YOUR INFORMATION — FYI

Accounting is not just for accountants. For example, a performing artist earns revenue from providing a service. Financial decisions must be made such as the cost of doing a performance, the percentage of revenue paid to a manager, travel expenses, and the cost of rehearsal space.

REMEMBER

In double-entry accounting, each transaction affects at least two accounts. At least one account will be debited and at least one account will be credited.

Journalizing Transactions That Affect Owner's Equity and Receiving Cash on Account — Lesson 3-3

PAID CASH FOR AN EXPENSE

August 12. Paid cash for rent, $300.00. Check No. 4.

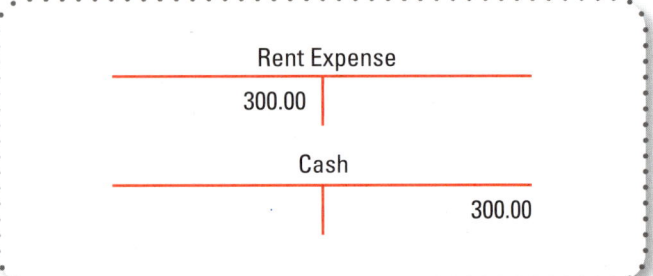

The source document for this transaction is Check No. 4. [CONCEPT: Objective Evidence] The analysis of this transaction is shown in the T accounts.

The expense account, Rent Expense, increases by a debit, $300.00. The asset account, Cash, decreases by a credit, $300.00.

The reason that Rent Expense is increased by a debit is discussed in the previous chapter. The owner's capital account has a normal credit balance. Decreases in the owner's capital account are shown as debits.

Because expenses decrease owner's equity, increases in expenses are recorded as debits. An expense account, therefore, has a normal debit balance.

Whenever cash is paid for an expense, the journal entry is similar to the entry discussed above. Therefore, the journal entry to record paying cash for utilities is also illustrated.

STEPS JOURNALIZING CASH PAID FOR AN EXPENSE

1. **Date.** Write the date, *12*, in the Date column.

2. **Debit.** Write the title of the account debited, *Rent Expense*, in the Account Title column. Write the debit amount, *$300.00*, in the Debit column.

3. **Credit.** On the next line, indented about 1 centimeter, write the title of the account credited, *Cash*, in the Account Title column. Write the credit amount, *$300.00*, in the Credit column.

4. **Source document.** Write the source document number, *C4*, in the Doc. No. column.

   For this entry, the total debits, $300.00, equal the total credits, $300.00.

FOR YOUR INFORMATION

FYI

Source documents can be critically important in tracking down errors. Businesses file their source documents so they can be referred to if it is necessary to verify information entered into the journals.

RECEIVED CASH ON ACCOUNT

August 18. Received cash on account from Oakdale School, $200.00. Receipt No. 2.

The source document for this transaction is Receipt No. 2. [CONCEPT: Objective Evidence] The analysis of this transaction is shown in the T accounts.

The asset account, Cash, increases by a debit, $200.00. The asset account, Accounts Receivable—Oakdale School, decreases by a credit, $200.00.

STEPS JOURNALIZING CASH RECEIVED ON ACCOUNT

1. **Date.** Write the date, *18*, in the Date column.

2. **Debit.** Write the title of the account debited, *Cash*, in the Account Title column. Write the debit amount, *$200.00*, in the Debit column.

3. **Credit.** On the next line, indented about 1 centimeter, write the title of the account credited, *Accounts Receivable—Oakdale School*, in the Account Title column. Write the credit amount, *$200.00*, in the Credit column.

4. **Source document.** Write the source document number, *R2*, in the Doc. No. column.
   For this entry, the total debits, $200.00, equal the total credits, $200.00.

> **REMEMBER**
>
> *Increases in expenses and in withdrawals decrease owner's equity. Decreases in owner's equity are recorded as debits. Therefore, increases in expenses and in withdrawals are recorded as debits.*

Journalizing Transactions That Affect Owner's Equity and Receiving Cash on Account — Lesson 3-3

PAID CASH TO OWNER FOR PERSONAL USE

August 18. Paid cash to owner for personal use, $125.00. Check No. 6.

The source document for this transaction is Check No. 6. [CONCEPT: Objective Evidence] The analysis of this transaction is shown in the T accounts.

The reason that Kim Park, Drawing increased by a debit is discussed in the previous chapter. Decreases in the owner's capital account are shown as debits. Because withdrawals decrease owner's equity, increases in withdrawals are recorded as debits. A withdrawal account, therefore, has a normal debit balance.

STEPS JOURNALIZING CASH PAID TO OWNER

 Date. Write the date, *18*, in the Date column.

 Debit. Write the title of the account debited, *Kim Park, Drawing*, in the Account Title column. Write the debit amount, *$125.00*, in the Debit column.

 Credit. On the next line, indented about 1 centimeter, write the title of the account credited, *Cash*, in the Account Title column. Write the credit amount, *$125.00*, in the Credit column.

 Source document. Write the source document number, *C6*, in the Doc. No. column.

For this entry, the total debits, $125.00, equal the total credits, $125.00.

PHOTODISC/GETTY IMAGES

End of Lesson REVIEW

AUDIT YOUR UNDERSTANDING

1. When cash is received from sales, which account is listed on the first line of the entry?
2. When cash is received from sales, which account is listed on the second line of the entry?
3. When services are sold on account, which account is listed on the second line of the entry?
4. When cash is paid for any reason, what abbreviation is used for the source document?
5. When cash is received on account, what abbreviation is used for the source document?

WORK TOGETHER 3-3

Journalizing transactions that affect owner's equity in a general journal

Use the chart of accounts and journal from Work Together 3-2. Your instructor will guide you through the following example.

Transactions:
Apr. 12. Paid cash for rent, $1,000.00. C4.
    13. Received cash from sales, $2,500.00. T13.
    14. Sold services on account to L. Rohe, $510.00. S1.
    19. Paid cash for electric bill, $148.00. C5.
    20. Received cash on account from L. Rohe, $255.00. R2.
    21. Paid cash to owner for personal use, $1,000.00. C6.

1. Journalize the transactions continuing on the next blank line of page 1 of the journal. Source documents are abbreviated as follows: check, C; receipt, R; sales invoice, S; calculator tape, T. Save your work to complete Work Together 3-4.

ON YOUR OWN 3-3

Journalizing transactions that affect owner's equity in a general journal

Use the chart of accounts and journal from On Your Own 3-2. Work this problem independently.

Transactions:
June 11. Paid cash for rent, $525.00. C4.
    12. Sold services on account to C. Lord, $700.00. S1.
    16. Received cash from sales, $2,300.00. T16.
    17. Paid cash for postage (Miscellaneous Expense), $37.00. C5.
    19. Received cash on account from C. Lord, $350.00. R2.
    20. Paid cash to owner for personal use, $850.00. C6.

1. Journalize the transactions continuing on the next blank line of page 1 of the journal. Source documents are abbreviated as follows: check, C; receipt, R; sales invoice, S; calculator tape, T. Save your work to complete On Your Own 3-4.

LESSON 3-4

Starting a New Journal Page

A COMPLETED JOURNAL PAGE

	GENERAL JOURNAL				PAGE 1	
DATE	ACCOUNT TITLE	DOC. NO.	POST. REF.	DEBIT	CREDIT	
20-- Aug. 1	Cash	R1		500000		1
	Kim Park, Capital				500000	2
3	Supplies	C1		27500		3
	Cash				27500	4
4	Prepaid Insurance	C2		120000		5
	Cash				120000	6
33 20	Supplies	M2		5000		33
34	Accounts Payable—Thomas Supply Co.				5000	34
35						35

A general journal page is complete when there is insufficient space to record any more entries. A partial view of TechKnow Consulting's completed page 1 of the general journal is shown.

TechKnow Consulting has one blank line remaining at the bottom of page 1. However, each journal entry requires at least two lines. If a journal entry is split between two different pages, the equality of debits and credits for the entry is not as easily verified. Also, to a person examining a single journal page, a split entry will appear incorrect.

Therefore, a journal entry should not be split and journalized on two different pages. If there is only one blank line remaining on a journal page, a new page is started.

PHOTODISC/GETTY IMAGES

SMALL BUSINESS SPOTLIGHT

Successful small business owners typically have the following characteristics: confidence to make decisions, determination to keep trying during hard times for the business, willingness to take risks, creativity to surpass the competition, and an inner need to achieve.

STARTING A NEW GENERAL JOURNAL PAGE

DATE	ACCOUNT TITLE	DOC. NO.	POST. REF.	DEBIT	CREDIT

GENERAL JOURNAL — PAGE 2

After one page of a general journal is filled, a new journal page is started. A new page is started by writing the page number in the space provided in the journal heading.

CULTURAL DIVERSITY

Professional Organizations

Professional organizations provide important social and economic benefits to their members. For example, the National Association of Black Accountants, Inc. (www.nabainc.org) is a professional organization. Members of this association are CPAs, accountants, and accounting students, as well as accounting professionals working in other business areas. The organizational purpose is to unite accountants and accounting students who have similar interests and ideals. Members must be committed to professional and academic excellence. They must possess a sense of professional and civic responsibility. They must also be concerned with enhancing opportunities for minorities in the accounting profession.

Activities of the National Association of Black Accountants, Inc. are diverse. They include free income tax preparation, student scholarships, high school and university career seminars, regional student conferences, and technical seminars and lectures. Other services of the organization include a speakers' bureau, a placement service, and publication of a journal and newsletter.

Critical Thinking

1. Professional interest groups for minorities often begin as a means of securing employment opportunities for their members. What other groups of accountants might benefit from having such an organization?

2. Search the website of the National Association of Black Accountants, Inc. and describe one of the programs available to student members.

Starting a New Journal Page — Lesson 3-4

STANDARD ACCOUNTING PRACTICES

	DATE	ACCOUNT TITLE	DOC. NO.	POST. REF.	DEBIT	CREDIT	
9	27	~~Miscellaneous Expense~~	~~C10~~		~~70 00~~		9
10		~~Cash~~				~~70 00~~	10
11	27	Utility Expense	C10		70 00		11
12		Cash				70 00	12
13	28	Supplies	C11		20 00		13
14		Cash				20 00	14
15	28	Cash	T28		1190 00		15
16		Sales				1190 00	16
17	31	Miscellaneous Expense	C12		20 00		17
18		Advertising			10 00		18
19		Cash				30 00	19
20							20
21							21
22							22

GENERAL JOURNAL — PAGE 14

In completing accounting work, TechKnow Consulting follows standard accounting practices. These practices include procedures for error corrections, abbreviating words, writing dollar and cents signs, and rulings.

1. Errors are corrected in a way that does not cause doubts about what the correct information is. If an error is recorded, cancel the error by neatly drawing a line through the incorrect item. Write the correct item immediately above the canceled item.
2. Sometimes an entire entry is incorrect and is discovered before the next entry is journalized. Draw neat lines through all parts of the incorrect entry. Journalize the entry correctly on the next blank lines.
3. Sometimes several correct entries are recorded after an incorrect entry is made. The next blank lines are several entries later. Draw neat lines through all incorrect parts of the entry. Record the correct items on the same lines as the incorrect items, directly above the canceled parts.
4. Words in accounting records are written in full when space permits. Words may be abbreviated only when space is limited. All items are written legibly.
5. Dollars and cents signs and decimal points are not used when writing amounts on ruled accounting paper. Sometimes a color tint or a heavy vertical rule is used on printed accounting paper to separate the dollars and cents columns.
6. Two zeros are written in the cents column when an amount is in even dollars, such as $500.00. If the cents column is left blank, doubts may arise later about the correct amount.
7. Neatness is very important in accounting records so that there is never any doubt about what information has been recorded. A ruler is used to draw lines.

End of Lesson REVIEW

AUDIT YOUR UNDERSTANDING

1. When is a general journal page complete?
2. If an entire entry is incorrect and is discovered before the next entry is journalized, how should the incorrect entry be corrected?
3. If several correct entries are recorded after an incorrect entry is made, how should the incorrect entry be corrected?

WORK TOGETHER 3-4

Journalizing transactions and starting a new general journal page

Use the general journal from Work Together 3-3. Your instructor will guide you through the following examples.

Transactions:
- Apr. 22. Paid cash for water bill (Utilities Expense), $205.00. C7.
- 23. Sold services on account to L. Rohe, $289.00. S2.
- 26. Received cash from sales, $1,670.00. T26.
- 27. Paid cash to owner for personal use, $650.00. C8.
- 27. Paid cash for supplies, $42.00. C9.
- 28. Paid cash for postage (Miscellaneous Expense), $53.00. C10.
- 29. Received cash on account from L. Rohe, $200.00. R3.
- 30. Received cash from sales, $544.00. T30.

1. Journalize the transactions for April 22 through 27. Source documents are abbreviated as follows: check, C; receipt, R; sales invoice, S; cash register tape, T.
2. Use page 2 of the journal to journalize the remaining transactions for April.

ON YOUR OWN 3-4

Journalizing transactions and starting a new general journal page

Use the general journal from On Your Own 3-3. Work this problem independently.

Transactions:
- June 23. Sold services on account to C. Lord, $255.00. S2.
- 24. Paid cash for advertising, $84.00. C7.
- 25. Received cash from sales, $950.00. T25.
- 26. Paid cash for delivery charges (Miscellaneous Expense), $25.00. C8.
- 26. Received cash on account from C. Lord, $150.00. R3.
- 27. Paid cash for postage (Miscellaneous Expense), $40.00. C9.
- 28. Paid cash for supplies, $42.00. C10.
- 30. Received cash from sales, $335.00. T30.

1. Journalize the transactions for June 23 through 26. Source documents are abbreviated as follows: check, C; receipt, R; sales invoice, S; cash register tape, T.
2. Use page 2 of the journal to journalize the remaining transactions for June.

Starting a New Journal Page

SUMMARY

After completing this chapter, you can:

1. Define accounting terms related to journalizing transactions.
2. Identify accounting concepts and practices related to journalizing transactions.
3. Record in a general journal transactions to set up a business.
4. Record in a general journal transactions to buy insurance for cash and supplies on account.
5. Record in a general journal transactions that affect owner's equity and receiving cash on account.
6. Start a new journal page.

EXPLORE ACCOUNTING

Prenumbered Documents

As one way to control the operations of the business, a company often will use prenumbered documents. Such a document is one that has the form number printed on it in advance. The most common example in everyday life is the personal check.

Businesses use several prenumbered documents. Examples include business checks, sales invoices, receipts, and memorandums.

The use of prenumbered documents allows a simple way to ensure that all documents are recorded. For example, when a business records the checks written during a period of time, all check numbers should be accounted for in numeric order. The person recording the checks must watch to see that no numbers are skipped. In this way, the business is more confident that all checks are recorded.

By using several types of prenumbered documents, the business helps ensure that all transactions are properly recorded.

Another way a business tries to control operations is through the use of batch totals. When many (sometimes hundreds) of documents are being recorded, the total amount can be used to help ensure that all documents are recorded.

For example, when sales invoices are recorded, the total of all the invoices is calculated prior to the invoices being recorded. Once all invoices are recorded, another total can be calculated. If the two totals are equal, it is assumed that all invoices have been recorded. If the totals do not equal, it may indicate that a document was skipped.

Research: With your instructor's permission, contact a local business and ask what prenumbered documents are used there. Determine how the business uses the documents to ensure that all documents are recorded properly.

3-1 APPLICATION PROBLEM

Journalizing transactions in a general journal

Dennis Gilbert owns a service business called D & G Company, which uses the following accounts.

Cash	Accts. Pay.—Scott Supplies	Miscellaneous Expense
Accts. Rec.—Covey Company	Dennis Gilbert, Capital	Rent Expense
Supplies	Dennis Gilbert, Drawing	Utilities Expense
Prepaid Insurance	Sales	

Transactions:

Feb. 1. Received cash from owner as an investment, $10,000.00. R1.
     4. Paid cash for supplies, $3,000.00. C1.

Instructions:

Journalize the transactions completed during February of the current year. Use page 1 of the journal given in the *Working Papers*. Source documents are abbreviated as follows: check, C; receipt, R. Save your work to complete Application Problem 3-2.

3-2 APPLICATION PROBLEM

Journalizing buying insurance, buying on account, and paying on account in a general journal

Use the chart of accounts and journal from Application Problem 3-1.

Transactions:

Feb. 6. Paid cash for insurance, $600.00. C2.
     7. Bought supplies on account from Scott Supplies, $2,000.00. M1.
     8. Paid cash on account to Scott Supplies, $1,000.00. C3.
    12. Paid cash on account to Scott Supplies, $1,000.00. C4.

Instructions:

Journalize the transactions. Source documents are abbreviated as follows: check, C; memorandum, M. Save your work to complete Application Problem 3-3.

Go Beyond the Book
For more information go to www.C21accounting.com

3-3 APPLICATION PROBLEM

Journalizing transactions that affect owner's equity in a general journal

Use the chart of accounts given in Application Problem 3-1 and the general journal from Application Problem 3-2.

Transactions:

Feb. 12. Paid cash for rent, $800.00. C5.
13. Received cash from sales, $500.00. T13.
14. Sold services on account to Covey Company, $450.00. S1.
15. Paid cash to owner for personal use, $2,800.00. C6.
18. Received cash from sales, $278.00. T18.
19. Paid cash for postage (Miscellaneous Expense), $64.00. C7.
21. Received cash on account from Covey Company, $250.00. R2.
22. Received cash from sales, $700.00. T22.
22. Paid cash for heating fuel bill, $329.00. C8.

Instructions:
Journalize the transactions. Source documents are abbreviated as follows: check, C; receipt, R; sales invoice, S; calculator tape, T. Save your work to complete Application Problem 3-4.

3-4 APPLICATION PROBLEM

Journalizing transactions and starting a new page of a general journal

Use the chart of accounts given in Application Problem 3-1 and the general journal from Application Problem 3-3.

Transactions:

Feb. 25. Received cash on account from Covey Company, $200.00. R3.
26. Paid cash for a delivery (Miscellaneous Expense), $25.00. C9.
26. Sold services on account to Covey Company, $800.00. S2.
26. Paid cash for supplies, $44.00. C10.
27. Paid cash for rent, $200.00. C11.
27. Paid cash for postage (Miscellaneous Expense), $37.00. C12.
28. Received cash from sales, $1,365.00. T28.
28. Paid cash to owner for personal use, $800.00. C13.

Instructions:

1. Journalize the transaction for February 25. Source documents are abbreviated as follows: check, C; receipt, R; sales invoice, S; calculator tape, T.
2. Use page 2 of the journal to journalize the rest of the transactions for February.

3-5 APPLICATION PROBLEM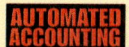

Journalizing transactions in a general journal

Hans Schultz owns a service business called YardCare, which uses the following accounts.

Cash
Accts. Rec.—Frank Morris
Supplies
Prepaid Insurance
Accts. Pay.—Midwest Supplies
Hans Schultz, Capital
Hans Schultz, Drawing
Sales
Advertising Expense
Utilities Expense

Transactions:

Apr. 1. Hans Schultz invested $2,500.00 of his own money in the business. Receipt No. 1.
3. Used business cash to purchase supplies costing $105.00. Wrote Check No. 1.
4. Wrote Check No. 2 for insurance, $240.00.
5. Purchased supplies for $75.00 over the phone from Midwest Supplies, promising to send the check next week. Memo. No. 1.
11. Sent Check No. 3 to Midwest Supplies, $75.00.
12. Sent a check for the electricity bill, $65.00. Check No. 4.
15. Wrote a $700.00 check to Mr. Schultz for personal use. Used Check No. 5.
16. Sold services for $358.00 to Frank Morris, who agreed to pay for them within 10 days. Sales Invoice No. 1.
17. Recorded cash sales of $1,287.00 from calculator tape T17.
18. Paid $90.00 for advertising. Wrote Check No. 6.
25. Received $358.00 from Frank Morris for the services performed last week. Wrote Receipt No. 2.

Instructions:
Journalize the transactions completed during April of the current year. Use page 1 of the journal given in the *Working Papers*. Record appropriate source document numbers.

3-6 MASTERY PROBLEM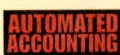

Journalizing transactions in a general journal

Jane Fernandez owns a service business called Jane's Car Wash, which uses the following accounts.

Cash	Accts. Pay.—Pine Supplies	Miscellaneous Expense
Accts. Rec.—Tony's Limos	Jane Fernandez, Capital	Rent Expense
Supplies	Jane Fernandez, Drawing	Repair Expense
Prepaid Insurance	Sales	Utilities Expense
Accts. Pay.—Atkin Supplies	Advertising Expense	

Transactions:

June 1. Received cash from owner as an investment, $16,000.00. R1.
 2. Paid cash for supplies, $300.00. C1.
 3. Paid cash for rent, $900.00. C2.
 4. Bought supplies on account from Atkin Supplies, $1,700.00. M1.
 5. Paid cash for electric bill, $146.00. C3.
 8. Paid cash on account to Atkin Supplies, $1,000.00. C4.
 8. Received cash from sales, $980.00. T8.
 8. Sold services on account to Tony's Limos, $450.00. S1.
 9. Paid cash for insurance, $1,200.00. C5.
 10. Paid cash for repairs, $388.00. C6.
 10. Received cash from sales, $476.00. T10.
 11. Paid cash for miscellaneous expense, $15.00. C7.
 11. Received cash from sales, $630.00. T11.
 12. Received cash from sales, $900.00. T12.
 15. Paid cash to owner for personal use, $400.00. C8.
 15. Received cash from sales, $850.00. T15.
 16. Paid cash for supplies, $1,100.00. C9.
 17. Received cash on account from Tony's Limos, $225.00. R2.
 17. Bought supplies on account from Pine Supplies, $600.00. M2.
 17. Received cash from sales, $500.00. T17.
 19. Received cash from sales, $650.00. T19.
 22. Bought supplies on account from Pine Supplies, $60.00. M3.
 22. Received cash from sales, $610.00. T22.
 23. Sold services on account to Tony's Limos, $582.00. S2.
 24. Paid cash for advertising, $125.00. C10.
 24. Received cash from sales, $300.00. T24.
 25. Received cash from sales, $770.00. T25.
 26. Paid cash for supplies, $90.00. C11.
 26. Received cash from sales, $300.00. T26.
 29. Received cash on account from Tony's Limos, $350.00. R3.
 30. Paid cash to owner for personal use, $450.00. C12.
 30. Received cash from sales, $500.00. T30.

Instructions:

1. The journals for Jane's Car Wash are given in the *Working Papers*. Use page 1 of the journal to journalize the transactions for June 1 through June 15. Source documents are abbreviated as follows: check, C; memorandum, M; receipt, R; sales invoice, S; calculator tape, T.

2. Use page 2 of the journal to journalize the transactions for the remainder of June.

3-7 CHALLENGE PROBLEM

Journalizing transactions using a variation of the general journal

Tony Wirth owns a service business called Wirth's Tailors, which uses the following accounts.

Cash	Accts. Pay.—Marker Supplies	Rent Expense
Accts. Rec.—Amy's Uniforms	Tony Wirth, Capital	Utilities Expense
Supplies	Tony Wirth, Drawing	
Prepaid Insurance	Sales	

Transactions:

June 1. Received cash from owner as an investment, $17,000.00. R1.
2. Paid cash for insurance, $3,000.00. C1.
3. Bought supplies on account from Marker Supplies, $2,500.00. M1.
4. Paid cash for supplies, $1,400.00. C2.
8. Paid cash on account to Marker Supplies, $1,300.00. C3.
9. Paid cash for rent, $800.00. C4.
12. Received cash from sales, $550.00. T12.
15. Sold services on account to Amy's Uniforms, $300.00. S1.
16. Paid cash for telephone bill, $70.00. C5.
22. Received cash on account from Amy's Uniforms, $300.00. R2.
25. Paid cash to owner for personal use, $900.00. C6.

Instructions:

The journal for Wirth's Tailors is given in the *Working Papers*. Wirth's Tailors uses a journal that is slightly different from the journal used in this chapter, as shown below. Use page 1 of the journal to journalize the transactions. Source documents are abbreviated as follows: check, C; memorandum, M; receipt, R; sales invoice, S; calculator tape, T.

General Journal

Page 1

Debit	Date	Account Title	Doc. No.	Post Ref.	Credit

APPLIED COMMUNICATION

Careful research about careers will help prepare you for making career choices. There are several U.S. government publications that provide detailed descriptions of many job titles. Two that are available in most public libraries are the *Dictionary of Occupational Titles (DOT)* and the *Occupational Outlook Handbook*.

Instructions: Go to the library and, using one of the two publications listed or any other appropriate resource, find the description for any accounting-related job. Record information you find, such as qualifications needed, job outlook, and earnings. Write one paragraph describing the pros and cons of working in such a job. Be sure to write a topic sentence and a conclusion.

CASES FOR CRITICAL THINKING

Case 1

During the summer, Willard Kelly does a variety of small jobs for many different people in the community to earn money. Mr. Kelly keeps all his money in a single checking account. He writes checks to pay for personal items and for business expenses. These payments include personal clothing, school supplies, gasoline for his car, and recreation. Mr. Kelly uses his check stubs as his accounting records. Are Mr. Kelly's accounting procedures and records correct? Explain your answer.

Case 2

Monica Zapata runs a personal shopper business. Her customers are busy professional men and women who call on Ms. Zapata to shop for personal items and gifts and even run personal errands such as taking clothing to the dry cleaner. Ms. Zapata always says she's too busy making money to keep records. Each day she accumulates receipts from purchases, checks and cash from customers, receipts for expenses such as fuel for her car, and her personal receipts. She puts all these items in a large box at the end of the day. At the end of the month, she sorts all these records, puts paper clips on similar items (such as all receipts for the month), and then files all the records until she has to do her income tax return in the spring. Ms. Zapata says it takes a long time to do her taxes because she doesn't remember what many of the pieces of paper represent. What change in business practices would you recommend to Ms. Zapata?

SCANS WORKPLACE COMPETENCY

Basic Skill: Writing

Concept: Employers frequently cite the ability to communicate as one of the most important skills they require in employees. When communicating thoughts, ideas, and information, it is important to be clear and concise so that the intended receiver of the communication understands the message.

Application: Proprietorships are the most common form of business organization in the United States with over 17 million proprietorships filing tax returns. Review the advantages and disadvantages of proprietorships in Chapter 1 and write a paragraph describing why you think proprietorships are the most common form of business organization.

USING SOURCE DOCUMENTS

Journalizing transactions

Cy Sawyer owns a service business called Cy's Repair Service, which uses the following accounts.

Cash	Accts. Pay.—Atlas Supplies	Miscellaneous Expense
Accts. Rec.—J. Hutton	Cy Sawyer, Capital	Rent Expense
Supplies	Cy Sawyer, Drawing	Utilities Expense
Prepaid Insurance	Sales	

Source documents related to the transactions for Cy's Repair Service for May are provided in the *Working Papers*.

Instructions

1. The general journal for Cy's Repair Service is given in the *Working Papers*. Use page 1 of the journal to journalize the transactions for May. Source documents are abbreviated as follows: check, C; memorandum, M; receipt, R; sales invoice, S; calculator tape, T.

ANALYZING BEST BUY'S FINANCIAL STATEMENTS

To calculate what percentage one amount is of another amount, you divide the smaller amount by the total that contains the amount. Using Best Buy as an example, Cash for 2007 = $1,205,000,000. Total assets for 2007 = $13,570,000,000. To calculate what percentage cash is of total assets, use the following formula: Cash, 1,205,000,000 ÷ total assets, 13,570,000,000. The answer is .0888, or 8.88%.

Instructions

1. Use the information on page B-5 in Appendix B. Find the amount of Receivables and Total Assets for Best Buy for 2006 and 2007. Calculate what percentage Receivables are of Total Assets for 2006 and 2007.
2. Did the percentage increase or decrease over this period of time?
3. If this percentage would increase rapidly, what could be happening?

Accounting SOFTWARE

TOOLBAR, MENUS, HELP, AND PROBLEM INSTRUCTIONS

Modern software usually has several features in common. These include a toolbar, menus, and a Help function. A toolbar is a set of icons or buttons that perform a single function, such as Open, Save, or Print. The kinds and number of toolbar buttons vary with the software. In addition to the toolbar buttons, there are menus that perform more detailed functions. Each menu item usually includes several options that display when the menu item is clicked. Different kinds of software have different kinds of menu options.

The Help menu provides information about how to perform different kinds of functions using the software. Experienced users of a particular kind of software rarely use the Help function. However, it can be very useful when you are starting out and need to look up how to do a particular task. There are often several different kinds of help available on the Help menu.

PEACHTREE ACTIVITY

1. Open (Restore) the data file for Mastery Problem 4-5 (filename: 04-5MP.ptb).
2. Click the Help menu. Note that several options are available. Click the different options to see what is available. Then, click Contents and Index and search for help on adding an account ("add account"). Write a brief description of the procedure.
3. Close the data file and exit the software.

TOOLBAR, MENUS, HELP, AND PROBLEM INSTRUCTIONS

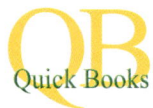

QuickBooks has toolbar, menu, and Help functions. A toolbar is a set of icons or buttons that perform a single function, such as Open, Save, or Print. The kinds and number of toolbar buttons vary with the software. In addition to the toolbar buttons, there are menus that perform more detailed functions. Each menu item usually includes several options that display when the menu item is clicked. Different kinds of software have different kinds of menu options.

The Help menu provides information about how to perform different kinds of functions using the software. Experienced users of a particular kind of software rarely use the Help function. However, it can be very useful when you are starting out and need to look up how to do a particular task. There are often several different kinds of help available on the Help menu.

QUICKBOOKS ACTIVITY

1. Open Mastery Problem 4-5 (filename: O'Kalla Lawn and Garden.qbw).
2. Click the Help menu. Note that several options are available. Click the different options to see what is available. Then, search for help on adding an account ("add account"). Write a brief description of the procedure.
3. Close the data file and exit the software.

BASIC SPREADSHEET TERMINOLOGY

A file containing an electronic spreadsheet is referred to as a *workbook*. A workbook can contain one or more work sheets, each containing the row and column cell structure in which text, numbers, and formulas are entered. A schedule or form created on a work sheet ready for data to be entered is referred to as a *template* or *data file*.

The Excel problem template files have at least two work sheets. One of the work sheets is labeled *Instructions*. The Instructions work sheet details the specific instructions for that problem. It is accessed by simply clicking the Instructions tab.

EXCEL ACTIVITY

1. Open the data file for Application Problem 5-2 (filename: F05-2.xls).
2. Click the Instructions tab and read the instructions for this problem. You will not complete this problem until Chapter 5.
3. Close the data file and exit the software.

HELP, PROBLEM INSTRUCTIONS, AND JOURNAL ENTRIES

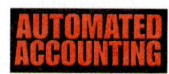

The *Automated Accounting* software has a Help menu with features similar to all other software. The software also has a function that displays instructions for specific problems. Click the Browser toolbar button. This opens the default browser and displays the specific step-by-step instructions for a problem. The instructions may be displayed at any time they are needed. However, it is usually easier to simply minimize the browser with the instructions displayed and then maximize the browser when an instruction is needed.

Just as in manual accounting, transactions are recorded in a journal. A 2-column general journal is used for all problems in Part 1. The journal is accessed by clicking the Journal toolbar button and the General Journal tab. You may move to the next entry field with the Tab key or position with the mouse.

Date: Key the date or increase or decrease it with the + or − keys.

Refer.: The source document number and identifying letter abbreviation are keyed in the Refer. column.

Account: You may key the account number, select the account by clicking the chart of accounts button, or key part of the account title.

Debit: Key the debit amount in the debit column. Use the Tab key to advance to the next line for an additional account title.

Credit: Key the credit amount in the credit column.

Post: After all parts of a transaction are entered, click the Post button or press Enter in the last field of the entry. This prepares the software for a new transaction.

AUTOMATED ACCOUNTING ACTIVITY

1. Open your Automated Accounting software.
2. Open the data file for Application Problem 3-5 (filename: F03-5.AA8).
3. Click the Help button, then click Help Contents and Index.
4. Search for Help on adding a new account.
5. Keep the data file open to complete Application Problem 3-5.

AUTOMATED ACCOUNTING APPLICATION PROBLEM 3-5

Open file F03-5.AA8 if it is not already open. Display the problem instructions and complete the problem.

AUTOMATED ACCOUNTING MASTERY PROBLEM 3-6

Open file F03-6.AA8. Display the problem instructions and complete the problem.

CHAPTER 4

Posting from a General Journal to a General Ledger

OBJECTIVES

After studying Chapter 4, you will be able to:

1. Define accounting terms related to posting from a general journal to a general ledger.
2. Identify accounting concepts and practices related to posting from a general journal to a general ledger.
3. Prepare a chart of accounts for a service business organized as a proprietorship.
4. Post amounts from a general journal to a general ledger.
5. Prove cash.
6. Analyze and journalize correcting entries.

KEY TERMS

- ledger
- general ledger
- account number
- file maintenance
- opening an account
- posting
- proving cash
- correcting entry

Point Your Browser
www.C21accounting.com

ACCOUNTING IN THE REAL WORLD

Amazon.com

Record Sales Volume at Amazon.com

Have you ever realized the day before a special occasion that you forgot to purchase a gift for someone? Have you ever thought of going online, purchasing a gift, and getting it delivered the very next day?

On December 24 of a recent year, more than 70,000 gift certificates were ordered on Amazon.com. These certificates were delivered, via e-mail, on December 25. Recently Amazon.com, headquartered in Seattle, experienced its busiest holiday season and set a single-day record for items ordered—averaging 24 items per second!

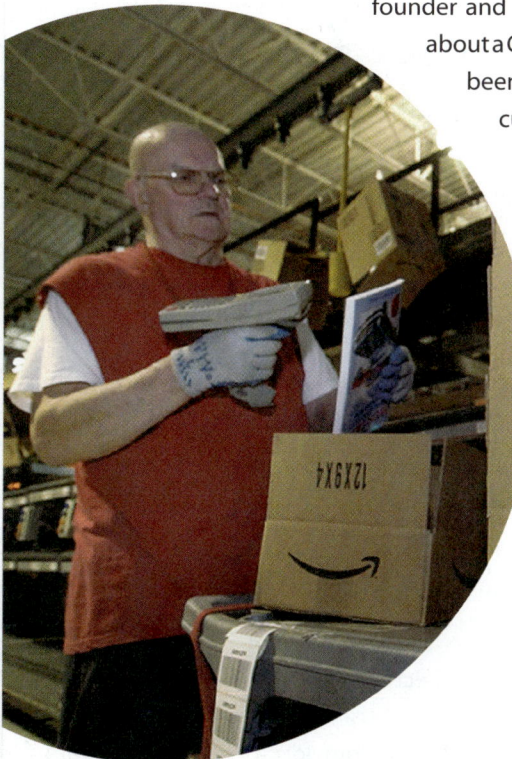

In a letter to stockholders, Jeffrey P. Bezos, the founder and CEO of Amazon.com, explained about a Customer Review feature that had been established. This feature allows customers to rate both products and vendors. Mr. Bezos noted that "negative reviews cost us some sales in the short run." Also, an Instant Order Update feature reminds customers that they have already ordered an item if they order the same item again. Mr. Bezos stated that this feature "slightly reduced sales."

Critical Thinking

1. If the Customer Review feature and the Instant Order Update feature both reduce sales, why would Amazon.com continue to make these features available to its customers?
2. What problems might occur when Amazon.com receives orders at the rate of 24 items per second?

Source: www.amazon.com and Letter to Shareholders in 2003 Annual Report

INTERNET ACTIVITY

Securities and Exchange Commission

Go to the homepage for the Securities and Exchange Commission (SEC) at www.sec.gov. The SEC was created through two Acts of Congress. Search the site to find out more about these two Acts. This information is usually found under the headings such as "About the SEC" and/or "What We Do."

Instructions

1. List the names of the two Acts of Congress that created the SEC.
2. Briefly summarize the purposes of these two Acts.

LESSON 4-1

Preparing a Chart of Accounts

ACCOUNT FORM

TechKnow Consulting records transactions in a general journal as described in Chapter 3. A journal is a permanent record of the debit and credit parts of each transaction with transactions recorded in chronological order. However, a journal does not show, in one place, all the changes in a single account.

If only a journal is used, a business must search through all journal pages to find items affecting a single account balance. For this reason, a form is used to summarize in one place all the changes to a single account. A separate form is used for each account.

CHARACTER COUNTS

Are Your Actions Legal?

"A man should be upright, not be kept upright." This famous statement by Marcus Aurelius suggests that, in a perfect world, everyone would always do the right thing. In the real world, however, governments have been forced to create complex systems of laws to force individuals to adhere to the social norm of right and wrong. We rely on these laws for our protection as well as the orderly operation of our society. For example, think about the chaos that might result if individuals could choose which side of the road to drive on! Many laws are common knowledge for individuals working in business:

- Employers may not discriminate on the basis of national origin.
- Customers may not be charged different prices for the same item.
- Taxes must be paid to the government.

Whether an action is legal is not always so obvious. Did you know:

- It may be illegal to sell certain items, such as computers and oil, to countries that violate global norms of conduct.
- An interviewer may not ask a prospective employee if he or she has children.
- Companies with more than $10 million in assets having more than 500 owners must file annual and other periodic reports with the government.

No one can be expected to know every law that might affect the operation of a business. To assist its managers, businesses hire lawyers to provide their managers with legal advice. Most large businesses have their own legal departments staffed with lawyers. Smaller businesses typically pay a retainer fee to an independent lawyer to provide legal advice when needed. All businesses should provide their managers with regular training on legal issues. Managers should be encouraged to consult the lawyers if there is any question whether an action might be illegal.

Instructions

Use an Internet or library source to prepare a list of questions that are illegal for an employer to ask during a job interview.

90   Chapter 4   Posting from a General Journal to a General Ledger

RELATIONSHIP OF A T ACCOUNT TO AN ACCOUNT FORM

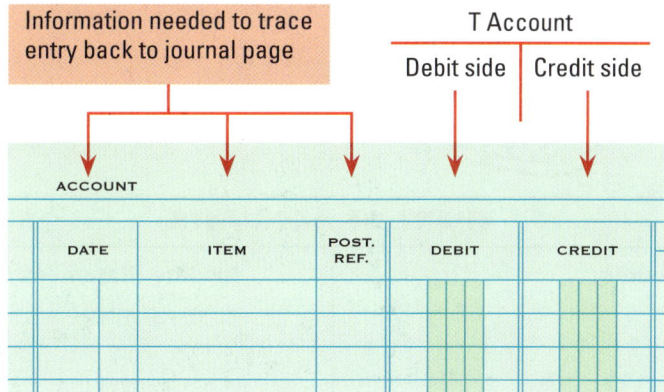

An account form is based on and includes the debit and credit sides of a T account. In addition to debit and credit columns, space is provided in the account form for recording the transaction date and journal page number. This information can be used to trace a specific entry back to where a transaction is recorded in a journal.

The major disadvantage of the account form shown is that no current, up-to-date account balance is shown. If this form is used, an up-to-date balance must be calculated each time the account is examined. When an account has a large number of entries, the balance is difficult and time consuming to calculate. Therefore, a more commonly used account form has Debit and Credit Balance columns as shown below.

Because the form has columns for the debit and credit balance, it is often referred to as the *balance-ruled account form*.

The account balance is calculated and recorded as each entry is recorded in the account. Recording information in an account is described later in this chapter. The T account is a useful device for analyzing transactions into debit and credit parts. However, the balance-ruled account form is more useful than the T account as a permanent record of changes to account balances. TechKnow Consulting uses the balance-ruled account form.

Preparing a Chart of Accounts   Lesson 4-1

CHART OF ACCOUNTS

TechKnow Consulting
7549 Broadway
Portland, OR 97202-2531

CHART OF ACCOUNTS

Balance Sheet Accounts

    (100) ASSETS
110 Cash
120 Petty Cash
130 Accounts Receivable—Oakdale School
140 Accounts Receivable—Campus Internet Cafe
150 Supplies
160 Prepaid Insurance

    (200) LIABILITIES
210 Accounts Payable—Supply Depot
220 Accounts Payable—Thomas Supply Co.

    (300) OWNER'S EQUITY
310 Kim Park, Capital
320 Kim Park, Drawing
330 Income Summary

Income Statement Accounts

    (400) REVENUE
410 Sales

    (500) EXPENSES
510 Advertising Expense
520 Insurance Expense
530 Miscellaneous Expense
540 Rent Expense
550 Supplies Expense
560 Utilities Expense

A group of accounts is called a **ledger**. A ledger that contains all accounts needed to prepare financial statements is called a **general ledger**. The name given to an account is known as an *account title*. The number assigned to an account is called an **account number**.

Preparing a Chart of Accounts

A list of account titles and numbers showing the location of each account in a ledger is known as a *chart of accounts*.

TechKnow Consulting's chart of accounts is shown above. For ease of use while studying the chapters in Part 1, TechKnow Consulting's chart of accounts is also shown on page 3.

Accounts in a general ledger are arranged in the same order as they appear on financial statements. TechKnow Consulting's chart of accounts shows five general ledger divisions: (1) Assets, (2) Liabilities, (3) Owner's Equity, (4) Revenue, and (5) Expenses.

ACCOUNT NUMBERS

    1   5   0   **Supplies**

General ledger division   Location within general ledger division

TechKnow Consulting assigns a three-digit account number to each account. For example, Supplies is assigned the number 150, as shown.

The first digit of each account number shows the general ledger division in which the account is located. For example, the asset division accounts are numbered in the 100s. Therefore, the number for the asset account, Supplies, begins with a 1.

The second two digits indicate the location of each account within a general ledger division. The 50 in the account number for Supplies indicates that the account is located between account number 140 and account number 160.

Assigning Account Numbers

TechKnow Consulting initially assigns account numbers by 10s so that new accounts can be added easily. Nine numbers are unused between each account on TechKnow Consulting's chart of accounts. For example, numbers 111 to 119 are unused between accounts numbered 110 and 120. New numbers can be assigned between existing account numbers without renumbering all existing accounts. The procedure for arranging accounts in a general ledger, assigning account numbers, and keeping records current is called **file maintenance**.

Unused account numbers are assigned to new accounts. TechKnow Consulting records payments for gasoline in Miscellaneous Expense. If Ms. Park found that the amount paid each month for gasoline had become a major expense, she might decide to use a separate account. The account might be titled Gasoline Expense. TechKnow Consulting arranges expense accounts in alphabetic order in its general ledger. Therefore, the new account would be inserted between Advertising Expense and Insurance Expense.

510	Advertising Expense	(Existing account)
	Gasoline Expense	**(New Account)**
520	Insurance Expense	(Existing account)

The number selected for the new account should leave some unused numbers on either side of it for other accounts that might need to be added. The middle, unused account number between existing numbers 510 and 520 is 515. Therefore, 515 is assigned as the account number for the new account.

510	Advertising Expense	(Existing account)
515	**Gasoline Expense**	**(New Account)**
520	Insurance Expense	(Existing account)

When an account is no longer needed, it is removed from the general ledger and the chart of accounts. For example, if TechKnow Consulting were to buy its own equipment and building, there would be no need for the rent expense account. The account numbered 540 would be removed, and that number would become unused and available to assign to another account if the need should arise.

When a new account is added at the end of a ledger division, the next number in a sequence of 10s is used. For example, suppose TechKnow Consulting needs to add another expense account, Water Expense, to show more detail about one of the utility expenses. The expense accounts are arranged in alphabetic order. Therefore, the new account would be added at the end of the expense section of the chart of accounts. The last used expense account number is 560, as shown on the chart of accounts. The next number in the sequence of 10s is 570, which is assigned as the number of the new account.

550	Supplies Expense	(Existing account)
560	Utilities Expense	(Existing account)
570	**Water Expense**	**(New Account)**

TechKnow Consulting has relatively few accounts in its general ledger and does not anticipate adding many new accounts in the future. Therefore, a three-digit account number adequately provides for the few account numbers that might be added. However, as the number of general ledger accounts increases, a business may change to four or more digits.

Charts of accounts with more than three digits are described in later chapters.

PHOTODISC/GETTY IMAGES

OPENING AN ACCOUNT IN A GENERAL LEDGER

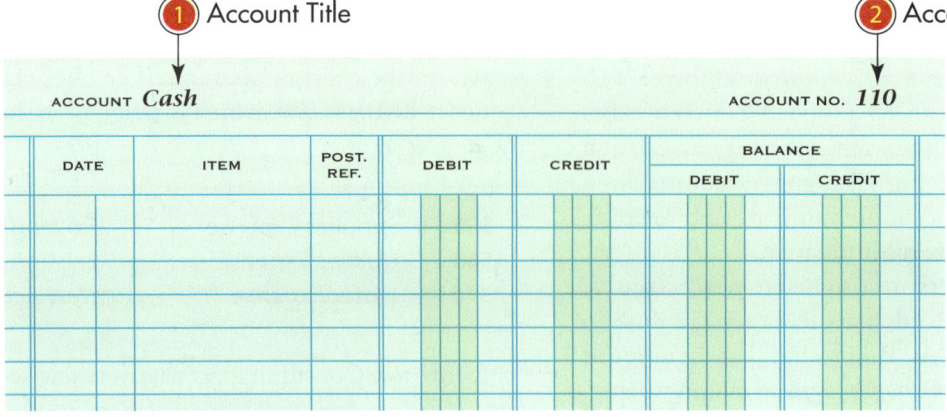

Writing an account title and number on the heading of an account is called **opening an account**. A general ledger account is opened for each account listed on a chart of accounts. Accounts are opened and arranged in a general ledger in the same order as on the chart of accounts.

Cash, account number 110, is the first account on TechKnow Consulting's chart of accounts. The cash account is opened using the steps shown below. The same procedure is used to open all accounts listed on TechKnow Consulting's chart of accounts.

STEPS OPENING AN ACCOUNT IN A GENERAL LEDGER

1. Write the account title, *Cash*, after the word *Account* in the heading.
2. Write the account number, *110*, after the words *Account No.* in the heading.

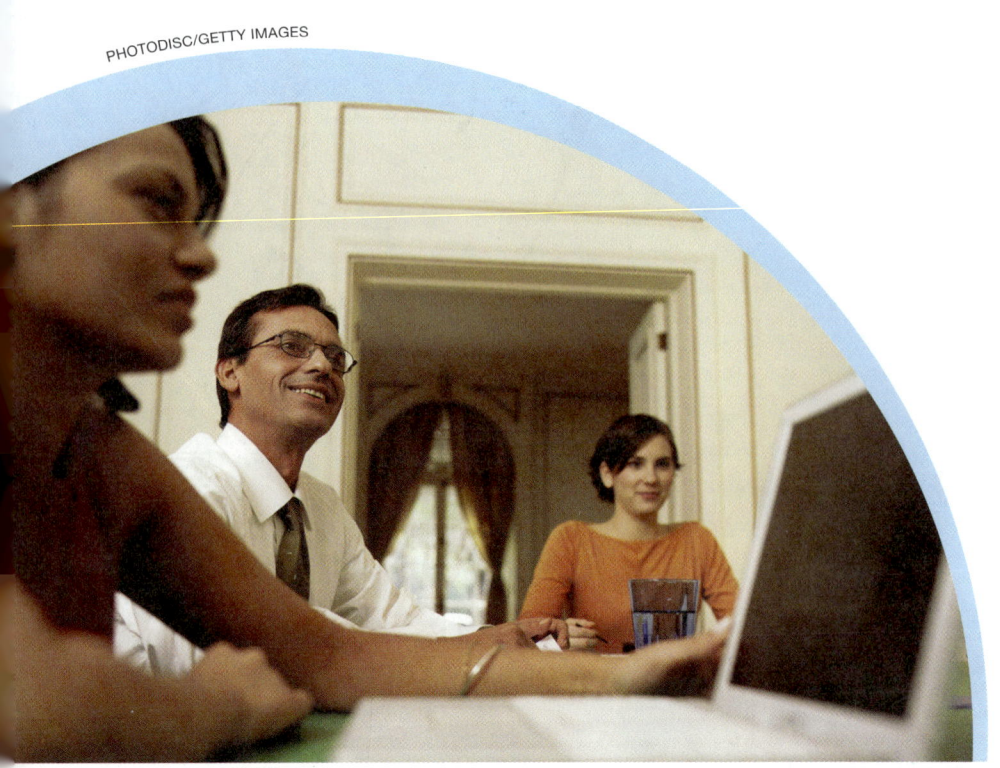

PHOTODISC/GETTY IMAGES

End of Lesson REVIEW

TERMS REVIEW

ledger
general ledger
account number
file maintenance
opening an account

AUDIT YOUR UNDERSTANDING

1. Describe the two parts of an account number.
2. List the two steps for opening an account.

WORK TOGETHER 4-1

Preparing a chart of accounts and opening an account

Forms are given in the *Working Papers*. Your instructor will guide you through the following examples.

Clara Ross owns a service business called Ross Company, which uses these accounts.

Accts. Pay.—Sherer Supplies	Miscellaneous Expense	Cash	Automobile Expense
Accts. Rec.—Tyler Link	Insurance Expense	Sales	Clara Ross, Capital
Accts. Pay.—Mid City Supplies	Prepaid Insurance	Supplies	Rent Expense
Accts. Rec.—Megan Alvarez	Clara Ross, Drawing	Supplies Expense	

1. Prepare a chart of accounts. Arrange expense accounts in alphabetical order. Use 3-digit account numbers and number the accounts within a division by 10s.
2. Two new accounts, Postage Expense and Utilities Expense, are to be added to the chart of accounts prepared in Instruction 1. Assign account numbers to the two new accounts.
3. Using the account form in the *Working Papers*, open Cash.

ON YOUR OWN 4-1

Preparing a chart of accounts and opening an account

Forms are given in the *Working Papers*. Work this problem independently.

Eric Roen owns a service business called Roen's Hair Care, which uses these accounts.

Accts. Pay.—Milton Company	Supplies Expense	Cash	Delivery Expense
Accts. Rec.—Superior Supplies	Insurance Expense	Sales	Accts. Pay.—North Star
Accts. Rec.—M. Faller	Prepaid Insurance	Telephone Expense	Supplies
Eric Roen, Drawing	Eric Roen, Capital		

1. Prepare a chart of accounts. Arrange expense accounts in alphabetical order. Use 3-digit account numbers and number the accounts within a division by 10s.
2. Two new accounts, Gasoline Expense and Water Expense, are to be added to the chart of accounts prepared in Instruction 1. Assign account numbers to the two new accounts.
3. Using the account form in the *Working Papers*, open Delivery Expense.

Preparing a Chart of Accounts

LESSON 4-2

Posting from a General Journal to a General Ledger

POSTING AN AMOUNT FROM THE DEBIT COLUMN OF A GENERAL JOURNAL

Transferring information from a journal entry to a ledger account is called **posting**. Posting sorts journal entries so that all debits and credits affecting each account are brought together in one place. For example, all changes to Cash are brought together in the cash account.

Each amount in the Debit and Credit columns of a general journal is posted to the account written in the Account Title column.

The numbers in the Post. Ref. columns of the general ledger account and the general journal serve three purposes: (1) An entry in an account can be traced to its source in a journal. (2) An entry in a journal can be traced to where it was posted in an account. (3) If posting is interrupted, the accounting personnel can easily see which entries in the general journal still need to be posted. A blank in the Post. Ref. column of the journal indicates that posting for that line still needs to be completed. Therefore, the posting reference is always recorded in the journal as the last step in the posting procedure.

STEPS — POSTING AN AMOUNT FROM A DEBIT COLUMN OF A GENERAL JOURNAL

1. Write the date, 20--, Aug. 1, in the Date column of the account, *Cash*.

2. Write the journal page number, *G1*, in the Post. Ref. column of the account. The letter *G* is an abbreviation for the general journal. *Post. Ref.* is an abbreviation for Posting Reference.

3. Write the debit amount, *$5,000.00*, in the Debit amount column of the account.

4. Write the new account balance, *$5,000.00*, in the Balance Debit column. Because this entry is the first in the Cash account, the previous balance is zero. The new account balance is calculated as shown.

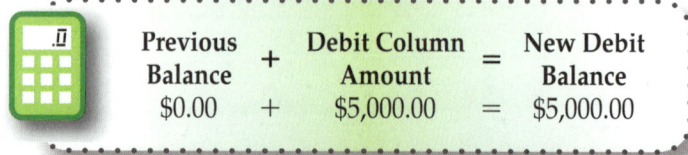

Previous Balance + Debit Column Amount = New Debit Balance
$0.00 + $5,000.00 = $5,000.00

5. Return to the journal and write the account number, *110*, in the Post. Ref. column of the journal.

POSTING AN AMOUNT FROM THE CREDIT COLUMN OF A GENERAL JOURNAL

As stated previously, each amount in the Debit and Credit columns of a general journal is posted to the account written in the Account Title column. The five steps used to post an amount from the Credit column are described below.

STEPS — POSTING AN AMOUNT FROM THE CREDIT COLUMN OF A GENERAL JOURNAL

1. Write the date, *20--, Aug. 1*, in the Date column of the account, *Kim Park, Capital*.
2. Write the journal page number, *G1*, in the Post. Ref. column of the account.
3. Write the credit amount, *$5,000.00*, in the Credit amount column of the account.
4. Write the new account balance, *$5,000.00*, in the Balance Credit column. Because this entry is the first in the capital account, the previous balance is zero. The new account balance is calculated as shown.
5. Return to the journal and write the account number, *310*, in the Post. Ref. column of the journal.

Previous Balance	+	Credit Column Amount	=	New Credit Balance
$0.00	+	$5,000.00	=	$5,000.00

Posting from a General Journal to a General Ledger • Lesson 4-2

POSTING A DEBIT AMOUNT TO AN ACCOUNT WITH A BALANCE

Only the first set of five steps is shown in the illustration. The second set of five steps is similar to the first set of steps and is described on page 99.

STEPS — POSTING A DEBIT AMOUNT TO AN ACCOUNT WITH A DEBIT BALANCE

1. Write the date, *7*, in the Date column of the account. The month and the year are written only once on a page of a ledger account unless the month or year changes.

2. Write the journal page number, *G1*, in the Post. Ref. column of the account.

3. Write the debit amount, *$500.00*, in the Debit amount column of the account.

 Previous Balance + Debit Column Amount = New Debit Balance
$275.00 + $500.00 = $775.00

4. Write the new balance, *$775.00*, in the Balance Debit column. When both the previous balance and a newly posted amount are debits, the new balance is a debit.

5. Return to the journal and write the account number, *150*, in the Post. Ref. column of the journal.

98   Chapter 4   Posting from a General Journal to a General Ledger

STEPS: POSTING A DEBIT AMOUNT TO AN ACCOUNT WITH A CREDIT BALANCE

1. Write the date, *11*, in the Date column of the account.
2. Write the journal page number, *G1*, in the Post. Ref. column of the account.
3. Write the debit amount, *$300.00*, in the Debit amount column of the account.
4. Write the new balance, *$200.00*, in the Balance Credit column. Whenever the credits in an account exceed the debits, the balance is a credit. Whenever the debits in an account exceed the credits, the balance is a debit.

> Previous Balance − Debit Column Amount = New Credit Balance
> $500.00 − $300.00 = $200.00

5. Return to the journal and write the account number, *210*, in the Post. Ref. column of the journal.

CULTURAL DIVERSITY

Accounting in Ancient Civilizations

In the ancient civilizations of Asia Minor and northern Africa, most citizens were illiterate. The scribe, who could read and write, became a very important person in the society. Of ancient Hebrew origin, the scribe has been called the forerunner of today's accountant.

Public scribes often recorded transactions as citizens arrived to do business. Most scribes recorded transactions on moist clay tablets that were then dried in the sun. Therefore, permanent records of transactions were not possible until scribes could write them down on clay tablets.

The Greeks invented coined money around 630 B.C., which facilitated assigning values to transactions.

The Babylonians in Asia Minor used an early form of banking. They transferred funds with a system resembling our modern-day checking accounts. This is believed to be one of the first uses of business documents.

These early practices provided the foundation for today's financial system and recordkeeping methods.

Critical Thinking

1. Estimate how many transactions might occur in a single day in a modern grocery store with which you are familiar.
2. List the number of different methods of payments that are accepted by modern grocery stores.

JOURNAL PAGE WITH POSTING COMPLETED

GENERAL JOURNAL PAGE 1

	DATE	ACCOUNT TITLE	DOC. NO.	POST. REF.	DEBIT	CREDIT	
1	20-- Aug. 1	Cash	R1	110	500000		1
2		Kim Park, Capital		310		500000	2
3	3	Supplies	C1	150	27500		3
4		Cash		110		27500	4
5	4	Prepaid Insurance	C2	160	120000		5
6		Cash		110		120000	6
7	7	Supplies	M1	150	50000		7
8		Accounts Payable—Supply Depot		210		50000	8
9	11	Accounts Payable—Supply Depot	C3	210	30000		9
10		Cash		110		30000	10
11	12	Cash	T12	110	29500		11
12		Sales		410		29500	12
13	12	Accounts Receivable—Oakdale School	S1	130	35000		13
14		Sales		410		35000	14
15	12	Rent Expense	C4	540	30000		15
16		Cash		110		30000	16
17	12	Utilities Expense	C5	560	4000		17
18		Cash		110		4000	18
19	13	Accounts Receivable—Campus Internet Cafe	R3	140	10000		19
20		Sales		410		10000	20
21	14	Advertising Expense	C7	510	7800		21
22		Cash		110		7800	22
23	14	Cash	T14	110	44500		23
24		Sales		410		44500	24
25	17	Petty Cash	C8	120	10000		25
26		Cash		110		10000	26
27	18	Cash	R2	110	20000		27
28		Accounts Receivable—Oakdale School		130		20000	28
29	18	Kim Park, Drawing	C6	320	12500		29
30		Cash		110		12500	30
31	18	Advertising Expense	C9	510	12500		31
32		Cash		110		12500	32
33	20	Supplies	M2	150	5000		33
34		Accounts Payable—Thomas Supply Co.		220		5000	34
35							35

Page 1 of TechKnow Consulting's August general journal, after all posting has been completed, is shown above. Notice that the Post. Ref. column is completely filled in with account numbers.

REMEMBER

Posting will go smoothly if you consistently follow the five steps of posting. The last step in posting is to put the account number in the Post. Ref. column of the general journal.

End of Lesson REVIEW

AUDIT YOUR UNDERSTANDING

TERM REVIEW

posting

1. List the five steps of posting from the general journal to the general ledger.
2. When both debit and credit amounts have been posted to an account, what determines whether the balance is a debit or a credit?

WORK TOGETHER 4-2

Posting to a general ledger

A completed journal and general ledger accounts are given in the *Working Papers*. Your instructor will guide you through the following example.

Leonard Witkowski owns a service business that uses the following accounts.

Assets
110 Cash
120 Accounts Receivable—Danielle Braastad
130 Supplies
140 Prepaid Insurance

Liabilities
210 Accounts Payable—Joshua's Supplies

Owner's Equity
310 Leonard Witkowski, Capital
320 Leonard Witkowski, Drawing

Revenue
410 Sales

Expenses
510 Rent Expense

1. Post all the entries in the general journal.

ON YOUR OWN 4-2

Posting to a general ledger

A completed journal and general ledger accounts are given in the *Working Papers*. Work this problem independently.

Heather Hasley owns a service business that uses the following accounts.

Assets
110 Cash
120 Accounts Receivable—Ken Garlie
130 Supplies
140 Prepaid Insurance

Liabilities
210 Accounts Payable—Bodden Company

Owner's Equity
310 Heather Hasley, Capital
320 Heather Hasley, Drawing

Revenue
410 Sales

Expenses
510 Advertising Expense

1. Post all the entries in the general journal.

LESSON 4-3
Completed General Ledger, Proving Cash, and Making Correcting Entries

GENERAL LEDGER WITH POSTING COMPLETED

ACCOUNT Cash **ACCOUNT NO.** 110

DATE	ITEM	POST. REF.	DEBIT	CREDIT	BALANCE DEBIT	BALANCE CREDIT
Aug. 1		G1	5000 00		5000 00	
3		G1		275 00	4725 00	
4		G1		1200 00	3525 00	
11		G1		300 00	3225 00	
12		G1	295 00		3520 00	
12		G1		300 00	3220 00	
12		G1		40 00	3180 00	
14		G1		78 00	3102 00	
14		G1	445 00		3547 00	
18		G1	200 00		3747 00	
18		G1		125 00	3622 00	
18		G1		125 00	3497 00	
19		G1		100 00	3397 00	
21		G2	995 00		4392 00	
27		G2		70 00	4322 00	
28		G2		200 00	4122 00	
28		G2	1190 00		5312 00	
31		G2		30 00	5282 00	
31		G2		500 00	4782 00	
31		G2	190 00		4972 00	
31		G2		8 00	4964 00	

ACCOUNT Petty Cash **ACCOUNT NO.** 120

DATE	ITEM	POST. REF.	DEBIT	CREDIT	BALANCE DEBIT	BALANCE CREDIT
Aug. 19		G1	100 00		100 00	

TechKnow Consulting's general ledger, after all posting from the August journal is completed, is shown here and on the next several pages.

The use of the accounts Income Summary, Insurance Expense, and Supplies Expense is described in Chapter 6.

A General Ledger after Posting Has Been Completed (continued)

A General Ledger after Posting Has Been Completed (continued)

A General Ledger after Posting Has Been Completed (concluded)

Completed General Ledger, Proving Cash, and Making Correcting Entries Lesson 4-3

PROVING CASH

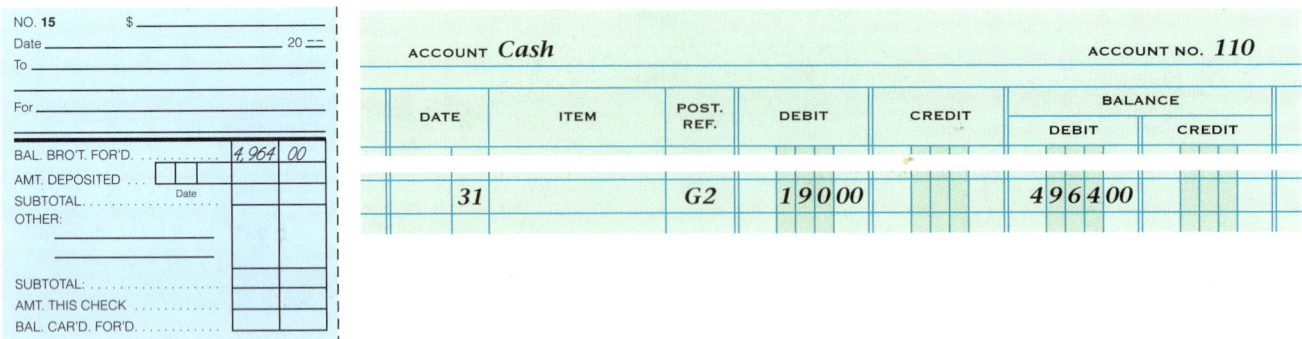

Determining that the amount of cash agrees with the balance of the cash account in the accounting records is called **proving cash**. Cash can be proved at any time TechKnow Consulting wishes to verify the accuracy of the cash records. However, TechKnow Consulting always proves cash at the end of a month. To prove cash, TechKnow Consulting compares the cash balance as shown in the checkbook with the cash balance in the cash account. If the two balances equal, cash is proved.

MEMORANDUM FOR A CORRECTING ENTRY

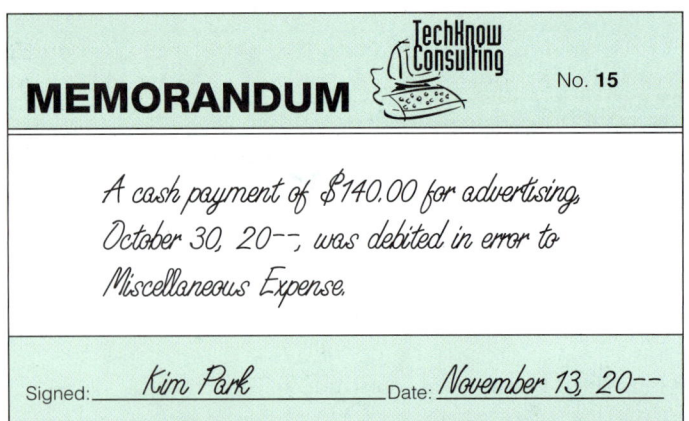

Errors can be made even though care is taken in recording transactions. Simple errors discovered before entries are posted may be corrected by ruling through the item, as described in Chapter 3. However, a transaction may have been improperly journalized and posted to the ledger. When an error in a journal entry has already been posted, the incorrect journal entry should be corrected with an additional journal entry. A journal entry made to correct an error in the ledger is called a **correcting entry**.

If an accounting error is discovered, a memorandum is prepared describing the correction to be made. The source document for a correcting entry is the memorandum.

JOURNAL ENTRY TO RECORD A CORRECTING ENTRY

November 13. Discovered that a payment of cash for advertising in October was journalized and posted in error as a debit to Miscellaneous Expense instead of Advertising Expense, $140.00. Memorandum No. 15.

Advertising Expense
140.00 |

Miscellaneous Expense
| 140.00

To correct the error, an entry is made to add $140.00 to the advertising expense account. The entry must also deduct $140.00 from the miscellaneous expense account. The correcting entry increases the advertising expense account balance and decreases the miscellaneous expense account balance.

Because the advertising expense account has a normal debit balance, Advertising Expense is debited for $140.00 to show the increase in this expense account. The miscellaneous expense account also has a normal debit balance. Therefore, Miscellaneous Expense is credited for $140.00 to show the decrease in this expense account.

The same four steps are followed when making a correcting entry as when making any journal entry.

STEPS JOURNALIZING A CORRECTING ENTRY

1. **Date.** Write the date, *13*, in the Date column.

2. **Debit.** Write the title of the account debited, *Advertising Expense*, in the Account Title column. Write the debit amount, *$140.00*, in the Debit column.

3. **Credit.** On the next line, indented about 1 centimeter, write the title of the account credited, *Miscellaneous Expense*, in the Account Title column. Write the credit amount, $140.00, in the Credit column.

4. **Source document.** On the first line of this entry, write the source document number, M15, in the Doc. No. column.

> **REMEMBER**
>
> Two zeroes are written in the cents column when an amount is in even dollars, such as $500.00. If the cents column is left blank, doubts may arise later about the correct amount.

Completed General Ledger, Proving Cash, and Making Correcting Entries

End of Lesson REVIEW

AUDIT YOUR UNDERSTANDING

1. Which two amounts are compared when proving cash?
2. What is a correcting entry?
3. When an amount is journalized and posted to an incorrect expense account, why is the amount of the correcting entry debited to the correct expense account?
4. When an amount is journalized and posted to an incorrect expense account, why is the amount of the correcting entry credited to the incorrect expense account?

TERMS REVIEW

proving cash
correcting entry

WORK TOGETHER 4-3

Journalizing correcting entries

A general journal is given in the *Working Papers*. Your instructor will guide you through the following example.

Transactions:
Nov. 1. Discovered that a transaction for supplies bought last month was journalized and posted in error as a debit to Prepaid Insurance instead of Supplies, $60.00. M15.
  1. Discovered that a transaction for rent expense for last month was journalized and posted in error as a debit to Repair Expense instead of Rent Expense, $550.00. M16.

1. Journalize each correcting entry discovered during November of the current year. Use page 21 of the general journal.

ON YOUR OWN 4-3

Journalizing correcting entries

A general journal is given in the *Working Papers*. Work this problem independently.

Transactions:
June 1. Discovered that a transaction for supplies bought last month was journalized and posted in error as a debit to Prepaid Insurance instead of Supplies, $150.00. M23.
  1. Discovered that a transaction for utilities expense for last month was journalized and posted in error as a debit to Miscellaneous Expense instead of Utilities Expense, $850.00. M24.

1. Journalize each correcting entry discovered during June of the current year. Use page 11 of the general journal.

SUMMARY

After completing this chapter, you can:

1. Define accounting terms related to posting from a general journal to a general ledger.
2. Identify accounting concepts and practices related to posting from a general journal to a general ledger.
3. Prepare a chart of accounts for a service business organized as a proprietorship.
4. Post amounts from a general journal to a general ledger.
5. Prove cash.
6. Analyze and journalize correcting entries.

EXPLORE ACCOUNTING

Chart of Accounts

Each company designs its chart of accounts to meet the needs of that company. TechKnow Consulting, the company described in this section of the textbook, has a relatively simple chart of accounts, with a small number of accounts. Therefore, TechKnow Consulting can use a three-digit account number for each account. A company with more accounts may need to use a four- or five-digit account number for each account. The numbering system used by the company should ensure that each account can be assigned a unique number.

When setting up a chart of accounts, a company does not have to use a straight series of numbers. If a company has several departments, it may choose to use account numbers such as 12-150. The first two digits (12) can be used to designate a specific department. The last three digits (150) identify a unique account within that department. If this company has many departments or many accounts within each department, it may have to increase the number of digits in the account, such as 123-4567.

A large corporation made up of smaller companies may have one chart of accounts for the entire corporation. If the managers of the corporation also want to be able to separate out the accounts for each company, they may choose to set up the account numbers in an xx-yyy-zzzz format. The first two digits (xx) would be a unique number for each company, the second set of numbers (yyy) refer to a department number, and the third set of numbers (zzzz) is a unique account.

Another example would be a company that manufactures goods for its customers. Such a company may want to include the job order number in each account number, so that it can easily trace the cost of each job.

As you can see, there is an infinite number of possible systems that can be followed when assigning account numbers. A company should consider future growth when first setting up a system so that it can avoid having to renumber accounts at a later date.

Group Activity: Develop a chart of accounts for an imaginary business. Write a detailed description of the company and a rationale for the account numbering system you have developed.

4-1 APPLICATION PROBLEM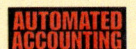

Preparing a chart of accounts and opening an account

Lillian Deters owns a service business called Deters Duplicating, which uses the following accounts.

Accounts Receivable—Teegan Walters	Lillian Deters, Capital	Postage Expense	Supplies
Accounts Receivable—Austin Kirnyczuk	Lillian Deters, Drawing	Charitable Expense	Sales
Accounts Payable—Dakota Company	Prepaid Insurance	Rent Expense	Cash
Accounts Payable—Falls Supply	Advertising Expense		

Instructions:

1. Prepare a chart of accounts similar to the one described in this chapter. Arrange expense accounts in alphabetical order. Use 3-digit account numbers and number the accounts within a division by 10s.
2. Two new accounts, Delivery Expense and Telephone Expense, are to be added to the chart of accounts prepared in Instruction 1. Assign account numbers to the two new accounts.
3. Using the forms in the *Working Papers*, open the Prepaid Insurance and the Postage Expense accounts.

4-2 APPLICATION PROBLEM

Posting to a general ledger

A completed general journal and general ledger accounts are given in the *Working Papers*. Alta Komoko owns a service business that uses the following accounts.

Assets
110 Cash
120 Accounts Receivable—Melanie Ford
130 Supplies
140 Prepaid Insurance

Liabilities
210 Accounts Payable—Bay Bridge Supply

Owner's Equity
310 Alta Komoko, Capital
320 Alta Komoko, Drawing

Revenue
410 Sales

Expenses
510 Advertising Expense

Instructions:

1. Post all entries in the general journal.
2. Prove cash. The balance on the next unused check stub is $1,647.00.

4-3 APPLICATION PROBLEM

Journalizing correcting entries

The following errors were discovered after the incorrect entries were already journalized and posted.

Transactions:

Apr. 1. Discovered that a transaction for utilities expense was journalized and posted in error as a debit to Repairs Expense instead of Utilities Expense, $265.00. M66.
5. Discovered that a cash investment by Manuel Ricardo, owner, was journalized and posted in error as a credit to Sales instead of Manuel Ricardo, Capital, $600.00. M67.
8. Discovered that a check received on account was journalized and posted in error as a credit to Accounts Receivable—Carol Jussila instead of Accounts Receivable—Cindy Joelson, $278.00. M68.

Instructions:
Journalize each correcting entry discovered during April of the current year. Use page 3 of a general journal given in the *Working Papers*.

4-4 MASTERY PROBLEM

Journalizing transactions and posting to a general ledger

Patrick O'Kalla owns a service business called O'Kalla Lawn and Garden. O'Kalla Lawn and Garden's general ledger accounts are given in the *Working Papers*.

Transactions:

Nov. 1. Received cash from owner as an investment, $5,500.00. R1.
3. Paid cash for supplies, $400.00. C1.
5. Received cash from sales, $900.00. T5.
6. Sold services on account to Merilda Domingo, $280.00. S1.
9. Paid cash for rent, $600.00. C2.
11. Paid cash for miscellaneous expense, $50.00. C3.
13. Bought supplies on account from Park Supplies, $240.00. M1.
13. Received cash from sales, $430.00. T13.
16. Paid cash for advertising, $143.00. C4.
18. Paid cash on account to Park Supplies, $140.00. C5.
20. Paid cash for electric bill, $230.00. C6.
20. Received cash on account from Merilda Domingo, $150.00. R2.
25. Paid cash for supplies, $150.00. C7.
27. Paid cash for supplies, $80.00. C8.
27. Received cash from sales, $2,100.00. T27.
30. Paid cash to owner for personal use, $500.00. C9.
30. Received cash from sales, $110.00. T30.

Instructions:

1. Open an account for Utilities Expense. Use the 3-digit numbering system described in the chapter.
2. Journalize the transactions completed during November of the current year. Use page 1 of a general journal. Source documents are abbreviated as follows: check, C; memorandum, M; receipt, R; sales invoice, S; calculator tape, T.
3. Post from the general journal to the general ledger.
4. Prove cash. The balance on the next unused check stub is $6,897.00.

4-5 CHALLENGE PROBLEM

Posting using a variation of the general journal

Frances Fessler owns a service business called HouseCare. HouseCare uses a general journal that is different from the general journal used in this chapter. HouseCare's March general journal and general ledger accounts (before posting) are given in the *Working Papers*.

Instructions:

1. Post from the general journal to the general ledger.
2. Prove cash. The balance on the next unused check stub is $3,575.00.

APPLIED COMMUNICATION

A fax machine allows a business to send documents anywhere in a matter of minutes using a telephone line. Today, most documents can also be transmitted by email if they are in an electronic format.

Most fax machines in offices are located in one or more central locations and used by a number of different workers for both sending and receiving documents. To facilitate directing the document to the intended receiver, it is usual practice to include a cover sheet in the fax transmission. The cover sheet should include the information below.

1. Names of the person sending the message and the person to receive the message.
2. Phone number of both sending and receiving fax machines.
3. Total number of pages being transmitted, including the cover sheet.

Instructions

1. Write a memorandum responding to the following scenario: Kim Park is at the bank, applying for a business loan. Ms. Park has just called you and asked that you fax her with the following information: TechKnow Consulting's asset, liability, owner's equity, sales, and expense accounts, and their current balances. In your memorandum, include an introductory sentence or paragraph and end with a concluding statement.
2. Prepare a cover sheet for transmitting a fax message. The bank's fax machine telephone number is 800-555-3333. Use your own name and personal telephone number or school telephone number.

CASES FOR CRITICAL THINKING

Case 1

Janna Sturm does not use a journal in her business records. She records the debits and credits for each transaction directly in the general ledger accounts. Is Ms. Sturm using the correct procedure? Explain your answer.

Case 2

Trent Marvets does the accounting work for his business. When posting, he first transfers all of the information to the general ledger accounts. Then he returns to the general journal and, all at one time, writes the account numbers in the Post. Ref. column of the journal. Diana Young also does the accounting work for her business. When posting, she writes all the account numbers in the Post. Ref. column of the general journal before she transfers any information to the accounts. Is Mr. Marvets or Ms. Young following the correct procedure? Explain your answer.

SCANS WORKPLACE COMPETENCY

Resource Competency: Organizing and Maintaining Information

Concept: Information is a precious resource of organizations. Businesses collect information about customers, competitors, resources, and economic conditions, as well as information about their own organization. To be useful, however, information must be organized in such a way that information can be accessed when needed. Software programs such as spreadsheets and databases are often used to organize and maintain information.

Application: Examine the employment advertisements in the Sunday edition of a major metropolitan newspaper. Study the listings for accounting-related positions and organize the information found. Focus on job responsibilities, educational requirements, experience requirements, and personal and software skills for each position. Then create a word processing table, spreadsheet file, or database to organize this information. Put at least ten different advertisements in the file you create. Add ten more the following week. Describe any trends you discover.

USING SOURCE DOCUMENTS

Journalizing transactions and posting to a general ledger

Darcia Tomzak owns a service business called Darcia's School of Dance. Darcia's School of Dance's general ledger accounts are given in the *Working Papers*.

Source documents related to the transactions for Darcia's School of Dance for July are provided in the *Working Papers*.

Instructions

1. The general journal for Darcia's School of Dance is given in the *Working Papers*. Use page 1 of the journal to journalize the transactions for July. Source documents are abbreviated as follows: check, C; memorandum, M; receipt, R; sales invoice, S; calculator tape, T.
2. Prove cash. The balance on the next unused check stub is $6,576.00.
3. Post from the general journal to the general ledger.

ANALYZING BEST BUY'S FINANCIAL STATEMENTS

In order to move into smaller markets, Best Buy has intentionally planned smaller stores, with 20,000 to 30,000 square feet as compared to the standard Best Buy showroom, which is 45,000 square feet. In order to calculate the average total retail square footage per U.S. Best Buy store, divide the total retail square footage by the number of stores. You will find this data in the 5-Year Financial Highlights on Appendix page B-2.

Instructions

1. Calculate the average total retail square footage per store for U.S. Best Buy stores for 2003 through 2007.
2. Is Best Buy succeeding on the goal of smaller stores?

Accounting SOFTWARE

CHART OF ACCOUNTS MAINTENANCE; JOURNALIZING TRANSACTIONS

As a business grows, it will become involved in new and more complex business transactions. Those transactions will require that the company add new accounts to its chart of accounts. File maintenance of a chart of account also involves deleting accounts that are no longer needed. In this chapter, you learned how to add a new account to a general ledger. The process of creating a new account in Peachtree is almost identical.

1. Select Maintain, Chart of Accounts from the menu bar.
2. Key the account number in the Account ID field and press Enter.
3. Key the account title in the Description field and press Enter.
4. Select Expenses in the Account Type field.
5. Click Save and then click Close.

PEACHTREE MASTERY PROBLEM 4-4

1. Open (Restore) file 04-5MP.ptb. Note that the filename is 04-5 even though the textbook problem is 4-4.
2. Before you start journalizing, add Account. No. 540, Utilities Expense to O'Kalla Lawn and Garden's Chart of Accounts. Journalize and post the November transactions, using General Journal Entry from the menu bar and selecting Tasks.
3. From the menu bar, select Reports, and then General Ledger to print the general journal.
4. Print the general ledger from the Select a Report window.

CHART OF ACCOUNTS MAINTENANCE; JOURNALIZING TRANSACTIONS

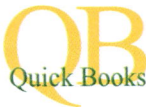

Maintaining a chart of accounts could include adding new accounts, changing an account title, or deleting an account. To display a chart of accounts, choose Chart of Accounts from the List menu. Once the chart of accounts is displayed, you can perform maintenance on it. In this chapter, you learned how to add a new account to a general ledger. The process of creating a new account in QuickBooks is almost identical.

1. Click on the Account dropdown box.
2. Click on New to bring up the Add New Account dialog box.
3. Select an account type and click on Continue.
4. Enter the account number, name, and any other appropriate information.
5. Click on Save and Close.

QUICKBOOKS MASTERY PROBLEM 4-4

1. Open the O'Kalla Lawn and Garden file if it is not already open.
2. Choose Make General Journal Entries from the Company menu, and enter the transactions.
3. Print the General Journal report from the Accountant & Taxes option from the Reports drop-down menu; choose Journal and date the report November 30.
4. Choose Company & Financial from the Reports drop-down menu; select Balance Sheet Standard, and print a report dated November 30.
5. Choose Make General Journal Entries from the Company menu and enter the transactions.
6. Print the General Journal report from the Accountant & Taxes option from the Reports drop-down menu; choose Journal and date the report November 30.
7. Choose Company & Financial from the Reports drop-down menu; select Balance Sheet Standard and print a report dated November 30.

BASIC SPREADSHEET SKILLS

A basic knowledge of electronic spreadsheets is required to complete the exercises in this textbook. What is "basic knowledge?" For purposes of the exercises in this textbook, you need to be able to do the following.

1. Open a workbook.
2. Enter numbers and text in a template.
3. Enter a formula.
4. Enter a SUM function.
5. Save the workbook.
6. Print a worksheet.
7. Switch between worksheets.

Each workbook contains an Instructions worksheet that contains the exercise number and title followed by a detailed list of instructions. A second worksheet contains a template that you will complete by entering numbers and text. Whenever a cell contains [F], that means that you are to create a formula in that cell.

EXCEL ACTIVITY
1. Access the spreadsheet files as instructed by your teacher.
2. Open several of these files to get acquainted with the style of the workbooks and the types of tasks that you will be performing.

CHART OF ACCOUNTS MAINTENANCE; JOURNALIZING TRANSACTIONS

Chart of Accounts Maintenance
Accounts can be added, deleted, or changed. The Account Maintenance window will appear when you choose the Maintain Accounts menu item from the Data drop-down list or click on the Accts. toolbar button.

Adding a New Account
1. Enter the account number in the Account column at the end of the list; then press the Tab key.
2. Enter the title for the new account.
3. For a departmentalized business, enter the department number.
4. Click the Add Account button.
5. Click the Close button to exit the Accounts window.

Changing an Account Title
1. Select the account that you wish to change.
2. Enter the correct account title or department number.
3. Click the Change button when the account title has been changed.

The account number cannot be changed. If an account number needs to be changed because of an incorrect account number, the account must be deleted and then added as a new account number.

Deleting an Account
1. Select the account that you wish to delete.
2. Click the Delete button. General ledger accounts cannot be deleted unless the account has a zero balance.
3. Click the OK button.

Posting Amounts to the General Ledger
In automated accounting, journal entries are automatically posted by clicking the Post button or pressing the Enter key after a transaction is entered in a journal.

AUTOMATED ACCOUNTING APPLICATION PROBLEM 4-1
Open file F04-1.AA8. Display the problem instructions and complete the problem.

AUTOMATED ACCOUNTING MASTERY PROBLEM 4-4
Open file F04-4Green.AA8. Display the problem instructions and complete the problem.

Posting from a General Journal to a General Ledger

CHAPTER 5

Cash Control Systems

OBJECTIVES

After studying Chapter 5, you will be able to:

1. Define accounting terms related to using a checking account and a petty cash fund.
2. Identify accounting concepts and practices related to using a checking account.
3. Prepare business papers related to using a checking account.
4. Reconcile a bank statement.
5. Journalize dishonored checks and electronic banking transactions.
6. Establish and replenish a petty cash fund.

KEY TERMS

- code of conduct
- checking account
- endorsement
- blank endorsement
- special endorsement
- restrictive endorsement
- postdated check
- bank statement
- dishonored check
- electronic funds transfer
- debit card
- petty cash
- petty cash slip

Point Your Browser
www.C21accounting.com

ACCOUNTING IN THE REAL WORLD

Hard Rock Cafe

Hard Rock Really Rocks

"Hard Rock isn't just a name; it's a culture." These words are used on the Hard Rock website to describe the company. The culture that is Hard Rock is summed up in its mission, which is "to spread the spirit of rock 'n roll by creating authentic experiences that rock." As anyone who has visited a Hard Rock Cafe can tell you, it *is* all about rock and roll.

Each of the 121 Hard Rock Cafes, located in over 40 countries, features rock and roll memorabilia—over 60,000 pieces in total, as well as classic American food and good music. And, if your dining experience was a pleasant one, you can take a piece of it home with you by shopping at the on-site stores for articles that range from collector pins to one-of-a-kind guitars.

The Hard Rock culture is also evident in its mottos: "Love All—Serve All"; "All Is One"; "Save the Planet"; and "Take Time to Be Kind." Hard Rock lives out these mottos by contributing to many charitable organizations designed to make the earth a safer, healthier, and better place to live.

Critical Thinking

1. At Hard Rock Cafe, customers use cash or credit cards to make purchases. What control problems may occur when employees accept cash for a sale?
2. What can Hard Rock do, in its own cafes, to help support its "Save the Planet" motto?

Source: www.hardrock.com

INTERNET ACTIVITY

Interest Rates

Banks offer many services, including savings accounts and loans. If you have a savings account with a bank, the bank pays you interest on the money in the account. If you take out a loan, you pay interest to the bank on the money you owe.

Go to the homepage for a bank of your choice.

Instructions

1. Find the range of interest the bank offers for its savings accounts.
2. Find the range of interest charged by the bank on an auto loan.
3. Compare the two rates. Why does the bank charge more interest on loans than it pays on savings accounts?

LESSON 5-1

Checking Accounts

HOW BUSINESSES USE CASH

In accounting, money is usually referred to as cash. Most businesses make major cash payments by check. However, small cash payments for items such as postage and some supplies may be made from a cash fund kept at the place of business.

Because cash transactions occur more frequently than other types of transactions, more chances occur to make recording errors affecting cash. Cash can be transferred from one person to another without any question about ownership. Also, cash may be lost as it is moved from one place to another.

As a safety measure, TechKnow Consulting keeps most of its cash in a bank. Because all cash receipts are placed in a bank, TechKnow Consulting has written evidence to support its accounting records. TechKnow Consulting can compare its record of checks written with the bank's record of checks paid. Greater control of TechKnow Consulting's cash and greater accuracy of its cash records result from these procedures.

CHARACTER COUNTS

Business Codes of Conduct

A statement that guides the ethical behavior of a company and its employees is called a **code of conduct**. Merck & Co., Inc., a leading pharmaceutical company, makes its code of conduct available to its employees, consultants, and the public. The document, titled "Our Values and Standards," begins by stating:

At Merck, our values and standards have always formed the basis of our success. They inspire trust and confidence on the part of the medical community, government officials, regulatory agencies, financial markets, our customers and patients—all who are essential to our success.

The code of conduct contains sections that focus on Merck's relationship with customers, employees, shareholders, suppliers, and communities/society. Each section contains specific guidance on Merck policies. Common questions and answers are provided to expand on these policies. Throughout the document, individuals are encouraged to seek the guidance of upper-level managers, the Legal Department, and the Office of Ethics if they are unsure whether their actions comply with the code of conduct.

Instructions

Obtain access to Merck's code of conduct at www.merck.com. Assuming you are a Merck employee, may you:

1. Give a physician a gift consisting of a medical textbook?
2. Use your cellular phone to discuss new research methods with another Merck employee?
3. Accept a supplier's invitation to attend the Super Bowl?

DEPOSITING CASH

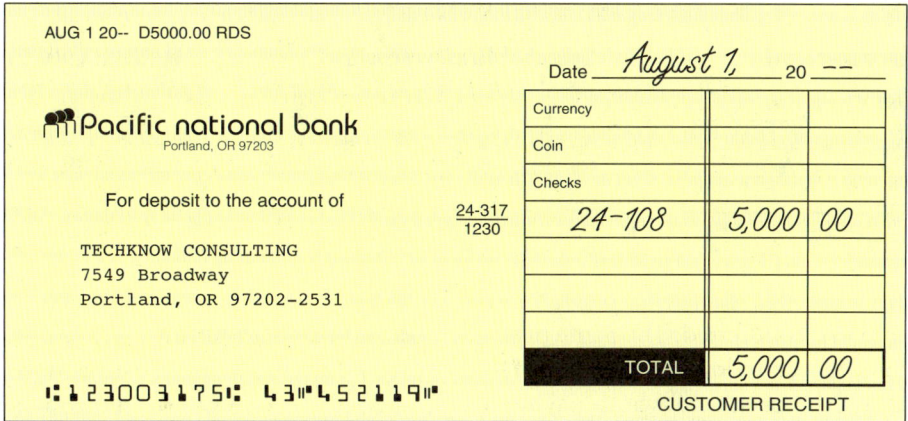

A business form ordering a bank to pay cash from a bank account is known as a check. A bank account from which payments can be ordered by a depositor is called a **checking account**.

When a checking account is opened, the bank customer must provide a signature on a signature card for the bank records. If several persons are authorized to sign checks, each person's signature must be on the signature card.

A bank customer prepares a deposit slip each time cash or checks are placed in a bank account. Deposit slips may differ slightly from one bank to another. Each bank designs its own deposit slips to fit the bank's recording machines. However, all deposit slips contain the same basic information.

Checks are listed on a deposit slip according to the bank routing number on each check. For example, the routing number 24-108 identifies the bank on which the $5,000.00 check is written.

When a deposit is made, a bank gives the depositor a receipt. Many banks use a copy of the deposit slip with a printed or stamped verification as the receipt. The printed verification, *Aug 1, 20-- D5000.00 RDS*, is printed along the top left edge of the deposit slip. This printed verification means that a total of $5,000.00 was deposited on August 1. The initials *RDS* next to the amount are those of the bank employee who accepted the deposit.

DEPOSIT RECORDED ON A CHECK STUB

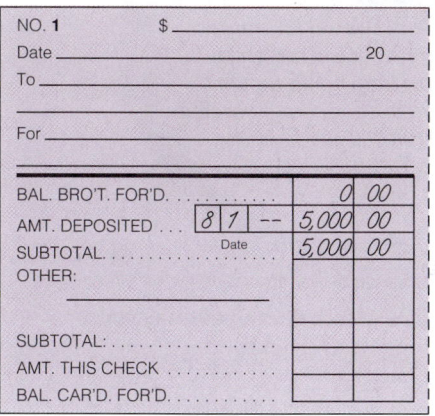

After the deposit is recorded on the check stub, a checkbook subtotal is calculated. The balance brought forward on Check Stub No. 1 is zero. The previous balance, $0.00, plus the deposit, $5,000.00, equals the subtotal, $5,000.00.

Cash receipts are journalized at the time cash is received. Later, the cash receipts are deposited in the checking account. Therefore, no journal entry is needed for deposits because the cash receipts have already been journalized.

BLANK ENDORSEMENT, SPECIAL ENDORSEMENT, AND RESTRICTIVE ENDORSEMENT

Blank Endorsement

> Endorse here
> X *Kim Park*
>
> DO NOT WRITE, STAMP, OR SIGN BELOW THIS LINE
> Reserved for Financial Institution Use

Special Endorsement

> Endorse here
> X *Pay to the order of*
> *Eleanor Johnson*
> *Kim Park*
>
> DO NOT WRITE, STAMP, OR SIGN BELOW THIS LINE
> Reserved for Financial Institution Use

Restrictive Endorsement

> Endorse here
> X For deposit only to
> the account of
> TECHKNOW CONSULTING
> *Kim Park*
>
> DO NOT WRITE, STAMP, OR SIGN BELOW THIS LINE
> Reserved for Financial Institution Use

Ownership of a check can be transferred. The name of the first owner is stated on a check following the words *Pay to the order of*. Therefore, the person to whom payment is to be made must indicate that ownership of the check is being transferred. One person transfers ownership to another person by signing on the back of a check. A signature or stamp on the back of a check transferring ownership is called an **endorsement**. Federal regulations require that an endorsement be confined to a limited amount of space that is indicated on the back of a check.

An endorsement should be signed exactly as the person's name appears on the front of the check. For example, a check made payable to K. A. Park is endorsed on the back as *K. A. Park*. Immediately below that endorsement, Ms. Park would write her official signature, *Kim Park*.

Ownership of a check might be transferred several times, resulting in several endorsements. Each endorser guarantees payment of the check. If a bank does not receive payment from the person who signed the check, each endorser is individually liable for payment.

Three types of endorsements are commonly used, each having a specific use in transferring ownership.

Blank Endorsement

An endorsement consisting only of the endorser's signature is called a **blank endorsement**. A blank endorsement indicates that the subsequent owner is whoever has the check.

If a check with a blank endorsement is lost or stolen, the check can be cashed by anyone who has possession of it. Ownership may be transferred without further endorsement. A blank endorsement should be used only when a person is at the bank ready to cash or deposit a check.

Special Endorsement

An endorsement indicating a new owner of a check is called a **special endorsement**. Special endorsements are sometimes known as *endorsements in full*.

Special endorsements include the words *Pay to the order of* and the name of the new check owner. Only the person or business named in a special endorsement can cash, deposit, or further transfer ownership of the check.

Restrictive Endorsement

An endorsement restricting further transfer of a check's ownership is called a **restrictive endorsement**. A restrictive endorsement limits use of the check to whatever purpose is stated in the endorsement.

Many businesses have a stamp prepared with a restrictive endorsement. When a check is received, it is immediately stamped with the restrictive endorsement. This prevents unauthorized persons from cashing the check if it is lost or stolen.

FOR YOUR INFORMATION

FYI

The Federal Deposit Insurance Corporation (FDIC) protects depositors from banks that fail. Bank deposits are generally covered up to $100,000 per depositor.

COMPLETED CHECK STUB AND CHECK

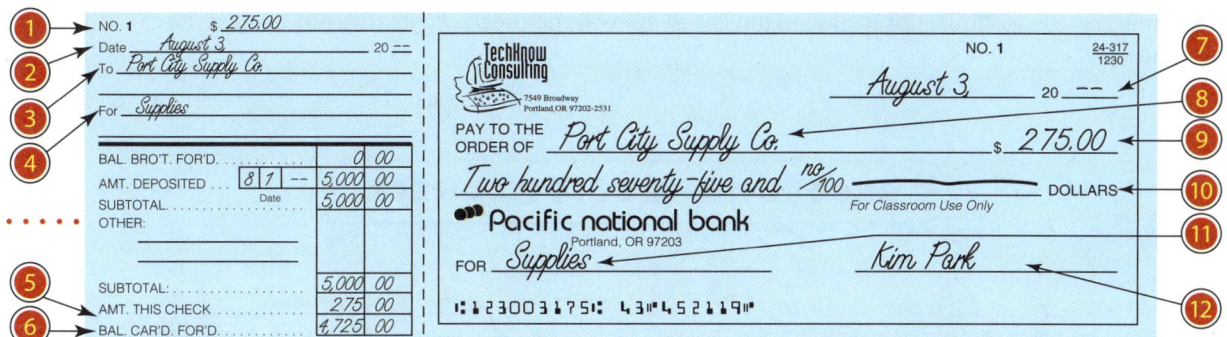

TechKnow Consulting uses printed checks with check stubs attached. Consecutive numbers are preprinted on TechKnow Consulting's checks. Consecutive numbers on checks provide an easy way of identifying each check. Also, the numbers help keep track of all checks to assure that none are lost or misplaced.

A check stub is a business's record of each check written for a cash payment transaction. [CONCEPT: Objective Evidence] To avoid forgetting to prepare a check stub, the check stub is prepared before the check is written.

After the check stub is completed, the check is written.

STEPS PREPARING CHECK STUBS AND CHECKS

① Write the amount of the check, *$275.00*, in the space after the dollar sign at the top of the stub.

② Write the date of the check, *August 3, 20--*, on the Date line at the top of the stub.

③ Write to whom the check is to be paid, *Port City Supply Co.*, on the To line at the top of the stub.

④ Record the purpose of the check, *Supplies*, on the For line.

⑤ Write the amount of the check, *$275.00*, in the amount column at the bottom of the stub on the line with the words "Amt. This Check."

⑥ Calculate the new checking account balance, *$4,725.00*, and record the new balance in the amount column on the last line of the stub. The new balance is calculated as shown.

	Subtotal	−	Amount of This Check	=	New Balance
	$5,000.00	−	$275.00	=	$4,725.00

PREPARING CHECKS

⑦ Write the date, *August 3, 20--*, in the space provided. The date should be the month, day, and year on which the check is issued. A check with a future date on it is called a **postdated check**. Most banks will not accept postdated checks because money cannot be withdrawn from a depositor's account until the date on the check.

⑧ Write to whom the check is to be paid, *Port City Supply Co.*, following the words "Pay to the order of." If the person to whom a check is to be paid is a business, use the business's name rather than the owner's name. [CONCEPT: Business Entity] If the person to whom the check is to be paid is an individual, use that person's name.

⑨ Write the amount in figures, *$275.00*, following the dollar sign. Write the figures close to the printed dollar sign. This practice prevents anyone from writing another digit in front of the amount to change the amount of the check.

⑩ Write the amount in words, *Two hundred seventy-five and no/100*, on the line with the word "Dollars." This written amount verifies the amount written in figures after the dollar sign. Begin the words at the extreme left. Draw a line through the unused space up to the word "Dollars." This line prevents anyone from writing in additional words to change the amount. If the amounts in words and in figures are not the same, a bank may pay only the amount in words. Often, when the amounts do not agree, a bank will refuse to pay the check. (*continued on next page*)

Checking Accounts   Lesson 5-1   **121**

11. Write the purpose of the check, *Supplies*, on the line labeled "For." (On some checks this space is labeled "Memo.") Some checks do not have a line for writing the purpose of the check.

12. Sign the check. A check should not be signed until each item on the check and its stub has been verified for accuracy.

RECORDING A VOIDED CHECK

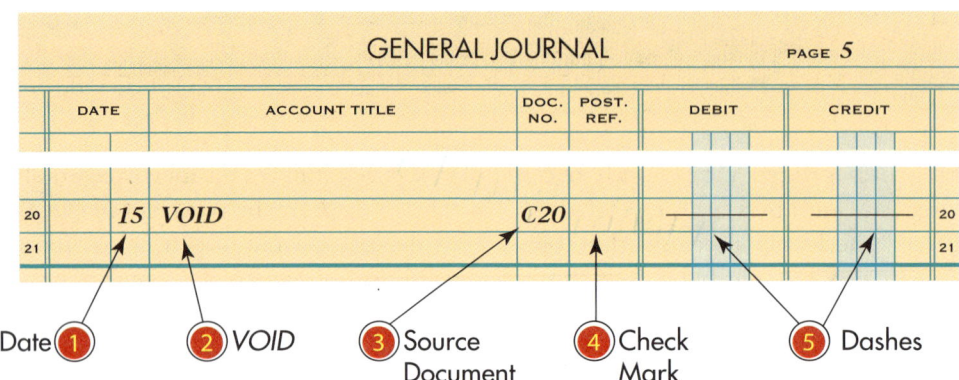

Banks usually refuse to accept altered checks. If any kind of error is made in preparing a check, a new check should be prepared. Because checks are prenumbered, all checks not used should be retained for the records. This practice helps account for all checks and assures that no checks have been lost or stolen.

A check that contains errors must be marked so that others will know that it is not to be used. The word *VOID* is written in large letters across both the check and its stub.

When TechKnow Consulting records a check in its general journal, the check number is placed in the journal's Doc. No. column. If a check number is missing from the Doc. No. column, there is a question whether all checks have been journalized. To assure that all check numbers are listed in the journal, TechKnow Consulting records voided checks in the general journal.

STEPS — RECORDING A VOIDED CHECK IN THE GENERAL JOURNAL

1. Record the date, *15*, in the Date column.
2. Write the word *VOID* in the Account Title column.
3. Write the check number, *C20*, in the Doc. No. column.
4. Place a check mark in the Post. Ref. column.
5. Place a dash in both the Debit and Credit columns.

> **REMEMBER**
> *Always complete the check stub before writing the check. Otherwise you may forget to record the amount of the check on the check stub.*

122   Chapter 5   Cash Control Systems

End of Lesson REVIEW

TERMS REVIEW

code of conduct
checking account
endorsement
blank endorsement
special endorsement
restrictive endorsement
postdated check

AUDIT YOUR UNDERSTANDING

1. List the three types of endorsements.
2. List the steps for preparing a check stub.
3. List the steps for preparing a check.

WORK TOGETHER 5-1

Endorsing and writing checks

Write the answers to the following problems in the *Working Papers*. Your instructor will guide you through the following examples. You are authorized to sign checks for Balsam Lake Accounting.

1. For each of these situations, prepare the appropriate endorsement.
    a. Write a blank endorsement.
    b. Write a special endorsement to transfer a check to Kelsey Sather.
    c. Write a restrictive endorsement to deposit a check in the account of Balsam Lake Accounting.
2. Record the balance brought forward on Check Stub No. 78, $1,805.75.
3. Record a deposit of $489.00 made on October 30 of the current year on Check Stub No. 78.
4. Prepare check stubs and write the following checks. Use October 30 of the current year as the date.
    a. Check No. 78 to Corner Garage for repairs, $162.00.
    b. Check No. 79 to St. Croix Supply for supplies, $92.00.

ON YOUR OWN 5-1

Endorsing and writing checks

Write the answers to the following problems in the *Working Papers*. Work these problems independently. You are authorized to sign checks for Centuria Hair Care.

1. For each of these situations, prepare the appropriate endorsement.
    a. Write a special endorsement to transfer a check to Kenneth Burleson.
    b. Write a restrictive endorsement to deposit a check in the account of Centuria Hair Care.
2. Record the balance brought forward on Check Stub No. 345, $2,106.53.
3. Record a deposit of $456.25 made on May 31 of the current year on Check Stub No. 345.
4. Prepare check stubs and write the following checks. Use May 31 of the current year as the date.
    a. Check No. 345 to Uniforms Plus for uniform rental, $355.00.
    b. Check No. 346 to HairWorld for supplies, $412.00.

LESSON 5-2

Bank Reconciliation

BANK STATEMENT

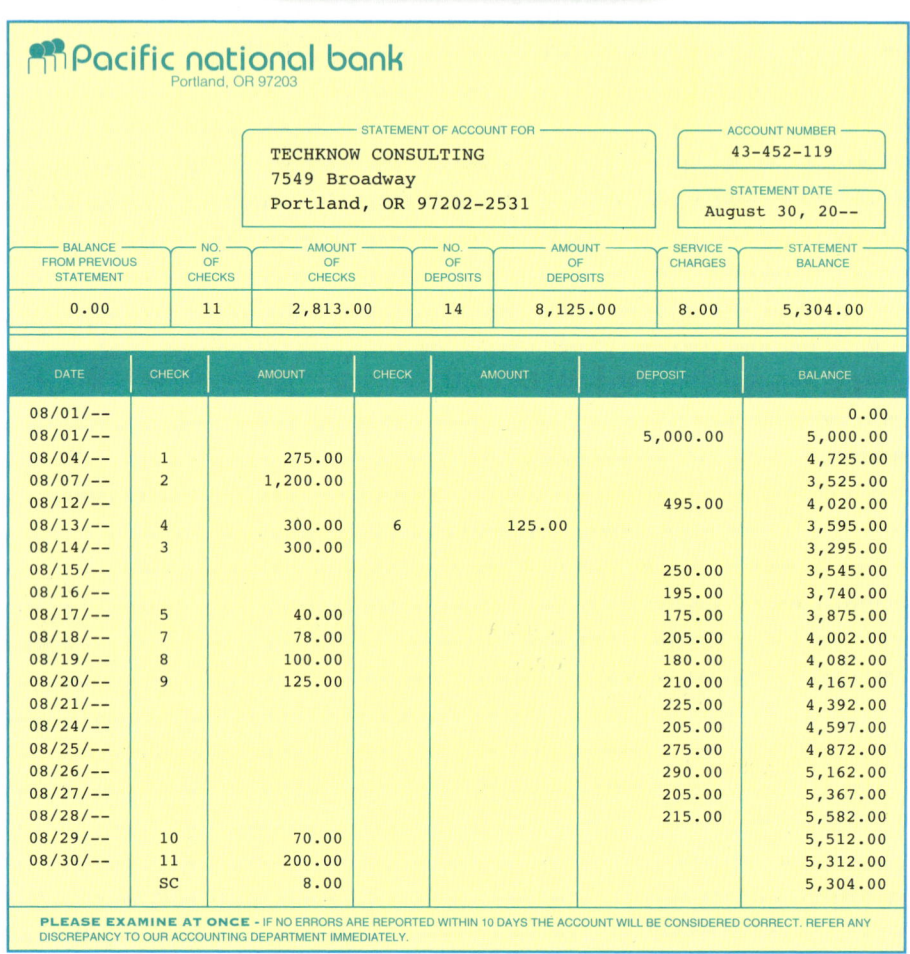

A report of deposits, withdrawals, and bank balances sent to a depositor by a bank is called a **bank statement**.

When a bank receives checks, the amount of each check is deducted from the depositor's account. The bank stamps the checks to indicate that the checks are canceled and are not to be transferred further. Canceled checks may be returned to a depositor with a bank statement or may be kept on record by the bank. Account service charges are also listed on a bank statement.

Although banks seldom make mistakes, occasionally a check or deposit might be recorded in a wrong account. If errors are discovered, the bank should be notified at once. However, a bank's records and a depositor's records may differ for several reasons:

1. A service charge may not have been recorded in the depositor's business records.
2. Outstanding deposits may be recorded in the depositor's records but not on a bank statement.
3. Outstanding checks may be recorded in the depositor's records but not on a bank statement.
4. A depositor may have made math or recording errors.

BANK STATEMENT RECONCILIATION

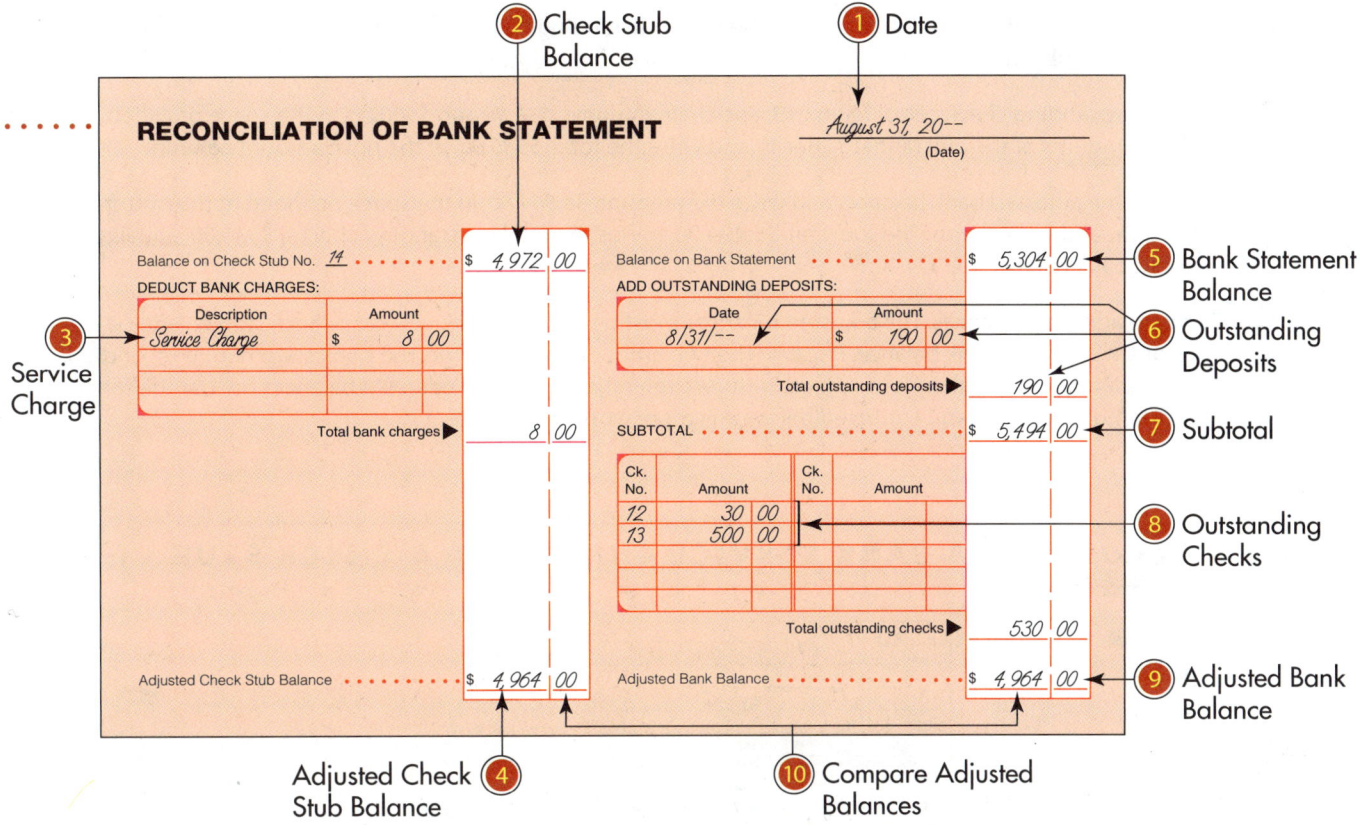

A bank statement is reconciled by verifying that information on a bank statement and a checkbook are in agreement. Reconciling immediately is an important aspect of cash control.

TechKnow Consulting's canceled checks are kept on record at the bank. The bank statement is used to determine the canceled checks. For each canceled check listed on the bank statement, a check mark is placed on the corresponding check stub. A check stub with no check mark indicates an outstanding check. Outstanding checks are those checks issued by a depositor but not yet reported on a bank statement. Outstanding deposits are those deposits made at a bank but not yet shown on a bank statement.

TechKnow Consulting receives a bank statement dated August 30 on August 31. TechKnow Consulting uses a reconciliation form printed on the back of the bank statement.

STEPS RECONCILING A BANK STATEMENT

1. Write the date on which the reconciliation is prepared, *August 31, 20--*.

2. In the left amount column, list the balance brought forward on Check Stub No. 14, the next unused check stub, *$4,972.00*.

3. In the space for bank charges, list any charges. The only such charge for TechKnow Consulting is the bank service charge, *$8.00*. The bank service charge is labeled "SC" on the bank statement.

4. Write the adjusted check stub balance, *$4,964.00*, in the space provided at the bottom of the left amount column. The balance on the check stub, $4,972.00, minus the bank's service charge, $8.00, equals the adjusted check stub balance, $4,964.00.

5. Write the ending balance shown on the bank statement, *$5,304.00*, in the right amount column. *(continued on next page)*

Bank Reconciliation Lesson 5-2 7

6. Write the date, *8/31/--*, and the amount, *$190.00*, of any outstanding deposits in the space provided. Add the outstanding deposits. Write the total outstanding deposits, *$190.00*, in the right amount column.

7. Add the ending bank statement balance to the total outstanding deposits. Write the total, *$5,494.00*, in the space for the Subtotal.

8. List the outstanding checks, Nos. *12* and *13*, and their amounts, *$30.00* and *$500.00*, in the space provided. Add the amounts of the outstanding checks, and write the total, *$530.00*, in the right amount column.

9. Calculate the adjusted bank balance, and write the amount, *$4,964.00*, in the space provided at the bottom of the right amount column. The subtotal, $5,494.00, minus the total outstanding checks, $530.00, equals the adjusted bank balance, $4,964.00.

10. Compare adjusted balances. The adjusted balances must be the same. The adjusted check stub balance is the same as the adjusted bank balance. Because the two amounts are the same, the bank statement is reconciled. The completed reconciliation form is filed for future reference. If the two adjusted balances are not the same, the error must be found and corrected before any more work is done.

RECORDING A BANK SERVICE CHARGE ON A CHECK STUB

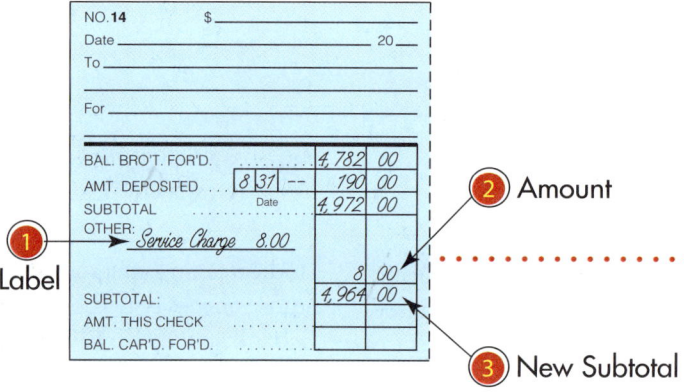

The bank deducts the service charge from TechKnow Consulting's checking account each month. Although TechKnow Consulting did not write a check for the bank service charge, this cash payment must be recorded in TechKnow Consulting's accounting records as a cash payment. TechKnow Consulting makes a record of a bank service charge on a check stub.

STEPS RECORDING A BANK SERVICE CHARGE ON A CHECK STUB

1. Write *Service Charge $8.00* on the check stub under the heading "Other."

2. Write the amount of the service charge, *$8.00*, in the amount column.

3. Calculate and record the new subtotal, *$4,964.00*, on the Subtotal line. A new Balance Carried Forward is not calculated until after Check No. 14 is written.

JOURNALIZING A BANK SERVICE CHARGE

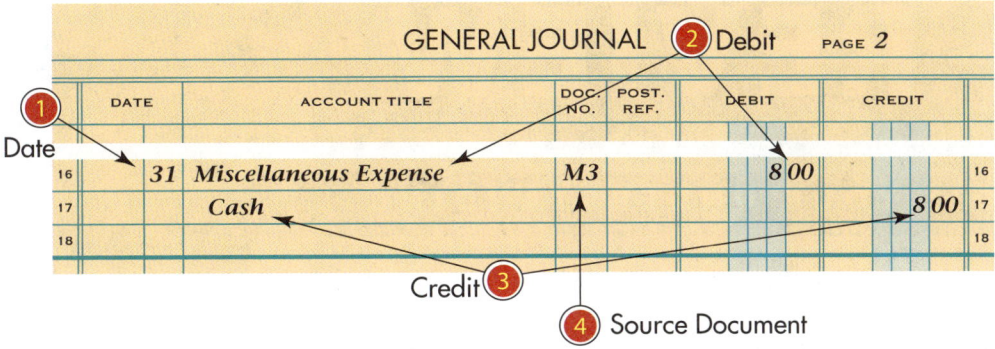

Because the bank service charge is a cash payment for which no check is written, TechKnow Consulting prepares a memorandum as the source document. TechKnow Consulting's bank service charges are relatively small and occur only once a month. Therefore, a separate ledger account for the expense is not used. Instead, TechKnow Consulting records the bank service charge as a miscellaneous expense.

A memorandum is the source document for a bank service charge transaction. [CONCEPT: Objective Evidence] The analysis of this transaction is shown in the T accounts.

The expense account, Miscellaneous Expense, is debited for $8.00 to show the decrease in owner's equity. The asset account, Cash, is credited for $8.00 to show the decrease in assets.

August 31. Received bank statement showing August bank service charge, $8.00. Memorandum No. 3.

STEPS — JOURNALIZING A BANK SERVICE CHARGE

1. **Date.** Write the date, *31*, in the Date column.

2. **Debit.** Write the title of the account to be debited, *Miscellaneous Expense*, in the Account Title column. Record the amount debited, *$8.00*, in the Debit column.

3. **Credit.** On the next line, indented about 1 centimeter, write the title of the account credited, *Cash*, in the Account Title column. Write the credit amount, *$8.00*, in the Credit column.

4. **Source document.** On the first line of the entry, write the source document number, *M3*, in the Doc. No. column.

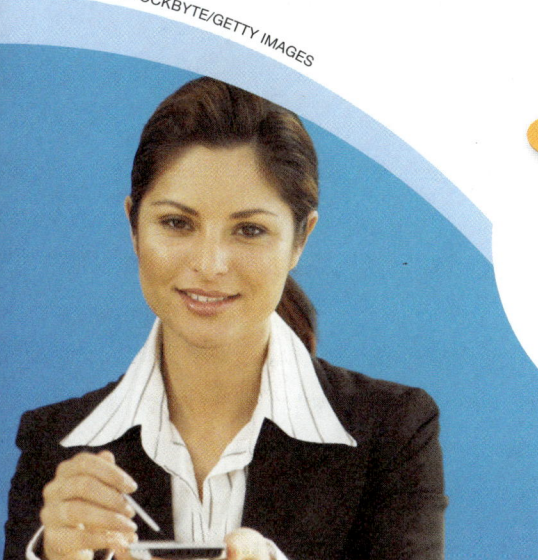

SMALL BUSINESS SPOTLIGHT

Three factors generally motivate people to start a new business: the desire to control their own destinies, the desire to work more closely with customers, and the desire to achieve substantial profits.

Bank Reconciliation

End of Lesson REVIEW

AUDIT YOUR UNDERSTANDING

1. List four reasons why a depositor's records and a bank's records may differ.
2. If a check mark is placed on the check stub of each canceled check, what does a check stub with no check mark indicate?

TERM REVIEW

bank statement

WORK TOGETHER 5-2

Reconciling a bank statement and recording a bank service charge

Forms are given in the *Working Papers*. Your instructor will guide you through the following examples.

On July 29 of the current year, DeepClean received a bank statement dated July 28. The following information is obtained from the bank statement and from the records of the business.

Bank statement balance	$1,528.00	Outstanding checks:	
Bank service charge	2.00	No. 103	$ 70.00
Outstanding deposit, July 28	150.00	No. 105	35.00
		Checkbook balance on Check Stub No. 106	1,575.00

1. Prepare a bank statement reconciliation. Use July 29 of the current year as the date.
2. Record the service charge on check stub No. 106.
3. Record the service charge on general journal page 14. Use Memorandum No. 44 as the source document.

ON YOUR OWN 5-2

Reconciling a bank statement and recording a bank service charge

Forms are given in the *Working Papers*. Work these problems independently.

On April 30 of the current year, Able Service Co. received a bank statement dated April 29. The following information is obtained from the bank statement and from the records of the business.

Bank statement balance	$3,184.00	Outstanding checks:	
Bank service charge	15.00	No. 115	$ 70.00
Outstanding deposits:		No. 117	313.00
April 29	360.00	No. 118	80.00
April 30	510.00		
		Checkbook balance on Check Stub No. 119	3,606.00

1. Prepare a bank statement reconciliation. Use April 30 of the current year as the date.
2. Record the service charge on check stub No. 119.
3. Record the service charge on general journal page 8. Use Memorandum No. 84 as the source document.

LESSON 5-3

Dishonored Checks and Electronic Banking

RECORDING A DISHONORED CHECK ON A CHECK STUB

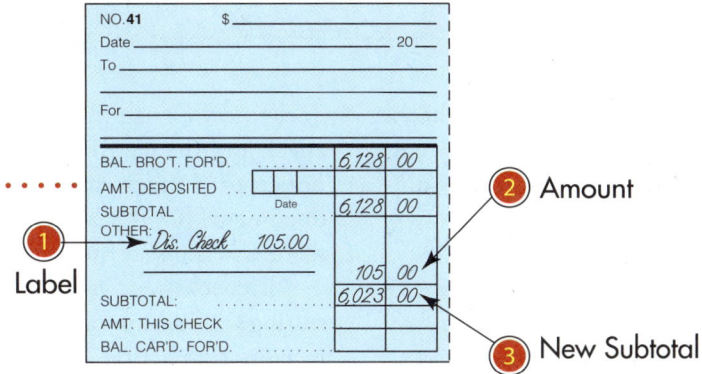

1. Label
2. Amount
3. New Subtotal

A check that a bank refuses to pay is called a **dishonored check**. Banks dishonor a check when the account of the person who wrote the check has insufficient funds to pay the check. Banks may also dishonor a check for other reasons: (1) The check appears to be altered. (2) The signature of the person who signed the check does not match the one on the signature card at the bank. (3) The amounts written in figures and in words do not agree. (4) The check is postdated. (5) The person who wrote the check has stopped payment on the check.

Issuing a check on an account with insufficient funds is illegal. Altering or forging a check is also illegal. A dishonored check may affect the credit rating of the person or business that issued the check. Checking accounts and records should be maintained in such a way that all checks will be honored when presented to the bank.

Sometimes money for a dishonored check can be collected directly from the person or business that wrote the check. Often, however, the value of a dishonored check cannot be recovered and becomes an expense to the business.

Most banks charge a fee for handling dishonored checks that have been previously accepted for deposit. This fee is an expense of the business receiving a dishonored check. TechKnow Consulting's bank charges a $35.00 fee for handling dishonored checks. TechKnow Consulting attempts to collect the $35.00 fee in addition to the amount of the dishonored check from the person or business that wrote the check.

When TechKnow Consulting receives a check, it records the check as a debit to **Cash** and deposits the check in the bank. When a check is dishonored, the bank deducts the amount of the check plus the fee, $35.00, from TechKnow Consulting's checking account. Therefore, TechKnow Consulting records a dishonored check as a cash payment transaction.

STEPS RECORDING A DISHONORED CHECK ON A CHECK STUB

1. Write *Dishonored check $105.00* on the line under the heading "Other." The amount is the amount of the dishonored check, $70.00, plus the service fee of $35.00.

2. Write the total of the dishonored check, *$105.00*, in the amount column.

3. Calculate and record the new subtotal, *$6,023.00*, on the Subtotal line. A new Balance Carried Forward is not calculated until after Check No. 41 is written.

JOURNALIZING A DISHONORED CHECK

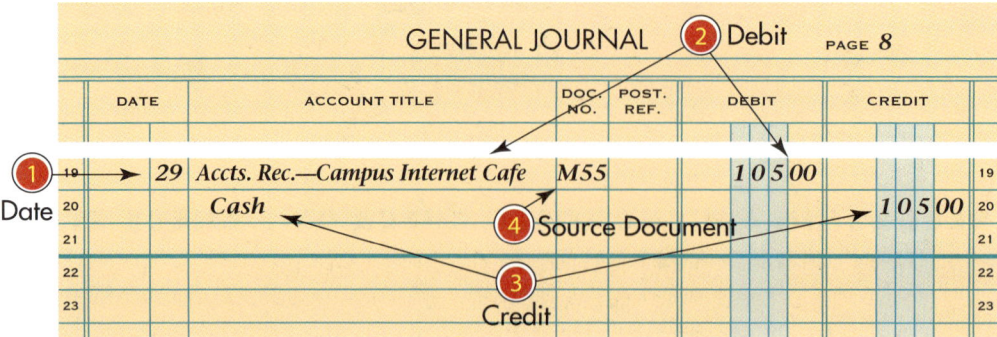

During August, TechKnow Consulting received no checks that were subsequently dishonored. However, in November TechKnow Consulting did receive a check from Campus Internet Cafe that was eventually dishonored.

> **November 29. Received notice from the bank of a dishonored check from Campus Internet Cafe, $70.00, plus $35.00 fee; total, $105.00. Memorandum No. 55.**

TechKnow Consulting receives a notice of the dishonored check and the fee from the bank. TechKnow attaches the notice to a memorandum, which is used as the source document. [CONCEPT: Objective Evidence] The analysis of this transaction is shown in the T accounts.

All checks received are deposited in TechKnow Consulting's checking account. The entry for each cash receipts transaction includes a debit to Cash. If a check is subsequently returned as dishonored, the previous cash debit for the amount of the check must be offset by a cash credit. The asset account, Cash, is credited for $105.00 to show the decrease in assets.

When TechKnow Consulting originally received the check from Campus Internet Cafe, Accounts Receivable—Campus Internet Cafe was credited to reduce the balance of the account. When TechKnow Consulting finds out that the check was not accepted by the bank, the account, Accounts Receivable—Campus Internet Cafe, must be increased to show that this amount, plus the bank charge, is still owed to TechKnow Consulting. The asset account, Accounts Receivable—Campus Internet Cafe, is debited for $105.00 to show the increase in assets.

S T E P S JOURNALIZING A DISHONORED CHECK

1. **Date.** Write the date, *29*, in the Date column.

2. **Debit.** Write the title of the account to be debited, *Accounts Receivable—Campus Internet Cafe*, in the Account Title column. Record the amount debited, *$105.00*, in the Debit column.

3. **Credit.** On the next line, indented about 1 centimeter, write the title of the account credited, *Cash*, in the Account Title column. Write the credit amount, *$105.00*, in the Credit column.

4. **Source document.** On the first line of this entry, write the source document number, *M55*, in the Doc. No. column.

> **REMEMBER**
>
> *Checking accounts and records should be maintained in such a way that all checks will be honored when presented to the bank.*

JOURNALIZING AN ELECTRONIC FUNDS TRANSFER

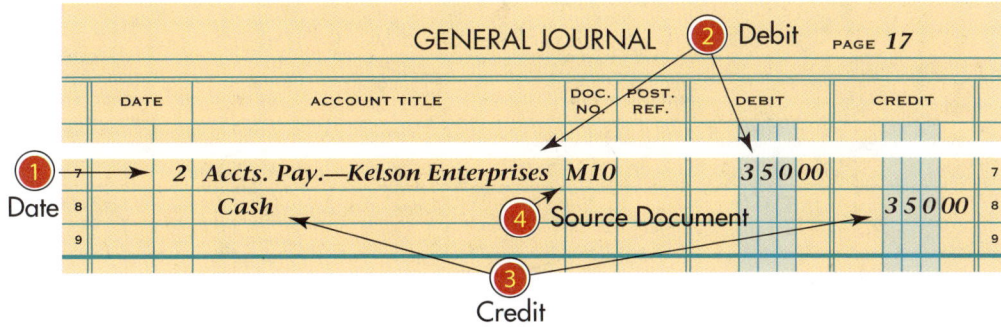

A computerized cash payments system that transfers funds without the use of checks, currency, or other paper documents is called **electronic funds transfer**. Many businesses use electronic funds transfer (EFT) to pay vendors. To use EFT, a business makes arrangements with its bank to process EFT transactions. Arrangements are also made with vendors to accept EFT payments on account. Then a transfer of funds from the business's account to the vendor's account can be completed via the Internet or a telephone call.

To control cash payments through EFT, the person responsible for requesting transfers should be given a password. The bank should not accept EFT requests from any person unable to provide an established password.

Superior Cleaning Service uses electronic funds transfer to make payments on account to vendors. The journal entry for making payments on account through EFT is the same as when a check is written. The only change is the source document used for the transaction. Superior Cleaning Service uses a memorandum as the source document for an EFT. A note is written on the memorandum to describe the transaction.

The source document for this transaction is Memorandum No. 10. [CONCEPT: Objective Evidence] The analysis of this transaction is shown in the T accounts.

The liability account, Accounts Payable—Kelson Enterprises, is decreased by a debit, $350.00. The asset account, Cash, is decreased by a credit, $350.00.

A cash payment made by EFT is recorded on the check stub as "Other." This procedure keeps the checkbook in balance during the time lag from when the EFT is made until receipt of the bank statement. The EFT payments are verified as part of the regular bank statement reconciliation process. EFT payments are identified in the Check column of the bank statement by the notation "EFT," rather than by a check number.

> **September 2.** Paid cash on account to Kelson Enterprises, $350.00, using EFT. Memorandum No. 10.

STEPS — JOURNALIZING AN ELECTRONIC FUNDS TRANSFER

1. **Date.** Write the date, 2, in the Date column.

2. **Debit.** Write the title of the account to be debited, *Accounts Payable—Kelson Enterprises*, in the Account Title column. Record the amount debited, *$350.00*, in the Debit column.

3. **Credit.** On the next line, indented about 1 centimeter, write the title of the account credited, *Cash*, in the Account Title column. Write the credit amount, *$350.00*, in the Credit column.

4. **Source document.** On the first line of this entry, write the source document number, *M10*, in the Doc. No. column.

JOURNALIZING A DEBIT CARD TRANSACTION

A bank card that automatically deducts the amount of a purchase from the checking account of the cardholder is called a **debit card**. There is one major difference between a debit card and a credit card. When a purchase is made with a debit card, the amount of the purchase is automatically deducted from the checking account of the cardholder. A debit card eliminates the need to write a check for the purchase. However, the effect is the same. The checking account balance is reduced by the amount of the purchase. A debit card also eliminates the need to carry a checkbook.

When using a debit card, it is important to remember to record all purchases to avoid errors in the checking account.

Superior Cleaning Service uses a debit card to make some purchases. Recording a cash payment made by a debit card is similar to recording a cash payment made by electronic funds transfer.

Superior Cleaning Service uses a memorandum as the source document for a debit card purchase. A note is written on the memorandum to describe the transaction.

September 5. Purchased supplies, $24.00, using debit card. Memorandum No. 12.

The source document for this transaction is Memorandum No. 12. [CONCEPT: Objective Evidence] The analysis of this transaction is shown in the T accounts.

The asset account, Supplies, is increased by a debit, $24.00. The asset account, Cash, is decreased by a credit, $24.00.

A cash payment made with a debit card is recorded on the check stub as "Other." This procedure keeps the checkbook in balance during the time lag from when the debit card payment is made until receipt of the bank statement. The debit card payments are verified as part of the regular bank statement reconciliation process. Debit card payments are identified as a Purchase on the bank statement, with the date, time, location, and the amount of the debit card transaction stated.

STEPS — JOURNALIZING A DEBIT CARD PURCHASE

1. **Date.** Write the date, *5*, in the Date column.

2. **Debit.** Write the title of the account to be debited, *Supplies*, in the Account Title column. Record the amount debited, *$24.00*, in the Debit column.

3. **Credit.** On the next line, indented about 1 centimeter, write the title of the account credited, *Cash*, in the Account Title column. Write the credit amount, *$24.00*, in the Credit column.

4. **Source document.** On the first line of this entry, write the source document number, *M12*, in the Doc. No. column.

132   Chapter 5   Cash Control Systems

End of Lesson REVIEW

AUDIT YOUR UNDERSTANDING

TERMS REVIEW

dishonored check
electronic funds transfer
debit card

1. List six reasons why a bank may dishonor a check.
2. What account is credited when electronic funds transfer is used to pay cash on account?
3. What account is credited when a debit card is used to purchase supplies?

WORK TOGETHER 5-3

Recording dishonored checks, electronic funds transfers, and debit card purchases

Write the answers to this problem in the *Working Papers*. Your instructor will guide you through the following example.

1. Enter the following transactions on page 6 of a general journal.

Transactions:
March 15. Received notice from the bank of a dishonored check from Christopher Ikola, $63.00, plus $10.00 fee; total, $73.00. Memorandum No. 121.
     16. Paid cash on account to Spinoza Enterprises, $135.00, using EFT. Memorandum No. 122.
     17. Purchased supplies, $31.00, using a debit card. Memorandum No. 123.

ON YOUR OWN 5-3

Recording dishonored checks, electronic funds transfers, and debit card purchases

Write the answers to this problem in the *Working Papers*. Work this problem independently.

1. Enter the following transactions on page 12 of a general journal.

Transactions:
June 12. Received notice from the bank of a dishonored check from Thomas Hofski, $65.00, plus $30.00 fee; total, $95.00. Memorandum No. 54.
     13. Paid cash on account to Alfonso Company, $243.00, using EFT. Memorandum No. 55.
     14. Purchased supplies, $65.00, using a debit card. Memorandum No. 56.

Dishonored Checks and Electronic Banking

LESSON 5-4

Petty Cash

ESTABLISHING A PETTY CASH FUND

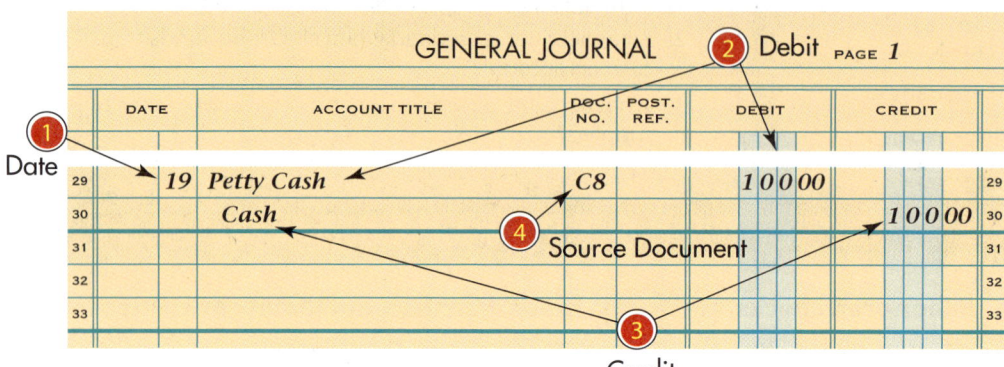

An amount of cash kept on hand and used for making small payments is called **petty cash**. A business usually has some small payments for which writing a check is not time or cost effective. Therefore, a business may maintain a separate cash fund for making small cash payments. The actual dollar amount considered to be a small payment differs from one business to another. Ms. Park has set $20.00 as the maximum amount to be paid at any one time from the petty cash fund.

The petty cash account is an asset with a normal debit balance. The balance of the petty cash account increases on the debit side and decreases on the credit side.

On August 19, Ms. Park decided that TechKnow Consulting needed a petty cash fund of $100.00. This amount should provide for small cash payments during a month.

> August 19. Paid cash to establish a petty cash fund, $100.00. Check No. 8.

The source document for this transaction is Check No. 8. [CONCEPT: Objective Evidence] The analysis is shown in the T accounts. Petty Cash is debited for $100.00 to show the increase in this asset account balance. Cash is credited for $100.00 to show the decrease in this asset account balance.

Ms. Park cashed the check and placed the $100.00 in a locked petty cash box at her place of business. Only she is authorized to make payments from the petty cash fund.

STEPS — ESTABLISHING A PETTY CASH FUND

1. **Date.** Write the date, *19*, in the Date column.
2. **Debit.** Write the title of the account to be debited, *Petty Cash*, in the Account Title column. Record the amount debited, *$100.00*, in the Debit column.
3. **Credit.** On the next line, indented about 1 centimeter, write the title of the account credited, *Cash*, in the Account Title column. Write the credit amount, *$100.00*, in the Credit column.
4. **Source document.** On the first line of this entry, write the source document number, *C8*, in the Doc. No. column.

MAKING PAYMENTS FROM A PETTY CASH FUND WITH A PETTY CASH SLIP

```
PETTY CASH SLIP              No. 1
Date:    August 19, 20--
Paid to: Tribune
For:     Newspaper Ad         $ 10.00
Account: Advertising Expense
              Approved: Kim Park
```

Each time a small payment is made from the petty cash fund, Ms. Park prepares a form showing the purpose and amount of the payment. A form showing proof of a petty cash payment is called a **petty cash slip**.

A petty cash slip shows the following information: (1) petty cash slip number; (2) date of petty cash payment; (3) to whom paid; (4) reason for the payment; (5) amount paid; (6) account in which amount is to be recorded; and (7) signature of person approving the petty cash payment.

The petty cash slips are kept in the petty cash box until the fund is replenished. No entries are made in the journal for the individual petty cash payments.

FINANCIAL LITERACY

Managing a Checking Account

The privilege of having a checking account brings with it the responsibility of managing that account. The cost of inefficient management can be high—especially if you write a "bad" check. A "bad" check, or insufficient-funds check, means that you don't have enough money in your account to cover the amount of the check written. If this happens, you may have to pay two fines, one to your bank and one to the company to whom you gave the bad check. These two fines could easily total over $100.

Managing a checking account is not difficult, but it involves recording all written checks, electronic funds transfers, and automatic payments; making regular deposits; recording all deposits, including electronic funds received; and reconciling your account each month.

Properly managing your checking account also means physically safeguarding your blank checks, your check registers, and monies waiting to be deposited. In addition, it requires safeguarding any account numbers and passwords used to log in to Internet banking sites.

Finally, efficiently managing a checking account means monitoring the costs and benefits of your account. Features of some accounts include interest on the balance, free electronic bill pay, Internet access to account information, electronic transfers between accounts, and free blank checks. Costs include monthly service fees, per-check charges, per-item charge on deposits, and overdraft charges.

Activities

1. Investigate the costs and features of checking accounts from three different banks. Present your findings to five people and ask each person which account would be best for his or her needs. Summarize your findings in a written report.

2. Visit a local bank and inquire about opening a checking account. Write a report outlining the steps involved.

REPLENISHING PETTY CASH

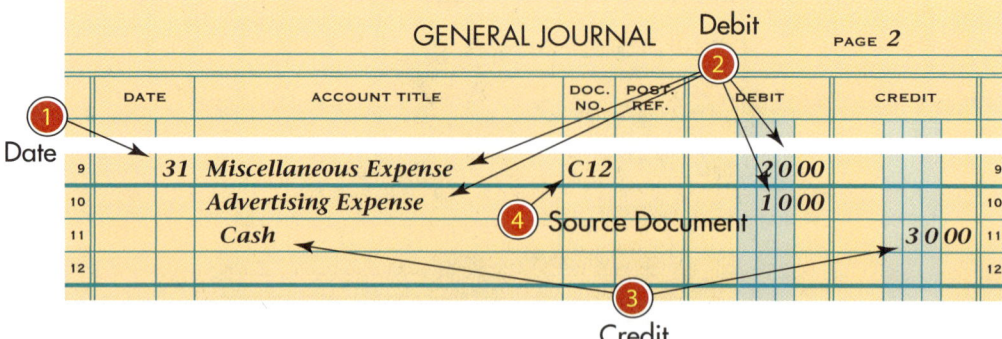

As petty cash is paid out, the amount in the petty cash box decreases. Eventually, the petty cash fund must be replenished and the petty cash payments recorded. TechKnow Consulting replenishes its petty cash fund whenever the amount on hand is reduced to $25.00. Also, the petty cash fund is always replenished at the end of each month so that all of the expenses are recorded in the month they are incurred.

Before petty cash is replenished, a proof of the fund must be completed.

Petty cash remaining in the petty cash fund	$ 70.00
Plus total of petty cash slips	+ 30.00
Equals petty cash fund	$100.00

The last line of the proof must show the same total as the original balance of the petty cash fund, $100.00. If petty cash does not prove, the errors must be found and corrected before any more work is done.

The proof shows that a total of $30.00 has been paid out of petty cash. An inspection of the petty cash slips shows that $20.00 has been paid for miscellaneous expenses and $10.00 has been paid for advertising. Therefore, an additional $30.00 must be placed in the fund. TechKnow Consulting will write a check to replenish the fund.

> *August 31. Paid cash to replenish the petty cash fund, $30.00: miscellaneous expense, $20.00; advertising, $10.00. Check No. 12.*

Unless the petty cash fund is permanently increased or decreased, the balance of the account is always the original amount of the fund. The check issued to replenish petty cash is a credit to **Cash** and does not affect **Petty Cash**. When the check is cashed, the money is placed in the petty cash box. The amount in the petty cash box changes, as shown below.

Amount in petty cash box before fund is replenished	$ 70.00
Amount from check issued to replenish petty cash	+ 30.00
Amount in petty cash box after fund is replenished	$100.00

The total amount in the petty cash box, $100.00, is again the same as the balance of the petty cash account.

STEPS — JOURNALIZING THE ENTRY TO REPLENISH PETTY CASH

1. **Date.** Write the date, *31*, in the Date column.

2. **Debit.** Write the title of the first account debited, *Miscellaneous Expense*, in the Account Title column. Write the amount to be debited to Miscellaneous Expense, *$20.00*, in the Debit column on the same line as the account title. Write the title of the second account debited, *Advertising Expense*, on the next line in the Account Title column. Record the amount to be debited to Advertising Expense, *$10.00*, in the Debit column on the same line as the account title.

3. **Credit.** On the next line, indented about 1 centimeter, write the title of the account credited, *Cash*, in the Account Title column. Write the credit amount, *$30.00*, in the Credit column.

4. **Source document.** Write the source document number, *C12*, in the Doc. No. column on the first line of the entry.

Business, Management & Administration

CAREERS IN ACCOUNTING

Tim DuFrene, Sole Proprietor

The average person will make at least three career changes over the course of his or her working life. Tim DuFrene fits that average precisely. He has found that accounting is a transferable skill that has served him well throughout his multiple careers.

When Tim took accounting courses in high school and college, he saw himself preparing for a career in banking. His first full-time job was, in fact, in a bank. Working first as a teller, he used his accounting skills to balance cash and reconcile accounts. Advancing to the position of loan officer, Tim relied on his accounting knowledge to review business plans of loan applicants.

After a few years in banking, Tim was drawn into his second professional field—industrial construction. After several years of learning and applying a craft, Tim began working his way into management. Once again, accounting was an important aspect of his work responsibilities. As a project superintendent, he oversaw the construction of various industrial projects throughout the United States. Important accounting aspects of that job included bidding for projects, assessing estimated costs, and setting project budgets.

After 25 years in his second career of industrial construction, Tim became tired of the extensive travel associated with his job and decided to pursue a lifelong dream of owning his own business—career #3. In 2001, he launched Han-D-Man, a home maintenance and repair business that he runs from his home office. As a sole proprietor, he found his accounting skills to be especially important in setting up his business and tracking billing and income, managing expenses, and satisfying tax requirements. Tim says, "Owning my own business has allowed me to interact with many people and improve their quality of life through providing them with more pleasant, functional surroundings. I enjoy having more freedom now to pursue my hobbies, travel, and spend more time with my wife and children. My knowledge of accounting enabled me to change careers and be successful."

Salary Range: Self-employed individuals in a service industry set their desired hourly rate based on their expertise and geographic area. The time required to bid jobs, collect fees, and travel between jobs means that a service provider does not bill all of his or her work time. Thus, a service provider may bill about 1,600 hours during a year. Hourly billing rates between $25.00 and $50.00 per hour and a 1,600-hour work year yield an annual salary of $40,000 to $80,000, less expenses.

Qualifications: Self-employed individuals need three types of skills: (1) communication skills to interact with clients, (2) organizational skills to schedule jobs and manage the business, and (3) a specific skill to sell in the marketplace.

Occupational Outlook: In a career such as Tim's, the sustained growth of the housing market will cause individual homeowners to need more home repairs.

End of Lesson REVIEW

AUDIT YOUR UNDERSTANDING

1. Why do businesses use petty cash funds?
2. Why is Cash and not Petty Cash credited when a petty cash fund is replenished?

TERMS REVIEW

petty cash
petty cash slip

WORK TOGETHER 5-4

Establishing and replenishing a petty cash fund

Write the answers to this problem in the *Working Papers*. Your instructor will guide you through the following example.

1. Journalize the following transactions completed during July of the current year. Use page 13 of a general journal. The abbreviation for check is C.

Transactions:
July 3. Paid cash to establish a petty cash fund, $250.00. C57.
    31. Paid cash to replenish the petty cash fund, $78.00: supplies, $25.00; miscellaneous expense, $8.00; repairs, $45.00. C97.

ON YOUR OWN 5-4

Establishing and replenishing a petty cash fund

Write the answers to this problem in the *Working Papers*. Work this problem independently.

1. Journalize the following transactions completed during August of the current year. Use page 15 of a general journal. The abbreviation for check is C.

Transactions:
Aug. 1. Paid cash to establish a petty cash fund, $200.00. C114.
    31. Paid cash to replenish the petty cash fund, $145.00: supplies, $72.00; advertising, $40.00; miscellaneous expense, $33.00. C157.

SUMMARY

After completing this chapter, you can:

1. Define accounting terms related to using a checking account and a petty cash fund.
2. Identify accounting concepts and practices related to using a checking account.
3. Prepare business papers related to using a checking account.
4. Reconcile a bank statement.
5. Journalize dishonored checks and electronic banking transactions.
6. Establish and replenish a petty cash fund.

EXPLORE ACCOUNTING

Cash Controls

Cash transactions occur more frequently than other types of transactions. Because cash is easily transferred from one person to another, a business must try to safeguard its cash to protect it and other assets from errors.

An unintentional error occurs when someone mistakenly records an incorrect amount or forgets to record a transaction. An intentional error occurs when someone intentionally records an incorrect amount or does not record a transaction in order to cover up fraud or theft. Good cash control procedures should guard against both types of errors.

One common method of controlling cash is to insist that all cash payments over a certain amount be paid by check. In addition, checks should be prenumbered so that it is easy to account for each check. The document number column of a journal can be used to ensure that all checks issued are recorded in the journal. Other cash controls are to have one person responsible for authorizing all checks, and requiring a source document in support of each cash payment.

One of the best ways to safeguard assets is to separate duties so that one employee does not have total control of an entire set of processes. For example, one employee could receive and record the receipt of cash on account; a second employee could make and record deposits; and a third employee could reconcile the bank statement. By separating the duties, it is less likely that errors will be made.

A company that does not have enough employees to institute the separation of duties concept may hire a certified public accountant (CPA) to perform some of these duties on a regular basis.

Research Assignment: Talk to a businessperson to determine what kinds of controls are in place in his or her business to safeguard cash. Schools, hospitals, charitable organizations, and government offices as well as retail, wholesale, and service businesses should have established controls that are being followed. Summarize and present your findings to your class.

5-1 APPLICATION PROBLEM

Endorsing and writing checks

You are authorized to sign checks for Accounting Tutors. Forms are given in the *Working Papers*.

Instructions:

1. For each of the following situations, prepare the appropriate endorsement.
   a. Write a blank endorsement.
   b. Write a special endorsement to transfer a check to Vu Kim.
   c. Write a restrictive endorsement to deposit a check in the account of Accounting Tutors.
2. Record the balance brought forward on Check Stub No. 390, $6,711.62.
3. Record a deposit of $1,244.25 made on September 30 of the current year on Check Stub No. 390.
4. Prepare check stubs and write the following checks. Use September 30 of the current year as the date.
   a. Check No. 390 to Williamson Street Supplies for supplies, $945.00.
   b. Check No. 391 to Spring Park Tribune for advertising, $112.00.
   c. Check No. 392 to Bryce Wilton for rent, $250.00.

5-2 APPLICATION PROBLEM

Reconciling a bank statement and recording a bank service charge

Forms are given in the *Working Papers*. On May 31 of the current year, Parties Plus received a bank statement dated May 30. The following information is obtained from the bank statement and from the records of the business.

Bank statement balance	$1,927.00
Bank service charge	20.00
Outstanding deposit, May 30	756.25
Outstanding checks:	
No. 310	421.76
No. 311	150.50
Checkbook balance on Check Stub No. 312	2,130.99

Instructions:

1. Prepare a bank statement reconciliation. Use May 31 of the current year as the date.
2. Record the service charge on check stub No. 312.
3. Record the service charge on general journal page 10. Use Memorandum No. 58 as the source document.

Go Beyond the Book
For more information go to
www.C21accounting.com

5-3 APPLICATION PROBLEM

Recording dishonored checks, electronic funds transfers, and debit card purchases

Enter the following transactions on page 8 of the general journal given in the *Working Papers*.

Transactions:

Jan. 25. Received notice from the bank of a dishonored check from Ralston Eubanks, $125.00, plus $30.00 fee; total, $155.00. Memorandum No. 333.
26. Paid cash on account to Reed Rosman, $289.00, using EFT. Memorandum No. 334.
27. Purchased supplies, $54.00, using a debit card. Memorandum No. 335.

5-4 APPLICATION PROBLEM

Establishing and replenishing a petty cash fund

Journalize the following transactions completed during November of the current year. Use page 22 of the general journal given in the *Working Papers*. The abbreviation for check is C.

Transactions:

Nov. 5. Paid cash to establish a petty cash fund, $300.00. C527.
30. Paid cash to replenish the petty cash fund, $165.00: supplies, $57.00; miscellaneous expense, $58.00; repairs, $40.00; postage (Postage Expense), $10.00. C555.

5-5 MASTERY PROBLEM

Reconciling a bank statement; journalizing a bank service charge, a dishonored check, and petty cash transactions

James Astrup owns a business called LawnMow. Selected general ledger accounts are given below.

110 Cash
115 Petty Cash
120 Accts. Rec.—Bruce Kassola
130 Supplies

140 Prepaid Insurance
320 James Astrup, Drawing
520 Miscellaneous Expense
530 Rent Expense

535 Repair Expense
540 Supplies Expense
550 Utilities Expense

Instructions:

1. Journalize the following transactions completed during August of the current year. Use page 20 of the general journal given in the *Working Papers*. Source documents are abbreviated as follows: check, C; memorandum, M; calculator tape, T.

Transactions:

Aug. 21. Paid cash to establish a petty cash fund, $300.00. C110.
24. Paid cash for repairs, $165.00. C111.
26. Paid cash for supplies, $60.00. C112.
27. Received notice from the bank of a dishonored check from Bruce Kassola, $140.00, plus $35.00 fee; total, $175.00. M33.
28. Paid cash for miscellaneous expense, $31.00. C113.
31. Paid cash to owner for personal use, $400.00. C114.
31. Paid cash to replenish the petty cash fund, $255.00: supplies, $125.00; miscellaneous expense, $130.00. C115.
31. Received cash from sales, $350.00. T31.

2. On August 31 of the current year, LawnMow received a bank statement dated August 30. Prepare a bank statement reconciliation. Use August 31 of the current year as the date. The following information is obtained from the August 30 bank statement and from the records of the business.

Bank statement balance	$2,721.00
Bank service charge	15.00
Outstanding deposit, August 31	350.00
Outstanding checks, Nos. 114 and 115	
Checkbook balance on Check Stub No. 116	2,431.00

3. Continue using the journal and journalize the following transaction:

Transaction:

Aug. 31. Received bank statement showing August bank service charge, $15.00. M34.

5-6 CHALLENGE PROBLEM Peachtree by Sage   QuickBooks

Reconciling a bank statement and recording a bank service charge

Use the bank statement, canceled checks, and check stubs for GolfPro given in the *Working Papers*.

Instructions:

1. Compare the canceled checks with the check stubs. For each canceled check, place a check mark next to the appropriate check stub number. For each deposit shown on the bank statement, place a check mark next to the deposit amount on the appropriate check stub.
2. Prepare a bank statement reconciliation. Use August 29 of the current year as the date.
3. Record the following transactions on page 8 of a general journal. The abbreviation for memorandum is M.

Transactions:

Sept. 1. Received bank statement showing August bank service charge, $5.00. M25.
  1. Received notice from the bank of a dishonored check from Sheldon Martindale, $170.00, plus $5.00 fee; total, $175.00. M26.

4. Record the bank service charge and dishonored check on Check Stub No. 165.

APPLIED COMMUNICATION

All businesses are affected to some degree by issues and events that occur in the areas in which the businesses are located. For example, a city may gain an industry that will employ many people for a long time. Or, a town might build new roads or schools.

Instructions: Collect three to five newspaper or magazine articles about issues in your area that you think will affect local businesses. For each article, prepare a written list of consequences that a business might encounter.

CASES FOR CRITICAL THINKING

Case 1

Iris Velez and Suzanne Merker have personal checking accounts for which they receive a bank statement every month. Ms. Merker does not prepare a reconciliation; instead she records the balance on the bank statement as her new checkbook balance. Ms. Velez prepares a bank statement reconciliation for each bank statement received. Is Ms. Velez or Ms. Merker following the better procedure? Explain.

Case 2

Dorset Company decides to establish a petty cash fund. The owner, Edna Dorset, wants to establish a $100.00 petty cash fund and limit payments to $20.00 or less. The manager, Roy Evans, suggests a petty cash fund of $3,000.00 limited to payments of $50.00 or less. Mr. Evans claims this limit will help him avoid writing so many checks. Do you agree with Ms. Dorset or Mr. Evans? Explain.

SCANS WORKPLACE COMPETENCY

Personal Qualities: Responsibility

Concept: Employers seek individuals who exert a high level of effort and persevere toward goal attainment.

Application: Make a list of your responsibilities in this accounting course; then assess whether you meet these responsibilities with a low, medium, or high level of effort. Make a plan for how you can improve your performance on those responsibilities that you are not already fulfilling at a high level of effort.

GRAPHING WORKSHOP

A bar chart of the assets, liabilities, and owner's equity of Moua Company is shown here. Analyze the chart to answer the following questions.

1. What was the amount of total assets in May?
2. In what month were liabilities the lowest?

ANALYZING BEST BUY'S FINANCIAL STATEMENTS

On a financial statement, the term "Cash and cash equivalents" includes more than just cash on hand. Checking accounts, savings accounts, and even some very short-term investments are also included in this total. Best Buy's financial statement on Appendix B page B-5 shows the total "Cash and cash equivalents" for Best Buy for each year.

Published financial statements include notes that explain some of the titles and amounts used in the statements. Note 1 for Best Buy's financial statements begins on page B-9. Read the second page of Note 1.

Instructions: List the amount of Best Buy's cash and cash equivalents for 2006 and 2007. Look at Note 1 and list what Best Buy considers to be "cash and cash equivalents."

PHOTODISC/GETTY IMAGES

Accounting SOFTWARE

BANK STATEMENT RECONCILIATION; JOURNALIZING TRANSACTIONS

Preparing a bank reconciliation is an easy task with accounting software. Peachtree presents a list of all the checks and deposits so that a simple click identifies whether each transaction has cleared. Peachtree performs all calculations and clearly indicates any difference between the book and bank balances. Knowing that bank service charges must be journalized, Peachtree automatically generates the journal entry when the bank reconciliation is processed. You are only required to enter is the amount of the bank charge and the number of the general ledger account to be debited.

PEACHTREE MASTERY PROBLEM 5-5
1. Open (Restore) file 05-5MP.ptb.
2. Journalize and post the August cash transactions, including the journal entry for a dishonored check. Remember to save after each transaction.
3. From the menu bar, select Tasks, then Account Reconciliation to reconcile the bank statement; print a report.

PEACHTREE CHALLENGE PROBLEM 5-6
1. Open (Restore) file 05-6CP.ptb.
2. To complete account reconciliation, use the bank statement, canceled checks, check stubs, and transactions for Golf Pro. Journalize cash transactions and a dishonored check transaction.
3. Reconcile the bank statement and print a report.

BANK STATEMENT RECONCILIATION; JOURNALIZING TRANSACTIONS

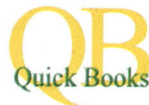

QuickBooks can be used to prepare the monthly bank reconciliation. The bank statement can be reconciled to the checkbook balance in the following steps:
1. Choose Reconcile from the Banking menu. When the Begin Reconciliation dialog box appears, make sure Cash shows in the Account field, and enter the correct ending date.
2. Key in the required data in the Begin Reconciliation dialog box. Click Continue.
3. The Reconcile – Cash dialog box will display. Click in the blank field next to the Date field for all checks and deposits that have already cleared through the bank and appear on the bank statement. Verify that the amount next to Difference is 0.00. Make any necessary corrections. Click Reconcile Now.
4. The Select Reconciliation Report dialog box will appear.
   Choose which reports you want displayed. Click Display. The reports will display.

QUICKBOOKS MASTERY PROBLEM 5-5
1. Open the LawnMow file.
2. Journalize the transactions completed during August.
3. Choose Reconcile from the Banking menu to reconcile the bank statement.
4. From the Reconcile – Cash dialog box, click the Reconcile Now button to view the Reconciliation Summary report. Print this report.

QUICKBOOKS CHALLENGE PROBLEM 5-6
1. Open the GolfPro file.
2. Prepare a bank reconciliation for GolfPro.
3. Print the Reconciliation Summary and Reconciliation Detail reports.
4. Journalize the transaction for the dishonored check.
5. Print a Journal report for GolfPro for August 28 through September 30.

BANK STATEMENT RECONCILIATION

A bank reconciliation is a relatively easy procedure, yet it is a powerful tool to identify errors in the accounting records. A bank reconciliation provides proof that cash disbursements and receipts have been recorded the same way in the accounting records of both the business and the bank.

The spreadsheet template for Chapter 5 presents a replica of the bank reconciliation shown in this chapter. You will enter the description and amount of any bank charges identified on the bank statement. These are the items that will require a journal entry to record in the accounting records. On the opposite side of the template, you will enter the date and amount of all outstanding deposits, and the check number and amount of all outstanding checks.

By creating formulas to calculate the adjusted balances, you will be able to use the template for other reconciliations. Because the number of outstanding deposits and checks may differ from month to month, it may be necessary to add additional rows to the template. Thus, you should use the SUM function to calculate the total of bank charges, outstanding deposits, and outstanding checks.

EXCEL APPLICATION PROBLEM 5-2
1. Open the F05-2 Excel data file.
2. Follow the step-by-step instructions in the Instructions work sheet to reconcile a bank statement using an Excel spreadsheet.

BANK STATEMENT RECONCILIATION; JOURNALIZING TRANSACTIONS

The automated accounting system may be used to prepare the monthly bank reconciliation. Information maintained by the software, such as the checkbook balance and checks that were written during the period, will be automatically provided to make the reconciliation process simpler and more accurate.

While the *Automated Accounting* Help system contains detailed instructions, the bank statement can be reconciled to the checkbook balance in the following steps:
1. Choose the Other Activities menu item from the Data menu, or click on the Other toolbar button.
2. When the Reconciliation window appears, click on the Clear button to erase any previous data.
3. Enter the bank credits, bank charges, bank statement balance, and outstanding deposit amounts.
4. Checks written during the period are displayed in the Checks from the Journals list box. Select the outstanding checks by pointing and double-clicking. Each selected check will appear in the Outstanding Checks list, and the Adjusted Bank Balance will automatically be updated.
5. Click the Report command button in the Reconciliation window to see the completed reconciliation.
6. Click the Close command button to dismiss the report window.
7. When the Bank Reconciliation reappears, click the OK command button to record your data and end the Bank Reconciliation process.

AUTOMATED ACCOUNTING APPLICATION PROBLEM 5-2
Open file F05-2.AA8. Display the problem instructions and complete the problem.

AUTOMATED ACCOUNTING MASTERY PROBLEM 5-5
Open file F05-5.AA8. Display the problem instructions and complete the problem.

REINFORCEMENT Activity 1—Part A

An Accounting Cycle for a Proprietorship: Journalizing and Posting Transactions

Reinforcement activities strengthen the learning of accounting concepts and procedures. Reinforcement Activity 1 is a single problem divided into two parts. Part A includes learning from Chapters 1 through 5. Part B includes learning from Chapters 6 through 8. An accounting cycle is completed in Parts A and B for a single business—Extreme Adventures.

EXTREME ADVENTURES

In May of the current year, Brian Dawson starts a service business called Extreme Adventures. The business provides adventure trips throughout the world, such as trekking in the Himalayas and helo skiing in Colorado. The business rents the facilities in which it operates, pays the utilities, and is responsible for maintenance. Extreme Adventures charges clients for each trip. Most of Extreme Adventures' sales are for cash. However, two private schools use Extreme Adventures for some physical education classes. These schools have an account with Extreme Adventures.

CHART OF ACCOUNTS

Extreme Adventures uses the following chart of accounts.

CHART OF ACCOUNTS

BALANCE SHEET ACCOUNTS
- (100) **ASSETS**
- 110 Cash
- 120 Petty Cash
- 130 Accts. Rec.—Matterhorn University
- 140 Accts. Rec.—Midwest College
- 150 Supplies
- 160 Prepaid Insurance
- (200) **LIABILITIES**
- 210 Accts. Pay.—Dunn Supplies
- 220 Accts. Pay.—Greenway Supplies
- (300) **OWNER'S EQUITY**
- 310 Brian Dawson, Capital
- 320 Brian Dawson, Drawing
- 330 Income Summary

INCOME STATEMENT ACCOUNTS
- (400) **REVENUE**
- 410 Sales
- (500) **EXPENSES**
- 510 Advertising Expense
- 520 Insurance Expense
- 530 Miscellaneous Expense
- 540 Rent Expense
- 550 Repair Expense
- 560 Supplies Expense
- 570 Utilities Expense

RECORDING TRANSACTIONS

Instructions:

1. Journalize the following transactions completed during May of the current year. Use page 1 of the general journal given in the *Working Papers*. Source documents are abbreviated as follows: check stub, C; memorandum, M; receipt, R; sales invoice, S; calculator tape, T.

   May 1. Received cash from owner as an investment, $15,000.00. R1.
   1. Paid cash for rent, $1,800.00. C1.
   2. Paid cash for electric bill, $105.00. C2.
   4. Paid cash for supplies, $450.00. C3.
   4. Paid cash for insurance, $1,200.00. C4.
   7. Bought supplies on account from Dunn Supplies, $900.00. M1.
   11. Paid cash to establish a petty cash fund, $250.00. C5.
   12. Received cash from sales, $475.00. T12.
   13. Paid cash for repairs, $250.00. C6.
   13. Paid cash for miscellaneous expense, $40.00. C7.
   13. Sold services on account to Midwest College, $225.00. S1.
   14. Paid cash for advertising, $300.00. C8.
   15. Paid cash to owner for personal use, $200.00. C9.
   15. Paid cash on account to Dunn Supplies, $500.00. C10.
   15. Sold services on account to Matterhorn University, $425.00. S2.
   18. Paid cash for miscellaneous expense, $95.00. C11.
   18. Received cash on account from Midwest College, $125.00. R2.

2. Post from the general journal to the general ledger.

3. Use page 2 of the general journal. Journalize the following transactions.

   May 19. Received cash from sales, $1,020.00. T19.
   20. Paid cash for repairs, $160.00. C12.
   20. Bought supplies on account from Greenway Supplies, $120.00. M2.
   21. Paid cash for water bill, $265.00. C13.
   25. Paid cash for supplies, $25.00. C14.
   25. Received cash from sales, $1,940.00. T25.
   26. Paid cash for miscellaneous expense, $37.00. C15.
   26. Received cash on account from Matterhorn University, $250.00. R3.
   28. Paid cash for telephone bill, $245.00. C16.
   28. Received cash from sales, $650.00. T28.

4. Extreme Adventures received a bank statement dated May 27. The following information is obtained from the bank statement and from the records of the business. Prepare a bank statement reconciliation. Use May 29 as the date.

Bank statement balance	$13,180.00
Bank service charge	15.00
Outstanding deposit, May 28	650.00
Outstanding checks:	
No. 14	25.00
No. 15	37.00
No. 16	245.00
Checkbook balance on Check Stub No. 17	$13,538.00

5. Continue using page 2 of the general journal, and journalize the following transactions.

   May 29. Received bank statement showing May bank service charge, $15.00. M3.

29. Paid cash for supplies, $30.00. C17.
31. Paid cash to replenish the petty cash fund, $165.00: miscellaneous expense, $120.00; repairs, $45.00. C18.
31. Paid cash to owner for personal use, $1,000.00. C19.
31. Received cash from sales, $1,355.00. T31.

6. Post from the general journal to the general ledger.
7. Prove cash. The beginning cash balance on May 1 is zero. The balance on the next unused check stub is $13,683.00.

The general ledger prepared in Reinforcement Activity 1—Part A is needed to complete Reinforcement Activity 1—Part B.

CHAPTER 6

Work Sheet for a Service Business

OBJECTIVES

After studying Chapter 6, you will be able to:

1. Define accounting terms related to a work sheet for a service business organized as a proprietorship.
2. Identify accounting concepts and practices related to a work sheet for a service business organized as a proprietorship.
3. Prepare a heading and a trial balance on a work sheet.
4. Plan adjustments for supplies and prepaid insurance.
5. Complete a work sheet for a service business organized as a proprietorship.
6. Identify selected procedures for finding and correcting errors in accounting records.

KEY TERMS

- fiscal period
- work sheet
- trial balance
- adjustments
- balance sheet
- income statement
- net income
- net loss

Point Your Browser
www.C21accounting.com

ACCOUNTING IN THE REAL WORLD

The AICPA

Professionalism and the AICPA

The American Institute of Certified Public Accountants (AICPA) is America's leading professional CPA organization, with more than 340,000 members who work for public accounting firms, multinational corporations, small businesses, not-for-profit organizations, governmental agencies, and educational institutions.

Certified Public Accountants—CPAs—who work for public accounting firms provide many services to their clients, such as auditing financial statements, forensic accounting (sometimes called fraud auditing), consulting services, information technology services, evaluating operating performance, international accounting, and tax and financial planning services.

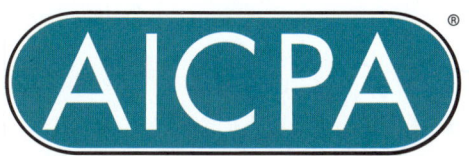

CPAs who are employed by corporations and businesses often work in finance and accounting departments as financial analysts and have the opportunity to rise up the ranks to positions such as controller and Chief Financial Officer (CFO), and even Chief Executive Officer (CEO). Others work in the areas of international finance, treasury, or internal auditing.

To find out more about CPA career opportunities, salary information, and the accounting profession, visit www.StartHereGoPlaces.com or www.aicpa.org, or e-mail the AICPA at educat@aicpa.org. In addition, each state has a CPA society or association that can provide you with more information. You can contact a state CPA society or association through the "CPA links" section of the AICPA web site.

Critical Thinking

1. If you were going to hire an accountant, why might you choose to hire a CPA?
2. If you were a CPA, why might you choose to join a professional association like the AICPA?

Source: www.aicpa.org

INTERNET ACTIVITY

AICPA Career Resources

Go to the homepage for the American Institute of Certified Public Accountants (AICPA) (www.aicpa.org). Search the site for information about career resources for students.

Instructions

1. List two resources provided by the AICPA designed to help students with career choices in the field of accounting.
2. Pick one of these two resources and examine it in more detail. List two interesting pieces of information you learned from this resource.

LESSON 6-1

Creating a Work Sheet

CONSISTENT REPORTING

General ledger accounts contain information needed by managers and owners. Before the information can be used, however, it must be analyzed, summarized, and reported in a meaningful way. The accounting concept *Consistent Reporting* is applied when the same accounting procedures are followed in the same way in each accounting period. [CONCEPT: Consistent Reporting] For example, in one year a delivery business might report the number of deliveries made. The next year, the same business reports the amount of revenue received for the deliveries made. The information for the two years cannot be compared because the business has not been consistent in reporting information about deliveries.

> A summary of preparing a work sheet is shown on the Work Sheet Overlay within this chapter.

FISCAL PERIODS

The length of time for which a business summarizes and reports financial information is called a **fiscal period** (also known as an accounting period). Businesses usually select a period of time for which to summarize and report financial information. The accounting concept *Accounting Period Cycle* is applied when changes in financial information are reported for a specific period of time in the form of financial statements. [CONCEPT: Accounting Period Cycle] Each business chooses a fiscal period length that meets its needs. Because federal and state tax reports are based on one year, most businesses use a one-year fiscal period. However, because TechKnow Consulting is a new business, Ms. Park wishes to have financial information reported frequently to help her make decisions. For this reason, TechKnow Consulting uses a one-month fiscal period.

A fiscal period can begin on any date. However, most businesses begin their fiscal periods on the first day of a month. TechKnow Consulting started business on August 1. Therefore, TechKnow Consulting's monthly fiscal period is for the period from August 1 through August 31, inclusive. Businesses often choose a one-year fiscal period that ends during a period of low business activity. In this way, the end-of-year accounting work comes at a time when other business activities are the lightest.

Financial information may be analyzed, summarized, and reported on any date a business needs the information. However, financial information is always summarized and reported at the end of a fiscal period.

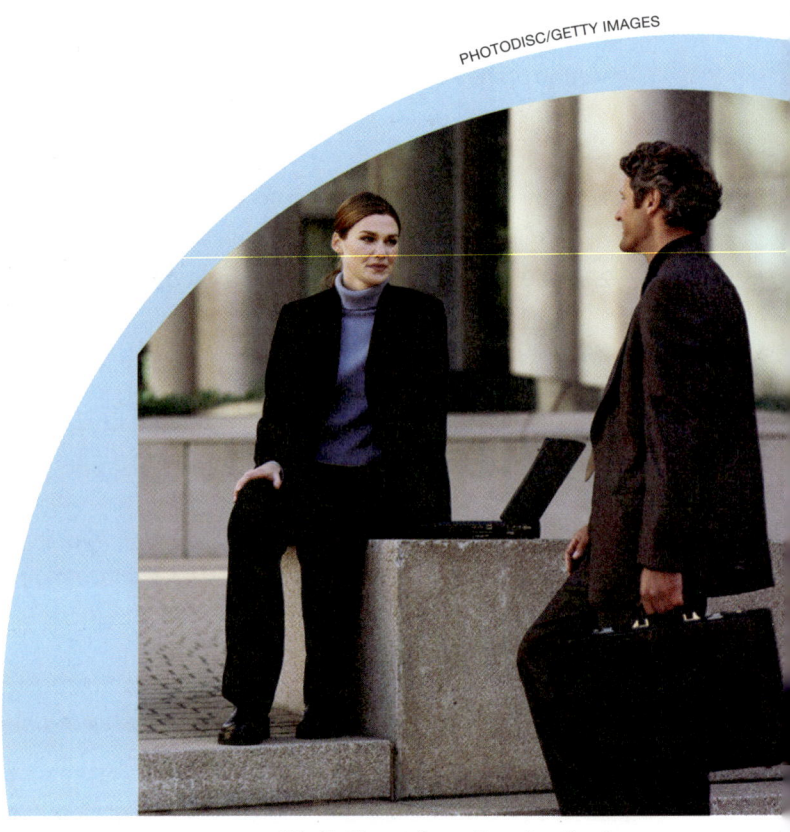

PHOTODISC/GETTY IMAGES

Work Sheet for a Service Business

152 Chapter 6

WORK SHEET

A columnar accounting form used to summarize the general ledger information needed to prepare financial statements is called a **work sheet.**

Accountants use a work sheet for four reasons: (1) to summarize general ledger account balances to prove that debits equal credits; (2) to plan needed changes to general ledger accounts to bring account balances up to date; (3) to separate general ledger account balances according to the financial statements to be prepared; and (4) to calculate the amount of net income or net loss for a fiscal period.

Journals and ledgers are permanent records of a business and are usually prepared in ink or printed by a computer. However, a work sheet is a planning tool and is not considered a permanent accounting record. Therefore, a work sheet is prepared in pencil.

PREPARING THE HEADING OF A WORK SHEET

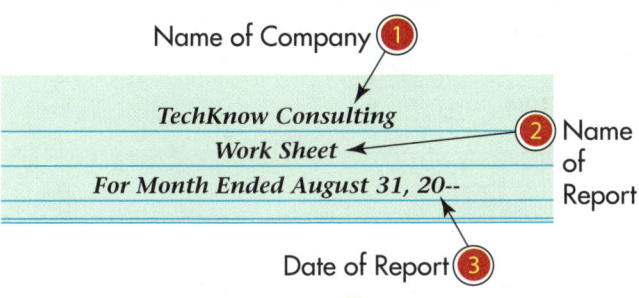

The heading on a work sheet consists of three lines and contains the name of the business, the name of the report, and the date of the report.

The date on TechKnow Consulting's work sheet indicates that the work sheet covers the 31 days from August 1 through and including August 31. If a work sheet were for a calendar year fiscal period, it might have a date stated as *For Year Ended December 31, 20--*.

CHARACTER COUNTS

Professional Codes of Conduct

Most professional organizations have a code of professional conduct to guide the actions of their members. One of the best-known codes of professional conduct is that of the American Institute of Certified Public Accountants (AICPA). A national organization of over 340,000 certified public accountants, the AICPA seeks to help its members provide professional services that benefit their employees, clients, and society. An important component of this mission is the AICPA Code of Professional Conduct.

The Code contains Rules of Conduct that its members must follow in their performance of professional services. The Rules address the topics of independence, integrity, objectivity, client relations, and colleague relations. Some Rules have Interpretations that provide further insight into the Rules. The Code is also supported by Ethics Rulings, a series of questions and answers that the AICPA elects to share with its members.

AICPA members who fail to adhere to the Code can be disciplined or expelled from the membership. Losing membership in the AICPA can result in serious consequences for a certified public accountant working in the profession.

Instructions

Access the AICPA's Code of Professional Conduct at www.aicpa.org. Citing the exact source of each answer, determine whether a member of the AICPA may:

1. Accept a gift from a client. (*Hint:* Search Independence Ethics Rulings)
2. Charge a client a fee based on the net income reported on the audited income statement. (*Hint:* Search Contingent Fees)
3. Advertise professional services in television commercials. (*Hint:* Search Other Professional Responsibilities and Practices, Advertising Interpretations)

PREPARING A TRIAL BALANCE ON A WORK SHEET

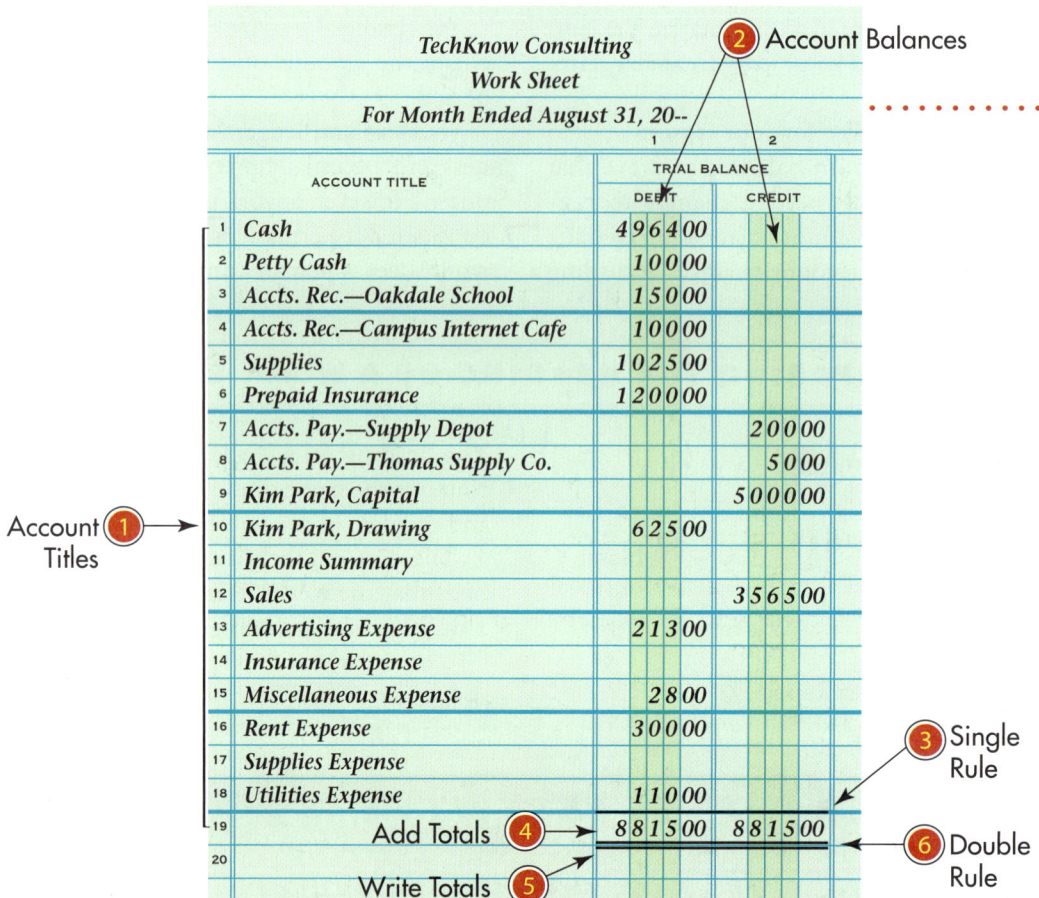

The total of all debit account balances must equal the total of all credit account balances. A proof of the equality of debits and credits in a general ledger is called a **trial balance.**

Information for the trial balance is taken from the general ledger. General ledger account titles are listed on a trial balance in the same order as they are listed on the chart of accounts. All the account titles are listed, even if some accounts do not have balances.

STEPS PREPARING A TRIAL BALANCE ON A WORK SHEET

1. Write the general ledger account titles in the work sheet's Account Title column.

2. Write the general ledger debit account balances in the Trial Balance Debit column. Write the general ledger credit account balances in the Trial Balance Credit column. If an account does not have a balance, the space in the Trial Balance columns is left blank.

3. Rule a single line across the two Trial Balance columns below the last line on which an account title is written. This single line shows that each column is to be added.

4. Add both the Trial Balance Debit and Credit columns. If the two column totals are the same, then debits equal credits in the general ledger accounts. If the two column totals are not the same, recheck the Trial Balance columns to find the error. Other parts of a work sheet are not completed until the Trial Balance columns are proved. Suggestions for locating errors are described later in this chapter.

5. Write each column's total below the single line.

6. Rule double lines across both Trial Balance columns. The double lines mean that the Trial Balance column totals have been verified as correct.

End of Lesson REVIEW

TERMS REVIEW

fiscal period
work sheet
trial balance

AUDIT YOUR UNDERSTANDING

1. What is written on the three-line heading on a work sheet?
2. What general ledger accounts are listed in the Trial Balance columns of a work sheet?

WORK TOGETHER 6-1

Recording the trial balance on a work sheet

Use the work sheet given in the *Working Papers*. Your instructor will guide you through the following example.

On February 28 of the current year, Golden Tan has the following general ledger accounts and balances. The business uses a monthly fiscal period.

Account Titles	Account Balances	
	Debit	Credit
Cash	$9,800.00	
Petty Cash	150.00	
Accounts Receivable—Ruby Prince	2,795.00	
Supplies	456.00	
Prepaid Insurance	750.00	
Accounts Payable—Richard Navarro		$ 555.00
Gary Baldwin, Capital		14,885.00
Gary Baldwin, Drawing	3,400.00	
Income Summary		
Sales		4,320.00
Advertising Expense	931.00	
Insurance Expense		
Miscellaneous Expense	378.00	
Supplies Expense		
Utilities Expense	1,100.00	

1. Prepare the heading and trial balance on a work sheet. Total and rule the Trial Balance columns. Save your work to complete Work Together 6-2.

Creating a Work Sheet

ON YOUR OWN 6-1

Recording the trial balance on a work sheet

Use the work sheet given in the *Working Papers*. Work this problem independently.

On December 31 of the current year, Copa's Copies has the following general ledger accounts and balances. The business uses a monthly fiscal period.

Account Titles	Account Balances	
	Debit	Credit
Cash	$6,800.00	
Petty Cash	75.00	
Accounts Receivable—Burt Strog	1,498.00	
Supplies	238.00	
Prepaid Insurance	325.00	
Accounts Payable—Janet Dao		$ 298.00
Jabbo West, Capital		7,443.00
Jabbo West, Drawing	1,700.00	
Income Summary		
Sales		4,140.00
Advertising Expense	456.00	
Insurance Expense		
Miscellaneous Expense	189.00	
Supplies Expense		
Utilities Expense	600.00	

1. Prepare the heading and trial balance on a work sheet. Total and rule the Trial Balance columns. Save your work to complete On Your Own 6-2.

LESSON 6-2: Planning Adjusting Entries on a Work Sheet

PLANNING ADJUSTMENTS ON A WORK SHEET

Sometimes a business will pay cash for an expense in one fiscal period, but the expense is not used until a later period. The expense should be reported in the same fiscal period that it is used to produce revenue. The accounting concept *Matching Expenses with Revenue* is applied when revenue from business activities and expenses associated with earning that revenue are recorded in the same accounting period. For example, TechKnow Consulting buys supplies in quantity in August, but some of the supplies are not used until September. Only the value of the supplies used in August should be reported as expenses in August. In this way, August revenue and the supplies expense associated with earning the August revenue are recorded in the same accounting period. [CONCEPT: Matching Expenses with Revenue]

In order to give accurate information on financial statements, some general ledger accounts must be brought up to date at the end of a fiscal period. For example, TechKnow Consulting debits an asset account, **Supplies**, each time supplies are bought. Supplies on hand are items of value owned by a business until the supplies are used. The value of supplies that are used becomes an expense to the business. However, recording an expense each time an individual supply, such as a pencil, is used would be impractical. Therefore, on August 31 the balance of the asset account, **Supplies**, is the value of all supplies bought rather than the value of only the supplies that have not yet been used. The amount of supplies that have been used must be deducted from the asset account, **Supplies**, and recorded in the expense account, **Supplies Expense**.

Likewise, the amount of insurance that has been used during the fiscal period is also an expense of the business. When the insurance premium for a year of insurance coverage is paid, the entire amount is debited to an asset account, **Prepaid Insurance**. Recording each day's amount of insurance used during August is impractical. Therefore, at the end of a fiscal period, the amount of the insurance coverage used must be deducted from the asset account, **Prepaid Insurance**, and recorded in the expense account, **Insurance Expense**.

Changes recorded on a work sheet to update general ledger accounts at the end of a fiscal period are called **adjustments**. The assets of a business, such as supplies and prepaid insurance, are used to earn revenue. The portions of the assets consumed in order to earn revenue become expenses of the business. The portions consumed are no longer assets but are now expenses. Therefore, adjustments must be made to both the asset and expense accounts for supplies and insurance. After the adjustments are made, the expenses incurred to earn revenue are reported in the same fiscal period as the revenue is earned and reported. [CONCEPT: Matching Expenses with Revenue]

A work sheet is used to plan adjustments. Changes are not made in general ledger accounts until adjustments are journalized and posted. The accuracy of the planning for adjustments is checked on a work sheet before adjustments are actually journalized.

Procedures for journalizing TechKnow Consulting's adjustments are described in Chapter 8.

> **REMEMBER**
>
> *The ending balance of the asset account, Supplies, should represent the amount of supplies remaining on hand at the end of the fiscal period. The amount of supplies used during the period should be recorded in the expense account, Supplies Expense.*

SUPPLIES ADJUSTMENT ON A WORK SHEET

On August 31, before adjustments, the balance of Supplies is $1,025.00, and the balance of Supplies Expense is zero, as shown in the T accounts.

BEFORE ADJUSTMENT

Supplies Expense

Supplies
Aug. 31 Bal. 1,025.00

On August 31, Ms. Park counted the supplies on hand and found that the value of supplies still unused on that date was $310.00. The value of the supplies used is calculated as follows.

Supplies Account Balance, August 31	−	Supplies on Hand, August 31	=	Supplies Used During August
$1,025.00	−	$310.00	=	$715.00

Four questions are asked in analyzing the adjustment for the asset account, Supplies.

1. **What is the balance of Supplies?** *$1,025.00*
2. **What should the balance be for this account?** *$310.00*
3. **What must be done to correct the account balance?** *Decrease $715.00*
4. **What adjustment is made?**
   Debit Supplies Expense, *$715.00*
   Credit Supplies, *$715.00*

The expense account, Supplies Expense, is increased by a debit, $715.00, the value of supplies used. The balance of Supplies Expense, $715.00, is the value of supplies used during the fiscal period from August 1 to August 31. [CONCEPT: Matching Expenses with Revenue]

AFTER ADJUSTMENT

Supplies Expense
Adj. (a)   715.00

Supplies
Aug. 31 Bal. 1,025.00 | Adj. (a)   715.00
(New Bal.   310.00)

The asset account, Supplies, is decreased by a credit, $715.00, the value of supplies used. The debit balance, $1,025.00, less the credit adjustment, $715.00, equals the new balance, $310.00. The new balance of Supplies is the same as the value of supplies on hand on August 31.

STEPS — RECORDING THE SUPPLIES ADJUSTMENT ON A WORK SHEET

1. Write the debit amount, *$715.00*, in the work sheet's Adjustments Debit column on the line with the account title *Supplies Expense*.

2. Write the credit amount, *$715.00*, in the Adjustments Credit column on the line with the account title *Supplies*.

3. Label the two parts of this adjustment with a small letter *a* in parentheses, *(a)*. The letter *a* identifies the debit and credit amounts as part of the same adjustment.

PREPAID INSURANCE ADJUSTMENT ON A WORK SHEET

On August 31, before adjustments, the balance of Prepaid Insurance is $1,200.00 and the balance of Insurance Expense is zero.

BEFORE ADJUSTMENT

Insurance Expense

Prepaid Insurance
Aug. 31 Bal.   1,200.00

On August 31, Ms. Park checked the insurance records and found that the value of insurance coverage remaining was $1,100.00. The value of the insurance coverage used during the fiscal period is calculated as follows.

Prepaid Insurance Balance, August 31	−	Insurance Coverage Remaining Unused, August 31	=	Insurance Coverage Used During August
$1,200.00	−	$1,100.00	=	$100.00

Four questions are asked in analyzing the adjustment for the asset account, Prepaid Insurance.

1. **What is the balance of** Prepaid Insurance? *$1,200.00*
2. **What should the balance be for this account?** *$1,100.00*
3. **What must be done to correct the account balance?** *Decrease $100.00*
4. **What adjustment is made?**
   Debit Insurance Expense, *$100.00*
   Credit Prepaid Insurance, *$100.00*

The expense account, Insurance Expense, is increased by a debit, $100.00, the value of insurance used. The balance of Insurance Expense, $100.00, is the value of insurance coverage used from August 1 to August 31. [CONCEPT: Matching Expenses with Revenue]

AFTER ADJUSTMENT

Insurance Expense
Adj. (b)   100.00

Prepaid Insurance
Aug. 31 Bal.   1,200.00 | Adj. (b)   100.00
(New Bal.   1,100.00)

The asset account, Prepaid Insurance, is decreased by a credit, $100.00, the value of insurance used. The debit balance, $1,200.00, less the credit adjustment, $100.00, equals the new balance, $1,100.00. The new balance of Prepaid Insurance is the same as the amount of insurance coverage unused on August 31.

STEPS — RECORDING THE PREPAID INSURANCE ADJUSTMENT ON A WORK SHEET

1. Write the debit amount, $100.00, in the work sheet's Adjustments Debit column on the line with the account title *Insurance Expense*.

2. Write the credit amount, $100.00, in the Adjustments Credit column on the line with the account title *Prepaid Insurance*.

3. Label the two parts of this adjustment with a small letter *b* in parentheses, *(b)*. The letter *b* identifies the debit and credit amounts as part of the same adjustment.

Planning Adjusting Entries on a Work Sheet

PROVING THE ADJUSTMENTS COLUMNS OF A WORK SHEET

TechKnow Consulting
Work Sheet
For Month Ended August 31, 20--

	ACCOUNT TITLE	TRIAL BALANCE DEBIT	TRIAL BALANCE CREDIT	ADJUSTMENTS DEBIT	ADJUSTMENTS CREDIT	
5	Supplies	1025.00			(a) 715.00	
6	Prepaid Insurance	1200.00			(b) 100.00	
14	Insurance Expense			(b) 100.00		
15	Miscellaneous Expense	28.00				
16	Rent Expense	300.00				
17	Supplies Expense			(a) 715.00		
18	Utilities Expense	110.00				← ① Single Rule
19		8815.00	8815.00	815.00	815.00	← ② Totals
						← ③ Double Rule

After all adjustments are recorded in a work sheet's Adjustments columns, the equality of debits and credits for the two columns is proved by totaling and ruling the two columns.

STEPS — PROVING THE ADJUSTMENTS COLUMNS OF A WORK SHEET

1. Rule a single line across the two Adjustments columns on the same line as the single line for the Trial Balance columns.

2. Add both the Adjustments Debit and Credit columns. If the two column totals are the same, then debits equal credits for these two columns, and the work sheet's Adjustments columns are in balance. Write each column's total below the single line. If the two Adjustments column totals are not the same, the Adjustments columns are rechecked and errors corrected before the work sheet is completed.

3. Rule double lines across both Adjustments columns. The double lines mean that the totals have been verified as correct.

GLOBAL PERSPECTIVE

International Weights and Measures

The primary system of measurement in the United States is the customary system. Among the units of measurement in the customary system are inches, feet, and quarts. The United States is among the few major industrial countries that do not use the metric system exclusively. Among the units of measurement in the metric system are centimeters, meters, and liters. The metric system is based on a decimal system—like U.S. currency. Some U.S. industries have converted to the metric system. Others specify measurements in both customary and metric systems.

To conduct international business, the U.S. has recognized the need to convert customary units to the metric system. For example, beverages are routinely packaged in liter containers. Although the U.S. is a global business leader, it has had to adjust to meet the needs of the rest of the world.

Critical Thinking

1. Look at five food packages. List the weights and measures indicated.

2. List arguments both for and against a proposal to convert all U.S. weights and measures to the metric system.

SUMMARY OF PREPARATION OF A WORK SHEET FOR A SERVICE BUSINESS

The following overlay summarizes the preparation of a work sheet. Follow the directions below in using the overlay.

1. Before using the overlay, be sure the pages and transparent overlays are arranged correctly. The correct arrangement is shown below.

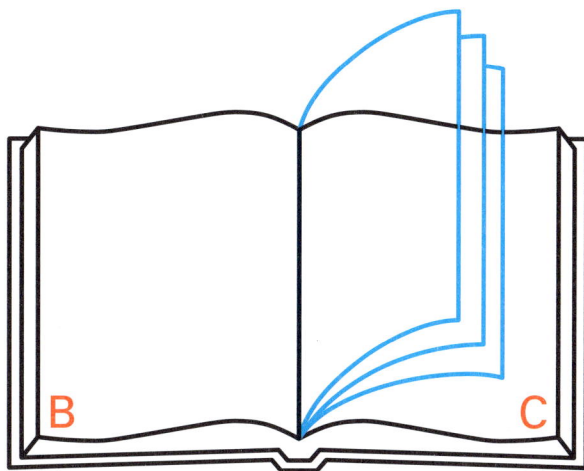

2. Place your book in a horizontal position. Study the steps on page C in preparing the work sheet. You will be able to read the text through the transparent overlays. When directed, carefully lift the transparent overlays and lay them over the work sheet as shown below.

A

PREPARING A WORK SHEET

To correctly use the insert, read the steps on page C. Apply the transparent overlays when directed to do so in the steps.

TechKnow Consulting
Work Sheet
For Month Ended August 31, 20--

	ACCOUNT TITLE	TRIAL BALANCE DEBIT	TRIAL BALANCE CREDIT	ADJUSTMENTS DEBIT	ADJUSTMENTS CREDIT	INCOME STATEMENT DEBIT	INCOME STATEMENT CREDIT	BALANCE SHEET DEBIT	BALANCE SHEET CREDIT	
1	Cash	4964 00								1
2	Petty Cash	100 00								2
3	Accts. Rec.—Oakdale School	150 00								3
4	Accts. Rec.—Campus Internet Cafe	100 00								4
5	Supplies	1025 00								5
6	Prepaid Insurance	1200 00								6
7	Accts. Pay.—Supply Depot		200 00							7
8	Accts. Pay.—Thomas Supply Co.		50 00							8
9	Kim Park, Capital		5000 00							9
10	Kim Park, Drawing	625 00								10
11	Income Summary									11
12	Sales		3565 00							12
13	Advertising Expense	213 00								13
14	Insurance Expense									14
15	Miscellaneous Expense	28 00								15
16	Rent Expense	300 00								16
17	Supplies Expense									17
18	Utilities Expense	110 00								18
19		8815 00	8815 00							19
20										20
21										21

B

End of Lesson REVIEW

AUDIT YOUR UNDERSTANDING

1. Explain how the concept of Matching Expenses with Revenue relates to adjustments.
2. List the four questions asked in analyzing an adjustment on a work sheet.

TERM REVIEW

adjustments

WORK TOGETHER 6-2

Planning adjustments on a work sheet

Use the work sheet from Work Together 6-1. Your instructor will guide you through the following examples.

1. Analyze the following adjustment information into debit and credit parts. Record the adjustments on the work sheet.

   Adjustment Information, February 28
   Supplies on hand $325.00
   Value of prepaid insurance   500.00

2. Total and rule the Adjustments columns. Save your work sheet to complete Work Together 6-3.

ON YOUR OWN 6-2

Planning adjustments on a work sheet

Use the work sheet from On Your Own 6-1. Work this problem independently.

1. Analyze the following adjustment information into debit and credit parts. Record the adjustments on the work sheet.

   Adjustment Information, December 31
   Supplies on hand $120.00
   Value of prepaid insurance   225.00

2. Total and rule the Adjustments columns. Save your work sheet to complete On Your Own 6-3.

Planning Adjusting Entries on a Work Sheet

LESSON 6-3: Extending Financial Statement Information on a Work Sheet

EXTENDING BALANCE SHEET ACCOUNT BALANCES ON A WORK SHEET

TechKnow Consulting
Work Sheet
For Month Ended August 31, 20--

	ACCOUNT TITLE	TRIAL BALANCE DEBIT	TRIAL BALANCE CREDIT	ADJUSTMENTS DEBIT	ADJUSTMENTS CREDIT	INCOME STATEMENT DEBIT	INCOME STATEMENT CREDIT	BALANCE SHEET DEBIT	BALANCE SHEET CREDIT	
1	Cash	4964 00						4964 00		1
2	Petty Cash	100 00						100 00		2
3	Accts. Rec.—Oakdale School	150 00						150 00		3
4	Accts. Rec.—Campus Internet Cafe	100 00						100 00		4
5	Supplies	1025 00			(a) 715 00			310 00		5
6	Prepaid Insurance	1200 00			(b) 100 00			1100 00		6
7	Accts. Pay.—Supply Depot		200 00						200 00	7
8	Accts. Pay.—Thomas Supply Co.		50 00						50 00	8
9	Kim Park, Capital		5000 00						5000 00	9
10	Kim Park, Drawing	625 00						625 00		10

② Debit Balances with Adjustments   ③ Credit Balances without Adjustments

At the end of each fiscal period, TechKnow Consulting prepares two financial statements from information on a work sheet. [CONCEPT: Accounting Period Cycle] The up-to-date account balances on a work sheet are extended to columns for the two financial statements.

A financial statement that reports assets, liabilities, and owner's equity on a specific date is called a **balance sheet**. The balance sheet accounts are the asset, liability, and owner's equity accounts. Up-to-date balance sheet account balances are extended to the Balance Sheet Debit and Credit columns of the work sheet.

STEPS: EXTENDING BALANCE SHEET ACCOUNT BALANCES ON A WORK SHEET

① Extend the balance of *Cash*, $4,964.00, to the Balance Sheet Debit column. The balance of *Cash* in the Trial Balance Debit column is up-to-date because no adjustment affects this account. Extend to the Balance Sheet Debit column the balances of all accounts with debit balances that are not affected by adjustments.

② Calculate the up-to-date adjusted balance of *Supplies*. The balance of *Supplies* in the Trial Balance Debit column is not up-to-date because it is affected by an adjustment. The debit balance, $1,025.00, minus the credit adjustment, $715.00, equals the up-to-date adjusted balance, $310.00. Extend the up-to-date balance, *$310.00*, to the Balance Sheet Debit column. Using the same procedure, calculate and extend the up-to-date adjusted balance of the other asset account affected by an adjustment, *Prepaid Insurance*.

③ Extend the up-to-date balance of *Accounts Payable—Supply Depot*, $200.00, to the Balance Sheet Credit column. The balance of *Accounts Payable—Supply Depot* in the Trial Balance Credit column is up-to-date because no adjustment affects this account. Extend to the Balance Sheet Credit column the balances of all accounts with credit balances that are not affected by adjustments.

EXTENDING INCOME STATEMENT ACCOUNT BALANCES ON A WORK SHEET

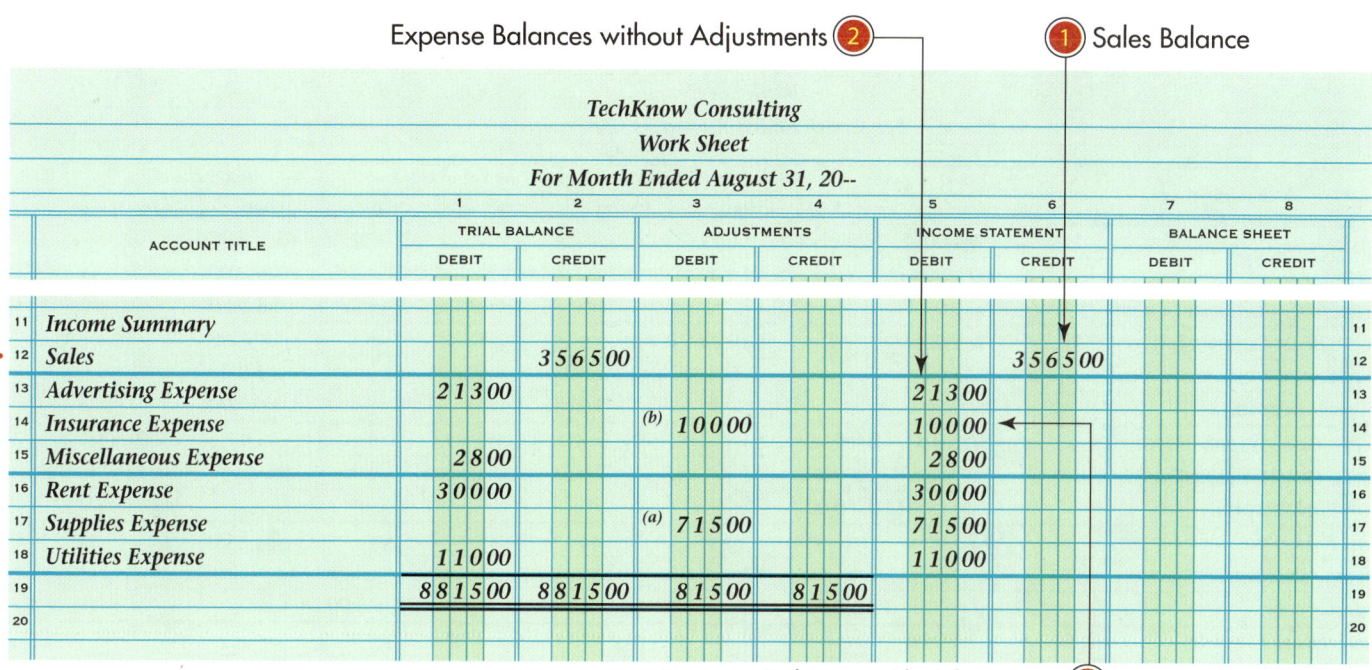

A financial statement showing the revenue and expenses for a fiscal period is called an **income statement.** TechKnow Consulting's income statement accounts are the revenue and expense accounts. Up-to-date income statement account balances are extended to the Income Statement Debit and Credit columns of the work sheet.

FOR YOUR INFORMATION — FYI

Use a ruler when extending amounts on a work sheet to keep track of the line you are on.

FOR YOUR INFORMATION — FYI

A work sheet is prepared in manual accounting to adjust the accounts and sort amounts needed to prepare financial statements. However, in automated accounting, adjustments are prepared from the trial balance, and the software automatically generates the financial statements with no need for a work sheet.

STEPS: EXTENDING INCOME STATEMENT ACCOUNT BALANCES ON A WORK SHEET

1. Extend the balance of *Sales*, $3,565.00, to the Income Statement Credit column. The balance of *Sales* in the Trial Balance Credit column is up-to-date because no adjustment affects this account.

2. Extend the balance of *Advertising Expense*, $213.00, to the Income Statement Debit column. The balance of *Advertising Expense* is up-to-date because no adjustment affects this account. Extend the balances of all expense accounts not affected by adjustments to the Income Statement Debit column.

3. Calculate the up-to-date adjusted balance of *Insurance Expense*. The balance of *Insurance Expense* in the Trial Balance Debit column is zero. This zero balance is not up-to-date because this account is affected by an adjustment. The debit balance, $0.00, plus the debit adjustment, $100.00, equals the adjusted balance, $100.00. Extend the up-to-date adjusted debit balance, *$100.00,* to the Income Statement Debit column. Using the same procedure, calculate and extend the up-to-date adjusted balance of each expense account affected by an adjustment.

Extending Financial Statement Information on a Work Sheet — Lesson 6-3

RECORDING NET INCOME, AND TOTALING AND RULING A WORK SHEET

TechKnow Consulting
Work Sheet
For Month Ended August 31, 20--

	ACCOUNT TITLE	TRIAL BALANCE		ADJUSTMENTS		INCOME STATEMENT		BALANCE SHEET		
		DEBIT	CREDIT	DEBIT	CREDIT	DEBIT	CREDIT	DEBIT	CREDIT	
1	Cash	4964 00						4964 00		1
2	Petty Cash	100 00						100 00		2
3	Accts. Rec.—Oakdale School	150 00						150 00		3
4	Accts. Rec.—Campus Internet Cafe	100 00						100 00		4
5	Supplies	1025 00			(a) 715 00			310 00		5
6	Prepaid Insurance	1200 00			(b) 100 00			1100 00		6
7	Accts. Pay.—Supply Depot		200 00						200 00	7
8	Accts. Pay.—Thomas Supply Co.		50 00						50 00	8
9	Kim Park, Capital		5000 00						5000 00	9
10	Kim Park, Drawing	625 00						625 00		10
11	Income Summary									11
12	Sales		3565 00				3565 00			12
13	Advertising Expense	213 00				213 00				13
14	Insurance Expense			(b) 100 00		100 00				14
15	Miscellaneous Expense	28 00				28 00				15
16	Rent Expense	300 00				300 00				16
17	Supplies Expense			(a) 715 00		715 00				17
18	Utilities Expense	110 00				110 00				18
19		8815 00	8815 00	815 00	815 00	1466 00	3565 00	7349 00	5250 00	19
20	Net Income					2099 00			2099 00	20
21						3565 00	3565 00	7349 00	7349 00	21

Single Rule ① Totals ② ⑤ Single Rule

③ Net Income   Totals ⑥   Double Rule ⑦

The difference between total revenue and total expenses when total revenue is greater is called **net income.** Before the work sheet is complete, net income must be calculated and the work sheet must be totaled and ruled. A summary of preparing a work sheet is shown on the Work Sheet Overlay.

STEPS: CALCULATING AND RECORDING NET INCOME ON A WORK SHEET; TOTALING AND RULING A WORK SHEET

1. Rule a single line across the four income statement and balance sheet columns.

2. Add both the Income Statement and Balance Sheet columns. Write the totals below the single line.

3. Calculate the net income. The Income Statement Credit column total, $3,565.00, minus the Income Statement Debit column total, $1,466.00, equals net income, $2,099.00. Write the amount of net income, *$2,099.00,* below the Income Statement Debit column total. Write the words *Net Income* on the same line in the Account Title column.

4. Extend the amount of net income, *$2,099.00,* to the Balance Sheet Credit column. Since the owner's equity account, *Kim Park, Capital,* increases by a credit, extend the net income amount to the Balance Sheet Credit column.

5. Rule a single line across the four Income Statement and Balance Sheet columns just below the net income amounts.

6. Add the subtotal and net income amount for each column to get proving totals for the Income Statement and Balance Sheet columns. Write the totals below the single line. Check the equality for each pair of columns.

7. Rule double lines across the Income Statement and Balance Sheet columns.

164 Chapter 6 Work Sheet for a Service Business

CALCULATING AND RECORDING A NET LOSS ON A WORK SHEET

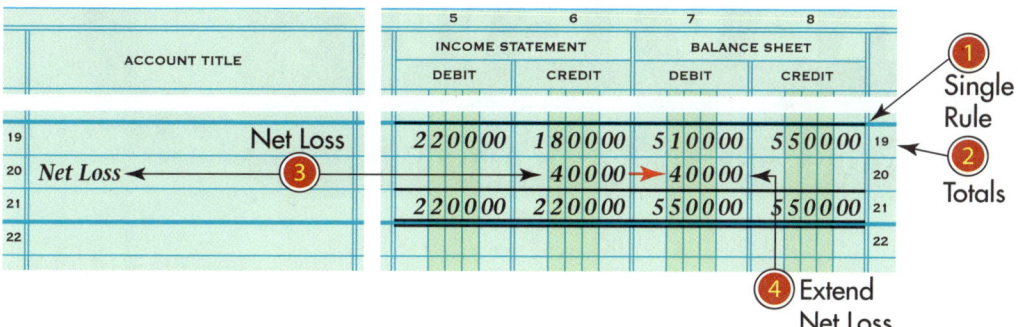

TechKnow Consulting's completed work sheet shows a net income. However, a business might have a net loss to report. The difference between total revenue and total expenses when total expenses are greater is called a **net loss.**

STEPS — CALCULATING AND RECORDING A NET LOSS ON A WORK SHEET

1. Rule a single line across the four Income Statement and Balance Sheet columns.

2. Add both the Income Statement and Balance Sheet columns. Write the totals below the single line.

3. Calculate the net loss. The Income Statement Debit column total, $2,200.00, minus the Income Statement Credit column total, $1,800.00, equals net loss, $400.00. The Income Statement Debit column total (expenses) is greater than the Income Statement Credit column total (revenue). Therefore, because expenses exceed revenue, there is a net loss. Write the amount of net loss, $400.00, below the Income Statement Credit column total. Write the words *Net Loss* on the same line in the Account Title column.

4. Extend the amount of net loss, $400.00, to the Balance Sheet Debit column on the same line as the words *Net Loss*. The owner's equity account, *Kim Park, Capital*, is decreased by a debit. Therefore, a net loss is extended to the Balance Sheet Debit column.

Extending Financial Statement Information on a Work Sheet

End of Lesson REVIEW

AUDIT YOUR UNDERSTANDING

1. Which accounts are extended into the Balance Sheet columns of the work sheet?
2. Which accounts are extended into the Income Statement columns of the work sheet?
3. In which Balance Sheet column do you record net income on the work sheet?
4. In which Balance Sheet column do you record net loss on the work sheet?

TERMS REVIEW

balance sheet
income statement
net income
net loss

WORK TOGETHER 6-3

Completing a work sheet

Use the work sheet from Work Together 6-2. Your instructor will guide you through the following examples.

1. Extend the up-to-date balances to the Balance Sheet and Income Statement columns.
2. Rule a single line across the Income Statement and Balance Sheet columns. Total each column. Calculate and record the net income or net loss. Label the amount in the Account Title column.
3. Total and rule the Income Statement and Balance Sheet columns.

ON YOUR OWN 6-3

Completing a work sheet

Use the work sheet from On Your Own 6-2. Work this problem independently.

1. Extend the up-to-date balances to the Balance Sheet or Income Statement columns.
2. Rule a single line across the Income Statement and Balance Sheet columns. Total each column. Calculate and record the net income or net loss. Label the amount in the Account Title column.
3. Total and rule the Income Statement and Balance Sheet columns.

LESSON 6-4: Finding and Correcting Errors on the Work Sheet

CORRECTING ACCOUNTING ERRORS ON THE WORK SHEET

Some errors in accounting records are not discovered until a work sheet is prepared. For example, a debit to supplies may not have been posted from a journal to the general ledger supplies account. The omission may not be discovered until the work sheet's trial balance does not balance. Also, information may be transferred incorrectly from general ledger accounts to the work sheet's trial balance. Additional errors may be made, such as recording adjustment information incorrectly or adding columns incorrectly. In addition, errors may be made in extending amounts to the Income Statement and Balance Sheet columns.

Any errors found on a work sheet should be corrected before any further work is completed. If an incorrect amount is found on a work sheet, erase the error and replace it with the correct amount. If an amount is written in an incorrect column, erase the amount and record it in the correct column.

CHECKING FOR TYPICAL CALCULATION ERRORS

When two column totals are not in balance, subtract the smaller total from the larger total to find the difference. Check the difference between the two amounts against the following guides.

1. **The difference is 1, such as $.01, $.10, $1.00, or $10.00.** For example, if the totals of the two columns are Debit, $14,657.00, and Credit, $14,658.00, the difference between the two columns is $1.00. The error is most likely in addition. Add the columns again.
2. **The difference can be divided evenly by 2.** For example, the difference between two column totals is $48.00, which can be divided by 2 with no remainder. Look for a $24.00 amount in the Trial Balance columns of the work sheet. If the amount is found, check to make sure it has been recorded in the correct Debit or Credit column. A $24.00 debit amount recorded in a credit column results in a difference between column totals of $48.00. If the error is not found on the work sheet, check the general ledger accounts and journal entries. An entry for $24.00 may have been recorded in an incorrect column in the journal or in an account.
3. **The difference can be divided evenly by 9.** For example, the difference between two columns is $45.00, which can be divided by 9 with no remainder. When the difference can be divided equally by 9, look for transposed numbers such as 54 written as 45 or 19 written as 91. Also, check for a "slide." A "slide" occurs when numbers are moved to the right or left in an amount column. For example, $12.00 is recorded as $120.00 or $350.00 is recorded as $35.00.
4. **The difference is an omitted amount.** Look for an amount equal to the difference. If the difference is $50.00, look for an account balance of $50.00 that has not been extended. Look for any $50.00 amount on the work sheet and determine if it has been handled correctly. Look in the accounts and journals for a $50.00 amount, and check if that amount has been handled correctly. Failure to record a $50.00 account balance will make a work sheet's column totals differ by $50.00.

CHECKING FOR ERRORS IN THE WORK SHEET

Check for Errors in the Trial Balance Column
1. Have all general ledger account balances been copied in the trial balance column correctly?
2. Have all general ledger account balances been recorded in the correct Trial Balance column?

Check for Errors in the Adjustments Columns
1. Do the debits equal the credits for each adjustment? Use the small letters that label each part of an adjustment to help check accuracy and equality of debits and credits.
2. Is the amount for each adjustment correct?

Check for Errors in the Income Statement and Balance Sheet Columns
1. Has each amount been copied correctly when extended to the Income Statement or Balance Sheet column?
2. Has each account balance been extended to the correct Income Statement or Balance Sheet column?
3. Has the net income or net loss been calculated correctly?
4. Has the net income or net loss been recorded in the correct Income Statement or Balance Sheet column?

For all three of these cases, correct any errors found and add the columns again.

CORRECTING AN ERROR IN POSTING TO THE WRONG ACCOUNT

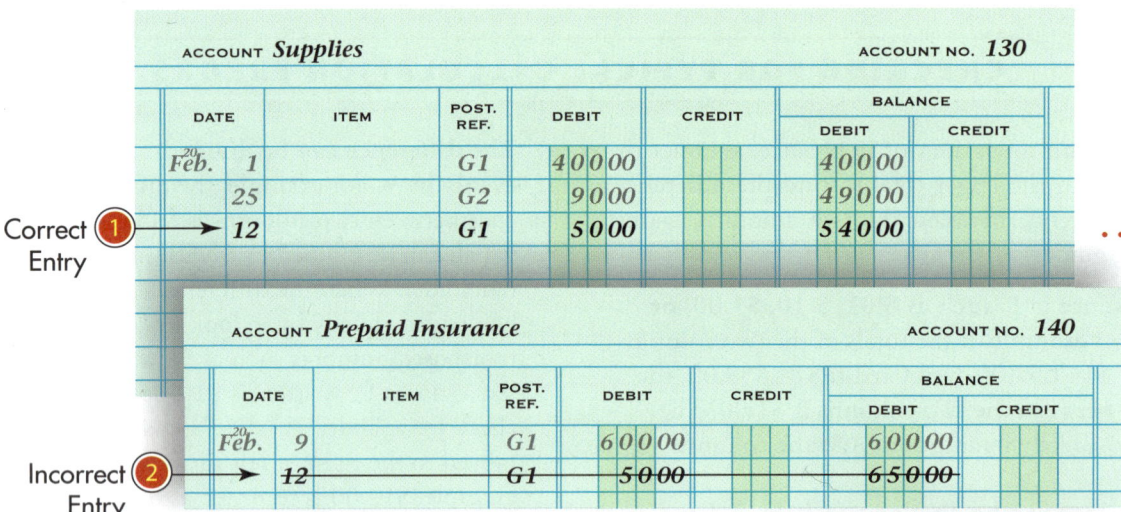

If a pair of work sheet columns does not balance and an error cannot be found on the work sheet, look for an error in posting from the journal to the general ledger accounts.

As each item in an account or a journal entry is verified, a check mark should be placed next to it. The check mark indicates that the item has been checked for accuracy.

1. Have all amounts that need to be posted actually been posted from the journal? To correct, complete the posting to the correct account. When posting is corrected, recalculate the account balance and correct it on the work sheet.
2. Have all amounts been posted to the correct accounts? To correct, follow these steps.

STEPS — CORRECTING AN ERROR IN POSTING TO THE WRONG ACCOUNT

1. Draw a line through the entire incorrect entry. Recalculate the account balance and correct the work sheet.

2. Record the posting in the correct account. Recalculate the account balance, and correct the work sheet.

168 Chapter 6 Work Sheet for a Service Business

CORRECTING AN INCORRECT AMOUNT AND AN AMOUNT POSTED TO THE WRONG COLUMN

Errors can be made in writing amounts in general ledger accounts. Errors in permanent records should never be erased. Erasures in permanent records raise questions about whether important financial information has been altered.

STEPS CORRECTING AN INCORRECT AMOUNT

1. Draw a line through the incorrect amount.
2. Write the correct amount just above the correction in the same space.
3. Recalculate the account balance, and correct the account balance on the work sheet.

CORRECTING AN AMOUNT POSTED TO THE WRONG COLUMN

4. Draw a line through the incorrect item in the account.
5. Record the posting in the correct amount column.
6. Recalculate the account balance, and correct the work sheet.

CHECKING FOR ERRORS IN JOURNAL ENTRIES

1. Do debits equal credits in each journal entry?
2. Is each journal entry amount recorded in the correct journal column?
3. Is information in the Account Title column correct for each journal entry?
4. Are all of the journal amount column totals correct?
5. Does the sum of debit column totals equal the sum of credit column totals in the journal?
6. Have all transactions been recorded?

Some suggestions for correcting errors in journal entries are described in Chapter 3.

PREVENTING ERRORS

The best way to prevent errors is to work carefully. Check the work at each step in an accounting procedure. Most errors occur in doing arithmetic, especially in adding columns. When possible, use a calculator. When an error is discovered, do no more work until the cause of the error is found and corrections are made.

Finding and Correcting Errors on the Work Sheet

End of Lesson REVIEW

AUDIT YOUR UNDERSTANDING

1. What is the first step in checking for arithmetic errors when two column totals are not in balance?
2. What is one way to check for an error caused by transposed numbers?
3. What term is used to describe an error that occurs when numbers are moved to the right or left in an amount column?

WORK TOGETHER 6-4

Finding and correcting errors in accounting records

Paul Coty has completed the September monthly work sheet for his business, LeafyLift. The work sheet and general ledger accounts are given in the *Working Papers*. Mr. Coty believes that he has made one or more errors in preparing the work sheet. He asks you to help him verify the work sheet. Your instructor will guide you through the following examples.

1. Examine the work sheet and the general ledger accounts. Make a list of the errors you find.
2. Correct any errors you find in the general ledger accounts.
3. Prepare a corrected work sheet.

ON YOUR OWN 6-4

Finding and correcting errors in accounting records

Nadine Fritz has completed the November monthly work sheet for her business, Your Personal Trainer. The work sheet and general ledger accounts are given in the *Working Papers*. Ms. Fritz believes that she has made one or more errors in preparing the work sheet. She asks you to help her verify the work sheet. Work this problem independently.

1. Examine the work sheet and the general ledger accounts. Make a list of the errors you find.
2. Correct any errors you find in the general ledger accounts.
3. Prepare a corrected work sheet.

SUMMARY

After completing this chapter, you can:

1. Define accounting terms related to a work sheet for a service business organized as a proprietorship.
2. Identify accounting concepts and practices related to a work sheet for a service business organized as a proprietorship.
3. Prepare a heading and a trial balance on a work sheet.
4. Plan adjustments for supplies and prepaid insurance.
5. Complete a work sheet for a service business organized as a proprietorship.
6. Identify selected procedures for finding and correcting errors in accounting records.

EXPLORE ACCOUNTING

Fiscal Periods

A fiscal period is the length of time for which a business summarizes and reports financial information. Since many companies are required to publish yearly annual reports, these companies choose a year for the fiscal period. In such a case, a company will prepare financial statements every year.

A fiscal year can be any consecutive 12-month period. The Internal Revenue Service (IRS) requires many companies to report taxable income for the fiscal year January 1 through December 31. A fiscal year beginning January 1 can also be called a calendar year. Because they use a calendar year for reporting taxable income, many companies choose to use the calendar year for issuing financial statements also.

However, there is no requirement to begin a fiscal year on January 1. Companies often choose a fiscal year that ends during a period of low business activity. Twelve consecutive months which end when business activities have reached the lowest point in their annual cycle are called a natural business year.

The following survey conducted on 600 businesses shows the number of companies that chose a fiscal year ending at the end of a specific month.

Fiscal Year End	No. of Companies
January	32
February	10
March	16
April	8
May	18
June	48
July	8
August	15
September	38
October	19
November	15
December	373

Activity: Assume you work for a company that makes snowmobiles. You must determine what fiscal year should be used. Make a written recommendation to the owner. Explain why your recommendation is preferable.

Source: Accounting Trends and Techniques, *2002, published by the American Institute of Certified Public Accountants.*

6-1 APPLICATION PROBLEM

Recording the trial balance on a work sheet

Use the work sheet given in the *Working Papers*. On June 30 of the current year, Roseville Rental has the following general ledger accounts and balances. The business uses a monthly fiscal period.

Account Titles	Account Balances	
	Debit	Credit
Cash	$11,620.00	
Petty Cash	100.00	
Accounts Receivable—Leslie Naples	855.00	
Supplies	690.00	
Prepaid Insurance	900.00	
Accounts Payable—Russell Goodland		$ 355.00
Sunthi Ling, Capital		12,926.00
Sunthi Ling, Drawing	500.00	
Income Summary		
Sales		2,270.00
Advertising Expense	340.00	
Insurance Expense		
Miscellaneous Expense	184.00	
Supplies Expense		
Utilities Expense	362.00	

Instructions:
Prepare the heading and trial balance on a work sheet. Total and rule the Trial Balance columns. Save your work to complete Application Problem 6-2.

6-2 APPLICATION PROBLEM

Planning adjustments on a work sheet

Use the work sheet from Application Problem 6-1.

Instructions:

1. Analyze the following adjustment information into debit and credit parts. Record the adjustments on the work sheet.

   Adjustment Information, June 30
Supplies on hand	$250.00
Value of prepaid insurance	750.00

2. Total and rule the Adjustments columns. Save your work to complete Application Problem 6-3.

Go Beyond the Book
For more information go to www.C21accounting.com

6-3 APPLICATION PROBLEM

Completing a work sheet

Use the work sheet from Application Problem 6-2.

Instructions:
1. Extend the up-to-date balances to the Balance Sheet or Income Statement columns.
2. Rule a single line across the Income Statement and Balance Sheet columns. Total each column. Calculate and record the net income or net loss. Label the amount in the Account Title column.
3. Total and rule the Income Statement and Balance Sheet columns.

6-4 APPLICATION PROBLEM

Finding and correcting errors in accounting records

Ervin Watkins has completed the April monthly work sheet for his business, EverClean. The work sheet and general ledger accounts are given in the *Working Papers*. Mr. Watkins believes that he has made one or more errors in preparing the work sheet. He asks you to help him verify the work sheet.

Instructions:
1. Examine the work sheet and the general ledger accounts. Make a list of the errors you find.
2. Correct any errors you find in the general ledger accounts.
3. Prepare a corrected work sheet.

6-5 MASTERY PROBLEM

Completing a work sheet

On April 30 of the current year, Bonita Bubbles has the following general ledger accounts and balances. The business uses a monthly fiscal period. A work sheet is given in the *Working Papers*.

Account Titles	Account Balances	
	Debit	**Credit**
Cash	$2,829.00	
Petty Cash	150.00	
Accounts Receivable—Bernard Corbett	511.00	
Supplies	855.00	
Prepaid Insurance	1,100.00	
Accounts Payable—Spooner Supplies		$ 500.00
Paulo Gutierrez, Capital		4,500.00
Paulo Gutierrez, Drawing	440.00	
Income Summary		
Sales		2,400.00
Advertising Expense	450.00	
Insurance Expense		
Miscellaneous Expense	190.00	
Rent Expense	375.00	
Supplies Expense		
Utilities Expense	500.00	

Work Sheet for a Service Business

Instructions:

1. Prepare the heading and trial balance on a work sheet. Total and rule the Trial Balance columns.
2. Analyze the following adjustment information into debit and credit parts. Record the adjustments on the work sheet.

   Adjustment Information, April 30
Supplies inventory	$220.00
Value of prepaid insurance	800.00

3. Total and rule the Adjustments columns.
4. Extend the up-to-date balances to the Balance Sheet or Income Statement columns.
5. Rule a single line across the Income Statement and Balance Sheet columns. Total each column. Calculate and record the net income or net loss. Label the amount in the Account Title column.
6. Total and rule the Income Statement and Balance Sheet columns.

6-6 CHALLENGE PROBLEM

Completing a work sheet

LawnPro Company had a small fire in its office. The fire destroyed some of the accounting records. On November 30 of the current year, the end of a monthly fiscal period, the following information was constructed from the remaining records and other sources. A work sheet is given in the *Working Papers*.

Remains of the general ledger:

Account Titles	Account Balances
Accounts Receivable—C. Gabriel	$ 825.00
Supplies	700.00
Don Arnodt, Drawing	300.00
Sales	3,800.00
Advertising Expense	200.00
Rent Expense	600.00
Utilities Expense	390.00

Information from the business's checkbook:

Cash balance on last unused check stub	$3,119.00
Total payments for miscellaneous expense	50.00
Total payments for insurance	400.00

Information obtained through inquiries to other businesses:

Owed to St. Croix Supplies	$1,500.00
Value of prepaid insurance, November 30	250.00

Information obtained by counting supplies on hand after the fire:

Supplies on hand	$ 200.00

Instructions:

1. From the information given, prepare a heading and reconstruct a trial balance on a work sheet. The owner's capital account balance is the difference between the total of all debit account balances minus the total of all credit account balances.
2. Complete the work sheet.

APPLIED COMMUNICATION

Accounting information is used by managers to make business decisions. But exactly what kind of decisions does the owner of a local business make? How does accounting information enable the manager to make better decisions?

Instructions: Identify a local business of personal interest to you. Write five questions you would ask the manager to learn how that person uses accounting information to make decisions. Interview the manager and write a one- or two-page summary of the interview.

CASE FOR CRITICAL THINKING

When posting amounts from a journal to general ledger accounts, a $10.00 debit to Supplies is mistakenly posted as a credit to Utilities Expense. Will this error be discovered when the work sheet is prepared? Explain.

AUDITING FOR ERRORS

The trial balance for Enfield Company is given below.

Account Titles	Account Balances	
	Debit	Credit
Cash	$ 4,391.00	
Petty Cash	300.00	
Accounts Receivable—Harned Co.		$2,950.00
Supplies	327.00	
Accounts Payable—Esby Inc.		1,250.00
Ervin Enfield, Capital	6,500.00	
Ervin Enfield, Drawing	600.00	
Income Summary		
Sales	2,500.00	
Advertising Expense	1,432.00	
Supplies Expense		
Rent Expense	250.00	
Totals	16,300.00	4,200.00

The debit column does not equal the credit column. The new bookkeeper knows that the amounts are correct but is not sure if the amounts are in the correct columns.

Instructions

1. Using what you know about the normal balance side of each account, find which amount(s) are in the wrong column.
2. On a separate piece of paper, copy the balances, putting them in the correct columns.
3. Total the columns to prove that debits now equal credits.

ANALYZING BEST BUY'S FINANCIAL STATEMENTS

The length of time for which a business summarizes and reports financial information is known as a *fiscal period*. Annual statements use a fiscal period equal to one year. However, the fiscal year does not necessarily have to begin on January 1 and end on December 31 (a calendar year). A company's fiscal year can begin on any date. Most companies choose a fiscal year that ends during a period of low business activity, often after a period of high activity, when inventories are low. Look at the second page of Note 1 to Best Buy's financial statements on Appendix B page B-10.

Instructions

1. When does Best Buy's fiscal year end?
2. Why do you think Best Buy's management feels that this is a good time for a fiscal year end?

Accounting SOFTWARE

TRIAL BALANCE AND ADJUSTING ENTRIES

Computer accounting systems do not use work sheets to plan adjustments. At any time, a trial balance can be printed that reports all general ledger account balances in debit and credit columns, just like the first two columns of the work sheet. Rather than being recorded in the adjustment columns of a work sheet, adjustments are entered individually using the general journal and posted to the general ledger.

A second trial balance should be printed to report the adjusted account balances. It is important that you review every report printed by a computer. Don't assume that anything produced by a computer is accurate. After recording adjustments, you should pay special attention to every account that required adjustment. Is the new Supplies account balance correct? Does the Insurance Expense account now have a balance?

PEACHTREE MASTERY PROBLEM 6-5

1. Open (Restore) file 06-5MP.ptb.
2. Journalize and post the adjusting entries.
3. Print trial balances before and after adjustments. NOTE: Although the instructions direct you to prepare a manual 8-column work sheet, it is not necessary to do this for this problem.

TRIAL BALANCE AND ADJUSTING ENTRIES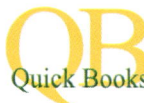

The work sheet was introduced in this chapter. The work sheet is used only in a manual accounting system. Computerized accounting systems do not produce a work sheet. Instead, a trial balance is printed to make sure that the debit account balances equal the credit account balances. The trial balance is used to plan the necessary adjustments. The adjusting entries are then entered into the system using general journal entries.

Once the adjusting entries have been made, another trial balance should be prepared. Although computer systems are very accurate, the new balances should be examined to determine if the correct adjusting entries were made. This can be done by checking to make sure the new balances in supplies and prepaid insurance reflect the amount of supplies on hand and the unexpired insurance.

QUICKBOOKS MASTERY PROBLEM 6-5

1. Open the Bonita Bubbles file.
2. Journalize the adjusting entries for April 30 using the general journal in your QuickBooks software to record the transactions.
3. Print a trial balance. NOTE: Although the instructions direct you to generate a balance sheet and profit and loss statement, it is not necessary to do this right now. You will do this in a later problem. However, you should generate a trial balance after the adjusting entries are recorded in order to check the accuracy of the adjusting process.

8-COLUMN WORK SHEET AND INSERTING AND DELETING ROWS

Imagine that you are preparing a paper work sheet and have completed entering all the account titles and trial balance amounts. Calculating the total for each column, you discover that you have missed entering the Petty Cash account. What would you do to correct this mistake?

Whether using a paper work sheet or an electronic spreadsheet template, the process of entering accounts and amounts may seem to be the same. However, the electronic spreadsheet has two important advantages. First, additional rows can easily be inserted to correct a mistake as described above. Second, column totals calculated using SUM functions eliminate the time and potential errors inherent with calculating these values with a calculator.

Inserting rows does not require that you modify a SUM function. The function easily adapts to new rows being entered on a work sheet. A SUM function such as =SUM(B10:B24) will automatically change to =SUM(B10:B25) when a row is inserted between rows 10 and 24. In the same manner, SUM functions will adjust when unused rows are deleted.

EXCEL APPLICATION PROBLEM 6-1
Open the F06-1 Excel data file. Follow the step-by-step instructions in the Instructions work sheet to make changes to an 8-column work sheet using an Excel spreadsheet.

This template can also be used to complete Application Problems 6-2 and 6-3.

EXCEL MASTERY PROBLEM 6-5
Open the F06-5 Excel data file. Follow the step-by-step instructions in the Instructions work sheet to make changes to an 8-column work sheet using an Excel spreadsheet.

TRIAL BALANCE AND ADJUSTING ENTRIES

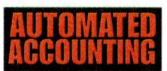

In automated accounting, the emphasis is on the analysis of the source documents and the preparation of timely and accurate journal entries and adjusting entries. These are the parts of the accounting cycle that require accounting personnel to apply the matching concept to ensure that revenues and expenses are recorded in the proper periods. The automated accounting system is programmed to post journal entries and to prepare trial balances, closing entries, and financial statements as needed. The accounting staff is freed from the more repetitive tasks associated with the accounting cycle and can concentrate on the analysis functions.

Work sheets are not used in Automated Accounting. However, it is still necessary to plan and journalize adjusting entries at the end of the fiscal period.

A trial balance is printed or displayed to show the current account balances. Adjustments are then planned and journalized and posted to bring general ledger accounts up to date.

AUTOMATED ACCOUNTING APPLICATION PROBLEM 6-2
Open file F06-2.AA8. Display the problem instructions and complete the problem.

AUTOMATED ACCOUNTING MASTERY PROBLEM 6-5
Open file F06-5.AA8. Display the problem instructions and complete the problem.

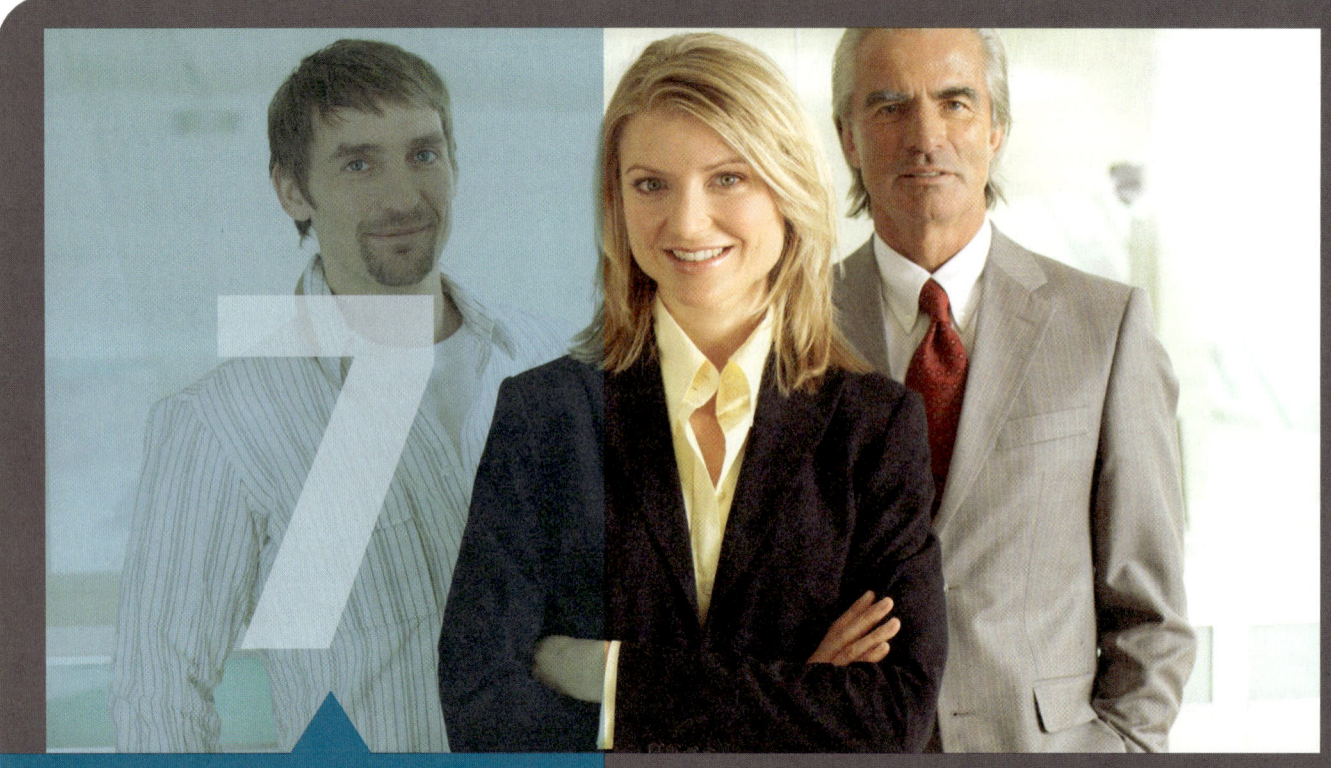

CHAPTER 7

Financial Statements for a Proprietorship

OBJECTIVES

After studying Chapter 7, you will be able to:

1. Define accounting terms related to financial statements for a service business organized as a proprietorship.
2. Identify accounting concepts and practices related to preparation of financial statements for a service business organized as a proprietorship.
3. Prepare an income statement for a service business organized as a proprietorship and analyze an income statement using component percentages.
4. Prepare a balance sheet for a service business organized as a proprietorship.

KEY TERMS

- stakeholders
- component percentage

Point Your Browser
www.C21accounting.com

ACCOUNTING IN THE REAL WORLD

American Eagle Outfitters

King of Jeans

If you have bought a pair of jeans at American Eagle (AE), you're not alone. American Eagle sells the most jeans of any U.S. specialty store brand. In 2006, the company sold over 6.5 million pairs of jeans. And, American Eagle doesn't sell only jeans. An AE T-shirt is sold every 10 seconds.

American Eagle describes the style of its brand as "laidback, current clothing" and targets 15-to-25-year-olds. It strives for high-quality merchandise while offering it at affordable prices. Their strategy seems to be working. Sales have increased from $1.39 billion in 2003 to $2.29 billion for the year ending February, 2007. These sales are from 911 stores in the U.S., Puerto Rico, and Canada as well as through ae.com.

In 2006, AE launched its new lifestyle brand under the name of Martin + OSA. This brand is described as being able to go from the workplace to leisure activities and is targeted at 25-to-40-year-olds. American Eagle hopes that this new brand will boost sales even more in the future.

Critical Thinking

1. What account titles might you find on a balance sheet for American Eagle?
2. Why would American Eagle start a new brand of sportswear focused on the 25-to-40-year-old market?

Source: www.ae.com

INTERNET ACTIVITY

Financial Statement Analysis

Choose two companies in the same industry. Go to the homepage for each company. Search each site for its most current financial statements.

Instructions

1. List the "Total Revenue," "Total Expenses," and "Net Income" or "Net Loss" for each company.
2. For each company, calculate and record the component percentages for total expenses and net income by dividing each item by the amount of net sales. Round percentage calculations to the nearest 0.1%.
3. Compare the component percentages for net income for each company. Which company has the better component percentage?

LESSON 7-1

Preparing an Income Statement

REPORTING FINANCIAL INFORMATION

The financial information needed by managers and owners to make good business decisions can be found in the general ledger accounts. However, the information in the general ledger is very detailed. Therefore, to make this general ledger information more usable, the information is summarized, organized, and reported to the owners and managers.

Also, all financial information must be reported if good business decisions are to be made. A financial statement with incomplete information is similar to a book with missing pages. The complete story is not told. If a business has both rent and utilities expenses but reports only the rent expense, managers will have incomplete information on which to base decisions. The accounting concept *Adequate Disclosure* is applied when financial statements contain all information necessary to understand a business's financial condition. [CONCEPT: Adequate Disclosure]

TechKnow Consulting prepares two financial statements: an income statement and a balance sheet. TechKnow Consulting always prepares financial statements at the end of each monthly fiscal period. [CONCEPT: Accounting Period Cycle]

When a business is started, it is expected that the business will continue to operate indefinitely. For example, Kim Park assumes that she will own and operate TechKnow Consulting for many years. When she retires, she expects to sell TechKnow Consulting to someone else, who will continue its operation. The accounting concept *Going Concern* is applied when financial statements are prepared with the expectation that a business will remain in operation indefinitely. [CONCEPT: Going Concern]

PHOTODISC/GETTY IMAGES

CHARACTER COUNTS

Identifying Stakeholders

Many states now require motorcyclists to wear helmets—a law unpopular with individuals who believe they should have the freedom of choice. Most people recognize that wearing a helmet provides the rider with extra protection in a crash. But why not allow a rider to accept the extra risk of riding without a helmet?

A well-known ethical model, the utilitarian theory, states that an ethical action is one that provides the greatest balance of good over harm. Any persons or groups who will be affected by an action are called **stakeholders**. The impact of the action on all stakeholders should be analyzed. Major stakeholders include owners, employees, customers, local communities, and society. Not every type of stakeholder will apply in each decision. However, the list of stakeholders provides a useful guide for individuals to search beyond themselves for the impact of their actions.

Examine the table below, which analyzes the impact on stakeholders involved in a motorcyclist's decision to ride without a helmet.

This analysis clearly demonstrates how a seemingly personal decision—wearing a helmet—can affect many people. Individuals must make their own conclusions from this analysis. State legislators who have voted for helmet laws believed that benefits to the motorcyclist failed to offset the negative impact on so many stakeholders. Individuals who opposed helmet laws believe the benefits to the individual offset the negative impact on all other stakeholders.

Instructions

Most colleges and universities have minimum academic standards for admission. Create a table that analyzes the positive and negative impact of admission standards. Are admission standards ethical?

Impact on Stakeholders of a Motorcyclist's Decision to Ride Without a Helmet		
Stakeholders	**Negative Impact**	**Positive Impact**
Motorcyclist	• Likely to have to pay higher insurance premiums. • May incur more serious injuries or death.	• Enjoys the freedom of riding without the confinement of a helmet.
Automobile drivers	• May suffer higher mental anguish if motorcyclist incurs more serious injuries.	• May drive more cautiously when near motorcyclists without helmets.
Relatives	• Personal lives and careers may be negatively affected if accident disables motorcyclist.	
Emergency personnel	• Risks to emergency personnel are greater because they are more aggressive when responding to serious accidents.	
Insurance companies	• Higher medical bills resulting from more serious injuries will hopefully be offset by charging higher insurance premiums.	
State	• May be subject to lawsuits by individuals who believe state was negligent in not passing a helmet law. • More serious accidents require more emergency personnel and equipment, thus spending limited resources.	
Society	• Government programs will pay for medical bills and disability payments not provided by the motorcyclist's insurance.	

INCOME STATEMENT INFORMATION ON A WORK SHEET

	ACCOUNT TITLE	INCOME STATEMENT DEBIT	INCOME STATEMENT CREDIT	BALANCE SHEET DEBIT	BALANCE SHEET CREDIT	
12	Sales		3565.00			12
13	Advertising Expense	213.00				13
14	Insurance Expense	100.00				14
15	Miscellaneous Expense	28.00				15
16	Rent Expense	300.00				16
17	Supplies Expense	715.00				17
18	Utilities Expense	110.00				18
19		1466.00	3565.00			19
20	Net Income	2099.00				20
21		3565.00	3565.00			21
22						22

An income statement reports financial information over a specific period of time, indicating the financial progress of a business in earning a net income or a net loss. Expenses are the amounts a business pays to operate the business and earn the revenue. The revenue earned and the expenses incurred to earn that revenue are reported in the same fiscal period. [CONCEPT: Matching Expenses with Revenue]

Information needed to prepare TechKnow Consulting's income statement is obtained from two places on the work sheet. Account titles are obtained from the work sheet's Account Title column. Account balances are obtained from the work sheet's Income Statement columns. The income statement for a service business has four sections: (1) heading, (2) revenue, (3) expenses, and (4) net income or net loss.

HEADING OF AN INCOME STATEMENT

TechKnow Consulting ①
Income Statement ②
For Month Ended August 31, 20-- ③

1. Name of Company
2. Name of Report
3. Date of Report

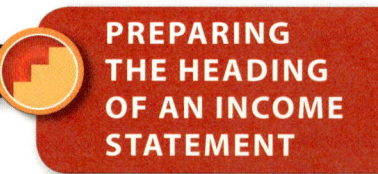

PREPARING THE HEADING OF AN INCOME STATEMENT

① Center the name of the company, *TechKnow Consulting*, on the first line.

② Center the name of the report, *Income Statement*, on the second line.

③ Center the date of the report, *For Month Ended August 31, 20--*, on the third line.

The income statement's date shows that this income statement reports information for the one-month period from August 1 through August 31.

REVENUE, EXPENSES, AND NET INCOME SECTIONS OF AN INCOME STATEMENT

STEPS — PREPARING THE REVENUE, EXPENSES, AND NET INCOME SECTIONS OF AN INCOME STATEMENT

1. Write the name of the first section, *Revenue:*, at the extreme left of the wide column on the first line.
2. Write the title of the revenue account, *Sales*, on the next line, indented about one centimeter.
3. Record the balance of the account, $3,565.00, on the same line in the second amount column.
4. Write the name of the second section, *Expenses:*, on the next line at the extreme left of the wide column.
5. Write the title of each expense account in the wide column, indented about one centimeter.
6. Record the balance of each expense account in the first amount column on the same line as the account title.
7. Rule a single line across the first amount column under the last expense account balance to indicate addition.
8. Write the words *Total Expenses* on the next blank line in the wide column, indented about one centimeter.
9. Record the amount of total expenses, *$1,466.00*, on the same line in the second amount column.
10. Calculate and verify the amount of net income.
    a. Calculate net income from information on the income statement, as shown.
    b. Compare the amount of net income, $2,099.00, with the net income on the work sheet. If the two amounts are not the same, an error has been made.

Total Revenue	−	Total Expenses	=	Net Income
$3,565.00	−	$1,466.00	=	$2,099.00

11. Rule a single line across the second amount column just below the amount of total expenses.
12. Write the words *Net Income* on the next line at the extreme left of the wide column.
13. On the same line, record the amount of net income, *$2,099.00*, in the second amount column.
14. Rule double lines across both amount columns below the amount of net income to show that the amount has been verified as correct.

Preparing an Income Statement

COMPONENT PERCENTAGE ANALYSIS OF AN INCOME STATEMENT

TechKnow Consulting
Income Statement
For Month Ended August 31, 20--

			% OF SALES
Revenue:			
Sales		3565 00	100.0
Expenses:			
Advertising Expense	213 00		
Insurance Expense	100 00		
Miscellaneous Expense	28 00		
Rent Expense	300 00		
Supplies Expense	715 00		
Utilities Expense	110 00		
Total Expenses		1466 00	41.1
Net Income		2099 00	58.9

For a service business, the revenue reported on an income statement is compared to two components: (1) total expenses and (2) net income. To make decisions about future operations, a manager analyzes relationships between these two income statement components and the total sales. The percentage relationship between one financial statement item and the total that includes that item is called a **component percentage**. On an income statement, component percentages are calculated by dividing the amount of each component by the total amount of sales. TechKnow Consulting calculates a component percentage for total expenses and net income. The relationship between each component and total sales is shown in a separate column on the income statement at the right of the amount columns.

Acceptable Component Percentages

For a component percentage to be useful, Ms. Park needs to know what component percentages are acceptable for businesses similar to TechKnow Consulting. Various industry organizations publish average percentages for similar businesses. In the future, Ms. Park could also compare TechKnow Consulting's component percentages from one fiscal period with the percentages of previous fiscal periods.

Total Expenses Component Percentage

The total expenses component percentage, based on information from the August income statement, is calculated as shown. For businesses similar to TechKnow Consulting, an acceptable total expenses component percentage is not more than 55.0%. Therefore, TechKnow Consulting's percentage, 41.1%, is less than 55.0% and is acceptable.

$$\frac{\text{Total Expenses}}{\$1,466.00} \div \frac{\text{Total Sales}}{\$3,565.00} = \frac{\text{Total Expenses Component Percentage}}{41.1\%}$$

Net Income Component Percentage

The net income component percentage, based on information from the August income statement, is calculated as shown. For businesses similar to TechKnow Consulting, an acceptable net income component percentage is not less than 45.0%. Therefore TechKnow Consulting's percentage, 58.9%, is greater than 45.0% and is acceptable.

$$\frac{\text{Net Income}}{\$2,099.00} \div \frac{\text{Total Sales}}{\$3,565.00} = \frac{\text{Net Income Component Percentage}}{58.9\%}$$

INCOME STATEMENT WITH TWO SOURCES OF REVENUE AND A NET LOSS

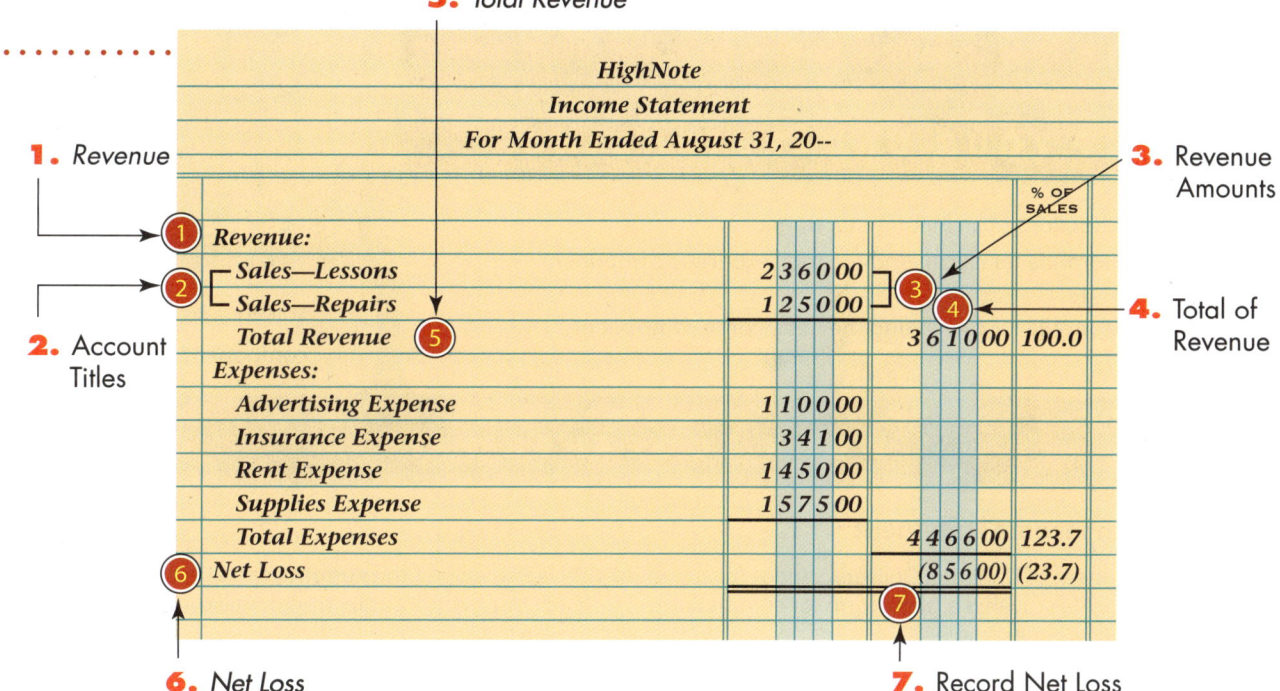

TechKnow Consulting receives revenue from only one source, the sale of services for setting up and troubleshooting computer networks. HighNote receives revenue from two sources, the sale of services for music lessons and the sale of services to repair musical instruments. The business's owner wants to know how much revenue is earned from each source. Therefore, the business uses two revenue accounts: Sales—Lessons and Sales—Repairs.

When an income statement is prepared for HighNote, both revenue accounts are listed. The revenue section of HighNote differs from the income statement prepared by TechKnow Consulting.

If total expenses exceed total revenue, a net loss is reported on an income statement. HighNote reported a net loss on its August income statement.

STEPS — PREPARING THE REVENUE SECTION OF AN INCOME STATEMENT WITH TWO SOURCES OF REVENUE

1. Write the section heading, *Revenue:*, at the left of the wide column.
2. Write the titles of both revenue accounts in the wide column, indented about one centimeter.
3. Record the balance of each account in the first amount column on the same line as the account title.
4. Total the two revenue account balances. Write the total amount on the next line in the second amount column.
5. Write the words *Total Revenue* in the wide column, indented about one centimeter on the same line as the total revenue amount.

PREPARING THE NET LOSS SECTION OF AN INCOME STATEMENT

6. Write the words *Net Loss* at the extreme left of the wide column.
7. Subtract the total expenses from the revenue to calculate the net loss. Record the amount of net loss in the second amount column in parentheses. An amount written in parentheses on a financial statement indicates a negative amount.

Preparing an Income Statement

End of Lesson REVIEW

AUDIT YOUR UNDERSTANDING

1. List the four sections of an income statement.
2. What is the formula for calculating the total expenses component percentage?
3. What is the formula for calculating the net income component percentage?

TERMS REVIEW

stakeholders

component percentage

WORK TOGETHER 7-1

Preparing an income statement

A partial work sheet of Darlene's Delivery Service for the month ended July 31 of the current year is given in the *Working Papers*. Also given is a blank form for completing an income statement. Your instructor will guide you through the following example.

1. Prepare an income statement for the month ended July 31 of the current year. Calculate and record the component percentages for total expenses and net income. Round percentage calculations to the nearest 0.1%.

ON YOUR OWN 7-1

Preparing an income statement

A partial work sheet of Cuts by Kelley for the month ended February 28 of the current year is given in the *Working Papers*. Also given is a blank form for completing an income statement. Work this problem independently.

1. Prepare an income statement for the month ended February 28 of the current year. Calculate and record the component percentages for total expenses and net income. Round percentage calculations to the nearest 0.1%.

LESSON 7-2

Balance Sheet Information on a Work Sheet

BALANCE SHEET

	ACCOUNT TITLE	BALANCE SHEET DEBIT	BALANCE SHEET CREDIT	
1	Cash	4 96 4 00		1
2	Petty Cash	1 00 00		2
3	Accounts Receivable—Oakdale School	1 50 00		3
4	Accounts Receivable—Campus Internet Cafe	1 00 00		4
5	Supplies	3 10 00		5
6	Prepaid Insurance	1 1 00 00		6
7	Accounts Payable—Supply Depot		2 00 00	7
8	Accounts Payable—Thomas Supply Co.		50 00	8
9	Kim Park, Capital		5 000 00	9
10	Kim Park, Drawing	6 25 00		10
19		7 34 9 00	5 25 0 00	19
20	Net Income		2 09 9 00	20
21		7 34 9 00	7 34 9 00	21

A balance sheet reports financial information on a specific date, indicating the financial condition of a business. The financial condition of a business refers to its financial strength. If a business has adequate available assets and few liabilities, that business is financially strong. If the business's financial condition is not strong, adverse changes in the economy might cause the business to fail.

Information about assets, liabilities, and owner's equity might be obtained from the general ledger accounts or from a work sheet. However, the information is easier to use if reported in an organized manner such as on a balance sheet.

Information needed to prepare TechKnow Consulting's balance sheet is obtained from two places on the work sheet. Account titles are obtained from the work sheet's Account Title column. Account balances are obtained from the work sheet's Balance Sheet columns.

A balance sheet has four sections: (1) heading, (2) assets, (3) liabilities, and (4) owner's equity.

HEADING OF A BALANCE SHEET

1. Name of Company
2. Name of Report
3. Date of Report

TechKnow Consulting
Balance Sheet
August 31, 20--

STEPS — PREPARING THE HEADING OF A BALANCE SHEET

1. Center the name of the company, *TechKnow Consulting*, on the first line.
2. Center the name of the report, *Balance Sheet*, on the second line.
3. Center the date of the report, *August 31, 20--*, on the third line.

Balance Sheet Information on a Work Sheet

ASSETS AND LIABILITIES SECTIONS OF A BALANCE SHEET

A balance sheet reports information about the elements of the accounting equation.

Assets = Liabilities + Owner's Equity

The assets are on the LEFT side of the accounting equation and on the LEFT side of TechKnow Consulting's balance sheet.

Two kinds of equities are reported on a balance sheet: (1) liabilities and (2) owner's equity. Liabilities and owner's equity are on the RIGHT side of the accounting equation and on the RIGHT side of TechKnow Consulting's balance sheet.

The information needed to prepare the assets section is obtained from the work sheet's Account Title column and the Balance Sheet Debit column. The information needed to prepare the liabilities section is obtained from the work sheet's Account Title column and the Balance Sheet Credit column.

STEPS PREPARING THE ASSETS AND LIABILITIES SECTIONS OF A BALANCE SHEET

1. Write the title of the first section, *Assets*, in the middle of the left wide column.

2. Write the titles of all asset accounts under the heading.

3. Record the balance of each asset account in the left amount column on the same line as the account title.

4. Write the title of the next section, *Liabilities*, in the middle of the right wide column.

5. Write the titles of all liability accounts under the heading.

6. Record the balance of each liability account in the right amount column on the same line as the account title.

7. Rule a single line across the right amount column under the last amount, to indicate addition.

8. Write the words *Total Liabilities* in the right wide column on the next blank line.

9. Record the total of all liabilities, $250.00, in the right amount column.

PHOTODISC/GETTY IMAGES

188 Chapter 7   Financial Statements for a Proprietorship

OWNER'S EQUITY SECTION OF A BALANCE SHEET

Only the amount of current capital is reported on TechKnow Consulting's balance sheet. The amounts needed to calculate the current capital are found in the work sheet's Balance Sheet columns. The amount of current capital is calculated as shown.

Capital Account Balance	+	Net Income	−	Drawing Account Balance	=	Current Capital
$5,000.00	+	$2,099.00	−	$625.00	=	$6,474.00

When a business has a net loss, current capital is calculated as shown. The current capital is reported on the balance sheet in the same way as when the business has a net income.

Capital Account Balance	−	Net Loss	−	Drawing Account Balance	=	Current Capital
$12,000.00	−	$200.00	−	$500.00	=	$11,300.00

STEPS PREPARING THE OWNER'S EQUITY SECTION OF A BALANCE SHEET

1. Write the title of the section, *Owner's Equity*, in the middle of the right wide column on the next line below "Total Liabilities."

2. Write the title of the owner's capital account, *Kim Park, Capital*, on the next line.

3. Record the current amount of owner's equity, *$6,474.00*, in the right amount column.

4. Rule a single line under the last amount in the longer left amount column. Rule a single line in the right amount column on the same line.

5. Write the words *Total Assets* on the next line, in the left wide column.

6. Record the amount of total assets, *$6,724.00*, in the left amount column.

7. Write the words *Total Liab. and Owner's Eq.* in the right wide column on the same line as Total Assets.

8. Record the amount of total liabilities and owner's equity, *$6,724.00*, in the right amount column.

9. Compare the totals of the two amount columns. The totals are the same, so the balance sheet is in balance.

10. Rule double lines across both the left and right amount columns just below the column totals to show that the totals have been verified as correct.

Balance Sheet Information on a Work Sheet Lesson 7-2 189

OWNER'S EQUITY REPORTED IN DETAIL ON A BALANCE SHEET

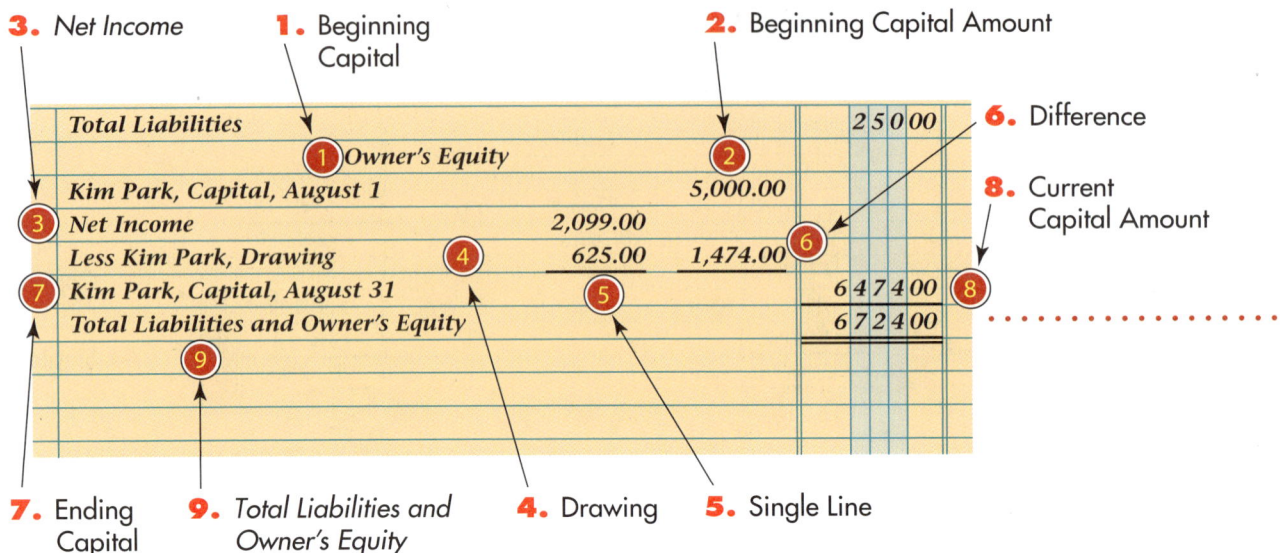

TechKnow Consulting's balance sheet reports the current capital on August 31 but does not show how this amount was calculated. TechKnow Consulting is a small business with relatively few changes in owner's equity to report. Therefore, Kim Park decided that the business does not need to report all the details in the owner's equity section. However, some businesses prefer to report the details about how owner's equity is calculated.

If TechKnow Consulting were to report details about owner's equity, the owner's equity section of the balance sheet would be prepared as shown in the illustration.

S T E P S PREPARING THE OWNER'S EQUITY SECTION REPORTED IN DETAIL ON A BALANCE SHEET

1. Write the words *Kim Park, Capital, August 1* on the first line under the words "Owner's Equity."

2. Record the owner's capital account balance on August 1, *$5,000.00*, in the wide column.

3. Write the words *Net Income* on the next line. Record the net income, *$2,099.00*, in the wide column to the left of the capital account balance.

4. Write the words *Less Kim Park, Drawing* on the next line. Record the balance of the drawing account, *$625.00*, in the wide column.

5. Rule a single line under the amount.

6. Subtract the balance of the drawing account from the net income. Record the difference, *$1,474.00*, in the wide column to the right of the drawing account balance.

7. Write the words *Kim Park, Capital, August 31* on the next line.

8. Add the August 1 capital amount, *$5,000.00*, and the difference between the net income and the drawing account, *$1,474.00*. Record the sum, *$6,474.00*, in the right amount column.

9. Write the words *Total Liabilities and Owner's Equity* on the next line. Record the amount of total liabilities and owner's equity, *$6,724.00*, in the right amount column.

> **REMEMBER**
>
> Capital is not copied from the work sheet to the balance sheet. Capital is calculated using beginning capital, plus net income or minus net loss, minus drawing.

190 Chapter 7 Financial Statements for a Proprietorship

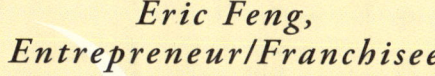

CAREERS IN ACCOUNTING

Eric Feng, Entrepreneur/Franchisee

Entrepreneurial spirit is the foundation of our economy. From Henry Ford to Sam Walton to Bill Gates, individuals have dreamed of controlling their destiny by starting their own business. These entrepreneurs identified a need in the marketplace and developed a product to fill that need. Through vision and determination, they created three of the best-known corporations in the world.

Eric Feng is an example of how an entrepreneurial spirit can launch a successful business. He says, "I wanted to be my own boss—a dream for many people—and we were no exception." Eric and his wife, Candy, came to the United States as foreign students to pursue advanced college degrees. Eric finished a master's degree in computer science, and Candy earned a degree in accounting. After several years of working for the local university, they decided it was time to turn their dream into reality.

"We took our first step when we decided to purchase a franchise for a quick-serve restaurant," Eric recalls. After researching numerous opportunities, they decided to pursue the purchase of an Arby's franchise. "We did not have any experience managing a company, much less a restaurant business, nor did we have any significant capital to invest in the business. What we did have, however, was our knowledge of accounting."

The Fengs prepared an extensive business plan that outlined in detail the amount of capital that would be required. The business plan included budgets of sales, expenses, and net income under several different sets of assumptions. They then submitted the business plan to the commercial loan officers of several local banks. "The loan officers at the National Bank of Commerce were confident enough in our business plan to provide us the financing we needed to make our dream come true. The reason, we were told later, was that we had a well-thought-out business plan that made good business sense. All business ventures involve risk. Thanks to the accounting and computer backgrounds we had, we were able to evaluate the business venture in financial accounting terms and demonstrate to the bank that it was a risk worth taking."

Like many entrepreneurs, the Fengs have expanded their operations beyond their initial restaurant. Now the owners of three Arby's units, Eric and Candy credit their success to their knowledge of accounting. "Business success is not a matter of luck. We owe what we have today to our knowledge of accounting and our insistence on quality in all we do."

Salary Range: Virtually unlimited, although the net income from a single unit of a franchise is limited by its physical size and location. However, like the Fengs, an entrepreneur can acquire many units of the same franchise.

Qualifications: Franchisors provide potential franchisees with information on qualifications, which may include specific levels of financial net worth, access to operating capital, and personal experience in the industry.

Occupational Outlook: On its web site (www.franchise.org), the International Franchise Association lists over 800 corporations that offer franchises. Each of these franchisors is actively seeking entrepreneurs to expand the number of company units in operation.

End of Lesson REVIEW

AUDIT YOUR UNDERSTANDING

1. List the four sections on a balance sheet.
2. What is the formula for calculating current capital?

WORK TOGETHER 7-2

Preparing a balance sheet

A partial work sheet of Ken's Carpet Cleaning for the month ended April 30 of the current year is given in the *Working Papers*. Also given is a blank form for completing a balance sheet. Your instructor will guide you through the following example.

1. Prepare a balance sheet for April 30 of the current year.

ON YOUR OWN 7-2

Preparing a balance sheet

A partial work sheet of Anne's Alterations for the month ended October 31 of the current year is given in the *Working Papers*. Also given is a blank form for completing a balance sheet. Work this problem independently.

1. Prepare a balance sheet for October 31 of the current year.

SUMMARY

After completing this chapter, you can:

1. Define accounting terms related to financial statements for a service business organized as a proprietorship.
2. Identify accounting concepts and practices related to preparation of financial statements for a service business organized as a proprietorship.
3. Prepare an income statement for a service business organized as a proprietorship and analyze an income statement using component percentages.
4. Prepare a balance sheet for a service business organized as a proprietorship.

EXPLORE ACCOUNTING

Comparative and Interim Financial Statements

A corporation that trades its stock on a U.S. stock exchange must submit an annual report to the Securities and Exchange Commission (SEC). The SEC has specific requirements as to what must be included in the financial statements.

One requirement is that the financial statements included in the annual report must show amounts for more than one year. The balance sheet must show ending balances for the current and the previous year. The income statement and statement of stockholder's equity must show amounts for the current year and the two previous years. Financial statements providing information for multiple fiscal periods are called *comparative financial statements*.

These statements make it possible for a user to compare performance from year to year. For example, the net income for the current year can be compared to the net income for the two previous years. In this way, the user can determine if there is a positive or negative trend occurring in net income. On the balance sheet, the ending cash balance for the current year can be compared to the ending cash balance from the previous year to determine if the amount of cash on hand is increasing or decreasing.

Businesses that are required to submit an annual report to the SEC must also submit a quarterly report. This report is not as detailed as the annual report, but it must include the financial statements for the quarter. Financial statements providing information for a time period shorter than the fiscal year are called *interim financial statements*. Users of financial information are able to evaluate the progress of the firm every three months rather than waiting an entire year. The importance of interim financial statements can be verified by the fact that the results reported in these statements are often summarized and reported in financial news sources, such as *The Wall Street Journal* and CNBC.

Activity: Contact a corporation near you. Ask if the business prepares interim financial statements and, if it does, find out how often these statements are prepared.

7-1 APPLICATION PROBLEM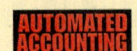

Preparing an income statement

A form is given in the *Working Papers*. The following information is obtained from the work sheet of Len's Laundry for the month ended August 31 of the current year.

ACCOUNT TITLE	INCOME STATEMENT DEBIT	INCOME STATEMENT CREDIT	BALANCE SHEET DEBIT	BALANCE SHEET CREDIT
Sales		6233 00		
Advertising Expense	800 00			
Insurance Expense	200 00			
Miscellaneous Expense	315 00			
Supplies Expense	450 00			
Utilities Expense	1495 00			
	3260 00	6233 00	10436 00	7463 00
Net Income	2973 00			2973 00
	6233 00	6233 00	10436 00	10436 00

Instructions:

1. Prepare an income statement for the month ended August 31 of the current year.
2. Calculate and record the component percentages for total expenses and net income. Round percentage calculations to the nearest 0.1%.

7-2 APPLICATION PROBLEM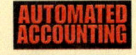

Preparing a balance sheet

A form is given in the *Working Papers*. The following information is obtained from the work sheet of Len's Laundry for the month ended August 31 of the current year.

ACCOUNT TITLE	BALANCE SHEET DEBIT	BALANCE SHEET CREDIT
Cash	7607 00	
Accts. Rec.—Natasha Goodlad	700 00	
Accts. Rec.—R. Henry	498 00	
Supplies	431 00	
Prepaid Insurance	200 00	
Accts. Pay.—Tri-County Supplies		381 00
Accts. Pay.—West End Supply Co.		555 00
Leonard Long, Capital		6527 00
Leonard Long, Drawing	1000 00	
Income Summary		
	10436 00	7463 00
Net Income		2973 00
	10436 00	10436 00

194 Chapter 7 Financial Statements for a Proprietorship

Instructions:
Prepare a balance sheet for August 31 of the current year.

7-3 MASTERY PROBLEM

Preparing financial statements with a net loss

Forms are given in the *Working Papers*. The following information is obtained from the work sheet of Rolstad Repair Service for the month ended September 30 of the current year.

	ACCOUNT TITLE	INCOME STATEMENT DEBIT	INCOME STATEMENT CREDIT	BALANCE SHEET DEBIT	BALANCE SHEET CREDIT	
1	Cash			6958 00		1
2	Petty Cash			150 00		2
3	Accts. Rec.—M. Hollerud			197 00		3
4	Supplies			780 00		4
5	Prepaid Insurance			800 00		5
6	Accts. Pay.—Tampa Supply				612 00	6
7	Ron Rolstad, Capital				9337 00	7
8	Ron Rolstad, Drawing			600 00		8
9	Income Summary					9
10	Sales		3269 00			10
11	Advertising Expense	450 00				11
12	Insurance Expense	157 00				12
13	Miscellaneous Expense	85 00				13
14	Supplies Expense	1400 00				14
15	Utilities Expense	1641 00				15
16		3733 00	3269 00	9485 00	9949 00	16
17	Net Loss		464 00	464 00		17
18		3733 00	3733 00	9949 00	9949 00	18

Instructions:

1. Prepare an income statement for the month ended September 30 of the current year.
2. Calculate and record the component percentages for total expenses and net loss. Place the percentage for net loss in parentheses to show that it is for a net loss. Round percentage calculations to the nearest 0.1%.
3. Prepare a balance sheet for September 30 of the current year.

7-4 CHALLENGE PROBLEM

Preparing financial statements with two sources of revenue and a net loss

Forms are given in the *Working Papers*. The information below is obtained from the work sheet of LawnMow for the month ended October 31 of the current year.

	ACCOUNT TITLE	INCOME STATEMENT DEBIT	INCOME STATEMENT CREDIT	BALANCE SHEET DEBIT	BALANCE SHEET CREDIT	
1	Cash			1 8 9 8 00		1
2	Accts. Rec.—Sandra Rohe			9 5 00		2
3	Supplies			6 5 0 00		3
4	Prepaid Insurance			1 2 0 00		4
5	Accts. Pay.—Corner Garage				5 8 00	5
6	Accts. Pay.—Broadway Gas				1 1 0 00	6
7	Accts. Pay.—Esko Repair				2 1 5 00	7
8	Ryo Morrison, Capital				4 0 0 0 00	8
9	Ryo Morrison, Drawing			1 0 0 00		9
10	Income Summary					10
11	Sales—Lawn Care		4 9 0 0 00			11
12	Sales—Shrub Care		2 5 0 0 00			12
13	Advertising Expense	3 9 0 00				13
14	Insurance Expense	4 0 0 00				14
15	Miscellaneous Expense	5 5 0 00				15
16	Rent Expense	3 3 0 0 00				16
17	Supplies Expense	3 2 0 0 00				17
18		7 8 4 0 00	7 4 0 0 00	3 9 4 3 00	4 3 8 3 00	18
19	Net Loss		4 4 0 00	4 4 0 00		19
20		7 8 4 0 00	7 8 4 0 00	4 3 8 3 00	4 3 8 3 00	20
21						21

Instructions:

1. Prepare an income statement for the month ended October 31 of the current year.
2. Calculate and record the component percentages for total expenses and net loss. Place the percentage for net loss in parentheses to show that it is for a net loss. Round percentage calculations to the nearest 0.1%.
3. Prepare a balance sheet for October 31 of the current year.

APPLIED COMMUNICATION

Assume that you are the owner of a proprietorship, and you have just hired a new assistant. In the past, your assistants have had difficulty understanding the importance of financial statements to your business.

Instructions: Write down what you would say to your assistant about the importance of income statements and balance sheets in making financial decisions. Your statements should be no longer than one or two paragraphs.

CASE FOR CRITICAL THINKING

Romelle Woods and Ahti Indihar each own small businesses. Ms. Woods prepares an income statement and balance sheet at the end of each day for her business, in order to make business decisions. Mr. Indihar prepares an income statement and balance sheet for his business only at the end of each one-year fiscal period, when preparing tax reports. Which owner is using the better procedure? Explain your answer.

GRAPHING WORKSHOP

The net income figures for three companies for three years are given below.

	2005	2006	2007
Atlas Company	15,000	17,000	14,000
Mertzel Company	13,000	15,000	17,000
Tampeau Company	16,000	14,000	13,000

Develop a graph that will best illustrate the difference in the net income for each company each year. Decide for yourself which type of graph to use.

ANALYZING BEST BUY'S FINANCIAL STATEMENTS

Best Buy's financial reports include a consolidated statement of earnings, which is shown in Appendix B page B-6. This statement reports revenue, expenses, and operating income similar to an income statement for a proprietorship. Best Buy's statement of earnings is more complex than the income statement described in this chapter. Besides reporting net income (called *net earnings*), it also reports "Earnings from continuing operations." The difference between these two amounts is caused by discontinuing or selling a portion of the company or because of changes in accounting procedures.

Instructions

1. What are Best Buy's net earnings for each of the three years?
2. What are Best Buy's earnings from continuing operations for each of the three years?
3. Note 2 to the financial statements is on page B-20. Note 2 tells about discontinuing or selling a portion of the company. Read Note 2. What portion of the company was sold that caused the difference between net earnings and earnings from continuing operations in 2004?

Accounting SOFTWARE

GENERATING FINANCIAL STATEMENTS

As an elementary student, you learned to add, subtract, multiply, and divide—the basic functions of math. In junior high and high school, you learned algebra and geometry—more complex and sophisticated levels of math.

Throughout this chapter, you have been learning the basic functions of accounting. When you use Peachtree to print an income statement and balance sheet, you will note some terms and headings that you have not yet learned, such as Cost of Goods Sold, Gross Profit, Current Assets, and Long-term Liabilities. Peachtree was developed assuming that you, the user, possess a more complete knowledge of accounting. Be patient; you will learn about these terms as you continue your accounting education.

PEACHTREE MASTERY PROBLEM 7-3

1. Open (Restore) file 07-3MP.ptb.
2. Print an income statement and balance sheet.

PEACHTREE CHALLENGE PROBLEM 7-4

1. Open (Restore) file 07-4CP.ptb.
2. Print an income statement and balance sheet.

GENERATING FINANCIAL STATEMENTS

Accounting terms vary from company to company. This chapter discussed the income statement, which shows net income or net loss. Another name for this statement is *profit and loss statement*. QuickBooks uses the title Profit & Loss to identify a statement that shows net income or net loss.

Financial statements also vary in format. The financial statements printed in QuickBooks may contain terms, such as current assets or current liabilities, that have not been covered in this course. These terms will be defined in a later chapter. Regardless of the terms used, the financial statements still provide the same basic information and can still be analyzed in the same way.

QUICKBOOKS MASTERY PROBLEM 7-3

Note: For all printouts, add a custom footer that includes your name and the problem number; print in portrait orientation

1. Open the Rolstad Repair Service file.
2. Print a profit and loss statement for the month ended September 30. Use the Reports menu and choose Company & Financial.
3. Modify the report to include component percentages for expenses and net loss as a percentage of sales.
4. Print a standard balance sheet as of September 30.

QUICKBOOKS CHALLENGE PROBLEM 7-4

1. Open the LawnMow file.
2. Print a profit and loss report for October 1 through October 31, including component percentages.
3. Generate a balance sheet for October 31.

GENERATING FINANCIAL STATEMENTS

Data and *information* are often considered synonymous terms. Accountants use the term *data* to refer to unorganized facts. In contrast, *information* is data that has been organized and is presented in a manner that can be understood by the reader.

An income statement organizes the current balances of revenue and expense accounts to inform the reader how effectively the business has operated during a fiscal period. For a business that has incurred a net loss, accountants have commonly reported negative amounts by using a hyphen in front of the number or by surrounding the number with parentheses.

Today's electronic spreadsheets provide accountants with an additional method of alerting the reader to a net loss. Negative values can also be displayed in red font. You have probably heard someone say "in the red" when referring to a business that is losing money. By allowing negative numbers to appear in red, the electronic spreadsheet uses this traditional association to further communicate that the business has incurred a net loss.

EXCEL MASTERY PROBLEM 7-3

1. Open the F07-3 Excel data file.
2. Follow the step-by-step instructions in the Instructions work sheet to change the cell format of the net loss amount.

GENERATING FINANCIAL STATEMENTS

One of the advantages of using accounting software is that once transaction data are entered, the software prepares financial statements automatically.

To display financial statements:

1. Click the Reports toolbar button, or choose the Report Selection menu item from the Report menu.
2. When the Report Selection dialog appears, choose the Financial Statements option from the Select a Report Group list.
3. Choose the financial statement report you would like to display from the Choose a Report to Display list.
4. Click the OK button.

The up-to-date account balances stored by the software are used to calculate and display the current financial statements. A component percentage is included for each dollar amount. Component percentages calculated on the income statement show the relationship of items to total sales.

The balance sheet reports information about assets, liabilities, and owner's equity on a specific date. Additional information about owner's equity can be obtained by selecting the Statement of Owner's Equity. This statement shows changes to the capital account during the period.

When a report is displayed in *Automated Accounting*, it can also be copied in word processor or spreadsheet format by pressing the Copy button at the bottom of the report window. The report can then be pasted into a word processing document or spreadsheet for additional processing or distribution. For example, if an income statement were pasted into a spreadsheet, amounts could be changed to perform "what-if" analysis, such as "What if sales increased by 25%: what would the effect on net income be?"

AUTOMATED ACCOUNTING APPLICATION PROBLEMS 7-1 AND 7-2

Open file F07-1.AA8. Display the problem instructions and complete the problems.

AUTOMATED ACCOUNTING CHALLENGE PROBLEM 7-4

Open file F07-4.AA8. Display the problem instructions and complete the problem.

CHAPTER 8

Recording Adjusting and Closing Entries for a Service Business

OBJECTIVES

After studying Chapter 8, you will be able to:

1. Define accounting terms related to adjusting and closing entries for a service business organized as a proprietorship.
2. Identify accounting concepts and practices related to adjusting and closing entries for a service business organized as a proprietorship.
3. Record adjusting entries for a service business organized as a proprietorship.
4. Record closing entries for a service business organized as a proprietorship.
5. Prepare a post-closing trial balance for a service business organized as a proprietorship.

KEY TERMS

- adjusting entries
- permanent accounts
- temporary accounts
- closing entries
- post-closing trial balance
- accounting cycle

Point Your Browser
www.C21accounting.com

ACCOUNTING IN THE REAL WORLD

The Walt Disney Company

Conservation Is Good Business at The Walt Disney Company

Say the word "Disney" and you may think of any one of hundreds of movies produced by Walt Disney Studios. You may think of a wild, exciting ride in one of the Disney theme parks around the world. You may even think of a fun-filled resort area within Walt Disney World in Orlando.

How many of you, however, would think of the environment when you hear the word "Disney"? In 1990, The Walt Disney Company introduced an initiative called "Environmentality." Disney Online describes Environmentality as "a fundamental ethic that blends business growth with the conservation of natural resources. Attention to the environment drives new business initiatives, demonstrating how environmental stewardship goes hand-in-hand with bottom-line cost savings." Environmentality goes beyond just complying with laws. It includes "purchasing recycled products, waste minimization, resource conservation, research and development, community involvement, and education" to make the program successful.

A 2003 report designed to highlight environmental accomplishments describes many examples of waste reductions and resource conservation. One example is a water-monitoring program in Disney's Animal Kingdom. The monitoring results identified areas where water usage could be reduced, saving an estimated 145,000,000 gallons of water each year.

Critical Thinking

1. List at least two reasons why The Walt Disney Company would be interested in such environmental measures.
2. If The Walt Disney Company purchased equipment to help measure water usage, would that equipment be classified as an asset, liability, or owner's equity on the balance sheet? Why?

Source: disney.go.com

INTERNET ACTIVITY

Closing Entries

Go to the homepage for a company or corporation of your choice. Search the site for the most recent annual report. Go to the income statement.

Instructions

1. Looking at the categories of revenues on the income statement, list the accounts that may be included in the company's entry to close the revenue accounts.
2. Looking at the categories of expenses on the income statement, list the accounts that may be included in the company's entry to close the expense accounts.

LESSON 8-1

Recording Adjusting Entries

ADJUSTING ENTRIES

TechKnow Consulting prepares a work sheet at the end of each fiscal period to summarize the general ledger information needed to prepare financial statements. [CONCEPT: Accounting Period Cycle] Financial statements are prepared from information on the work sheet. [CONCEPT: Adequate Disclosure]

TechKnow Consulting's adjustments are analyzed and planned on a work sheet. However, these adjustments must be journalized so they can be posted to the general ledger accounts. Journal entries recorded to update general ledger accounts at the end of a fiscal period are called **adjusting entries**.

Adjusting entries are recorded on the next journal page following the page on which the last daily transactions for the month are recorded.

ADJUSTING ENTRY FOR SUPPLIES

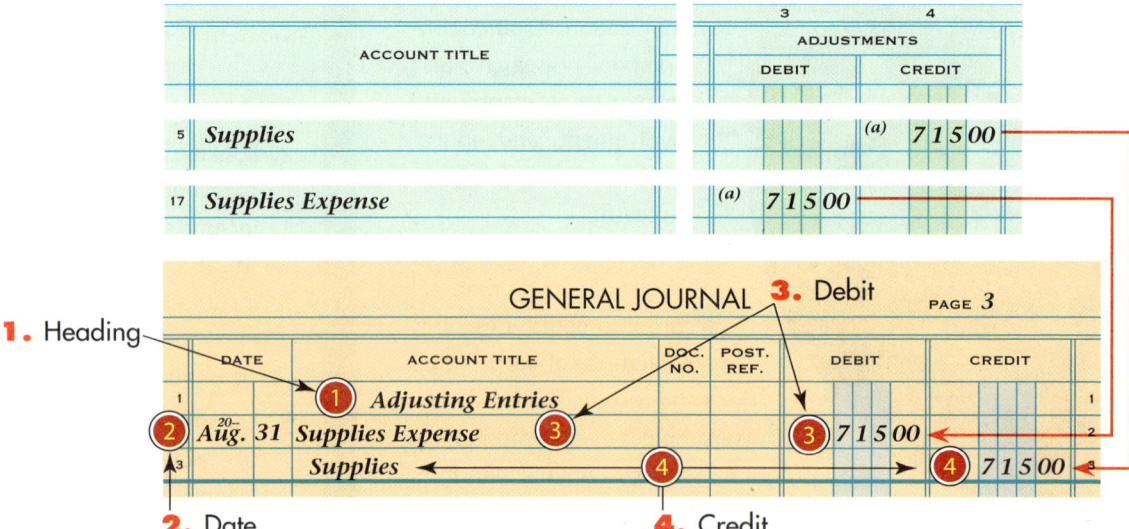

The information needed to journalize the adjusting entry for Supplies is obtained from lines 5 and 17 of the work sheet, as shown in the illustration. The entry must be recorded in a journal and posted to the general ledger accounts affected by the entry.

The effect of posting the adjusting entry for supplies to the general ledger accounts is shown in the T accounts.

Supplies Expense has an up-to-date balance of $715.00, which is the value of the supplies used during the fiscal period. [CONCEPT: Matching Expenses with Revenue]

Supplies has a new balance of $310.00, which is the cost of the supplies on hand at the end of the fiscal period.

```
         Supplies Expense
Adj. (a)      715.00  |

             Supplies
Bal.        1,025.00  | Adj. (a)   715.00
(New Bal.    310.00)
```

202 Chapter 8 Recording Adjusting and Closing Entries for a Service Business

STEPS ADJUSTING ENTRY FOR SUPPLIES

1. Write the heading, *Adjusting Entries*, in the middle of the Account Title column of the general journal. Because no source document is prepared for adjusting entries, the entries are identified with a heading in the general journal. The heading explains all of the adjusting entries that follow. Therefore, the heading is written only once for all adjusting entries.

2. Write the date, *20--, Aug. 31*, in the Date column.

3. Write the title of the account debited, *Supplies Expense*, in the Account Title column. Record the debit amount, *$715.00*, in the Debit column on the same line as the account title.

4. Write the title of the account credited, *Supplies*, on the next line in the Account Title column. Record the credit amount, *$715.00*, in the Credit column on the same line as the account title.

CHARACTER COUNTS

Can I Say This on My Resume?

Kendra Wheeler applied for a payroll clerk job with Hampton Group. She slightly exaggerated her work experience on her resume. She felt uncomfortable with this decision, but she was desperate to get a job.

Based on the resume, Kendra was hired. After one year, she received above-average ratings during her annual review. Then, her boss met Kendra's former supervisor and learned the truth.

Was Kendra's action unethical? Let's apply the ethical model to this situation.

1. *Recognize you are facing an ethical dilemma.* Kendra should have realized that her uncomfortable feelings were a sign that her actions might not be ethical.

2. *Identify the action taken or the proposed action.* Kendra could have stated her qualifications honestly. However, she elected to exaggerate her work experience. That action will be evaluated in the following steps.

3. *Analyze the action.*

   a. *Is the action illegal?* No. Overstating qualifications is not illegal, but the employer could terminate her employment.

   b. *Does the action violate company or professional standards?* No. Kendra was neither an employee of the company nor a member of any profession at the time she was hired.

   c. *Who is affected, and how, by the action?*

Impact on Stakeholders of Exaggerating Work Experience on a Resume		
Stakeholders	**Negative**	**Positive**
Kendra	• She might be terminated. • If retained, she could have difficulty being promoted.	• She obtained employment.
Other applicants	• More highly qualified applicants lost an employment opportunity.	
Hampton Group	• The company lost the opportunity of receiving the benefits of a more qualified employee. • If Kendra is terminated, the company must train another employee. • If Kendra is retained, managers may hesitate to give Kendra responsibilities necessary for the efficient operation of the company.	

4. *Determine if the action is ethical.* Kendra's action was not ethical. Exaggerating her resume provided her with a short-term benefit. However, this benefit does not outweigh the negative impact on other applicants and the Hampton Group. In fact, Kendra's action could possibly cause her more harm in the long run.

Recording Adjusting Entries

ADJUSTING ENTRY FOR PREPAID INSURANCE

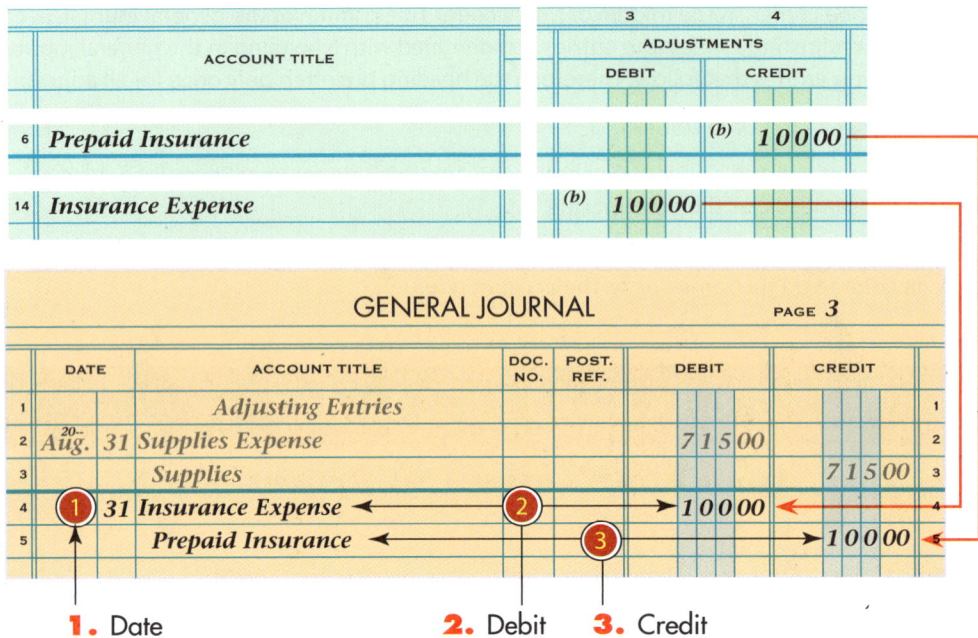

1. Date 2. Debit 3. Credit

The information needed to journalize the adjusting entry for **Prepaid Insurance** is obtained from lines 6 and 14 of the work sheet. The entry must be recorded in a journal and posted to the general ledger accounts affected by the entry.

The effect of posting the adjusting entry for **Prepaid Insurance** to the general ledger accounts is shown in the T accounts.

Insurance Expense	
Adj. (b) 100.00	

Prepaid Insurance	
Bal. 1,200.00	Adj. (b) 100.00
(New Bal. 1,100.00)	

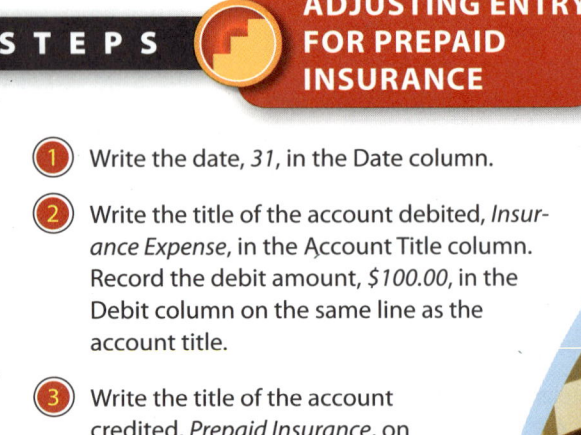

STEPS — ADJUSTING ENTRY FOR PREPAID INSURANCE

1. Write the date, *31*, in the Date column.

2. Write the title of the account debited, *Insurance Expense*, in the Account Title column. Record the debit amount, *$100.00*, in the Debit column on the same line as the account title.

3. Write the title of the account credited, *Prepaid Insurance*, on the next line in the Account Title column. Record the credit amount, *$100.00*, in the Credit column on the same line as the account title.

PHOTODISC/GETTY IMAGES

End of Lesson REVIEW

AUDIT YOUR UNDERSTANDING

1. Why are adjusting entries journalized?
2. Where is the information obtained to journalize adjusting entries?
3. What accounts are increased from zero balances after adjusting entries for supplies and prepaid insurance are journalized and posted?

TERM REVIEW

adjusting entries

WORK TOGETHER 8-1

Journalizing and posting adjusting entries

A partial work sheet of Darlene's Delivery Service for the month ended July 31 of the current year is given in the *Working Papers*. Also given are the general journal and general ledger accounts. The general ledger accounts do not show all details for the fiscal period. The balance shown in each account is the account's balance before adjusting entries are posted. Your instructor will guide you through the following example.

1. Use page 4 of the general journal. Journalize and post the adjusting entries. Save your work to complete Work Together 8-2.

ON YOUR OWN 8-1

Journalizing and posting adjusting entries

A partial work sheet of Cuts by Kelley for the month ended February 28 of the current year is given in the *Working Papers*. Also given are a journal and general ledger accounts. The general ledger accounts do not show all details for the fiscal period. The balance shown in each account is the account's balance before adjusting entries are posted. Work this problem independently.

1. Use page 8 of the general journal. Journalize and post the adjusting entries. Save your work to complete On Your Own 8-2.

LESSON 8-2

Recording Closing Entries

NEED FOR PERMANENT AND TEMPORARY ACCOUNTS

Accounts used to accumulate information from one fiscal period to the next are called **permanent accounts**. Permanent accounts are also referred to as *real accounts*. Permanent accounts include the asset and liability accounts and the owner's capital account. The ending account balances of permanent accounts for one fiscal period are the beginning account balances for the next fiscal period.

Accounts used to accumulate information until it is transferred to the owner's capital account are called **temporary accounts**. Temporary accounts are also referred to as *nominal accounts*. Temporary accounts include the revenue, expense, and owner's drawing accounts plus the income summary account. Temporary accounts show changes in the owner's capital for a single fiscal period. Therefore, at the end of a fiscal period, the balances of temporary accounts are summarized and transferred to the owner's capital account. The temporary accounts begin a new fiscal period with zero balances.

NEED FOR CLOSING TEMPORARY ACCOUNTS

Journal entries used to prepare temporary accounts for a new fiscal period are called **closing entries**. The temporary account balances must be reduced to zero at the end of each fiscal period. This procedure prepares the temporary accounts for recording information about the next fiscal period. Otherwise, the amounts for the next fiscal period would be added to amounts for previous fiscal periods. [CONCEPT: Matching Expenses with Revenue] The net income for the next fiscal period would be difficult to calculate because amounts from several fiscal periods remain in the accounts. Therefore, the temporary accounts must start each new fiscal period with zero balances.

To close a temporary account, an amount equal to its balance is recorded in the account on the side opposite to its balance. For example, if an account has a credit balance of $3,565.00, a debit of $3,565.00 is recorded to close the account.

PHOTODISC/GETTY IMAGES

206 Chapter 8 Recording Adjusting and Closing Entries for a Service Business

NEED FOR THE INCOME SUMMARY ACCOUNT

Whenever a temporary account is closed, the closing entry must have equal debits and credits. If an account is debited for $3,000.00 to close the account, some other account must be credited for the same amount. A temporary account titled **Income Summary** is used to summarize the closing entries for the revenue and expense accounts.

The income summary account is unique because it does not have a normal balance side. The balance of this account is determined by the amounts posted to the account at the end of a fiscal period. When revenue is greater than total expenses, resulting in a net income, the income summary account has a credit balance, as shown in the T account.

Income Summary	
Debit	Credit
Total expenses	Revenue (greater than expenses)
	(Credit balance is the net income.)

When total expenses are greater than revenue, resulting in a net loss, the income summary account has a debit balance, as shown in the T account.

Income Summary	
Debit	Credit
Total expenses (greater than revenue)	Revenue
(Debit balance is the net loss.)	

Thus, whether the balance of the income summary account is a credit or a debit depends upon whether the business earns a net income or incurs a net loss. Because **Income Summary** is a temporary account, the account is also closed at the end of a fiscal period when the net income or net loss is recorded.

TechKnow Consulting records four closing entries: (1) an entry to close income statement accounts with credit balances; (2) an entry to close income statement accounts with debit balances; (3) an entry to record net income or net loss and close **Income Summary**; and (4) an entry to close the owner's drawing account.

Information needed to record the four closing entries is found in the Income Statement and Balance Sheet columns of the work sheet.

> **REMEMBER**
>
> TechKnow Consulting makes four closing entries: (1) Close income statement accounts with credit balances. (2) Close income statement accounts with debit balances. (3) Record net income or loss in the owner's capital account and close Income Summary. (4) Close the owner's drawing account.

> **FOR YOUR INFORMATION**
>
> **FYI**
>
> Most small businesses use the calendar year as their fiscal year because it matches the way in which the owners have to file their personal income tax returns.

Recording Closing Entries

CLOSING ENTRY FOR AN INCOME STATEMENT ACCOUNT WITH A CREDIT BALANCE

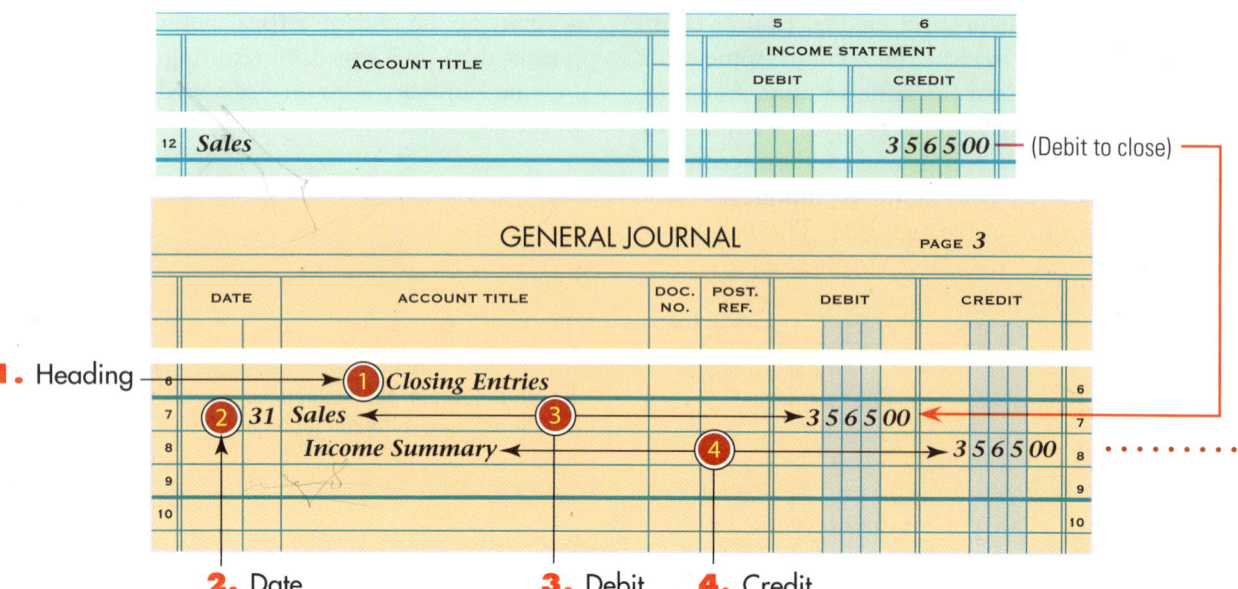

1. Heading
2. Date
3. Debit
4. Credit

TechKnow Consulting has one income statement account with a credit balance, Sales. This credit balance must be reduced to zero to prepare the account for the next fiscal period. To reduce the balance to zero, Sales is debited for the amount of the balance. Because debits must equal credits for each journal entry, some other account must be credited. The account used for the credit part of this closing entry is Income Summary.

The effect of this closing entry on the general ledger accounts is shown in the T accounts.

Sales			
Closing	3,565.00	Bal.	3,565.00
		(New Bal. zero)	

Income Summary	
	Closing (revenue) 3,565.00

The balance of Sales is now zero, and the account is ready for the next fiscal period. The credit balance of Sales is transferred to Income Summary.

> **FOR YOUR INFORMATION**
> # FYI
> *The reasons for recording closing entries can be compared to a trip odometer. Closing entries are recorded to prepare the temporary accounts for the next fiscal period by reducing their balances to zero. Likewise, a trip odometer must be reset to zero to begin recording the miles for the next trip.*

STEPS — CLOSING ENTRY FOR AN INCOME STATEMENT ACCOUNT WITH A CREDIT BALANCE

1. Write the heading, *Closing Entries*, in the middle of the Account Title column of the general journal. For TechKnow Consulting, this heading is placed in the general journal on the first blank line after the last adjusting entry.

2. Write the date, *31*, on the next line in the Date column.

3. Write the title of the account debited, *Sales*, in the Account Title column. Record the debit amount, *$3,565.00*, in the Debit column on the same line as the account title.

4. Write the title of the account credited, *Income Summary*, on the next line in the Account Title column. Record the credit amount, *$3,565.00*, in the Credit column on the same line as the account title.

CLOSING ENTRY FOR INCOME STATEMENT ACCOUNTS WITH DEBIT BALANCES

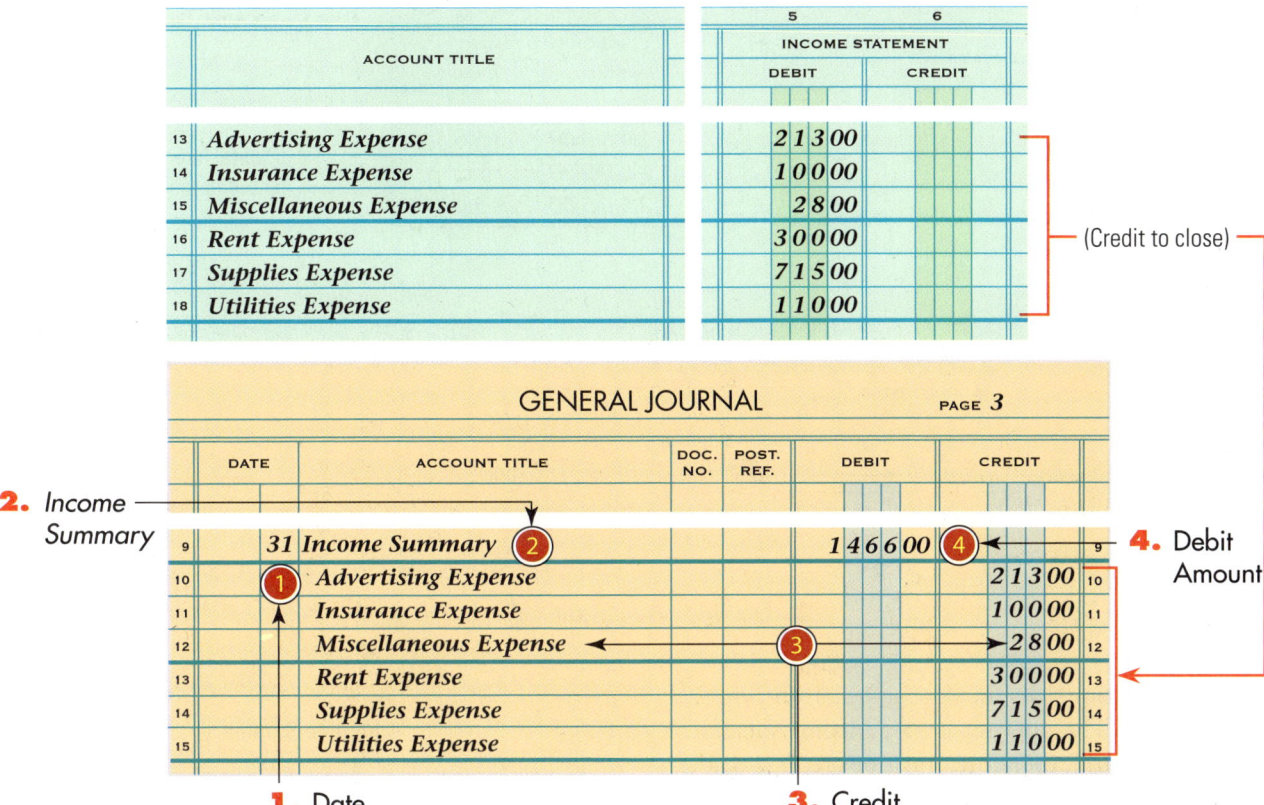

TechKnow Consulting has six income statement accounts with debit balances. The six expense accounts have normal debit balances at the end of a fiscal period. The balances of the expense accounts must be reduced to zero to prepare the accounts for the next fiscal period. Each expense account is credited for an amount equal to its balance. Income Summary is debited for the total of all the expense account balances. The amount debited to Income Summary is not entered in the amount column until all expenses have been journalized and the total amount calculated.

The effect of this closing entry on the general ledger accounts is shown in the T accounts. The balance of each expense account is returned to zero, and the accounts are ready for the next fiscal period. The balance of Income Summary is the net income for the fiscal period, $2,099.00.

Recording Closing Entries   Lesson 8-2   **209**

CLOSING ENTRY TO RECORD NET INCOME OR LOSS AND CLOSE THE INCOME SUMMARY ACCOUNT

TechKnow Consulting's net income appears on line 20 of the work sheet. The amount of net income increases the owner's capital and, therefore, must be credited to the owner's capital account. The balance of the temporary account, Income Summary, must be reduced to zero to prepare the account for the next fiscal period.

The effect of this closing entry on the general ledger accounts is shown in the T accounts. The debit to the income summary account, $2,099.00, reduces the account balance to zero and prepares the account for the next fiscal period. The credit, $2,099.00, increases the balance of the owner's capital account, Kim Park, Capital.

Income Summary			
Closing (expenses)	1,466.00	Closing (revenue)	3,565.00
Closing	2,099.00	(New Bal. zero)	

Kim Park, Capital			
		Bal.	5,000.00
		Closing (net inc.)	2,099.00
		(New Bal.	7,099.00)

If a business incurs a net loss, the closing entry is a debit to the owner's capital account and a credit to the income summary account.

STEPS — CLOSING ENTRY TO RECORD NET INCOME OR LOSS AND CLOSE THE INCOME SUMMARY ACCOUNT

① Write the date, 31, on the next line in the Date column.

② Write the title of the account debited, Income Summary, in the Account Title column. Record the debit amount, $2,099.00, in the Debit column on the same line as the account title.

③ Write the title of the account credited, Kim Park, Capital, on the next line in the Account Title column. Record the credit amount, $2,099.00, in the Credit column on the same line as the account title.

REMEMBER

Amounts for closing entries are taken from the Income Statement and Balance Sheet columns of the work sheet.

210 Chapter 8 Recording Adjusting and Closing Entries for a Service Business

CLOSING ENTRY FOR THE OWNER'S DRAWING ACCOUNT

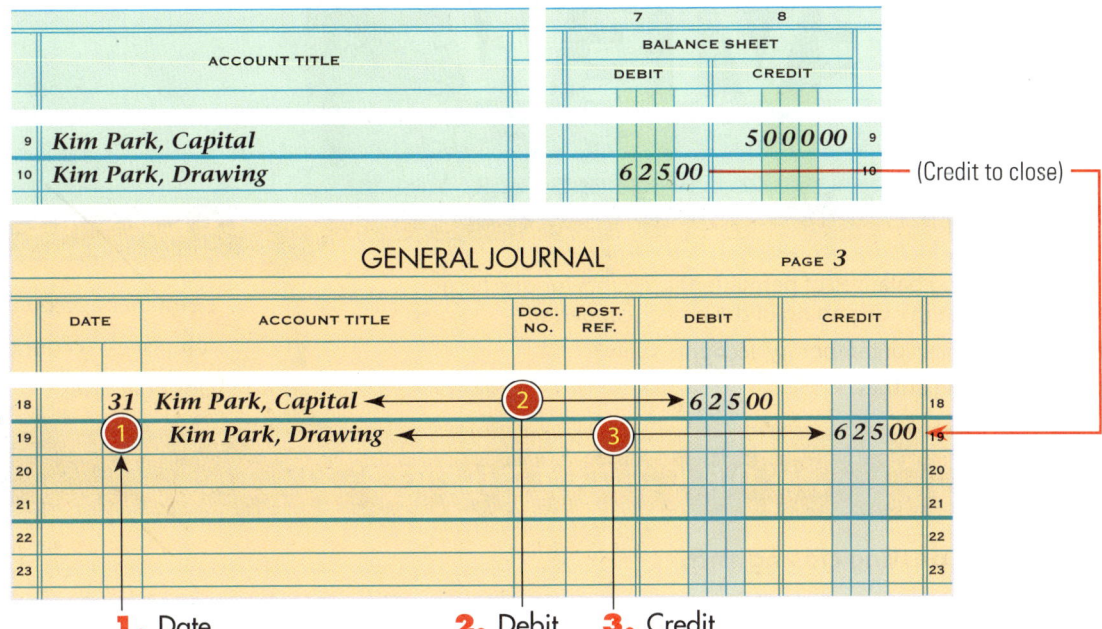

1. Date   2. Debit   3. Credit

Withdrawals are assets that the owner takes out of a business and which decrease the amount of the owner's equity. The drawing account is a temporary account that accumulates information separately for each fiscal period. Therefore, the drawing account balance is reduced to zero at the end of one fiscal period to prepare the account for the next fiscal period.

The drawing account is neither a revenue nor an expense account. Therefore, the drawing account is not closed through Income Summary. The drawing account balance is closed directly to the owner's capital account.

The effect of the entry to close the drawing account is shown in the T accounts.

The drawing account has a zero balance and is ready for the next fiscal period. The capital account's new balance, $6,474.00, is verified by comparing the balance to the amount of capital shown on the balance sheet prepared at the end of the fiscal period. The capital account balance shown on TechKnow Consulting's balance sheet in Chapter 7 is $6,474.00. The two amounts are the same, and the capital account balance is verified.

Kim Park, Capital			
Closing (drawing) 625.00	Bal.	5,000.00
	Net Income	2,099.00
	(New Bal.	6,474.00)

Kim Park, Drawing	
Bal. 625.00	Closing 625.00
(New Bal. zero)	

STEPS CLOSING ENTRY FOR THE OWNER'S DRAWING ACCOUNT

1. Write the date, *31*, in the Date column.

2. Write the title of the account debited, *Kim Park, Capital*, in the Account Title column. Record the debit amount, *$625.00*, in the Debit column on the same line as the account title.

3. Write the title of the account credited, *Kim Park, Drawing*, in the Account Title column. Record the credit amount, *$625.00*, in the Credit column on the same line as the account title.

Recording Closing Entries

End of Lesson REVIEW

AUDIT YOUR UNDERSTANDING

1. What do the ending balances of permanent accounts for one fiscal period represent at the beginning of the next fiscal period?
2. What do the balances of temporary accounts show?
3. List the four closing entries.

TERMS REVIEW

permanent accounts
temporary accounts
closing entries

WORK TOGETHER 8-2

Journalizing and posting closing entries

Use the general journal and general ledger accounts from Work Together 8-1. A partial work sheet for the month ended July 31 of the current year is given in the *Working Papers*. Your instructor will guide you through the following example.

1. Continue on the same general journal page. Journalize and post the closing entries. Save your work to complete Work Together 8-3.

ON YOUR OWN 8-2

Journalizing and posting closing entries

Use the general journal and general ledger accounts from On Your Own 8-1. A partial work sheet for the month ended February 28 of the current year is given in the *Working Papers*. Work this problem independently.

1. Continue on the same general journal page. Journalize and post the closing entries. Save your work to complete On Your Own 8-3.

LESSON 8-3

Preparing a Post-Closing Trial Balance

GENERAL LEDGER ACCOUNTS AFTER ADJUSTING AND CLOSING ENTRIES ARE POSTED

ACCOUNT **Cash**   ACCOUNT NO. **110**

DATE	ITEM	POST. REF.	DEBIT	CREDIT	BALANCE DEBIT	BALANCE CREDIT
31		G2	190 00		4 972 00	
31		G2		8 00	4 964 00	

ACCOUNT **Petty Cash**   ACCOUNT NO. **120**

DATE	ITEM	POST. REF.	DEBIT	CREDIT	BALANCE DEBIT	BALANCE CREDIT
20-- Aug. 19		G1	100 00		100 00	

ACCOUNT **Accounts Receivable—Oakdale School**   ACCOUNT NO. **130**

DATE	ITEM	POST. REF.	DEBIT	CREDIT	BALANCE DEBIT	BALANCE CREDIT
20-- Aug. 12		G1	350 00		350 00	
18		G1		200 00	150 00	

ACCOUNT **Accounts Receivable—Campus Internet Cafe**   ACCOUNT NO. **140**

DATE	ITEM	POST. REF.	DEBIT	CREDIT	BALANCE DEBIT	BALANCE CREDIT
20-- Aug. 13		G1	100 00		100 00	

ACCOUNT **Supplies**   ACCOUNT NO. **150**

DATE	ITEM	POST. REF.	DEBIT	CREDIT	BALANCE DEBIT	BALANCE CREDIT
20-- Aug. 3		G1	275 00		275 00	
7		G1	500 00		775 00	
20		G1	50 00		825 00	
28		G2	200 00		1 025 00	
31		G3		715 00	310 00	

TechKnow Consulting's general ledger, after the adjusting and closing entries are posted, is shown here and on the next several pages. When an account has a zero balance, lines are drawn in both the Balance Debit and Balance Credit columns. The lines assure a reader that a balance has not been omitted.

Preparing a Post-Closing Trial Balance

A General Ledger after Adjusting and Closing Entries Are Posted (continued)

ACCOUNT Advertising Expense — ACCOUNT NO. 510

DATE	ITEM	POST. REF.	DEBIT	CREDIT	BALANCE DEBIT	BALANCE CREDIT
Aug. 14		G1	78 00		78 00	
18		G1	125 00		203 00	
31		G2	10 00		213 00	
31		G3		213 00	—	—

ACCOUNT Insurance Expense — ACCOUNT NO. 520

DATE	ITEM	POST. REF.	DEBIT	CREDIT	BALANCE DEBIT	BALANCE CREDIT
Aug. 31		G3	100 00		100 00	
31		G3		100 00	—	—

ACCOUNT Miscellaneous Expense — ACCOUNT NO. 530

DATE	ITEM	POST. REF.	DEBIT	CREDIT	BALANCE DEBIT	BALANCE CREDIT
Aug. 31		G2	20 00		20 00	
31		G2	8 00		28 00	
31		G3		28 00	—	—

ACCOUNT Rent Expense — ACCOUNT NO. 540

DATE	ITEM	POST. REF.	DEBIT	CREDIT	BALANCE DEBIT	BALANCE CREDIT
Aug. 12		G1	300 00		300 00	
31		G3		300 00	—	—

ACCOUNT Supplies Expense — ACCOUNT NO. 550

DATE	ITEM	POST. REF.	DEBIT	CREDIT	BALANCE DEBIT	BALANCE CREDIT
Aug. 31		G3	715 00		715 00	
31		G3		715 00	—	—

ACCOUNT Utilities Expense — ACCOUNT NO. 560

DATE	ITEM	POST. REF.	DEBIT	CREDIT	BALANCE DEBIT	BALANCE CREDIT
Aug. 12		G1	40 00		40 00	
27		G2	70 00		110 00	
31		G3		110 00	—	—

A General Ledger after Adjusting and Closing Entries Are Posted (concluded)

POST-CLOSING TRIAL BALANCE

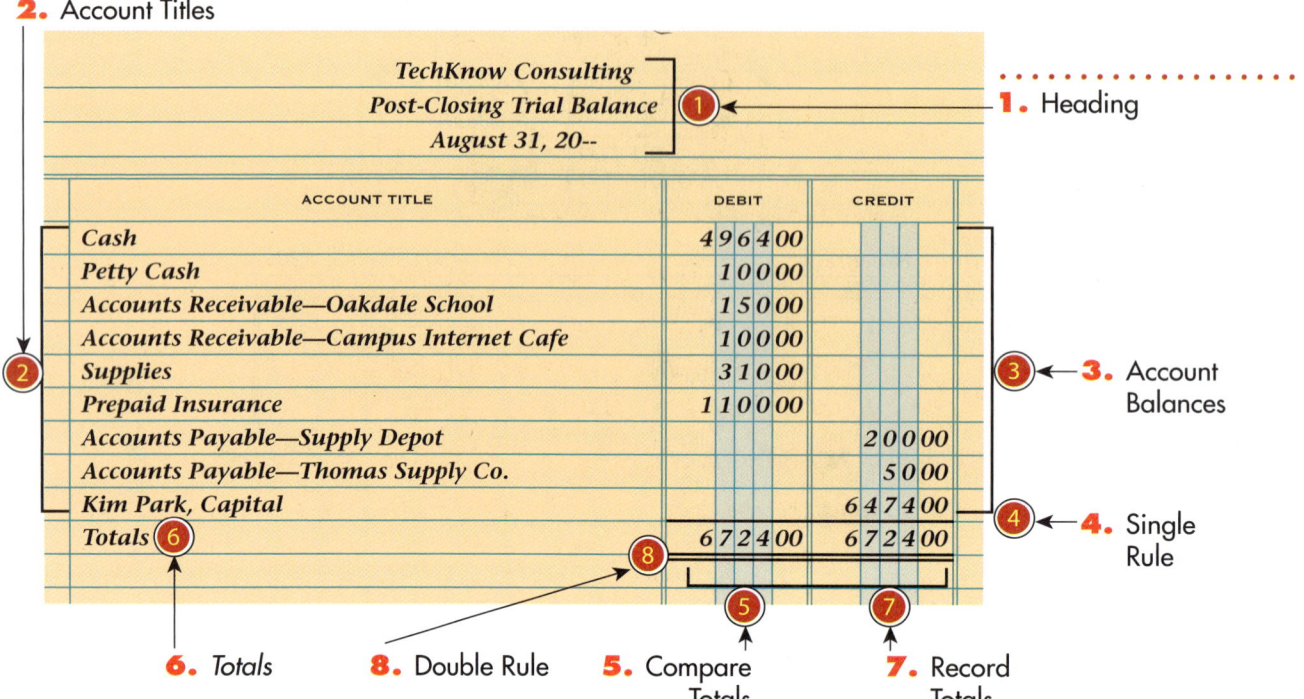

After the closing entries are posted, TechKnow Consulting verifies that debits equal credits in the general ledger accounts by preparing a trial balance. A trial balance prepared after the closing entries are posted is called a **post-closing trial balance**.

Only general ledger accounts with balances are included on a post-closing trial balance. The permanent accounts (assets, liabilities, and owner's capital) have balances and do appear on a post-closing trial balance. Because the temporary accounts (income summary, revenue, expense, and drawing) are closed and have zero balances, they do not appear on a post-closing trial balance.

The total of all debits must equal the total of all credits in a general ledger. The totals of both columns on TechKnow Consulting's post-closing trial balance are the same, $6,724.00. TechKnow Consulting's post-closing trial balance shows that the general ledger account balances are in balance and ready for the new fiscal period.

STEPS — PREPARING A POST-CLOSING TRIAL BALANCE

1. Write the heading on three lines.
2. Write the titles of all general ledger accounts with balances in the Account Title column.
3. On the same line with each account title, write each account's balance in either the Debit or Credit column.
4. Rule a single line across both amount columns below the last amount, and add each amount column.
5. Compare the two column totals. The two column totals must be the same. If the two column totals are not the same, the errors must be found and corrected before any more work is completed.
6. Write the word *Totals* on the line below the last account title.
7. Write the column totals, $6,724.00, below the single line.
8. Rule double lines across both amount columns to show that the totals have been verified as correct.

216 Chapter 8 Recording Adjusting and Closing Entries for a Service Business

ACCOUNTING CYCLE FOR A SERVICE BUSINESS

Chapters 1 through 8 describe TechKnow Consulting's accounting activities for a one-month fiscal period. The series of accounting activities included in recording financial information for a fiscal period is called an **accounting cycle**. [CONCEPT: Accounting Period Cycle]

For the next fiscal period, the cycle begins again at Step 1.

STEPS IN AN ACCOUNTING CYCLE

1. Source documents are checked for accuracy, and transactions are analyzed into debit and credit parts.
2. Transactions, from information on source documents, are recorded in the general journal.
3. Journal entries are posted to the general ledger.
4. A work sheet, including a trial balance, is prepared from the general ledger.
5. Financial statements are prepared from the work sheet.
6. Adjusting and closing entries are journalized from the work sheet.
7. Adjusting and closing entries are posted to the general ledger.
8. A post-closing trial balance of the general ledger is prepared.

REMEMBER

The word *post* means after. The Post-Closing Trial Balance is *prepared* after *closing entries*.

Preparing a Post-Closing Trial Balance Lesson 8-3 217

Business, Management & Administration

CAREERS IN ACCOUNTING

Anna McNeese Price, Future Certified Financial Planner

When Anna McNeese Price started college, entering the field of accounting wasn't part of her career plan. Through high school she worked at a mental health facility and enjoyed the personal contact she had with the clients in the physical therapy department. But an interest in business (and a sudden lack of interest in biology) led her to change majors as a college sophomore.

After considering the different business degrees offered, she decided to go into accounting. Anna recalls, "I knew I was interested in business, and I thought accounting would be the most challenging. I also heard about the great job market, and since I was going through school during the height of the WorldCom/Enron scandals, any degree that could guarantee job placement was attractive."

But her desire to affect lives personally didn't seem to mix with the large corporate jobs that recruiters from the "Big Four" firms were offering. So when one of her professors told her about a part-time job working for Ernie George, a certified financial planner, Anna saw an opportunity to experience a different type of career.

By working closely with Mr. George and his assistant, Anna has been able to use her accounting background to better understand the stock market and what it takes to advise people on how to invest their money. She has found that as a certified financial planner, Mr. George has a close personal relationship with his clients and is able to make the impact that she dreamed of in her early college career.

"I will finish my bachelor's of accountancy next year and immediately enroll in the Master of Taxation program," Anna explains. "Within five years of graduation, I hope to have obtained my certified public accountant (CPA) and certified financial planner (CFP) certifications and go into private practice as a certified financial planner with professional tax expertise."

Salary Range: Median annual earnings of personal financial advisors were $62,700 in 2004, according to the *Occupational Outlook Handbook*. Over 25% of financial planners earn more than $100,000. (Source: Bureau of Labor Statistics, U.S. Department of Labor, *Occupational Outlook Handbook, 2006–07 Edition*; Financial Analysts and Personal Financial Advisors, on the Internet at www.bls.gov/oco/ocos259.htm [visited January 15, 2007].)

Qualifications: A college degree is required, and professional certification is recommended. Financial planners must have good communication skills. Because many financial planners are self-employed, they must also possess the skills necessary to manage a business.

Occupational Outlook: More and more people are choosing alternative ways to plan for retirement. The complexity of the stock market and the tax laws (which can limit how much you can save) have increased the need for professionals who can give sound advice to individuals interested in investing.

End of Lesson REVIEW

AUDIT YOUR UNDERSTANDING

TERMS REVIEW

post-closing trial balance
accounting cycle

1. Why are lines drawn in both the Balance Debit and Balance Credit columns when an account has a zero balance?
2. Which accounts go on the post-closing trial balance?
3. Why are temporary accounts omitted from a post-closing trial balance?

WORK TOGETHER 8-3

Preparing a post-closing trial balance

Use the general ledger accounts from Work Together 8-2. Your instructor will guide you through the following example. A form to complete a post-closing trial balance is given in the *Working Papers*.

1. Prepare a post-closing trial balance for Darlene's Delivery Service on July 31 of the current year.

ON YOUR OWN 8-3

Preparing a post-closing trial balance

Use the general ledger accounts from On Your Own 8-2. Work this problem independently. A form to complete a post-closing trial balance is given in the *Working Papers*.

1. Prepare a post-closing trial balance for Cuts by Kelley on February 28 of the current year.

Preparing a Post-Closing Trial Balance

SUMMARY

After completing this chapter, you can:

1. Define accounting terms related to adjusting and closing entries for a service business organized as a proprietorship.
2. Identify accounting concepts and practices related to adjusting and closing entries for a service business organized as a proprietorship.
3. Record adjusting entries for a service business organized as a proprietorship.
4. Record closing entries for a service business organized as a proprietorship.
5. Prepare a post-closing trial balance for a service business organized as a proprietorship.

EXPLORE ACCOUNTING

Public Accounting Firms

One type of business that helps other businesses with accounting issues is known as a *public accounting firm*.

The independent reviewing and issuing of an opinion on the reliability of accounting records is known as *auditing*.

When performing an audit for a client, the accounting firm looks closely at the client's financial statements and the way the client records transactions. The auditor's job is to determine if the financial statements fairly present the financial position of the client. The auditor issues an opinion, which is a statement as to whether the financial statements follow standard accounting rules (GAAP). (GAAP stands for *G*enerally *A*ccepted *A*ccounting *P*rinciples.) This "opinion" is used by bankers deciding to lend money to the company. It is also used by investors when making investment decisions.

Auditing, however, is just one of many services provided by public accounting firms. Other services include tax preparation, tax advice, payroll services, bookkeeping services, financial statement preparation, and consulting services. These other services often make up a higher percentage of business for the accounting firm than performing audits.

Many accounting firms report that they are getting more requests for consulting services than for other services they can provide.

In many cases, consulting is also the area that produces the largest profit margin for the public accounting firm. Therefore, some firms are actively advertising their ability to provide management consulting services for clients.

Activity: Contact a public accounting firm in your area. Research what services the firm provides and which service area (if any) is growing. Present your findings to your class.

8-1 APPLICATION PROBLEM

Journalizing and posting adjusting entries

A journal and general ledger accounts for Len's Laundry are given in the *Working Papers*. A partial work sheet for the month ended April 30 of the current year is shown below.

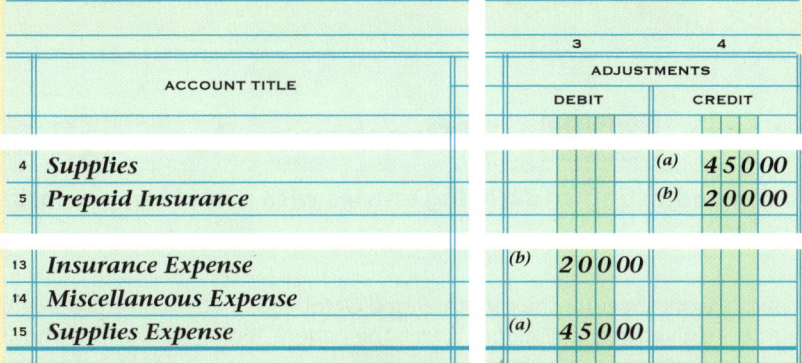

	ACCOUNT TITLE	ADJUSTMENTS DEBIT	ADJUSTMENTS CREDIT
4	Supplies		(a) 45000
5	Prepaid Insurance		(b) 20000
13	Insurance Expense	(b) 20000	
14	Miscellaneous Expense		
15	Supplies Expense	(a) 45000	

Use page 12 of the journal. Journalize and post the adjusting entries. Save your work to complete Application Problem 8-2.

8-2 APPLICATION PROBLEM

Journalizing and posting closing entries

Use the journal and general ledger accounts for Len's Laundry from Application Problem 8-1. A partial work sheet for the month ended April 30 of the current year is shown below.

	ACCOUNT TITLE	INCOME STATEMENT DEBIT	INCOME STATEMENT CREDIT	BALANCE SHEET DEBIT	BALANCE SHEET CREDIT
1	Cash			7 6 0 7 00	
2	Accounts Receivable—Natasha Goodlad			7 0 0 00	
3	Accounts Receivable—R. Henry			4 9 8 00	
4	Supplies			4 3 1 00	
5	Prepaid Insurance			2 0 0 00	
6	Accounts Payable—Tri-County Supplies				3 8 1 00
7	Accounts Payable—West End Supply Co.				5 5 5 00
8	Leonard Long, Capital				6 5 2 7 00
9	Leonard Long, Drawing			1 0 0 0 00	
10	Income Summary				
11	Sales		6 2 3 3 00		
12	Advertising Expense	8 0 0 00			
13	Insurance Expense	2 0 0 00			
14	Miscellaneous Expense	3 1 5 00			
15	Supplies Expense	4 5 0 00			
16	Utilities Expense	1 4 9 5 00			
17		3 2 6 0 00	6 2 3 3 00	10 4 6 3 00	7 4 6 3 00
18	Net Income	2 9 7 3 00			2 9 7 3 00
19		6 2 3 3 00	6 2 3 3 00	10 4 6 3 00	10 4 3 6 00

Continue on the same journal page. Journalize and post the closing entries. Save your work to complete Application Problem 8-3.

Recording Adjusting and Closing Entries for a Service Business

8-3 APPLICATION PROBLEM

Preparing a post-closing trial balance

Use the general ledger accounts for Len's Laundry from Application Problem 8-2. A form to complete a post-closing trial balance is given in the *Working Papers*.

Prepare a post-closing trial balance for Len's Laundry on April 30 of the current year.

8-4 MASTERY PROBLEM

Journalizing and posting adjusting and closing entries with a net loss; preparing a post-closing trial balance

Rolstad Repair Service's partial work sheet for the month ended October 31 of the current year is given below. The general ledger accounts are given in the *Working Papers*. The general ledger accounts do not show all details for the fiscal period. The Balance shown in each account is the account's balance before adjusting and closing entries are posted.

ACCOUNT TITLE	ADJUSTMENTS DEBIT	ADJUSTMENTS CREDIT	INCOME STATEMENT DEBIT	INCOME STATEMENT CREDIT	BALANCE SHEET DEBIT	BALANCE SHEET CREDIT
1 Cash					6958 00	
2 Petty Cash					150 00	
3 Accts. Rec.—M. Hollerud					197 00	
4 Supplies		(a) 1400 00			780 00	
5 Prepaid Insurance		(b) 157 00			800 00	
6 Accts. Pay.—Tampa Supply						612 00
7 Ron Rolstad, Capital						9337 00
8 Ron Rolstad, Drawing					600 00	
9 Income Summary						
10 Sales				3269 00		
11 Advertising Expense			450 00			
12 Insurance Expense	(b) 157 00		157 00			
13 Miscellaneous Expense			85 00			
14 Supplies Expense	(a) 1400 00		1400 00			
15 Utilities Expense			1641 00			
16	1557 00	1557 00	3733 00	3269 00	9485 00	9949 00
17 Net Loss				464 00	464 00	
18			3733 00	3733 00	9949 00	9949 00

Instructions:

1. Use page 20 of the journal. Journalize and post the adjusting entries.
2. Continue to use page 20 of the journal. Journalize and post the closing entries.
3. Prepare a post-closing trial balance.

8-5 CHALLENGE PROBLEM

Journalizing and posting adjusting and closing entries with two revenue accounts and a net loss; preparing a post-closing trial balance

LawnMow's partial work sheet for the month ended September 30 of the current year is given below. The general ledger accounts are given in the *Working Papers*. The general ledger accounts do not show all details for the fiscal period. The Balance shown in each account is the account's balance before adjusting and closing entries are posted.

	ACCOUNT TITLE	ADJUSTMENTS DEBIT	ADJUSTMENTS CREDIT	INCOME STATEMENT DEBIT	INCOME STATEMENT CREDIT	BALANCE SHEET DEBIT	BALANCE SHEET CREDIT
1	Cash					1898 00	
2	Accts. Rec.—Sandra Rohe					95 00	
3	Supplies		(a) 320 00			650 00	
4	Prepaid Insurance		(b) 40 00			120 00	
5	Accts. Pay.—Corner Garage						58 00
6	Accts. Pay.—Broadway Gas						110 00
7	Accts. Pay.—Esko Repair						215 00
8	Ryo Morrison, Capital						4000 00
9	Ryo Morrison, Drawing					100 00	
10	Income Summary						
11	Sales—Lawn Care				4900 00		
12	Sales—Shrub Care				2500 00		
13	Advertising Expense			390 00			
14	Insurance Expense	(b) 40 00		40 00			
15	Miscellaneous Expense			550 00			
16	Rent Expense			3300 00			
17	Supplies Expense	(a) 320 00		320 00			
18		360 00	360 00	7840 00	7400 00	3943 00	4383 00
19	Net Loss				440 00	440 00	
20				7840 00	7840 00	4383 00	4383 00

Instructions:

1. Use page 18 of the journal. Journalize and post the adjusting entries.
2. Continue to use page 18 of the journal. Journalize and post the closing entries.
3. Prepare a post-closing trial balance.
4. Ryo Morrison, owner of LawnMow, is disappointed that his business incurred a net loss for September of the current year. Mr. Morrison would have preferred not to have to reduce his capital by $440.00. He knows that you are studying accounting, so Mr. Morrison asks you to analyze his work sheet for September. Based on your analysis of the work sheet, what would you suggest might have caused the net loss for LawnMow? What steps would you suggest so that Mr. Morrison can avoid a net loss in future months?

APPLIED COMMUNICATION

Service businesses are the fastest growing part of our business world. Social and economic changes create needs for new and different kinds of service businesses to satisfy customer demands.

For example, the growing popularity of the World Wide Web led to the creation of service businesses that design Web pages. These businesses create text, graphics, animation, and links for business and private clients. Another example of a new type of service business is a personal services business that runs errands or stands in long lines for clients. As lifestyles become busier and busier, some people do not have the time to take care of all their personal errands. Service businesses have appeared to fill this need.

Instructions: Using library, online, or other information resources, write a one-page report on a new or unusual service business that you would be interested in working for or owning.

CASES FOR CRITICAL THINKING

Case 1

Gretel Bakken forgot to journalize and post the adjusting entry for prepaid insurance at the end of the June fiscal period. What effect will this omission have on the records of Ms. Bakken's business as of June 30? Explain your answer.

Case 2

Vincente Burgos states that his business is so small that he just records supplies and insurance as expenses when he pays for them. Thus, at the end of a fiscal period, Mr. Burgos does not record adjusting and closing entries for his business. Do you agree with his accounting procedures? Explain your answer.

SCANS WORKPLACE COMPETENCY

Thinking Skill: Seeing things in the mind's eye

Concept: Effective employees can visualize how every part of a company contributes to the success of the whole company, from maintenance workers to the chief executive officer. Now that you have finished the study of a complete accounting cycle, you should better understand how each part of the cycle contributes to the whole cycle.

Application: Describe the importance of the work each of the following employees does. Explain how errors would affect the reporting of the company.

a. Employee who reconciles the bank statement.
b. Employee who determines the amount of supplies on hand at the end of the fiscal period.
c. Employee who posts the journal entries.
d. Employee who calculates and records the adjusting entries.
e. Employee who records the closing entries.

AUDITING FOR ERRORS

The closing entries for Greenlund Enterprises are given below. Assuming all account balances are correct, review the entries. List any errors you find.

Date	Account Title	Doc No.	Post Ref.	General Debit	General Credit
20-- May 31	Income Summary			32,000	
	Sales				32,000
31	Income Summary			6,200	
	Insurance Expense			900	
	Rent Expense				2,500
	Supplies Expense				1,200
	Utilities Expense				3,400
31	Lionel Greenlund, Capital			38,200	
	Income Summary				38,200
31	Lionel Greenlund, Capital			4,500	
	Lionel Greenlund, Drawing				4,500

ANALYZING BEST BUY'S FINANCIAL STATEMENTS

Refer to Best Buy's consolidated statements of earnings on Appendix B page B-6. To calculate what percentage an item increased or decreased from one year to another, calculate the difference between the two amounts and divide this difference by the amount for the earlier year. For example, the percentage of increase in revenue from 2005 to 2006 would be calculated as follows: ($30,848,000,000 − $27,433,000,000) ÷ $27,433,000,000 = 12.45%.

Instructions

1. What is Best Buy's revenue (sales) for each of the three years? Is this a favorable or unfavorable trend?
2. Calculate the percentage of increase in revenue from 2006 to 2007.
3. How does the increase from 2006 to 2007 compare to the increase from 2005 to 2006?

Accounting SOFTWARE

CLOSING ENTRIES; POST-CLOSING TRIAL BALANCE

Accounting software does not require that you journalize closing entries. Rather, you can use a wizard to assist you in closing the accounts. A wizard is a series of windows that collect the information necessary to perform a specific task. Based on the information you enter, the wizard performs the selected functions automatically.

A wizard is especially useful for functions that are very complicated or rarely performed. In the case of closing entries, computerized accounting systems are only closed at the end of a fiscal year. Because you only perform this process once a year, it is helpful to have a wizard to assist you.

Once Peachtree closes an account, you no longer have the ability to examine or modify journal entries made in that fiscal year. For this reason, Peachtree allows you to have two fiscal years open at one time. This strategy provides you with ample opportunity to ensure that your journal entries from the past fiscal year are correct while you continue to record transactions for the current fiscal year.

PEACHTREE MASTERY PROBLEM 8-4

1. Open (Restore) file 08-4MP.ptb.
2. Journalize and post the adjusting and closing entries in Peachtree's general journal. Use the closing entries wizard to record the closing entries.
3. Print the October 31 general ledger.
4. Print a post-closing trial balance.

PEACHTREE CHALLENGE PROBLEM 8-5

1. Open (Restore) file 08-5CP.ptb.
2. Journalize and post the adjusting and closing entries in Peachtree's general journal. Use the closing entries wizard to record the closing entries.
3. Print the September 30 general ledger.
4. Print a post-closing trial balance.

CLOSING ENTRIES; POST-CLOSING TRIAL BALANCE

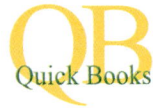

QuickBooks automatically closes all revenue and expense accounts into a summary account. However, the user must make entries to close this summary account into the capital account and to close the drawing account into the capital account.

Similar to manual accounting, it is a good idea to run a trial balance after the closing entries have been made and posted. Although computer systems are very accurate, the new balances should be examined to determine if the correct closing entries were made. The capital account should show the new ending balance, and all revenue and expense accounts should have a zero balance.

QUICKBOOKS MASTERY PROBLEM 8-4

1. Open the Rolstad Repair Service file and record the adjusting entries dated October 31.
2. Print a Profit & Loss report for October 1-31.
3. Print a Balance Sheet report and a Trial Balance report for the month ending October 31. Use the Accountant & Taxes Reports menu to print the Trial Balance report.
4. Using the information in the Trial Balance and the Profit & Loss reports, record the closing entries.
5. Print a Journal report containing both the adjusting and closing entries. Use October 31 for the date.
6. Print a post-closing trial balance from the Accountant & Taxes Reports menu.

QUICKBOOKS CHALLENGE PROBLEM 8-5

1. Open the LawnMow file and record the September 30 adjusting entries.
2. Print a Profit & Loss report for September 1-30.
3. Print a Balance Sheet report and Trial Balance report for the month ending September 30. Use the Accountant & Taxes Reports menu to print the Trial Balance report.
4. Using the information in the Trial Balance and the Profit & Loss reports, record the closing entries.
5. View and print a Journal report containing both the adjusting and closing entries, using September 30 for the To and From dates.
6. Print a post-closing trial balance from the Account & Taxes Reports menu.
7. Record the closing entries and print a post-closing trial balance.

CHARTS AND GRAPHS

A post-closing trial balance verifies that debits equal credits after posting adjustments and closing the accounts. The schedule reports the account balances of all permanent accounts at the beginning of the next fiscal period.

What if a manager asked you to provide a report of assets at the beginning of a fiscal period? Before preparing the answer, you should determine how the manager intends to use the information. Does the manager need to know the exact amount of every asset account? If so, a schedule of the asset accounts from the post-closing trial balance would provide the manager with the requested information.

However, the manager may not need to know the exact dollar amount of each asset. Instead, the manager may need only a general perception of the relative amount of each asset owned by the business. In this case, creating a chart of the data will provide the manager with better information than a detailed schedule of accounts.

EXCEL MASTERY PROBLEM 8-4

1. Complete Mastery Problem 8-4 using your Working Papers or accounting software. Prepare a post-closing trial balance.
2. In a new spreadsheet, list the asset accounts in one column and their balances in the next column.
3. Experiment with creating different types of charts of these accounts and balances (pie chart, bar chart, or line chart, for example).

CLOSING ENTRIES; POST-CLOSING TRIAL BALANCE

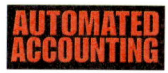

In an automated accounting system, closing entries are generated and posted by the software. The software automatically closes net income to the owner's capital account after closing the revenue and expense accounts. The drawing account is closed as well.

To perform a period-end closing:

1. Choose Generate Closing Journal Entries from the Options menu.
2. Click Yes to generate the closing entries.
3. The general journal will appear, containing the journal entries.
4. Click the Post button.

In *Automated Accounting*, once closing entries are posted, the journal entries of the period cannot be accessed to make corrections if errors are found later. Therefore, it is always a good practice to save your file before closing entries are generated; the letters *BC* (for *Before Closing*) can be added to the filename. After the closing entries are generated, add the letters *AC* (for *After Closing*) to the filename and save the file again. When this procedure is followed, if it is necessary to correct a journal entry, the file with *BC* in its name can be opened and corrected, and closing entries can be generated again.

AUTOMATED ACCOUNTING MASTERY PROBLEM 8-4
Open file F08-4.AA8. Display the problem instructions and complete the problem.

AUTOMATED ACCOUNTING CHALLENGE PROBLEM 8-5
Open file F08-5.AA8. Display the problem instructions and complete the problem.

REINFORCEMENT Activity 1—Part B

An Accounting Cycle for a Proprietorship: End-of-Fiscal-Period Work

The general ledger prepared in Reinforcement Activity 1—Part A is needed to complete Reinforcement Activity 1—Part B. Reinforcement Activity 1—Part B includes end-of-fiscal-period activities studied in Chapters 6 through 8.

WORK SHEET

INSTRUCTIONS:

8. Prepare a trial balance on the work sheet given in the Working Papers. Use a one-month fiscal period ended May 31 of the current year.

9. Analyze the following adjustment information into debit and credit parts. Record the adjustments on the work sheet.

Adjustment Information, May 31	
Supplies on hand	$ 625.00
Value of prepaid insurance	1,100.00

10. Total and rule the Adjustments columns.
11. Extend the up-to-date account balances to the Balance Sheet and Income Statement columns.
12. Complete the work sheet.

FINANCIAL STATEMENTS

INSTRUCTIONS:

13. Prepare an income statement. Figure and record the component percentages for sales, total expenses, and net income. Round percentage calculations to the nearest 0.1%.
14. Prepare a balance sheet.

ADJUSTING ENTRIES

INSTRUCTIONS:

15. Use page 3 of the general journal. Journalize and post the adjusting entries.

CLOSING ENTRIES

INSTRUCTIONS:

16. Continue using page 3 of the general journal. Journalize and post the closing entries.

POST-CLOSING TRIAL BALANCE

INSTRUCTIONS:

17. Prepare a post-closing trial balance.

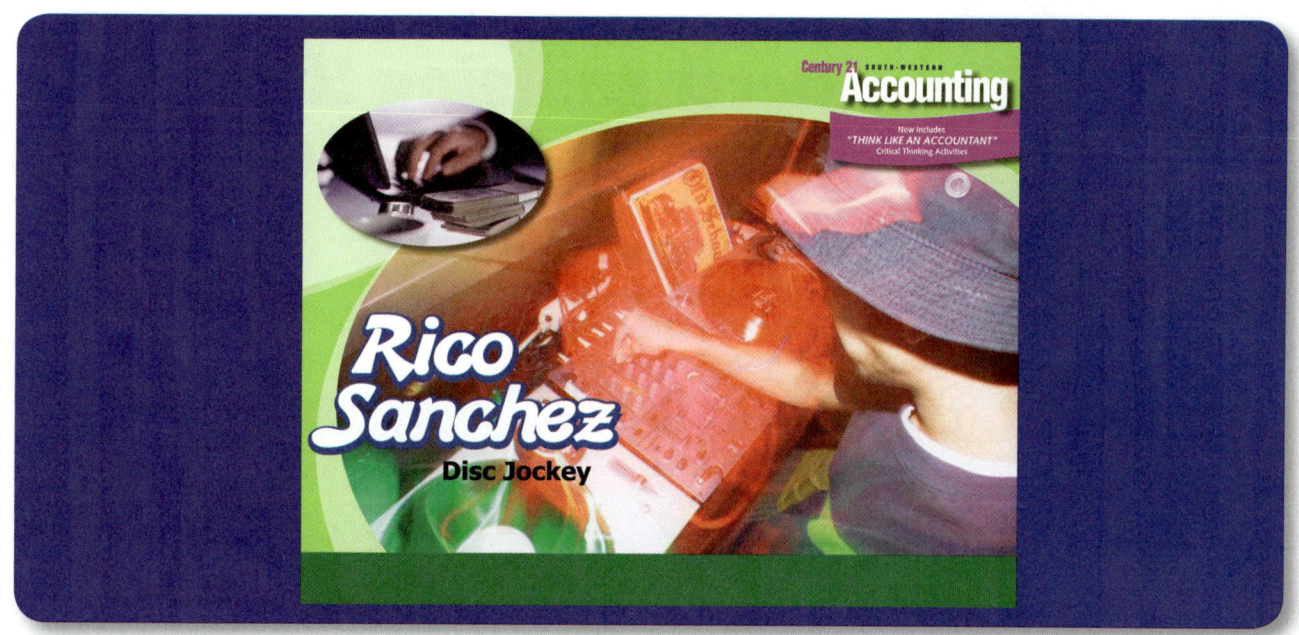

This simulation covers the transactions completed by Rico Sanchez, Disc Jockey, a service business organized as a proprietorship. On September 1 of the current year, Rico Sanchez, Disc Jockey, begins business. The owner, Rico Sanchez, performs as a disc jockey at clubs and private parties. He also specializes in karaoke when requested.

The activities included in the accounting cycle for Rico Sanchez, Disc Jockey, are listed below. The company uses a general journal and a general ledger similar to those described for TechKnow in Cycle 1.

This simulation is available in manual and in automated versions, for use with *Automated Accounting* software.

The following activities are included in this simulation:

1. Journalizing transactions in a general journal.
2. Preparing a bank statement reconciliation and recording a bank service charge.
3. Proving cash.
4. Posting from a general journal to a general ledger.
5. Preparing a trial balance on a work sheet.
6. Recording adjustments on a work sheet.
7. Completing a work sheet.
8. Preparing financial statements (income statement and balance sheet).
9. Journalizing and posting adjusting entries.
10. Journalizing and posting closing entries.
11. Preparing a post-closing trial balance.
12. Completing Think Like an Accountant Financial Analysis activity.

An Accounting Cycle for a Proprietorship: End-of-Fiscal-Period Work

PART 2
Accounting for a Merchandising Business Organized as a Corporation

▽ Chapter 9	Journalizing Purchases and Cash Payments
▽ Chapter 10	Journalizing Sales and Cash Receipts Using Special Journals
▽ Chapter 11	Posting to General and Subsidiary Ledgers
▽ Chapter 12	Preparing Payroll Records
▽ Chapter 13	Payroll Accounting, Taxes, and Reports
▽ Chapter 14	Distributing Dividends and Preparing a Work Sheet for a Merchandising Business
▽ Chapter 15	Financial Statements for a Corporation
▽ Chapter 16	Recording Adjusting and Closing Entries for a Corporation

THE BUSINESS—HOBBY SHACK, INC.

Hobby Shack, Inc., the business described in Part 2, is a retail merchandising business organized as a corporation. The business purchases and sells a wide variety of craft and hobby items such as silk flowers, ceramics, paints, and jewelry. Hobby Shack purchases its merchandise directly from businesses that manufacture the items. Hobby Shack rents the building in which the business is located.

PHOTOS: DIGITAL VISION, STOCKBYTE, PHOTODISC, TETRA IMAGES (ALL GETTY IMAGES)

HOBBY SHACK, INC., CHART OF ACCOUNTS

GENERAL LEDGER

Balance Sheet Accounts

(1000) ASSETS
- 1100 Current Assets
- 1110 Cash
- 1120 Petty Cash
- 1130 Accounts Receivable
- 1135 Allowance for Uncollectible Accounts
- 1140 Merchandise Inventory
- 1145 Supplies—Office
- 1150 Supplies—Store
- 1160 Prepaid Insurance
- 1200 Plant Assets
- 1205 Office Equipment
- 1210 Accumulated Depreciation—Office Equipment
- 1215 Store Equipment
- 1220 Accumulated Depreciation—Store Equipment

(2000) LIABILITIES
- 2100 Current Liabilities
- 2110 Accounts Payable
- 2120 Federal Income Tax Payable
- 2130 Employee Income Tax Payable
- 2135 Social Security Tax Payable
- 2140 Medicare Tax Payable
- 2145 Sales Tax Payable
- 2150 Unemployment Tax Payable—Federal
- 2155 Unemployment Tax Payable—State
- 2160 Health Insurance Premiums Payable
- 2165 U.S. Savings Bonds Payable
- 2170 United Way Donations Payable
- 2180 Dividends Payable

(3000) STOCKHOLDERS' EQUITY
- 3110 Capital Stock
- 3120 Retained Earnings
- 3130 Dividends
- 3140 Income Summary

Income Statement Accounts

(4000) OPERATING REVENUE
- 4110 Sales
- 4120 Sales Discount
- 4130 Sales Returns and Allowances

(5000) COST OF MERCHANDISE
- 5110 Purchases
- 5120 Purchases Discount
- 5130 Purchases Returns and Allowances

(6000) OPERATING EXPENSES
- 6105 Advertising Expense
- 6110 Cash Short and Over
- 6115 Credit Card Fee Expense
- 6120 Depreciation Expense—Office Equipment
- 6125 Depreciation Expense—Store Equipment
- 6130 Insurance Expense
- 6135 Miscellaneous Expense
- 6140 Payroll Taxes Expense
- 6145 Rent Expense
- 6150 Salary Expense
- 6155 Supplies Expense—Office
- 6160 Supplies Expense—Store
- 6165 Uncollectible Accounts Expense
- 6170 Utilities Expense
- 6200 Income Tax Expense
- 6205 Federal Income Tax Expense

SUBSIDIARY LEDGERS

Accounts Receivable Ledger
- 110 Country Crafters
- 120 Cumberland Center
- 130 Fairview Church
- 140 Playtime Childcare
- 150 Village Crafts
- 160 Washington Schools

Accounts Payable Ledger
- 210 American Paint
- 220 Ceramic Supply
- 230 Crown Distributing
- 240 Floral Designs
- 250 Gulf Craft Supply
- 260 Synthetic Arts

The charts of accounts for Hobby Shack, Inc., are illustrated here for ready reference as you study Part 2 of this textbook.

CHAPTER 11

CHAPTER 12

CHAPTER 15

CHAPTER 16

CHAPTER 9
Journalizing Purchases and Cash Payments

OBJECTIVES

After studying Chapter 9, you will be able to:

1. Define accounting terms related to purchases and cash payments for a merchandising business.
2. Identify accounting concepts and practices related to purchases and cash payments for a merchandising business.
3. Journalize purchases of merchandise using a purchases journal.
4. Journalize cash payments and cash discounts using a cash payments journal.
5. Prepare a petty cash report and journalize the reimbursement of the petty cash fund.
6. Total, prove, and rule a cash payments journal and start a new cash payments journal page.
7. Journalize purchases returns and allowances and other transactions using a general journal.

KEY TERMS

- merchandise
- merchandising business
- retail merchandising business
- wholesale merchandising business
- corporation
- share of stock
- capital stock
- stockholder
- special journal
- cost of merchandise
- markup
- vendor
- purchase on account
- purchases journal
- special amount column
- purchase invoice
- terms of sale
- cash payments journal
- cash discount
- purchases discount
- general amount column
- list price
- trade discount
- contra account
- cash short
- cash over
- purchases return
- purchases allowance
- debit memorandum

Point Your Browser
www.C21accounting.com

ACCOUNTING IN THE REAL WORLD

OfficeMax

Purchasing Synergies Benefit OfficeMax and Boise Office Solutions

Like the trees it manages, Boise Cascade Corporation has grown and evolved from its roots as a wood products company in Boise, Idaho. Building on its strength as a manufacturer of wood building products and paper, Boise established Boise Office Solutions to provide office supplies and furniture directly to businesses, government offices, and educational institutions.

In its 2002 annual report, Boise stated, "Boise Office Solutions' primary goal is profitable growth. This means winning new customers, selling more products to existing customers, and controlling operating costs."

Boise took a bold step to achieve that goal through the 2003 acquisition of OfficeMax, an office products company with nearly 1,000 retail outlets. The acquisition more than doubled sales in Boise's office products distribution business.

The company expects to use its combined purchasing power to lower the cost of the office products purchased from other manufacturers and to eliminate duplicate distribution facilities and marketing efforts. Boise expects the combined companies to achieve synergy benefits of $160 million a year.

Critical Thinking

1. How can purchasing more units of an item enable a company to purchase that item at a reduced cost?
2. Can you think of any two other companies that could reduce their operating costs by combining their businesses?

Source: www.bc.com

INTERNET ACTIVITY

C Corporations, S Corporations, and LLCs

There are several factors to consider when organizing a corporation. One of these is to determine what type of corporation you want to organize. Search the Internet for an explanation of each of the following types of corporations: C Corporation, S Corporation, and a Limited Liability Company (LLC).

Instructions

1. List the benefits and disadvantages of a C Corporation.
2. List the benefits and disadvantages of an S Corporation.
3. List the benefits and disadvantages of a Limited Liability Company.

LESSON 9-1: Journalizing Purchases Using a Purchases Journal

MERCHANDISING BUSINESSES

TechKnow Consulting, the business described in Part 1, is a service business; it sells services for a fee. However, many other businesses purchase goods to sell. Goods that a business purchases to sell are called **merchandise**. A business that purchases and sells goods is called a **merchandising business**. A merchandising business that sells to those who use or consume the goods is called a **retail merchandising business**. A business that buys and resells merchandise to retail merchandising businesses is called a **wholesale merchandising business**. Service and merchandising businesses use many of the same accounts. A merchandising business has additional accounts on the balance sheet and income statement to account for the purchase and sale of merchandise.

BUSINESS STRUCTURES

Forming a Corporation

Many businesses need amounts of capital that cannot be easily provided by a proprietorship. These businesses choose to organize using another form of business. An organization with the legal rights of a person and which many persons may own is called a **corporation**. A corporation is formed by receiving approval from a state or federal agency. Each unit of ownership in a corporation is called a **share of stock**. Total shares of ownership in a corporation are called **capital stock**. An owner of one or more shares of a corporation is called a **stockholder**.

A corporation is a business organization that has the legal rights of a person. A corporation can own property, incur liabilities, and enter into contracts in its own name. A corporation may also sell ownership in itself. A person becomes an owner of a corporation by purchasing shares of stock.

The principal difference between the accounting records of proprietorships and corporations is in the capital accounts. Proprietorships have a single capital and drawing account for the owner. A corporation has separate capital accounts for the stock issued and for the earnings kept in the business, which will be explained in more detail in Chapter 16. As in proprietorships, information in a corporation's accounting system is kept separate from the personal records of its owners. [CONCEPT: Business Entity] Periodic financial statements must be sent to the stockholders of the corporation to report the financial activities of the business.

Critical Thinking

1. The names of many corporations include the words *Corporation*, *Incorporated*, *Corp.*, or *Inc.* in their names. Based on their names, identify several corporations in your area.
2. Why do you think many very large companies are organized as corporations?

THE BUSINESS—HOBBY SHACK, INC.

Janice Kellogg decided to quit her full-time job and turn her ceramic hobby into a retail hobby business. She developed a plan to rent space in a shopping center and operate Hobby Shack six days a week. Hobby Shack would sell a wide variety of art and hobby supplies to individuals, schools, and businesses. Janice planned to expand the merchandise she offers, rent store and office equipment, and employ other individuals to work in the store. However, Janice did not personally have the capital to implement her plan. But with the help of a small group of investors, Janice formed a corporation called Hobby Shack, Inc. Each stockholder received a number of shares of stock based on the amount invested.

Unlike a proprietorship, a corporation exists independent of its owners. Janice expects the Hobby Shack to continue beyond her lifetime and plans to give her shares of stock to her children. [CONCEPT: Going Concern]

USING SPECIAL JOURNALS

A business with a limited number of daily transactions may record all entries in one journal. A business with many daily transactions may choose to use a separate journal for each kind of transaction. A journal used to record only one kind of transaction is called a **special journal**. Hobby Shack uses five journals to record daily transactions:

1. Purchases journal—for all purchases of merchandise on account
2. Cash payments journal—for all cash payments
3. Sales journal—for all sales of merchandise on account
4. Cash receipts journal—for all cash receipts
5. General journal—for all other transactions

Recording transactions in a sales journal and a cash receipts journal is described in Chapter 10.

CHARACTER COUNTS

Walking on Ethical Ice

Lockheed Martin is an international corporation engaged in the production of advanced technology systems. The company's largest customers are the U.S. Department of Defense and other U.S. federal government agencies.

Lockheed Martin is working to be a leader in ethical conduct. In its code of conduct, "Setting the Standard," the company provides its employees with detailed guidance on making ethical decisions. One method of assisting its employees to make ethical decisions is to provide a list of statements that are warning signs of unethical behavior, such as the following:

"Well, maybe just this once."
"No one will ever know."
"It doesn't matter how it gets done as long as it gets done."
"It sounds too good to be true."
"Everyone does it."
"Shred that document."
"We can hide it."
"No one will get hurt."
"What's in it for me?"
"This will destroy the competition."
"We didn't have this conversation."

Instructions

Think of statements you hear that are warning signs of unethical behavior.

Source: www.lockheedmartin.com

Journalizing Purchases Using a Purchases Journal LESSON 9-1

PURCHASING MERCHANDISE

The price a business pays for goods it purchases to sell is called **cost of merchandise**. The selling price of merchandise must be greater than the cost of merchandise for a business to make a profit. The amount added to the cost of merchandise to establish the selling price is called **markup**. Revenue earned from the sale of merchandise includes both the cost of merchandise and markup. Only the markup increases capital. Accounts for the cost of merchandise are kept in a separate division of the general ledger. The cost of merchandise division is shown in Hobby Shack's chart of accounts on page 231.

In addition to purchasing merchandise to sell, a merchandising business also buys supplies and other assets for use in the business. A business from which merchandise is purchased or supplies or other assets are bought is called a **vendor**.

The account used for recording the cost of merchandise is titled Purchases. Purchases is classified as a cost account because it is in the cost of merchandise division in the chart of accounts. Purchases is a temporary account. Because the cost of merchandise reduces capital when the merchandise is purchased, Purchases has a normal debit balance. Therefore, the purchases account increases by a debit and decreases by a credit, as shown in the T account.

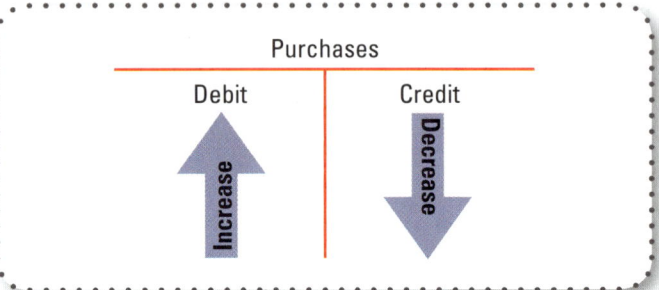

PURCHASES ON ACCOUNT

The cost account, Purchases, is used only to record the cost of merchandise purchased. No other items bought, such as supplies, are recorded in the purchases account. These items are recorded in other accounts, such as Supplies. Merchandise and other items bought are recorded and reported at the price agreed upon at the time the transactions occur. The accounting concept *Historical Cost* is applied when the actual amount paid for merchandise or other items bought is recorded. [CONCEPT: Historical Cost]

A transaction in which the merchandise purchased is to be paid for later is called a **purchase on account**. Some businesses that purchase on account from only a few vendors keep a separate general ledger account for each vendor. Businesses that purchase on account from many vendors will have many accounts for vendors. To avoid a bulky general ledger, the total amount owed to all vendors can be summarized in a single general ledger account.

A liability account that summarizes the amounts owed to all vendors is titled Accounts Payable. Hobby Shack uses an accounts payable account. The liability account, Accounts Payable, has a normal credit balance. Therefore, the accounts payable account increases by a credit and decreases by a debit, as shown in the T account.

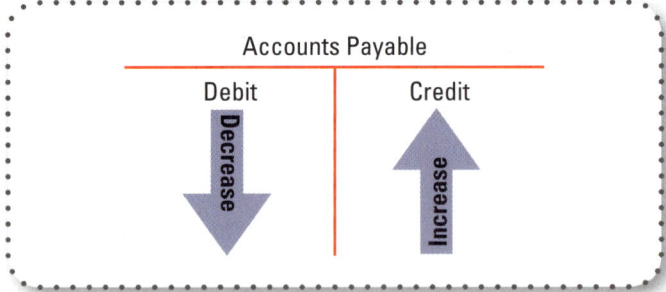

PURCHASES JOURNAL

		PURCHASES JOURNAL			PAGE	
	DATE	ACCOUNT CREDITED	PURCH. NO.	POST. REF.	PURCHASES DR. ACCTS. PAY. CR.	
1						1
2						2

A special journal used to record only purchases of merchandise on account is called a **purchases journal**. A purchase on account transaction is recorded on only one line of Hobby Shack's purchases journal. The amount column has two account titles in its heading: *Purchases Dr.* and *Accts. Pay. Cr.* A journal amount column headed with an account title is called a **special amount column**. Special amount columns are used for frequently occurring transactions. All of Hobby Shack's purchase on account transactions involve a debit to Purchases and a credit to Accounts Payable. Therefore, Hobby Shack's special amount column in the purchases journal includes those accounts in the heading.

Using special amount columns eliminates writing general ledger account titles in the Account Title column. Recording entries in a journal with special amount columns saves time.

REMEMBER

All purchase on account transactions are recorded in the purchases journal. If a purchase is made for cash, the transaction is NOT recorded in the purchases journal.

Journalizing Purchases Using a Purchases Journal

PURCHASE INVOICE

When a vendor sells merchandise to a buyer, the vendor prepares a form showing what has been sold. A form describing the goods sold, the quantity, and the price is known as an invoice. An invoice used as a source document for recording a purchase on account transaction is called a **purchase invoice**. [CONCEPT: Objective Evidence]

A purchase invoice lists the quantity, the description, the price of each item, and the total amount of the invoice. A purchase invoice provides the information needed for recording a purchase on account.

Hobby Shack takes the following actions when a purchase invoice is received.

STEPS RECEIVING A PURCHASE INVOICE

 Stamp the date received, *11/02/--*, and Hobby Shack's purchase invoice number, *P83*, in the upper right corner.

This date should not be confused with the vendor's date on the invoice, *10/26*. Hobby Shack assigns numbers in sequence to easily identify all purchase invoices. The number stamped on the invoice, *P83*, is the number assigned by Hobby Shack to this purchase invoice. This number should not be confused with the invoice number, *2389*, assigned by the vendor. Each vendor uses a different numbering system. Therefore, vendor invoice numbers could not be recorded in sequence, which would make it impossible to detect a missing invoice.

② Place a check mark by each of the amounts in the Total column to show that the items have been received and that amounts have been checked and are correct.

③ The person who checked the invoice should initial below the total amount in the Total column.

④ Review the vendor's terms. An agreement between a buyer and a seller about payment for merchandise is called the **terms of sale**. The terms of sale on the invoice are 30 days. These terms mean that payment is due within 30 days from the vendor's date of the invoice. The invoice is dated October 26. Therefore, payment must be made by November 25.

238 Chapter 9 Journalizing Purchases and Cash Payments

PURCHASING MERCHANDISE ON ACCOUNT

November 2. Purchased merchandise on account from Crown Distributing, $2,039.00. Purchase Invoice No. 83.

Purchases	
2,039.00	

Accounts Payable	
	2,039.00

A purchase on account transaction increases the amount owed to a vendor. This transaction increases the purchases account balance and increases the accounts payable account balance. Because the purchases account has a normal debit balance, Purchases is debited for $2,039.00 to show the increase in this cost account. The accounts payable account has a normal credit balance. Therefore, Accounts Payable is credited for $2,039.00 to show the increase in this liability account.

STEPS JOURNALIZING A PURCHASE OF MERCHANDISE ON ACCOUNT

1. Write the date, *20--, Nov. 2*, in the Date column.

2. Write the vendor name, *Crown Distributing*, in the Account Credited column.

3. Write the purchase invoice number, *83*, in the Purch. No. column.

4. Write the amount of the invoice, *$2,039.00*, in the special amount column. This single amount is both a debit to *Purchases* and a credit to *Accounts Payable*. Therefore, it is not necessary to write the title of either general ledger account.

The way Hobby Shack keeps a record of the amount owed to each vendor is described in Chapter 11.

FOR YOUR INFORMATION

FYI

Gross Domestic Product (GDP) is the total dollar value of all final goods and services produced by resources located in the United States (regardless of who owns the resources) during one year's time.

Journalizing Purchases Using a Purchases Journal   Lesson 9-1   **239**

TOTALING AND RULING A PURCHASES JOURNAL

Hobby Shack always rules its purchases journal at the end of each month, even if the page for the month is not full.

Hobby Shack uses the following six steps in ruling its purchases journal at the end of each month.

STEPS — TOTALING AND RULING A PURCHASES JOURNAL

1. Rule a single line across the amount column under the last entry.

2. Write the date, *30*, in the Date column.

3. Write the word *Total* in the Account Credited column.

4. Add the amount column. Verify the total by re-adding the column in reverse order.

5. Write the total, *$17,148.08*, directly below the single line in the amount column.

6. Rule double lines across the amount column directly below the total amount to show that the total has been verified as correct.

Posting from a purchases journal is described in Chapter 11.

PHOTODISC/GETTY IMAGES

End of Lesson REVIEW

TERMS REVIEW

- merchandise
- merchandising business
- retail merchandising business
- wholesale merchandising business
- corporation
- share of stock
- capital stock
- stockholder
- special journal
- cost of merchandise
- markup
- vendor
- purchase on account
- purchases journal
- special amount column
- purchase invoice
- terms of sale

AUDIT YOUR UNDERSTANDING

1. What kinds of transactions are recorded in a purchases journal?
2. For what are special amount columns in a journal used?
3. Why are there two account titles in the amount column of the purchases journal?
4. What is the advantage of having special amount columns in a journal?

WORK TOGETHER 9-1

Journalizing purchases using a purchases journal

The purchases journal for Lambert Hardware is given in the *Working Papers*. Your instructor will guide you through the following examples.

1. Using the current year, journalize these transactions on page 10 of the purchases journal. Purchase invoices are abbreviated as P.

   Transactions:
   Oct. 2. Purchased merchandise on account from American Tools, $1,230.00. P116.
   7. Purchased merchandise on account from Harris Manufacturing, Inc., $480.00. P117.
   11. Purchased merchandise on account from Keasler Supply, $780.00. P118.

2. Total and rule the purchases journal.

ON YOUR OWN 9-1

Journalizing purchases using a purchases journal

The purchases journal for Classic Gifts, Inc., is given in the *Working Papers*. Work this problem independently.

1. Using the current year, journalize these transactions on page 11 of the purchases journal. Purchase invoices are abbreviated as P.

   Transactions:
   Nov. 4. Purchased merchandise on account from Ulman Supply, Inc., $670.00. P149.
   9. Purchased merchandise on account from Else Silver Co., $2,345.00. P150.
   18. Purchased merchandise on account from Pratt Paints, $1,150.00. P151.

2. Total and rule the purchases journal.

Journalizing Purchases Using a Purchases Journal

LESSON 9-2

Journalizing Cash Payments Using a Cash Payments Journal

CASH PAYMENTS JOURNAL

					GENERAL		ACCOUNTS PAYABLE DEBIT	PURCHASES DISCOUNT CREDIT	CASH CREDIT
DATE	ACCOUNT TITLE	CK. NO.	POST. REF.		DEBIT	CREDIT			
					1	2	3	4	5

A special journal used to record only cash payment transactions is called a **cash payments journal**. Only those columns needed to record cash payment transactions are included in Hobby Shack's cash payments journal. A cash payments journal may be designed to accommodate a business's frequent cash payment transactions. Since all cash payment transactions affect the cash account, a special amount column is provided for this general ledger account. In addition, Hobby Shack has many cash payment transactions affecting the accounts payable account. Therefore, a special amount column is provided in the cash payments journal for this general ledger account.

Normally, the total amount shown on a purchase invoice is the amount that a customer is expected to pay. To encourage early payment, however, a vendor may allow a deduction from the invoice amount. A deduction that a vendor allows on the invoice amount to encourage prompt payment is called a **cash discount**. A cash discount on purchases taken by a customer is called a **purchases discount**. When a purchases discount is taken, the customer pays less than the invoice amount previously recorded in the purchases account. Taking purchases discounts reduces the customer's cost of merchandise purchased. Because it often takes purchase discounts, Hobby Shack uses a cash payments journal with a Purchases Discount Credit column.

A journal amount column that is not headed with an account title is called a **general amount column**. Hobby Shack's cash payments journal has General Debit and General Credit columns for cash payment transactions that do not occur often, such as monthly rent.

All cash payments made by Hobby Shack are recorded in a cash payments journal. The source document for most cash payments is the check issued. A few payments, such as bank service charges, are made as direct withdrawals from the company's bank account. For payments not using a check, the source document is a memorandum. Most of Hobby Shack's cash payments are to vendors and for expenses that are paid by check.

> **REMEMBER**
>
> Only cash payment transactions are recorded in the cash payments journal.

CASH PAYMENT OF AN EXPENSE

November 2. Paid cash for advertising, $150.00. Check No. 292.

Hobby Shack usually pays for an expense at the time the transaction occurs.

This cash payment increases the advertising expense account balance and decreases the cash account balance. The expense account **Advertising Expense** has a normal debit balance and increases by a debit of $150.00. The asset account **Cash** also has a normal debit balance and decreases by a credit of $150.00.

STEPS: JOURNALIZING A CASH PAYMENT OF AN EXPENSE

1. Write the date, 20--, Nov. 2, in the Date column.
2. Write the account title, *Advertising Expense*, in the Account Title column.
3. Write the check number, *292*, in the Ck. No. column.
4. Write the debit amount to Advertising Expense, *$150.00*, in the General Debit column.
5. Write the credit amount, *$150.00*, in the Cash Credit column.

BUYING SUPPLIES FOR CASH

November 5. Paid cash for office supplies, $94.00. Check No. 293.

Hobby Shack buys supplies for use in the business. Supplies are not recorded in the purchases account because supplies are not intended for sale. Cash register tapes and price tags are examples of supplies used in a business.

This transaction increases the office supplies account balance and decreases the cash account balance. The steps for journalizing buying supplies for cash are similar to journalizing paying cash for an expense.

Journalizing Cash Payments Using a Cash Payments Journal — Lesson 9-2   **243**

CASH PAYMENTS FOR PURCHASES

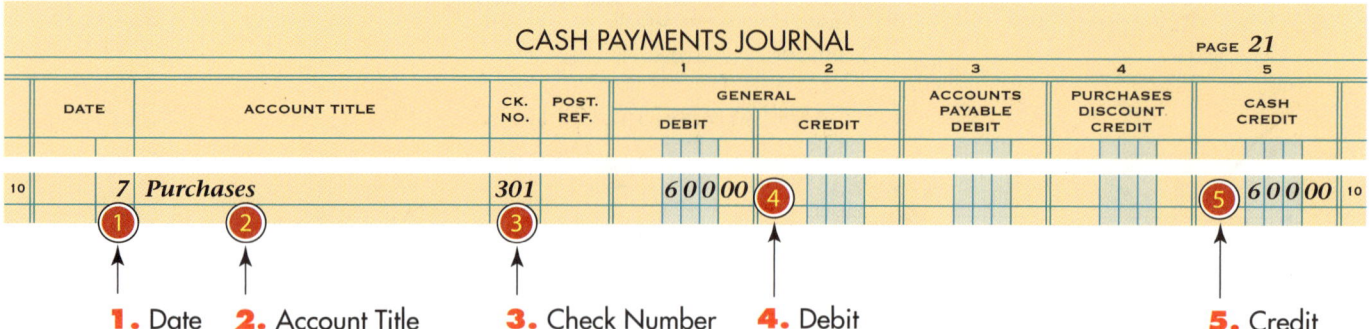

1. Date
2. Account Title
3. Check Number
4. Debit
5. Credit

Businesses usually purchase merchandise on account. However, vendors may not extend credit to all of their customers. Thus, these businesses must pay the vendor with a check before the merchandise is either shipped or delivered.

Trade Discount

Most manufacturers and wholesalers print catalogs and maintain Internet sites that describe their products. Generally, the prices listed are the manufacturers' suggested retail prices. The retail price listed in a catalog or on an Internet site is called a **list price**. When a merchandising business purchases a number of products from a manufacturer, the price frequently is quoted as "list price less trade discount." A reduction in the list price granted to customers is called a **trade discount**. Trade discounts are also used to quote different prices for different quantities purchased without changing catalog or list prices.

When a trade discount is granted, the seller's invoice shows the actual amount charged. This amount after the trade discount has been deducted from the list price is referred to as the *invoice amount*. Only the invoice amount is used in a journal entry. [CONCEPT: Historical Cost] No journal entry is made to show the amount of a trade discount.

Cash Purchases

Hobby Shack pays cash for 10 ceramic molds with an invoice amount of $600.00, the list price less a trade discount. Because the transaction involves a cash payment, it is recorded in the cash payments journal. Only purchases on account are recorded in the purchases journal.

November 7. Purchased merchandise for cash, $600.00. Check No. 301.

The list price for the 10 ceramic molds is $1,500.00. The invoice price is the list price, less a 60% trade discount. The total invoice amount is calculated in two steps, as follows.

244   Chapter 9   Journalizing Purchases and Cash Payments

CASH PAYMENTS ON ACCOUNT WITH PURCHASES DISCOUNTS

1. Date
2. Vendor Name
3. Check Number
4. Purchase Invoice Amount
5. Purchases Discount
6. Purchase Invoice Amount Less the Purchases Discount

A cash discount is stated as a percentage deducted from the invoice amount. For example, *2/10, n/30* is a common term of sale, which is read *two ten, net thirty. Two ten* means that 2% of the invoice amount may be deducted if the invoice is paid within 10 days of the invoice date. *Net thirty* means that the total invoice amount must be paid within 30 days.

Purchases discounts are recorded in a general ledger account titled Purchases Discount. An account that reduces a related account on a financial statement is called a **contra account**. Purchases Discount is a contra account to Purchases and is included in the cost of merchandise division of the general ledger. On an income statement, Purchases Discount is deducted from the balance of its related account, Purchases.

Since contra accounts are deductions from their related accounts, contra account normal balances are opposite the normal balances of their related accounts. The normal balance for Purchases is a debit. Therefore, the normal balance for Purchases Discount, a contra account to Purchases, is a credit. Trade discounts are not recorded; however, cash discounts are recorded as purchases discounts because they decrease the recorded invoice amount.

November 8. Paid cash on account to Gulf Craft Supply, $488.04, covering Purchase Invoice No. 82 for $498.00, less 2% discount, $9.96. Check No. 302.

The way Hobby Shack keeps a record of the amount paid to each vendor is described in Chapter 11.

The steps, numbered above, are described on the top of page 246.

STEP 1:
Purchase Invoice Amount × Purchases Discount Rate = Purchases Discount
$498.00 × 2% = $9.96

STEP 2:
Purchase Invoice Amount − Purchases Discount = Cash Amount After Discount
$498.00 − $9.96 = $488.04

Journalizing Cash Payments Using a Cash Payments Journal

STEPS JOURNALIZING A CASH PAYMENT ON ACCOUNT WITH PURCHASES DISCOUNT

1. Write the date, *8*, in the Date column.
2. Write the account title of the vendor, *Gulf Craft Supply*, in the Account Title column.
3. Write the check number, *302*, in the Ck. No. column.
4. Write the debit amount to Accounts Payable, *$498.00*, in the Accounts Payable Debit column.
5. Write the credit amount, *$9.96*, in the Purchases Discount Credit column.
6. Write the credit amount, *$488.04*, in the Cash Credit column.

CASH PAYMENTS ON ACCOUNT WITHOUT PURCHASES DISCOUNTS

1. Date 2. Vendor Name 3. Check Number 4. Total Purchase Invoice Amount 5. Total Purchase Invoice Amount

Some vendors do not offer purchases discounts. Sometimes a business does not have the cash available to take advantage of a purchases discount. In both cases, the full purchase invoice amount is paid.

Hobby Shack purchased merchandise on account from American Paint on October 25. American Paint's credit terms are n/30. Therefore, Hobby Shack will pay the full amount of the purchase invoice, $2,650.00, within 30 days of the invoice date, October 25.

> **November 13.** Paid cash on account to American Paint, $2,650.00, covering Purchase Invoice No. 77. Check No. 303.

STEPS JOURNALIZING A CASH PAYMENT OF AN EXPENSE

1. Write the date, *13*, in the Date column.
2. Write the vendor account title, *American Paint*, in the Account Title column.
3. Write the check number, *303*, in the Ck. No. column.
4. Write the debit amount to Accounts Payable, *$2,650.00*, in the Accounts Payable Debit column.
5. Write the credit amount, *$2,650.00*, in the Cash Credit column.

End of Lesson REVIEW

TERMS REVIEW

cash payments journal
cash discount
purchases discount
general amount column
list price
trade discount
contra account

AUDIT YOUR UNDERSTANDING

1. Why would a vendor offer a cash discount to a customer?
2. What is recorded in the general amount columns of the cash payments journal?
3. What is the difference between purchasing merchandise and buying supplies?
4. What is meant by terms of sale 2/10, n/30?

WORK TOGETHER 9-2

Journalizing cash payments using a cash payments journal

The cash payments journal for Franklin Lumber is given in the *Working Papers*. Your instructor will guide you through the following example.

1. Using the current year, journalize these transactions on page 10 of a cash payments journal. The checks used as source documents are abbreviated as C.

Transactions:

Oct. 1. Paid cash for telephone bill, $85.00. C321.
    7. Paid cash for office supplies, $52.00. C322.
   11. Paid cash to GMT Hardware for merchandise with a list price of $800.00, less a 60% trade discount. C323.
   17. Paid cash on account to West Supply covering Purchase Invoice No. 199 for $3,420.00, less 2% discount. C324.
   19. Paid cash on account to Quill Forest Products covering Purchase Invoice No. 182 for $4,380.00. No cash discount was offered. C325.

ON YOUR OWN 9-2

Journalizing cash payments using a cash payments journal

The cash payments journal for Rapid Auto Supply is given in the *Working Papers*. Work this problem independently.

1. Using the current year, journalize these transactions on page 11 of the cash payments journal. The checks used as source documents are abbreviated as C.

Transactions:

Nov. 2. Paid cash for the electric bill, $248.00. C432.
    6. Paid cash for office supplies, $142.00. C433.
    9. Paid cash to Zebra Metals for merchandise with a list price of $3,400.00, less a 40% trade discount. C434.
   12. Paid cash on account to Racing Images covering Purchase Invoice No. 543 for $4,230.00, less 2% discount. C435.
   14. Paid cash on account to SPL Renovations covering Purchase Invoice No. 182 for $2,573.00. No cash discount was offered. C436.

LESSON 9-3

Performing Additional Cash Payments Journal Operations

PETTY CASH REPORT

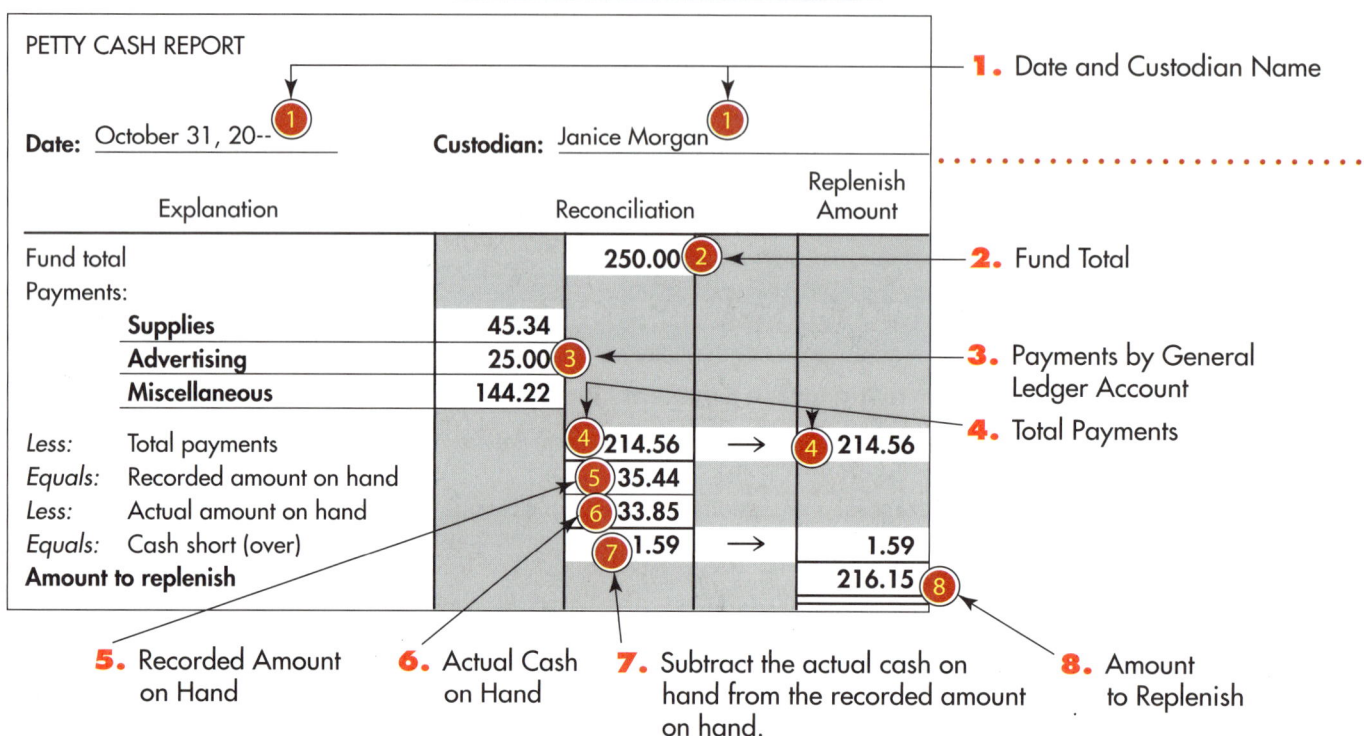

A petty cash fund enables a business to pay cash for small expenses without writing a check, as described in Chapter 5.

Errors may be made when making payments from a petty cash fund. These errors cause a difference between actual cash on hand and the record of the amount of cash that should be on hand. A petty cash on hand amount that is less than a recorded amount is called **cash short**. A petty cash on hand amount that is more than a recorded amount is called **cash over**.

The custodian prepares a petty cash report when the petty cash fund is to be replenished.

STEPS PREPARING A PETTY CASH REPORT

1. Write the date, *October 31, 20--*, and custodian name, *Janice Morgan*, in the report heading.
2. Write the fund total, *$250.00*, from the general ledger account.
3. Summarize petty cash payments by totals for each general ledger account.
4. Calculate and write the total payments, *$214.56*, in the Reconciliation and Replenish Amount columns.
5. Calculate and write the recorded amount on hand, *$35.44* ($250.00 − $214.56).
6. Write the actual amount of cash on hand, *$33.85*, in the Reconciliation column.
7. Subtract the actual amount on hand, *$33.85*, from the recorded amount on hand, *$35.44*, and write the amount, *$1.59*, in the Reconciliation and Replenish Amount columns. Note that petty cash is short by $1.59. The actual amount of petty cash on hand is $1.59 less than the recorded amount.
8. Write the total of the replenish amount, *$216.15*.

REPLENISHING A PETTY CASH FUND

PETTY CASH REPORT

Date: November 18, 20-- Custodian: Janice Morgan

Explanation		Reconciliation		Replenish Amount
Fund total		250.00		
Payments:				
	Supplies—Office	32.33		
	Advertising	50.00		
	Miscellaneous	128.50		
Less:	Total payments	210.83	→	210.83
Equals:	Recorded amount on hand	39.17		
Less:	Actual amount on hand	41.34		
Equals:	Cash short (over)	(2.17)	→	(2.17)
Amount to replenish				208.66

4. Expense Amounts   **6.** Total Cash Payment

CASH PAYMENTS JOURNAL — PAGE 21

DATE	ACCOUNT TITLE	CK. NO.	POST. REF.	GENERAL DEBIT	GENERAL CREDIT	ACCOUNTS PAYABLE DEBIT	PURCHASES DISCOUNT CREDIT	CASH CREDIT
18	Supplies—Office	310		32 33				208 66
	Advertising Expense			50 00				
	Miscellaneous Expense			128 50				
	Cash Short and Over				2 17			

1. Date   **2.** Account Titles   **3.** Check Number   **5.** Cash Short as a Debit, Cash Over as a Credit

Petty cash short and petty cash over are recorded in an account titled **Cash Short and Over**. The account is a temporary account. At the end of the fiscal year, the cash short and over account is closed to Income Summary.

The balance of Cash Short and Over can be either a debit or credit. However, the balance is usually a debit because the petty cash fund is more likely to be short than over. A cash shortage adds to the cost of operating a business. Thus, the account is classified as an operating expense. Note that in Step 5, the amount of petty cash over is recorded in the General Credit column. If petty cash were short, the amount would be recorded in the General Debit column.

Cash Short and Over	
Debit	Credit
Cash short	Cash over

November 18. Paid cash to replenish the petty cash fund, $208.66: office supplies, $32.33; advertising, $50.00; miscellaneous, $128.50; cash over, $2.17. Check No. 310.

The petty cash fund is replenished for the amount paid out, $210.83, less cash over, $2.17. This total amount, $208.66, restores the fund's cash balance to its original amount, $250.00 ($210.83 − $2.17 + $41.34 cash on hand).

TOTALING, PROVING, AND RULING A CASH PAYMENTS JOURNAL PAGE TO CARRY TOTALS FORWARD

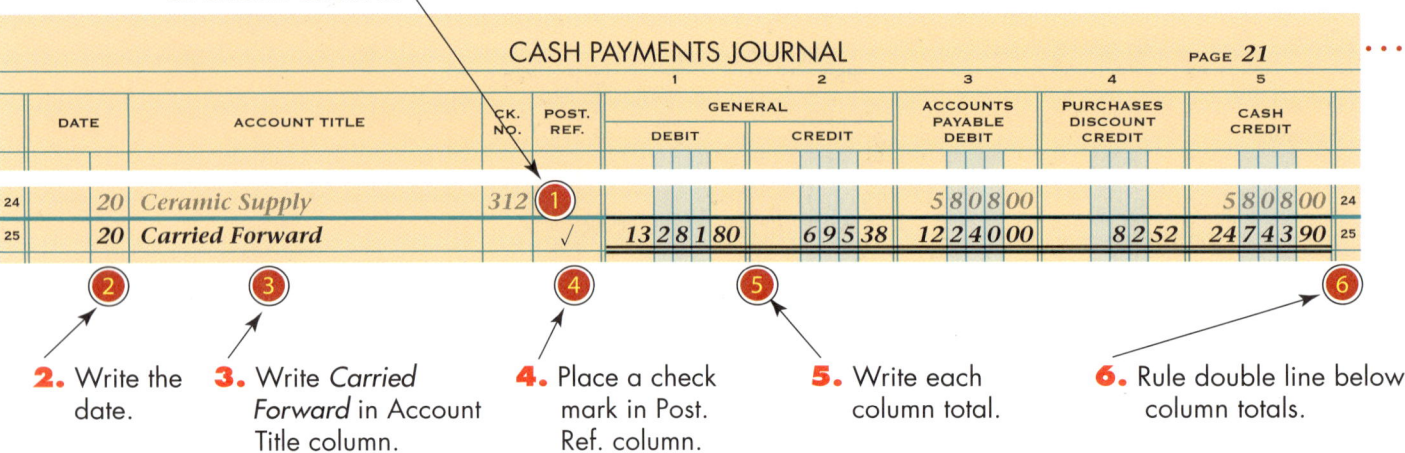

1. Rule a single line across all amount columns.
2. Write the date.
3. Write *Carried Forward* in Account Title column.
4. Place a check mark in Post. Ref. column.
5. Write each column total.
6. Rule double line below column totals.

A journal is proved and ruled whenever a journal page is filled and always at the end of a month.

After all November 20 entries are recorded, page 21 of Hobby Shack's cash payments journal is filled. Column totals of page 21 are totaled and proved before being forwarded to page 22. The proof that Hobby Shack's debit totals equal the credit totals on page 21 of the journal is shown.

If the total debits do not equal the total credits, the errors must be found and corrected before any more work is completed.

After a journal page has been totaled and proved, the journal is ruled in preparation for forwarding to the next page.

Column Title	Debit Column Totals	Credit Column Totals
General Debit	$13,281.80	
General Credit		$ 695.38
Accounts Payable Debit	12,240.00	
Purchases Discount Credit		82.52
Cash Credit		24,743.90
Totals	$25,521.80	$25,521.80

STEPS FOR RULING A CASH PAYMENTS JOURNAL

1. Rule a single line across all amount columns directly below the last entry to indicate that all the columns are to be added.
2. On the next line, write the date, *20*, in the Date column.
3. Write the words *Carried Forward* in the Account Title column.
4. Place a check mark in the Post. Ref. column to show that nothing on this line needs to be posted.
5. Write each column total below the single line.
6. Rule double lines below the column totals across all amount columns to show that the totals have been verified as correct.

250   Chapter 9   Journalizing Purchases and Cash Payments

STARTING A NEW CASH PAYMENTS JOURNAL PAGE

The totals from the previous journal page are carried forward to the next journal page.

The totals are recorded on the first line of the new page.

STEPS STEPS FOR FORWARDING TOTALS TO A NEW JOURNAL PAGE

1. Write the journal page number, *22*, at the top of the journal.
2. Write the date, *20--, Nov. 20*, in the Date column.
3. Write the words *Brought Forward* in the Account Title column.
4. Place a check mark in the Post. Ref. column to show that nothing on this line needs to be posted.
5. Record the column totals brought forward from page 21 of the journal.

GLOBAL PERSPECTIVE

Accountancy in Africa

The accounting profession in Africa has been influenced by the European colonial powers that formerly governed there. Most African nations gained independence in the mid-twentieth century.

In Nigeria, Kenya, Ghana, and Zimbabwe (formerly under British rule), accounting is seen as a tool for financial management and is oriented toward the needs of the enterprise. Tax authorities are concerned with account items that can be valued in different ways, such as fixed assets, inventories, and depreciation.

In Togo, Rwanda, and Gambia (formerly ruled by France), accountancy is regulated by charts of accounts that standardize financial transactions and annual financial statements.

In Angola, Cape Verde, and São Tomé and Principe (formerly ruled by Portugal), the accounting system also is based on charts of accounts that provide rules and regulations for companies. There are no professional accounting organizations in many African countries.

In the expanding economies of many developing African countries, the belief is that it is important to have well-qualified and experienced accountants and a sound accounting framework to sustain economic growth.

Critical Thinking

1. What should an investor consider when comparing financial statements of companies in Kenya and Gambia?
2. What would be the advantages of having a professional accounting organization in a country that does not currently have one?

Performing Additional Cash Payments Journal Operations

TOTALING, PROVING, AND RULING A CASH PAYMENTS JOURNAL AT THE END OF A MONTH

1. Rule a single line across all amount columns.

					CASH PAYMENTS JOURNAL			PAGE 22
					1	2	3	4	5
	DATE	ACCOUNT TITLE	CK. NO.	POST. REF.	GENERAL		ACCOUNTS PAYABLE DEBIT	PURCHASES DISCOUNT CREDIT	CASH CREDIT
					DEBIT	CREDIT			
1	Nov. 20	Brought Forward		✓	13 281 80	695 38	12 240 00	82 52	24 743 90	1
8	29	Advertising Expense	319		1 500 00				1 500 00	8
9	30	Floral Designs	320				1 650 00	33 00	1 617 00	9
10	30	Rent Expense	321		600 00				600 00	10
11	30	Totals			16 462 99	1 390 75	17 984 00	154 84	32 901 40	11

2. Write the date.

3. Write *Totals* in Account Title column.

4. Write each column total.

5. Rule double line across all amount columns.

Equality of debits and credits in a journal is proved at the end of each month. Proof for Hobby Shack's cash payments journal for November is shown.

Column Title	Debit Column Totals	Credit Column Totals
General Debit	$16,462.99	
General Credit		$ 1,390.75
Accounts Payable Debit	17,984.00	
Purchases Discount Credit		154.84
Cash Credit		32,901.40
Totals	$34,446.99	$34,446.99

The two totals, $34,446.99, are equal. Equality of debits and credits in Hobby Shack's cash payments journal for November is proved.

After a cash payments journal has been totaled and proved at the end of the month, the journal is ruled.

STEPS STEPS FOR RULING A CASH PAYMENTS JOURNAL AT THE END OF THE MONTH

1. Rule a single line across all amount columns directly below the last entry to indicate that all the columns are to be added.
2. On the next line write the date, *30*, in the date column.
3. Write the word *Totals* in the Account Title column.
4. Write each column total below the single line.
5. Rule double lines across all amount columns to show that the totals have been verified as correct.

Posting from a cash payments journal is described in Chapter 11.

End of Lesson REVIEW

AUDIT YOUR UNDERSTANDING

TERMS REVIEW

cash short

cash over

1. When journalizing a cash payment to replenish petty cash, what is entered in the Account Title column of the cash payments journal?
2. What is the usual balance of the account Cash Short and Over? Zero
3. List the five steps for ruling a cash payments journal at the end of the month.

WORK TOGETHER 9-3

Performing other cash payments journal operations

The cash payments journals and petty cash report for Keller Lighting are given in the *Working Papers*. Your instructor will guide you through the following examples. The abbreviation for a check is C.

1. Rule page 5 of the cash payments journal using March 27 of the current year.
2. Begin page 6 of a cash payments journal.
3. Kevin Tomlinson is the custodian of a $200.00 petty cash account. On March 31, he had receipts for the following total payments: supplies—office, $45.23; supplies—store, $66.18; and miscellaneous, $49.25. A cash count shows $40.59 in the petty cash box. Prepare the petty cash report.
4. Record the replenishment of the fund on March 31. C536.
5. Total, prove, and rule the cash payments journal.

ON YOUR OWN 9-3

Performing other cash payments journal operations

The cash payments journals and petty cash report for Magic Music are given in the *Working Papers*. Work this problem independently. The abbreviation for a check is C.

1. Rule page 11 of the cash payments journal using June 28 of the current year.
2. Begin page 12 of a cash payments journal.
3. Jerri Harris is the custodian of a $250.00 petty cash account. On June 30, she had receipts for the following total payments: supplies—office, $56.21; supplies—store, $48.27; miscellaneous, $36.17; and repairs, $82.25. A cash count shows $26.48 in the petty cash box. Prepare the petty cash report.
4. Record the replenishment of the fund on June 30. C627.
5. Total, prove, and rule the cash payments journal.

LESSON 9-4: Journalizing Other Transactions Using a General Journal

GENERAL JOURNAL

Not all transactions can be recorded in special journals. Those transactions that cannot be recorded in a special journal are recorded in a general journal. For example, when Hobby Shack buys supplies on account, the transaction cannot be recorded in any of the special journals. Because the transaction is not a cash payment, it cannot be recorded in the cash payments journal. Since the transaction is not a purchase of merchandise on account, it cannot be recorded in the purchases journal.

> **REMEMBER**
>
> If a transaction cannot be recorded in one of the special journals, it must be recorded in the general journal.

MEMORANDUM FOR BUYING SUPPLIES ON ACCOUNT

When Hobby Shack buys store supplies on account, an invoice is received from the vendor. This invoice is similar to the purchase invoice received when merchandise is purchased. To assure that no mistake is made, a memorandum is attached to the invoice, noting that the invoice is for store supplies and not for purchases.

> **FOR YOUR INFORMATION — FYI**
>
> Office supplies purchased by an office supplies company to sell to its customers should be recorded as a merchandise purchase. However, office supplies bought by the company for use by employees in its store or office should be recorded as store supplies or office supplies.

HOBBY SHACK, INC.
MEMORANDUM
NO. 52
DATE November 6, 20--

Attached invoice is for store supplies bought on account.

254 • Chapter 9 • Journalizing Purchases and Cash Payments

BUYING SUPPLIES ON ACCOUNT

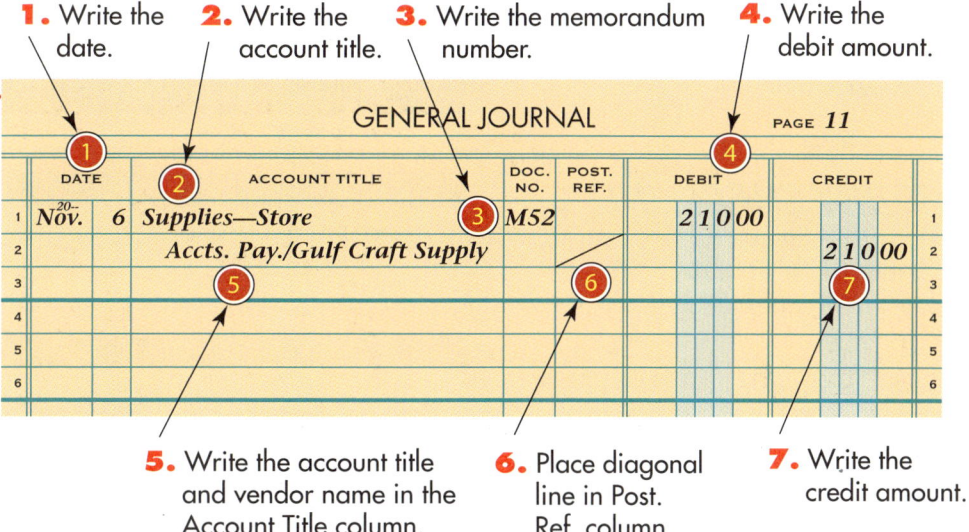

1. Write the date.
2. Write the account title.
3. Write the memorandum number.
4. Write the debit amount.
5. Write the account title and vendor name in the Account Title column.
6. Place diagonal line in Post. Ref. column.
7. Write the credit amount.

November 6. Bought store supplies on account from Gulf Craft Supply, $210.00. Memorandum No. 52.

Hobby Shack usually buys supplies for cash. Occasionally, however, Hobby Shack buys some supplies on account.

This transaction increases the store supplies account balance and increases the accounts payable account balance. The asset account Supplies—Store has a normal debit balance and increases by a $210.00 debit. The liability account Accounts Payable has a normal credit balance and increases by a $210.00 credit.

The equality of debits and credits for each general journal entry is checked after each entry is recorded. For this entry, the amount of the debit entry, $210.00, is the same as the amount of the credit entry, $210.00. Therefore, debits equal credits for this entry.

STEPS — JOURNALIZING BUYING SUPPLIES ON ACCOUNT

1. Write the date, *20--, Nov. 6*, in the Date column.
2. Write the account title, *Supplies—Store*, in the Account Title column.
3. Write the memorandum number, *M52*, in the Doc. No. column.
4. Write the debit amount to Supplies—Store, *$210.00*, in the Debit column on the same line as the account title.
5. On the next line indented about one centimeter, write the account title and vendor name, *Accts. Pay./Gulf Craft Supply*, in the Account title column. Place a diagonal line between the two account titles.
6. Place a diagonal line in the Post. Ref. column on the same line to show that the single credit amount is posted to two accounts. Posting of a single amount in the general journal to two accounts is described in Chapter 11.
7. Write the credit amount to Accts. Pay./Gulf Craft Supply, *$210.00*, in the Credit column on the same line as the account titles.

Journalizing Other Transactions Using a General Journal   Lesson 9-4

DEBIT MEMORANDUM FOR PURCHASES RETURNS AND ALLOWANCES

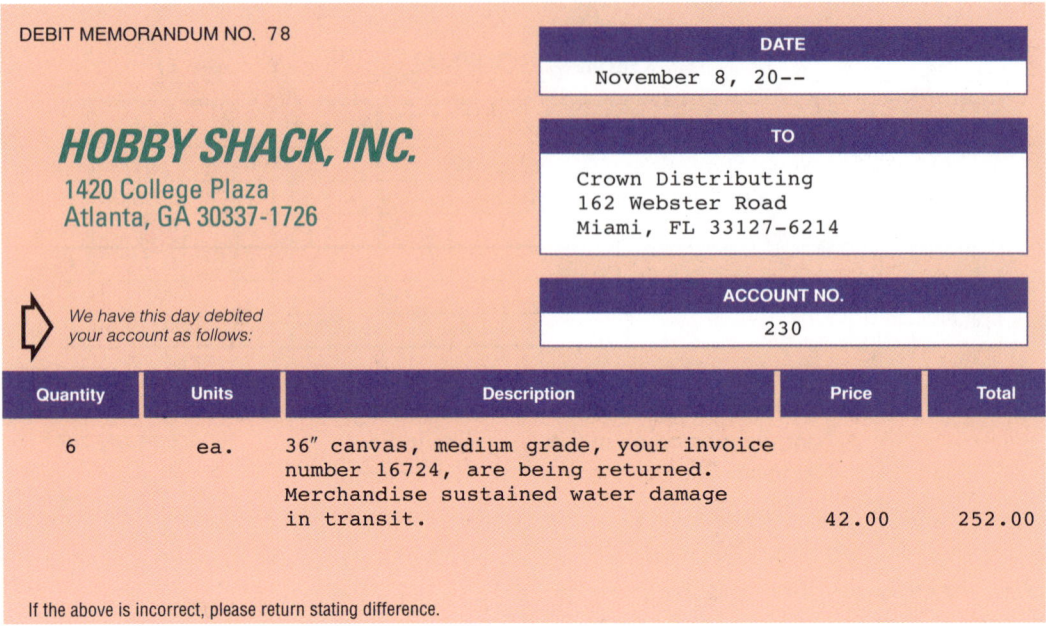

A customer may not want to keep merchandise that is inferior in quality or is damaged when received. A customer may be allowed to return part or all of the merchandise purchased. Credit allowed for the purchase price of returned merchandise, resulting in a decrease in the customer's accounts payable, is called a **purchases return**.

When merchandise is damaged but still usable or is of a different quality than that ordered, the vendor may let the customer keep the merchandise at a reduced price. Credit allowed for part of the purchase price of merchandise that is not returned, resulting in a decrease in the customer's accounts payable, is called a **purchases allowance**.

A purchases return or allowance should be confirmed in writing. A form prepared by the customer showing the price deduction taken by the customer for returns and allowances is called a **debit memorandum**. The form is called a debit memorandum because the customer records the amount as a debit (deduction) to the vendor account to show the decrease in the amount owed.

The customer may use a copy of the debit memorandum as the source document for journalizing purchases returns and allowances. However, the customer may wait for written confirmation from the vendor and use that confirmation as the source document. Hobby Shack issues a debit memorandum for each purchases return or allowance. This debit memorandum is used as the source document for purchases returns and allowances transactions. [CONCEPT: Objective Evidence] The transaction can be recorded immediately without waiting for written confirmation from the vendor. The original of the debit memorandum is sent to the vendor. A copy is kept by Hobby Shack.

Some businesses credit the purchases account for the amount of a purchases return or allowance. However, better information is provided if these amounts are credited to a separate account titled Purchases Returns and Allowances. A business can track the amount of purchases returns and allowances in a fiscal period if a separate account is used for recording them. The account enables a business to evaluate the effectiveness of its merchandise purchasing activities.

JOURNALIZING PURCHASES RETURNS AND ALLOWANCES

Purchases returns and allowances decrease the amount of purchases. Therefore, Purchases Returns and Allowances is a contra account to Purchases. Thus, the normal account balance of Purchases Returns and Allowances is a credit, the opposite of the normal account balance of Purchases, a debit.

The account is in the cost of merchandise division of Hobby Shack's chart of accounts.

Accounts Payable
252.00	

Purchases Returns and Allowances
	252.00

November 28. Returned merchandise to Crown Distributing, $252.00, covering Purchase Invoice No. 80. Debit Memorandum No. 78.

STEPS JOURNALIZING PURCHASES RETURNS AND ALLOWANCES

1. Write the date, *28*, in the Date column.

2. Write the account title and vendor name, *Accounts Pay./Crown Distributing*, in the Account Title column. A diagonal line is placed between the two accounts.

3. Place a diagonal line in the Post. Ref. column to show that the single debit amount is posted to two accounts.

4. Write the debit memorandum number, *DM78*, in the Doc. No. column.

5. Write the amount, *$252.00*, in the Debit column of the first line.

6. On the next line indented about 1 centimeter, write *Purchases Returns and Allow.* in the Account Title column.

7. Write the amount, *$252.00*, in the Credit column of the second line.

FOR YOUR INFORMATION

FYI

Using the debit memorandum as a source document is a proper accounting procedure only if the business is confident that the vendor will honor the request for the purchases return or allowance.

Journalizing Other Transactions Using a General Journal

End of Lesson REVIEW

AUDIT YOUR UNDERSTANDING

1. What journal is used to record transactions that cannot be recorded in special journals?
2. Why is a memorandum used as the source document when supplies are bought on account?
3. Why are two account titles written for the credit amount when supplies are bought on account?
4. When is the equality of debits and credits proved for a general journal?
5. If purchases returns and allowances are a decrease in purchases, why are returns and allowances credited to a separate account?
6. What is a primary difference between a purchases return and a purchases allowance?
7. When is a debit memorandum a proper source document for a purchases return or allowance?

TERMS REVIEW

purchases return
purchases allowance
debit memorandum

WORK TOGETHER 9-4

Journalizing other transactions using a general journal

A general journal for Rood Electric is given in the *Working Papers*. Your instructor will guide you through the following example.

1. Using the current year, journalize the following transactions on page 8 of the general journal. Source documents are abbreviated as follows: memorandum, M; debit memorandum, DM. Save your work to complete On Your Own 9-4.

Transactions:
Oct. 5. Bought store supplies on account from Designer Supplies, $180.00. M35.
   7. Returned merchandise to Hendrix Products, $540.00. DM65.

ON YOUR OWN 9-4

Journalizing other transactions using a general journal

Use the general journal that you started for Work Together 9-4. Work this problem independently.

1. Using the current year, journalize the following transactions, continuing on the next blank line of page 8 of the general journal. Source documents are abbreviated as follows: memorandum, M; debit memorandum, DM.

Transactions:
Oct. 11. Bought office supplies on account from Office Express, $240.00. M36.
   14. Returned merchandise to Fretz Industries, $1,239.00. DM66.

SUMMARY

After completing this chapter, you can:

1. Define accounting terms related to purchases and cash payments for a merchandising business.
2. Identify accounting concepts and practices related to purchases and cash payments for a merchandising business.
3. Journalize purchases of merchandise using a purchases journal.
4. Journalize cash payments and cash discounts using a cash payments journal.
5. Prepare a petty cash report and journalize the reimbursement of the petty cash fund.
6. Total, prove, and rule a cash payments journal and start a new cash payments journal page.
7. Journalize purchases returns and allowances and other transactions using a general journal.

EXPLORE ACCOUNTING

Can Accounting Change the Course of History?

According to accounting historians, the start of the Industrial Revolution was delayed by nearly a century by restrictions on the use of the corporate form of organization. Events in Britain had a profound impact on the development of global commerce.

The scientific knowledge that was required to spur the Industrial Revolution began to emerge in the eighteenth century. The massive financial resources necessary to develop new industries could not be generated using partnerships, the traditional form of business organization. The British Parliament developed laws permitting the corporate form of organization, including limited liability for stockholders, as a means to enable these new industries to generate financial resources.

The financial collapse of one corporation caused Parliament to reverse the corporation laws. Financial losses, mismanagement, and improper accounting caused the financial collapse of the South Sea Company. The ensuing personal financial losses of investors generated a public outcry against the corporation laws. The South Sea Bubble Act of 1720 eliminated limited liability, effectively restricting the formation of corporations. Only a limited number of businesses, granted special charters by the British Parliament, were able to form as corporations during the remainder of the century.

During the early nineteenth century, a series of court cases and law changes gradually loosened the rules governing the granting of limited liability. Finally, the 1862 Companies Act completely removed all restrictions, permitting the corporate form of organization used today. Accounting historians believe that the spread of the Industrial Revolution was helped by the growing acceptance of the corporate form of organization.

Instructions: Research the start and growth of a major corporation in your state or region. Prepare a short report that discusses how the company generated the capital required to begin and expand the business. Would the company have been successful had it not been able to form as a corporation?

9-1 APPLICATION PROBLEM

Journalizing purchases using a purchases journal

Eupora Electric is a small appliance store.

Instructions:

1. Journalize the following transactions completed during September of the current year. Use page 9 of the purchases journal given in the *Working Papers*. The purchase invoices used as source documents are abbreviated as P.

Transactions:

Sept. 2. Purchased merchandise on account from Woodland Appliances, $2,600.00. P54.
       6. Purchased merchandise on account from Quality Wholesalers, $1,460.00. P55.
     12. Purchased merchandise on account from East Gate Appliances, $1,850.00. P56.
     18. Purchased merchandise on account from Winston, Inc., $2,300.00. P57.
     26. Purchased merchandise on account from Woodland Appliances, $3,800.00. P58.

2. Total and rule the purchases journal at the end of the month.

9-2 APPLICATION PROBLEM

Journalizing cash payments using a cash payments journal

Second Base is a sports equipment store that sells discontinued and damaged items.

Instructions:
Journalize the following transactions completed during November of the current year. Use page 22 of the cash payments journal given in the *Working Papers*. Source documents are abbreviated as follows: check, C; purchase invoice, P. Save your work to complete Application Problem 9-4.

Transactions:

Nov. 1. Paid cash for telephone bill, $96.00. C241.
     4. Paid cash on account to The Pro Shop, $1,250.00, covering P367, less 2% discount. C242.
     6. Paid cash for advertising, $75.00. C243.
     9. Paid cash on account to Athletic Center, $925.00, covering P362. No cash discount was offered. C244.
   11. Paid cash for office supplies, $50.00. C245.
   13. Paid cash to Tennis City for merchandise with a list price of $1,850.00, less a 50% trade discount. C246.
   18. Paid cash for store supplies, $125.00. C247.
   21. Purchased merchandise for cash from Trevor Industries, $250.00. C248.
   23. Purchased merchandise for cash from Paris Mfg. Co., $750.00, less a 60% trade discount. C249.
   25. Paid cash on account to Best Clothing, $925.00, covering P363. No cash discount was offered. C250.
   27. Paid cash on account to Trophy Sports, $2,100.00, covering P373, less 2% discount. C251.

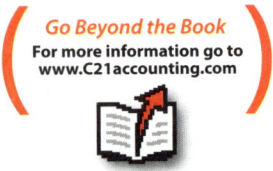

9-3 APPLICATION PROBLEM

Preparing a petty cash report

Kevin Tomlinson is the custodian of a $200.00 petty cash fund. On January 31 he had receipts for the following payments.

Payee	Description	Amount
City Office Supply	Computer disks	$ 5.95
KEWQ Radio	Voice fee for radio advertisement	50.00
Rocket Computers	Fix laser printer	45.95
Hooksville PTA	Advertisement in monthly newsletter	10.00
John Simmons	Pick up recyclable materials	8.00
Myers Hardware	Nails to repair outdoor sign	2.50
Books and More	Mouse pad	6.15

Instructions:

1. Classify each expense into one of the general ledger accounts used by Hobby Shack in this chapter.
2. Calculate the total of expenses by account.
3. Prepare the petty cash report given in the *Working Papers*. A cash count shows $70.67 in the petty cash box.

9-4 APPLICATION PROBLEM

Performing additional cash payments journal operations

Second Base is a sports equipment store that sells discontinued and damaged items. The cash payments journal used in Application Problem 9-2 is needed to complete this problem.

Instructions:

1. Total the amount columns of cash payments journal page 22 from Application Problem 9-2. Prove the equality of debits and credits.
2. Rule the cash payments journal.
3. Begin page 23 of a cash payments journal.
4. Wendy Morris is the custodian of a $250.00 petty cash account. On November 30, she had receipts for the following total payments: supplies—office, $45.31; supplies—store, $54.62; repairs, $75.82; and miscellaneous, $41.67. A cash count shows $31.05 in the petty cash box. Prepare the petty cash report.
5. Record the replenishment of the fund on November 30. C252.
6. Total the amount columns of the cash payments journal. Prove the equality of debits and credits.
7. Rule the cash payments journal.

9-5 APPLICATION PROBLEM

Journalizing other transactions using a general journal

Jenny's Designs is a bridal shop.

Instructions:
Journalize the following transactions completed during October of the current year. Use page 10 of the general journal given in the *Working Papers*. Source documents are abbreviated as follows: memorandum, M; debit memorandum, DM.

Transactions:
Oct. 5. Bought store supplies on account from Displays Warehouse, $275.00. M39.
      9. Returned merchandise to Hendrix Products, $640.00. DM25.
     13. Bought office supplies on account from Office Express, $215.00. M40.
     18. Returned merchandise to T-J Designs, $390.00. DM26.
     25. Bought store supplies on account from Classic Fixtures, $180.00. M41.

9-6 MASTERY PROBLEM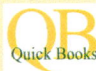

Journalizing purchases, cash payments, and other transactions

Mercury Computers sells computer parts and accessories.

Instructions:
1. Using the journals given in the *Working Papers*, journalize the following transactions completed during July of the current year. Use page 7 of a purchases journal, page 13 of a cash payments journal, and page 11 of a general journal. Source documents are abbreviated as follows: check, C; memorandum, M; purchase invoice, P; debit memorandum, DM.

Transactions:
Jul. 2. Purchased merchandise on account from Woodland Computers, $2,600.00. P354.
     4. Paid cash on account to Pacific Industries, $1,400.00, covering P367, less 2% discount. C242.
     6. Purchased merchandise on account from NewWave Electronics, $2,560.00. P355.
     8. Paid cash to WCKF Radio for advertising, $750.00. C243.
     8. Bought store supplies on account from Willcut & Bishop, $125.00. M39.
     9. Paid cash on account to American Semiconductor, $2,690.00, covering P352. No cash discount was offered. C244.
    10. Paid cash to Southern Bell for telephone bill, $136.00. C245.
    11. Paid cash on account to Woodland Computers, $2,600.00, covering P354, less 2% discount. C246.
    12. Returned merchandise to NewWave Electronics, $1,640.00. DM25.
    12. Purchased merchandise on account from Helms Supply, $550.00. P356.
    13. Paid cash to Edmondson Supply for office supplies, $126.00. C247.
    14. Paid cash to Deanes Electronics for merchandise with a list price of $3,480.00, less a 60% trade discount. C248.
    15. Bought office supplies on account from Office Express, $106.00. M40.
    15. Purchased merchandise on account from Keel, Inc., $3,480.00. P357.
    16. Paid cash on account to Farris Cable, $329.00, covering P353. No cash discount was offered. C249.
    18. Purchased merchandise for cash from Columbus Industries, $429.00. C250.
    20. Purchased merchandise for cash from Mena Mfg. Co., $260.00, less a 40% trade discount. C251.
    22. Paid cash on account to Keel, Inc., $3,480.00, covering P357, less 2% discount. C252.
    24. Paid cash to Williams Stores for store supplies, $94.00. C253.
    25. Paid cash on account to NewWave Electronics, $920.00, covering P355 less DM25. C254.
    27. Purchased merchandise on account from Woodland Computers, $3,200.00. P358.
    30. Returned merchandise to Woodland Computers, $120.00. DM26.

2. Total the amount columns of cash payments journal page 13. Prove the equality of debits and credits and rule the cash payments journal to carry the totals forward.
3. Record the totals brought forward from cash payments journal page 13 to line 1 of page 14 of the cash payments journal.
4. Journalize the following transactions.

Transactions:

Jul. 31. Paid cash on account to Helms Supply, $550.00, covering P356. No discount was offered. C255.
31. Paid cash to reimburse the petty cash fund, $181.75: supplies—office, $23.45; supplies—store, $84.32; miscellaneous, $74.34; and cash over, $0.36. C256.

5. Total and rule page 7 of the purchases journal.
6. Total the amount columns of cash payments journal page 14. Prove the equality of debits and credits of cash payments journal page 14.
7. Rule page 14 of the cash payments journal.

9-7 CHALLENGE PROBLEM

Journalizing purchases, cash payments, and other transactions

Fitness Connection is an exercise equipment store.

Instructions:

1. Using the journals given in the *Working Papers*, journalize the following transactions completed during November of the current year. Use page 12 of a purchases journal, page 26 of a cash payments journal, and page 11 of a general journal. Record the appropriate source documents in the journals.

Transactions:

Nov. 1. Wrote Check No. 363 for the monthly rent of $1,300.00.
2. Bought $120.00 worth of store supplies on account from Meda Store Supplies, recorded on Memo 43, with 2/10, n/30 payment terms.
3. Received an invoice, stamped Purchase Invoice 84, for merchandise on account from Central Fitness for $2,150.00, less a 60% trade discount.
4. Paid $150.00 to Pitman Industries with Check No. 364 for merchandise.
6. Wrote Check No. 365 for $1,020.00 to Pacer Equipment for Purchase Invoice 82's payment on account.
8. Returned $260.00 of the merchandise purchased on Purchase Invoice 84 to Central Fitness, recorded on Debit Memorandum 54.
9. Purchased $2,900.00 of merchandise on account from Trackmaster on Purchase Invoice 85, with 2/10, n/30 payment terms.
10. Paid $52.00 to myOffice for office supplies with Check No. 366.
11. Paid the balance of Purchase Invoice 84 less Debit Memorandum 54, to Central Fitness with Check No. 367, taking advantage of the 2/10, n/30 payment terms.
12. Wrote Check No. 368 for $290.00 to pay the monthly insurance premium.
16. Paid Trackmaster the amount owed on Purchase Invoice 85, writing Check No. 369.
29. Paid Meda Store Supplies for the Nov. 2 purchase of store supplies with Check No. 370.
30. Replenished the petty cash fund by writing Check No. 371 to the custodian for $207.00. Receipts were submitted for the following: office supplies, $48.00; store supplies, $24.00; advertising, $68.00; and miscellaneous, $66.00.

2. Evaluate and then write a response to the following questions.
   a. The cash payments journal used in this problem has only three special amount columns. Under what circumstances would you recommend that additional special amount columns be added to a cash payments journal?
   b. When insurance premiums are paid, should the debit entry be to the asset account, Prepaid Insurance, or to the expense account, Insurance Expense? Are there circumstances where either entry could be correct? Explain.

APPLIED COMMUNICATION

When you purchase merchandise for your business, you are considered a customer. Sometimes a customer might have a problem or complaint about the product. There are several ways to go about resolving the problem. One suggestion is to write to the person or company selling the product.

Instructions: Assume that you bought stereo speakers using the Internet site of a consumer electronics company. Unfortunately, the speakers make a strange static noise. Write a persuasive e-mail message to the company requesting a refund or a new set of speakers. Identify (1) information related to the purchase, such as invoice number and date, (2) the problem with the speakers, and (3) a request for a refund or a new set of speakers.

CASES FOR CRITICAL THINKING

Case 1

Trent Mercer owns and operates a music store in a mature shopping mall. When the largest store in the mall (often referred to as the *anchor*) moved two years ago, the traffic in the shopping center dramatically decreased. Mr. Mercer has an opportunity to move the business to a popular new shopping mall. Additional capital, however, is required to move and operate the business in a new location. The local bank has agreed to lend the money needed. His CPA has suggested that he consider forming a corporation and raise the necessary capital by selling capital stock to a small group of local investors. Should Mr. Mercer (1) borrow the money from the bank or (2) raise capital by creating a corporation? Explain your answer.

Case 2

Sophia Perez is a high school student who works part time in a local sports equipment store. As part of her duties, she records daily transactions in a journal. One day she asks the owner, "You use the purchase invoice as your source document for recording purchases of merchandise on account. You use a memorandum as your source document for recording the entry when supplies are bought on account. Why don't you use the invoice for both entries?" How would you respond to this question?

SCANS WORKPLACE COMPETENCY

Thinking Skill: Creative Thinking

Concept: Every business encounters problems that require new solutions. Methods of cutting costs, new promotions to increase sales, and changes in merchandising and product mix all require creative solutions. Employees who can "think outside the box" and generate new creative ideas are important resources to any company.

Application: Choose a retail merchandising business with which you are familiar. Study as much of the business as is visible to you. Generate new ideas that you think could increase sales for the company.

USING SOURCE DOCUMENTS

Journalizing purchases, cash payments, and other transactions from source documents

Messler Sailing sells sailboats, parts, and accessories. Source documents related to the purchases and cash payments of Messler Sailing for October are provided in the *Working Papers*.

Instructions

1. Using journals given in the *Working Papers*, journalize the transactions for October of the current year. Use page 10 of a purchases journal, page 15 of a cash payments journal, and page 14 of a general journal. Source documents are abbreviated as follows: check, C; memorandum, M; purchase invoice, P; debit memorandum, DM.
2. Total and rule the purchases journal.
3. Total the amount columns of cash payments journal page 15. Prove the equality of debits and credits and rule the cash payments journal.

ANALYZING BEST BUY'S FINANCIAL STATEMENTS

Best Buy has two types of stock—preferred and common. The company's Board of Directors must first authorize the issuance of each stock. The company then sells (issues) its stock on stock exchanges and can distribute shares to employees. On occasion, the company may repurchase shares, reducing the number of shares outstanding.

Instructions

1. Using page B-5 in Appendix B in this text, refer to Best Buy's balance sheet to determine the number of shares of preferred stock authorized, issued, and outstanding.
2. Identify the number of shares of common stock authorized, issued, and outstanding for 2007.

Accounting SOFTWARE

PURCHASES AND CASH PAYMENTS

Special journals eliminate the need for you to write most debit and credit account titles. Peachtree uses a different method to increase your efficiency when entering similar transactions, such as cash payments. Rather than using a cash payments journal, Peachtree has a unique input screen to record cash payments.

Cash payments should be made only to vendors that have been set up in Peachtree. When you are setting up a vendor, Peachtree requires that you enter the general ledger account to be debited when a payment is made to the vendor. For example, when "Castle Advertising" is set up, you would identify that cash payments should be debited to Advertising Expense. Thus, when entering a cash payment to Castle Advertising, Peachtree accesses the vendor's information and debits Advertising Expense. Peachtree also knows that cash payments require a credit to Cash. A window that displays the journal entry can be viewed before posting the transaction.

PEACHTREE MASTERY PROBLEM 9-6
1. Open (Restore) file 09-6MP.ptb.
2. Record purchases and cash payments. Use the July transactions to journalize and post to the purchase journal and cash disbursements journal in Peachtree.
3. Print the cash disbursements journal from the Reports menu (select Accounts Payable, Cash Disbursements Journal).
4. Print the purchases journal from the Report List.

PEACHTREE CHALLENGE PROBLEM 9-7
1. Open (Restore) file 09-7CP.ptb.
2. Journalize and post the November transactions in Peachtree's Purchase Journal and Cash Disbursements Journal.
3. Print the purchase journal.
4. Print the cash disbursements journal.

PURCHASES AND CASH PAYMENTS

QuickBooks does not use special journals. Instead, QuickBooks uses special screens designed to help make specific entries. These screens include one for entering bills, which is used to enter purchases on account, and one for paying bills, which is used to enter payments on account.

When you enter a purchase on account in QuickBooks, a vendor must be identified. That vendor must have already been entered into the company file. The software will credit both Accounts Payable and the specific vendor account. At the same time, an account to debit must be identified. For example, if buying supplies on account, the account—Supplies—would be identified in the entry and automatically debited. When a payment on account is entered, the software will automatically debit both Accounts Payable and the vendor, and credit Cash.

QUICKBOOKS MASTERY PROBLEM 9-6
1. Open the Mercury Computers file.
2. Journalize purchases, cash payments, and other transactions completed in July, using QuickBooks. Enter the Bills and Pay Bills windows for purchases and payments on account.
3. Print a Journal report using July 1 and July 31 as the dates.
4. Choose Vendors & Payables from the Reports menu, and print an Unpaid Bills Detail Report for July 31.

QUICKBOOKS CHALLENGE PROBLEM 9-7
1. Open the Fitness Connection file.
2. Journalize purchases, cash payments, and other transactions completed during November.
3. Print a Journal report, using November 1 and 30 for the dates.
4. Print an Unpaid Bills Detail report for November 30.

DISPLAYING CALCULATED AMOUNTS

When you think about a worksheet formula, it's natural to expect that the formula will perform a mathematical calculation using two or more numbers. However, a formula does not necessarily have to add, subtract, multiply, or divide.

When creating a petty cash report on an Excel worksheet, you will need to display a calculated amount in more than one cell. This task is accomplished with a single-cell formula or cell reference.

Assume the total amount of payments made out of the petty cash fund is calculated in cell D15. To complete the form, you want to display this amount in cell F15 to show how the amount to be replenished is calculated. The solution is to enter the formula +D15 in cell F15. The formula simply shows the same amount calculated in cell D15.

EXCEL APPLICATION PROBLEM 9-3
Open the F09-3 Excel data file. Follow the step-by-step instructions in the Instructions worksheet.
Note: This spreadsheet template may also be used to complete Instruction 4 of Application Problem 9-4.

PURCHASES AND CASH PAYMENTS

A merchandising business has many frequently occurring transactions that would require many entries in the general journal. Therefore, special journals are used to simplify the recording of these repetitive transactions. All transactions involving the payment of cash are recorded in the cash payments journal. All purchases of merchandise on account are recorded in the purchases journal.

Entering Purchases on Account in the Purchases Journal
1. Enter the transaction date and press Tab.
2. Enter the invoice number in the Refer. column and press Tab.
3. Enter the amount of the invoice in the Purchases Debit column and press Tab. The Accounts Payable credit amount is calculated and displayed automatically.
4. Choose a vendor name from the drop-down list.
5. Click the Post button.

Entering Cash Payments in the Cash Payments Journal
1. Enter the transaction date and press Tab. (Remember that the date can be increased and decreased by the + and − keys.)
2. Enter the check number in the Refer. column and press Tab.
3. For general debit or credit amounts, enter the account number and amount to debit or credit in the Debit or Credit columns. Enter other amounts in the special columns.
4. If making a payment on account, enter the Accounts Payable debit amount and choose the vendor from the drop-down vendor list. The Cash credit is automatically calculated and displayed by the computer.
5. If the transaction is correct, click the Post button.

AUTOMATED ACCOUNTING APPLICATION PROBLEM 9-2
Open file F09-2.AA8. Display the problem instructions and complete the problem.

AUTOMATED ACCOUNTING MASTERY PROBLEM 9-6
Open file F09-6.AA8. Display the problem instructions and complete the problem.

CHAPTER 10

Journalizing Sales and Cash Receipts Using Special Journals

OBJECTIVES

After studying Chapter 10, you will be able to:

1. Define accounting terms related to sales and cash receipts for a merchandising business.
2. Identify accounting concepts and practices related to sales and cash receipts for a merchandising business.
3. Journalize sales on account using a sales journal.
4. Journalize cash receipts using a cash receipts journal.
5. Record sales returns and allowances using a general journal.

KEY TERMS

- customer
- sales tax
- sales journal
- cash sale
- credit card sale
- point-of-sale (POS) terminal
- terminal summary
- batch report
- batching out
- cash receipts journal
- sales discount
- sales return
- sales allowance
- credit memorandum

Point Your Browser
www.C21accounting.com

ACCOUNTING IN THE REAL WORLD

Best Buy

Best Buy—Increasing Sales Results

A sluggish economy had caused consumer spending to drop, especially in the sales of desktop computers and CDs. Growth in comparable store sales—the sales at stores open for more than a year—were disappointing. This was not the ideal time to assume leadership of a leading specialty retailer of consumer electronics, personal computers, entertainment software, and appliances. But that is exactly what faced Bradbury H. Anderson as he became the new chief executive officer of Best Buy.

So how did Best Buy overcome this challenge? It went digital. Recognizing changes in consumer preferences, Best Buy increased its assortment of digital cameras and digital, LCD, and projection TVs. Mr. Anderson and his new management team undertook other strategic plans to reduce product costs and store expenses. These changes enabled Best Buy to achieve a 2.5% increase in comparable store sales, a 13% increase in total revenue, and an 8% increase in net income.

Critical Thinking

1. How can a company have a 13% increase in total revenue with just a 2.5% increase in comparable store sales?
2. For any local company, such as a fast-food restaurant, suggest changes in the products they offer that you believe could increase sales.

Source: www.bestbuy.com

INTERNET ACTIVITY

State Sales Tax Rates

Go to the homepage for the Federation of Tax Administrators (www.taxadmin.org) or search the Internet for state sales tax rates. Look for a chart or table that compares the sales tax rate for each state.

Instructions

1. Make a chart comparing the sales tax rate for your state with the sales tax rate for 10 other states.
2. Highlight the highest and lowest rates.

LESSON 10-1

Journalizing Sales on Account Using a Sales Journal

SALES TAX

Purchases and sales of merchandise are the two major activities of a merchandising business. A person or business to whom merchandise or services are sold is called a **customer**. Hobby Shack sells merchandise to a variety of customers, including individuals, schools, and churches. Hobby Shack uses the special journals described in this chapter to record transactions related to sales.

Laws of most states and some cities require that a tax be collected from customers for each sale made. A tax on a sale of merchandise or services is called a **sales tax**. Sales tax rates are usually stated as a percentage of sales. Regardless of the tax rates used, accounting procedures are the same.

Businesses must file reports with the proper government unit and pay the amount of sales tax collected. Every business collecting a sales tax needs accurate records of the amount of (1) total sales and (2) total sales tax collected. The amount of sales tax collected is a business liability until paid to the government agency. Therefore, the sales tax amount is recorded in a separate liability account titled Sales Tax Payable, which has a normal credit balance.

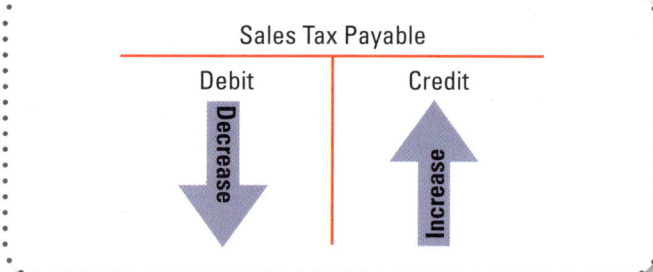

CHARACTER COUNTS

Integrity—Doing What's Right

What does the word *integrity* mean to you? The word is derived from a Latin word meaning "wholeness," "completeness," and "purity." Many companies include an interpretation of integrity in their code of conduct.

"We always try to do the right thing." —Procter & Gamble

"To say what we mean, to deliver what we promise, to fulfill our commitments, and to stand for what is right." —Lockheed Martin

"We do the right thing without compromise. We avoid even the appearance of impropriety." —Intel

Companies with integrity have an absolute commitment to do what is right in all business activities. Integrity is ultimately the most critical component to long-term business success. A business that fails to act with integrity will soon find it difficult to hire employees, deal with suppliers, and enjoy repeat customers.

The American Institute of Certified Public Accountants recognizes that integrity is critical for maintaining public confidence in its members' professional services. "Integrity is an element of character fundamental to professional recognition. It is the quality from which the public trust derives and the benchmark against which a member must ultimately test all decisions."

Instructions

In private, write down five qualities that you believe people of high integrity possess. Using a typical grading schedule (A+, A, A–, etc.), identify how you believe your friends, teachers, and others would rate your integrity. Do you have integrity as defined by the three companies above?

SALES OF MERCHANDISE ON ACCOUNT

A sale of merchandise may be (1) on account or (2) for cash. A sale of merchandise increases the revenue of a business. Regardless of when payment is made, the revenue should be recorded at the time of a sale, not on the date cash is received. For example, on June 15 Hobby Shack sells merchandise on account to a customer. The customer pays Hobby Shack for the merchandise on July 12. Hobby Shack records the revenue on June 15, the date of the sale. The accounting concept *Realization of Revenue* is applied when revenue is recorded at the time goods or services are sold. [CONCEPT: Realization of Revenue]

A sale for which cash will be received at a later date is known as a sale on account. A sale on account is also referred to as a charge sale. Hobby Shack summarizes the total due from all charge customers in a general ledger account titled Accounts Receivable. Accounts Receivable is an asset account with a normal debit balance. Therefore, the accounts receivable account is increased by a debit and decreased by a credit.

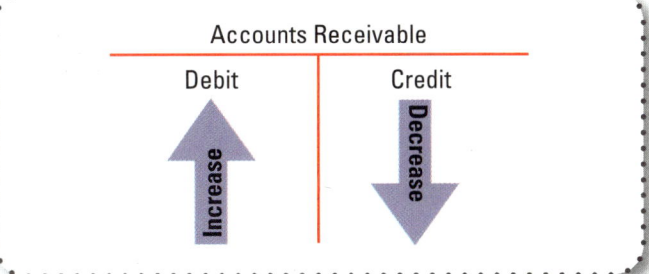

BUSINESS STRUCTURES

Advantages and Disadvantages of a Corporation

Organizing a corporation is as simple as filing an application with the appropriate state agency. The approved application establishes the corporation as a legal entity, giving the corporation many of the same legal rights and risks as individuals, including owning assets, borrowing money, paying taxes, and being sued.

The corporate form of business organization has several advantages over a sole proprietorship:

- *Limited liability*. The liability of stockholders is limited to their investment in the corporation.
- *Supply of capital*. Individuals are more willing to invest in a corporation because their personal assets are protected by limited liability.

However, there are also some disadvantages to a corporation:

- *Shared decision making*. Significant business decisions must be approved by a vote of the stockholders.
- *Shared profits*. The earnings of the corporation are divided among the stockholders.
- *Taxation*. The earnings of a corporation may be subject to federal and state income taxes. When the earnings of the corporation are distributed to the stockholders, individual stockholders may also have to pay income taxes on the distributions. Thus, the earnings of a corporation can be taxed twice, a concept known as double taxation.

Proper planning can offer stockholders the advantage of limited liability while avoiding the disadvantage of double taxation. Thus, although the organization application can be prepared without the help of an attorney or accountant, consulting with these professionals is recommended.

Critical Thinking

1. Think of two businesses you might be interested in starting. Describe whether the proprietorship or corporation form of organization would be better suited for this business.

2. Often a person who has started a proprietorship and run it successfully for many years sells the business to a corporation. Why would a corporation be interested in buying such a business?

SALES JOURNAL

					1	2	3	
	DATE	ACCOUNT DEBITED	SALE NO.	POST. REF.	ACCOUNTS RECEIVABLE DEBIT	SALES CREDIT	SALES TAX PAYABLE CREDIT	
1								1
2								2

Hobby Shack uses a special journal to record only sales of merchandise on account transactions. A special journal used to record only sales of merchandise on account is called a **sales journal**.

The special amount columns in this sales journal are Accounts Receivable Debit, Sales Credit, and Sales Tax Payable Credit. With these special amount columns, each sale on account transaction can be recorded on one line of the sales journal.

SALES INVOICE

HOBBY SHACK, INC.
1420 College Plaza
Atlanta, GA 30337-1726

Sold to: Village Crafts
120 Mountain Road
Marietta, GA 30060-1320

Cust. No. 150

No. 76
Date 11/3/--
Terms 30 days

Stock No.	Description	Quantity	Unit Price	Amount
4422	Deer and fawn bisque	25	12.00	300.00
7710	Lighthouse, 6" -- bisque	30	8.00	240.00
			Subtotal	540.00
Customer's Signature Max Schindler		Salesclerk S.A.	Sales Tax	32.40
			Total	572.40

When merchandise is sold on account, the seller prepares a form showing what has been sold. A form describing the goods or services sold, the quantity, and the price is known as an *invoice*. An invoice used as a source document for recording a sale on account is known as a *sales invoice*. [CONCEPT: Objective Evidence] A sales invoice is also referred to as a *sales ticket* or a *sales slip*.

The seller considers an invoice for a sale on account to be a sales invoice. The same invoice is considered by the customer to be a purchase invoice.

In the case of Hobby Shack, three copies of a sales invoice are prepared. The original copy is given to the customer. The second copy goes to Hobby Shack's shipping department. The third copy is used as the source document for the sale on account transaction. [CONCEPT: Objective Evidence] Sales invoices are numbered in sequence. Number 76 is the number of the sales invoice issued to Village Crafts.

Hobby Shack operates in a state with a 6% sales tax rate. The total amount of the sale of merchandise in the invoice above is calculated as follows.

Price of Goods	×	Sales Tax Rate	=	Sales Tax
$540.00	×	6%	=	$32.40
Price of Goods	+	Sales Tax	=	Total Amount
$540.00	+	$32.40	=	$572.40

Chapter 10   Journalizing Sales and Cash Receipts Using Special Journals

SALE ON ACCOUNT

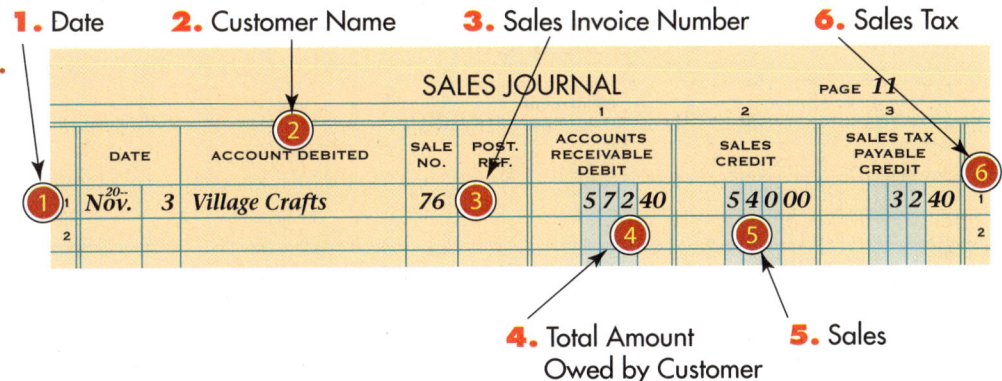

Hobby Shack sells on account only to businesses. Other customers must either pay cash or use a credit card.

November 3. Sold merchandise on account to Village Crafts, $540.00, plus sales tax, $32.40; total, $572.40. Sales Invoice No. 76.

A sale on account transaction increases the amount to be collected later from a customer. Payment for this sale will be received at a later date. However, the sale is recorded at the time the sale is made because the sale has taken place and payment is due to Hobby Shack. [CONCEPT: Realization of Revenue]

Because Accounts Receivable has a normal debit balance, Accounts Receivable is debited for the total sales and sales tax, $572.40, to show the increase in this asset account. Sales has a normal credit balance. Therefore, Sales is credited for the price of the goods, $540.00, to show the increase in this revenue account. The sales tax payable account also has a normal credit balance. Therefore, Sales Tax Payable is credited for the amount of sales tax, $32.40, to show the increase in this liability account.

STEPS JOURNALIZING A SALE ON ACCOUNT

1. Write the date, *20--, Nov. 3*, in the Date column.

2. Write the customer name, *Village Crafts*, in the Account Debited column. The debit and credit amounts are recorded in special amount columns. Therefore, writing the titles of the general ledger accounts in the Account Debited column is not necessary. However, the name of the customer is written in the Account Debited column to show from whom the amount is due. Hobby Shack's procedures for keeping records of the amounts to be collected from each customer are described in Chapter 11.

3. Write the sales invoice number, *76*, in the Sale No. column.

4. Write the total amount owed by the customer, *$572.40*, in the Accounts Receivable Debit column.

5. Write the sales amount, *$540.00*, in the Sales Credit column.

6. Write the sales tax amount, *$32.40*, in the Sales Tax Payable Credit column.
    Some states exempt schools and other organizations from paying sales tax. A sale to a tax-exempt organization would be recorded using the same amount in the Sales Credit and Accounts Receivable Debit columns. No amount would be entered in the Sales Tax Payable Credit column.

Journalizing Sales on Account Using a Sales Journal   Lesson 10-1   273

TOTALING, PROVING, AND RULING A SALES JOURNAL

SALES JOURNAL   PAGE 11

	DATE	ACCOUNT DEBITED	SALE NO.	POST. REF.	ACCOUNTS RECEIVABLE DEBIT	SALES CREDIT	SALES TAX PAYABLE CREDIT	
1	Nov. 3	Village Crafts	76		572 40	540 00	32 40	1
2	5	Fairview Church	77		1 908 00	1 908 00		2
3	9	Washington Schools	78		572 00	572 00		3
4	11	Country Crafters	79		768 50	725 00	43 50	4
5	16	Playtime Childcare	80		1 752 18	1 653 00	99 18	5
6	19	Village Crafts	81		2 549 30	2 405 00	144 30	6
7	24	Cumberland Center	82		158 00	158 00		7
8	24	Washington Schools	83		334 00	334 00		8
9	29	Country Crafters	84		453 68	428 00	25 68	9
10	30	Totals			9 068 06	8 723 00	345 06	10

At the end of each month, Hobby Shack totals, proves, and rules its sales journal. The procedures for proving and ruling a sales journal are the same as the procedures described for Hobby Shack's cash payments journal in Chapter 9.

The proof for Hobby Shack's sales journal is calculated as follows.

Col. No.	Column Title	Debit Totals	Credit Totals
1	Accounts Receivable Debit	$9,068.06	
2	Sales Credit		$8,723.00
3	Sales Tax Payable Credit		345.06
	Totals	$9,068.06	$9,068.06

The two totals, $9,068.06, are equal. Equality of debits and credits in Hobby Shack's sales journal for November is proved.

Posting from a sales journal is described in Chapter 11.

FOR YOUR INFORMATION

FYI

Many states exempt food and drug sales for all customers. some states even exempt clothing sales from sales tax.

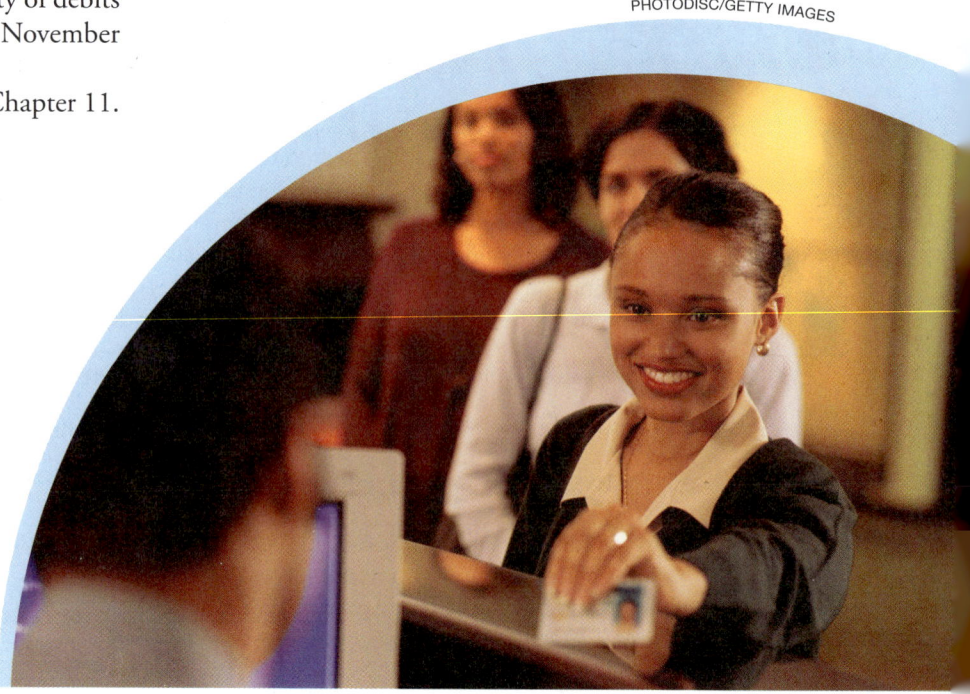

PHOTODISC/GETTY IMAGES

End of Lesson REVIEW

AUDIT YOUR UNDERSTANDING

1. How does a merchandising business differ from a service business?
2. How are sales tax rates usually stated?
3. Why is sales tax collected considered a liability?
4. What is the title of the general ledger account used to summarize the total amount due from all charge customers?

TERMS REVIEW

customer
sales tax
sales journal

WORK TOGETHER 10-1

Journalizing sales on account; proving and ruling a sales journal

The sales journal for Distinctive Appliances is given in the *Working Papers*. Your instructor will guide you through the following examples.

1. Using the current year, journalize the following transactions on page 9 of the sales journal. The sales invoice source document is abbreviated as S.

Transactions:

Sept. 1. Sold merchandise on account to Adrian Makowski, $800.00, plus sales tax, $48.00; total, $848.00. S104.
    11. Sold merchandise on account to Columbus City Schools, $875.00. Columbus City Schools is exempt from sales taxes. S105.
    28. Sold merchandise on account to Swiss Delight, $1,460.00, plus sales tax, $87.60; total, $1,547.60. S106.

2. Total, prove, and rule the sales journal.

ON YOUR OWN 10-1

Journalizing sales on account; proving and ruling a sales journal

The sales journal for Parris Supplies is given in the *Working Papers*. Work this problem independently.

1. Using the current year, journalize the following transactions on page 6 of the sales journal. The sales invoice source document is abbreviated as S.

Transactions:

Jun. 5. Sold merchandise on account to Peter Gallaher, $650.00, plus sales tax, $39.00; total, $689.00. S410.
    12. Sold merchandise on account to Spann Auto Supply, $590.00, plus sales tax, $35.40; total, $625.40. S411.
    24. Sold merchandise on account to Fleming College, $545.00. Fleming College is exempt from sales taxes. S412.

2. Total, prove, and rule the sales journal.

LESSON 10-2

Journalizing Cash Receipts Using a Cash Receipts Journal

PROCESSING SALES TRANSACTIONS

Hobby Shack sells most of its merchandise for cash. A sale in which cash is received for the total amount of the sale at the time of the transaction is called a **cash sale**. Hobby Shack also sells merchandise to customers who have a bank-approved credit card. A sale in which a credit card is used for the total amount of the sale at the time of the transaction is called a **credit card sale**. Major bank-approved credit cards include VISA, MasterCard, and Discover Card. A customer who uses a credit card promises to pay the amount due for the credit card transaction to the bank issuing the credit card.

Some small businesses continue to use the traditional cash register to process sales transactions. After entering the price marked on each item sold, the sales clerk pushes a button instructing the cash register to total the sale, including any sales tax, and produce a cash register receipt for the customer. A typical cash register receipt is shown on the next page. At the end of every day, the cash register prints a summary of the sales recorded. The summary is adequate for journalizing the sales transaction, but it is unable to provide the business with information about what merchandise was sold, when it was sold, and to which customers.

Hobby Shack installed a modern version of a cash register. A computer used to collect, store, and report all the information of a sales transaction is called a **point-of-sale (POS) terminal**. Before any sale is entered, the number, description, price, and quantity on hand of each item of merchandise are stored in the POS terminal. When processing a sale, the sales clerk uses a scanning device to scan the universal product code (UPC) symbol on the item.

The POS terminal matches the number represented by the UPC symbol with the merchandise number to obtain the description and price of the merchandise. When all the merchandise has been scanned, the sales clerk enters the customer's method of payment. For a cash sale, the sales clerk enters the cash tendered by the customer and the POS terminal computes the amount of change. For a credit card sale, the customer swipes the credit card in the card scanner. The POS system produces a receipt that contains detailed information about the sale. A customer receipt from a POS terminal is shown on the next page.

Periodically, Hobby Shack instructs the point-of-sale terminal to print a report of all cash and credit card sales. The report that summarizes the cash and credit card sales of a point-of-sale terminal is called a **terminal summary**. Hobby Shack uses the terminal summary as the source document for recording sales in its journals. [CONCEPT: Objective Evidence] A terminal summary is shown on the next page.

At any time, the POS system can produce a variety of informational reports to help management make decisions. For example:

1. A report of sales by sales clerk would assist management to analyze a sales clerk's efficiency.
2. A report of sales by time of day would assist management in scheduling sales clerks to match busy periods.
3. A report of merchandise having a quantity on hand below a predetermined reorder point alerts management to purchase additional merchandise.

UPC (Universal Product Code) symbol on merchandise is scanned to enter data into a point-of-sale (POS) terminal

```
         Antique Shop
       123 Eagle Street
         Hanson, Iowa

                         13.23
                          2.45
                          2.45
                         10.34
   Subtotal              28.47
   Tax                    1.71
   Total                 30.18
```

Cash register receipt from a traditional cash register

```
                    Hobby Shack, Inc.
                    1420 College Plaza
                     Atlanta, Georgia

latex paint, blue 1 oz.
    5 @ $1.45                        7.25
paint brush, 3/4 glaze
    3 @ $3.25                        9.75
Subtotal 1                          17.00
Tax                                  1.02
TOTAL                               18.02

                      VISA RECEIPT
Jan Windham                XXXXXXXX1122
Exp 02/--                    Ref3534423
04/01/--
Register #: 002      Cashier #: 010

                  Thanks, Come Again
```

Point-of-sale (POS) terminal receipt

TERMINAL SUMMARY Hobby Shack, Inc.	
Code:	34
Date:	11/27/--
Time:	18:24
Visa	*034*
Sales	295.38
Sales Tax	17.72
Total	313.10
MasterCard	*042*
Sales	107.21
Sales Tax	6.43
Total	113.64
Cash	*152*
Sales	5,057.41
Sales Tax	303.45
Total	5,360.86
Totals	
Sales	5,460.00
Sales Tax	327.60
Total	5,787.60

Terminal summary printed by POS terminal, used as source document for journalizing cash and credit card sales

```
              BATCH REPORT
MERCHANT      02938493   234
TERMINAL      923874
DATE          04/03/--  TIME 18:45
BATCH         45

VISA
COUNT       =         007
SALES       = $    325.23
RETURNS     = $     12.13
NET         = $    313.10

MASTERCARD
COUNT       =         003
SALES       = $    145.86
RETURNS     = $     32.22
NET         = $    113.64

TOTALS
COUNT       =         010
SALES       = $    471.09
RETURNS     = $     44.35
NET         = $    426.74

CONTROL NUMBER: 0938904235343
```

Batch Report for credit card sales printed by POS terminal (as discussed on page 278)

Journalizing Cash Receipts Using a Cash Receipts Journal

PROCESSING CREDIT CARDS

Sales information for credit card sales is stored in the POS terminal. When Hobby Shack produces the terminal summary, it also instructs the point-of-sale terminal to print a report of credit card sales. A report of credit card sales produced by a point-of-sale terminal is called a **batch report**. A batch report can be detailed, showing each credit card sale, or it can provide a summary of the number and total of sales by credit card type. The process of preparing a batch report of credit card sales from a point-of-sale terminal is called **batching out**. A batch report for credit card sales is shown on the previous page.

Hobby Shack has contracted with its bank, First American, to process its credit card sales. When Hobby Shack batches out, the POS terminal electronically transmits a summary batch report to First American. The bank combines the batch reports for all of its customers and submits the information to the nearest Federal Reserve Bank. The funds are transferred among the banks issuing the credit cards, similar to the way checks are transferred between banks.

For example, suppose a customer having a VISA card issued by Capital National Bank buys $500.00 worth of merchandise from Hobby Shack. When Hobby Shack batches out, an electronic message is sent to First American with the credit card number and amount of the sale. When the Federal Reserve Bank receives the information, $500.00 is transferred from Capital National's account to First American's account. First American then credits Hobby Shack's account for the sale. The cash is deposited in Hobby Shack's account 2–3 business days after the sale. However, Hobby Shack records the transaction on the date it occurs.

CASH RECEIPTS JOURNAL

					GENERAL		ACCOUNTS RECEIVABLE CREDIT	SALES CREDIT	SALES TAX PAYABLE CREDIT	SALES DISCOUNT DEBIT	CASH DEBIT
	DATE	ACCOUNT TITLE	DOC. NO.	POST. REF.	DEBIT	CREDIT					
1											
2											
3											

Hobby Shack, Inc., has many transactions involving the receipt of cash. Because of the number of transactions, Hobby Shack uses a special journal for recording only cash receipts. A special journal used to record only cash receipt transactions is called a **cash receipts journal**.

Only those columns needed to record cash receipt transactions are included in Hobby Shack's cash receipts journal. Since all cash receipt transactions affect the cash account, a special column is provided for this general ledger account. In addition, Hobby Shack has many cash receipt transactions affecting the accounts receivable account, the sales account, and the sales tax payable account. Therefore, special columns are provided in Hobby Shack's cash receipts journal for these general ledger accounts.

To encourage early payment, Hobby Shack allows customers who purchase merchandise on account to take a deduction from the invoice amount. A cash discount on sales taken by a customer is called a **sales discount**. When a sales discount is taken, the customer pays less than the invoice amount previously recorded in the sales account. Sales discounts reduce the amount of cash Hobby Shack receives on sales on account. Because customers often take these discounts, Hobby Shack's cash receipts journal has a special column titled Sales Discount Debit. Because of these special columns, most of Hobby Shack's cash receipt transactions can be recorded on one line in the cash receipts journal. Cash receipts that do not occur often are recorded in the General columns.

CASH AND CREDIT CARD SALES

Hobby Shack's POS terminal combines cash and credit card sales in the terminal summary. The total of the terminal summary is recorded as a single cash sales transaction.

November 4. Recorded cash and credit card sales, $5,460.00, plus sales tax, $327.60; total, $5,787.60. Terminal Summary 34.

At the end of each week, Hobby Shack batches out and prints a terminal summary. The POS terminal assigns the summary a sequential number. The terminal summary is used by Hobby Shack as the source document for weekly cash and credit card sales transactions. [CONCEPT: Objective Evidence] Sales are also totaled at the end of each month so Hobby Shack can analyze monthly sales.

Management is responsible for determining how often the business should batch out, deposit cash, and record sales in the sales journal. Most businesses perform these tasks at the end of every business day. (The weekly processing demonstrated in this textbook was selected to simplify the textbook illustrations and problems.)

Because the asset account, **Cash**, has a normal debit balance, **Cash** is debited for the total sales and sales tax, $5,787.60, to show the increase in this asset account. The sales account has a normal credit balance. Therefore, **Sales** is credited for the total price of all goods sold, $5,460.00, to show the increase in this revenue account. The sales tax payable account also has a normal credit balance. Therefore, **Sales Tax Payable** is credited for the total sales tax, $327.60, to show the increase in this liability account.

STEPS: JOURNALIZING CASH AND CREDIT CARD SALES

1. Write the date, *20--, Nov. 4*, in the Date column.
2. Place a check mark in the Account Title column to show that no account title needs to be written. The debit and credit amounts will be recorded in special amount columns.
3. Write the terminal summary document number, *TS34*, in the Doc. No. column.
4. Place a check mark in the Post. Ref. column to show that amounts on this line are not to be posted individually.
5. Write the sales amount, *$5,460.00*, in the Sales Credit column.
6. Write the sales tax amount, *$327.60*, in the Sales Tax Payable Credit column.
7. Write the cash amount, *$5,787.60*, in the Cash Debit column.

Journalizing Cash Receipts Using a Cash Receipts Journal • Lesson 10-2 • 279

CASH RECEIPTS ON ACCOUNT

1. Date 2. Customer's Name 3. Receipt Number 4. Credit 5. Debit

When cash is received on account from a customer, Hobby Shack prepares a receipt. The receipts are prenumbered so that all receipts can be accounted for. Receipts are prepared in duplicate. The original receipt is given to the customer. The copy of the receipt is used as the source document for the cash receipt on account transaction. [CONCEPT: Objective Evidence]

> **November 6. Received cash on account from Country Crafters, $2,162.40, covering S69. Receipt No. 90.**

A cash receipt on account transaction decreases future amounts to be collected from a customer. This transaction increases the cash account balance and decreases the accounts receivable account balance. Because the cash account has a normal debit balance, **Cash** is debited for the amount of cash received, $2,162.40, to show the increase in this asset account. The accounts receivable account also has a normal debit balance. Therefore, **Accounts Receivable** is credited for $2,162.40 to show the decrease in this asset account.

Hobby Shack's procedures for keeping records of the amounts received from customers are described in Chapter 11. Posting procedures are also described in Chapter 11.

FOR YOUR INFORMATION

F Y I

All cash receipts are recorded in a cash receipts journal. Most cash receipts are for (1) cash received from customers on account and (2) cash and credit card sales.

STEPS JOURNALIZING CASH RECEIPTS ON ACCOUNT

1. Write the date, *6*, in the Date column.
2. Write only the customer's name, *Country Crafters*, in the Account Title column. The debit and credit amounts are entered in special amount columns. Therefore, the titles of the two general ledger accounts do not need to be written in the Account Title column.
3. Write the receipt number, *R90*, in the Doc. No. column.
4. Write the credit amount, *$2,162.40*, in the Accounts Receivable Credit column.
5. Write the debit amount, *$2,162.40*, in the Cash Debit column.

CALCULATING CASH RECEIPTS ON ACCOUNT WITH SALES DISCOUNT

To encourage early payment for a sale on account, a deduction on the invoice amount may be allowed. A deduction that a vendor allows on the invoice amount to encourage prompt payment is known as a cash discount. A cash discount on sales is called a sales discount. When a sales discount is taken, a customer pays less cash than the invoice amount previously recorded in the sales account.

To encourage prompt payment, Hobby Shack gives credit terms of 2/10, n/30. When a customer pays the amount owed within 10 days, the sales invoice amount is reduced 2%. Otherwise, the net amount is due in 30 days.

On October 30, Hobby Shack sold merchandise on account to Cumberland Center for $1,200.00. On November 7, Hobby Shack received payment for this sale on account within the discount period. Because the payment is received within the discount period, the amount received is reduced by the amount of the sales discount.

Sales Invoice Amount	×	Sales Discount Rate	=	Sales Discount
$1,200.00	×	2%	=	$24.00

FINANCIAL LITERACY

Credit Cards

Buying goods with a credit card is a great way to take advantage of sales or to purchase an unplanned necessity such as an appliance. However, this convenience has a price—the interest that is applied to any unpaid balance on the account.

Interest rates and credit terms vary from card to card, so it is important to investigate and compare before choosing a card. Find out how the interest is calculated and when the interest starts on a purchase. For some companies, interest starts on the day of purchase. Sometimes interest doesn't start until 20 to 25 days after the end of a billing cycle. If you pay your bill in full by the due date, no interest will be charged. If you are charged interest, it is usually calculated based on the average daily unpaid balance of your account.

Some credit card companies entice you to switch to their card by offering very low introductory interest rates—but only for a specific period of time. Once the introductory period expires, the interest rate increases.

Other companies offer cash back or other rewards such as miles or points that can be used for the purchase of airline tickets or other items. Again, these programs vary greatly between credit cards. Make sure you understand the terms of such reward programs.

Credit cards can be a wonderful convenience as long as you understand the rules of the card you choose.

Activities

1. Using the Internet or other resources, compare the interest rates on two credit cards. If either card offers an introductory rate, find out the terms of the introductory rate and the interest rate after the introductory period is over. Present your findings in written form.

2. Using the Internet or other resources, find out how the interest is calculated for two different credit cards. Summarize your findings in a written report.

Journalizing Cash Receipts Using a Cash Receipts Journal

JOURNALIZING CASH RECEIPTS ON ACCOUNT WITH SALES DISCOUNTS

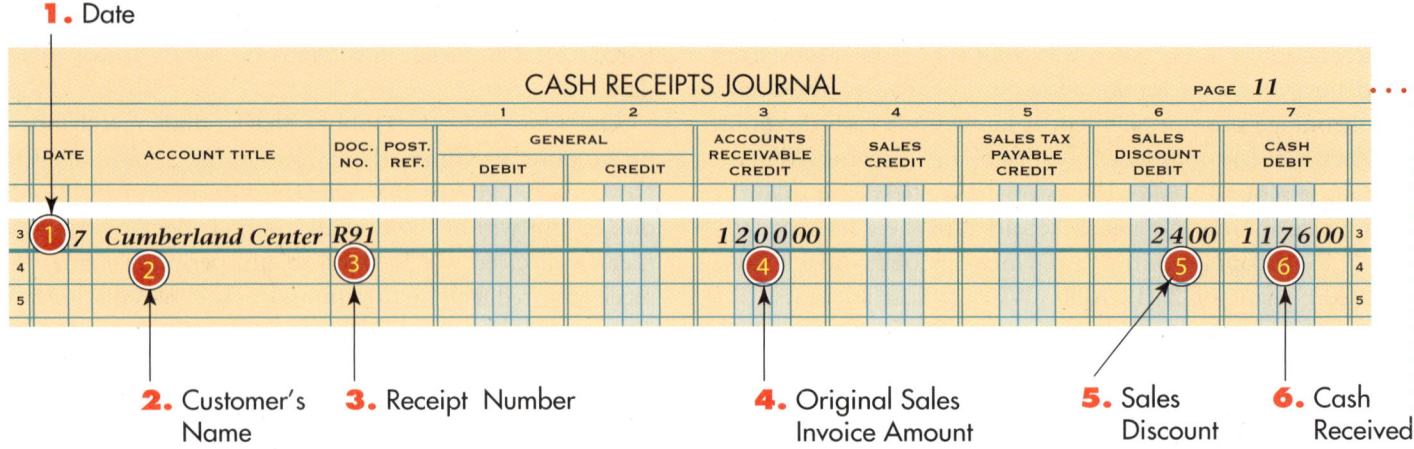

Sales discounts are recorded in a general ledger account titled Sales Discount. Since sales discounts decrease sales, the account Sales Discount is a contra account to Sales.

A business could debit Sales for the amount of the sales discount. However, better information is provided if these amounts are debited to Sales Discount. A separate account provides business managers with more information to evaluate whether a sales discount is a cost-effective method of encouraging early payments of sales on account.

> **November 7.** Received cash on account from Cumberland Center, $1,176.00, covering Sales Invoice No. 74 for $1,200.00, less 2% discount, $24.00. Receipt No. 91.

```
        Cash
Nov. 7  1,176.00  |

     Accounts Receivable
                  | Nov. 7  1,200.00

      Sales Discount
Nov. 7  24.00     |
```

If a customer does not pay the amount owed within the sales discount period, the full invoice amount is due. If Cumberland Center had not taken the sales discount, the journal entry would be a debit to Cash, $1,200.00, and a credit to Accounts Receivable, $1,200.00.

STEPS — JOURNALIZING CASH RECEIPTS ON ACCOUNT WITH SALES DISCOUNTS

1. Write the date, *7*, in the Date column.
2. Write the customer's name, *Cumberland Center*, in the Account Title column.
3. Write the receipt number, *R91*, in the Doc. No. column.
4. Write the original invoice amount, *$1,200.00*, in the Accounts Receivable Credit column.
5. Write the amount of sales discount, *$24.00*, in the Sales Discount Debit column.
6. Write the debit to *Cash*, *$1,176.00*, in the Cash Debit column.

TOTALING, PROVING, AND RULING A CASH RECEIPTS JOURNAL

						CASH RECEIPTS JOURNAL						PAGE 11	
						1	2	3	4	5	6	7	
	DATE	ACCOUNT TITLE	DOC. NO.	POST. REF.		GENERAL		ACCOUNTS RECEIVABLE CREDIT	SALES CREDIT	SALES TAX PAYABLE CREDIT	SALES DISCOUNT DEBIT	CASH DEBIT	
						DEBIT	CREDIT						
22	30	✓	T38	✓					1380 00	82 80		1462 80	22
23	30	Totals						9540 00	27532 50	1648 80	52 50	38668 80	23
24													24

The procedures for totaling, proving, and ruling a cash receipts journal are the same as the procedures described for Hobby Shack's cash payments journal in Chapter 9. The use of the General Debit and General Credit columns is described in Part 3.

The proof for Hobby Shack's cash receipts journal for November is calculated as shown below. The two totals, $38,721.30, are equal. Equality of debits and credits is proved.

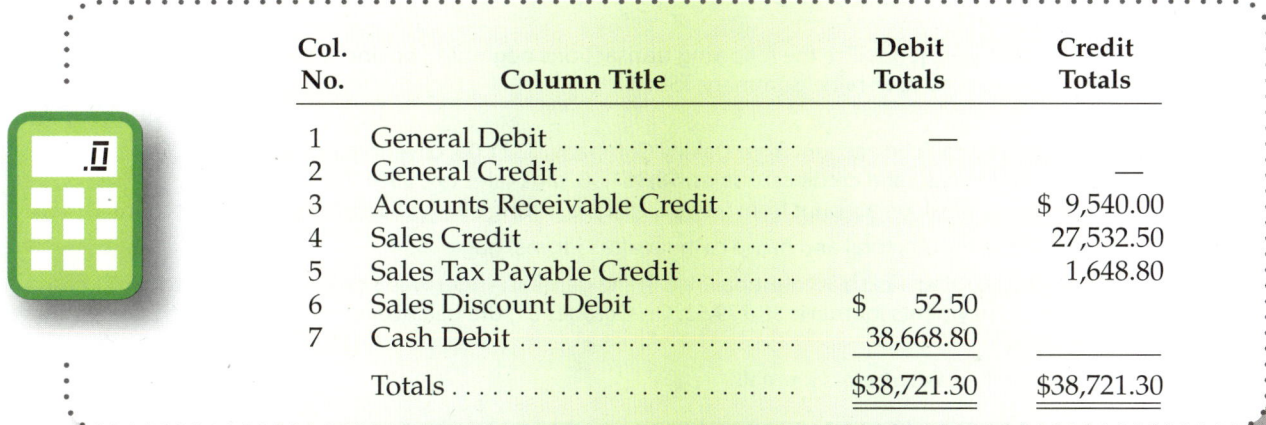

Col. No.	Column Title	Debit Totals	Credit Totals
1	General Debit	—	
2	General Credit		—
3	Accounts Receivable Credit		$ 9,540.00
4	Sales Credit		27,532.50
5	Sales Tax Payable Credit		1,648.80
6	Sales Discount Debit	$ 52.50	
7	Cash Debit	38,668.80	
	Totals	$38,721.30	$38,721.30

PROVING CASH AT THE END OF A MONTH

After the cash receipts journal is proved at the end of each month, cash is proved. Hobby Shack's cash proof at the end of November is calculated as shown.

The balance on the next unused check stub is $23,414.84. Since the balance on the next unused check stub is the same as the cash proof, cash is proved.

Cash on hand at the beginning of the month	$17,647.44
(Nov. 1 balance of general ledger cash account)	
Plus total cash received during the month	38,668.80
(Cash Debit column total, cash receipts journal)	
Equals total	$56,316.24
Less total cash paid during the month	32,901.40
(Cash Credit column total, cash payments journal, Chapter 9)	
Equals cash balance on hand at end of the month	$23,414.84
Checkbook balance on the next unused check stub	$23,414.84

Journalizing Cash Receipts Using a Cash Receipts Journal Lesson 10-2

End of Lesson REVIEW

TERMS REVIEW

cash sale
credit card sale
point-of-sale (POS) terminal
terminal summary
batch report
batching out
cash receipts journal
sales discount

AUDIT YOUR UNDERSTANDING

1. What is the difference in the receipt received by a customer from a cash register versus a point-of-sale terminal?
2. What are the two types of batch reports?
3. Who transfers funds between banks involved in the credit card sales?

WORK TOGETHER 10-2

Journalizing cash receipts; proving and ruling a cash receipts journal

Cash receipts journal page 16 for Graphics Co. is given in the *Working Papers*. Your instructor will guide you through the following examples.

1. Using the current year, journalize the following transactions beginning on line 1. Source documents are abbreviated as follows: receipt, R; terminal summary, TS.

Transactions:

Oct. 4. Received cash on account from Oakley Company, $371.00, covering S96. R144.
    13. Recorded cash and credit card sales, $8,361.60, plus sales tax, $501.70; total, $8,863.30. TS43.
    30. Received cash on account from Sierra Supply, covering S97 for $5,989.00, less 2% discount. R145.

2. For the end of the month, total and prove cash receipts journal page 16.
3. Prove cash. The October 1 cash account balance in the general ledger was $11,764.96. The October 31 cash credit total in the cash payments journal is $8,779.53. On October 31, the balance on the next unused check stub was $18,088.95.
4. Rule page 16 of the cash receipts journal.

ON YOUR OWN 10-2

Journalizing cash receipts; proving and ruling a cash receipts journal

Cash receipts journal page 17 for Holloman Auto Parts is given in the *Working Papers*. Work this problem independently.

1. Using the current year, journalize the following transactions beginning on line 1. Source documents are abbreviated as follows: receipt, R; terminal summary, TS.

Transactions:

Nov. 2. Received cash on account from Wakeman Auto, $425.00, covering S298. R312.
    13. Recorded cash and credit card sales, $3,254.30, plus sales tax, $189.55; total, $3,443.85. TS48.
    27. Received cash on account from Cooley Used Cars, covering S295 for $1,459.00, less 2% discount. R313.

2. For the end of the month, total and prove cash receipts journal page 17.
3. Prove cash. The November 1 cash account balance in the general ledger was $2,848.10. The November 30 cash credit total in the cash payments journal is $4,284.25. On November 30, the balance on the next unused check stub was $3,862.52.
4. Rule page 17 of the cash receipts journal.

LESSON 10-3

Recording Transactions Using a General Journal

CREDIT MEMORANDUM FOR SALES RETURNS AND ALLOWANCES

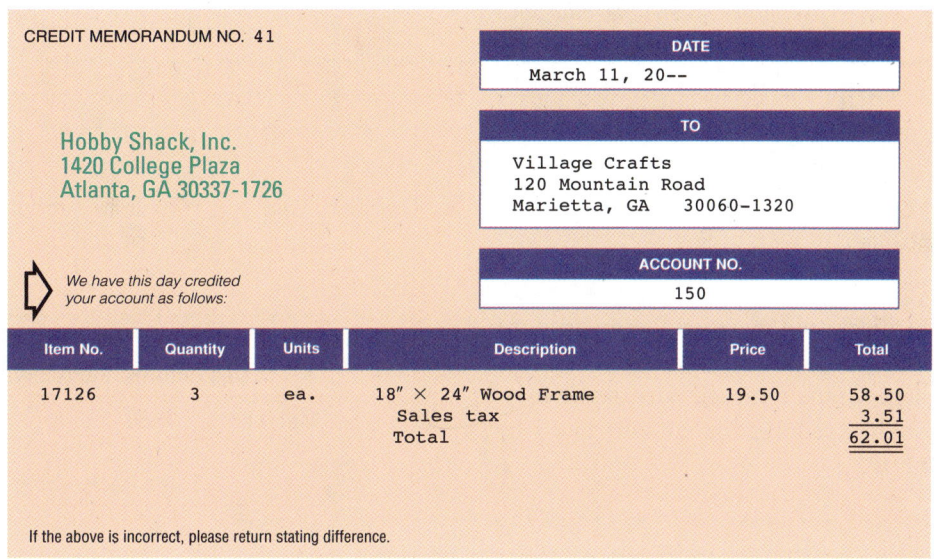

In Chapter 9, purchases-related transactions other than purchases and cash payments were recorded in a general journal. Hobby Shack has a sales-related transaction that is recorded in a general journal rather than either the sales or the cash receipts journals.

Sales Returns and Allowances

Most merchandising businesses expect to have some merchandise returned. A customer may have received the wrong item or damaged goods. A customer may return merchandise for a credit on account or a cash refund. Credit allowed a customer for the sales price of returned merchandise, resulting in a decrease in the vendor's accounts receivable, is called a **sales return**.

Credit may be granted to a customer without requiring the return of merchandise. Credit also may be given because of a shortage in a shipment. Credit allowed a customer for part of the sales price of merchandise that is not returned, resulting in a decrease in the vendor's accounts receivable, is called a **sales allowance**.

A vendor usually informs a customer in writing when a sales return or a sales allowance is granted. A form prepared by the vendor showing the amount deducted for returns and allowances is called a **credit memorandum**. The original of a credit memorandum is given to the customer. The copy is used as the source document for recording the sales returns and allowances transaction. [CONCEPT: Objective Evidence]

Sales returns and sales allowances decrease the amount of sales. Therefore, the account Sales Returns and Allowances is a contra account to the revenue account Sales. Thus, the normal account balance of Sales Returns and Allowances is a debit, the opposite of the normal balance of Sales, a credit.

A business could debit the sales account for the amount of a return or allowance. However, better information is provided if these amounts are debited to Sales Returns and Allowances. This contra account enables management to quickly identify if the amount of sales returns and allowances compared to sales is greater than expected.

JOURNALIZING SALES RETURNS AND ALLOWANCES

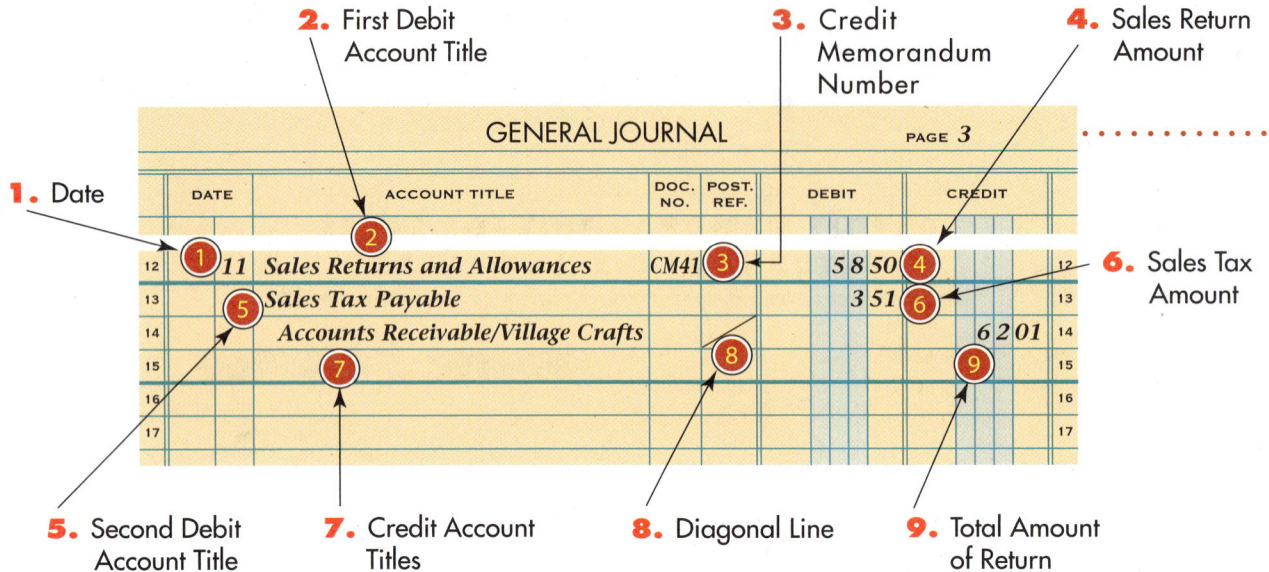

On March 8, Hobby Shack sold merchandise on account to Village Crafts for $503.50 ($475.00 sales plus $28.50 sales tax). Later, Village Crafts returned part of the merchandise. The sales return reduces the amount owed by Village Crafts by $62.01.

> **March 11.** Granted credit to Village Crafts for merchandise returned, $58.50, plus sales tax, $3.51, from S160; total, $62.01. Credit Memorandum No. 41.

Sales Returns and Allowances	
Mar. 11 58.50	

Sales Tax Payable	
Mar. 11 3.51	Mar. 8 28.50

Accounts Receivable	
Mar. 8 503.50	Mar. 11 62.01

STEPS JOURNALIZING SALES RETURNS AND ALLOWANCES

① Write the date, *11*, in the Date column.

② Write *Sales Returns and Allowances* in the Account Title column.

③ Write *CM* and the credit memorandum number, *41*, in the Doc. No. column.

④ Write the amount of the sales return, *$58.50*, in the Debit column.

⑤ Write *Sales Tax Payable* on the next line in the Account Title column.

⑥ Write the sales tax amount, *$3.51*, in the Debit column.

⑦ On the next line, indented about 1 centimeter, write the accounts to be credited, *Accounts Receivable/Village Crafts*, in the Account Title column. Hobby Shack's procedures for keeping records of the amounts to be collected from each customer are described in Chapter 11.

⑧ Draw a diagonal line in the Post. Ref. column.

⑨ Write the total accounts receivable amount, *$62.01*, in the Credit column.

End of Lesson REVIEW

AUDIT YOUR UNDERSTANDING

TERMS REVIEW

sales return
sales allowance
credit memorandum

1. What is the difference between a sales return and a sales allowance?
2. What is the source document for journalizing sales returns and allowances?
3. What general ledger accounts are affected, and how, by a sales returns and allowances transaction?
4. Why are sales returns and allowances not debited to the Sales account?

WORK TOGETHER 10-3

Journalizing sales returns and allowances using a general journal

The general journal for Cline Interiors is given in the *Working Papers*. Your instructor will guide you through the following examples.

1. Using the current year, journalize the following transactions on page 6 of a general journal. Source documents are abbreviated as: credit memorandum, CM; sales invoice, S.

Transactions:

June 3. Granted credit to Wilbanks and Associates for merchandise returned, $457.00, plus sales tax, $36.56, from S356; total, $493.56. CM41.
6. Granted credit to Westfall High School for damaged merchandise, $67.00 (no sales tax), from S345. CM42.

ON YOUR OWN 10-3

Journalizing sales returns and allowances using a general journal

The general journal for City Lighting is given in the *Working Papers*. Work this problem independently.

1. Using the current year, journalize the following transactions on page 7 of a general journal. Source documents are abbreviated as: credit memorandum, CM; sales invoice, S.

Transactions:

July 3. Granted credit to Carver High School for damaged merchandise, $46.00 (no sales tax), from S642. CM86.
4. Granted credit to Karen's Fine Gifts for merchandise returned, $425.00, plus sales tax, $25.50, from S623; total, $450.50. CM87.

SUMMARY

After completing this chapter, you can:

1. Define accounting terms related to sales and cash receipts for a merchandising business.
2. Identify accounting concepts and practices related to sales and cash receipts for a merchandising business.
3. Journalize sales on account using a sales journal.
4. Journalize cash receipts using a cash receipts journal.
5. Journalize sales returns and allowances using a general journal.

EXPLORE ACCOUNTING

Journalizing Sales Discounts

Most sales of a merchandising business are to individuals for cash or credit card. Individual customers are expected to pay the full amount of the invoice at the time of the sale. In contrast, sales on account to business customers may involve a cash discount, such as 2/10, n/30. As discussed in Chapter 9, businesses often receive cash discounts to encourage early payment for a sale on account.

Sales on account that involve both sales taxes and a cash discount present an interesting accounting problem. Assume Country Crafters purchases $100.00 of merchandise, plus $6.00 sales tax, for a total sale of $106.00, with 2/10, n/30 payment terms. Nine days later, Country Crafters pays $103.88 in full payment of the invoice. How should the cash receipt be journalized?

Because the payment is received within the discount period, the sales amount is reduced by the amount of the sales discount, $2.12. The amount of sales tax should also be reduced because the amount of the sale is reduced. Thus, the following journal entry should be recorded:

Cash	103.88	
Sales Tax Payable	.12	
Sales Discount	2.00	
Accounts Receivable		106.00

The net sales amount is $98.00—the original $100.00 sales less a 2% discount of $2.00. The net sales tax payable is $5.88—the original $6.00 sales tax less a 2% discount of $0.12. The end result is that a $98.00 sale was made on which $5.88 sales tax ($98.00 × 6%) was collected.

It is critically important for accounting employees to be familiar with sales tax laws in the states in which their companies do business. Each state regulates how sales taxes should be paid. In some states, state regulations require that sales taxes be paid only on actual sales realized—$5.88 for this transaction. Merchandising businesses in these states might modify the cash receipts journal to include a Sales Tax Payable Debit column.

In some states, sales taxes must be paid on the original invoice amount of sale—$6.00 for this transaction. In these states, a sales discount would not result in a reduction in the sales tax liability. The following journal entry would be recorded:

Cash	103.88	
Sales Discount	2.12	
Accounts Receivable		106.00

Instructions: With your instructor's permission, contact several local businesses to determine how they account for cash discounts on sales on account. Specifically, ask the manager (1) does the business offer cash discounts and (2) how do sales returns impact the amount of sales tax paid to the state.

10-1 APPLICATION PROBLEM

Journalizing sales on account; proving and ruling a sales journal

Audio Engineering is an electronics store specializing in sound systems.

Instructions:

1. Journalize the following transactions completed during September of the current year on page 10 of the sales journal given in the *Working Papers*. The sales invoice source document is abbreviated as S.

Transactions:

Sep. 2. Sold merchandise on account to Ketchum Clothing, $457.50, plus sales tax, $27.45; total, $484.95. S134.
     5. Sold merchandise on account to Norton Industries, $345.00, plus sales tax, $20.70; total, $365.70. S135.
    10. Sold merchandise on account to Jackson City Schools, $426.00. Jackson City Schools is exempt from paying sales tax. S136.
    17. Sold merchandise on account to Riley & Slay, CPAs, $522.00, plus sales tax, $31.32; total, $553.32. S137.
    23. Sold merchandise on account to Meadowbrook Church, $453.00. Meadowbrook Church is exempt from paying sales tax. S138.
    30. Sold merchandise on account to Tang Construction, $512.00, plus sales tax, $30.72; total, $542.72. S139.

2. Total, prove, and rule page 10 of the sales journal.

10-2 APPLICATION PROBLEM

Journalizing cash receipts; proving and ruling a cash receipts journal

In Focus is a camera and film shop.

Instructions:

1. Journalize the following transactions completed during August of the current year on page 15 of the cash receipts journal given in the *Working Papers*. Source documents are abbreviated as follows: receipt, R; terminal summary, TS.

Transactions:

Aug. 1. Received cash on account from Reader Advertising, $345.60, covering S357. R288.
     3. Recorded cash and credit card sales, $2,534.00, plus sales tax, $145.54; total, $2,679.54. TS28.
     8. Received cash on account from WXGS Television, $312.60, covering S358. R289.
    10. Recorded cash and credit card sales, $2,650.00, plus sales tax, $140.80; total, $2,790.80. TS29.
    15. Received cash on account from Lambert News, covering S360 for $204.30, less 2% discount. R290.
    17. Recorded cash and credit card sales, $2,372.00, plus sales tax, $132.43; total, $2,504.43. TS30.
    24. Received cash on account from Kelly Modeling Agency, $236.96, covering S359. R291.
    24. Recorded cash and credit card sales, $3,180.00, plus sales tax, $170.80; total, $3,350.80. TS31.
    30. Received cash on account from JGN Industries, covering S361 for $201.40, less 2% discount. R292.
    31. Recorded cash and credit card sales, $2,100.00, plus sales tax, $104.25; total, $2,204.25. TS32.

2. Total and prove the equality of debits and credits for cash receipts journal page 15.

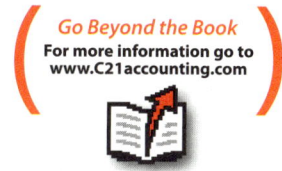

Go Beyond the Book
For more information go to
www.C21accounting.com

3. Prove cash. The August 1 cash account balance in the general ledger was $2,548.25. The August 31 cash credit total in the cash payments journal was $15,485.25. On August 31, the balance on the next unused check stub was $1,885.56.
4. Rule page 15 of the cash receipts journal.

10-3 APPLICATION PROBLEM

Journalizing sales returns and allowances using a general journal

VanHorn Designs sells custom logo products.

Instructions:
1. Journalize the following transactions affecting sales completed during July of the current year. Use page 14 of the general journal given in the *Working Papers*. Source documents are abbreviated as follows: credit memorandum, CM; receipt, R; sales invoice, S.

Transactions:
July 2. Granted credit to Tahai Industries for merchandise returned, $253.00, plus sales tax, $15.18, from S456; total, $268.18. CM61.
   4. Granted credit to Allergy Associates for damaged merchandise, $235.00, plus sales tax, $14.10, from S455; total, $249.10. CM62.
   12. Granted credit to Jefferson School for damaged merchandise, $134.25, from S458. CM63.

10-4 MASTERY PROBLEM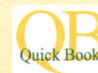

Journalizing sales and cash receipts transactions; proving and ruling journals

Aqua Center installs and maintains swimming pools and spas.
Use page 19 of a sales journal, page 20 of a cash receipts journal, and page 14 of a general journal. Balances brought forward are provided on line 1 of each journal in the *Working Papers*.

Instructions:
1. Journalize the following transactions completed during the remainder of October in the appropriate journal. The sales tax rate is 4%. Source documents are abbreviated as follows: receipt, R; sales invoice, S; terminal summary, TS.

Transactions:
Oct. 26. Received cash on account from Slumber Inns, covering S435 for $1,356.00, less a 2% discount. R293.
   27. Sold merchandise on account to County Hospital, $489.50, plus sales tax, $19.58; total, $509.08. S443.
   28. Recorded cash and credit card sales, $4,315.00, plus sales tax, $126.60; total, $4,441.60. TS44.
   29. Received cash on account from Summit Lodge, $467.24, covering S438. R294.
   29. Granted credit to Slumber Inns for merchandise returned, $124.00, plus sales tax, $4.96, from S293; total, $128.96. CM54.
   30. Sold merchandise on account to Southeastern University, $3,643.50. Southeastern University is exempt from sales tax. S444.
   31. Recorded cash and credit card sales, $1,232.00, plus sales tax, $42.22; total, $1,274.22. TS45.

2. Total and prove the equality of debits and credits for the sales journal.
3. Rule the sales journal.
4. Total and prove the equality of debits and credits for the cash receipts journal.
5. Prove cash. The October 1 cash account balance in the general ledger was $4,483.25. The October 31 cash credit total in the cash payments journal was $39,315.22. On October 31, the balance on the next unused check stub was $8,918.50.
6. Rule the cash receipts journal.

10-5 CHALLENGE PROBLEM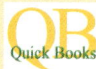

Journalizing transactions; proving and ruling special journals

Zone 6 is a lawn and garden store.

Instructions:

1. Journalize in the appropriate journal the following transactions completed during May of the current year. Use page 5 of a purchases and sales journal, page 8 of a cash payments journal, page 9 of a cash receipts journal, and page 7 of a general journal given in the *Working Papers*. The sales tax rate is 8%. Calculate and add the appropriate sales tax amount to each sale. Source documents are abbreviated as follows: check, C; credit memorandum, CM; purchase invoice, P; receipt, R; sales invoice, S; terminal summary, TS.

Transactions:

May 1. Paid cash for rent, $1,400.00. C344.
3. Paid cash for electric bill, $186.00. C345.
3. Granted credit to Slippery Rock Inn for merchandise returned, $235.00, plus sales tax, $18.80, from S493; total, $253.80. CM67.
3. Purchased merchandise on account from Angelo Lawn Supplies, $1,340.00. P91.
4. Bought $120.00 worth of store supplies on account from Mosby Store Supplies, recorded on Memo 43, with 2/10, n/30 payment terms.
4. Paid cash on account to Northeast Nurseries, $7,632.00, covering P87. C346.
4. Sold merchandise on account to First National Bank, $546.00, plus sales tax. S567.
5. Bought office supplies for cash, $35.45. C347.
5. Paid cash for some merchandise, $89.40. C348.
6. Recorded cash and credit card sales, $3,235.00, plus sales tax of $239.40. TS23.
7. Received an invoice, stamped Purchase Invoice 92, for merchandise on account from Forde Collectibles for $3,250.00, less a 60% trade discount.
7. Houston Landscaping paid its $545.65 balance, less 2% discount. R490.
8. Bought office supplies on account from Office Mart, $81.60. M44.
10. Returned $260.00 of the merchandise purchased on Purchase Invoice 92 to Forde Collectibles, recorded on Debit Memorandum 23.
11. Paid the remaining balance of Purchase Invoice 92, less Debit Memorandum 23, to Forde Collectibles with Check No. 349, taking advantage of the 2/10, n/30 payment terms.
13. Cash and credit card sales for the week were $3,216.00, plus sales tax of $206.70. TS24.
14. Jackson Public Schools bought merchandise on account for $450.00. S568.
16. Purchased $2,900.00 of merchandise on account from Tom's Sod Farm on Purchase Invoice 93, with 2/10, n/30 payment terms.
17. Paid cash on account to Office Mart, $81.60, covering M44. C350.
20. Cash and credit card sales for the week were $2,554.00, plus sales tax, $184.23. TS25.
22. First National Bank paid $589.68 cash on its account, covering S567. R491.
23. SDR Investment Trust bought merchandise on account for $1,456.00, plus sales tax. S569.
23. Purchased merchandise on account from LawnScapes, Inc., $4,488.00. P94.
25. Paid $102.00 cash for advertising. C351.
27. Cash and credit card sales for the week were $2,742.00, plus sales tax, $184.25. TS26.
29. Slippery Rock Inn paid $2,345.64 on its account, covering S493. R492.
29. Granted credit to SDR Investment Trust for damaged merchandise, $45.00, plus sales tax, from S455. CM68.
31. Paid cash to replenish the petty cash fund, $361.60: office supplies, $74.40; store supplies, $85.00; advertising, $105.00; miscellaneous, $96.00. C352.
31. Recorded cash and credit card sales, $768.00, plus sales tax, $49.45. TS27.

2. Total the purchases, cash payments, sales, and cash receipts journals.
3. Prove the equality of debits and credits for the cash payments, sales, and cash receipts journals.
4. Prove cash. The May 1 cash account balance in the general ledger was $2,464.60. On May 31, the balance on the next unused check stub was $8,406.44.
5. Rule the purchases, cash payments, sales, and cash receipts journals.

APPLIED COMMUNICATION

The tendency for prices to increase over time is referred to as *inflation*. Increasing prices reduce what an individual or company can purchase with the same amount of money.

Instructions: The following table represents the prices for selected consumer goods in 1990. Copy the table and add a column for the current year and a column for the percent of change. Use the newspaper and identify current prices for the products listed. Determine the percentage change in the price of each item. If an item decreased in price, can you explain the reason for the decrease?

Comparison of Prices for Selected Consumer Items

Item	1990 Price
19-inch color television	$149.00
Cassette tape	13.50
Milk (gallon)	1.99
Ground beef (pound)	1.69
Eggs, medium (dozen)	.99
Raisin bran	1.99
Film, 24 exposures	3.88
Theater ticket	6.50
Motor oil (quart)	.84
Refrigerator (19.1 cu. ft.)	790.00

CASE FOR CRITICAL THINKING

Roshonda Compton, an accountant for an office supplies store, has noted a major increase in overdue amounts from charge customers. All invoice amounts from sales on account are due within 30 days. The amounts due have reduced the amount of cash available for the day-to-day operation of the business. Ms. Compton recommends that the business (1) stop all sales on account and (2) begin accepting bank credit cards. The owner is reluctant to accept the recommendations because the business might lose some reliable customers who do not have credit cards. Also, the business will have increased expenses because of the credit card fee. How would you respond to Ms. Compton's recommendations? What alternatives might the owner consider?

SCANS WORKPLACE COMPETENCY

Basic Skill: Reading

Concept: Employers need employees at all levels who can read well. Reading includes locating, understanding, and interpreting written information. The written information may be in documents such as manuals, graphs, schedules, or even in software "Help" windows.

Application: Open a software application with which you are familiar, such as word processing, spreadsheet, or accounting software. Using either printed documentation or the Help function of the software, locate a software feature with which you are not familiar. Read the document and create a file in which you can practice applying this previously unknown feature. Write a statement about situations in which this new feature could save time.

USING SOURCE DOCUMENTS

Journalizing sales and cash receipts transactions; proving and ruling journals

Golfer's Paradise sells golf and other recreational equipment. Source documents related to the sales and cash receipts are provided in the *Working Papers*.

Sales journal page 18, cash receipts journal page 24, and general journal page 15 for Golfer's Paradise are given in the *Working Papers*. Balances brought forward are provided on line 1 of each journal.

Instructions

1. Journalize the transactions shown in the source documents in the appropriate journal. The sales tax rate is 8%.
2. Total and prove the equality of debits and credits for the sales journal.
3. Rule the sales journal.
4. Total and prove the equality of debits and credits for the cash receipts journal.
5. Prove cash. The November 1 cash account balance in the general ledger was $2,551.18. The November 30 cash credit total in the cash payments journal was $49,158.84. On November 30, the balance on the next unused check stub was $5,106.41.
6. Rule the cash receipts journal.

ANALYZING BEST BUY'S FINANCIAL STATEMENTS

Comparable store sales—the sales at stores open for more than a year—is one of the best measures of financial success for a retail business. An increase in comparable store sales can be achieved by a combination of raising unit sales prices and selling more units. Regardless of the reason, an increase in comparable store sales demonstrates that the company's products are in demand.

Instructions

1. Use Best Buy's 5-Year Financial Highlights on page B-2 in Appendix B to identify the comparable store sales change for 2005–2007.
2. Use the 5-Year Financial Highlights to identify the types and number of stores open at the end of 2006 and 2007.

Accounting SOFTWARE

SALES AND CASH RECEIPTS

Accounting software enables you to create a sales invoice by entering sales information directly into the computer. Peachtree provides you with a computer screen that closely resembles a paper sales invoice. Peachtree enhances the process by assigning a document number, automatically entering a transaction date, providing you with a list of customers and inventory items, and calculating the total sale. These features increase the efficiency of creating a sales invoice and reduce the number of errors.

PEACHTREE MASTERY PROBLEM 10-4
1. Open (Restore) file 10-4MP.ptb.
2. Use the Receipts task to journalize and record cash receipts transactions. (Peachtree will automatically debit Cash; the offsetting credit goes to Sales or the account you specify.)
3. Use the Sales/Invoicing task to record a credit sale. (Peachtree automatically debits the customer's account and Accounts Receivable; the credit side defaults to Sales.)
4. Use the Credit Memos task to record sales returns. This transaction will post to the Sales Journal.
5. Print the sales journal from the Reports, Accounts Receivable Report List.
6. Print the cash receipts journal from the Report List.

PEACHTREE CHALLENGE PROBLEM 10-5
1. Open (Restore) file 10-5CP.ptb.
2. Record sales and cash receipts. The sales tax rate is 8%.
3. Print the purchase journal, cash disbursements journal, sales journal, and cash receipts journal.

SALES AND CASH RECEIPTS

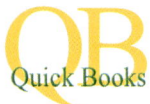

New screens will be used to record receiving cash on account, selling merchandise on account, recording cash and credit card sales, granting credit for sales returns, and making cash payments. By filling in all the data required on these screens, the report generated will have much more information than can be provided by special journals. QuickBooks also provides many shortcuts to make entering the data more efficient and accurate. Dropdown lists are available for account titles and customer and vendor names. The software program automatically fills in much of the data on many screens.

QUICKBOOKS MASTERY PROBLEM 10-4
1. Open the Aqua Center file.
2. Use the Receive Payment option from the Customers menu to record payments on account.
3. Use the Create Invoices option from the Customers menu to record sales on account.
4. Use the Enter Sales Receipts window to record cash and credit card sales.
5. Record customer returns in the Create Credit Memos/Refunds feature.
6. Print a Journal report.

QUICKBOOKS CHALLENGE PROBLEM 10-5
1. Open the Zone file.
2. Use the Enter Bills and Pay Bills features to record purchases, payments, and vendor returns on account.
3. Use the Receive Payments and Create Invoices features to record cash receipts and sales on account.
4. Use the Create Credit Memos/Returns feature to record customer returns.
5. Use the Write Checks feature to record cash payments.
6. Use the Enter Sales Receipts feature to record cash and credit card sales.
7. Print a Journal report, a Customer Balance Summary report, a Vendor Balance Summary report, and a Trial Balance report.

SORTING AND FILTERING DATA

Effective managers use sales information to understand sales trends and target potential customers. In other words, sales information should be used to help increase sales. The sales journal reports sales for a period of time. Knowing the customers involved in the largest sales can provide managers with ideas to increase sales to other customers. Managers can learn how these sales were made and apply that knowledge when making sales to other customers.

Electronic spreadsheets have the ability to sort and filter data. Data can be sorted in ascending or descending order by numbers or text. Filters display the information that meets certain criteria, such as amounts that are greater than 10,000.

OPTIONAL SPREADSHEET ACTIVITY
Open the file F10-OPT. Complete the instructions provided to sort and filter the sales data.

SALES AND CASH RECEIPTS

To record transactions in the sales journal
1. Enter the transaction date.
2. Enter the invoice number in the Refer. column.
3. Enter the amount of the invoice in the Sales Credit column. The Accounts Receivable debit amount is calculated and displayed automatically.
4. If the transaction involves sales tax, enter the amount in the Sales Tax Credit column.
5. Choose a customer name from the Customer drop-down list.
6. Click the Post button.

The cash receipts journal is used to enter all cash receipt transactions. The debit to cash is automatically calculated and displayed by the computer. There are two types of cash receipts:
- Cash and credit card sales are cash receipts that do not affect Accounts Receivable.
- Receipts on account are cash receipts that do affect Accounts Receivable.

To record transactions in the cash receipts journal
1. Enter the transaction date.
2. Enter the transaction reference.
3. If recording a cash or credit card sale, enter the sales amount of the merchandise sold. Enter the amount of sales tax in the Sales Tax Payable Credit column. The debit to Cash is automatically calculated and displayed.
4. If recording a receipt on account, enter the amount in the A.R. Credit column. Choose the customer from the Customer drop-down list.
5. Click the Post button.

AUTOMATED ACCOUNTING APPLICATION PROBLEM 10-2
Open file F10-2.AA8. Display the problem instructions and complete the problem.

AUTOMATED ACCOUNTING MASTERY PROBLEM 10-4
Open file F10-4.AA8. Display the problem instructions and complete the problem.

CHAPTER 11

Posting to General and Subsidiary Ledgers

OBJECTIVES

After studying Chapter 11, you will be able to:

1. Define accounting terms related to posting to ledgers.
2. Identify accounting practices related to posting to ledgers.
3. Post separate items from a purchases, cash payments, and general journal to an accounts payable ledger.
4. Post separate items from a sales, cash receipts, and general journal to an accounts receivable ledger.
5. Post separate items from a cash payments and general journal to a general ledger.
6. Post special journal column totals to a general ledger.
7. Journalize and post correcting entries affecting customer accounts.

KEY TERMS

- subsidiary ledger
- accounts payable ledger
- accounts receivable ledger
- controlling account
- schedule of accounts payable
- schedule of accounts receivable

Point Your Browser
www.C21accounting.com

ACCOUNTING IN THE REAL WORLD

eBay, Inc.

eBay Conquers the Online Marketplace

Cleaning out your closet and finding things you don't need? Don't trash it, eBay it!

From its beginning in 1995, eBay has become an integral part of today's society, boasting 222 million registered users as of December 31, 2006. Innovative thinking has fueled eBay's dynamic growth of its online marketplace, where individuals and businesses bought and sold a staggering $52 billion worth of goods during 2006.

eBay is more than just an online marketplace. The company has been quick to identify and purchase companies that have developed services that take advantage of the Internet. PayPal, purchased in 2002, provides a platform for the online payment of eBay transactions. Purchased in 2005, Skype provides voice and video communications. Shopping.com provides comparison shopping for new products, and Rent.com lists apartments from more than 20,000 properties.

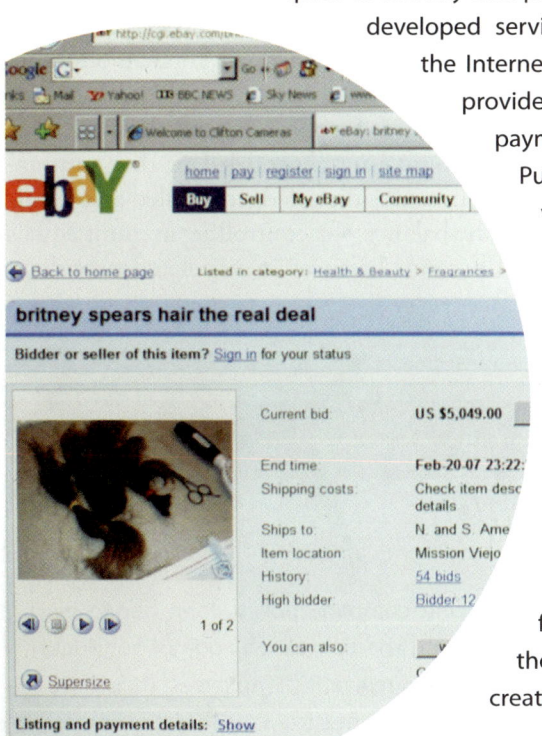

With every change in its business, eBay must change its accounting system. New accounts and different methods for combining those accounts are required to create financial statements.

Critical Thinking

1. Many businesses begin as a sole proprietorship and later transform into a corporation. What changes might occur in the chart of accounts when a business changes from being a sole proprietorship to a corporation?
2. Identify another business that has experienced changes in its corporate structure. What motivated the change(s)?

Source: http://pages.ebay.com/aboutebay/thecompany/companyoverview.html

INTERNET ACTIVITY

AICPA—Student Resources

Go to the homepage for the American Institute of Certified Public Accountants (AICPA) (www.aicpa.org).

Instructions

1. Search for "Accounting Fun Facts." Find and list three of the fun facts given.
2. Click on the "About the AICPA" link. Under the "Frequently Asked Questions (FAQ)" link, read through the questions and answers. List one question and summarize the answer to the question.

LESSON 11-1: Posting to an Accounts Payable Ledger

LEDGERS AND CONTROLLING ACCOUNTS

A business's size, number of transactions, and type of transactions determine the number of ledgers used in an accounting system.

General Ledger
Hobby Shack's general ledger chart of accounts is on page 231. However, because of the business's size and the number and type of transactions, Hobby Shack also uses additional ledgers in its accounting system.

Subsidiary Ledgers
A business needs to know the amount owed each vendor as well as the amount to be collected from each charge customer. Therefore, a separate account is needed for each vendor and each customer. Hobby Shack keeps a separate ledger for vendors and a separate ledger for customers.

Each separate ledger is summarized in a single general ledger account. A ledger that is summarized in a single general ledger account is called a **subsidiary ledger**. A subsidiary ledger containing only accounts for vendors from whom merchandise or other items are purchased on account is called an **accounts payable ledger**. A subsidiary ledger containing only accounts for charge customers is called an **accounts receivable ledger**. Total amounts are summarized in single general ledger accounts: Accounts Payable for vendors and Accounts Receivable for charge customers. An account in a general ledger that summarizes all accounts in a subsidiary ledger is called a **controlling account**. The balance of a controlling account equals the total of all account balances in its related subsidiary ledger.

CHARACTER COUNTS

Whose Computer Is It Really?

John Melton is an accounting manager at Stegall Industries. John frequently walks through his department to make himself readily available for his employees to ask questions and provide feedback. With increasing frequency, John has observed that his employees have Internet auction sites open while they are working on their computers. Concerned that productivity in his department is suffering, he is considering installing some sort of monitoring system to gather evidence of the employees' computer usage.

In accordance with company policy, John began his planning by examining the company's code of conduct. Two statements appear relevant: "Employees should be treated with mutual respect, free from the threat of harassment and discrimination."

"Employees may occasionally use company computer systems, such as Internet and e-mail, for personal use. Such use should be on a limited basis and should not result in a measurable cost to the Company."

Instructions
Use the ethical model to evaluate John's proposed action to monitor his employees' Internet usage. Do you have any recommendations for John?

ACCOUNTS PAYABLE LEDGER AND GENERAL LEDGER CONTROLLING ACCOUNT

Hobby Shack assigns a vendor number to each account in the accounts payable ledger. A three-digit number is used. The first digit identifies the division in which the controlling account appears in the general ledger. The second two digits show each account's location within a subsidiary ledger. Accounts are assigned by 10s, beginning with the second digit. Accounts in the subsidiary ledgers can be located by either number or name.

The vendor number for American Paint is 210. The first digit, *2*, shows that the controlling account is a liability, Accounts Payable. The second and third digits, *10*, show the vendor number assigned to American Paint.

The procedure for adding new accounts to subsidiary ledgers is the same as described for TechKnow Consulting's general ledger in Chapter 4. Accounts are arranged in alphabetical order within the subsidiary ledgers. New accounts are assigned an unused middle number. If the proper alphabetical order places a new account as the last account, the next number in the sequence of 10s is assigned. Hobby Shack's chart of accounts for the subsidiary ledgers is on page 231.

When the balance of a vendor account in an accounts payable ledger is changed, the balance of the controlling account, Accounts Payable, is also changed. The total of all vendor account balances in the accounts payable ledger equals the balance of the controlling account, Accounts Payable.

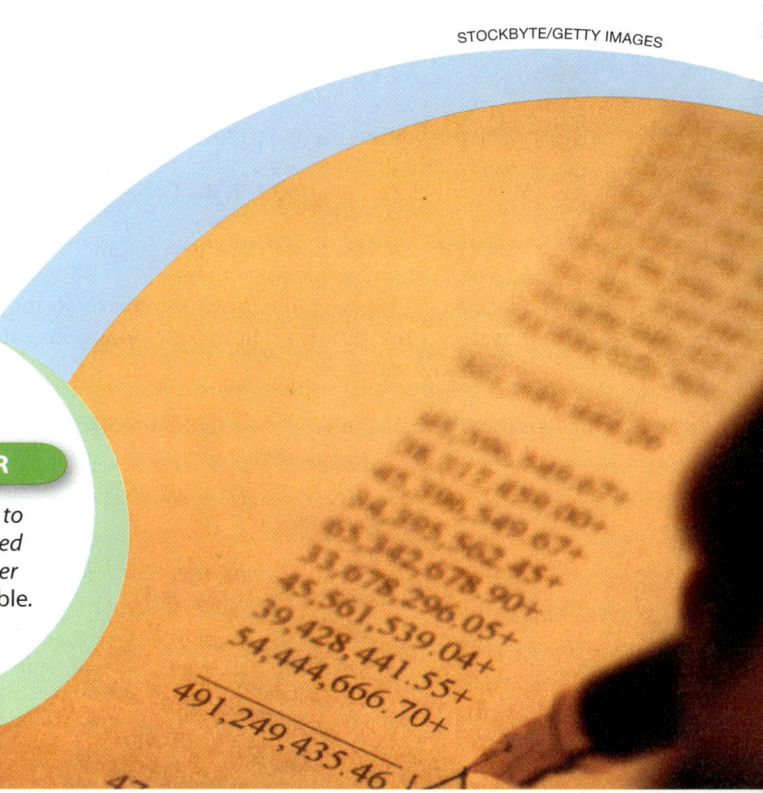

STOCKBYTE/GETTY IMAGES

REMEMBER

The total amount owed to all vendors is summarized in a single general ledger account, Accounts Payable.

Posting to an Accounts Payable Ledger   Lesson 11-1

ACCOUNTS PAYABLE LEDGER FORMS

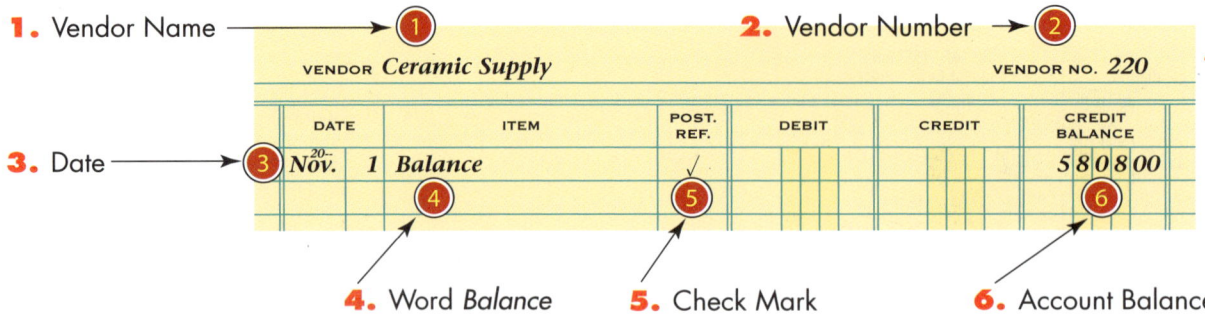

1. Vendor Name
2. Vendor Number
3. Date
4. Word *Balance*
5. Check Mark
6. Account Balance

Hobby Shack uses a 3-column accounts payable subsidiary account form. Information to be recorded in the accounts payable ledger includes the date, posting reference, debit or credit amount, and new account balance. Accounts payable are liabilities and have normal credit balances. Therefore, a Debit Balance column is usually not included in the accounts payable ledger accounts.

Each new account is opened by:

1. Writing the vendor name on the heading of the ledger account.
2. Writing the vendor number on the heading of the ledger account.

The vendor name is obtained from the first purchase invoice received. The vendor number is assigned using the three-digit numbering system previously described.

Some businesses record both the vendor name and vendor address on the ledger form. However, the address information is usually kept in a separate name and address file. This practice eliminates having to record the vendor address on the ledger form each time a new ledger page is opened or the address changes.

The number of entries that may be recorded on each account form depends on the number of lines provided. When all lines have been used, a new page is prepared. The vendor name, vendor number, and account balance are recorded on the new page.

On November 1, Hobby Shack prepared a new page for Ceramic Supply in the accounts payable ledger because the existing page was full. On that day, the account balance was $5,808.00.

STEPS STARTING A NEW PAGE IN THE ACCOUNTS PAYABLE LEDGER

1. Write the vendor name, *Ceramic Supply*, on the Vendor line.
2. Write the vendor number, *220*, on the Vendor No. line.
3. Write the date, *20--, Nov. 1*, in the Date column.
4. Write the word *Balance* in the Item column.
5. Place a check mark in the Post. Ref. column to show that the amount has been carried forward from a previous page rather than posted from a journal.
6. Write the balance, *$5,808.00*, in the Credit Balance column.

> **REMEMBER**
>
> *A new vendor account is opened by writing the vendor name and vendor number on the heading of the ledger account and placing it in alphabetical order.*

POSTING FROM A PURCHASES JOURNAL TO AN ACCOUNTS PAYABLE LEDGER

Each entry in the purchases journal affects the account of the vendor named in the Account Credited column. The amount on each line of a purchases journal is posted as a credit to a vendor account in the accounts payable ledger. Hobby Shack posts frequently to the accounts payable ledger. Posting frequently keeps each vendor account balance up to date.

STEPS POSTING FROM A PURCHASES JOURNAL TO AN ACCOUNTS PAYABLE LEDGER

1. Write the date, *20--, Nov. 2*, in the Date column of the vendor account.

2. Write the journal page number, *P11*, in the Post. Ref. column of the account. When several journals are used, an abbreviation is used to show the journal from which the posting is made. *P* is the abbreviation used for the purchases journal. The abbreviation *P11* means page 11 of the purchases journal.

3. Write the credit amount, *$2,039.00*, in the Credit column of the account for *Crown Distributing*.

4. Add the amount in the Credit column to the previous balance in the Credit Balance column. (*Crown Distributing* has no previous balance; therefore, $0 + $2,039.00 = $2,039.00.) Write the new account balance, *$2,039.00*, in the Credit Balance column.

5. Write the vendor number, *230*, in the Post. Ref. column of the journal. The vendor number shows that the posting for this entry is complete.

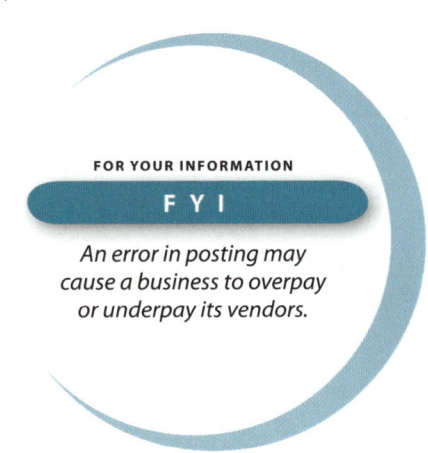

FOR YOUR INFORMATION

FYI

An error in posting may cause a business to overpay or underpay its vendors.

Posting to an Accounts Payable Ledger Lesson 11-1 **301**

POSTING FROM A CASH PAYMENTS JOURNAL TO AN ACCOUNTS PAYABLE LEDGER

Each entry in the Accounts Payable Debit column of a cash payments journal affects a vendor account. Individual amounts in the Accounts Payable Debit column are posted frequently to the proper vendor account in the accounts payable ledger. Posting frequently keeps each vendor account balance up to date.

STEPS: POSTING FROM A CASH PAYMENTS JOURNAL TO AN ACCOUNTS PAYABLE LEDGER

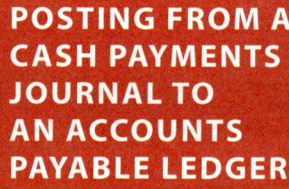

1. Write the date, 7, in the Date column of the vendor account.

2. Write the journal page number, CP21, in the Post. Ref. column of the account. The abbreviation CP21 means page 21 of the cash payments journal.

3. Write the debit amount, $1,050.00, in the Debit column of the vendor account.

4. Subtract the amount in the Debit column from the previous balance in the Credit Balance column ($4,866.00 − $1,050.00 = $3,816.00). Write the new balance, $3,816.00, in the Credit Balance column.

5. Write the vendor number, 260, in the Post. Ref. column of the cash payments journal.

POSTING CREDIT AND DEBIT ENTRIES FROM A GENERAL JOURNAL TO AN ACCOUNTS PAYABLE LEDGER

Entries in a general journal may affect account balances in a general ledger and an accounts payable ledger. Posting from a general journal to a general ledger is described on pages 317–318.

STEPS: POSTING DEBIT AND CREDIT ENTRIES FROM A GENERAL JOURNAL TO AN ACCOUNTS PAYABLE LEDGER

POSTING A CREDIT ENTRY FOR SUPPLIES BOUGHT ON ACCOUNT

1. Write the date, *Nov. 6*, in the Date column of the vendor account.
2. Write the general journal page number, *G11*, in the Post. Ref. column of the account. The abbreviation *G11* means page 11 of the general journal.
3. Write the amount, *$210.00*, in the Credit column of the vendor account.
4. Add the amount in the Credit column to the previous balance in the Credit Balance column ($498.00 + $210.00 = $708.00). Write the new balance, *$708.00*, in the Credit Balance column.
5. Write the vendor number, *250*, to the right of the diagonal line in the Post. Ref. column of the general journal.

POSTING A DEBIT ENTRY FOR A PURCHASES RETURN OR ALLOWANCE

1. Write the date, *28*, in the Date column of the vendor account.
2. Write the general journal page number, *G11*, in the Post. Ref. column of the account.
3. Write the amount, *$252.00*, in the Debit column of the vendor account.
4. Subtract the amount in the Debit column from the previous balance in the Credit Balance column ($2,039.00 − $252.00 = $1,787.00). Write the new balance, *$1,787.00*, in the Credit Balance column.
5. Write the vendor number, *230*, to the right of the diagonal line in the Post. Ref. column of the general journal.

Posting to an Accounts Payable Ledger

COMPLETED ACCOUNTS PAYABLE LEDGER

VENDOR American Paint **VENDOR NO.** 210

DATE	ITEM	POST. REF.	DEBIT	CREDIT	CREDIT BALANCE
Nov. 20-- 1	Balance	✓			2 650 00
13		P11		3 768 00	6 418 00
13		CP21	2 650 00		3 768 00
20		P11		3 377 88	7 145 88

VENDOR Ceramic Supply **VENDOR NO.** 220

DATE	ITEM	POST. REF.	DEBIT	CREDIT	CREDIT BALANCE
Nov. 20-- 1	Balance	✓			5 808 00
5		P11		4 147 20	9 955 20
20		CP21	5 808 00		4 147 20

VENDOR Crown Distributing **VENDOR NO.** 230

DATE	ITEM	POST. REF.	DEBIT	CREDIT	CREDIT BALANCE
Nov. 20-- 2		P11		2 039 00	2 039 00
28		G11	252 00		1 787 00

VENDOR Floral Designs **VENDOR NO.** 240

DATE	ITEM	POST. REF.	DEBIT	CREDIT	CREDIT BALANCE
Nov. 20-- 1	Balance	✓			744 00
23		CP22	744 00		—
24		G11		1 650 00	1 650 00
26		G11		996 00	2 646 00
30		CP22	1 650 00		996 00

VENDOR Gulf Craft Supply **VENDOR NO.** 250

DATE	ITEM	POST. REF.	DEBIT	CREDIT	CREDIT BALANCE
Nov. 20-- 1	Balance	✓			498 00
6		G11		210 00	708 00
8		CP21	498 00		210 00
23		G11		690 00	900 00

VENDOR Synthetic Arts **VENDOR NO.** 260

DATE	ITEM	POST. REF.	DEBIT	CREDIT	CREDIT BALANCE
Nov. 20-- 1	Balance	✓			1 050 00
5		P11		3 816 00	4 866 00
7		CP21	1 050 00		3 816 00

Hobby Shack's accounts payable ledger has been posted for the month of November.

PROVING THE ACCOUNTS PAYABLE LEDGER

Hobby Shack, Inc.
Schedule of Accounts Payable
November 30, 20--

American Paint	7 145 88
Ceramic Supply	4 147 20
Crown Distributing	1 787 00
Floral Designs	996 00
Gulf Craft Supply	900 00
Synthetic Arts	3 816 00
Total Accounts Payable	18 792 08

A controlling account balance in a general ledger must equal the sum of all account balances in a subsidiary ledger. Hobby Shack proves subsidiary ledgers at the end of each month.

A listing of vendor accounts, account balances, and total amount due all vendors is called a **schedule of accounts payable**. A schedule of accounts payable is prepared after all entries in a journal are posted. The balance of Accounts Payable in the general ledger is $18,792.08. The total of the schedule of accounts payable is $18,792.08. Because the two amounts are the same, the accounts payable ledger is proved.

GLOBAL PERSPECTIVE

The International Business Day

American business offices normally operate Monday through Friday, eight hours a day, with a 30- to 60-minute lunch break. This is not necessarily true in other countries, however. In the People's Republic of China, for example, employees usually work Monday through Saturday, eight hours a day, with lunch from 1:00 p.m. to 2:00 p.m.

When doing business internationally, both time zone differences and cultural factors affecting the business day must be taken into consideration. For example, in Spain, many businesses close at 2:00 p.m. so that employees may eat lunch with their families. The office reopens at 5:00 p.m. and stays open until about 8:00 p.m. Spain is in a time zone that is five hours ahead of Eastern Standard Time (EST), the time zone along the eastern coast of the United States. If doing business with a company in Spain, it would not be a good idea to try to call at 9:00 a.m. EST because the business might just be closing for lunch. A better time to call Spain from the EST time zone would be between noon and 3:00 p.m.

Critical Thinking

1. What are some ways you could reference time zones if you had to make frequent international phone calls?

2. If you work for a company with offices and customers all over the world, how could that affect the way you schedule projects?

Posting to an Accounts Payable Ledger   Lesson 11-1   **305**

End of Lesson REVIEW

TERMS REVIEW

- subsidiary ledger
- accounts payable ledger
- accounts receivable ledger
- controlling account
- schedule of accounts payable

AUDIT YOUR UNDERSTANDING

1. What is the relationship between a controlling account and a subsidiary ledger?
2. In which column of the cash payments journal are the amounts that are posted individually to the accounts payable ledger?

WORK TOGETHER 11-1

Posting to an accounts payable ledger

Partial purchases, cash payments, and general journals for Graphics, Inc., are given in the *Working Papers*. Also given in the *Working Papers* are accounts payable ledger account forms for selected accounts and a blank form for a schedule of accounts payable. Your instructor will guide you through the following examples.

1. Start a new page for an accounts payable ledger account for Regal Designs. The account number is 240 and the balance on October 1 of the current year is $877.00.
2. Post the Accounts Payable Credit entry on line 7 of the purchases journal to the accounts payable account for Regal Designs.
3. Post the Accounts Payable Debit entry on line 15 of the cash payments journal to the accounts payable account for Electro-Graphics Supply.
4. Post the credit entry on line 5 of the general journal to the accounts payable account for Electro-Graphics Supply. Post the debit entry on line 6 of the general journal to the accounts payable account for Art and Things.
5. Prepare a schedule of accounts payable for Graphics, Inc., on October 31 of the current year for these selected accounts. Accounts Payable balance in the general ledger on October 31 is $6,558.20. Save your work to complete Work Together 11-2, 11-3, and 11-4.

ON YOUR OWN 11-1

Posting to an accounts payable ledger

Partial purchases, cash payments, and general journals for Amatera, Inc., are given in the *Working Papers*. Also given in the *Working Papers* are accounts payable ledger account forms for selected accounts and a blank form for a schedule of accounts payable. Work this problem independently.

1. Start a new page for an accounts payable ledger account for Swann Industries. The account number is 240 and the balance on September 1 of the current year is $1,248.00.
2. Post the Accounts Payable Credit entry on line 11 of the purchases journal to the accounts payable account for Swann Industries.
3. Post the Accounts Payable Debit entry on line 19 of the cash payments journal to the accounts payable account for Miller Supply.
4. Post the credit entry on line 5 of the general journal to the accounts payable account for Miller Supply. Post the debit entry on line 6 of the general journal to the accounts payable account for Franklin Mfg. Corp.
5. Prepare a schedule of accounts payable for Amatera, Inc., on September 30 of the current year for these selected accounts. Accounts Payable balance in the general ledger on September 30 is $9,142.25. Save your work to complete On Your Own 11-2, 11-3, and 11-4.

LESSON 11-2

Posting to an Accounts Receivable Ledger

ACCOUNTS RECEIVABLE LEDGER AND GENERAL LEDGER CONTROLLING ACCOUNT

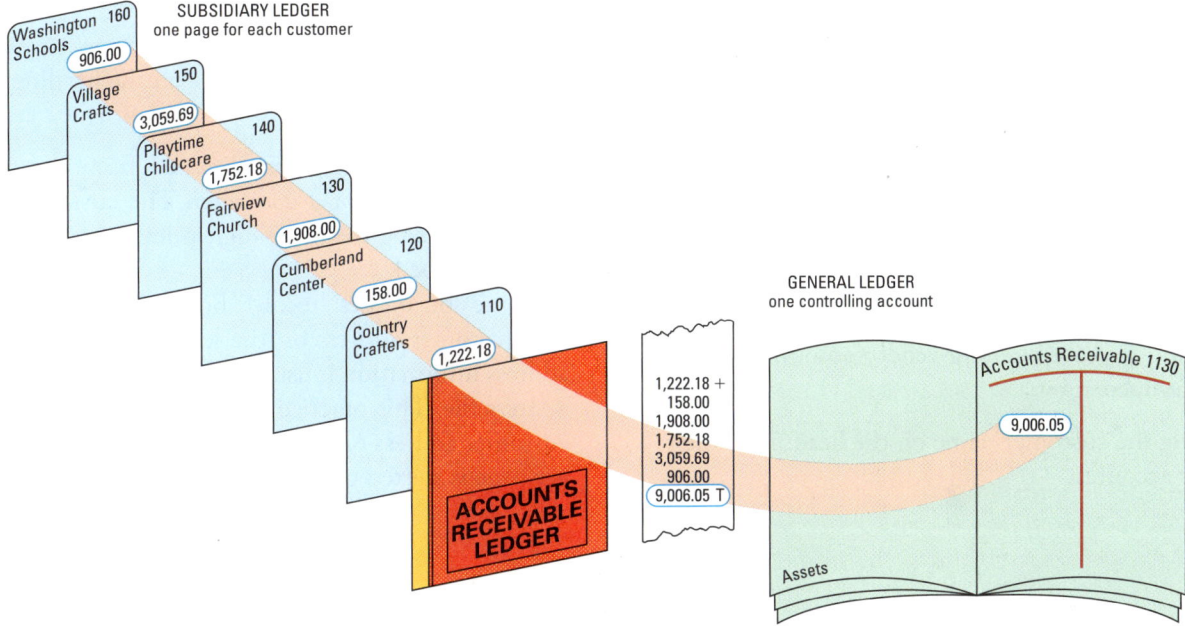

Hobby Shack assigns a customer number to each account in the accounts receivable ledger. A three-digit number is used.

The customer number for Country Crafters is 110. The first digit, *1*, shows that the controlling account is an asset, Accounts Receivable. The second and third digits, *10*, show the customer number assigned to Country Crafters.

When the balance of a customer account in an accounts receivable ledger is changed, the balance of the controlling account, Accounts Receivable, is also changed. The total of all customer account balances in the accounts receivable ledger equals the balance of the controlling account, Accounts Receivable.

> **REMEMBER**
>
> *The total amount to be collected from all charge customers is summarized in a single general ledger account, Accounts Receivable.*

Posting to an Accounts Receivable Ledger Lesson 11-2 **307**

ACCOUNTS RECEIVABLE LEDGER FORMS

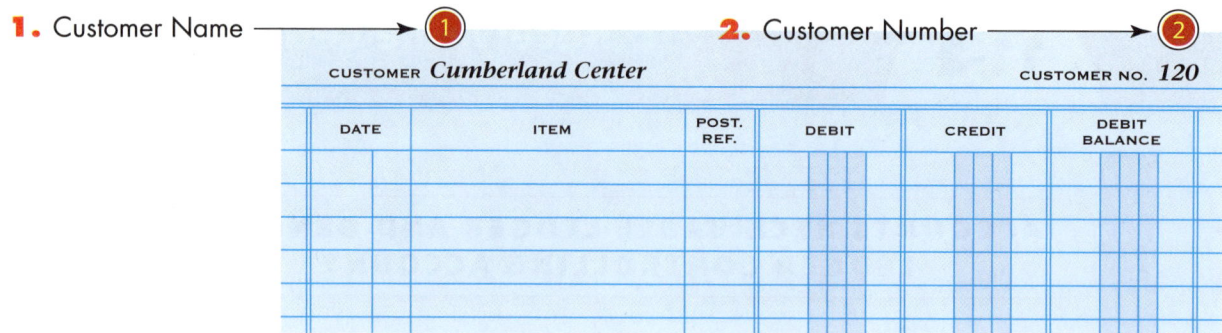

1. Customer Name
2. Customer Number

Hobby Shack uses a 3-column accounts receivable subsidiary account form. The accounts receivable account form is similar to the one used for the accounts payable ledger. Accounts receivable are assets, and assets have normal debit balances. Therefore, the form used in the accounts receivable ledger has a Debit Balance column instead of a Credit Balance column.

Procedures for opening customer accounts are similar to those used for opening vendor accounts. Each new account is opened by:

1. Writing the customer name on the heading of the ledger account.
2. Writing the customer number on the heading of the ledger account.

The customer name is obtained from the first sales invoice prepared for a customer. The customer number is assigned using the three-digit numbering system previously described.

Some businesses record both the customer name and customer address on the ledger form. However, the address information is usually kept in a separate name and address file. This practice eliminates having to record the customer address on the ledger form each time a new ledger page is started or the address changes.

FOR YOUR INFORMATION

FYI

When an account that is no longer used is removed from the accounts receivable ledger, that customer number is available for assignment to a new customer.

POSTING FROM A SALES JOURNAL TO AN ACCOUNTS RECEIVABLE LEDGER

1. Date
2. Journal Page Number
3. Debit
4. Account Balance
5. Customer Number

Each amount in a sales journal's Accounts Receivable Debit column is posted to the accounts receivable ledger. Each amount is posted as a debit to the customer account listed in the Account Debited column. Hobby Shack posts frequently to the accounts receivable ledger so that each customer account will show an up-to-date balance.

The controlling account in the general ledger, Accounts Receivable, is also increased by this entry. At the end of the month, the journal's Accounts Receivable Debit column total is posted to the controlling account, Accounts Receivable.

STEPS — POSTING FROM A SALES JOURNAL TO AN ACCOUNTS RECEIVABLE LEDGER

1. Write the date, *3*, in the Date column of the account.

2. Write the sales journal page number, *S11*, in the Post. Ref. column of the account. *S* is the abbreviation used for the sales journal.

3. Write the debit amount, *$572.40*, in the Debit column of the customer account.

4. Add the amount in the Debit column to the previous balance in the Debit Balance column ($318.00 + $572.40 = $890.40). Write the new account balance, *$890.40*, in the Debit Balance column.

5. Write the customer number, *150*, in the Post. Ref. column of the sales journal. The customer number shows that the posting for this entry is complete.

FOR YOUR INFORMATION

FYI

Individual amounts in the Accounts Receivable Debit column are posted frequently to customer accounts in the accounts receivable ledger.

Posting to an Accounts Receivable Ledger   Lesson 11-2

POSTING FROM A CASH RECEIPTS JOURNAL TO AN ACCOUNTS RECEIVABLE LEDGER

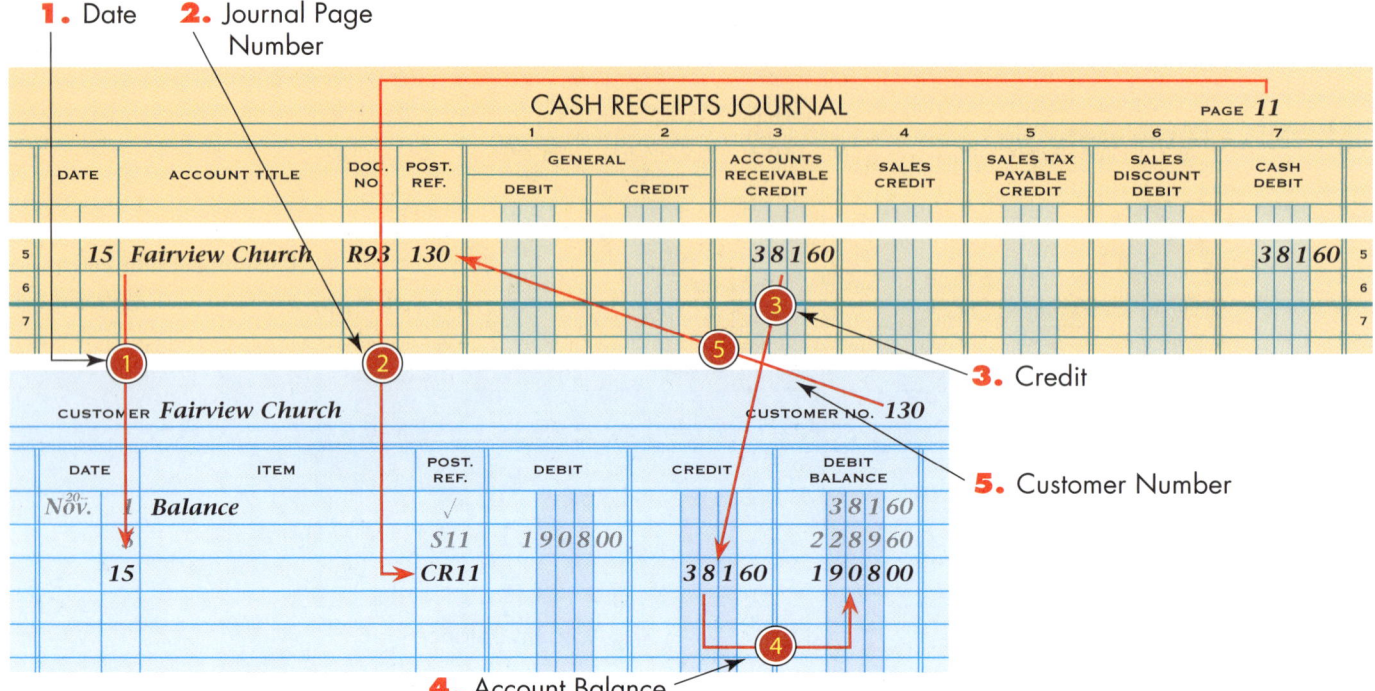

Each entry in the Accounts Receivable Credit column affects the customer named in the Account Title column. Each amount listed in the Accounts Receivable Credit column is posted to the proper customer account in the accounts receivable ledger. Hobby Shack posts frequently to the accounts receivable ledger so that each customer account will show an up-to-date balance.

STEPS — POSTING FROM A CASH RECEIPTS JOURNAL TO AN ACCOUNTS RECEIVABLE LEDGER

1. Write the date, *15*, in the Date column of the account.

2. Write the cash receipts journal page number, *CR11*, in the Post. Ref. column of the account. *CR* is the abbreviation for the cash receipts journal.

3. Write the credit amount, *$381.60*, in the Credit column of the customer account.

4. Subtract the amount in the Credit column from the previous balance in the Debit Balance column ($2,289.60 − $381.60 = $1,908.00). Write the new balance, *$1,908.00*, in the Debit Balance column.

5. Write the customer number, *130*, in the Post. Ref. column of the cash receipts journal.

STOCKBYTE/GETTY IMAGES

POSTING A CREDIT ENTRY FROM A GENERAL JOURNAL TO AN ACCOUNTS RECEIVABLE LEDGER

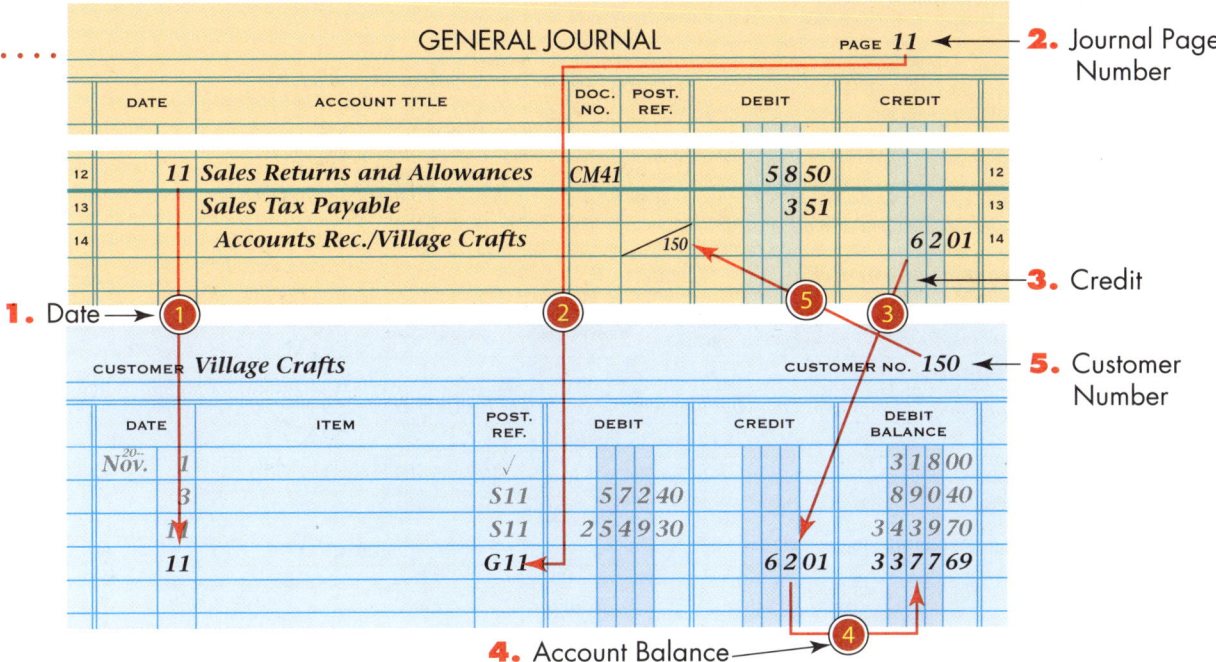

1. Date
2. Journal Page Number
3. Credit
4. Account Balance
5. Customer Number

Entries in a general journal may affect account balances in a general ledger and an accounts receivable ledger. Posting from a general journal to a general ledger is described on pages 317–318.

STEPS: POSTING A CREDIT ENTRY FOR SALES RETURNS AND ALLOWANCES FROM A GENERAL JOURNAL TO AN ACCOUNTS RECEIVABLE LEDGER

1. Write the date, *Nov. 11*, in the Date column of the customer account.
2. Write the general journal page number, *G11*, in the Post. Ref. column of the account. The abbreviation *G11* means page 11 of the general journal.
3. Write the amount, *$62.01*, in the Credit column of the customer account.
4. Subtract the amount in the Credit column from the previous balance in the Debit Balance column ($3,439.70 − $62.01 = $3,377.69). Write the new balance, *$3,377.69*, in the Debit Balance column.
5. Write the customer number, *150*, to the right of the diagonal line in the Post. Ref. column of the general journal.

INGRAM PUBLISHING/GETTY IMAGES

Posting to an Accounts Receivable Ledger Lesson 11-2 **311**

COMPLETED ACCOUNTS RECEIVABLE LEDGER

CUSTOMER Country Crafters   **CUSTOMER NO.** 110

DATE	ITEM	POST. REF.	DEBIT	CREDIT	DEBIT BALANCE
Nov. 1	Balance	✓			2 1 6 2 40
6		CR11		2 1 6 2 40	—
11		S11	7 6 8 50		7 6 8 50
29		S11	4 5 3 68		1 2 2 2 18

CUSTOMER Cumberland Center   **CUSTOMER NO.** 120

DATE	ITEM	POST. REF.	DEBIT	CREDIT	DEBIT BALANCE
Nov. 1	Balance	✓			4 1 8 9 20
7		CR11		1 2 0 0 00	2 9 8 9 20
24		S11	1 5 8 00		3 1 4 7 20
25		CR11		2 9 8 9 20	1 5 8 00

CUSTOMER Fairview Church   **CUSTOMER NO.** 130

DATE	ITEM	POST. REF.	DEBIT	CREDIT	DEBIT BALANCE
Nov. 1	Balance	✓			3 8 1 60
5		S11	1 9 0 8 00		2 2 8 9 60
15		CR11		3 8 1 60	1 9 0 8 00

CUSTOMER Playtime Childcare   **CUSTOMER NO.** 140

DATE	ITEM	POST. REF.	DEBIT	CREDIT	DEBIT BALANCE
Nov. 1	Balance	✓			1 1 4 4 80
16		S11	1 7 5 2 18		2 8 9 6 98
18		CR11		1 1 4 4 80	1 7 5 2 18

CUSTOMER Village Crafts   **CUSTOMER NO.** 150

DATE	ITEM	POST. REF.	DEBIT	CREDIT	DEBIT BALANCE
Nov. 1	Balance	✓			3 1 8 00
3		S11	5 7 2 40		8 9 0 40
11		S11	2 5 4 9 30		3 4 3 9 70
11		G11		6 2 01	3 3 7 7 69
19		CR11		3 1 8 00	3 0 5 9 69

CUSTOMER Washington Schools   **CUSTOMER NO.** 160

DATE	ITEM	POST. REF.	DEBIT	CREDIT	DEBIT BALANCE
Nov. 1	Balance	✓			2 5 4 4 00
9		S11	5 7 2 00		3 1 1 6 00
12		CR11		2 5 4 4 00	5 7 2 00
24		S11	3 3 4 00		9 0 6 00

Hobby Shack's accounts receivable ledger has been posted for the month of November.

PROVING THE ACCOUNTS RECEIVABLE LEDGER

Hobby Shack, Inc.
Schedule of Accounts Receivable
November 30, 20--

Country Crafters	1 2 2 2 18
Cumberland Center	1 5 8 00
Fairview Church	1 9 0 8 00
Playtime Childcare	1 7 5 2 18
Village Crafts	3 0 5 9 69
Washington Schools	9 0 6 00
Total Accounts Receivable	**9 0 0 6 05**

A listing of customer accounts, account balances, and total amount due from all customers is called a **schedule of accounts receivable**. A schedule of accounts receivable is prepared after all entries in a journal are posted. The balance of Accounts Receivable in the general ledger is $9,006.05. The total of the schedule of accounts receivable is $9,006.05. Because the two amounts are the same, the accounts receivable ledger is proved.

FINANCIAL LITERACY

Account Reconciliations

"I don't ever reconcile my accounts. I just trust the bank." Many people feel this way about reconciling checking accounts. Yet mistakes can be made—even by the bank.

Savings accounts as well as checking accounts should be reconciled regularly. Internet account access makes it possible to reconcile your accounts frequently. This can uncover errors more quickly—therefore preventing overdraft charges that otherwise may be applied.

Many banks include a reconciliation form on the back of the monthly statements sent to each account owner. The forms give directions for completing the reconciliation. The steps are: (1) Go through the statement, marking deposits and checks that have cleared the bank and recording any charges and/or automatic withdrawals/deposits that are listed on the statement. (2) List the account balance as printed on the bank statement. (3) Add any deposits made that have not cleared the bank. (4) Subtract any checks that have been written but have not cleared the bank. (5) Verify that the new subtotal equals the balance as recorded in your records.

If you find errors in your records, make the necessary corrections and clearly note the reason for the correction. This will make it easier to understand the corrections if you need to refer to them in the future.

Activities

1. Survey 10 people to determine if they regularly perform an account reconciliation. If so, ask them how often they find an error that they made and how often they find an error made by their bank. Report your findings to your class in a presentation.

2. Interview a bank employee who helps clients with bank reconciliations. Ask him or her what are the most common errors made by the account owner and by the bank. Summarize your findings in a written report.

Posting to an Accounts Receivable Ledger

End of Lesson REVIEW

AUDIT YOUR UNDERSTANDING

1. To which accounts are the separate amounts in the sales journal posted individually?
2. In which column of the cash receipts journal are the amounts that are posted individually to the accounts receivable ledger?
3. What accounts are listed on a schedule of accounts receivable?

TERM REVIEW

schedule of accounts receivable

WORK TOGETHER 11-2

Posting to an accounts receivable ledger

Partial sales and cash receipts journals for Graphics, Inc. are given in the *Working Papers*. Also given in the *Working Papers* are one blank accounts receivable ledger account form and a blank form for preparation of a schedule of accounts receivable. You will also need the general journal from Work Together 11-1. Your instructor will guide you through the following examples.

1. Start a new page for an accounts receivable ledger account for Brandee Sparks. The account number is 140, and the balance for October 1 of the current year is $212.00.
2. Post the Accounts Receivable Debit entry on line 5 of the sales journal to the accounts receivable account for Brandee Sparks.
3. Post the Accounts Receivable Credit entry on line 9 of the cash receipts journal to the accounts receivable account for Alfredo Lopez.
4. Post the credit entry on line 3 of the general journal to the accounts receivable account for David Bishop. *[skip]*
5. Prepare a schedule of accounts receivable for Graphics, Inc., on October 31 of the current year. Accounts Receivable balance in the general ledger on October 31 is $2,530.22. Save your work to complete Work Together 11-4.

ON YOUR OWN 11-2

Posting to an accounts receivable ledger

Partial sales and cash receipts journals for Amatera, Inc. are given in the *Working Papers*. Also given in the *Working Papers* are one blank accounts receivable ledger account form and a blank form for preparation of a schedule of accounts receivable. You will also need the general journal from On Your Own 11-1. Work this problem independently.

1. Start a new page for an accounts receivable ledger account for Davis Sullivan. The account number is 140, and the balance for September 1 of the current year is $564.00.
2. Post the Accounts Receivable Debit entry on line 8 of the sales journal to the accounts receivable account for Davis Sullivan.
3. Post the Accounts Receivable Credit entry on line 21 of the cash receipts journal to the accounts receivable account for Harris Evans.
4. Post the credit entry on line 3 of the general journal to the accounts receivable account for Mary Burgin.
5. Prepare a schedule of accounts receivable for Amatera, Inc., on September 30 of the current year. Accounts Receivable balance in the general ledger on September 30 is $5,986.80. Save your work to complete On Your Own 11-4.

LESSON 11-3

Posting from Journals to a General Ledger

STARTING A NEW PAGE FOR AN ACCOUNT IN A GENERAL LEDGER

1. Account Title
2. Account Number
3. Date
4. Word *Balance*
5. Check Mark
6. Balance

The number of entries that may be recorded on each general ledger account form depends on the number of lines provided. When all lines have been used, a new page is prepared. The account name, account number, and account balance are recorded on the new page.

On November 1, Hobby Shack prepared a new page for Cash in the general ledger because the existing page was full. On that day, the account balance was $17,647.44.

STEPS — STARTING A NEW PAGE FOR A GENERAL LEDGER ACCOUNT

1. Write the account title, *Cash*, at the top of the page.
2. Write the account number, *1110*, at the top of the page.
3. Write the date, *20--, Nov. 1*, in the Date column.
4. Write the word *Balance* in the Item column.
5. Place a check mark in the Post. Ref. column to show that the amount has been carried forward from a previous page rather than posted from a journal.
6. Write the balance, *$17,647.44*, in the Balance Debit column.

PHOTOGRAPHER'S CHOICE RF/GETTY IMAGES

POSTING FROM THE GENERAL AMOUNT COLUMNS OF A CASH PAYMENTS JOURNAL TO A GENERAL LEDGER

Amounts in cash payments journal entries are recorded in either general amount columns or special amount columns. Each amount in the General columns of a cash payments journal is posted individually to the general ledger account written in the Account Title column. However, only the monthly total of each special amount column is posted to a general ledger account.

STEPS POSTING FROM THE GENERAL AMOUNT COLUMNS OF A CASH PAYMENTS JOURNAL TO A GENERAL LEDGER

1. Write the date, *7*, in the Date column of the account.

2. Write the journal page number, *CP21*, in the Post. Ref. column of the account. The abbreviation *CP21* means page 21 of the cash payments journal.

3. Write the debit amount, *$600.00*, in the account's Debit column. (A credit amount would be written in the Credit column.)

4. Add the amount in the Debit column to the previous balance in the Balance Debit column ($600.00 + $154,840.92 = $155,440.92). Write the new account balance, *$155,440.92*, in the Balance Debit column of the account.

5. Write the general ledger account number, *5110*, in the Post. Ref. column of the cash payments journal.

REMEMBER

Separate amounts listed in special amount columns of a special journal are not posted individually to the general ledger—only the totals are posted.

Chapter 11   Posting to General and Subsidiary Ledgers

POSTING A DEBIT ENTRY FROM A GENERAL JOURNAL TO A GENERAL LEDGER

STEPS — POSTING A DEBIT AMOUNT FROM A GENERAL JOURNAL TO A GENERAL LEDGER

1. Write the date, *6*, in the Date column of the account.

2. Write the general journal page number, *G11*, in the Post. Ref. column of the account. The abbreviation *G11* means page 11 of the general journal.

3. Write the amount, *$210.00*, in the Debit column of the account.

4. Calculate and write the new account balance, *$6,138.00*, in the Balance Debit column of the account.

5. Write the general ledger account number, *1150*, in the Post. Ref. column of the general journal.

FOR YOUR INFORMATION

FYI

Accuracy is very important in accounting. Following the proper sequence of steps for posting increases the accuracy of the task.

Posting from Journals to a General Ledger · Lesson 11-3

POSTING A CREDIT ENTRY FROM A GENERAL JOURNAL TO A GENERAL LEDGER

Transactions recorded in a general journal can affect both subsidiary ledger and general ledger accounts. Buying supplies on account, for example, results in a credit to Accounts Payable. The purchase should also be recorded as a credit in the subsidiary ledger account of the vendor, Gulf Craft Supply.

The diagonal line in the Post. Ref. column allows the posting reference of both the general ledger and subsidiary ledger account to be recorded.

STEPS: POSTING A CREDIT AMOUNT FROM A GENERAL JOURNAL TO A GENERAL LEDGER

1. Write the date, *6*, in the Date column of the account.

2. Write the general journal page number, *G11*, in the Post. Ref. column of the account.

3. Write the amount, *$210.00*, in the Credit column of the account.

4. Calculate and write the new account balance, *$13,194.00*, in the Balance Credit column of the account.

5. Write the general ledger account number, *2110*, to the left of the diagonal line in the Post. Ref. column of the general journal. The vendor account number, *250*, written to the right of the diagonal line, was described on page 303.

SMALL BUSINESS SPOTLIGHT

The major ways of starting a new small business are:
1. Buy an existing business.
2. Buy a franchise.
3. Start a business from scratch.

End of Lesson REVIEW

AUDIT YOUR UNDERSTANDING

1. Which amounts in a general journal are posted individually?
2. List the five steps for posting to a general ledger account.

WORK TOGETHER 11-3

Posting to a general ledger

Use the partial cash payments and general journals from Work Together 11-1. General ledger account forms are given in the *Working Papers*. Your instructor will guide you through the following examples.

1. Start a new page for a general ledger account for Supplies—Office. The account number is 1145, and the balance for October 1 of the current year is $3,824.00.
2. Post the October 19 General Debit entry of the cash payments journal to the appropriate general ledger account.
3. Post the October 12 general journal entry to the appropriate general ledger accounts.
4. Post the October 26 general journal entry to the appropriate general ledger accounts.
5. Post the October 28 general journal entry to the appropriate general ledger accounts. Save the general ledger accounts to complete Work Together 11-4.

ON YOUR OWN 11-3

Posting to a general ledger

Use the partial cash payments and general journals from On Your Own 11-1. General ledger account forms are given in the *Working Papers*. Work this problem independently.

1. Start a new page for a general ledger account for Supplies—Store. The account number is 1150, and the balance for September 1 of the current year is $3,158.00.
2. Post the September 21 General Debit entry of the cash payments journal to the appropriate general ledger account.
3. Post the September 15 general journal entry to the appropriate general ledger accounts.
4. Post the September 27 general journal entry to the appropriate general ledger accounts.
5. Post the September 29 general journal entry to the appropriate general ledger accounts. Save the general ledger accounts to complete On Your Own 11-4.

Posting from Journals to a General Ledger

LESSON 11-4
Posting Special Journal Totals to a General Ledger

POSTING TOTALS OF A SALES JOURNAL TO A GENERAL LEDGER

2. Journal Page Number

1. Date

3. Column Total

4. Account Balance

5. Account Number

STEPS POSTING EACH SPECIAL AMOUNT COLUMN TOTAL OF A SALES JOURNAL

1. Write the date, *30*, in the Date columns of the accounts.
2. Write the sales journal page number, *S11*, in the Post. Ref. columns of the accounts.
3. For each column and account, write the column total in the Debit or Credit column of the account.
4. For each account, calculate and write the new account balance in the Balance Debit or Credit column.
5. In the sales journal, write the general ledger account number in parentheses below each column total.

POSTING THE TOTAL OF A PURCHASES JOURNAL TO A GENERAL LEDGER

A purchases journal is totaled and ruled at the end of each month as described in Chapter 9. The total amount of the purchases journal is then posted to two general ledger accounts, Purchases and Accounts Payable.

STEPS POSTING THE TOTAL OF A PURCHASES JOURNAL TO THE TWO GENERAL LEDGER ACCOUNTS

1. Write the date, *30*, in the Date columns of the accounts.

2. Write the purchases journal page number, *P11*, in the Post. Ref. columns of the accounts. The abbreviation *P11* means page 11 of the purchases journal.

3. For each account, write the purchases journal column total, *$17,148.08*, in the Debit or Credit column.

4. For each account, calculate and write the new account balance in the Balance Debit or Credit column.

5. Return to the purchases journal and write the purchases general ledger account number, *(5110)*, and the accounts payable general ledger account number, *(2110)*, in parentheses below the column total.

Posting Special Journal Totals to a General Ledger   Lesson 11-4   321

POSTING SPECIAL AMOUNT COLUMN TOTALS OF A CASH RECEIPTS JOURNAL TO A GENERAL LEDGER

At the end of each month, equality of debits and credits is proved for a cash receipts journal. Cash is then proved as described in Chapter 10. After cash is proved, the cash receipts journal is ruled as described in Chapter 10. The total of each special amount column is then posted to the corresponding general ledger account.

STEPS POSTING EACH SPECIAL AMOUNT COLUMN TOTAL OF A CASH RECEIPTS JOURNAL

1. Write the date, *30*, in the Date columns of the accounts.
2. Write the cash receipts journal page number, *CR11*, in the Post. Ref. columns of the accounts. The abbreviation *CR11* means page 11 of the cash receipts journal.
3. For each special amount column and account, write the special amount column total in the Debit or Credit column of the account.
4. For each account, calculate and write the new account balance in the Balance Debit or Credit column.
5. Return to the cash receipts journal and write the general ledger account number in parentheses below each special amount column total.

CULTURAL DIVERSITY

Timeless Tools

Throughout history, people of different cultures and civilizations have devised tools for counting, calculating, and recordkeeping.

The Jibaro Indians living in the Amazon rain forest in South America use the most basic counting tools of all—their fingers. Jibaros use phrases to express the numbers five and ten that translate to "I have finished one hand" and "I have finished both hands."

A more complex device of ancient origin is the abacus. The abacus is a calculating device that developed in several different cultures. The Babylonians in Asia Minor had an early form of abacus, as did the Egyptians in northern Africa. The first abacus was known in China as early as the 6th century B.C. This abacus was a flat piece of wood divided into squares. Its use spread to the rest of the Asian world.

The abacus may be used to add, subtract, multiply, and divide. Twelfth-century Chinese mathematicians used the abacus to solve algebraic equations. Today some highly skilled people, particularly of Asian descent, still use the abacus for calculations.

Recordkeepers in the Incan civilization (in present-day Peru) memorized business transactions and recited them when necessary. Incan recordkeepers used small ropes of different colors and sizes and knotted and joined them in different ways to help remember financial data. These ropes, called *quipu*, were one of the earliest means of recording transactions.

Accounting tools have changed over the course of history. They will continue to evolve with future advances in technology.

Critical Thinking

1. What tools do most accounting workers today use for calculations?
2. Discuss whether the use of modern calculating tools results in the creation of more complex accounting transactions.

Posting Special Journal Totals to a General Ledger

POSTING SPECIAL AMOUNT COLUMN TOTALS OF A CASH PAYMENTS JOURNAL TO A GENERAL LEDGER

The cash payments journal is totaled and ruled at the end of each month as described in Chapter 9. The total of each special column is then posted to a general ledger account. The total of each special amount column is posted to the account named in the journal's column headings.

The totals of the General amount columns are not posted. Each amount in these columns was posted individually to a general ledger account. To indicate that these totals are not to be posted, a check mark is placed in parentheses below each column total.

STEPS POSTING THE TOTALS OF EACH SPECIAL AMOUNT COLUMN TO THE GENERAL LEDGER ACCOUNT

1. Write the date, *30*, in the Date columns of the accounts.
2. Write the cash payments journal page number, *CP22*, in the Post. Ref. columns of the accounts.
3. For each special amount column and account, write the special amount column total in the Debit or Credit column of the account.
4. For each account, calculate and write the new account balance in the Balance Debit or Credit column.
5. Return to the cash payments journal and write the general ledger account number in parentheses below each special amount column total.

ORDER OF POSTING FROM SPECIAL JOURNALS

Items affecting customer or vendor accounts are posted periodically during the month. Hobby Shack posts frequently so that the balances of the subsidiary ledger accounts will be up to date. Since general ledger account balances are needed only when financial statements are prepared, the general ledger accounts are posted less often during the month. All items, including the totals of special columns, must be posted before a trial balance is prepared. Hobby Shack posts special amount column totals monthly.

The journals should be posted in the following order:

1. Sales journal.
2. Purchases journal.
3. General journal.
4. Cash receipts journal.
5. Cash payments journal.

DIGITAL VISION/GETTY IMAGES

FOR YOUR INFORMATION
FYI

It is important to post the journals in the proper sequence. However, sometimes the entries will be out of chronological order. For example, if subsidiary accounts are posted for the week ended June 24, it is possible for a June 23 entry from the sales journal to appear before a June 20 entry from the cash receipts journal.

End of Lesson REVIEW

AUDIT YOUR UNDERSTANDING

1. For which columns of a special journal are the column totals posted to the general ledger?
2. In what order should special journals be posted to the general ledger?

WORK TOGETHER 11-4

Posting special journal totals to a general ledger

Use the journals that were used for Work Together 11-1 and 11-2. General ledger accounts are given in the *Working Papers*. Your instructor will guide you through the following examples.

1. Post the October 31 column totals of the sales journal.
2. Post the October 31 column total of the purchases journal.
3. Post the October 31 column totals of the cash receipts journal.
4. Post the October 31 column totals of the cash payments journal.

ON YOUR OWN 11-4

Posting special journal totals to a general ledger

Use the journals that were used for On Your Own 11-1 and 11-2. General ledger accounts are given in the *Working Papers*. Work this problem independently.

1. Post the September 30 column totals of the sales journal.
2. Post the September 30 column total of the purchases journal.
3. Post the September 30 column totals of the cash receipts journal.
4. Post the September 30 column totals of the cash payments journal.

LESSON 11-5

Correcting Errors in Subsidiary Ledger Accounts

JOURNALIZING CORRECTING ENTRIES AFFECTING CUSTOMER ACCOUNTS

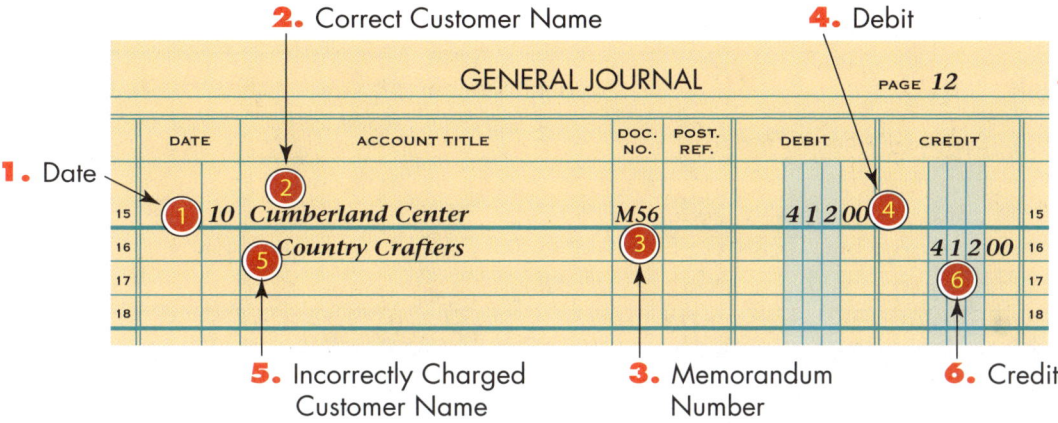

Errors may be made in recording amounts in subsidiary ledgers that do not affect the general ledger controlling account. For example, a sale on account may be recorded to the wrong customer in the sales journal. The column total posted from the sales journal to the general ledger is correct. The accounts receivable account shows the correct balance. However, two of the customer accounts in the accounts receivable ledger show incorrect balances.

> **December 10.** Discovered that a sale on account to Cumberland Center on December 3 was incorrectly charged to the account of Country Crafters, $412.00. Memorandum No. 56.

The correcting entry recorded in the general journal involves only subsidiary ledger accounts. Cumberland Center's account is debited for $412.00 to record the charge sale in the correct account. Country Crafters' account is credited for $412.00 to cancel the incorrect entry.

STEPS JOURNALIZING CORRECTING ENTRIES AFFECTING CUSTOMER ACCOUNTS

1. Write the date, *10*, in the Date column of a general journal.
2. Write the name of the correct customer, *Cumberland Center*, in the Account Title column.
3. Write the memorandum number, *M56*, in the Doc. No. column.
4. Write the amount, *$412.00*, in the Debit column.
5. Indent and write the name of the incorrectly charged customer, *Country Crafters*, on the next line in the Account Title column.
6. Write the amount, *$412.00*, in the Credit column.

Correcting Errors in Subsidiary Ledger Accounts Lesson 11-5

POSTING CORRECTING ENTRIES AFFECTING CUSTOMER ACCOUNTS

With one exception, the steps for posting a journal entry to correct customer accounts are the same as posting other transactions to subsidiary ledgers. However, a diagonal line is not needed in the Post. Ref. column to separate the references to the general ledger and subsidiary ledger account. Because the transaction does not affect a general ledger account, only a reference to the subsidiary ledger account is entered in the Post. Ref. column of the general journal.

STEPS — POSTING CORRECTING ENTRIES AFFECTING CUSTOMER ACCOUNTS

1. Write the date, *10*, in the Date column of each customer account.
2. Write the general journal page number, *G12*, in the Post. Ref. column of the account.
3. Write the amount, *$412.00*, in the appropriate Debit or Credit column of each customer account.
4. For each account, calculate and write the new account balance in the Debit Balance column.
5. Write the appropriate customer numbers in the Post. Ref. column of the general journal.

FOR YOUR INFORMATION — FYI

Recording a correcting entry establishes what accountants refer to as an audit trail. The original (incorrect) entry is retained in the accounting records. The reason for the correcting entry and the name of the employee who authorized the correction are recorded on the memo supporting the correcting entry. Thus, accountants can follow the history of the transactions to ensure that the net effect of the transactions is accurate.

Chapter 11   Posting to General and Subsidiary Ledgers

End of Lesson REVIEW

AUDIT YOUR UNDERSTANDING

1. What is the source document for a correcting entry affecting customer accounts?
2. How does a correcting entry affecting customer accounts impact the general ledger accounts?
3. How does posting a correcting entry affecting customer accounts differ from recording other general journal entries that impact subsidiary ledger accounts?

WORK TOGETHER 11-5

Journalizing and posting correcting entries affecting customer accounts

The general journal and accounts receivable ledger accounts for Cline Interiors are given in the *Working Papers*. Your instructor will guide you through the following examples.

1. Using the current year, journalize the following transaction on page 6 of a general journal. The memorandum source document is abbreviated as M.

Transaction:
  June 3. Discovered that a sale on account to Howell Clinic on May 25, S346, was incorrectly charged to the account of Howsley Dance Studio, $414.99. M57.

2. Post the items to the accounts receivable ledger.

ON YOUR OWN 11-5

Journalizing and posting correcting entries affecting customer accounts

The general journal and accounts receivable ledger accounts for Gentry, Inc., are given in the *Working Papers*. Work this problem independently.

1. Using the current year, journalize the following transaction on page 7 of a general journal. The memorandum source document is abbreviated as M.

Transaction:
  July 4. Discovered that a sale on account to Kellogg Co., on June 28, S143, was incorrectly charged to the account of Keller Corp., $715.98. M76.

2. Post the items to the accounts receivable ledger.

SUMMARY

After completing this chapter, you can:

1. Define accounting terms related to posting to ledgers.
2. Identify accounting practices related to posting to ledgers.
3. Post separate items from a purchases, cash payments, and general journal to an accounts payable ledger.
4. Post separate items from a sales, cash receipts, and general journal to an accounts receivable ledger.
5. Post separate items from a cash payments and general journal to a general ledger.
6. Post special journal column totals to a general ledger.
7. Journalize and post correcting entries affecting customer accounts.

EXPLORE ACCOUNTING

Categories of Internal Control

Posting transactions from a journal to both the general ledger and subsidiary ledgers presents opportunities for errors. Hobby Shack can fail to record a sales transaction to a customer's account. If the customer does not pay the amount owed, Hobby Shack may never collect the accounts receivable. To avoid errors and their resulting losses, businesses should institute effective internal controls.

Internal controls may be categorized in three phases: (1) preventive, (2) detective, and (3) corrective. A preventive control prevents the individual from making the error. Establishing and following consistent procedures for posting transactions is a preventive control. A detective control detects or finds the error. Preparing a trial balance is a detective control. A corrective control restores the business back to normal if an error occurs. Insurance, such as a fidelity bond on a cashier, is a corrective control.

Businesses with an adequate number of employees should split duties among several employees to reduce the chances of error. This segregation of duties enables one employee to check the work of another. For example, one employee should post transactions to the general ledger while another employee should post transactions to the subsidiary ledger.

Discussion

1. Describe internal control procedures that you have observed either as an employee or as a customer. Identify each procedure as (1) preventive, (2) detective, or (3) corrective.
2. Discuss whether a policeman monitoring a highway with radar is a preventive or detective control of the speed limit.

11-1 APPLICATION PROBLEM

Posting to an accounts payable ledger

Selected entries from the purchases, cash payments, and general journals for Healthy Nutrition, a health food store, are given in the *Working Papers*.

Instructions:

1. Start new pages for the following vendor accounts in the accounts payable ledger. Record the balances as of October 1 of the current year.

Vendor No.	Vendor Name	Account Balance
210	Cornucopia, Inc.	$3,090.00
220	Healthy Foods	5,064.00
230	Nutrition Center	—
240	Office Center	—
250	Sports Nutrition	4,512.00

2. Post the separate items recorded in the purchases, cash payments, and general journals to the appropriate accounts payable ledger accounts. Post in chronological order by date.

3. Prepare a schedule of accounts payable. Compare the total of the schedule with the balance of the controlling account, Accounts Payable, $13,352.00. If the totals are not the same, find and correct the errors.

11-2 APPLICATION PROBLEM

Posting to an accounts receivable ledger

Selected entries from the sales, cash receipts, and general journals for Healthy Nutrition are given in the *Working Papers*.

Instructions:

1. Start new pages for the following customer accounts in the accounts receivable ledger. Record the balances as of October 1 of the current year.

Customer No.	Customer Name	Account Balance
110	Children's Center	$4,416.00
120	Eastman Sports Arena	2,220.00
130	Maple Tree Club	3,528.00
140	Southwest Community Club	—

2. Post the separate items recorded in the sales, cash receipts, and general journals to the appropriate accounts receivable ledger accounts. Post in chronological order by date.

3. Prepare a schedule of accounts receivable. Compare the total of the schedule with the balance of the controlling account, Accounts Receivable, $8,293.44. If the totals are not the same, find and correct the errors.

11-3 APPLICATION PROBLEM

Posting to a general ledger

Selected entries from the cash payments and general journals for Hartley Corporation are given in the *Working Papers*.

Instructions:

1. Start new pages for the following accounts in the general ledger. Record the balances as of November 1 of the current year.

General Ledger Account No.	Account Title	Balance
1110	Cash	$ 21,960.00
1130	Accounts Receivable	8,420.64
1150	Supplies—Office	4,416.00
1170	Prepaid Insurance	1,870.00
2110	Accounts Payable	15,396.00
2120	Sales Tax Payable	1,615.20
4110	Sales	206,904.00
4120	Sales Discount	2,051.23
5110	Purchases	115,800.00
5120	Purchases Discount	1,845.22
6160	Rent Expense	12,000.00

2. Post the separate general ledger items recorded in the cash payments and general journals. Save your work to complete Application Problem 11-4.

11-4 APPLICATION PROBLEM

Posting special journal column totals to a general ledger

The sales, purchases, and cash receipts journals for Hartley Corporation are given in the *Working Papers*. Use the general ledger accounts and cash payments journal from Application Problem 11-3.

Instructions:
Post the totals of the special columns of the sales, purchases, cash receipts, and cash payments journals.

11-5 APPLICATION PROBLEM

Journalizing and posting correcting entries affecting customer accounts

The general journal and accounts receivable ledger accounts for Placid Marina are given in the *Working Papers*.

Instructions:

1. Using the current year, journalize the following transactions on page 6 of a general journal. Source documents are abbreviated as: sales invoices, S; memorandum, M.

Transactions:

July 14. Discovered that a sale on account to Mark Ford on July 5, S534, was incorrectly charged to the account of Andrew Forde, $253.32. M37.
    15. Discovered that a sale on account to Sandy Patterson on July 8, S567, was incorrectly charged to the account of Daniel Patrick, $384.50. M38.

2. Post the items to the accounts receivable ledger.

11-6 MASTERY PROBLEM

Posting to general and subsidiary ledgers

The journals, subsidiary ledgers, and selected general ledger accounts for Auto Restoration, Inc., are given in the *Working Papers*.

Instructions:

1. Post the separate items in the following journals to the general and subsidiary ledgers. Use the current year. Note that some postings will be out of order by date because posting of individual amounts is not being done weekly.
   a. Sales journal to the accounts receivable ledger.
   b. Purchases journal to the accounts payable ledger.
   c. General journal to the accounts payable, accounts receivable, and general ledger.
   d. Cash receipts journal to the accounts receivable ledger.
   e. Cash payments journal to the accounts payable and general ledgers.
2. Post the totals of the special amount columns of the sales, purchases, cash receipts, and cash payments journals.
3. Prepare a schedule of accounts payable and a schedule of accounts receivable. Compare the totals of the schedules with the balances of the controlling accounts, Accounts Payable and Accounts Receivable, in the general ledger. If the totals are not the same, find and correct the errors.

11-7 CHALLENGE PROBLEM

Journalizing and posting business transactions

The general, accounts payable, and accounts receivable ledgers for Custom Golf Land are given in the *Working Papers*.

Instructions:

1. Journalize the following transactions completed during October of the current year. Use page 11 of a sales journal, purchases journal, general journal, and cash receipts journal. Use page 21 of a cash payments journal. Add an 8% sales tax to all sales transactions. Source documents are abbreviated as follows: check, C; memorandum, M; purchase invoice, P; receipt, R; sales invoice, S; terminal summary, TS.

Transactions:

Oct. 2. Wrote a check for rent, $1,150.00. C265.
    3. Received an invoice from Vista Golf Co. for merchandise purchased on account, $1,950.00. P71.
    4. Paid for merchandise, $142.80. C266.
    6. A check was received in payment on account from Viola Davis, $829.44, covering S45. R43.
    7. Eagle Golf Equipment was paid on account, $2,358.00, covering P67. C267.
    7. Cash and credit card sales, $5,676.00. TS31.
       Posting. Post the items that are to be posted individually.
    11. Merchandise was sold on account to Doris McCarley, $306.00. S49.

13. Store supplies were bought on account from Golf Source, $258.00. M34.
14. Cash and credit card sales, $5,808.00. TS32.
    Posting. Post the items that are to be posted individually.
17. Wrote a check for electric bill, $220.20. C268.
20. Wrote a check to Vista Golf Co. on account, $3,216.00, less 2% discount, covering P68. C269.
21. Recorded cash and credit card sales, $5,376.00. TS33.
    Posting. Post the items that are to be posted individually.
23. Design Golf was paid on account, $2,916.00, covering P69. C270.
24. Barry Fuller bought merchandise on account, $1,315.00. S50.
24. Received payment on account from Leona Silva, $285.12, covering S46. R44.
25. Merchandise was purchased on account from Pro Golf Supply, $1,542.00. P72.
27. A check was received in payment on account from David Bench, $972.00, covering S47. R45.
28. Received an invoice from Design Golf for merchandise purchased on account, $2,790.00. P73.
28. Merchandise was sold on account to Leona Silva, $1,314.00. S51.
28. Recorded cash and credit card sales, $5,556.00. TS34.
    Posting. Post the items that are to be posted individually.
30. Discovered that a sale on account to David Bench on October 28, S51, was incorrectly charged to the account of Leona Silva, $1,419.12. M35.
30. Replenish the petty cash fund, $251.00: office supplies, $40.00; store supplies, $51.00; advertising, $62.00; miscellaneous, $98.00. C271.
31. Recorded cash and credit card sales, $1,680.00. TS35.
    Posting. Post the items that are to be posted individually.

2. Prove and rule the sales journal. Post the totals of the special columns.
3. Total and rule the purchases journal. Post the total.
4. Prove the equality of debits and credits for the cash receipts and cash payments journals.
5. Prove cash. The balance on the next unused check stub is $38,140.56.
6. Rule the cash receipts journal. Post the totals of the special columns.
7. Rule the cash payments journal. Post the totals of the special columns.
8. Prepare a schedule of accounts payable and a schedule of accounts receivable. Prove the accuracy of the subsidiary ledgers by comparing the schedule totals with the balances of the controlling accounts in the general ledger. If the totals are not the same, find and correct the errors.
9. In states that have sales taxes, businesses are required to collect taxes on their sales and submit the taxes to the state. This additional activity requires considerable extra effort: keeping a separate record of the taxes collected at the time of sale, maintaining a separate account for the sales taxes collected, Sales Taxes Payable, and recording the collection and payment of the sales taxes in the account. These additional activities place an additional administrative burden on businesses, especially small businesses with few employees.

   Can you think of a procedure that would not require the separate record for collecting and accounting for sales taxes, yet comply with a state's requirement to collect and submit sales taxes based on sale of merchandise sold? Write a brief response providing an alternative approach to collecting and paying sales taxes.

APPLIED COMMUNICATION

Instructions: Write a letter to the Cute and Cuddly Corporation explaining that you are returning an order of stuffed toys because of poor workmanship. You would like to receive a refund for the full amount of the order, $350.25. Explain that you are providing a copy of the invoice, and ask for written confirmation of the processing of the refund. Include information that will allow the Cute and Cuddly Corp. to comply with your request.

CASE FOR CRITICAL THINKING

Larry Hayes observes his accountant at work and says, "You post each individual accounts receivable entry in the journal. Then you post the totals of the Accounts Receivable columns. You are posting these entries twice, which will make the records wrong." The accountant does not agree that the posting procedure is incorrect. Is Mr. Hayes or his accountant correct? Why?

AUDITING FOR ERRORS

Veronica Harper has just completed posting sales and cash receipts transactions to the general and subsidiary ledgers. According to the company's internal control procedures, you are assigned the task of checking her work.

Instructions: Three accounts receivable ledger accounts are shown below. Assume that the posting references and the amounts are correct. From your knowledge of the sales and cash receipts journals, determine whether any of the amounts are recorded in the incorrect column. List any incorrect amounts and calculate new ending balances for the accounts.

CUSTOMER Gerald Adams **CUSTOMER NO.** 110

DATE	ITEM	POST. REF.	DEBIT	CREDIT	DEBIT BALANCE
July 1	Balance	✓			624 25
16		S7	554 53		1 178 78
25		CR12	624 25		1 803 03

CUSTOMER Betty Daigre **CUSTOMER NO.** 120

DATE	ITEM	POST. REF.	DEBIT	CREDIT	DEBIT BALANCE
July 1	Balance	✓			2 315 48
24		S7		230 24	2 085 24

CUSTOMER Jackson Miller **CUSTOMER NO.** 130

DATE	ITEM	POST. REF.	DEBIT	CREDIT	DEBIT BALANCE
July 1	Balance	✓			2 946 22
5		CR7	1 758 95		4 705 17
22		S7		2 946 22	1 758 95

ANALYZING BEST BUY'S FINANCIAL STATEMENTS

Graphics are an effective method of communicating financial information. A stacked bar chart is especially useful in communicating the amounts presented in an income statement. The chart shows the relative amounts for each fiscal year as well as the overall trend in sales.

Instructions

1. Prepare a spreadsheet containing selected information from Best Buy's Consolidated Statements of Earnings on page B-6 in Appendix B. If spreadsheet software is not available, use a sheet of paper with 4 columns. In the first column, beginning in the second row, enter the following headings:

   Cost of goods sold

   Selling, general, and administrative expenses

   Operating income

2. Across the first row, beginning in the second column, enter the years 2007 to 2005.
3. Prepare a stacked column (bar) graph of the data.
4. What amount is represented by each year's bar?

Posting to General and Subsidiary Ledgers

Accounting SOFTWARE

CHECKING ACCURACY IN JOURNAL ENTRIES

There are many opportunities to make errors when entering and posting transactions in a manual accounting system. Many of these errors will never occur when using a computerized accounting system. For instance, by using a computerized system, you can be assured that a sale to a customer will be posted to that customer's account.

Peachtree has additional controls to help identify input errors. For example, Peachtree will not allow you to enter a sale on account to a customer that does not exist in the system. The program will not allow you to enter a transaction where the debit and credit amounts are not equal. A transaction date of February 30 will not be accepted.

But no accounting software can prevent you from entering the wrong customer, purchasing the wrong part, or writing a check for the wrong amount. Peachtree provides a variety of reports to help you review your transactions and identify any errors. Transaction journals and trial balances of accounts receivable and accounts payable should be reviewed carefully to help detect any errors.

PEACHTREE MASTERY PROBLEM 11-6
1. Open (Restore) file 11-6MP.ptb.
2. Print the purchase journal, cash disbursements journal, sales journal, cash receipts journal, general ledger, vendor ledgers (accounts payable ledger), and customer ledgers (accounts receivable ledger).

PEACHTREE CHALLENGE PROBLEM 11-7
1. Open (Restore) file 11-7CP.ptb.
2. Journalize and post the transactions completed during October. Add an 8% sales tax to all sales transactions.
3. Print the sales journal, cash receipts journal, purchase journal and cash disbursements journal.
4. Print the vendor ledgers, customer ledgers, and the general ledger.
5. Prove the accuracy of the subsidiary ledgers by comparing the totals with the balances of the controlling accounts in the general ledger.

CHECKING ACCURACY IN JOURNAL ENTRIES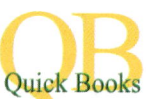

Accounting software packages can quickly print out volumes of journals, reports, and financial statements. The old adage "garbage in, garbage out" is especially pertinent when using an automated accounting system. The journals, reports, and financial statements are only as good as the data entered into the system.

Most accounting software programs have a variety of safeguards, or controls, to help limit the number and kinds of errors that can be entered. For example, QuickBooks will not allow a journal transaction to be saved if the debits do not equal the credits. Instead, an error message will be displayed, and a correction must be made. Other controls may include requiring a customer name whenever accounts receivable is used in a transaction or using dropdown lists to avoid typing errors.

However, no software program can eliminate all entry errors. Dropdown boxes don't prevent the user from selecting the wrong account. Making sure debits and credits are equal doesn't help if both amounts are incorrect. Therefore, journals, reports, and financial statements must be reviewed carefully to determine accuracy.

QUICKBOOKS MASTERY PROBLEM 11-6
1. Open the Auto Restoration Inc. file.
2. Print a Customer Balance Summary report, a Vendor Balance report, and a Trial Balance report using October 1 and October 31 for the From and To dates.

QUICKBOOKS CHALLENGE PROBLEM 11-7
1. Open the Custom Golf Land file.
2. Journalize the transactions completed during October. Use the Receive Payments and Create Invoices features for cash receipts and sales on account.
3. Use Enter Bills and Pay Bills for purchases and payments on account. Manually enter the amount of the purchase discount for the October 20 transaction.
4. Use the Write Checks feature on all other cash payments.
5. Use the Enter Sales Receipts option to record cash and credit card sales. Use the Make General Journal Entries window for all other transactions.
6. Use 8% sales tax rate for all sales transactions.
7. Print a Journal report, a Customer Balance Summary report, a Vendor Balance Summary report, and a Trial Balance report.

DOWNLOADING FILES INTO A SPREADSHEET

Today's computer accounting systems provide a wide variety of reports of accounts receivable and accounts payable transactions. Yet even the most sophisticated system may not be able to predict every information need of a business. For this reason, accounting systems enable you to download information using a file format that is recognized by other software, including electronic spreadsheets.

Files are often downloaded as comma or tab delimited files. A comma or tab is used to separate each piece of data in the file. An electronic spreadsheet uses the comma or tab to identify and place the data into the columns and rows of the spreadsheet. Once the data are imported, any of the tools of an electronic spreadsheet can used to analyze and report the data.

OPTIONAL SPREADSHEET ACTIVITY
Open the file F11-OPT. Complete the instructions provided to import a comma delimited file.

CORRECTING ERRORS IN JOURNAL ENTRIES

In manual accounting, errors can be made even though care is taken in recording transactions. Likewise, in automated accounting, an incorrect entry can be journalized and posted. Account numbers or dollar amounts can be transposed, or the wrong customer, vendor, or general ledger account selected. If an error has been made, it is necessary to locate and correct the inaccurate journal entry.

Finding a Journal Entry
1. Click the desired journal tab: General, Purchases, Sales, Cash Payments, or Cash Receipts.
2. Choose Find from the Edit menu bar.
3. Enter the date, reference, name, or amount you want to find in the Find What text box. Click OK.
4. If a matching transaction is found, it will be highlighted in the journal.

Changing or Deleting Journal Transactions
1. Select (highlight) the specific transaction text box that you wish to change or delete.
2. To change the transaction, enter the correction and click the Post command button. To delete the entire transaction, choose the Delete command button.

AUTOMATED ACCOUNTING APPLICATION PROBLEM 11-5
Open file F11-5.AA8. Display the problem instructions and complete the problem.

AUTOMATED ACCOUNTING CHALLENGE PROBLEM 11-7
Open file F11-7.AA8. Display the problem instructions and complete the problem.

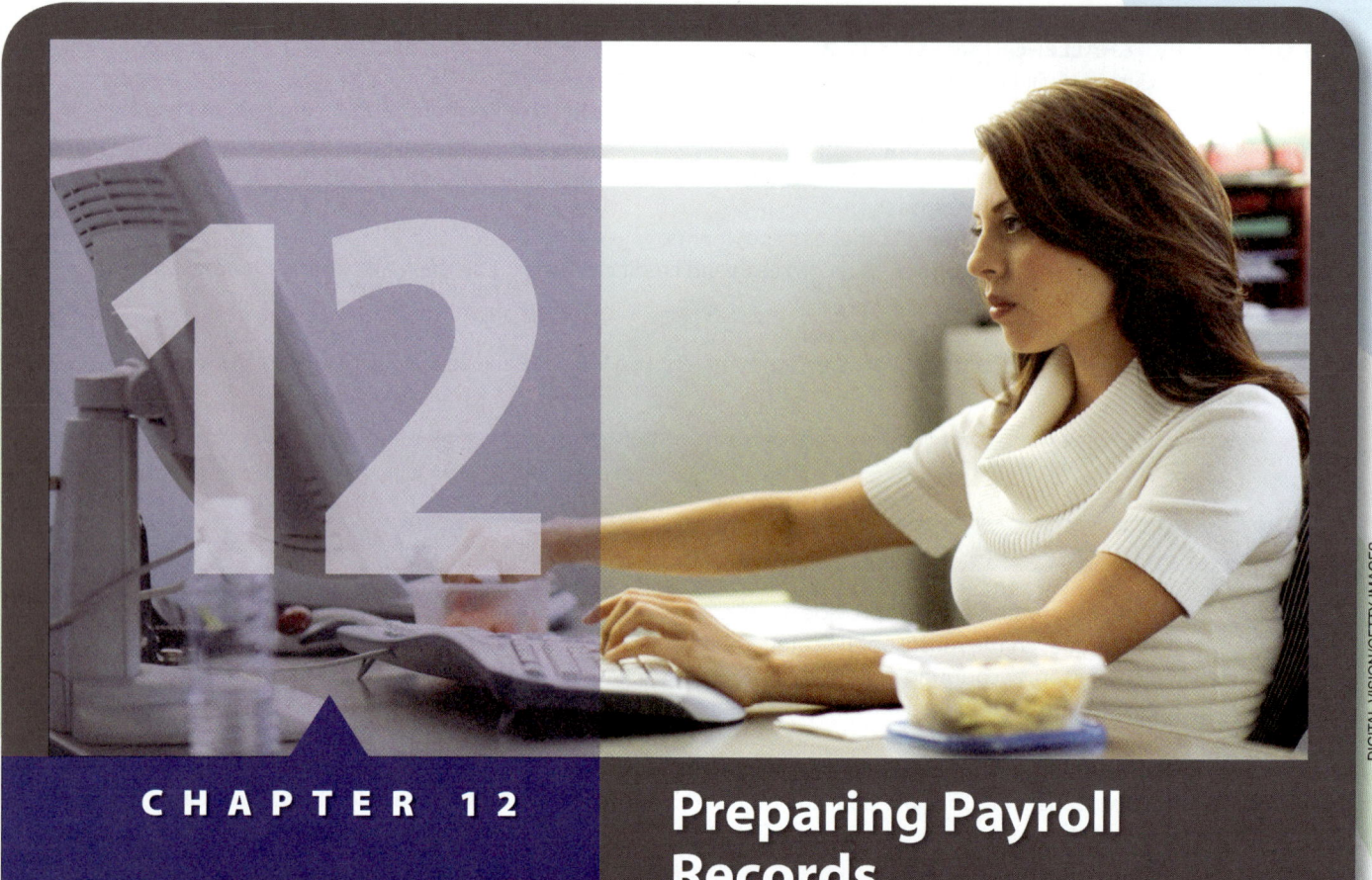

CHAPTER 12

Preparing Payroll Records

OBJECTIVES

After studying Chapter 12, you will be able to:

1. Define accounting terms related to payroll records.
2. Identify accounting practices related to payroll records.
3. Complete a payroll time card.
4. Calculate payroll taxes.
5. Complete a payroll register and an employee earnings record.
6. Prepare payroll checks.

KEY TERMS

- salary
- pay period
- payroll
- total earnings
- payroll taxes
- withholding allowance
- social security tax
- Medicare tax
- tax base
- payroll register
- net pay
- employee earnings record

Point Your Browser
www.C21accounting.com

ACCOUNTING IN THE REAL WORLD

The Green Bay Packers

The Payroll Playbook of the Green Bay Packers

The Green Bay Packers have one of the richest and most enduring traditions of any professional franchise in any sport. Who hasn't watched the Packer faithful cheer their team to victory in snow-covered Lambeau Field? Twelve championships and three Super Bowls have been won under the leadership of legendary coaches like Vince Lombardi.

But did you know that the Green Bay Packers has been a publicly owned, nonprofit corporation since 1923? And, like every other corporation, the Green Bay Packers must pay its employees, withhold payroll taxes and benefits, and submit employee reports to the government.

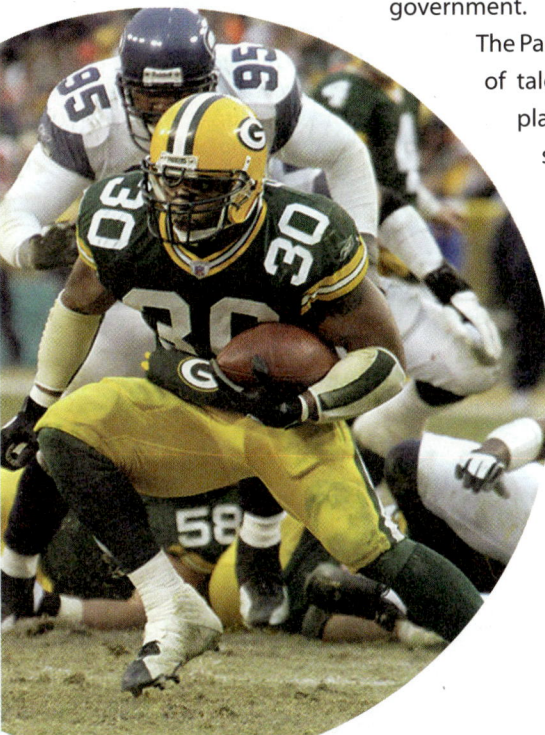

The Packers employ a diverse group of talented individuals, including players, coaches, trainers, and scouts. However, many of its employees work off the field. From purchasing materials for the concession stands to planning advertising campaigns, individuals with a wide variety of talents are required for the Packers to continue as a viable corporation.

Critical Thinking

1. Identify at least 10 off-field jobs that might be available with the Green Bay Packers.
2. How might payment of wages be different among the various types of employees?

Source: www.packers.com

INTERNET ACTIVITY

Child Labor Laws

Go to the web site for the Department of Labor, Youth Rules (www.youthrules.dol.gov). Search the site for information about child labor laws.

Instructions

1. Make a chart showing which jobs youth can do at age 13 or younger, age 14, age 16, and age 18.
2. Make a chart showing what hours youth can work at age 14–15 and age 16.

LESSON 12-1

Preparing Payroll Time Cards

PAYING EMPLOYEES

Hobby Shack employs several people to work in the business. These employees record the time they work for Hobby Shack each day. Periodically, Hobby Shack pays its employees for the number of hours each employee has worked. The money paid for employee services is called a **salary**. The period covered by a salary payment is called a **pay period**. A business may decide to pay employee salaries every week, every two weeks, twice a month, or once a month. Hobby Shack uses a semimonthly pay period. Employees are paid twice a month, on the 15th and last day of each month.

The total amount earned by all employees for a pay period is called a **payroll**. The payroll is reduced by state and federal taxes and other deductions, such as health insurance, to determine the amount paid to all employees. Special payroll records support the recording of payroll transactions in a journal. The business also uses these records to inform employees of their annual earnings and to prepare payroll reports for the government.

FOR YOUR INFORMATION
FYI

Salaries are usually stated as a fixed amount on a weekly, biweekly, semimonthly, or monthly basis. Salaried workers do not normally receive overtime pay. Money paid to employees on an hourly, daily, or even weekly basis is often referred to as wages. In practice, the terms wages *and* salary *are often used interchangeably.*

CHARACTER COUNTS

Is It Discrimination or Poor Judgment?

Your group at CyberMarket has an opening for a research analyst. You are on the search committee to pick candidates to be interviewed. Your company has a code of conduct that states the company will not discriminate on the basis of "race, color, religion, national origin, sex, sexual orientation or group affiliation, age, disability, or veteran status." In a recent meeting, committee members gave the following reasons for wanting to eliminate two candidates.

Candidate A: "She graduated from college before I was born. She can't possibly know anything about our business."

Candidate B: "The ad said two to five years of experience, but we really need someone with more than two years of experience."

Instructions

Use the ethical model to help evaluate hiring decisions based on each of the statements above. Use online sources, as appropriate, to determine whether any actions are illegal.

ANALYZING A PAYROLL TIME CARD

Hobby Shack

EMPLOYEE NO. _____3_____
NAME _____Rick E. Selby_____
PAY PERIOD ENDED _____December 15, 20--_____

MORNING		AFTERNOON		OVERTIME		HOURS	
IN	OUT	IN	OUT	IN	OUT	REG	OT
7:58	12:02	12:59	5:06				

A payroll system must include an accurate record of the time each employee has worked. Several methods are used for keeping time records. One of the more frequently used methods is a time card. Time cards are used as the basic source of information to prepare a payroll.

Some time cards require employees to record only the total hours worked each day. Employees who record the total hours worked each day usually complete time cards by hand.

A business may use a time card that requires employees to record their arrival and departure times. Hobby Shack uses a time clock to record the daily arrival and departure times of its employees.

The time card shown here is for Rick E. Selby. Mr. Selby's employee number is at the top of the card. Below the employee number are the employee name and the ending date of the pay period.

Hobby Shack's time cards have three sections (Morning, Afternoon, and Overtime) with In and Out columns under each section. When Mr. Selby reported for work on December 1, he inserted the card in the time clock. The clock recorded his time of arrival, 7:58, on the first line of the time card. The other entries on this line indicate that he left for lunch at 12:02. He returned at 12:59 and left for the day at 5:06.

Hobby Shack calculates overtime pay for each employee who works more than 8 hours in one day. No employee works more than 5 days in any one week.

FOR YOUR INFORMATION

FYI

Larger companies can afford more expensive systems to record employee arrival and departure times. A popular system requires employees to scan a personal identification card through a card scanner. At the end of the pay period, the system prints a report similar to the time card.

Preparing Payroll Time Cards — Lesson 12-1

CALCULATING EMPLOYEE HOURS WORKED

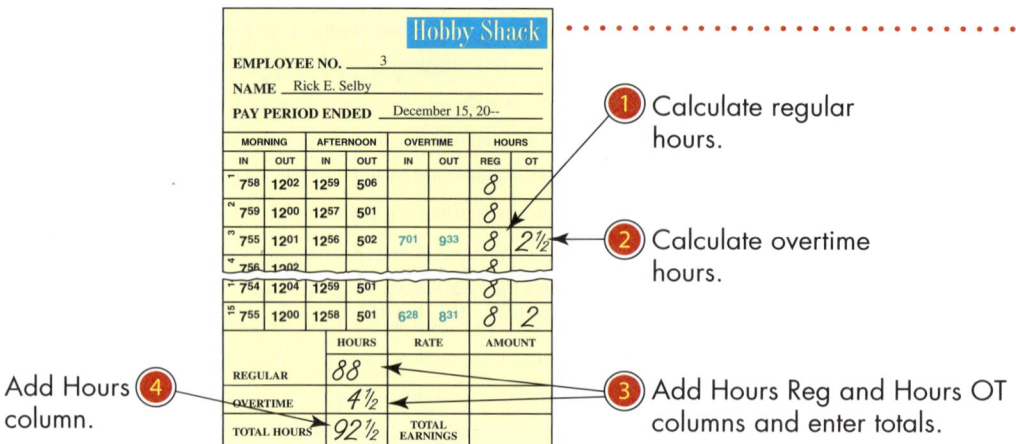

1. Calculate regular hours.
2. Calculate overtime hours.
3. Add Hours Reg and Hours OT columns and enter totals.
4. Add Hours column.

The first task in preparing a payroll is to calculate the number of hours worked by each employee. When calculating hours worked, Hobby Shack rounds arrival and departure times to the nearest quarter hour.

STEPS CALCULATING EMPLOYEE HOURS WORKED

1. Calculate the number of regular hours for each day and enter the amounts in the Hours Reg column. Mr. Selby works 8 hours during a normal day. The hours worked on December 3, the third line of the time card, are calculated using the arrival and departure times imprinted on the time card.

   The hours worked in the morning and afternoon are calculated separately. The morning departure time of 12:01 is rounded to the nearest quarter hour, 12:00. The rounded arrival time, 8:00, subtracted from the departure time, 12:00,

	Departure Time	−	Arrival Time	=	Hours Worked
Morning:					
Time card	12:01		7:55		
Nearest quarter hour	12:00	−	8:00	=	4:00
Afternoon:					
Time card	5:02		12:56		
Nearest quarter hour	5:00	−	1:00	=	4:00
Total regular hours worked on December 3					8:00

equals the morning hours worked. Hours worked of 4:00 means that Mr. Selby worked 4 hours and no (00) minutes. The total regular hours worked, 8, is recorded in the Hours Reg column.

2. Calculate the number of overtime hours for each day and enter the amounts in the Hours OT column. Overtime hours for December 3 are calculated using the same procedure as for regular hours.

	Departure Time	−	Arrival Time	=	Hours Worked
Time card	9:33		7:01		
Nearest quarter hour	9:30	−	7:00	=	2:30

   The hours worked of 2:30 means that Mr. Selby worked 2 hours and 30 minutes (½ hour) of overtime.

3. Add the hours worked in the Hours Reg and Hours OT columns and enter the totals in the spaces provided at the bottom of the time card. Mr. Selby worked 88 regular hours (8 hours × 11 days) and 4½ overtime hours during the semimonthly pay period.

4. Add the Hours column to calculate the total hours. Enter the total in the Hours column at the bottom of the time card. Mr. Selby worked 88 regular hours and 4½ overtime hours for a total of 92½ hours.

CALCULATING EMPLOYEE TOTAL EARNINGS

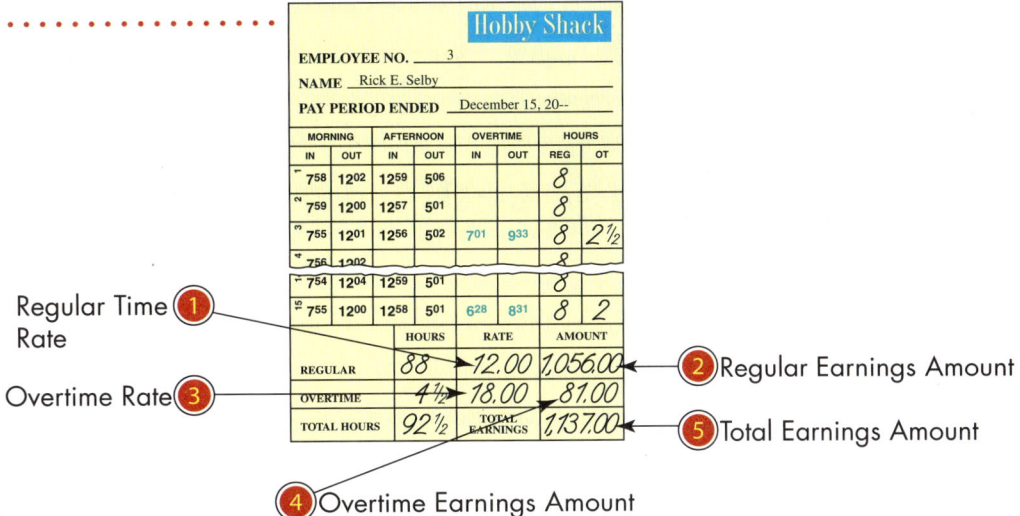

1. Regular Time Rate
2. Regular Earnings Amount
3. Overtime Rate
4. Overtime Earnings Amount
5. Total Earnings Amount

Once the total regular and overtime hours are determined, employee earnings can be calculated. The total pay due for a pay period before deductions is called **total earnings**. Total earnings are sometimes referred to as gross pay or gross earnings.

Hobby Shack owes Mr. Selby $1,137.00 for his work during the pay period ending December 15. However, taxes and other deductions must be subtracted from total earnings to determine the actual amount Hobby Shack will pay Mr. Selby.

STEPS CALCULATING AN EMPLOYEE'S TOTAL EARNINGS

1. Enter the rate for regular time in the Rate column. Mr. Selby's regular hourly rate is *$12.00*.

2. Calculate the regular earnings by multiplying regular hours times the regular rate. Enter the amount of regular earnings, *$1,056.00*, in the Regular Amount space.

3. Enter the rate for overtime, *$18.00*, in the Rate column. Mr. Selby is paid $1^{1}/_{2}$ times his regular rate for overtime work.

4. Calculate the overtime earnings by multiplying overtime hours times the overtime rate. Enter the amount of overtime earnings, *$81.00*, in the Overtime Amount space.

5. Add the Amount column to calculate the total earnings. Enter the amount of total earnings, *$1,137.00*, in the Total Earnings space.

Regular Hours	×	Regular Rate	=	Regular Earnings
88	×	$12.00	=	$1,056.00

Regular Rate	×	$1^{1}/_{2}$	=	Overtime Rate
$12.00	×	$1^{1}/_{2}$	=	$18.00

Overtime Hours	×	Overtime Rate	=	Overtime Earnings
$4^{1}/_{2}$	×	$18.00	=	$81.00

Preparing Payroll Time Cards

End of Lesson REVIEW

AUDIT YOUR UNDERSTANDING

1. What is a payroll?
2. How many hours were worked by a Hobby Shack employee who arrived at 8:29 and departed at 12:02?
3. How does Hobby Shack calculate overtime earnings?
4. What are the total earnings of a Hobby Shack employee who worked 44 hours in a week and earns $11.00 per hour?

TERMS REVIEW

salary
pay period
payroll
total earnings

WORK TOGETHER 12-1

Calculating total earnings

Information taken from employee time cards is provided in the *Working Papers*. Your instructor will guide you through the following example.

1. For each employee, calculate the amount of regular, overtime, and total earnings. Overtime hours are paid at $1\frac{1}{2}$ times the regular rate.

ON YOUR OWN 12-1

Calculating total earnings

Information taken from employee time cards is provided in the *Working Papers*. Work this problem independently.

1. For each employee, calculate the amount of regular, overtime, and total earnings. Overtime hours are paid at $1\frac{1}{2}$ times the regular rate.

LESSON 12-2: Determining Payroll Tax Withholding

PAYROLL TAXES

Taxes based on the payroll of a business are called **payroll taxes**. A business is required by law to withhold certain payroll taxes from employee salaries. All payroll taxes are based on employee total earnings. Therefore, accurate and detailed payroll records must be maintained. Errors in payroll records could cause incorrect payroll tax payments. Federal and state governments may charge a business a penalty for failure to pay correct payroll taxes when they are due. Payroll taxes withheld represent a liability for the employer until payment is made to the government.

Employee Income Tax

A business must withhold federal income taxes from employee total earnings. Federal income taxes withheld must be forwarded periodically to the federal government. Federal income tax is withheld from employee earnings in all 50 states. Employers in many states also are required to withhold state, city, or county income taxes from employee earnings.

BUSINESS STRUCTURES

Selecting a Corporate Form

There are several forms of corporations, each designed to meet the specific needs of its stockholders. The appropriate form is generally dependent on the size of the business and may be changed as the business grows.

1. *General Corporations*. Corporations that have more than 30 stockholders or offer to sell stock to the public must organize as a general or "C" corporation. These corporations must have a board of directors, conduct annual stockholders meetings, and publish financial reports with certain government agencies, such as the Securities and Exchange Commission. Large, well-known companies, such as Wal-Mart and General Motors, are C Corporations.

2. *Close Corporations*. In some states, corporations having fewer than 30 stockholders may elect to be a close corporation. This form of corporation reduces the governance requirements of a C Corporation. For example, a board of directors or annual stockholder meetings may not be required. Less than half of the states recognize this form of corporation.

3. *Subchapter S Corporation*. Named for the related section of the Internal Revenue Code, the Subchapter S or "S" Corporation is a special tax status available to C corporations. Unlike with C Corporations, distributions of earnings are not taxed to the stockholders, thus eliminating the "double taxation" of corporate earnings and distributions. Having 75 or fewer stockholders is the primary requirement for electing S corporation status.

Critical Thinking

1. You plan to expand your small proprietorship with an investment from several family members who will be stockholders. Which form of corporation would you probably use?

2. Considering your answer to question 1, what is the advantage to you? To your investors?

EMPLOYEE'S WITHHOLDING ALLOWANCE CERTIFICATE

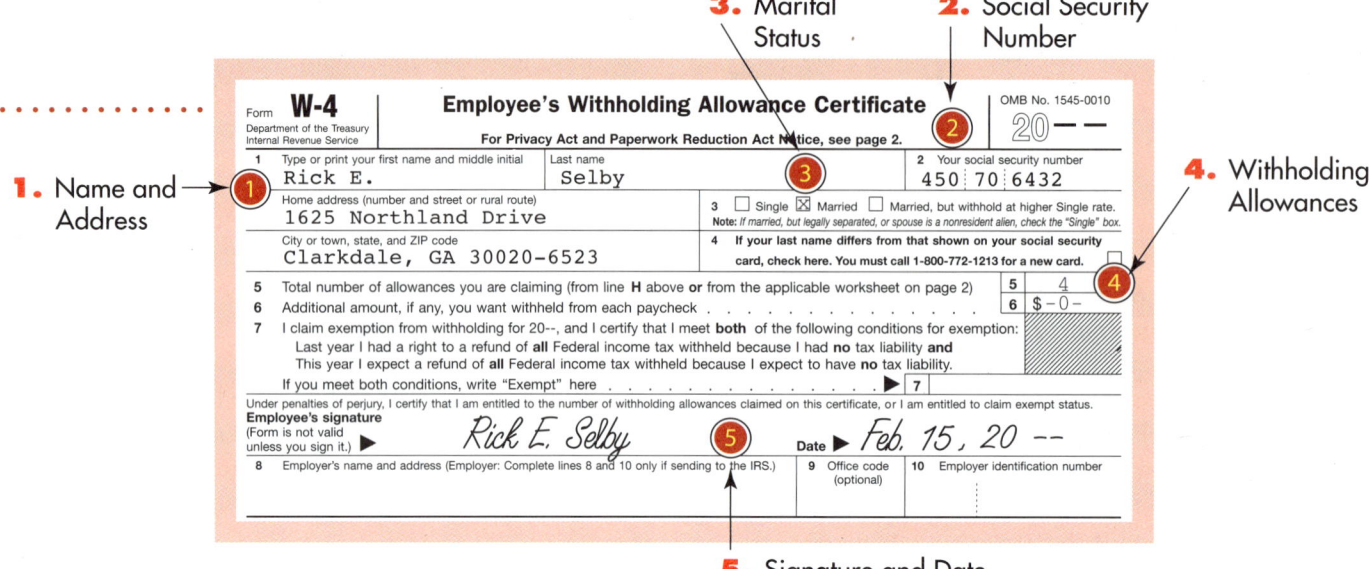

The information used to determine the amount of income tax withheld is identified on Form W-4, Employee's Withholding Allowance Certificate. A deduction from total earnings for each person legally supported by a taxpayer, including the employee, is called a **withholding allowance**. Employers are required to have a current Form W-4 on file for all employees. The amount of income tax withheld is based on employee marital status and number of withholding allowances. A married employee will have less income tax withheld than a single employee with the same total earnings. The larger the number of withholding allowances claimed, the smaller the amount of income tax withheld.

Most employees are required to have federal income taxes withheld from their salaries. An exemption from withholding is available for certain low-income and part-time employees. The employee must meet the requirements listed in item 7 of the Form W-4. However, individuals cannot claim exemption from withholding if (1) their income exceeds $750 and includes more than $250 of unearned income such as interest and dividends and (2) another person can claim them as a dependent on their tax return.

> **FOR YOUR INFORMATION**
> **FYI**
>
> Each employee must have a social security number. Current law ensures that most infants who are at least one year old by the end of a tax year will have a social security number. Therefore, most employees will have received their social security number as a child. Employees without social security numbers can apply for a number at the nearest Social Security office.

> **FOR YOUR INFORMATION**
> **FYI**
>
> Employees are responsible for contacting their employer when the number of their dependents changes. A new W-4 form should be completed and a copy of the form sent to the Internal Revenue Service.

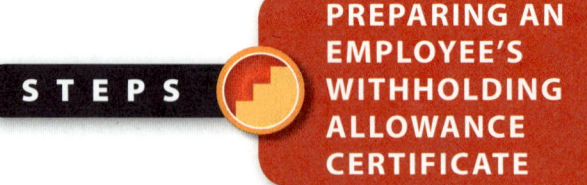

PREPARING AN EMPLOYEE'S WITHHOLDING ALLOWANCE CERTIFICATE

1. Write the employee's name and address.
2. Write the employee's social security number.
3. Check the appropriate marital status block. Mr. Selby checked the married box for item 3.
4. Write the total number of withholding allowances claimed. Mr. Selby claimed four withholding allowances, one each for himself, his wife, and his two children.
5. The employee signs and dates the form.

EMPLOYEE'S INCOME TAX WITHHOLDING—SINGLE PERSONS

SINGLE Persons—SEMIMONTHLY Payroll Period

If the wages are—		And the number of withholding allowances claimed is—										
At least	But less than	0	1	2	3	4	5	6	7	8	9	10
		The amount of income tax to be withheld is—										
$0	$115	$0	$0	$0	$0	$0	$0	$0	$0	$0	$0	$0
115	120	1	0	0	0	0	0	0	0	0	0	0
120	125	1	0	0	0	0	0	0	0	0	0	0
125	130	2	0	0	0	0	0	0	0	0	0	0
130	135	2	0	0	0	0	0	0	0	0	0	0
235	240	13	0	0	0	0	0	0	0	0	0	0
240	245	13	0	0	0	0	0	0	0	0	0	0
245	250	14	1	0	0	0	0	0	0	0	0	0
250	260	14	2	0	0	0	0	0	0	0	0	0
260	270	15	3	0	0	0	0	0	0	0	0	0
540	560	51	32	18	5	0	0	0	0	0	0	0
560	580	54	35	20	7	0	0	0	0	0	0	0
580	600	57	38	22	9	0	0	0	0	0	0	0
600	620	60	41	24	11	0	0	0	0	0	0	0
620	640	63	44	26	13	0	0	0	0	0	0	0
640	660	66	47	28	15	2	0	0	0	0	0	0
660	680	69	50	31	17	4	0	0	0	0	0	0
680	700	72	53	34	19	6	0	0	0	0	0	0
700	720	75	56	37	21	8	0	0	0	0	0	0
720	740	78	59	40	23	10	0	0	0	0	0	0
740	760	81	62	43	25	12	0	0	0	0	0	0
760	780	84	65	46	27	14	1	0	0	0	0	0
780	800	87	68	49	29	16	3	0	0	0	0	0
800	820	90	71	52	32	18	5	0	0	0	0	0
820	840	93	74	55	35	20	7	0	0	0	0	0
840	860	96	77	58	38	22	9	0	0	0	0	0
860	880	99	80	61	41	24	11	0	0	0	0	0
880	900	102	83	64	44	26	13	0	0	0	0	0
900	920	105	86	67	47	28	15	2	0	0	0	0
920	940	108	89	70	50	31	17	4	0	0	0	0
940	960	111	92	73	53	34	19	6	0	0	0	0
960	980	114	95	76	56	37	21	8	0	0	0	0
980	1,000	117	98	79	59	40	23	10	0	0	0	0
1,000	1,020	120	101	82	62	43	25	12	0	0	0	0
1,020	1,040	123	104	85	65	46	27	14	2	0	0	0
1,040	1,060	126	107	88	68	49	29	16	4	0	0	0
1,060	1,080	129	110	91	71	52	32	18	6	0	0	0
1,080	1,100	132	113	94	74	55	35	20	8	0	0	0
1,100	1,120	135	116	97	77	58	38	22	10	0	0	0
1,120	1,140	138	119	100	80	61	41	24	12	0	0	0
1,140	1,160	141	122	103	83	64	44	26	14	1	0	0
1,160	1,180	144	125	106	86	67	47	28	16	3	0	0
1,180	1,200	147	128	109	89	70	50	31	18	5	0	0
1,200	1,220	150	131	112	92	73	53	34	20	7	0	0
1,220	1,240	153	134	115	95	76	56	37	22	9	0	0
1,240	1,260	156	137	118	98	79	59	40	24	11	0	0
1,260	1,280	159	140	121	101	82	62	43	26	13	0	0
1,280	1,300	163	143	124	104	85	65	46	28	15	2	0
1,300	1,320	168	146	127	107	88	68	49	30	17	4	0
1,320	1,340	173	149	130	110	91	71	52	33	19	6	0

The amount of federal income tax withheld from each employee's total earnings is determined from withholding tables prepared by the Internal Revenue Service. These withholding tables are revised each year and are available from the Internal Revenue Service in Publication 15 (Circular E), Employer's Tax Guide. The withholding tables shown in this chapter are those available when this textbook was prepared.

Tables are prepared for various payroll periods—monthly, semimonthly, biweekly, weekly, and daily. Single persons are taxed at different levels of income than married persons. Therefore, one table is available for single persons and another table is available for married persons for each pay period.

Hobby Shack's pay period is semimonthly, so Hobby Shack uses the semimonthly withholding tables.

EMPLOYEE'S INCOME TAX WITHHOLDING—MARRIED PERSONS

MARRIED Persons—SEMIMONTHLY Payroll Period

① Select the appropriate table.

If the wages are—		And the number of withholding allowances claimed is—										
At least	But less than	0	1	2	3	4	5	6	7	8	9	10
		The amount of income tax to be withheld is—										
720	740	40	27	14	1	0	0	0	0	0	0	0
740	760	42	29	16	3	0	0	0	0	0	0	0
760	780	44	31	18	5	0	0	0	0	0	0	0
780	800	46	33	20	7	0	0	0	0	0	0	0
800	820	48	35	22	9	0	0	0	0	0	0	0
820	840	50	37	24	11	0	0	0	0	0	0	0
840	860	52	39	26	13	0	0	0	0	0	0	0
860	880	54	41	28	15	2	0	0	0	0	0	0
880	900	56	43	30	17	4	0	0	0	0	0	0
900	920	58	45	32	19	6	0	0	0	0	0	0
920	940	60	47	34	21	8	0	0	0	0	0	0
940	960	63	49	36	23	10	0	0	0	0	0	0
960	980	66	51	38	25	12	0	0	0	0	0	0
980	1,000	69	53	40	27	14	1	0	0	0	0	0
1,000	1,020	72	55	42	29	16	3	0	0	0	0	0
1,020	1,040	75	57	44	31	18	5	0	0	0	0	0
1,040	1,060	78	59	46	33	20	7	0	0	0	0	0
1,060	1,080	81	61	48	35	22	9	0	0	0	0	0
1,080	1,100	84	64	50	37	24	11	0	0	0	0	0
1,100	1,120	87	67	52	39	26	13	0	0	0	0	0
1,120	1,140	90	70	54	41	28	15	2	0	0	0	0
1,140	1,160	93	73	56	43	30	17	4	0	0	0	0
1,160	1,180	96	76	58	45	32	19	6	0	0	0	0
1,180	1,200	99	79	60	47	34	21	8	0	0	0	0
1,200	1,220	102	82	63	49	36	23	10	0	0	0	0
1,220	1,240	105	85	66	51	38	25	12	0	0	0	0
1,240	1,260	108	88	69	53	40	27	14	1	0	0	0
1,260	1,280	111	91	72	55	42	29	16	3	0	0	0
1,280	1,300	114	94	75	57	44	31	18	5	0	0	0
1,300	1,320	117	97	78	59	46	33	20	7	0	0	0
1,320	1,340	120	100	81	62	48	35	22	9	0	0	0
1,340	1,360	123	103	84	65	50	37	24	11	0	0	0
1,360	1,380	126	106	87	68	52	39	26	13	0	0	0
1,380	1,400	129	109	90	71	54	41	28	15	2	0	0
1,400	1,420	132	112	93	74	56	43	30	17	4	0	0
1,420	1,440	135	115	96	77	58	45	32	19	6	0	0
1,440	1,460	138	118	99	80	60	47	34	21	8	0	0
1,460	1,480	141	121	102	83	63	49	36	23	10	0	0
1,480	1,500	144	124	105	86	66	51	38	25	12	0	0
1,500	1,520	147	127	108	89	69	53	40	27	14	1	0
1,820	1,840	195	175	156	137	117	98	78	59	46	33	21
1,840	1,860	198	178	159	140	120	101	81	62	48	35	23
1,860	1,880	201	181	162	143	123	104	84	65	50	37	25
1,880	1,900	204	184	165	146	126	107	87	68	52	39	27
1,900	1,920	207	187	168	149	129	110	90	71	54	41	29

② Locate employee's total earnings.

③ Intersection of wages and number of withholding allowances column.

STEPS DETERMINING AN EMPLOYEE'S INCOME TAX WITHHOLDING

① Select the appropriate table. Married Persons—Semimonthly Payroll Period is selected to determine income tax withholding for employee Rick E. Selby.

② Locate the employee's total earnings between the appropriate lines of the At Least and But Less Than columns. Mr. Selby's total earnings for the pay period ended December 15, 20--, are $1,137.00. Locate the line At Least $1,120.00 But Less Than $1,140.00.

③ Follow the selected wages line across to the column headed by the employee's number of withholding allowances. The amount listed at the intersection of the wages line and number of withholding allowances column is the employee's amount of income tax withholding. Mr. Selby's federal income tax withholding, with total earnings of $1,137.00 and withholding allowances of four, is $28.00 for the semimonthly pay period ended December 15, 20--.

EMPLOYEE SOCIAL SECURITY AND MEDICARE TAX

The Federal Insurance Contributions Act (FICA) provides for a federal system of old-age, survivors, disability, and hospital insurance. A federal tax paid for old-age, survivors, and disability insurance is called **social security tax**. A federal tax paid for hospital insurance is called **Medicare tax**. Each of these taxes is accounted for and reported separately.

Social security and Medicare taxes are paid by both employees and employer. Employers are required to withhold and deposit the employees' part of the taxes and pay a matching amount of these taxes.

Social security tax is calculated on employee earnings up to a maximum paid in a calendar year. The maximum amount of earnings on which a tax is calculated is called a **tax base**. Congress sets the tax base and the tax rates for social security tax. An act of Congress can change the tax base and tax rate at any time. The social security tax rate and base used in this text are 6.2% of earnings up to a maximum of $87,000.00 in each calendar year.

Between January 1 and December 15, Mr. Selby's earnings are less than the social security tax base. Therefore, Mr. Selby's social security tax deduction for the semimonthly pay period ended December 15, 20--, is calculated as shown.

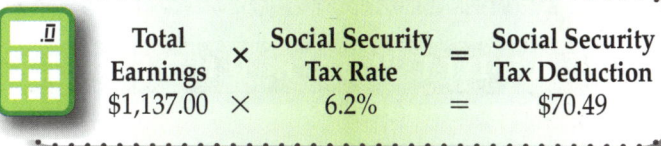

Total Earnings	×	Social Security Tax Rate	=	Social Security Tax Deduction
$1,137.00	×	6.2%	=	$70.49

Medicare does not have a tax base. Therefore, Medicare tax is calculated on total employee earnings. The Medicare tax rate used in this text is 1.45% of total employee earnings.

Rick E. Selby's Medicare tax deduction for the semimonthly pay period ended December 15, 20--, is calculated as shown.

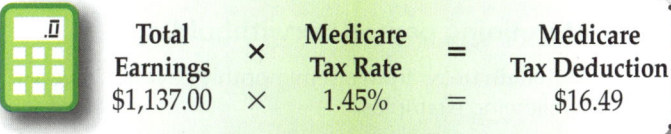

Total Earnings	×	Medicare Tax Rate	=	Medicare Tax Deduction
$1,137.00	×	1.45%	=	$16.49

FOR YOUR INFORMATION

FYI

Accounting procedures are the same regardless of changes in the tax base and tax rate. The social security tax rate and the tax base shown above are assumed for all payroll calculations in this textbook.

REMEMBER

When an employee's earnings exceed the tax base, no more social security tax is deducted.

Determining Payroll Tax Witholding

End of Lesson REVIEW

AUDIT YOUR UNDERSTANDING

1. Where does an employer get the information used to determine the amount of federal income tax to withhold from employees' earnings?
2. Employee federal income tax withholdings are based on what two factors?
3. Does the employer or employee pay social security tax and Medicare tax?

TERMS REVIEW

payroll taxes
withholding allowance
social security tax
Medicare tax
tax base

WORK TOGETHER 12-2

Determining payroll tax withholding

Information taken from a semimonthly payroll is given in the *Working Papers*. Your instructor will guide you through the following examples.

1. For each employee, determine the federal income tax that must be withheld. Use the tax withholding tables in this lesson.
2. Calculate the amount of social security tax and Medicare tax that must be withheld for each employee. Use a social security tax rate of 6.2% and a Medicare tax rate of 1.45%. None of the employees has accumulated earnings greater than the tax base.

ON YOUR OWN 12-2

Determining payroll tax withholding

Information taken from a semimonthly payroll is given in the *Working Papers*. Work this problem independently.

1. For each employee, determine the federal income tax that must be withheld. Use the tax withholding tables in this lesson.
2. Calculate the amount of social security tax and Medicare tax that must be withheld for each employee. Use a social security tax rate of 6.2% and a Medicare tax rate of 1.45%. None of the employees has accumulated earnings greater than the tax base.

LESSON 12-3

Preparing Payroll Records

PAYROLL REGISTER

Callouts:
1. Pay Period Date
2. Payment Date
3. Employee Personal Data
4. Earnings
5. Federal Income Tax
6. Social Security Tax
7. Medicare Tax
8. Health Insurance
9. Other Deductions
10. Total Deductions
11. Net Pay
12. Total, Prove, and Rule
13. Check Number

PAYROLL REGISTER

SEMIMONTHLY PERIOD ENDED December 15, 20--   DATE OF PAYMENT December 15, 20--

	EMPL. NO.	EMPLOYEE'S NAME	MARITAL STATUS	NO. OF ALLOWANCES	EARNINGS REGULAR	OVERTIME	TOTAL	DEDUCTIONS FEDERAL INCOME TAX	SOC. SEC. TAX	MEDICARE TAX	HEALTH INSURANCE	OTHER	TOTAL	NET PAY	CHECK NO.
1	2	Aranda, Susan A.	M	2	968 00		968 00	38 00	60 02	14 04	45 00	B 10 00	167 06	800 94	482
2	5	Drew, Paul S.	S	1	550 00		550 00	32 00	34 10	7 98	38 00		112 08	437 92	483
3	1	Kellogg, Janice P.	M	1	1760 00	150 00	1910 00	187 00	118 42	27 70	38 00	UW 20 00	391 12	1518 88	484
4	6	Mendel, Ann M.	S	1	240 00		240 00		14 88	3 48			18 36	221 64	485
5	3	Selby, Rick E.	M	4	1056 00	81 00	1137 00	28 00	70 49	16 49	60 00	B 10 00 UW 10 00	194 98	942 02	486
6	4	Young, Justin L.	S	1	906 40		906 40	86 00	56 20	13 14	38 00	B 15 00 UW 10 00	218 34	688 06	487
7		Totals			5480 40	231 00	5711 40	371 00	354 11	82 83	219 00	B 35 00 UW 40 00	1101 94	4609 46	

A business form used to record payroll information is called a **payroll register**. A payroll register summarizes the payroll for one pay period and shows total earnings, payroll withholdings, and net pay of all employees. Hobby Shack prepares a separate payroll register for each semimonthly payroll.

STEPS PREPARING A PAYROLL REGISTER

1. Enter the last date of the semimonthly payroll period, *December 15, 20--*, at the top of the payroll register.

2. Enter the date of payment, *December 15, 20--*, also at the top of the payroll register.

3. For each employee, enter employee number, name, marital status, and number of allowances. This information is taken from personnel records. Entries for Rick E. Selby are on line 5 of the register.

4. Enter regular earnings, overtime earnings, and total earnings for each employee in columns 1, 2, and 3 of the payroll register. This information is taken from each employee's time card.

Preparing Payroll Records   Lesson 12-3   **351**

⑤ Enter in column 4 the federal income tax withheld from each employee. Mr. Selby's federal tax withholding is $28.00.

⑥ Enter in column 5 of the payroll register the social security tax withheld from each employee. Mr. Selby's social security tax deduction, *$70.49*, is recorded in column 5 of the payroll register. Mr. Selby's total earnings for the year have not exceeded the social security tax base, so his total earnings for the pay period are taxed.

⑦ Enter in column 6 the Medicare tax withheld from each employee. Mr. Selby's Medicare tax deduction is *$16.49*.

⑧ Enter in column 7 the health insurance premium deductions. Full-time employees of Hobby Shack participate in a group health insurance plan to take advantage of lower group rates. Mr. Selby's semimonthly health insurance premium is *$60.00*. Premiums are set by the insurance company and are usually based on the employee marital status and whether coverage is for an individual or a family. Some health insurance premiums may be based on the number of individuals covered.

⑨ Enter in column 8 all other employee payroll deductions. The Other column is used to record voluntary deductions requested by an employee. Entries are identified by code letters. Hobby Shack uses the letter *B* to identify amounts withheld for buying U.S. Savings Bonds. *UW* is used to identify amounts withheld for employee contributions to United Way. Mr. Selby has authorized Hobby Shack to withhold *$10.00* each pay period to buy U.S. Savings Bonds for him. Mr. Selby has also authorized that *$10.00* be withheld as a contribution to the United Way.

⑩ After all deductions are entered in the payroll register, add all the deduction amounts for each employee and enter the totals in column 9. Mr. Selby's total deductions, *$194.98*, are calculated as shown.

Federal Income Tax	+	Social Security Tax	+	Medicare Tax	+	Health Insurance	+	Other	=	Total Deductions
$28.00	+	$70.49	+	$16.49	+	$60.00	+	$20.00	=	$194.98

⑪ Determine the net pay for each employee. The total earnings paid to an employee after payroll taxes and other deductions is called **net pay**. Subtract the total deductions, column 9, from total earnings, column 3, to determine net pay. Enter net pay in column 10. Mr. Selby's net pay, *$942.02*, is calculated as shown.

Total Earnings	−	Total Deductions	=	Net Pay
$1,137.00	−	$194.98	=	$942.02

⑫ Total, prove, and rule the payroll register. Total each amount column. Subtract the Total Deductions column from the Total Earnings column. The result should equal the total of the Net Pay column. If the totals do not agree, the errors must be found and corrected. Proving the accuracy of Hobby Shack's payroll register for the pay period ended December 15, 20--, is shown.

Total Earnings	−	Total Deductions	=	Net Pay
$5,711.40	−	$1,101.94	=	$4,609.46

The net pay, $4,609.46, is the same as the total of the Net Pay column. The payroll register is proved. After the payroll register is proved, rule double lines below all amount column totals to show the totals have been verified as correct.

⑬ Payroll checks are written after payroll calculations are verified and a manager approves the payroll. Write the payroll check numbers in the Check No. column.

EMPLOYEE EARNINGS RECORDS

A business must send a quarterly report to federal and state governments showing employee taxable earnings and taxes withheld from employee earnings. Detailed information about each employee's earnings is summarized in a single record for each employee. A business form used to record details affecting payments made to an employee is called an **employee earnings record**. An employee's earnings and deductions for each pay period are summarized on one line of the employee earnings record. A new earnings record is prepared for each employee each quarter. Rick E. Selby's earnings record for the fourth quarter is shown.

The steps for completing the employee earnings record are on the next page.

FOR YOUR INFORMATION

FYI

The federal income tax withholding tables on pages 347–348 contain a column for 0 dependents. How can an employee have 0 dependents if the employee is a dependent? Some employees claim fewer dependents than they are allowed—even as low as zero—to increase the amount of tax withheld. An employee who has other taxable income, such as interest and dividends, can use payroll withholding to pay the additional income taxes owed on this income. As a result, the employee avoids having a large income tax payment when the tax return is filed.

Preparing Payroll Records   Lesson 12-3   **353**

STEPS PREPARING AN EMPLOYEE EARNINGS RECORD

1 Enter the last day of the yearly quarter, *December 31, 20--*, at the top of the earnings record.

2 Enter the employee's number, name, marital status, withholding allowances, hourly rate, social security number, and position in the provided space. This information is taken from the employee's personnel records.

3 Enter the fiscal year's accumulated earnings for the beginning of the current quarter. This information is taken from the ending accumulated earnings for the previous quarter. Mr. Selby's accumulated earnings for the first three quarters ended September 30 are *$18,432.00*. The Accumulated Earnings column of the employee earnings record shows the accumulated earnings since the beginning of the fiscal year.

4 Enter the ending date of the pay period being recorded, *12/15*.

5 Enter the earnings, deductions, and net pay in the columns of the employee earnings record. This information is taken from the current pay period's payroll register.

6 Add the current pay period's total earnings to the previous period's accumulated earnings. Mr. Selby's accumulated earnings as of December 15 are calculated as shown.

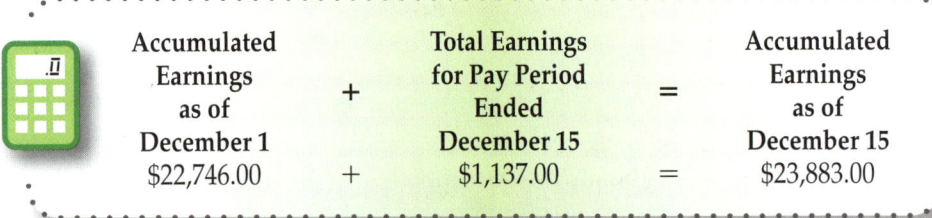

The Accumulated Earnings column shows the total earnings for Mr. Selby since the first of the year. The amounts in the Accumulated Earnings column supply an up-to-date reference for an employee's year-to-date earnings. When employee earnings reach the tax base, certain payroll taxes do not apply. For example, social security taxes are paid only on the first $87,000 of earnings.

7 At the end of each quarter, total and prove the earnings record for each employee. Calculate quarterly totals for each amount column. Subtract the Total Deductions column from the Total Earnings column. The result should equal the total of the Net Pay column. If the totals do not agree, the errors must be found and corrected. Proving the accuracy of Mr. Selby's fourth quarterly totals is shown.

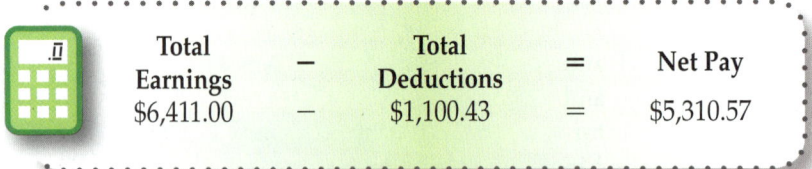

The net pay, *$5,310.57*, is compared to the total of the Net Pay column. The earnings record is proved because these amounts are equal. These totals are needed to prepare required government reports.

> **REMEMBER**
>
> *Total earnings, not net pay, are added to the previous accumulated earnings amount on the earnings record. Total earnings is the amount compared to the tax base to determine whether social security taxes should be withheld.*

End of Lesson REVIEW

TERMS REVIEW

payroll register

net pay

employee earnings record

AUDIT YOUR UNDERSTANDING

1. What does the payroll register summarize?
2. How is net pay calculated?
3. Why do companies complete employee earnings records?

WORK TOGETHER 12-3

Preparing payroll records

Selected payroll data for Antique Shop are provided in a payroll register in the *Working Papers*. Your instructor will guide you through the following examples.

1. Complete the payroll register entries for Judy Hensley and Mike McCune for the semimonthly pay period ended July 15, 20--. Use the tax withholding tables shown in Lesson 12-2. Use tax rates of 6.2% for social security tax and 1.45% for Medicare tax. Neither employee has reached the tax base. For each employee, withhold $60.00 for health insurance and $15.00 for U.S. Savings bonds, per pay period.
2. Total all the amount columns of the payroll register. Prove the payroll register.
3. Prepare a quarterly earnings record for Ms. Hensley for the quarter ended September 30, 20--, and enter the July 15 payroll information. Ms. Hensley's employee number is 5; rate of pay is $13.00; social security number is 543-69-0123; position is sales clerk. Accumulated earnings at the end of the second quarter are $13,520.00. Save your work to complete Work Together 12-4.

ON YOUR OWN 12-3

Preparing payroll records

Selected payroll data for Prosser Company are provided in a payroll register in the *Working Papers*. Work this problem independently.

1. Complete the payroll register entries for Allen P. Best and Tammy S. Edwards for the semimonthly pay period ended July 15, 20--. Use the tax withholding tables shown in Lesson 12-2. Use tax rates of 6.2% for social security tax and 1.45% for Medicare tax. For each employee, withhold $60.00 for health insurance and $10.00 for U.S. Savings Bonds per pay period. For Ms. Edwards, also withhold $20.00 for United Way per pay period.
2. Total all the amount columns of the payroll register. Prove the payroll register.
3. Prepare a quarterly earnings record for Mr. Best for the quarter ended September 30, 20--, and enter the July 15 payroll information. Mr. Best's employee number is 4; rate of pay is $12.25; social security number is 301-69-1427; position is sales clerk. Accumulated earnings at the end of the second quarter are $28,692.00. Save your work to complete On Your Own 12-4.

LESSON 12-4

Preparing Payroll Checks

PAYROLL BANK ACCOUNT

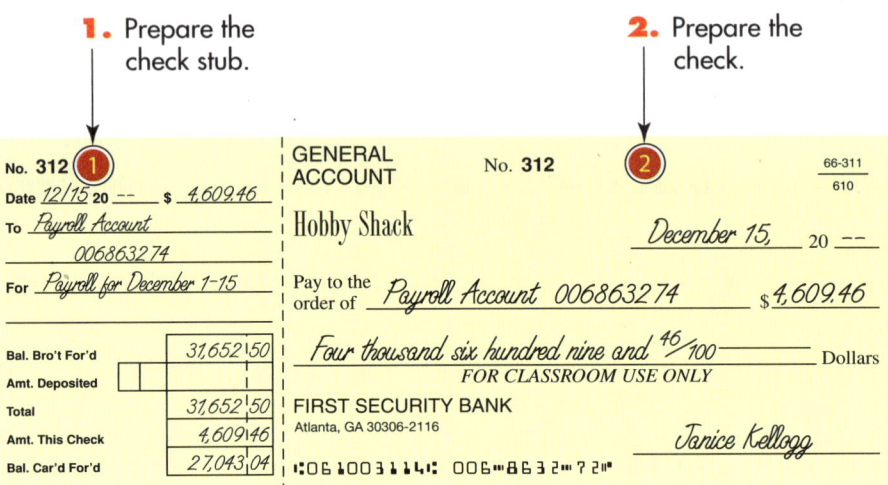

1. Prepare the check stub.
2. Prepare the check.

Hobby Shack pays its employees with checks written on a special payroll checking account. A check for the total net pay is written on Hobby Shack's general checking account. The check is deposited in the payroll checking account.

A separate checking account for payroll checks helps to protect and control payroll payments. The exact amount needed to pay the payroll is deposited in the special payroll checking account. If amounts on checks are altered or unauthorized payroll checks are prepared, the amount in the special payroll account would be insufficient to cover all the checks. Thus, the bank and Hobby Shack would be alerted quickly to an unauthorized payroll check. Also, since payroll checks are drawn on the separate account, any balance in this account will correspond to the sum of outstanding payroll checks.

STEPS PREPARING A CHECK FOR TOTAL NET PAY

1. Prepare the check stub. The date of the check is *12/15*. The amount, *$4,609.46*, is the total of the Net Pay column of the payroll register. The check is payable to *Payroll Account 006863274*, Hobby Shack's special payroll checking account. The payment is for the payroll period from December 1 to 15. Calculate and record the new general checking account balance.

2. Prepare the check from the information on the check stub. Hobby Shack's check is drawn on the company's general account and is signed by Janice Kellogg.

REMEMBER

Using a separate checking account for payroll checks provides internal control and helps to prevent fraud.

EMPLOYEE'S PAYROLL CHECK

1. Enter on check stub information from payroll register.
2. Prepare employee's payroll check for net amount of earnings.

The information used to prepare payroll checks is taken from a payroll register. A special payroll check form is used that has a detachable stub for recording earnings and amounts deducted. Employees keep the stubs for a record of deductions and cash received.

STEPS — PREPARING AN EMPLOYEE'S PAYROLL CHECK

1. Prepare the check stub of each employee's payroll check. Enter information from the payroll register.
2. Prepare each employee's payroll check payable for the amount of net pay for the pay period. Rick E. Selby's net pay for the pay period ended December 15, 20--, is $942.02.

ELECTRONIC FUNDS TRANSFER

A computerized cash payments system that transfers funds without the use of checks, currency, or other paper documents is known as electronic funds transfer (EFT). Some businesses deposit employee net pay directly to each employee bank account by using EFT. When EFT is used, the bank's computer deducts the amount of net pay from the business's bank account and adds the amount to each employee bank account. The payroll must still be calculated, but individual checks are not written and do not have to be distributed. Under this system, each employee receives a statement of earnings and deductions similar to the detachable stub on a payroll check.

PHOTODISC/GETTY IMAGES

Preparing Payroll Checks — Lesson 12-4

End of Lesson REVIEW

AUDIT YOUR UNDERSTANDING

1. Why does Hobby Shack have a separate checking account for payroll checks?
2. What is the source of the information that is recorded on each employee's payroll check stub?
3. How do payroll procedures differ for employees who request that their pay be deposited through electronic funds transfer?

WORK TOGETHER 12-4

Preparing payroll checks

Use the payroll register from Work Together 12-3. In the *Working Papers* are three blank checks: one General Account check and two Payroll Account checks. Your instructor will guide you through the following examples.

1. Prepare Antique Shop's General Account check for the pay period ended July 15, 20--. The payment date is July 15. Balance brought forward from the previous check is $16,542.00. The Payroll Account number is 0639583. Sign your name as the manager of Antique Shop.
2. For the pay period ended July 15, 20--, prepare payroll checks for Judy Hensley and Mike McCune. The payment date is July 15. Sign your name as the manager of Antique Shop. Record the two payroll check numbers in the payroll register.

ON YOUR OWN 12-4

Preparing payroll checks

Use the payroll register from On Your Own 12-3. In the *Working Papers* are three blank checks: one General Account check and two Payroll Account checks. Work this problem independently.

1. Prepare Prosser Company's General Account check for the pay period ended July 15, 20--. The payment date is July 15. Balance carried forward from the previous check is $12,421.90. The Payroll Account number is 146-7219-6. Sign your name as the manager of Prosser Company.
2. For the pay period ended July 15, 20--, prepare payroll checks for Allen P. Best and Tammy S. Edwards. The payment date is July 15. Sign your name as the manager of Prosser Company. Record the two payroll checks in the payroll register.

SUMMARY

After completing this chapter, you can:

1. Define accounting terms related to payroll records.
2. Identify accounting practices related to payroll records.
3. Complete a payroll time card.
4. Calculate payroll taxes.
5. Complete a payroll register and an employee earnings record.
6. Prepare payroll checks.

Go Beyond the Book
For more information go to www.C21accounting.com

EXPLORE ACCOUNTING

Employee vs. Independent Contractor

A business sometimes contracts with individuals to perform specified services for the business. Determining whether such an individual is an employee or a self-employed independent contractor is an important issue.

If the person is found to be an employee, the employer must withhold and submit employee income tax, social security tax, and Medicare tax to the Internal Revenue Service (IRS). The employer must pay an equal amount of social security and Medicare tax. Also, the employer will pay unemployment taxes (discussed in Chapter 13) and be subject to various employer reporting requirements.

A person who is found to be a self-employed independent contractor must pay an amount of social security and Medicare tax that is equivalent to both the employer and employee taxes.

If an employer incorrectly treats an employee as a self-employed independent contractor, the penalties can be severe. Therefore, it is important to a business to make an accurate determination of the status of all individuals performing work for the business. The IRS has provided guidelines to help businesses make the distinction. Every individual who performs services subject to the will and control of an employer both as to what shall be done and how it shall be done is considered an employee for withholding purposes. The major determining factor is whether the employer has the legal right to control both the method and result of the services. If the business has the right to control only the result of the service performed and not the means and methods of accomplishing the result, the individual is probably a self-employed independent contractor.

Research: Review federal tax publications or interview local businesses on the issues below. Then prepare a written or oral report to present to your class. (1) Why is it important to determine an individual's status? What is at stake for the individual, the employer, and the IRS? (2) What are the advantages and disadvantages of determining an individual to be an employee or independent contractor—to the individual? to the employer? to the IRS?

12-1 APPLICATION PROBLEM

Preparing payroll time cards

Employee time cards are given in the *Working Papers*.

Instructions:
1. Calculate the regular, overtime, and total hours worked by each employee. Any hours over the regular 8-hour day are considered overtime. Record the hours on the time cards.
2. Determine the regular, overtime, and total earnings for each employee. The overtime rate is $1\frac{1}{2}$ times the regular rate. Complete the time cards.

12-2 APPLICATION PROBLEM

Determining payroll tax withholding

Information taken from the semimonthly payroll register is given in the *Working Papers*.

Instructions:
1. Determine the federal income tax that must be withheld for each of the eight employees. Use the tax withholding tables shown in Lesson 12-2.
2. Calculate the amount of social security tax and Medicare tax that must be withheld for each employee using 6.2% and 1.45% tax rates, respectively. None of the eight employees has accumulated earnings greater than the tax base.

12-3 APPLICATION PROBLEM *Microsoft Office*

Preparing a payroll register

The information for the semimonthly pay period October 1–15 of the current year is given in the *Working Papers*.

Instructions:
Complete a payroll register for Perez Company. The date of payment is October 15. Use the tax withholding tables shown in Lesson 12-2 for the income tax withholding for each employee. Calculate social security and Medicare taxes withholding using 6.2% and 1.45% tax rates, respectively. None of the employees has accumulated earnings greater than the social security tax base.

12-4 APPLICATION PROBLEM *Microsoft Office*

Preparing an employee earnings record

Grady R. Hurley's earnings for the six semimonthly pay periods in July, August, and September of the current year are given in the *Working Papers*. Deductions and net pay have been completed for July and August.

The following additional data about Grady R. Hurley are needed to complete the employee earnings record.

1. Employee number: 28
2. Marital status: married
3. Withholding allowances: 2
4. Rate of pay: regular, $15.00
5. Social security number: 462-81-5823
6. Position: service manager
7. Accumulated earnings for the end of second quarter: $15,750.00
8. Deductions from total earnings:
   a. Health insurance: $60.00 each semimonthly pay period
   b. U.S. Savings Bonds: $20.00 each semimonthly pay period
   c. Federal income tax: determined each pay period by using the withholding tables in Lesson 12-2
   d. Social security taxes: 6.2% of total earnings each pay period
   e. Medicare taxes: 1.45% of total earnings each pay period

Instructions:
1. Calculate and record the accumulated earnings for the July and August pay periods.
2. Complete the earnings record for the pay periods ended September 15 and September 30.
3. Total all amount columns on the earnings record.
4. Verify the accuracy of the completed employee earnings record. The Quarter Total for Regular and Overtime Earnings should equal the Quarter Total for Net Pay plus Total Deductions. The Quarter Total for Total Earnings should equal the end-of-quarter Accumulated Earnings minus the beginning-of-quarter Accumulated Earnings.

12-5 APPLICATION PROBLEM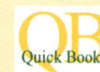

Preparing payroll checks

Royal Appliances' net payroll for the semimonthly pay period ended May 15, 20--, is $7,498.80. Payroll checks are prepared May 15, 20--. Blank checks are provided in the *Working Papers*.

Instructions:
1. Prepare a General Account check for the total amount of the net pay. Make the check payable to Payroll Account 018-65-4237, and sign your name as manager of Royal Appliances. The beginning check stub balance is $10,138.95.
2. Prepare payroll checks for two employees of Royal Appliances. Payroll information for the two employees is as follows. Sign your name as a manager of Royal Appliances.

   a. Wanda M. Curtis
      Check No. 823
      Regular Earnings $740.00
      Overtime Earnings   40.00
      Deductions:
         Federal Income Tax $ 33.00
         Social Security Tax   48.36
         Medicare Tax   11.31
         Health Insurance   35.00

   b. Kevin R. Hayes
      Check No. 827
      Regular Earnings $920.00
      Overtime Earnings   30.00
      Deductions:
         Federal Income Tax $ 23.00
         Social Security Tax   58.90
         Medicare Tax   13.78
         Health Insurance   60.00
         Savings Bond   20.00

12-6 MASTERY PROBLEM

Preparing a semimonthly payroll

The following information for Arrow Company is for the semimonthly pay period August 16–31 of the current year. Forms are given in the *Working Papers*.

EMPL. NO.	EMPLOYEE'S NAME	MARITAL STATUS	NO. OF ALLOWANCES	EARNINGS REGULAR	EARNINGS OVERTIME	DEDUCTIONS HEALTH INSURANCE	DEDUCTIONS SAVINGS BONDS
5	Acron, Peter C.	M	3	1 126 40	115 20	60 00	10 00
7	Barenis, Mary P.	S	1	1 155 00		25 00	
6	Epps, John P.	M	2	792 00		40 00	10 00
1	Goforth, Alice A.	S	2	1 135 20	77 40	40 00	
8	Hiett, Franklin B.	M	3	1 188 00		60 00	10 00
9	Land, Keith	S	1	954 60		25 00	10 00
2	Malone, Lillie L.	S	1	1 083 60		25 00	
4	Rivers, Linda K.	M	2	1 091 20	93 00	40 00	
10	Sowell, Jacob S.	M	2	1 161 60		40 00	10 00
3	Vole, Ryan V.	M	5	1 075 00		80 00	10 00

Preparing Payroll Records

Instructions:

1. Prepare a payroll register. The date of payment is August 31. Use the income tax withholding tables shown in Lesson 12-2 to find the income tax withholding for each employee. Calculate social security and Medicare tax withholdings using 6.2% and 1.45% tax rates, respectively. None of the employees has accumulated earnings greater than the social security tax base.
2. Prepare a check for the total amount of the net pay. Make the check payable to Payroll Account 59-721-65, and sign your name as the manager of Arrow Company. The beginning check stub balance is $16,216.90.
3. Prepare payroll checks for Peter C. Acron, Check No. 1692, and Franklin B. Hiett, Check No. 1696. Sign your name as the manager of Arrow Company. Record the two payroll check numbers in the payroll register.

12-7 CHALLENGE PROBLEM

Calculating piecework wages

Production workers in factories are frequently paid on the basis of the number of units they produce. This payroll method is referred to as the *piecework incentive wage plan*. Most piecework incentive wage plans include a guaranteed hourly rate to employees regardless of the number of units they produce. This guaranteed hourly rate is referred to as the *base rate*.

Time and motion study engineers usually determine the standard time required for producing a single unit. Assume, for example, that time studies determine that one-third of an hour is the standard time required to produce a unit. Then the standard rate for an 8-hour day would be 24 units (8 hours divided by 1/3 hour = 24 units per day). If a worker's daily base pay is $96.00, the incentive rate per unit is $4.00 ($96.00 divided by 24 units × $4.00 per unit). Therefore, the worker who produces 24 or fewer units per day is paid the base pay, $96.00. However, each worker is paid an additional $4.00 for each unit over 24 produced each day.

Draker Furniture Company has eight employees in production departments that are paid on a piecework incentive wage plan. The following standard and incentive wage rates are listed by department.

Department	Standard Production per Employee	Incentive Rate per Unit
Cutting	32 units per day	$3.50
Assembly	20 units per day	$5.75
Finishing	45 units per day	$2.00

A payroll register is given in the *Working Papers*. Each employee worked eight hours a day during the semimonthly pay period, May 1–15. Payroll records for May 1–15 are summarized in the following table.

Employee No.	Employee Name	Marital Status	No. of Allowances	Guaranteed Daily Rate	Units Produced per Day — Pay Period May 1–15								
					2	3	4	5	6	9	10	11	12	13
Cutting Department														
C3	Bell, Julie M.	M	4	$112.00	33	30	28	32	32	32	32	33	35	33
C6	Hairston, Gary P.	M	2	$112.00	29	35	29	32	31	33	32	33	30	30
C9	Reeves, John M.	S	1	$112.00	31	30	35	34	34	31	35	28	31	32
Assembly Department														
A2	Bullock, Amy C.	S	2	$115.00	22	20	20	20	22	22	22	22	23	20
A6	Green, Steven P.	S	1	$115.00	20	23	23	20	22	21	20	20	20	20
A9	Prine, Jacob R.	M	4	$115.00	23	22	21	22	22	21	22	22	20	23
Finishing Department														
F5	Gerez, Dave A.	M	2	$90.00	39	47	38	47	43	41	40	41	39	46
F2	Kyle, Ryan G.	S	1	$90.00	41	43	47	38	42	39	43	39	43	39

Instructions:

Prepare a payroll register. The earnings column Incentive is used instead of Overtime. The date of payment is May 15. Use the income tax withholding tables shown in Lesson 12-2. Calculate the employee social security and Medicare tax withholdings using 6.2% and 1.45% tax rates, respectively. None of the employees has health insurance or other deductions. None of the employees has accumulated earnings greater than the social security tax base.

APPLIED COMMUNICATION

The employees of Kaden Company currently use time cards and a time clock to record their arrival and departure times. Management plans to replace the time clock with a device that reads a magnetic strip on the back of each employee's name badge. The badge is scanned by a reader in the same manner that credit cards are scanned. Because the badge reader is connected to a computer, the information is recorded directly to a computer file. Thus, the new system will enable management to make daily analyses of employee hours and productivity. This information should allow managers to make more timely decisions and increase profits.

Instructions: Assume you work in the payroll department for Kaden Company. Write a memo to the employees informing them of the new system. Because some employees may not be happy with this new system, be sure to include reasons why the policy is being implemented.

CASE FOR CRITICAL THINKING

Vadillo Lumber currently requires each employee to inform the accounting clerk of the total hours worked each day during the pay period. The total number of hours worked by all employees has been steadily increasing during the prior pay periods. The new store manager has suggested that a time clock be installed to record arrival and departure times. The accounting clerk believes the current system is satisfactory. Do you agree with the new manager or the accounting clerk? Explain your response.

GRAPHING WORKSHOP

Distribution of Gross Wages

The chart depicts data from the payroll register of Alectra Corporation. Analyze the graph to answer the following questions.

1. What was the largest payroll deduction?
2. What percent of employees' wages are withheld for taxes?
3. What amount is represented by the entire pie graph?

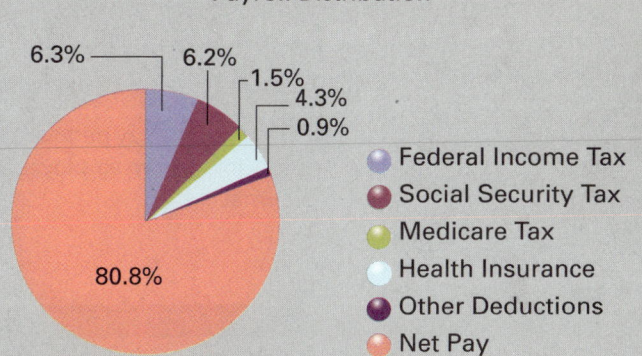

ANALYZING BEST BUY'S FINANCIAL STATEMENTS

Annual reports contain a report by management designed to inform potential investors and business partners about how the financial statements were prepared. The report describes, in detail, accounting and management policies that are followed to ensure that the amounts on the financial statements can be relied upon for making business decisions.

Instructions: Use Management's Report on the Financial Statements and Management's Report on Internal Control over Financial Reporting on page B-4 in Appendix B to answer the following questions.

1. Who is responsible for the preparation of Best Buy's financial statements?
2. What is the system of internal control designed to do?
3. Can internal controls prevent or detect all misstatements?

Accounting SOFTWARE

RECORDING PAYROLL

Review the payroll calculations for: (1) gross wages, (2) federal income tax withholding, (3) FICA taxes, considering whether the employee has reached the tax base, (4) Medicare taxes, and (5) net wages. Peachtree can perform all the calculations required to prepare payroll checks.

Before preparing payroll checks, an employee's personal record must be up to date. The personal record contains the employee's regular and overtime wage rates, filing status (single or married), withholding allowances, and any optional deductions. When the number of hours worked is entered, Peachtree calculates all required amounts and prints the payroll check. The journal entry is automatically recorded when the payroll check is printed. Peachtree records each payroll check as a separate journal entry.

PEACHTREE APPLICATION PROBLEM 12-5
1. Open (Restore) file 12-5AP.ptb.
2. Use Peachtree's Payments task to journalize the May 15 transactions to establish the payroll account for the amount of the net payroll; post the Payments entry.
3. Record the May 15 paychecks for the two employees. Post the Payments entries.

PEACHTREE MASTERY PROBLEM 12-6
1. Open (Restore) file 12-6MP.ptb.
2. Prepare a payroll register.
3. Record the check for the net payroll for the pay period August 16-31.
4. Journalize and post payroll checks for the two employees.
5. Print the cash disbursements journal.

RECORDING PAYROLL

The benefit of an automated payroll package is that it usually calculates all the deductions and the net pay for each employee. In QuickBooks, the payroll function is a special package to which a company can subscribe.

A company that does not subscribe to the payroll function will still use QuickBooks for payroll but will have to calculate the deductions and net pay manually. The payroll check will be entered into QuickBooks similar to other checks, which will automatically make a journal entry for the check. Since each employee will receive a separate check, a separate entry will be made for each employee. This is different from the method illustrated in this chapter, where the payroll register totals are used to journalize the payroll.

QUICKBOOKS APPLICATION PROBLEM 12-5
1. Open the Royal Appliances file if it is not already open.
2. Record the deposit in the Payroll account using the Make Deposits feature.
3. Write the payroll checks using the Write Checks feature for the two employees.
4. Print a Journal report for May 1 through May 15.

QUICKBOOKS MASTERY PROBLEM 12-6
1. Open the Arrow Company file.
2. Record the payroll deposit.
3. Write the payroll checks for the two employees.
4. Print a Journal report for August 16 through August 31.

USING THE ROUND FUNCTION

Can 4.00 + 3.00 equal 6.99? It can on an electronic spreadsheet! Users of such spreadsheets typically apply cell formatting to display dollar amounts to two-decimal-place accuracy. If they do not account for rounding, this kind of error can occur.

Shown below are two employees' FICA tax calculations. Each actual number in the first column is rounded to display to the nearest cent when it is displayed in the second column. This is done by using the ROUND function. The function =ROUND(Cell, Number of places) rounds the contents of the Cell to a specified Number of decimals. Thus, the function doesn't just display a number to a specified decimal-place accuracy, it actually rounds the number.

To get a correct total of the individual rounded amounts in Cell C5, simply add the rounded amounts in cells C3 and C4. You may use +C3+C4 or SUM(C3:C4), but do not round the total.

	A	B	C	D
1		Actual	Formatted (to two	=ROUND (to two
2		Number	decimal places)	decimal places)
3	Sanders, Jim	3.996	$4.00	4.00
4	Keller, Danielle	2.997	$3.00	3.00
5	Totals	6.993	$6.99	7.00

EXCEL APPLICATION PROBLEM 12-3
Open the F12-3 Excel data file. Follow the step-by-step instructions in the Instructions worksheet.

EXCEL APPLICATION PROBLEM 12-4
Open the F12-4 Excel data file. Follow the step-by-step instructions in the Instructions worksheet.

RECORDING PAYROLL

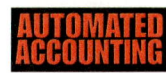

In an automated payroll system, the computer is used to maintain the employee database, to record payroll transactions at the end of each pay period, to calculate withholding taxes, and to create all the related journal entries. The employee database identifies each employee by employee number. Other data required for each employee includes the employee's name, social security number, marital status, number of withholding allowances, pay rate, and voluntary deductions. Employee accounts may be added, changed, or deleted from the accounting system.

Entering Payroll Transactions
1. Click the Other toolbar button.
2. Click the Payroll tab.
3. Enter the date of the check.
4. Select the employee from the employee drop-down list.
5. Verify that the check number displayed is correct, or key the correct number.
6. For salaried employees, the salary amount will be automatically displayed. For hourly employees, enter the regular and overtime hours worked during the current payroll period.
7. Click the Calculate Taxes button to direct the software to calculate the employee taxes.
8. Enter the employee's voluntary deductions.
9. Click OK to generate and display the payroll check.
10. Click the Close button to dismiss the check and continue, or click Print to print the check.

AUTOMATED ACCOUNTING MASTERY PROBLEM 12-6
Open file F12-6.AA8. Display the problem instructions and complete the problem.

CHAPTER 13

Payroll Accounting, Taxes, and Reports

OBJECTIVES

After studying Chapter 13, you will be able to:

1. Define accounting terms related to payroll accounting, taxes, and reports.
2. Identify accounting concepts and practices related to payroll accounting, taxes, and reports.
3. Analyze payroll transactions and record a payroll.
4. Record employer payroll taxes.
5. Prepare selected payroll tax reports.
6. Pay and record withholding and payroll taxes.

KEY TERMS

- federal unemployment tax
- state unemployment tax
- lookback period

Point Your Browser
www.C21accounting.com

ACCOUNTING IN THE REAL WORLD

Google

Employee Benefits at Google

Innovative thinking comes from creative minds. Technology companies must continually develop new products and applications for those products in order to stay competitive in today's rapidly changing marketplace. To maintain a creative workforce, companies must create a comfortable work environment that encourages and rewards creativity.

Google offers many innovative benefits designed to make its employees' lives healthier, less complicated, and simply more fun. Beyond traditional medical, vacation, and retirement benefits, employees at Google's Mountain View, California headquarters can ride to work in a shuttle that serves the San Francisco area. Once at work, employees can:

- Drop their children off at the Kinderplex, Google's own child care center.
- Eat a free lunch or dinner cooked by gourmet chefs.
- Visit a doctor or receive a massage.
- Have their laundry dry cleaned.
- Exercise in the gym.

Google is family friendly. New mothers receive 12 weeks of paid (75%) maternity leave. Fathers also receive between 2 and 6 weeks of parental leave. New parents are reimbursed for up to $500 for take-out meals during the first four weeks the new baby is home. Google also provides financial assistance to pay the legal and other fees in the adoption of a child.

From ski trips to parking-lot roller hockey, Google makes working fun.

Critical Thinking

1. Google has offices all over the world. Identify three services you would suggest any company offer that would uniquely serve employees living in your city or state.
2. Why do you think Google employees are offered financial planning classes?

Source: www.google.com

INTERNET ACTIVITY

IRS Forms Online

(NOTE: You will need to have Adobe Acrobat Reader on your computer to complete this activity.)

The Internal Revenue Service (IRS) makes some tax forms available online. Go to the homepage for the IRS (www.irs.gov). Click on "Forms and Publications." A W-4 Form is the form you fill out for your employer when you are hired. A 1040EZ Form is the form you use to file your income tax return each year.

Instructions

1. Search the site for a W-4 Form. Print out the form.
2. Search the site for a 1040EZ Form. Print out the form.
3. List one additional form that is available on the IRS site.

LESSON 13-1

Recording a Payroll

DIFFERENT FORMS OF PAYROLL INFORMATION

Payroll information for each pay period is recorded in a payroll register. Each pay period the payroll information for each employee is also recorded on each employee earnings record. Separate payroll accounts for each employee are not kept in the general ledger. Instead, accounts are kept in the general ledger to summarize total earnings and deductions for all employees.

The payroll register and employee earnings records provide all the payroll information needed to prepare payroll and payroll tax reports. Journal entries are made to record the payment of the payroll and the employer payroll taxes. In addition, various quarterly and annual payroll tax reports are required to report the payment of payroll taxes.

CHARACTER COUNTS

Your Call May Be Recorded

Janice Whitehead has just been fired for violating her employer's code of conduct. Over the last few months, Janice has been using her office phone to call former classmates to inform them of an upcoming class reunion. She believes her firing is unethical and is considering legal action against the company.

Cobb Manufacturing has the following statement in its code of conduct:

"Company telephones are to be used exclusively for company business. Employees needing to make personal phone calls should use their personal cellular phones."

During an ethics training program, employees were informed that the company uses a pen register. The device creates a list of all outgoing calls and the length of each call. Janice signed a statement that she understood the company has a "no tolerance" approach toward topics discussed in the training program.

Instructions

Was it ethical for Cobb Manufacturing to fire Janice for making personal phone calls?

PAYROLL REGISTER

PAYROLL REGISTER

SEMIMONTHLY PERIOD ENDED December 15, 20-- DATE OF PAYMENT December 15, 20--

	EMPL. NO.	EMPLOYEE'S NAME	MARITAL STATUS	NO. OF ALLOWANCES	EARNINGS REGULAR (1)	EARNINGS OVERTIME (2)	EARNINGS TOTAL (3)	FEDERAL INCOME TAX (4)	SOC. SEC. TAX (5)	MEDICARE TAX (6)	HEALTH INSURANCE (7)	OTHER (8)		TOTAL (9)	NET PAY (10)	CHECK NO.	
1	2	Aranda, Susan A.	M	2	968 00		968 00	38 00	60 02	14 04	45 00	B	10 00	167 06	800 94	482	1
2	5	Drew, Paul S.	S	1	550 00		550 00	32 00	34 10	7 98	38 00			112 08	437 92	483	2
3	1	Kellogg, Janice P.	M	1	1760 00	150 00	1910 00	187 00	118 42	27 70	38 00	UW	20 00	391 12	1518 88	484	3
4	6	Mendel, Ann M.	S	1	240 00		240 00		14 88	3 48				18 36	221 64	485	4
5	3	Selby, Rick E.	M	4	1056 00	81 00	1137 00	28 00	70 49	16 49	60 00	B UW	10 00 10 00	194 98	942 02	486	5
6	4	Young, Justin L.	S	1	906 40		906 40	86 00	56 20	13 14	38 00	B UW	15 00 10 00	218 34	688 06	487	6
7		Totals			5480 40	231 00	5711 40	371 00	354 11	82 83	219 00	B UW	35 00 40 00	1101 94	4609 46		7

Similar to a special journal, the column totals of a payroll register provide the debit and credit amounts needed to journalize a payroll.

As you will learn in this chapter, the payroll journal entry is based on the totals of the Earnings Total column, each deduction column, and the Net Pay column. The totals of the Earnings Regular, Earnings Overtime, and Deductions Total columns are not used to journalize the payroll.

FINANCIAL LITERACY

Taxes

An old saying goes, "Only two things are certain in life—death and taxes!" Depending on where you live, you may encounter a few or many different taxes. In the United States, there is a federal tax on the income you earn. Some states also impose a tax on personal income. Many states and some cities have a sales tax, but the list of taxable items varies greatly. Some states and cities charge a sales tax on nearly everything, while others may exclude specific items such as food, clothing, medical items, etc. If you own property, you may have to pay a state property tax and/or a city property tax.

The major purpose of most taxes is to provide funds for services supplied by the government such as schools, roadways, emergency services, water and sewer systems, public transportation systems, and public parks.

However, some taxes are designed to encourage us to behave in certain ways. If the United States government wants us to save more money, it can make certain payments to savings and investment accounts tax deductible, which means those amounts are not subject to tax. If the government wants to encourage home ownership, it can make interest on home mortgages tax deductible.

Activities

1. Using tables provided by the Internal Revenue Service for the most current year (which can be found on the Internet), determine how much federal income tax would be due from a single taxpayer with no additional deductions, who earned $26,000.

2. Write a report on your state's sales tax, including the amount of the tax and what items are subject to this tax. If your state does not have a sales tax, pick a neighboring state that has a sales tax.

Recording a Payroll Lesson 13-1 369

ANALYZING PAYMENT OF A PAYROLL

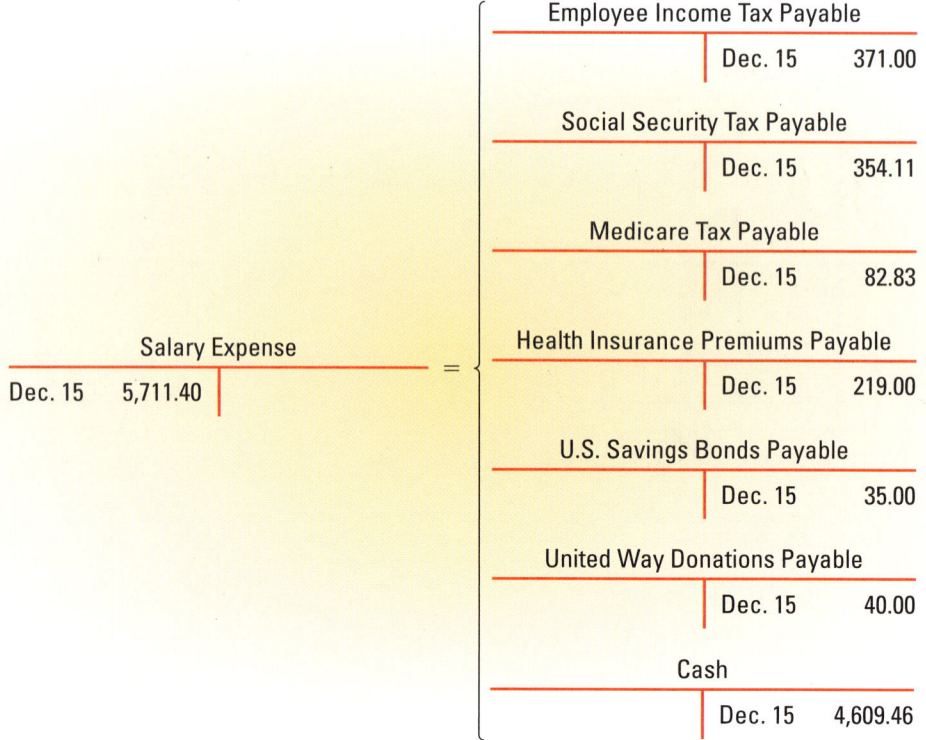

Data about Hobby Shack's semimonthly pay period ended December 15, obtained from the payroll register, are summarized in the T accounts.

The Total Earnings column total, $5,711.40, is the salary expense for the period. **Salary Expense** is debited for this amount.

The Federal Income Tax column total, $371.00, is the amount withheld from employee salaries for federal income tax. The amount withheld is a liability of the business until the taxes are sent to the federal government. **Employee Income Tax Payable** is credited for $371.00 to record this liability.

The Social Security Tax column total, $354.11, is the amount withheld for social security tax. The amount is a liability of the business until the tax is paid to the government. **Social Security Tax Payable** is credited for $354.11.

The Medicare Tax column total, $82.83, is the amount withheld for Medicare tax. The amount is a liability of the business until the tax is paid to the government. **Medicare Tax Payable** is credited for $82.83.

The Health Insurance column total, $219.00, is the amount withheld for health insurance premiums. The amount is a liability of the business until the premiums are paid to the insurance company. **Health Insurance Premiums Payable** is credited for $219.00 to record this liability.

Two types of Other deductions are recorded in Hobby Shack's payroll register. The $35.00 Other column total identified with the letter *B* is withheld to buy savings bonds for employees. The $40.00 total identified with the letters *UW* is withheld for employee United Way pledges. Until these amounts have been paid by the employer, they are liabilities of the business. **U.S. Savings Bonds Payable** is credited for $35.00. **United Way Donations Payable** is credited for $40.00.

The Net Pay column total, $4,609.46, is the net amount paid to employees. **Cash** is credited for $4,609.46. A check for the total net pay amount, $4,609.46, is written on Hobby Shack's general checking account and is deposited in a special payroll checking account. Individual payroll checks are then written on the special payroll checking account.

JOURNALIZING PAYMENT OF A PAYROLL

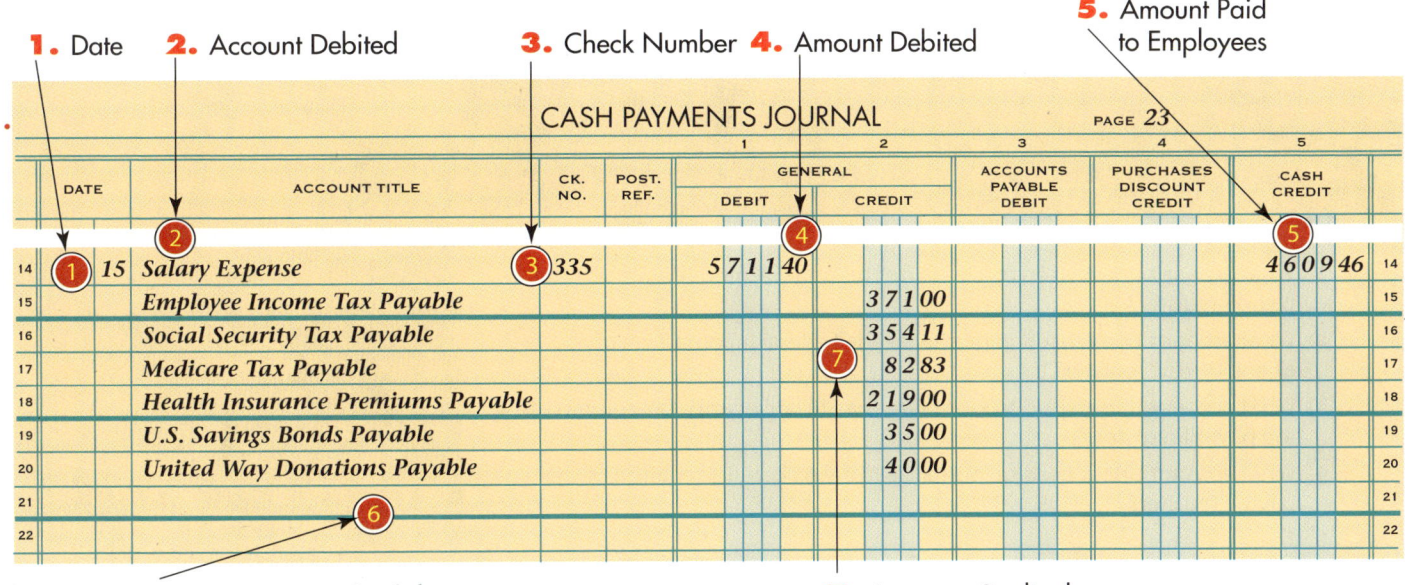

Hobby Shack journalized the company's payroll for the semimonthly period ended December 15, 20--.

December 15. Paid cash for semimonthly payroll, $4,609.46 (total payroll, $5,711.40, less deductions: employee income tax, $371.00; social security tax, $354.11; Medicare tax, $82.83; health insurance premiums, $219.00; U.S. Savings Bonds, $35.00; United Way donations, $40.00). Check No. 335.

Amounts recorded in the General columns of a cash payments journal are posted individually to general ledger accounts. The credit to Cash, $4,609.46, is not posted separately to the cash account. The amount is included in the journal's Cash Credit column total that is posted at the end of the month. The same procedures are followed to post this journal entry to the appropriate accounts as were described in Chapter 11.

STEPS JOURNALIZING PAYMENT OF A PAYROLL

1. Write the date, *15*, in the Date column.
2. Write the title of the account debited, *Salary Expense*, in the Account Title column.
3. Write the check number, *335*, in the Ck. No. column.
4. Write the amount debited to Salary Expense, *$5,711.40*, in the General Debit column.
5. On the same line, write the total amount paid to employees, *$4,609.46*, in the Cash Credit column.
6. On the next six lines, write the titles of the accounts credited, *Employee Income Tax Payable, Social Security Tax Payable, Medicare Tax Payable, Health Insurance Premiums Payable, U.S. Savings Bonds Payable*, and *United Way Donations Payable*, in the Account Title column.
7. On the same six lines, write the amounts credited to the corresponding liability accounts, *$371.00, $354.11, $82.83, $219.00, $35.00*, and *$40.00*, in the General Credit column.

REMEMBER

Total Earnings is the debit amount for Salary Expense. Net Pay is the credit amount for cash.

Recording a Payroll Lesson 13-1

End of Lesson REVIEW

AUDIT YOUR UNDERSTANDING

1. What account title is used to journalize the Total Earnings column of the payroll register?
2. What account title is used to journalize the Federal Income Tax column of the payroll register?
3. What account title is used to journalize the Social Security Tax column of the payroll register?
4. What account title is used to journalize the Medicare Tax column of the payroll register?

WORK TOGETHER 13-1

Recording a payroll

Metro Company's payroll register has the following totals for the semimonthly pay period, July 1–15 of the current year. T accounts and a cash payments journal page are provided in the *Working Papers*. Your instructor will guide you through the following examples.

Total Earnings	Federal Income Tax Withheld	Social Security Tax Withheld	Medicare Withheld
$12,600.00	$1,186.00	$781.20	$182.70

1. Use the T accounts provided to analyze Metro's July 1–15 payroll.
2. Journalize the payment of Metro's July 1–15 payroll on page 15 of the cash payments journal. The payroll was paid by Check No. 455 on July 15 of the current year.

ON YOUR OWN 13-1

Recording a payroll

Butler Company's payroll register has the following totals for the semimonthly pay period, August 16–31 of the current year. T accounts and a cash payments journal page are provided in the *Working Papers*. Work this problem independently.

Total Earnings	Federal Income Tax Withheld	Social Security Tax Withheld	Medicare Withheld
$14,260.00	$1,562.00	$884.12	$206.77

1. Use the T accounts provided to analyze Butler's August 16–31 payroll.
2. Journalize the payment of Butler's August 16–31 payroll on page 16 of a cash payments journal. The payroll was paid by Check No. 628 on August 31 of the current year.

LESSON 13-2

Recording Employer Payroll Taxes

CALCULATING EMPLOYER PAYROLL TAXES

Employers must pay to the government the taxes withheld from employee earnings. Hobby Shack has withheld federal income tax, social security tax, and Medicare tax from employee salaries. The amounts withheld are liabilities to the business until they are actually paid to the government. In addition, employers must pay several of their own payroll taxes. Employer payroll taxes are business expenses.

Most employers must pay four separate payroll taxes. These taxes are (1) social security tax, (2) Medicare tax, (3) federal unemployment tax, and (4) state unemployment tax. Employer payroll taxes expense is based on a percentage of employee earnings.

Employer Social Security and Medicare Taxes

The social security and Medicare taxes are the only payroll taxes paid by both the employees and the employer. Hobby Shack withheld $354.11 in social security tax and $82.83 in Medicare tax from employee wages for the pay period ended December 15. Hobby Shack owes the same amount of social security and Medicare taxes as the amount withheld from employees. Therefore, Hobby Shack's social security and Medicare taxes for the pay period ended December 15 are also $354.11 and $82.83 respectively.

Congress sets the social security and Medicare tax rates for employees and employers. Periodically, Congress may change the tax rates and tax base. The social security tax rate and base used in this text are 6.2% of earnings up to a maximum of $87,000.00 in each calendar year. Medicare does not have a tax base. Therefore, Medicare tax is calculated on total employee earnings. The Medicare tax rate used in this text is 1.45% of total employee earnings.

REDCHOPSTICKS/GETTY IMAGES

> **REMEMBER**
>
> Employers must pay four taxes on employee earnings—social security tax, Medicare tax, federal unemployment tax, and state unemployment tax.

Recording Employer Payroll Taxes

UNEMPLOYMENT TAXABLE EARNINGS

HOBBY SHACK
Taxable Earnings
for December 15, 20--, Pay Period

	Accumulated Earnings as of Nov. 30, 20--	Total Earnings for Dec. 15, 20-- Pay Period	Unemployment Taxable Earnings
Aranda, Susan A.	$21,115.00	$ 968.00	—
Drew, Paul S.	5,595.25	550.00	$550.00 ②
Kellogg, Janice P.	39,840.00	1,910.00	—
Mendel, Ann M.	2,030.00	240.00	240.00
Selby, Rick E.	22,746.00	1,137.00	—
Young, Justin L.	19,816.00	906.40	—
			③ $790.00

1. Enter accumulated earnings and total earnings for each employee.

2. Enter unemployment taxable earnings.

3. Total the unemployment taxable earnings column.

Federal unemployment insurance laws require that employers pay taxes for unemployment compensation. These tax funds are used to pay workers' benefits for limited periods of unemployment and to administer the unemployment compensation program.

The total earnings subject to unemployment tax is referred to as *unemployment taxable earnings*. The unemployment tax is applied to the first $7,000.00 earned by each employee for each calendar year. The amount of unemployment taxable earnings for Hobby Shack's pay period ended December 15, 20--, is shown in the illustration.

STEPS CALCULATING UNEMPLOYMENT TAXABLE EARNINGS

① For each employee, enter accumulated earnings as of November 30 and total earnings for the December 15 pay period. These amounts are taken from each employee earnings record. Rick E. Selby's accumulated earnings as of November 30, *$22,746.00*, are recorded in the first column. His total earnings for the December 15 pay period, *$1,137.00*, are recorded in the second column.

② Enter unemployment taxable earnings for the pay period in the Unemployment Taxable Earnings column for employees whose accumulated earnings are less than $7,000.00. The November 30 accumulated earnings for Paul S. Drew, *$5,595.25*, plus the December 15 earnings, *$550.00*, equal $6,145.25 and are less than $7,000.00. Therefore, his total earnings for the December 15 pay period, *$550.00*, are subject to unemployment tax and are recorded in the Unemployment Taxable Earnings column. Since the accumulated earnings for Mr. Selby are greater than $7,000.00, none of his current earnings are subject to unemployment tax. Thus, the amount of unemployment taxable earnings recorded in the third column is zero, which is represented by a dash.

③ Total the Unemployment Taxable Earnings column. This total amount, *$790.00*, is used to calculate the unemployment tax.

UNEMPLOYMENT TAXES

Hobby Shack pays two unemployment taxes, federal unemployment tax and state unemployment tax.

Federal Unemployment Tax

A federal tax used for state and federal administrative expenses of the unemployment program is called **federal unemployment tax**. The federal unemployment tax is 6.2% of the first $7,000.00 earned by each employee. An employer generally can deduct from federal unemployment payments the amounts paid to state unemployment funds. This deduction cannot be more than 5.4% of taxable earnings. The effective federal unemployment tax rate in most states is, therefore, 0.8% on the first $7,000.00 earned by each employee. (Federal, 6.2% − deductible for state, 5.4% = 0.8%.) All of the unemployment tax on the first $7,000.00 of salary is paid by the employer.

Hobby Shack's federal unemployment tax for the pay period ended December 15, 20--, is calculated as shown.

Unemployment Taxable Earnings	×	Federal Unemployment Tax Rate	=	Federal Unemployment Tax
$790.00	×	0.8%	=	$6.32

State Unemployment Tax

A state tax used to pay benefits to unemployed workers is called **state unemployment tax**. The Social Security Act specifies certain standards for unemployment compensation laws. Therefore, a high degree of uniformity exists in state unemployment laws. However, details of state unemployment laws do differ. Because of these differences, employers must know the requirements of the states in which they operate.

Many states require that employers pay unemployment tax of 5.4% on the first $7,000.00 earned by each employee. The unemployment taxable earnings used to calculate the federal unemployment tax are also used to calculate the state unemployment tax. Hobby Shack's state unemployment tax for the pay period ended December 15, 20--, is calculated as shown.

Unemployment Taxable Earnings	×	State Unemployment Tax Rate	=	State Unemployment Tax
$790.00	×	5.4%	=	$42.66

JOURNALIZING EMPLOYER PAYROLL TAXES

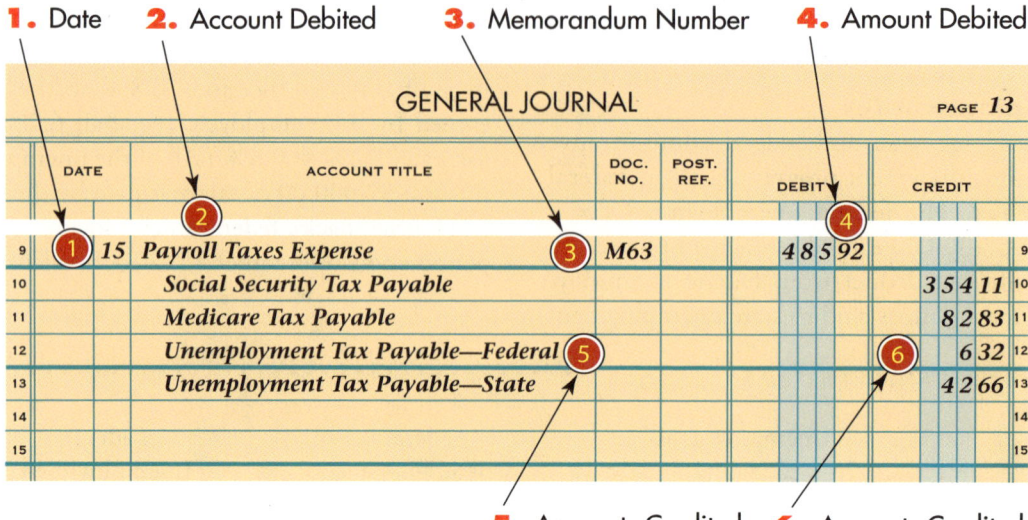

Employer payroll taxes are paid to the government at a later date. However, the liability is incurred when salaries are paid. Therefore, the transaction to record employer payroll taxes expense is journalized on the same date the payroll is journalized. The salary expense and the employer payroll taxes expense are, therefore, both recorded in the same accounting period.

> *December 15. Recorded employer payroll taxes expense, $485.92, for the semimonthly pay period ended December 15. Taxes owed are: social security tax, $354.11; Medicare tax, $82.83; federal unemployment tax, $6.32; state unemployment tax, $42.66. Memorandum No. 63.*

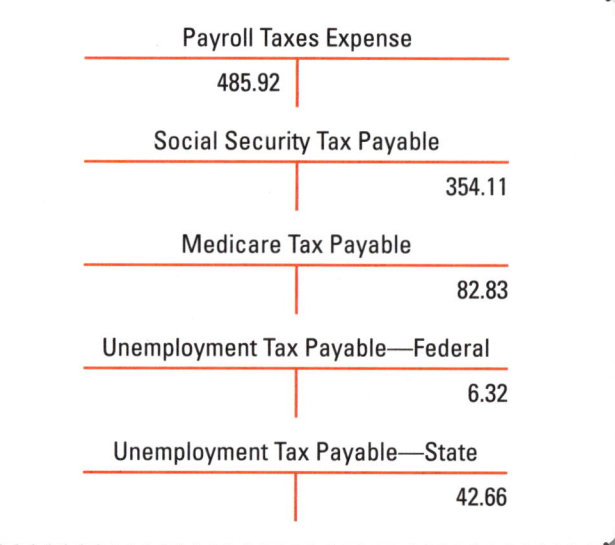

Payroll Taxes Expense is debited for $485.92 to show the increase in the balance of this expense account. Four liability accounts are credited to show the increase in payroll tax liabilities.

Amounts recorded in the general journal are posted individually to general ledger accounts. The same procedures are followed to post this journal entry to the appropriate accounts as were described in Chapter 11.

STEPS JOURNALIZING EMPLOYER PAYROLL TAXES

1. Write the date, *15*, in the Date column.
2. Write the title of the expense account debited, *Payroll Taxes Expense*, in the Account Title column.
3. Write the memorandum number, *M63*, in the Doc. No. column.
4. Write the debit amount, *$485.92*, in the Debit column.
5. Write the titles of the liability accounts credited, *Social Security Tax Payable, Medicare Tax Payable, Unemployment Tax Payable—Federal,* and *Unemployment Tax Payable—State,* on the next four lines of the Account Title column, indented about 1 centimeter.
6. Write the credit amounts, *$354.11, $82.83, $6.32,* and *$42.66*, respectively, in the Credit column.

End of Lesson REVIEW

AUDIT YOUR UNDERSTANDING

TERMS REVIEW

federal unemployment tax
state unemployment tax

1. What is the tax rate Hobby Shack must pay on employees for each of the following taxes: social security, Medicare, federal unemployment, and state unemployment?
2. What is the amount of each employee's earnings that is subject to federal and state unemployment taxes at Hobby Shack?

WORK TOGETHER 13-2

Recording employer payroll taxes

Payroll information taken from employee earnings records is given below. A form and general journal page are provided in the *Working Papers*. Your instructor will guide you through the following examples.

Employee Name	Accumulated Earnings, April 30	Total Earnings for May 1–15 Pay Period
Beltran, Tamela C.	$5,100.00	$637.50
Cintron, Irma V.	7,350.00	920.00

1. Calculate the amount of earnings subject to unemployment taxes. Unemployment taxes are owed on the first $7,000.00 of earnings for each employee.
2. Calculate the amount of employer payroll taxes owed for the May 1–15 pay period. Use the employer payroll tax rates shown in this chapter.
3. Journalize the employer's payroll taxes for the May 1–15 pay period on May 15 of the current year. Use general journal page 10 and Memorandum No. 46.

ON YOUR OWN 13-2

Recording employer payroll taxes

Payroll information taken from employee earnings records is given below. A form and general journal page are provided in the *Working Papers*. Work this problem independently.

Employee Name	Accumulated Earnings, May 31	Total Earnings for June 1–15 Pay Period
Caldwell, Sarah H.	$6,020.00	$ 580.00
Easley, Benjamin P.	5,450.00	620.00
Franks, John J.	8,420.00	1,000.00

1. Calculate the amount of earnings subject to unemployment taxes. Unemployment taxes are owed on the first $7,000.00 of earnings for each employee.
2. Calculate the amount of employer payroll taxes owed for the June 1–15 pay period. Use the employer payroll tax rates shown in this chapter.
3. Journalize the employer's payroll taxes for the June 1–15 pay period on June 15 of the current year. Use general journal page 12 and Memorandum No. 83.

LESSON 13-3

Reporting Withholding and Payroll Taxes

EMPLOYER ANNUAL REPORT TO EMPLOYEES OF TAXES WITHHELD

a Control number	22222	Void ☐	For Official Use Only ▶ OMB No. 1545-0008		
b Employer identification number 31-0429632			1 Wages, tips, other compensation 24,843.00	2 Federal income tax withheld 648.00	
c Employer's name, address, and ZIP code Hobby Shack, Inc. 1420 College Plaza Atlanta, GA 30337-1726			3 Social security wages 24,843.00	4 Social security tax withheld 1,540.27	
			5 Medicare wages and tips 24,843.00	6 Medicare tax withheld 360.22	
			7 Social security tips	8 Allocated tips	
d Employee's social security number 450-70-6432			9 Advance EIC payment	10 Dependent care benefits	
e Employee's first name and initial Rick E.	Last name Selby		11 Nonqualified plans	12a See instructions for box 12	
			13 Statutory employee ☐ Retirement plan ☐ Third-party sick pay ☐	12b	
1625 Northland Drive Clarkdale, GA 30020-6523			14 Other	12c	
				12d	
f Employee's address and ZIP code					
15 State	Employer's state ID number	16 State wages, tips, etc.	17 State income tax	18 Local wages, tips, etc.	19 Local income tax	20 Locality name

Form **W-2** Wage and Tax Statement

20--

Copy A For Social Security Administration — Send this entire page with Form W-3 to the Social Security Administration; photocopies are **not** acceptable.

Cat. No. 10134D

Department of the Treasury—Internal Revenue Service
For Privacy Act and Paperwork Reduction Act Notice, see back of Copy D.

Each employer who withholds income tax, social security tax, and Medicare tax from employee earnings must furnish each employee with an annual report of these withholdings. The report shows total year's earnings and the amounts withheld for taxes for an employee. These amounts are obtained from the employee earnings records. The report is prepared on the Internal Revenue Service Form W-2, Wage and Tax Statement. The Form W-2 prepared by Hobby Shack for Rick E. Selby is shown.

Employers are required to furnish Form W-2 to each employee by January 31 of the next year. If an employee ends employment before December 31, Form W-2 must be furnished within 30 days of the last date of employment.

Four copies (A to D) of Form W-2 are prepared for each employee. Copies B and C are given to the employee. The employee attaches Copy B to a personal federal income tax return and keeps Copy C for a personal record. The employer sends Copy A to the Social Security Administration and keeps Copy D for the business's records.

Businesses in states with state income tax must prepare additional copies of Form W-2. The employee attaches the additional copy to the personal state income tax return.

EMPLOYER'S QUARTERLY FEDERAL TAX RETURN

1. Heading

Form 941 (Rev. January 2004)
Department of the Treasury
Internal Revenue Service (99)

Employer's Quarterly Federal Tax Return
► See separate instructions revised January 2004 for information on completing this return.
Please type or print.

Enter state code for state in which deposits were made **only** if different from state in address to the right (see page 2 of separate instructions).

Name (as distinguished from trade name): Hobby Shack, Inc.
Trade name, if any:
Address (number and street): 1420 College Plaza
Date quarter ended: December 31, 20--
Employer identification number: 31-0429632
City, state, and ZIP code: Atlanta GA 30337-1726

OMB No. 1545-0029
T / FF / FD / FP / I / T

If address is different from prior return, check here ►

A If you **do not have to file** returns in the future, check here ► ☐ and enter date final wages paid ►
B If you are a seasonal employer, see **Seasonal employers** on page 1 of the instructions and check here ► ☐

1	Number of employees in the pay period that includes March 12th ►	1	16
2	Total wages and tips, plus other compensation (see separate instructions)	2	32,980 00
3	Total income tax withheld from wages, tips, and sick pay	3	2,168 00
4	Adjustment of withheld income tax for preceding quarters of **this calendar year**	4	- 0 -
5	Adjusted total of income tax withheld (line 3 as adjusted by line 4)	5	2,168 00
6	Taxable social security wages . . . 6a 32,980 00 × 12.4% (.124) =	6b	4,089 52
	Taxable social security tips . . . . 6c - 0 - × 12.4% (.124) =	6d	- 0 -
7	Taxable Medicare wages and tips . . 7a 32,980 00 × 2.9% (.029) =	7b	956 42
8	Total social security and Medicare taxes (add lines 6b, 6d, and 7b). **Check here if wages are not subject to social security and/or Medicare tax** . . . . . ► ☐	8	5,045 94
9	Adjustment of social security and Medicare taxes (see instructions for required explanation) Sick Pay $_____ ± Fractions of Cents $_____ ± Other $_____ =	9	- 0 -
10	Adjusted total of social security and Medicare taxes (line 8 as adjusted by line 9)	10	5,045 94
11	**Total taxes** (add lines 5 and 10)	11	7,213 94
12	Advance earned income credit (EIC) payments made to employees (see instructions)	12	- 0 -
13	Net taxes (subtract line 12 from line 11). **If $2,500 or more, this must equal line 17, column (d) below (or line D of Schedule B (Form 941))**	13	7,213 94
14	Total deposits for quarter, including overpayment applied from a prior quarter	14	7,213 94
15	**Balance due** (subtract line 14 from line 13). See instructions	15	- 0 -
16	**Overpayment.** If line 14 is more than line 13, enter excess here ► $_____ and check if to be: ☐ Applied to next return **or** ☐ Refunded.		

- **All filers:** If line 13 is less than $2,500, **do not** complete line 17 **or** Schedule B (Form 941).
- **Semiweekly schedule depositors:** Complete Schedule B (Form 941) and check here . . . ► ☐
- **Monthly schedule depositors:** Complete line 17, columns (a) through (d), and check here . . . ► ☒

17	Monthly Summary of Federal Tax Liability. (Complete **Schedule B (Form 941)** instead, if you were a semiweekly schedule depositor.)
(a) First month liability	(b) Second month liability	(c) Third month liability	(d) Total liability for quarter
2,271.44	2,394.70	2,547.80	7,213.94

Third Party Designee: Do you want to allow another person to discuss this return with the IRS (see separate instructions)? ☐ Yes. Complete the following. ☒ No
Designee's name ►
Phone no. ( )
Personal identification number (PIN)

Sign Here: Under penalties of perjury, I declare that I have examined this return, including accompanying schedules and statements, and to the best of my knowledge and belief, it is true, correct, and complete.
Signature ► *Janice Kellogg*
Print Your Name and Title ► Janice Kellogg, Manager
Date ► 1/24/--

For Privacy Act and Paperwork Reduction Act Notice, see back of Payment Voucher.   Cat. No. 17001Z   Form **941** (Rev. 1-2004)

Callouts:
1. Heading
2. Number of Employees
3. Total Quarterly Earnings
4. Income Tax Withheld
5. Employee and Employer Social Security and Medicare Taxes
6. Total Social Security plus Medicare Taxes
7. Total Taxes
8. Total Taxes for Each Month
9. Total Taxes

PREPARING EMPLOYER'S QUARTERLY FEDERAL TAX RETURN

Each employer is required by law to periodically report the payroll taxes withheld from employee salaries and the employer payroll taxes due the government. Some reports are submitted quarterly and others, annually.

Each employer must file a quarterly federal tax return showing the federal income tax, social security tax, and Medicare tax due the government. This information is submitted every three months on Form 941, Employer's Quarterly Federal Tax Return. Form 941 is filed before the last day of the month following the end of a calendar quarter. Hobby Shack's Form 941 for the quarter ended December 31 is shown on the previous page. The information needed to prepare Form 941 is obtained from employee earnings records.

STEPS — PREPARING AN EMPLOYER'S QUARTERLY FEDERAL TAX RETURN

1. Enter the company name, address, employer identification number, and the date the quarter ended in the heading section of Form 941.

2. Enter the number of employees, *6*, on line 1.

3. Enter total quarterly earnings, *$32,980.00*, on line 2. This amount is the sum of the fourth quarter total earnings of all employees. Total earnings, *$32,980.00*, is also recorded on lines 6a and 7a.

4. Enter the income tax withheld, *$2,168.00*, on line 3. The amount is the total of the fourth quarter federal income tax withheld from all employees. The same amount is entered on line 5.

5. Enter the quarterly employee and employer social security taxes, *$4,089.52*, and Medicare taxes, *$956.42*, on lines 6b and 7b, respectively. The taxes due are calculated as shown.

	Total Earnings	×	Tax Rate	=	Tax
Social Security	$32,980.00	×	12.4%	=	$4,089.52
Medicare	$32,980.00	×	2.9%	=	$ 956.42

The 12.4% tax rate is the sum of the employee 6.2% and the employer 6.2% social security tax rates. The 2.9% tax rate is the sum of the employee 1.45% and the employer 1.45% Medicare tax rates.

6. Enter the total social security tax plus Medicare tax, *$5,045.94* ($4,089.52 + $956.42 = $5,045.94), on line 8. Since Hobby Shack has no adjustment to its taxes, the total is also entered on line 10.

7. Enter the total taxes, *$7,213.94*, on lines 11 and 13. Hobby Shack is required to pay the federal government the sum of the federal income tax withheld and the employee and employer's shares of the social security tax and Medicare tax.

8. Enter on lines 17a, 17b, and 17c the total amounts of employee income tax withheld and employee and employer social security and Medicare taxes for each month of the quarter. For the month of December, the amount of taxes owed is calculated as shown and recorded on line 17c.

	Federal Income Tax Withheld	+	Employee Social Security and Medicare Tax	+	Employer Social Security and Medicare Tax	=	Federal Tax Liability
Dec. 1–15	$371.00	+	$436.94	+	$436.94	=	$1,244.88
Dec. 16–31	$386.00	+	$458.46	+	$458.46	=	$1,302.92
Totals	$757.00	+	$895.40	+	$895.40	=	$2,547.80

9. Enter the total quarterly withholding and payroll taxes, *$7,213.94*, on line 17d. This total is the sum of the three monthly totals reported on line 17 ($2,271.44 + $2,394.70 + $2,547.80 = $7,213.94).

EMPLOYER ANNUAL REPORTING OF PAYROLL TAXES

DO NOT STAPLE OR FOLD

a Control number: 33333	**1** Wages, tips, other compensation: 104,525.00	**2** Federal income tax withheld: 6,790.00
b Kind of Payer: 941 [X]	**3** Social security wages: 104,525.00	**4** Social security tax withheld: 6,480.55
c Total number of Forms W-2	**5** Medicare wages and tips: 104,525.00	**6** Medicare tax withheld: 1,515.61
e Employer identification number: 31-0429632	**7** Social security tips	**8** Allocated tips
f Employer's name: Hobby Shack, Inc. 1420 College Plaza Atlanta, GA 30337-1726	**9** Advance EIC payments	**10** Dependent care benefits
	11 Nonqualified plans	**12** Deferred compensation
	13 For third-party sick pay use only	
	14 Income tax withheld by payer of third-party sick pay	
15 State / Employer's state ID number	**16** State wages, tips, etc.	**17** State income tax
	18 Local wages, tips, etc.	**19** Local income tax
Contact person: Janice Kellogg	Telephone number: (404) 555-9368	For Official Use Only
Email address: jkellogg@hobbyshack.com	Fax number	

Under penalties of perjury, I declare that I have examined this return and accompanying documents, and, to the best of my knowledge and belief, they are true, correct, and complete.

Signature ▶ *Janice Kellogg*   Title ▶ *Manager*   Date ▶ 2/27/--

Form **W-3** Transmittal of Wage and Tax Statements   20--   Department of the Treasury / Internal Revenue Service

Send this entire page with the entire Copy A page of Form(s) W-2 to the Social Security Administration. Photocopies are not acceptable.

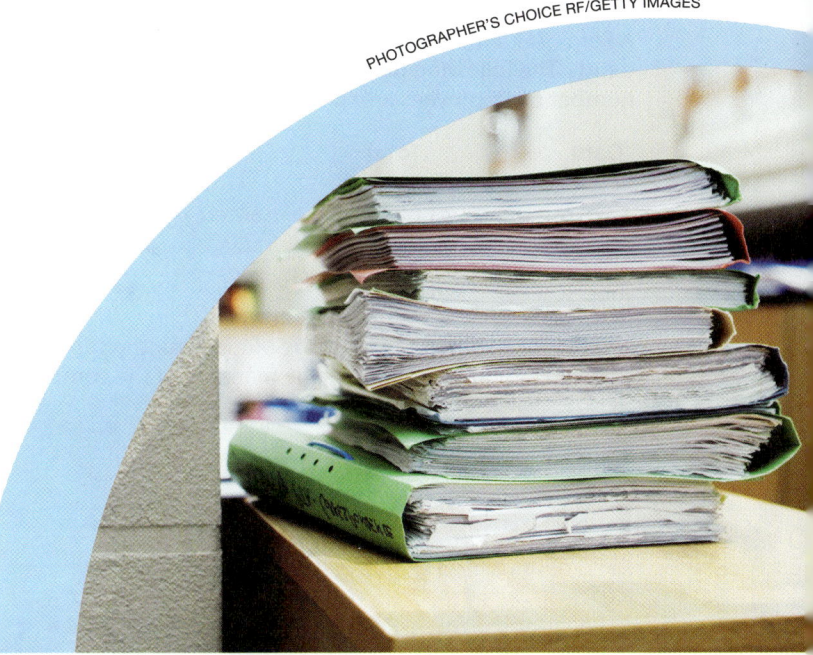

PHOTOGRAPHER'S CHOICE RF/GETTY IMAGES

Form W-3, Transmittal of Wage and Tax Statements, is sent to the Social Security Administration by February 28 each year. Form W-3 reports the previous year's earnings and payroll taxes withheld for all employees. Attached to Form W-3 is Copy A of each employee Form W-2. Employers with more than 250 employees must send the information to the Internal Revenue Service in computer files rather than the actual Forms W-2 and W-3.

At the end of a calendar year, employers must also report to the federal and state governments a summary of all earnings paid to employees during the twelve months.

Reporting Withholding and Payroll Taxes   Lesson 13-3   381

End of Lesson REVIEW

AUDIT YOUR UNDERSTANDING

1. When must employers furnish a W-2 statement to their employees?
2. What taxes are included in the quarterly federal tax return filed by the employer?

WORK TOGETHER 13-3

Reporting withholding and payroll taxes

A Form 941, Employer's Quarterly Federal Tax Return, is given in the *Working Papers*. Your instructor will guide you through the following example. The following data is for Audio Solutions.

Date Paid	Total Earnings	Federal Income Tax Withheld	Employee Social Security Tax Withheld	Employee Medicare Tax Withheld
Jan. 31	$10,440.00	$731.00	$647.28	$151.38
Feb. 28	10,960.00	767.00	679.52	158.92
Mar. 31	12,400.00	868.00	768.80	179.80

a. Company address: 625 Sandpiper Street, Ormond Beach, Florida 32074-4060
b. Employer identification number: 70-7818356
c. Number of employees: 6

1. Prepare a Form 941 for Audio Solutions for the first quarter of the current year. Use the preparation date of April 24. Sign your name as the manager of the company.

ON YOUR OWN 13-3

Reporting withholding and payroll taxes

A Form 941, Employer's Quarterly Federal Tax Return, is given in the *Working Papers*. Work this problem independently. The following data is for Audio Solutions. The company address, employer identification number, and number of employees are the same as in Work Together 13-3.

Date Paid	Total Earnings	Federal Income Tax Withheld	Employee Social Security Tax Withheld	Employee Medicare Tax Withheld
Apr. 30	$11,760.00	$823.00	$729.12	$170.52
May 31	11,820.00	827.00	732.84	171.39
June 30	10,900.00	763.00	675.80	158.05

1. Prepare a Form 941 for Audio Solutions for the second quarter of the current year. Use the preparation date of July 22. Sign your name as the manager of the company.

LESSON 13-4: Paying Withholding and Payroll Taxes

PAYING THE LIABILITY FOR EMPLOYEE INCOME TAX, SOCIAL SECURITY TAX, AND MEDICARE TAX

Employers must pay to the federal, state, and local governments all payroll taxes withheld from employee earnings as well as the employer payroll taxes. The payment of payroll taxes with the government is referred to as a *deposit*. Two amounts determine how often deposits are made to the federal government: (1) the amount of payroll taxes collected during the current deposit period and (2) the amount of payroll taxes owed during a prior 12-month period. The 12-month period that ends on June 30th of the prior year is called the **lookback period**. The Internal Revenue Service provides businesses with the following flowchart to assist them in determining when to make tax deposits.

When to Deposit Form 941 Employment Taxes

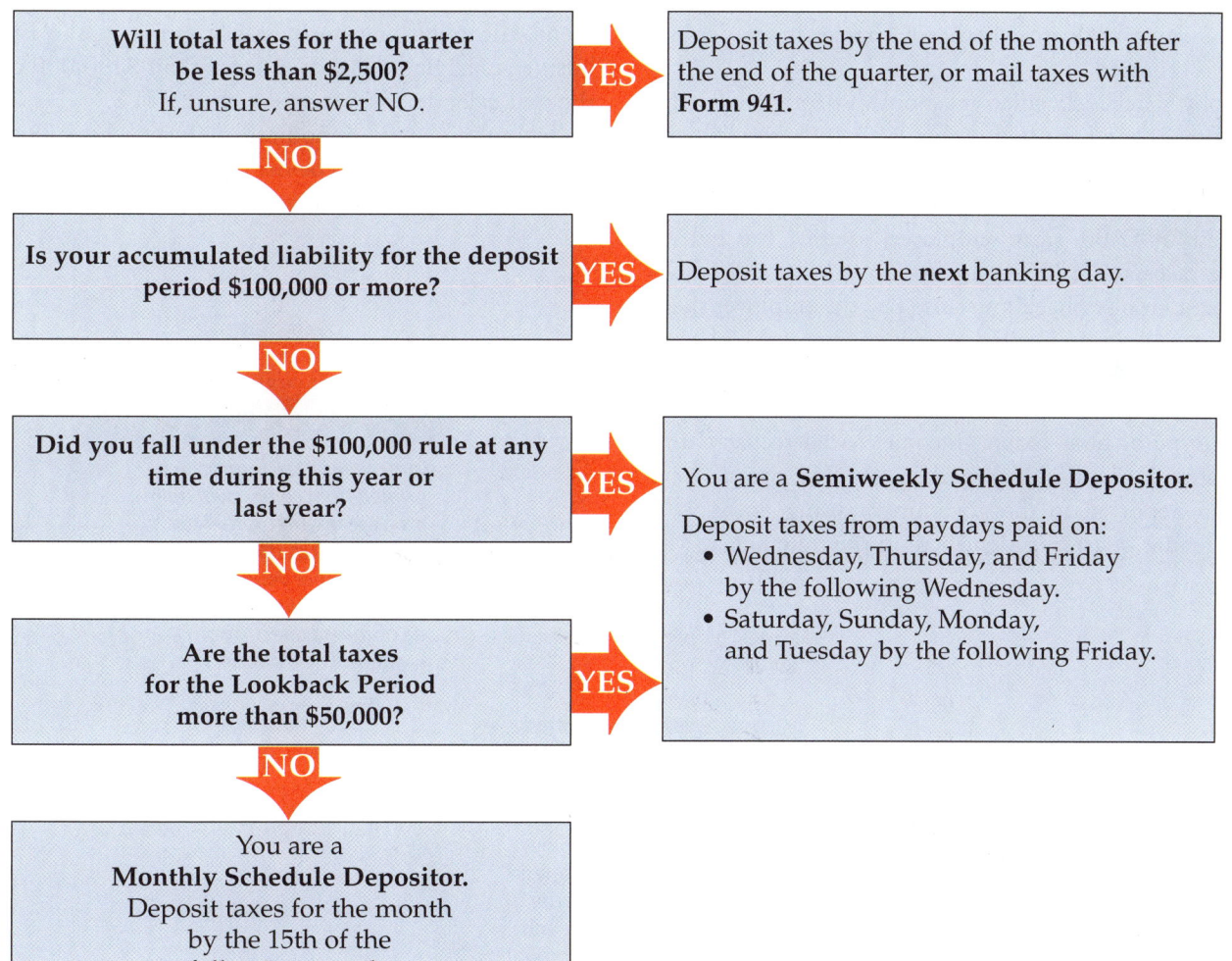

Paying Withholding and Payroll Taxes

Lesson 13-4   383

FORM 8109, FEDERAL DEPOSIT COUPON

New employers are monthly schedule depositors for the first calendar year of business. The Internal Revenue Service issues a monthly Form 8109 coupon book to new employers. After a lookback period is established, the business must evaluate whether a change in its deposit period is required.

Hobby Shack is classified as a monthly depositor. So, the payroll taxes are deposited with a local authorized financial institution by the 15th day of the following month, accompanied by Form 8109. In December, Hobby Shack withheld $757.00 from employee salaries for federal income taxes and $895.40 for social security and Medicare taxes. Hobby Shack must also pay the employer share of the payroll taxes. The federal tax payment, $2,547.80, is sent January 15 to an authorized bank with Form 8109 as shown.

The type of tax—federal income, social security, and Medicare—is identified by marking the 941 circle. These taxes are reported to the government using Form 941. The calendar quarter is identified on the right side of the form.

Deposits can also be made using the Electronic Federal Tax Payment System (EFTPS). Using either a personal computer or telephone, the business can have the deposit transferred directly from its bank account to the government. Although any business can enroll in the EFTPS, businesses having deposits of more than $200,000 during the past calendar year must use the EFTPS.

Tax rules change periodically. Always check the most current tax information before calculating any tax amount and the tax deposit requirements.

FOR YOUR INFORMATION

FYI

Some federal tax forms can be printed from copies available on the Internet. Other tax forms, such as the W-2, W-3, and 8109, are designed to be machine readable and must be obtained directly from the Internal Revenue Service.

REMEMBER

Social security tax and Medicare tax are the only payroll taxes paid by both the employer and employee. A business pays the same amount of social security tax and Medicare tax as the amount withheld from employees.

JOURNALIZING PAYMENT OF LIABILITY FOR EMPLOYEE INCOME TAX, SOCIAL SECURITY TAX, AND MEDICARE TAX

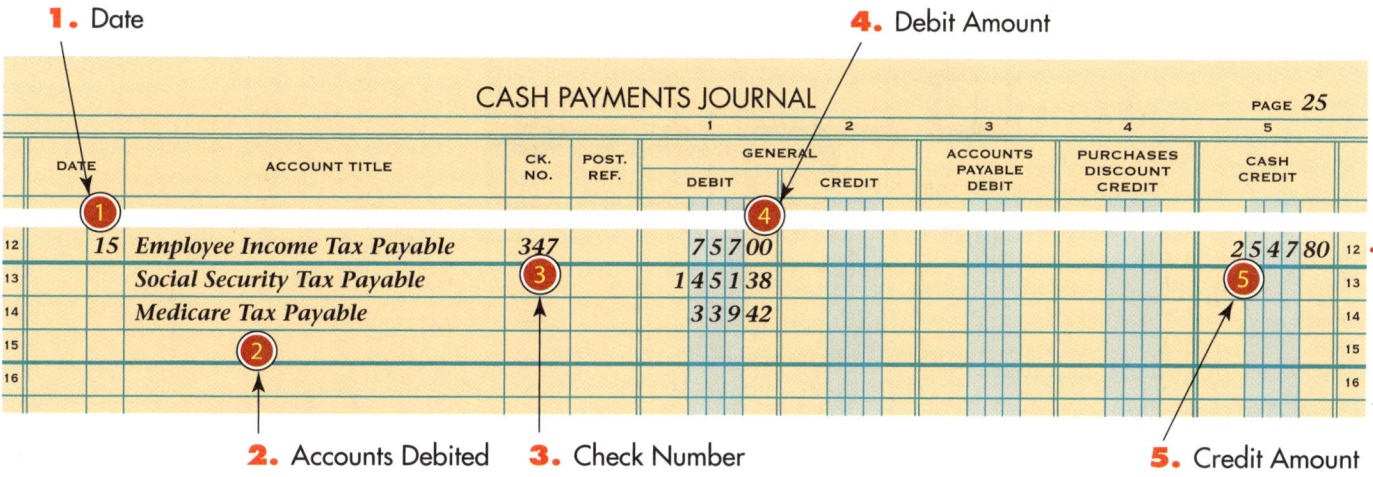

January 15. Paid cash for liability for employee income tax, $757.00; social security tax, $1,451.38; and Medicare tax, $339.42; total, $2,547.80. Check No. 347.

STEPS: JOURNALIZING A PAYMENT OF LIABILITY FOR EMPLOYEE INCOME TAX, SOCIAL SECURITY TAX, AND MEDICARE TAX

1. Write the date, *15*, in the Date column.
2. Write the titles of the three accounts debited, *Employee Income Tax Payable, Social Security Tax Payable*, and *Medicare Tax Payable*, in the Account Title column.
3. Write the check number, *347*, in the Ck. No. column.
4. Write the three debit amounts, *$757.00, $1,451.38,* and *$339.42*, in the General Debit column.
5. Write the amount of the credit to *Cash, $2,547.80*, in the Cash Credit column.

The balances of the liability accounts are reduced by this transaction. Therefore, Employee Income Tax Payable is debited for $757.00. Social Security Tax Payable is debited for $1,451.38. Medicare Tax Payable is debited for $339.42. The balance of Cash is decreased by a credit for the total payment, $2,547.80.

FOR YOUR INFORMATION

FYI

Semimonthly pay periods are paid twice a month. Biweekly pay periods are paid every two weeks.

Paying Withholding and Payroll Taxes — Lesson 13-4

PAYING THE LIABILITY FOR FEDERAL UNEMPLOYMENT TAX

Federal unemployment insurance is paid by the end of the month following each quarter if the liability amount is more than $100. However, all unemployment tax liabilities outstanding at the end of a calendar year should be paid. Federal unemployment tax is paid to the federal government by making a tax deposit with an authorized bank. The deposit for federal unemployment tax is similar to the deposit required for income tax, social security tax, and Medicare tax. Form 8109, Federal Tax Deposit Coupon accompanies the unemployment tax deposit.

The total of federal unemployment taxes paid during a calendar year is reported on Form 940. Hobby Shack's federal unemployment tax liability at the end of December 31 is $34.60. Hobby Shack's Form 8109 for the fourth quarter is shown. The type of tax, federal unemployment tax, is identified by marking the 940 circle since this tax is reported to the government using Form 940. The calendar quarter is identified on the right side of the form.

JOURNALIZING PAYMENT OF LIABILITY FOR FEDERAL UNEMPLOYMENT TAX

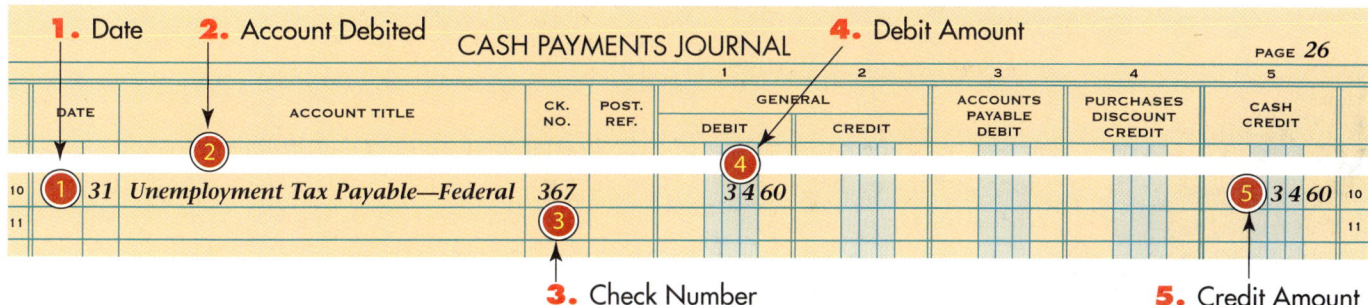

January 31. Paid cash for federal unemployment tax liability for quarter ended December 31, $34.60. Check No. 367.

The balance of the liability account is reduced by this transaction. Therefore, Unemployment Tax Payable—Federal is debited for $34.60. The balance of the asset account, Cash, is decreased by a credit for the payment, $34.60.

STEPS — JOURNALIZING A PAYMENT OF LIABILITY FOR FEDERAL UNEMPLOYMENT TAX

1. Write the date, *31*, in the Date column.
2. Write the title of the account debited, *Unemployment Tax Payable—Federal*, in the Account Title column.
3. Write the check number, *367*, in the Ck. No. column.
4. Write the debit amount, *$34.60*, in the General Debit column.
5. Write the amount of the credit to Cash, *$34.60*, in the Cash Credit column.

JOURNALIZING PAYMENT OF LIABILITY FOR STATE UNEMPLOYMENT TAX

The same steps are followed as for federal unemployment tax. State requirements for reporting and paying state unemployment taxes vary. In general, employers are required to pay the state unemployment tax during the month following each calendar quarter.

January 31. Paid cash for state unemployment tax liability for quarter ended December 31, $233.55. Check No. 368.

Paying Withholding and Payroll Taxes

CAREERS IN ACCOUNTING

Business, Management & Administration

Wally Wood, Managing Partner of Accounting Firm

Stop a farmer as he harvests his crop. Ask him how he decided to become a farmer and you are likely to hear, "I was born to be a farmer. My grandfather started this farm. My father worked this farm. I've never thought of doing anything else."

Likewise, Wally Wood was born into the accounting profession. Wally began working part-time for his father, K. Dale Wood, CPA, in 1973 at the age of 16. He started his accounting career doing write-up work for clients, recording their accounting transactions in accounting records, and preparing their financial statements. He also began preparing short tax returns.

After graduating from high school, he became a full-time employee of his father's accounting firm while majoring in accounting at the local university. "After about two years, due to circumstances beyond our control, I became the in-charge on several tax and small write-up clients. By the time I graduated from college, I was responsible for the majority of the tax and write-up clients."

Soon after graduating from college and passing the CPA examination, Wally became a partner in the firm, now called Wood and Wood, Ltd. Within three years, before the age of 30, Wally became managing partner of the firm. As the managing partner, Wally is ultimately responsible for the quality of all services provided by the firm. A managing partner also markets the firm's services to obtain new clients. Like the owner of any small business, the managing partner manages the firm's employees, technology, equipment, and accounting records.

The firm recently expanded by buying another CPA firm, becoming Wood, Wood and Taylor, Ltd. Wally notes, "As a small firm, we are uniquely positioned to provide personalized tax, audit, and consulting services to our clients, including individuals, small businesses, and government agencies. We also perform peer reviews for other accounting firms, evaluating their work to ensure that proper accounting and auditing standards are being applied."

As managing partner of an accounting firm, Wally recognizes his obligation to be involved in the growth and governance of his profession. As a member of several committees of his state society of certified public accountants, he is working to ensure that accountants provide quality services to their clients.

Salary Range: According to the 2005 salary survey conducted by financial recruiting company Robert Half International, directors (partners) of small public accounting firms earned between $69,000 and $87,750 a year. Graduate degrees and professional certifications can increase these salaries by up to 10 percent.

Qualifications: Starting your own accounting firm requires a combination of expertise and experience. After earning a Certified Public Accountant license, you should obtain several years' experience in another accounting firm.

Occupational Outlook: The Sarbanes-Oxley Act of 2002 has dramatically increased the demand for accountants who can establish, document, and evaluate the internal accounting controls required to prepare accurate financial statements. Clients continue to need tax planning and other consulting services.

End of Lesson REVIEW

AUDIT YOUR UNDERSTANDING

TERM REVIEW

lookback period

1. For a monthly schedule depositor, when are payroll taxes paid to the federal government?
2. What are two different uses for Form 8109?

WORK TOGETHER 13-4

Paying withholding and payroll taxes

A cash payments journal page is given in the *Working Papers*. Your instructor will guide you through the following examples. The following payroll data is for Digital Supplies for the monthly pay period ended March 31 of the current year.

Date Paid	Federal Income Tax Withheld	Employee Social Security Tax Withheld	Employee Medicare Tax Withheld
Mar. 31	$1,386.00	$1,322.05	$309.25

Credit balances on March 31 for the unemployment tax accounts for the first quarter are as follows: Unemployment Tax Payable—Federal, $511.75; Unemployment Tax Payable—State, $3,454.34. Digital Supplies pays both unemployment taxes each quarter.

1. Prepare a journal entry for payment of the withheld taxes. Digital Supplies is a monthly schedule depositor. Journalize Check No. 383 on cash payments journal page 14 using the date the taxes are due to the federal government.
2. Prepare journal entries for payment of the federal and state unemployment taxes liability. Assume both checks were prepared on the due date for the federal tax deposit. Check Nos. 401 and 402.

ON YOUR OWN 13-4

Paying withholding and payroll taxes

A cash payments journal page is given in the *Working Papers*. Work this problem independently. The following payroll data is for River Hardware for the monthly pay period ended June 30 of the current year.

Date Paid	Federal Income Tax Withheld	Employee Social Security Tax Withheld	Employee Medicare Tax Withheld
June 30	$1,052.00	$1,004.40	$234.95

Credit balances on June 30 for the unemployment tax accounts for the second quarter are as follows: Unemployment Tax Payable—Federal, $274.80; Unemployment Tax Payable—State, $1,922.40. River Hardware pays both unemployment taxes each quarter, regardless of the amount owed.

1. Prepare a journal entry for payment of the withheld taxes. River Hardware is a monthly schedule depositor. Journalize Check No. 678 on cash payments journal page 19 using the date the taxes are due to the federal government.
2. Prepare journal entries for payment of the federal and state unemployment taxes liability. Assume both checks were prepared on the due date for the federal tax deposit. Check Nos. 711 and 712.

SUMMARY

After completing this chapter, you can:
1. Define accounting terms related to payroll accounting, taxes, and reports.
2. Identify accounting concepts and practices related to payroll accounting, taxes, and reports.
3. Analyze payroll transactions and record a payroll.
4. Record employer payroll taxes.
5. Prepare selected payroll tax reports.
6. Pay and record withholding and payroll taxes.

EXPLORE ACCOUNTING

Net Income vs. Taxable Income

Financial statements should provide important information that is accurate, reliable, comparable, and consistent. Over the years, a set of principles and concepts for maintaining accounting records and preparing financial statements has been developed. These guidelines are known as Generally Accepted Accounting Principles (GAAP). Most businesses use GAAP in preparing their financial statements and determining their net income.

The Internal Revenue Service (IRS) is responsible for collecting money to operate the federal government. Federal income taxes are calculated as a percentage of business or individual income. To accomplish its task, the IRS prepares Internal Revenue Service Regulations.

The objectives of the accounting profession and business community, however, are not necessarily the same as those of the federal government and the IRS. For example, a GAAP concept, Matching Expenses with Revenue, requires that the cost of business equipment be allocated over the usable life of the equipment. However, to encourage businesses to replace equipment more rapidly, IRS Regulations may permit the cost of equipment to be allocated more rapidly. Thus, in a certain year the expense for allocating cost would be greater for tax purposes than for financial reporting purposes. These types of differences create different amounts reported as net income for financial reporting purposes and for tax reporting purposes.

Thus, most businesses follow GAAP in preparing their financial statements but must follow IRS Regulations in preparing their tax returns. As a result, net income on financial statements generally differs from taxable income reported on tax returns.

Research: Examine several company annual reports. Study the financial statements and the notes connected with those statements. Is there any information indicating a difference between net income reported on the financial statements and taxable income for tax purposes? What are they, if any?

13-1 APPLICATION PROBLEM

Recording a payroll

Dana's payroll register has the following totals for two semimonthly pay periods, July 1–15 and July 16–31 of the current year.

Period	Total Earnings	Deductions					Net Pay
		Federal Income Tax	Social Security Tax	Medicare Tax	Other	Total	
July 1–15	$6,970.00	$685.00	$432.14	$101.07	B $180.00	$1,398.21	$5,571.79
July 16–31	6,040.00	572.00	374.48	87.58	B 150.00	1,184.06	4,855.94

Other Deductions: B—U.S. Savings Bonds

Instructions:
Journalize payment of the two payrolls on page 15 of the cash payments journal given in the *Working Papers*. The first payroll was paid by Check No. 547 on July 15 of the current year. The second payroll was paid by Check No. 568 on July 31 of the current year.

13-2 APPLICATION PROBLEM

Recording employer payroll taxes

Use Malone's selected payroll information for the two semimonthly pay periods, April 1–15 and April 16–30 of the current year. Forms and a general journal are given in the *Working Papers*.

Employee Name	Accumulated Earnings, March 31	Total Earnings for April 1–15 Pay Period	Total Earnings for April 16–30 Pay Period
Bolser, Frank T.	$4,860.00	$ 810.00	$ 795.00
Denham, Beth R.	5,670.00	945.00	980.00
Harjo, Teresa S.	7,500.00	1,250.00	1,250.00
Knutzen, John L.	3,720.00	620.00	635.00
Prescott, Laura F.	4,560.00	760.00	740.00
Schmidt, Ian T.	6,900.00	1,150.00	1,125.00

Employer payroll tax rates are as follows: social security, 6.2%; Medicare, 1.45%; federal unemployment, 0.8%; state unemployment, 5.4%. Unemployment taxes are owed on the first $7,000.00 of earnings for each employee.

Instructions:
1. Calculate the amount of earnings subject to unemployment taxes for the April 1–15 pay period. Note that Ian T. Schmidt has accumulated earnings on March 31 of $6,900.00. Therefore, only $100.00 ($7,000.00 − $6,900.00) of his April 1–15 earnings is subject to unemployment tax.
2. Calculate the employer payroll tax amounts for the April 1–15 pay period.

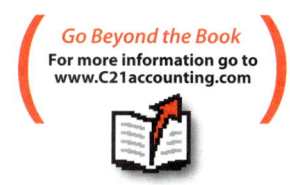

Go Beyond the Book
For more information go to
www.C21accounting.com

Payroll Accounting, Taxes, and Reports — Chapter 13 — 391

3. Journalize the employer payroll taxes on page 16 of a general journal. Use the date of April 15 of the current year. The source document is Memorandum No. 69.
4. Calculate the employer payroll taxes for the April 16–30 pay period. Calculate April 15 accumulated earnings by adding total earnings for the April 1–15 pay period to the March 31 accumulated earnings. Note that only part of Beth R. Denham's earnings for April 16–30 are subject to unemployment tax.
5. Journalize the employer payroll taxes on page 16 of a general journal. Use the date of April 30 of the current year. The source document is Memorandum No. 76.

13-3 APPLICATION PROBLEM

Reporting withholding and payroll taxes

The following payroll data is for Eagle Toys for the second quarter of the current year.

Date Paid	Total Earnings	Federal Income Tax Withheld	Employee Social Security Tax Withheld	Employee Medicare Tax Withheld
Apr. 30	$ 9,166.00	$654.00	$568.29	$132.91
May 31	10,382.00	687.00	643.68	150.54
June 30	9,872.00	718.00	612.06	143.14

Additional data:
1. Company address: 784 McDonald Street, Mesa, AZ 85201-5874
2. Employer identification number: 80-7818356
3. Number of employees: 5
4. Federal tax payments have been made on May 15, June 15, and July 15.

Instructions:
Prepare the Form 941, Employer's Quarterly Federal Tax Return, given in the *Working Papers*. Use the date July 21. Sign your name as the manager of the company. Amounts on lines 13 and 17d may not equal, due to rounding.

13-4 APPLICATION PROBLEM

Paying withholding and payroll taxes

The following payroll data is for Zimmerman Company for the first quarter of the current year.

Period	Total Earnings	Federal Income Tax Withheld
March	$17,560.00	$1,548.00
First Quarter	$52,210.00	—

In addition, total earnings are subject to 6.2% employee and 6.2% employer social security tax, plus 1.45% employee and 1.45% employer Medicare tax. The federal unemployment tax rate is 0.8% and the state unemployment tax rate is 5.4% of total earnings. No total earnings have exceeded the tax base for calculating unemployment taxes.

Instructions:
1. Calculate the appropriate liability amount of social security and Medicare taxes for March. Journalize the payment of the withheld taxes on page 8 of the cash payments journal given in the *Working Papers*. The taxes were paid by Check No. 813 on April 15 of the current year.

2. Calculate the appropriate federal unemployment tax liability for the first quarter. Journalize payment of this liability in the cash payments journal. The tax was paid by Check No. 830 on April 30 of the current year.

3. Calculate the appropriate state unemployment tax liability for the first quarter. Journalize payment of this liability in the cash payments journal. The tax was paid by Check No. 831 on April 30 of the current year.

13-5 MASTERY PROBLEM

Journalizing payroll transactions

Keller Systems, Inc., completed payroll transactions during the period May 1 to June 15 of the current year. Payroll tax rates are as follows: social security, 6.2%; Medicare, 1.45%; federal unemployment, 0.8%; state unemployment, 5.4%. The company buys savings bonds for employees as accumulated withholdings reach the necessary amount to purchase a bond. No total earnings have exceeded the tax base for calculating unemployment taxes. Keller Systems is a monthly schedule depositor for payroll taxes.

Instructions:

1. Journalize the following transactions on page 14 of the cash payments journal and page 10 of the general journal given in the *Working Papers*. Source documents are abbreviated as follows: check, C, and memorandum, M.

Transactions:

May 15. Paid cash for April's payroll tax liability. Withheld taxes from April payrolls: employee income tax, $532.00; social security tax, $634.88; and Medicare tax, $148.48. C421.
   15. Paid cash for semimonthly payroll. Total earnings, $5,250.00; withholdings: employee income tax, $273.00; U.S. Savings Bonds, $60.00 (calculate the social security and Medicare deductions). C422.
   15. Recorded employer payroll taxes expense for the May 15 payroll. M42.
   15. Paid cash for U.S. Savings Bonds for employees, $300.00. C423.
   31. Paid cash for semimonthly payroll. Gross wages, $5,310.00; withholdings: employee income tax, $276.00; U.S. Savings Bonds, $60.00. C461.
   31. Recorded employer payroll taxes expense for the May 31 payroll. M46.
   31. Paid cash for federal unemployment tax liability for quarter ended March 31, $245.76. C462.
   31. Paid cash for state unemployment tax liability for quarter ended March 31, $1,658.88. C463.
June 15. Paid cash for the May liability for employee income tax, social security tax, and Medicare tax, C487. (Calculate the social security and Medicare tax liabilities by multiplying total earnings for the period by 12.4% for social security tax and 2.9% for Medicare tax.)
   15. Paid cash for semimonthly payroll. Gross wages, $5,280.00; withholdings: employee income tax, $274.00; U.S. Savings Bonds, $75.00. C488.
   15. Recorded employer payroll taxes expense. M53.

2. Prove and rule the cash payments journal.

13-6 CHALLENGE PROBLEM

Journalizing and posting payroll transactions

Golf Design, Inc., completed payroll transactions during the period January 1 to April 30 of the current year. Payroll tax rates are as follows: social security, 6.2%; Medicare, 1.45%; federal unemployment, 0.8%; and state unemployment, 5.4%. The company buys savings bonds for employees as the accumulated withholdings reach the necessary amount to purchase a bond. No total earnings have exceeded the tax base for calculating unemployment taxes.

The balances in the general ledger as of January 1 of the current year are recorded in the *Working Papers*.

Payroll Accounting, Taxes, and Reports   Chapter 13   **393**

Chart of Accounts

Account Number	Account Title
2120	Employee Income Tax Payable
2130	Social Security Tax Payable
2140	Medicare Tax Payable
2150	Unemployment Tax Payable—Federal
2160	Unemployment Tax Payable—State
2180	U.S. Savings Bonds Payable
6150	Payroll Taxes Expense
6170	Salary Expense

Instructions:

1. Journalize the following transactions on page 1 of the cash payments journal and the general journal given in the Working Papers. Payroll withholdings for employee income tax and U.S. Savings Bonds are provided. Calculate other payroll withholdings using the tax rates provided. Source documents are abbreviated as follows: check, C, and memorandum, M.

Transactions:

Jan. 2. Wrote a check for 15 U.S. Savings Bonds at $25.00 each for employees. C195.
15. Paid the December liability for employee income tax, social security tax, and Medicare tax. C204.
31. Wrote a check for federal unemployment tax liability for quarter ended December 31. C210.
31. Wrote a check for state unemployment tax liability for quarter ended December 31. C211.
31. Paid January payroll (total payroll, $12,200.00, less deductions: employee income tax, $805.00; U.S. Savings Bonds, $125.00). C216.
31. Recorded employer payroll taxes expense. M98.
Posting. Post the items that are to be posted individually.

Feb. 15. Wrote a check for January liability for employee income tax and for social security tax and Medicare tax. C222.
28. Paid February payroll (total payroll, $12,360.00, less deductions: employee income tax, $816.00; U.S. Savings Bonds, $125.00). C232.
28. Recorded employer payroll taxes expense. M107.
Posting. Post the items that are to be posted individually.

2. Prove and rule cash payments journal page 1. Carry the column totals forward to page 2 of the cash payments journal.

3. Journalize the following transactions on page 2 of the cash payments journal and continuing on page 1 of the general journal.

Transactions:

Mar. 15. Wrote a check for February liability for employee income tax, social security tax, and Medicare tax. C237.
31. Paid March payroll (total payroll, $11,860.00, less deductions: employee income tax, $783.00; U.S. Savings Bonds, $125.00). C258.
31. Recorded employer payroll taxes expense. M116.
Posting. Post the items that are to be posted individually.

Apr. 1. Paid cash for 15 U.S. Savings Bonds at $25.00 each for employees. C259.
15. Wrote a check for March liability for employee income tax, social security tax, and Medicare tax. C270.
30. Wrote a check for federal unemployment tax liability for quarter ended March 31. C276.
30. Wrote a check for state unemployment tax liability for quarter ended March 31. C277.
Posting. Post the items that are to be posted individually.

4. Prove and rule cash payments journal page 2.

APPLIED COMMUNICATION

One of the unwritten rules of business is that payroll information is private and confidential. People usually do not want their co-workers to know how much they are paid. This common business practice presents a challenge for employees responsible for payroll accounting. Payroll workers handle many different types of data. The payroll department records personal information about employees, such as addresses and social security numbers, and verifies and totals time cards. In addition, each pay period, payroll accountants calculate each employee's earnings, deductions, and net pay. It is important for payroll employees to be trustworthy and able to maintain confidentiality.

Instructions: In the form of a memorandum, write a statement of a company's policy regarding the confidentiality of payroll information. The memorandum should be addressed to the employees of the payroll department.

CASE FOR CRITICAL THINKING

Wyatt Company has decided to hire a sales representative. The business can afford to pay the representative a salary of only $30,000.00. The accounting assistant informs the manager that hiring the representative will cost the business more than the $30,000.00 salary. Do you agree with the accounting assistant? Explain your response.

AUDITING FOR ERRORS

In June, the liability for federal and state unemployment tax for Excelsior Corporation is recorded at about the same amount as for previous months. Jackie Blette suggests that it usually begins to decrease in June, except when many new graduates are hired that month. You have been asked to investigate the payroll data to discover whether there is a problem.

Instructions

1. Why would the liability for unemployment tax begin to decline in June?
2. If there is an error in the unemployment liability amounts, what is the likely cause?
3. Examine the information below and on a separate sheet of paper write the correct amounts for the unemployment tax liabilities.

Accumulated Earnings Jan.–May	June Total Earnings	Federal Unemployment Tax	State Unemployment Tax
$4,260.00	$ 810.00	$ 6.48	$43.74
5,200.00	1,100.00	8.80	59.40
6,450.00	1,250.00	10.00	67.50
6,800.00	1,350.00	10.80	72.90
3,600.00	1,200.00	9.60	64.80

ANALYZING BEST BUY'S FINANCIAL STATEMENTS

Best Buy plans for current-year claims against it as well as any claims that might occur in the future. Best Buy estimates an amount for claims it expects to pay in the future that relate to activities of the current fiscal year.

Instructions: Use the Insurance section in Note 1 of Best Buy's financial statements in Appendix B, page B-14, to answer the following questions.

1. How does Best Buy insure against losses?
2. For what types of losses does Best Buy self-insure?
3. Does Best Buy purchase insurance?
4. How does Best Buy estimate its claims?
5. How are accrued claims reported on the March 3, 2007 financial statements?

Accounting SOFTWARE

RECORDING PAYROLL TAXES

The government does not send an invoice for the amount of payroll taxes due. Businesses must keep accurate records of the payroll taxes withheld and employer payroll taxes to ensure the correct amount is paid. The payroll tax liability accounts provide a record of all payroll taxes due. The balance in the account is the amount that should be paid to the government.

Peachtree provides two methods to obtain the outstanding balances of general ledger accounts. A report of general ledger accounts presents each transaction and the ending balance of every account. Another window reports only the monthly total debits and credits and balance for a single account.

PEACHTREE MASTERY PROBLEM 13-5
1. Open (Restore) file 13-5MP.ptb.
2. Journalize and post the May 15 and May 31 transactions in the cash disbursements journal. Use the general journal to record the employer payroll taxes expense for May 15 and May 31.
3. Before you journalize and post the June 15 transactions, remember to change the accounting periods (Tasks, System, Change Accounting Period).
4. Journalize and post the June 15 transactions. Use the general journal for the payroll tax expense transactions.
5. Print the May 15 through June 15 cash disbursements journal.

PEACHTREE CHALLENGE PROBLEM 13-6
1. Open (Restore) file 13-6CP.ptb.
2. Journalize and post the payroll transactions. Use the general journal to record the employer payroll taxes expense.
3. Print the January through April cash disbursements journal.
4. Print the January 2 through March general journal.
5. Print the January through April general ledger.

RECORDING PAYROLL TAXES

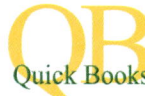

When paying payroll taxes and other payroll liabilities in this chapter, the amounts were clearly stated in the transaction. In a company, there are no bills received stating payroll liability amounts and due date. The payroll employee must determine how much needs to be paid for each liability and when the amount is due. The electronic records contain all the data needed to determine the correct amounts, but they must be accessed in order to be of help. QuickBooks has several ways to determine the balance of various accounts.

A trial balance can be run to show the balance in each account. In most cases, the balance of the account is the amount that is due the government for the payroll tax liability. To get more detail, a general ledger can be printed or displayed. The general ledger can be displayed in two forms—one showing only the account balances and one showing all the entries in each account along with the account balance.

QUICKBOOKS MASTERY PROBLEM 13-5
1. Open the Keller Systems Inc file.
2. Journalize the transactions completed during May 15 through June 15. Use the Write Checks option for all cash payments. Use the Make General Journal Entries window for all other transactions.
3. Print a Journal report. Use May 15 and June 15 for the dates.

QUICKBOOKS CHALLENGE PROBLEM 13-6
1. Open the Golf Design Inc file.
2. Journalize the transactions completed during January through April.
3. Print a Journal report. Use January 1 and April 30 for the dates.

CALCULATING UNEMPLOYMENT TAX

Determining the amount of unemployment taxable earnings can be difficult. The calculation is especially difficult in the pay period in which an employee's accumulated earnings reach $7,000. Mistakes can easily be made calculating these amounts. The solution is to create a template on an electronic spreadsheet.

A formula using a combination of IF and MIN functions is required to calculate unemployment taxable earnings. An IF function compares two numbers and enters one of two values in the cell. The syntax of the IF function is =IF(logical_test, true_value, false_value). A MIN function calculates the minimum of two or more values. The syntax of the MIN function is =MIN(value1, value2, …)

Suppose an employee's accumulated earnings are $6,200 (cell C8) and earnings for the pay period are $500 (cell D8). The function to calculate the unemployment taxable earnings would be

=IF(C8>7000,0,MIN(D8,7000-C8))

The logical_test is false; C8 is not greater than $7,000. Therefore, the MIN function then calculates the lesser of (1) $500 in D8 or (2) $800, the difference between $7,000 and the accumulated earnings, $6,200. As you can see, using IF functions can be complex and will require you to have a full understanding how unemployment taxes are calculated.

OPTIONAL SPREADSHEET ACTIVITY
Open the file F13-OPT. Follow the step-by-step instructions in the Instructions worksheet to use the IF and MIN functions to calculate unemployment taxable earnings.

RECORDING PAYROLL TAXES

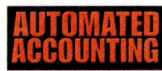

In an automated payroll system, the computer is used to maintain the employee database, to record payroll transactions at the end of each pay period, and to display and print various payroll reports.

Generating Payroll Journal Entries
Automated Accounting can generate the current payroll journal entry.
1. Choose the Current Payroll Journal Entry menu item from the Options menu. Note that you must first have a payroll entered into the system before payroll journal entries can be generated.
2. When the confirmation dialog box appears, click Yes.
3. Click the Post button.

Generating the Employer's Payroll Taxes Journal Entries
Automated Accounting can also generate the current payroll taxes journal entry.
1. Choose the Employer's Payroll Taxes menu item from the Options menu.
2. When the confirmation dialog box appears, click Yes.
3. Click the Post button.

AUTOMATED ACCOUNTING MASTERY PROBLEM 13-5
Open file F13-5.AA8. Display the problem instructions and complete the problem.

REINFORCEMENT Activity 2—Part A

An Accounting Cycle for a Corporation: Journalizing and Posting Transactions

Reinforcement Activity 2 reinforces learning from Part 2, Chapters 9 through 16. Activities cover a complete accounting cycle for a merchandising business organized as a corporation. Reinforcement Activity 2 is a single problem divided into two parts. Part A includes learning from Chapters 9 through 13. Part B includes learning from Chapters 14 through 16.

The accounting work of a single merchandising business for the last month of a yearly fiscal period is used in this reinforcement activity. The records kept and reports prepared, however, illustrate the application of accounting concepts for all merchandising businesses.

MEDICAL SERVICES COMPANY (MSC)

Medical Services Company (MSC), a merchandising business, is organized as a corporation. The business sells a complete line of medical accessories, from crutches to lift chairs. MSC is located in a medical office plaza adjacent to the hospital and is open for business Monday through Saturday. A monthly rent is paid for the building. MSC accepts credit cards from customers.

CHART OF ACCOUNTS

MSC uses the chart of accounts shown on the next page.

JOURNALS AND LEDGERS

The journals and ledgers used by MSC are listed below. Models of the journals and ledgers are shown in the textbook chapters indicated.

Journals and Ledgers	Chapter
Purchases journal	9
Cash payments journal	9
General journal	9
Sales journal	10
Cash receipts journal	10
Accounts payable ledger	11
Accounts receivable ledger	11
General ledger	11

CHART OF ACCOUNTS
GENERAL LEDGER

Balance Sheet Accounts

(1000) ASSETS
1100 Current Assets
1110 Cash
1120 Petty Cash
1130 Accounts Receivable
1135 Allowance for Uncollectible Accounts
1140 Merchandise Inventory
1145 Supplies—Office
1150 Supplies—Store
1160 Prepaid Insurance
1200 Plant Assets
1210 Office Equipment
1220 Accumulated Depreciation—Office Equipment
1230 Store Equipment
1240 Accumulated Depreciation—Store Equipment
(2000) LIABILITIES
2100 Current Liabilities
2110 Accounts Payable
2115 Federal Income Tax Payable
2120 Employee Income Tax Payable
2130 Social Security Tax Payable
2135 Medicare Tax Payable
2140 Sales Tax Payable
2150 Unemployment Tax Payable—Federal
2160 Unemployment Tax Payable—State
2170 Health Insurance Premiums Payable
2180 U.S. Savings Bonds Payable
2190 United Way Donations Payable
2195 Dividends Payable
(3000) OWNERS' EQUITY
3110 Capital Stock
3120 Retained Earnings
3130 Dividends
3140 Income Summary

Income Statement Accounts

(4000) OPERATING REVENUE
4110 Sales
4120 Sales Discount
4130 Sales Returns and Allowances
(5000) COST OF MERCHANDISE
5110 Purchases
5120 Purchases Discount
5130 Purchases Returns and Allowances
(6000) OPERATING EXPENSES
6110 Advertising Expense
6115 Cash Short and Over
6120 Credit Card Fee Expense
6125 Depreciation Expense—Office Equipment
6130 Depreciation Expense—Store Equipment
6135 Insurance Expense
6140 Miscellaneous Expense
6150 Payroll Taxes Expense
6160 Rent Expense
6165 Repairs Expense
6170 Salary Expense
6175 Supplies Expense—Office
6180 Supplies Expense—Store
6185 Uncollectible Accounts Expense
6190 Utilities Expense
(7000) INCOME TAX EXPENSE
7105 Federal Income Tax Expense

SUBSIDIARY LEDGERS

Accounts Receivable Ledger

110 Bratton Clinic
120 Clegg Medical Center
130 Glenmore School
140 Jamacus Clinic
150 Odom Daycare
160 Treet Retirement Home

Accounts Payable Ledger

210 Armstrong Medical
220 Cross Office Supply
230 Evans Supply
240 Ogden Instruments
250 Spencer Industries
260 Ziegler, Inc.

RECORDING TRANSACTIONS

The December 1 account balances for the general and subsidiary ledgers are given in the *Working Papers*.

Instructions:

1. Journalize the following transactions completed during December of the current year. Use page 12 of a sales journal, page 12 of a purchases journal, page 12 of a general journal, page 12 of a cash receipts journal, and page 23 of a cash payments journal. MSC offers sales terms of 2/10, n/30. The sales tax rate is 6%. Source documents are abbreviated as follows: check, C; memorandum, M; purchase invoice, P; receipt, R; sales invoice, S; terminal summary, TS; debit memorandum, DM; credit memorandum, CM.

   Dec. 1. Paid cash for rent, $1,200.00. C372.
   2. Paid cash for electric bill, $346.20. C373.
   2. Received cash on account from Clegg Medical Center, covering S64 for $413.40, less 2% sales discount. R92.
   3. Paid cash for miscellaneous expense, $72.00. C374.
   3. Paid cash on account to Spencer Industries, covering P73 for $580.00, less 2% discount. C375.
   4. Sold merchandise on account to Bratton Clinic, $450.00, plus sales tax, $27.00; total, $477.00. S67.
   5. Recorded cash and credit card sales, $5,796.00, plus sales tax, $347.76; total, $6,143.76. TS45.
      Posting. Post the items that are to be posted individually. Post the journals in this order: sales journal, purchases journal, general journal, cash receipts journal, and cash payments journal.
   7. Sold merchandise on account to Glenmore School, $462.00. Glenmore School is exempt from sales tax. S68.
   7. Received cash on account from Treet Retirement Home, $432.48, covering S65. R93.
   8. Bought office supplies on account from Cross Office Supply, $351.60. M43.
   9. Purchased merchandise on account from Ogden Instruments, $2,250, less a 40% trade discount. P77.
   9. Bought store supplies on account from Ziegler, Inc., $330.00. M44.
   10. Paid cash for office supplies, $174.00. C376.
   11. Paid cash on account to Evans Supply, $1,170.00, covering P74. C377.
   11. Purchased merchandise on account from Spencer Industries, $1,032.00. P78.
   12. Paid cash for store supplies, $264.00. C378.
   12. Recorded cash and credit card sales, $7,125.00, plus sales tax, $427.50; total, $7,552.50. TS46.
      Posting. Post the items that are to be posted individually.
   14. Purchased merchandise on account from Evans Supply, $3,276.00. P79.
   14. Sold merchandise on account to Odom Daycare, $170.00, plus sales tax, $10.20; total, $180.20. S69.
   14. Paid cash for advertising, $415.00. C379.
   15. Returned $226.00 of merchandise to Evans Supply from P79, $226.00. DM4.
   15. Paid cash on account to Armstrong Medical, $1,272.00, covering P75. C380.
   15. Received cash on account from Jamacus Clinic, $821.50, covering S66. R94.
   15. Sold merchandise on account to Clegg Medical Center, $490.00, plus sales tax, $29.40; total, $519.40. S70.
   15. Paid cash for liability for employee income tax, $342.00, social security tax, $767.00, and Medicare tax, $179.38; total, $1,288.38. C381.
   15. Paid cash for semimonthly payroll, $2,313.85 (total payroll, $2,930.00, less deductions: employee income tax, $162.00; social security tax, $181.66; Medicare tax, $42.49; health insurance, $170.00; U.S. Savings Bonds, $30.00; United Way donations, $30.00). C382.
   15. Recorded employer payroll taxes, $248.95, for the semimonthly pay period ended December 15. Taxes owed are: social security tax, $181.66; Medicare tax, $42.49; federal unemployment tax, $3.20; and state unemployment tax, $21.60. M45.
   19. Recorded cash and credit card sales, $6,925.00, plus sales tax, $415.50; total, $7,340.50. TS47.
      Posting. Post the items that are to be posted individually.
   23. Paid cash on account to Ogden Instruments, $2,200.00, covering P76. C383.
   24. Received cash on account from Odom Daycare, covering S69 for $180.20, less 2% discount. R95.
   24. Granted credit to Clegg Medical Center for merchandise returned, $120.00, plus sales tax, $7.20, from S70; total, $127.20. CM5.
   26. Recorded cash and credit card sales, $6,980.00, plus sales tax, $418.80; total, $7,398.80. TS48.
      Posting. Post the items that are to be posted individually.

MSC's bank charges a fee for handling the collection of credit card sales deposited during the month. The credit card fee is deducted from MSC's bank account. The amount is then shown on the bank statement. The credit card fee is recorded in the cash payments journal as a reduction in cash.

    Dec. 28. Recorded credit card fee expense, $342.00. M46. (Debit Credit Card Fee Expense; credit Cash.)

2. Prove and rule page 23 of the cash payments journal.
3. Carry the column totals forward to page 24 of the cash payments journal.
4. Journalize the following transactions.

    Dec. 30. Purchased merchandise on account from Armstrong Medical, $1,940.00. P80.
          31. Paid cash to replenish the petty cash fund, $145.20: office supplies, $35.00; store supplies, $19.00; advertising, $64.00; miscellaneous, $26.00; cash short, $1.20. C384.
          31. Paid cash for semimonthly payroll, $2,462.32 (total payroll, $3,120.00, less deductions: employee income tax, $189.00; social security tax, $193.44; Medicare tax, $45.24; health insurance, $170.00; U.S. Savings Bonds, $30.00; United Way donations, $30.00). C385.
          31. Recorded employer payroll taxes, $263.48, for the semimonthly pay period ended December 31. Taxes owed are: social security tax, $193.44: Medicare tax, $45.24; federal unemployment tax, $3.20; and state unemployment tax, $21.60. M47.
          31. Recorded cash and credit card sales, $3,890.00, plus sales tax, $233.40; total, $4,123.40. TS49.
    Posting. Post the items that are to be posted individually.

5. Prove and rule the sales journal. Post the totals of the special columns.
6. Total and rule the purchases journal. Post the total.
7. Prove the equality of debits and credits for the cash receipts and cash payments journals.
8. Prove cash. The balance on the next unused check stub is $40,126.14.
9. Rule the cash receipts journal. Post the totals of the special columns.
10. Rule the cash payments journal. Post the totals of the special columns.
11. Prepare a schedule of accounts receivable and a schedule of accounts payable. Prove the accuracy of the subsidiary ledgers by comparing the schedule totals with the balances of the controlling accounts in the general ledger. If the totals are not the same, find and correct the errors.

The ledgers used in Reinforcement Activity 2—Part A are needed to complete Reinforcement Activity 2—Part B.

CHAPTER 14

Distributing Dividends and Preparing a Work Sheet for a Merchandising Business

OBJECTIVES

After studying Chapter 14, you will be able to:

1. Define accounting terms related to distributing dividends and preparing a work sheet for a merchandising business.
2. Identify accounting concepts and practices related to distributing dividends and preparing a work sheet for a merchandising business.
3. Journalize the declaration and payment of a dividend.
4. Begin a work sheet for a merchandising business.
5. Plan work sheet adjustments for merchandise inventory, supplies, prepaid expenses, uncollectible accounts, and depreciation.
6. Calculate federal income tax and plan the work sheet adjustment for federal income tax.
7. Complete a work sheet for a merchandising business.

KEY TERMS

- retained earnings
- dividends
- board of directors
- declaring a dividend
- merchandise inventory
- uncollectible accounts
- allowance method of recording losses from uncollectible accounts
- book value
- book value of accounts receivable
- current assets
- plant assets
- depreciation expense
- estimated salvage value
- straight-line method of depreciation
- accumulated depreciation
- book value of a plant asset

Point Your Browser
www.C21accounting.com

ACCOUNTING IN THE REAL WORLD

Lowe's

Lowe's—the Good Neighbor

Welcome to the neighborhood! That's the reaction Lowe's wants when it opens a store in your neighborhood. Lowe's is working to make home improvement more convenient for its customers. By providing the right products at the right price, whether in local stores or at Lowes.com, the company seeks to make it easy for its customers to improve the quality and value of their homes.

Lowe's is also investing in its community. The company provides relief supplies to victims of natural disasters, financial support for Habitat for Humanity, and educational grants to K-12 public education systems.

Community involvement is important to the employees at Lowe's. The company encourages volunteerism through Lowe's Heroes, a program focused on home safety. Looking out for your neighbor—that's what being a good neighbor is all about.

Critical Thinking

1. Beyond having quality products at a fair price, how do Lowe's and other home improvement companies assist customers to improve their homes?
2. How should Lowe's account for a donation of lumber to a Habitat for Humanity house?

Source: www.lowes.com

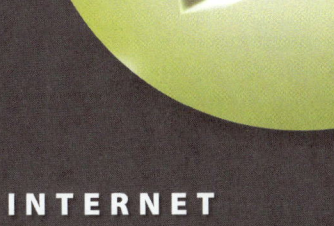

INTERNET ACTIVITY

Finding Stock Prices

Many company web sites give a history of the stock prices for the company's stock. Go to the homepage for a company of your choice. Look under a heading such as "About Us" or "Investor Relations" to find information about the price of the company's stock.

Instructions

1. Find the closing stock price from the previous day's trading.
2. Find the highest price for which the stock sold on the previous day.
3. Find the lowest price for which the stock sold on the previous day.

LESSON 14-1

Distributing Corporate Earnings to Stockholders

FINANCIAL INFORMATION

Management decisions about future business operations are often based on financial information. This information shows whether a profit is being made or a loss is being incurred. Profit or loss information helps an owner or manager determine future changes. Financial information is also needed to prepare required tax reports.

Hobby Shack uses a fiscal year that begins on January 1 and ends on December 31. Therefore, Hobby Shack summarizes its financial information on December 31 of each year.

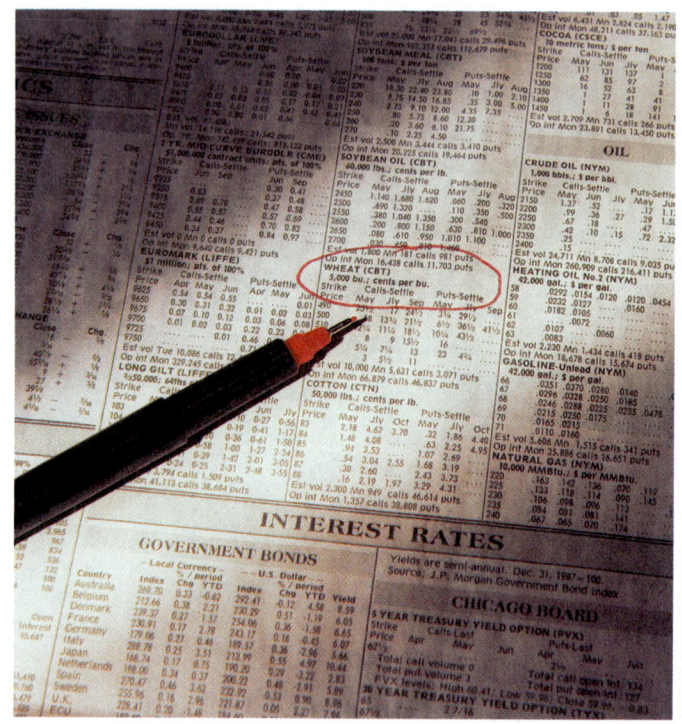

CHARACTER COUNTS

He's Guilty!

A company that believes one of its employees is stealing may obtain the services of a Certified Fraud Examiner (CFE). The CFE is trained to examine accounting records and obtain other evidence related to the alleged theft. CFEs often serve as expert witnesses in court. The Code of Professional Ethics of the Association of Certified Fraud Examiners provides its members with guidance on how to serve as an expert witness. The Code states that the CFE should obtain evidence that provides a reasonable basis for his or her opinion. However, the CFE should never express an opinion on the guilt or innocence of any person.

Instructions

Access the ACFE Code of Professional Ethics of the Association of Certified Fraud Examiners at www.cfenet.com. Citing the section, what other advice does the Code provide a CFE when serving as an expert witness?

STOCKHOLDERS' EQUITY ACCOUNTS USED BY A CORPORATION

(3000) STOCKHOLDERS' EQUITY
3110 Capital Stock
3120 Retained Earnings
3130 Dividends
3140 Income Summary

A corporation's ownership is divided into units. Each unit of ownership in a corporation is known as a *share of stock*. An owner of one or more shares of a corporation is known as a *stockholder*. Each stockholder is an owner of a corporation.

Owners' equity accounts for a corporation normally are listed under a major chart of accounts division titled Stockholders' Equity.

Most corporations have many stockholders. It is not practical to have a separate owner's equity account for each stockholder. Instead, a single owners' equity account, titled **Capital Stock**, is used for the investment of all owners.

A second stockholders' equity account is used to record a corporation's earnings. Net income increases a corporation's total stockholders' equity. Some income may be retained by a corporation for business expansion. An amount earned by a corporation and not yet distributed to stockholders is called **retained earnings**. Retained Earnings is the title of the account used to record a corporation's earnings.

Some income may be given to stockholders as a return on their investments. A third stockholders' equity account is used to record the distribution of a corporation's earnings to stockholders. Earnings distributed to stockholders are called **dividends**. A corporation's dividend account is a temporary account similar to a proprietorship's drawing account. Each time a dividend is declared, an account titled Dividends is debited. At the end of each fiscal period, the balance in the dividends account is closed to Retained Earnings.

> **REMEMBER**
> Dividends *is a temporary account that is closed to* Retained Earnings *at the end of the fiscal period.*

Distributing Corporate Earnings to Stockholders

DECLARING A DIVIDEND

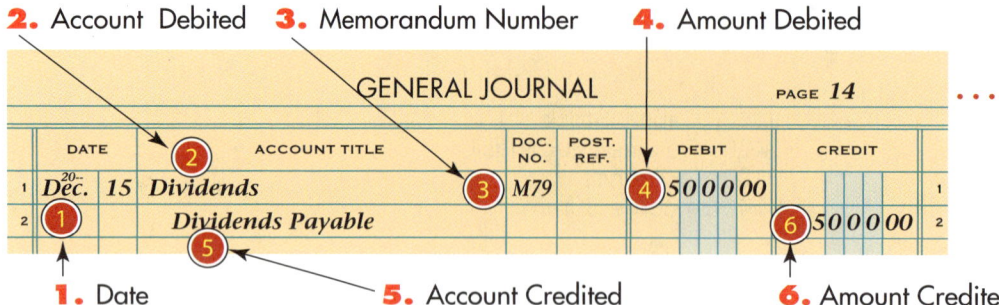

A group of persons elected by the stockholders to manage a corporation is called a **board of directors**. Dividends can be distributed to stockholders only by formal action of a corporation's board of directors. [CONCEPT: Business Entity]

Action by a board of directors to distribute corporate earnings to stockholders is called **declaring a dividend**. Dividends normally are declared on one date and paid on a later date. If a board of directors declares a dividend, the corporation is then obligated to pay the dividend. The dividend is a liability that must be recorded in the corporation's accounts.

Hobby Shack declares dividends each March 15, June 15, September 15, and December 15. The dividends are then paid on the 15th of the following month.

The stockholders' equity account, Dividends, has a normal debit balance and is increased by a $5,000.00 debit. Dividends Payable is credited for $5,000.00 to show the increase in this liability account.

December 15. Hobby Shack's board of directors declared a quarterly dividend of $2.00 per share; capital stock issued is 2,500 shares; total dividend, $5,000.00. Date of payment is January 15. Memorandum No. 79.

Dividends	
3/15 Decl.	5,000.00
6/15 Decl.	5,000.00
9/15 Decl.	5,000.00
12/15 Decl.	**5,000.00**

Dividends Payable			
4/15 Paid	5,000.00	3/15 Decl.	5,000.00
7/15 Paid	5,000.00	6/15 Decl.	5,000.00
10/15 Paid	5,000.00	9/15 Decl.	5,000.00
		12/15 Decl.	**5,000.00**

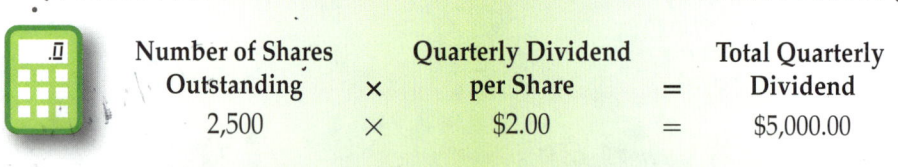

Number of Shares Outstanding	×	Quarterly Dividend per Share	=	Total Quarterly Dividend
2,500	×	$2.00	=	$5,000.00

STEPS — JOURNALIZING DECLARING A DIVIDEND

1. Write the date, *20--, Dec. 15*, in the Date column.
2. Write the title of the account debited, *Dividends*, in the Account Title column.
3. Write the memorandum number, *M79*, in the Doc. No. column.
4. Write the debit amount, *$5,000.00*, in the Debit column.
5. Write the title of the account credited, *Dividends Payable*, on the next line of the Account Title column, indented about 1 centimeter.
6. Write the credit amount, *$5,000.00*, in the Credit column.

PAYING A DIVIDEND

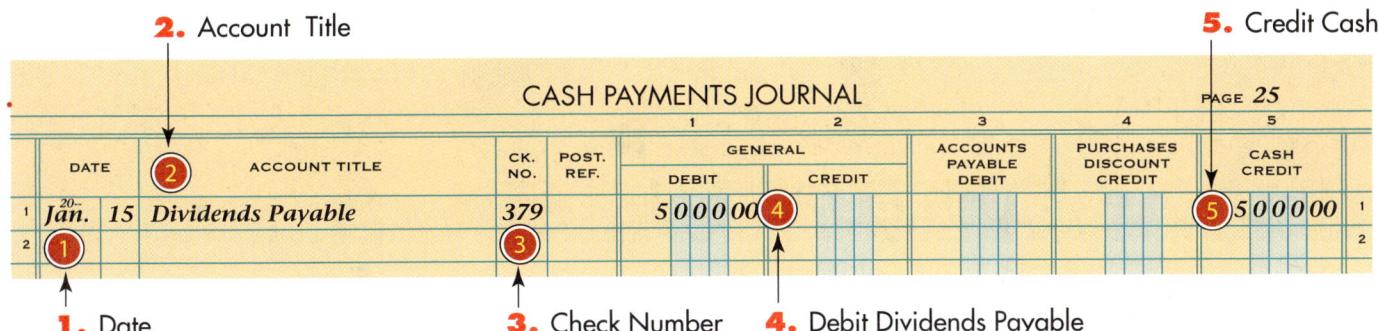

Hobby Shack issues one check for the amount of the total dividend to be paid. This check is deposited in a special dividend checking account. A separate check for each stockholder is drawn on this special account. The special account avoids a large number of cash payments journal entries and also reserves cash specifically for paying dividends.

A check is often made payable to an agent, such as a bank. The agent then handles the details of sending dividend checks to individual stockholders.

Dividends Payable			
4/15 Paid	5,000.00	3/15 Decl.	5,000.00
7/15 Paid	5,000.00	6/15 Decl.	5,000.00
10/15 Paid	5,000.00	9/15 Decl.	5,000.00
1/15 Paid	5,000.00	12/15 Decl.	5,000.00

Cash			
		1/15 Paid	5,000.00

January 15. Paid cash for quarterly dividend declared December 15, $5,000.00. Check No. 379.

When this entry is posted, the dividends payable account has a zero balance.

STEPS JOURNALIZING THE PAYMENT OF DIVIDENDS

1. Write the date, *20--, Jan. 15*, in the Date column.
2. Write the account title, *Dividends Payable*, in the Account Title column.
3. Write the check number, *379*, in the Ck. No. column.
4. Write the debit amount, *$5,000.00*, in the General Debit column.
5. Write the credit amount, *$5,000.00*, in the Cash Credit column.

FOR YOUR INFORMATION

FYI

Dividends are declared on one date and paid on a later date. Only stockholders owning the stock on the date of record specified by the board of directors receive the dividend. Stockholders owning the stock on the date of record receive the entire dividend, regardless of how long they have owned the stock.

End of Lesson REVIEW

AUDIT YOUR UNDERSTANDING

1. Under what major chart of accounts division are the owners' equity accounts for a corporation normally listed?
2. How many accounts are kept for the investment of all owners of a corporation?
3. What account does a corporation use to record earnings not yet distributed to stockholders?
4. What action is required before a corporation can distribute income to its stockholders?

TERMS REVIEW

retained earnings
dividends
board of directors
declaring a dividend

WORK TOGETHER 14-1

Journalizing dividends

Journals are given in the *Working Papers*. Your instructor will guide you through the following examples.

Coastal Aquatics completed the following transactions during December of the current year and January of the next year.

Transactions:
- Dec. 15. The board of directors declared a dividend of $3.00 per share; capital stock issued is 1,750 shares. M162.
- Jan. 15. Paid cash for dividend declared December 15. C687.

1. Use page 14 of a general journal. Journalize the dividend declared on December 15.
2. Use page 21 of a cash payments journal. Journalize payment of the dividend on January 15.

ON YOUR OWN 14-1

Journalizing dividends

Journals are given in the *Working Papers*. Work this problem independently.

Sonoma Treasures completed the following transactions during December of the current year and January of the next year.

Transactions:
- Dec. 15. The board of directors declared a dividend of $1.00 per share; capital stock issued is 21,000 shares. M321.
- Jan. 15. Paid cash for dividend declared December 15. C721.

1. Use page 22 of a general journal. Journalize the dividend declared on December 15.
2. Use page 24 of a cash payments journal. Journalize payment of the dividend.

LESSON 14-2

Beginning an 8-Column Work Sheet for a Merchandising Business

A columnar accounting form on which the financial information needed to prepare financial statements is summarized is known as a *work sheet*. A work sheet is used to plan adjustments and summarize the information necessary to prepare financial statements. The steps used to prepare a work sheet are similar for proprietorships and corporations.

ENTERING A TRIAL BALANCE ON A WORK SHEET

To prepare a work sheet, a trial balance is first entered in the Trial Balance columns. All general ledger accounts and balances are listed in the same order as they appear in the general ledger. Trial Balance columns are totaled to prove equality of debits and credits.

The worksheet for Hobby Shack is different from the work sheet completed for TechKnow in Chapter 6. Unlike a service business, a merchandising business will have an account for merchandise inventory. A corporation's accounts are similar to those of a proprietorship except for the capital stock, retained earnings, dividends, and federal income tax accounts.

PLANNING ADJUSTMENTS ON A WORK SHEET

Some general ledger accounts need to be brought up to date before financial statements are prepared. Accounts are brought up to date by planning and entering adjustments on a work sheet. Adjustments are planned in the Adjustments columns of a work sheet. Adjustments recorded on a work sheet are for planning purposes only. The general ledger account balances are not changed until entries are journalized and posted. Journal entries made to bring general ledger accounts up to date are known as *adjusting entries*.

Hobby Shack's adjustments for supplies and prepaid insurance are the same as those for TechKnow described in Chapter 6. Hobby Shack also makes adjustments to these accounts: (1) Merchandise Inventory, (2) Uncollectible Accounts Expense, (3) Depreciation Expense, and (4) Federal Income Tax Expense.

The adjustment for merchandise inventory is unique to a merchandising business. Adjustments for uncollectible accounts expense and depreciation expense could also be made by a service business. The adjustment for federal income tax is unique to corporations. This adjustment is not made for a proprietorship because taxes are paid by the owner, not the business.

SMALL BUSINESS SPOTLIGHT

Small businesses represent approximately 99 percent of employers, employ nearly 50 percent of non-government employees, and are responsible for about two-thirds to three-quarters of net new jobs, according to the Office of Advocacy of the U.S. Small Business Administration.

RECORDING A TRIAL BALANCE ON A WORK SHEET

ACCOUNT Cash **1.** Account Titles **ACCOUNT NO.** 1110

DATE	ITEM	POST. REF.	DEBIT	CREDIT	BALANCE DEBIT	BALANCE CREDIT
Dec. 20-- 1	Balance	✓			2 826 0 00	
31		CR12	3 718 0 80		6 544 0 80	
31		CP24		3 636 0 52	2 908 0 28	

2. Account Balances

Hobby Shack, Inc.
Work Sheet
For Year Ended December 31, 20--

	ACCOUNT TITLE	TRIAL BALANCE DEBIT	TRIAL BALANCE CREDIT
1	Cash	2 908 0 28	
2	Petty Cash	3 0 0 00	
3	Accounts Receivable	14 6 9 8 40	
4	Allow. for Uncoll. Accts.		1 2 7 52
5	Merchandise Inventory	140 4 8 0 00	
6	Supplies—Office	3 4 8 0 00	
7	Supplies—Store	3 9 4 4 00	
8	Prepaid Insurance	5 8 0 0 00	
9	Office Equipment	35 8 6 4 50	
10	Acc. Depr.—Office Equipment		6 4 9 7 00
11	Store Equipment	40 8 4 9 50	
12	Acc. Depr.—Store Equipment		5 0 6 9 00
13	Accounts Payable		11 5 8 3 03
14	Federal Income Tax Payable		
40	Insurance Expense		
41	Miscellaneous Expense	2 5 6 4 90	
42	Payroll Taxes Expense	9 1 0 5 00	
43	Rent Expense	18 0 0 0 00	
44	Salary Expense	104 5 2 5 00	
45	Supplies Expense—Office		
46	Supplies Expense—Store		
47	Uncollectible Accounts Expense		
48	Utilities Expense	3 8 2 0 00	
49	Federal Income Tax Expense	18 0 0 0 00	
50		670 8 6 1 59	670 8 6 1 59

3. Total, prove and rule the debit and credit columns.

STEPS RECORDING A TRIAL BALANCE ON A WORK SHEET

1. Write the title of each general ledger account in the work sheet's Account Title column in the same order they appear in the general ledger. All accounts are listed regardless of whether there is a balance or not. Listing all accounts reduces the possibility of overlooking an account that needs to be brought up to date.

2. Write the balance of each account in the appropriate work sheet's Trial Balance Debit or Credit column. The amounts are taken from the general ledger accounts.

3. Total, prove, and rule the Trial Balance Debit and Credit columns of the work sheet.

ANALYZING AND RECORDING SUPPLIES ADJUSTMENTS

The balance of Supplies—Office in the trial balance, $3,480.00, is the cost of office supplies on hand at the beginning of the year plus the office supplies purchased during the year. The supplies on hand on December 31 are counted and determined to be $750.00. The difference is the value of office supplies used during the year, which is an expense.

Likewise, the balance of Supplies—Store in the trial balance, $3,944.00, is the cost of store supplies on hand at the beginning of the year plus the store supplies purchased during the year. The value of store supplies on hand on December 31 is determined to be $1,034.00.

Analyzing Supplies Adjustments

Four questions are asked to analyze the adjustments for the supplies accounts.

1. **What is the balance of the Supplies accounts?**
   Supplies—Office, *$3,480.00*
   Supplies—Store, *$3,944.00*
2. **What should the balance be for these accounts?**
   Supplies—Office, *$750.00*
   Supplies—Store, *$1,034.00*
3. **What must be done to correct the account balances?**
   Decrease Supplies—Office, *$2,730.00 ($3,480.00 − 750.00)*
   Decrease Supplies—Store, *$2,910.00 ($3,944.00 − 1,034.00)*
4. **What adjustment is made?**
   Debit:
   Supplies Expense—Office, *$2,730.00*
   Supplies Expense—Store, *$2,910.00*
   Credit:
   Supplies—Office, *$2,730.00*
   Supplies—Store, *$2,910.00*

The supplies adjustments are shown in the T accounts. The December 31 balance shown in faded type is the balance before the adjustments.

```
           Supplies Expense—Office
Adj. (a)        2,730.00

              Supplies—Office
Dec. 31 Bal.    3,480.00   Adj. (a)    2,730.00
(Adj. Bal.       750.00)

           Supplies Expense—Store
Adj. (b)        2,910.00

              Supplies—Store
Dec. 31 Bal.    3,944.00   Adj. (b)    2,910.00
(Adj Bal.       1,034.00)
```

Beginning an 8-Column Work Sheet for a Merchandising Business

RECORDING SUPPLIES ADJUSTMENTS ON A WORK SHEET

STEPS — RECORDING WORK SHEET ADJUSTMENTS FOR SUPPLIES

1. Write the debit amounts in the Adjustments Debit column on the lines with the appropriate account titles: $2,730.00 with *Supplies Expense—Office* and $2,910.00 with *Supplies Expense—Store*.

2. Write the credit amounts in the Adjustments Credit column on the lines with the appropriate account titles: $2,730.00 with *Supplies—Office* and $2,910.00 with *Supplies—Store*.

3. Label the two parts of the *Supplies—Office* adjustment with a small letter *a* in parentheses, *(a)*. Label the two parts of the *Supplies—Store* adjustment with a small letter *b* in parentheses, *(b)*.

DIGITAL VISION/GETTY IMAGES

ANALYZING AND RECORDING A PREPAID INSURANCE ADJUSTMENT

Insurance premiums are debited to a prepaid insurance account when paid. During the year, Hobby Shack paid $5,800.00 of insurance premiums.

Analyzing a Prepaid Insurance Adjustment

Hobby Shack determined that the value of prepaid insurance on December 31 is $2,630.00. Therefore, the value of insurance used during the year is $3,170.00 ($5,800.00 − $2,630.00). This difference is the amount of insurance expense for the year. Prepaid Insurance is credited and Insurance Expense is debited at the end of the fiscal period for the value of insurance used.

The prepaid insurance adjustment is shown in the T accounts. The December 31 balance shown in faded type is the balance before the adjustment.

1. **What is the balance of** Prepaid Insurance?
   $5,800.00
2. **What should the balance be for this account?**
   $2,630.00
3. **What must be done to correct the account balance?**
   Decrease $3,170.00 ($5,800.00 − $2,630.00)
4. **What adjustment is made?**
   Debit Insurance Expense, *$3,170.00*
   Credit Prepaid Insurance, *$3,170.00*

Insurance Expense	
Adj. (c) 3,170.00	

Prepaid Insurance	
Dec. 31 Bal. 5,800.00	Adj. (c) 3,170.00
(New Bal. 2,630.00)	

Recording a Prepaid Insurance Adjustment

3. Labels **2.** Debit **1.** Credit

STEPS RECORDING WORK SHEET ADJUSTMENTS FOR PREPAID INSURANCE

1. Enter the amount of insurance used, $3,170.00, in the Adjustments Credit column on the Prepaid Insurance line of the work sheet.

2. Enter the same amount, $3,170.00, in the Adjustments Debit column on the Insurance Expense line of the work sheet.

3. Label the two parts of the adjustment with a small letter c in parentheses, (c).

End of Lesson REVIEW

AUDIT YOUR UNDERSTANDING

1. What accounts are used for the adjustment to office supplies?
2. What accounts are used for the adjustment to prepaid insurance?

WORK TOGETHER 14-2

Beginning an 8-column work sheet for a merchandising business

A partially completed work sheet for Coastal Aquatics is given in the *Working Papers*. Four general ledger accounts are shown below. Your instructor will guide you through the following examples.

1. Enter the accounts and account balances on the following lines.

Line	Account	Account Balance
3	Accounts Receivable	$ 15,485.25
13	Accounts Payable	18,482.28
29	Sales	845,828.09
32	Purchases	389,184.01

2. Total, prove, and rule the trial balance.
3. From a physical count of the following, December 31 balances are determined to be:

Supplies—Office	$657.15
Supplies—Store	633.11
Prepaid Insurance	800.00

Analyze adjustments that need to be made for the accounts above and enter the adjustments on the work sheet. Label the adjustments *(a)–(c)*. Save your work to complete Work Together 14-3.

ON YOUR OWN 14-2

Beginning an 8-column work sheet for a merchandising business

A partially completed work sheet for Sonoma Treasures is given in the *Working Papers*. Four general ledger accounts are shown below. Work this problem independently.

1. Enter the accounts and account balances on the following lines.

Line	Account	Account Balance
8	Prepaid Insurance	$ 12,000.00
25	Capital Stock	210,000.00
30	Sales Discount	715.25
43	Rent Expense	30,000.00

2. Total, prove, and rule the trial balance.
3. From a physical count of the following, December 31 balances are determined to be:

Supplies—Office	$ 633.61
Supplies—Store	983.36
Prepaid Insurance	3,000.00

Analyze adjustments that need to be made for the accounts above and enter the adjustments on the work sheet. Label the adjustments *(a)–(c)*. Save your work to complete On Your Own 14-3.

LESSON 14-3: Planning and Recording a Merchandise Inventory Adjustment

MERCHANDISE INVENTORY

In addition to supplies and prepaid insurance, Hobby Shack needs to adjust the merchandise inventory account. Planning the adjustment is similar to the adjustment for supplies. However, the adjusting entry includes a new account.

The amount of goods on hand for sale to customers is called **merchandise inventory**. The general ledger account in which merchandise inventory is recorded is titled Merchandise Inventory. Merchandise Inventory is an asset account with a normal debit balance.

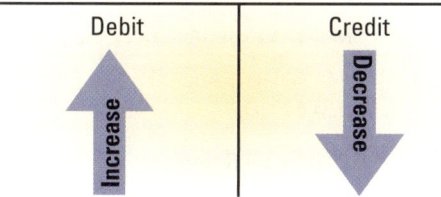

Hobby Shack's merchandise inventory account on January 1, the beginning of the fiscal year, has a debit balance of $140,480.00.

Merchandise Inventory	
Jan. 1 Bal. 140,480.00	

The balance of the merchandise inventory account on December 31, the end of the fiscal year, is the same amount, $140,480.00. The January 1 and December 31 balances are the same because no entries have been made in the account during the fiscal year. The changes in inventory resulting from purchases and sales transactions have not been recorded in the merchandise inventory account.

During a fiscal period, the amount of merchandise on hand increases each time merchandise is purchased. However, all purchases are recorded in the purchases account. The amount of merchandise on hand decreases each time merchandise is sold. However, all sales are recorded in the sales account. This procedure makes it easier to determine the total purchases and sales during a fiscal period. The merchandise inventory account balance, therefore, must be adjusted to reflect the changes resulting from purchases and sales during a fiscal period.

STOCKBYTE/GETTY IMAGES

ANALYZING AND RECORDING A MERCHANDISE INVENTORY ADJUSTMENT

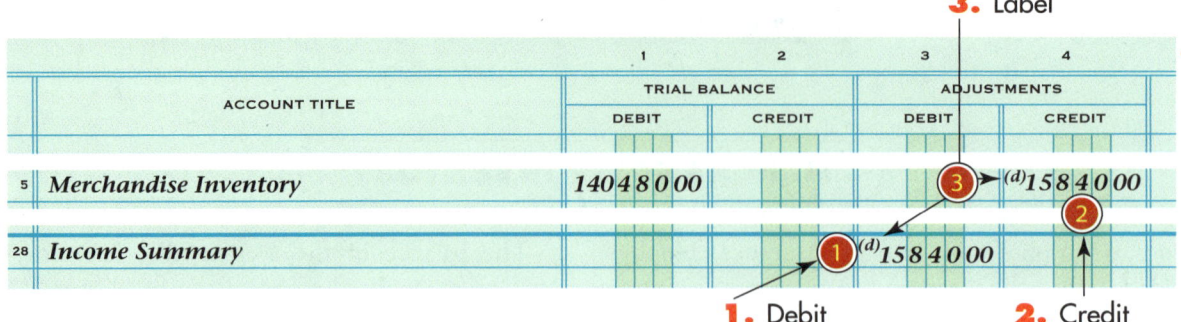

The two accounts used to adjust the merchandise inventory are Merchandise Inventory and Income Summary.

Before the adjustment, the merchandise inventory account has a January 1 debit balance of $140,480.00. The merchandise inventory account balance, however, is not up-to-date. The actual count of merchandise on December 31 shows that the inventory is valued at $124,640.00. Therefore, the merchandise inventory account balance must be adjusted to show the current value of merchandise on hand.

Most accounts needing adjustment at the end of a fiscal period have a related temporary account. For example, when the account Prepaid Insurance is adjusted, Insurance Expense is the related expense account, a temporary account. Merchandise Inventory, however, does not have a related expense account. Therefore, Income Summary, a temporary account, is used to adjust the merchandise inventory account at the end of a fiscal period.

Four questions are asked in analyzing the adjustment for merchandise inventory.

1. **What is the balance of** Merchandise Inventory?
   $140,480.00
2. **What should the balance be for this account?**
   $124,640.00
3. **What must be done to correct the account balance?**
   Decrease $15,840.00
4. **What adjustment is made?**
   Debit Income Summary, $15,840.00
   Credit Merchandise Inventory, $15,840.00

Merchandise Inventory			
Jan. 1 Bal.	140,480.00	Adj. (d)	15,840.00
(New Bal.	124,640.00)		
Income Summary			
Adj. (d)	15,840.00		

Income Summary is debited and Merchandise Inventory is credited for $15,840.00. The beginning debit balance of Merchandise Inventory, *$140,480.00*, minus the adjustment credit amount, *$15,840.00*, equals the ending debit balance of Merchandise Inventory, *$124,640.00*.

STEPS — RECORDING A WORK SHEET ADJUSTMENT FOR MERCHANDISE INVENTORY

1. Write the debit amount, *$15,840.00*, in the Adjustments Debit column on the line with the account title *Income Summary*.

2. Write the credit amount, *$15,840.00*, in the Adjustments Credit column on the line with the account title *Merchandise Inventory*.

3. Label the two parts of this adjustment with a small letter *d* in parentheses, *(d)*.

ANALYZING AN ADJUSTMENT WHEN ENDING MERCHANDISE INVENTORY IS GREATER THAN BEGINNING MERCHANDISE INVENTORY

If the amount of merchandise inventory on hand is greater than the January 1 balance of Merchandise Inventory, opposite entries would be made—debit Merchandise Inventory and credit Income Summary. For example, Venable Company's merchandise inventory account on January 1 has a debit balance of $294,700.00. The count of merchandise on December 31 shows that the inventory is valued at $298,900.00. The merchandise on hand is $4,200.00 greater than the January 1 balance of Merchandise Inventory.

Four questions are asked in analyzing the adjustment for merchandise inventory.

1. **What is the balance of** Merchandise Inventory?
   $294,700.00
2. **What should the balance be for this account?**
   $298,900.00
3. **What must be done to correct the account balance?**
   Increase $4,200.00
4. **What adjustment is made?**
   Debit Merchandise Inventory, *$4,200.00*
   Credit Income Summary, *$4,200.00*

The merchandise inventory adjustment is shown in the T accounts.

```
              Merchandise Inventory
Jan. 1 Bal.      294,700.00
Adj. (d)           4,200.00
(New Bal.        298,900.00)

                 Income Summary
                              |  Adj. (d)   4,200.00
```

Merchandise Inventory is debited and Income Summary is credited for $4,200.00. The beginning debit balance of Merchandise Inventory, $294,700.00, plus the adjustment debit amount, $4,200.00, equals the ending debit balance of Merchandise Inventory, $298,900.00.

> **REMEMBER**
>
> When an account that requires adjusting does not have a related expense account, the temporary account Income Summary is used.

End of Lesson REVIEW

AUDIT YOUR UNDERSTANDING

1. In what order should general ledger accounts be listed on a work sheet?
2. What accounts are used for the adjustment for merchandise inventory?
3. What adjusting entry is entered on a work sheet when the ending merchandise inventory is less than the beginning value?
4. When is the temporary account Income Summary used?

TERM REVIEW

merchandise inventory

WORK TOGETHER 14-3

Analyzing and recording an adjustment for merchandise inventory

Use the work sheet from Work Together 14-2. Your instructor will guide you through the following example.

1. From a physical count of merchandise inventory, the December 31 balance is determined to be $234,904.20. Analyze the merchandise inventory adjustment and enter the adjustment on the work sheet. Label the adjustment *(d)*. Save your work to complete Work Together 14-4.

ON YOUR OWN 14-3

Analyzing and recording an adjustment for merchandise inventory

Use the work sheet from On Your Own 14-2. Work this problem independently.

1. From a physical count of merchandise inventory, the December 31 balance is determined to be $261,089.97. Analyze the merchandise inventory adjustment and enter the adjustment on the work sheet. Label the adjustment *(d)*. Save your work to complete On Your Own 14-4.

LESSON 14-4: Planning and Recording an Allowance for Uncollectible Accounts Adjustment

ALLOWANCE METHOD OF RECORDING LOSSES FROM UNCOLLECTIBLE ACCOUNTS

Uncollectible Accounts Expense		Accounts Receivable		Allowance for Uncollectible Accounts	
Debit	Credit	Debit	Credit	Debit	Credit
Increase	Decrease	Increase	Decrease	Decrease	Increase

With each sale on account, a business takes a risk that customers will not pay their accounts. Accounts receivable that cannot be collected are called **uncollectible accounts**. This risk is a cost of doing business that should be recorded as an expense in the same accounting period that the revenue is earned. Accurate financial reporting requires that expenses be recorded in the fiscal period in which the expenses contribute to earning revenue. [CONCEPT: Matching Expenses with Revenue]

At the end of a fiscal year, a business does not know which customer accounts will become uncollectible. If a business knew exactly which accounts would become uncollectible, it could credit Accounts Receivable and each customer account for the uncollectible amounts and debit Uncollectible Accounts Expense for the same amounts.

To solve this accounting problem, a business can calculate and record an estimated amount of uncollectible accounts expense. Estimating uncollectible accounts expense at the end of a fiscal period accomplishes two objectives:

1. It reports a balance sheet amount for Accounts Receivable that reflects the amount the business expects to collect in the future.
2. It recognizes the expense of uncollectible accounts in the same period in which the related revenue is recorded.

To record estimated uncollectible accounts, an adjusting entry is made affecting two accounts. The estimated amount of uncollectible accounts is debited to Uncollectible Accounts Expense and credited to an account titled Allowance for Uncollectible Accounts.

An account that reduces a related account is known as a *contra account*. Allowance for Uncollectible Accounts is a contra account to its related asset account, Accounts Receivable.

Crediting the estimated value of uncollectible accounts to a contra account is called the **allowance method of recording losses from uncollectible accounts**. The difference between an asset's account balance and its related contra account balance is called **book value**. The difference between the balance of Accounts Receivable and its contra account, Allowance for Uncollectible Accounts, is called the **book value of accounts receivable**. The book value of accounts receivable, which is reported on the balance sheet, represents the total amount of accounts receivable the business expects to collect in the future.

A contra account is usually assigned the next number of the account number sequence after its related account in the chart of accounts. Hobby Shack's Accounts Receivable account is numbered 1130 and the Allowance for Uncollectible Accounts contra account is numbered 1135.

ESTIMATING UNCOLLECTIBLE ACCOUNTS EXPENSE

Total Sales on Account	×	Percentage	=	Estimated Uncollectible Accounts Expense
$124,500.00	×	1%	=	$1,245.00

Many businesses use a percentage of total sales on account to estimate uncollectible accounts expense. Each sale on account represents a risk of loss from an uncollectible account. Therefore, if the estimated percentage of loss is accurate, the amount of uncollectible accounts expense will be accurate regardless of when the actual losses occur.

Since a sale on account creates a risk of loss, estimating the percentage of uncollectible accounts expense for the same period matches sales revenue with the related uncollectible accounts expense. [CONCEPT: Matching Expenses with Revenue]

Hobby Shack estimates uncollectible accounts expense by calculating a percentage of total sales on account. A review of Hobby Shack's previous experience in collecting sales on account shows that actual uncollectible accounts expense has been about 1% of total sales on account. The company's total sales on account for the year is $124,500.00. Thus, Hobby Shack estimates that $1,245.00 of the current fiscal year's sales on account will eventually be uncollectible.

FOR YOUR INFORMATION

FYI

Allowance for Bad Debts *and* Allowance for Doubtful Accounts *are account titles sometimes used instead of* Allowance for Uncollectible Accounts.

FINANCIAL LITERACY

Personal Budgets

Mention the word "budget" to most people and many negative thoughts come to mind. However, a budget does not have to be restrictive or inflexible. In fact, a budget may give you more freedom.

A budget is merely a plan that helps you achieve your goals. When getting ready to prepare a budget, you not only need to gather income and expense data, but you also need to determine and prioritize your goals. For example, suppose you want to take a trip during spring break, but you also like to have all the latest clothing styles. If you can't do both, which is more important to you? No one can answer this question for you. Financial goals are very personal.

One of the major benefits of a budget is that any "leftover" money you have is used to fund your goals in their order of priority. This may mean that instead of spending money on the latest fashions, you may choose to save it to fund your spring-break trip—but only because you determined the trip was more important. You are in control, and your budget can change as your goals change.

Think of a budget as a flexible spending plan that helps you achieve your goals, and you will be more likely to follow your budget and actually be able to take that trip!

Activities

1. One way to gather expense data for your budget is to write down all of your expenses for a period of time. Do this for one week. Try to pick a typical week, and remember to include all expenses. Then categorize what you've spent into "needs" and "wants."

2. Survey five adults. Ask each one if he or she has a budget. If that person has a budget, ask if he or she follows it. What does he or she feel are the advantages and disadvantages of having a budget? Summarize your findings in a written report.

ANALYZING AND RECORDING AN ADJUSTMENT FOR UNCOLLECTIBLE ACCOUNTS EXPENSE

3. Label
2. Debit
1. Credit

The percentage of total sales on account method of estimating uncollectible accounts expense assumes that a portion of every sale on account dollar will become uncollectible. Hobby Shack has estimated that 1% of its $124,500.00 sales on account, or $1,245.00, will eventually become uncollectible.

At the end of a fiscal period, an adjustment for uncollectible accounts expense is planned on a work sheet.

The Allowance for Uncollectible Accounts balance in the Trial Balance Credit column, $127.52, is the allowance estimate from the previous fiscal period that has not yet been identified as uncollectible.

When the allowance account has a previous credit balance, the amount of the adjustment is added to the previous balance.

This new balance of the allowance account, $1,372.52, is the estimated amount of accounts receivable that will eventually become uncollectible. This amount, subtracted from the accounts receivable account balance, $14,698.40, is the book value of accounts receivable. Notice in the T accounts that Accounts Receivable is not affected by this adjustment. Also notice that Uncollectible Accounts Expense did not have a balance before the adjustment.

Hobby Shack estimates that it will collect $13,325.88 from its outstanding accounts receivable.

STEPS — RECORDING A WORK SHEET ADJUSTMENT FOR UNCOLLECTIBLE ACCOUNTS

1. Enter the estimated uncollectible amount, $1,245.00, in the Adjustments Credit column on the *Allowance for Uncollectible Accounts* line of the work sheet.

2. Enter the same amount, $1,245.00, in the Adjustments Debit column on the *Uncollectible Accounts Expense* line of the work sheet.

3. Label the two parts of this adjustment with a small letter *e* in parentheses, *(e)*.

Planning and Recording an Allowance for Uncollectible Accounts Adjustment — Lesson 14-4

End of Lesson REVIEW

AUDIT YOUR UNDERSTANDING

1. Why is an uncollectible account recorded as an expense rather than a reduction in revenue?
2. When do businesses normally estimate the amount of their uncollectible accounts expense?
3. What two objectives will be accomplished by recording an estimated amount of uncollectible accounts expense?
4. Why is *Allowance for Uncollectible Accounts* called a *contra account*?
5. How is the book value of accounts receivable calculated?

TERMS REVIEW

uncollectible accounts

allowance method of recording losses from uncollectible accounts

book value

book value of accounts receivable

WORK TOGETHER 14-4

Analyzing and recording an adjustment for uncollectible accounts expense

Use the work sheet from Work Together 14-3. Your instructor will guide you through the following example.

1. Coastal Aquatics estimates uncollectible accounts expense as 0.5% of its total sales on account. During the current year, Coastal Aquatics had sales on account of $424,000.00. Record the uncollectible accounts expense adjustment on the work sheet. Label the adjustment *(e)*. Save your work to complete Work Together 14-5.

ON YOUR OWN 14-4

Analyzing and recording an adjustment for uncollectible accounts expense

Use the work sheet from On Your Own 14-3. Work this problem independently.

1. Sonoma Treasures estimates uncollectible accounts expense as 0.4% of its total sales on account. During the current year, Sonoma Treasures had sales on account of $462,500.00. Record the uncollectible accounts expense adjustment on the work sheet. Label the adjustment *(e)*. Save your work to complete On Your Own 14-5.

LESSON 14-5

Planning and Recording Depreciation Adjustments

CATEGORIES OF ASSETS

Most businesses use two broad categories of assets in their operations. Cash and other assets expected to be exchanged for cash or consumed within a year are called **current assets**. Assets that will be used for a number of years in the operation of a business are called **plant assets**. Some of Hobby Shack's plant assets are computers, cash registers, sales display cases, and furniture.

Businesses may have three major types of plant assets—equipment, buildings, and land. Hobby Shack records its equipment in two different equipment accounts—Office Equipment and Store Equipment. Because it rents the building and the land where the business is located, Hobby Shack does not need plant asset accounts for buildings and land. [CONCEPT: Adequate Disclosure]

Depreciating Plant Assets

A business buys plant assets to use in earning revenue. Hobby Shack bought a new lighted display case. Hobby Shack knows that the display case will be useful only for a limited period of time. After several years, most display cases become worn from use and no longer attractively display the products. Hobby Shack will replace worn display cases with newer models. Thus, each display case has a limited useful life to the business.

In order to match revenue with the expenses used to earn the revenue, the cost of a plant asset should be expensed over the plant asset's useful life. A portion of a plant asset's cost is transferred to an expense account in each fiscal period that a plant asset is used to earn revenue. [CONCEPT: Matching Expenses with Revenue] The portion of a plant asset's cost that is transferred to an expense account in each fiscal period during a plant asset's useful life is called **depreciation expense**.

Three factors are considered in calculating the annual amount of depreciation expense for a plant asset.

1. *Original Cost.* The original cost of a plant asset includes all costs paid to make the asset usable to a business. These costs include the price of the asset, delivery costs, and any necessary installation costs.

2. *Estimated Salvage Value.* Generally, a business removes a plant asset from use and disposes of it when the asset is no longer usable. The amount that will be received for an asset at the time of its disposal is not known when the asset is bought. Thus, the amount that may be received at disposal must be estimated. The amount an owner expects to receive when a plant asset is removed from use is called **estimated salvage value**. Estimated salvage value may also be referred to as *residual value* or *scrap value*.

3. *Estimated Useful Life.* The total amount of depreciation expense is distributed over the estimated useful life of a plant asset. When a plant asset is bought, the exact length of useful life is not known. Therefore, the number of years of useful life must be estimated. Two factors affect the useful life of a plant asset: (1) physical depreciation and (2) functional depreciation. Physical depreciation is caused by wear from use and deterioration from aging and weathering. Functional depreciation occurs when a plant asset becomes inadequate or obsolete. An asset is inadequate when it can no longer satisfactorily perform the needed service. An asset is obsolete when a newer asset can operate more efficiently or produce better service.

CALCULATING DEPRECIATION EXPENSE AND BOOK VALUE

Straight-Line Depreciation

Charging an equal amount of depreciation expense for a plant asset in each year of useful life is called the **straight-line method of depreciation**.

Hobby Shack summarizes the depreciation expense for each plant asset to calculate the total depreciation expense recorded on the work sheet.

On January 2, 20X1, Hobby Shack bought a lighted display case for $1,250.00, with an estimated salvage value of $250.00 and an estimated useful life of 5 years. Using the straight-line method of depreciation, the annual depreciation expense, $200.00, is the same for each year in which the asset is used.

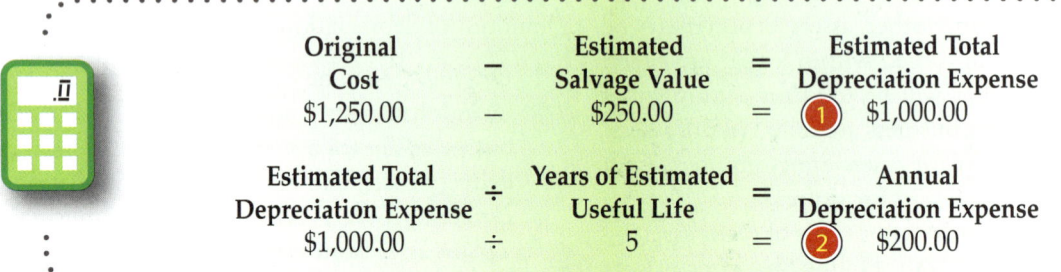

STEPS — CALCULATING ANNUAL DEPRECIATION EXPENSE

1. Subtract the asset's estimated salvage value from the asset's original cost. This difference is the estimated total depreciation expense for the asset's entire useful life.

2. Divide the estimated total depreciation expense by the years of estimated useful life. The result is the annual depreciation expense.

Calculating Accumulated Depreciation

The total amount of depreciation expense that has been recorded since the purchase of a plant asset is called **accumulated depreciation**. The amount accumulates each year of the plant asset's useful life.

First, the depreciation expense that has accumulated over all prior years is determined. Second, the depreciation expense for the current year is calculated. Third, the prior accumulated depreciation and the current depreciation expense are added.

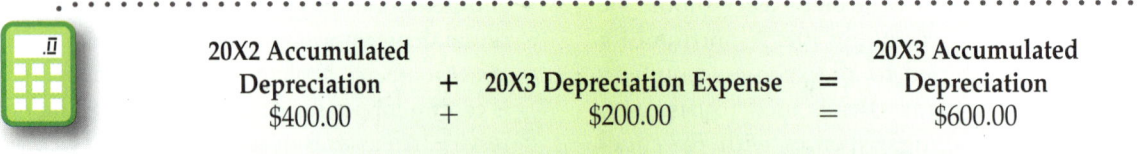

Calculating Book Value

The original cost of a plant asset minus accumulated depreciation is called the **book value of a plant asset**. The book value is calculated by subtracting the accumulated depreciation from the original cost of the asset.

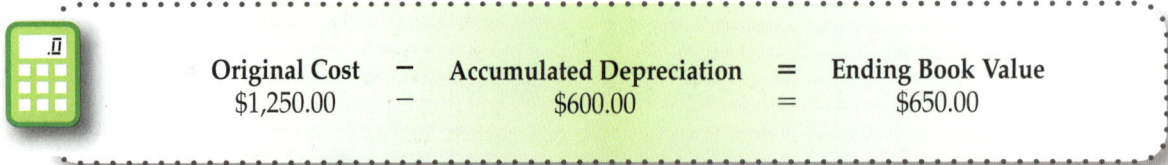

Procedures for recording the accumulated depreciation and book value of individual assets are presented in Chapter 18.

ANALYZING AND RECORDING ADJUSTMENTS FOR DEPRECIATION EXPENSE

At the end of the fiscal year, Hobby Shack calculates the depreciation expense for each plant asset. Hobby Shack determined that total depreciation expense is $6,540.00 for office equipment and $5,250.00 for store equipment. Adjustments are planned in the Adjustments columns of the work sheet.

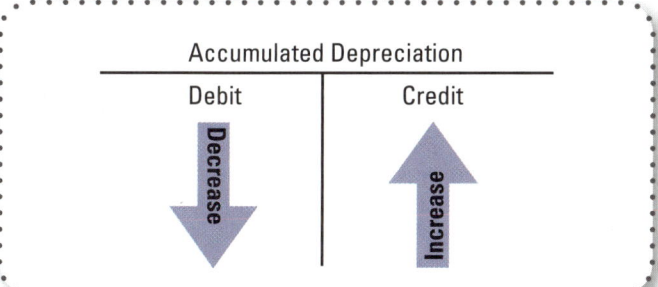

It is important to retain original cost information for plant assets. Therefore, rather than credit the plant asset account, depreciation is recorded in the contra asset account Accumulated Depreciation.

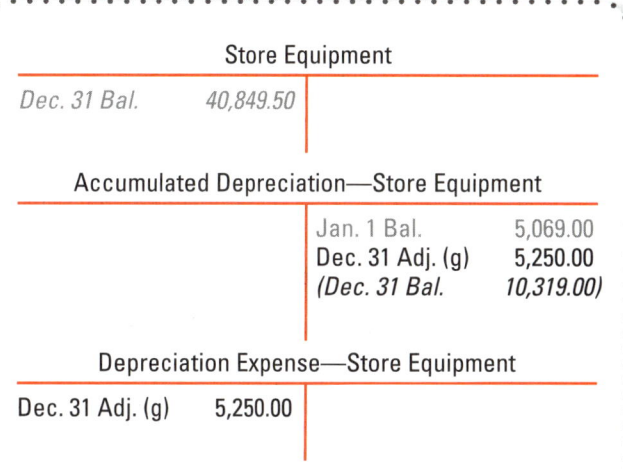

At any time, the book value of plant assets can be calculated by subtracting Accumulated Depreciation from its related plant asset account.

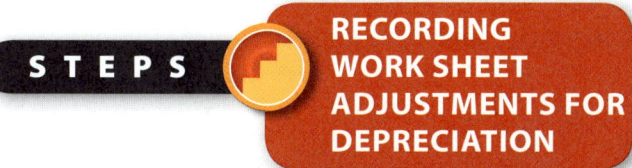

RECORDING WORK SHEET ADJUSTMENTS FOR DEPRECIATION

1. Write the debit amounts in the Adjustments Debit column on the lines with the appropriate account titles: $6,540.00 with *Depreciation Expense—Office Equipment* and $5,250.00 with *Depreciation Expense—Store Equipment*.

2. Write the credit amounts in the Adjustments Credit column on the lines with the appropriate account titles: $6,540.00 with *Accumulated Depreciation—Office Equipment* and $5,250.00 with *Accumulated Depreciation—Store Equipment*.

3. Label the two parts of the Office Equipment adjustment with a small letter *f* in parentheses, *(f)*. Label the two parts of the Store Equipment adjustment with a small letter *g* in parentheses, *(g)*.

Planning and Recording Depreciation Adjustments   Lesson 14-5

End of Lesson REVIEW

TERMS REVIEW

current assets
plant assets
depreciation expense
estimated salvage value
straight-line method of depreciation
accumulated depreciation
book value of a plant asset

AUDIT YOUR UNDERSTANDING

1. What are the two categories of assets?
2. What three factors are used to calculate a plant asset's annual depreciation expense?

WORK TOGETHER 14-5

Planning and recording adjustments for depreciation

Use the work sheet from Work Together 14-4. Your instructor will guide you through the following example.

1. Calculate depreciation expense for a computer printer costing $1,600.00; estimated salvage value, $100.00, useful life, 5 years.
2. Calculate the book value of the computer printer at the end of its second year of service.
3. On December 31, Coastal Aquatics determined the total depreciation expense: office equipment, $6,120.00; store equipment, $5,060.00. Plan the work sheet adjustments and label the adjustments *(f)* and *(g)*. Save your work to complete Work Together 14-6.

ON YOUR OWN 14-5

Planning and recording adjustments for depreciation

Use the work sheet from On Your Own 14-4. Work this problem independently.

1. Calculate depreciation expense for a display rack costing $2,350.00; estimated salvage value, $600.00, useful life, 7 years.
2. Calculate the book value of the display rack at the end of its third year of service.
3. On December 31, Sonoma Treasures determined the total depreciation expense: office equipment, $5,184.00; store equipment, $6,480.00. Plan the work sheet adjustments and label the adjustments *(f)* and *(g)*. Save your work to complete On Your Own 14-6.

LESSON 14-6

Calculating Federal Income Tax and Completing a Work Sheet

FEDERAL INCOME TAX EXPENSE ADJUSTMENT

Corporations anticipating annual federal income taxes of $500.00 or more are required to pay their estimated taxes each quarter. Estimated income tax is paid in quarterly installments in April, June, September, and December. However, the actual federal income tax owed is calculated at the end of a fiscal year. Based on the actual income tax owed for a year, a corporation must file an annual return. Any additional tax owed that was not paid in quarterly installments must be paid when the final return is filed.

Early in the current year, Hobby Shack estimated $18,000.00 federal income tax for the year. Hobby Shack paid $4,500.00 in each quarterly installment for a total of $18,000.00. Each tax payment is recorded as a debit to Federal Income Tax Expense and a credit to Cash.

Federal income tax is an expense of a corporation. However, the amount of tax depends on net income before the tax is recorded.

Federal Income Tax Expense is an expense account. The account appears under a major division titled *Income Tax Expense* in Hobby Shack's chart of accounts. Federal Income Tax Payable, a liability account, appears under the heading *Current Liabilities*.

In order to make adjustments to federal income tax, you must first determine the net income before federal income tax expense. To calculate, follow these steps:

1. Complete all other adjustments on a work sheet.
2. Extend all amounts except Federal Income Tax Expense to the Income Statement or Balance Sheet columns.
3. On a separate sheet of paper, total the work sheet's Income Statement columns.
4. Calculate the difference between the Income Statement Debit column total and the Income Statement Credit column total. This difference between the totals of these two income statement columns is the net income before federal income tax expense.

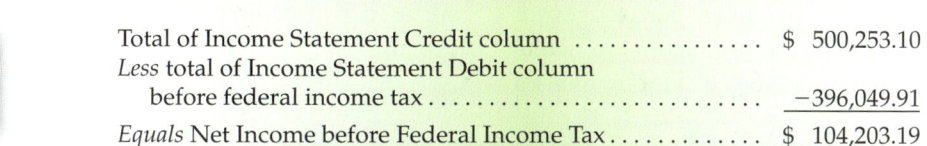

Total of Income Statement Credit column .... $ 500,253.10
Less total of Income Statement Debit column
    before federal income tax .... −396,049.91
Equals Net Income before Federal Income Tax .... $ 104,203.19

CALCULATING FEDERAL INCOME TAX

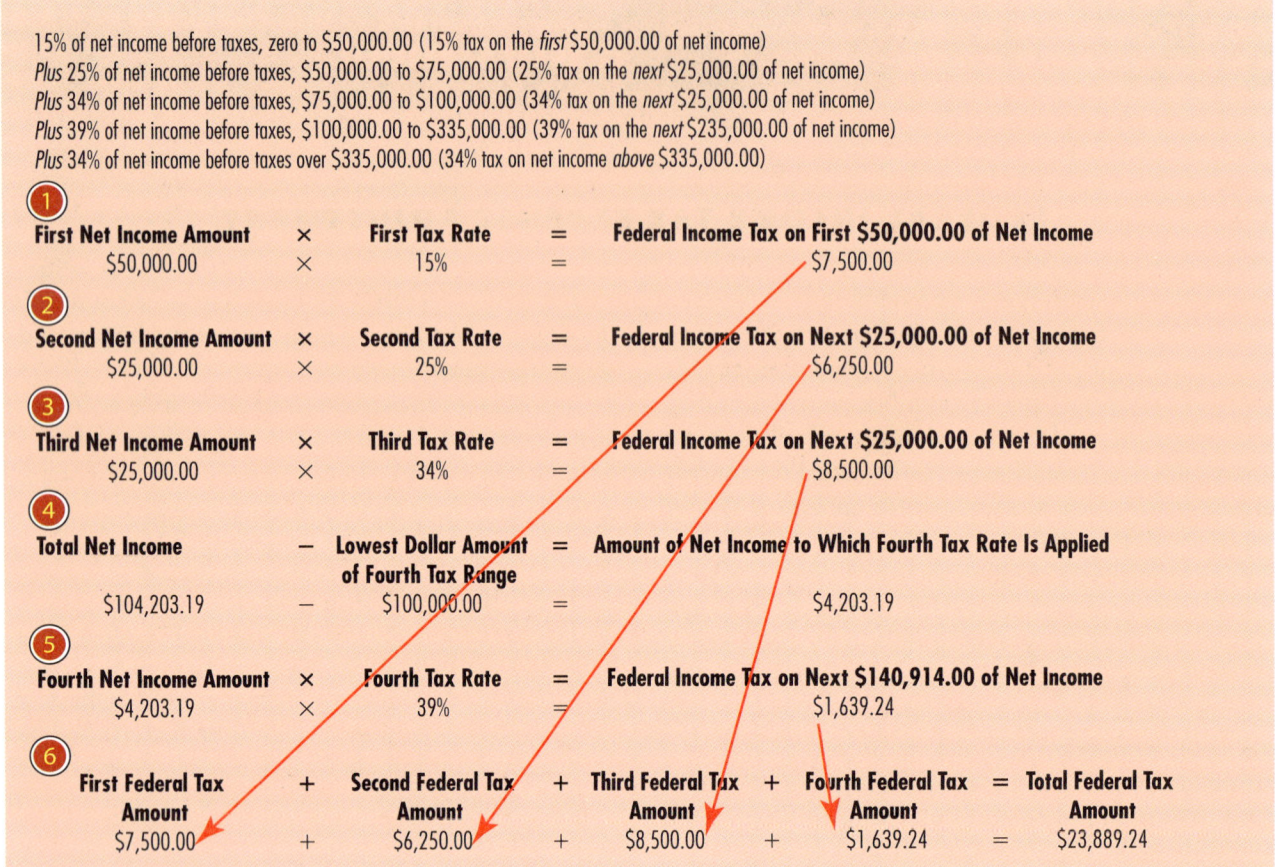

The amount of federal income tax expense a corporation must pay is calculated using a tax rate table furnished by the Internal Revenue Service. Different tax percentages are applied to different portions of the net income to determine the total federal income tax owed. Hobby Shack's net income before federal income tax is $104,203.19. Corporation tax rates in effect when this text was written are used to calculate Hobby Shack's federal income tax expense.

STEPS — CALCULATING FEDERAL INCOME TAX

1. Multiply $50,000.00 by a tax rate of 15% to calculate the first federal income tax amount. This is the tax Hobby Shack must pay on its first $50,000.00 of net income.

2. Multiply $25,000.00 by a tax rate of 25% to calculate the second federal income tax amount. This is the tax Hobby Shack must pay on the next $25,000.00 of net income.

3. Multiply $25,000.00 by a tax rate of 34% to calculate the third federal income tax amount. This is the tax Hobby Shack must pay on the next $25,000.00 of net income.

4. The tax rate of 39% applies to all net income that falls in the range of $100,000.00 to $335,000.00. Hobby Shack's net income is $104,203.19. When the net income does not equal or exceed the highest dollar amount given in a range, the amount of net income to which the tax rate is applied is determined by subtracting the lowest dollar amount in the range from the total net income. ($104,203.19 − $100,000.00 = $4,203.19)

5. Multiply $4,203.19 by a tax rate of 39% to calculate the fourth federal income tax amount, $1,639.24. This is the tax Hobby Shack must pay on the remainder of its net income.

6. Add the four tax amounts together to determine Hobby Shack's federal income tax expense for the fiscal year.

RECORDING THE FEDERAL INCOME TAX ADJUSTMENT

ACCOUNT TITLE	TRIAL BALANCE DEBIT	TRIAL BALANCE CREDIT	ADJUSTMENTS DEBIT	ADJUSTMENTS CREDIT	INCOME STATEMENT DEBIT	INCOME STATEMENT CREDIT	BALANCE SHEET DEBIT	BALANCE SHEET CREDIT	
9 Office Equipment	35864 50						35864 50		9
10 Acc. Depr.—Office Equipment		6497 00		(f) 6540 00				13037 00	10
11 Store Equipment	40849 50						40849 50		11
12 Acc. Depr.—Store Equipment		5069 00		(g) 5250 00				10319 00	12
13 Accounts Payable		11583 03						11583 03	13
14 Federal Income Tax Payable			①	(h) 5889 24				③ 5889 24	14
46 Supplies Expense—Store			(b) 2910 00		2910 00				46
47 Uncollectible Accounts Expense			(e) 1245 00		1245 00				47
48 Utilities Expense	3820 00				3820 00				48
49 Federal Income Tax Expense	18000 00		① (h) 5889 24		③ 23889 24				49
50	670861 59	670861 59	43574 24	43574 24					50
51				②					51

1. Calculate and enter the federal income tax adjustment.

2. Total and rule the adjustment columns.

3. Extend the account balances.

STEPS — RECORDING A WORK SHEET ADJUSTMENT FOR FEDERAL INCOME TAX EXPENSE

① Calculate the amount of the federal income tax expense adjustment. The adjustment is the difference between the federal income tax for the year and the taxes paid during the year.

Federal Income Tax....................................	$23,889.24
Less Total of Quarterly Installments.....................	−18,000.00
Equals Federal Income Tax Adjustment..................	$ 5,889.24

Enter the federal income tax expense adjustment, *$5,889.24*, in the Adjustments Credit column on the *Federal Income Tax Payable* line of the work sheet. Enter the same amount in the Adjustments Debit column of the *Federal Income Tax Expense* line of the work sheet. Label both parts of the adjustment *(h)*.

② Total and rule the Adjustments columns.

③ Extend the *Federal Income Tax Expense* account balance, *$23,889.24*, to the Income Statement Debit column. Extend the amount for *Federal Income Tax Payable*, *$5,889.24*, to the Balance Sheet Credit column.

Federal Income Tax Expense

4/15	4,500.00
6/15	4,500.00
9/15	4,500.00
12/15	4,500.00
(12/15 Bal.	18,000.00)
12/31 Adj. (h)	5,889.24
(New Bal.	23,889.24)

Federal Income Tax Payable

	12/31 Adj. (h)	5,889.24

Calculating Federal Income Tax and Completing a Work Sheet

COMPLETING A WORK SHEET

After the adjustment for federal income tax expense has been recorded, the work sheet is ready to be completed. Income Statement column totals are used to calculate net income after federal income tax.

Hobby Shack follows the same procedures for completing a work sheet as described for TechKnow in Chapter 6, with the exception of the Income Summary account. TechKnow sells a service, not merchandise. Therefore, TechKnow has no amount recorded in the Income Summary account, a related account used to adjust Merchandise Inventory. Hobby Shack sells merchandise. Therefore, the Income Summary account is used as the related account to adjust Merchandise Inventory. The merchandise inventory adjustment reflects the increases and decreases in the amount of goods on hand resulting from purchases and sales. Therefore, the amount recorded in Income Summary is extended to the work sheet's Income Statement Debit or Credit column. An Income Summary debit amount is extended to the Income Statement Debit column. An Income Summary credit amount is extended to the Income Statement Credit column.

Hobby Shack's completed work sheet for the year ended December 31, 20--, is shown on pages 432–433.

STEPS COMPLETING A WORK SHEET

1. Total the Income Statement and Balance Sheet columns.

2. Write the words *Net Income after Federal Income Tax* on line 51 of the work sheet. Calculate and enter the net income after federal income tax, $80,313.95, in the Income Statement Debit column on this new line of the work sheet.

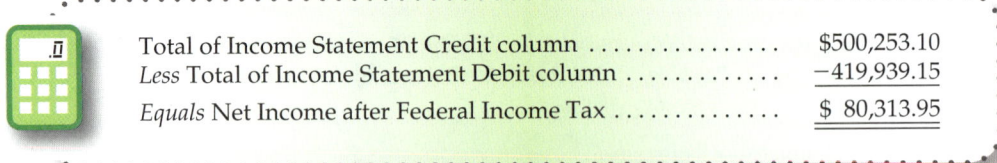

Total of Income Statement Credit column................	$500,253.10
Less Total of Income Statement Debit column.............	−419,939.15
Equals Net Income after Federal Income Tax..............	$ 80,313.95

3. Extend the net income after federal income tax amount, $80,313.95, to the Balance Sheet Credit column.

4. Total the four Income Statement and Balance Sheet columns. Determine that the totals of each pair of columns are in balance.

5. Rule double lines across the Income Statement and Balance Sheet columns to show that the totals have been verified as correct.

CAREERS IN ACCOUNTING

Everlyn Johnson, Small Business Owner

By the age of 18, you will have gained experiences that will change your life in ways you might never imagine. These experiences may come from an extracurricular activity, a part-time job, or a hobby, and they may influence the direction of your career or retirement.

For Everlyn Johnson, the youthful experience that would affect her life was learning to sew. Her mother taught her the basics when Everlyn was 11. Advancing from quilts to doll clothes to her prom dress, Everlyn learned that human sciences (formerly home economics) would lead her to a fulfilling career. Earning bachelor's, master's, and doctoral degrees in the area, Dr. Johnson worked with her state's cooperative extension service for over 27 years. In her role as a county agent, she was responsible for educating the public on home living skills—including sewing. Later she advanced to a position where she was responsible for gathering and communicating current knowledge and research with other county agents.

Most people plan to relax in their retirement. But not Dr. Johnson. She says, "I constantly heard people say that they wish they knew how to sew. I saw a niche that needed filling and decided I was the person to fulfill it." So after just three years of retirement, Everlyn decided to open a fabric store.

One of her first tasks to prepare for the store opening was to enroll in an income tax course at the local university. She recalls, "I felt the tax course would help me do a better job of keeping the records of the business and would ensure that I planned the business to take advantage of tax laws." Then she started doing her homework, meeting with a variety of small business owners to learn the rewards and pitfalls of small business ownership.

Everlyn visited fabric stores outside her market area. "The owners of many stores painted less than a rosy picture of the prospect of opening a store," she remarks. "I felt they were missing something—that main ingredient that would make the store successful. Then I visited two stores that were constantly conducting sewing classes. It was clear to see that these classes were the key to the success of the stores. Perfect!" Having spent most of her career teaching classes, Everlyn now plans sewing classes, teaching some herself, to serve her customers and to promote the sale of fabric and accessories in her store.

Salary: Approximately $70,000, depending on experience.

Qualifications: A master's degree requires one year of university courses beyond the bachelor's degree. Most doctoral programs require another four years of university study and research.

Occupational Outlook: The budgetary constraints of county, state, and federal governments have reduced the financial resources devoted to cooperative education. Thus, the opportunities for individuals in this career have been declining. However, in Dr. Johnson's situation, she was able to use her background to move into a successful business venture.

A COMPLETED 8-COLUMN WORK SHEET

Hobby Shack, Inc.
Work Sheet
For Year Ended December 31, 20--

	ACCOUNT TITLE	TRIAL BALANCE DEBIT	TRIAL BALANCE CREDIT	ADJUSTMENTS DEBIT	ADJUSTMENTS CREDIT	INCOME STATEMENT DEBIT	INCOME STATEMENT CREDIT	BALANCE SHEET DEBIT	BALANCE SHEET CREDIT	
1	Cash	2908028						2908028		1
2	Petty Cash	30000						30000		2
3	Accounts Receivable	1469840						1469840		3
4	Allow. for Uncoll. Accts.		12752		(e) 124500				137252	4
5	Merchandise Inventory	14048000			(d) 1584000			12464000		5
6	Supplies—Office	348000			(a) 273000			75000		6
7	Supplies—Store	394400			(b) 291000			103400		7
8	Prepaid Insurance	580000			(c) 317000			263000		8
9	Office Equipment	3586450						3586450		9
10	Acc. Depr.—Office Equipment		649700		(f) 654000				1303700	10
11	Store Equipment	4084950						4084950		11
12	Acc. Depr.—Store Equipment		506900		(g) 525000				1031900	12
13	Accounts Payable		1158303						1158303	13
14	Federal Income Tax Payable				(h) 588924				588924	14
15	Employee Income Tax Payable		75700						75700	15
16	Social Security Tax Payable		145138						145138	16
17	Medicare Tax Payable		39942						39942	17
18	Sales Tax Payable		255670						255670	18
19	Unemployment Tax Payable—Federal		3460						3460	19
20	Unemployment Tax Payable—State		23355						23355	20
21	Health Insurance Premiums Payable		100800						100800	21
22	U.S. Savings Bonds Payable		6000						6000	22
23	United Way Donations Payable		7000						7000	23
24	Dividends Payable		500000						500000	24
25	Capital Stock		12500000						12500000	25
26	Retained Earnings		1076129						1076129	26
27	Dividends	2000000						2000000		27
28	Income Summary			(d) 1584000		1584000				28

#	Account	Trial Balance Debit	Trial Balance Credit	Adjustments Debit	Adjustments Credit	Income Statement Debit	Income Statement Credit	Balance Sheet Debit	Balance Sheet Credit
29	Sales		49512000				49512000		
30	Sales Discount	25848				25848			
31	Sales Returns and Allowances	312728				312728			
32	Purchases	20996000				20996000			
33	Purchases Discount		164815				164815		
34	Purch. Returns and Allowances		348495				348495		
35	Advertising Expense	360000				360000			
36	Cash Short and Over	1925				1925			
37	Credit Card Fee Expense	338500				338500			
38	Depr. Exp.—Office Equipment			(f) 654000		654000			
39	Depr. Exp.—Store Equipment			(g) 525000		525000			
40	Insurance Expense			(c) 317000		317000			
41	Miscellaneous Expense	256490				256490			
42	Payroll Taxes Expense	910500				910500			
43	Rent Expense	1800000				1800000			
44	Salary Expense	10452500				10452500			
45	Supplies Expense—Office			(a) 273000		273000			
46	Supplies Expense—Store			(b) 291000		291000			
47	Uncollectible Accounts Expense			(e) 124500		124500			
48	Utilities Expense	382000				382000			
49	Federal Income Tax Expense	1800000		(h) 588924		2388924			
50		67086159	67086159	4357424	4357424	41993915	50025310	26984668	18953273
51	Net Income after Federal Income Tax					8031395			8031395
52						50025310	50025310	26984668	26984668

Calculating Federal Income Tax and Completing a Work Sheet Lesson 14-6

A 10-COLUMN WORK SHEET (LEFT PAGE)

1. Trial balance
2. Adjustments
3. Extend Adjusted Balances

Hobby Shack, Inc.
Work Sheet
For Year Ended December 31, 20--

	ACCOUNT TITLE	1 TRIAL BALANCE DEBIT	2 TRIAL BALANCE CREDIT	3 ADJUSTMENTS DEBIT	4 ADJUSTMENTS CREDIT	5 ADJUSTED TRIAL BALANCE DEBIT	6 ADJUSTED TRIAL BALANCE CREDIT
1	Cash	290 80 28				290 80 28	
2	Petty Cash	300 00				300 00	
3	Accounts Receivable	146 98 40				146 98 40	
4	Allow. for Uncoll. Accts.		127 52		(e) 1245 00		1372 52
5	Merchandise Inventory	14048 00 00			(d)15840 00	12464 00 00	
6	Supplies—Office	3480 00			(a) 2730 00	750 00	
7	Supplies—Store	3944 00			(b) 2910 00	1034 00	
8	Prepaid Insurance	5800 00			(c) 3170 00	2630 00	
9	Office Equipment	35864 50				35864 50	
10	Acc. Depr.—Office Equipment		6497 00		(f) 6540 00		13037 00
11	Store Equipment	40849 50				40849 50	
12	Acc. Depr.—Store Equipment		5069 00		(g) 5250 00		10319 00
13	Accounts Payable		11583 03				11583 03
14	Federal Income Tax Payable				(h) 5889 24		5889 24
24	Dividends Payable		5000 00				5000 00
25	Capital Stock		125000 00				125000 00
26	Retained Earnings		10761 29				10761 29
27	Dividends	20000 00				20000 00	
28	Income Summary			(d)15840 00		15840 00	
29	Sales		495120 00				495120 00
30	Sales Discount	258 48				258 48	
31	Sales Returns and Allowances	3127 28				3127 28	
32	Purchases	209960 00				209960 00	
33	Purchases Discount		1648 15				1648 15
34	Purch. Returns and Allowances		3484 95				3484 95
35	Advertising Expense	3600 00				3600 00	
36	Cash Short and Over	19 25				19 25	
37	Credit Card Fee Expense	3385 00				3385 00	
38	Depr. Exp.—Office Equipment			(f) 6540 00		6540 00	
39	Depr. Exp.—Store Equipment			(g) 5250 00		5250 00	
40	Insurance Expense			(c) 3170 00		3170 00	
41	Miscellaneous Expense	2564 90				2564 90	
42	Payroll Taxes Expense	9105 00				9105 00	
43	Rent Expense	18000 00				18000 00	
44	Salary Expense	104525 00				104525 00	
45	Supplies Expense—Office			(a) 2730 00		2730 00	
46	Supplies Expense—Store			(b) 2910 00		2910 00	
47	Uncollectible Accounts Expense			(e) 1245 00		1245 00	
48	Utilities Expense	3820 00				3820 00	
49	Federal Income Tax Expense	18000 00		(h) 5889 24		23889 24	
50		670861 59	670861 59	43574 24	43574 24	689785 83	689785 83
51	Net Income after Federal Income Tax						
52							

4. Total, prove, and rule

434 Chapter 14   Distributing Dividends and Preparing a Work Sheet for a Merchandising Business

A 10-COLUMN WORK SHEET (RIGHT PAGE)

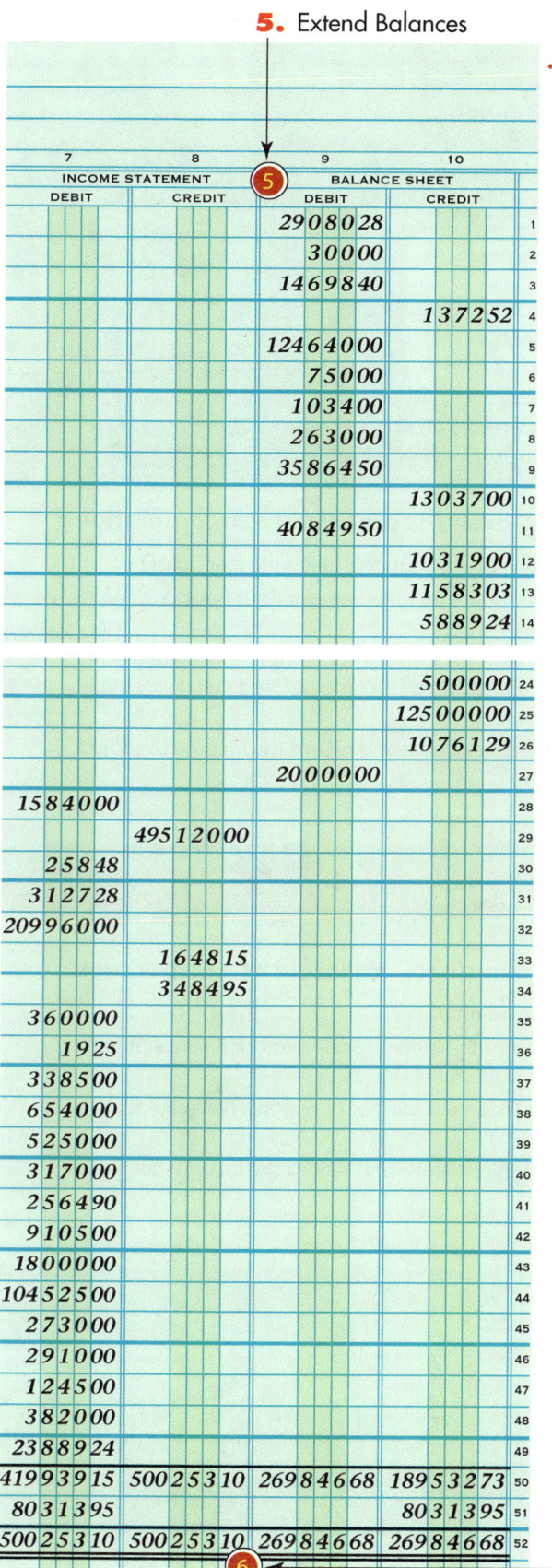

5. Extend Balances

6. Calculate net income; total, prove, and rule

Some large businesses with many accounts to be adjusted at the end of a fiscal period may use a 10-column work sheet. A 10-column work sheet includes an additional pair of amount columns titled Adjusted Trial Balance.

Any business with adjustments to make at the end of a fiscal period could use either an 8-column or a 10-column work sheet. However, completing two extra amount columns when most of the account balances are not adjusted requires extra time and work. Account balances not adjusted must be extended from the Trial Balance columns to the Adjusted Trial Balance columns; whereas, with an 8-column work sheet, account balances not adjusted are extended directly to the Balance Sheet or Income Statement columns.

STEPS — COMPLETING A 10-COLUMN WORK SHEET

1. Record the trial balance on the work sheet.
2. Plan the adjustments on the work sheet.
3. Extend the balances in the Trial Balance Debit and Credit columns to the Adjusted Trial Balance Debit and Credit columns. Calculate up-to-date adjusted balances for all accounts affected by adjustments.
4. Total, prove, and rule the Adjusted Trial Balance Debit and Credit columns.
5. Extend the amounts in the Adjusted Trial Balance Debit and Credit columns to the appropriate Income Statement and Balance Sheet columns.
6. Calculate net income and total, prove, and rule the Income Statement and Balance Sheet columns in the same way as on an 8-column work sheet.

REMEMBER

A 10-column work sheet is often used by large merchandising companies with many accounts to be adjusted.

Calculating Federal Income Tax and Completing a Work Sheet · Lesson 14-6

End of Lesson REVIEW

AUDIT YOUR UNDERSTANDING

1. In what column is the Income Summary amount extended?
2. To which Balance Sheet column is a net loss amount extended?
3. What extra step is required when a 10-column work sheet is prepared instead of an 8-column work sheet?

WORK TOGETHER 14-6

Completing an 8-column work sheet for a merchandising business organized as a corporation

Use the work sheet from Work Together 14-5. Your instructor will guide you through the following examples.

1. Extend all amounts except Federal Income Tax Expense to the appropriate Income Statement or Balance Sheet columns. Do not total the columns.
2. On the form provided in the *Working Papers*, total the work sheet's Income Statement columns. Calculate the difference between the debit and credit totals. This difference becomes the net income before federal income tax expense.
3. Using the tax table shown in this chapter, calculate federal income tax expense and record the income tax adjustment on the work sheet. Label the adjustment *(h)*.
4. Complete the work sheet.

ON YOUR OWN 14-6

Completing an 8-column work sheet for a merchandising business organized as a corporation

Use the work sheet from On Your Own 14-5. Work this problem independently.

1. Extend all amounts except Federal Income Tax Expense to the appropriate Income Statement or Balance Sheet columns. Do not total the columns.
2. On the form provided in the *Working Papers*, total the work sheet's Income Statement columns. Calculate the difference between the debit and credit totals.
3. Using the tax table shown in this chapter, calculate federal income tax expense and record the income tax adjustment on the work sheet. Label the adjustment *(h)*.
4. Complete the work sheet.

SUMMARY

After completing this chapter, you can:

1. Define accounting terms related to distributing dividends and preparing a work sheet for a merchandising business.
2. Identify accounting concepts and practices related to distributing dividends and preparing a work sheet for a merchandising business.
3. Journalize the declaration and payment of a dividend.
4. Begin a work sheet for a merchandising business.
5. Plan work sheet adjustments for merchandise inventory, supplies, prepaid expenses, uncollectible accounts, and depreciation.
6. Calculate federal income tax and plan the work sheet adjustment for federal income tax.
7. Complete a work sheet for a merchandising business.

Go Beyond the Book
For more information go to www.C21accounting.com

EXPLORE ACCOUNTING

Accounting Systems Design

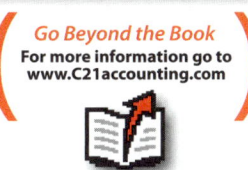

An important role of accountants is to prepare financial statements for businesses. In addition, many accountants design accounting systems used to prepare the various financial reports important to successful business operations.

An accounting system should be designed to meet the needs of the business it serves. Factors to consider are size of the company, number of facility locations, geographic area of operations (local, statewide, national, international), number of employees, and type of organization (service, merchandising, manufacturing). Also to be considered are the intended uses of the information: traditional financial statements (income statement, balance sheet, cash flow statement), income tax information, management decision information, management control information, and product pricing information.

An accounting system is built around a chart of accounts, which provides the organizational system around which information will be collected, filed, and made available for various types of financial reports.

A small business owned and operated by one person may not need detailed information. However, as a business grows in size and complexity, more detailed information is required. Large international businesses need very complex accounting systems with thousands of accounts to furnish management with the information needed to make decisions and the data for various reports required by governments and other agencies. As businesses grow, accountants constantly look for ways to provide better information. Thus, accountants play a key role in the successful growth of a business.

Activity: Assume Hobby Shack has made the decision to change from a merchandising business to a manufacturing business. It will create its own ceramic molds that will enable it to produce its own line of ceramic images. As the accountant, how would you recommend the chart of accounts be modified to meet the changing needs of the company?

14-1 APPLICATION PROBLEM

Journalizing dividends

Drake Corporation completed the following transactions during December of the current year and January of the next year.

Instructions:

1. Use page 17 of a general journal. Journalize the dividend declared on December 15.
2. Use page 28 of a cash payments journal. Journalize payment of the dividend on January 15.

Transactions:

Dec. 15. The board of directors declared a dividend of $1.50 per share; capital stock issued is 2,100 shares. M258.

Jan. 15. Paid cash for dividend declared December 15. C721.

14-2 APPLICATION PROBLEM

Beginning an 8-column work sheet for a merchandising business

A partially completed work sheet for Branson Amusement Company is given in the *Working Papers*. Four general ledger accounts are shown below.

Instructions:

1. Enter the accounts and account balances on the following lines.

Line	Account	Account Balance
6	Supplies—Office	$ 5,210.98
13	Accounts Payable	17,558.16
33	Purchases Discount	5,155.28
44	Salary Expense	193,971.80

2. Total, prove, and rule the trial balance.
3. From a physical count of the following, December 31 balances are determined to be:

Supplies—Office	$489.73
Supplies—Store	701.19
Prepaid Insurance	500.00

Analyze the supplies and prepaid insurance adjustments and enter the adjustments on the work sheet. Label the adjustments *(a)–(c)*. Save your work to complete Application Problem 14-3.

14-3 APPLICATION PROBLEM

Analyzing and recording a merchandise inventory adjustment on a work sheet

Use the work sheet prepared in Application Problem 14-2.

Instructions:

1. From a physical count of merchandise inventory, the December 31 balance is determined to be $226,766.38. Analyze the merchandise inventory adjustment and enter the adjustment on the work sheet. Label the adjustment *(d)*. Save your work to complete Application Problem 14-4.

14-4 APPLICATION PROBLEM

Analyzing and recording an allowance for uncollectible accounts adjustment on a work sheet

Use the work sheet prepared in Application Problem 14-3.

Instructions:

1. Branson Amusement Company estimates uncollectible accounts expense as 0.8% of its total sales on account. During the current year, Branson had credit sales of $248,500.00. As of December 31, record the uncollectible accounts expense adjustment on the work sheet and label the adjustment *(e)*. Save your work to complete Application Problem 14-5.

14-5 APPLICATION PROBLEM

Planning and recording adjustments for depreciation

Use the work sheet prepared in Application Problem 14-4.

Instructions:

1. Wave Dive Company tests scuba equipment. Calculate depreciation expense for scuba testing equipment costing $10,540.00; estimated salvage value, $2,500.00; useful life, 3 years.
2. Calculate the book value of the scuba testing equipment at the end of its second year of service.
3. On December 31, Branson Amusement Company determined total depreciation expense: office equipment, $5,850.00; store equipment, $5,250.00. Plan the work sheet adjustments and label the adjustments *(f)* and *(g)*. Save your work to complete Application Problem 14-6.

14-6 APPLICATION PROBLEM

Calculating federal income tax and completing an 8-column work sheet for a merchandising business

Use the work sheet prepared in Application Problem 14-5.

Instructions:

1. Extend all amounts except Federal Income Tax Expense to the appropriate Income Statement or Balance Sheet columns. Do not total the columns.
2. On the form provided in the *Working Papers*, calculate the net income before federal income tax expense.
3. Using the tax table shown in this chapter, calculate federal income tax expense and record the income tax adjustment on the work sheet. Label the adjustment *(h)*.
4. Finish the work sheet.

14-7 MASTERY PROBLEM   Peachtree by Sage   QuickBooks

Preparing an 8-column work sheet for a merchandising business

The trial balance for Carol's Closet as of December 31 of the current year is recorded on a work sheet in the *Working Papers*.

Instructions:

1. Analyze the following adjustment information collected on December 31 and record the adjustments on the work sheet. Label each adjustment using labels *(a)* through *(g)*.

   a. Office supplies inventory $1,407.00
   b. Store supplies inventory 570.11
   c. Merchandise inventory 238,830.61
   d. Uncollectible accounts are 1.2% of credit sales of: 458,200.00
   e. Value of prepaid insurance 2,000.00
   f. Estimate of office equipment depreciation 5,216.00
   g. Estimate of store equipment depreciation 4,820.00

2. Using the tax table shown in this chapter, calculate federal income tax expense and record the income tax adjustment on the work sheet. Label the adjustment *(h)*.

3. Complete the work sheet.

14-8 CHALLENGE PROBLEM

Preparing a 10-column work sheet for a merchandising business

Hillside Ski Shop's trial balance as of December 31 of the current year is recorded on a work sheet in the *Working Papers*.

Instructions:

1. Analyze the following adjustment information collected on December 31 and record the adjustments on the work sheet. Label each adjustment using labels *(a)* through *(g)*.

   a. Office supplies inventory $343.42
   b. Store supplies inventory 309.41
   c. Merchandise inventory 167,000.46
   d. Uncollectible accounts are 1.0% of credit sales of: 158,900.00
   e. Value of prepaid insurance 3,000.00
   f. Estimate of office equipment depreciation 3,890.00
   g. Estimate of store equipment depreciation 3,460.00

2. Using the tax table shown in this chapter, calculate federal income tax expense and record the income tax adjustment on the work sheet. Label the adjustment *(h)*.

3. Complete the work sheet.

APPLIED COMMUNICATION

Sometimes a credit customer does not pay off the amount due on an account receivable by the deadline specified in the terms of the sale on account. In this situation, a business wants to (1) receive the amount owed and (2) preserve a long-term relationship so there can be repeated sales to that customer.

Instructions: Write a first-notice letter to a customer who has not yet paid an amount due. Balance your business's need to receive payment with the desire to keep the customer's goodwill now and in the future. Use a supportive opening and closing.

CASE FOR CRITICAL THINKING

After completing a work sheet, Park's Boutique finds that garment bags worth $600.00 were overlooked in the supplies inventory. Jerry Park suggests that the oversight does not have any effect on balancing the Income Statement and Balance Sheet columns of the work sheet. He adds that the oversight will be corrected when the store supplies are counted at the end of the next fiscal period. The accountant recommends that the work sheet be redone to reflect the recalculated supplies inventory. Do you agree with Mr. Park or the accountant? Explain your answer.

AUDITING FOR ERRORS

Martin Grotte has just completed the year-end work sheet for Lancing Corporation. Part of the work sheet is shown below.

Account Title	Trial Balance Debit	Trial Balance Credit	Adjustments Debit	Adjustments Credit
Accounts Receivable	42,518.25			
Allow. for Uncoll. Accts.		251.66		(e) 496.41
Merchandise Inventory	251,486.36		(d) 9,548.25	
Supplies—Office	5,141.84			(a) 4,154.22
Supplies—Store	3,148.28			(b) 2,974.22
Prepaid Insurance	6,000.00			(c) 5,000.00
Office Equipment	28,550.00			
Acc. Depr.—Office Equipment		12,480.00		(f) 5,210.00
Store Equipment	58,940.00			
Acc. Depr.—Store Equipment		16,420.00		(g) 8,420.00
Federal Income Tax Payable				(h) 45,813.38
Sales		992,818.10		
Utilities Expense	5,485.22			
Federal Income Tax Expense	60,000.00		(h) 45,813.38	

Martin used the following information to prepare the work sheet adjustments:
a. Uncollectible accounts are estimated to be 0.5% of gross sales (the amount of sales before discounts and returns and allowances are subtracted).
b. Office supplies inventory on hand, $987.62.
c. Store supplies inventory on hand, $174.06.
d. Merchandise inventory on hand, $241,938.11.
e. The six-month insurance premium was paid on July 1.
f. Office equipment has a 5-year useful life and a $2,500 salvage value.
g. Store equipment has a 7-year useful life and a $3,500 salvage value.

Instructions

Audit the work sheet to determine if the work sheet adjustments were recorded properly. Prepare a list that describes any errors you discover and how they should be corrected.

ANALYZING BEST BUY'S FINANCIAL STATEMENTS

Investors use a ratio known as the *dividend yield* when making investment decisions. The dividend yield is calculated as follows:

$$\text{Dividend Yield} = \frac{\text{Dividend per Share}}{\text{Market Price per Share}}$$

Companies with large dividend yields (greater than 3%) are typically considered to be *income stocks*, meaning that investors own the stock primarily to earn the dividend. In contrast, companies with small dividend yields (less than 2%) are often referred to as *growth stocks*, meaning that investors are counting on the market value of the stock to increase over time.

Instructions: Use Best Buy's Statement of Changes in Shareholders' Equity on page B-8 in Appendix B to answer the following questions.

1. Calculate the 2006 dividend yield for Best Buy, assuming the current market price is $50.00 per share.
2. Would you classify Best Buy as an income or growth stock?

Accounting SOFTWARE

JOURNALIZING ADJUSTING ENTRIES

Peachtree has a working trial balance report that is similar to a work sheet. The report presents each account, the account balance as of the end of the last fiscal period, and the current balance.

Like the work sheet, the printed working trial balance has blank debit and credit columns where adjustments can be planned. The completed report provides the support for adjustments of allowance for uncollectible accounts, inventory, prepaid insurance, and accumulated depreciation accounts. After the adjustments are entered in Peachtree, an income statement is printed to obtain the required pretax net income amount needed for calculating federal income taxes.

PEACHTREE APPLICATION PROBLEM 14-1
1. Open (Restore) file 14-1AP.ptb.
2. Journalize and post the dividend declared on December 15 in the general journal.
3. Change the accounting periods from Period 12 to Period 13.
4. Using the Write Checks task, journalize and post the payment of the dividend on January 16.
5. Print the December 15 general journal.
6. Print the January 15 cash disbursements journal.

PEACHTREE MASTERY PROBLEM 14-7
1. Open (Restore) file 14-7MP.ptb.
2. Journalize and post the adjusting entries in the general journal.
3. Display or print Peachtree's general ledger trial balance to see the account balances.
4. Print the December 31 general journal, the income statement and the balance sheet.

JOURNALIZING ADJUSTING ENTRIES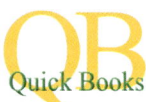

As discussed in this chapter, many corporations pay cash dividends to their shareholders. The number of shareholders receiving checks could number in the thousands. Similar to how many companies use a special payroll account, some companies deposit the total amount of the cash dividend to a special dividend bank account. The check to each shareholder is written from that special dividend account.

Also covered in this chapter is the calculating and recording of adjusting entries. If a work sheet is not used, the adjusting entries must be planned using other means. A trial balance can be printed out and used to plan the adjusting entries. The trial balance, however, will not provide the amount of pretax net income needed to calculate the federal income tax adjustment. To determine this amount, it is necessary to enter all the other adjusting entries, print out a profit & loss statement, and use the net income amount on that profit & loss statement to calculate the adjusting entry for federal income taxes.

QUICKBOOKS APPLICATION PROBLEM 14-1
1. Open the Drake Corporation file.
2. Record the dividend transactions. Use the Write Checks option for all cash payments; use the Make General Journal Entries window for all other transactions.
3. Print a Journal report, using December 15 and January 15 for the dates. Change column widths as needed to display all of the data.

QUICKBOOKS MASTERY PROBLEM 14-7
1. Open the Carol's Closet file.
2. Journalize the adjusting entries, using the Make General Journal Entries window for all transactions.
3. View a Profit & Loss Standard report, using January 1 and December 31 for the dates; close without printing.
4. Print a Journal report for Carol's Closet, using December 1 and December 31 for the dates.
5. Print a Trial Balance report, using December 31 for the dates.

LOGICAL RELATIONSHIPS

In Chapter 9, you learned that a formula can consist of a reference to a single cell. A formula can also determine the logical relationship between two numbers. Some common logical relationships are equal to (=), less than, (<), greater than or equal to (>=), and not equal to (<>).

Debit and credit columns of a worksheet must be equal. As the numbers get larger, it becomes more likely that you may miss an error. Examine the following section of a worksheet.

	A	B	C
56	Utilities Expense	4,051.06	0.00
57	Fed. Income Tax Expense	48,000.00	0.00
58		1,058,513.74	1,059,513.74
59	Net Inc. after Fed. Income Tax		
60			

How long did it take you to detect that the column totals are not equal? Rather than relying on yourself to determine if the columns are equal, you can enter a formula, such as +B58=C58, to compare the two amounts. If the amounts are equal, the cells will display TRUE; if the amounts are not equal, FALSE.

EXCEL APPLICATION PROBLEM 14-2
Open the F14-2–F14-3 Excel data file. Follow the instructions for Application Problem 14-2 and the step-by-step instructions in the Instructions worksheet. Use the logical functions to ensure that the Trial Balance column totals are equal.

EXCEL APPLICATION PROBLEMS 14-3 to 14-6
Open the F14-2–F14-3 Excel data file. Follow the instructions for Application Problems 14-3 to 14-6 and the step-by-step instructions in the Instructions worksheet. Use the logical functions to ensure that each pair of column totals are equal.

CREATING CHARTS AND GRAPHS

Charts and graphs provide a picture of numeric data. To be effective, charts and graphs should be clearly labeled. They are commonly used to track sales goals, monitor expenses, identify trends, and make forecasts.

Different styles of graphs are used to display different types of financial information. A pie graph is used to illustrate parts of a whole, such as cost of goods sold, operating expenses, and net income as percentages of net sales. Bar graphs are used to show the relative size of related items, such as expenses. Line graphs are used to illustrate trends, such as net sales or net income over a period of years.

To prepare a graph based on financial data when a data file is open, choose the Graph Selection menu item from the Reports menu or click the Graphs toolbar button. Then click the type of graph you would like to display.

AUTOMATED ACCOUNTING GRAPHING PROBLEM (OPTIONAL)
1. Open the data file that is your solution to Automated Accounting Problem F11-5. There is no Help file available for this optional graphing problem.
2. Click the Graphs toolbar button.
3. Click the Income Statement button to display a graph of the income statement.
4. View the other graphs available. Note that some are not very meaningful because this particular problem does not have a wide range of data available for graphing.
5. Exit Automated Accounting without saving your file.

CHAPTER 15

Financial Statements for a Corporation

OBJECTIVES

After studying Chapter 15, you will be able to:

1. Define accounting terms related to financial statements for a merchandising business organized as a corporation.
2. Identify accounting concepts and practices related to financial statements for a merchandising business organized as a corporation.
3. Prepare an income statement for a merchandising business organized as a corporation.
4. Analyze an income statement using component percentages and financial ratios.
5. Prepare a statement of stockholders' equity for a merchandising business organized as a corporation.
6. Prepare a balance sheet for a merchandising business organized as a corporation.

KEY TERMS

- net sales
- cost of merchandise sold
- gross profit on sales
- financial ratio
- earnings per share
- price-earnings ratio
- statement of stockholders' equity
- par value
- current liabilities
- long-term liabilities
- supporting schedule

Point Your Browser
www.C21accounting.com

ACCOUNTING IN THE REAL WORLD

Gap, Inc.

The Evolution of Gap, Inc.

Many of today's most notable companies had very humble beginnings. Gap, Inc., began in 1969 when Don and Doris Fisher opened a clothing store in San Francisco. The company grew quickly, becoming a publicly traded company in just seven years.

The company expanded beyond its Gap store concept in 1983 by purchasing Banana Republic, a small safari and travel clothing company. Gap further extended its penetration into the clothing market by introducing the Old Navy brand in 1994. The rest, as they say, is history. With over 3,000 stores, Gap, Inc., is now a major force in the apparel industry.

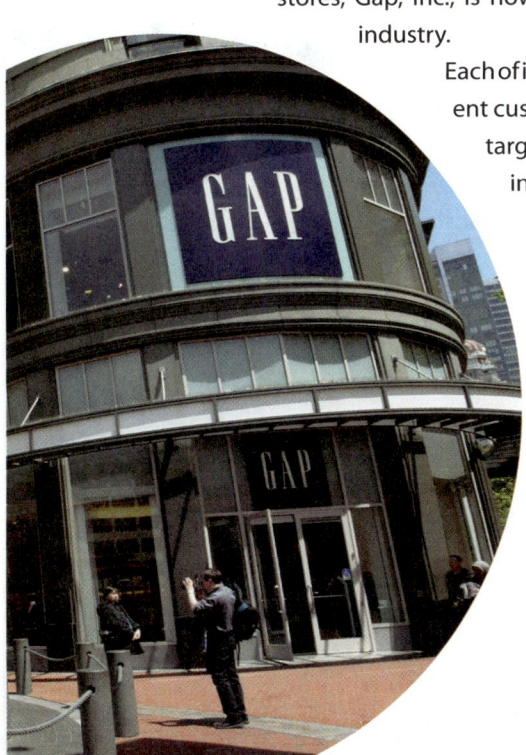

Each of its clothing brands targets different customers. The original Gap brand targets style-conscious customers in the casual specialty market. Banana Republic targets men and women who want more sophisticated seasonal fashions, shoes, personal care products, intimate apparel, and gifts for the home. Old Navy is more value focused, providing families with great fashions at affordable prices.

Critical Thinking

1. Should a single set of financial statements be prepared for Gap Inc., or should financial statements be prepared for each brand?
2. How would the chart of accounts differ among the three brands?

Source: www.gapinc.com

INTERNET ACTIVITY

EDGAR—Part 1

Go to the homepage for the Securities and Exchange Commission (SEC) (www.sec.gov). The SEC provides almost instant access to forms filed with the SEC. Investors can access these forms through a system called EDGAR. Click on "Filings and Forms (EDGAR)." Search the site to find out more about EDGAR.

Instructions

1. Each letter in "EDGAR" is an abbreviation for a word. List the word connected with each letter in EDGAR.
2. Briefly state how EDGAR helps investors.

LESSON 15-1

Preparing an Income Statement

USES OF FINANCIAL STATEMENTS

Financial statements provide the primary source of information needed by owners and managers to make decisions on the future activity of a business. All financial information must be reported in order to make sound business decisions. The financial statements should provide information about a business's financial condition, changes in this financial condition, and the progress of operations. [CONCEPT: Adequate Disclosure]

Comparing financial condition and progress for more than one fiscal period also helps owners and managers make sound business decisions. Therefore, financial information must be reported the same way from one fiscal period to the next. [CONCEPT: Consistent Reporting]

Hobby Shack prepares three financial statements to report financial progress and condition. A corporation prepares an income statement and a balance sheet similar to those used by a proprietorship. A corporation also prepares a statement of stockholders' equity.

CHARACTER COUNTS

Can You Share Client Names?

After working six years with a national public accounting firm, Raymond Steele decided to venture out on his own. Raymond's new firm, Steele Consulting, specializes in helping companies that are facing severe financial difficulties. When delivering proposals to potential clients, Raymond proudly lists the names of his current clients.

The Code of Professional Conduct for the American Institute of Certified Public Accountants "prohibits a member in public practice from disclosing confidential information without the client's consent." Raymond is aware of the rule but believes he is not violating this rule.

Instruction

Access the AICPA Code of Professional Conduct. Determine if Raymond's actions violate the confidentiality rule. (Hint: Remember that the Code includes rules, interpretations, and ethics rulings.)

CAREERS IN ACCOUNTING

Ken Harrison, Computer and Information Systems Manager

As a high school student, Ken Harrison knew he didn't want to do the same thing for his entire career. Ken recalls, "I was the only one in my college freshman orientation group who firmly knew their intended major. 'Accounting!' I proudly responded to our group leader." Ken had been advised that an accounting degree was a good background for law school. However, when presented with attractive accounting job offers in the first semester of his senior year, he thought that "perhaps law school could wait!"

Ken began his career with PricewaterhouseCoopers. During five years in public accounting, he was exposed to numerous accounting issues and became acquainted with the upper-level managers and officers of his clients.

Networking in his profession and community has brought Ken numerous opportunities. At age 28, he was offered the chief financial officer (CFO) position for a start-up general aviation company. Later, as its general manager, he was involved in sales, marketing, human resources, finance, and information technology. "As a successful entrepreneurial business, our little company soon became the target of larger companies in the industry. I hadn't studied much about mergers and acquisitions in college, but 'deal making' soon became a requirement." The sale of the company to a much larger out-of-state corporation, which brought in their own leadership, resulted in Ken's position being eliminated.

Another opportunity soon appeared—to go to work for a publicly held client who needed a CPA familiar with mergers and acquisitions. Seven years later, when Ken's personal desires turned to a more humanitarian calling, he accepted the CFO position of an international not-for-profit organization working to provide impoverished people with the skills and means to improve their lives. In that role, he experienced different and interesting challenges, including travel to many developing countries. "Who would have imagined an accounting degree would take me to remote Africa!" he remarks.

Ken is now working in state government for another former colleague. He explains, "Our mission is to help improve business processes of the state government by installing and supporting an enterprise resource planning (ERP) system." Ken helps direct 80 individuals who assist the users of the ERP throughout the government.

Salary Range: Earnings for computer and information systems managers vary by specialty and level of responsibility. The median annual salary for these managers was $92,570 in 2004 (Bureau of Labor Statistics, *Occupational Outlook Handbook, 2006-07*, at www.bls.gov [visited January 15, 2007]).

Qualifications: Ken believes networking is the key to opportunity. Developing relationships with colleagues and individuals in professional and civic organizations will open doors to opportunities in the most unexpected places. A Certified Public Accountant (CPA) license and public accounting experience provide a solid foundation. Communication skills and a willingness to work in every aspect of the organization, from sales to technology, are important to take advantage of job opportunities.

Occupational Outlook: The U.S. Department of Labor expects jobs for computer and information systems managers to increase much faster than the national average for all occupations. The continued application of technology to business operations will increase the number of jobs that use computer technology, thus requiring more individuals to manage the technology.

INCOME STATEMENT INFORMATION ON A WORK SHEET

Hobby Shack, Inc.
Work Sheet
For Year Ended December 31, 20--

	ACCOUNT TITLE	TRIAL BALANCE DEBIT	TRIAL BALANCE CREDIT	ADJUSTMENTS DEBIT	ADJUSTMENTS CREDIT	INCOME STATEMENT DEBIT	INCOME STATEMENT CREDIT	BALANCE SHEET DEBIT	BALANCE SHEET CREDIT	
5	Merchandise Inventory	140480 00			(d) 158400			126400		5
29	Sales		4951200				4951200			29
30	Sales Discount	25848				25848				30
31	Sales Returns and Allowances	312728				312728				31
32	Purchases	2099600				2099600				32
33	Purchases Discount		164815				164815			33
34	Purch. Returns and Allowances		348495				348495			34
35	Advertising Expense	360000				360000				35
36	Cash Short and Over	1925				1925				36
37	Credit Card Fee Expense	338500				338500				37
38	Depr. Exp.—Office Equipment			(f) 654000		654000				38
39	Depr. Exp.—Store Equipment			(g) 525000		525000				39
40	Insurance Expense			(c) 317000		317000				40
41	Miscellaneous Expense	256490				256490				41
42	Payroll Taxes Expense	910500				910500				42
43	Rent Expense	1800000				1800000				43
44	Salary Expense	1045 2500				1045 2500				44
45	Supplies Expense—Office			(a) 273000		273000				45
46	Supplies Expense—Store			(b) 291000		291000				46
47	Uncollectible Accounts Expense			(e) 124500		124500				47
48	Utilities Expense	382000				382000				48
49	Federal Income Tax Expense	1800000		(h) 588924		2388924				49
50		67086159	67086159	4357424	4357424	41993915	50025310	26984668	18953273	50
51	Net Income after Federal Income Tax					8031395			8031395	51
52						50025310	50025310	26984668	26984668	52

An income statement is used to report a business's financial progress. Merchandising businesses report revenue, cost of merchandise sold, gross profit on sales, expenses, and net income or loss. Current and previous income statements can be compared to determine the reasons for increases or decreases in net income. This comparison is helpful in making management decisions about future operations.

Information from a completed work sheet is used to prepare an income statement. Amounts in all revenue and expense accounts and **Merchandise Inventory** are reported on an income statement.

The income statement of a merchandising business has three main sections: (1) revenue section, (2) cost of merchandise sold section, and (3) expenses section.

REVENUE SECTION OF AN INCOME STATEMENT FOR A MERCHANDISING BUSINESS

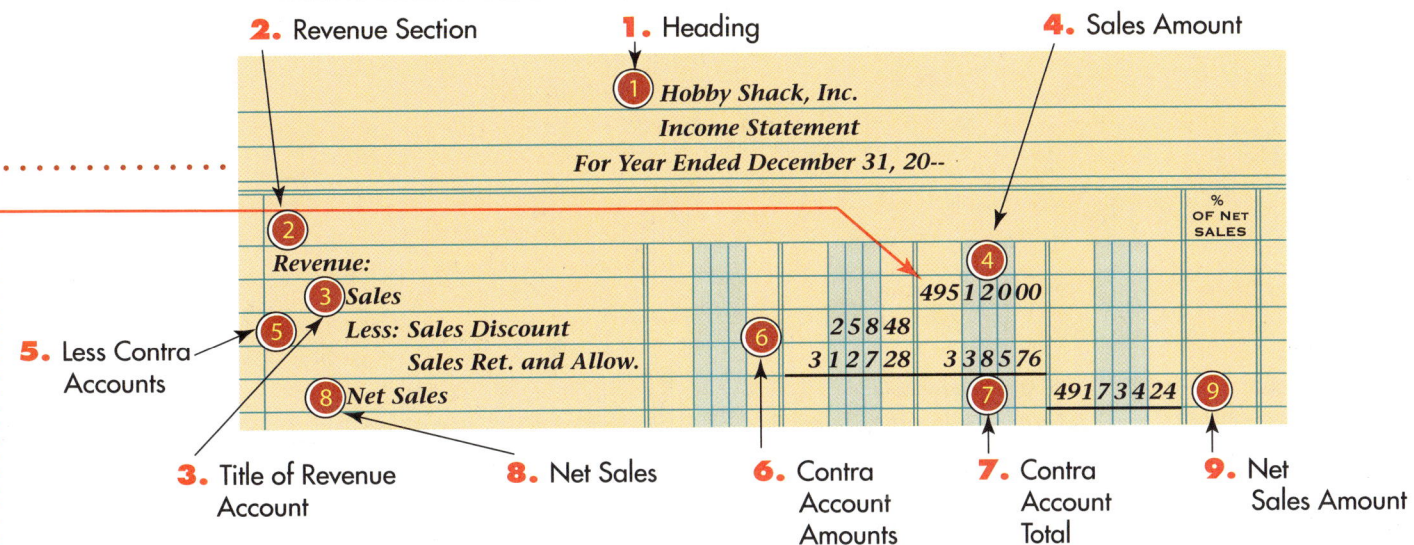

Hobby Shack's income statement differs from TechKnow's income statement shown in Part 1. Hobby Shack has more accounts to report on the income statement. The account Sales and its contra accounts, Sales Discount and Sales Returns and Allowances, are reported in the Revenue section. Total sales less sales discount and sales returns and allowances is called **net sales**.

STEPS — PREPARING THE REVENUE SECTION OF AN INCOME STATEMENT

1. Write the income statement heading on three lines.

2. Write the name of this section, *Revenue:*, at the extreme left of the wide column on the first line.

3. Write the title of the revenue account, *Sales*, on the next line, indented about one centimeter.

4. Write the balance of the sales account, $495,120.00, in the third amount column.

5. Write *Less:* on the next line, indented about one centimeter, followed by *Sales Discount* and *Sales Returns and Allowances* on the next line.

6. Write the balances of the sales discount account, $258.48, and sales returns and allowances account, $3,127.28, in the second amount column.

7. Add sales discounts, $258.48, and sales returns and allowances, $3,127.28, and write the amount, $3,385.76, in the third amount column.

8. Write *Net Sales* on the next line, indented about one centimeter.

9. Subtract the total of the contra accounts, $3,385.76, from sales, $495,120.00, to calculate net sales, $491,734.24. Write this amount in the fourth amount column.

Preparing an Income Statement   Lesson 15-1   449

COST OF MERCHANDISE SOLD SECTION OF AN INCOME STATEMENT FOR A MERCHANDISING BUSINESS

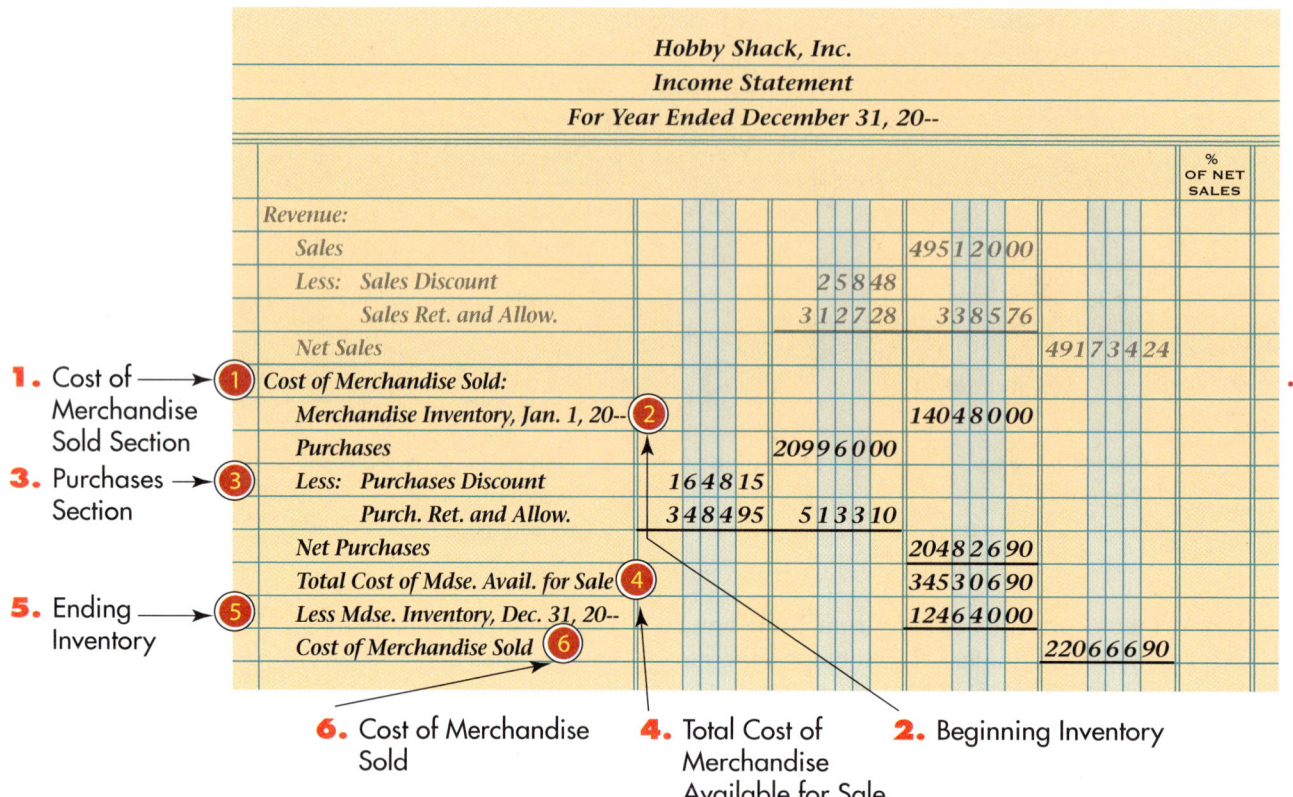

6. Cost of Merchandise Sold
4. Total Cost of Merchandise Available for Sale
2. Beginning Inventory

The original price of all merchandise sold during a fiscal period is called the **cost of merchandise sold**. [CONCEPT: Historical Cost] Cost of merchandise sold is also known as *cost of goods sold* or *cost of sales*.

STEPS — PREPARING THE COST OF MERCHANDISE SOLD SECTION OF AN INCOME STATEMENT

1. Write the name of this section, *Cost of Merchandise Sold:*, at the extreme left of the wide column.

2. Write the beginning inventory found in the Trial Balance Debit column of the work sheet.
   a. Indent about one centimeter on the next line and write *Merchandise Inventory, Jan. 1, 20--*.
   b. Write the beginning merchandise inventory balance, $140,480.00, in the third amount column.

3. Prepare the Purchases section.
   a. Indent about one centimeter on the next line and write *Purchases*. Enter the purchases amount, $209,960.00, in the second amount column.
   b. Write *Less:* on the next line, indented about one centimeter, followed by *Purchases Discount* and *Purchases Returns and Allowances* on the next line. It is permissible to abbreviate long titles when necessary.
   c. Write the balances of the purchases discount account, $1,648.15, and purchases returns and allowances account, $3,484.95, in the first amount column.
   d. Add purchases discounts, $1,648.15, and purchases returns and allowances, $3,484.95, and write the amount, $5,133.10, in the second amount column.
   e. Write *Net Purchases* on the next line, indented about one centimeter.
   f. Subtract the total of the contra accounts, $5,133.10, from purchases, $209,960.00, to calculate net purchases, $204,826.90. Write this amount in the third amount column.

450 Chapter 15   Financial Statements for a Corporation

④ Calculate the total cost of merchandise available for sale.
   a. Indent about one centimeter on the next line, and write *Total Cost of Merchandise Available for Sale*.
   b. Add the beginning merchandise inventory balance, *$140,480.00*, and net purchases, *$204,826.90*, to calculate the total cost of merchandise available for sale, *$345,306.90*. Write this amount in the third amount column.

⑤ Write the ending inventory found in the Balance Sheet Debit column of the work sheet.
   a. Indent about one centimeter on the next line, and write *Less Merchandise Inventory, Dec. 31, 20--*.
   b. Write the ending merchandise inventory balance, *$124,640.00*, found in the Balance Sheet Debit column of the work sheet, in the third amount column.

⑥ Calculate the cost of merchandise sold.
   a. Indent about one centimeter on the next line, and write *Cost of Merchandise Sold*.
   b. Subtract the ending merchandise inventory balance, *$124,640.00*, from the total cost of merchandise available for sale, *$345,306.90*, to calculate the cost of merchandise sold, *$220,666.90*. Write the amount in the fourth amount column.

Most calculated amounts reported on a financial statement have a related description. Net sales and net purchases are two examples. However, the totals of the sales contra accounts, $3,385.76, and the purchases contra accounts, $5,133.10, are not described. Instead, the reader of the financial statement is expected to understand the amount by its physical position on the statement. Each amount is immediately to the right of an amount column ruled with a single line.

The single ruled line indicates that the column is being totaled. The amount adjacent to the column is the sum of that column.

				% OF NET SALES
Hobby Shack, Inc.				
Income Statement				
For Year Ended December 31, 20--				
Revenue:				
Sales			49512000	
Less: Sales Discount		25848		
Sales Ret. and Allow.		312728	338576	
Net Sales				49173424

Total of adjacent column

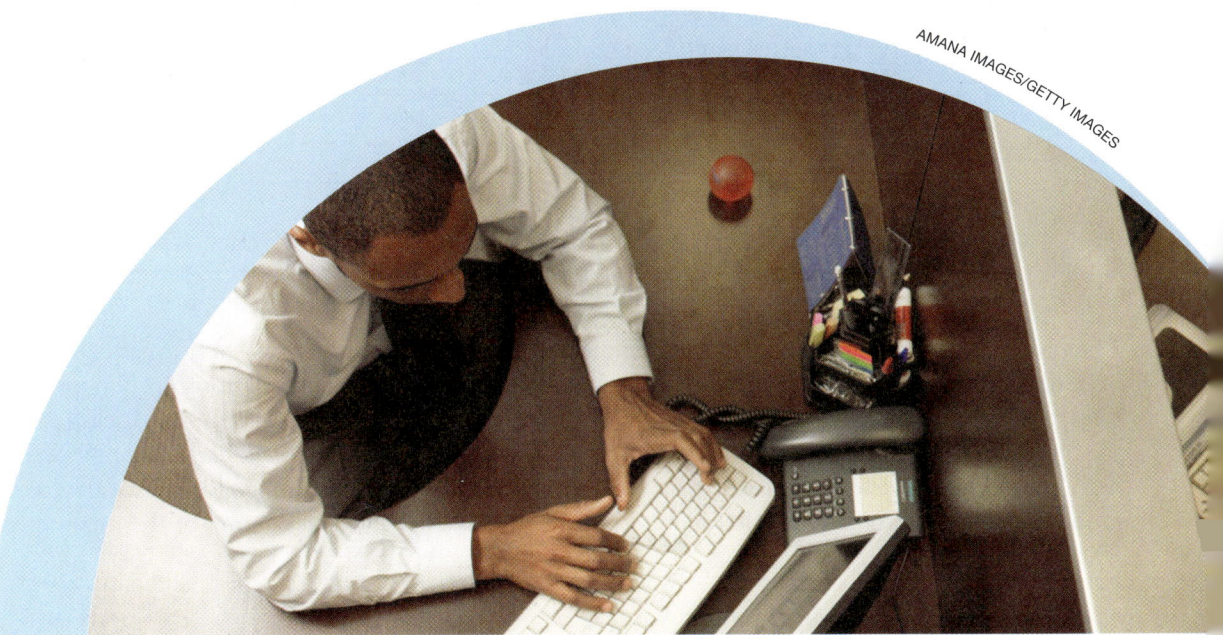

Preparing an Income Statement

COMPLETING AN INCOME STATEMENT FOR A MERCHANDISING BUSINESS

Hobby Shack, Inc.
Income Statement
For Year Ended December 31, 20--

				% NET OF SALES
Revenue:				
Sales			4951 20 00	
Less: Sales Discount		2 58 48		
Sales Ret. and Allow.		3 127 28	3 385 76	
Net Sales			4917 34 24	100.0
Cost of Merchandise Sold:				
Merchandise Inventory, Jan. 1, 20--			140 480 00	
Purchases		2099 60 00		
Less: Purchases Discount	1 648 15			
Purch. Ret. and Allow.	3 484 95	5 133 10		
Net Purchases			2048 26 90	
Total Cost of Mdse. Avail. for Sale			3453 06 90	
Less Mdse. Inventory, Dec. 31, 20--			1246 40 00	
Cost of Merchandise Sold			2206 66 90	44.9
Gross Profit on Sales			2710 67 34	55.1
Expenses:				
Advertising Expense		36 000 00		
Cash Short and Over		19 25		
Credit Card Fee Expense		3 385 00		
Depr. Exp.—Office Equipment		6 540 00		
Depr. Exp.—Store Equipment		5 250 00		
Insurance Expense		3 170 00		
Miscellaneous Expense		2 564 90		
Payroll Taxes Expense		9 105 00		
Rent Expense		18 000 00		
Salary Expense		104 525 00		
Supplies Expense—Office		2 730 00		
Supplies Expense—Store		2 910 00		
Uncollectible Accounts Expense		1 245 00		
Utilities Expense		3 820 00		
Total Expenses			1668 64 15	33.9
Net Income before Federal Income Tax			1042 03 19	21.2
Less Federal Income Tax Expense			238 89 24	
Net Income after Federal Income Tax			803 13 95	

1. Gross Profit on Sales
2. Expenses Section
3. Net Income before Federal Income Tax
4. Less Federal Income Tax Expense
5. Net Income after Federal Income Tax
6. Double Lines
7. Component Percentage

The revenue remaining after cost of merchandise sold has been deducted is called **gross profit on sales**. Management uses gross profit on sales as a measure for how effectively the business is performing in its primary functions of buying and selling merchandise. Calculating a ratio between gross profit on sales and net sales enables management to compare its performance to prior fiscal periods. The percentage relationship between one financial statement item and the total that includes that item is known as a *component percentage*. Hobby Shack calculates a component percentage for most calculated amounts reported in the fourth column of the income statement.

452   Chapter 15   Financial Statements for a Corporation

STEPS COMPLETING AN INCOME STATEMENT

1. Calculate the gross profit on sales.
   a. Write *Gross Profit on Sales* on the next line at the extreme left of the wide column.
   b. Write the gross profit on sales amount, $271,067.34, in the second amount column. (Total revenue, $491,734.24, less cost of merchandise sold, $220,666.90, equals gross profit on sales, $271,067.34.)

2. Prepare the expenses section. Use the information from the Income Statement Debit column of the work sheet.
   a. Write the name of this section, *Expenses:*, at the extreme left of the wide column.
   b. On the next line, indented about one centimeter, list the expense account titles, one per line, in the order in which they appear on the work sheet.
   c. Write the amount of each expense account balance in the third amount column.
   d. Indent about one centimeter, and write Total Expenses on the next line in the wide column below the last expense account title.
   e. Total the individual expense amounts and write the total, $166,864.15, in the fourth amount column on the total line.

3. Calculate the net income before federal income tax.
   a. Write *Net Income before Federal Income Tax* on the next line at the extreme left of the wide column.
   b. Write the amount, $104,203.19, in the fourth amount column. (Gross profit on sales, $271,067.34, less total expenses, $166,864.15, equals net income before federal income tax, $104,203.19.)

4. Write *Less Federal Income Tax Expense* on the next line at the extreme left of the wide column. Write the amount, $23,889.24, on the same line in the fourth amount column.

5. Calculate net income after federal income tax.
   a. Write *Net Income after Federal Income Tax* on the next line at the extreme left of the wide column.
   b. Write the amount, $80,313.95, in the fourth amount column. (Net income before federal income tax, $104,203.19, less federal income tax expense, $23,889.24, equals net income after federal income tax, $80,313.95.)
   c. Verify accuracy by comparing the amount of net income after federal income tax calculated on the income statement, $80,313.95, with the amount on the work sheet, $80,313.95. The two amounts must be the same.

6. Rule double lines across the four amount columns to show that the income statement has been verified as correct.

7. Calculate a component percentage for each amount in the fourth amount column through the Net Income before Federal Income Tax. Divide the amount of each component by the amount of net sales. Round each component percentage to the nearest 0.1%. Write the component percentage in the % of Net Sales column.

Income Statement Component	Amount	÷	Net Sales	=	Component Percentage
Cost of Merchandise Sold	$220,666.90	÷	$491,734.24	=	44.9%
Gross Profit on Sales	$271,067.34	÷	$491,734.24	=	55.1%
Total Expenses	$166,864.15	÷	$491,734.24	=	33.9%
Net Income before Federal Income Tax	$104,203.19	÷	$491,734.24	=	21.2%

End of Lesson REVIEW

AUDIT YOUR UNDERSTANDING

1. What is the major difference between the income statement for a merchandising business and a service business?
2. How is the cost of merchandise sold calculated?
3. How can the amount of net income calculated on the income statement be verified?

TERMS REVIEW

net sales
cost of merchandise sold
gross profit on sales

WORK TOGETHER 15-1

Preparing an income statement for a merchandising business

The work sheet for Interstate Tires, Inc., for the year ended December 31 of the current year is given in the *Working Papers*. Your instructor will guide you through the following examples.

1. Prepare an income statement.
2. Calculate and record on the income statement the following component percentages: (a) cost of merchandise sold, (b) gross profit on sales, (c) total expenses, and (d) net income before federal income tax. Round percentage calculations to the nearest 0.1%. Save your work to complete Work Together 15-2.

ON YOUR OWN 15-1

Preparing an income statement for a merchandising business

Osborn Corporation's work sheet for the year ended December 31 of the current year is given in the *Working Papers*. Work this problem independently.

1. Prepare an income statement.
2. Calculate and record on the income statement the following component percentages: (a) cost of merchandise sold, (b) gross profit on sales, (c) total expenses, and (d) net income before federal income tax. Round percentage calculations to the nearest 0.1%. Save your work to complete On Your Own 15-2.

LESSON 15-2

Analyzing an Income Statement

USING COMPONENT PERCENTAGES

A percentage relationship between one financial statement item and the total that includes that item is known as a *component percentage*. For Hobby Shack, a merchandising business, every sales dollar reported on the income statement includes four components: (1) cost of merchandise sold, (2) gross profit on sales, (3) total expenses, and (4) net income before income tax. To help make decisions about future operations, Hobby Shack analyzes relationships between these four income statement components and sales. Hobby Shack calculates a component percentage for each of the four components. The relationship between each component and sales is shown in a separate column on the income statement.

Acceptable Component Percentages

	Acceptable Industry Standards	Hobby Shack Component Percentages
Sales	100%	100%
Cost of merchandise sold	not more than 46.0%	44.9%
Gross profit on sales	not less than 54.0%	55.1%
Total expenses	not more than 35.0%	33.9%
Net income before federal income tax	not less than 19.0%	21.2%

For a component percentage to be useful, a business must know acceptable percentages. This information is determined by making comparisons with prior fiscal periods as well as with industry standards published by industry organizations. Based on these sources, Hobby Shack determines acceptable component percentages for the current fiscal period. Each percentage represents the amount of each sales dollar that is considered acceptable. For example, Hobby Shack determines that the cost of merchandise sold should be no more than 46.0%, or 46 cents, of each sales dollar.

FOR YOUR INFORMATION

FYI

Unacceptable component percentages serve as a warning that management action is necessary. Calculating and reporting component percentages is an example of how accounting information can help management planning and decision making. Effective managers rely on the information provided from accounting records.

ANALYSIS OF COMPONENT PERCENTAGES

Hobby Shack compares four of its component percentages to its acceptable component percentages. The four component percentages are for cost of merchandise sold, gross profit on sales, total expenses, and net income before federal income tax.

Cost of Merchandise Sold Component Percentage

The cost of merchandise sold is a major cost and must be kept as low as possible. Analysis of Hobby Shack's component percentages shows that the cost of merchandise sold is 44.9% of sales.

The component percentage for cost of merchandise sold, *44.9%*, is less than the maximum acceptable percentage, *46.0%*. Therefore, Hobby Shack's component percentage for cost of merchandise sold is considered acceptable.

Gross Profit on Sales Component Percentage

Gross profit must be large enough to cover total expenses and the desired amount of net income. Acceptable industry standards show that at least 54 cents, or 54.0%, of each sales dollar should result in gross profit. Hobby Shack's component percentage for gross profit on sales is 55.1%.

The component percentage for gross profit on sales, *55.1%*, is not less than the minimum acceptable percentage, *54.0%*. Therefore, Hobby Shack's component percentage for gross profit on sales is considered acceptable.

Total Expenses Component Percentage

Total expenses must be less than gross profit on sales to provide a desirable net income. Acceptable industry standards show that no more than 35 cents, or 35.0%, of each sales dollar should be devoted to total expenses. Hobby Shack's component percentage for total expenses is 33.9%.

The component percentage for total expenses, *33.9%*, is not more than the maximum acceptable percentage, *35.0%*. Therefore, Hobby Shack's component percentage for total expenses is considered acceptable.

Net Income before Federal Income Tax Component Percentage

The component percentage for net income before federal income tax shows the progress being made by a business. Acceptable industry standards show that at least 19 cents, or 19.0%, of each sales dollar should result in net income. Hobby Shack's component percentage for net income is 21.25%.

The component percentage for net income, *21.2%*, is not less than the minimum acceptable percentage, *19.0%*. Therefore, Hobby Shack's component percentage for net income is considered acceptable.

REMEMBER

The cost of merchandise sold and total expenses reduce owner's equity. For this reason, a business wants actual component percentages of these financial statement totals to be less than the acceptable component percentage. A business wants the gross profit on sales and net income before federal income tax to be as high as possible. Thus, a business wants the actual component percentage for these financial statement totals to be higher than the acceptable component percentages.

ANALYZING AN INCOME STATEMENT SHOWING A NET LOSS

Cloth Circuit
Income Statement
For Year Ended December 31, 20--

				% OF NET SALES
Revenue:				
Sales			848,184.10	
Cost of Merchandise Sold			485,763.95	58.0
Gross Profit on Sales			351,956.98	42.0
Expenses:				
Advertising Expense		32,550.00		
Credit Card Fee Expense		5,118.20		
Utilities Expense		5,184.00		
Total Expenses			393,726.94	47.0
Net Loss before Federal Income Tax			(41,769.96)	(5.0)
Plus Federal Income Tax Benefit			6,265.49	
Net Loss after Federal Income Tax			(35,504.47)	

When a business's total expenses are greater than the gross profit on sales, the difference is known as a *net loss*. Cloth Circuit's total expenses, $393,726.94, less gross profit on sales, $351,956.98, equals net loss before federal income taxes, $41,769.96. The net loss before federal income taxes, $41,769.96, is written in parentheses in the fourth amount column on the line with the words *Net Loss before Federal Income Taxes*. An amount written in parentheses on a financial statement indicates a negative amount.

Cloth Circuit's managers can compare its component percentages to acceptable component percentages. The component percentage for cost of merchandise sold, *58.0%*, is less than Cloth Circuit's maximum acceptable component percentage, *60.0%*. The component percentage for gross profit on sales, *42.0%*, is greater than the minimum acceptable component percentage, *40.0%*. These component percentages indicate that management is doing a good job controlling the cost of merchandise inventory.

The component percentage for total expenses, *47.0%*, is more than the maximum acceptable component percentage, *37.0%*. Because a net loss occurred, the component percentage for net income before federal income tax, *(5.0%)*, means that Cloth Circuit lost 5.0 cents on each sales dollar. These component percentages indicate that management is not effective in controlling its expenses.

To return to profitability, management must take action to reduce its expenses. Advertising and salary expense are the two largest expenses that management could quickly control. Rent expense, although one of the three largest expenses, is more difficult to control in the short term since most lease agreements are signed for a year or more.

FOR YOUR INFORMATION

FYI

A corporation having a net loss before federal income taxes can file for a tax refund from the federal government. To qualify for this benefit, the corporation must have paid at least an equal amount of federal income taxes in the previous three years. Cloth Circuit calculates its tax refund using the same tax schedule Hobby Shack used to calculate its federal income tax expense. Cloth Circuit's tax benefit, $6,265.49, is shown as a positive amount, thus reducing the amount of the net loss to $35,504.47.

ACTIONS TO CORRECT UNACCEPTABLE COMPONENT PERCENTAGES

The goal of any business is to earn an acceptable net income. When component percentages are not acceptable, regardless of whether a net income or net loss occurred, management action is necessary.

Unacceptable Component Percentage for Gross Profit on Sales

The component percentage for gross profit on sales is directly related to sales revenue and cost of merchandise sold. An unacceptable component percentage for gross profit on sales requires one of three actions: (1) increase sales revenue, (2) decrease cost of merchandise sold, or (3) increase sales revenue and also decrease cost of merchandise sold.

Increasing sales revenue while keeping the cost of merchandise sold the same will increase gross profit on sales. To increase sales revenue, management may consider increasing the markup on merchandise purchased for sale. However, a business must be cautious on the amount of the markup increase. If the increase in markup is too large, a decrease in sales revenue could occur for two reasons: (1) the sales price is beyond what customers are willing to pay or (2) the sales price is higher than what competing businesses charge for the same merchandise.

Decreasing the cost of merchandise sold while keeping the sales revenue the same will also increase gross profit on sales. To decrease cost of merchandise sold, management should review purchasing practices. For example, would purchasing merchandise in larger quantities or from other vendors result in a lower cost?

Combining a small increase in sales revenue and a small decrease in the cost of merchandise sold may also result in an acceptable component percentage for gross profit on sales.

Unacceptable Component Percentage for Total Expenses

Each expense account balance must be reviewed to determine if major increases have occurred. This review should include comparisons with prior fiscal periods as well as with industry standards. Actions must then be taken to reduce any expenses for which major increases have occurred or that are beyond industry standards.

Unacceptable Component Percentage for Net Income before Federal Income Tax

If the component percentages for cost of merchandise sold, gross profit on sales, and total expenses are brought within acceptable ranges, net income before federal income tax will also be acceptable.

FOR YOUR INFORMATION

F Y I

Net income after federal income tax is typically referred to as net income.

DIGITAL VISION/GETTY IMAGES

FINANCIAL RATIOS

Individual amounts reported on an income statement have little meaning without being compared to another amount. Suppose a company has net income before federal income taxes of $1,000,000.00. Is the company successful? Only by calculating the net income before federal income taxes component percentage could this question begin to be answered.

Comparisons between other financial items can also provide valuable information about the financial performance of a business. A comparison between two items of financial information is called a **financial ratio**. Most financial ratios include at least one amount reported on the financial statements.

Earnings per Share

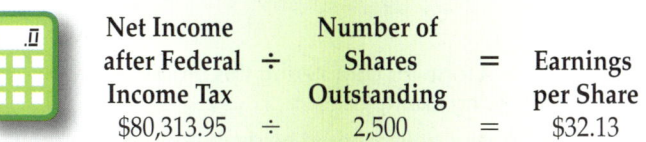

The amount of net income after federal income tax belonging to a single share of stock is called **earnings per share**. The ratio is calculated by dividing net income after federal income taxes by the number of shares outstanding.

Earnings per share is one of the most widely recognized measures of a corporation's financial performance. The financial ratio is often referred to as *EPS*. Unlike component percentages, earnings per share cannot be compared to industry standards. Instead, earnings per share is compared to (1) prior year's earnings per share or (2) the market price of the stock.

Price-Earnings Ratio

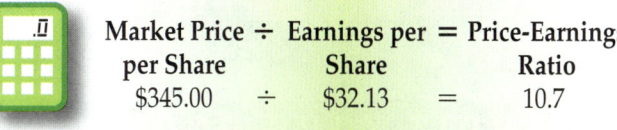

The relationship between the market value per share and earnings per share of a stock is called the **price-earnings ratio**. The ratio is calculated as the market price per share divided by the earnings per share as determined by the stock markets. The ratio is often referred to as the *P-E ratio*.

The price-earnings ratio provides investors with information concerning the price of the stock relative to the earnings. Low price-earnings ratios are typically associated with slow growth companies, such as public utilities. Companies expected to have dynamic growth in future earnings typically have a high price-earnings ratio.

Online sources of financial information highlight the earnings per share and price-earnings ratio over several years. Investors can analyze the trends in the earnings per share to project future earnings of the company. Then, using historical price-earnings ratios, investors can predict future market prices of the company's stock.

FOR YOUR INFORMATION

FYI

Some financial ratios are unique to companies in a particular industry. For example, a critical financial ratio for the airline industry is revenue per passenger mile, calculated as sales divided by total passenger miles. Managers of airline companies rely on this ratio to measure how effectively the airline is pricing its tickets.

End of Lesson REVIEW

AUDIT YOUR UNDERSTANDING

1. For a merchandising business, every sales dollar includes what four components?
2. How does a company determine acceptable component percentages?
3. What is the result if total expenses are greater than gross profit on sales?

TERMS REVIEW

financial ratio
earnings per share
price-earnings ratio

WORK TOGETHER 15-2

Analyzing an income statement

Use the income statement for Interstate Tires, Inc., from Work Together 15-1. A form for completing this problem is given in the *Working Papers*. Your instructor will guide you through the following examples.

1. Interstate Tires determines that no more than 53 cents, or 53.0%, of each sales dollar should be devoted to cost of merchandise sold. Compare the actual component percentage for cost of merchandise sold to the acceptable percentage. Indicate if the actual component percentage is acceptable or unacceptable. If it is unacceptable, suggest an action that corrects it.
2. Acceptable auto parts industry standards show that at least 47 cents, or 47.0%, of each sales dollar should result in gross profit. For Interstate Tires, compare the actual component percentage for gross profit on sales to the acceptable percentage. Indicate if the actual component percentage is acceptable or unacceptable. If it is unacceptable, suggest an action that corrects it.
3. Interstate Tires currently has 110,000 of shares outstanding with a market price of $13.75 per share. Calculate the earnings per share and price-earnings ratio.

ON YOUR OWN 15-2

Analyzing an income statement

Use the income statement for Osborn Corporation from On Your Own 15-1. A form for completing this problem is given in the *Working Papers*. Work this problem independently.

1. Acceptable game industry standards show that no more than 30 cents, or 30.0%, of each sales dollar should be devoted to total expenses. For Osborn Corporation, compare the actual component percentage for total expenses to the acceptable percentage. Indicate if the actual component percentage is acceptable or unacceptable. If it is unacceptable, suggest an action that corrects it.
2. Acceptable game industry standards show that at least 15 cents, or 15.0%, of each sales dollar should result in net income before federal income tax. For Osborn Corporation, compare the actual component percentage for net income before federal income tax to the acceptable percentage. Indicate if the actual component percentage is acceptable or unacceptable. If it is unacceptable, suggest an action that corrects it.
3. Osborn Corporation currently has 8,000 shares outstanding with a market price of $104.50 per share. Calculate the earnings per share and price-earnings ratio.

LESSON 15-3: Preparing a Statement of Stockholders' Equity

CAPITAL STOCK SECTION OF THE STATEMENT OF STOCKHOLDERS' EQUITY

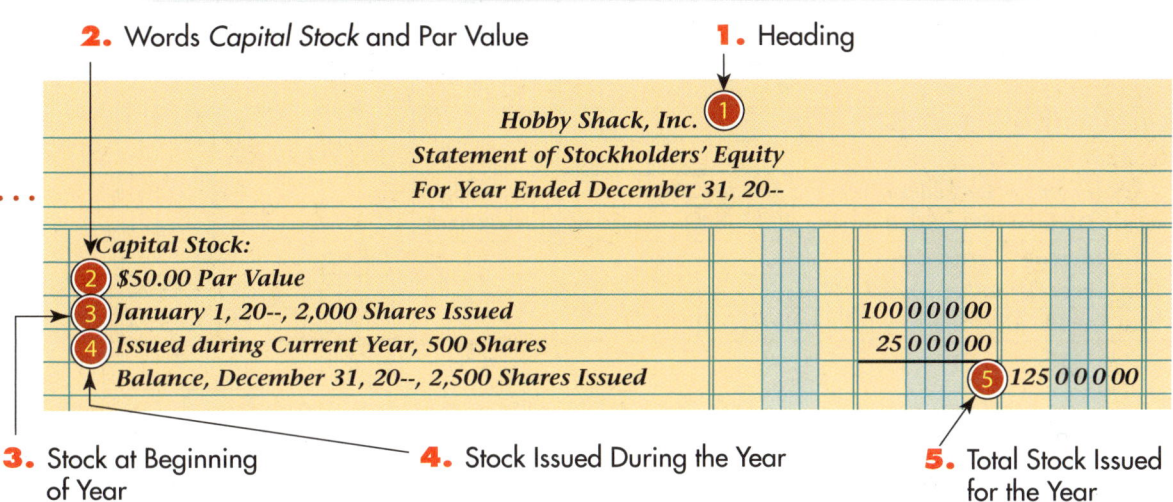

1. Heading
2. Words *Capital Stock* and Par Value
3. Stock at Beginning of Year
4. Stock Issued During the Year
5. Total Stock Issued for the Year

A financial statement that shows changes in a corporation's ownership for a fiscal period is called a **statement of stockholders' equity**. A statement of stockholders' equity contains two major sections: (1) capital stock and (2) retained earnings.

The amount of capital stock issued as of the beginning of the year is the beginning balance of the capital stock account. Any additional stock transactions recorded in the general ledger during the fiscal year would be added to calculate the amount of stock issued during the fiscal year. Thus, the amounts in the capital stock section of the statement of stockholders' equity are obtained from the general ledger account, Capital Stock.

Each share of stock issued by a corporation has a monetary value. A value assigned to a share of stock and printed on the stock certificate is called **par value**.

STEPS PREPARING THE CAPITAL STOCK SECTION OF A STATEMENT OF STOCKHOLDERS' EQUITY

1. Write the heading: company name, *Hobby Shack, Inc.*; statement name, *Statement of Stockholders' Equity*; and fiscal period, *For Year Ended December 31, 20--*, in the statement heading.

2. Write the heading *Capital Stock:* and on the next line write the par value of the stock, *$50.00 Par Value*, indented about 1 centimeter.

3. Write the number of shares, *2,000*, and dollar amount, *$100,000.00*, of stock issued as of the beginning of the year.

4. Write the number of shares, *500*, and dollar amount, *$25,000.00*, of stock issued during the year.

5. Calculate the total dollar amount of stock issued as of the end of the year, *$125,000.00*, by adding the dollar amount of beginning stock, *$100,000.00*, and the dollar amount of shares issued during the year, *$25,000.00*.

RETAINED EARNINGS SECTION OF THE STATEMENT OF STOCKHOLDERS' EQUITY

Net income increases a corporation's total capital. Some income may be retained by a corporation for business expansion. Some income may be distributed as dividends to provide stockholders with a return on their investments. During the year, Hobby Shack's board of directors declared $20,000.00 in dividends.

Amounts used to prepare the statement of stockholders' equity are obtained from the income statement and balance sheet columns of the work sheet shown in Chapter 14.

STEPS — PREPARING THE RETAINED EARNINGS SECTION OF A STATEMENT OF STOCKHOLDERS' EQUITY

1. Write the heading *Retained Earnings*.

2. Write the beginning balance of Retained Earnings, $10,761.29, from the Balance Sheet Credit column, indented about 1 centimeter.

3. Write the net income after federal income tax, $80,313.95, from the Income Statement Debit column.

4. Write the amount of dividends, $20,000.00, from the Balance Sheet Debit column.

5. Subtract dividends, $20,000.00, from net income after federal income tax, $80,313.95, to calculate the increase in retained earnings, $60,313.95.

6. Add the beginning balance of retained earnings, $10,761.29, and the increase in retained earnings, $60,313.95, to calculate the ending balance of retained earnings, $71,075.24.

7. Add the ending amounts of capital stock, $125,000.00, and retained earnings, $71,075.24, to calculate the total amount of stockholders' equity, $196,075.24.

462 • Chapter 15 Financial Statements for a Corporation

End of Lesson REVIEW

AUDIT YOUR UNDERSTANDING

1. What financial information does a statement of stockholders' equity report?
2. What are the two major sections of a statement of stockholders' equity?
3. Where is the information found to prepare the capital stock section of a statement of stockholders' equity?
4. Where is the beginning balance of retained earnings found?
5. How does a corporation distribute a portion of income to stockholders?
6. Where is the amount of dividends found?

TERMS REVIEW

statement of stockholders' equity
par value

WORK TOGETHER 15-3

Preparing a statement of stockholders' equity

Use the work sheet and income statement for Interstate Tires, Inc., from Work Together 15-2. A form for the statement of stockholders' equity is given in the *Working Papers*. Your instructor will guide you through the following example.

1. Prepare a statement of stockholders' equity for the current year. As of January 1, Interstate Tires, Inc., had issued 100,000 shares of capital stock with a par value of $1.00 per share. During the fiscal year, the corporation issued 10,000 additional shares of capital stock. Save your work to complete Work Together 15-4.

ON YOUR OWN 15-3

Preparing a statement of stockholders' equity

Use the work sheet and income statement for Osborn Corporation from On Your Own 15-2. A form for the statement of stockholders' equity is given in the *Working Papers*. Work this problem independently.

1. Prepare a statement of stockholders' equity for the current year. As of January 1, Osborn Corporation had issued 7,500 shares of capital stock with a par value of $25.00 per share. During the fiscal year, the corporation issued 500 additional shares of stock. Save your work to complete On Your Own 15-4.

LESSON 15-4

Preparing a Balance Sheet

BALANCE SHEET INFORMATION ON A WORK SHEET

Hobby Shack, Inc.
Work Sheet
For Year Ended December 31, 20--

	ACCOUNT TITLE	TRIAL BALANCE DEBIT	TRIAL BALANCE CREDIT	ADJUSTMENTS DEBIT	ADJUSTMENTS CREDIT	INCOME STATEMENT DEBIT	INCOME STATEMENT CREDIT	BALANCE SHEET DEBIT	BALANCE SHEET CREDIT	
1	Cash	29080 28						29080 28		1
2	Petty Cash	300 00						300 00		2
3	Accounts Receivable	14698 40						14698 40		3
4	Allow. for Uncoll. Accts.		127 52		(e) 1245 00				1372 52	4
5	Merchandise Inventory	140480 00			(d) 15840 00			124640 00		5
6	Supplies—Office	3480 00			(a) 2730 00			750 00		6
7	Supplies—Store	3944 00			(b) 2910 00			1034 00		7
8	Prepaid Insurance	5800 00			(c) 3170 00			2630 00		8
9	Office Equipment	35864 50						35864 50		9
10	Acc. Depr.—Office Equipment		6497 00		(f) 6540 00				13037 00	10
11	Store Equipment	40849 50						40849 50		11
12	Acc. Depr.—Store Equipment		5069 00		(g) 5250 00				10319 00	12
13	Accounts Payable		11583 03						11583 03	13
14	Federal Income Tax Payable				(h) 5889 24				5889 24	14
15	Employee Income Tax Payable		757 00						757 00	15
16	Social Security Tax Payable		1451 38						1451 38	16
17	Medicare Tax Payable		399 42						399 42	17
18	Sales Tax Payable		2556 70						2556 70	18
19	Unemployment Tax Payable—Federal		34 60						34 60	19
20	Unemployment Tax Payable—State		233 55						233 55	20
21	Health Insurance Premiums Payable		1008 00						1008 00	21
22	U.S. Savings Bonds Payable		60 00						60 00	22
23	United Way Donations Payable		70 00						70 00	23
24	Dividends Payable		5000 00						5000 00	24

A corporation's balance sheet reports assets, liabilities, and stockholders' equity on a specific date. [CONCEPT: Accounting Period Cycle] Some management decisions can best be made after owners have analyzed the balance sheet. For example, balance sheet information would enable management to determine whether the corporation should incur additional liabilities to acquire additional plant assets.

The information used to prepare a balance sheet is obtained from two sources: (1) the Balance Sheet columns of a work sheet and (2) the owners' equity statement.

Procedures for preparing Hobby Shack's balance sheet are similar to those used by TechKnow in Part 1. A balance sheet may be prepared in account form or report form. As described in Chapter 7, TechKnow uses the account form. Hobby Shack uses the report form.

CURRENT ASSETS SECTION OF A BALANCE SHEET

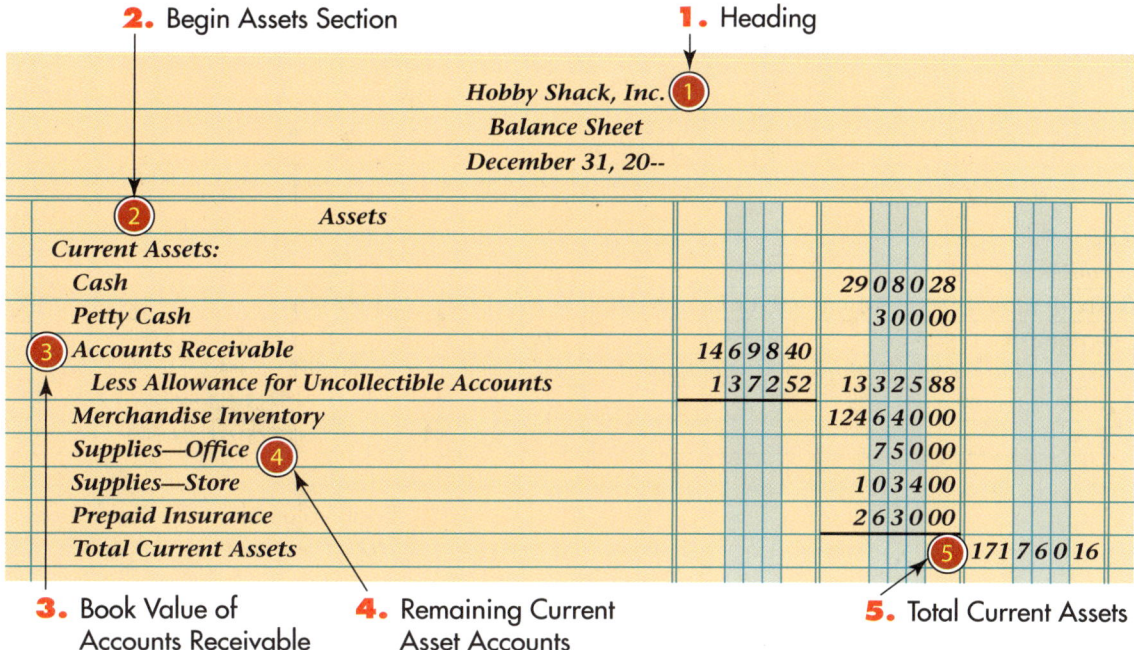

1. Heading
2. Begin Assets Section
3. Book Value of Accounts Receivable
4. Remaining Current Asset Accounts
5. Total Current Assets

Hobby Shack classifies its assets as current assets and plant assets. A business owning both current and plant assets usually lists them under separate headings on a balance sheet. Some of Hobby Shack's asset accounts have related contra accounts that reduce the related account on the balance sheet. The difference between an asset's account balance and its related contra account balance is known as *book value*. An asset's book value is reported on a balance sheet by listing three amounts: (1) the balance of the asset account, (2) the balance of the asset's contra account, and (3) the book value.

STEPS PREPARING THE CURRENT ASSETS SECTION OF A BALANCE SHEET

 Write the balance sheet heading on three lines.

 Begin preparing the assets section of the balance sheet. Use information from the work sheet.
  a. Write the section title, *Assets*, on the first line in the middle of the wide column.
  b. Write the section title, *Current Assets:*, on the next line at the extreme left of the wide column.
  c. Beginning on the next line, indented about one centimeter, write the *Cash* and *Petty Cash* account titles in the order in which they appear on the work sheet.
  d. Write the balance of each asset account in the second column.

 Calculate the book value of accounts receivable.
  a. Write *Accounts Receivable* on the next line, indented about one centimeter.
  b. Write the total amount of accounts receivable, $14,698.40, in the first amount column.
  c. Write *Less Allowance for Uncollectible Accounts* on the next line, indented about two centimeters.
  d. Write the amount of the allowance for uncollectible accounts, $1,372.52, in the first amount column.
  e. Subtract the allowance for uncollectible accounts, $1,372.52, from the total amount of accounts receivable, $14,698.40, to calculate the book value of accounts receivable, $13,325.88. Write the amount in the second amount column on the same line.

④ Write the remaining current asset account titles and amounts.

 Calculate total current assets.
  a. Write *Total Current Assets* on the next line, indented about one centimeter.
  b. Add the amounts in the second amount column and write the total, $171,760.16, in the third amount column.

Preparing a Balance Sheet

PLANT ASSETS SECTION OF A BALANCE SHEET

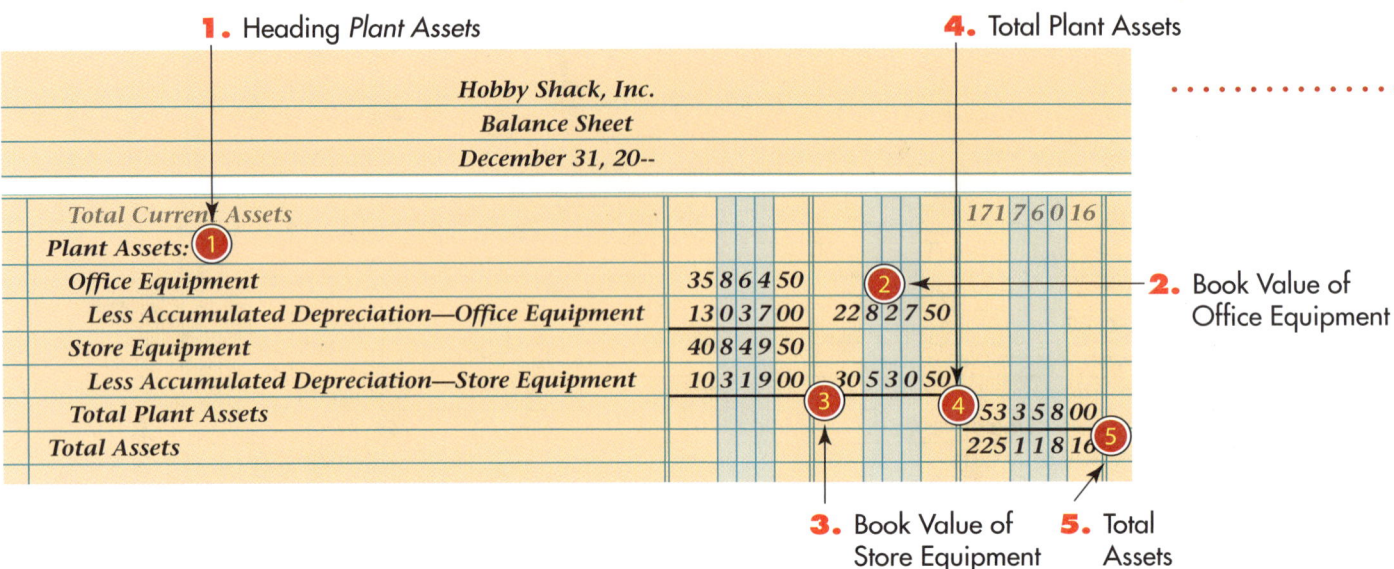

STEPS — PREPARING THE PLANT ASSETS SECTION OF A BALANCE SHEET

1. Write the heading *Plant Assets* on the next line at the extreme left of the wide column.

2. Calculate the book value of office equipment using information from the work sheet.
   a. Write *Office Equipment* on the next line, indented about one centimeter.
   b. Write the total amount of office equipment, *$35,864.50*, in the first amount column.
   c. Write *Less Accumulated Depreciation—Office Equipment* on the next line, indented about two centimeters.
   d. Write the amount of the accumulated depreciation—office equipment, *$13,037.00*, in the first amount column.
   e. Subtract the accumulated depreciation—office equipment, *$13,037.00*, from the total amount of office equipment, *$35,864.50*, to calculate the book value of office equipment, *$22,827.50*. Write the amount in the second amount column on the same line.

3. Use the same procedure to calculate the book value of store equipment.

4. Calculate total plant assets.
   a. Write *Total Plant Assets* on the next line, indented about one centimeter.
   b. Add the amounts in the second amount column and write the total, *$53,358.00*, in the third amount column.

5. Calculate total assets.
   a. Write *Total Assets* on the next line at the extreme left of the wide column.
   b. Add the current and plant asset totals and write the amount, *$225,118.16*, on the same line in the third amount column.

STOCKBYTE/GETTY IMAGES

LIABILITIES SECTION OF A BALANCE SHEET

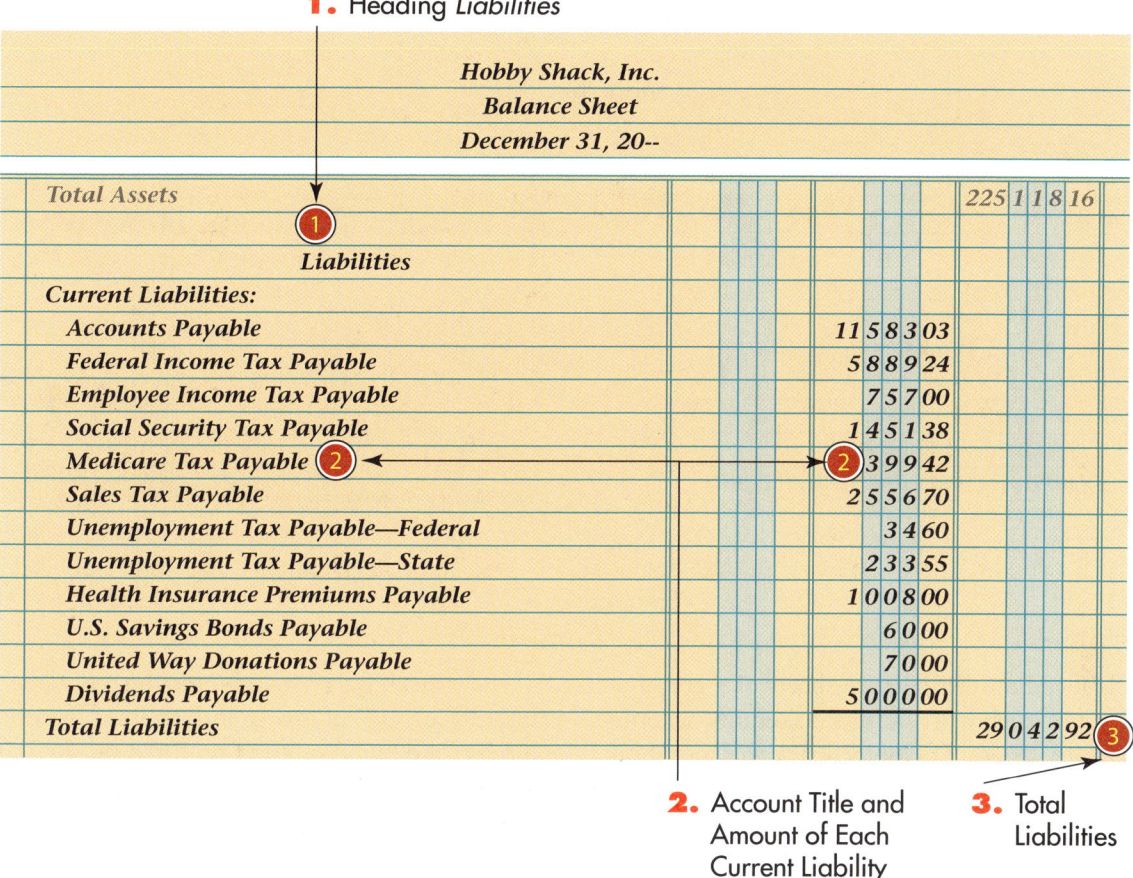

1. Heading *Liabilities*
2. Account Title and Amount of Each Current Liability
3. Total Liabilities

Liabilities are classified according to the length of time until they are due. Liabilities due within a short time, usually within a year, are called **current liabilities**.

Liabilities owed for more than a year are called **long-term liabilities**. An example of a long-term liability is Mortgage Payable. On December 31 of the current year, Hobby Shack does not have any long-term liabilities.

To prepare the liabilities section of the balance sheet, use information from the work sheet.

STEPS PREPARING THE LIABILITIES SECTION OF A BALANCE SHEET

1. Write the section title, *Liabilities*, on the next line in the middle of the wide column.

2. Write the title *Current Liabilities:* on the next line at the extreme left of the wide column.
   a. Beginning on the next line, indented about one centimeter, write the liability account titles in the order in which they appear on the work sheet.
   b. Write the balance of each liability account in the second amount column.

3. Calculate total liabilities.
   a. Write *Total Liabilities* on the next line below the last liability account title at the extreme left of the wide column.
   b. Write the total liabilities, $29,042.92, on the same line in the third amount column.

FOR YOUR INFORMATION

FYI

A company having both current liabilities and long-term liabilities would include headings and totals for each category. The process is similar to preparing the assets section of a balance sheet.

Preparing a Balance Sheet · Lesson 15-4 · **467**

STOCKHOLDERS' EQUITY SECTION OF A BALANCE SHEET

A major difference between balance sheets of a corporation and a proprietorship is the owners' equity section. The owners' equity section of Hobby Shack's balance sheet is labeled *Stockholders' Equity*. Some corporations use the same label, *Owners' Equity*, as proprietorships. Either label is acceptable.

The stockholders' equity section contains the total amounts of capital stock and retained earnings. These amounts are calculated and reported on the statement of stockholders' equity.

Hobby Shack's completed balance sheet is shown on the following page.

STEPS PREPARING THE STOCKHOLDERS' EQUITY SECTION OF A BALANCE SHEET

1. Write the heading *Stockholders' Equity* on the next line centered in the wide column.

2. Write the title and amount of *Capital Stock*, $125,000.00, calculated on the statement of stockholders' equity.

3. Write the title and amount of *Retained Earnings*, $71,075.24, calculated on the statement of stockholders' equity.

4. Add the amount of capital stock, $125,000.00, and retained earnings, $71,075.24, to calculate the total of stockholders' equity, $196,075.24.

5. Add the amount of total liabilities, $29,042.92, and total stockholders' equity, $196,075.24, to calculate the total of liabilities and stockholders' equity, $225,118.16. Verify accuracy by comparing the total amount of assets and the total amount of liabilities and stockholders' equity. These two amounts must be the same.

6. Draw double rules across the three columns at the end of the Assets section and the Stockholders' Equity section to show that assets equal liabilities plus owners' equity.

REMEMBER

Total assets must equal the total of liabilities and stockholders' equity. If these totals are not equal, identify the errors before preparing adjusting and closing entries.

COMPLETED BALANCE SHEET

<table>
<tr><td colspan="4" align="center">Hobby Shack, Inc.
Balance Sheet
December 31, 20--</td></tr>
<tr><td colspan="4" align="center">Assets</td></tr>
<tr><td>Current Assets:</td><td></td><td></td><td></td></tr>
<tr><td> Cash</td><td></td><td>29 080 28</td><td></td></tr>
<tr><td> Petty Cash</td><td></td><td>300 00</td><td></td></tr>
<tr><td> Accounts Receivable</td><td>14 698 40</td><td></td><td></td></tr>
<tr><td>   Less Allowance for Uncollectible Accounts</td><td>1 372 52</td><td>13 325 88</td><td></td></tr>
<tr><td> Merchandise Inventory</td><td></td><td>124 640 00</td><td></td></tr>
<tr><td> Supplies—Office</td><td></td><td>750 00</td><td></td></tr>
<tr><td> Supplies—Store</td><td></td><td>1 034 00</td><td></td></tr>
<tr><td> Prepaid Insurance</td><td></td><td>2 630 00</td><td></td></tr>
<tr><td> Total Current Assets</td><td></td><td></td><td>171 760 16</td></tr>
<tr><td>Plant Assets:</td><td></td><td></td><td></td></tr>
<tr><td> Office Equipment</td><td>35 864 50</td><td></td><td></td></tr>
<tr><td>   Less Accumulated Depreciation—Office Equipment</td><td>13 037 00</td><td>22 827 50</td><td></td></tr>
<tr><td> Store Equipment</td><td>40 849 50</td><td></td><td></td></tr>
<tr><td>   Less Accumulated Depreciation—Store Equipment</td><td>10 319 00</td><td>30 530 50</td><td></td></tr>
<tr><td> Total Plant Assets</td><td></td><td></td><td>53 358 00</td></tr>
<tr><td>Total Assets</td><td></td><td></td><td>225 118 16</td></tr>
<tr><td colspan="4" align="center">Liabilities</td></tr>
<tr><td>Current Liabilities:</td><td></td><td></td><td></td></tr>
<tr><td> Accounts Payable</td><td></td><td>11 583 03</td><td></td></tr>
<tr><td> Federal Income Tax Payable</td><td></td><td>5 889 24</td><td></td></tr>
<tr><td> Employee Income Tax Payable</td><td></td><td>757 00</td><td></td></tr>
<tr><td> Social Security Tax Payable</td><td></td><td>1 451 38</td><td></td></tr>
<tr><td> Medicare Tax Payable</td><td></td><td>399 42</td><td></td></tr>
<tr><td> Sales Tax Payable</td><td></td><td>2 556 70</td><td></td></tr>
<tr><td> Unemployment Tax Payable—Federal</td><td></td><td>34 60</td><td></td></tr>
<tr><td> Unemployment Tax Payable—State</td><td></td><td>233 55</td><td></td></tr>
<tr><td> Health Insurance Premiums Payable</td><td></td><td>1 008 00</td><td></td></tr>
<tr><td> U.S. Savings Bonds Payable</td><td></td><td>60 00</td><td></td></tr>
<tr><td> United Way Donations Payable</td><td></td><td>70 00</td><td></td></tr>
<tr><td> Dividends Payable</td><td></td><td>5 000 00</td><td></td></tr>
<tr><td>Total Liabilities</td><td></td><td></td><td>29 042 92</td></tr>
<tr><td colspan="4" align="center">Stockholders' Equity</td></tr>
<tr><td>Capital Stock</td><td></td><td>125 000 00</td><td></td></tr>
<tr><td>Retained Earnings</td><td></td><td>71 075 24</td><td></td></tr>
<tr><td>Total Stockholders' Equity</td><td></td><td></td><td>196 075 24</td></tr>
<tr><td>Total Liabilities and Stockholders' Equity</td><td></td><td></td><td>225 118 16</td></tr>
</table>

Preparing a Balance Sheet

SUPPORTING SCHEDULES FOR A BALANCE SHEET

A report prepared to give details about an item on a principal financial statement is called a **supporting schedule**. A supporting schedule is sometimes referred to as a *supplementary report* or an *exhibit*.

Hobby Shack prepares two supporting schedules to accompany the balance sheet. The supporting schedules are a schedule of accounts payable and a schedule of accounts receivable. A balance sheet shows only the accounts payable total amount. The account balance for each vendor is not shown. When detailed information is needed, a supporting schedule of accounts payable is prepared, showing the balance for each vendor. A balance sheet also shows only the accounts receivable total amount. When information about the account balance for each customer is needed, a supporting schedule of accounts receivable is prepared. Hobby Shack's supporting schedules on December 31 are similar to the supporting schedules for November 30 shown in Chapter 11.

BUSINESS STRUCTURES

Who Owns the Corporation?

A share of stock is a unit of ownership in a corporation. Stock may be purchased by individuals, investment companies, pension funds, institutions, banks, and other companies. Publicly traded stocks are bought and sold on stock exchanges throughout the world. Ownership of a corporation's stock entitles the owner to distributions of earnings if there are dividends declared. Many stock owners, however, buy stock with the expectation that the stock will increase in value and they can then sell the stock at a profit.

Stock ownership also entitles the owner to vote at stockholders' meetings, where important issues regarding the corporation may be decided. The membership of the board of directors of the corporation is also determined at stockholders' meetings. Sometimes individuals or other stock owners will attempt to gain a majority holding of a company's stock in order to take control of the company.

Sometimes investors determine which corporation's stock they will purchase based on political or social issues. For example, one investor might buy stocks only of companies that have good reputations on environmental issues. Others might buy stocks only of companies that have good policies regarding racial or gender discrimination.

Critical Thinking

1. If you were buying stock as an investment for your retirement years, would you be more concerned with the future resale value of the stock or its dividends? Would the answer be different for 18-year-olds and 60-year-olds?

2. What are some other kinds of social issues that might be important considerations for some people in purchasing corporate stock?

End of Lesson REVIEW

AUDIT YOUR UNDERSTANDING

1. How does Hobby Shack classify its assets?
2. What three items are listed on the balance sheet for an account having a related contra asset account?
3. What is an example of a long-term liability?
4. Where are the amounts obtained for the stockholders' equity section of the balance sheet?
5. What are two supporting schedules that might accompany a balance sheet?

TERMS REVIEW

current liabilities
long-term liabilities
supporting schedule

WORK TOGETHER 15-4

Preparing a balance sheet for a corporation

Use Interstate Tires' work sheet and statement of stockholders' equity from Work Together 15-3. A form for the balance sheet is given in the *Working Papers*. Your instructor will guide you through the following examples.

1. Prepare a balance sheet for the current year.

ON YOUR OWN 15-4

Preparing a balance sheet for a corporation

Use Osborn Corporation's work sheet and statement of stockholders' equity from On Your Own 15-3. A form for the balance sheet is given in the *Working Papers*. Work this problem independently.

1. Prepare a balance sheet for the current year.

Preparing a Balance Sheet

SUMMARY

After completing this chapter, you can:

1. Define accounting terms related to financial statements for a merchandising business organized as a corporation.
2. Identify accounting concepts and practices related to financial statements for a merchandising business organized as a corporation.
3. Prepare an income statement for a merchandising business organized as a corporation.
4. Analyze an income statement using component percentages and financial ratios.
5. Prepare a statement of stockholders' equity for a merchandising business organized as a corporation.
6. Prepare a balance sheet for a merchandising business organized as a corporation.

EXPLORE ACCOUNTING

Alternative Fiscal Years

Most small companies use a fiscal year that is the same as the calendar year, January 1 to December 31. However, there may be several reasons why a different fiscal period would be beneficial. If the calendar year end comes in the middle of a high sales period, a fiscal year ending at this time can be more difficult. All employees are extremely busy with sales and shipping. Because of this activity, accurately identifying sales, inventory, and accounts receivable is more difficult. If the calendar year end comes just before the high sales period begins, an analysis of the company's financial condition will not be as favorable. The company may have borrowed money to buy a high level of inventory, so the company has higher debt and high inventory levels. Therefore, some companies choose to use a natural business year as the fiscal year, as discussed in Chapter 6.

FanciFoods is a corporation that makes and sells decorative cakes, cookies, and candies. Approximately 90% of its sales are made between November 1 and February 15 because of the three holidays of Thanksgiving, Christmas, and Valentine's Day. The company spends six months—May to November—preparing for its heavy sales period. The company has selected April 1 to March 31 as its fiscal year. By March 31, inventory is low, most accounts receivable have been collected, and the company has not yet replaced inventory to begin preparing for the next season. Thus, this is an ideal time to end the fiscal period. Inventory is easier to count, the level of accounts receivable is lower, and more employees are available to help with the closing activities.

Research: What other types of companies may find it beneficial to use a fiscal year different from the calendar year? What would be the ideal fiscal period for these companies? You may wish to find a local business that has a fiscal period different from the calendar year. If so, determine the reasons for selecting the fiscal period it now uses.

15-1 APPLICATION PROBLEM

Preparing an income statement for a merchandising business

A work sheet for Historic Doors, Inc., for the year ended December 31 of the current year is given in the *Working Papers*.

Instructions:

1. Prepare an income statement.
2. Calculate and record on the income statement the following component percentages: (a) cost of merchandise sold, (b) gross profit on sales, (c) total expenses, and (d) net income before federal income tax. Round percentage calculations to the nearest 0.1%.

15-2 APPLICATION PROBLEM

Analyzing component percentages and financial ratios

The income statement for Custom Jewelry, Inc., and a form for completing this problem are given in the *Working Papers*. The managers of Custom Jewelry have established the following target component percentages:

Cost of Merchandise Sold	35.0%
Gross Profit on Sales	65.0%
Expenses	40.0%
Net Income before Federal Income Tax	25.0%

Instructions:

1. Compare the actual component percentages to the target percentage. Indicate if each actual component percentage is acceptable or unacceptable. If a percentage is unacceptable, suggest a possible action to correct the unacceptable component percentage.
2. Custom Jewelry has 110,000 shares of stock outstanding on December 31. The company's market price is $13.75 per share. Calculate the earnings per share and price-earnings ratio.

15-3 APPLICATION PROBLEM

Preparing a statement of stockholders' equity

A form for completing this problem is given in the *Working Papers*.

Instructions:

1. Prepare a statement of stockholders' equity for Classic Interiors, Inc., for the fiscal year ended on December 31 of the current year. Use the following additional information.

Capital stock outstanding on January 1	50,000 shares
Capital stock issued during the year	10,000 shares
Capital stock par value	$5.00
Retained earnings, January 1	$59,485.50
Dividends declared during year	$66,000.00
Net income after federal income tax	$110,635.34

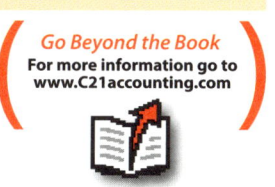

15-4 APPLICATION PROBLEM

Preparing a balance sheet for a corporation

Henderson Corporation's partial work sheet for the year ended December 31 of the current year is given in the *Working Papers*. A form for completing this problem is also given in the *Working Papers*. The December 31 balance in retained earnings reported on the statement of stockholders' equity is $97,294.85.

Instructions:
1. Prepare a balance sheet in report form.

15-5 MASTERY PROBLEM

Preparing financial statements

The work sheet for Lighting Center, Inc., for the year ended December 31 of the current year and forms for completing this problem are given in the *Working Papers*.

Instructions:
1. Prepare an income statement. Calculate and record the following component percentages: (a) cost of merchandise sold, (b) gross profit on sales, (c) total expenses, and (d) net income or loss before federal income tax. Round percentage calculations to the nearest 0.1%.
2. Prepare a statement of stockholders' equity. The company had 90,000 shares of $1.00 par value stock outstanding on January 1. The company issued an additional 10,000 shares during the year.
3. Prepare a balance sheet in report form.
4. Calculate the earnings per share and price-earnings ratio. The current market price of the stock is $28.50.

15-6 CHALLENGE PROBLEM

Analyzing component percentages and financial ratios

Instructions:
1. Obtain the financial statements of two corporations in similar industries. Calculate the income statement component percentages, earnings per share, and price-earnings ratio of each corporation. The current market price of each stock can be obtained from a newspaper or online. *Note: Annual reports may be available in your classroom, school library, or public library. They can also be found online.*
2. Contrast the component percentages of the companies. Identify which company you believe is performing better.

APPLIED COMMUNICATION

A long written report should contain numerous headings. A heading enables the reader to focus on the primary idea of the next section. An outline is a special document that lists only the headings of a report. By reviewing an outline before and after reading a report, the reader can gain a better understanding of the relationship among the topics being presented.

Each chapter of this textbook is similar to a long report. Headings are used to separate and emphasize major concepts.

Instructions: Prepare an outline of this chapter.

CASE FOR CRITICAL THINKING

Christy Burch and Myung Lim, business managers, compared their current income statement with the income statement of a year ago. They noted that sales were 12.0% higher than a year ago. They also noted that the total expenses were 20.0% higher than a year ago. What type of analysis should be done to determine whether the increase in expenses is justified?

GRAPHING WORKSHOP

Evaluating Department Sales

Collinsville Home Center made a strategic decision in 2002 to carry a line of home appliances. The following graph depicts sales for the company's three departments for the recent eight-year period. Analyze the graph to answer the following questions.

1. Describe the sales growth in the Appliances department.
2. State the approximate total company sales for 2007.
3. Describe the performance of the Lumber Department.

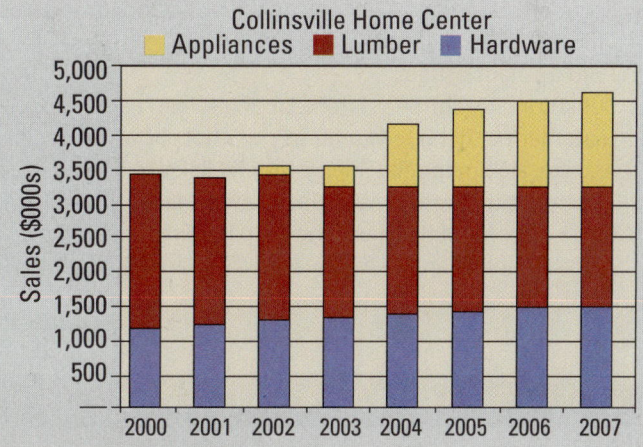

ANALYZING BEST BUY'S FINANCIAL STATEMENTS

Gross profit on sales is the amount of revenue remaining after the cost of merchandise has been deducted. Best Buy's gross profit on sales, labeled simply as "gross profit" on its income statement, has increased dramatically over the past three fiscal periods, a very favorable trend. But sales have also increased, making it difficult to determine how effectively Best Buy has been controlling its cost of merchandise sold.

The component percentage for gross profit on sales is also referred to as the *gross margin* or *gross profit rate*.

Instructions

1. Use Best Buy's Financial Highlights on page B-2 in Appendix B to identify the gross profit rate for 2005–2007.
2. Is the trend in the gross profit rate favorable or unfavorable?
3. Demonstrate how amounts on Best Buy's Consolidated Statement of Earnings, on page B-6, were used to calculate the gross profit rate for 2007.

Accounting SOFTWARE

FINANCIAL STATEMENTS

Component percentages are an essential tool for understanding financial statements. Peachtree includes component percentages on many, but not all, of its financial statements.

What if a manager requests that you add the component percentages to a report? Peachtree provides you with an easy method for accomplishing this task. With the report displayed on the screen, you can instruct Peachtree to export the financial statement to an electronic spreadsheet file.

This feature provides you with two important benefits. First, formulas can be entered to quickly and accurately calculate the component percentages. Second, the financial statement printed from the electronic spreadsheet will have a more professional appearance than might have been available otherwise.

PEACHTREE MASTERY PROBLEM 15-5

1. Open (Restore) file 15-5MP.ptb.
2. Print an income statement. Calculate the component percentages for (a) cost of merchandise sold, (b) gross profit on sales, (c) total expenses, and (d) net income or loss before federal income tax. Round percentage calculations to the nearest 0.1%.
3. Print a balance sheet.
4. Substitute Peachtree's statement of retained earnings for the statement of stockholders' equity. Peachtree's Statement of Retained Earnings does not show the beginning Capital Stock balance of $100,000. Add that balance to the Ending Retained Earnings Balance so that Peachtree's statement agrees with the manually-prepared statement that would have been completed in the Working Papers.
5. As an optional activity, use the Help feature to learn how to export the income statement to an electronic spreadsheet. Then use formulas to calculate additional component percentages. Format the spreadsheet.

FINANCIAL STATEMENTS

QuickBooks is a very useful software program for recording transactions and producing reports and financial statements. It is not as helpful when it comes to trying to look into the future and answer questions, such as "How much will the net income be if the revenues increase by 25% and expenses only increase 10%?"

This type of question is better answered by electronic spreadsheet software. Thus, in order to answer the question, the current accounting data would have to be exported into the electronic spreadsheet program. QuickBooks has a function that allows data to be transferred to an electronic spreadsheet program.

In addition to answering "what if" questions such as that above, exporting data into a spreadsheet also makes it possible to change a report's appearance or contents without affecting your QuickBooks data.

QUICKBOOKS MASTERY PROBLEM 15-5

1. Open the Lighting Center Inc. file.
2. Print the Profit & Loss Standard report, using January 1 and December 31 for the dates.
3. Add component percentages calculated as a percentage of income to the report. Change the report subtitle to "For Year Ended December 31." Print the report.
4. To create a year-end balance sheet in QuickBooks, it is necessary to make a closing entry to close the equity account Dividends to retained earnings. Print a Trial Balance report to use as the basis for journalizing the closing transaction.
5. Use the Make General Journal Entries window to journalize the closing entry, using December 31 for the date.
6. Print a Journal report and a Balance Sheet Standard report, using December 31 for the dates.
7. As an optional activity, use the Help feature to learn how to export the income statement to an electronic spreadsheet. Then use formulas to calculate additional component percentages. Format the spreadsheet.

FORMATTING FINANCIAL STATEMENTS

Indenting section and account titles on a financial statement helps the reader identify the major sections of the statement. For example, having all the expenses indented under the Expense title clearly identifies these accounts as expenses.

The traditional method for indenting on an electronic spreadsheet was to have a series of thin columns on the left of the template. Each column allowed for one indentation. Modern electronic spreadsheets have tools that allow you to increase and decrease the indentation of text within a cell. Using these tools eliminates the need for many thin columns and allows you to easily change the level of indentation.

EXCEL APPLICATION PROBLEM 15-1
Open the F15-1 Excel data file. Follow the step-by-step instructions in the Instructions work sheet to calculate component percentages and indent text within cells for a better appearance.

EXCEL APPLICATION PROBLEM 15-3
Open the F15-3 Excel data file. Follow the step-by-step instructions in the Instructions work sheet to complete the statement of stockholders' equity.

FINANCIAL STATEMENTS

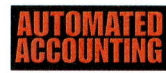

Sometimes it is not enough to simply display or print a financial statement. It might be desirable to paste a copy of the income statement or balance sheet in a memo or report. There could be an advantage in copying and pasting a financial statement in a spreadsheet where different assumptions could be tried to see how the business could be improved. For example, you might change the cost of purchases and see what effect the change has on net income.

Automated Accounting has a Copy function in the report window that allows you to copy the displayed financial statement in either a word processing or a spreadsheet format. When the report is displayed, click the Copy button. You then must choose either a word processing or a spreadsheet format. The report is saved on the operating system's Clipboard. You can then open an existing word processing document or start a new one, click the Paste tool on the toolbar or select Edit Paste, and the report is copied into a word processing document.

To make columns align, it is necessary to reformat the entire report in a monotype font, such as Courier New, so that each character occupies the same amount of space. A similar process is used to copy a report to a spreadsheet.

Optional Automated Accounting Problem
Open file F15-CP.AA8. Display the problem instructions and complete the problem.

CHAPTER 16

Recording Adjusting and Closing Entries for a Corporation

OBJECTIVES

After studying Chapter 16, you will be able to:
1. Identify accounting concepts and practices related to adjusting and closing entries for a merchandising business organized as a corporation.
2. Record adjusting entries.
3. Record closing entries for income statement accounts.
4. Record closing entry for dividends.
5. Prepare a post-closing trial balance.

Point Your Browser
www.C21accounting.com

ACCOUNTING IN THE REAL WORLD

Apple

Apple Spreads Its Wings

Recent world history would be incomplete without a reference to three computers—Apple II, Macintosh, and iMac—that pushed computer technology beyond the standard of their day.

The Apple II was the first personal computer to gain wide distribution and put the Apple Computer company on the technology map. The Macintosh introduced the graphical interface and mouse technologies we now take for granted. The iMac merged digital audio and video into traditional computer technology to enable stunning editing of video and audio files.

Although Apple's foundation is in computers, the company has spread its wings into related technology markets. The widely successful iPod is the driving force in the popular digital music player market. iTunes was the first Internet site to offer legal, digital copies of music files. Together, iPod and iTunes have revolutionized how people access and play music.

Apple has clearly demonstrated that it can be a player in any market that requires the innovative application of computer technology.

Critical Thinking

1. Identify other companies that have extended their product lines beyond their original market.
2. Identify at least five expenses Apple incurs to support its iTunes business.

Source: www.apple.com, www.apple-history.com

INTERNET ACTIVITY

EDGAR—Part 2

Go to the homepage for EDGAR (www.sec.gov/edgar.shtml). Click on "Search for Company Filings," and then click on "Latest Filings."

Instructions

1. Look at the most recent filing (top of the list) and record the company name and the date and time the filing was accepted.
2. Click the "Back" button to return to "Search the EDGAR Database" page. Again, click on "Latest Filings." Scroll down the list to find the company filing you recorded in instruction 1. Count and record the number of additional filings that are listed.

LESSON 16-1

Recording Adjusting Entries

ADJUSTING ENTRIES RECORDED FROM A WORK SHEET

General ledger account balances are changed only by posting journal entries. Two types of journal entries change general ledger account balances at the end of a fiscal period: (1) Adjusting entries bring general ledger account balances up to date. (2) Closing entries prepare temporary accounts for the next fiscal period. [CONCEPT: Matching Expenses with Revenue] Adjusting entries recorded in a work sheet are journalized in a general journal. Hobby Shack begins the adjusting entries on a new general journal page. The adjusting entries are entered in the Debit and Credit columns of the general journal.

STEPS RECORDING ADJUSTING ENTRIES IN A GENERAL JOURNAL

1. Write the heading, *Adjusting Entries,* in the middle of the general journal's Account Title column. This heading explains all of the adjusting entries that follow. Therefore, indicating a source document is unnecessary. The first adjusting entry is recorded on the first two lines below the heading.

2. For the first adjusting entry in the work sheet Adjustments columns, write the date, *Dec. 31, 20--*, in the Date column.

3. Scan down the Adjustments column of the work sheet to identify the first adjustment, *(e)*, to *Allowance for Uncollectible Accounts*. Identify the debit and credit parts of this entry.

4. Write the title of the account debited in the Account Title column.

5. Write the debit adjustment amount in the Debit column.

6. Write the title of the account credited in the Account Title column, indented about 1 centimeter.

7. Write the credit adjustment amount in the Credit column.

8. Continue down the Adjustments columns, repeating Steps 4 through 7 for each of the additional adjustments.

REMEMBER
Remember to start a new general journal page for adjusting entries.

CHARACTER COUNTS

Insider Trading

Ben Levine works in the research unit of a large chemical company. His group has recently discovered a new chemical process that will revolutionize how household cleaning products are manufactured. The discovery should have a significant positive impact on his company's profitability and its stock price.

Ben purchases shares of his company every month through a payroll deduction program. He is considering using a large portion of his savings to buy additional shares of the company. Since you are the ethics officer of the company, he has asked your opinion on his proposed stock purchase.

Instructions

Access the *Code of Business Conduct* of Dow at www.dow.com. Using this code of conduct as a guide, provide Ben with guidance on his proposed stock purchase. Can Ben continue his monthly purchases?

ADJUSTING ENTRY FOR ALLOWANCE FOR UNCOLLECTIBLE ACCOUNTS

	GENERAL JOURNAL				PAGE 15
DATE	ACCOUNT TITLE	DOC. NO.	POST. REF.	DEBIT	CREDIT
	Adjusting Entries				
20-- Dec. 31	Uncollectible Accounts Expense			1 245 00	
	Allowance for Uncoll. Accounts				1 245 00

Hobby Shack estimated that $1,245.00 of the current fiscal year's sales on account will eventually be uncollectible. The amount is added to the existing balance in Allowance for Uncollectible Accounts, $127.52. The adjusted balance of Allowance for Uncollectible Accounts, $1,372.52, is the amount of the current accounts receivable that Hobby Shack expects to become uncollectible.

The effect of posting the adjusting entry (e) for Uncollectible Accounts is shown in the T accounts. The debit to **Uncollectible Accounts Expense** recognizes this as an expense for the fiscal period.

Allowance for Uncollectible Accounts

	Bal. 127.52
	Adj. (e) 1,245.00
	(New Bal. 1,372.52)

Uncollectible Accounts Expense

Adj. (e) 1,245.00	

ADJUSTING ENTRY FOR MERCHANDISE INVENTORY

	GENERAL JOURNAL				PAGE 15
DATE	ACCOUNT TITLE	DOC. NO.	POST. REF.	DEBIT	CREDIT
31	Income Summary			15 840 00	
	Merchandise Inventory				15 840 00

The merchandise inventory account has a January 1 debit balance of $140,480.00. The inventory was counted at the end of the fiscal period and determined to cost $124,640.00. Adjustment *(d)* for $15,840.00 reduces the cost of inventory, $140,480.00, to $124,640.00. The effect of posting the adjusting entry for merchandise inventory is shown in the T accounts.

Merchandise Inventory

Bal. 140,480.00	Adj. (d) 15,840.00
(New Bal. 124,640.00)	

Income Summary

Adj. (d) 15,840.00	

ADJUSTING ENTRY FOR SUPPLIES—OFFICE

	GENERAL JOURNAL				PAGE 15	
DATE	ACCOUNT TITLE	DOC. NO.	POST. REF.	DEBIT	CREDIT	
31	Supplies Expense—Office			2 73 0 00		6
	Supplies—Office				2 73 0 00	7

Hobby Shack counted $750.00 of office supplies on hand at the end of the fiscal period. The balance of Supplies—Office in the trial balance, $3,480.00, is the cost of office supplies on hand at the beginning of the year plus the office supplies purchased during the year. Adjustment *(a)* for $2,730.00 reduces the balance in Supplies—Office from $3,480.00 to $750.00.

The effect of posting the adjusting entry for office supplies is shown in the T accounts. The debit to Supplies Expense—Office recognizes the amount of supplies used during the period as an expense.

Supplies—Office
| Bal. | 3,480.00 | Adj. (a) | 2,730.00 |
| (New Bal. | 750.00) | | |

Supplies Expense—Office
| Adj. (a) | 2,730.00 | | |

ADJUSTING ENTRY FOR SUPPLIES—STORE

	GENERAL JOURNAL				PAGE 15	
DATE	ACCOUNT TITLE	DOC. NO.	POST. REF.	DEBIT	CREDIT	
31	Supplies Expense—Store			2 91 0 00		8
	Supplies—Store				2 91 0 00	9

Hobby Shack also counted $1,034.00 of store supplies on hand at the end of the fiscal period. Adjustment *(b)* for $2,910.00 reduces the balance in Supplies—Store, $3,944.00, to the current cost of store supplies on hand, $1,034.00. The effect of posting the adjusting entry for store supplies inventory is shown in the T accounts. The debit to Supplies Expense—Store recognizes the amount of supplies used during the period as an expense.

Supplies—Store
| Bal. | 3,944.00 | Adj. (b) | 2,910.00 |
| (New Bal. | 1,034.00) | | |

Supplies Expense—Store
| Adj. (b) | 2,910.00 | | |

Recording Adjusting Entries

ADJUSTING ENTRY FOR PREPAID INSURANCE

	GENERAL JOURNAL				PAGE 15
DATE	ACCOUNT TITLE	DOC. NO.	POST. REF.	DEBIT	CREDIT
10 31	Insurance Expense			3 1 7 0 00	
11	Prepaid Insurance				3 1 7 0 00

During the fiscal period, Hobby Shack paid $5,800.00 for future insurance coverage. At the end of the fiscal year, Hobby Shack determined that the value of prepaid insurance on December 31 is $2,630.00. Adjustment *(c)* reduces **Prepaid Insurance** by $3,170.00, the value of insurance used during the year.

The effect of posting the adjusting entry for **Prepaid Insurance** is shown in the T accounts. The debit to **Insurance Expense** recognizes the amount of insurance used during the fiscal period as an expense.

```
             Prepaid Insurance
Bal.             5,800.00   Adj. (c)    3,170.00
(New Bal.        2,630.00)

             Insurance Expense
Adj. (c)         3,170.00
```

ADJUSTING ENTRY FOR DEPRECIATION—OFFICE EQUIPMENT

	GENERAL JOURNAL				PAGE 15
DATE	ACCOUNT TITLE	DOC. NO.	POST. REF.	DEBIT	CREDIT
12 31	Depreciation Exp.—Office Equip.			6 5 4 0 00	
13	Accum. Depr.—Office Equip.				6 5 4 0 00

Hobby Shack estimated its depreciation of office equipment during the fiscal year to be $6,540.00. Adjustment *(f)* increases **Accum. Depr.—Office Equip.** by $6,540.00, resulting in a new balance of $13,037.00.

The effect of posting the adjusting entry for office equipment depreciation is shown in the T accounts. The debit to **Depreciation Exp.—Office Equip.** recognizes the depreciation as an expense for the fiscal period.

ADJUSTING ENTRY FOR DEPRECIATION—STORE EQUIPMENT

	GENERAL JOURNAL				PAGE 15	
DATE	ACCOUNT TITLE	DOC. NO.	POST. REF.	DEBIT	CREDIT	
14	31	Depreciation Exp.—Store Equip.			5 2 5 0 00		14
15		Accum. Depr.—Store Equip.				5 2 5 0 00	15

Hobby Shack estimated its depreciation of store equipment during the fiscal year to be $5,250.00. Adjustment *(g)* increases Accum. Depr.—Store Equip. by $5,250.00, resulting in a new balance of $10,319.00.

The effect of posting the adjusting entry for store equipment depreciation is shown in the T accounts. The debit to Depreciation Exp.—Store Equip. recognizes the depreciation as an expense for the fiscal period.

```
Accum. Depr.—Store Equip.
                   Bal.        5,069.00
                   Adj. (g)    5,250.00
                   (New Bal.  10,319.00)

Depreciation Exp.—Store Equip.
Adj. (g)   5,250.00
```

ADJUSTING ENTRY FOR FEDERAL INCOME TAXES

	GENERAL JOURNAL				PAGE 15	
DATE	ACCOUNT TITLE	DOC. NO.	POST. REF.	DEBIT	CREDIT	
16	31	Federal Income Tax Expense			5 8 8 9 24		16
17		Federal Income Tax Payable				5 8 8 9 24	17

Hobby Shack made four quarterly estimated payments of $4,500.00. The actual federal income tax expense, $23,889.24, was calculated based on the company's net income before federal income tax. Hobby Shack must make an extra payment of $5,889.24 to pay its tax liability. Adjustment *(h)* increases Federal Income Tax Expense by $5,889.24, resulting in a new balance of $23,889.24. The adjustment also creates the $5,889.24 tax liability.

The effect of posting the adjusting entry for federal income tax is shown in the T accounts.

```
Federal Income Tax Payable
                   Adj. (h)    5,889.24
                   (New Bal.   5,889.24)

Federal Income Tax Expense
Bal.        18,000.00
Adj. (h)     5,889.24
(New Bal.   23,889.24)
```

End of Lesson REVIEW

AUDIT YOUR UNDERSTANDING

1. When adjusting entries are journalized, why is no source document recorded?
2. What adjusting entry is recorded for a merchandising business that is not recorded for a service business?
3. What balance sheet account is increased from a zero balance after adjusting entries are journalized and posted?

WORK TOGETHER 16-1

Journalizing adjusting entries

The work sheet for Discount Books, Inc., is given in the *Working Papers*. Your instructor will guide you through the following example.

1. Record the appropriate adjusting entries on page 18 of a general journal provided in the *Working Papers*. Use December 31 of the current year as the date. Save your work to complete Work Together 16-2.

ON YOUR OWN 16-1

Journalizing adjusting entries

The work sheet for Sturgis Supply, Inc., is given in the *Working Papers*. Work this problem independently.

1. Record the appropriate adjusting entries on page 24 of a general journal provided in the *Working Papers*. Use December 31 of the current year as the date. Save your work to complete On Your Own 16-2.

LESSON 16-2: Recording Closing Entries for Income Statement Accounts

Closing entries for a corporation are made from information in a work sheet. Closing entries for revenue and expense accounts are similar to those for proprietorships. A corporation's closing entries to close net income and temporary equity accounts are also similar to those for a proprietorship. However, these closing entries affect different accounts. A corporation records four closing entries:

1. A closing entry for income statement accounts with credit balances (revenue and contra cost accounts)
2. A closing entry for income statement accounts with debit balances (cost, contra revenue, and expense accounts)
3. A closing entry to record net income or net loss in the retained earnings account and close the income summary account
4. A closing entry for the dividends account

THE INCOME SUMMARY ACCOUNT

At the end of a fiscal period, the temporary accounts are closed to prepare the general ledger for the next fiscal period. [CONCEPT: Matching Expenses with Revenue] To close a temporary account, an amount equal to its balance is recorded on the side opposite the balance.

Amounts needed for the closing entries are obtained from the Income Statement and Balance Sheet columns of the work sheet and from the statement of stockholders' equity. Closing entries are recorded in the general journal.

Chapter 8 discusses the difference between permanent accounts and temporary accounts. Permanent accounts, also referred to as *real accounts*, include the asset and liability accounts as well as the owners' capital accounts. The ending account balances of permanent accounts for one fiscal period are the beginning account balances for the next fiscal period. Temporary accounts, also referred to as *nominal accounts*, include the revenue, cost, expense, and dividend accounts.

Another temporary account is used to summarize the closing entries for revenue, cost, and expenses. The account is titled Income Summary because it is used to summarize information about net income. Income Summary is used only at the end of a fiscal period to help prepare other accounts for a new fiscal period.

The income summary account is unique because it does not have a normal balance side. The balance of this account is determined by the amounts posted to the account at the end of a fiscal period. When revenue is greater than total expenses, resulting in a net income, the income summary account has a credit balance, as shown in the T account.

REMEMBER

The income summary account is used only at the end of the fiscal period to help prepare other accounts for a new fiscal period.

CLOSING ENTRY FOR ACCOUNTS WITH CREDIT BALANCES

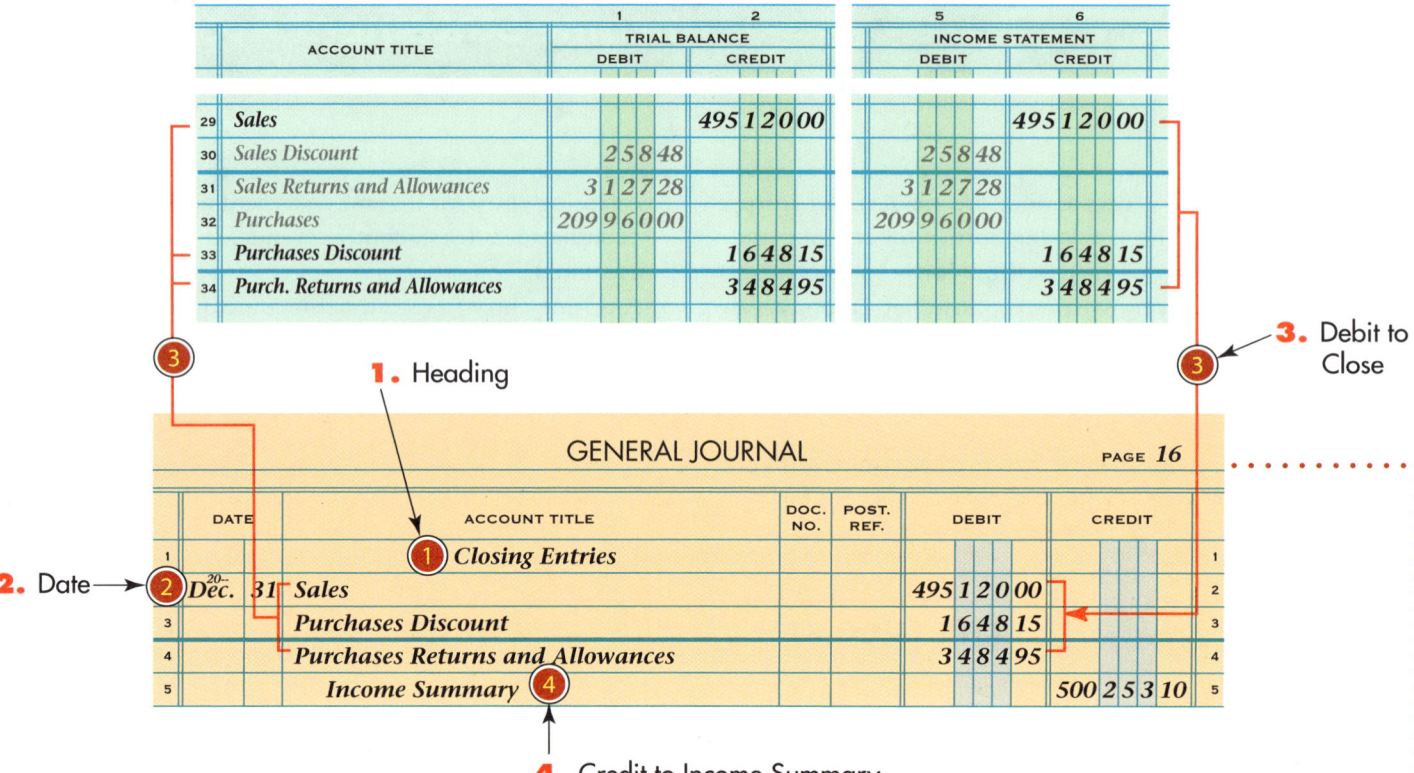

Hobby Shack's work sheet has three income statement accounts with credit balances. One account, Sales, is a revenue account. The other two accounts, Purchases Discount and Purchases Returns and Allowances, are contra cost accounts. Each account has a normal credit balance that must be reduced to zero to prepare the account for the next fiscal period. [CONCEPT: Matching Expenses with Revenue]

To reduce each balance to zero, each account is debited for the amount of the balance. The impact of the closing entry on the sales account is shown in the T account.

Sales			
Closing	495,120.00	Bal.	495,120.00
		(New Bal. zero)	

Income Summary is credited for $500,253.10, the total of the three debits in this closing entry.

The balance in Income Summary will be adjusted by other closing entries.

STEPS — CLOSING INCOME STATEMENT ACCOUNTS WITH CREDIT BALANCES

1. Write the heading, *Closing Entries*, in the middle of the general journal's Account Title column on a new page. This heading explains all of the closing entries that follow. Therefore, indicating a source document is unnecessary. The first closing entry is recorded on the first four lines below the heading.

2. Write the date, *Dec. 31, 20--*, in the Date column.

3. Write the account title of each revenue and contra cost account in the Account Title column. Write the balance of each revenue and contra cost account in the Debit column.

4. Write the title of the account credited, *Income Summary*, in the Account Title column, indented about 1 centimeter. Write the amount, *$500,253.10*, in the Credit column.

488 Chapter 16   Recording Adjusting and Closing Entries for a Corporation

CLOSING ENTRY FOR INCOME STATEMENT ACCOUNTS WITH DEBIT BALANCES

Hobby Shack's work sheet has many income statement accounts with debit balances—contra revenue accounts, Purchases, and the expense accounts. These debit balances must be reduced to zero to prepare the accounts for the next fiscal period. [CONCEPT: Matching Expenses with Revenue] To reduce the balances to zero, the accounts are credited for the amount of their balances. Income Summary is debited for the total amount.

STEPS — CLOSING INCOME STATEMENT ACCOUNTS WITH DEBIT BALANCES

1. Write the date, *31*, in the Date column.
2. Write the title of the account debited, *Income Summary*, in the Account Title column. The debit to *Income Summary* is not entered in the amount column until all contra revenue, cost, and expense balances have been journalized and the total amount calculated.
3. Write the account title of each contra revenue, cost, and expense account in the Account Title column, each indented about 1 centimeter. Write the balance of each cost and expense account in the Credit column.
4. Add the credit amounts for this entry. Write the total of the credited accounts, *$404,099.15*, in the Debit column on the same line as the account title *Income Summary*.

Recording Closing Entries for Income Statement Accounts

SUMMARY OF CLOSING ENTRY FOR INCOME STATEMENT ACCOUNTS WITH DEBIT BALANCES

The second closing entry reduces the balance of the contra revenue, Purchases, and expense accounts to a zero balance. The effect of the closing entry on Purchases is shown in the T account.

Purchases	
Bal. 209,960.00	Closing 209,960.00
(New Bal. zero)	

After recording this closing entry, Income Summary has three amounts:

1. A debit of $15,840.00, the amount of the merchandise inventory adjustment
2. A credit of $500,253.10, the amount of the entry to close the revenue and contra cost accounts
3. A debit of $404,099.15, the amount of the entry to close the contra revenue, cost, and expense accounts

Income Summary	
Adj. (mdse. inv.) 15,840.00	Closing (credit amounts) 500,253.10
Closing (debit accounts) 404,099.15	(New Bal. 80,313.95)

The credit balance of Income Summary, *$80,313.95*, is equal to the net income amount shown on the work sheet. However, Income Summary is not closed as part of this closing entry. Instead, the account is closed with the third closing entry when net income is recorded.

FSTOP/GETTY IMAGES

FOR YOUR INFORMATION

FYI

A document that outlines the mission and goals of a corporation is known as a strategic plan. *The management of a corporation uses the strategic plan as a guiding light to ensure that all business decisions work toward achieving its goals.*

SMALL BUSINESS

SPOTLIGHT

Buying a franchise is a popular way to start a small business. Franchises are particularly appealing to people with less experience because the failure rate is much lower than that of other new businesses. Advantages of purchasing a franchise include the franchise's proven reputation, established customers, and time-tested business procedures. Disadvantages include the franchisee's sometimes-limited control over the new business and the relatively high initial fees attached to the purchase of a franchise.

CLOSING ENTRY TO RECORD NET INCOME

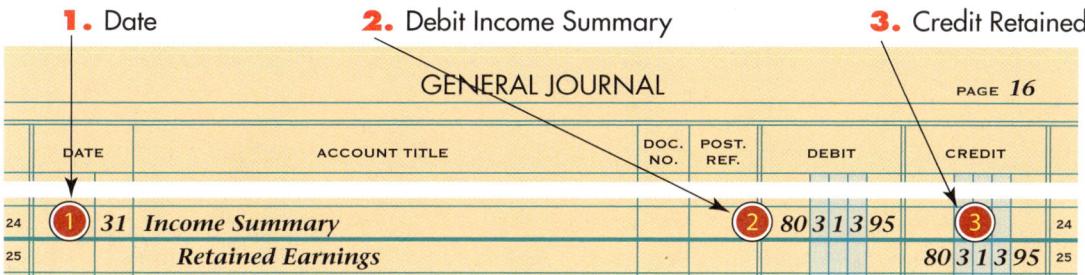

After closing entries for the income statement accounts are posted, Income Summary has a credit balance of $80,313.95. This credit balance equals the net income calculated on the work sheet.

A corporation's net income should be recorded in the retained earnings account at the end of the fiscal year. After the closing entry is posted, Income Summary has a zero balance.

The new balance in retained earnings, $91,075.24, does not yet equal the amount reported on the statement of stockholders' equity. The fourth closing entry is required to adjust Retained Earnings to the correct amount.

Income Summary			
Adj. (mdse. inv.)	15,840.00	Closing (credit accounts)	500,253.10
Closing (debit accounts)	404,099.15		
Closing (retained earnings)	80,313.95	(New Bal. zero)	

Retained Earnings			
		Bal.	10,761.29
		Closing (Income Summary)	80,313.95
		(New Bal.	91,075.24)

CLOSING ENTRY FOR DIVIDENDS

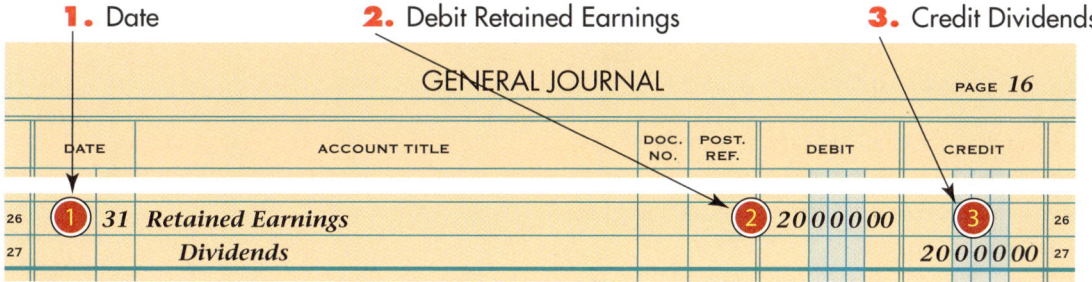

Because dividends decrease the earnings retained by a corporation, the dividends account is closed to Retained Earnings. After the closing entry for the dividends account is posted, Dividends has a zero balance. The amount of the dividends, $20,000.00, has reduced the balance of Retained Earnings. The new balance in Retained Earnings, $71,075.24, now equals the amount reported on the statement of stockholders' equity. Therefore, the retained earnings account is now up to date.

Retained Earnings			
Closing (dividends)	20,000.00	Bal.	10,761.29
		Closing (Income Summary)	80,313.95
		(New Bal.	71,075.24)

Dividends			
Bal.	20,000.00	Closing (dividends)	20,000.00
(New Bal. zero)			

Recording Closing Entries for Income Statement Accounts

COMPLETED CLOSING ENTRIES FOR A CORPORATION RECORDED IN A JOURNAL

GENERAL JOURNAL PAGE 16

DATE		ACCOUNT TITLE	DOC. NO.	POST. REF.	DEBIT	CREDIT	
		Closing Entries					1
Dec. 20--	31	Sales			495 1 2 0 00		2
		Purchases Discount			1 6 4 8 15		3
		Purchases Ret. and Allow.			3 4 8 4 95		4
		Income Summary				500 2 5 3 10	5
	31	Income Summary			404 0 9 9 15		6
		Sales Discount				2 5 8 48	7
		Sales Returns and Allow.				3 1 2 7 28	8
		Purchases				209 9 6 0 00	9
		Advertising Expense				3 6 0 0 00	10
		Cash Short and Over				1 9 25	11
		Credit Card Fee Expense				3 3 8 5 00	12
		Depr. Exp.—Office Equipment				6 5 4 0 00	13
		Depr. Exp.—Store Equipment				5 2 5 0 00	14
		Insurance Expense				3 1 7 0 00	15
		Miscellaneous Expense				2 5 6 4 90	16
		Payroll Taxes Expense				9 1 0 5 00	17
		Rent Expense				18 0 0 0 00	18
		Salary Expense				104 5 2 5 00	19
		Supplies Expense—Office				2 7 3 0 00	20
		Supplies Expense—Store				2 9 1 0 00	21
		Uncollectible Accounts Expense				1 2 4 5 00	22
		Utilities Expense				3 8 2 0 00	23
		Federal Income Tax Expense				23 8 8 9 24	24
	31	Income Summary			80 3 1 3 95		25
		Retained Earnings				80 3 1 3 95	26
	31	Retained Earnings			20 0 0 0 00		27
		Dividends				20 0 0 0 00	28

Hobby Shack's general journal appears as shown above, after all closing entries have been recorded.

The next step would be to post the adjusting and closing entries to the general ledger.

FOR YOUR INFORMATION

FYI

If a corporation has a net loss, Income Summary has a debit balance. Retained Earnings would then be debited and Income Summary credited for the net loss amount.

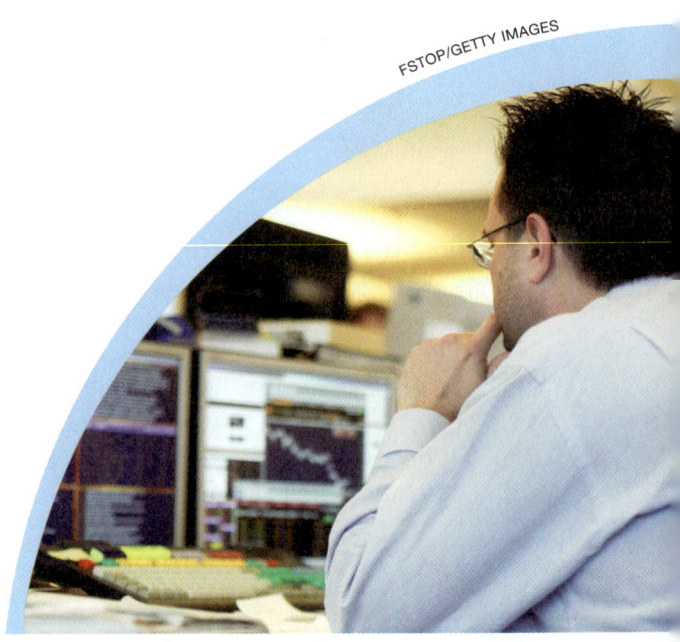
FSTOP/GETTY IMAGES

End of Lesson REVIEW

AUDIT YOUR UNDERSTANDING

1. Where is the information obtained for journalizing closing entries for revenue, cost, and expenses?
2. What is the name of the temporary account that is used to summarize the closing entries for revenue, cost, and expenses?

WORK TOGETHER 16-2

Journalizing closing entries

Use the work sheet of Discount Books, Inc., from Work Together 16-1. A general journal is given in the *Working Papers*. Your instructor will guide you through the following example.

1. Record the following closing entries on page 19 of the general journal.
   a. Close the income statement accounts with credit balances.
   b. Close the income statement accounts with debit balances.
   c. Close Income Summary.
   d. Close the dividend account.

ON YOUR OWN 16-2

Journalizing closing entries

Use the work sheet of Sturgis Supply, Inc., from On Your Own 16-1. A general journal is given in the *Working Papers*. Work this problem independently.

1. Record the following closing entries on page 25 of the general journal.
   a. Close the income statement accounts with credit balances.
   b. Close the income statement accounts with debit balances.
   c. Close Income Summary.
   d. Close the dividend account.

LESSON 16-3

Preparing a Post-Closing Trial Balance

COMPLETED GENERAL LEDGER AFTER ADJUSTING AND CLOSING ENTRIES ARE POSTED

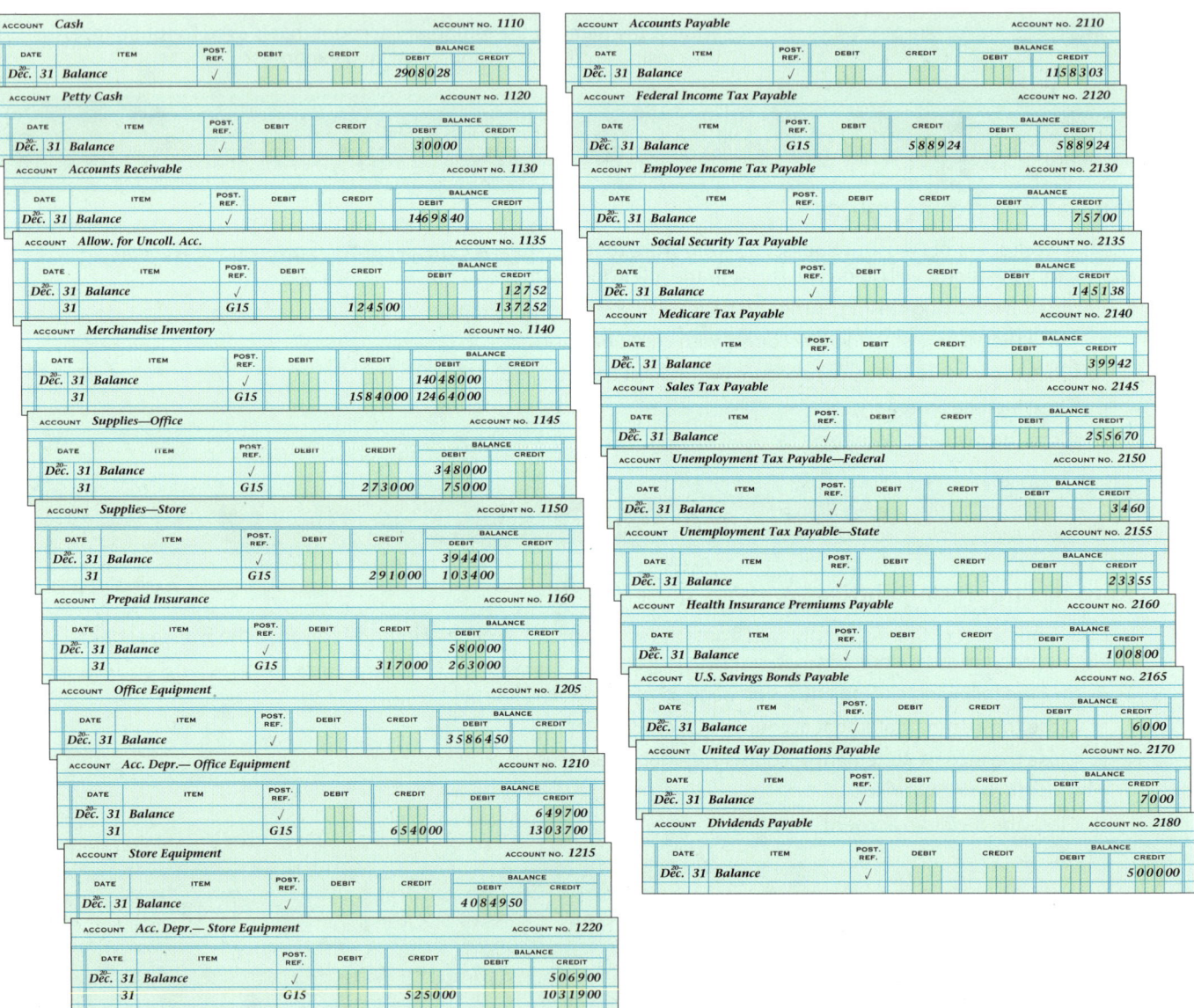

Hobby Shack's completed general ledger after adjusting and closing entries are posted is shown above and on the following page.

Balance sheet accounts (asset, liability, and capital accounts) have up-to-date balances to begin the new fiscal period.

Income statement accounts (revenue, cost, and expense accounts) have zero balances to begin the new fiscal period. [CONCEPT: Matching Expenses with Revenue]

COMPLETED GENERAL LEDGER AFTER ADJUSTING AND CLOSING ENTRIES ARE POSTED (CONCLUDED)

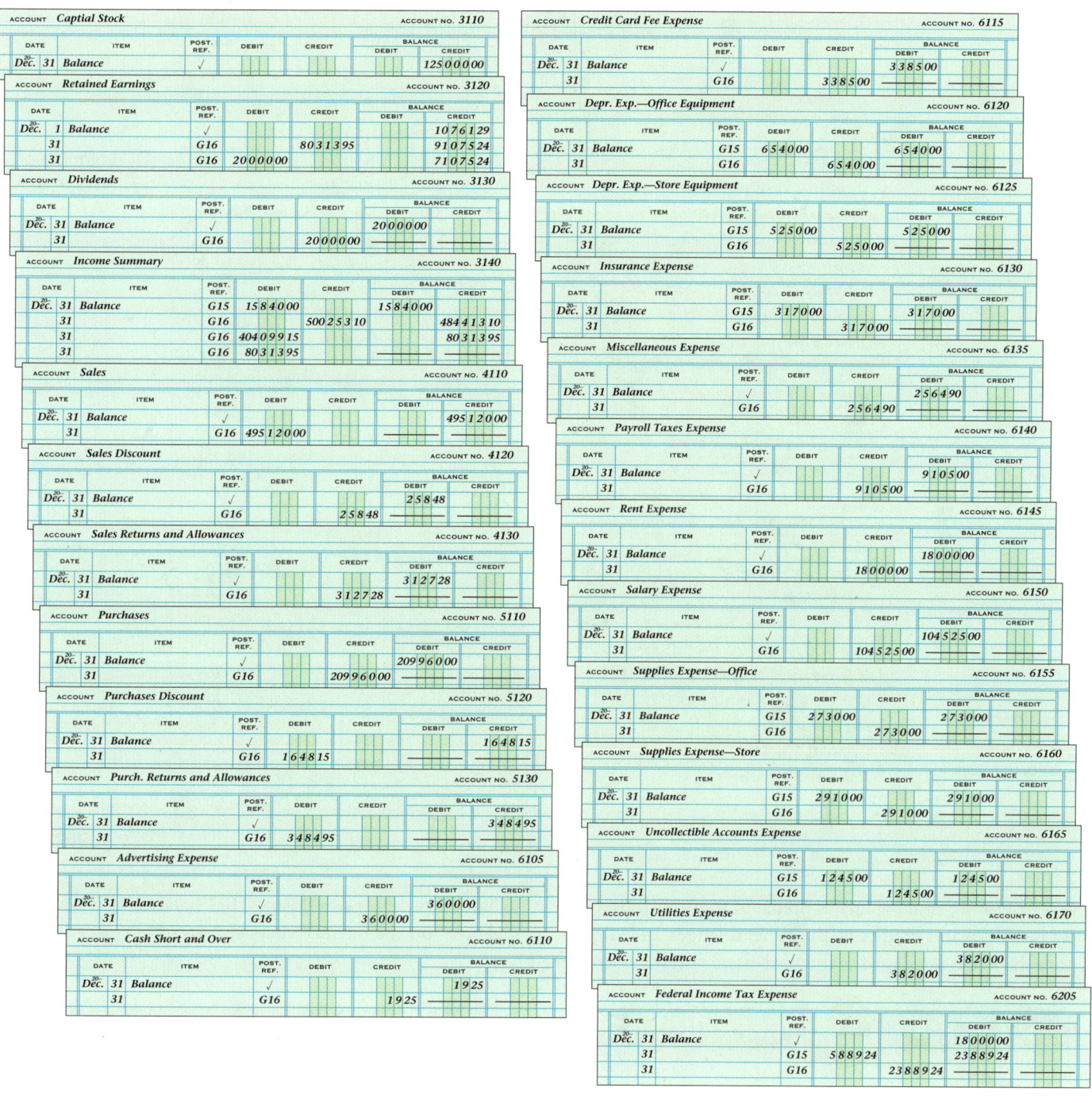

Preparing a Post-Closing Trial Balance

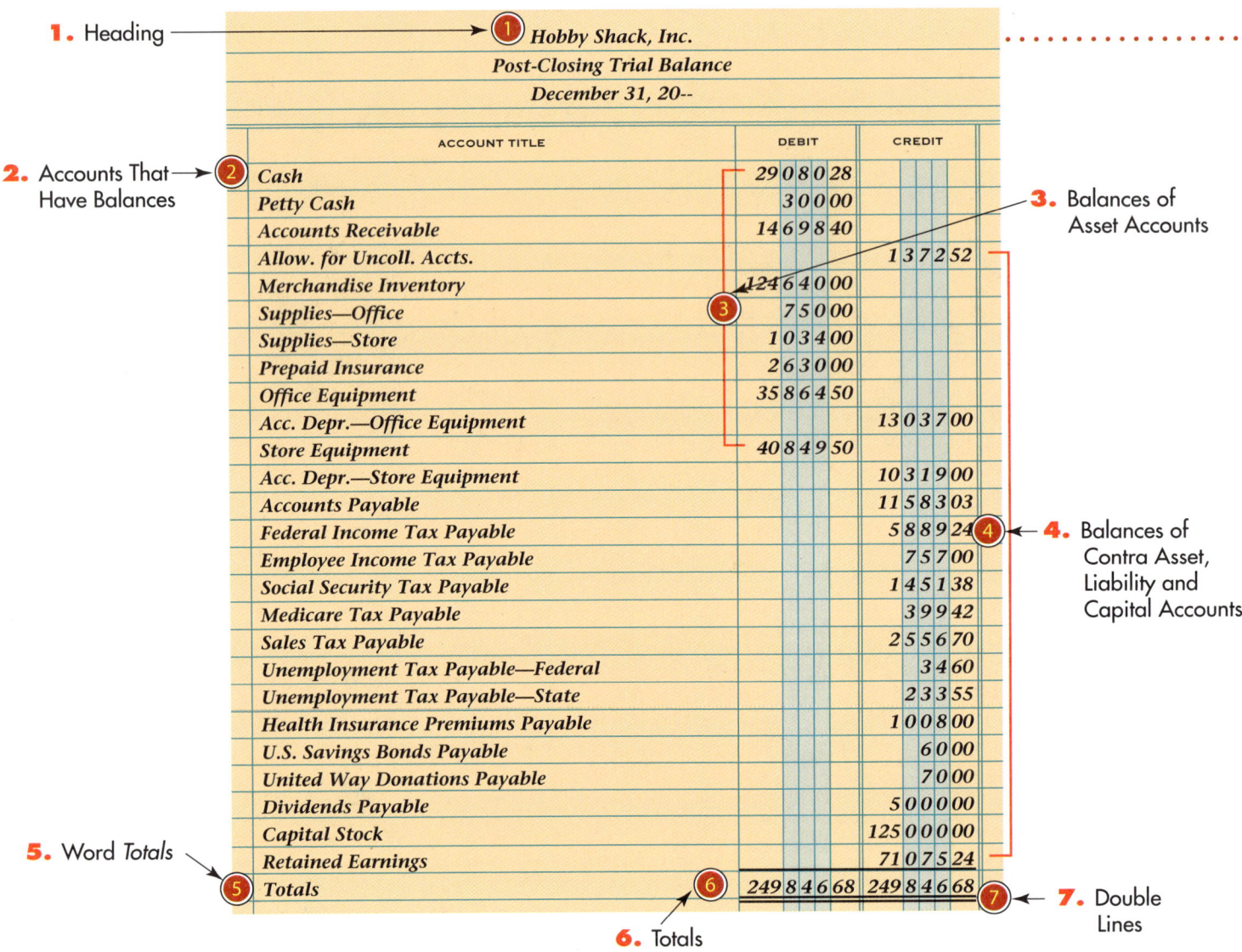

A post-closing trial balance is prepared to prove the equality of debits and credits in the general ledger and to prepare the general ledger for the next fiscal period. Account balances on the post-closing trial balance agree with the balances on the balance sheet shown in Chapter 15.

STEPS PREPARING A POST-CLOSING TRIAL BALANCE

1. Write the post-closing trial balance heading on three lines.
2. List all general ledger accounts that have balances in the Account Title column.
3. Write the balance of each asset account in the Debit column. Write the balance of each contra account in the Credit column.
4. Write the balance of each liability and capital account in the Credit column.
5. Write the word *Totals* on the next line below the last account title.
6. Total the columns and write the totals, $249,846.68, on the Totals line.
7. Verify equality. Rule double lines below both column totals.

ACCOUNTING CYCLE FOR A MERCHANDISING BUSINESS ORGANIZED AS A CORPORATION

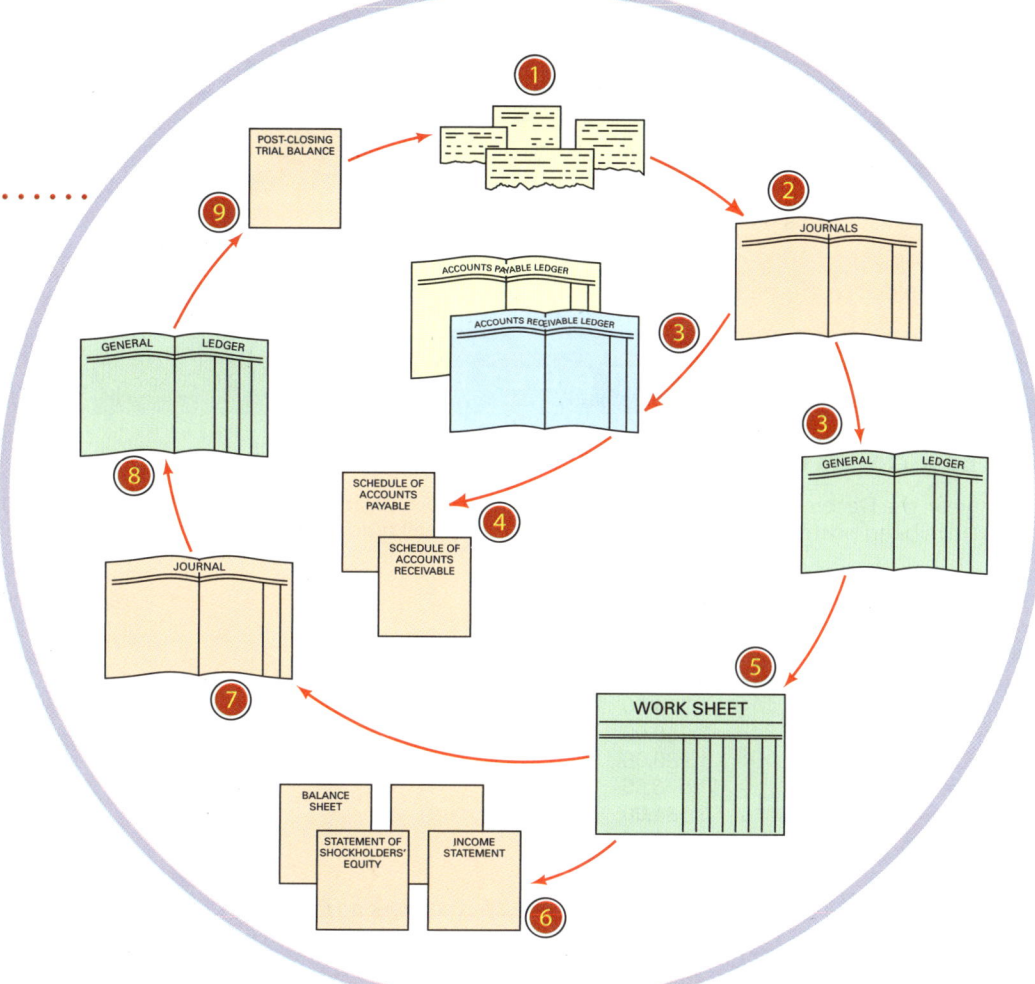

Service and merchandising businesses use a similar accounting cycle. The accounting cycles are also similar for a proprietorship and a corporation. Variations occur when subsidiary ledgers are used. Variations also occur in preparing financial statements.

STEPS — ACCOUNTING CYCLE FOR A MERCHANDISING BUSINESS

1. Source documents are checked for accuracy, and transactions are analyzed into debit and credit parts.
2. Transactions, from information on source documents, are recorded in journals.
3. Journal entries are posted to the accounts payable ledger, the accounts receivable ledger, and the general ledger.
4. Schedules of accounts payable and accounts receivable are prepared from the subsidiary ledgers.
5. A work sheet, including a trial balance, is prepared from the general ledger.
6. Financial statements are prepared from the work sheet.
7. Adjusting and closing entries are journalized from the work sheet.
8. Adjusting and closing entries are posted to the general ledger.
9. A post-closing trial balance of the general ledger is prepared.

Preparing a Post-Closing Trial Balance   Lesson 16-3   497

End of Lesson REVIEW

AUDIT YOUR UNDERSTANDING

1. Which accounts are listed on a post-closing trial balance?
2. What is the purpose of preparing a post-closing trial balance?
3. In what order should accounts be listed on a post-closing trial balance?

WORK TOGETHER 16-3

Preparing a post-closing trial balance

For the current year, the December 31 balances for Visual Art Center's balance sheet accounts after adjusting and closing entries have been posted are given below. Your instructor will guide you through the following example.

Account	Balance
Cash	$ 21,810.20
Petty Cash	350.00
Accounts Receivable	8,398.80
Merchandise Inventory	190,980.00
Supplies—Office	1,314.00
Supplies—Store	2,268.00
Prepaid Insurance	1,980.00
Accounts Payable	11,676.50
Sales Tax Payable	1,584.00
Capital Stock	100,000.00
Retained Earnings	113,840.50

1. Prepare a post-closing trial balance on the form provided in the *Working Papers*.

ON YOUR OWN 16-3

Preparing a post-closing trial balance

For the current year, the December 31 balances for Welding Supply's balance sheet accounts after adjusting and closing entries have been posted are given below. Work this problem independently.

Account	Balance
Cash	$ 26,485.00
Petty Cash	500.00
Accounts Receivable	15,487.00
Allow. for Uncoll. Accts.	1,457.00
Merchandise Inventory	134,152.00
Supplies	741.00
Prepaid Insurance	1,000.00
Equipment	25,487.00
Acc. Dep.—Equipment	12,450.00
Accounts Payable	13,154.00
Federal Income Tax Payable	2,489.00
Sales Tax Payable	1,548.00
Dividends Payable	5,000.00
Capital Stock	50,000.00
Retained Earnings	117,754.00

1. Prepare a post-closing trial balance on the form provided in the *Working Papers*.

SUMMARY

After completing this chapter, you can:

1. Identify accounting concepts and practices related to adjusting and closing entries for a merchandising business organized as a corporation.
2. Record adjusting entries.
3. Record closing entries for income statement accounts.
4. Record closing entry for dividends.
5. Prepare a post-closing trial balance.

EXPLORE ACCOUNTING

Freight Charges

When a business purchases merchandise from a vendor, ordinarily a third-party freight company is used to deliver the merchandise from the seller (vendor) to the buyer (purchasing business). As part of the terms of sale, the buyer and seller must agree on who is responsible for the freight charges. Those terms will be listed on the seller's sales invoice as either FOB shipping point or FOB destination. *FOB* is an abbreviation for the phrase "Free on Board." *FOB shipping point* means that the buyer is responsible for the freight charges. *FOB destination* means that the seller is responsible for the freight charges. *Shipping point* is the location where the freight company receives the merchandise from the seller. *Destination* refers to the receiving point of the buyer.

The accounting entries for freight charges can be complicated when one business is responsible for the freight charges according to the terms of sale, but the other business pays the freight company. For example, terms of sale may be FOB shipping point, meaning that the buyer is responsible for the freight charges. However, the freight company may require payment in advance. Therefore, the seller pays the freight company for the freight charges.

Four different situations may occur:

1. FOB shipping point, seller pays freight company
2. FOB shipping point, buyer pays freight company
3. FOB destination, seller pays freight company
4. FOB destination, buyer pays freight company

Research: Investigate this issue by reviewing collegiate Principles of Accounting or Intermediate Accounting textbooks. Also, you might interview a merchandising business manager to determine how the business accounts for freight charges. After completing your research, write a report on the issue of freight charges that would clearly explain the correct accounting procedures to a new accounting department employee.

16-1 APPLICATION PROBLEM

Journalizing adjusting entries

A partial work sheet for Cellar Books, Inc., for the year ended December 31 is given in the *Working Papers*.

Instructions:
1. Record the appropriate adjusting entries on page 22 of the general journal provided in the *Working Papers*. Use December 31 of the current year as the date.

16-2 APPLICATION PROBLEM

Journalizing closing entries

Use the partial work sheet for Cellar Books, Inc., given in Problem 16-1.

Instructions:
Prepare the following closing entries on page 23 of the general journal provided in the *Working Papers*.
1. Close the income statement accounts with credit balances.
2. Close the income statement accounts with debit balances.
3. Close Income Summary.
4. Close the dividend account.

16-3 APPLICATION PROBLEM

Preparing a post-closing trial balance

For the current year, the December 31 balances for the balance sheet accounts of Cellar Books, Inc., after adjusting and closing entries have been posted are given below.

Account	Balance	Account	Balance
Cash	$ 16,485.00	Federal Income Tax Payable	$ 3,660.23
Petty Cash	400.00	Employee Income Tax Payable	1,248.20
Accounts Receivable	41,483.15	Social Security Tax Payable	903.96
Allow. for Uncoll. Accts.	2,406.15	Medicare Tax Payable	211.41
Merchandise Inventory	246,598.05	Sales Tax Payable	2,458.25
Supplies—Office	329.62	Unemployment Tax Payable—Federal	28.00
Supplies—Store	326.81	Unemployment Tax Payable—State	189.00
Prepaid Insurance	2,000.00	Health Insurance Premiums Payable	400.00
Office Equipment	38,458.25	U.S. Savings Bonds Payable	25.00
Acc. Dep.—Office Equipment	23,960.00	United Way Donations Payable	40.00
Store Equipment	41,478.50	Dividends Payable	3,000.00
Acc. Dep.—Store Equipment	31,100.00	Capital Stock	60,000.00
Accounts Payable	19,948.80	Retained Earnings	237,980.38

Instructions:
1. Prepare a post-closing trial balance on the form provided in the *Working Papers*.

16-4 APPLICATION PROBLEM

Journalizing and posting adjusting and closing entries; preparing a post-closing trial balance

Use the partial work sheet of Wilson Paint, Inc., for the year ended December 31 of the current year, on page 502. The general ledger accounts and their balances as well as forms for completing this problem are in the *Working Papers*.

Instructions:
1. Journalize the adjusting entries using page 22 of a general journal.
2. Post the adjusting entries.
3. Journalize the closing entries using page 23 of a general journal.
4. Post the closing entries.
5. Prepare a post-closing trial balance.

16-5 MASTERY PROBLEM

Journalizing and posting adjusting and closing entries; preparing a post-closing trial balance

Use the partial work sheet of Northern Lights for the year ended December 31 of the current year, on page 503. The general ledger accounts and their balances as well as forms for completing this problem are in the *Working Papers*.

Instructions:
1. Journalize the adjusting entries using page 18 of a general journal.
2. Post the adjusting entries.
3. Journalize the closing entries using page 19 of a general journal.
4. Post the closing entries.
5. Prepare a post-closing trial balance.

Partial Work Sheet for Application Problem 16-4 (Wilson Paint, Inc.)

#	ACCOUNT TITLE	TRIAL BALANCE DEBIT	TRIAL BALANCE CREDIT	ADJUSTMENTS DEBIT	ADJUSTMENTS CREDIT	INCOME STATEMENT DEBIT	INCOME STATEMENT CREDIT
1	Cash	15 482 00					
2	Petty Cash	500 00					
3	Accounts Receivable	42 158 80					
4	Allow. for Uncoll. Accts.		684 20		(e) 3 560 00		
5	Merchandise Inventory	274 535 33		(d) 1 483 60			
6	Supplies—Office	6 158 84			(a) 5 847 10		
7	Supplies—Store	5 548 55			(b) 4 918 50		
8	Prepaid Insurance	8 000 00			(c) 7 200 00		
9	Office Equipment	22 158 66					
10	Acc. Depr.—Office Equipment		4 848 00		(f) 3 580 00		
11	Store Equipment	34 158 11					
12	Acc. Depr.—Store Equipment		12 480 00		(g) 6 140 00		
13	Accounts Payable		15 487 99				
14	Federal Income Tax Payable				(h) 1 356 14		
15	Employee Income Tax Payable		1 125 58				
16	Social Security Tax Payable		903 96				
17	Medicare Tax Payable		211 41				
18	Sales Tax Payable		2 345 99				
19	Unemployment Tax Pay.—Federal		25 60				
20	Unemployment Tax Pay.—State		172 80				
21	Health Insurance Premiums Payable		350 00				
22	U.S. Savings Bonds Payable		50 00				
23	United Way Donations Payable		60 00				
24	Dividends Payable		5 000 00				
25	Capital Stock		125 000 00				
26	Retained Earnings		136 843 68				
27	Dividends	20 000 00					
28	Income Summary			(d) 1 483 60			1 483 60
29	Sales		724 183 99				724 183 99
30	Sales Discount	1 694 48				1 694 48	
31	Sales Returns and Allowances	4 189 64				4 189 64	
32	Purchases	331 805 18				331 805 18	
33	Purchases Discount		3 418 47				3 418 47
34	Purch. Returns and Allowances		4 684 69				4 684 69
35	Advertising Expense	14 518 00				14 518 00	
36	Cash Short and Over		4 60				4 60
37	Credit Card Fee Expense	12 180 00				12 180 00	
38	Depr. Exp.—Office Equipment			(f) 3 580 00		3 580 00	
39	Depr. Exp.—Store Equipment			(g) 6 140 00		6 140 00	
40	Insurance Expense			(c) 7 200 00		7 200 00	
41	Miscellaneous Expense	6 481 00				6 481 00	
42	Payroll Taxes Expense	14 184 60				14 184 60	
43	Rent Expense	20 150 00				20 150 00	
44	Salary Expense	168 483 60				168 483 60	
45	Supplies Expense—Office			(a) 5 847 10		5 847 10	
46	Supplies Expense—Store			(b) 4 918 50		4 918 50	
47	Uncollectible Accounts Expense			(e) 3 560 00		3 560 00	
48	Utilities Expense	5 484 97				5 484 97	
49	Federal Income Tax Expense	30 000 00		(h) 1 356 14		31 356 14	
50		1037 876 36	1037 876 36	34 085 34	34 085 34	641 777 81	733 770 75
51	Net Income after Federal Income Tax					91 992 94	
52						733 770 75	733 770 75

Partial Work Sheet for Mastery Problem 16-5 (Northern Lights)

	ACCOUNT TITLE	TRIAL BALANCE DEBIT	TRIAL BALANCE CREDIT	ADJUSTMENTS DEBIT	ADJUSTMENTS CREDIT	INCOME STATEMENT DEBIT	INCOME STATEMENT CREDIT
1	Cash	5 124 12					
2	Petty Cash	250 00					
3	Accounts Receivable	14 843 30					
4	Allow. for Uncoll. Accts.		124 55		(e) 2 120 00		
5	Merchandise Inventory	154 318 22			(d) 3 488 14		
6	Supplies—Office	3 415 58			(a) 3 148 66		
7	Supplies—Store	6 184 56			(b) 5 348 84		
8	Prepaid Insurance	700 00			(c) 600 00		
9	Office Equipment	21 482 66					
10	Acc. Depr.—Office Equipment		6 480 00		(f) 3 580 00		
11	Store Equipment	40 481 66					
12	Acc. Depr.—Store Equipment		18 480 00		(g) 6 140 00		
13	Accounts Payable		8 418 36				
14	Federal Income Tax Payable				(h) 965 64		
15	Employee Income Tax Payable		458 00				
16	Social Security Tax Payable		528 24				
17	Medicare Tax Payable		123 54				
18	Sales Tax Payable		1 415 30				
19	Unemployment Tax Pay.—Federal		4 00				
20	Unemployment Tax Pay.—State		27 00				
21	Health Insurance Premiums Payable		250 00				
22	U.S. Savings Bonds Payable		40 00				
23	United Way Donations Payable		60 00				
24	Dividends Payable		400 00				
25	Capital Stock		80 000 00				
26	Retained Earnings		89 761 21				
27	Dividends	16 000 00					
28	Income Summary			(d) 3 488 14		3 488 14	
29	Sales		514 815 35				514 815 35
30	Sales Discount	2 154 94				2 154 94	
31	Sales Returns and Allowances	6 184 74				6 184 74	
32	Purchases	301 548 60				301 548 60	
33	Purchases Discount		2 154 65				2 154 65
34	Purch. Returns and Allowances		2 889 41				2 889 41
35	Advertising Expense	2 491 95				2 491 95	
36	Cash Short and Over	5 25				5 25	
37	Credit Card Fee Expense	8 154 62				8 154 62	
38	Depr. Exp.—Office Equipment			(f) 3 580 00		3 580 00	
39	Depr. Exp.—Store Equipment			(g) 6 140 00		6 140 00	
40	Insurance Expense			(c) 600 00		600 00	
41	Miscellaneous Expense	410 00				410 00	
42	Payroll Taxes Expense	14 184 60				14 184 60	
43	Rent Expense	15 400 00				15 400 00	
44	Salary Expense	102 240 30				102 240 30	
45	Supplies Expense—Office			(a) 3 148 66		3 148 66	
46	Supplies Expense—Store			(b) 5 348 84		5 348 84	
47	Uncollectible Accounts Expense			(e) 2 120 00		2 120 00	
48	Utilities Expense	4 154 51				4 154 51	
49	Federal Income Tax Expense	4 000 00		(h) 965 64		4 965 64	
50		730 029 61	730 029 61	30 791 28	30 791 28	491 720 79	519 859 41
51	Net Income after Federal Income Tax					28 138 62	
52						519 859 41	519 859 41

Recording Adjusting and Closing Entries for a Corporation

16-6 CHALLENGE PROBLEM

Inventory auditing challenges

For most businesses, merchandise inventory is a major portion of the business's assets. Therefore, reporting an accurate amount on the financial statements is important to accurate financial reporting. Whether a member of the business's accounting staff or an outside auditor audits the merchandise inventory of the business, determining an accurate count of the merchandise inventory is very important. Different types of merchandise present different kinds of challenges for the auditor.

a. *Actual count, common costs:* A sports store has 50 tennis rackets, all the same model. The rackets should be counted and multiplied times the cost per racket to determine the inventory value.

b. *Actual count, unique costs:* An automobile dealer has 60 new automobiles. Since each automobile probably has a unique and significant cost, the cost of each automobile should be totaled to determine the inventory value.

c. *Sampling:* A hardware store has many machine bolts. Since the value of each is low and there are many items, a small quantity may be counted or weighed. Then estimate the total cost based on the sample size or weight.

d. *Measuring/calculating:* An oil company stores crude oil in large tanks. The depth of the oil in the tank can be measured with a measuring rod; then the circumference of the tank can be measured. The total volume of crude oil can be calculated, then divided by the volume of one barrel of crude oil to determine the total barrels. This number can then be multiplied by the cost per barrel of crude oil.

Instructions:

How would you determine the value of the following inventory items? Record your answers in the *Working Papers*.

1. Grain in a grain elevator
2. Lumber in a lumber yard
3. Diamond rings in a jewelry store
4. Nails in a home improvement store

APPLIED COMMUNICATION

Public speakers are judged by the ability of the audience to remember important points of their presentation. Effective public speakers use a variety of techniques to encourage the audience to listen to their message.

Instructions: Contact an instructor in your school or a local businessperson you have heard speak at school or community functions. Ask the person to describe the techniques used to help the audience listen and remember the message. Write a short report summarizing these techniques. Be prepared to present your report orally in class.

CASE FOR CRITICAL THINKING

Antwan Jones, a new accounting clerk, has just experienced his first closing of a fiscal period. He questions why the adjustments on the work sheet have to be recorded in a general journal. Antwan maintains that the adjustments can simply be posted from the work sheet. As the senior accounting clerk, how would you respond to his statement?

SCANS WORKPLACE COMPETENCY

Thinking Skills: Knowing how to learn

Concept: One way to learn new concepts is to build on knowledge already acquired. For example, you might learn how to create your own filing system after using a filing system created by someone else.

Application: Describe how the financial statements and adjusting and closing entries for a corporation differ from those of a proprietorship. Could a proprietorship prepare a statement of stockholders' equity?

AUDITING FOR ERRORS

Editing an Accounting Policies Manual

The Sarbanes-Oxley Act requires publicly traded corporations to document and test their accounting systems. The documentation for Mateen Supply Corporation contains the following section on the preparation of closing entries. Identify the errors in this section of Mateen's accounting systems documentation.

Closing Entries

After the worksheet has been completed and verified, journal entries are recorded to close temporary accounts. Three entries are recorded:

1. Sales and contra purchases accounts are debited for their year-end balances. The total of the accounts is credited to Income Summary.

2. Purchasing and expense accounts are credited for their year-balances. The total of the accounts is debited to Income Summary.

3. If the company had a net income, record a debit to Income Summary for the difference of the closing entries recorded in steps 1 and 2. If the company had a net loss, record a credit to Income Summary for this difference. In either case, record the same amount to Retained Earnings to balance the entry.

ANALYZING BEST BUY'S FINANCIAL STATEMENTS

Generally accepted accounting principles require several forms of earnings per share to be reported. Earnings per share from the normal operations of the business is presented first. The effect on earnings per share from unusual, nonrecurring events is added or deducted. The net of these items is the earnings per share that is typically reported in the financial news.

Instructions: Use Best Buy's Consolidated Statements of Earnings on page B-6 in Appendix B to answer the following questions.

1. What is the label given to the net earnings per share amount, and what are its components?
2. What earnings per share amount would be reported in the financial news for the most recent fiscal year?

Accounting SOFTWARE

GROUPING FINANCIAL STATEMENT REPORTS

Peachtree has a feature that allows you to create and print a group of reports. Creating a group is as easy as selecting each report and giving the group a name. The group appears in the report menu along with the other reports you have become accustomed to printing.

PEACHTREE APPLICATION PROBLEM 16-4
1. Open (Restore) file 16-4AP.ptb.
2. Journalize and post the adjusting entries.
3. Print the income statement, and compare the amounts with the work sheet.
4. Journalize and post the closing entries.
5. Print the December 31 general journal, the general ledger, and the post-closing trial balance.

PEACHTREE MASTERY PROBLEM 16-5
1. Open (Restore) file 16-5MP.ptb.
2. Journalize and post the adjusting entries.
3. Print the income statement, and compare the amounts with the work sheet.
4. Journalize and post the closing entries.
5. Print the general ledger and post-closing trial balance.

GROUPING FINANCIAL STATEMENT REPORTS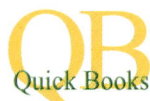

One way QuickBooks supports efficiency is by allowing common tasks to be completed quickly. QuickBooks can be programmed to memorize the format of any financial statement and also to group financial statements together. When it is time to prepare financial statements, the user can print the entire group with a minimum of commands.

QUICKBOOKS APPLICATION PROBLEM 16-4
1. Open the Wilson Paint Inc. file.
2. Journalize the adjusting entries using the Make General Journal Entries window.
3. Print a Profit & Loss Standard report using January 1 and December 31 for the dates.
4. To create a year-end balance sheet in QuickBooks, it is necessary to make a closing entry to close the equity account Dividends to Retained Earnings. Print a Trial Balance report to use for the closing transaction.
5. Use the General Journal Entries window to journalize the closing entry dated December 31.
6. Print a Journal report, a Balance Sheet Standard report, and a Trial Balance report.
7. As an optional activity, group the financial statement reports and print them. Then, record the closing entries and print a post-closing trial balance.

QUICKBOOKS MASTERY PROBLEM 16-5
1. Open the Northern Lights file.
2. Journalize the adjusting entries using the Make General Journal Entries window.
3. Print a Profit & Loss Standard report using January 1 and December 31 for the dates.
4. Journalize the closing entry for Dividends using the Make General Journal Entries window.
5. Print a Journal report, a Balance Sheet Standards report, and a Trial Balance report. The trial balance will show only balance sheet accounts so you will need to edit the Report Title field to read "Post-Closing Trial Balance." Edit the Subtitle field to read "As of December 31."

FORMATTING GRIDLINES ON REPORTS

What do a football field and journal paper have in common? Each has many lines to help provide structure to its activity. Lines on the football field guide players where to run and mark the end zones. Journal paper lines guide accountants where to write account information and related amounts. These lines also help readers accurately locate information on a journal.

Spreadsheets also display row and column lines, called *gridlines*, to provide you with this structure as you enter text and numbers in a template. Unfortunately, these lines do not automatically appear on printed output.

Lines can be added to an electronic spreadsheet using two methods. A single command will print all gridlines. This quick solution may be overwhelming as the lines surrounding every cell will be printed. In contrast, the Borders tool allows you to insert a variety of line styles exactly where you want them–you decide what lines will provide readers with the structure they need.

EXCEL APPLICATION PROBLEM 16-3
Open the F16-3 Excel data file. Follow the step-by-step instructions in the Instructions work sheet. Use the Borders tool to insert horizontal and vertical lines to provide structure to the trial balance.

ADJUSTING ENTRIES, CLOSING ENTRIES, AND POST-CLOSING TRIAL BALANCE

Adjusting Entries
At the end of a fiscal period, many accounts need to be adjusted to recognize changes and expenses of the fiscal period. Adjusting entries are recorded in the general journal. The reference used for adjusting entries is *Adj.Ent*. After all adjusting entries have been entered and posted, the file should be saved with the letters *BC* in the filename. *BC* stands for *Before Closing*. Once closing entries are posted, it is very difficult to correct any errors that may have been made during the fiscal period. Therefore, having a file saved before the closing entries ensures that a before-closing file exists if corrections are necessary.

Closing Entries
In an automated accounting system, closing entries are generated and posted by the software. *Automated Accounting* automatically prepares all closing entries with the Generate Closing Journal Entries option from the Options menu. Once generated, the journal entries should be examined for accuracy and then posted.

Post-Closing Trial Balance
After closing entries are journalized and posted, a general ledger trial balance report is selected from the Reports menu. Because the closing entries have been posted, this trial balance is a post-closing trial balance.

AUTOMATED ACCOUNTING APPLICATION PROBLEM 16-4
Open file F16-4.AA8. Display the problem instructions and complete the problem.

AUTOMATED ACCOUNTING MASTERY PROBLEM 16-5
Open file F16-5.AA8. Display the problem instructions and complete the problem.

REINFORCEMENT Activity 2—Part B

An Accounting Cycle for a Corporation: End-of-Fiscal-Period Work

The ledgers used in Reinforcement Activity 2—Part A are needed to complete Reinforcement Activity 2—Part B. Reinforcement Activity 2—Part B includes those accounting activities needed to complete the accounting cycle of Medical Services Company (MSC).

END-OF-FISCAL-PERIOD WORK

INSTRUCTIONS:

12. Prepare a trial balance on a work sheet. Use December 31 of the current year as the date.
13. Complete the work sheet using the following adjustment information:
    a. Office supplies inventory $476.60
    b. Store supplies inventory 817.00
    c. Merchandise inventory 33,278.01
    d. Uncollectible accounts are 2.0% of credit sales of $65,000.00
    e. Value of prepaid insurance $500.00
    f. Estimate of office equipment depreciation 3,520.00
    g. Estimate of store equipment depreciation 2,240.00
14. Using the tax table shown in Chapter 14, calculate federal income tax expense and record the income tax adjustment on the work sheet.
15. Prepare an income statement. Figure and record the following component percentages of net sales: (a) cost of merchandise sold, (b) gross profit on sales, (c) total expenses, and (d) net income or loss before federal income tax. Round percentage calculations to the nearest 0.1%.
16. Prepare a statement of stockholders' equity. The company had 9,500 shares of $1.00 par value stock outstanding on January 1. The company issued an additional 500 shares during the year.
17. Prepare a balance sheet in report form.
18. Calculate the earnings per share and price-earnings ratio. The current market price of the stock is $87.50.
19. Use page 13 of a general journal. Journalize and post the adjusting entries.
20. Use page 14 of a general journal. Journalize and post the closing entries.
21. Prepare a post-closing trial balance.

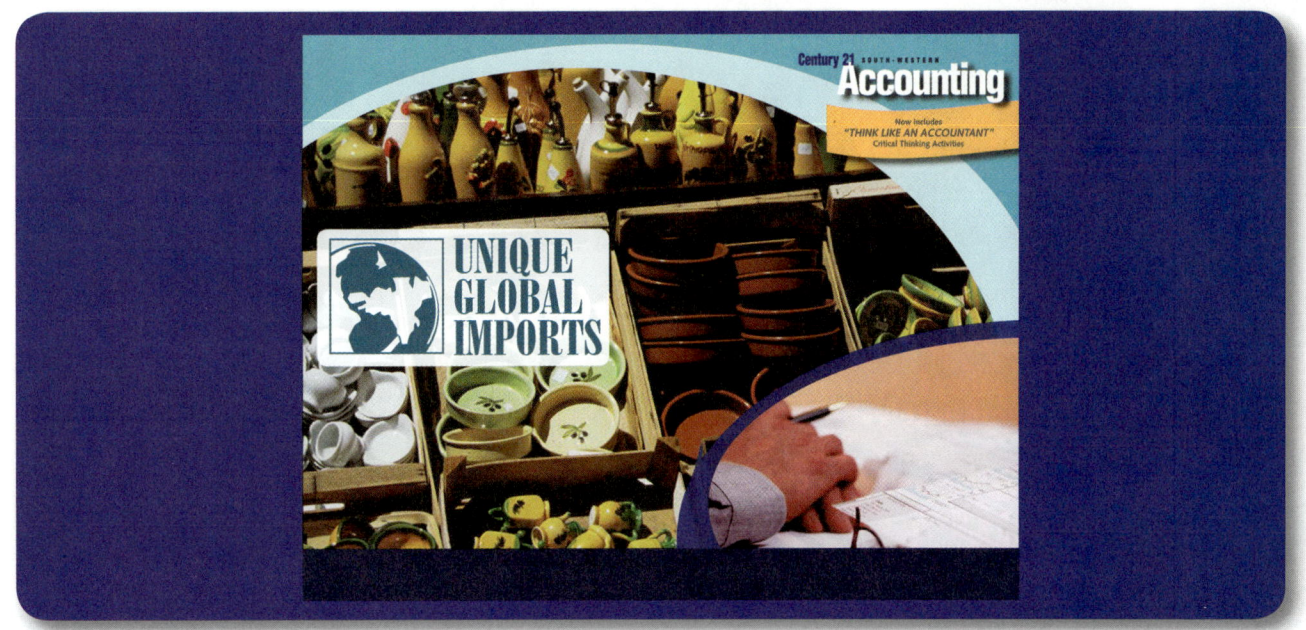

This simulation covers the realistic transactions completed by Unique Global Imports. The business sells imported goods, including fabrics, clothing, furniture, and decorative accessories.

Transactions are recorded in special journals similar to the ones used by Hobby Shack, Inc., in this accounting cycle. The activities included in the accounting cycle for Unique Global Imports are listed below.

This real-life business simulation comes with source documents. It is available in manual and automated versions. The automated version is used with *Automated Accounting* software.

The following activities are included in the Unique Global Imports simulation:

1. Recording transactions in special journals from source documents.
2. Posting items to be posted individually to a general ledger and subsidiary ledgers.
3. Recording a payroll in a payroll register. Updating the employee earnings records. Recording payroll journal entries.
4. Posting column totals to a general ledger.
5. Preparing schedules of accounts receivable and accounts payable from subsidiary ledgers.
6. Preparing a trial balance on a work sheet.
7. Planning adjustments and completing a work sheet.
8. Preparing financial statements.
9. Journalizing and posting adjusting entries.
10. Journalizing and posting closing entries.
11. Preparing a post-closing trial balance.
12. Preparing a post-closing trial balance.
13. Completing Think Like an Accountant Financial Analysis.

PART 3: Accounting for a Merchandising Business Organized as a Corporation—Adjustments and Valuation

▽ Chapter 17	Accounting for Uncollectible Accounts Receivable
▽ Chapter 18	Accounting for Plant Assets and Depreciation
▽ Chapter 19	Accounting for Inventory
▽ Chapter 20	Accounting for Notes and Interest
▽ Chapter 21	Accounting for Accrued Revenue and Expenses
▽ Chapter 22	End-of-Fiscal-Period Work for a Corporation

THE BUSINESS—RESTAURANT SUPPLY CO.

Restaurant Supply Co., the business described in Part 3, is a retail merchandising business organized as a corporation. The business purchases and sells a wide variety of cooking and restaurant supplies and equipment. Restaurant Supply purchases its merchandise directly from the manufacturers and distributors. Restaurant Supply rents the building in which the business is located.

CHAPTER 17

CHAPTER 18

CHAPTER 19

RESTAURANT SUPPLY CO. CHART OF ACCOUNTS

GENERAL LEDGER

Balance Sheet Accounts

(1000) ASSETS
- 1100 Current Assets
- 1105 Cash
- 1110 Petty Cash
- 1115 Notes Receivable
- 1120 Interest Receivable
- 1125 Accounts Receivable
- 1130 Allowance for Uncollectible Accounts
- 1135 Merchandise Inventory
- 1140 Supplies
- 1145 Prepaid Insurance
- 1200 Plant Assets
- 1205 Office Equipment
- 1210 Accumulated Depreciation—Office Equipment
- 1215 Store Equipment
- 1220 Accumulated Depreciation—Store Equipment

(2000) LIABILITIES
- 2100 Current Liabilities
- 2105 Notes Payable
- 2110 Interest Payable
- 2115 Accounts Payable
- 2120 Employee Income Tax Payable
- 2125 Federal Income Tax Payable
- 2130 Social Security Tax Payable
- 2135 Medicare Tax Payable
- 2140 Sales Tax Payable
- 2145 Unemployment Tax Payable—Federal
- 2150 Unemployment Tax Payable—State
- 2155 Health Insurance Premiums Payable
- 2160 Dividends Payable

(3000) STOCKHOLDERS' EQUITY
- 3105 Capital Stock
- 3110 Retained Earnings
- 3115 Dividends
- 3120 Income Summary

Income Statement Accounts

(4000) OPERATING REVENUE
- 4105 Sales
- 4110 Sales Discount
- 4115 Sales Returns and Allowances

(5000) COST OF MERCHANDISE
- 5105 Purchases
- 5110 Purchases Discount
- 5115 Purchases Returns and Allowances

(6000) OPERATING EXPENSES
- 6105 Advertising Expense
- 6110 Cash Short and Over
- 6115 Credit Card Fee Expense
- 6120 Depreciation Expense—Office Equipment
- 6125 Depreciation Expense—Store Equipment
- 6130 Insurance Expense
- 6135 Miscellaneous Expense
- 6140 Payroll Taxes Expense
- 6145 Rent Expense
- 6150 Repair Expense
- 6155 Salary Expense
- 6160 Supplies Expense
- 6165 Uncollectible Accounts Expense
- 6170 Utilities Expense

(7000) OTHER REVENUE
- 7105 Gain on Plant Assets
- 7110 Interest Income

(8000) OTHER EXPENSES
- 8105 Interest Expense
- 8110 Loss on Plant Assets

(9000) INCOME TAX EXPENSE
- 9105 Federal Income Tax Expense

The chart of accounts for Restaurant Supply Co. is illustrated here for ready reference as you study Part 3 of this textbook.

CHAPTER 20

CHAPTER 21

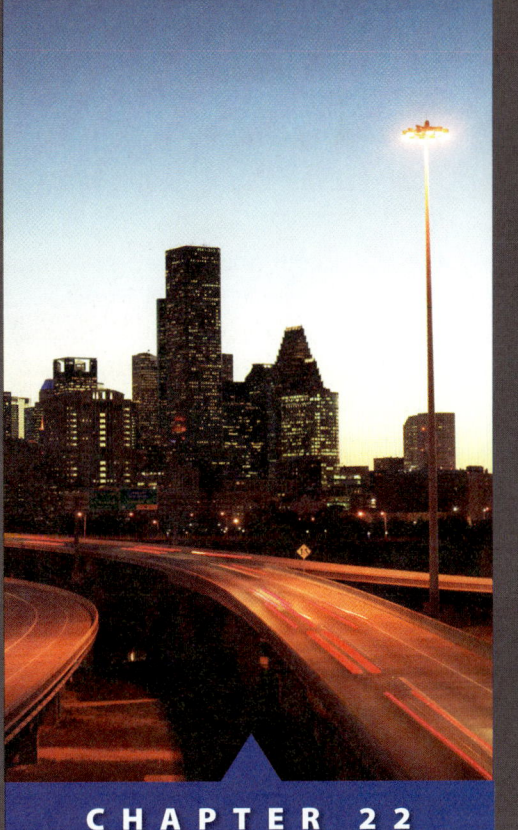

CHAPTER 22

CHAPTER 17

Accounting for Uncollectible Accounts Receivable

OBJECTIVES

After studying Chapter 17, you will be able to:

1. Define accounting terms related to uncollectible accounts.
2. Identify accounting concepts and practices related to uncollectible accounts.
3. Calculate, journalize, and post estimated uncollectible accounts expense.
4. Journalize and post entries related to writing off and collecting uncollectible accounts receivable.

KEY TERMS

- writing off an account

Point Your Browser
www.C21accounting.com

ACCOUNTING IN THE REAL WORLD

Performance Food Group

Dining Out with Performance Food Group

You can't drive down the road and find a restaurant by its name. But chances are you have eaten recently at a restaurant that purchased its food from Performance Food Group (PFG). The company is one of the leading food distributors in the United States.

PFG purchases food products from manufacturers and produces its own line of ready-to-eat products. The company delivers these products to more than 47,000 customers that include restaurants, schools, cafeterias, healthcare facilities, and grocery stores. To provide superior service, PFG sells to some customers on account.

Unfortunately, the food service business can be challenging, even for entrepreneurs with experience in the industry. As a result, some of PFG's customers cannot pay their accounts. PFG is unable to collect approximately 0.1% of its sales, or approximately $5.5 million per year.

Critical Thinking

1. Using the information provided, estimate PFG's annual sales.
2. What account is used to record the period estimate of future uncollectible accounts? What is the classification of this account?

Source: www.pfgc.com

INTERNET ACTIVITY

EDGAR—Part 3

Go to the homepage for EDGAR (www.sec.gov/edgar/searchedgar/webusers.htm). Click on "Companies & Other Filers." Search the EDGAR database for the most recent 10K report from Dell, Inc. (Enter "Dell Inc" for company name, click on "Find Companies," and then scroll down and click on "10-K" in the first column.) The 10-K form is very similar to and contains much of the same information as the annual report.

Instructions

1. Find the balance sheet and record the net amount of Accounts Receivable.
2. Find the "Notes" to the financial statements and record the amount of "gross accounts receivable" and the amount of "allowance for doubtful accounts."

LESSON 17-1

Uncollectible Accounts

A business sells on account to encourage sales. Customers can buy merchandise even though they will not have the cash needed to pay the account until days or months later.

A business that sells on account expects full payment within the terms of sale. Before selling to a customer on account, management should perform a thorough credit check on a customer.

A credit customer's financial condition may decline over time. Business customers may experience increased competition or a catastrophic event, such as a weather disaster. Individual customers may lose their employment. Regardless of the reason, creditworthy customers may later be unable to pay their accounts. Accounts receivable that cannot be collected are known as *uncollectible accounts*.

THE BUSINESS—RESTAURANT SUPPLY CO.

Miguel Lopez, Keisha Tomkins, and Joseph Weisbaum worked as chefs at restaurants in a trendy part of the city. They all had dreams of owning their own businesses, but they tired of the long hours involved in restaurant operations. Since they had experience using cooking tools and equipment, they explored the restaurant supply business and decided to form a corporation to sell to restaurants. Because of widespread consumer interest in cooking, they also make cash and credit card sales to individual customers. They sell on account to restaurants and catering operations.

The chart of accounts on page 511 is similar to that of the corporation in Part 2. However, Restaurant Supply has two new sections in the chart of accounts: Other Revenue and Other Expenses. The accounts in these sections are income statement accounts that are used for interest they pay on loans or earn on extended credit terms for customers. They also have accounts for recording gains and losses on plant assets they sell, trade, or discard.

CHARACTER COUNTS

Lifelong Learning

When you are ill, you expect your doctor to know the latest methods and medicines to restore your health. Businesses should expect nothing less from their accountants. Therefore, accountants must constantly improve their knowledge and skills to provide their clients, employees, and the public with the highest level of professional service.

The code of conduct for every major accounting organization includes some reference to lifelong learning. Many organizations require their members to complete a specified number of continuing education credits annually. For example, most certified public accountants must complete 40 hours of continuing education every year. This education may be in the form of self-study courses, college courses, seminars, or conferences.

Instructions

Access the code of conduct from the American Institute of Certified Public Accountants (AICPA), the Institute of Internal Auditors (IIA), the Institute of Management Accountants (IMA), and the Association of Certified Fraud Examiners (ACFE). Identify what each code states about lifelong learning.

ESTIMATING AND RECORDING UNCOLLECTIBLE ACCOUNTS EXPENSE

Allowing customers to buy now and pay later is an effective method for increasing sales. Unfortunately, some customers may later become unable or unwilling to pay their account. These uncollectible accounts must be recorded as an expense.

The allowance method of recording losses from uncollectible accounts attempts to match the expense of uncollectible accounts in the same fiscal year the related sales are recorded. At the end of the fiscal year, the business does not know which specific accounts will become uncollectible. Therefore, an estimate of the uncollectible accounts is recorded to the contra asset account Allowance for Uncollectible Accounts and the expense account Uncollectible Accounts Expense. [CONCEPT: Matching Expenses with Revenue]

Restaurant Supply estimates uncollectible accounts expense by calculating a percentage of total sales on account. A review of Restaurant Supply's previous experience in collecting sales on account shows that actual uncollectible accounts expense has been about 1.0% of total sales on account. The company's total sales on account for the year is $1,287,330.00. Thus, Restaurant Supply estimates that $12,873.30 of the current fiscal period's sales on account will eventually be uncollectible.

Total Sales on Account	× Percentage	=	Estimated Uncollectible Accounts Expense
$1,287,330.00 ×	1.0%	=	$12,873.30

FOR YOUR INFORMATION
FYI

A credit check might involve an analysis of the customer's financial statements, a review of reports from national credit agencies, and interviews with other businesses that sell to the customer on account.

BUSINESS STRUCTURES

Dissolving a Corporation

Because the corporation is the most complex form of business, dissolution involves many legal procedures. Thus, the board of directors should seek the legal advice of an attorney.

In some states, the Secretary of State may take action to dissolve a corporation if one or more of the three following conditions exists: (1) The corporation is 60 days late in paying franchise taxes. (2) The corporation does not file its annual report within 60 days of the due date. (3) The corporation does not have a registered agent or office for 60 days or more.

Judicial proceedings may be brought against a corporation if the corporation acts beyond the powers it has been granted or engages in illegal activity. These proceedings may force the corporation to give up its charter.

Once a corporation is dissolved, the liquidation process can begin. Noncash assets usually are sold, and the proceeds are used to pay creditors. The procedure for selling noncash assets is similar to that for proprietorships. However, because a corporation's earnings are taxable, the gains and losses on the sales of noncash assets are subject to taxation. Therefore, additional tax reports for the corporation must be filed.

Critical Thinking
What do you think are some circumstances that might lead a corporation to dissolve voluntarily?

Uncollectible Accounts   Lesson 17-1

ANALYZING AND JOURNALIZING AN ADJUSTMENT FOR UNCOLLECTIBLE ACCOUNTS EXPENSE

The percentage of total sales on account method of estimating uncollectible accounts expense assumes that a portion of every sale on account dollar will become uncollectible. Restaurant Supply has estimated that 1% of its $1,287,330.00 sales on account, or $12,873.30, will eventually become uncollectible.

At the end of a fiscal period, an adjustment for uncollectible accounts expense is planned on a work sheet. The Allowance for Uncollectible Accounts balance in the Trial Balance Credit column, $280.00, is the allowance estimate from the previous fiscal period that has not yet been identified as uncollectible.

When the allowance account has a previous credit balance, the amount of the adjustment is added to the previous balance. This new balance of the allowance account is the estimated amount of accounts receivable that will eventually become uncollectible.

Uncollectible Accounts Expense	
Dec. 31 Adj. 12,873.30	

Allowance for Uncollectible Accounts	
	Bal. 280.00
	Dec. 31 Adj. 12,873.30
	(New Bal. 13,153.30)

STEPS ANALYZING AND JOURNALIZING AN ADJUSTMENT FOR UNCOLLECTIBLE ACCOUNTS EXPENSE

1. Enter the estimated uncollectible amount, $12,873.30, in the Adjustments Credit column on the *Allowance for Uncollectible Accounts* line of the work sheet. Label the adjustment *(b)* with a small letter in parentheses.

2. Enter the same amount, $12,873.30, in the Adjustments Debit column on the *Uncollectible Accounts Expense* line of the work sheet. Label the adjustment using the same letter, *(b)*.

3. Use the debit and credit amounts on the work sheet to record an adjusting entry in a general journal.

POSTING AN ADJUSTING ENTRY FOR UNCOLLECTIBLE ACCOUNTS EXPENSE

GENERAL JOURNAL PAGE 15

	DATE	ACCOUNT TITLE	DOC. NO.	POST. REF.	DEBIT	CREDIT	
1		*Adjusting Entries*					1
4	31	Uncollectible Accounts Expense		6165	12 873 30		4
5		Allow. for Uncollectible Accts.		1130		12 873 30	5

ACCOUNT **Accounts Receivable** ACCOUNT NO. **1125**

DATE	ITEM	POST. REF.	DEBIT	CREDIT	BALANCE DEBIT	BALANCE CREDIT
Dec. 31		S49	84 451 25		142 624 50	
31		CR54		64 284 20	78 340 30	

1. Debit

2. Credit

ACCOUNT **Allowance for Uncollectible Accounts** ACCOUNT NO. **1130**

DATE	ITEM	POST. REF.	DEBIT	CREDIT	BALANCE DEBIT	BALANCE CREDIT
Dec. 22		G14	810 00		280 00	
31		G15		12 873 30		13 153 30

ACCOUNT **Uncollectible Accounts Expense** ACCOUNT NO. **6165**

DATE	ITEM	POST. REF.	DEBIT	CREDIT	BALANCE DEBIT	BALANCE CREDIT
Dec. 31		G15	12 873 30		12 873 30	

The adjustment for uncollectible accounts expense planned on the work sheet is recorded as an adjusting entry in the general journal. The adjusting entry is then posted to the general ledger.

The adjusting entry affects two of the three accounts related to accounts receivable. After the adjustment, Allowance for Uncollectible Accounts has a credit balance of $13,153.30. The balance of this contra account is an estimate of outstanding accounts receivable that will become uncollectible during the next fiscal period.

The debit balance of Uncollectible Accounts Expense, $12,873.30, is the estimated uncollectible accounts resulting from sales on account during the current fiscal year.

The adjusting entry does not affect the balance of Accounts Receivable. Accounts Receivable has a debit balance of $78,340.30 before and after the adjusting entry is posted. The book value of accounts receivable on December 31, $65,187.00, is an estimate of the amount of the December 31 balance of accounts receivable Restaurant Supply expects to collect during the next fiscal year.

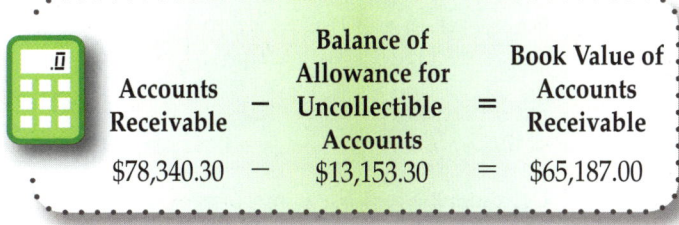

Accounts Receivable − Balance of Allowance for Uncollectible Accounts = Book Value of Accounts Receivable

$78,340.30 − $13,153.30 = $65,187.00

Uncollectible Accounts Lesson 17-1 **517**

End of Lesson REVIEW

AUDIT YOUR UNDERSTANDING

1. How are uncollectible accounts recorded?
2. Explain why an adjustment for uncollectible accounts is an application of the *Matching Expenses with Revenue* concept.
3. How is the account Accounts Receivable affected by the estimate of uncollectible accounts?

WORK TOGETHER 17-1

Estimating and journalizing entries for uncollectible accounts expense

A general journal, work sheet, and selected general ledger accounts for Velson Company are given in the *Working Papers*. Your instructor will guide you through the following examples.

1. Velson Company estimates uncollectible accounts expense as 0.3% of its total sales on account. During the current year, Velson had credit sales of $2,152,000.00. The balance in Allowance for Uncollectible Accounts before adjustment is an $853.00 credit. Record the December 31 uncollectible accounts expense adjustment on a work sheet. Label the adjustment *(e)*.
2. Journalize the adjusting entry on page 13 of a general journal.
3. Post the adjusting entry to the general ledger.

ON YOUR OWN 17-1

Estimating and journalizing entries for uncollectible accounts expense

A general journal, work sheet, and selected general ledger accounts for McCaffery Industries are given in the *Working Papers*. Work this problem independently.

1. McCaffery Industries estimates uncollectible accounts expense as 0.4% of its total sales on account. During the current year, McCaffery had credit sales of $1,548,050.00. The balance in Allowance for Uncollectible Accounts before adjustment is a $216.00 credit. Record the December 31 uncollectible accounts expense adjustment on a work sheet. Label the adjustment *(e)*.
2. Journalize the adjusting entry on page 26 of a general journal.
3. Post the adjusting entry to the general ledger.

LESSON 17-2

Writing Off and Collecting Uncollectible Accounts Receivable

JOURNALIZING WRITING OFF AN UNCOLLECTIBLE ACCOUNT RECEIVABLE

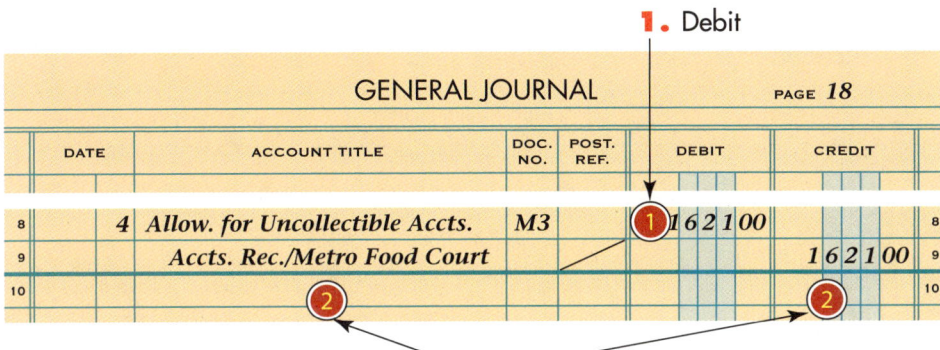

1. Debit
2. Credit and Customer's Name

When a customer account is determined to be uncollectible, a journal entry is made to cancel the uncollectible account. This entry cancels the uncollectible amount from the general ledger account Accounts Receivable as well as the customer account in the accounts receivable subsidiary ledger. Canceling the balance of a customer account because the customer does not pay is called **writing off an account**.

After months of unsuccessful collection efforts, Restaurant Supply decides that the past-due account of Metro Food Court is uncollectible.

> **January 4.** Wrote off Metro Food Court's past-due account as uncollectible, $1,621.00. Memorandum No. 3.

Because the account of Metro Food Court has been determined to be uncollectible, the $1,621.00 is now an actual uncollectible amount. Therefore, the amount of the uncollectible account is deducted from the allowance account.

Accounts Receivable is credited to reduce the balance due from customers. Metro Food Court's account is also credited to cancel the debit balance of the account. Metro Food Court's account is written off.

The book value of accounts receivable is the same both before and after writing off an uncollectible account. This is true because the same amount is deducted from both the accounts receivable and the allowance accounts.

GENERAL LEDGER
Allowance for Uncollectible Accounts

Jan. 4	1,621.00	Bal.	13,153.30
		(New Bal.	11,532.30)

Accounts Receivable

Bal.	78,340.30	Jan. 4	1,621.00
(New Bal.	76,719.30)		

ACCOUNTS RECEIVABLE LEDGER
Metro Food Court

Bal.	1,621.00	Jan. 4	1,621.00
(New Bal.	zero)		

	Before Account Written Off	After Account Written Off
Accounts Receivable	$ 78,340.30	$76,719.30
Allowance for Uncollectible Accounts	–13,153.30	–11,532.30
Book Value	$ 65,187.00	$ 65,187.00

POSTING AN ENTRY TO WRITE OFF AN UNCOLLECTIBLE ACCOUNT RECEIVABLE

The journal entry to write off an uncollectible account affects the two general ledger accounts Accounts Receivable and Allowance for Uncollectible Accounts, and the customer account. The words *Written off* are written in the Item column of the customer account to show the full credit history for the customer.

STEPS — POSTING AN ENTRY TO WRITE OFF AN UNCOLLECTIBLE ACCOUNT RECEIVABLE

1. Post the debit, $1,621.00, to *Allowance for Uncollectible Accounts* in the general ledger.
2. Post the credit, $1,621.00, to *Accounts Receivable* in the general ledger.
3. Post the credit, $1,621.00, to the customer account, *Metro Food Court*, in the accounts receivable ledger.
4. Write the words *Written off* in the Item column of the customer account.

REOPENING AN ACCOUNT PREVIOUSLY WRITTEN OFF

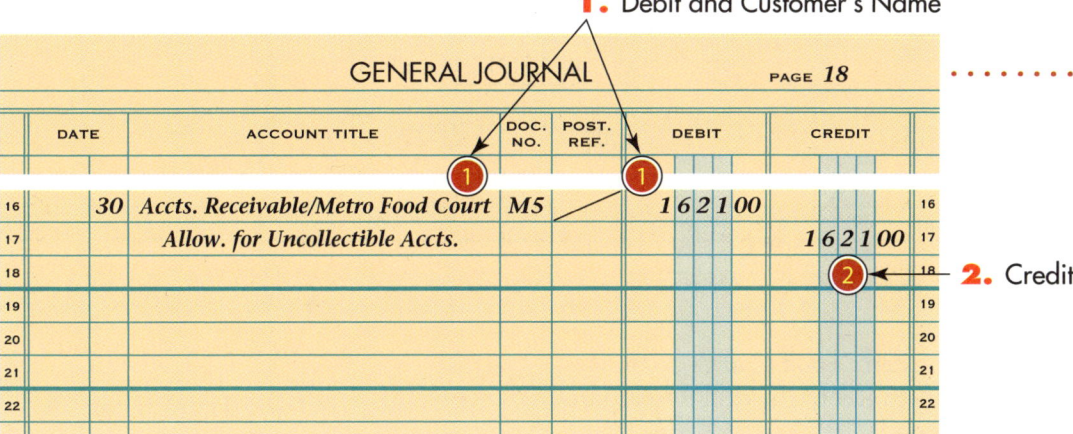

A business writes off a specific account receivable after determining that the account probably will not be collected. Occasionally, after an account has been written off, the customer pays the delinquent account. Several accounts must be changed to recognize payment of a written-off account receivable.

> **January 30.** Received cash in full payment of Metro Food Court's account, previously written off as uncollectible, $1,621.00. Memorandum No. 5 and Receipt No. 12.

GENERAL LEDGER
Accounts Receivable

Bal.	78,340.30	Jan. 4	1,621.00
Jan. 30	1,621.00		
(New Bal.	78,340.30)		

Allowance for Uncollectible Accounts

Jan. 4	1,621.00	Bal.	13,153.30
		Jan. 30	1,621.00
		(New Bal.	13,153.30)

ACCOUNTS RECEIVABLE LEDGER
Metro Food Court

Bal.	1,621.00	Jan. 4	1,621.00
Jan. 30	1,621.00		
(New Bal.	1,621.00)		

Several accounts must be changed to show that Metro Food Court did pay its account. The accounts also should be changed to show a complete credit history of Metro Food Court's dealings with Restaurant Supply Co.

Two journal entries are recorded for the collection of a written-off account receivable: (1) a general journal entry to reopen the customer account and (2) a cash receipts journal entry to record the cash received on account.

To show an accurate credit history, Metro Food Court's account is reopened. Accounts Receivable is debited for $1,621.00 to replace the amount previously written off in the general ledger account. Allowance for Uncollectible Accounts is credited for $1,621.00 to replace the amount that was removed when Metro Food Court's account was previously written off. Also, Metro Food Court's account in the accounts receivable ledger is debited for $1,621.00. This entry to reopen the account is the exact reverse of the entry to write off Metro Food Court's account.

STEPS — REOPENING AN ACCOUNT PREVIOUSLY WRITTEN OFF

1. Enter a debit, *$1,621.00*, to *Accounts Receivable*. Place a diagonal line after the account title and enter the customer's name, *Metro Food Court*. Place a diagonal line in the Post. Ref. column.

2. Enter a credit, *$1,621.00*, to *Allowance for Uncollectible Accounts*.

RECORDING CASH RECEIVED FOR AN ACCOUNT PREVIOUSLY WRITTEN OFF

	DATE	ACCOUNT TITLE	DOC. NO.	POST. REF.	GENERAL DEBIT	GENERAL CREDIT	ACCOUNTS RECEIVABLE CREDIT	SALES CREDIT	SALES TAX PAYABLE CREDIT	SALES DISCOUNT DEBIT	CASH DEBIT	
21	30	Metro Food Court	R12				1 621 00				1 621 00	21
22												22

CASH RECEIPTS JOURNAL — PAGE 54

After the entry to reopen Metro Food Court's account is recorded, an entry is made to record the cash received on Metro Food Court's account.

> **January 30.** Received cash in full payment of Metro Food Court's account, previously written off as uncollectible, $1,621.00. Memorandum No. 5 and Receipt No. 12.

The entry in the cash receipts journal is the same as for any other collection of accounts receivable.

GENERAL LEDGER
Cash
| Jan. 30 | 1,621.00 | |

Accounts Receivable
| Bal. | 78,340.30 | Jan. 4 | 1,621.00 |
| Jan. 30 | 1,621.00 | Jan. 30 | 1,621.00 |

ACCOUNTS RECEIVABLE LEDGER
Metro Food Court
Bal.	1,621.00	Jan. 4	1,621.00
Jan. 30	1,621.00	Jan. 30	1,621.00
		(New Bal.	zero)

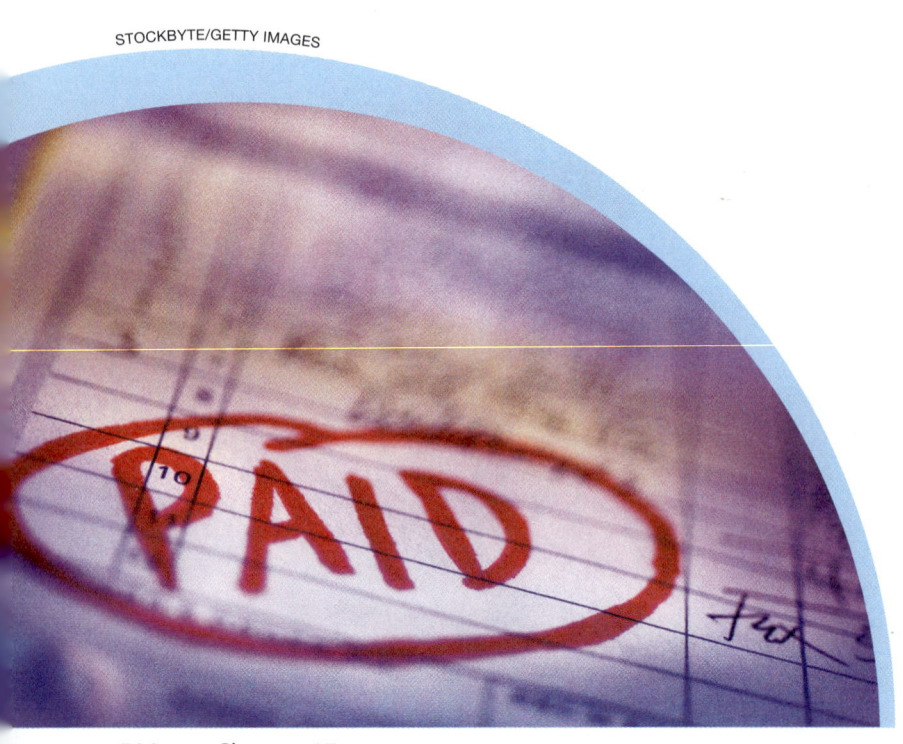
STOCKBYTE/GETTY IMAGES

POSTING ENTRIES FOR COLLECTING A WRITTEN-OFF ACCOUNT RECEIVABLE

STEPS: POSTING ENTRIES FOR COLLECTING A WRITTEN-OFF ACCOUNT RECEIVABLE

1. Post the general journal entry to the general ledger.
2. Post the debit portion of the general journal entry to the customer account.
3. Write the words *Reopen account* in the Item column of the customer account.
4. Post the cash receipts journal entry to the customer account.

Writing Off and Collecting Uncollectible Accounts Receivable   Lesson 17-2   **523**

End of Lesson REVIEW

AUDIT YOUR UNDERSTANDING

1. Why is Allowance for Uncollectible Accounts debited when a customer account is written off?
2. Does the book value of accounts receivable differ before and after writing off an account? Explain.
3. Why is a customer account reopened when the account is paid after being previously written off?

TERM REVIEW

writing off an account

WORK TOGETHER 17-2

Recording entries related to uncollectible accounts receivable

The journals and selected ledger accounts for Cross Company are given in the *Working Papers*. Your instructor will guide you through the following examples.

1. Journalize the following transactions completed during November of the current year. Use page 15 of a general journal and page 24 of a cash receipts journal.

Transactions:

Nov. 2. Wrote off Davidson Corp.'s past-due account as uncollectible, $849.00. M245.
    3. Wrote off JGF Industries' past-due account as uncollectible, $2,488.00. M247.
    4. Wrote off Sansing Co.'s past-due account as uncollectible, $609.00. M251.
    14. Received cash in full payment of Lynchburg Co.'s account, previously written off as uncollectible, $1,548.00. M258 and R415.
    29. Received cash in full payment of JGF Industries' account, previously written off as uncollectible, $2,488.00. M261 and R429.

2. Post each entry to the customer accounts in the accounts receivable ledger.
3. Post general journal entries to the general ledger.

ON YOUR OWN 17-2

Recording entries related to uncollectible accounts receivable

The journals and selected ledger accounts for Potera Company are given in the *Working Papers*. Work this problem independently.

1. Journalize the following transactions completed during October of the current year. Use page 11 of a general journal and page 15 of a cash receipts journal.

Transactions:

Oct. 5. Wrote off Angela White's past-due account as uncollectible, $159.00. M45.
    8. Wrote off Peter Ewing's past-due account as uncollectible, $612.00. M47.
    12. Received cash in full payment of Mike Novak's account, previously written off as uncollectible, $853.00. M51 and R313.
    16. Wrote off Tim Haley's past-due account as uncollectible, $238.00. M58.
    23. Received cash in full payment of Peter Ewing's account, previously written off as uncollectible, $612.00. M61 and R345.

2. Post each entry to the customer accounts in the accounts receivable ledger.
3. Post general journal entries to the general ledger.

SUMMARY

After completing this chapter, you can:

1. Define accounting terms related to uncollectible accounts.
2. Identify accounting concepts and practices related to uncollectible accounts.
3. Calculate, journalize, and post estimated uncollectible accounts expense.
4. Journalize and post entries related to writing off and collecting uncollectible accounts receivable.

EXPLORE ACCOUNTING

Accounting Estimates Use Interesting Assumptions

Accountants use many accounting estimates to adjust the historical cost of certain transactions to better reflect the company's financial condition.

One of the most interesting accounting estimates concerns a payroll-related expense known as post-retirement benefits other than pensions. Some companies offer their employees free services, such as health care, during their retirement. For many years, companies have expensed these costs when the services were actually provided and paid for in cash. Accounting rules recently changed to require that these costs be recognized as an expense over the employee's years of work. The promise of free health care during retirement is part of the total benefits that the company provides an employee in exchange for the employee's services.

For example, Watanabe Industries has promised free health care to its retired employees and their family members under 21 years of age. Carmen Suarez is expected to work for Watanabe Industries for 30 years. Health care costs for Carmen, her husband, and any future children during her retirement are currently estimated to be $30,000. Rather than expense the $30,000 when the bills are paid during Carmen's retirement, the new accounting rule requires that the $30,000 be expensed over Carmen's 30 years of service. Therefore, $1,000 will be expensed each year.

To estimate the projected benefit, assumptions must be made regarding the following items: (1) percentage annual growth rate in health care costs, (2) life expectancy, (3) retirement age, (4) number of children, and (5) interest costs. Management's assumptions can dramatically affect accounting estimates. Companies that prepare public financial statements have independent auditors examine the assumptions used to compute accounting estimates to assure that these assumptions are reasonable.

Research: Research the annual growth rate of health care costs. Do you believe this growth rate will continue? Identify factors that might cause further increases or decreases in growth rate.

17-1 APPLICATION PROBLEM

Estimating and journalizing entries for uncollectible accounts expense

A general journal, partial work sheet, and selected general ledger accounts for Kellogg, Inc., are given in the *Working Papers*.

Instructions:

1. Kellogg, Inc., estimates uncollectible accounts expense as 1.0% of its total sales on account. During the current year, Kellogg had credit sales of $3,426,000.00. The balance in Allowance for Uncollectible Accounts before adjustment is a $534.00 credit. Record the uncollectible accounts expense adjustment on a work sheet. Label the adjustment *(e)*.
2. Journalize the adjusting entry on page 25 of a general journal.
3. Post the adjusting entry to the general ledger.

17-2 APPLICATION PROBLEM

Recording entries related to uncollectible accounts receivable

The journals and selected ledger accounts for Waldron Company are given in the *Working Papers*.

Instructions:

1. The following transactions related to accounts receivable occurred during September of the current year. Journalize the transactions using page 14 of a general journal and page 19 of a cash receipts journal.

Transactions:

Sept. 5. Wrote off Jackson Company's past-due account as uncollectible, $124.00. M234.
      7. Received cash in full payment of Davis Industries' account, previously written off as uncollectible, $185.00. M235 and R339.
     14. Wrote off Lancing, Inc.'s past-due account as uncollectible, $215.00. M238.
     19. Wrote off Sanders Mfg.'s past-due account as uncollectible, $842.00. M243.
     27. Received cash in full payment of Jackson Company's account, previously written off as uncollectible, $124.00. M251 and R362.

2. Post each entry to the customer accounts in the accounts receivable ledger.
3. Post each entry in the general journal to the general ledger.

PURESTOCK/GETTY IMAGES

17-3 APPLICATION PROBLEM

Recording entries related to uncollectible accounts receivable

The journals and selected ledger accounts for Weatherly Co. are given in the *Working Papers*.

Instructions:

1. The following transactions related to accounts receivable occurred during February of the current year. Journalize the transactions using page 4 of a general journal and page 2 of a cash receipts journal.

Transactions:

Feb. 3. Received a $1,458.00 check from Bearden Co. in full payment of its account. The account was written off in the previous month based on a newspaper story that indicated the company was about to close. M24 and R134.
    7. Monique Pearce, controller of Hampton Industries, just called, stating that the company had serious cash flow problems and would not be able to pay its $2,584.00 account balance. M25.
   10. Received a letter from Rankin Co.'s legal counsel, stating that the company was in the process of filing bankruptcy. The letter gave little hope that Weatherly would collect Rankin's $948.00 account. M28.
   12. Received a check from Camden Enterprises in full payment of its $1,784.00 account. The account was written off in January after months of efforts to collect the account. M31 and R142.
   21. A letter from Wilmont Co.'s receiving department supervisor, Daymon Lewis, stated that Wilmont refuses to pay for a prior year shipment of product for $548.00. The supervisor contends that the products were spoiled on arrival and were discarded. M34.
   27. Received a letter and check in the mail from Monique Pearce of Hampton Industries. Two weeks ago the company was purchased by another company and therefore has access to cash to pay its debt. M35 and R159.

2. Post each entry to the customer accounts in the accounts receivable ledger.
3. Post each entry in the general journal to the general ledger.

17-4 MASTERY PROBLEM

Recording entries for uncollectible accounts

Selected accounts receivable and general ledger accounts for Sing Industries are given in the *Working Papers*. The following transactions relating to uncollectible accounts receivable occurred during the final quarter of the current fiscal year.

Instructions:

1. Journalize the following transactions completed during October using page 20 of a general journal. Post the transactions to the customer accounts and general ledger accounts.

Transactions:

Oct. 8. Wrote off Keller Corporation's past-due account as uncollectible, $648.25. M243.
   19. Wrote off Gason Company's past-due account as uncollectible, $948.00. M252.

2. Journalize the following transactions completed during November using page 22 of a general journal and page 24 of a cash receipts journal. Prove the cash receipts journal. Post the transactions and the total of the Accounts Receivable Credit column to the customer accounts and general ledger accounts.

Transactions:

Nov. 9. Wrote off Baker Co.'s past-due account as uncollectible, $815.00. M267.
   18. Received cash in full payment of Keller Corporation's account, previously written off as uncollectible, $648.25. M274 and R453.
   23. Received cash in full payment of Pearson Industries' account, previously written off as uncollectible, $251.80. M281 and R476.

3. Journalize the following transactions for December. Use page 24 of a general journal and page 26 of a cash receipts journal. Prove the cash receipts journal. Post the transactions and the total of the Accounts Receivable Credit column to the customer accounts and general ledger accounts.

Transactions:

Dec. 4. Wrote off Franklin, Inc.'s past-due account as uncollectible, $1,458.00. M291.
     10. Received cash in full payment of Baker Corp.'s account, previously written off as uncollectible, $815.00. M293 and R489.
     29. Received cash in full payment of Gason Company's account, previously written off as uncollectible, $948.00. M297 and R502.

4. Journalize the December 31 adjusting entry for estimated uncollectible accounts expense for the year. Use page 26 of the general journal. Uncollectible accounts expense is estimated as 0.5% of total sales on account. Total sales on account for the year were $1,654,800.00. Post the transaction to the general ledger accounts.

17-5   CHALLENGE PROBLEM

Recording entries for uncollectible accounts

Information from the accounting records of Rosedale Company concerning uncollectible accounts during the past five years follows (presented in thousands of dollars).

	20X1	20X2	20X3	20X4	20X5
Sales on account	$575	$700	$850	$1,050	$1,200
Ending Accounts Receivable	50	60	80	90	100
Uncollectible Accounts Expense	8	8	15	15	15
Ending Allowance for Uncollectible Accounts	5	1	4	3	1
Accounts written off	10	13	14	18	19
Accounts collected after being written off	1	1	2	2	2

Yu-lan Cheng, the controller of the company, has asked you to evaluate the prior annual adjustments to Allowance for Uncollectible Accounts. If the company expects to have sales of $1,400,000.00 next year, what amount would you suggest be expensed to Uncollectible Accounts Expense? Support your answer.

APPLIED COMMUNICATION

For many years, the accounting staff at St. Charles Furniture has written off uncollectible accounts receivable by debiting Uncollectible Accounts Expense and crediting Accounts Receivable. Despite relatively constant sales and collections on account, the annual amount of Uncollectible Accounts Expense has fluctuated between $5,000.00 and $90,000.00 during the past six years. Management admits that the amount of accounts written off depends largely on the time the managers have devoted to evaluating accounts receivable for possible collection problems.

Instructions: Prepare a memorandum to Tomas Gonzalez, president of St. Charles Furniture, explaining the correct way to account for uncollectible accounts receivable. The memorandum should persuade him to implement a change from the current accounting procedure.

CASE FOR CRITICAL THINKING

Some businesses have a policy of accepting only cash sales. Depending on economic conditions or the time of year, many potential customers may not be able to pay with currency, check, or debit card. Businesses with cash-only policies will lose those potential sales. As has been discussed in previous chapters, other businesses encourage more sales by selling on account to customers with approved credit. The key decision is defining what is approved credit. Employees responsible for meeting the sales goals of a business might choose one set of standards for approving credit. Employees responsible for maintaining merchandise inventory and filling orders might choose a different set of standards for approving credit. What role, if any, do you believe that accounting employees should play in setting a company's standards for approving credit? What contributions can accounting employees make to discussions about credit standards?

GRAPHING WORKSHOP

Predicting Uncollectible Accounts

Each year Hitesh Nizami, the controller for Southern Electronics, evaluates the percentage to be used to estimate uncollectible accounts expense. The company adopted a more liberal credit policy, resulting in a significant but acceptable increase in the accounts that were actually written off.

1. In what year did the company implement its new credit policy?
2. What percentage would you recommend Hitesh use to calculate the 2005 adjustment for allowance for uncollectible accounts? Justify your answer.

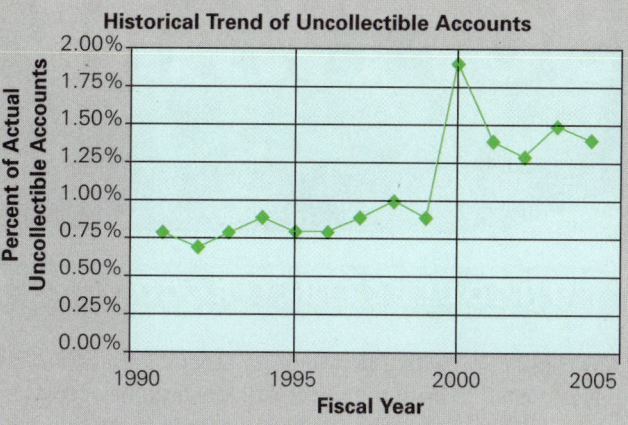

ANALYZING BEST BUY'S FINANCIAL STATEMENTS

A standard set of financial ratios has been developed to help individuals understand financial statements. Not every ratio, however, can be applied to every company. Best Buy customers must pay for their purchases with cash or a credit card. Thus, Best Buy does not have any trade accounts receivable. The small amount of accounts receivable reported on Best Buy's Consolidated Balance Sheets results from miscellaneous transactions.

For companies that do have trade accounts receivable, the accounts receivable turnover ratio measures how quickly a company is collecting its trade accounts receivable (A/R). The ratio is calculated as shown below:

$$\text{Accounts Receivable Turnover} = \frac{\text{Sales}}{(\text{Beginning balance of A/R} + \text{Ending balance of A/R}) \div 2}$$

Dividing the sum of the beginning and ending accounts receivable by 2 approximates the average accounts receivable for the fiscal year.

The accounts receivable turnover for Hershey Foods Corporation, based on its 2006 fiscal year financial statements, is calculated below (www.hersheys.com):

$$\text{A/R Turnover} = \frac{\$4,944,230,000}{(\$507,119,000 + \$522,673,000) \div 2} = 9.60 \text{ times}$$

Dividing 365 by the turnover ratio yields a financial ratio known as the *number of days' sales in receivables*. Hershey Foods' number of days' sales in receivables is 38.0 days. Thus, the average account is collected in approximately 38 days.

Instructions

1. What is the amount of accounts receivable for Best Buy reported on its fiscal year 2006 and 2007 financial statements on Appendix B page B-5?
2. Calculate the accounts receivable turnover and number of days' sales in receivables for the Procter & Gamble Company. The company reported $4,185 and $5,725 million of accounts receivable on June 30, 2005 and 2006, respectively, and sales of $68,222 million for fiscal year 2006. (www.pg.com)

Accounting SOFTWARE

UNCOLLECTIBLE ACCOUNTS RECEIVABLE

Any transaction with a customer, whether it's a sale or cash receipt, results in transactions being posted to both the general ledger and the accounts receivable ledger. Writing off a customer's account is no different. Not only is the transaction posted to the general ledger, but the outstanding invoice in the customer's account must also be written off as uncollectible.

How does a business determine if an account is uncollectible? The process often begins with preparing an aging of accounts receivable report, which is a list of outstanding invoices. This report classifies outstanding invoices by the time each is overdue, such as 1 to 30 days overdue, 30 to 60 days overdue, 60 to 90 days overdue, and over 90 days overdue.

PEACHTREE APPLICATION PROBLEM 17-2
1. Open (Restore) file 17-2AP.ptb.
2. Use the Receipts task to write off the customer accounts.
3. To record payment of previously written-off amounts, go to the menu and select Tasks, Sales Invoicing, and the appropriate account. Remember to post when you have completed the transaction. Complete all the transactions.
4. Print the sales journal, cash receipts journal, and the customer ledger.
5. Print the accounts receivable and allowance for uncollectible accounts from the general ledger.

PEACHTREE APPLICATION PROBLEM 17-3
1. Open (Restore) file 17-3AP.ptb.
2. Journalize the entries related to accounts receivable using the sales journal and cash receipts journal.
3. Print the sales journal, cash receipts journal, and customer ledger.
4. Print the accounts receivable and allowance for uncollectible accounts in the general ledger.

UNCOLLECTIBLE ACCOUNTS RECEIVABLE

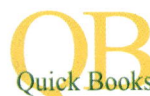

There are no special systems in QuickBooks software for handling the recording of uncollectible accounts. The transactions for recording uncollectible accounts are recorded in journals just as in a manual accounting system.

QuickBooks does, however, have some additional features that make the tracking of uncollectible accounts more efficient. One of these features is the ability to print out a report that lists the accounts receivables according to how old they are. This report is sometimes called an *Aging Schedule of Accounts Receivable*. This schedule can usually be set up to list if an account is current, 1 to 30 days overdue, 30 to 60 days overdue, 60 to 90 days overdue, 90 to 120 days overdue, and over 120 days overdue.

QUICKBOOKS APPLICATION PROBLEM 17-2
1. Open the Waldron Company file.
2. Journalize the transactions; use the Create Credit Memos/Refunds window to write off customer invoices.
3. Use the Make General Journal Entries window to record the reinstatement of previously written-off invoices and receipts from customers in payment.
4. Print a Journal report using September 1 and September 30 as the dates.
5. Print a Customer Balance Detail report using January 1 and September 30 for the dates.

QUICKBOOKS APPLICATION PROBLEM 17-3
1. Open the Weatherly Company file.
2. Journalize the transactions related to accounts receivable; use the Create Credit Memos/Refunds window to write off customer invoices.
3. Use the Make General Journal Entries window to record the reinstatement of previously written-off invoices and to record receipts from customers in payment of the invoices.
4. Print a Journal report using February 1 and February 28 as the dates.
5. Print a Customer Balance Detail report.

FORMATTING THE DISPLAY OF RATIOS

The relationship of two amounts can provide managers with useful information for making business decisions. For example, the ratio of accounts written off to sales on account provides important information about the actual rate of uncollectible accounts receivable.

Most accountants believe that only the first three digits of a ratio are meaningful for making business decisions. Suppose you learned that your credit manager had been able to reduce the ratio of accounts written off to sales on account to 1.23%. Would you think differently about the credit manager's performance if you knew that the ratio was actually 1.234567%?

Electronic spreadsheets make it easy for you to modify the format of a cell to display any number of decimal places. Displaying amounts with proper formatting makes printed schedules more useful.

EXCEL CHALLENGE PROBLEM 17-5
Open the F17-5OPT Excel data file. Follow the step-by-step instructions in the Instructions worksheet. Use the Format Cells feature to display ratios with the proper number of decimal places.

UNCOLLECTIBLE ACCOUNTS RECEIVABLE

There are no special systems in the Automated Accounting software for handling the recording of uncollectible accounts. Instead, transactions for uncollectible accounts are recorded in journals, just as in a manual accounting system. There are four kinds of entries described in this chapter that can be recorded using the Automated Accounting software:

1. *Adjusting Entry for Uncollectible Accounts:* This entry is recorded in the general journal with a debit to Uncollectible Accounts Expense and a credit to Allowance for Uncollectible Accounts.
2. *Writing Off an Account Receivable:* This entry is also recorded in the general journal. The entry includes a debit to Allowance for Uncollectible Accounts and a credit to Accounts Receivable and the customer's account. When the general ledger account number for Accounts Receivable is keyed in the Account Title field, a drop-down list for selecting the individual customer's account will appear. A separate entry for the Customer account is not recorded.
3. *Collecting a Previously Written-Off Account Receivable:* This transaction requires two entries: (a) an entry in the general journal to re-open the account and (b) an entry in the cash receipts journal to record the receipt of cash.

AUTOMATED ACCOUNTING APPLICATION PROBLEM 17-2
Open file F17-2.AA8. Display the problem instructions and complete the problem.

AUTOMATED ACCOUNTING MASTERY PROBLEM 17-4
Open file F17-4.AA8. Display the problem instructions and complete the problem.

CHAPTER 18

Accounting for Plant Assets and Depreciation

OBJECTIVES

After studying Chapter 18, you will be able to:

1. Define accounting terms related to plant assets, depreciation, and property tax expense.
2. Identify accounting concepts and practices related to accounting for plant assets, depreciation, and property tax expense.
3. Record the buying of a plant asset and the paying of property tax.
4. Calculate depreciation expense and book value using the straight-line method of depreciation.
5. Prepare plant asset records and journalize annual depreciation expense.
6. Record entries related to disposing of plant assets.
7. Calculate depreciation expense using the double declining-balance method of depreciation.

KEY TERMS

- real property
- personal property
- assessed value
- plant asset record
- gain on plant assets
- loss on plant assets
- declining-balance method of depreciation

Point Your Browser
www.C21accounting.com

ACCOUNTING IN THE REAL WORLD

Carnival Cruise Lines

Carnival Invests in Fun

Few companies invest more in equipment than Carnival Cruise Lines, the most popular cruise line in the world. Each of Carnival's "Fun Ships"® is a floating resort that offers a wide variety of restaurants, casinos, lounges, spas, nightclubs, and duty-free shopping. Ports of call allow passengers the opportunity to explore port cities in the Caribbean, Alaska, Mexico, and Canada, just to name a few.

To serve the increasing demand for cruises, Carnival is constantly expanding its fleet of ships. At up to $500 million per ship, the cost of the cruise ships is one of Carnival's most significant expenses. Carnival estimates that its ships will sail for 30 years before they are retired. Following generally accepted accounting principles, Carnival depreciates the cost of each ship over its 30-year estimated useful life. Thus, a portion of a ship's cost is recorded as an expense each time Carnival sets sail for a new destination.

Critical Thinking

1. A properly maintained ship can easily last more than 30 years. Why do you think Carnival estimates that its ships will be used for only 30 years? (Hint: What is the estimated life of your car?)
2. Suppose Carnival installs a teen club in a ship that was added to the fleet 10 years ago. How should the cost of this enhancement be accounted for?

Source: www.carnival.com

INTERNET ACTIVITY

Notes to the Financial Statements— Depreciation Methods

Go to the homepage for Carnival Cruise Lines (www.carnival.com) and Royal Caribbean Cruise Lines (www.royalcaribbean.com). Search for the latest annual report for each company. The annual report is usually found under the heading "About Us" or "Investor Relations." In the annual report, usually after the financial statements, you will find the notes to the financial statements. Using these notes (probably Note #1 or #2), look for the information about depreciating their ships.

Instructions

1. For each company, state the method of depreciation used to depreciate the ships.
2. For each company, state the number of years used in estimating the "useful life" of the ships.

LESSON 18-1

Buying Plant Assets and Paying Property Tax

Assets that will be used for a number of years in the operation of a business are known as *plant assets*. A business may have several types of plant assets, including equipment, buildings, and land. Businesses often subdivide plant assets into more focused categories and create an account for each category. For example, a company may divide its equipment into office, store, warehouse, and transportation equipment.

Restaurant Supply Co. owns its equipment but rents the building and the land where the business is located. Therefore, Restaurant Supply has only accounts for equipment. To provide more detailed financial information, Restaurant Supply records its equipment in two different equipment accounts—Office Equipment and Store Equipment. [CONCEPT: Adequate Disclosure]

Most plant assets are useful for only a limited period of time. Over time, most equipment wears out and can no longer perform its functions. Other equipment, such as computers, becomes technologically outdated. Regardless of the reason, the cost of a plant asset should be depreciated over its useful life. Each plant asset account should have a related accumulated depreciation account—a contra asset account—to accumulate the annual depreciation expense of the plant assets in the account.

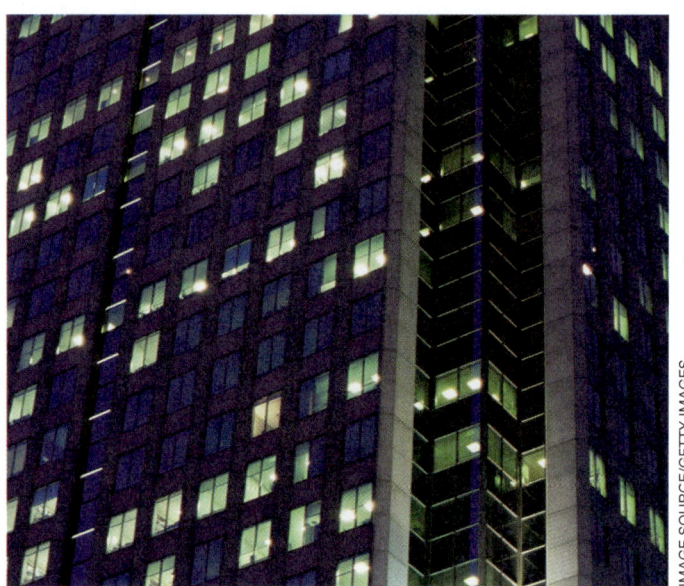

IMAGE SOURCE/GETTY IMAGES

CHARACTER COUNTS

Keeping Your Employees Busy

Gabriel Peña is a receptionist for Traylor Technologies. After the company installed voice mail, Gabriel's workload became lighter, so his supervisor, Amy Sanchez, assigned Gabriel additional responsibilities, including some accounting tasks. Even with these assignments, Gabriel is not always busy. Amy does not assign him additional work because she doesn't have the time to provide more training or supervision. Therefore, to fill the time, Gabriel plays computer games.

Instructions

Do an Internet search using "Hilton Hotels" and "Code of Conduct." Read the Hilton Code of Conduct. Then, use the ethical model to determine if Amy's supervision of Gabriel represents ethical behavior.

PHOTO: BLEND IMAGES/GETTY IMAGES

RECORDING THE BUYING OF A PLANT ASSET

1. Account Title
2. Cost of the Plant Asset
3. Cash Paid
4. Post

Procedures for recording the buying of a plant asset are similar to procedures for recording the buying of current assets such as supplies. The amount paid for a plant asset is debited to a plant asset account with a title such as Store Equipment. [CONCEPT: Historical Cost]

January 3, 20X1. Paid cash for a display case, $3,250.00. Check No. 4.

The entry in the General Debit column of the cash payments journal is posted individually to the account named in the Account Title column.

STEPS — JOURNALIZING AND POSTING THE BUYING OF A PLANT ASSET

1. Write the plant asset account, *Store Equipment*, in the Account Title column of the cash payments journal.
2. Enter the cost of the plant asset, *$3,250.00*, in the General Debit column.
3. Enter the same amount, *$3,250.00*, in the Cash Credit column.
4. Post the entry in the general debit column to the general ledger.

FOR YOUR INFORMATION — FYI

Because of its permanent nature, land is generally not subject to depreciation. Buildings, after years of use, eventually become unusable. A building may be torn down and a new building constructed on the same land. However, since land can be used indefinitely, it is considered permanent and is not depreciated.

Buying Plant Assets and Paying Property Tax · Lesson 18-1

CALCULATING AND PAYING PROPERTY TAX

For tax purposes, state and federal governments define two kinds of property—real and personal. Land and anything attached to the land is called **real property**. Real property is sometimes referred to as *real estate*. All property not classified as real property is called **personal property**. For tax purposes, these definitions apply whether the property is owned by a business or an individual.

The value of an asset determined by tax authorities for the purpose of calculating taxes is called the **assessed value**. Assessed value is usually based on the judgment of persons referred to as assessors. Assessors are elected by citizens or are specially trained employees of a governmental unit.

Most governmental units with taxing power have a tax based on the value of real property. The real property tax is used on buildings and land. Some governmental units also tax personal property such as cars, boats, trailers, and airplanes.

A governmental taxing unit determines a tax rate to use in calculating taxes. The tax rate is multiplied by an asset's assessed value, not the value recorded on a business's records.

Classic Parts, Inc., owns real property that has been assessed for a total of $60,000.00. The city tax rate is 1.2%.

Assessed Value	×	Tax Rate	=	Annual Property Tax
$60,000.00	×	1.2%	=	$720.00

February 1. Classic Parts, Inc., paid cash for property tax, $720.00. Check No. 69.

Payment of property taxes is necessary if a firm is to continue in business. Therefore, Classic Parts, Inc., classifies property tax as an operating expense.

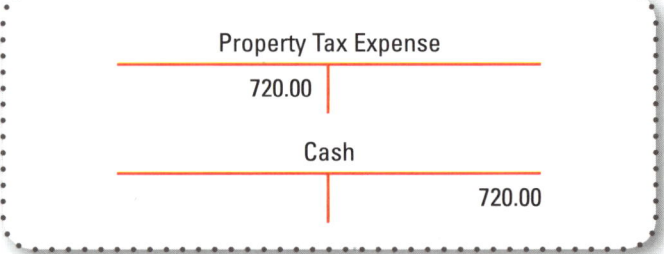

FOR YOUR INFORMATION

FYI

The assessed value of an asset may not be the same as the value on the business's or individual's records. The assessed value is assigned to an asset for tax purposes only. Often the assessed value is only a part of the true value of the asset.

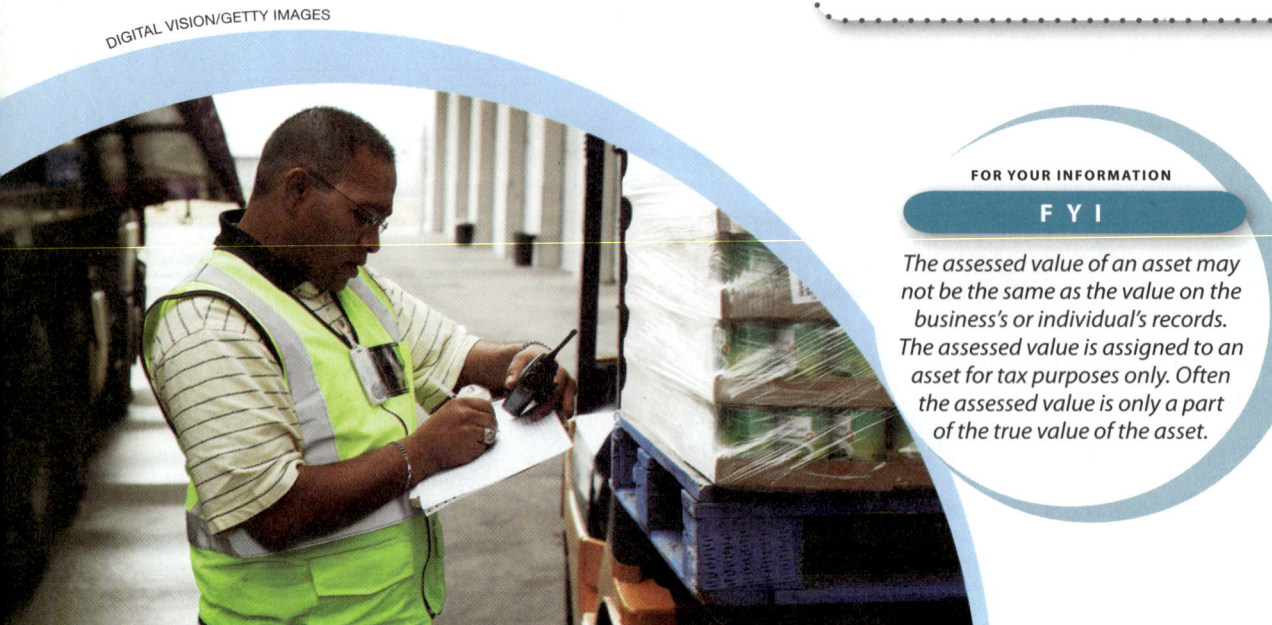

End of Lesson REVIEW

TERMS REVIEW

real property
personal property
assessed value

AUDIT YOUR UNDERSTANDING

1. What accounts are affected, and how, when cash is paid for office equipment?
2. What items are included in real property?
3. Who determines the assessed value of plant assets?

WORK TOGETHER 18-1

Journalizing buying plant assets and paying property tax

The cash payments journal and selected general ledger accounts for Singh Paint Store are given in the *Working Papers*. Your instructor will guide you through the following examples.

1. Journalize the following transactions completed during the current year. Use page 1 of a cash payments journal. The abbreviation for a check is C.

Transactions:
- Jan. 3. Paid cash for a paint mixer, $500.00. C142.
- 5. Paid cash for an office chair, $400.00. C145.
- Feb. 26. Paid property taxes on real property with an assessed value of $80,000.00. The tax rate in the city where the property is located is 3.0% of assessed value. C182.
- July 2. Paid cash for a filing cabinet, $260.00. C216.

2. Post the general columns of the cash payments journal.

ON YOUR OWN 18-1

Journalizing buying plant assets and paying property tax

The cash payments journal and selected general ledger accounts for Herrera Tile Center are given in the *Working Papers*. Work this problem independently.

1. Journalize the following transactions completed during the current year. Use page 1 of a cash payments journal. The abbreviation for a check is C.

Transactions:
- Jan. 2. Paid cash for a computer printer, $1,800.00. C215.
- 5. Paid cash for a tile cutter, $520.00. C216.
- Feb. 24. Paid property taxes on real property with an assessed value of $72,000.00. The tax rate in the city where the property is located is 2.5% of assessed value. C232.
- Mar. 13. Paid cash for a dolly, $325.00. C283.

2. Post the general columns of the cash payments journal.

LESSON 18-2: Calculating Depreciation Expense

STRAIGHT-LINE DEPRECIATION

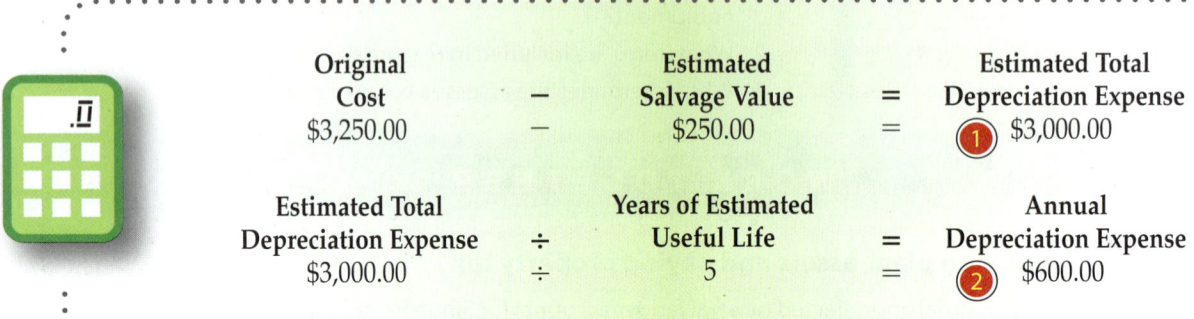

Plant assets are expected to be used in the business for many years. Generally accepted accounting principles require that the cost of a plant asset be expensed over the plant asset's useful life. [CONCEPT: Matching Expenses with Revenues] The annual expense is recorded in Depreciation Expense and the contra asset account Accumulated Depreciation.

Several methods for calculating depreciation expense are available. The easiest and most widely used method is known as the *straight-line method of depreciation*. The method requires the business to know the cost of the plant asset and to estimate two amounts:

1. The amount the business expects to receive when a plant asset is removed from use, known as the *estimated salvage value*.
2. The number of years a plant asset is expected to be used, known as the *estimated useful life*.

The straight-line method of depreciation charges an equal amount of depreciation expense in each full year in which the asset is used.

On January 3, 20X1, Restaurant Supply bought a lighted display case for $3,250.00 with an estimated salvage value of $250.00 and an estimated useful life of 5 years.

> **FOR YOUR INFORMATION**
> **FYI**
> The estimated useful life should be based on prior experience with similar assets and on available guidelines. Trade associations frequently publish guidelines for specialized plant assets. The Internal Revenue Service also publishes depreciation guidelines for plant assets.

STEPS — CALCULATING ANNUAL DEPRECIATION EXPENSE

① Subtract the asset's estimated salvage value from the asset's original cost. This difference is the estimated total depreciation expense for the asset's entire useful life.

② Divide the estimated total depreciation expense by the years of estimated useful life. The result is the annual depreciation expense.

CALCULATING DEPRECIATION EXPENSE FOR PART OF A YEAR

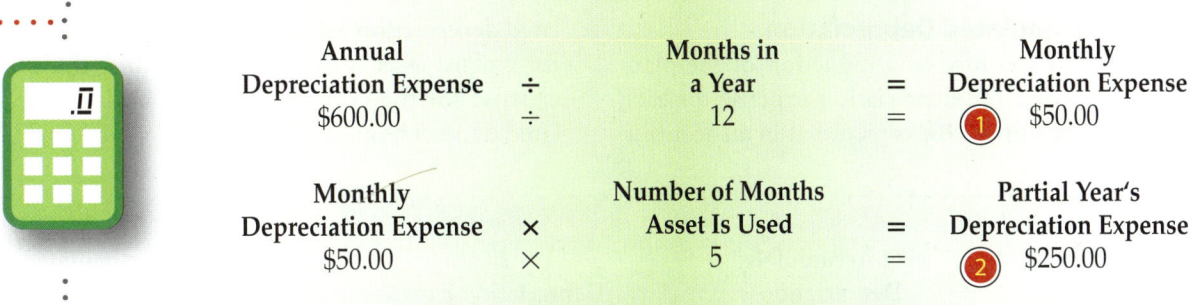

A month is the smallest unit of time used to calculate depreciation. A plant asset may be placed in service at a date other than the first day of a fiscal period. In such cases, a business may elect to calculate depreciation expense to the nearest first of a month. A partial year's depreciation may also be recorded in the year the plant asset is sold or disposed of.

Restaurant Supply bought a point-of-sale terminal on August 2, 20X1. The annual straight-line depreciation expense is $600.00. The depreciation expense is $250.00 for the remaining 5 months of the year in which Restaurant Supply used the computer.

STEPS CALCULATING PARTIAL YEAR'S DEPRECIATION EXPENSE

1. Divide the annual depreciation expense by 12, the number of months in a year. The result is the monthly depreciation expense.

2. Multiply the monthly depreciation expense by the number of months the plant asset is used in a year. The result is the partial year's depreciation expense.

The five years' depreciation expense is illustrated below. In the first year, a partial year's depreciation is recorded: August 1, 20X1 to December 31, 20X1—five months. If the asset had been purchased August 16 or later, only four months' depreciation would be expensed because the date would be closer to September 1 than August 1. In the next four years, a full year's depreciation, $600.00, would be expensed each year. In 20X6, the original five-year useful life ends July 31, so seven months' depreciation would be recorded.

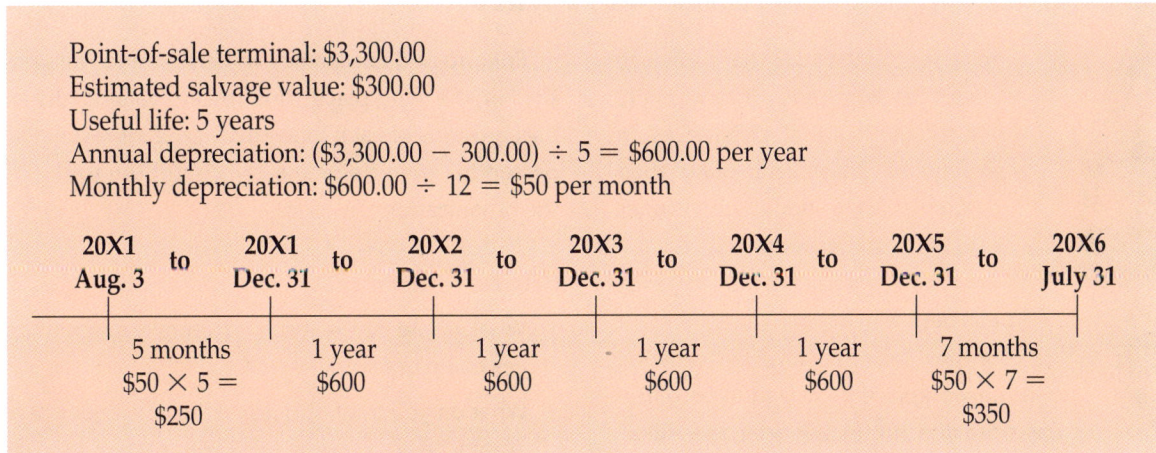

Plant assets may continue to be used after their estimated useful lives have ended; however, no additional depreciation is recorded.

CALCULATING ACCUMULATED DEPRECIATION AND BOOK VALUE

Calculating Accumulated Depreciation

Depreciation is not recorded as a reduction of the plant asset account. Instead, the depreciation expense for each year of a plant asset's useful life is recorded in an accumulated depreciation account. The accumulated depreciation for a plant asset is calculated by adding the depreciation expense for the current year to the prior year's accumulated depreciation.

20X2 Accumulated Depreciation	+	20X3 Depreciation Expense	=	20X3 Accumulated Depreciation
$1,200.00	+	$600.00	=	$1,800.00

Calculating Book Value

The original cost of a plant asset minus accumulated depreciation is known as the *book value of a plant asset*. The book value is calculated by subtracting the accumulated depreciation from the original cost of the plant asset. The ending book value is the beginning book value for the next year.

Original Cost	−	Accumulated Depreciation	=	Ending Book Value
$3,250.00	−	$1,800.00	=	$1,450.00

The book value can also be calculated by subtracting the year's depreciation from that year's beginning book value. Either method of calculating a book value is acceptable because both methods calculate the same amount.

CULTURAL DIVERSITY

Valuing Diversity in the Workplace

Employees in the U.S. have diverse cultural backgrounds. This diversity reflects the cultural differences in society. All employees bring their cultural backgrounds and values with them to the workplace.

Cultural differences do not exist only between people from different countries. They may arise with anyone in the workplace perceived to be different from the norm. Consider the differences in employees who are younger or older than average, who are physically challenged, or who speak English as a second language.

Enlightened companies will encourage "valuing diversity" in the workplace. This means valuing the cultural backgrounds of each individual. It means respecting each person for what he or she can contribute to the goals of the organization.

Critical Thinking

1. What would be the result if culturally different employees could not work together?
2. What do you think should be the consequence for an employee who cannot work with other employees of different cultural backgrounds?

End of Lesson REVIEW

AUDIT YOUR UNDERSTANDING

1. Which accounting concept is being applied when depreciation expense is recorded for plant assets?
2. What three amounts are used to calculate a plant asset's annual depreciation expense using the straight-line method of depreciation?

WORK TOGETHER 18-2

Calculating depreciation

Depreciation tables for Fairbrother, Inc., are given in the *Working Papers*. Your instructor will guide you through the following example.

1. Fairbrother, Inc., bought the following assets during 20X1. Complete a depreciation table for each asset using the straight-line depreciation method. If the asset was not bought at the beginning of 20X1, calculate the depreciation expense for the part of 20X1 in which the company owned the asset. Save your work to complete Work Together 18-3.

Transactions:
Jan. 3. Bought a computer monitor costing $560.00; estimated salvage value, $60.00; estimated useful life, 5 years.
Oct. 19. Bought a notebook computer, $2,750.00; estimated salvage value, $350.00; estimated useful life, 4 years.

ON YOUR OWN 18-2

Calculating depreciation

Depreciation tables for Wrench Co. are given in the *Working Papers*. Work this problem independently.

1. Wrench Co. bought the following assets during 20X1. Complete a depreciation table for each asset using the straight-line depreciation method. If the asset was not bought at the beginning of 20X1, calculate the depreciation expense for the part of 20X1 in which the company owned the asset. Save your work to complete On Your Own 18-3.

Transactions:
Jan. 6. Bought a sound system costing $5,600.00; estimated salvage value, $400.00; estimated useful life, 8 years.
May 22. Bought a shredder, $1,250.00; estimated salvage value, $50.00; estimated useful life, 5 years.

LESSON 18-3

Journalizing Depreciation Expense

PREPARING PLANT ASSET RECORDS

PLANT ASSET RECORD No. **62**		General Ledger Account No.	**1215**
Description	**Display Case**	General Ledger Account	**Store Equipment**
Date Bought	**January 3, 20X1**	Serial Number **D2679-26**	Original Cost **$3,250.00**
Estimated Useful Life	**5 years**	Estimated Salvage Value **$250.00**	Depreciation Method **Straight-line**

Disposed of: Discarded _____ Sold _____ Traded _____
Date _____ Disposal Amount _____

YEAR	ANNUAL DEPRECIATION EXPENSE	ACCUMULATED DEPRECIATION	ENDING BOOK VALUE
20X1	$600.00	$ 600.00	$2650.00
20X2	600.00	1,200.00	2,050.00
20X3	600.00	1,800.00	1,450.00
20X4	600.00	2,400.00	850.00
20X5	600.00	3,000.00	250.00

Continue record on back of card

A separate record is kept for each plant asset. An accounting form on which a business records information about each plant asset is called a **plant asset record**.

Plant asset records may vary in arrangement for different businesses, but most records contain similar information. Restaurant Supply's plant asset record has three sections. Section 1 is prepared when a plant asset is bought. Section 2 provides space for recording the disposition of the plant asset. When the asset is disposed of, this information will be filled in. Section 3 provides space for recording annual depreciation expense and the changing book value of the asset each year it is used.

At the end of each fiscal period, Restaurant Supply brings each plant asset record up to date by recording three amounts: (1) annual depreciation expense, (2) accumulated depreciation, and (3) ending book value.

The amount recorded in the Annual Depreciation Expense column is the amount calculated for each year. These amounts may be different if the asset is bought or sold at a time other than near the fiscal year beginning or end.

Accumulated depreciation for the first year is the annual depreciation expense for the first year. In later years, accumulated depreciation is the depreciation expense that has accumulated over all prior years added to that year's annual depreciation expense.

The ending book value is the original cost less that year's accumulated depreciation.

STEPS — PREPARING A PLANT ASSET RECORD

1. Write the information in Section 1 when the plant asset is purchased.

2. Do not write in Section 2 until the asset is disposed of.

3. Each year the asset is owned, record the year's annual depreciation expense in Section 3. Calculate and record accumulated depreciation and ending book value.

JOURNALIZING ANNUAL DEPRECIATION EXPENSE

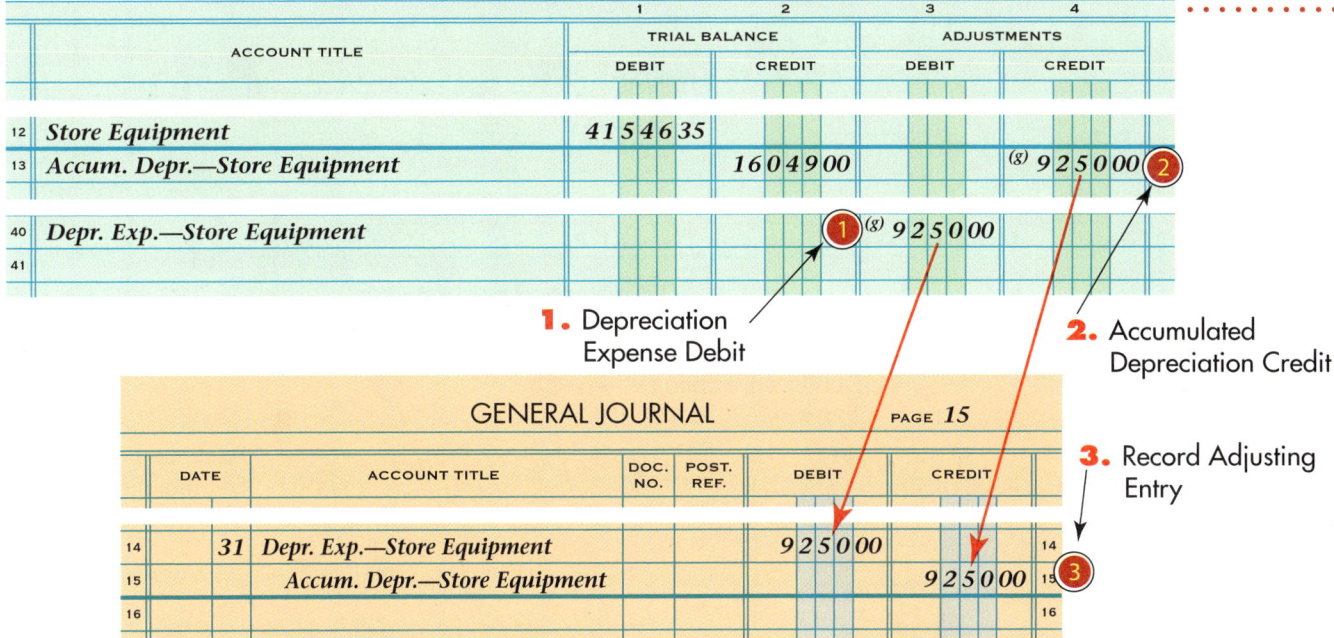

1. Depreciation Expense Debit
2. Accumulated Depreciation Credit
3. Record Adjusting Entry

At the end of the fiscal year, Restaurant Supply calculates the depreciation expense for each plant asset. The depreciation expense for each asset is recorded on its plant asset record. Next, the total depreciation expense is calculated for all plant assets recorded in the same plant asset account.

Restaurant Supply determined that total depreciation expense for store equipment is $9,250.00. An adjustment is planned in the Adjustments columns of the work sheet. Using this information, an adjusting entry is then recorded in a general journal.

It is important to retain original cost information for plant assets. Rather than credit the plant asset account, depreciation is recorded to the contra asset account Accumulated Depreciation.

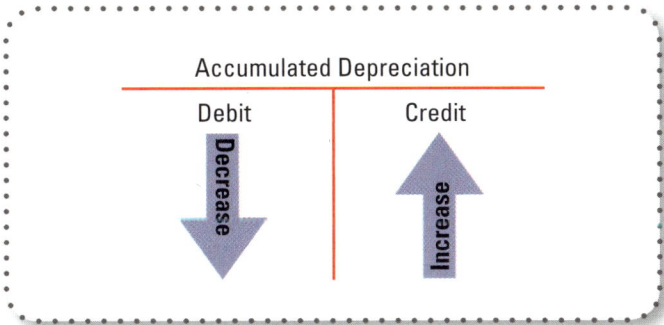

At any time, the book value of plant assets can be calculated by subtracting Accumulated Depreciation from the plant asset account.

ANALYZING AND JOURNALIZING ANNUAL DEPRECIATION EXPENSE

1. Write the total annual depreciation expense, $9,250.00, in the Adjustments Debit column on the *Depreciation Expense—Store Equipment* line of the work sheet. Label the adjustment (g), with a small letter in parentheses.

2. Write the same amount, $9,250.00, in the Adjustments Credit column on the *Accumulated Depreciation—Store Equipment* line of the work sheet. Label the adjustment using the same letter, (g).

3. Use the debit and credit accounts on the work sheet to record an adjusting entry in a general journal.

Journalizing Depreciation Expense   Lesson 18-3   **543**

POSTING AN ADJUSTING ENTRY FOR DEPRECIATION EXPENSE

The adjustment for depreciation expense planned on the work sheet is recorded as an adjusting entry in the general journal. The adjusting entry is then posted to the general ledger.

After posting, Store Equipment has a debit balance showing the original cost of all store equipment. The contra account Accumulated Depreciation—Store Equipment has a credit balance showing the accumulated depreciation recorded to date.

The debit balance of Depreciation Expense—Store Equipment is the portion of the cost of plant assets allocated to expense during the fiscal period.

STEPS: POSTING AN ADJUSTING ENTRY FOR DEPRECIATION EXPENSE

1. Post the debit, $9,250.00, to *Depreciation Expense—Store Equipment*.
2. Post the credit, $9,250.00, to *Accumulated Depreciation—Store Equipment*.

REMEMBER

An adjusting entry is made to record the depreciation expense for each category of plant assets. Restaurant Supply also records an adjusting entry for Depreciation Expense—Office Equipment and Accumulated Depreciation—Office Equipment.

End of Lesson REVIEW

AUDIT YOUR UNDERSTANDING

TERM REVIEW

plant asset record

1. What method is used to record accumulated depreciation while also retaining original cost information for plant assets?
2. How does an adjusting entry for depreciation expense change the balance of the asset account?

WORK TOGETHER 18-3

Journalizing depreciation

Use the depreciation tables from Work Together 18-2. Additional forms are given in the *Working Papers*. Your instructor will guide you through the following examples.

1. Complete each plant asset record for the years 20X1 through 20X3. Use the following additional information.

Description	General Ledger Account	Date Bought	Plant Asset No.	Serial No.
Computer Monitor	1215-Store Equipment	Jan. 3	241	51-4882
Notebook Computer	1205-Office Equipment	Oct. 19	242	GY1281

2. On December 31, Fairbrother, Inc., determined that total depreciation expense for office equipment was $4,230.00. Plan the work sheet adjustment and label the adjustment *(f)*. Record the adjusting entry on page 20 of a general journal and post the entry to the general ledger. Save your work to complete Work Together 18-4.

ON YOUR OWN 18-3

Journalizing depreciation

Use the depreciation tables from On Your Own 18-2. Additional forms are given in the *Working Papers*. Work this problem independently.

1. Complete each plant asset record from the years 20X1 through 20X3. Use the following additional information:

Description	General Ledger Account	Date Bought	Plant Asset No.	Serial No.
Sound System	1215-Store Equipment	Jan. 6	353	12488BF2
Shredder	1205-Office Equipment	May 22	354	34-432-2

2. On December 31, Wrench Co. determined that total depreciation expense for store equipment was $9,880.00. Plan the work sheet adjustment and label the adjustment *(g)*. Record the adjusting entry on page 18 of a general journal and post the entry to the general ledger. Save your work to complete On Your Own 18-4.

LESSON 18-4

Disposing of Plant Assets

SALE OF A PLANT ASSET FOR BOOK VALUE

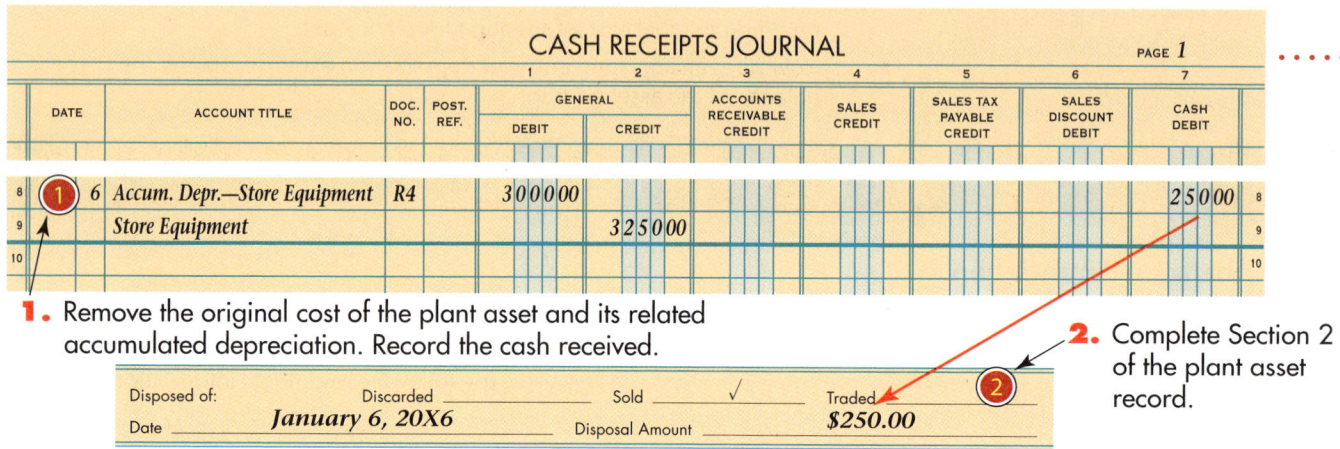

When a plant asset is no longer useful to a business, the asset may be disposed of. The old plant asset may be sold, traded for a new asset, or discarded.

When a plant asset is disposed of, a journal entry is recorded that achieves the following:

1. Removes the original cost of the plant asset and its related accumulated depreciation.
2. Recognizes any cash or other asset received for the old plant asset.
3. Recognizes any gain or loss on the disposal.

> January 6, 20X6. Received cash from sale of display case, $250.00: original cost, $3,250.00; total accumulated depreciation through December 31, 20X5, $3,000.00. Receipt No. 4.

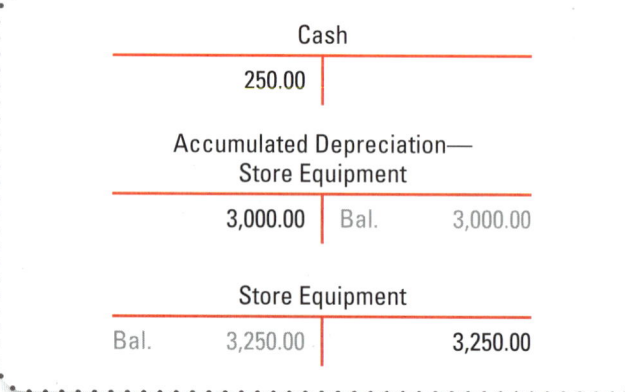

Cash received		$250.00
Less: Book value of asset sold:		
Cost	$3,250.00	
Accum. Depr.	3,000.00	250.00
Gain (loss) on sale of plant asset		$ 0.00

The amount of gain or loss, if any, is calculated by subtracting the book value from the cash received. The display case was sold for its book value. Therefore, no gain or loss exists.

STEPS — RECORDING SALE OF A PLANT ASSET FOR BOOK VALUE

1. Record an entry in the cash receipts journal to remove the original cost, $3,250.00, from *Store Equipment* and $3,000.00 from *Accumulated Depreciation—Store Equipment*. Record the cash received from the sale, $250.00, as a debit to *Cash*.

2. Check the type of disposal, *Sold*, and write the date, *January 6, 20X6*, and disposal amount, $250.00, in Section 2 of the plant asset record.

RECORDING A PLANT ASSET'S DEPRECIATION EXPENSE FOR A PARTIAL YEAR

1. Debit the depreciation expense account.

GENERAL JOURNAL PAGE 4

DATE	ACCOUNT TITLE	DOC. NO.	POST. REF.	DEBIT	CREDIT
20X7 Apr. 4	Depr. Exp.—Store Equipment	M31		① 60 00	
	Accum. Depr.—Store Equipment				② 60 00

3. Update Section 3 of the plant asset record.

2. Credit the accumulated depreciation account.

YEAR	ANNUAL DEPRECIATION EXPENSE	ACCUMULATED DEPRECIATION	ENDING BOOK VALUE
20X5	240.00	1,200.00	600.00
20X6	240.00	1,440.00	360.00
20X7	③ 60.00	1,500.00	300.00

A plant asset may be sold at any time during the asset's useful life. When a plant asset is sold, its depreciation from the beginning of the current fiscal year to the date of disposal must be recorded.

On April 4, 20X7, Restaurant Supply intends to sell a safe that was bought on January 12, 20X1, for $1,800.00. Annual depreciation expense for the safe is $240.00. Depreciation recorded through December 31, 20X6, is $1,440.00.

The method to calculate a partial year's depreciation is the same as calculating depreciation when an asset is purchased during the fiscal year. The monthly depreciation expense is multiplied by the number of months the asset is used during the current fiscal year. Depreciation is calculated for each month prior to the month the plant asset is sold. Thus, Restaurant Supply will depreciate the safe for three months, January through March.

April 4, 20X7. Recorded a partial year's depreciation on a safe to be sold, $60.00. Memorandum No. 31.

The depreciation is also recorded on the plant asset record for the safe.

RECORDING A PARTIAL YEAR'S DEPRECIATION

① Record a debit, $60.00, to *Depreciation Expense—Store Equipment* in the general journal.

② Record a credit, $60.00, to *Accumulated Depreciation—Store Equipment* in the general journal.

③ Record the depreciation expense in Section 3 of the plant asset record for the safe. Calculate and record accumulated depreciation and ending book value.

SALE OF A PLANT ASSET FOR MORE THAN BOOK VALUE

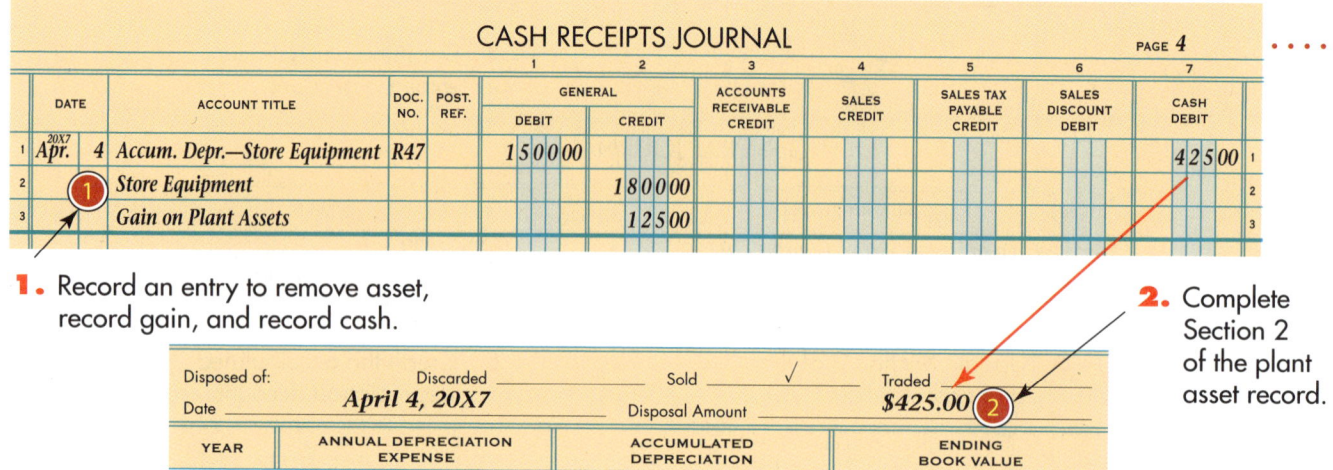

1. Record an entry to remove asset, record gain, and record cash.
2. Complete Section 2 of the plant asset record.

Revenue that results when a plant asset is sold for more than book value is called **gain on plant assets**. Restaurant Supply is selling a safe for $425.00. After the partial year's depreciation is recorded, a journal entry is made to record the sale of the safe.

> April 4, 20X7. Received cash from sale of safe, $425.00: original cost, $1,800.00; accumulated depreciation through April 4, 20X7, $1,500.00. Receipt No. 47.

The gain or loss on the sale of a plant asset is the book value subtracted from cash received.

Cash received		$425.00
Less: Book value of asset sold:		
Cost	$1,800.00	
Accum. Depr.	1,500.00	300.00
Gain (loss) on sale of plant asset		$125.00

The gain realized on the disposal of a plant asset is credited to a revenue account titled Gain on Plant Assets.

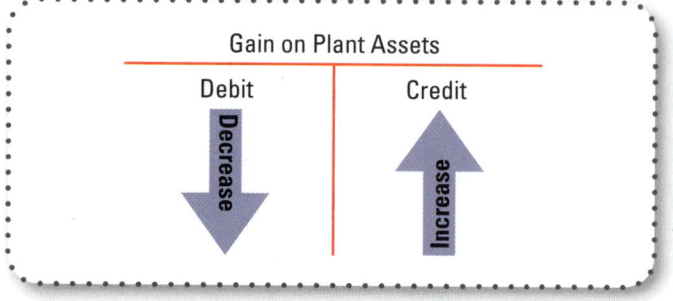

A gain from the sale of plant assets is not an operating revenue. Therefore, Gain on Plant Assets is listed in a classification titled "Other Revenue" in the chart of accounts.

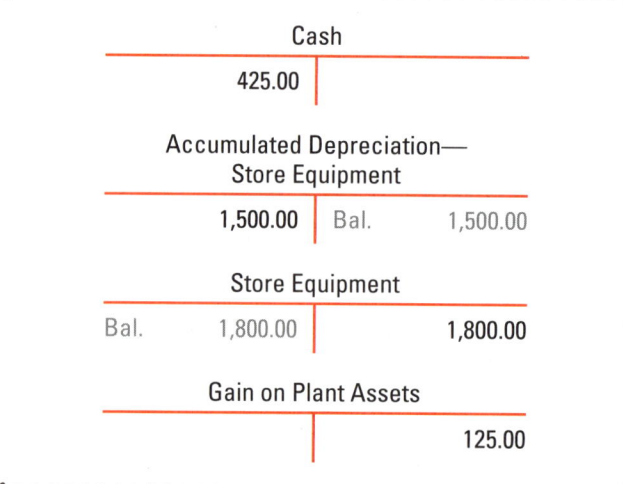

STEPS — RECORDING SALE OF A PLANT ASSET FOR MORE THAN BOOK VALUE

1. Record an entry in the cash receipts journal to remove the original cost, $1,800.00, from *Store Equipment* and $1,500.00 from *Accumulated Depreciation—Store Equipment*. Record the gain on the sale, $125.00, as a credit to *Gain on Plant Assets*. Record the cash received from the sale, $425.00, as a debit to *Cash*.
2. Check the type of disposal, *Sold*, and write the date, *April 4, 20X7*, and disposal amount, $425.00, in Section 2 of the plant asset record for the safe.

SALE OF A PLANT ASSET FOR LESS THAN BOOK VALUE

DATE	ACCOUNT TITLE	DOC. NO.	POST. REF.	GENERAL DEBIT	GENERAL CREDIT	ACCOUNTS RECEIVABLE CREDIT	SALES CREDIT	SALES TAX PAYABLE CREDIT	SALES DISCOUNT DEBIT	CASH DEBIT
20X7 Oct. 6	Accum. Depr.—Office Equipment	R281		1500 00						150 00
	Loss on Plant Assets			250 00						
	Office Equipment				1900 00					

1. Record an entry to dispose of the asset, record a loss on plant assets, and record cash.

Disposed of: Discarded _____ Sold ✓ Traded _____
Date __October 6, 20X7__ Disposal Amount __$150.00__

2. Complete Section 2 of the plant asset record.

The loss that results when a plant asset is sold for less than book value is called **loss on plant assets**. Restaurant Supply sold a computer after three years of use. After the partial year's depreciation is recorded, a journal entry is made to record the sale of the computer.

> October 6, 20X7. Received cash from sale of a computer, $150.00: original cost, $1,900.00; total accumulated depreciation through October 1, 20X7, $1,500.00. Receipt No. 281.

The gain or loss on the sale of a plant asset is the book value subtracted from cash received.

Cash received		$ 150.00
Less: Book value of asset sold:		
Cost	$1,900.00	
Accum. Depr.	1,500.00	400.00
Gain (loss) on sale of plant asset		$(250.00)

The loss realized on the disposal of a plant asset is debited to an other expense account titled Loss on Plant Assets.

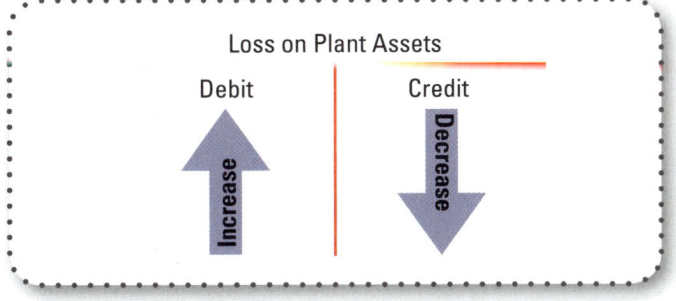

A loss from the sale of plant assets is not an operating expense. Therefore, Loss on Plant Assets is listed in a classification titled "Other Expenses" in the chart of accounts.

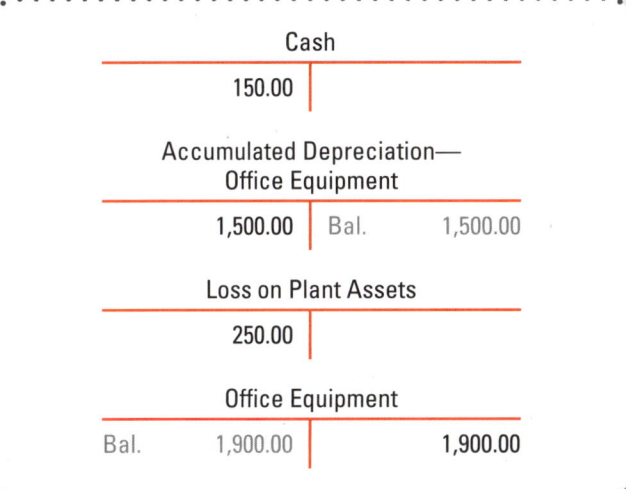

STEPS — RECORDING SALE OF A PLANT ASSET FOR LESS THAN BOOK VALUE

1. Record an entry in the cash receipts journal to remove the original cost, $1,900.00, from *Office Equipment* and $1,500.00 from *Accumulated Depreciation—Office Equipment*. Record the loss on the sale, $250.00, as a debit to *Loss on Plant Assets*. Record the cash received from the sale, $150.00, as a debit to *Cash*.

2. Check the type of disposal, *Sold*, and write the date, *Oct. 6, 20X7*, and disposal amount, *$150.00*, in Section 2 of the plant asset record for the computer.

Disposing of Plant Assets   Lesson 18-4

End of Lesson REVIEW

AUDIT YOUR UNDERSTANDING

1. What is recorded on plant asset records for plant assets that have been disposed of?
2. When an asset is disposed of after the beginning of the fiscal year, what entry may need to be recorded before an entry is made for the discarding of a plant asset?
3. What is the formula to calculate the gain or loss on the sale of a plant asset?
4. In what account classification is Loss on Plant Assets listed?

TERMS REVIEW

gain on plant assets

loss on plant assets

WORK TOGETHER 18-4

Recording the disposal of plant assets

Use the plant asset records from Work Together 18-3. Your instructor will guide you through the following examples.

1. For each of the following transactions completed in 20X4, journalize an entry for additional depreciation, if needed. Use page 11 of a general journal given in the *Working Papers*. Source documents are abbreviated as follows: memorandum, M; receipt, R.

Transactions:
- Jan. 6. Received cash for sale of a computer monitor, plant asset No. 241, $290.00. R4.
- Jul. 12. Received cash for sale of a notebook computer, plant asset No. 242, $800.00. M67 and R203.

2. Use page 1 of a cash receipts journal to record the disposal of each plant asset.
3. Make appropriate notations in the plant asset records.

ON YOUR OWN 18-4

Recording the disposal of plant assets

Use the plant asset records from On Your Own 18-3. Work this problem independently.

1. For each of the following transactions completed in 20X4, journalize an entry for additional depreciation, if needed. Use page 10 of a general journal given in the *Working Papers*. Source documents are abbreviated as follows: memorandum, M; receipt, R.

Transactions:
- Jan. 2. Received cash for sale of a sound system, plant asset No. 353, $4,000.00. R11.
- Oct. 3. Received cash for sale of a shredder, plant asset No. 354, $325.00. M82 and R255.

2. Use page 8 of a cash receipts journal to record the disposal of each plant asset.
3. Make appropriate notations in the plant asset records.

LESSON 18-5: Declining-Balance Method of Depreciation

CALCULATING DEPRECIATION USING THE DOUBLE DECLINING-BALANCE METHOD

Plant Asset: Truck
Depreciation Method: Double Declining-Balance
Original Cost: $25,000.00
Estimated Salvage Value: $2,500.00
Estimated Useful Life: 5 years

Year	Beginning Book Value	Declining-Balance Rate ①	Annual Depreciation	Ending Book Value
1	$25,000.00	40%	② $10,000.00	③ $15,000.00
2	④ 15,000.00	40%	6,000.00	9,000.00

4. Transfer the book value to the following year.

1. Calculate rate.

2. Determine the annual depreciation expense.

3. Determine the ending book value.

The straight-line method charges an equal amount of depreciation expense each year. However, many plant assets depreciate more in the early years of useful life than in later years. For example, a truck's value will decrease more in the first year than in later years. Therefore, charging more depreciation expense in the early years may be more accurate than charging the same amount each year. [CONCEPT: Matching Expenses with Revenue]

Multiplying the book value by a constant depreciation rate at the end of each fiscal period is called the **declining-balance method of depreciation**.

The declining-balance depreciation rate is a multiple of the straight-line rate. Many businesses use a declining-balance rate that is two times the straight-line rate. This method of depreciation is referred to as the *double declining-balance method*.

STEPS: CALCULATING DEPRECIATION USING THE DOUBLE DECLINING-BALANCE METHOD

① Calculate the double declining-balance rate. An example of a plant asset with a five-year life is shown.

Estimated Depreciation Expense	÷	Years of Estimated Useful Life	=	Straight-line Rate of Depreciation
100%	÷	5	=	20%

Straight-line Rate of Depreciation	×		=	Double Declining-balance Rate
20%	×	2	=	40%

② Multiply the double declining-balance rate by the beginning book value to determine the annual depreciation expense for a given year ($25,000.00 × 40% = $10,000.00).

③ Subtract the annual depreciation expense from the beginning book value to determine the ending book value ($25,000.00 − $10,000.00 = $15,000.00).

④ Transfer the ending book value to the beginning book value for the following year. Calculating the depreciation expense in the last year of an asset's life is described on the next page.

Declining-Balance Method of Depreciation

CALCULATING THE LAST YEAR'S DEPRECIATION EXPENSE

Plant Asset: Truck
Depreciation Method: Double Declining-Balance
Original Cost: $25,000.00
Estimated Salvage Value: $2,500.00
Estimated Useful Life: 5 years

Year	Beginning Book Value	Declining-Balance Rate	Annual Depreciation	Ending Book Value
1	$25,000.00	40%	$10,000.00	$15,000.00
2	15,000.00	40%	6,000.00	9,000.00
3	9,000.00	40%	3,600.00	5,400.00
4	5,400.00	40%	2,160.00	3,240.00
5	① 3,240.00	—	② 740.00	③ 2,500.00
Total Depreciation			$22,500.00	

1. Transfer the book value.

2. Determine the last year's depreciation.

3. Verify the ending book value.

Although the depreciation rate is the same each year, the annual depreciation expense declines from one year to the next.

A plant asset is never depreciated below its estimated salvage value. Therefore, in the last year, only enough depreciation expense is recorded to reduce the book value of the plant asset to its salvage value.

Sometimes in the last year of a plant asset's useful life, the formula for the double declining-balance method of depreciation results in an ending book value greater than the estimated salvage value. In other words, the depreciation formula does not create enough accumulated depreciation to reduce the book value down to what is a relatively small estimated salvage value.

When this situation exists, most companies that use the declining-balance method of depreciation switch to the straight-line method sometime during the life of the plant asset. To determine when to switch to the straight-line method of depreciation, each year a company compares the annual depreciation expense calculated using the straight-line method to the annual depreciation expense calculated using the declining-balance method. If the annual depreciation expense using the straight-line method is greater than the annual depreciation expense using the declining-balance method, the company should use the straight-line method.

STEPS CALCULATING THE LAST YEAR'S DEPRECIATION EXPENSE

① Transfer the ending book value from Year 4 to the beginning book value of Year 5.

② Subtract the salvage value of the plant asset from the beginning book value to determine the depreciation expense for the last year of useful life ($3,240.00 − $2,500.00 = $740.00).

③ Verify that the ending book value is equal to the salvage value.

> **REMEMBER**
>
> *Unlike the straight-line method, the declining-balance method does not use the estimated salvage value to calculate depreciation. The estimated salvage value is used only to limit the last year's depreciation expense.*

COMPARISON OF TWO METHODS OF DEPRECIATION

Plant Asset: Computer
Depreciation Method: Comparison of Two Methods

Original Cost: $4,000.00
Estimated Salvage Value: $500.00
Estimated Useful Life: 5 years

Year	Straight-Line Method			Double Declining-Balance Method		
	Beginning Book Value	Annual Depreciation	Ending Book Value	Beginning Book Value	Annual Depreciation	Ending Book Value
1	$4,000.00	$700.00	$3,300.00	$4,000.00	$1,600.00	$2,400.00
2	3,300.00	700.00	2,600.00	2,400.00	960.00	1,440.00
3	2,600.00	700.00	1,900.00	1,440.00	576.00	864.00
4	1,900.00	700.00	1,200.00	864.00	345.60	518.40
5	1,200.00	700.00	500.00	518.40	18.40	500.00
Total Depreciation	—	$3,500.00	—	—	$3,500.00	—

Regardless of the depreciation method used, the total depreciation expense over the useful life of a plant asset is the same. The accounts used in the journal entries to record depreciation expense and the sale of plant assets are also the same.

Each depreciation method is acceptable according to generally accepted accounting principles. The straight-line method is easy to calculate. The same amount of depreciation expense is recorded for each year of estimated useful life.

The double declining-balance method is slightly more complicated. This method records a greater depreciation expense in the early years than the straight-line method. The declining-balance method is referred to as an *accelerated depreciation method*. The method accelerates the recording of depreciation in the early years of the asset's useful life.

BUSINESS STRUCTURES

Piercing the Corporate Veil

A major advantage of a corporation is the limited liability for its owners. This protection from liability is sometimes referred to as a *corporate veil*, or shield. It protects the personal assets of stockholders from creditors' claims.

To benefit from the corporate veil, however, stockholders must keep corporate affairs completely separate from their personal affairs. If this separation is maintained, only the corporation's assets are available for payment of creditors' claims. If the owners do not maintain this separation and, for example, pay personal bills with corporate funds, the corporate protection may be lost.

A court "pierces the corporate veil" when it imposes personal liability for corporate debts on shareholders active in the management of a corporation. For example, owners might pay themselves excessive salaries or other benefits.

If this type of abuse occurs and creditors are not being paid, the court will pierce the corporate veil and hold owners active in management personally liable to creditors.

Critical Thinking

Why would courts consider paying personal expenses from corporate funds to be a reason for piercing the corporate veil?

Declining-Balance Method of Depreciation

End of Lesson REVIEW

AUDIT YOUR UNDERSTANDING

1. When calculating depreciation expense using the declining-balance method, what number stays constant each fiscal period?
2. What is the declining-balance method that uses twice the straight-line rate?
3. What change occurs in the annual depreciation expense calculated using the declining-balance method?
4. An asset is never depreciated below what amount?

TERM REVIEW

declining-balance method of depreciation

WORK TOGETHER 18-5

Calculating depreciation using the double declining-balance depreciation method

Depreciation tables for Clearwater Clothiers are given in the *Working Papers*. Your instructor will guide you through the following example.

1. Complete a depreciation table for each of the following plant assets purchased during the current year. Use the double declining-balance depreciation method. Round amounts to the nearest cent.

Date	Description	Original Cost	Estimated Salvage Value	Estimated Useful Life
Jan. 4	Truck	$22,000.00	$2,200.00	4 years
Jan. 6	Cash Register	$1,200.00	$100.00	5 years
Jan. 7	Clothing Rack	$500.00	$50.00	8 years

ON YOUR OWN 18-5

Calculating depreciation using the double declining-balance depreciation method

Depreciation tables for Teton Skis are given in the *Working Papers*. Work this problem independently.

1. Complete a depreciation table for each of the following plant assets purchased during the current year. Use the double declining-balance depreciation method. Round amounts to the nearest cent.

Date	Description	Original Cost	Estimated Salvage Value	Estimated Useful Life
Jan. 2	Ski Rack	$1,200.00	$100.00	5 years
Jan. 4	Delivery Truck	$25,000.00	$2,000.00	3 years
Jan. 6	Filing Cabinet	$600.00	$50.00	4 years

SUMMARY

After completing this chapter, you can:

1. Define accounting terms related to plant assets, depreciation, and property tax expense.
2. Identify accounting concepts and practices related to accounting for plant assets, depreciation, and property tax expense.
3. Record the buying of a plant asset and the paying of property tax.
4. Calculate depreciation expense and book value using the straight-line method of depreciation.
5. Prepare plant asset records and journalize annual depreciation expense.
6. Record entries related to disposing of plant assets.
7. Calculate depreciation expense using the double declining-balance method of depreciation.

EXPLORE ACCOUNTING

Accounting for Leases

Leasing has become a popular alternative to purchasing a new car. The customer, called the *lessee*, has use of the car during the lease period. At the end of the lease term, the car dealer, called the *lessor*, may give the lessee the option to purchase the car.

The accounting for a lease and the buying of an asset on account are very different. Normally, a leased asset is not recorded on the balance sheet as a plant asset, and the future lease payments are not recorded as a liability. Lease payments are charged to Rent Expense when paid. In contrast, an asset bought on account is recorded on the balance sheet as a plant asset and the total payments are recorded as a liability. Each month, Depreciation Expense is charged and the interest expense is recorded on the monthly note payment. In addition, the liability account is debited; the cash and accumulated depreciation accounts are credited. Thus, the decision to lease or buy plant assets can have a dramatic impact on the financial statements of a company.

Accountants often apply the concept of substance over form when accounting for economic transactions. *Substance* refers to the underlying nature of the transaction. *Form* considers only the appearance of the transaction. FASB (Financial Accounting Standards Board) Statement No. 13, Accounting for Leases, provides accountants with guidelines for evaluating lease agreements. If one of four criteria is met, the lease is recorded as if the asset were purchased, referred to as a *capital lease*.

Research: Investigate the terms of leases offered by a local car dealership and an apartment complex. Identify factors, such as lease term and maintenance, that differ between the two leases. Disregarding the rules of FASB Statement No. 13, would you consider the substance of either lease to be a purchase of the asset?

18-1 APPLICATION PROBLEM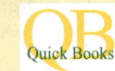

Journalizing buying plant assets and paying property tax

The cash payments journal and selected general ledger accounts for Umeki Food Source are given in the *Working Papers*.

Instructions:

1. Journalize the following transactions completed during the current year. The abbreviation for a check is C.

Transactions:

Jan. 4. Paid cash for office desk, $700.00. C334.
     5. Paid cash for a freezer, $4,200.00. C337.
Feb. 24. Paid property taxes on real property with an assessed value of $240,000.00. The tax rate in the city where the property is located is 1.4% of assessed value. C411.
May 12. Paid cash for shopping carts, $1,250.00. C534.

2. Post the general columns of the cash payments journal.

18-2 APPLICATION PROBLEM

Calculating straight-line depreciation

Planter Stores depreciates plant assets using the straight-line depreciation method. If the asset was not bought at the beginning of 20X1, calculate the depreciation expense for the part of 20X1 during which the company owned the asset.

Instructions:

1. Prepare a depreciation table for each of the following plant assets bought by Planter Stores during 20X1. Depreciation tables are given in the *Working Papers*. Save your work to complete Application Problem 18-3.

Transactions:

Jan. 4. Bought a cooler costing $1,400.00; estimated salvage value, $350.00; estimated useful life, 7 years; plant asset No. 311; serial number, 47367BX34.
Mar. 30. Bought an office chair, $500.00; estimated salvage value, $50.00; estimated useful life, 5 years; plant asset No. 312; serial number, 1727X6B3.
Aug. 2. Bought a sale sign, $350.00; estimated salvage value, $50.00; estimated useful life, 5 years; plant asset no. 313; serial number, BC762761.

18-3 APPLICATION PROBLEM

Preparing plant asset records

Instructions:

1. Using the depreciation tables prepared in Application Problem 18-2, prepare a plant asset record for each plant asset. Plant asset records are given in the *Working Papers*. Record the depreciation and book values for 20X1–20X4. Save the plant asset records for use in Application Problem 18-5.

Go Beyond the Book
For more information go to
www.C21accounting.com

18-4 APPLICATION PROBLEM

Journalizing annual depreciation expense

Instructions:

1. On December 31, Ester Engineering, Inc., determined that total depreciation expense for office equipment was $4,320.00. Plan the work sheet adjustment and label the adjustment *(f)*. Record the adjusting entry on page 14 of a general journal and post the transaction to the general ledger. Forms are given in the *Working Papers*.

18-5 APPLICATION PROBLEM

Recording the disposal of plant assets

During 20X5, Planter Stores had the following transactions involving the sale of plant assets. Use the plant asset records completed in Application Problem 18-3. Journals are given in the *Working Papers*.

Transactions:
- Jan. 6. Received cash for sale of an office chair, plant asset No. 312, $250.00. R4.
- Mar. 29. Received cash for sale of a sale sign, plant asset No. 313, $130.00. M3 and R53.
- July 8. Received cash for sale of a cooler, plant asset No. 311, $300.00. M34 and R125.

Instructions:

1. For each plant asset disposed of in 20X5, journalize an entry for additional depreciation, if needed. Use page 3 of a general journal. Source documents are abbreviated as follows: check, C; memorandum, M; receipt, R.
2. Use page 3 of a cash receipts journal to record the disposal of each plant asset.
3. Make appropriate notations in the plant asset records.

18-6 APPLICATION PROBLEM

Calculating depreciation using the double declining-balance depreciation method

Instructions:

1. Depreciation tables are given in the *Working Papers*. Complete a depreciation table for each of the following plant assets purchased during the current year. Use the double declining-balance depreciation method. Round amounts to the nearest cent.

Date	Description	Original Cost	Estimated Salvage Value	Estimated Useful Life
Jan. 3	Display Case	$1,600.00	$200.00	8 years
Jan. 5	Truck	$30,000.00	$2,500.00	4 years
Jan. 8	Mixer	$2,400.00	$300.00	5 years

18-7 MASTERY PROBLEM

Recording transactions for plant assets

Hillside Resort records plant assets in two accounts: Room Furnishings, Account No. 1205, and Equipment, Account No. 1215. Room furnishings are depreciated using the double declining-balance method. Equipment is depreciated using the straight-line method. Forms are given in the *Working Papers*.

Instructions:

1. Record the following transactions completed during 20X1 on page 1 of a cash payments journal.

Transactions:

Jan. 5. Bought a dining table: cost, $2,200.00; estimated salvage value, $200.00; estimated useful life, 5 years; plant asset No. 892; serial number, 903452. C435.
Feb. 26. Paid property taxes on plant assets assessed at $1,600,000.00. The tax rate is 0.8%. C534.
Apr. 5. Bought an air purifier for the office: cost, $1,300.00; estimated salvage value, $100.00; estimated useful life, 6 years; plant asset No. 893; serial number, BE35CC. C577.

2. Complete Section 1 of a plant asset record for each new plant asset.
3. Prepare a depreciation table for each new plant asset.
4. Complete Section 3 of the plant asset records for 20X1–20X4.
5. Record the following transactions completed during 20X5. Use page 2 of a cash receipts journal and page 18 of a general journal.

Transactions:

Jan. 6. Received cash for sale of a dining table, plant asset No. 892, $300.00. R4.
Jul. 2. Received cash for sale of an air purifier, plant asset No. 893, $200.00. M31 and R77.
Dec. 31. Recorded the adjusting entry for depreciation expense—room furnishings. Total 20X5 depreciation expense of room furnishings was $38,520.00.

6. Complete the plant asset records for each plant asset sold during 20X5.

18-8 CHALLENGE PROBLEM

Calculating a partial year's depreciation using the double declining-balance method

Yann Landscaping uses the double declining-balance depreciation method for its equipment. Because many purchases are made during the year, Yann must calculate a partial year's depreciation in the first year. Yann uses the same method to calculate a partial year's depreciation as was described for Restaurant Supply in this chapter. The annual depreciation expense is divided by 12 to calculate a monthly depreciation. The monthly depreciation is then multiplied by the number of months the plant asset was owned during the year. For subsequent years, the annual depreciation is calculated using the normal method—book value multiplied by the depreciation rate.

Instructions:

1. Depreciation tables are given in the *Working Papers*. Prepare depreciation tables for the following assets purchased in 20X1. Round to the nearest cent.

Transactions:

Apr. 2. Bought a lift, $3,600.00; estimated salvage value, $250.00; estimated useful life, 5 years.
July 24. Purchased a lawnmower, $5,400.00; estimated salvage value, $300.00; estimated useful life, 4 years.

APPLIED COMMUNICATION

Public accountants often work with persons who do not understand the concept of depreciation. Although these individuals realize that equipment wears out and loses its value over time, they do not understand why depreciation is shown as an expense on the income statement.

Keyondra Lynch owns a business that manages several apartment buildings. The business had a net loss of $25,000.00 last year, largely because of $300,000.00 in building depreciation expense. The business also generated over $200,000.00 in cash. Ms. Lynch is confused by the financial statements and asks, "Did I make any money or not?"

Instructions: Write a letter to Ms. Lynch, explaining the concept of depreciation. Explain how her business can both "lose money" (incur expenses) yet have a positive cash flow (pay no cash for certain expenses).

CASE FOR CRITICAL THINKING

Miguel Quintanilla, owner of a business, does not record depreciation expense for the business's plant assets. Mr. Quintanilla says that he does not make actual cash payments for depreciation. Therefore, he records an expense for the use of plant assets only when cash is paid for a plant asset. Do you agree with Mr. Quintanilla's method? Explain.

AUDITING FOR ERRORS

Jaudon Industries recently purchased two new plant assets. Danielle Hess, accounting clerk, has prepared the following depreciation schedule for the assets.

Plant Asset: Copier Machine
Depreciation Method: Straight-line
Original Cost: $6,000.00
Estimated Salvage Value: $1,000.00
Estimated Useful Life: 5 years

Year	Beginning Book Value	Annual Depreciation	Accumulated Depreciation	Ending Book Value
20X1	$6,000.00	$1,200.00	$1,200.00	$4,800.00
20X2	$4,800.00	$1,200.00	$2,400.00	$3,600.00
20X3	$3,600.00	$1,200.00	$3,600.00	$2,400.00
20X4	$2,400.00	$1,200.00	$4,800.00	$1,200.00
20X5	$1,200.00	$1,200.00	$6,000.00	$0.00

Plant Asset: Computer System
Depreciation Method: Declining-balance
Original Cost: $8,000.00
Estimated Salvage Value: $1,000.00
Estimated Useful Life: 5 years

Year	Beginning Book Value	Annual Depreciation	Accumulated Depreciation	Ending Book Value
20X1	$8,000.00	$2,800.00	$2,800.00	$5,200.00
20X2	$5,200.00	$2,080.00	$4,880.00	$3,120.00
20X3	$3,120.00	$1,248.00	$6,128.00	$1,872.00
20X4	$1,872.00	$748.80	$6,876.80	$1,123.20
20X5	$1,123.20	$449.28	$7,326.08	$673.92

Instructions: Determine the accuracy of each depreciation schedule. Identify any corrections that Danielle should make.

ANALYZING BEST BUY'S FINANCIAL STATEMENTS

Merchandising businesses often rent buildings from companies that specialize in building management. Any modifications made to the building become the property of the building owner at the end of the lease. These fixed assets are known as *leasehold improvements*.

Instructions

1. Review Best Buy's annual report in Appendix B of this text. Referring to Note 1 beginning on page B-9, what method of depreciation does Best Buy use to depreciate property and equipment?
2. How does Best Buy determine the useful life of leasehold improvements?

Accounting for Plant Assets and Depreciation

Accounting SOFTWARE

PLANT ASSETS AND DEPRECIATION

In information technology terms, the ability of users to perform a specific task is known as *functionality*. Most software companies offer their product with the basic functionality, such as recording journal entries, sales, and cash disbursements, that is needed by all businesses. Additional functionality, such as payroll, fixed assets, credit card processing, and e-commerce, can be purchased separately if needed.

A company with only a few fixed assets may find it easier and more economical to keep their fixed asset records on an electronic spreadsheet. The amount of depreciation expense to be recorded would be calculated by the spreadsheet and recorded in the accounting system using a journal entry.

PEACHTREE APPLICATION PROBLEM 18-1
1. Open (Restore) file 18-1AP.ptb.
2. Journalize and post the transactions related to acquiring plant assets and paying property taxes. Use the Write Checks task; you do not need to change accounting periods.
3. Print the office equipment and store equipment general ledger accounts from Period 1 through Period 5.
4. Print the Property Tax account for February.

PEACHTREE APPLICATION PROBLEM 18-4
1. Open (Restore) file 18-4AP.ptb.
2. Record entries related to depreciation expense. Record and post $4,320 as the adjusting entry in the general journal for the total depreciation expense for office equipment.
3. Print the December 31 general journal, the general ledger's Office Equipment and Accumulated Depreciation–Office Equipment accounts, and the general ledger's Depreciation Expense—Office Equipment account.

PLANT ASSETS AND DEPRECIATION

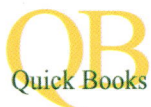

The information about plant assets is used to prepare depreciation schedules and to prepare the adjusting entries for depreciation. In QuickBooks, when a new plant asset is acquired, a new plant asset record must be established. The information to be recorded includes the name of the asset, the seller's name, the date acquired, the amount, the serial number of the asset (if available), and the title of the account that will be debited. When the asset is sold or retired, the plant asset record must be updated to show the asset disposal. Information recorded at this time includes: the date of sale or disposal; the amount of cash received for the asset; and other information if the asset was traded for a new asset. QuickBooks requires you to calculate the amount of depreciation for each plant asset and to enter all depreciation entries into the general journal.

QUICKBOOKS APPLICATION PROBLEM 18-1
1. Open the Umeki Food Source file if it is not already open.
2. Use the Write Checks window to record entries, creating an item for each new asset purchased in the Fixed Asset Item List option. Record all transactions related to acquiring plant assets, preparing fixed plant asset records, and paying property taxes.
3. Print a Journal report using January 1 and May 31 as the dates.
4. Print a Fixed Asset Listing report.

QUICKBOOKS APPLICATION PROBLEM 18-4
1. Open the Ester Engineering Inc file.
2. Journalize the depreciation expense in the Make General Journal Entries window. Print a Journal report using December 31 for the dates.

CALCULATING DEPRECIATION EXPENSE

The many calculations required by a depreciation schedule make this task a perfect application for an electronic spreadsheet. Armed with your understanding of how depreciation is calculated, you would begin by creating the formulas for the first year. Those formulas could be copied down the columns to quickly complete the schedule. You also need a good understanding of how formulas are copied. By default, formula cell references are *relative references*, meaning that the column and row of a cell reference change when the formula is copied. In contrast, the column and row of *absolute references* do not change when copied.

When creating the formulas for annual depreciation expense using the straight-line method, you will need to reference the cells containing the original cost, salvage value, and useful life. These cell references are the same whether calculating depreciation for year 1 or year 5. Therefore, identifying these cells as absolute references will enable you to copy the year 1 formula for each year on the schedule.

EXCEL APPLICATION PROBLEM 18-2
Open the F18-2 Excel data file. Follow the step-by-step instructions in the Instructions worksheet. Use absolute references to create the formulas for annual depreciation expense.

EXCEL APPLICATION PROBLEM 18-3
Open the F18-3 Excel data file. Follow the step-by-step instructions in the Instructions worksheet.

EXCEL APPLICATION PROBLEM 18-6
Open the F18-6 Excel data file. Follow the step-by-step instructions in the Instructions worksheet.

PLANT ASSETS AND DEPRECIATION

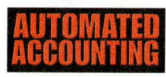

In order for the accounting system to prepare depreciation schedules, complete information must be entered for each plant asset.
1. Click the Accounts toolbar button.
2. Click the Plant Assets tab.
3. To add a new asset:
   a. Enter the asset number.
   b. Complete the data fields in the text boxes—asset name, date acquired, useful life, original cost, and salvage value.
   c. Enter the appropriate accumulated depreciation and depreciation expense account numbers.
   d. Select the desired depreciation method from the drop-down list.
   e. Click Add Asset.
4. To change or delete data for an existing plant asset:
   a. Select the asset by clicking the text box containing the data you wish to change.
   b. Enter the correct data and click the Change Asset button, or click the Delete button to remove the asset from the database.

Generating and Posting Depreciation Adjusting Entries
At the end of the fiscal period (month or year), the computerized accounting system will generate the adjusting entries from the information in the plant asset records. To generate and post the adjusting entries:
1. Choose Depreciation Adjusting Entries from the Options menu.
2. Click Yes to generate the depreciation adjusting entries.
3. Click the Post button. The general journal will appear, containing the posted journal entry. Verify the accuracy of the entry and click the Close button.

AUTOMATED ACCOUNTING APPLICATION PROBLEM 18-2
Open file F18-2.AA8. Display the problem instructions and complete the problem.

AUTOMATED ACCOUNTING MASTERY PROBLEM 18-7
Open file F18-7.AA8. Display the problem instructions and complete the problem.

CHAPTER 19

Accounting for Inventory

OBJECTIVES

After studying Chapter 19, you will be able to:

1. Define accounting terms related to inventory.
2. Identify accounting concepts and practices related to inventory.
3. Prepare a stock record.
4. Determine the cost of merchandise inventory using the fifo, lifo, and weighted-average inventory costing methods.
5. Estimate the cost of merchandise inventory using the gross profit method of estimating inventory.

KEY TERMS

- periodic inventory
- perpetual inventory
- inventory record
- stock record
- stock ledger
- first-in, first-out inventory costing method
- last-in, first-out inventory costing method
- weighted-average inventory costing method
- gross profit method of estimating inventory

Point Your Browser
www.C21accounting.com

ACCOUNTING IN THE REAL WORLD

Fender Guitars

Fender Guitars Are Everywhere

When you enter a music store searching for that perfect guitar, you expect to be able to choose from an extensive variety of guitars. You want a style and color that reflects your personality, an awesome sound, and a great price. Equally important, you want a brand name that is respected by musicians worldwide.

Beginning with its legendary Telecaster®, Fender has produced renowned electric guitars for more than 50 years. The company now offers a wide variety of electric basses and amplifiers.

Have you ever wondered how small music stores can afford to have such an extensive selection of guitars and amplifiers? The money required to maintain this level of inventory is beyond the financial resources of the typical music store.

To solve this problem, Fender has established relationships with various floor-planning companies that provide reasonable financing to Fender dealers. The dealers can purchase product beyond their financial resources, and pay for the product as it is sold. The floor-plan methodology enables Fender's dealers to provide their customers with a full range of product from which to select. In addition, the inventory can be very easily replenished.

Critical Thinking

1. Manufacturers in other industries, including automobiles, motorcycles, and appliances, often floor-plan inventory for their distributors. What do these industries have in common with musical instruments?
2. How does the floor-plan method benefit customers who do not live in large metropolitan areas?

Source: www.fender.com

INTERNET ACTIVITY

Notes to the Financial Statements—Inventory Costing Methods

Go to the homepage for Wal-Mart (www.walmart.com) and Target Corporation (www.target.com). Search for the latest annual report for each company. The annual report is usually found under the heading "About Us" or "Investor Relations." In the annual report, usually after the financial statements, you will find the notes to the financial statements. Using these notes (probably Note #1 or #2), look for the information about inventory.

Instructions

1. For each company, state which note contains the information about inventory.
2. For each company, find the method(s) used to calculate the cost of inventory (fifo, lifo, or weighted average.)

LESSON 19-1: Determining the Quantity of Merchandise Inventory

WHY MERCHANDISE INVENTORY IS IMPORTANT

Merchandise inventory on hand is typically the largest asset of a merchandising business. Successful businesses must have merchandise available for sale that customers want. A business therefore needs controls that assist managers in maintaining a merchandise inventory of sufficient quantity, variety, and price.

The cost of merchandise inventory is reported on both the balance sheet and the income statement. An accurate cost of merchandise inventory is required to correctly report current assets and retained earnings on the balance sheet. The accuracy of the inventory cost will also assure that gross profit and net income are reported correctly on the income statement. [CONCEPT: Adequate Disclosure]

> **SMALL BUSINESS SPOTLIGHT**
>
> Every state has a Small Business Development Center (SBDC) office, which provides a wide range of consulting services and seminars. Funded by state and federal governments, SBDCs are directed by the Small Business Administration and state university personnel.

CHARACTER COUNTS

Hotlines

The accounting scandals of the early 21st century led the U.S. Congress to pass legislation designed to protect investors by improving the accuracy and reliability of financial reporting. The bill, known as the Sarbanes-Oxley Act of 2002 (SOX), contains a section that requires management to make a written statement about the effectiveness of its internal control system. External auditors must test the internal control system to ensure that management's conclusions are appropriate.

In an effective internal control system, employees and other stakeholders must be able to communicate possible ethics violations. A phone number that allows an individual to provide confidential information regarding possible ethics violations is called a *hotline*. An effective hotline must ensure an individual that:

1. Management takes hotline calls seriously.
2. The information provided will be maintained on an anonymous or confidential basis.
3. No retaliation or harassment will be tolerated.

Instructions

Dow's EthicsLine is available to Dow employees to report possible violations of its *Code of Business Conduct* (www.dow.com). Describe how EthicsLine is designed to meet the three criteria presented above.

THE MOST EFFICIENT QUANTITY OF INVENTORY

To determine the most efficient quantity of inventory, a business makes frequent analysis of purchases, sales, and inventory records. Many businesses fail because too much or too little merchandise inventory is kept on hand. A business that stocks merchandise that does not satisfy the demand of its customers is also likely to fail.

A merchandise inventory that is larger than needed may decrease the net income of a business for several reasons.

1. Excess inventory requires that a business spend money for expensive store and warehouse space.
2. Excess inventory uses capital that could be invested in other assets to earn a profit for the business.
3. Excess inventory requires that a business spend money for expenses, such as taxes and insurance premiums, which increase with the cost of the merchandise inventory.
4. Excess inventory may become obsolete and unsalable.

Merchandise inventory that is smaller than needed may also decrease the net income of a business for several reasons.

1. Sales may be lost to competitors if items wanted by customers are not on hand.
2. Sales may be lost to competitors if there is an insufficient variety of merchandise to satisfy customers.
3. When a business frequently orders small quantities of an item, the price paid is often more per unit than when merchandise is ordered in large quantities.

METHODS USED TO DETERMINE THE QUANTITY OF MERCHANDISE INVENTORY

The quantity of items in inventory at the end of a fiscal period must be determined in order to calculate the cost of merchandise sold.

Two principal methods are used to determine the quantity of each item of merchandise on hand.

1. A merchandise inventory determined by counting, weighing, or measuring items of merchandise on hand is called a **periodic inventory**. A periodic inventory is also referred to as a *physical inventory*.
2. A merchandise inventory determined by keeping a continuous record of increases, decreases, and balance on hand is called a **perpetual inventory**. A perpetual inventory is also referred to as a *book inventory*.

Because controlling the quantity of merchandise inventory is so important to a business's success, many methods of keeping inventory records are used. Today, most companies use computers to keep track of the inventory on hand.

Keeping track of merchandise inventory also involves knowing the ideal quantity for each kind of merchandise in inventory. To ensure having the appropriate quantity, companies frequently establish an ideal minimum quantity and an ideal reorder quantity. When the minimum quantity is reached, new merchandise is ordered.

Minimum quantity levels must be established with consideration for how long it may take to receive new inventory. Otherwise, merchandise may not be available when a customer wants to buy it. Those who order new merchandise must also be aware of the ideal quantities to order to get the best prices and trade discounts.

BLEND IMAGES/GETTY IMAGES

INVENTORY RECORD

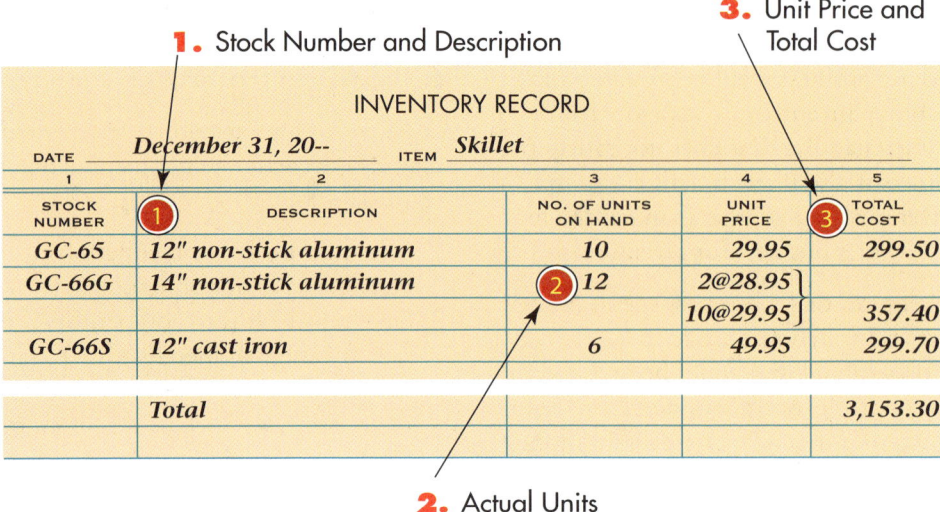

Counting, weighing, or measuring merchandise on hand for a periodic inventory is commonly referred to as "taking an inventory." Employees count each item of inventory and record the quantities on special forms. To assure an accurate and complete count, a business will typically be closed during the periodic inventory.

Businesses frequently establish their fiscal period to end when inventory is at a minimum because it takes less time to count a smaller inventory. For example, a department store may take an inventory at the end of December. The amount of merchandise on hand is smaller because of holiday sales. Few purchases of additional merchandise are made in December after the holiday sales. All of these activities make the merchandise inventory smaller at the end of December.

A form used during a periodic inventory to record information about each item of merchandise on hand is called an **inventory record**. The inventory record has space to record the stock number, description, number of units on hand, unit price, and total cost of each item.

Columns 1–3 are completed when the business is taking an inventory. Columns 4–5 are completed after the taking of inventory. The methods used to determine the unit prices are discussed later in this chapter.

> **FOR YOUR INFORMATION**
>
> **FYI**
>
> Taking an inventory is an involved and expensive task. An efficient inventory count requires extensive management planning and employee training. Some businesses hire independent companies that specialize in taking inventories to assist in planning for and counting the inventory.

STEPS PREPARING AN INVENTORY RECORD

1. Write the stock number and description before the periodic inventory begins.

2. Write the actual count in the No. of Units on Hand column.

3. Write the unit price and calculate the total cost after the physical inventory is completed. These columns are usually completed by the accounting department.

566   Chapter 19   Accounting for Inventory

STOCK RECORD

\multicolumn{3}{c}{STOCK RECORD}

Description Skillet, 14" cast iron   **Stock No.** GC-66
Reorder 20   **Minimum** 10   **Location** Rack C-24

1	2	3	4	5	6	7
INCREASES			DECREASES			BALANCE
DATE	PURCHASE INVOICE NO.	QUANTITY	DATE	SALES INVOICE NO.	QUANTITY	QUANTITY
			Oct. 10		5	9
Nov. 2	968	20				29
	①		Nov. 12	1726	4	25
			Nov. 29	1792	2	23
			Dec. 6	1841	3	20 ③
				②		

1. Purchase Information **2.** Sales Information **3.** New Balance on Hand

Some businesses keep inventory records that show continuously the quantity on hand for each kind of merchandise. A form used to show the kind of merchandise, quantity received, quantity sold, and balance on hand is called a **stock record**. A separate stock record is prepared for each kind of merchandise on hand. A file of stock records for all merchandise on hand is called a **stock ledger**.

A perpetual inventory system provides day-to-day information about the quantity of merchandise on hand. The minimum balance allowed before a reorder must be placed is also shown on each stock record. The minimum balance is the quantity that will typically last until the ordered merchandise can be received from the vendors. When the quantity falls below the minimum, additional merchandise is ordered in the quantity shown on the reorder line of the stock record. A stock record shows the quantity but usually not the cost of the merchandise.

Purchase information is recorded in the Increases columns when additional merchandise is received. Sales information is recorded in the Decreases columns when merchandise is sold. The new balance on hand is recorded after each purchase and sale.

When a perpetual inventory is kept, errors may be made in recording or calculating amounts. Also, some stock records may be incorrect because merchandise is taken from stock and not recorded on stock records. A business should take a periodic inventory at least once a fiscal period. The perpetual records are corrected to reflect the actual quantity on hand as determined by the periodic inventory.

PERPETUAL INVENTORY USING A COMPUTER

Many merchandising businesses use a computer to keep perpetual inventory records. The point-of-sale terminals at the customer check-out counters are connected to the computer. The terminals read the Universal Product Codes (UPC) marked on products.

The stock ledger is stored in the computer. When a UPC is read at the terminal, the product description and the sales price are retrieved from the stock ledger and displayed on the terminal. The computer reduces the units on hand to reflect the item sold. The computer may also periodically check the quantities in the stock ledger and print a list of items that need to be reordered.

End of Lesson REVIEW

AUDIT YOUR UNDERSTANDING

1. Why do successful businesses need an effective inventory system?
2. Identify four reasons why a merchandise inventory that is larger than needed may decrease the net income of a business.
3. When are periodic inventories normally taken?
4. How do inventory levels affect the period a business selects for its fiscal year? Why?
5. How is the accuracy of a perpetual inventory checked?

TERMS REVIEW

periodic inventory
perpetual inventory
inventory record
stock record
stock ledger

WORK TOGETHER 19-1

Preparing a stock record

A stock record for Sound Station is given in the *Working Papers*. Your instructor will guide you through the following example.

1. Enter the following transactions on the stock record of Stock No. W-394, 16-gauge speaker wire. Source documents are abbreviated as follows: purchase invoice, P; sales invoice, S.

   Transactions:
   Oct. 3. Sold 250 feet of W-394 speaker wire. S2543.
   27. Purchased 750 feet of W-394 speaker wire. P1542.
   29. Sold 300 feet of W-394 speaker wire. S2654.
   Dec. 4. Sold 170 feet of W-394 speaker wire. S2801.

ON YOUR OWN 19-1

Preparing a stock record

A stock record for Frames-R-Us is given in the *Working Papers*. Work this problem independently.

1. Enter the following transactions on the stock record of Stock No. M-253, an 8″ × 10″ white metal frame. Source documents are abbreviated as follows: purchase invoice, P; sales invoice, S.

   Transactions:
   Nov. 4. Sold 10 M-253 picture frames. S590.
   16. Sold 25 M-253 picture frames. S624.
   22. Received 50 M-253 picture frames. P223.
   Dec. 9. Sold 15 M-253 picture frames. S645.

LESSON 19-2

Determining the Cost of Merchandise Inventory

FIRST-IN, FIRST-OUT INVENTORY COSTING METHOD

3. Units Needed to Equal the Total Units on Hand

4. Unit Price Times Fifo Units

Purchase Dates	Units Purchased	Unit Price	Total Cost	FIFO Units on Hand	FIFO Cost
January 1, beginning inventory	10	$18.80	$188.00		
February 16, purchases	6	19.60	117.60		
April 17, purchases	14	20.40	285.60		
September 5, purchases	12	21.40	256.80	③ 10	④ $214.00
November 22, purchases	8	21.50	172.00	② 8	172.00
Totals	50		$1,020.00	① 18	$386.00 ⑤

2. Units from the Most Recent Purchase

1. Total Units on Hand

5. Total Fifo Cost

After the quantities of merchandise on hand are counted, purchase invoices are used to find merchandise unit prices. The total costs are then calculated using the quantities and unit prices recorded on the inventory records. Most businesses use one of three inventory costing methods: (1) first-in, first-out, (2) last-in, first-out, or (3) weighted-average.

Restaurant Supply uses the most recent invoices for purchases to determine the unit price of an item in inventory. The earliest invoices for purchases, therefore, are used to determine the cost of merchandise sold. Using the price of merchandise purchased first to calculate the cost of merchandise sold first is called the **first-in, first-out inventory costing method**. The first-in, first-out method is frequently abbreviated as *fifo*.

On December 31, a periodic inventory of 12-inch aluminum skillets, Model No. GS-67, showed 18 units on hand. Using the fifo method, the 18 units would show a total cost of $386.00.

STEPS COSTING INVENTORY USING THE FIFO METHOD

① Enter the total number of units on hand, *18*.

② From the most recent purchase, November 22, enter the number of units purchased, *8*. In some cases, the number of units of the most recent purchase will be greater than or equal to the total number of units on hand. In such a case, enter the total number of units on hand and do not complete Step 3 below.

③ From the next most recent purchase, September 5, enter the number of units, *10*, needed for the fifo units to equal the total number on hand, 18. Continue with the next invoices as needed.

④ Multiply the unit price of each appropriate purchase by the fifo units on hand to determine the fifo cost.

⑤ Add the individual fifo costs to determine the fifo cost of the total number of units in ending inventory.

Determining the Cost of Merchandise Inventory

LAST-IN, FIRST-OUT INVENTORY COSTING METHOD

Using the price of merchandise purchased last to calculate the cost of merchandise sold first is called the **last-in, first-out inventory costing method**. The last-in, first-out method is frequently abbreviated as *lifo*. This method is based on the idea that the most recent costs of merchandise should be charged against current revenue. [CONCEPT: Matching Expenses with Revenue]

Using the lifo method, each item on the inventory records is recorded at the earliest prices paid for the merchandise.

The earliest prices for the 18 skillets would consist of the 10 units in the January 1 beginning inventory. The next earliest purchase, February 16, of 6 units is then used to cost 6 units in ending inventory. The remaining 2 units in ending inventory are costed using the next earliest purchase, April 17. On the inventory record, the 18 units would show a total cost of $346.40.

STEPS COSTING INVENTORY USING THE LIFO METHOD

① Enter the total number of units on hand, *18*.

② Enter the number of units in beginning inventory, *10*. In some cases, the number of units of beginning inventory will be greater than or equal to the total number of units on hand. In such a case, enter the total number of units on hand and do not complete Steps 3 and 4 below.

③ From the earliest purchase, February 16, enter the number of units purchased, *6*.

④ From the next earliest purchase, April 17, enter the number of units, *2*, needed for the lifo units to equal the total number of units on hand, 18.

⑤ Multiply the unit price of the beginning inventory by the lifo units on hand to determine the lifo cost for beginning inventory. Repeat this process for each appropriate purchase.

⑥ Add the lifo cost for the beginning inventory and each appropriate purchase to determine the lifo cost of the total number of units in ending inventory.

> **REMEMBER**
>
> *In the lifo method, the latest purchases are assumed to be sold first (first-out). Therefore, ending inventory consists of the units purchased the earliest, and the earliest purchase invoice costs are used to value the ending inventory.*

WEIGHTED-AVERAGE INVENTORY COSTING METHOD

Purchases			Total Cost
Date	Units	Unit Price	
January 1, beginning inventory	10	$18.80	$188.00
February 16, purchases	6	19.60	117.60
April 17, purchases	14	20.40	285.60
September 5, purchases	12	21.40	256.80
November 22, purchases	8	21.50	172.00
Totals	50		$1,020.00

1. Total Cost of Inventory Available

Total of Beginning Inventory and Purchases ÷ Total Units = Weighted-Average Price per Unit
$1,020.00 ÷ 50 = $20.40

2. Weighted-Average Price per Unit

Units in Ending Inventory × Weighted-Average Price per Unit = Cost of Ending Inventory
18 × $20.40 = $367.20

3. Cost of Ending Inventory

Using the average cost of beginning inventory plus merchandise purchased during a fiscal period to calculate the cost of merchandise sold is called the **weighted-average inventory costing method**. The average unit price of the total inventory available is calculated. This average unit price is used to calculate both ending inventory and cost of merchandise sold. The average cost of merchandise is then charged against current revenue. [CONCEPT: Matching Expenses with Revenue]

Using the weighted-average method, the inventory is costed at the average price per unit of the beginning inventory plus the cost of all purchases during the fiscal year. On the inventory record, the 18 units would show a total cost of $367.20.

STEPS — COSTING INVENTORY USING THE WEIGHTED-AVERAGE METHOD

1. Calculate the total cost of beginning inventory and each purchase, *$1,020.00*, by multiplying the units by each unit price.

2. Calculate the weighted-average price per unit, *$20.40*, by dividing the total cost, *$1,020.00*, by the number of units available, *50*.

3. Calculate the cost of ending inventory, *$367.20*, by multiplying the weighted-average price per unit, *$20.40*, by the units in ending inventory, *18*.

FOR YOUR INFORMATION — FYI

A business usually determines the order in which products are sold, based on the type of inventory. A grocery store, for example, must sell its earliest purchases first. A hardware store, however, could sell its most recent purchases first. The inventory costing method used to calculate the cost of merchandise sold should not, however, be determined by the order in which items are sold. A business should choose the inventory costing method that provides its managers with the best accounting information.

Determining the Cost of Merchandise Inventory

CALCULATING THE COST OF MERCHANDISE SOLD

The cost of ending inventory determined using any of the three inventory costing methods can be used to calculate the cost of merchandise sold. The cost of ending inventory is subtracted from the total cost of units available for sale. Although the formula is the same, under each inventory costing method the amount determined will be different. Restaurant Supply uses the fifo method. Therefore, the fifo cost of $386.00 is subtracted from the total cost of merchandise available for sale, $1,020.00, to calculate the cost of merchandise sold of $634.00.

Cost of Merchandise Available for Sale	−	Fifo Cost of Ending Inventory	=	Cost of Merchandise Sold
$1,020.00	−	$386.00	=	$634.00

COMPARISON OF INVENTORY METHODS

	Fifo	Lifo	Weighted Average
Cost of Merchandise Sold:			
Merchandise Inventory, Jan. 1	$ 188.00	$ 188.00	$ 188.00
Net Purchases	832.00	832.00	832.00
Merchandise Available for Sale	$ 1,020.00	$ 1,020.00	$ 1,020.00
Less Ending Inventory, Dec. 31	386.00	346.40	367.20
Cost of Merchandise Sold	$ 634.00	$ 673.60	$ 652.80
In a period of rising prices:			
Relative Cost of Ending Inventory	highest	lowest	intermediate
Relative Cost of Merchandise Sold	lowest	highest	intermediate

In a period of rising prices, the fifo method gives the highest possible ending inventory cost and the lowest cost of merchandise sold. The lifo method gives the lowest possible ending inventory cost and the highest cost of merchandise sold. The weighted-average method gives ending inventory cost and cost of merchandise sold between fifo and lifo. As the cost of merchandise sold increases, gross profit and net income decrease. Thus, net income is highest under the fifo method, lowest under the lifo method, and intermediate under the weighted-average method.

In a period of declining prices, the results for the fifo and lifo methods are reversed.

All three inventory costing methods are acceptable accounting practices. A business should select one method and use that same method continuously for each fiscal period. If a business changed inventory costing methods, part of the difference in gross profit and net income would be caused by the change in methods. To provide financial statements that can be analyzed and compared with statements of other fiscal periods, the same inventory costing method should be used each fiscal period. [CONCEPT: Consistent Reporting]

End of Lesson REVIEW

TERMS REVIEW

first-in, first-out inventory costing method

last-in, first-out inventory costing method

weighted-average inventory costing method

AUDIT YOUR UNDERSTANDING

1. When the fifo method is used, how is the cost of each kind of ending merchandise inventory determined?
2. On what idea is the lifo method based?
3. In a period of rising prices, which inventory costing method gives the highest cost of merchandise sold?
4. Why should a business select one inventory costing method and use that same method continuously for each fiscal period?

WORK TOGETHER 19-2

Determining the cost of inventory using the fifo, lifo, and weighted-average inventory costing methods

Inventory costing information for Riverville Electronics is given in the *Working Papers*. Your instructor will guide you through the following example.

1. Calculate the cost of ending inventory using the fifo, lifo, and weighted-average methods. There are 16 units in ending inventory.

ON YOUR OWN 19-2

Determining the cost of inventory using the fifo, lifo, and weighted-average inventory costing methods

Inventory costing information for Venture Plumbing is given in the *Working Papers*. Work this problem independently.

1. Calculate the cost of ending inventory using the fifo, lifo, and weighted-average methods. There are 24 units in ending inventory.

Determining the Cost of Merchandise Inventory

LESSON 19-3

Estimating Inventory

GROSS PROFIT METHOD OF ESTIMATING INVENTORY

STEP 1: Beginning inventory, January 1 .... $ 142,536.20
    Plus   net purchases for January 1 to January 31 ..... + 42,452.80
    Equals cost of merchandise available for sale .... $ 184,989.00

STEP 2: Net sales for January 1 to January 31 .... $ 99,340.00
    Times previous year's gross profit percentage .... × 40.00%
    Equals estimated gross profit on operations .... $ 39,736.00

STEP 3: Net sales for January 1 to January 31 .... $ 99,340.00
    Less   estimated gross profit on operations .... − 39,736.00
    Equals estimated cost of merchandise sold .... $ 59,604.00

STEP 4: Cost of merchandise available for sale .... $ 184,989.00
    Less   estimated cost of merchandise sold .... − 59,604.00
    Equals estimated ending merchandise inventory ..... $ 125,385.00

Restaurant Supply Co.
Income Statement
For Month Ended January 31, 20--

			% of Net Sales
Operating Revenue:			
Net Sales		$ 99,340.00	100.0
Cost of Merchandise Sold:			
Beginning Inventory, January 1	$142,536.20		
Net Purchases	42,452.80		
Merchandise Available for Sale	$184,989.00		
Less Est. Ending Inv., January 31	125,385.00		
Cost of Merchandise Sold		59,604.00	60.0
Gross Profit on Operations		$ 39,736.00	40.0
Operating Expenses		30,298.70	30.5
Net Income		$ 9,437.30	9.5

Estimating inventory by using the previous year's percentage of gross profit on operations is called the **gross profit method of estimating inventory**. The gross profit method is often used to estimate the cost of the ending inventory reported on monthly financial statements. The gross profit method is a less expensive method of calculating inventory costs than taking a periodic inventory or maintaining a perpetual inventory system.

Four values are needed to perform the four-step process. Actual net sales and net purchases amounts are obtained from the general ledger. The beginning inventory amount is obtained from the prior period's financial statements. The gross profit percentage is estimated by management based on the previous year's actual percentage, adjusted for any significant changes in economic conditions.

ESTIMATING INVENTORY FOR OTHER MONTHS

When the gross profit method of estimating inventory is used for months other than the first month of the fiscal period, the process is the same as that just illustrated. Net sales and purchases amounts are obtained from the general ledger. For the sales account, the previous month's ending balance is subtracted from the current month's ending balance to calculate the amount of sales for just the current month. The same process is used for the purchases account. The beginning inventory for the month is the same as the ending inventory from the previous month. Note that both the beginning and ending inventory amounts will be based on estimated amounts.

FINANCIAL LITERACY

Synopsis of Investments

There is much pressure on individuals to save for retirement. Where do you start? If you have money available to put away for retirement, where should you invest it to get the best return? There are many investment options available to today's workers.

One kind of fund is called an Individual Retirement Account (IRA). There are several forms of IRAs. A deductible IRA means that the investor does not have to pay tax on the money deposited or on the interest earned on the account until it is withdrawn at retirement. A non-deductible IRA means that the investor does pay tax on the money deposited but does not pay tax on the interest earned on the account until it is withdrawn at retirement. A Roth IRA is one where the person pays tax on the amount deposited but never has to pay tax on the interest earned on the account.

A certificate of deposit (CD) is an investment product offered by banks. Interest is paid on the CD on a specific date in the future. The term of the CD can range from 30 days to more than five years. If you want to share directly in the success of a corporation, you may purchase shares of stock in that company. Each share of stock represents an ownership interest. Your investment can reward you either in the form of dividends or by an increase in the value of your shares of stock. Another investment is to purchase the bond of a company or government entity, which is similar to a loan that pays periodic interest. The repayment of the principal amount occurs at a specified date in the future.

If you want to invest in stocks and bonds but don't want to deal directly with each company, you can invest in a mutual fund, which means you buy shares in an entity designed to collect the investments from many investors. In turn, these funds are invested in the stocks and bonds of many companies by fund managers.

Activities

1. Contact a financial planner. Ask his or her advice on how much is needed to start investing and what types of investments are appropriate for someone your age. Prepare a written summary of your findings.

2. Pick two publicly traded companies in the same industry. Track each company's stock price daily for two weeks. Summarize your findings in a chart or graph.

End of Lesson REVIEW

AUDIT YOUR UNDERSTANDING

1. When neither a perpetual system is maintained nor a periodic inventory is taken, how can an ending merchandise inventory be determined that is accurate enough for a monthly income statement?
2. What amounts are needed to estimate ending merchandise inventory?
3. What amount is used for beginning inventory for a month that is not the first month of a fiscal period?

TERM REVIEW

gross profit method of estimating inventory

WORK TOGETHER 19-3

Estimating ending inventory using the gross profit method

A form for making estimated inventory calculations and a form for completing an income statement are given in the *Working Papers*. Your instructor will guide you through the following examples.

1. Use the following information obtained from the records and management of Evans Company to estimate the cost of the ending inventory on June 30.

Estimated beginning inventory, June 1	$154,800.00
Actual net purchases for June	$ 47,800.00
Actual net sales for June	$245,000.00
Estimated gross profit percentage	45.0%
Actual operating expenses for June	$ 76,930.00

2. Prepare an income statement for the month ended June 30 of the current year.

ON YOUR OWN 19-3

Estimating ending inventory using the gross profit method

A form for making estimated inventory calculations and a form for completing an income statement are given in the *Working Papers*. Work this problem independently.

1. Use the following information obtained from the records and management of Luke Enterprises to estimate the cost of the ending inventory on April 30.

Estimated beginning inventory, April 1	$24,500.00
Actual net purchases for April	$12,100.00
Actual net sales for April	$56,000.00
Estimated gross profit percentage	55.0%
Actual operating expenses for April	$17,920.00

2. Prepare an income statement for the month ended April 30 of the current year.

SUMMARY

After completing this chapter, you can:
1. Define accounting terms related to inventory.
2. Identify accounting concepts and practices related to inventory.
3. Prepare a stock record.
4. Determine the cost of merchandise inventory using the fifo, lifo, and weighted-average inventory costing methods.
5. Estimate the cost of merchandise inventory using the gross profit method of estimating inventory.

EXPLORE ACCOUNTING

Costing a CD Can Make Your Head Spin

Determining the cost of an item of inventory, often referred to as *costing* an item, is a relatively easy task for a merchandising business. However, costing can be a complex task for the company that manufactures the item.

Consider the challenge of a music company costing a music CD. Stardust Music has signed a new group, SeaMist, to its first contract. Included in the cost of the CD is all the labor required to produce the CD. Stardust Music will pay SeaMist $1.50 for every CD sold. Studio artists, however, were paid a fixed fee totaling $30,000.

If Stardust Music sells 100,000 CDs, its labor cost will be $180,000, or $1.80 per CD—$150,000 to SeaMist and $30,000 to the studio artists. If the CD is an unexpected smash hit, selling 300,000 CDs, Stardust's labor cost will be $480,000, or $1.60 per CD—$450,000 to SeaMist and $30,000 for the studio artists.

The artist cost, $1.50 per CD, is referred to as a *variable cost*. The total artist cost varies, depending on the number of units sold. The studio artist cost of $30,000 is referred to as a *fixed cost* because the total studio artist cost is fixed (constant), regardless of the number of units sold.

When preparing the first monthly financial statement after the release of SeaMist's CD, Stardust's accountants must assign a labor cost to SeaMist's CD. What amount should be used? $1.80? $1.60? Another amount?

Accountants must make good sales estimates and constantly reevaluate these estimates to calculate the most accurate cost information possible. Accountants must constantly communicate with the sales staff to update sales projections.

Required: Calculate the total and unit labor costs for SeaMist's second CD using the following assumptions: (1) SeaMist receives $1.75 per CD. (2) Studio artists cost $60,000. (3) A famous guest artist used on one track receives $30,000 plus $0.10 for every CD sold. Prepare estimates for 400,000; 500,000; and 600,000 unit sales.

19-1 APPLICATION PROBLEM

Preparing a stock record

A stock record for Mountain Pool & Spa is given in the *Working Papers*.

Instructions:
Enter the following transactions on the stock record of a 450-gallon spa, model no. HT-450. The units cost $1,299.00 and are sold for $2,599.00. Source documents are abbreviated as follows: purchase invoice, P; sales invoice, S.

Transactions:
Feb. 4. Sold 1 model no. HT-450 spa to Jan Ellis, n/30. S2433.
28. Sold 2 model no. HT-450 spas to Lake County Hospital, 2/10, n/30. S2478.
Mar. 10. Received 5 units of model no. HT-450 spas from SunSpa Manufacturing, 2/10, n/30. P789.
24. Sold 1 model no. HT-450 spa to John Pierce, n/30. S2502.

19-2 APPLICATION PROBLEM

Determining the cost of inventory using the fifo, lifo, and weighted-average inventory costing methods

Forms for costing inventory for Orlando Supply are given in the *Working Papers*. There are 172 units in ending inventory.

Purchase Date	Quantity	Unit Price
January 1, beginning inventory	90	$2.00
March 13, purchases	78	2.10
June 8, purchases	80	2.25
September 16, purchases	84	2.30
December 22, purchases	88	2.40

Instructions:
Calculate the cost of ending inventory using the fifo, lifo, and weighted-average methods.

19-3 APPLICATION PROBLEM

Estimating ending inventory using the gross profit method

Use the following information obtained from the records and management of Fultz Industries. A form for making inventory calculations and a form for completing an income statement are given in the *Working Papers*.

Instructions:

1. Estimate the cost of the ending inventory on March 31.

Estimated beginning inventory, March 1	$ 98,700.00
Actual net purchases for March	$ 45,800.00
Actual net sales for March	$186,000.00
Estimated gross profit percentage	58.0%
Actual operating expenses for March	$ 80,352.00

2. Prepare an income statement for the month ended March 31 of the current year.

19-4 MASTERY PROBLEM

Determining the cost of inventory using the fifo, lifo, and weighted-average inventory costing methods

Fratisi Company began the year with 8 units of its model P-234 electronic switch in beginning inventory. Each unit sells for $9.95. The following transactions involving model P-234 occurred during the year. Forms are given in the *Working Papers*. Source documents are abbreviated as follows: purchase invoice, P; sales invoice, S.

Transactions:
- Jan. 6. Purchased 20 units from Master Electronics for $5.12 per unit, 2/10, n/30. P154.
- Apr. 5. Sold 22 units to Evan Construction, n/30. S1998.
- 14. Purchased 20 units from Master Electronics for $5.18 per unit, 2/10, n/30. P223.
- Jul. 28. Sold 25 units to Pette Hardware, n/30. S2245.
- Aug. 3. Purchased 20 units from Master Electronics for $5.23 per unit, 2/10, n/30. P298.
- Dec. 2. Sold 15 units to Century Homebuilders, n/30. S2848.
- 12. Purchased 20 units from Master Electronics for $5.27 per unit, 2/10, n/30. P332.

Instructions:

1. Enter the transactions on the stock record and determine the number of units in ending inventory.
2. Calculate the cost of ending inventory using the fifo, lifo, and weighted-average methods.
3. Which of the inventory costing methods resulted in the highest cost of merchandise sold? Merchandise available for sale is the total cost of beginning inventory plus all purchases during the year.

19-5 CHALLENGE PROBLEM

Determining the cost of merchandise inventory destroyed in a fire

A fire completely destroyed the warehouse of Murphy Electronics Company on the night of May 12 of the current year. The accounting records of the company and $1,890.00 of merchandise inventory were salvaged. The company does not maintain a perpetual inventory system. The insurance company therefore has requested an estimate of the merchandise inventory destroyed in the fire. Forms are given in the *Working Papers*. The following income statement is for the previous fiscal year.

Murphy Electronics Company
Income Statement
For Year Ended April 30, 20--

Operating Revenue:		
Net Sales		$645,217.90
Cost of Merchandise Sold:		
Beginning Inventory, May 1 (prior year)	$ 33,298.45	
Net Purchases	322,564.03	
Merchandise Available for Sale	$355,862.48	
Less Ending Inv., April 30	34,543.98	
Cost of Merchandise Sold		321,318.50
Gross Profit on Operations		$323,899.40
Operating Expenses		284,535.22
Net Income		$ 39,364.18

The following additional financial information is obtained from the current year's accounting records.

Net purchases, May 1 to May 12	$ 6,754.03
Net sales, May 1 to May 12	22,432.87
Operating expenses, May 1 to May 12	9,875.40

Instructions:

1. Calculate the prior year's gross profit on operations as a percentage of net sales. Round the percentage calculation to the nearest 0.1 percent.
2. Use the percentage calculated in Instruction 1 and the current year's financial information to calculate an estimate of the total merchandise inventory as of May 12.
3. To calculate the cost of the inventory destroyed in the fire, subtract the cost of the merchandise inventory that was not destroyed from the estimate of the total merchandise inventory as of May 12.
4. Prepare an income statement for the period May 1 through May 12.

The insurance company maintains that it is liable for paying only the book value of the inventory destroyed by fire. Murphy Electronics Company maintains that the insurance company should pay the replacement cost of the destroyed inventory.

Instructions:

5. What is meant by the book value and the replacement value of the inventory?
6. Murphy Electronics Company uses the fifo inventory costing method. How does using fifo affect the difference between the book value and the replacement value of the destroyed inventory?
7. What should determine which value the insurance company uses?

APPLIED COMMUNICATION

Arrange with your instructor to call the manager of a local merchandising company. Ask the manager questions concerning how the company maintains a count and cost of its merchandise inventory. Suggested questions include:

1. Does the company maintain a perpetual inventory system?
2. How often does the company take an inventory?
3. Who counts the inventory during a periodic inventory?
4. What method is used to cost the ending inventory?
5. If a perpetual inventory is used, how closely do the year-end quantities match the periodic counts?

CASES FOR CRITICAL THINKING

Case 1

Ballston Company uses the fifo method of costing its merchandise inventory. The manager is considering a change to the lifo method. Costs have increased steadily over the past three years. What effect will the change have on the following items? (1) The amount of net income on the income statement. (2) The amount of income taxes to be paid. (3) The quantity of each item of merchandise that must be kept in stock. Why?

Case 2

The Pet Center stocks many kinds of merchandise. The store has always taken a periodic inventory at the end of a fiscal year. The store has not kept a perpetual inventory because of the cost. However, the manager wants a reasonably accurate cost of merchandise inventory at the end of each month. The manager needs the amount to prepare monthly income statements and to help in making decisions about the business. What would you recommend?

SCANS WORKPLACE COMPETENCY

Personal Quality: Sociability

Concept: Sociability involves understanding, friendliness, adaptability, empathy, and politeness in new and on-going group settings. It includes asserting oneself in familiar and unfamiliar social situations, relating well to others, responding appropriately as a situation might require, and taking an interest in what others say and do.

Application: Consider each element in the concept of sociability. Rate yourself on each element. List ways you could improve. Discuss whether there are workplace situations that require greater or lesser degrees of sociability.

DIGITAL VISION/GETTY IMAGES

Accounting for Inventory — Chapter 19

GRAPHING WORKSHOP

Employees responsible for purchasing inventory can be tempted to accept bribes from unscrupulous vendors. In exchange for the bribe, the employee favors the vendor in future purchasing decisions. This fraud is known as a *kickback*. Because the bribe is not recorded in the accounting records, it can be difficult to detect.

Marcus Salazar suspects one of his purchasing agents may be involved in a kickback scheme. To gather support for his suspicion, he has created graphs that depict the quantity and price paid for purchases of each inventory item from each vendor. An increase in the number of units purchased from a vendor, together with an increase in price, is a red flag of a kickback, since the vendor must raise the price to pay for the kickback.

The graphs for model AX-43 motors are shown below.

The first graph shows the monthly purchase quantity (in thousands) for each vendor. The second graph shows the unit price charged by vendor.

Assist Marcus in interpreting this data by answering the following questions.

1. From which vendor did the number of units purchased tend to increase over time?
2. How did the unit prices change for the vendor with increasing purchases? Support your answer.
3. Could there be a valid explanation why the buyer might purchase more from a vendor despite an increase in the unit price?

ANALYZING BEST BUY'S FINANCIAL STATEMENTS

The managers at Best Buy need to constantly monitor the amount of inventory available for sale. Having too little inventory can cause the company to miss sales if the product is out of stock. Holding too much inventory increases its operating expenses. A financial ratio that evaluates the amount of inventory available for sale is known as the *inventory turnover ratio*. The ratio is calculated as follows:

$$\text{Inventory Turnover} = \frac{\text{Cost of Goods Sold}}{(\text{Beginning Inventory} + \text{Ending Inventory}) \div 2}$$

Dividing the sum of the beginning and ending inventory by 2 approximates the average inventory for the fiscal year. The inventory turnover for Wendy's International, based on its 2006 fiscal year financial statements, is calculated below:

$$\text{Inventory Turnover} = \frac{\$1{,}352{,}312{,}000}{(\$30{,}252{,}000 + \$29{,}798{,}000) \div 2} = 45$$

Dividing 365 by the turnover ratio yields a financial ratio known as *days' sales in inventory*. Wendy's number of days' sales in inventory is 8.1 days. Thus, the average item remains in its inventory for approximately 8 days (www.wendys.com).

Instructions

1. Using the financial information in Appendix B of this text, calculate Best Buy's inventory turnover ratio and number of days' sales in inventory for 2007.
2. Why would the inventory turnover ratios for Best Buy and Wendy's differ?

Accounting
SOFTWARE

MERCHANDISE INVENTORY

Generally accepted accounting principles require that a business use a recognized method for determining the cost of merchandise inventory. The FIFO, LIFO, and weighted-average methods are all recognized methods. Two variations of each method are also acceptable.

In this chapter, the cost of the units in ending inventory was determined at the end of a fiscal period. This method of applying FIFO, LIFO, and weighted-average is known as a *periodic method*—the calculation is made only at the end of a period. The *perpetual method* results in the cost of inventory sold being determined every time an item is sold. Thus, the perpetual variation keeps a continual count of the number and cost of the units in inventory.

Periodic and perpetual methods of FIFO, LIFO, and weighted-average inventories result in different values for ending inventory and the cost of goods sold. For this reason, generally accepted accounting principles require the consistent use of an inventory method. Peachtree uses the perpetual FIFO method of costing inventory and produces an Item Costing report to account for how every purchase and sale affects the value of inventory items.

PEACHTREE MASTERY PROBLEM 19-4
1. Open (Restore) file 19-4MP.ptb.
2. Journalize and post the transactions for the purchase and sale of inventory.
3. Print the purchase journal from January 6 to December 12.
4. Print the sales journal from April 5 to December 2.
5. Print the Item Costing report from January 1 to December 31.

MERCHANDISE INVENTORY

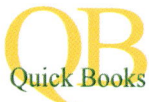

In QuickBooks, an inventory record is created for each item in inventory. The inventory record can include the item number, description, unit of measure, reorder point, quantity on hand, preferred vendor, cost, and selling price. When you purchase more of an item or sell it, the inventory record is automatically updated.

As discussed in this chapter, inventory can be accounted for on a periodic or perpetual basis. Also, inventory can be assigned a value based on a FIFO, LIFO, or weighted-average costing method. QuickBooks uses the perpetual basis and the weighted-average costing method.

In an automated accounting system, inventory reports can be produced anytime. These reports can be customized to contain all the information that is needed at the time. If the quantity of an item drops below the reorder point, QuickBooks will remind the user that it is time to reorder that inventory item.

QUICKBOOKS MASTERY PROBLEM 19-4
1. Open the Fratisi Company file.
2. Record the purchase of inventory by choosing the Enter Bills option from the Vendors menu.
3. Select Create Invoices from the Customers menu to record merchandise sales on account.
4. Choose Inventory from the Reports menu and Select Inventory Valuation Detail. Use January 1 and December 31 for the dates and print the report.

CALCULATING MERCHANDISE INVENTORY

"If the number of units in beginning inventory is less than the units on hand, enter the units in beginning inventory. Otherwise, enter the number of units on hand." This statement illustrates one of the decisions you must make in costing merchandise inventory using the LIFO method. Electronic spreadsheets can help you make these decisions. Through the use of its IF function, the electronic spreadsheet can compare two numbers and enter one of two values in the cell.

The syntax of the IF function is =IF(logical_test, true_value, false_value). Suppose there are 10 units (cell C17) in beginning inventory and 18 units (cell F22) on hand. The IF function to calculate the units from the beginning inventory would be:

=IF(C17< F22, C17, F22)

This function would calculate the value 10—it is true that C17 is less than F22, thus the true_value, 10 in cell C17, is calculated by the IF function.

Creating IF functions for a LIFO or FIFO template requires a full understanding of the logic of each inventory costing method. The logical tests for other purchases can become rather complex.

EXCEL APPLICATION PROBLEM 19-2
Open the F19-2 Excel data file. Follow the step-by-step instructions in the Instructions worksheet.

EXCEL APPLICATION PROBLEM 19-3
Open the F19-3 Excel data file. Follow the step-by-step instructions in the Instructions worksheet.

EXCEL MASTERY PROBLEM 19-4
Open the F19-4 Excel data file. Follow the step-by-step instructions in the Instructions worksheet.

AUTOMATED MERCHANDISE INVENTORY

A computerized inventory system provides better access to accurate information about the inventory. Managers need information about which items are selling, the number of items currently in inventory, and when to reorder an item.

All inventory transactions are recorded in the Other Activities Inventory window. These transactions include sales, purchases ordered, purchases received, and sales and purchases returns.

To enter inventory transactions:
1. Click the Other toolbar button.
2. Click the appropriate tab and enter the information about the purchase order, purchase invoice, or sales invoice; then click OK.
   a. Click Purch. Order if you are ordering items.
   b. Click Purch. Invoice if you are entering the receipt of merchandise purchased from a purchase invoice.
   c. Click Sales Invoice if you are entering the sale of merchandise from a sales invoice.

AUTOMATED ACCOUNTING APPLICATION PROBLEM 19-2
Open file F19-2.AA8. Display the problem instructions and complete the problem.

AUTOMATED ACCOUNTING MASTERY PROBLEM 19-4
Open file F19-4.AA8. Display the problem instructions and complete the problem.

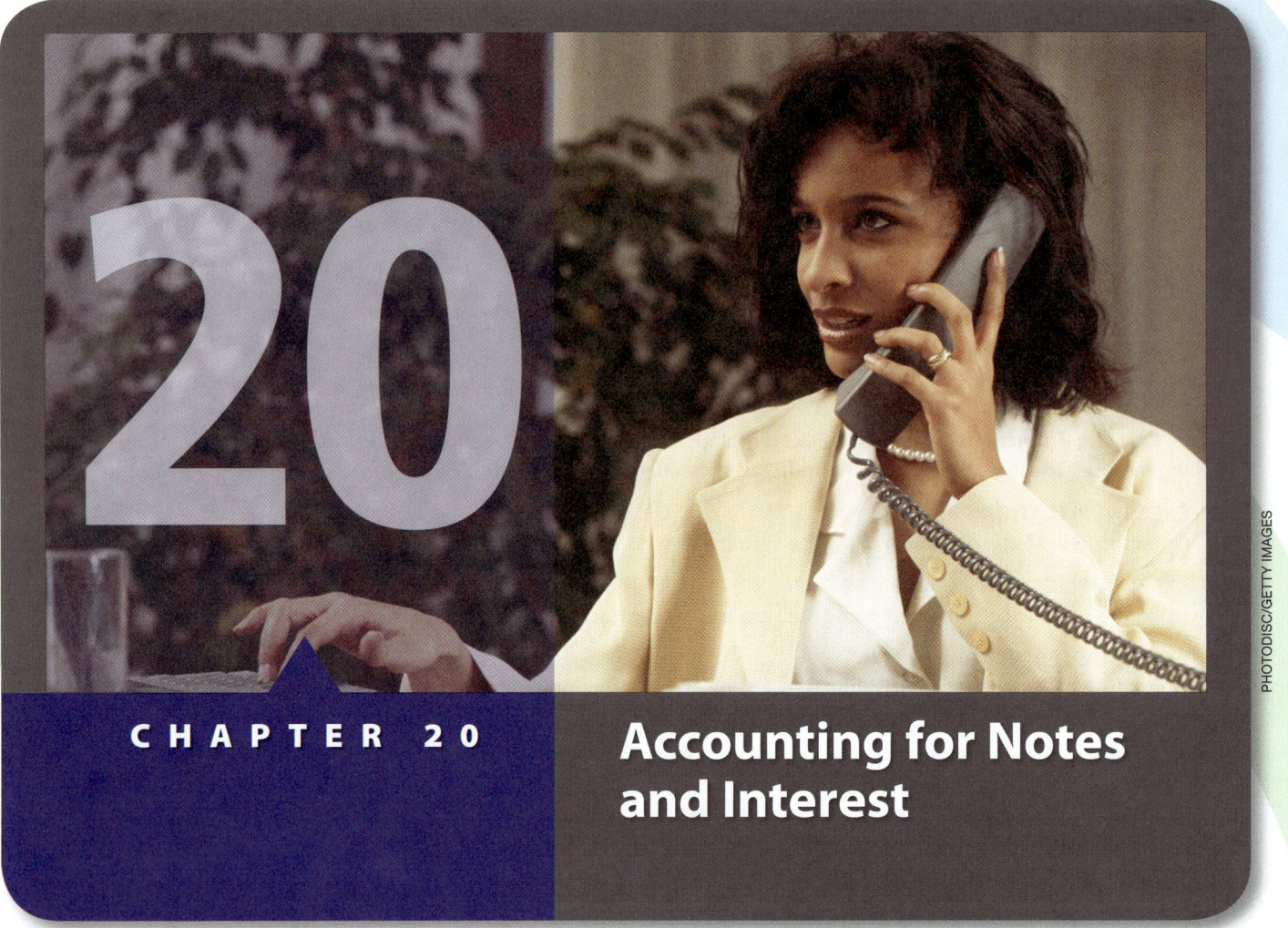

CHAPTER 20

Accounting for Notes and Interest

OBJECTIVES

After studying Chapter 20, you will be able to:

1. Define accounting terms related to notes and interest.
2. Identify accounting concepts and practices related to notes and interest.
3. Calculate interest and maturity dates for notes.
4. Analyze and record transactions for notes payable.
5. Analyze and record transactions for notes receivable.

KEY TERMS

- number of a note
- date of a note
- payee of a note
- time of a note
- principal of a note
- interest rate of a note
- maturity date of a note
- maker of a note
- promissory note
- creditor
- notes payable
- interest
- maturity value
- current liabilities
- interest expense
- notes receivable
- interest income
- dishonored note

Point Your Browser
www.C21accounting.com

ACCOUNTING IN THE REAL WORLD

Bank of America

Achieving Dreams with the Bank of America

Your first home. A new car. Opening your own business. Sending a child to college.

Many of the dreams we share require that we borrow money. That's how Bank of America helps people achieve their dreams. Through a national network of more than 16,000 ATMs and 5,700 branches, Bank of America is there to ensure that individuals, companies, and even government agencies have access to financial resources and services.

Bank of America is in the business of loaning money to its customers. In return, Bank of America expects the borrower to periodically pay interest on the loan until the loan matures. Interest income for a bank is equivalent to inventory sales of a retail company.

The timing of when interest is earned and recorded in the accounts is a significant issue for any bank. Interest income is earned each day a loan is outstanding, regardless of when the borrower pays the interest. As a result, banks must record the interest income earned, but not yet collected, in order for its financial statements to be in accordance with generally accepted accounting principles.

Critical Thinking

1. Banks make loans to individuals, companies, and many other groups, including cities. Why would a city need to borrow money?
2. If you borrow money, how is the interest rate usually stated?

Source: www.bankofamerica.com

INTERNET ACTIVITY

Federal Reserve

Go to the homepage for the Federal Reserve System (www.federalreserve.gov). The Federal Reserve's duties fall into four broad categories.

Instructions

1. List the four broad categories of duties of the Federal Reserve.
2. The United States is divided into 12 Federal Reserve districts. Find the district in which your school is located. List the district number and the headquarter city.

LESSON 20-1

Promissory Notes

WHEN LENDING AND BORROWING ARE NECESSARY

Cash is the primary medium of exchange for business transactions. [CONCEPT: Unit of Measurement] Cash is used to purchase merchandise and to pay salaries and other expenses. In turn, businesses receive cash when they sell their products or services and collect payment. The cash received can be used to purchase more merchandise and continue to pay salaries and other expenses. Thus, the business cycle continues.

Sometimes a business receives more cash from sales than is needed to pay for purchases and expenses. A business may deposit the extra cash in a bank for a short period. At other times, the receipt of cash from sales does not occur at the same time and in amounts sufficient to pay for needed purchases and expenses. When this occurs, a business needs to borrow additional cash or make arrangements with its vendors to delay payment for a period of time. Generally, when a bank or other business lends money to another business, the loan agreement is made in writing.

CHARACTER COUNTS

Only Full-Time Workers Receive Benefits

At the Backyard Gourmet, most employees work less than 30 hours per week. However, only employees who work a minimum of 30 hours per week are eligible for the company's health insurance plan. Thus, only the company's managers and officers are covered by health insurance. Lashonda Ethridge, a CPA and member of the American Institute of Certified Public Accountants, has just been hired as the company's chief financial officer. Having just learned of the company's hiring practices, she is considering resigning her position.

Instructions

Assume that Backyard Gourmet does not have a code of conduct. Use the ethical model to evaluate the company's hiring practices. Do you have any recommendations for Lashonda?

USES OF PROMISSORY NOTES

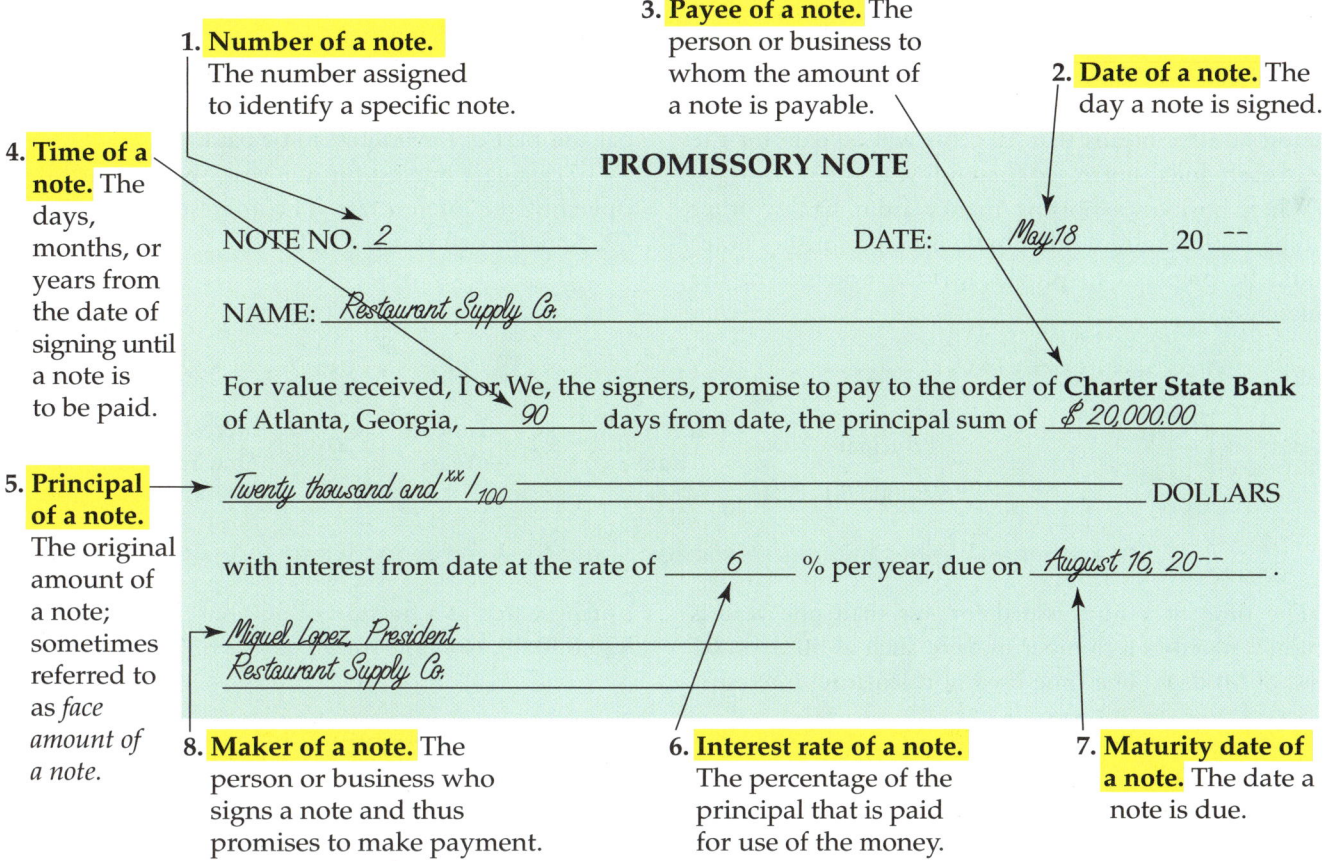

1. **Number of a note.** The number assigned to identify a specific note.
2. **Date of a note.** The day a note is signed.
3. **Payee of a note.** The person or business to whom the amount of a note is payable.
4. **Time of a note.** The days, months, or years from the date of signing until a note is to be paid.
5. **Principal of a note.** The original amount of a note; sometimes referred to as *face amount of a note*.
6. **Interest rate of a note.** The percentage of the principal that is paid for use of the money.
7. **Maturity date of a note.** The date a note is due.
8. **Maker of a note.** The person or business who signs a note and thus promises to make payment.

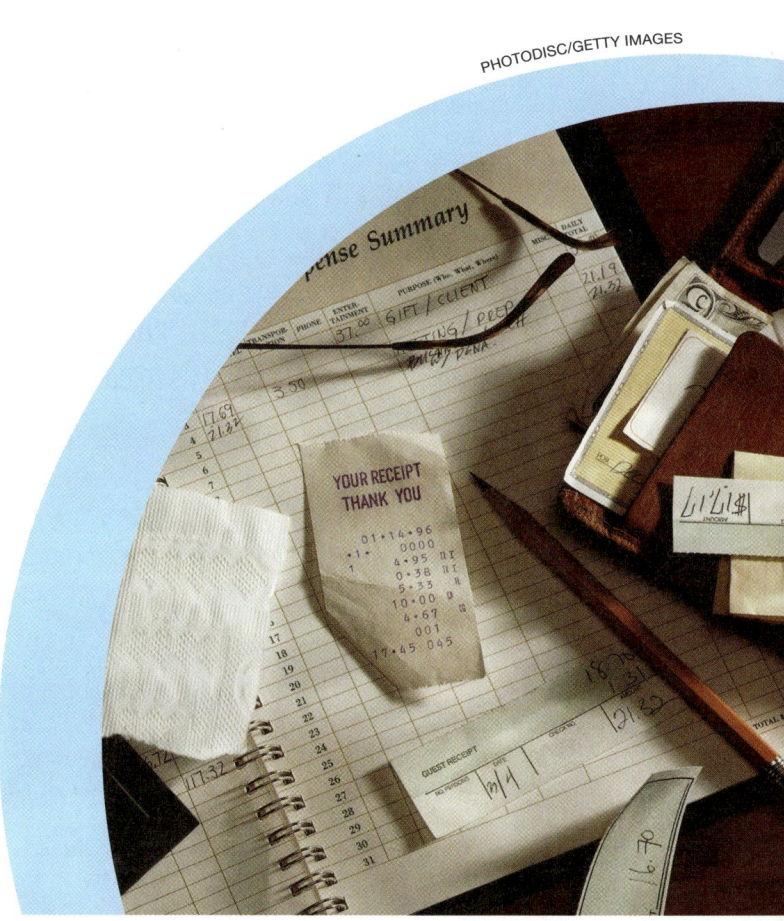

A written and signed promise to pay a sum of money at a specified time is called a **promissory note**. A person or organization to whom a liability is owed is called a **creditor**. Promissory notes signed by a business and given to a creditor are called **notes payable**. A note payable is frequently referred to as a *note*.

Promissory notes are used when money is borrowed for a period of time from a bank or other lending agency. Sometimes a business requests a note from a customer who wants credit beyond the usual time given for sales on account. Notes have an advantage over oral promises and accounts receivable or payable. Notes can be useful in a court of law as written evidence of a debt.

INTEREST ON PROMISSORY NOTES

An amount paid for the use of money for a period of time is called **interest**. Banks and other lending institutions charge interest on money loaned to their customers. The interest rate is stated as a percentage of the principal. Interest at 10% means that 10 cents will be paid for the use of each dollar borrowed for a full year.

When businesses borrow money from banks, other lending institutions, or other businesses, promissory notes should be prepared to provide written evidence of the transaction.

Sometimes partial payments on a note are made each month. This arrangement is particularly true when an individual buys a car and signs a note for the amount owed. Each monthly payment includes part of the principal and part of the interest to be paid.

To calculate interest for one year, the principal is multiplied by the interest rate. The interest on a $20,000.00, 6% note for one year is $1,200.00.

Principal	×	Interest Rate	×	Time in Years	=	Interest for One Year
$20,000.00	×	6%	×	1	=	$1,200.00

The time of a note issued for less than one year is typically stated as a number of days, such as 30 days, 60 days, or 90 days. The time used in calculating interest is usually stated as a fraction of 360 days. The interest on a $20,000.00, 6% note for 90 days is $300.00.

Principal	×	Interest Rate	×	Time as Fraction of Year	=	Interest for Fraction of Year
$20,000.00	×	6%	×	$\frac{90}{360}$	=	$300.00

The amount that is due on the maturity date of a note is called the **maturity value**. A 90-day note with a principal of $20,000.00 and interest rate of 6% will have a maturity value of $20,300.00.

Principal	+	Interest	=	Maturity Value
$20,000.00	+	$300.00	=	$20,300.00

IMAGE SOURCE/GETTY IMAGES

MATURITY DATE OF PROMISSORY NOTES

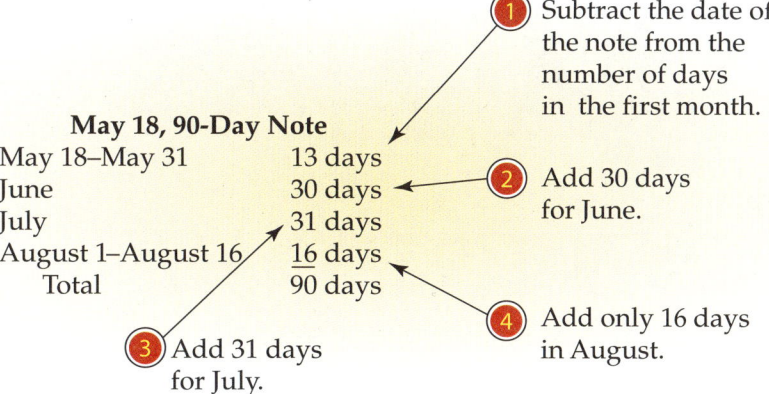

May 18, 90-Day Note

May 18–May 31	13 days
June	30 days
July	31 days
August 1–August 16	16 days
Total	90 days

1. Subtract the date of the note from the number of days in the first month.
2. Add 30 days for June.
3. Add 31 days for July.
4. Add only 16 days in August.

The time between the date a note is signed and the date a note is due is typically expressed in days. The maturity date is calculated by counting the exact number of days. The date on which the note is written is not counted, but the maturity date is counted. For example, a 90-day note dated May 18 is due on August 16.

STEPS CALCULATING THE MATURITY DATE OF A NOTE

1. Calculate the number of days remaining in May, *13*, by subtracting the date of the note, *18*, from the number of days in May, *31*.

2. Calculate the number of days remaining in the term of the note, *77*, by subtracting the number of days in the previous month, *13*, from the term of the note, *90*. Because *77* is greater than the number of days in June, *30*, add all of the days in June.

3. Calculate the number of days remaining in the term of the note, *47*, by subtracting the number of days in the previous months, *43 (13 + 30)*, from the term of the note, *90*. Because *43* is greater than the number of days in July, *31*, add all of the days in July.

4. Calculate the number of days remaining in the term of the note, *16*, by subtracting the number of days in the previous months, *74 (13 + 30 + 31)*, from the term of the note, *90*. Because *16* is less than the number of days in August, *31*, add only 16 days in August.

FOR YOUR INFORMATION

FYI

An interest rate can be entered on a calculator or electronic spreadsheet by using either the Percent key (%) or the decimal equivalent of the interest rate. For example, 12% could be keyed as 0.12.

FOR YOUR INFORMATION

FYI

Agencies of the federal government generally use a 365-day year when calculating interest. Consumer interest is also generally calculated on a 365-day year. However, many banks use a 360-day year when calculating interest. Therefore, the interest calculations in this textbook use a 360-day year.

End of Lesson REVIEW

TERMS REVIEW

number of a note
date of a note
payee of a note
time of a note
principal of a note
interest rate of a note
maturity date of a note
maker of a note
promissory note
creditor
notes payable
interest
maturity value

AUDIT YOUR UNDERSTANDING

1. What conditions would cause a business to have extra cash to deposit in a bank, yet at another time of year need to borrow extra cash from a bank?
2. What is the advantage of a promissory note over an account receivable?
3. What does interest at 10% mean?
4. How is interest calculated for a fraction of a year?

WORK TOGETHER 20-1

Calculating interest, maturity dates, and maturity values for promissory notes

Write the answers to the following problem in the *Working Papers*. Your instructor will guide you through the following example.

1. For each of the following promissory notes, calculate (a) the interest on the note, (b) the maturity date of the note, and (c) the maturity value of the note. Save your work to complete Work Together 20-2.

Date	Principal	Interest Rate	Time
March 3	$6,000.00	6%	90 days
March 18	$2,000.00	9%	60 days

ON YOUR OWN 20-1

Calculating interest, maturity dates, and maturity values for promissory notes

Write the answers to the following problem in the *Working Papers*. Work this problem independently.

1. For each of the following promissory notes, calculate (a) the interest on the note, (b) the maturity date of the note, and (c) the maturity value of the note. Save your work to complete On Your Own 20-2.

Date	Principal	Interest Rate	Time
June 8	$20,000.00	8%	180 days
June 12	$10,000.00	6%	90 days

LESSON 20-2

Notes Payable

SIGNING A NOTE PAYABLE

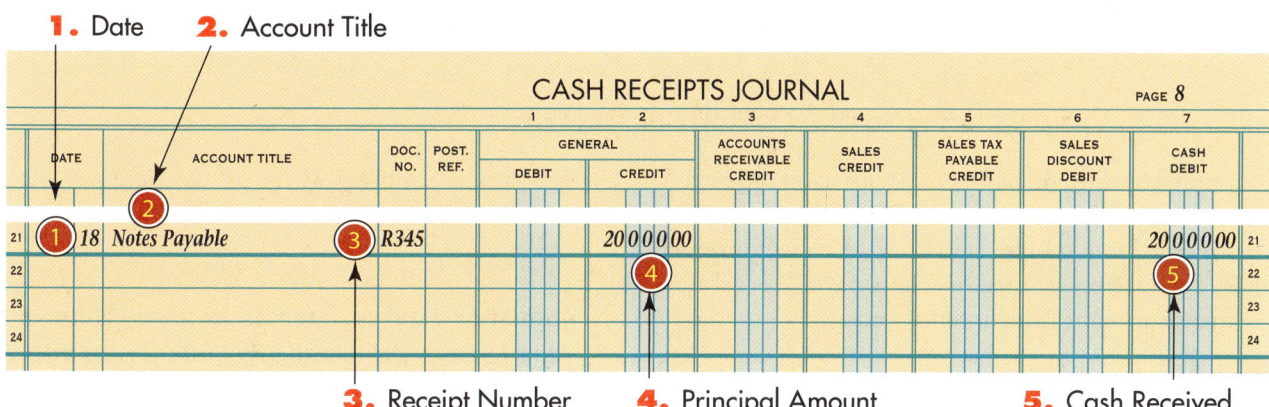

1. Date
2. Account Title
3. Receipt Number
4. Principal Amount
5. Cash Received

Liabilities due within a short time, usually within a year, are called **current liabilities**. Because notes payable generally are paid within one year, they are classified as current liabilities.

When a business signs a note payable, the principal or face amount of the note is credited to a liability account titled Notes Payable.

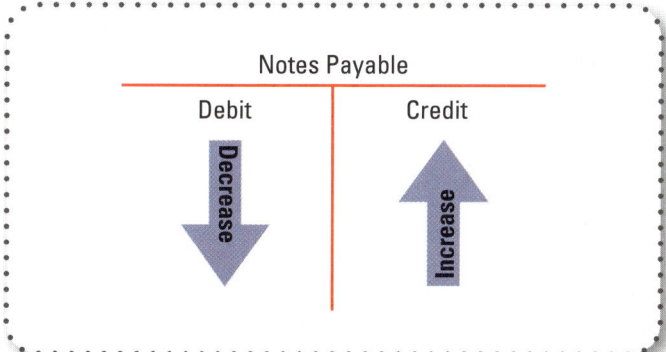

Restaurant Supply arranges to borrow money from its bank. A note payable is signed with the bank as evidence of the debt. The bank issues a check or deposits the principal amount of the note in Restaurant Supply's checking account.

May 18. Signed a 90-day, 6% note, $20,000.00. Receipt No. 345.

The bank retains the original of the note until Restaurant Supply pays the maturity value. A receipt is prepared to show the receipt of the principal amount of the note. [CONCEPT: Objective Evidence]

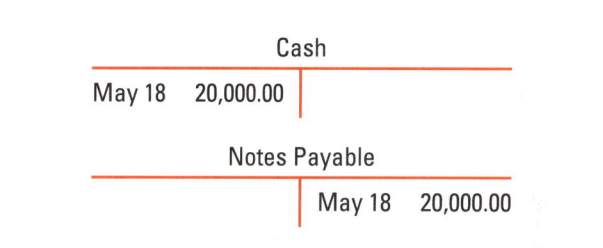

No entry is made for interest until a later date when the interest is paid.

STEPS — JOURNALIZING THE RECEIPT OF CASH FROM A NOTE PAYABLE

1. Write the date, *18*, in the Date column of the cash receipts journal.
2. Write the account title, *Notes Payable*, in the Account Title column.
3. Write the receipt number, *R345*, in the Doc. No. column.
4. Write the principal amount, *$20,000.00*, in the General Credit column.
5. Write the same amount, *$20,000.00*, in the Cash Debit column.

PAYING PRINCIPAL AND INTEREST ON A NOTE PAYABLE

When a note payable reaches its maturity date, the maker of the note pays the maturity value to the payee. The interest accrued on money borrowed is called **interest expense**. The interest accrued on a note payable is debited to an expense account titled Interest Expense.

Restaurant Supply paid the 90-day note payable it had signed on May 18.

August 16. Paid cash for the maturity value of the May 18 note: principal, $20,000.00, plus interest, $300.00; total, $20,300.00. Check No. 721.

Interest expense is a financial expense rather than an expense of the business's normal operations. Therefore, Interest Expense is listed in a classification titled *Other Expenses* in a chart of accounts.

STEPS — JOURNALIZING A CASH PAYMENT FOR THE MATURITY VALUE OF A NOTE PAYABLE

1. Write the date, *16*, in the Date column of the cash payments journal.
2. Write the account title, *Notes Payable*, in the Account Title column.
3. Write the check number, *721*, in the Ck. No. column.
4. Write the note's principal amount, *$20,000.00*, in the General Debit column.
5. Write the account title, *Interest Expense*, in the Account Title column on the next line.
6. Write the interest expense amount, *$300.00*, in the General Debit column.
7. Write the amount of cash paid, *$20,300.00*, in the Cash Credit column on the first line of the entry.

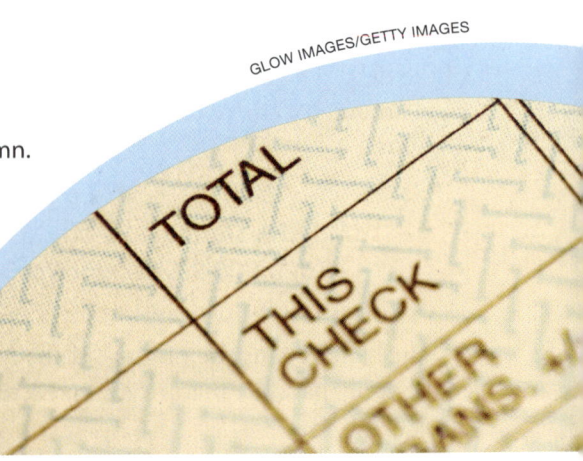

SIGNING A NOTE PAYABLE FOR AN EXTENSION OF TIME

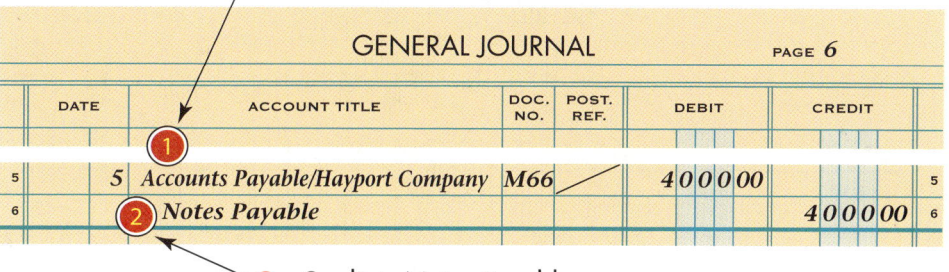

A business may ask for an extension of time if it is unable to pay an account when due. The vendor may ask the business to sign a note payable. The note payable does not pay the amount owed to the vendor. However, the form of the liability is changed from an account payable to a note payable. When this entry is posted, the balance of the accounts payable account for Hayport Company will be zero. One liability, Accounts Payable, is replaced by another liability, Notes Payable.

June 5. Restaurant Supply signed a 90-day, 12% note to Hayport Company for an extension of time on its account payable, $4,000.00. Memorandum No. 66.

GENERAL LEDGER
Accounts Payable

| June 5 | 4,000.00 | Bal. | 4,000.00 |

Notes Payable

| | | June 5 | 4,000.00 |

ACCOUNTS PAYABLE LEDGER
Hayport Company

| June 5 | 4,000.00 | Bal. | 4,000.00 |

STEPS: JOURNALIZING SIGNING A NOTE PAYABLE FOR AN EXTENSION OF TIME

1. Record a debit, $4,000.00, to *Accounts Payable/Hayport Company* in the general journal.
2. Record a credit, $4,000.00, to *Notes Payable*.

REMEMBER

When a note payable is signed for an extension of time on account, both the general ledger account, Accounts Payable, and the subsidiary ledger account are changed to a note payable. Therefore, both accounts must be debited to remove the amount from the accounts.

FOR YOUR INFORMATION — FYI

There are advantages to accepting a note from a customer for an extension of time. In addition to serving as legal evidence of the debt, accepting a note may avoid having an account become uncollectible if additional time is all the customer needs in order to pay the account eventually. The business accepting the note will also earn interest on the overdue account, usually at a relatively high interest rate. Also, in some industries, these notes can be sold for cash if that cash is needed to meet operating expenses.

PAYING A NOTE PAYABLE ISSUED FOR AN EXTENSION OF TIME

				GENERAL		ACCOUNTS PAYABLE DEBIT	PURCHASES DISCOUNT CREDIT	CASH CREDIT	
	DATE	ACCOUNT TITLE	CK. NO.	POST. REF.	DEBIT	CREDIT			
3	3	Notes Payable	722		4 0 0 0 00				4 1 2 0 00	3
4		Interest Expense			1 2 0 00					4

CASH PAYMENTS JOURNAL PAGE 11

The entry to record the cash payment at the maturity date of a note payable is the same regardless of the reason the note was signed.

September 3. Paid cash for the maturity value of the note payable to Hayport Company: principal, $4,000.00, plus interest, $120.00; total, $4,120.00. Check No. 722.

```
             Notes Payable
Sept. 3    4,000.00  |  Jan. 5   4,000.00

             Interest Expense
Sept. 3      120.00  |

                  Cash
                     |  Sept. 3   4,120.00
```

CULTURAL DIVERSITY

Ancient China

By approximately 1000 cb/, the Chinese had developed one of the most sophisticated accounting systems in the world. The Chao Dynasty ruled China from 1122 to 256 cb/ During this time, the dynasty oversaw territorial expansion and a Golden Age in literature and philosophy. The famous philosopher Confucius lived during this dynasty. Confucius was said to have been a government recordkeeper.

During the Chao Dynasty, the Chinese used a system of currency and had a central bank. The Office of the Superintendent of Records furnished compilations of receipts and payments. It also kept maps and records of production tools used. Many of the accounting and record keeping tasks that affect businesses and governments today can be traced back to systems established in ancient China.

Critical Thinking

1. Early civilizations did not have currency. How do you think people would buy and sell goods and services without currency?
2. If you owned a store, what kinds of records would you want to keep about your sales?

End of Lesson REVIEW

TERMS REVIEW

current liabilities

interest expense

AUDIT YOUR UNDERSTANDING

1. Why are notes payable generally classified as current liabilities?
2. What accounts are affected, and how, when a business signs a note payable for an extension of time on an account payable?

WORK TOGETHER 20-2

Journalizing notes payable transactions

The journals for Landings, Inc., are provided in the *Working Papers*. Your instructor will guide you through the following examples.

1. Using the current year, journalize the following transactions. Use page 3 of a general journal and page 5 of a cash receipts journal. Source documents are abbreviated as follows: check, C; receipt, R; memorandum, M.

Transactions:
Mar. 3. Signed a 90-day, 6% note, for $6,000.00 with First National Bank. R279.
18. Signed a 60-day, 9% note with DryCreek Company for an extension of time on this account payable, $2,000.00. M288.

2. Journalize the following transactions on page 9 of a cash payments journal. Use the maturity dates and maturity values calculated in Work Together 20-1.

Transactions:
Paid cash for the maturity value of the $2,000.00 note. C255.
Paid cash for the maturity value of the $6,000.00 note. C263.

ON YOUR OWN 20-2

Journalizing notes payable transactions

The journals for Modisto Corporation are provided in the *Working Papers*. Work this problem independently.

1. Using the current year, journalize the following transactions. Use page 10 of a general journal and page 20 of a cash receipts journal. Source documents are abbreviated as follows: check, C; receipt, R; memorandum, M.

Transactions:
June 8. Signed a 180-day, 8% note, for $20,000.00 with First National Bank. R361.
12. Signed a 90-day, 6% note with Best Company for an extension of time on this account payable, $10,000.00. M165.

2. Journalize the following transactions on page 17 of a cash payments journal. Use the maturity dates and maturity values calculated in On Your Own 20-1.

Transactions:
Paid cash for the maturity value of the $10,000.00 note. C601.
Paid cash for the maturity value of the $20,000.00 note. C882.

LESSON 20-3

Notes Receivable

ACCEPTING A NOTE RECEIVABLE FROM A CUSTOMER

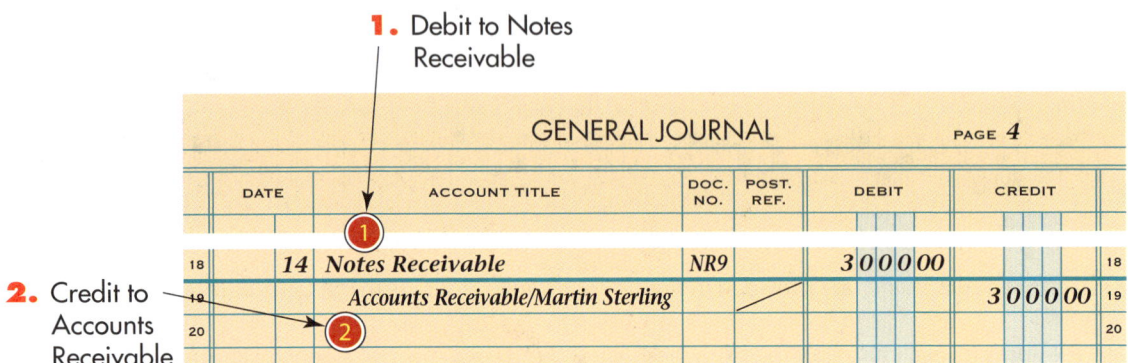

Promissory notes that a business accepts from customers are called **notes receivable**. Notes receivable are usually paid within one year. Therefore, they are classified as current assets.

A customer who is unable to pay an account on the due date may request additional time. The business should require the customer to sign a note. A note does not pay the amount the customer owes. However, the form of the asset is changed from an account receivable to a note receivable. The promissory note is a written confirmation of the amount owed, which provides the business with evidence of the debt in case legal action is required to collect.

When a customer signs a note, the principal amount of the note is debited to an asset account titled Notes Receivable. One asset, Accounts Receivable, is replaced by another asset, Notes Receivable.

When this entry is posted, the balance of the accounts receivable account for Mr. Sterling is zero.

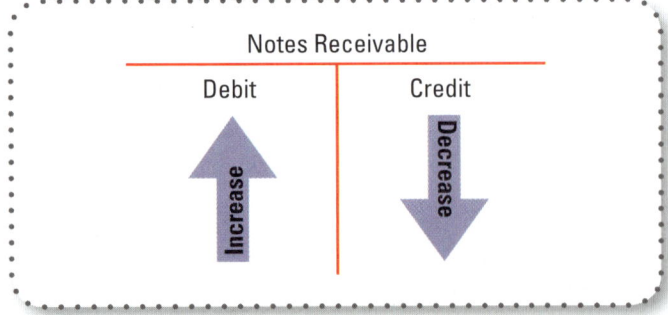

April 14. Accepted a 90-day, 8% note from Martin Sterling for an extension of time on his account, $3,000.00. Note Receivable No. 9.

STEPS — JOURNALIZING ACCEPTING A NOTE FOR AN EXTENSION OF TIME ON AN ACCOUNT RECEIVABLE

1. Record a debit to *Notes Receivable* for the amount of the note, $3,000.00, in the general journal.

2. Record a credit to *Accounts Receivable/Martin Sterling* for the same amount, $3,000.00.

COLLECTING PRINCIPAL AND INTEREST ON A NOTE RECEIVABLE

1. Date
2. First Account Title
3. Receipt Number
4. Principal Amount
5. Second Account Title
6. Interest Amount
7. Maturity Value

When a note receivable reaches its maturity date, the payee receives the maturity value from the maker. The interest earned on money loaned is called **interest income**. The interest earned on a note receivable is credited to a revenue account titled Interest Income.

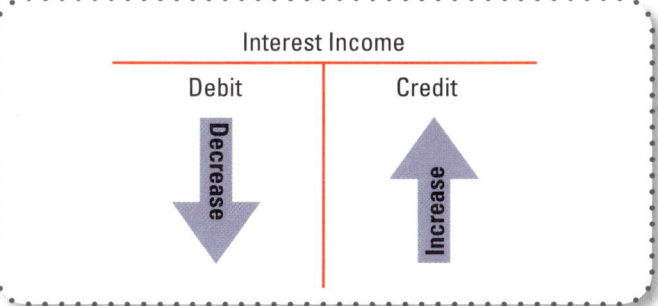

Interest income is investment revenue rather than revenue from normal operations. Therefore, Interest Income is listed in a classification titled *Other Revenue* in a chart of accounts.

Restaurant Supply received cash for the principal and interest of the note signed by Mr. Sterling on April 14.

> July 13. Received cash for the maturity value of Note Receivable No. 9, a 90-day, 8% note: principal, $3,000.00, plus interest, $60.00; total, $3,060.00. Receipt No. 562.

Interest income is calculated using the same method as that used for notes payable. The principal is multiplied by the interest rate and the fraction of the year ($3,000.00 × 8% × 90/360) to calculate interest income, $60.00.

After the entry is recorded, the original of Note Receivable No. 9 is marked *Paid*. The original is given to Mr. Sterling and a copy is kept by Restaurant Supply.

STEPS JOURNALIZING CASH RECEIVED FOR MATURITY VALUE OF A NOTE RECEIVABLE

1. Write the date, *13*, in the Date column of the cash receipts journal.
2. Write the account title, *Notes Receivable*, in the Account Title column.
3. Write the receipt number, *R562*, in the Doc. No. column.
4. Write the principal amount, *$3,000.00*, in the General Credit column.
5. On the next line, write the account title, *Interest Income*, in the Account Title column.
6. Calculate and write the interest income amount, *$60.00*, in the General Credit column.
7. Write the maturity value, *$3,060.00*, in the Cash Debit column on the first line of the entry.

Notes Receivable — Lesson 20-3

RECORDING A DISHONORED NOTE RECEIVABLE

1. Debit to Accounts Receivable

	GENERAL JOURNAL				PAGE 5
DATE	ACCOUNT TITLE	DOC. NO.	POST. REF.	DEBIT	CREDIT
6	① Accounts Receivable/Jill Davis	M92		612.00	
	② Notes Receivable				600.00
	Interest Income ③				12.00

2. Credit to Notes Receivable

3. Credit to Interest Income

A note that is not paid when due is called a **dishonored note**. The balance of the notes receivable account should show only the total amount of notes that probably will be collected. The amount of a dishonored note receivable should be removed from the notes receivable account.

The amount of the note plus interest income earned on the note is still owed by the customer. Therefore, the total amount owed should be debited to the accounts receivable account in the general ledger. The amount owed should also be debited to the customer account in the accounts receivable ledger. This information may be important if the customer requests credit in the future or if collection is achieved later.

> *May 6. Jill Davis dishonored Note Receivable No. 12, a 90-day, 8% note, maturity value due today: principal, $600.00; interest, $12.00; total, $612.00. Memorandum No. 92.*

The interest income on the note has been earned as of the maturity date even though the note has not been paid. Jill Davis owes the principal amount of the note plus the interest earned. Therefore, the maturity value, *$612.00*, is debited to Accounts Receivable and to Jill Davis's account in the accounts receivable ledger. One asset, Notes Receivable, is replaced by another asset, Accounts Receivable.

GENERAL LEDGER
Accounts Receivable
| May 6 | 612.00 | |

Notes Receivable
| Feb. 5 | 600.00 | May 6 | 600.00 |

Interest Income
| | | May 6 | 12.00 |

ACCOUNTS RECEIVABLE LEDGER
Jill Davis
| May 6 | 612.00 | |

Restaurant Supply does not write off Ms. Davis's account when the note is dishonored. The company continues to try to collect the account.

Later, Restaurant Supply may decide that the account cannot be collected. At that time, the balance of the account will be written off as an uncollectible account. Allowance for Uncollectible Accounts will be debited, and Accounts Receivable and Jill Davis's account will be credited.

STEPS — JOURNALIZING A DISHONORED NOTE RECEIVABLE

① Record a debit to *Accounts Receivable/Jill Davis* for the total maturity value of the note, *$612.00*, in the general journal.

② Record a credit to *Notes Receivable* for the principal amount of the dishonored note, *$600.00*.

③ Record a credit to *Interest Income* for the interest earned on the note, *$12.00*.

Business, Management & Administration

CAREERS IN ACCOUNTING

Missie T. Talbot, Law Firm Office Manager

Missie T. Talbot first became interested in accounting when she elected to take her first accounting course as a high school junior. She had always enjoyed working with numbers. During the first accounting class, she learned how to write checks properly, open a bank account, and balance a checking account—skills she believes every high school student should learn. Realizing that she enjoyed accounting, Missie elected to take a second year of high school accounting. She recalls, "We were able to set up our own company, record all the cash receipts, write checks, and perform the accounting procedures involved with running a business. I found the task a rewarding experience."

After graduation, she enrolled in accounting and data processing courses in college. Her accounting knowledge enabled her to become a bookkeeper for a forestry equipment manufacturer. She was later promoted to office manager while still performing her bookkeeping responsibilities. A family move led her to become an accounts payable clerk for a contact lens manufacturer and distributor. In that position, she prepared sales tax returns for over six states and many local taxing authorities, along with monthly, quarterly, and year-end closings.

Missie says, "During this time, my husband and I were approached by a corporation in Dallas to open and operate a dry cleaner. After considerable discussion and relying on my bookkeeping knowledge, we decided to go for it." Organized in 1992 as a sole proprietorship, the business was a grand success because all garments were cleaned for the same low price. Within two years, they opened another location in their hometown.

Successful businesses often catch the attention of investors. When Missie and her husband sold their business to investors, she became the office manager and paraprofessional for T. E. Lott & Company, PA, a regional accounting firm. There she prepared the monthly financial statements, quarterly payroll tax returns, sales tax reports, and payroll checks for its clients.

Missie is now the firm administrator for the law firm of Gholson, Hicks and Nichols, PA. She is responsible for the financial management of the firm and supervises its 16 staff members. She believes that "without the basics of accounting that I received in high school, I know that I would not be here in this law firm today."

Missie credits her high school math teacher, Mrs. Mythle Hodges, for encouraging her to stick with math and accounting. "I do regret never completing my college degree—but it's never too late!"

Salary Range: The median annual earnings of office support supervisors and managers were $41,030 in 2004. The middle 50 percent earned between $31,860 and $53,110, according to the *Occupational Outlook Handbook*. (Bureau of Labor Statistics, U.S. Department of Labor, *Occupational Outlook Handbook*, 2006–07 Edition, Secretaries and Administrative, on the Internet at www.bls.gov/oco/ocos127.htm.)

Qualifications: An office manager must possess a wide variety of skills, including communication, technology, and organizational skills. Accounting courses in high school and college are highly desirable.

Occupational Outlook: As the economy becomes more service oriented, more job opportunities will become available in the offices of small service businesses.

End of Lesson REVIEW

AUDIT YOUR UNDERSTANDING

1. When a business asks a customer to sign a note receivable for an extension of time on the customer's account receivable, how do the amount and form of the business asset change?
2. In which chart of accounts classification is Interest Income listed?
3. What accounts are affected, and how, when a customer dishonors a note receivable?
4. Why is interest income recorded at the time a note is dishonored even though cash has not been received?

TERMS REVIEW

notes receivable

interest income

dishonored note

WORK TOGETHER 20-3

Journalizing notes receivable transactions

The journals for Cruz Corporation are provided in the *Working Papers*. Your instructor will guide you through the following example.

1. Using the current year, journalize the following transactions. Use page 2 of a general journal and page 3 of a cash receipts journal. Source documents are abbreviated as follows: note receivable, NR; receipt, R; memorandum, M.

Transactions:
Feb. 2. Accepted a 90-day, 8% note from Paul Gary for an extension of time on his account, $1,800.00. NR17.
    18. Received cash for the maturity value of NR14, a 60-day, 9% note for $500.00. R67.
    27. Kirk Adams dishonored NR9, a 90-day, 9% note, for $400.00. M25.

ON YOUR OWN 20-3

Journalizing notes receivable transactions

The journals for Reality, Inc., are provided in the *Working Papers*. Work this problem independently.

1. Using the current year, journalize the following transactions. Use page 3 of a general journal and page 5 of a cash receipts journal. Source documents are abbreviated as follows: note receivable, NR; receipt, R; memorandum, M.

Transactions:
Mar. 4. Accepted a 90-day, 10% note from Kim Pratt for an extension of time on her account, $2,500.00. NR24.
    18. Received cash for the maturity value of NR18, a 60-day, 12% note for $1,500.00. R68.
    26. T. J. Cross dishonored NR15, a 90-day, 10% note, for $1,800.00. M21.

SUMMARY

After completing this chapter, you can:

1. Define accounting terms related to notes and interest.
2. Identify accounting concepts and practices related to notes and interest.
3. Calculate interest and maturity dates for notes.
4. Analyze and record transactions for notes payable.
5. Analyze and record transactions for notes receivable.

EXPLORE ACCOUNTING

Low Interest or Cash Back?

"For a limited time, receive 1.9% financing or $2,000 cash back on your new car!" We often hear car dealers offer customers incentives of below-market financing or a cash refund. Each option provides the customer with a monetary value. The below-market financing spreads this value—a reduced monthly payment—over a period of time. The cash refund is received when the car is purchased.

Should the customer's choice have an impact on the way the sales transaction is recorded by the car dealer? Hammond Motors has two cars with sticker prices of $18,000.00. Pedro Diaz purchased one car, paying $3,000.00 down and financing the remaining $15,000.00 over 4 years at the 1.9% interest rate. Tatsu Hamazaki purchased the other car, paying only $1,000.00 down and using her $2,000.00 cash back option to reduce her 12% note to $15,000.00. Using this information, it appears that Hammond Auto sold Pedro's car for $18,000.00 and Tatsu's car for $16,000.00. It also appears that both customers are responsible for $15,000.00 notes receivable.

However, accountants believe that, regardless of which sales incentive is offered, the value of the incentive should be deducted from the sales price. Accounting rules require that the recorded amount of below-market loans be reduced by the value of the incentive. This process, known as *imputing interest*, adjusts the note receivable to an amount that will yield a market rate of interest over the life of the note. Using the imputing interest rules, the below-market financing provided Pedro Diaz with a $2,000.00 benefit. Thus, Hammond Auto must record a $2,000.00 credit to Discount on Notes Receivable. The credit to Sales for Pedro's car, therefore, is only $15,000.00.

Instructions: Identify a below-market financing or cash refund currently being offered by an auto dealer. If you were purchasing the car, which offer would you accept? Without knowing the accounting rules for imputing interest, how could you make an informed decision?

20-1 APPLICATION PROBLEM

Calculating interest, maturity dates, and maturity values for promissory notes

Information regarding Shinoda, Inc., is provided in the *Working Papers*.

Instructions:

1. For each of the following promissory notes, calculate (a) the interest on the note, (b) the maturity date of the note, and (c) the maturity value of the note. Save your work to complete Application Problem 20-2.

Date	Principal	Interest Rate	Time
April 6	$10,000.00	12%	180 days
April 12	$600.00	9%	60 days
April 15	$5,000.00	10%	90 days
April 23	$3,000.00	14%	60 days

20-2 APPLICATION PROBLEM

Journalizing notes payable transactions

The journals for Webster Company are provided in the *Working Papers*.

Instructions:

1. Using the current year, journalize each of the following transactions using page 4 of a general journal and page 6 of a cash receipts journal. Source documents are abbreviated as follows: receipt, R; memorandum, M.

Transactions:

Apr. 6. Signed a 180-day, 12% note for $10,000.00 with First American Bank. R127.
   12. Signed a 60-day, 9% note with Milligan Company for an extension of time on this account payable, $600.00. M32.
   15. Signed a 90-day, 10% note for $5,000.00 with First National Bank. R142.
   23. Signed a 60-day, 14% note with Yeatman Industries for an extension of time on this account payable, $3,000.00. M42.

2. Journalize the following transactions on page 9 of a cash payments journal. Use the maturity dates and maturity values calculated in Application Problem 20-1. The abbreviation for a check is C.

Transactions:

Paid cash for the maturity value of the $600.00 note dated April 12. C310.
Paid cash for the maturity value of the $3,000.00 note dated April 23. C318.
Paid cash for the maturity value of the $5,000.00 note dated April 15. C456.
Paid cash for the maturity value of the $10,000.00 note dated April 6. C645.

(**Go Beyond the Book**
For more information go to
www.C21accounting.com)

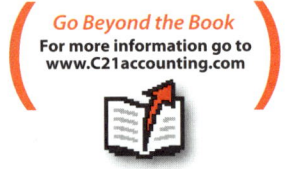

20-3 APPLICATION PROBLEM

Journalizing notes receivable transactions

The journals for Compression Services are provided in the *Working Papers*.

Instructions:

1. Using the current year, journalize the following transactions. Use page 14 of a general journal and page 10 of a cash receipts journal. Source documents are abbreviated as follows: notes receivable, NR; receipt, R; memorandum, M.

Transactions:

Jul. 5. Accepted a 90-day, 12% note from Peter Lamb for an extension of time on his account, $3,000.00. NR25.
    11. Received cash for the maturity value of NR20, a 60-day, 9% note for $800.00. R321.
    15. Accepted a 90-day, 10% note from Pam Sellers for an extension of time on her account, $2,400.00. NR26.
    21. Josh Kemp dishonored NR16, a 90-day, 12% note, for $3,500.00. M62.
    22. Received cash for the maturity value of NR17, a 90-day, 10% note for $1,000.00. R339.
    27. Phil Pellum dishonored NR18, a 90-day, 15% note, for $2,500.00. M63.

20-4 APPLICATION PROBLEM

Journalizing notes receivable transactions

Savath Rajady, the credit manager of Jenkin Company, encourages customers of past-due accounts to sign notes receivable. Mr. Rajady informs customers that future sales on account will be accepted only if the customers sign a note and subsequently pay the note with interest. Using this strategy, most of Jenkin's customers agree to sign notes. Jenkin Company requires all customers to sign 90-day, 18% notes.

Instructions:

1. Journalize the following transactions completed by Jenkin Company during the current year. The journals are provided in the *Working Papers*. Use page 18 of a general journal and page 11 of a cash receipts journal. Source documents are abbreviated as follows: notes receivable, NR; receipt, R; memorandum, M.

Transactions:

Nov. 3. Savath Rajady visited the offices of AutoCare Industries. AutoCare's president agreed to sign a note for $3,000.00. NR63.
    14. Received a check for $2,090.00 from Teltor Company. The payment covers a $2,000.00 note, number 52. R245.
    28. A $4,000.00, 18%, 90-day note receivable from Sanford Company was due today, but no check has been received. Savath Rajady attempted to call the company but discovered that its phone has been disconnected. M69.

20-5 MASTERY PROBLEM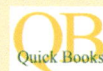

Journalizing notes payable and notes receivable transactions

The following transactions related to notes payable and notes receivable were completed by Amory Company during July of the current year. Journals are provided in the *Working Papers*.

Transactions:

Jul. 2. Signed a 90-day, 10% note for $5,000.00 with Commercial National Bank. R51.
   7. Accepted a 90-day, 10% note from Nan Abert for an extension of time on her account, $1,500.00. NR9.
   9. Received cash for the maturity value of NR4, a 60-day, 9% note for $1,600.00. R62.
   12. Accepted a 90-day, 10% note from Tom Burns for an extension of time on his account, $400.00. NR10.
   17. Received cash for the maturity value of NR5, a 60-day, 9% note for $800.00. R65.
   23. Signed a 180-day, 8% note for $8,000.00 with American National Bank. R74.
   24. Gibson Co. dishonored NR2, a 90-day, 12% note, for $3,000.00. M43.
   28. Received cash for the maturity value of NR3, a 90-day, 12% note for $4,500.00. R79.
   29. Signed a 60-day, 12% note with Daily Supply for an extension of time on this account payable, $2,500.00. M44.

Instructions:

1. Journalize each transaction, using page 7 of a general journal and page 6 of a cash receipts journal. Source documents are abbreviated as follows: check, C; receipt, R; memorandum, M; note receivable, NR.
2. Determine the maturity date and maturity value of each note signed by Amory Company.
3. Journalize the following transactions on page 9 of a cash payments journal. Use the maturity dates and maturity values calculated in previous steps.

Transactions:

Paid cash for the maturity value of the $2,500.00 note dated July 29. C417.
Paid cash for the maturity value of the $5,000.00 note dated July 2. C610.
Paid cash for the maturity value of the $8,000.00 note dated July 23. C821.

20-6 CHALLENGE PROBLEM

Recording notes receivable stated in months

On June 18, James Whiley signed a $10,000.00 note payable with National Bank of Cressville. At his request, the bank drafted the note for a 3-month term, payable on September 18, with 15% interest. Mr. Whiley proudly stated, "Since my company began in 1972, we have never had to borrow money for more than 90 days." The loan officer, believing that Mr. Whiley did not fully understand the terms of the note, explained that the company would be responsible for interest for the number of days between June 18 and September 18. That number, he continued, would be slightly more than 90 days.

Instructions:

1. Use the forms given in the *Working Papers*. Determine the maturity value of the note on September 18. Use the actual number of days from June 18 in your calculation.
2. Mr. Whiley expected to pay only 90 days of interest on the note. Determine the maturity value of the note assuming interest is charged for only 90 days.
3. Assume the bank allows Mr. Whiley to pay only the interest amount calculated in Instruction 2, even though the money will be borrowed for more than 90 days. Determine the actual interest rate of the note.
4. Should the bank allow Mr. Whiley to pay for only 90 days' interest?

APPLIED COMMUNICATION

As an accountant for Hasler Corporation, you have been asked to assist the president in making a presentation to the board of directors. The president wants to report the 4-year growth in sales of four major products. The following table presents product sales (in thousands of dollars) from 20X1 to 20X4.

	20X1	20X2	20X3	20X4
Lumber	$253	$316	$324	$315
Hardware	166	182	169	175
Carpet	153	176	189	201
Housewares	122	112	114	103

Instructions: Prepare a graph displaying the data presented in the table. Determine what type of graph (pie, line, bar, stacked-bar) best communicates the sales trend of each product. If available, use the graph or chart feature of a spreadsheet program to create the graph.

CASE FOR CRITICAL THINKING

TayVon Johnson, a new accounting department employee, questions the practice of recording interest income when a note is dishonored. Instead, he believes that the interest earned on the note should be recorded only if and when the account is subsequently paid. Is this alternative method acceptable? Why or why not?

GRAPHING WORKSHOP

Every week Sandie Oswalt, Vice-President, compares the certificate of deposit (CD) rates for her bank, National Bank, to three local competing banks. Sandie uses the information to decide when and by how much to raise or lower National Bank's CD rates.

Use the graph to answer the following questions. Support your answers.

1. Is the National Bank competitive with short-term (90 day or less) CDs?
2. Is the National Bank competitive with long-term (1 year or more) CDs?
3. Which bank has the least variation in its CD rates?

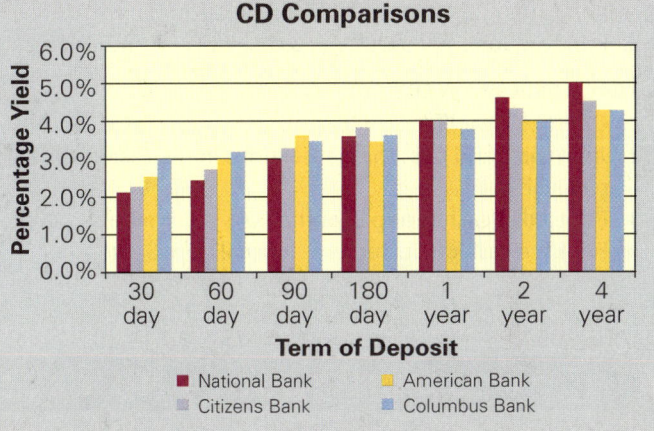

ANALYZING BEST BUY'S FINANCIAL STATEMENTS

Just as no two individuals are exactly the same, no two companies are exactly the same. Management decisions, such as the ownership of property and equipment, the types and amounts of inventory, and customer credit policies, all cause the economic events of each company to be different.

The summary of these economic events is reflected in financial statements. Financial statements should enable the reader to learn the important financial information of the company. Thus, just as each company is different, each company's financial statements are different.

Many companies have large levels of long-term debt and, as a result, report interest expense on their income statements. Compared with other companies, Best Buy has a relatively low level of long-term debt and incurs a small amount of interest expense.

Instructions: Refer to Best Buy's financial statements on pages B-5 and B-7 in Appendix B of this textbook.

1. What are Best Buy's long-term liabilities and debt as a percent of total liabilities and shareholders' equity for fiscal year 2007?
2. What was the amount of cash paid for interest expense in fiscal year 2007 as reported on the Consolidated Statements of Cash Flows?

Accounting SOFTWARE

NOTES PAYABLE AND RECEIVABLE

Peachtree keeps records of every purchase on account from each vendor. At any time, a business can see a listing of the outstanding invoices owed to a vendor. When the business pays the account, the payment is applied against specific outstanding invoices in the vendor's account. This method of maintaining an accounts payable ledger is known as an *open item system*.

When a business pays an outstanding invoice with a note payable, the outstanding invoice in the vendor's account should be marked as paid. Therefore, Peachtree has you record the signing of a note payable using the same window you would use if the business paid the invoice with a check.

Similarly, the receipt of cash from the signing of a note payable is recorded in a window normally used to record the receipt of cash from sales or the collection of accounts receivable. Changes in the default general ledger accounts are necessary to ensure the transaction is journalized properly.

PEACHTREE APPLICATION PROBLEM 20-2
1. Open (Restore) file 20-2AP.ptb.
2. Journalize and post each of the transactions covering the signing of notes payable and the payment of cash for a notes payable.
3. Print the April 6 to April 15 cash receipts journal.
4. Print the April 12 to April 23 purchase journal.
5. Print the June 11 to October 3 cash disbursements journal.

PEACHTREE MASTERY PROBLEM 20-5
1. Open (Restore) file 20-5MP.ptb.
2. Journalize and post the transactions in the cash disbursements journal related to notes payable and notes receivable.
3. Print July's cash receipts journal, sales journal, and purchase journal.
4. Print the cash disbursements journal from September 27 to January 19.

NOTES PAYABLE AND RECEIVABLE

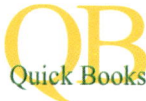

Using an accounting software package to record notes payable and notes receivable is very similar to recording these transactions in a manual accounting system.

The entry to record signing a note payable in exchange for cash or other assets is entered in the Make Deposits window. The entry to record signing a note payable for an extension of time on an account is entered in the Enter Bills window. The entry to record the payment of a note payable is entered in the Write Checks window.

Notes receivable are handled in a similar manner. The entry to record accepting a note receivable from a customer for an extension of time is entered in the Receive Payments window. The entry to record the receipt of cash from a note receivable is entered in the Make Deposits window.

While QuickBooks does not calculate maturity dates or maturity values, it does have a calculator feature available. To open the calculator, click in the amount field and either press = or enter a number followed by +, −, *, /, or =. A paper tape, much like the paper tape in a calculator, will appear, and your calculations will appear on the tape. To enter the calculation result in the field, press Enter or Tab, or click anywhere outside the lines of the tape.

QUICKBOOKS APPLICATION PROBLEM 20-2
1. Open the Webster Company file.
2. To record a note payable for cash, use the Make Deposits option from the Banking menu. To record a note payable to extend payment terms, choose the Enter Bills option from the Vendors menu. Record the signing of a note payable and the payment of cash for a note payable.
3. Print a Journal report using April 1 and October 31 for the dates.

QUICKBOOKS MASTERY PROBLEM 20-5
1. Open the Amory Company file.
2. Journalize the notes payable and notes receivable transactions for July.
3. Journalize the transactions for later months for notes paid at maturity using the Write Checks window to record the transactions.
4. Print a Journal report using July 1 and January 31 of the following year for the dates.

CALCULATING DATES FOR NOTES

Mitchell Nelson was born on the 33,131st day of the 20th century. Why would Mitchell or anyone else care about this number? Electronic spreadsheets use sequential numbers, beginning with January 1, 1900, to perform date calculations. A variety of date and time functions allows you to determine dates, such as the age of a person or the due date of a note payable.

Open a blank worksheet and enter Mitchell's birthday of 9/15/1990 in cell A1. The spreadsheet displays the date but stores the 33,131 in the cell. Let's assume today's date is January 1, 2009. How old is Mitchell on that date? To find out, enter 1/01/2009 in cell A2; then enter the following formula in cell A3: =(A2 − A1)/365. Subtracting Mitchell's birthday from today's value calculates his age in days; dividing this number by 365 completes the calculation of his age in years. The age displayed is 18.30959. Mitchell is 18 years old.

When does a 135-day note signed on 6/17/2010 mature? Enter the date in cell B1 and enter the formula +B1+135 in cell B2. The spreadsheet recognizes you are working with dates and automatically formats the new cell as a date—10/30/2010. But the number that is stored in the cell is actually 40,481.

Not sure you believe it? Format the four cells using a number or currency format and see it for yourself.

EXCEL APPLICATION PROBLEM 20-1
Open the F20-1 Excel data file. Follow the step-by-step instructions in the Instructions worksheet.

CALCULATING NOTES AND INTEREST

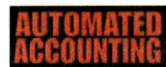

The Planning Tools in *Automated Accounting* perform specific types of interest and loan calculations.

The Notes and Interest Planner is used to calculate maturity date, amount of interest, and the maturity value of the note. A business can use the planner to calculate the total amount to be received or paid (maturity value) of its notes receivable or notes payable. The planner may also be used to determine the exact due date of a note when the term is stated as a number of days or months. To use the Notes and Interest Planner:

1. Click the Tools toolbar button.
2. Click the Notes and Interest tab.
3. In the Time Basis box, select the time basis to be used by clicking on the appropriate option button. (This textbook uses a 360-day year.)
4. Enter the data and press the Tab key to move among the text boxes. The calculated results for Maturity Date of Note, Amount of Interest, and Maturity Value will appear at the bottom of the Planning dialog box.
5. Click on the Report button to produce a schedule of the results. Once displayed, the report may be printed or copied to the clipboard for pasting into a spreadsheet or word processor.
6. Click the Close button to exit the report and return to the planner.
7. Click the Close button or press ESC to exit the planner.

AUTOMATED ACCOUNTING APPLICATION PROBLEM 20-1
Open file F20-1.AA8. Display the problem instructions and complete the problem.

AUTOMATED ACCOUNTING MASTERY PROBLEM 20-5
Open file F20-5.AA8. Display the problem instructions and complete the problem.

OPTIONAL ACTIVITY
On your own, explore the other planning tools. For example, you could use the Savings Planner to calculate the monthly deposit required to save enough to buy a car in the future.

REINFORCEMENT Activity 3—Part A

An Accounting Cycle for a Corporation: Journalizing and Posting Transactions

Reinforcement Activity 3 reinforces learning from Parts 2 and 3. Activities cover a complete accounting cycle for a merchandising business organized as a corporation. Reinforcement Activity 3 is a single problem divided into two parts. Part A includes learning from Part 2 and Chapters 17 through 20 of Part 3. Part B includes learning from Chapters 21 and 22.

The accounting work of a single merchandising business for the last month of a yearly fiscal period is used in this reinforcement activity. The records kept and reports prepared, however, illustrate the application of accounting concepts for all merchandising businesses.

SPARKLE, INC.

Sparkle, Inc., a merchandising business, is organized as a corporation. The business sells a complete line of cleaning and maintenance supplies, mostly to business customers. Sparkle is located within an industrial park and is open for business Monday through Saturday. A monthly rent is paid for the building. Sparkle sells to some businesses on account and accepts cash or credit cards from small business owners.

CHART OF ACCOUNTS

Sparkle uses the chart of accounts shown on the next page.

JOURNALS AND LEDGERS

The journals, ledgers, and forms used by Sparkle are listed below. Models of these items are shown in the textbook chapters indicated.

Journals and Ledgers	Chapter
Purchases journal	9
Cash payments journal	9
General journal	9
Sales journal	10
Cash receipts journal	10
Accounts payable ledger	11
Accounts receivable ledger	11
General ledger	11
Plant asset record	18

CHART OF ACCOUNTS
GENERAL LEDGER

Balance Sheet Accounts

(1000) ASSETS
1100 Current Assets
1105 Cash
1110 Petty Cash
1115 Notes Receivable
1120 Interest Receivable
1125 Accounts Receivable
1130 Allowance for Uncollectible Accounts
1135 Merchandise Inventory
1140 Supplies
1145 Prepaid Insurance
1200 Plant Assets
1205 Office Equipment
1210 Accumulated Depreciation—Office Equipment
1215 Warehouse Equipment
1220 Accumulated Depreciation—Warehouse Equipment
(2000) LIABILITIES
2100 Current Liabilities
2105 Notes Payable
2110 Interest Payable
2115 Accounts Payable
2120 Federal Income Tax Payable
2125 Employee Income Tax Payable
2130 Social Security Tax Payable
2135 Medicare Tax Payable
2140 Sales Tax Payable
2145 Unemployment Tax Payable—Federal
2150 Unemployment Tax Payable—State
2155 Health Insurance Premiums Payable
2160 Dividends Payable
(3000) OWNER'S EQUITY
3105 Capital Stock
3110 Retained Earnings
3115 Dividends
3120 Income Summary

Income Statement Accounts

(4000) OPERATING REVENUE
4105 Sales
4110 Sales Discount
4115 Sales Returns and Allowances
(5000) COST OF MERCHANDISE
5105 Purchases
5110 Purchases Discount
5115 Purchases Returns and Allowances
(6000) OPERATING EXPENSES
6105 Advertising Expense
6110 Cash Short and Over
6115 Credit Card Fee Expense
6120 Depreciation Expense—Office Equipment
6125 Depreciation Expense—Warehouse Equipment
6130 Insurance Expense
6135 Miscellaneous Expense
6140 Payroll Taxes Expense
6145 Rent Expense
6150 Repairs Expense
6155 Salary Expense
6160 Supplies Expense
6165 Uncollectible Accounts Expense
6170 Utilities Expense
(7000) OTHER REVENUE
7105 Gain on Plant Assets
7110 Interest Income
(8000) OTHER EXPENSES
8105 Interest Expense
8110 Loss on Plant Assets
(9000) INCOME TAX EXPENSE
9105 Federal Income Tax Expense

SUBSIDIARY LEDGERS

Accounts Receivable Ledger
110 Baker & Associates
120 Felton Industries
130 Hilldale School
140 Horton Company
150 Nelson Co.
160 Ruocco Plastics

Accounts Payable Ledger
210 Buntin Supply Company
220 Draper Company
230 Glenson Company
240 Hinsdale Supply Co.
250 SHF Corp.
260 Walbash Manufacturing

RECORDING TRANSACTIONS

The December 1, 20X4, account balances for the general and subsidiary ledgers are given in the *Working Papers*.

Instructions:

1. Journalize the following transactions completed during December, 20X4. Use page 12 of a sales journal, page 12 of a purchases journal, page 12 of a general journal, page 12 of a cash receipts journal, and page 23 of a cash payments journal. Sparkle offers sales terms of 2/10, n/30. The sales tax rate is 6%. Source documents are abbreviated as follows: check, C; memorandum, M; purchase invoice, P; receipt, R; sales invoice, S; terminal summary, TS; debit memorandum, DM; credit memorandum, CM; NR, note receivable; NP, note payable.

   Dec. 1. Paid cash for rent, $1,750.00. C578.
   2. Received cash on account from Ruocco Plastics, covering S637 for $3,250.00. R671.
   3. Paid cash on account to Walbash Manufacturing, covering P324 for $620.00, less 2% discount. C579.
   3. Paid cash for the maturity value of NP31, a 180-day, 9% note for $10,000.00 to First American Bank. C580.
   5. Bought a printer/scanner for the office: cost, $1,200.00; estimated salvage value, $200.00; estimated useful life, 3 years; plant asset No. 998; serial number, MNT-9343. C581. Open a plant asset record for this office equipment. Sparkle Inc. uses the straight-line method of depreciation. C581.
   5. Sold merchandise on account to Horton Company, $500.00, plus sales tax. S657.
   6. Recorded cash and credit card sales, $5,430.00, plus sales tax, $325.80; total, $5,755.80. TS49.
   6. Bought supplies on account from Draper Company, $362.40. M45.
   Posting. Post the items that are to be posted individually. Always post the journals in this order: sales journal, purchases journal, general journal, cash receipts journal, and cash payments journal.
   7. Accepted a 90-day, 10% note from Nelson Co. for an extension of time on its account, $3,600.00. NR34.
   8. Purchased merchandise on account from Glenson Company, $4,518.00. P332.
   9. Sold merchandise on account to Ruocco Plastics, $480.00, plus sales tax. S658.
   9. Wrote off Felton Industries' past-due account as uncollectible, $2,460.00. M46.
   10. Paid cash for supplies, $223.00. C582.
   12. Received cash on account from Horton Company, covering S657 for $530.00, less 2% discount. R672.
   12. Purchased merchandise on account from Hinsdale Supply Co., $6,812.00. P333.
   13. Recorded cash and credit card sales, $5,987.00, plus sales tax, $359.22; total, $6,346.22. TS50.
   Posting. Post the items that are to be posted individually.
   14. Received cash for sale of a hand truck, plant asset No. 432, $1,400.00. M47 and R673.
   14. Returned merchandise purchased from Glenson Company on P332, $198.00. DM34.
   15. Paid cash liability for employee income tax, $324.00; social security tax, $742.00; and Medicare tax, $162.35. C583.
   15. Paid cash for semimonthly payroll, $2,256.27 (total payroll, $2,820.00, less deductions: employee income tax, $158.00; social security tax, $174.84; Medicare tax, $40.89; health insurance, $190.00). C584.
   15. Recorded employer payroll taxes, $250.45, for the semimonthly pay period ended December 15. Taxes owed are: social security tax, $174.84; Medicare tax, $40.89; federal unemployment tax, $4.48; and state unemployment tax, $30.24. M48.
   16. Purchased merchandise on account from Buntin Supply Company, $4,833.00. P334.
   17. Paid cash for electric bill, $346.20. C585.
   17. Paid cash on account to Glenson Company, covering P332 for $4,518.00, less 2% discount. C586.
   18. Received cash in full payment of Baker & Associates' account, previously written off as uncollectible, $948.00. M49 and R674.
   19. Paid cash for miscellaneous expense, $72.00. C587.
   20. Sold merchandise on account to Hilldale School, $1,560.00. Hilldale School is exempt from sales tax. S659.
   20. Recorded cash and credit card sales, $3,554.00, plus sales tax, $213.24; total, $3,767.24. TS51.
   Posting. Post the items that are to be posted individually.
   21. Paid cash for merchandise, $357.00. C588.
   22. Granted credit to Ruocco Plastics for merchandise returned, $120.00; plus sales tax, $7.20; $127.20 total. CM15.
   23. Paid cash on account to Hinsdale Supply Co., covering P333 for $6,812.00. C589.
   26. Received cash for the maturity value of NR32, a 90-day, 12% note for $5,800.00. R675.
   27. Recorded cash and credit card sales, $2,337.00, plus sales tax, $140.22; total, $2,477.22. TS52.
   Posting. Post the items that are to be posted individually.
   28. Sold merchandise on account to Horton Company, $2,500.00, plus sales tax. S660.

28. Purchased merchandise on account from Draper Company, $6,148.00. P335.
28. Signed a 90-day, 10% note, for $6,000.00 with Commercial National Bank. NP33 and R676.
28. Received cash for sale of a computer printer, plant asset No. 667, $150.00. M50 and R677. Update the plant asset record and record the sale.
29. Paid $500.00 on the outstanding balance of the SHF Corp. account. C590.
30. Ruocco Plastics dishonored NR33, a 60-day, 12% note, for $3,000.00. M51.
30. Recorded credit card fee expense, $418.00. M52.
31. Paid cash to replenish the petty cash fund, $84.96: supplies, $12.50; advertising, $50.00; miscellaneous, $22.37; cash short, $.09. C591.
31. Paid cash for semimonthly payroll, $2,206.86 (total payroll, $2,760.00, less deductions: employee income tax, $152.00; social security tax, $171.12; Medicare tax, $40.02; health insurance, $190.00. C592.
31. Recorded employer payroll taxes, $242.14, for the semimonthly pay period ended December 31. Taxes owed are: social security tax, $171.12: Medicare tax, $40.02; federal unemployment tax, $4.00; and state unemployment tax, $27.00. M53.
31. Recorded cash and credit card sales, $465.00, plus sales tax, $27.90; total, $492.90. TS53.

Posting. Post the items that are to be posted individually.

2. Prove and rule the sales journal. Post the totals of the special columns.
3. Total and rule the purchases journal. Post the total.
4. Prove the equality of debits and credits for the cash receipts and cash payments journals.
5. Prove cash. The balance on the next unused check stub is $8,100.70.
6. Rule the cash receipts journal. Post the totals of the special columns.
7. Rule the cash payments journal. Post the totals of the special columns.
8. Prepare a schedule of accounts receivable and a schedule of accounts payable. Prove the accuracy of the subsidiary ledgers by comparing the schedule totals with the balances of the controlling accounts in the general ledger. If the totals are not the same, find and correct the errors.

The ledgers used in Reinforcement Activity 3—Part A are needed to complete Reinforcement Activity 3—Part B.

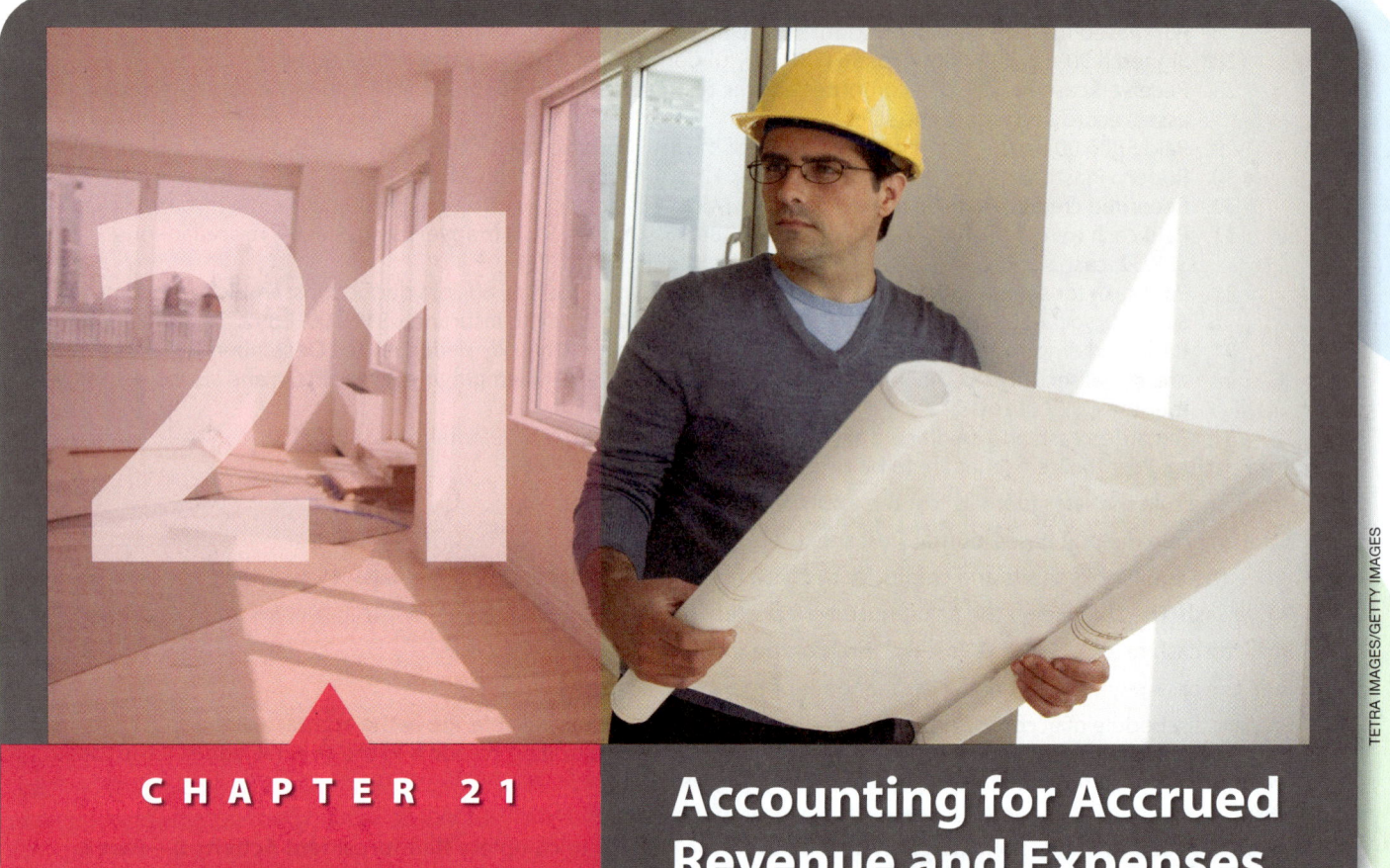

CHAPTER 21

Accounting for Accrued Revenue and Expenses

OBJECTIVES

After studying Chapter 21, you will be able to:

1. Define accounting terms related to accrued revenue and accrued expenses.
2. Identify accounting concepts and practices related to accrued revenue and accrued expenses.
3. Record adjusting, closing, and reversing entries for accrued revenue.
4. Record adjusting, closing, and reversing entries for accrued expenses.

KEY TERMS

- accrued revenue
- intellectual property
- accrued interest income
- reversing entry
- accrued expenses
- accrued interest expense

Point Your Browser
www.C21accounting.com

ACCOUNTING IN THE REAL WORLD

USA Today

Deferred Revenue at *USA Today*

You've probably heard someone use the phrase "timing is everything." This phrase has a special meaning to the accountants at *USA Today*, a division of Gannett Co., Inc.

USA Today collects fees for advertising before the advertisements appear. Customers pay subscriptions for paper delivery or online editions as much as a year in advance. Receiving these fees does not, however, mean that *USA Today* can record the amounts as current revenue. In accordance with generally accepted accounting principles, advertising fees are recorded as revenue when the advertising is printed or placed on a web site. In the same manner, subscription fees are recorded as revenue when purchased newspapers are delivered.

When preparing financial statements, accountants at *USA Today* must analyze the money collected from advertising and subscriptions to determine what amount should be recorded as revenue.

Critical Thinking

1. Suppose you purchase a $150.00 annual subscription to *USA Today* on November 1. How much should *USA Today* recognize as revenue on its December financial statements?
2. Would your answer to question 1 differ if the customer selected online delivery of *USA Today*?

Source: http://library.corporate-ir.net/library/84/846/84662/items/233865/06AnnualReport.pdf

INTERNET ACTIVITY

Mission Statements

Go to the homepage for Ben and Jerry's Ice Cream (www.benandjerrys.com). Search for Ben and Jerry's Mission Statement.

Instructions

1. List Ben and Jerry's Mission Statement in full.
2. Expand your search by reading about Ben and Jerry's commitment to the environment. List one interesting fact that you find.

LESSON 21-1

Accrued Revenue

ACCOUNTING FOR INTEREST AT THE FISCAL YEAR END

Generally accepted accounting principles (GAAP) require that revenue and expenses be recorded in the accounting period in which revenue is earned and expenses are incurred. [CONCEPT: Matching Expenses with Revenue] Some revenues, however, are earned each day but are usually recorded only when cash is actually received. For example, interest is earned for each day a note receivable is held.

However, the interest may not be received until the maturity date of the note. Likewise, some expenses may be incurred before they are actually paid. A note payable incurs interest expense each day the note is outstanding. However, the interest generally is not paid until the note's maturity date. At the end of the fiscal period, adjusting entries are recorded for these revenues and expenses.

Revenue earned in one fiscal period but not received until a later fiscal period is called **accrued revenue**. At the end of a fiscal period, accrued revenue is recorded by an adjusting entry. [CONCEPT: Realization of Revenue] The adjusting entry for accrued revenue increases a revenue account. The adjusting entry also increases a receivable account. The income statement will then report all revenue earned for the period, even though some of the revenue has not yet been received. The balance sheet will report all the assets, including the accrued revenue receivable. [CONCEPT: Adequate Disclosure]

CHARACTER COUNTS

Guarding Intellectual Property

Is it ethical to download free music from the Internet? This hotly debated issue provides interesting insight into our society and individuals' ability to make ethical decisions. Have you heard people attempt to justify copying music? "It doesn't cost the artists anything." "They're so rich anyway." "I can't afford to purchase the music I like." "If it's on the Internet, I can download it."

Any product that is protected by patents, trademarks, and copyrights is called **intellectual property**. Music, videos, and computer software are examples of intellectual property. Regardless of how individuals attempt to justify downloading free music from the Internet, there is no escaping the fact that these downloads are illegal.

Businesses recognize that the unauthorized copying of computer software is also illegal. Many companies address this issue in their code of conduct.

Instructions

Do an Internet search to access "Everyday Values," the code of conduct for Harley-Davidson, Inc. What guidance does Harley-Davidson provide its employees about copying software for both business and personal use?

Source: http://investor.harley-davidson.com/downloads/CG_CodeConduct.pdf.

ANALYZING AN ADJUSTMENT FOR ACCRUED INTEREST INCOME

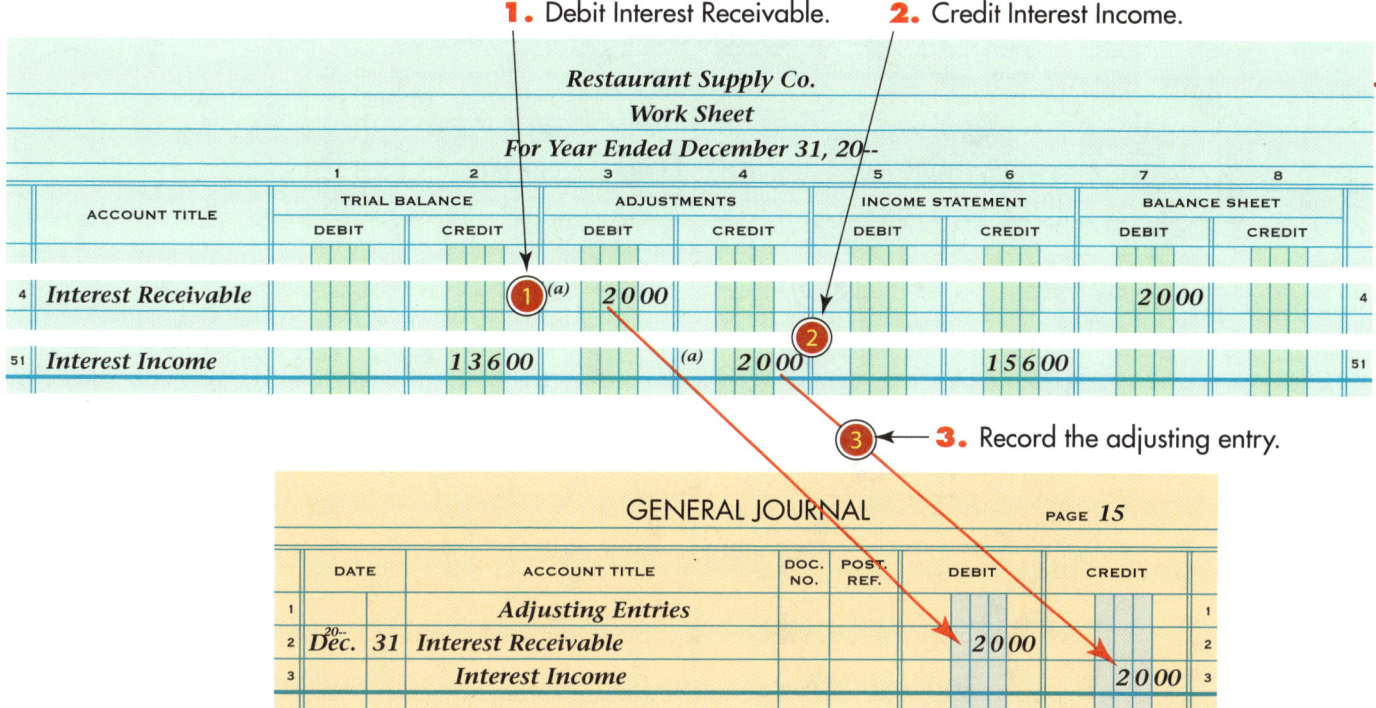

1. Debit Interest Receivable.
2. Credit Interest Income.
3. Record the adjusting entry.

At the end of each fiscal period, Restaurant Supply examines the notes receivable on hand. The amount of interest income earned but not yet collected is calculated. Interest earned but not yet received is called **accrued interest income**. On December 31, Restaurant Supply has one note receivable on hand, a 90-day, 6%, $2,000.00 note dated November 1. An adjusting entry must be made to record the amount of interest earned to date on this note.

The time period from November 1 through December 31 is 60 days. Therefore, the interest earned on the note is calculated for 60/360 of a year.

Interest Receivable is debited for $20.00 to show the interest income that has accrued at the end of the fiscal period. This revenue will not be collected until the next fiscal period.

The credit of $20.00 is added to the previous balance in Interest Income. The new account balance, $156.00, is the total amount of interest income earned during the fiscal period.

STEPS — RECORDING AN ADJUSTMENT FOR ACCRUED INTEREST INCOME

1. Write the accrued interest income amount, $20.00, in the Adjustments Debit column on the Interest Receivable line of the work sheet. Label the adjustment with a small letter *a* in parentheses, *(a)*.
2. Write the same amount, $20.00, in the Adjustments Credit column on the Interest Income line of the work sheet. Label the adjustment using the same letter, *(a)*.
3. Use the debit and credit amounts on the work sheet to record an adjusting entry in the general journal.

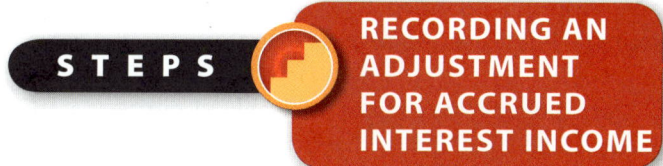

Principal × Interest Rate × Time as Fraction of Year = Accrued Interest Income

$2,000.00 × 6% × 60/360 = $20.00

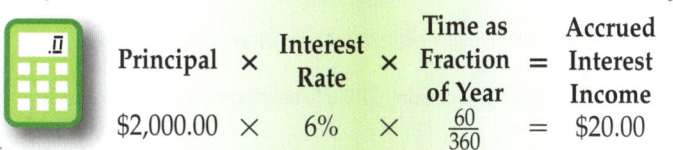

Interest Receivable
Dec. 31 Adj. 20.00

Interest Income
Dec. 31 Bal. 136.00
Dec. 31 Adj. 20.00
(New Bal. 156.00)

Accrued Revenue   Lesson 21-1   617

POSTING AN ADJUSTING ENTRY FOR ACCRUED INTEREST INCOME

The adjustment for accrued interest income planned on a work sheet is recorded as an adjusting entry in a general journal. The adjusting entry is then posted to the general ledger.

After posting, the interest receivable account has a debit balance of $20.00 and will appear on the balance sheet as a current asset. This debit balance is the accrued interest income earned but not yet collected at the end of the year. The interest income account has a credit balance of $156.00 and will appear on the income statement as other revenue. This amount is the total interest income for the year.

STEPS: POSTING AN ADJUSTING ENTRY FOR ACCRUED INTEREST INCOME

1. Post the debit, $20.00, to *Interest Receivable*.
2. Post the credit, $20.00, to *Interest Income*.

REMEMBER

The interest receivable account appears in the Current Assets section of the balance sheet. The interest income account appears in the Other Revenue section of the income statement.

REVERSING ENTRY FOR ACCRUED INTEREST INCOME

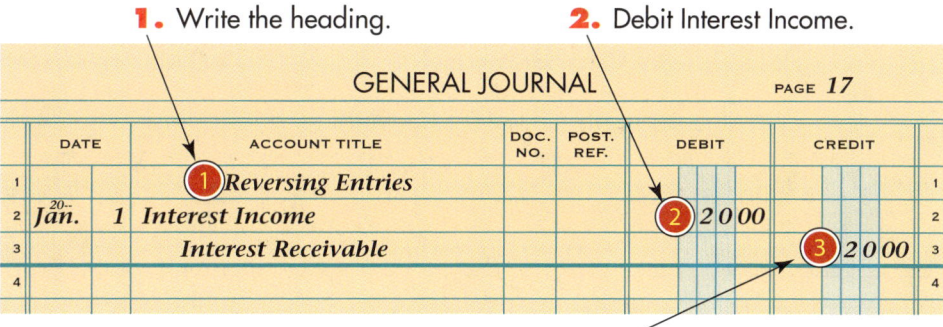

On December 31, Interest Income is closed as part of the regular closing entry for income statement accounts with credit balances. Interest Income is debited for $156.00 to reduce the account balance to zero.

Adjusting entries for accrued revenues have an effect on transactions that will be recorded in the following fiscal period. On the maturity date of the outstanding 90-day note receivable, Restaurant Supply will receive interest of $30.00.

However, an adjusting entry was made to record the amount of interest earned last year, $20.00. Thus, $20.00 of the $30.00 total interest income has already been recorded as revenue. The remaining $10.00 of the $30.00 total interest will be earned during the current fiscal period.

It is inconvenient to determine how much, if any, of cash received from notes receivable relates to interest accrued during the prior fiscal period. To avoid this inconvenience, an entry is made at the beginning of the new fiscal period to reverse the adjusting entry. An entry made at the beginning of one fiscal period to reverse an adjusting entry made in the previous fiscal period is called a **reversing entry**.

Interest Income			
Dec. 31 Closing	156.00	Dec. 31 Bal.	136.00
Jan. 1 Rev.	20.00	Dec. 31 Adj.	20.00
(New Bal.	20.00)		

Interest Receivable			
Dec. 31 Adj.	20.00	Jan. 1 Rev.	20.00
(New Bal. zero)			

The reversing entry is the opposite of the adjusting entry. The entry creates a debit balance of $20.00 in Interest Income. A debit balance is the opposite of the normal balance of Interest Income. When the full amount of interest is received, the $30.00 will be credited to Interest Income, resulting in a $10.00 credit balance ($30.00 credit − $20.00 debit), the amount of interest earned in the new year.

The reversing entry reduced the balance in Interest Receivable to zero. When the interest is received, no entry will be made to Interest Receivable. Instead, the total amount of interest received will be credited to Interest Income.

STEPS REVERSING AN ADJUSTING ENTRY FOR ACCRUED INTEREST INCOME

1. Write the heading, *Reversing Entries*, in the middle of the general journal's Account Title column. This heading explains all the reversing entries that follow. Therefore, indicating a source document is unnecessary.

2. Record a debit, *$20.00*, to *Interest Income*.

3. Record a credit, *$20.00*, to *Interest Receivable*.

Accrued Revenue

COLLECTING A NOTE RECEIVABLE ISSUED IN A PREVIOUS FISCAL PERIOD

1. Credit for Principal
2. Credit for Total Interest
3. Debit for Maturity Value
4. Post amounts in General columns.

On January 30, Restaurant Supply received the maturity value of the only note receivable on hand on December 31, the end of the previous fiscal year.

January 30. Received cash for the maturity value of a 90-day, 6% note: principal, $2,000.00, plus interest, $30.00; total, $2,030.00. Receipt No. 9.

Cash			
Jan. 30 Rec'd	2,030.00		
Notes Receivable			
Nov. 1	2,000.00	Jan. 30 Rec'd	2,000.00
Interest Income			
Dec. 31 Closing	156.00	Dec. 31 Bal.	136.00
Jan. 1 Rev.	20.00	Dec. 31 Adj.	20.00
		Jan. 30 Rec'd	30.00
		(New Bal.	10.00)

The total interest, $30.00, was earned during two fiscal periods—$20.00 during the previous fiscal period and $10.00 during the current fiscal period. The reversing entry created a $20.00 debit balance in Interest Income. After the $30.00 credit is posted, Interest Income has a credit balance of $10.00, the amount of interest earned during the current fiscal period.

STEPS: COLLECTING A NOTE RECEIVABLE ISSUED IN A PREVIOUS FISCAL PERIOD

1. Record a credit to *Notes Receivable* in the General Credit column of the cash receipts journal for the principal of the note, *$2,000.00*.
2. Record a credit to *Interest Income* in the General Credit column for the total interest, *$30.00*.
3. Record a debit in the Cash Debit column for the maturity value of the note, *$2,030.00*.
4. Post the amounts in the General columns.

End of Lesson REVIEW

TERMS REVIEW

- accrued revenue
- intellectual property
- accrued interest income
- reversing entry

AUDIT YOUR UNDERSTANDING

1. Which accounting concept is being applied when an adjusting entry is made at the end of the fiscal period to record accrued revenue?
2. Why does a business use reversing entries as part of its procedures for accounting for accrued interest income?

WORK TOGETHER 21-1

Journalizing and posting entries for accrued revenue

The accounting forms for the following problem are in the *Working Papers*. Your instructor will guide you through the following examples.

On December 31 of the current year, Marris Corporation has one note receivable outstanding, a 120-day, 12%, $4,000.00 note dated November 16.

1. Plan the adjustment on a work sheet. Label the adjustment *(a)*.
2. Journalize and post the adjusting entry for accrued interest income on December 31. Use page 14 of a general journal.
3. Journalize and post the closing entry for interest income using page 14 of a general journal.
4. Journalize and post the January 1 reversing entry for accrued interest income on page 15 of a general journal.
5. Journalize the receipt of cash for the maturity value of the note on March 16, Receipt No. 32. Use page 16 of a cash receipts journal. Post the amounts in the General columns.

ON YOUR OWN 21-1

Journalizing and posting entries for accrued revenue

The accounting forms for the following problem are in the *Working Papers*. Work this problem independently.

On December 31 of the current year, ExMark, Inc., has one note receivable outstanding, a 90-day, 10%, $6,000.00 note dated December 1.

1. Plan the adjustment on a work sheet. Label the adjustment *(a)*.
2. Journalize and post the adjusting entry for accrued interest income on December 31. Use page 14 of a general journal.
3. Journalize and post the closing entry for interest income using page 14 of a general journal.
4. Journalize and post the January 1 reversing entry for accrued interest income on page 15 of a general journal.
5. Journalize the receipt of cash for the maturity value of the note on March 1, Receipt No. 65. Use page 19 of a cash receipts journal. Post the amounts in the General columns.

LESSON 21-2

Accrued Expenses

ANALYZING AN ADJUSTMENT FOR ACCRUED INTEREST EXPENSE

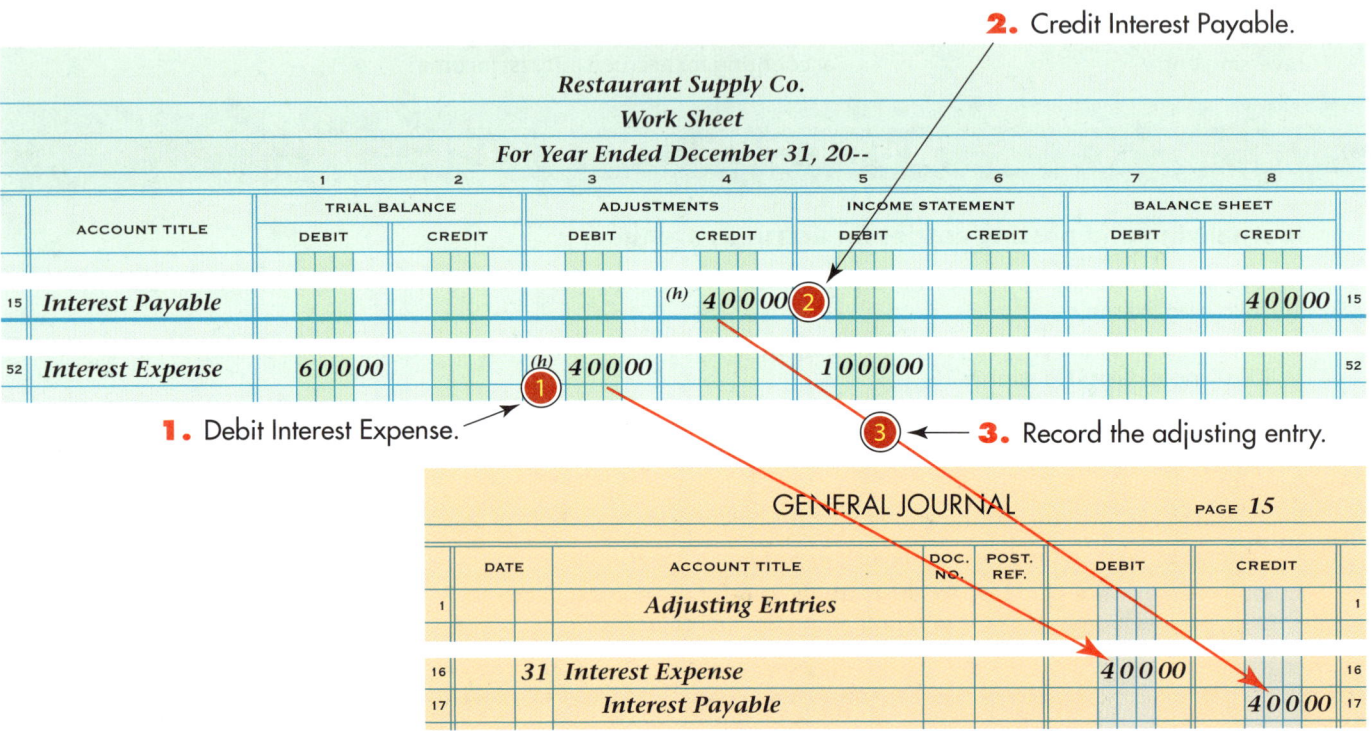

1. Debit Interest Expense.
2. Credit Interest Payable.
3. Record the adjusting entry.

Expenses incurred in one fiscal period but not paid until a later fiscal period are called **accrued expenses**. At the end of a fiscal period, accrued expense is recorded by an adjusting entry. [CONCEPT: Matching Expenses with Revenue] The adjusting entry increases an expense account. The adjusting entry also increases a payable account.

Interest incurred but not yet paid is called **accrued interest expense**. On December 31, Restaurant Supply has one note payable outstanding, a 180-day, 12%, $10,000.00 note dated September 2. Restaurant Supply owes $400.00 interest for the 120 days from September 2 through December 31.

Principal × Interest Rate × Time as Fraction of Year = Accrued Interest Expense

$10,000.00 × 12% × 120/360 = $400.00

Interest Expense is debited for $400.00 to show the increase in the balance of this other expense account. The new balance of Interest Expense, $1,000.00, is the total amount of interest expense incurred during the fiscal period.

The credit to Interest Payable creates a $400.00 account balance that represents the interest owed on December 31 that will be paid in the next fiscal period.

POSTING AN ADJUSTING ENTRY FOR ACCRUED INTEREST EXPENSE

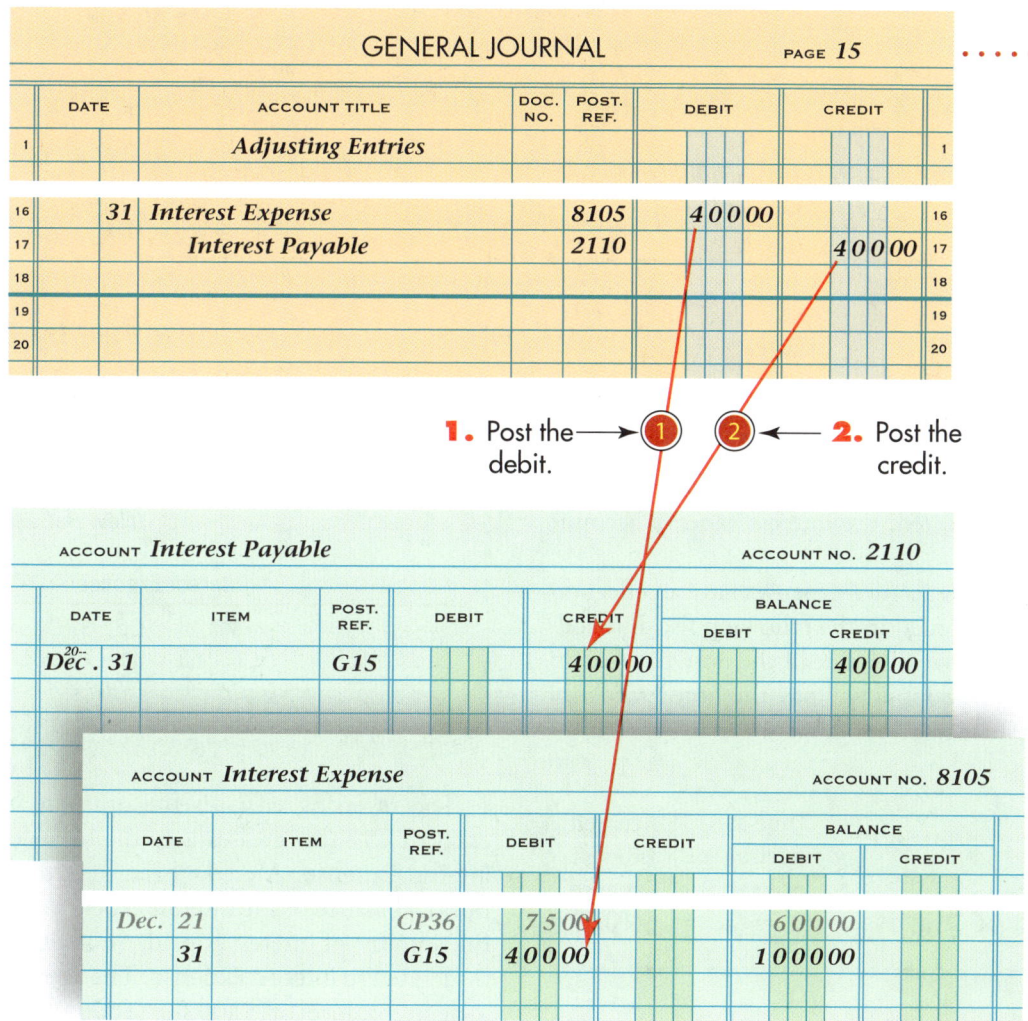

1. Post the debit.
2. Post the credit.

The adjustment for accrued interest expense planned on a work sheet is recorded as an adjusting entry in a general journal. The adjusting entry is then posted to the general ledger.

After posting, the interest payable account has a credit balance of $400.00 and will appear on the December 31 balance sheet as a current liability. This credit balance is the accrued interest expense incurred but not yet paid at the end of the year.

The interest expense account has a debit balance of $1,000.00 and will appear on the income statement for the year ended December 31 as an other expense. This amount is the total interest expense for the year.

STEPS: POSTING AN ADJUSTING ENTRY FOR ACCRUED INTEREST EXPENSE

1. Post the debit, $400.00, to *Interest Expense*.
2. Post the credit, $400.00, to *Interest Payable*.

REMEMBER

The adjusting entry for accrued interest expense affects both the income statement and the balance sheet. The income statement will report all expenses for the period even though some of the expenses have not yet been paid. The balance sheet will report all liabilities, including the accrued expenses payable. (CONCEPT: Adequate Disclosure)

Accrued Expenses   Lesson 21-2   **623**

REVERSING ENTRY FOR ACCRUED INTEREST EXPENSE

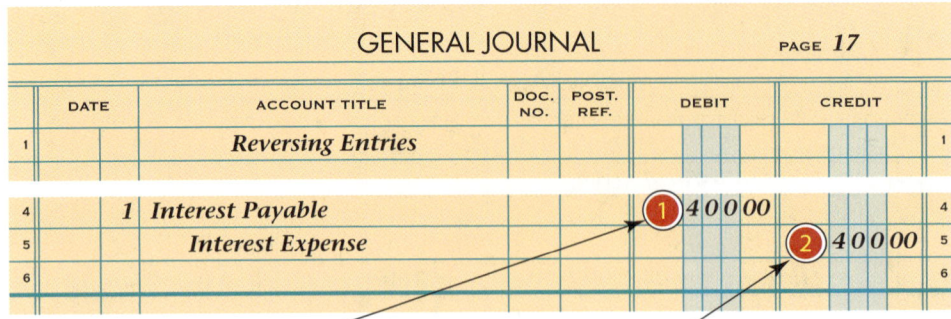

1. Debit Interest Payable. 2. Credit Interest Expense.

On December 31, Interest Expense is closed as part of the regular closing entries. Interest Expense is credited for $1,000.00 to reduce the account balance to zero. After the closing entry is posted, the interest expense account is closed.

Adjusting entries for accrued expenses have an effect on transactions to be recorded in the following fiscal period. For example, on the maturity date of the note payable on March 1, Restaurant Supply will pay the note's maturity value, including interest of $600.00.

	Interest Payable	
Jan. 1 Rev.	400.00	Dec. 31 Adj. 400.00
		(New Bal. zero)

	Interest Expense	
Dec. 31 Bal.	600.00	Dec. 31 Closing 1,000.00
Dec. 31 Adj.	400.00	Jan. 1 Rev. 400.00
		(New Bal. 400.00)

Principal	×	Interest Rate	×	Time as Fraction of Year	=	Accrued Interest Expense
$10,000.00	×	12%	×	$\frac{120}{360}$	=	$400.00

However, an adjusting entry was made to record the amount of accrued interest expense last year, $400.00. Thus, $400.00 of the $600.00 total interest expense was incurred and recorded in the previous year. The remaining $200.00 was incurred during the current year.

Determining how much of the cash paid is for accrued interest expense and how much applies to the current year is an inconvenience. To avoid this inconvenience, a reversing entry is made at the beginning of the new fiscal period.

The reversing entry is the opposite of the adjusting entry. The entry creates a credit balance of $400.00 in Interest Expense. A credit balance is the opposite of the normal balance of the interest expense account. When the full amount of interest is paid, $600.00, this amount will be debited to Interest Expense. The account will then have a debit balance of $200.00 ($600.00 debit − $400.00 credit), the amount of interest expense incurred in the new year.

The reversing entry to Interest Payable reduces that account to a zero balance. Thus, when the interest is paid, no debit entry will be required to recognize payment of the balance of Interest Payable. The total amount of interest paid will be debited to Interest Expense.

STEPS — REVERSING AN ADJUSTING ENTRY FOR ACCRUED INTEREST EXPENSE

1. Record a debit, $400.00, to *Interest Payable* in the general journal.
2. Record a credit, $400.00, to *Interest Expense*.

PAYING A NOTE PAYABLE SIGNED IN A PREVIOUS FISCAL PERIOD

March 1. Paid cash for the maturity value of the September 2 note: principal, $10,000.00, plus interest, $600.00; total, $10,600.00. Check No. 916.

The total interest, $600.00, was incurred during two fiscal periods—$400.00 during the previous fiscal period and $200.00 during the current fiscal period. The reversing entry created a $400.00 credit balance in Interest Expense. After the $600.00 debit is recorded, Interest Expense has a debit balance of $200.00, the amount of interest expense incurred during the current fiscal period.

STEPS: PAYING A NOTE PAYABLE SIGNED IN A PREVIOUS FISCAL PERIOD

1. Record a debit to *Notes Payable* in the General Debit column for the principal of the note, $10,000.00.
2. Record a debit to *Interest Expense* in the General Debit column for the total interest, $600.00.
3. Record a credit to *Cash* in the Cash Credit column for the maturity value of the note, $10,600.00.
4. Post the amounts in the General columns.

Accrued Expenses   Lesson 21-2

EFFECT OF NOT USING REVERSING ENTRIES

If Restaurant Supply did not use a reversing entry for accrued interest expense, $400.00 of the interest would be reported twice. The $400.00 amount is recorded once as an adjusting entry to Interest Expense in the previous fiscal period. The amount is recorded a second time as part of the $600.00 debit to Interest Expense in the current fiscal period when the note is paid.

The double charge might be avoided if accounting personnel are careful to divide the interest amount when the note is paid. The part of the interest chargeable to the previous fiscal period, $400.00, would be recorded as a debit in Interest Payable. The part chargeable to the current fiscal period, $200.00, is recorded as a debit in Interest Expense.

Restaurant Supply prefers to use reversing entries. Restaurant Supply's accounting personnel do not have to remember to check an entry each time a note is paid to determine if interest should be divided. Restaurant Supply, like other companies that use reversing entries, records a reversing entry whenever an adjusting entry creates a balance in an asset or liability account that initially had a zero balance.

BUSINESS STRUCTURES

Selling a Corporation's Stock

Many small corporations are owned by a few individuals, the original investors who founded the corporation. Sometimes these corporations require greater investments in order to expand to meet the needs of the marketplace or to achieve greater success. One way for a corporation to expand is to make a public offering of its stock. When a corporation issues new stock and the public buys it, the corporation receives the additional investment, minus any commissions, legal fees, and other costs of issuing stock. New offerings of stock are usually sold by investment bankers who have expertise in new stock offerings.

A public corporation which already has stock issued that is owned by the general public can also issue additional shares of stock to the public to attract funds for expansion, new product offerings, research, and many other purposes.

New stock offerings are sold in what is called *primary markets* and usually require the services of an investment banker.

A corporation's existing stock is sold by another means. Stock that has already been issued and sold may be sold again by whoever owns it. This is generally done through a stockbroker who buys and sells stock in a stock market. In the United States, the two national stock exchanges are the New York Stock Exchange (www.nyse.com) and the American Stock Exchange (www.amex.com). There are also regional stock exchanges in several large cities, such as Chicago and Philadelphia. In addition, Nasdaq (www.nasdaq.com) is a network of brokers who trade securities.

Critical Thinking

1. Do you think that issuing new stock is a guaranteed method of acquiring new funds? Why or why not?
2. Select a major corporation and study its stock listings in the newspaper or on the Internet for several days or weeks. What trends do you notice?

End of Lesson REVIEW

TERMS REVIEW

accrued expenses
accrued interest expense

AUDIT YOUR UNDERSTANDING

1. Why should accrued expenses be recorded by an adjusting entry before financial statements are prepared at the end of a fiscal period?
2. What accounts are affected, and how, by the reversing entry for accrued interest expense?

WORK TOGETHER 21-2

Journalizing and posting entries for accrued expenses

The accounting forms for this problem are in the *Working Papers*. Your instructor will guide you through the following examples.

On December 31 of the current year, Powers Corporation has one note payable outstanding, a 90-day, 12%, $2,000.00 note dated December 1.

1. Plan the adjustment on a work sheet. Label the adjustment *(h)*.
2. Journalize and post the adjusting entry for accrued interest expense on December 31. Use page 14 of a general journal.
3. Journalize and post the closing entry for interest expense on page 14 of a general journal.
4. Journalize and post the January 1 reversing entry for accrued interest expense on page 15 of a general journal.
5. Journalize the payment of cash for the maturity value of the note on March 1, Check No. 543. Use page 25 of a cash payments journal. Post the amounts in the General columns.

ON YOUR OWN 21-2

Journalizing and posting entries for accrued expenses

The accounting forms for this problem are in the *Working Papers*. Work this problem independently.

On December 31 of the current year, Latham Industries has one note payable outstanding, a 180-day, 9%, $5,000.00 note dated October 17.

1. Plan the adjustment on a work sheet. Label the adjustment *(h)*.
2. Journalize and post the adjusting entry for accrued interest expense on December 31. Use page 14 of a general journal.
3. Journalize and post the closing entry for interest expense using page 14 of a general journal.
4. Journalize and post the January 1 reversing entry for accrued interest expense on page 15 of a general journal.
5. Journalize the payment of cash for the maturity value of the note on April 15, Check No. 668. Use page 30 of a cash payments journal. Post the amounts in the General columns.

SUMMARY

After completing this chapter, you can:

1. Define accounting terms related to accrued revenue and accrued expenses.
2. Identify accounting concepts and practices related to accrued revenue and accrued expenses.
3. Record adjusting, closing, and reversing entries for accrued revenue.
4. Record adjusting, closing, and reversing entries for accrued expenses.

Go Beyond the Book
For more information go to www.C21accounting.com

EXPLORE ACCOUNTING

Annual Reports—Financial Information and More

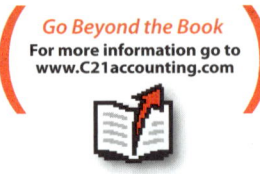

Corporations publish annual reports to communicate the results of operations to interested parties, such as stockholders, creditors, and government agencies. The typical annual report is a colorful, soft-cover brochure printed on glossy paper and 40 to 60 pages in length. Most companies post a copy of this report on their web site. The reports are grouped in two sections:

1. *Management's Analysis and Discussion.* This section provides management with an opportunity to promote the corporation. Through the use of pictures, graphs, and narrative, management can highlight the achievements of the past fiscal year and present its plans. Some corporations report on how the volunteer work of their employees is having a positive impact in their communities. Discussions of environmental and recycling programs could demonstrate how the corporation is socially responsible.

    The ultimate objective of any corporation is to increase the market price of its stock, thereby raising stockholders' investment. By "putting its best foot forward" in this section, management can increase the demand for the corporation's products and stock, thus increasing the stock's price.

2. *Financial Statements.* The financial statements section contains several items in addition to basic financial statements. Most of the additional items are required by GAAP or the Securities and Exchange Commission. As a result, these items are similar among corporations.

    a. *Notes to the Financial Statements.* The notes contain additional, detailed information about items presented on the financial statements. For example, the note related to long-term debt would include the projected loan repayments for the next five years.

    b. *Auditor's Report.* The report of the independent auditor states that a public accounting firm has tested the financial statements for accuracy and fair presentation. The report gives the reader confidence to use the financial statements to make business decisions.

    c. *Financial Analysis.* Summary financial information, such as total assets, net income, and common financial ratios, are presented for several years.

Instructions: Access an annual report using a library or the Internet and prepare a detailed outline of its contents. Summarize the major topics in management's analysis and discussion. Did management do a good job of "putting its best foot forward?" Would you recommend that a friend purchase the corporation's stock? Support your answers.

PHOTO: PHOTOGRAPHER'S CHOICE/GETTY IMAGES

21-1 APPLICATION PROBLEM

Journalizing and posting entries for accrued revenue

The accounting forms for this problem are in the *Working Papers*.
On December 31 of the current year, Velma Parts Company has one note receivable outstanding, a 120-day, 10%, $8,100.00 note dated November 6.

Instructions:
1. Plan the adjustment on a work sheet. Label the adjustment *(a)*.
2. Journalize and post the adjusting entry for accrued interest income on December 31. Use page 14 of a general journal.
3. Journalize and post the closing entry for interest income using page 14 of a general journal.
4. Journalize and post the January 1 reversing entry for accrued interest income on page 15 of a general journal.
5. Journalize the receipt of cash for the maturity value of the note on March 6, Receipt No. 457. Use page 8 of a cash receipts journal. Post the amounts in the General columns of the cash receipts journal.

21-2 APPLICATION PROBLEM

Journalizing and posting entries for accrued expenses

The accounting forms for this problem are in the *Working Papers*.
On December 31 of the current year, Delmar Plumbing Supply has one note payable outstanding, a 180-day, 10%, $12,000.00 note dated December 1.

Instructions:
1. Plan the adjustment on a work sheet. Label the adjustment *(h)*.
2. Journalize and post the adjusting entry for accrued interest expense on December 31. Use page 14 of a general journal.
3. Journalize and post the closing entry for interest expense using page 14 of a general journal.
4. Journalize and post the January 1 reversing entry for accrued interest expense on page 15 of a general journal.
5. Journalize the payment of cash for the maturity value of the note on May 30, Check No. 756. Use page 27 of a cash payments journal. Post the amounts in the General columns of the cash payments journal.

21-3 APPLICATION PROBLEM

Journalizing and posting entries for accrued expenses

The accounting forms for this problem are in the *Working Papers*.
On October 14 of the current year, Patti's Dress Shop signed a $10,000.00 note with National Bank of Columbus. The note term is 180 days at 12% interest.

Instructions:
1. Plan the adjustment on a work sheet for the fiscal year ended December 31. Label the adjustment *(h)*.
2. Journalize and post the transactions to accrue, close, and reverse interest-related accounts at the fiscal year-end. Use page 16 of a general journal for December 31 transactions and page 17 for the January 1 transactions.
3. Journalize the payment of cash for the maturity value of the note paid on April 12 with Check No. 377. Use page 23 of a cash payments journal. Post the amounts in the General columns of the cash payments journal.

21-4 MASTERY PROBLEM

Journalizing and posting entries for accrued interest revenue and expense

The accounting forms for Youngblood, Inc., are given in the *Working Papers*. The balances are recorded as of December 31 of the current year before adjusting entries. Youngblood, Inc., completed the following transactions related to notes receivable and notes payable during the current year and the following year. The first two transactions have already been journalized and posted. One note receivable and one note payable are the only notes on hand at the end of the fiscal period. Source documents are abbreviated as follows: receipt, R; check, C; note receivable, NR.

Transactions:
20X1
- Nov. 11. Accepted a 90-day, 12% note from Centre Plaza for an extension of time on their account, $900.00. NR10.
- Dec. 6. Signed a 120-day, 8% note, $7,200.00 with First American Bank. R336.

20X2
- Feb. 9. Received cash for the maturity value of NR10. R336.
- Apr. 5. Paid cash for the maturity value of the First American Bank note. C612.

Instructions:
1. Plan the adjustments on a work sheet. Label the interest income adjustment *(a)* and the interest expense adjustment *(h)*.
2. Journalize and post the adjusting entries for accrued interest income and accrued interest expense on December 31. Use page 15 of a general journal.
3. Journalize and post the closing entries for interest income and interest expense. Continue to use page 15 of a general journal.
4. Journalize and post the reversing entries for accrued interest income and accrued interest expense. Use page 16 of a general journal.
5. Journalize the receipt of cash for the maturity value of NR10. Use page 16 of a cash receipts journal. Post the amounts in the General columns of the cash receipts journal.
6. Journalize the cash payment for the maturity value of the note payable. Use page 28 of a cash payments journal. Post the amounts in the General columns of the cash payments journal.

21-5 CHALLENGE PROBLEM

Journalizing and posting entries for accrued interest revenue and expenses

The accounting forms for Blackwell Corporation are given in the *Working Papers*. The balances are recorded as of December 31 of the current year before adjusting entries. Blackwell Corporation completed the following transactions related to notes receivable and notes payable during the current year and the following year. The first two transactions have already been journalized and posted. These notes are the only notes outstanding on December 31, 20X1, the fiscal year-end.

Transactions:
20X1
- Dec. 8. Margaret Snider signed a 90-day, 18% note for an extension of time on her account, $900.00. NR56.
- 15. Signed a 180-day, 12% note with American National Bank, $10,000.00. R416.

20X2
- Mar. 8. Margaret Snider dishonored NR56, maturity value due today. M98.
- 12. Paid off the American National Bank note ahead of the maturity date. American National charges interest only for the number of days the note is outstanding, with no early payment penalty. C645.

Instructions:

1. Plan the adjustments on a work sheet. Label the interest income adjustment *(a)* and the interest expense adjustment *(h)*.
2. Journalize and post the transactions to accrue, close, and reverse interest-related accounts at the fiscal year-end. Use page 16 of a general journal for December 31 transactions and page 17 for January 1 transactions.
3. Journalize the 20X2 transactions using page 18 of a general journal and page 15 of a cash payments journal. Post the Credit column of the general journal and the amounts in the General columns of the cash payments journal.

APPLIED COMMUNICATION

Employers often screen prospective employees for written communication skills. As an applicant, you may be asked to write a short essay. Therefore, it is important for you to practice preparing documents that clearly communicate a message, demonstrate proper usage of grammar rules, and project a professional image.

Instructions: Write a one-page memo to Gerard Spikes, Controller of Jenkins Company, that gives your opinion on one of the following questions: (1) Why is a basic knowledge of accounting important for all employees of a company, even for those not directly involved in accounting? (2) Why should the company help its employees to continue their formal education by paying for one technical or college course each year?

CASE FOR CRITICAL THINKING

At the end of each fiscal period, Kimura Corporation prepares adjusting entries to record accrued interest expense. However, the company does not record reversing entries for the accrued interest expense. At the end of the current fiscal year, Kimura had a $3,000.00, 90-day, 10% note payable outstanding, signed November 1. Kimura made the following journal entries related to the note.

Signed Note Nov. 1
  Cash.................... $3,000.00
    Notes Payable $3,000.00
Adj. Entry Dec. 31
  Interest Expense 50.00
    Interest Payable.....   50.00

Closing Entry Dec. 31
  Income Summary 50.00
    Interest Expense 50.00
Paid Note Jan. 30
  Notes Payable 3,000.00
  Interest Payable........   50.00
  Interest Expense 25.00
    Cash...................   3,075.00

Isabel Lugo, an accounting supervisor, says that generally accepted accounting principles require that reversing entries be used in conjunction with adjusting entries for accrued expenses. Thus, Ms. Lugo says Kimura must begin using reversing entries for all accrued expenses. Is she correct? Do the procedures Kimura has been using result in incorrect financial statements? Explain.

ANALYZING BEST BUY'S FINANCIAL STATEMENTS

Reward Zone, Best Buy's customer loyalty program, awards discount certificates to members, based on their purchases. The value of the discount certificate must be recorded as an accrued liability until the customer redeems the certificate. Use the Sales Incentives section in the Notes to Consolidated Financial Statements on page B-16 in Best Buy's annual report in Appendix B.

Instructions

1. What account title is used to record discount certificates on the Consolidated Balance Sheets on page B-5?
2. What impact would the recorded debit have on the income statement when a discount certificate is issued?

Accounting for Accrued Revenue and Expenses

Accounting SOFTWARE

ACCRUED REVENUE AND EXPENSES

One of the most valuable assets of any business is its financial information. The actions that ensure that a business can quickly restore its access to and use its financial data is referred to as a *disaster recovery plan*. Creating a backup copy of financial data is one of the most common components of a disaster recovery plan. Peachtree has a menu option for creating a backup copy. Backup copies should be stored on a removable storage device and, preferably, stored at a remote location. Of course, after transactions are recorded in the restored backup copy, a new backup copy needs to be made.

PEACHTREE MASTERY PROBLEM 21-4
1. Open (Restore) file 21-4MP.ptb.
2. Journalize and post the adjusting entries for accrued interest income and accrued expense on December 31.
3. Journalize and post the closing entries for interest income and interest expense.
4. Journalize the post the reversing entries for accrued interest income and accrued interest expense.
5. Journalize and post the receipt of cash for the maturity value of NR10.
6. Journalize the cash payment for the maturity value of the note payable.
7. Print the December 31 to January 1 general journal, the February 9 cash receipts journal, the April 5 cash disbursements journal, and the general ledger from December 1 to April 30.

PEACHTREE CHALLENGE PROBLEM 21-5
1. Open (Restore) file 21-5CP.ptb.
2. Journalize and post the adjusting, closing, and reversing entries for interest-related accounts.
3. Journalize and post the 2006 transactions.
4. Print the general journal, the cash receipts journal, the cash disbursements journal, and the general ledger.

ACCRUED REVENUE AND EXPENSES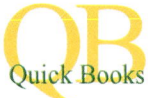

When using accounting software, critical financial information about the company is stored in an electronic file. QuickBooks allows the user to make a backup copy of the company's data. If there is a problem with the original file, the backup copy can be used. Any transactions recorded since the last backup was made will be lost. Therefore, if any entries are recorded, a backup copy should be made at the end of the day.

It is important to store the backup file on something other than the computer on which the original file is stored. It is also preferable to keep the removable storage device at a remote location.

QUICKBOOKS MASTERY PROBLEM 21-4
1. Open the Youngblood Inc file if it is not already open.
2. Journalize the reversing entries for accrued interest income and accrued interest expense as of January 1, 20X2.
3. Use the Make Deposits window to record the receipt of payment from Centre Plaza.
4. Print a journal report.

QUICKBOOKS CHALLENGE PROBLEM 21-5
1. Open the Blackwell Corporation file if it is not already open.
2. Journalize the adjusting entries for accrued interest income and expense as of December 31, 20X1.
3. Journalize the reversing entries for interest income and expense as of January 1, 20X2.
4. Calculate the maturity value of NR56. Record the dishonored note using the Make General Journal Entries window.
5. Calculate the maturity value of the note from First National Bank as of March 12, 20X2, and record the payment.
6. Print the Journal report using December 31, 20X1 and March 31, 20X2 as the dates.

REPORTING FINANCIAL INFORMATION

Annual reports of many public companies contain summary financial information for 10 years. This information provides investors with a rich history of the company's operating results and financial strength.

Absorbing 10 years of financial information can be overwhelming if that information is presented in a table. Charts provide a better approach of reporting this information. Line graphs are particularly adept at indicating trends.

Electronic spreadsheets provide a variety of tools to modify the chart's appearance. From adding titles to changing the scale of an axis, you can enhance the chart to ensure that the story of the financial information is clearly communicated.

OPTIONAL SPREADSHEET ACTIVITY
Open the F21-OPT Excel data file. Follow the step-by-step instructions in the Instructions work sheet. This problem is not related to a specific problem in the textbook; however, it is related to the Explore Accounting feature in this chapter.

ENTRIES FOR ACCRUED REVENUE AND EXPENSES

To complete the accounting cycle, adjusting entries are entered and verified for accuracy. The financial statements are generated and then closing entries are generated and posted by the software. On the first day of the next fiscal period, some adjusting entries for accrued revenue and expense items affecting the next fiscal period are reversed by recording reversing entries.

Closing entries are made to close all temporary accounts at the end of the accounting period. *Automated Accounting* automatically prepares and posts closing entries.

To generate closing entries:
1. Choose Generate Closing Journal Entries from the Options menu.
2. Click Yes to generate the closing entries.
3. The general journal will appear, containing the journal entries.
4. Check the entries for accuracy, then click the Post button.
5. To display a post-closing trial balance report:
   a. Click on the Reports toolbar button, or choose the Reports Selection menu item from the Reports menu.
   b. Select the Ledger Reports option button from the Report Selection dialog box.
   c. Choose Trial Balance report.

Revenue and expense items that affect two fiscal periods are adjusted at the end of a fiscal period and then reversed at the beginning of the next fiscal period. Reversing entries are recorded in the general journal the same way as adjusting entries. Use *Rev.Ent.* as the reference.

AUTOMATED ACCOUNTING MASTERY PROBLEM 21-4
Open file F21-4.AA8. Display the problem instructions and complete the problem.

CHAPTER 22

End-of-Fiscal-Period Work for a Corporation

OBJECTIVES

After studying Chapter 22, you will be able to:

1. Define accounting terms related to financial statements for a merchandising business organized as a corporation.
2. Identify accounting concepts and practices related to financial statements and end-of-fiscal-period entries for a merchandising business organized as a corporation.
3. Plan end-of-fiscal-period adjustments for a merchandising business organized as a corporation.
4. Calculate federal income tax, plan an adjustment for federal income tax expense, and complete a work sheet.
5. Prepare and analyze an income statement for a merchandising business organized as a corporation.
6. Prepare a statement of stockholders' equity for a merchandising business organized as a corporation.
7. Prepare and analyze a balance sheet for a merchandising business organized as a corporation.
8. Record adjusting, closing, and reversing entries for a merchandising business organized as a corporation.

KEY TERMS

- long-term liabilities
- working capital
- current ratio

Point Your Browser
www.C21accounting.com

ACCOUNTING IN THE REAL WORLD

Chico's

Store Efficiency Fuels Chico's Growth

Chico's FAS, Inc., is a specialty retailer of private-label, sophisticated, casual-to-dressy clothing. The company focuses on women who are 35 years old and up, with moderate to higher incomes. This focus has enabled the company to achieve dramatic growth since opening its first store in 1983. With sales of $1,646,482,000 in fiscal year 2006, the company now operates over 920 stores under its Chico's and White House | Black Market brands.

Chico's sales growth has also been achieved by improving the efficiency of each store. Similar to other retail businesses, Chico's tracks the change in its total sales per store. This financial ratio, often referred to as same-store sales, is calculated by dividing the change in sales by the prior period's sales. Chico's achieved same-store sales growth of 2.1% in its fiscal year 2006.

Chico's takes this analysis a step further by measuring its sales per square foot. Average net sales per selling square foot grew from below $700 in fiscal year 1999 to over $950 per square foot in fiscal year 2006.

Critical Thinking

1. Suggest three steps a clothing retailer can take to increase its sales per square foot.
2. What measure could Chico's managers use to evaluate the efficiency of its store employees?

Source: www.chicos.com

INTERNET ACTIVITY

Fiscal Year End

Go to the homepage for Home Depot (www.homedepot.com) and Lowe's (www.lowes.com).

Instructions

1. List the last day of the fiscal period for each company.
2. Are the dates similar for both companies? Why might these two companies have a similar year end?

LESSON 22-1

Preparing a Work Sheet for a Corporation

PREPARING FINANCIAL STATEMENTS

The preparation of financial statements begins with the work sheet. Account titles and balances are entered on the work sheet. Any adjustments to account balances are entered in the Adjustments columns. Restaurant Supply records adjustments affecting several accounts, including notes receivable, notes payable, allowance for uncollectible accounts, merchandise inventory, supplies, and depreciation. Since Restaurant Supply is a corporation, an adjustment is also planned for federal income tax expense.

The completed work sheet is used to prepare the financial statements. The income statement is prepared from amounts in the Income Statement columns of the work sheet. Restaurant Supply uses ratios to analyze its performance relative to industry standards and prior year's performance.

The amount of net income, selected balance sheet accounts, and other accounting information is used to prepare the statement of stockholders' equity. Summary amounts on this statement and account balances in the work sheet's Balance Sheet columns are used to prepare a balance sheet. Restaurant Supply uses ratios to evaluate its financial strength relative to expected measures.

In preparation for recording transactions during the next period, adjusting entries are journalized to record the work sheet adjustments in the accounts. After recording closing and reversing entries, the accounts are ready to record transactions for the next fiscal period. Businesses use work sheets to plan adjustments and provide information needed to prepare financial statements. Restaurant Supply may prepare a work sheet at any time financial statements are needed. However, Restaurant Supply always prepares a work sheet and financial statements at the end of a fiscal year. [CONCEPT: Accounting Period Cycle]

CHARACTER COUNTS

The Newspaper Test

A code of conduct should provide employees with a guide for making an ethical decision. The ethical model presented in Chapter 2 provides employees with a structured method of evaluating all the implications of an action. Yet, even with these aids, employees can still find it difficult to make a decision.

Some companies provide their employees with a simple set of questions.

The most popular question is: "Would I be comfortable if my actions were reported in the newspaper?" If employees are uncomfortable with their actions becoming public knowledge, chances are their actions are unethical. At the very least, the employees should realize that they should consult their company's ethics officer and legal department.

Instructions

Use the Internet to access the code of conduct for Lockheed Martin, the Coca-Cola Company, and Shell Oil Company. Prepare a list of questions that could help you determine if an action is ethical.

USE OF A WORK SHEET

Entering a Trial Balance on a Work Sheet
To prepare a work sheet, a trial balance is first entered in the Trial Balance columns. All general ledger accounts are listed in the same order as they appear in the general ledger. Trial Balance columns are totaled to prove equality of debits and credits.

Planning Adjustments on a Work Sheet
Some general ledger accounts need to be brought up to date before financial statements are prepared. Accounts are brought up to date by planning and entering adjustments on a work sheet. Two methods are used to determine the amount of each adjustment.

For some accounts, the calculated amount of the increase in the account is also the amount used in the work sheet adjustment. These adjustments include:

1. Interest Income
2. Uncollectible Accounts Expense
3. Depreciation Expense—Office Equipment
4. Depreciation Expense—Store Equipment
5. Interest Expense

Other accounts require calculating the end-of-period balance. The current balance is subtracted from the calculated end-of-period account balance to determine the amount of the adjustment. Thus, the work sheet adjustment brings the account balance up to date. These adjustments include:

1. Merchandise Inventory
2. Supplies
3. Prepaid Insurance
4. Federal Income Tax Expense

Examples of both types of adjustments are shown on the following page. Adjustments generally are made in the order that accounts are listed on a work sheet.

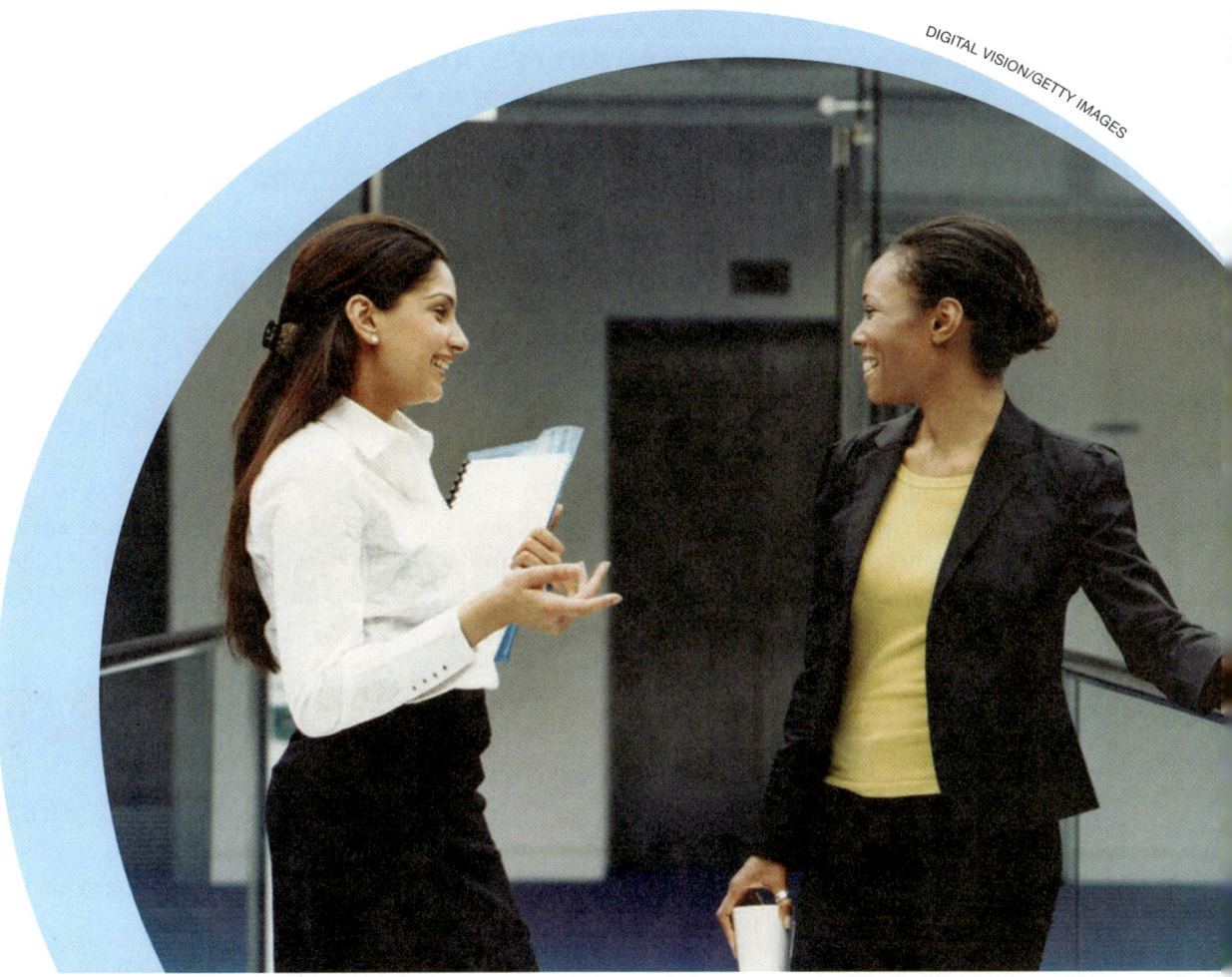

INTEREST INCOME ADJUSTMENT

1. Debit Interest Receivable

ACCOUNT TITLE	TRIAL BALANCE DEBIT	TRIAL BALANCE CREDIT	ADJUSTMENTS DEBIT	ADJUSTMENTS CREDIT
4 Interest Receivable			(a) 20 00	
51 Interest Income		136 00		(a) 20 00

2. Credit Interest Income

Interest income earned during the current fiscal period but not yet received needs to be recorded. Two accounts are used for the adjustment for accrued interest income: Interest Receivable and Interest Income. An analysis of Restaurant Supply's adjustment for accrued interest income is described in Chapter 21. The estimate of accrued interest income is the amount used in the work sheet adjustment.

STEPS — PLANNING A WORK SHEET ADJUSTMENT FOR INTEREST INCOME

1. Enter the accrued interest income amount, $20.00, in the Adjustments Debit column on the *Interest Receivable* line of the work sheet. Label the adjustment *(a)*.

2. Enter the same amount, $20.00, in the Adjustments Credit column on the *Interest Income* line. Label the adjustment *(a)*.

SUPPLIES ADJUSTMENT

1. Credit Supplies

ACCOUNT TITLE	TRIAL BALANCE DEBIT	TRIAL BALANCE CREDIT	ADJUSTMENTS DEBIT	ADJUSTMENTS CREDIT
8 Supplies	8 745 25			(d) 7 837 00
47 Supplies Expense			(d) 7 837 00	

2. Debit Supplies Expense

The balance of Supplies in the trial balance, $8,745.25, is the cost of supplies on hand at the beginning of the year plus the supplies purchased during the year. The supplies on hand on December 31 are counted and determined to be $908.25. To bring the account up to date, the balance of Supplies needs to be decreased by $7,837.00 ($8,745.25 − $908.25), the cost of supplies used during the year. Supplies Expense is debited, and Supplies is credited for the amount of the decrease.

STEPS — PLANNING A WORK SHEET ADJUSTMENT FOR SUPPLIES

1. Enter the amount of supplies used, $7,837.00, in the adjustments credit column on the *Supplies* line of the work sheet. Label the adjustment *(d)*.

2. Enter the same amount, $7,837.00, in the Adjustments Debit column on the *Supplies Expense* line of the work sheet. Label the adjustment *(d)*.

FEDERAL INCOME TAX ADJUSTMENT

ACCOUNT TITLE	TRIAL BALANCE		ADJUSTMENTS	
	DEBIT	CREDIT	DEBIT	CREDIT
18 *Federal Income Tax Payable*				(i) 4 5 7 8 18
54 *Federal Income Tax Expense*	8 0 0 0 0 00		(i) 4 5 7 8 18	

2. Credit Federal Income Tax Payable

1. Debit Federal Income Tax Expense

Detailed instructions for preparing the federal income tax adjustment were presented in Chapter 14. The first step is to calculate the corporation's net income before federal income tax. This procedure can be summarized in four steps:

1. Complete all adjustments other than federal income taxes.
2. Extend all the accounts except Federal Income Tax Expense to the Income Statement or Balance Sheet columns.
3. Calculate temporary totals of the Income Statement accounts in the Income Statement columns.
4. The difference between the two Income Statement columns, excluding the estimated federal income taxes, is the net income or loss before income taxes.

The amount of federal income tax is calculated using tax rates provided by the Internal Revenue Service. The tax rate varies, depending on the amount of net income earned. Restaurant Supply's net income before income tax expense is $259,815.85. The tax rates are given in the table on the next page.

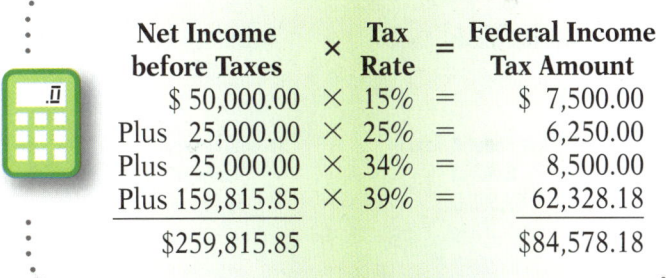

Net Income before Taxes	×	Tax Rate	=	Federal Income Tax Amount
$ 50,000.00	×	15%	=	$ 7,500.00
Plus 25,000.00	×	25%	=	6,250.00
Plus 25,000.00	×	34%	=	8,500.00
Plus 159,815.85	×	39%	=	62,328.18
$259,815.85				$84,578.18

The estimated tax payments already made are subtracted from the total federal income tax expense to calculate the adjustment for federal income tax expense.

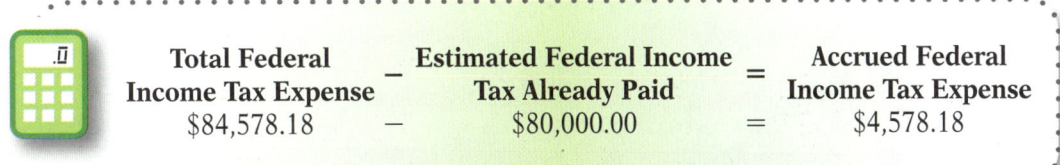

Total Federal Income Tax Expense − Estimated Federal Income Tax Already Paid = Accrued Federal Income Tax Expense
$84,578.18 − $80,000.00 = $4,578.18

STEPS PLANNING A WORK SHEET ADJUSTMENT FOR FEDERAL INCOME TAX EXPENSE

① Enter the federal income tax expense adjustment amount, $4,578.18, in the Adjustments Debit column on the *Federal Income Tax Expense* line of the work sheet. Label the adjustment *(i)*.

② Enter the same amount, $4,578.18, in the Adjustments Credit column on the *Federal Income Tax Payable* line of the work sheet. Label the adjustment *(i)*.

STOCKBYTE/GETTY IMAGES

Preparing a Work Sheet for a Corporation

15% of net income before taxes, zero to $50,000.00 (15% tax on the *first* $50,000.00 of net income)
Plus 25% of net income before taxes, $50,000.00 to $75,000.00 (25% tax on the *next* $25,000.00 of net income)
Plus 34% of net income before taxes, $75,000.00 to $100,000.00 (34% tax on the *next* $25,000.00 of net income)
Plus 39% of net income before taxes, $100,000.00 to $335,000.00 (39% tax on the *next* $225,000.00 of net income)
Plus 34% of net income before taxes over $335,000.00 (34% tax on net income *above* $335,000.00)

Step 1:
| First Net Income Amount | × | First Tax Rate | = | Federal Income Tax on First $50,000.00 of Net Income |
| $50,000.00 | × | 15% | = | $7,500.00 |

Step 2:
| Second Net Income Amount | × | Second Tax Rate | = | Federal Income Tax on Next $25,000.00 of Net Income |
| $25,000.00 | × | 25% | = | $6,250.00 |

Step 3:
| Third Net Income Amount | × | Third Tax Rate | = | Federal Income Tax on Next $25,000.00 of Net Income |
| $25,000.00 | × | 34% | = | $8,500.00 |

Step 4:
| Total Net Income | − | Lowest Dollar Amount of Fourth Tax Range | = | Amount of Net Income to Which Fourth Tax Rate Is Applied |
| $259,815.85 | − | $100,000.00 | = | $159,815.85 |

Step 5:
| Fourth Net Income Amount | × | Fourth Tax Rate | = | Federal Income Tax on Next $159,815.85 of Net Income |
| $159,815.85 | × | 39% | = | $62,328.18 |

Step 6:
| First Federal Tax Amount | + | Second Federal Tax Amount | + | Third Federal Tax Amount | + | Fourth Federal Tax Amount | = | Total Federal Tax Amount |
| $7,500.00 | + | $6,250.00 | + | $8,500.00 | + | $62,328.18 | = | $84,578.18 |

PURESTOCK/GETTY IMAGES

COMPLETING A WORK SHEET

1. Total the income statement and balance sheet columns.

ACCOUNT TITLE	TRIAL BALANCE DEBIT	TRIAL BALANCE CREDIT	ADJUSTMENTS DEBIT	ADJUSTMENTS CREDIT	INCOME STATEMENT DEBIT	INCOME STATEMENT CREDIT	BALANCE SHEET DEBIT	BALANCE SHEET CREDIT	
14 Notes Payable		10 000 00						10 000 00	14
15 Interest Payable				(h) 400 00				400 00	15
16 Accounts Payable		24 950 35						24 950 35	16
17 Employee Income Tax Payable		2 049 00						2 049 00	17
18 Federal Income Tax Payable				(i) 4 578 18				4 578 18	18
52 Interest Expense	600 00		(h) 400 00		1 000 00				52
53 Loss on Plant Assets	1 400 00				1 400 00				53
54 Federal Income Tax Expense	80 000 00		(i) 4 578 18		84 578 18				54
55	2264 522 37	2264 522 37	58 198 48	58 198 48	1957 009 33	2132 247 00	346 274 52	1710 368 5	55
56 Net Income after Federal Income Tax					175 237 67			175 237 67	56
57					2132 247 00	2132 247 00	346 274 52	346 274 52	57

2. Calculate and enter the net income after federal income tax.

5. Draw double lines.

4. Calculate the column totals.

3. Extend the net income amount.

After the adjustment for federal income tax expense has been recorded, the work sheet is ready to be completed. Income Statement column totals are used to calculate net income after federal income tax. Restaurant Supply's completed work sheet is shown on the following two pages.

STEPS COMPLETING A WORK SHEET

1 Total the Income Statement and Balance Sheet columns.

2 Write the words *Net Income after Federal Income Tax* on line 56 of the work sheet. Calculate and enter the net income after federal income tax, $175,237.67, in the Income Statement Debit column on this new line of the work sheet.

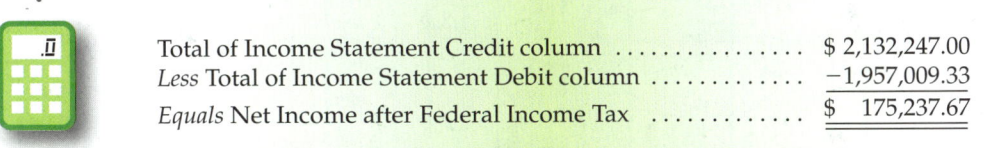

Total of Income Statement Credit column	$ 2,132,247.00
Less Total of Income Statement Debit column	−1,957,009.33
Equals Net Income after Federal Income Tax	$ 175,237.67

3 Extend the net income after federal income tax amount, $175,237.67, to the Balance Sheet Credit column.

4 Total the four Income Statement and Balance Sheet columns. Determine that the totals of each pair of columns are in balance.

5 Rule double lines across the Income Statement and Balance Sheet columns to show that the totals have been verified as correct.

Preparing a Work Sheet for a Corporation Lesson 22-1 **641**

COMPLETED WORK SHEET

Restaurant Supply Co.
Work Sheet
For Year Ended December 31, 20--

#	ACCOUNT TITLE	TRIAL BALANCE DEBIT	TRIAL BALANCE CREDIT	ADJUSTMENTS DEBIT	ADJUSTMENTS CREDIT	INCOME STATEMENT DEBIT	INCOME STATEMENT CREDIT	BALANCE SHEET DEBIT	BALANCE SHEET CREDIT
1	Cash	11203 10						11203 10	
2	Petty Cash	250 00						250 00	
3	Notes Receivable	2000 00						2000 00	
4	Interest Receivable			(a) 20 00				20 00	
5	Accounts Receivable	78340 30						78340 30	
6	Allowance for Uncollectible Accts.		280 00		(b)12873 30				13153 30
7	Merchandise Inventory	142536 20		(c) 5290 00				147826 20	
8	Supplies	8745 25			(d) 7837 00			908 25	
9	Prepaid Insurance	13800 00			(e) 11600 00			2200 00	
10	Office Equipment	31980 32						31980 32	
11	Accum. Depr.—Office Equipment		18760 00		(f) 6350 00				25110 00
12	Store Equipment	41546 35						41546 35	
13	Accum. Depr.—Store Equipment		16049 00		(g) 9250 00				25299 00
14	Notes Payable		10000 00						10000 00
15	Interest Payable				(h) 400 00				400 00
16	Accounts Payable		24950 35						24950 35
17	Employee Income Tax Payable		2049 00						2049 00
18	Federal Income Tax Payable				(i) 4578 18				4578 18
19	Social Security Tax Payable		1767 76						1767 76
20	Medicare Tax Payable		427 24						427 24
21	Sales Tax Payable		4980 00						4980 00
22	Unemployment Tax Payable—Federal		38 00						38 00
23	Unemployment Tax Payable—State		244 00						244 00
24	Health Insurance Premiums Payable		560 00						560 00
25	Dividends Payable		7500 00						7500 00
26	Capital Stock		150000 00						150000 00
27	Retained Earnings		34980 02						34980 02
28	Dividends	30000 00						30000 00	
29	Income Summary				(c) 5290 00		5290 00		
30	Sales		210989 43				210989 43		
31	Sales Discount	6958 20				6958 20			

#	Account Title	Trial Balance Debit	Trial Balance Credit	Adjustments Debit	Adjustments Credit	Income Statement Debit	Income Statement Credit	Balance Sheet Debit	Balance Sheet Credit
32	Sales Returns and Allowances	2405940				2405940			
33	Purchases	12123 21 50				12123 21 50			
34	Purchases Discount		1109420				1109420		
35	Purchases Returns and Allowances		514250				514250		
36	Advertising Expense	2432225				2432225			
37	Cash Short and Over	1423				1423			
38	Credit Card Fee Expense	1534244				1534244			
39	Depr. Expense—Office Equipment			(f) 635000		635000			
40	Depr. Expense—Store Equipment			(g) 925000		925000			
41	Insurance Expense			(e) 1160000		1160000			
42	Miscellaneous Expense	3002443				3002443			
43	Payroll Taxes Expense	2931005				2931005			
44	Rent Expense	6000000				6000000			
45	Repair Expense	454313				454313			
46	Salary Expense	39384428				39384428			
47	Supplies Expense			(d) 783700		783700			
48	Uncollectible Accounts Expense			(b) 1287330		1287330			
49	Utilities Expense	2138094				2138094			
50	Gain on Plant Assets		67000				67000		
51	Interest Income		13600		(a) 2000		15600		
52	Interest Expense	60000		(h) 40000		100000			
53	Loss on Plant Assets	140000				140000			
54	Federal Income Tax Expense	8000000		(i) 457818		8457818			
55		22645 22 37	22645 22 37	5819848	5819848	195700933	213224700	171036 85	
56	Net Income after Federal Income Tax					1752 37 67			1752 37 67
57						213224700	213224700	34627452	34627452

Preparing a Work Sheet for a Corporation

End of Lesson REVIEW

AUDIT YOUR UNDERSTANDING

1. Describe the two methods used to determine the amount of an adjustment on a work sheet.
2. Summarize the four steps to calculate net income before federal income taxes.

WORK TOGETHER 22-1

Preparing a work sheet for a corporation

Webster Corporation's work sheet is given in the *Working Papers*. Your instructor will guide you through the following example.

1. For the current year ended December 31, record the adjustments on the work sheet using the following information. Do not total the Adjustments columns.

Accrued interest income	$ 275.00
Uncollectible accounts expense estimated as 1.5% of sales on account.	
Sales on account for year, $490,000.00.	
Merchandise inventory	90,116.30
Supplies inventory	252.08
Value of prepaid insurance	3,071.60
Annual depreciation expense—office equipment	2,800.00
Annual depreciation expense—store equipment	1,700.60
Accrued interest expense	555.16

2. Using the tax table shown in this chapter, calculate federal income tax expense and record the income tax adjustment on the work sheet. Complete the work sheet. Save your work to complete Work Together 22-2.

ON YOUR OWN 22-1

Preparing a work sheet for a corporation

Osborn Corporation's work sheet is given in the *Working Papers*. Work this problem independently.

1. For the current year ended December 31, record the adjustments on the work sheet using the following information. Do not total the Adjustments columns.

Accrued interest income	$ 160.00
Uncollectible accounts expense estimated as 0.8% of sales on account.	
Sales on account for year, $914,000.00.	
Merchandise inventory	197,992.26
Supplies inventory	802.50
Value of prepaid insurance	1,200.00
Annual depreciation expense—office equipment	6,440.00
Annual depreciation expense—store equipment	8,250.00
Accrued interest expense	300.00

2. Using the tax table shown in this chapter, calculate federal income tax expense and record the income tax adjustment on the work sheet. Complete the work sheet. Save your work to complete On Your Own 22-2.

LESSON 22-2

Preparing an Income Statement

INCOME STATEMENT

Restaurant Supply Co.
Income Statement
For Year Ended December 31, 20--

				% OF NET SALES
Operating Revenue:				
Sales			21098930	
Less: Sales Discount		695820		
Sales Returns and Allowances		2405940	3101760	
Net Sales				20788 76 70	100.0
Cost of Merchandise Sold:				
Merchandise Inventory, Jan. 1, 20--			14253620	
Purchases		121232150		
Less: Purchases Discount	1109420			
Purchases Returns and Allow.	514250	1623670		
Net Purchases			119608480	
Total Cost of Mdse. Avail. for Sale			133862100	
Less Mdse. Inventory, Dec. 31, 20--			14782620	
Cost of Merchandise Sold				119079480	57.3
Gross Profit on Operations				88808190	42.7
Operating Expenses:				
Advertising Expense			2432225	
Cash Short and Over			1423	
Credit Card Fee Expense			1534244	
Depr. Expense—Office Equipment			635000	
Depr. Expense—Store Equipment			925000	
Insurance Expense			1160000	
Miscellaneous Expense			3002443	
Payroll Taxes Expense			2931005	
Rent Expense			6000000	
Repair Expense			454313	
Salary Expense			39384428	
Supplies Expense			783700	
Uncollectible Accounts Expense			1287330	
Utilities Expense			2138094	
Total Operating Expenses				62669205	30.1
Income from Operations				26138985	12.6
Other Revenue:				
Gain on Plant Assets			67000	
Interest Income			15600	
Total Other Income				82600	
Other Expenses:				
Interest Expense			100000	
Loss on Plant Assets			140000	
Total Other Expenses				240000	
Net Deduction					157400	0.1
Net Income before Federal Income Tax				25981585	12.5
Less Federal Income Tax Expense				8457818	
Net Income after Federal Income Tax				17523767	

USES OF AN INCOME STATEMENT

An income statement reports the financial progress of a business during a fiscal period. [CONCEPT: Accounting Period Cycle] Revenue, cost of merchandise sold, gross profit on operations, operating expenses, and net income or net loss are reported on an income statement. [CONCEPT: Adequate Disclosure] To help make decisions about current and future operations, Restaurant Supply also analyzes relationships between revenue and expense items. Based on this analysis, Restaurant Supply reports component percentages for all major income statement items.

Restaurant Supply's income statement is very similar to Hobby Shack's income statement, shown in Part 2. Both companies report net sales, net purchases, gross profit on operations, and income from operations. However, Restaurant Supply has two additional types of accounts that are reported on the income statement: (1) gains and losses from the sale of plant assets and (2) accruals for interest receivable and payable. These accounts are reported after income from operations.

STEPS — NEW ELEMENTS IN THE INCOME STATEMENT FOR RESTAURANT SUPPLY

1. Income from operations, $261,389.85, is the income earned only from normal business activities. Restaurant Supply's normal business activities are selling kitchen equipment and supplies. Revenue from the sales of plant assets, $670.00, and interest earned on notes receivable, $156.00, are not normal operating activities. Therefore, these accounts are reported after income from operations in a section labeled *Other Revenue*.

2. The interest expense on notes payable, $1,000.00, and the loss from the sales of plant assets, $1,400.00, are not normal operating activities. Therefore, these accounts are reported after income from operations in a section labeled *Other Expenses*.

3. The difference between other revenue and other expenses, $1,574.00, is reported as a net addition or net deduction. The difference is added to or deducted from income from operations to determine the net income before federal income tax.

GLOBAL PERSPECTIVE

International Quality Standards

The quality of products is a major concern for industry, especially when trading those products among nations. In order for some products to be used in other nations, they must be standardized. In this sense, a standard is a technical specification or other precise criteria used consistently in the production of a product.

Companies who intend to sell their products globally must produce them in compliance with the standards set for the industry. International standardization has been established for many fields, including information processing and communications, textiles, packaging, energy production, shipbuilding, and banking and financial services. Standardization will continue to grow in importance for all sectors of business activity.

Critical Thinking

1. How would your company benefit from international quality standards if it were buying the same product from different vendors in different countries?
2. Could meeting international quality standards give a company a competitive advantage?

646   Chapter 22   End-of-Fiscal-Period Work for a Corporation

ANALYZING AN INCOME STATEMENT

Income Statement Items	Acceptable Component Percentages	Actual Component Percentages
Net sales	100.0%	100.0%
Cost of merchandise sold	not more than 58.0%	57.3%
Gross profit on operations	not less than 42.0%	42.7%
Total operating expenses	not more than 35.0%	30.1%
Income from operations	not less than 7.0%	12.6%
Net deduction	not more than 0.1%	0.1%
Net income before federal income tax	not less than 6.9%	12.5%

For a business to determine whether it is progressing satisfactorily, results of operations are compared with industry standards and/or previous fiscal periods. By analyzing revenues, costs, and expenses, management can gain information that it can use to improve future operations.

The percentage relationship between one financial statement item and the total that includes that item is known as a *component percentage*. Restaurant Supply prepares component percentages for six major items on its income statement, as shown in the illustration. Restaurant Supply uses net sales as the base for calculating component percentages.

The amount of each item on the income statement is divided by the amount of net sales. Thus, each component percentage shows the percentage that item is of net sales. For example, the cost of merchandise sold component percentage indicates that Restaurant Supply spent 57.3 cents out of each $1.00 of sales for the merchandise sold.

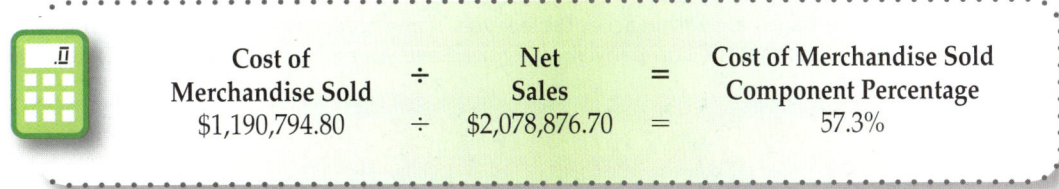

Cost of Merchandise Sold ÷ Net Sales = Cost of Merchandise Sold Component Percentage
$1,190,794.80 ÷ $2,078,876.70 = 57.3%

Acceptable Component Percentages

Based on comparisons with industry standards as well as previous accounting periods, Restaurant Supply has determined acceptable component percentages for each major item of cost and expense on its income statement.

If the component percentage of any cost or expense item for a fiscal period exceeds the acceptable percentage, that cost or expense is reviewed further to determine the reason. After determining the reason why a cost or expense exceeded the acceptable percentage, ways are sought to bring the expense within acceptable limits.

FOR YOUR INFORMATION

FYI

Component percentages are not calculated for federal income tax expense and net income after federal income tax. Corporations do not have much control over the amount of federal income taxes to be paid. Thus, the net income before federal income tax is the best measure the corporation has to assess its profitability.

End of Lesson REVIEW

AUDIT YOUR UNDERSTANDING

1. Why are other revenue and other expenses reported separately from sales, cost of merchandise sold, and operating expenses on the income statement?
2. What information is shown by component percentages on an income statement?

WORK TOGETHER 22-2

Preparing an income statement for a corporation

The completed work sheet for Webster Corporation and a blank income statement form are given in the *Working Papers*. Your instructor will guide you through the following examples.

1. Prepare an income statement for the current year. Calculate and record the following component percentages: (a) cost of merchandise sold; (b) gross profit on operations; (c) total operating expenses; (d) income from operations; (e) net addition or deduction resulting from other revenue and expenses; and (f) net income before federal income tax. Round percentage calculations to the nearest 0.1%.
2. The acceptable component percentages are given in the *Working Papers*. Analyze the income statement by determining if component percentages are within acceptable levels. If any component percentage is not within an acceptable level, suggest steps that the company should take. Save your work to complete Work Together 22-3.

ON YOUR OWN 22-2

Preparing an income statement for a corporation

The completed work sheet you prepared for Osborn Corporation and a blank income statement form are given in the *Working Papers*. Work this problem independently.

1. Prepare an income statement for the current year. Calculate and record the following component percentages: (a) cost of merchandise sold; (b) gross profit on operations; (c) total operating expenses; (d) income from operations; (e) net addition or deduction resulting from other revenue and expenses; and (f) net income before federal income tax. Round percentage calculations to the nearest 0.1%.
2. The acceptable component percentages are given in the *Working Papers*. Analyze the income statement by determining if component percentages are within acceptable levels. If any component percentage is not within an acceptable level, suggest steps that the company should take. Save your work to complete On Your Own 22-3.

LESSON 22-3
Preparing a Statement of Stockholders' Equity and Balance Sheet

STATEMENT OF STOCKHOLDERS' EQUITY

1. **Write Heading** → ① Restaurant Supply Co.
Statement of Stockholders' Equity
For Year Ended December 31, 20--

2. **Prepare Capital Stock Section** → ②

3. **Prepare Retained Earnings Section** → ③

Capital Stock:			
$1.00 Per Share			
January 1, 20--, 15,000 Shares Issued		15 000 00	
Issued during Current Year, None		0 00	
Balance, December 31, 20--, 15,000 Shares Issued			15 000 00
Retained Earnings:			
Balance, January 1, 20--		34 980 02	
Net Income after Federal Income Tax for 20--	17 523 767		
Less Dividends Declared during 20--	3 000 000		
Net Increase during 20--		14 523 767	
Balance, December 31, 20--			180 217 69
Total Stockholders' Equity, December 31, 20--			195 217 69

The statement of stockholders' equity shows changes in a corporation's ownership for a fiscal period. A statement of stockholders' equity contains two major sections: (1) capital stock and (2) retained earnings.

The capital stock section reports the amount of capital stock issued at the start of the year and any shares issued during the year. Information about the par value and the number of shares is also presented.

The lower section of the statement reports the changes in retained earnings. Net income after federal income taxes increases retained earnings. In contrast, dividends reduce retained earnings. The net difference of these amounts is added to beginning retained earnings to calculate the balance at the fiscal year end.

Detailed instructions for preparing the statement of stockholders' equity were presented in Chapter 15 and are summarized below.

STEPS PREPARING A STATEMENT OF STOCKHOLDERS' EQUITY

① Write the heading: company name, *Restaurant Supply Co.*; statement name, *Statement of Stockholders' Equity*; and fiscal period, *For Year Ended December 31, 20--*, in the statement heading.

② Use information in the accounting records and account balances on the work sheet to prepare the capital stock section of the statement.

③ Use account balances on the work sheet and the amount of net income after federal income tax reported on the income statement to prepare the retained earnings section of the statement.

BALANCE SHEET

Restaurant Supply Co.
Balance Sheet
December 31, 20--

Assets			
Current Assets:			
Cash		11 203 10	
Petty Cash		250 00	
Notes Receivable		2 000 00	
Interest Receivable		20 00	
Accounts Receivable	78 340 30		
Less Allowance for Uncollectible Accounts	13 153 30	65 187 00	
Merchandise Inventory		147 826 20	
Supplies		908 25	
Prepaid Insurance		2 200 00	
Total Current Assets			229 594 55
Plant Assets:			
Office Equipment	31 980 32		
Less Accumulated Depreciation—Office Equipment	25 110 00	6 870 32	
Store Equipment	41 546 35		
Less Accumulated Depreciation—Store Equipment	25 299 00	16 247 35	
Total Plant Assets			23 117 67
Total Assets			252 712 22
Liabilities			
Current Liabilities:			
Notes Payable		10 000 00	
Interest Payable		400 00	
Accounts Payable		24 950 35	
Employee Income Tax Payable		2 049 00	
Federal Income Tax Payable		4 578 18	
Social Security Tax Payable		1 767 76	
Medicare Tax Payable		427 24	
Sales Tax Payable		4 980 00	
Unemployment Tax Payable—Federal		38 00	
Unemployment Tax Payable—State		244 00	
Health Insurance Premiums Payable		560 00	
Dividends Payable		7 500 00	
Total Liabilities			57 494 53
Stockholders' Equity			
Capital Stock		15 000 00	
Retained Earnings		180 217 69	
Total Stockholders' Equity			195 217 69
Total Liabilities and Stockholders' Equity			252 712 22

PREPARING A BALANCE SHEET

A corporation's balance sheet reports assets, liabilities, and stockholders' equity on a specific date. [CONCEPT: Accounting Period Cycle] A balance sheet is prepared from information found in the Balance Sheet columns of the work sheet and on the statement of stockholders' equity.

Detailed procedures for preparing a balance sheet were presented in Chapter 15. These procedures are summarized below by the three primary account classifications.

Assets

Restaurant Supply classifies its assets as current assets and plant assets. Cash and other assets expected to be exchanged for cash or consumed within a year are known as *current assets*. Assets that will be used for a number of years in the operation of a business are known as *plant assets*. A business owning both current and plant assets usually lists them under separate headings on a balance sheet.

Some of Restaurant Supply's asset accounts have related contra accounts that reduce the related account on the balance sheet. The difference between an asset's account balance and its related contra account balance is known as *book value*. An asset's book value is reported on a balance sheet by listing three amounts: (1) the balance of the asset account, (2) the balance of the asset's contra account, and (3) book value.

Liabilities

Liabilities are classified according to the length of time until they are due. Liabilities due within a short time, usually within a year, are known as *current liabilities*. All of Restaurant Supply's liabilities are current liabilities because they come due within a year.

Liabilities owed for more than a year are called **long-term liabilities**. An example of a long-term liability is Mortgage Payable. On December 31 of the current year, Restaurant Supply does not have any long-term liabilities.

Stockholders' Equity

The stockholders' equity section contains the total amounts of capital stock and retained earnings. These amounts are calculated and reported on the statement of stockholders' equity, as well as on the balance sheet.

> **FOR YOUR INFORMATION**
> **FYI**
>
> A company having both current liabilities and long-term liabilities would include headings and totals for each category. The process is similar to preparing the asset section of a balance sheet.

Preparing a Statement of Stockholders' Equity and Balance Sheet

ANALYZING A BALANCE SHEET

To continue operating successfully, a business must have adequate financial resources to buy additional merchandise, pay employee salaries, and pay for other operating expenses. Financial strength analysis measures the level of financial resources. The balance sheet is the primary source of data to determine the financial strength of a business.

Restaurant Supply analyzes its financial strength to assist the company in planning for future periods and to ensure that adequate resources are available to operate the business. Creditors and investors also use financial strength analysis to determine if the company is a good credit and investment risk. Before a creditor sells merchandise to a company on account, the creditor must believe that the company will later pay for the merchandise. A company that is considered to be a poor credit risk is usually a bad investment for an investor.

Working Capital

The amount of total current assets less total current liabilities is called **working capital**. The amount is stated in dollars. Working capital is a measure of the financial resources available for the daily operations of the business. Restaurant Supply's working capital is calculated as shown below.

Working capital should not be confused with cash. Restaurant Supply does not have $172,100.02 of excess cash. However, Restaurant Supply does have $172,100.02 of financial resources that are available for use in daily operations at the beginning of the next fiscal year.

Total Current Assets	−	Total Current Liabilities	=	Working Capital
$229,594.55	−	$57,494.53	=	$172,100.02

Current Ratio

Although working capital is a useful measure, working capital does not permit a business to compare itself to its industry or to provide a convenient relative measurement from year to year.

A more useful measure results from comparing the amount of total current assets to total current liabilities. A comparison between two numbers showing how many times one number exceeds the other is known as a *ratio*. A ratio that shows the numeric relationship of current assets to current liabilities is called the **current ratio**. The current ratio is a measure of a company's ability to pay its current liabilities when due. Creditors use the ratio to determine if merchandise should be sold to a company on account. Restaurant Supply's current ratio is calculated as shown.

Restaurant Supply's current ratio is stated as 4.0 to 1, which means that total current assets are 4.0 times total current liabilities.

Based on previous experience, industry guidelines, and the need to maintain sufficient merchandise inventory, Restaurant Supply considers a current ratio between 3.0 to 1 and 4.5 to 1 to be acceptable. On December 31 of the current year, Restaurant Supply's current ratio, 4.0 to 1, is acceptable. This year's current ratio indicates a favorable condition of financial strength.

Total Current Assets	÷	Total Current Liabilities	=	Current Ratio
$229,594.55	÷	$57,494.53	=	4.0 to 1

DIGITAL VISION/GETTY IMAGES

End of Lesson REVIEW

TERMS REVIEW

long-term liabilities
working capital
current ratio

AUDIT YOUR UNDERSTANDING

1. What is an example of a long-term liability?
2. What is working capital?
3. Why is the current ratio a useful measure of financial strength?

WORK TOGETHER 22-3

Preparing a statement of stockholders' equity and balance sheet for a corporation

Use the work sheet and income statement for Webster Corporation from Work Together 22-2. Forms are given in the *Working Papers*. Your instructor will guide you through the following example.

1. Prepare a statement of stockholders' equity for the current year. As of January 1, Webster Corporation had issued 9,000 shares of capital stock with a par value of $10.00 per share. During the fiscal year, the corporation issued 1,000 additional shares of capital stock.
2. Prepare a balance sheet for the current year.
3. Calculate Webster Corporation's (a) working capital and (b) current ratio.
4. Determine if these items are within acceptable levels. The corporation considers working capital in excess of $150,000.00 and a current ratio between 2.0 to 1 and 3.0 to 1 to be acceptable indications of financial strength. Save your work to complete Work Together 22-4.

ON YOUR OWN 22-3

Preparing a statement of stockholders' equity and balance sheet for a corporation

Use the work sheet and income statement for Osborn Corporation from On Your Own 22-2. Forms are given in the *Working Papers*. Work this problem independently.

1. Prepare a statement of stockholders' equity for the current year. As of January 1, Osborn Corporation had issued 45,000 shares of capital stock with a par value of $1.00 per share. During the fiscal year, the corporation issued 5,000 additional shares of stock.
2. Prepare a balance sheet for the current year.
3. Calculate Osborn Corporation's (a) working capital and (b) current ratio.
4. Determine if these items are within acceptable levels. The corporation considers working capital in excess of $100,000.00 and a current ratio between 5.0 to 1 and 6.0 to 1 to be acceptable indications of financial strength. Save your work to complete On Your Own 22-4.

Preparing a Statement of Stockholders' Equity and Balance Sheet

LESSON 22-4

Adjusting, Closing, and Reversing Entries for a Corporation

ADJUSTING ENTRIES

GENERAL JOURNAL — PAGE 15

	DATE		ACCOUNT TITLE	DOC. NO.	POST. REF.	DEBIT	CREDIT	
1			*Adjusting Entries*					1
2	Dec. 20--	31	Interest Receivable			20 00		2
3			Interest Income				20 00	3
4		31	Uncollectible Accounts Expense			1287 30		4
5			Allowance for Uncoll. Accts.				1287 30	5
6		31	Merchandise Inventory			5290 00		6
7			Income Summary				5290 00	7
8		31	Supplies Expense			7837 00		8
9			Supplies				7837 00	9
10		31	Insurance Expense			11600 00		10
11			Prepaid Insurance				11600 00	11
12		31	Depreciation Exp.—Office Equip.			6350 00		12
13			Accum. Depr.—Office Equip.				6350 00	13
14		31	Depreciation Exp.—Store Equip.			9250 00		14
15			Accum. Depr.—Store Equip.				9250 00	15
16		31	Interest Expense			400 00		16
17			Interest Payable				400 00	17
18		31	Federal Income Tax Expense			4578 18		18
19			Federal Income Tax Payable				4578 18	19
20								20

After financial statements are prepared, adjusting and closing entries are journalized and posted. A post-closing trial balance is then prepared to prove the equality of debits and credits in the general ledger after adjusting and closing entries have been posted. The steps for preparing a post-closing trial balance are the same as discussed in Chapter 16. Finally, reversing entries are journalized and posted.

A corporation's adjusting entries are made from the Adjustments columns of a work sheet. To assure that each work sheet adjustment is journalized, record the entries in the order of the letters assigned to each adjustment on the work sheet.

Restaurant Supply's work sheet is shown in Lesson 22-1.

CLOSING ENTRIES FOR A CORPORATION

Closing entries for a corporation are made from information in a work sheet. A corporation records four closing entries:

1. Closing entry for income statement accounts with credit balances (revenue and contra cost accounts).
2. Closing entry for income statement accounts with debit balances (cost, contra revenue, and expense accounts).
3. Closing entry to record net income or net loss in the retained earnings account and close the income summary account.
4. Closing entry for the dividends account.

CLOSING ENTRY FOR ACCOUNTS WITH CREDIT BALANCES

1. Enter the balance of every Income Statement credit account in the debit column.

DATE	ACCOUNT TITLE	DOC. NO.	POST. REF.	DEBIT	CREDIT
	Closing Entries				
Dec. 31	Sales			2 109 894 30	
	Purchases Discount			11 094 20	
	Purchases Returns and Allow.			5 142 50	
	Gain on Plant Assets			670 00	
	Interest Income			156 00	
	Income Summary				2 126 957 00

GENERAL JOURNAL PAGE 16

2. Enter the total of debit entries as a credit to Income Summary.

The income statement credit balance accounts consist of the revenue (Sales, Gain on Plant Assets, and Interest Income) and the contra cost accounts (Purchases Discount and Purchases Returns and Allowances). Information needed for closing income statement credit balance accounts is obtained from the work sheet. Closing entries are recorded on a new page of the general journal.

STEPS — JOURNALIZING A CLOSING ENTRY FOR ACCOUNTS WITH CREDIT BALANCES

1. Except for *Income Summary*, enter the balance of every account found in the Income Statement credit column of the work sheet as a debit entry in a general journal.

2. Enter the total of the debit entries, $2,126,957.00, as a credit to *Income Summary*.

Adjusting, Closing, and Reversing Entries for a Corporation Lesson 22-4

CLOSING ENTRY FOR ACCOUNTS WITH DEBIT BALANCES

1. Enter Income Summary.
2. Enter the balance of every Income Statement debit account in the credit column.
3. Enter the total as a debit to Income Summary.

The income statement debit balance accounts consist of the contra revenue accounts (Sales Discount and Sales Returns and Allowances), the cost (Purchases), and all expense accounts. Information needed for closing income statement debit balance accounts is obtained from the work sheet's Income Statement Debit column.

Because Cash Short and Over has a debit balance in this fiscal period, the account balance amount is closed to Income Summary with the debit balance accounts.

STEPS — JOURNALIZING A CLOSING ENTRY FOR ACCOUNTS WITH DEBIT BALANCES

1. Enter the account title *Income Summary*.
2. Enter the balance of every account found in the Income Statement debit column of the work sheet as a credit entry in a general journal.
3. Enter the total of the credit entries, $1,957,009.33, as a debit to *Income Summary*.

CLOSING ENTRY TO RECORD NET INCOME

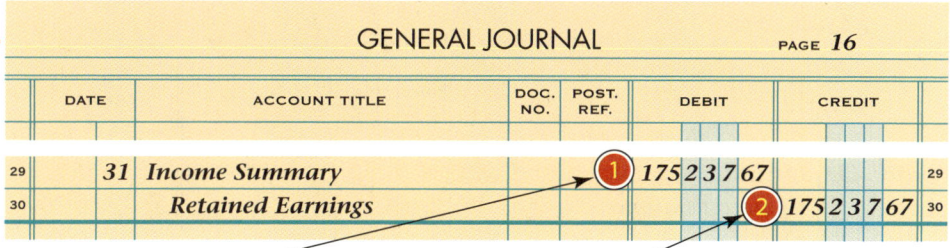

1. Debit Income Summary.   2. Credit Retained Earnings.

After closing entries for the income statement accounts are posted, Income Summary has a credit balance of $175,237.67. This credit balance equals the net income calculated on the work sheet.

As reported on the statement of stockholders' equity, the net income of a corporation increases retained earnings. Closing the balance of Income Summary actually increases the Retained Earnings account by the amount of net income. After the closing entry is posted, Income Summary has a zero balance.

A corporation having a net loss will have a debit balance in Income Summary. Retained Earnings would then be debited and Income Summary credited for the net loss amount. The entry would reduce the balance of Retained Earnings.

STEPS — JOURNALIZING A CLOSING ENTRY FOR NET INCOME TO RETAINED EARNINGS

1. Record a debit to *Income Summary* for the amount of net income, $175,237.67.
2. Record a credit to *Retained Earnings* for the same amount, $175,237.67.

CLOSING ENTRY FOR DIVIDENDS

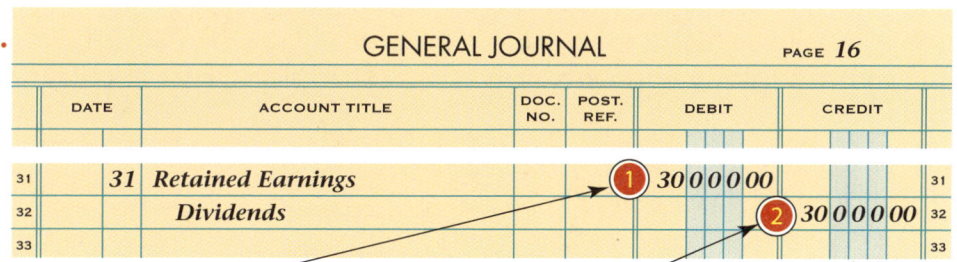

1. Debit Retained Earnings.   2. Credit Dividends.

Dividends reduce the earnings retained by a corporation, as reported on the Statement of Stockholders' Equity. The closing entry reduces the balance in the Retained Earnings account by the amount of the dividends.

STEPS — JOURNALIZING A CLOSING ENTRY FOR DIVIDENDS

1. Record a debit to *Retained Earnings* for the amount of dividends, $30,000.00.
2. Record a credit to *Dividends* for the same amount, $30,000.00.

REVERSING ENTRIES

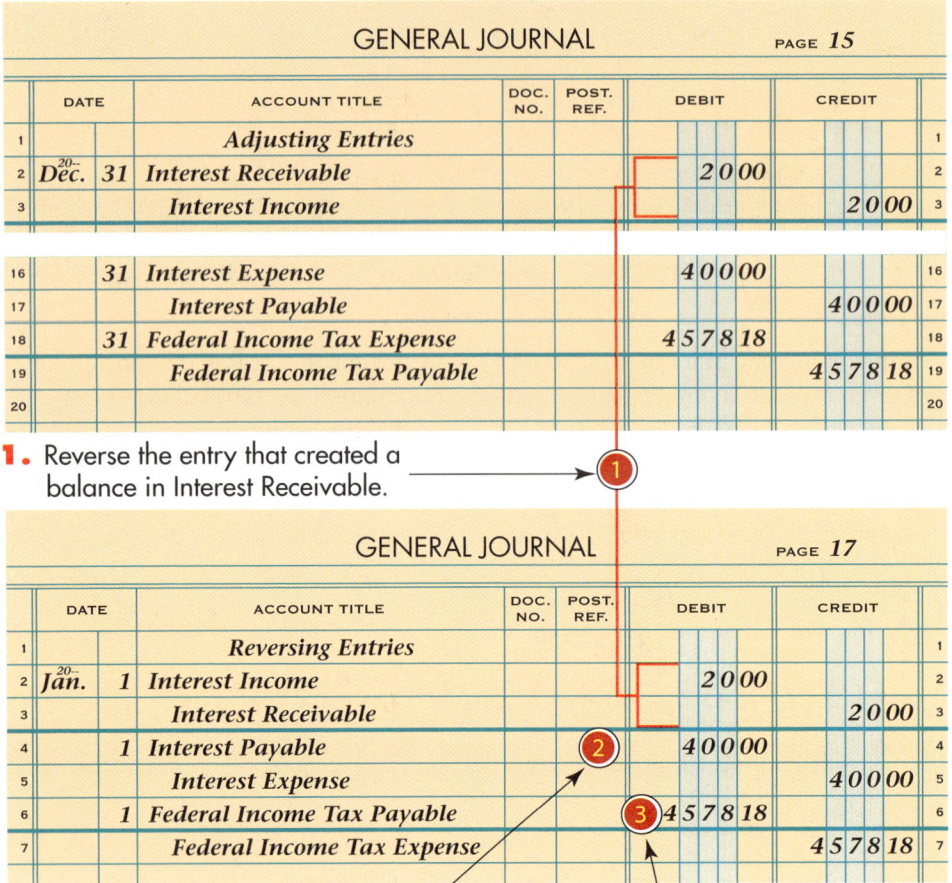

1. Reverse the entry that created a balance in Interest Receivable.

2. Reverse the entry that created a balance in Interest Payable.

3. Reverse the entry that created a balance in Federal Income Tax Payable.

If an adjusting entry creates a balance in an asset or liability account, the adjusting entry should be reversed. A review of Restaurant Supply's adjusting entries shows that three adjusting entries created a balance in an asset or liability account.

1. The adjusting entry for accrued interest income created a balance in the interest receivable account.
2. The adjusting entry for accrued interest expense created a balance in the interest payable account.
3. The adjusting entry for federal income tax expense created a balance in the federal income tax payable account.

STEPS JOURNALIZING REVERSING ENTRIES

① Reverse the entry that created a balance in *Interest Receivable*.

② Reverse the entry that created a balance in *Interest Payable*.

③ Reverse the entry that created a balance in *Federal Income Tax Payable*.

REMEMBER

A post-closing trial balance is prepared to prove the equality of debits and credits in the general ledger after adjusting and closing entries have been posted, but before reversing entries are posted.

658   Chapter 22   End-of-Fiscal-Period Work for a Corporation

ACCOUNTING CYCLE FOR A MERCHANDISING BUSINESS ORGANIZED AS A CORPORATION

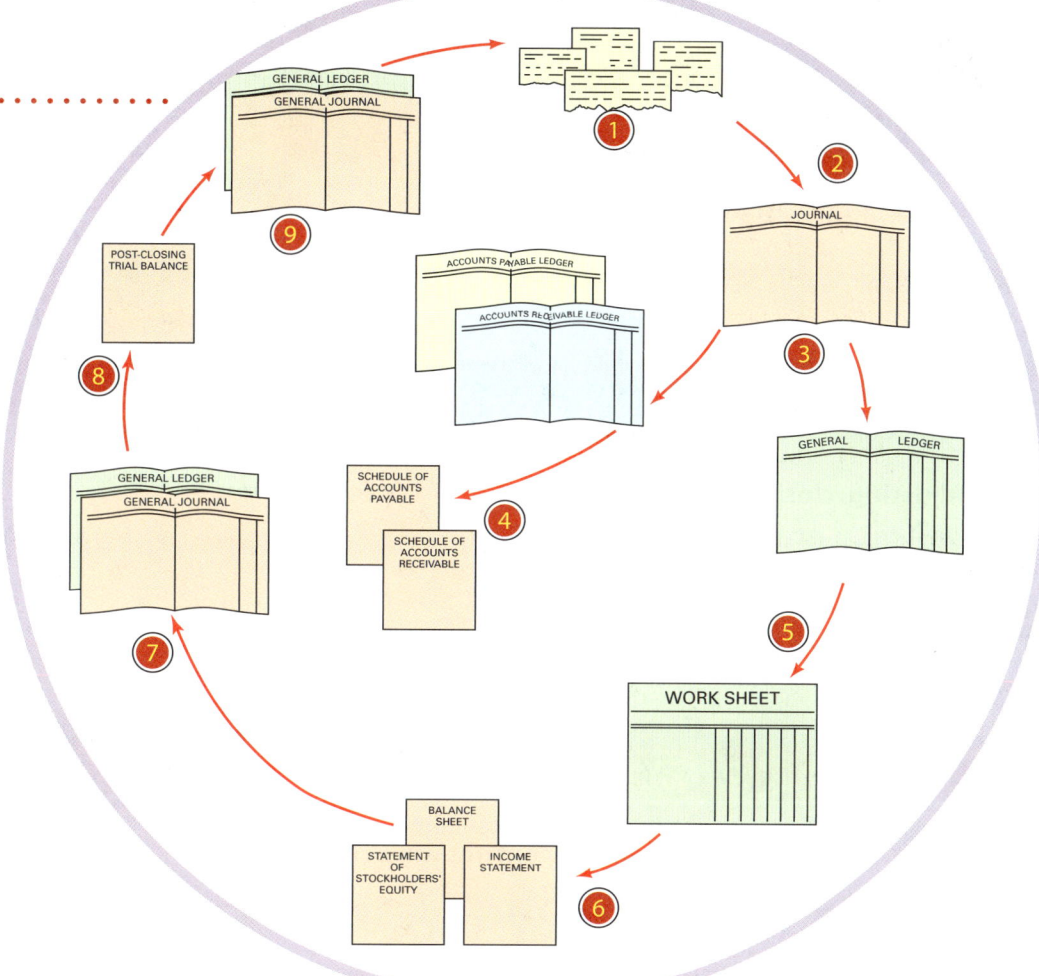

The accounting cycles are similar for merchandising businesses, regardless of how the businesses are organized. Variations occur in preparing financial statements. Variations also occur when reversing entries are recorded.

STEPS — ACCOUNTING CYCLE FOR A MERCHANDISING BUSINESS ORGANIZED AS A CORPORATION

1. Source documents are checked for accuracy, and transactions are analyzed into debit and credit parts.
2. Transactions, from information on source documents, are recorded in journals.
3. Journal entries are posted to the accounts payable, accounts receivable, and general ledgers.
4. Schedules of accounts payable and accounts receivable are prepared from the subsidiary ledgers.
5. A work sheet, including a trial balance and an adjustment for federal income tax expense, is prepared from the general ledger.
6. Financial statements are prepared from the work sheet.
7. Adjusting and closing entries are journalized from the work sheet and posted to the general ledger.
8. A post-closing trial balance of the general ledger is prepared.
9. Reversing entries are journalized and posted to the general ledger.

Adjusting, Closing, and Reversing Entries for a Corporation Lesson 22-4

End of Lesson REVIEW

AUDIT YOUR UNDERSTANDING

1. What is used to prove the equality of debits and credits in the general ledger?
2. What are the four closing entries for a corporation?
3. What accounts are closed to Retained Earnings?

WORK TOGETHER 22-4

Journalizing adjusting, closing, and reversing entries for a corporation

Use the work sheet and financial statements from Work Together 22-3. General journal pages are given in the *Working Papers*. Your instructor will guide you through the following examples.

1. For the current year, journalize the adjusting entries using page 15 of a general journal.
2. For the current year, journalize the closing entries using page 16 of a general journal.
3. For the following year, journalize the reversing entries using page 17 of a general journal.

ON YOUR OWN 22-4

Journalizing adjusting, closing, and reversing entries for a corporation

Use the work sheet and financial statements from On Your Own 22-3. General journal pages are given in the *Working Papers*. Work this problem independently.

1. For the current year, journalize the adjusting entries using page 18 of a general journal.
2. For the current year, journalize the closing entries using page 19 of a general journal.
3. For the following year, journalize the reversing entries using page 20 of a general journal.

SUMMARY

After completing this chapter, you can:

1. Define accounting terms related to financial statements for a merchandising business organized as a corporation.
2. Identify accounting concepts and practices related to financial statements and end-of-fiscal-period entries for a merchandising business organized as a corporation.
3. Plan end-of-fiscal-period adjustments for a merchandising business organized as a corporation.
4. Calculate federal income tax, plan an adjustment for federal income tax expense, and complete a work sheet.
5. Prepare and analyze an income statement for a merchandising business organized as a corporation.
6. Prepare a statement of stockholders' equity for a merchandising business organized as a corporation.
7. Prepare and analyze a balance sheet for a merchandising business organized as a corporation.
8. Record adjusting, closing, and reversing entries for a merchandising business organized as a corporation.

EXPLORE ACCOUNTING

Audits Provide Stockholders with Positive Assurance

Stockholders want assurance that the financial statements of their corporation accurately present its financial condition and results of operations. To provide this assurance, corporations hire independent public accountants to audit the financial statements. These accountants, referred to as *auditors*, provide a written opinion that informs stockholders whether the financial statements can be relied upon for making informed business decisions.

Auditors examine documents, journals, ledgers, and other accounting records to collect evidence that supports five declarations, or assertions, about each amount in the financial statements. Each assertion addresses a unique quality about the amount in the financial statements. These assertions are summarized as follows.

1. *Existence or Occurrence.* All assets and liabilities actually exist, and all income statement transactions actually occurred during the period.
2. *Completeness.* All assets and liabilities that exist have been reported, and all revenue and expense events have been recorded.
3. *Rights and Obligations.* All assets and liabilities are those of the corporation and not of its owners or another corporation.
4. *Valuation or Allocation.* Transactions are reported using amounts that correctly reflect the value of the item or event.
5. *Presentation and Disclosure.* Accounts are properly classified, described, and disclosed in conformity with generally accepted accounting principles.

Instructions: Create a table that shows how the five financial statement assertions relate to any one particular amount reported on the financial statements.

22-1 APPLICATION PROBLEM

Preparing a work sheet for a corporation

Donovan Lumber Corporation's work sheet is given in the *Working Papers*.

Instructions:

1. For the current year ended December 31, record the adjustments on the work sheet using the following information. Do not total the Adjustments columns. Save your work to complete Application Problem 22-2.

Adjustment Information, December 31

Accrued interest income	$ 315.00
Uncollectible accounts expense estimated as 1.0% of sales on account.	
Sales on account for year, $685,000.00.	
Merchandise inventory	81,284.50
Supplies inventory	1,847.50
Value of prepaid insurance	4,180.00
Annual depreciation expense—office equipment	3,128.00
Annual depreciation expense—store equipment	3,389.00
Accrued interest expense	300.00

2. Using the tax table shown in this chapter, calculate federal income tax expense and record the income tax adjustment on the work sheet. Complete the work sheet. Save your work to complete Application Problem 22-2.

22-2 APPLICATION PROBLEM

Preparing an income statement for a corporation

Use the work sheet from Application Problem 22-1 and the financial analysis form provided in the *Working Papers* to complete this problem. Save your work to complete Application Problem 22-3.

Instructions:

1. Prepare an income statement for Donovan Lumber Corporation for the fiscal year ending December 31 of the current year.

2. Calculate and record the following component percentages: (a) cost of merchandise sold; (b) gross profit on operations; (c) total operating expenses; (d) income from operations; (e) net addition or deduction from other revenue and expenses; and (f) net income before federal income tax. Round percentage calculations to the nearest 0.1%.

3. Analyze the corporation's income statement by determining if component percentages are within acceptable levels. If any component percentage is not within an acceptable level, suggest steps that the company should take. The corporation considers the following component percentages acceptable.

Cost of merchandise sold	Not more than 70.0%
Gross profit on operations	Not less than 30.0%
Total operating expenses	Not more than 25.0%
Income from operations	Not less than 5.0%
Net deduction from other revenue and expenses	Not more than 0.1%
Net income before federal income tax	Not less than 4.9%

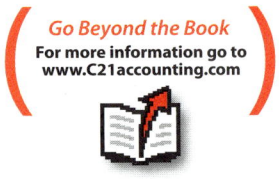

22-3 APPLICATION PROBLEM

Preparing a statement of stockholders' equity and balance sheet for a corporation

Use the work sheet and income statement from Application Problems 22-1 and 22-2 to complete this problem. Save your work to complete Application Problem 22-4.

Instructions:

1. Prepare a statement of stockholders' equity for Donovan Lumber Corporation for the fiscal year ended on December 31 of the current year. Use the following additional information.

January 1 balance of capital stock account (8,000 shares issued for $5.00 per share)	$40,000.00
Shares issued during the year	2,000 shares

2. Prepare a balance sheet for Donovan Lumber Corporation as of December 31 of the current year.
3. Calculate the corporation's (a) working capital and (b) current ratio.
4. Determine if these items are within acceptable levels. The corporation considers the following levels acceptable. Save your work to complete Application Problem 22-4.

Working capital	Not less than $100,000.00
Current ratio	Between 3.0 to 1 and 3.5 to 1

22-4 APPLICATION PROBLEM

Journalizing adjusting, closing, and reversing entries for a corporation

Use the work sheet and financial statements from Application Problem 22-3 to complete this problem.

Instructions:

1. For the current year, journalize the adjusting entries using page 15 of a general journal.
2. For the current year, journalize the closing entries using page 16 of a general journal.
3. For the following year, journalize the reversing entries using page 17 of a general journal.

22-5 MASTERY PROBLEM

Preparing a work sheet, financial statements, and end-of-fiscal-period entries for a corporation

Accounting forms are given in the *Working Papers*. Benford Corporation completed the following transactions during December of the current year and January of the next year.

Instructions:

1. Prepare Benford Corporation's work sheet for the current year ended December 31. Record the adjustments on the work sheet using the following information.

Adjustment Information, December 31

Accrued interest income	$ 80.00
Uncollectible accounts expense estimated as 0.6% of sales on account.	
Sales on account for year, $945,000.00.	
Merchandise inventory	283,028.08
Supplies inventory	998.99
Value of prepaid insurance	2,000.00
Annual depreciation expense—office equipment	5,480.00
Annual depreciation expense—store equipment	5,060.00
Accrued interest expense	312.50

Federal income tax is calculated using the tax table presented in this chapter.

2. Prepare an income statement. Calculate and record the following component percentages: (a) cost of merchandise sold; (b) gross profit on operations; (c) total operating expenses; (d) income from operations; (e) net addition or deduction from other revenue and expenses; and (f) net income before federal income tax. Round percentage calculations to the nearest 0.1%.

3. Analyze the corporation's income statement by determining if component percentages are within acceptable levels. If any component percentage is not within an acceptable level, suggest steps that the company should take. The corporation considers the following component percentages acceptable.

Cost of merchandise sold	Not more than 70.0%
Gross profit on operations	Not less than 30.0%
Total operating expenses	Not more than 25.0%
Income from operations	Not less than 5.0%
Net deduction from other revenue and expenses	Not more than 0.1%
Net income before federal income tax	Not less than 4.9%

4. Prepare a statement of stockholders' equity. Use the following additional information.

January 1 balance of capital stock account (14,000 shares issued for $10.00 per share)	$140,000.00
Shares issued during the year	1,000 shares

5. Prepare a balance sheet.

6. Calculate the corporation's (a) working capital and (b) current ratio. Determine if these items are within acceptable levels. The corporation considers the following levels acceptable.

Working capital	Not less than $150,000.00
Current ratio	Between 3.0 to 1 and 4.0 to 1

7. Journalize the adjusting entries using page 15 of a general journal.
8. Journalize the closing entries using page 16 of a general journal.
9. Journalize the reversing entries using page 17 of a general journal.

22-6 CHALLENGE PROBLEM

Analyzing financial strength

Instructions:

1. Obtain the financial statements of two corporations from two different industries. Calculate the amount of working capital and the current ratio of each corporation.

2. Discuss the usefulness of each measure of financial strength between the companies in each industry and among the different industries.

3. The current ratio is often considered to be acceptable within a specified range. Investigate why a current ratio being too high might be undesirable.

APPLIED COMMUNICATION

You have learned a wide variety of facts and concepts about accounting for service and merchandising businesses and for proprietorships, corporations, and the business world. Regardless of your future educational and career goals, this knowledge will provide you with a sound foundation to become a productive member of society.

Instructions: Prepare an essay to discuss how your knowledge of accounting will be useful to you in the future. How will accounting help you to complete your education, obtain a job, start a business, make personal investment decisions, and be successful in other facets of your life?

CASE FOR CRITICAL THINKING

The president of Reyes Company asked the accounting department to provide information to help management improve the company's net income. Accountant Pemlata Rathi suggests that an income statement showing all the revenue and expense amounts should provide all the information needed to analyze the company's results of operations. Do you agree? If not, what additional information do you recommend?

GRAPHING WORKSHOP

Stock prices are often presented in a high-low-close graph. The vertical line represents the range—the high and low price—in which the stock traded during the fiscal year. The following graph shows that Burnett Company's stock reached a high of $40 per share some time during 20X1. However, during the year the stock fell to as low as $30 per share. The small tab within each line shows the market price on the last day of the fiscal year—the close price.

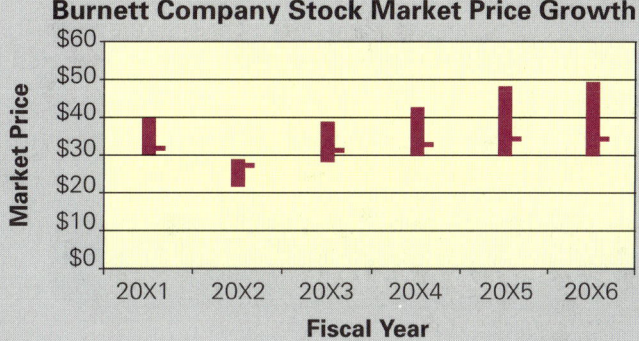

In its annual report, the president of Burnett Company made the following statement:
   "In 20X2, we implemented a strategic plan to reverse the decline in the market price of the company's stock. The installation of a new information system has increased sales and reduced the costs of purchasing materials and services. As evidenced by the steady increase in the stock price, stockholders who retained their investment in the company have been rewarded with significant appreciation in the value of their investments."

Instructions: Evaluate the president's statement. Does the information in the high-low-close graph support the president's analysis?

ANALYZING BEST BUY'S FINANCIAL STATEMENTS

A statement of shareholders' equity reports changes in each of the capital accounts. The amount of stock issued and repurchased is reported as changes in the common stock account. The company's operations for the year are reflected as changes in the retained earnings account.

Instructions
1. Use Best Buy's Consolidated Statements of Changes in Shareholders' Equity on page B-8 in Appendix B of this textbook to identify the changes in the retained earnings account for fiscal years 2005–2007.
2. Describe the change, if any, in the amount of dividends per share for the fiscal years 2005–2007.

Accounting SOFTWARE

END-OF-FISCAL-PERIOD WORK FOR A CORPORATION

It is common practice for businesses to set limits on the amount of unpaid sales on account to each customer. Businesses have learned these credit limits help limit bad debt expenses. A method or process that achieves a desired result for many businesses is referred to as *best practice*. In your accounting education, you have learned many best practices, such as the use of work sheets, special journals, and sales discounts.

Peachtree uses best practices for maintaining customer information and selling to customers. First, you can establish default options for all customers, including credit terms, credit limits, shipment methods, and finance charges. When a new customer is entered into Peachtree, the customer is initially assigned the default options. You can then change any of the options for that customer. For example, if your business offers most customers 2/10, n/30 credit terms, these terms would be entered in the default options. If you wanted to offer a particular customer different terms, those new terms would be entered into that customer's information.

PEACHTREE MASTERY PROBLEM 22-5
1. Open (Restore) file 22-5MP.ptb.
2. Print a Profit & Loss Standard report using January 1 and December 31 as the dates.
3. View a Trial Balance report for December 31. Use the report to help journalize the closing entry for Dividends.
4. Print a Balance Sheet Standard report dated December 31.

END-OF-FISCAL-PERIOD WORK FOR A CORPORATION

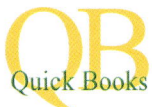

QuickBooks allows the user to customize lists, forms, and financial statements to meet the needs of each company. When creating lists, such as customers, vendors, employees, and inventory items, extra fields can be added. For example, a Sales Region field can be added to the customer list. This field can then be used to sort sales by region of the country.

Invoices, credit memos, sales receipts, statements, and other forms can be customized in several ways. Columns can be added, the format can be changed, columns can appear on the form when entering data but be hidden on the printed form, text can be automatically added to a form, or the style, color, and size of the font can be changed.

Reports can be modified in several ways. An income statement, for example, can be designed to show revenue month by month or week by week for the entire accounting period. Financial statements can show amounts for the previous period along with amounts for the current period.

QUICKBOOKS MASTERY PROBLEM 22-5
1. Open the Benford Corporation file if it is not already open.
2. Journalize and post the adjusting entries.
3. Print an income statement.
4. Print a statement of retained earnings.
5. Print a balance sheet.
6. Journalize and post the closing entries.
7. Print the December 31 to January 1 (of the following year) general journal.

CHARTS AND GRAPHS

Large work sheets can be difficult to print. Using default print settings, the template for this chapter prints, section by section, over six pages. You would have to tape the pages together to create a document that you could review. Obviously, such a method of printing a large work sheet is unacceptable in business today.

Electronic spreadsheets provide you with numerous tools to modify how a document is printed. One of the most powerful tools is called *scaling*. If you have ever used a copy machine to reduce a document to a certain percentage of its normal size, you have scaled a document.

The level of scaling can be entered as a percentage, or the electronic spreadsheet can determine the required scaling for you. By instructing the computer to print the document by a certain number of pages wide and pages tall, the computer automatically determines the required level of scaling.

EXCEL APPLICATION PROBLEM 22-1
Open the F22-1 Excel data file. Follow the step-by-step instructions in the Instructions work sheet. Scale the template to print one page wide and two pages tall.

EXCEL APPLICATION PROBLEM 22-3
Open the F22-1 Excel data file. Follow the step-by-step instructions in the Instructions work sheet.

END-OF-FISCAL-PERIOD WORK FOR A CORPORATION

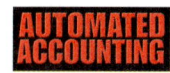

Adjusting entries must be planned and then entered into the software. The first step is to display or print a trial balance and use the data on that report to plan the adjusting entries. The adjusting entries are then journalized in the general journal and posted. The same reference, such as *Adj.Ent.*, should be used for each adjusting entry.

Financial statements are generated by the software by clicking the Reports toolbar button and then selecting the desired reports. The reports may be displayed, printed, or copied in word processing or spreadsheet format for pasting into another document or spreadsheet. Financial statements should be generated before closing entries are recorded and posted.

Closing entries can be generated automatically by the software. Click Options on the menu and select Generate Closing Entries. The closing entries are then displayed in the general journal and should be checked and then posted. Note that it is important to save a copy of the file before closing entries (use *BC* in the filename) so that the file can be opened in case corrections are needed. Another version of the file should be saved after closing entries (use *AC* in the filename).

After closing entries are posted, reversing entries are recorded in the general journal. The same reference, such as *Rev.Ent.*, should be used for each reversing entry.

AUTOMATED MASTERY PROBLEM 22-5
Open file F22-5.AA8. Display the problem instructions and complete the problem.

REINFORCEMENT Activity 3—Part B

An Accounting Cycle for a Corporation: End-of-Fiscal-Period Work

The general ledger used in Reinforcement Activity 3—Part A is needed to complete Reinforcement Activity 3—Part B.

END-OF-FISCAL-PERIOD WORK

INSTRUCTIONS:

9. Record the 20X4 depreciation on the plant asset record of plant asset no. 998.
10. Prepare a trial balance as of December 31, 20X4, on a work sheet.
11. Complete the work sheet using the following adjustment information:

    a. Outstanding notes receivable consist of NR34, a 90-day, 10% note accepted from Nelson Co. on December 7, 20X4, for an extension of time on its account, $3,600.00.
    b. Uncollectible accounts expense is estimated as 4.0% of sales on account. Sales on account for the year, $90,000.
    c. Merchandise inventory $80,491.95
    d. Supplies inventory $425.05
    e. Value of prepaid insurance $600.00
    f. Estimate of office equipment depreciation $6,520.00
    g. Estimate of warehouse equipment depreciation $4,210.00
    h. Outstanding notes payable consist of (1) NP32, a 90-day, 12% note for $10,000.00 signed on November 16, 20X4, and (2) NP33, a 90-day, 10% note for $6,000.00 signed on December 28, 20X4.

12. Calculate federal income tax expense and record the adjustment on the work sheet.
13. Prepare an income statement. Calculate and record the following component percentages: (a) cost of merchandise sold; (b) gross profit on operations; (c) total operating expenses; (d) income from operations; (e) net addition or deduction from other revenue and expenses; and (f) net income before federal income tax. Round percentage calculations to the nearest 0.1%.
14. Analyze the corporation's income statement by determining if component percentages are within acceptable levels. If any component percentage is not within an acceptable level, suggest steps that the company should take. The corporation considers the following component percentages acceptable:

    Cost of merchandise sold: Not more than 62.0%
    Income from operations: Not less than 10.0%
    Gross profit on operations: Not less than 38.0%
    Net deduction from other revenue and expenses: Not more than 0.5%
    Total operating expenses: Not more than 28.0%
    Net income before federal income tax: Not less than 9.5%

15. Calculate the earnings per share and price-earnings ratio. Current market price is $225.00.
16. Prepare a statement of stockholders' equity. The company had 3,000 shares of $10.00 par-value stock outstanding on January 1. The company did not issue any additional shares during the year.
17. Prepare a balance sheet in report form.
18. Journalize and post the adjusting entries. Use page 13 of a general journal.
19. Journalize and post the closing entries. Use page 14 of a general journal.
20. Prepare a post-closing trial balance.
21. Journalize and post the reversing entries. Use page 15 of a general journal.

Electro, Inc., is a merchandising business organized as a corporation. The company specializes in selling electronic items, including computers and audio and video systems and accessories. This simulation includes the realistic transactions completed by Electro, Inc., in the month of December, including end-of-fiscal-year activities.

Source documents are provided for transactions that are recorded in special journals and a general journal, similar to the ones used by Restaurant Supply Co. in Part 3.

This real-life business simulation is available in manual and automated versions. The automated version is used with Automated Accounting software.

The following activities are included in the Electro, Inc. simulation:

1. Recording transactions in special journals from source documents.
2. Posting items to be posted individually to a general ledger and subsidiary ledger.
3. Posting column totals to a general ledger.
4. Preparing schedules of accounts receivable and accounts payable from subsidiary ledgers.
5. Preparing a trial balance on a work sheet.
6. Planning adjustments and completing a work sheet.
7. Preparing financial statements.
8. Journalizing and posting adjusting entries.
9. Journalizing and posting closing entries.
10. Preparing a post-closing trial balance.
11. Journalizing and posting reversing entries.
12. Think Like an Accountant Financial Analysis Activity

PART 4
Additional Accounting Procedures

▽ **Chapter 23** Accounting for Partnerships
▽ **Chapter 24** Recording International and Internet Sales

THE BUSINESS— GIFTPAK COMPANY

GiftPak Company is the business that will be used in Chapters 23 and 24 in Part 4 to illustrate the chapter concepts. The company is a partnership that sells gift baskets with both national and international sales. The company also sells merchandise on the Internet through its web site. GiftPak rents the building that it uses for its operations.

PHOTO: IMAGE SOURCE/GETTY IMAGES

CHAPTER 23

GIFTPAK COMPANY CHART OF ACCOUNTS

GENERAL LEDGER

Balance Sheet Accounts

(1000) ASSETS
1100 Current Assets
1110 Cash
1120 Petty Cash
1130 Accounts Receivable
1135 Allowance for Uncollectible Accounts
1137 Time Drafts Receivable
1140 Merchandise Inventory
1150 Supplies
1160 Prepaid Insurance
1200 Plant Assets
1210 Office Equipment
1215 Accumulated Depreciation—Office Equipment

(2000) LIABILITIES
2100 Current Liabilities
2110 Accounts Payable

(3000) OWNERS' EQUITY
3110 Sawyer Hess, Capital
3120 Sawyer Hess, Drawing
3130 Kendra Sullivan, Capital
3140 Kendra Sullivan, Drawing
3150 Income Summary

Income Statement Accounts

(4000) OPERATING REVENUE
4110 Sales
4115 Sales Returns and Allowances
4120 Sales Discount

(5000) COST OF MERCHANDISE
5110 Purchases
5115 Purchases Returns and Allowances
5120 Purchases Discount

(6000) OPERATING EXPENSES
6110 Advertising Expense
6120 Credit Card Fee Expense
6130 Depreciation Expense—Office Equipment
6135 Insurance Expense
6140 Miscellaneous Expense
6150 Rent Expense
6160 Supplies Expense
6170 Uncollectible Accounts Expense

The chart of accounts for GiftPak Company is illustrated above for ready reference as you study Part 4 of this textbook.

CHAPTER 24

CHAPTER 23

Accounting for Partnerships

OBJECTIVES

After studying Chapter 23, you will be able to:

1. Define accounting terms related to forming, dissolving, and distributing the earnings of a partnership.
2. Identify accounting concepts and practices related to forming, dissolving, and distributing the earnings of a partnership.
3. Journalize entries related to forming, dissolving, and distributing the earnings of a partnership.
4. Calculate the distribution of partnership earnings.
5. Prepare a distribution of net income statement for a business organized as a partnership.
6. Prepare an owners' equity statement for a business organized as a partnership.

KEY TERMS

- partnership
- partner
- partnership agreement
- distribution of net income statement
- owners' equity statement
- liquidation of a partnership
- realization
- limited liability partnership (LLP)

Point Your Browser
www.C21accounting.com

ACCOUNTING IN THE REAL WORLD

Cold Stone Creamery®

Today's Business World—Cold Stone Creamery®

Do you love ice cream? Donald and Susan Sutherland's passion for ice cream led them to open Cold Stone Creamery® in Tempe, Arizona, in 1988. The Sutherlands make their ice cream daily, using only the finest ingredients. But what makes Cold Stone Creamery® unique is how the ice cream is prepared. As customers watch, their desired mix-ins are blended with the ice cream on a frozen granite stone and served in a fresh-baked waffle cone.

The success of Cold Stone Creamery® motivated the Sutherlands to begin franchising their concept in 1995. With nearly 1,400 franchise stores in operation in 2007 and many more in development, Cold Stone Creamery® was ranked #12 in Entrepreneur Magazine's 2007 100 Fastest Growing Franchises (Entrepreneur.com).

In exchange for an initial investment, Cold Store Creamery® franchisees receive step-by-step guidance in choosing a site, negotiating the lease, transforming the store, and, most important, learning how to create the best ice cream creations at the Cold Store Creamery® Ice Cream University.

Critical Thinking

1. What other kinds of support and training might be provided to a franchisee?
2. If you were going to start a business with someone else, how would you choose your partner?

Source: www.coldstonecreamery.com

INTERNET ACTIVITY

Partnership Agreements

Search the Internet for information about partnership agreements.

Instructions

1. List the purpose of a partnership agreement.
2. List at least four items that should be included in a partnership agreement.

LESSON 23-1

Forming a Partnership

PARTNERSHIPS

TechKnow Consulting, the business described in Part 1, is a proprietorship, a small business owned by one person. Hobby Shack, Inc., and Restaurant Supply Co., the businesses described in Parts 2 and 3, are organized as corporations. Businesses that require the skills and capital of more than one person, but that do not wish to be organized as a corporation, may choose another form of business. A business in which two or more persons combine their assets and skills is called a **partnership**. Each member of a partnership is called a **partner**. As in other forms of ownership, reports and financial records of the business are kept separate from the personal records of the partners. [CONCEPT: Business Entity]

A partnership prepares four financial statements. It prepares an income statement and a balance sheet similar to those used by a proprietorship or corporation. It also prepares two additional financial statements. One statement reports the distribution of net income or net loss for each partner. The other statement reports the changes in owners' equity for the fiscal period.

THE BUSINESS—GIFTPAK COMPANY

Sawyer Hess and Kendra Sullivan own a partnership called GiftPak Company. The business purchases gourmet foods and novelty gifts and packages these items into gift boxes and baskets. The company accepts orders through its web site and has customers in other countries.

The partners do all the work in the company; there are no employees. Partners are not employees, and the money that partners receive from a partnership is not considered salaries. Therefore, GiftPak Company does not need accounts for recording salaries and payroll taxes.

CHARACTER COUNTS

Setting the Tone at the Top

A certain company's code of conduct prohibits employees from accepting gifts, favors, or entertainment that would influence their sound business decisions. Despite the rule, the company president is known to accept lavish gifts from suppliers. Do you think the employees will be motivated to adhere to the code of conduct?

The employees at the top of a company—managers, officers, and directors—must provide leadership in making ethical decisions. Among the many ways companies can "set the tone at the top" is to have a special code of conduct for members of the board of directors.

Instructions
Access the *Code of Conduct for Kellogg Company Directors* at http://investor.kelloggs.com. Determine whether directors can own stock in companies that do business with Kellogg Company.

PARTNERSHIP AGREEMENTS

PARTNERSHIP AGREEMENT

THIS CONTRACT is made and entered into this thirty-first day of December, 20--, by and between Sawyer Hess and Kendra Sullivan, of Glendive, MT.

WITNESSETH: That the said parties have this date formed a partnership to engage in and conduct a business under the following stipulations which are a part of this contract. The partnership will begin operation January 1, 20--.

FIRST: The business shall be conducted under the name of GiftPak Company, located initially at 234 North River Avenue, Glendive, MT 59330.

SECOND: The investment of each partner is: Sawyer Hess: Cash of $15,000. Kendra Sullivan: Cash of $10,000 and office equipment with a value of $5,000; total investment, $15,000.

THIRD: Both partners are to (a) participate in all general policy-making decisions, (b) devote full time and attention to the partnership business, and (c) engage in no other business enterprise without the written consent of the other partner. Mr. Hess is to be general manager of the business's operations.

FOURTH: Neither partner is to become a surety or bonding agent for anyone without the written consent of the other partner.

FIFTH: The partners will share equally in all profits and losses of the partnership.

SIXTH: No partner is to withdraw assets without the other partner's written consent.

SEVENTH: All partnership transactions are to be recorded in accordance with standard and generally accepted accounting procedures and concepts. The partnership records are to be open at all times for inspection by either partner.

EIGHTH: In case of either partner's death or legal disability, the equity of the partners is to be determined as of the time of the death or disability of the one partner. The continuing partner is to have first option to buy the deceased/disabled partner's equity at recorded book value.

NINTH: This partnership agreement is to continue indefinitely unless (a) terminated by death of one partner, (b) terminated by either partner giving the other partner written notice at least ninety (90) days prior to the termination date, or (c) terminated by written mutual agreement signed by both partners.

TENTH: At the termination of this partnership agreement, the partnership's assets, after all liabilities are paid, will be distributed according to the balance in partners' capital accounts.

IN WITNESS WHEREOF, the parties to this contract have set their hands and seals on the date and year written.

Signed: *Sawyer Hess* (Seal) Date December 31, 20--

Signed: *Kendra Sullivan* (Seal) Date December 31, 20--

A written agreement setting forth the conditions under which a partnership is to operate is called a **partnership agreement**. Legally, a partnership agreement may be either written or oral. However, a written agreement may limit misunderstandings in the future; therefore, a partnership agreement should be in writing. It should include the name of the business and the partners, the investments of each partner, the duties and responsibilities of each partner, how profits and losses are to be divided, what happens if a partner dies, how the partnership is to be dissolved, and the duration of the agreement.

Forming a Partnership

INITIAL INVESTMENTS BY OWNERS

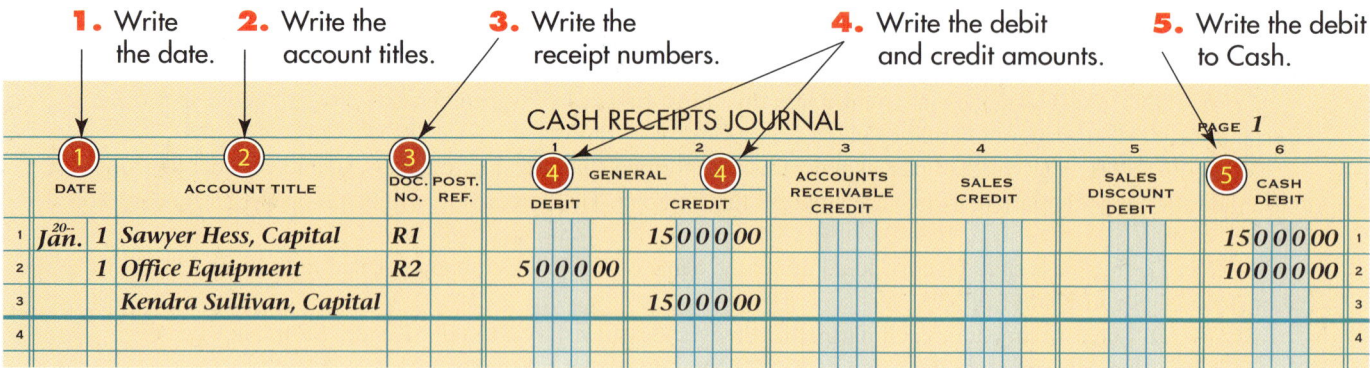

GiftPak's partnership agreement calls for Sawyer Hess to contribute cash and for Kendra Sullivan to contribute cash and office equipment to the new partnership. A separate journal entry is made for each partner's initial investment.

January 1. Received cash from partner, Sawyer Hess, as an initial investment, $15,000.00. Receipt No. 1.

The asset account, Cash, increases by a debit, $15,000.00. The owner's capital account, Sawyer Hess, Capital, increases by a credit, $15,000.00.

January 1. Received cash, $10,000.00, and office equipment valued at $5,000.00, from partner, Kendra Sullivan, as an initial investment. Receipt No. 2.

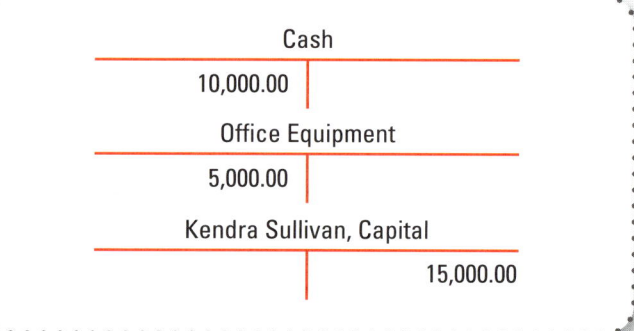

The asset account, Cash, increases by a debit, $10,000.00. The asset account, Office Equipment, increases by a debit, $5,000.00. The owner's capital account, Kendra Sullivan, Capital, increases by a credit, $15,000.00.

STEPS — JOURNALIZING RECEIPT OF PARTNERS' INITIAL INVESTMENTS

1. Write the date, *20--, Jan. 1*, in the Date column.

2. Write the account titles in the Account Title column. For Sawyer Hess's investment, write the account to be credited, *Sawyer Hess, Capital*. For Kendra Sullivan's investment, write the account to be debited, *Office Equipment*. Also write the account to be credited, *Kendra Sullivan, Capital*.

3. Write the receipt numbers, *R1* and *R2*, in the Doc. No. column.

4. Write the amounts in the General Debit and Credit columns. The only credit amount for Sawyer Hess is $15,000 for the cash investment. For Kendra Sullivan's investment, the debit amount is $5,000.00 for the office equipment. The credit amount for Kendra Sullivan is $15,000.00 for the total investment.

5. Write the debits to *Cash*, *$15,000.00* and *$10,000.00*, in the Cash Debit column.

WITHDRAWAL OF CASH BY PARTNER

1. Write the date.
2. Write the account debited.
3. Write the check number.
4. Write the debit amount.
5. Write the credit amount.

During a fiscal period, partners may take assets out of the partnership in anticipation of the net income for the period. As in a proprietorship, assets taken out of a business for the personal use of an owner are known as *withdrawals*. The two assets generally taken out of a merchandising business are cash and merchandise. The partnership agreement may limit the amount of assets that may be withdrawn.

Withdrawals reduce the amount of a business's capital. The account titles of the partners' drawing accounts are Sawyer Hess, Drawing and Kendra Sullivan, Drawing. Since capital accounts have credit balances, partners' drawing accounts have normal debit balances. Therefore, the drawing accounts increase by a debit and decrease by a credit, as shown in the T accounts.

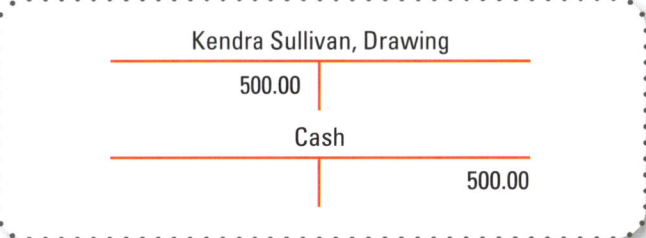

The owner's drawing account, Kendra Sullivan, Drawing, has a normal debit balance because withdrawals decrease owner's equity. Therefore, increases in withdrawals are recorded by a debit, $500.00. The asset account, Cash, decreases by a credit, $500.00.

Withdrawals could be recorded as debits directly to the partners' capital accounts. However, withdrawals are normally recorded in separate accounts so that the total amounts are easily determined for each accounting period.

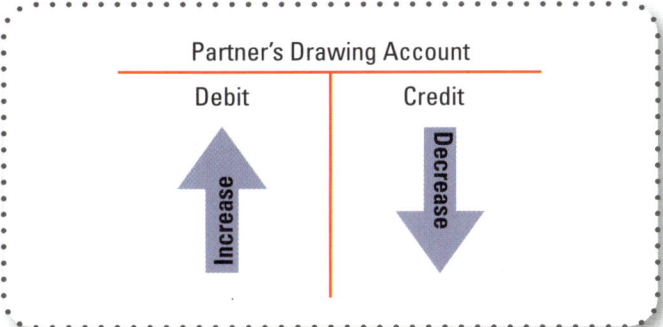

January 15. Kendra Sullivan, partner, withdrew cash for personal use, $500.00. Check No. 10.

STEPS: JOURNALIZING WITHDRAWALS OF CASH BY PARTNERS

1. Write the date, *15*, in the Date column.
2. Write the title of the account debited, *Kendra Sullivan, Drawing*, in the Account Title column.
3. Write the check number, *10*, in the Ck. No. column.
4. Write the debit amount, *$500.00*, in the General Debit column.
5. Write the credit amount, *$500.00*, in the Cash Credit column.

Forming a Partnership

WITHDRAWAL OF MERCHANDISE BY PARTNER

A partner usually withdraws cash for personal use. However, a partner may also withdraw merchandise for personal use. This merchandise withdrawal increases the account balance of Sawyer Hess, Drawing and decreases the purchases account balance.

January 15. Sawyer Hess, partner, withdrew merchandise for personal use, $200.00. Memorandum No. 1.

Sawyer Hess's drawing account increases by a debit, $200.00. The cost account, Purchases, decreases by a credit, $200.00. This transaction is recorded in the general journal.

STEPS — JOURNALIZING WITHDRAWALS OF MERCHANDISE BY PARTNERS

1. Write the date, 20--, Jan. 15, in the Date column.
2. Write the account title, *Sawyer Hess, Drawing*, in the Account Title column.
3. Write the memorandum number, *M1*, in the Doc. No. column.
4. Write the debit amount, *$200.00*, in the Debit column on the same line as the account title.
5. On the next line, indented about one centimeter, write the account title, *Purchases*, in the Account Title column.
6. Write the credit amount, *$200.00*, in the Credit column on the same line as the account title.

End of Lesson REVIEW

AUDIT YOUR UNDERSTANDING

TERMS REVIEW

partnership
partner
partnership agreement

1. What two financial statements prepared by a partnership are similar to those prepared by a proprietorship?
2. List at least three items that should be included in a partnership agreement.
3. What accounts are debited and credited when a partner withdraws cash from the partnership?

WORK TOGETHER 23-1

Journalizing partners' investments and withdrawals

Cash receipts, cash payments, and general journals are given in the *Working Papers*. Your instructor will guide you through the following examples.

B and B Diving completed the following transactions during March of the current year.

Transactions:
Mar. 1. Received cash of $22,000.00 and office supplies valued at $3,000.00 from partner, Robert Billings, as an initial investment. Receipt No. 1.
   1. Received cash from partner, Susan Billings, as an initial investment, $25,000.00. Receipt No. 2.
   30. Susan Billings, partner, withdrew cash for personal use, $600.00. Check No. 23.
   30. Robert Billings, partner, withdrew merchandise for personal use, $600.00. Memorandum No. 4.

1. Use page 1 of a cash receipts journal. Journalize the investments on March 1.
2. Use page 1 of a cash payments journal and page 3 of a general journal. Journalize the withdrawals on March 30.

ON YOUR OWN 23-1

Journalizing partners' investments and withdrawals

Cash receipts, cash payments, and general journals are given in the *Working Papers*. Work this problem independently.

Northern Lights completed the following transactions during September of the current year.

Transactions:
Sept. 1. Received cash of $45,000.00 and inventory valued at $5,000.00 from partner, Loane Le, as an initial investment. Receipt No. 1.
   1. Received cash from partner, Wheatonia Makebu, as an initial investment, $30,000.00 Receipt No. 2.
   30. Loane Le, partner, withdrew cash for personal use, $1,000.00. Check No. 65.
   30. Wheatonia Makebu, partner, withdrew merchandise for personal use, $1,500.00. Memorandum No. 6.

1. Use page 1 of a cash receipts journal. Journalize the investments on September 1.
2. Use page 1 of a cash payments journal and page 9 of a general journal. Journalize the withdrawals on September 30.

Forming a Partnership

LESSON 23-2

Distribution of Net Income and Owners' Equity Statements

DISTRIBUTION OF NET INCOME STATEMENT

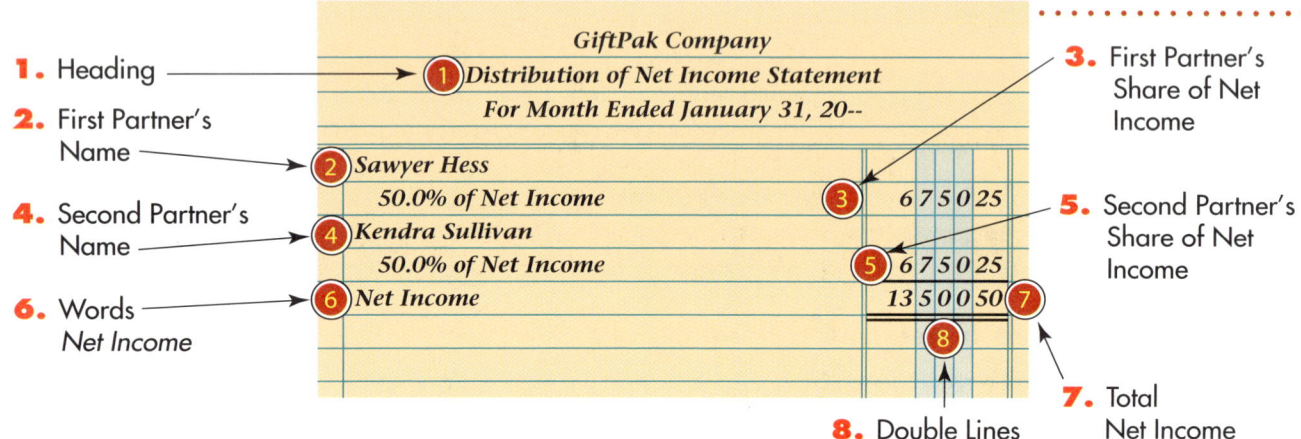

A partnership's net income or net loss may be divided in any way agreed upon by the partners in their partnership agreement. Sawyer Hess and Kendra Sullivan, partners in GiftPak Company, agreed to share net income or net loss equally.

A partnership's distribution of net income or net loss is usually shown on a separate financial statement. A partnership financial statement showing net income or loss distribution to partners is called a **distribution of net income statement**.

The income statement for a partnership is prepared in the same way as an income statement for a proprietorship, described in Chapter 7. GiftPak Company's income statement shows a net income of $13,500.50 for the month ended January 31. This net income is used to prepare the distribution of net income statement.

STEPS PREPARING A DISTRIBUTION OF NET INCOME STATEMENT

1. Write the heading of the distribution of net income statement on three lines.

2. Write one partner's name, *Sawyer Hess*, on the first line at the extreme left.

3. Indent about one centimeter on the next line, and write Sawyer Hess's share of net income as a percentage, *50.0% of Net Income*. Write Mr. Hess's share of net income, *$6,750.25* (50.0% × $13,500.50), in the amount column on the same line.

4. Write the other partner's name, *Kendra Sullivan*, on the next line.

5. Indent about one centimeter on the next line, and write Kendra Sullivan's share of net income as a percentage, *50.0% of Net Income*. Write Ms. Sullivan's share of net income, *$6,750.25* (50.0% × $13,500.50), in the amount column on the same line.

6. Write *Net Income* on the next line at the extreme left of the wide column.

7. Add the distribution of net income and write the total amount, *$13,500.50*, in the amount column. Verify accuracy by comparing the total amount, *$13,500.50*, with the net income reported on the income statement, *$13,500.50*. The two amounts must be the same.

8. Rule double lines across the amount column to show that the distribution of net income statement has been verified as correct.

DISTRIBUTION OF NET INCOME STATEMENT WITH UNEQUAL DISTRIBUTION OF EARNINGS

Custom Cabinets Distribution of Net Income Statement For Year Ended December 31, 20--	
Beth Castillo	
60.0% of Net Income	38 520 00
Jana Kenyon	
40.0% of Net Income	25 680 00
Net Income	64 200 00

Regardless of how earnings are shared, the steps in preparing a distribution of net income statement are the same. The only difference is the description of how the earnings are to be shared by the partners.

Beth Castillo and Jana Kenyon are partners in a business. Because Ms. Castillo spends more time in the business than Ms. Kenyon, the partners agree to share net income or loss unequally. Ms. Castillo gets 60.0% of net income or loss. Ms. Kenyon gets 40.0% of net income or loss. With a net income of $64,200.00, Ms. Castillo receives 60.0%, or $38,520.00. Ms. Kenyon receives 40.0%, or $25,680.00.

CULTURAL DIVERSITY

Business Culture and Accountancy in Russia

The changeover of Russia's economy from socialism to free enterprise has strongly influenced Russian business culture. Employees, who for generations have depended on the government to fulfill their needs, now have the opportunity to get ahead individually. Russian business culture—the way Russians do business—is changing gradually. An example of this change can be seen in the accounting profession.

In the emerging Russian market economy, the person performing the role of accountant is called an "economist." These employees have a degree in "economics" and years of experience. Employees performing the role of "bookkeeper" have lower status and lower pay. The chief bookkeeper, however, has a prominent position because of his or her responsibility for the accuracy of financial statements.

The accounting profession in Russia is devising a regulatory framework based upon similar frameworks in existing market economies. Regulations are being written that include precise definitions for accounting terms. Regulations on the qualifications of auditors also are being developed.

Critical Thinking

1. What are the advantages if the accounting standards in Russia are similar to those in the rest of the world?

2. What factors might require that some accounting standards differ from those in other countries?

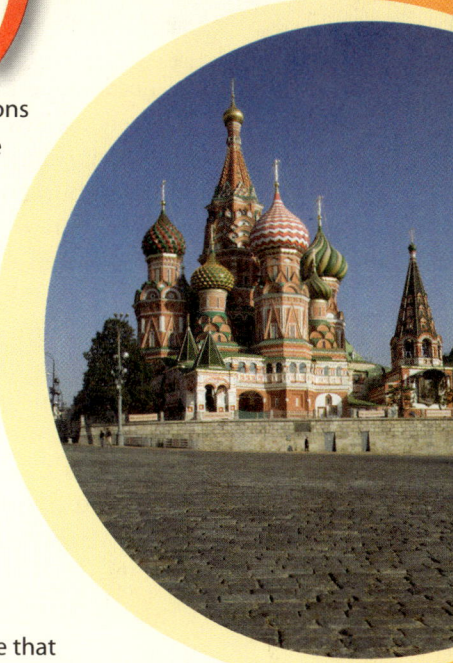

PHOTO: NATIONAL GEOGRAPHIC/GETTY IMAGES

Distribution of Net Income and Owners' Equity Statements

PARTNERS' CAPITAL AND DRAWING ACCOUNTS

ACCOUNT Sawyer Hess, Capital					ACCOUNT NO. 3110	
DATE	ITEM	POST. REF.	DEBIT	CREDIT	BALANCE	
					DEBIT	CREDIT
Jan. 1 20--		CR1		15 000 00		15 000 00

ACCOUNT Sawyer Hess, Drawing					ACCOUNT NO. 3120	
DATE	ITEM	POST. REF.	DEBIT	CREDIT	BALANCE	
					DEBIT	CREDIT
Jan. 15 20--		G1	200 00		200 00	

ACCOUNT Kendra Sullivan, Capital					ACCOUNT NO. 3130	
DATE	ITEM	POST. REF.	DEBIT	CREDIT	BALANCE	
					DEBIT	CREDIT
Jan. 1 20--		CR1		15 000 00		15 000 00

ACCOUNT Kendra Sullivan, Drawing					ACCOUNT NO. 3140	
DATE	ITEM	POST. REF.	DEBIT	CREDIT	BALANCE	
					DEBIT	CREDIT
Jan. 15 20--		CP1	500 00		500 00	

The amount of net income earned is important to business owners. Owners are also interested in changes that occur in owners' equity during a fiscal period. A financial statement that summarizes the changes in owners' equity during a fiscal period is called an **owners' equity statement**. Business owners can review an owners' equity statement to determine if owners' equity is increasing or decreasing and what is causing the change. Three factors can change owners' equity: (1) additional investments, (2) withdrawals, and (3) net income or net loss.

An owners' equity statement shows information about changes in each partner's capital during a fiscal period. Information needed to prepare an owners' equity statement is obtained from the distribution of net income statement, shown on page 680, and the general ledger capital and drawing accounts shown above. The distribution of net income statement shows each partner's share of net income or net loss. Three kinds of information are obtained from each partner's capital and drawing account:

(1) beginning capital amount,
(2) any additional investments made during the fiscal period, and
(3) each partner's withdrawal of assets during the fiscal period.

OWNERS' EQUITY STATEMENT

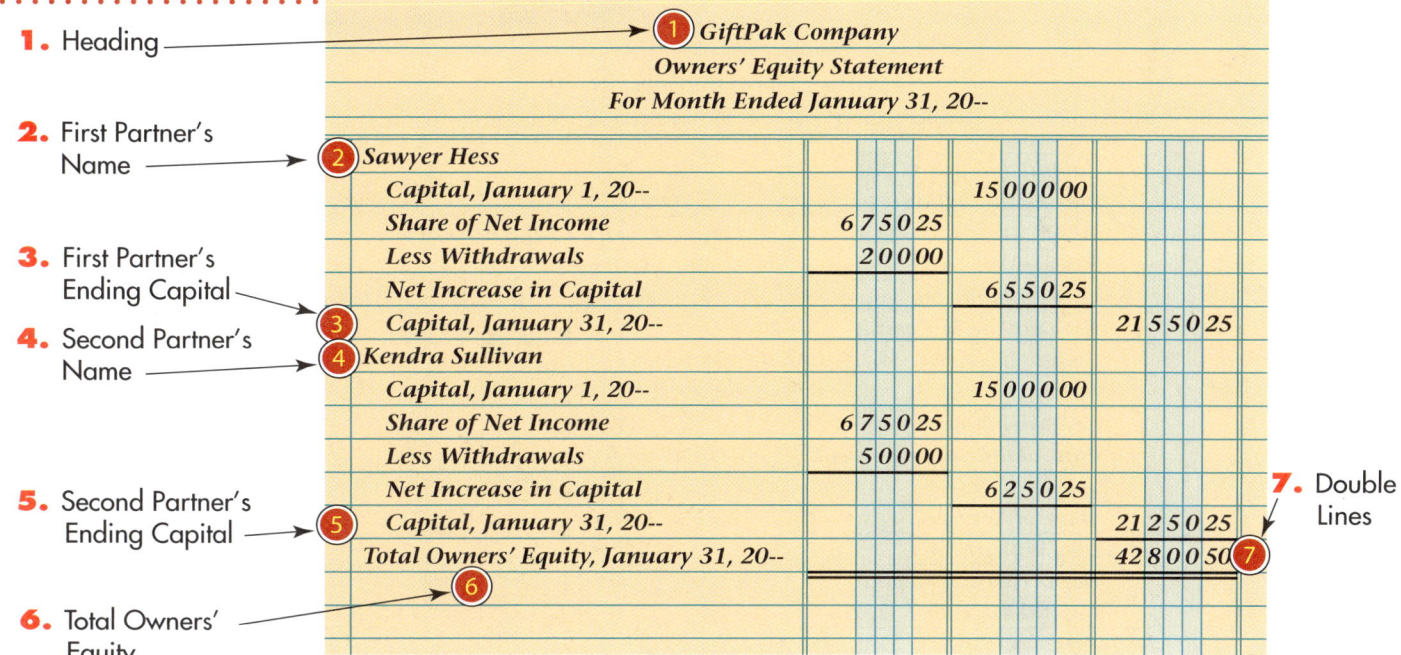

Neither Sawyer Hess nor Kendra Sullivan invested any additional capital during the month ended January 31 after the initial investments on January 1. Both partners withdrew either cash or merchandise during the month.

Some businesses include the owners' equity statement information as part of the balance sheet. An example of this method of reporting changes in owner's equity is shown in Chapter 7.

STEPS PREPARING AN OWNERS' EQUITY STATEMENT

① Write the heading of the owners' equity statement on three lines.

② Write the name *Sawyer Hess* on the first line at the extreme left.

③ Calculate the net increase in capital and ending capital amount for Sawyer Hess.
   a. Indent about one centimeter on the next line, and write *Capital, January 1, 20--*. Write the amount $15,000.00 in the second amount column. (This amount is obtained from the capital account.)
   b. Indent about one centimeter on the next line, and write *Share of Net Income*. Write the amount $6,750.25 in the first amount column. (This amount is obtained from the distribution of net income statement.)
   c. Indent about one centimeter on the next line, and write *Less Withdrawals*. Write the amount $200.00 in the first amount column. (This amount is obtained from the drawing account.)
   d. Indent about one centimeter on the next line, and write *Net Increase in Capital*. Write the amount $6,550.25 in the second amount column. ($6,750.25 − $200.00 = $6,550.25)
   e. Indent about one centimeter on the next line, and write *Capital, January 31, 20--*. Write the amount $21,550.25 in the third amount column. ($15,000.00 + $6,550.25 = $21,550.25)

④ Write the name *Kendra Sullivan* on the next line at the extreme left of the wide column.

⑤ Calculate the net increase in capital and ending capital amount for Kendra Sullivan. Follow Step 3.

⑥ Write *Total Owners' Equity, January 31, 20--* on the next line at the extreme left of the wide column. Write the amount $42,800.50 in the third amount column.

⑦ Rule double lines across the three amount columns to show that the totals have been verified as correct.

Distribution of Net Income and Owners' Equity Statements

OWNERS' EQUITY STATEMENT WITH AN ADDITIONAL INVESTMENT AND A NET LOSS

Cloth Circuit Owners' Equity Statement For Year Ended December 31, 20--			
Mark Gavin			
Capital, January 1, 20--	12520000		
Plus Additional Investment	1200000		
Total		13720000	
Share of Net Loss	284000		
Plus Withdrawals	1776000		
Net Decrease in Capital		2060000	
Capital, December 31, 20--			11660000
Judy Oliver			
Capital, January 1, 20--	12340000		
Plus Additional Investment	1200000		
Total		13540000	
Share of Net Loss	284000		
Plus Withdrawals	1812000		
Net Decrease in Capital		2096000	
Capital, December 31, 20--			11444000
Total Owners' Equity, December 31, 20--			23104000

On December 31, the capital accounts of Mark Gavin and Judy Oliver showed additional investments of $12,000.00 each. Also, the income statement for their company, Cloth Circuit, showed a net loss of $5,680.00. The partners agreed to share net income or net loss equally. The owners' equity statement above shows the net loss as a deduction from the owners' capital.

BALANCE SHEET FOR A PARTNERSHIP

GiftPak Company Balance Sheet January 31, 20--		
Total Liabilities		1027611
Owners' Equity		
Sawyer Hess, Capital	2155025	
Kendra Sullivan, Capital	2125025	
Total Owners' Equity		4280050
Total Liabilities and Owners' Equity		5307661

The asset and liability sections of a balance sheet for a partnership are prepared in the same way as the asset and liability sections of a balance sheet for a proprietorship. The only section that is different is the equity section. The equity section lists the capital account for each partner. The balances of these two accounts are added together and listed as Total Owners' Equity. Total Liabilities and Total Owners' Equity are added together to determine Total Liabilities and Owners' Equity.

FOR YOUR INFORMATION

FYI

Partnerships must file tax returns with the IRS to report how income was divided among the partners.

End of Lesson REVIEW

TERMS REVIEW

distribution of net income statement

owners' equity statement

AUDIT YOUR UNDERSTANDING

1. What information used to prepare an owners' equity statement is obtained from the distribution of net income statement?
2. What information used to prepare an owners' equity statement is obtained from the partners' capital and drawing accounts?
3. What is the procedure for calculating an owner's end-of-year capital?

WORK TOGETHER 23-2

Preparing distribution of net income and owners' equity statements

B and B Diving is a partnership owned by Susan and Robert Billings. Information from B and B's worksheet and income statement is given below. Forms for completing these problems are given in the *Working Papers*. Your instructor will guide you through the following examples.

Net Income for the month ended March 31	$29,600.00
Robert Billings, Capital March 1 balance	25,000.00
Susan Billings, Capital March 1 balance	25,000.00
Robert Billings, Drawing March 31 balance	600.00
Susan Billings, Drawing March 31 balance	600.00

1. Prepare a distribution of net income statement for B and B Diving. Net income or loss is to be shared equally.
2. Using the balances of the general ledger capital and drawing accounts from the work sheet, prepare an owners' equity statement for B and B Diving. No additional investments were made.

ON YOUR OWN 23-2

Preparing distribution of net income and owners' equity statements

Northern Lights is a partnership owned by Loane Le and Wheatonia Makebu. Information from Northern Lights' worksheet and income statement is given below. Forms for completing these problems are given in the *Working Papers*. Work this problem independently.

Net Income for the month ended September 30	$58,800.00
Leone Le, Capital September 1 balance	35,000.00
Wheatonia Makebu, Capital September 1 balance	28,000.00
Leone Le, Drawing September 30 balance	4,500.00
Wheatonia Makebu, Drawing September 30 balance	2,600.00

1. Prepare a distribution of net income statement for Northern Lights. Net income or loss is to be distributed 60% to Mr. Le and 40% to Ms. Makebu.
2. Using the balances of the general ledger capital and drawing accounts from the work sheet, prepare an owners' equity statement for Northern Lights. No additional investments were made.

LESSON 23-3

Dissolving a Partnership

ACCOUNT BALANCES BEFORE REALIZATION

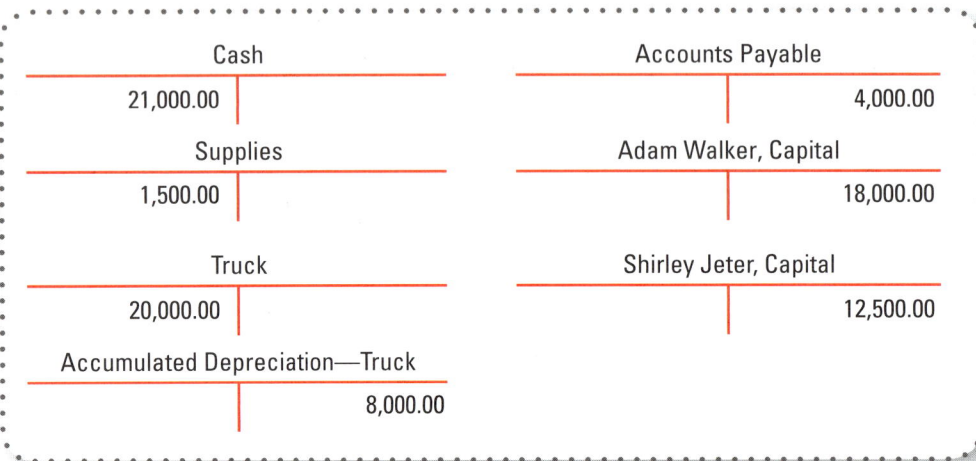

If a partnership goes out of business, its assets are distributed to the creditors and partners. The process of paying a partnership's liabilities and distributing remaining assets to the partners is called **liquidation of a partnership**.

Cash received from the sale of assets during liquidation of a partnership is called **realization**. Typically, when a partnership is liquidated, the noncash assets are sold, and the available cash is used to pay the creditors. Any remaining cash is distributed to the partners according to each partner's total equity.

On July 31, Adam Walker and Shirley Jeter liquidated their partnership. At that time, financial statements were prepared and adjusting and closing entries were journalized and posted. After the end-of-fiscal-period work was completed, the partnership had account balances as shown in the T accounts above.

GAIN ON REALIZATION

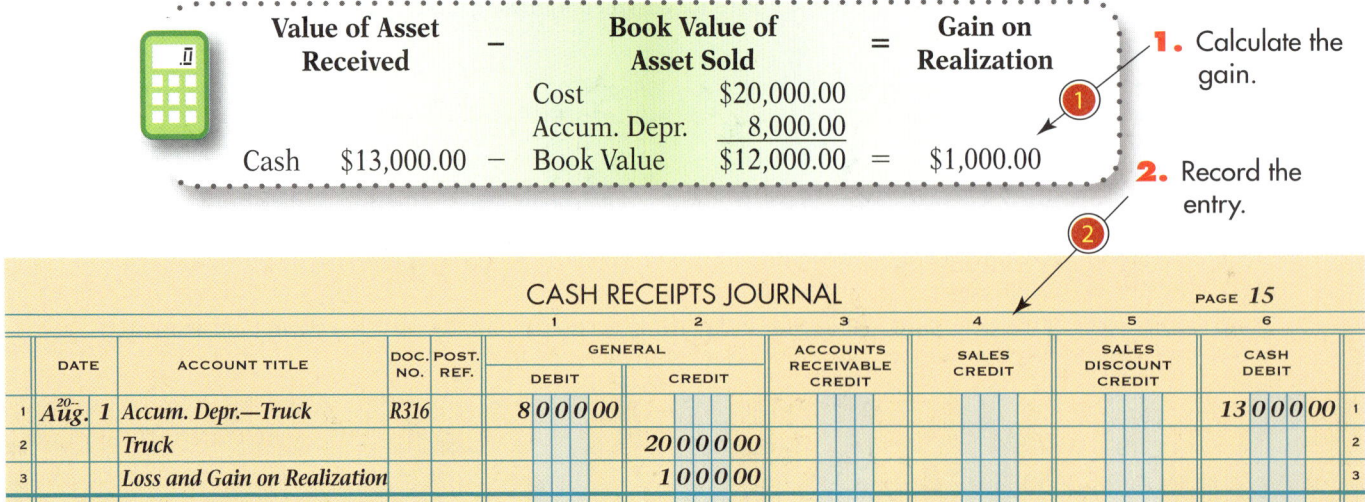

1. Calculate the gain.
2. Record the entry.

686 Chapter 23 · Accounting for Partnerships

RECOGNIZING A GAIN ON REALIZATION

Noncash assets might be sold for more than the recorded book value. When this happens, the amount received in excess of the book value is recorded as a gain on realization. The gain is recorded as a credit in an account titled Loss and Gain on Realization.

> August 1, 20--. Received cash from sale of truck, $13,000.00: original cost, $20,000.00; total accumulated depreciation recorded to date, $8,000.00. Receipt No. 316.

The partnership's gain on the sale of the truck is calculated as shown.

STEPS — RECOGNIZING A GAIN ON REALIZATION

1. Calculate the gain on the sale of the asset, *$1,000.00* ($13,000.00 cash received − $12,000.00 book value of asset).
2. Record the entry in the cash receipts journal, as shown on the previous page.

LOSS ON REALIZATION

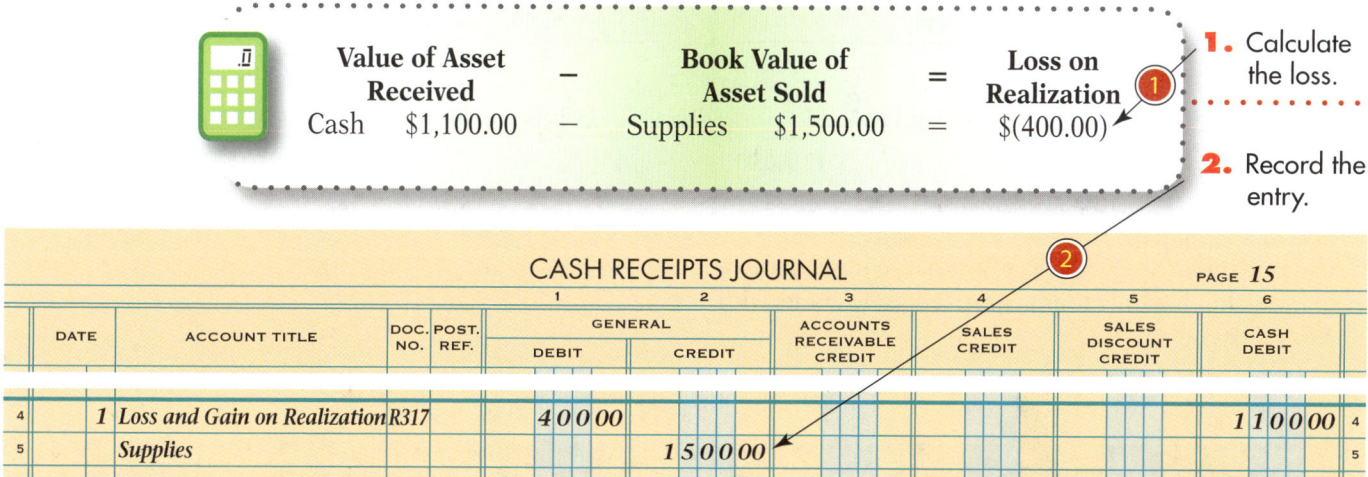

Sometimes during liquidation, the sale of an asset brings in less cash than the recorded book value.

> August 1. Received cash from sale of supplies, $1,100.00; balance of supplies account, $1,500.00. Receipt No. 317.

The journal entry to record this transaction is shown. After both liquidation entries have been journalized, the credit balance of Loss and Gain on Realization, $600.00, is the amount received in excess of the value of the truck and supplies combined.

STEPS — RECOGNIZING A LOSS ON REALIZATION

1. Calculate the loss on the sale of the asset, *$400.00* ($1,500.00 book value of supplies − $1,100.00 cash received).
2. Record the entry in the cash receipts journal.

FYI

A partnership usually tries to sell the business before it begins the process of liquidation.

Dissolving a Partnership

LIQUIDATING LIABILITIES

	CASH PAYMENTS JOURNAL						PAGE 15
				1 GENERAL	2 GENERAL	3 ACCOUNTS PAYABLE DEBIT	4 PURCHASES DISCOUNT CREDIT	5 CASH CREDIT
DATE	ACCOUNT TITLE	CK. NO.	POST. REF.	DEBIT	CREDIT			
Aug. 4 20--	✓	422				4 000 00		4 000 00

The partnership's available cash is used to pay creditors. The entry is recorded in the cash payments journal as shown.

August 4, 20--. Paid cash to all creditors for the amounts owed, $4,000.00. Check No. 422.

ACCOUNT BALANCES AFTER LIQUIDATION OF NONCASH ASSETS AND PAYMENT OF LIABILITIES

Cash			Shirley Jeter, Capital	
Bal. 31,100.00				Bal. 12,500.00

Adam Walker, Capital			Loss and Gain on Realization	
	Bal. 18,000.00			Bal. 600.00

When this transaction has been journalized and posted, the partnership has only four general ledger accounts with balances as shown.

BUSINESS STRUCTURES

Limited Liability Partnerships

A partnership that combines the advantages of the partnership and the corporation, while avoiding their disadvantages, is called a **limited liability partnership (LLP)**. At least two members, or partners, are necessary to form an LLP. The primary advantage of the LLP is that it does not pay separate income tax. LLP partners allocate profits and losses among themselves, according to the partnership agreement.

All members in the LLP have "limited" liability for the debts of the business. This means that none of the personal assets of the members are subject to the claims of business creditors.

The LLP follows partnership rules for dissolution. If one member drops out, all others must formally agree to continue the business.

Many major accounting firms have changed to the LLP form of business organization in an effort to limit the costs associated with malpractice liability.

Critical Thinking
What other professions might organize as LLPs to limit the costs associated with malpractice liability?

DISTRIBUTING LOSS OR GAIN ON REALIZATION TO PARTNERS

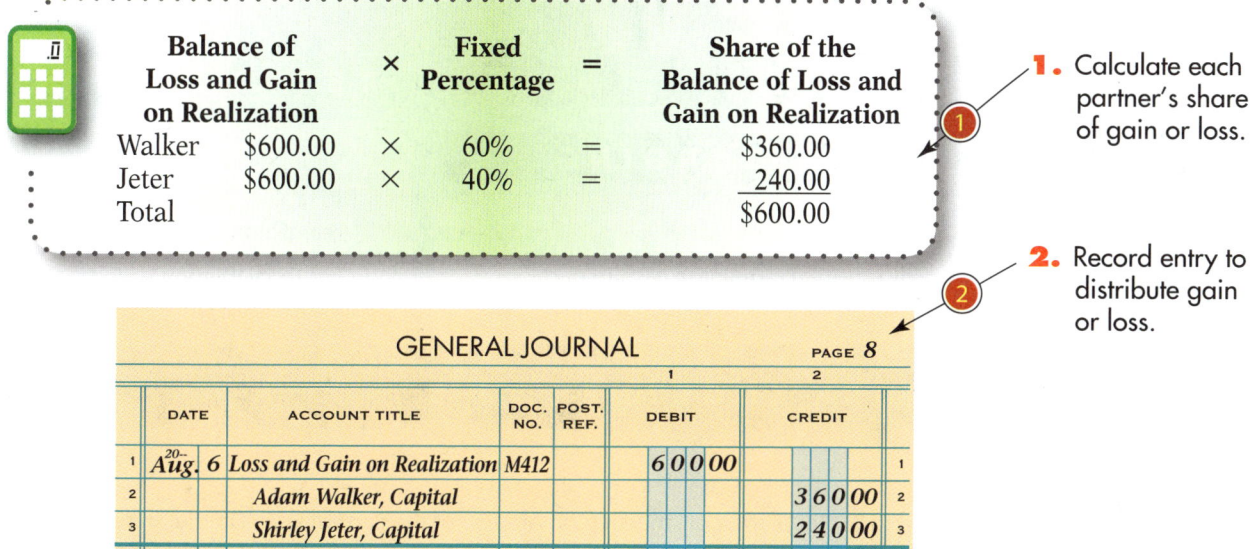

1. Calculate each partner's share of gain or loss.

2. Record entry to distribute gain or loss.

When all creditors have been paid, the balance of Loss and Gain on Realization is distributed to the partners. A credit balance indicates a gain on realization. A debit balance indicates a loss. The distribution is based on the method of distributing net income or net loss as stated in the partnership agreement. The percentages for the Walker and Jeter partnership are Adam Walker, 60%, and Shirley Jeter, 40%. The distribution of the balance of Loss and Gain on Realization is calculated as shown.

> August 6, 20--. Recorded distribution of gain on realization: to Adam Walker, $360.00; to Shirley Jeter, $240.00. Memorandum No. 412.

If a loss on realization is distributed to the partners, Loss and Gain on Realization is credited to close the account. Each partner's capital account is debited for the partner's share of the loss on realization.

DISTRIBUTING REMAINING CASH TO PARTNERS

Any remaining cash is distributed to the partners. The cash is distributed according to each partner's capital account balance, regardless of the method used to distribute net income or net loss.

> August 6. Recorded final distribution of remaining cash to partners: to Adam Walker, $18,360.00; to Shirley Jeter, $12,740.00. Check Nos. 423 and 424.

After this journal entry is journalized (as shown) and posted, all of the partnership's general ledger accounts will have zero balances. The partnership is liquidated.

Dissolving a Partnership — Lesson 23-3

End of Lesson REVIEW

AUDIT YOUR UNDERSTANDING

1. What is meant by the term "realization"?
2. What accounts are debited when distributing remaining cash to partners during liquidation?

TERMS REVIEW

liquidation of a partnership

realization

limited liability partnership (LLP)

WORK TOGETHER 23-3

Liquidation of a partnership

Jason Edson and Peggy Karam agreed to liquidate their partnership on April 30 of the current year. On that date, after financial statements were prepared and closing entries were posted, the general ledger accounts had the balances shown in the *Working Papers*.

A cash receipts journal, page 6, a cash payments journal, page 8, and a general journal, page 4, are provided in the *Working Papers*. Your instructor will guide you through the following examples.

Transactions:

May 1. Received cash from sale of office equipment, $6,000.00. R86.
  1. Received cash from sale of supplies, $950.00. R87.
  3. Received cash from sale of truck, $7,500.00. R88.
  5. Paid cash to all creditors for amounts owed. C116.
  6. Distributed loss or gain to Jason Edson, 60%; to Peggy Karam, 40%. M21.
  6. Distributed remaining cash to partners. C117 and C118.

1. Journalize the transactions.

ON YOUR OWN 23-3

Liquidation of a partnership

Daska Madura and Lawrence Neary agreed to liquidate their partnership on May 31 of the current year. On that date, after financial statements were prepared and closing entries were posted, the general ledger accounts had the balances shown in the *Working Papers*.

A cash receipts journal, page 8, a cash payments journal, page 10, and a general journal, page 5, are provided in the *Working Papers*. Work this problem independently.

Transactions:

June 1. Received cash from sale of office equipment, $800.00. R96.
  1. Received cash from sale of supplies. $1,600.00. R97.
  3. Received cash from sale of truck, $5,400.00. R98.
  5. Paid cash to all creditors for amounts owed. C125.
  6. Distributed loss or gain to Daska Madura, 60%; to Lawrence Neary, 40%. M29.
  6. Distributed remaining cash to partners. C126 and C127.

1. Journalize the transactions.

SUMMARY

After completing this chapter, you can:

1. Define accounting terms related to forming, dissolving, and distributing the earnings of a partnership.
2. Identify accounting concepts and practices related to forming, dissolving, and distributing the earnings of a partnership.
3. Journalize entries related to forming, dissolving, and distributing the earnings of a partnership.
4. Calculate the distribution of partnership earnings.
5. Prepare a distribution of net income statement for a business organized as a partnership.
6. Prepare an owners' equity statement for a business organized as a partnership.

EXPLORE ACCOUNTING

Business Forms

Properly designed business forms can accomplish several important purposes for a company. Business forms may (1) initiate action, (2) exercise control, (3) provide essential accounting information, and (4) provide information to multiple users. Consider how a sales invoice accomplishes these purposes.

1. *Initiate action.* The major action initiated in a sales invoice is the collection of the amount owed by a customer for merchandise received. Information needed to accomplish this action is the customer's name and address; stock number, description, quantity, unit price, and total amounts owed for items purchased; the seller's name and address; date of the invoice; and terms of sale, such as 2/10, n/30.

2. *Exercise control.* The seller needs to insure that all merchandise shipped is properly invoiced to the customer and that the information on the invoice is correct. A seller's invoices should be sequentially numbered to insure that all invoices are accounted for. The invoice date and terms permit the seller to file the invoice by the due date so that the company can follow up if payment is not received.

   The sales clerk's initials show who made the sale so that person can be consulted if there are any questions. If the merchandise is delivered in person, the customer's signature confirms the delivery. If the merchandise is delivered by a freight company, the freight company normally requires a signature to verify delivery.

3. *Provide essential accounting information.* To account for the merchandise sold, the accounting department needs the description, unit price, and total amounts of merchandise; name, address, and customer number; and invoice date and terms of sale.

4. *Provide information to multiple users.* Several individuals or departments need some or all of the information on a business form. A company may color-code multiple copies of its sales invoice. For example, the first copy (white) goes to the customer. The second copy (yellow) goes to the seller's shipping department. The third copy (salmon) goes to the seller's accounts receivable department. Although different businesses may use different colors, the use of color-coding insures that the appropriate copy goes to the correct user.

Required: With your instructor's permission, visit a local business and request a copy of one of its business forms. Identify the items on the form that achieve important purposes for the company.

23-1 APPLICATION PROBLEM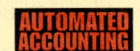

Journalizing partners' investments and withdrawals

Cash receipts, cash payments, and general journals are given in the *Working Papers*. Kopy King completed the following transactions during April of the current year.

Transactions:

Apr. 1. Received cash of $2,000.00 and equipment valued at $33,000.00 from partner, Wilhelm Mellberg, as an investment. Receipt No. 1.
   1. Received cash from partner, Julie Jenson, as an initial investment, $30,000.00. Receipt No. 2.
   30. Julie Jenson, partner, withdrew cash for personal use, $3,600.00. Check No. 66.
   30. Wilhelm Mellberg, partner, withdrew merchandise for personal use, $4,800.00. Memorandum No. 10.

Instructions:

1. Use page 1 of a cash receipts journal. Journalize the investments on April 1.
2. Use page 5 of a cash payments journal and page 12 of a general journal. Journalize the withdrawals on April 30.

23-2 APPLICATION PROBLEM

Preparing distribution of net income and owners' equity statements (net income)

Janet Kelly and Paul Sharp are partners in a merchandising business, Kelly Appliances. Forms for completing this problem are given in the *Working Papers*. The following information was taken from the records on December 31 of the current year.

Partner	Balance of Capital Account January 1	Balance of Drawing Account	Distribution of Net Income
Kelly	$159,000.00	$17,550.00	60.0%
Sharp	$142,600.00	$18,800.00	40.0%

Instructions:

1. On December 31, the partnership had a net income of $83,260.00. Prepare a distribution of net income statement for the partnership.
2. Prepare an owners' equity statement for Kelly Appliances. No additional investments were made.

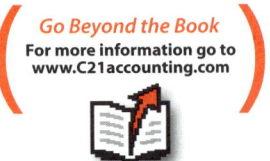

23-3 APPLICATION PROBLEM

Preparing an owners' equity statement (net loss)

Judy Fulton and Lee Terry are partners in a merchandising business, Elegant Cosmetics. Forms for completing this problem are given in the *Working Papers*. The following information was taken from the records on December 31 of the current year.

Partner	Balance of Capital Account January 1	Balance of Drawing Account	Distribution of Net Loss
Fulton	$124,300.00	$13,950.00	$3,750.00
Terry	$118,000.00	$14,900.00	$3,750.00

Instructions:

1. Prepare an owners' equity statement for Elegant Cosmetics. Additional investments made during the year: Judy Fulton, $12,000.00; Lee Terry, $10,000.00.

23-4 APPLICATION PROBLEM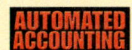

Liquidating a partnership

Donald Winn and Judy Reed agreed to liquidate their partnership on July 30 of the current year. On that date, after financial statements were prepared and closing entries were posted, the general ledger accounts had the following balances.

Cash	$ 5,000.00
Supplies	500.00
Office Equipment	10,000.00
Accumulated Depreciation—Office Equipment	5,500.00
Truck	17,000.00
Accumulated Depreciation—Truck	12,200.00
Accounts Payable	500.00
Donald Winn, Capital	7,300.00
Judy Reed, Capital	7,000.00

The following transactions occurred during July of the current year.

Transactions:

July 1. Received cash from sale of office equipment, $4,000.00. R114.
  1. Received cash from sale of supplies, $200.00. R115.
  3. Received cash from sale of truck, $5,000.00. R116.
  5. Paid cash to all creditors for amounts owed. C156.
  6. Distributed balance of Loss and Gain on Realization to Donald Winn, 65%; to Judy Reed, 35%. M34.
  6. Distributed remaining cash to partners. C157 and C158.

Instructions:

1. Journalize the transactions. Use page 13 of a cash receipts journal, page 13 of a cash payments journal, and page 7 of a general journal.

Accounting for Partnerships   Chapter 23   693

23-5 MASTERY PROBLEM

Recording partners' investments and withdrawals, preparing financial statements, and liquidating a partnership

Darren and Karen Greenlund are partners in a business called GreenGarden. Journals and forms for completing this problem are given in the *Working Papers*. GreenGarden completed the following transactions during July of the current year.

Transactions:

July 15. Received cash from partner, Darren Greenlund, as an investment, $10,000.00. Receipt No. 87.
15. Received cash of $3,000.00 and equipment valued at $8,000.00 from partner, Karen Greenlund, as an investment. Receipt No. 88.
31. Karen Greenlund, partner, withdrew merchandise for personal use, $1,000.00. Memorandum No. 61.
31. Darren Greenlund, partner, withdrew cash for personal use, $800.00. Check No. 321.

Instructions:

1. Use page 13 of a cash receipts journal. Journalize the investments on July 15.
2. Use page 19 of a cash payments journal and page 23 of a general journal. Journalize the withdrawals on July 31.

Information from GreenGarden's worksheet and income statement for the month ended July 31 is given below.

Net Income for the month ended July 31	$14,600.00
Darren Greenlund, Capital July 1 balance	32,310.00
Karen Greenlund, Capital July 1 balance	28,880.00

Instructions:

3. Prepare a distribution of net income statement for Green Garden. Net income or loss is to be distributed equally to the partners.
4. Using the balances of the general ledger capital accounts, prepare an owners' equity statement for GreenGarden. The investments made on July 15 are the only additional investments made by the partners this month. The withdrawals made on July 31 are the only withdrawals made by the partners this month.

The Greenlunds decided to liquidate GreenGarden and retire on July 31. On that date, after financial statements were prepared and closing entries were posted, the general ledger accounts had the following balances.

Cash	$90,490.00
Merchandise Inventory	2,000.00
Equipment	15,000.00
Accumulated Depreciation—Equipment	10,000.00
Accounts Payable	2,500.00
Darren Greenlund, Capital	48,810.00
Karen Greenlund, Capital	46,180.00

The following transactions occurred on July 31 of the current year.

Transactions:

a. Received cash from the sale of merchandise inventory, $1,800.00. R89.
b. Received cash from the sale of equipment, $7,000.00. R90.
c. Paid cash to all creditors for amounts owed. C322.
d. Distributed balance of Loss and Gain on Realization to the partners on an equal basis. M62.
e. Distributed remaining cash to partners. C323 and C324.

Instructions:

5. Journalize the transactions. Continue on the next available line of the journals used in instructions 1 and 2.

23-6 CHALLENGE PROBLEM

Preparing a distribution of net income statement and owners' equity statement (unequal distribution of net loss; additional investment)

Kaye Skousen and Timothy Tripp are partners in a merchandising business, Jewelry Joint. Forms for completing this problem are given in the *Working Papers*. The following information was taken from the records on December 31 of the current year.

Partner	Balance of Capital Account January 1	Balance of Drawing Account	Distribution of Net Loss
Skousen	$125,294.00	$18,000.00	65.0%
Tripp	$101,961.00	$16,300.00	35.0%

Instructions:

1. On December 31, the partnership had a net loss of $32,340.00. Prepare a distribution of net income statement for the partnership.
2. Prepare an owners' equity statement for Jewelry Joint. Additional investments made during the year: Kaye Skousen, $11,000.00; Timothy Tripp, $9,500.00.

APPLIED COMMUNICATION

Since reports are valuable communication tools used to make decisions, they must be clearly written.

Instructions: Research the advantages and disadvantages of three types of business ownership: proprietorship, partnership, and corporation. Write a clear, concise report on your findings.

CASE FOR CRITICAL THINKING

Rena Jacques and George Nadler are partners in a paint and decorating store. The store operates on a yearly fiscal period. At the end of each year, an accountant is hired to prepare financial statements. At the end of each month during the year, Ms. Jacques prepares a work sheet. The work sheet is prepared to determine if the business made or lost money that month. The accountant suggests that monthly financial statements also be prepared. Ms. Jacques believes, however, that the monthly work sheet is sufficient to determine how the business is doing. Do you agree with Ms. Jacques or the accountant? Why?

SCANS WORKPLACE COMPETENCY

Systems Competency: Monitors and Corrects Performance

Concept: A workplace consists of many different systems, from the human resources system to the computer network to the order fulfillment system. Every employee needs to understand the system in which he or she works. Managers of a system need to distinguish trends, predict impacts on systems operations, diagnose deviations in systems' performance, and correct malfunctions in a system.

Application: Your company has just introduced a new product with predictions that it will be enormously popular and increase sales 50% after a large advertising campaign. List the systems that could be affected by a sudden large increase in demand for the company's products. Suggest ways this increased demand can be handled.

AUDITING FOR ERRORS

Wendy Winger and Leo Zenisek are partners in Old World Bakery. The following information was taken from the records on December 31 of the current year.

Partner	Balance of Capital Account January 1	Balance of Drawing Account	Distribution of Net Income
Winger	$15,000.00	$2,300.00	40.0%
Zenisek	$12,000.00	$1,100.00	60.0%

On December 31, the partnership had a net income of $14,500.00. No additional investments were made.

The following statements were prepared using the information above. Audit the statements. Prepare a list that describes any errors you discover and how they should be corrected.

Old World Bakery
Distribution of Net Income Statement
December 31, 20--

Wendy Winger	
40.0% of Net Income	7 250 00
Leo Zenisek	
60.0% of Net Income	7 250 00
Net Income	14 500 00

Old World Bakery
Owners' Equity Statement
For Year Ended December 31, 20--

Wendy Winger			
Capital Balance, January 1, 20--		51 000 00	
Share of Net Income	7 250 00		
Less Withdrawals	2 300 00		
Increase in Capital		4 950 00	
Capital, December 31, 20--			46 050 00
Leo Zenisek			
Capital Balance, January 1, 20--		12 000 00	
Share of Net Income	7 250 00		
Less Withdrawals	1 100 00		
Increase in Capital		8 350 00	
Capital, December 31, 20--			20 350 00
Total Owners' Equity, December 31, 20--			66 400 00

ANALYZING BEST BUY'S FINANCIAL STATEMENTS

Look at the equity section of Best Buy's consolidated balance sheets on Appendix B page B-5 in this textbook.

Instructions: How would this section be different if Best Buy were a partnership owned by two partners instead of a corporation?

Accounting SOFTWARE

MEMORIZED JOURNAL ENTRIES

Peachtree strives to make entering journal entries as efficient as possible. For many transactions, such as a credit sale, you don't even have to enter a debit or credit--Peachtree assigns the appropriate account titles based on previously entered customer default options.

In contrast, some journal entries, such as accruals, must be entered using a general journal. These transactions require that you identify each debit and credit account. Over time, you might wonder if there is a way that you can eliminate the need to enter these accounts.

Peachtree's memorized transaction feature is the solution. Imagine entering the debit and credit accounts (but no amounts) of a general journal entry you record frequently. You can save this transaction as a memorized transaction. Then, when entering a general journal entry, you can select the appropriate entry from a list of memorized journal entries. With the accounts titles automatically identified, you only have to enter the amounts to save the entry.

The more often a journal entry is recorded, the more efficient you will be by creating a memorized journal entry. Of equal importance, the chance of entering an incorrect account title is reduced because you do not enter this information each time an entry is recorded.

OPTIONAL PEACHTREE ACTIVITY
Identify five general journal entries that could be entered as memorized journal entries.

MEMORIZED JOURNAL ENTRIES

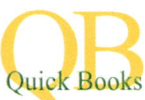

Much of the work of a computerized accounting system is focused on recording transactions. Some of these transactions are repeated, possibly several times a day. The QuickBooks "memorize a transaction" function allows the user to enter a transaction one time and then memorize it for later use.

When a memorized transaction is created, it can be set up to be automatically entered into the system on a set schedule. The user can also call up a memorized transaction to enter it into the system. A reminder can also be set up to prompt the user to enter a recurring transaction.

Reminders are another QuickBooks feature designed to increase efficiency and accuracy. QuickBooks can be programmed to remind the user to send out invoices, pay the payroll, print checks, make deposits, and perform other functions.

A good example of the use of reminders and memorized transactions could be applied to the adjusting entry for supplies. The entry could be memorized, with the amounts omitted since the amount will change each period. A reminder can be set to prompt the user to enter the adjusting entry at the end of each fiscal period. Once reminded, the user can recall the memorized adjusting entry and insert the amount of supplies used that period.

OPTIONAL QUICKBOOKS ACTIVITY
Identify five general journal entries that could be entered as memorized journal entries.

MERGING AND CENTERING TITLES

Throughout this textbook you have used Excel templates in which document titles were centered over several columns. For example, the corporation's name and statement title are usually centered over the statement.

The Merge and Center tool allows you to combine a group of adjacent cells into a single cell. Any text to be displayed in the combined cell should be entered in the upper left cell of the range.

Once the cells are merged, you can do anything you would do to any other cell: change the font size or color, right or left justify, or add a border. Selecting the Merge and Center tool again returns the cells to their original condition.

EXCEL APPLICATION PROBLEM 23-2
Open the F23-2 Excel data file. Follow the step-by-step instructions in the Instructions work sheet. Merge and center each financial statement heading.

CUSTOMIZING THE AUTOMATED ACCOUNTING SYSTEM

Many of the functions of the accounting cycle are performed automatically by the Automated Accounting system after journal entries are recorded and posted. Journal entry, ledger reports, financial statement, payroll, plant asset, and closing entries are generated automatically. The options that determine the nature of these reports and entries are determined by the settings in the Company Info. Window, which is accessed from the Custom toolbar button.

Company Name: The name of the company is entered in the Company name text box. The company name is displayed and printed as part of the heading for each report.

Problem Name: The problem name entered in this textbox is printed at the top of every report along with the user name. The problem name also appears in the title bar of the Automated Accounting main window.

Departments: The Departments drop-down list allows you to select from three options: None, 2, or 3 to set the number of departments in the business. In this course, none of the problems involve a departmentalized business, so None is selected.

Business Organization: The type of business organization selected determines the format and nature of financial statements. If Partnership Equal Distribution is selected, the automatic closing entries will distribute net income equally between the partners' capital accounts. If Partnership Unequal Distribution is selected, the closing entries to close Income Summary and distribute net income to the partners' capital accounts must be journalized and posted.

Features: Turning on the various features enables the use of plant assets, payroll, inventory, and/or budgeting systems. Employee deductions for the Payroll system can be entered under Voluntary Deductions.

Type of Business: The type of business selected determines the format of the income statement.

Income Statement: The Report by Month and Year option will show both the current month and the current year on the income statement. There must be enough data available to make this option meaningful. The problems in this textbook use the Report by Fiscal Period.

Accounting System: The Standard option is selected for all the problems in this textbook. The Voucher option is an alternative to an accounts payable system.

Computer Checks: If Accounts Payable Checks is turned on, checks will be created each time a cash payment that involves a vendor is entered. If the Payroll Checks option is turned on, paychecks will be created each time a payroll transaction is entered for an employee.

AUTOMATED ACCOUNTING APPLICATION PROBLEM 23-1
Open file F23-1.AA8. Display the problem instructions and complete the problem.

AUTOMATED ACCOUNTING APPLICATION PROBLEM 23-4
Open file F23-4.AA8. Display the problem instructions and complete the problem.

CHAPTER 24

Recording International and Internet Sales

OBJECTIVES

After studying Chapter 24, you will be able to:

1. Define accounting terms related to international sales.
2. Identify accounting concepts and practices related to international and Internet sales.
3. Record transactions for international sales.
4. Record transactions for Internet sales.

KEY TERMS

- exports
- imports
- contract of sale
- letter of credit
- bill of lading
- commercial invoice
- draft
- sight draft
- time draft
- trade acceptance

Point Your Browser
www.C21accounting.com

ACCOUNTING IN THE REAL WORLD

Honeywell

Honeywell Around the World

"You can't see most of our products, but you can count on them." This is a quote from the Honeywell web site. Sometimes the products we don't think about or can't see are some of the most important products for our safety and comfort.

Honeywell manufactures collision avoidance and traffic control systems for the aerospace industry. They also make wing-ice and wind-shear sensors and landing systems. Most of us will never see these products, but we rely on them to help get us safely to our destination. Honeywell also makes controls to keep airport facilities efficient, safe, and comfortable. Again, most of us will never see these products, but we count on them to keep us comfortable as we travel.

Honeywell has manufacturing facilities and affiliates around the world, including the Asia Pacific region, Europe, the Middle East, Africa, Latin America, Brazil, and Mexico. It is estimated that Honeywell employs nearly 62,000 people outside North America.

Critical Thinking

1. Name at least two challenges Honeywell faces because of its world-wide operations.
2. Name at least two benefits Honeywell has because of its world-wide operations.

Source: www.honeywell.com

INTERNET ACTIVITY

Foreign Exchange Rates

There are several Internet sites designed to help you convert foreign currency. Perform an Internet search for the phrase "foreign currency." Find a site that converts currency.

Instructions

1. Pick the currency of a foreign country. List the exchange rate for that currency.
2. If you gave the exchange organization 100 U.S. dollars, how much foreign currency would you receive?

LESSON 24-1

Recording International Sales

INTERNATIONAL SALES

Sales in the international market have become a major source of revenue for both small and large businesses. Improved technology has helped support international trade. It is no longer necessary to talk to your vendor or customer via telephone. E-mail, fax, and the Internet have made it possible to do business without as much concern about time zones and business hours around the world.

Goods or services shipped out of a seller's home country to a foreign country are called **exports**. Goods or services bought from a foreign country and brought into a buyer's home country are called **imports**.

Businesses may be able to import materials or services that are not available or are less expensive than within their own country. Thus, many companies have entered into the export and import markets to maintain their competitiveness and provide the products and services to meet customer demand.

GiftPak Company imports merchandise such as Swiss chocolate and Chinese tea from a variety of countries. GiftPak also exports its gift boxes and baskets to customers around the world. Selling merchandise to individuals or other businesses within one's own country, generally referred to as *domestic sales*, is much simpler than international sales.

CHARACTER COUNTS

Become an Ethics Officer

While researching the ethics activities in this textbook, you have reviewed the codes of conduct for several companies. You have seen references to individuals with titles such as ethics officer, governance manager, or compliance officer. These individuals are charged with ensuring that the company has an effective ethics policy, educating employees on the code of conduct, and resolving ethical issues reported by employees.

Have you considered a career in business ethics? Beyond earning a college education, you would need to constantly increase your knowledge of business ethics and corporate governance. One resource of information available to ethics officers is the Ethics Resource Center (ERC), a nonprofit organization devoted to helping individuals and organizations act with integrity. The ERC provides a wide range of resources to help ethics officers. The ERC is also involved in ethics education for students.

Instructions

Access the Ethics Resource Center at www.ethics.org. Prepare a list of the various resources available to ethics officers. How does the ERC help provide ethics education to students?

INTERNATIONAL SALES COMPARED WITH DOMESTIC SALES

Most domestic sales are sold for cash or on account after reviewing and approving a customer's credit. Because all transactions in the United States are covered by the same universal commercial laws and the same accounting standards, many transactions are based on trust. A customer with approved credit orders merchandise. The merchandise is shipped, and an invoice is sent by the vendor. After receiving the merchandise and invoice, the customer pays the vendor.

However, because of the increased complexities of international sales, several issues must be considered. The lack of uniform commercial laws among countries makes settlement of disputes more difficult. Greater distances and sometimes more complex transportation methods increase the time to complete the transaction. Because it may be difficult to determine a customer's financial condition and to take legal action if a customer does not pay, the risk of uncollected amounts is increased. Unstable political conditions in some countries may affect the ability to receive payments from those countries. Therefore, most businesses dealing in exports and/or imports follow a general process in international trade that ensures that the vendor receives payment for merchandise sold and the customer receives the merchandise ordered.

PROCESSING AN INTERNATIONAL SALE

A document that details all the terms agreed to by seller and buyer for a sales transaction is called a **contract of sale**. The contract includes a description and quantity of merchandise, price, point of delivery, packing and marking instructions, shipping information, insurance provisions, and method of payment.

GiftPak Company, located in Glendive, Montana, contracts to sell merchandise to Santiago Company in Mexico City, Mexico. The contract price is $5,000.00 in U.S. dollars, and merchandise is to be delivered to Mexico City. The Santiago Company is to pay transportation charges.

A letter issued by a bank guaranteeing that a named individual or business will be paid a specified amount provided stated conditions are met is called a **letter of credit**. The contract of sale between GiftPak and Santiago specified a letter of credit as the method of payment.

Santiago prepared an application with its bank, Banco Nacional de México, to issue a letter of credit. Banco Nacional de México approved Santiago's application and issued the letter of credit. Banco Nacional de México forwarded the letter of credit to GiftPak's bank, First Bank in Glendive.

First Bank delivered the letter of credit to GiftPak. GiftPak reviewed the letter of credit to ensure that the provisions in the letter agreed with the contract of sale. GiftPak then shipped the merchandise.

PHOTODISC/GETTY IMAGES

> **FOR YOUR INFORMATION**
>
> **FYI**
>
> The International Chamber of Commerce publishes "Incoterms" to attempt to coordinate international sales. This set of international rules interprets common sales terms used in foreign trade that are adopted by most international trade associations.

Recording International Sales

COLLECTING PAYMENT FOR AN INTERNATIONAL SALE

In order for GiftPak to collect payment, three documents specified in the letter of credit must be submitted to First Bank: (1) a bill of lading, (2) a commercial invoice, and (3) a draft.

A receipt signed by the authorized agent of a transportation company for merchandise received that also serves as a contract for the delivery of the merchandise is called a **bill of lading**. The transportation company sends the bill of lading to GiftPak when the merchandise is shipped. GiftPak then prepares the other two documents. A statement prepared by the seller of merchandise addressed to the buyer showing a detailed listing and description of merchandise sold, including prices and terms, is called a **commercial invoice**. A written, signed, and dated order from one party ordering another party, usually a bank, to pay money to a third party is called a **draft**. A draft is sometimes referred to as a *bill of exchange*. A draft payable on sight when the holder presents it for payment is called a **sight draft**.

First Bank examines the documents submitted by GiftPak to ensure that all terms of sale are in compliance with the letter of credit. First Bank then forwards the documents to Santiago's bank, Banco Nacional de México. Banco Nacional de México examines the documents to ensure they are in compliance with the terms and conditions of the letter of credit. When Banco Nacional de México determines that all documents are in compliance, it deducts the amount of the sight draft from Santiago's account and sends that amount, $5,000.00, to GiftPak's bank, First Bank.

Banco Nacional de México then forwards the documents to Santiago Company. By presenting the bill of lading and letter of credit to the transportation company, Santiago can receive the merchandise.

FOR YOUR INFORMATION
FYI

The United States federal government does not collect a sales tax. However, many countries of the world, including most of the major industrial powers, do collect what is referred to as a value added tax, or VAT. A value added tax is basically a national sales tax.

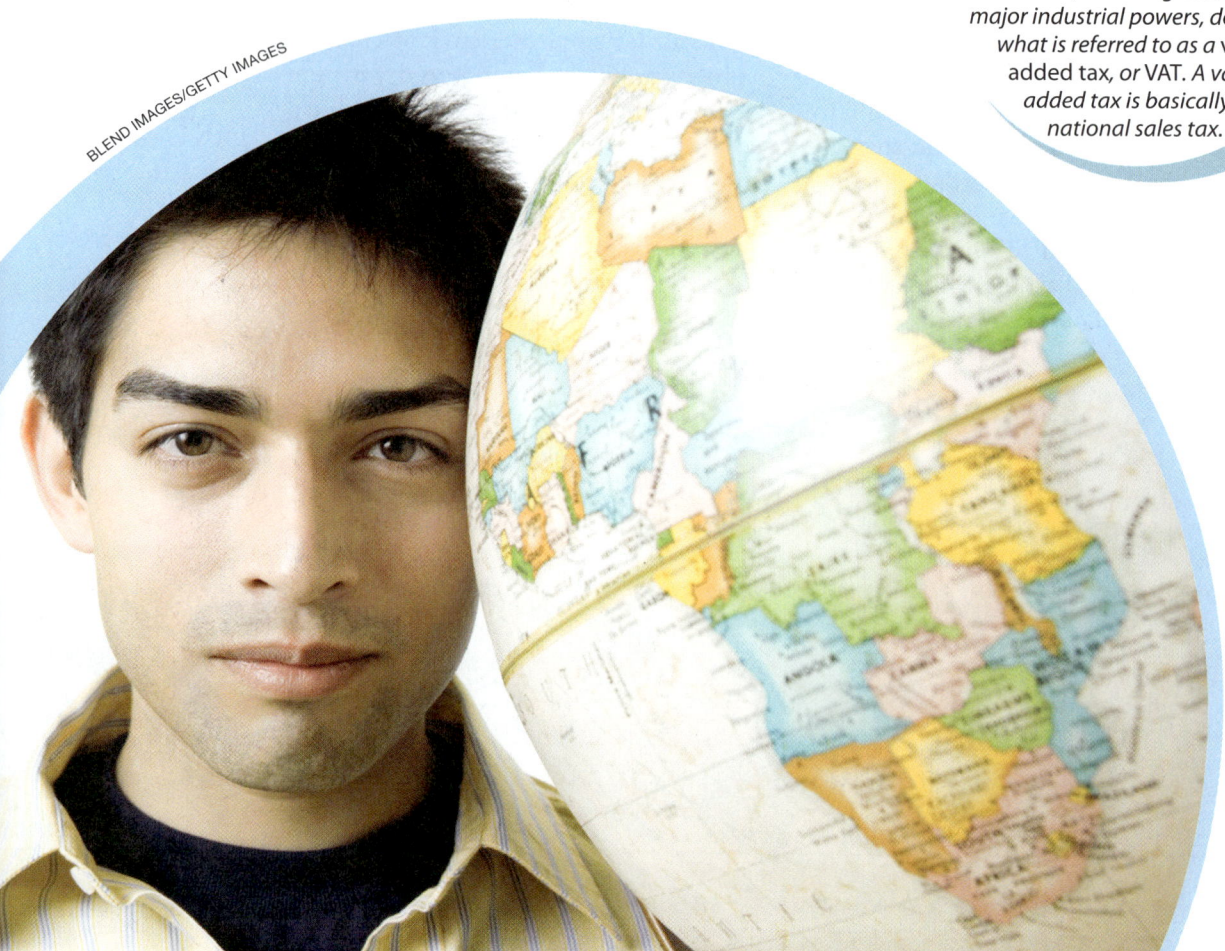

GLOBAL PERSPECTIVE

Foreign Currency

As our world becomes smaller and global trade increases, U.S. businesses become more involved in transactions with foreign businesses. These transactions can be stated in terms of U.S. dollars or in the currency of the other country. If the transaction involves foreign currency, a U.S. business must convert the foreign currency into U.S. dollars before the transaction can be recorded. [CONCEPT: Unit of Measurement]

The value of foreign currency may change daily. In the United States, the exchange rate is the value of foreign currency in relation to the U.S. dollar. Banks, online services, and many daily newspapers list current exchange rates.

The exchange rate is stated in terms of one unit of foreign currency. Using Argentina as an example, assume that one Argentine peso is worth 0.33820 U.S. dollar (or about 34 U.S. cents). This rate would be used when exchanging Argentine pesos for U.S. dollars.

A conversion formula can be used to find out how many foreign currency units can be purchased with one U.S. dollar. The formula is:

÷ exchange rate = foreign currency per U.S. dollar
1 dollar ÷ 0.33820 = 2.9568 pesos per dollar

To convert an amount in Argentine pesos to U.S. dollars, divide the amount of pesos by the number of pesos per dollar as shown.

350 Argentine pesos ÷ 2.9568 pesos per U.S. dollar
= $118.37 US

Instructions

1. Current exchange rates change constantly. Do an Internet search and report the current exchange rate for the Argentine peso.

2. If the exchange rate for one Japanese yen is .0085143 U.S. dollar, what U.S. dollar amount would be recorded for a receipt of 5,200 Japanese yen?

3. If the exchange rate for one European euro is 1.08944 U.S. dollars, what amount would be recorded for a receipt of 197 euros?

JOURNALIZING AN INTERNATIONAL SALE

After receiving payment from Banco Nacional de México, First Bank deposits the payment for the sale in GiftPak's account and sends GiftPak a deposit slip for the amount deposited. After receiving the deposit slip from First Bank, GiftPak prepares a memorandum as a source document for the cash received. The sale is then recorded as a cash sale.

Sales taxes are normally paid only on sales to the final consumer. GiftPak's sale is to Santiago Company, a merchandising company. Therefore, sales tax is not collected.

The sales and collection process GiftPak followed assured GiftPak of receiving payment for its sale and Santiago Company of receiving the merchandise it ordered.

April 1. Recorded international cash sale, $5,000.00. Memorandum 45.

FOR YOUR INFORMATION
FYI

Visitors to foreign countries with a value added tax (VAT) typically are required to pay the VAT. However, if items purchased exceed a specified amount, a refund of a portion of the VAT can be requested.

STEPS — RECORDING AN ENTRY FOR AN INTERNATIONAL SALE

1. Write the date, 20--, Apr. 1, in the Date column.
2. Place a check mark in the Account Title column to indicate that no account title needs to be entered.
3. Write the source document number, *M45*, in the Doc. No. column.
4. Place a check mark in the Post. Ref. column to indicate that the amounts on this line are not posted individually.
5. Write the sale amount, *$5,000.00*, in the Sales Credit column.
6. Write the sale amount, *$5,000.00*, in the Cash Debit column.

PHOTODISC/GETTY IMAGES

JOURNALIZING TIME DRAFTS

GiftPak Company sold $6,000.00 of merchandise to Simov Co., located in Istanbul, Turkey. The contract of sale with Simov was similar to the contract with Santiago Company, with one exception. GiftPak agreed to delay receipt of payment 60 days. A draft that is payable at a fixed or determinable future time after it is accepted is called a **time draft**.

The sales process with Simov is the same as with Santiago, except GiftPak submits with the documentation a time draft due 60 days from the date the draft is accepted. On May 10, all documentation for the Simov sale is verified to be correct by the seller's and buyer's banks, and GiftPak's time draft is accepted.

After verifying the documentation, Simov's bank, Bank of Istanbul, returns the accepted time draft to GiftPak and forwards the other documents to Simov Co. Simov can receive the merchandise by presenting the bill of lading and letter of credit to the transportation company.

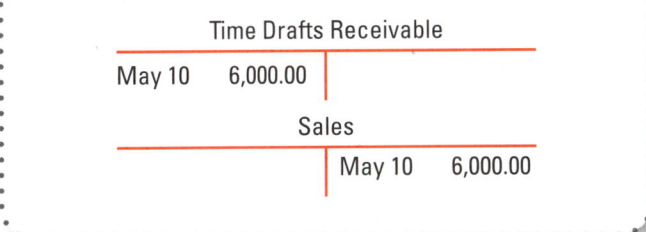

May 10. Received a 60-day time draft from Simov Co. for an international sale, $6,000.00. Time Draft No. 12.

STEPS JOURNALIZING A TIME DRAFT

1. Write the date, *10*, in the Date column.
2. Write *Time Drafts Receivable* in the Account Title column.
3. Write *TD* and the time draft number, *12*, in the Doc. No. column.
4. Write the sale amount, *$6,000.00*, in the Debit column.
5. On the next line, indent and write *Sales* in the Account Title column.
6. Write the sale amount, *$6,000.00*, in the Credit column.

FOR YOUR INFORMATION

FYI

The minimum value added tax (VAT) in the European Community is 15%; however, there is no additional local sales tax. The Philippines has a 10% VAT that applies to the sale, barter, or exchange of goods, properties, or services. Thailand applies a 7% VAT to selected beverages.

Recording International Sales Lesson 24-1

JOURNALIZING CASH RECEIPTS FROM TIME DRAFTS

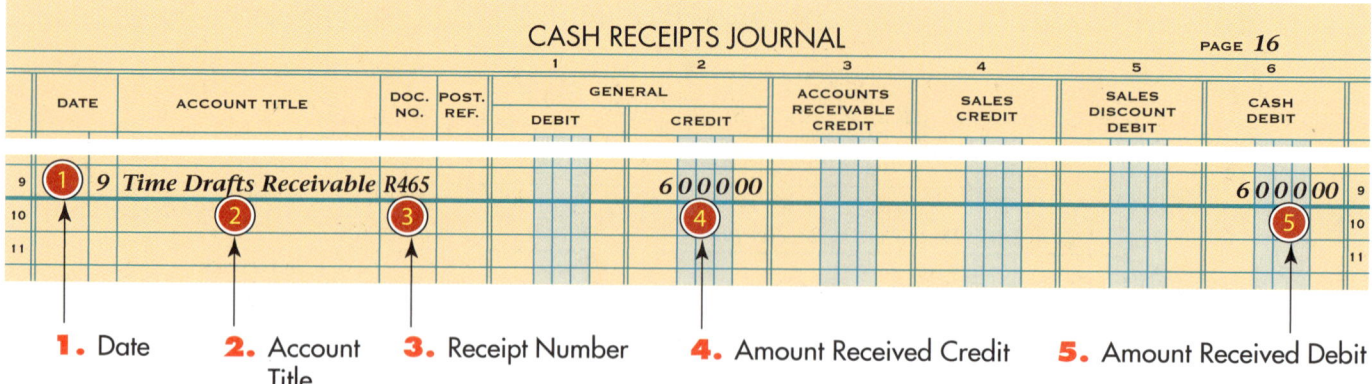

1. Date
2. Account Title
3. Receipt Number
4. Amount Received Credit
5. Amount Received Debit

When Simov's time draft is due and presented to its bank, Bank of Istanbul, the bank pays the draft. The payment process is the same as the payment of Santiago Company's sight draft.

> July 9. Received cash for the value of Time Draft No. 12, $6,000.00. Receipt No. 465.

Cash	
July 9 6,000.00	

Time Drafts Receivable	
May 10 6,000.00	July 9 6,000.00

The process used by GiftPak Company for international sales relies upon letters of credit from banks to assure receipt of payment for those sales. Occasionally, GiftPak grants an extension of time for payment to long-time international customers by submitting a time draft.

Trade Acceptances

A form signed by a buyer at the time of a sale of merchandise in which the buyer promises to pay the seller a specified sum of money, usually at a stated time in the future, is called a **trade acceptance**.

A trade acceptance is similar to a draft except a draft is generally paid by a bank and a trade acceptance is paid by the buyer. A seller generally has much more assurance of receiving payment from a bank than from a buyer. Because of the many complexities, few businesses use trade acceptances in international sales. Some businesses, however, use trade acceptances for domestic sales to very reliable customers.

STEPS JOURNALIZING CASH RECEIVED FROM A TIME DRAFT

1. Write the date, 9, in the Date column.
2. Write *Time Drafts Receivable* in the account title column.
3. Write the source document number, *R465*, in the Doc. No. column.
4. Write the amount received, $6,000.00, in the General Credit column.
5. Write the same amount, $6,000.00, in the Cash Debit column.

> **REMEMBER**
>
> A sight draft and a time draft are similar. Both methods of international sales require the buyer's bank to guarantee the cash payment for the sale. The primary difference between a sight draft and a time draft is the timing of the payment. Cash payment of a time draft is delayed for a period of time after the delivery of the goods to the buyer.

End of Lesson REVIEW

TERMS REVIEW

- exports
- imports
- contract of sale
- letter of credit
- bill of lading
- commercial invoice
- draft
- sight draft
- time draft
- trade acceptance

AUDIT YOUR UNDERSTANDING

1. What are some of the issues that must be considered before making international sales?
2. What two purposes does a bill of lading serve?
3. How does a sight draft differ from a time draft?
4. Why do many companies dealing in international sales rely upon letters of credit from banks?
5. How does a trade acceptance differ from a draft?

WORK TOGETHER 24-1

Journalizing international sales transactions

The cash receipts and general journals for Marlon Exports, Ltd. are given in the *Working Papers*. Your instructor will guide you through the following examples.

1. Using the current year, journalize the following international sales on page 9 of a cash receipts journal and page 5 of a general journal. Sales tax is not charged on these sales. Source documents are abbreviated as follows: memorandum, M; time draft, TD; receipt, R.

   Transactions

   May 1. Recorded an international cash sale, $14,000.00. M323.
       5. Received a 30-day time draft from Ying Shen for an international sale, $18,000.00. TD32.
       9. Received cash for the value of Time Draft No. 10, $21,000.00. R221.

2. Prove and rule the cash receipts journal.

ON YOUR OWN 24-1

Journalizing international sales transactions

The cash receipts and general journals for Hakim Handicrafts are given in the *Working Papers*. Work this problem independently.

1. Using the current year, journalize the following international sales on page 17 of a cash receipts journal and page 9 of a general journal. Sales tax is not charged on these sales. Source documents are abbreviated as follows: memorandum, M; time draft, TD; receipt, R.

   Transactions

   Sep. 3. Recorded an international cash sale, $9,400.00. M256.
       5. Received a 45-day time draft from Ledah Patel for an international sale, $7,800.00. TD81.
       6. Received cash for the value of Time Draft No. 73, $13,500.00. R211.

2. Prove and rule the cash receipts journal.

Recording International Sales

LESSON 24-2

Recording Internet Sales

INTERNET SALES

More and more companies are turning to the Internet as an additional way of selling goods and services. Internet shopping provides customers the opportunity to browse the products offered by a company, compare competitors' products, and do so at a time and place convenient to the customer.

Selling goods over the Internet, however, also presents some challenges to the seller. The web site developed must be easy to navigate and safe to use. Customers must feel that the web site uses up-to-date security procedures to protect credit card information as it is being transmitted. The selling company must also be able to accept credit card sales, which means it must contract with a bank to offer this service or with a company that will offer this service to businesses for a fee.

GiftPak has prepared a web site that will accept credit card orders and transmit the sales information for immediate shipping and billing. An order confirmation is also immediately sent to the buyer, containing information about the order and expected shipping date.

Internet sales at GiftPak must be completed with a credit card. At the end of each day, GiftPak will be able to print out a terminal summary similar to the terminal summary discussed in Chapter 10. The terminal summary is used as the source document for recording online sales.

PHOTOGRAPHER'S CHOICE RF/GETTY IMAGES

FOR YOUR INFORMATION

FYI

Credit card companies are taking measures to protect online shoppers. Some companies offer a safe-shopping option, which allows the credit card holder to instantly obtain a temporary credit card account number good only for one purchase.

FOR YOUR INFORMATION

FYI

Companies such as PayPal offer services to online customers and sellers. For customers, these companies offer sites that use the most modern methods to safeguard credit card information as it is transmitted online. For sellers, these companies offer the availability of credit card sales with less cost and red tape.

JOURNALIZING AN INTERNET SALE

May 1. Recorded Internet credit card sales, $891.00. Terminal Summary 45.

GiftPak Company processes its credit card sales at the end of each day. At the same time, the information is electronically transmitted to First Bank, with whom GiftPak has contracted to process its credit card sales. This information is transferred to the Federal Reserve Bank and processed in a manner similar to checks. Therefore, GiftPak considers these sales to be cash sales.

The asset account Cash has a normal debit balance and is debited for the amount of the credit card sales, $891.00. The sales account has a normal credit balance. Therefore, Sales is credited for the amount of the sales, $891.00.

FOR YOUR INFORMATION

FYI

In order to process bank credit cards such as Visa and MasterCard, a business must set up a merchant account with a bank. The business pays a fee to the bank for processing credit card sales.

STEPS   RECORDING AN ENTRY FOR AN INTERNET SALE

1. Write the date, *20--, May 1,* in the Date column.
2. Place a check mark in the Account Title column to indicate that no account title needs to be entered.
3. Write the source document number, *TS45*, in the Doc. No. column.
4. Place a check mark in the Post. Ref. column to indicate that the amounts on this line are not posted individually.
5. Write the sale amount, *$891.00*, in the Sales Credit column.
6. Write the sale amount, *$891.00*, in the Cash Debit column.

Recording Internet Sales

End of Lesson REVIEW

AUDIT YOUR UNDERSTANDING

1. What are two reasons why a customer might prefer online shopping?
2. Why is a bank credit card sale treated the same as a cash sale?

WORK TOGETHER 24-2

Journalizing Internet sales transactions

The cash receipts journal for Teddy Bears Galore is given in the *Working Papers*. Your instructor will guide you through the following examples.

1. Using the current year, journalize the following Internet sales on page 5 of a cash receipts journal.

Transactions

Mar. 5. Recorded Internet credit card sales, $2,432.00. Terminal Summary 331.
    12. Recorded Internet credit card sales, $3,010.00. Terminal Summary 332.
    19. Recorded Internet credit card sales, $1,550.00. Terminal Summary 333.

ON YOUR OWN 24-2

Journalizing Internet sales transactions

The cash receipts journal for Labels World is given in the *Working Papers*. Work this problem independently.

1. Using the current year, journalize the following Internet sales on page 9 of a cash receipts journal.

Transactions

May 7. Recorded Internet credit card sales, $352.00. Terminal Summary 44.
    12. Recorded Internet credit card sales, $187.00. Terminal Summary 45.
    20. Recorded Internet credit card sales, $319.00. Terminal Summary 46.

SUMMARY

After completing this chapter, you can:

1. Define accounting terms related to international sales.
2. Identify accounting concepts and practices related to international and Internet sales.
3. Record transactions for international sales.
4. Record transactions for Internet sales.

EXPLORE ACCOUNTING

How Credit Card Systems Work

To promote sales, Chimes Music Store accepts major credit cards, such as Visa, MasterCard, American Express, and Discover. To process these sales, Chimes Music contracted with a processing center to install and maintain its credit card system.

When a customer presents Chimes with a credit card, the card is scanned and the amount of purchase is entered in a credit card reader. The reader uses phone lines to contact the processing center. If the processing center determines that the customer has an adequate amount of unused credit, the transaction is approved and a sales receipt is printed. At the same time, the transaction is added to daily totals maintained by the processing center. After the customer signs the credit card receipt, both the customer and business keep a copy.

At the end of the day, Chimes enters a command to instruct the system to close its account. The credit card reader prints a summary receipt that lists the total number and amount of sales by credit card company. The processing center notifies each credit card company of its daily total. The credit card companies then make electronic funds transfers to Chimes Music's bank account. This process often requires several days to complete.

Both the processing center and the credit card companies charge Chimes with a fee for processing credit card sales. These charges are accumulated, and a monthly fee is charged directly to Chimes Music's bank account.

Research: Credit card processing companies can use different equipment and procedures to process credit card sales. Ask a local retailer to describe its credit card processing system. Prepare a report that describes the equipment and procedures used as well as the fees charged. Contrast the system you observed with Chimes Music's system. Which system is better? How could the system you researched be improved?

24-1 APPLICATION PROBLEM

Journalizing international sales transactions

The cash receipts and general journals for Parker Exports, Ltd. are given in the *Working Papers*.

Instructions:

1. Journalize the following international sales completed by Parker Exports, Ltd. during June of the current year. Use page 10 of a cash receipts journal and page 6 of a general journal. Sales tax is not charged on these sales. Source documents are abbreviated as follows: memorandum, M; time draft, TD; receipt, R.

Transactions:

June 1. Recorded an international cash sale, $12,000.00. M82.
 5. Received a 30-day time draft from Bella Lamas for an international sale, $13,000.00. TD32.
 9. Received cash for the value of Time Draft No. 24, $16,000.00. R116.
 12. Received a 60-day time draft from Pablo Fuentes for an international sale, $8,000.00. TD33.
 19. Received cash for the value of Time Draft No. 21, $22,000.00. R117.
 21. Recorded an international cash sale, $17,500.00. M83.
 25. Received a 30-day time draft from Rodrigo Soto for an international sale, $24,000.00. TD34.

2. Prove and rule the cash receipts journal.

24-2 APPLICATION PROBLEM

Journalizing Internet sales transactions

The cash receipts journal for Sports Memorabilia is given in the *Working Papers*.

Instructions:

1. Journalize the following Internet sales completed by Sports Memorabilia during August of the current year. Use page 15 of a cash receipts journal. Source documents are abbreviated as follows: Terminal Summary, TS.

Transactions:

Aug. 6. Recorded Internet credit card sales, $909.00. TS116.
 13. Recorded Internet credit card sales, $1,480.00. TS117.
 20. Recorded Internet credit card sales, $1,147.00. TS118.
 27. Recorded Internet credit card sales, $2,843.00. TS119.

2. Total and rule the cash receipts journal.

(Go Beyond the Book
For more information go to
www.C21accounting.com)

24-3 MASTERY PROBLEM

Recording international and Internet sales

Argo Corporation has both international and Internet sales.

Instructions:

1. Journalize the following transactions affecting sales and cash receipts completed during February of the current year. Use page 2 of a general journal and a cash receipts journal. Source documents are abbreviated as follows: memorandum, M; receipt, R; time draft, TD; terminal summary, TS.

Transactions:
Feb. 5. Received a 30-day time draft from Akeo Doi for an international sale, $5,000.00. TD10.
     8. Recorded Internet credit card sales, $12,300.00. TS23.
    12. Recorded an international cash sale, $10,500.00. M8.
    14. Received cash for the value of Time Draft No. 4, $23,000.00. R35.
    18. Recorded Internet credit card sales, $18,400.00. TS24.
    21. Received cash for the value of Time Draft No. 7, $8,000.00. R37.
    24. Recorded an international cash sale, $13,500.00. M12.
    27. Recorded Internet credit card sales, $9,200.00. TS25.
    28. Received a 30-day time draft from Sachi Nozaki for international sale of merchandise, $6,000.00. TD11.

2. Prove and rule the cash receipts journal.

24-4 CHALLENGE PROBLEM

Recording international sales and converting foreign currency

International sales can be stated in terms of U.S. dollars or in the foreign currency. The transaction statements below are stated in terms of the foreign currency of the customer.

Instructions:

1. Journalize the following transactions affecting sales. Use the foreign currency exchange rates given in the table below to translate the amount of the sales into U.S. dollars. Use page 11 of a cash receipts journal. Source documents are abbreviated as follows: memorandum, M.

Transactions:
June 1. Recorded international cash sale, 7,026 Chinese yuan. M46.
     8. Recorded international cash sale, 13,782 Mexican pesos. M49.
    14. Recorded international cash sale, 1,364 New Zealand dollars. M55.
    19. Recorded international cash sale, 354 European euros. M57.
    28. Recorded international cash sale, 3,174,060 Zimbabwe dollars. M68.

Currency	1 U.S. Dollar Equals…
Chinese Yuan	8.26650 Yuan
European Euro	.78796 Euro
Mexican Peso	11.48500 Pesos
New Zealand Dollar	1.43616 New Zealand Dollars
Zimbabwe Dollar	5,290.10 Zimbabwe Dollars

2. Prove and rule the cash receipts journal.

APPLIED COMMUNICATION

Internet sites must be easy to use and provide the customer with the information needed to make buying decisions.

Instructions: Investigate the web sites of two businesses. Write a report stating which site you feel is more customer friendly. Be sure to support your opinion with facts and examples.

CASE FOR CRITICAL THINKING

Julie Lindstrom is the bookkeeper for a small company that imports handcrafted items from foreign countries. Most of its suppliers are individuals who sell handmade crafts. All purchases are stated in the currency of the supplier's country but paid in U.S. dollars. When Julie pays the suppliers for their goods, she must look up the exchange rate in effect at the time and convert the foreign currency into U.S. dollars.

Most of the suppliers are not knowledgeable about the current exchange rates. Julie calculates the amount of U.S. dollars owed to each supplier, but she then rounds down to the lower whole dollar. She reasons that this saves time for both parties by eliminating "cents" from all transactions. Is this the correct procedure? What would you say to Julie about her policy?

GRAPHING WORKSHOP

Data regarding unit sales of Import/Export World are given in the table below.

Instructions: For each year, create a pie graph showing the amount of unit sales in each country.

	China	Italy	Bolivia	Germany	Total Sales
Year 1	10,000	5,000	8,000	15,000	38,000
Year 2	25,000	4,000	10,000	18,000	57,000

ANALYZING BEST BUY'S FINANCIAL STATEMENTS

When a company does business in a foreign country, it often deals in the currency of that country. When financial statements are prepared, the company must convert these amounts to U.S. dollars. Note 1 to Best Buy's financial statements on Appendix pages B-9 through B-20 explains how many different financial statement items are presented.

Instructions

1. When Best Buy translates foreign currency into U.S. dollars, what rate is used when listing the amounts for assets and liabilities?
2. When Best Buy translates its results of operations and cash flows into U.S. dollars, what rate is used?

Accounting SOFTWARE

PEACHTREE REMINDERS AND ALERTS

Today's computerized accounting systems are designed to do more than organize transactions and prepare financial statements. These systems also provide features to help you get organized.

Imagine starting your computer each morning and receiving a list of items that require your attention. You might begin by looking at your "to-do" list, notes you create for yourself to remind you of tasks to be performed. Then, examine your list of "events," such as the time and location of a meeting, the deadline for a report, or a desired date to contact a potential customer. As you enter a new event, Peachtree asks you identify the number of days before the event will be listed. For example, your event list might include a meeting scheduled for tomorrow while also listing an important report due in one week.

PEACHTREE MASTERY PROBLEM 24-3

1. Open (Restore) file 24-3MP.ptb.
2. Journalize the international sales involving a time draft using the Make General Journal Entries window.
3. Use the Enter Sales Receipts window to journalize Internet sales.
4. Use the Enter Sales Receipts window to journalize international sales.
5. Use the Make Deposits window to journalize the receipt of time draft payments.
6. Print a Journal report using February 1 and February 28 for the dates.

QUICKBOOKS PORTABLE FILES

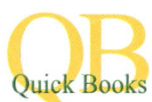

A previous chapter discussed the importance of making a backup copy of accounting data stored electronically. Backup files contain all of the financial data for the company and can be quite large.

If you need to email or transport the financial data to a different location, it is not reasonable to use the backup file because of its size. A better solution is provided by QuickBooks. A portable file is a compact version of company's file and is small enough to be sent via email or saved to a portable media device.

If the person receiving the portable file is only looking at the data and will not be changing any data, no special considerations need to be made. However, if that person will be changing the data, no additional changes should be made to the main company files. When the portable file with changes is received by the company, it is not possible to merge the portable file back into the company files. Instead, the new, changed portable file will be used in place of the old company file.

QUICKBOOKS MASTERY PROBLEM 24-3

1. Open the Argo Corporation file.
2. Journalize the transactions affecting sales and cash receipts completed during February in the appropriate journal.
3. Print the general journal and cash receipts journal.

OPTIONAL QUICKBOOKS ACTIVITY

If directed by your instructor, make a portable file from your solution to Mastery Problem 24-3 and email it to your instructor.

FORMATS FOR CURRENCY

As a student of accounting, you have become accustomed to writing amounts in dollars and cents. On a spreadsheet, monetary amounts are almost always presented using a number, currency, or accounting format with two decimal places.

In today's global economy, accountants need to create workbooks that can accurately translate U.S. dollars to any of the world's many currencies. For example, one U.S. dollar may equal 8.2665 Chinese Yuan or 0.78796 European Euro.

Electronic spreadsheets allow you to display amounts to 30 or more decimal places. Although it is unlikely you will ever need that level of accuracy, it demonstrates the flexibility of today's electronic spreadsheets.

EXCEL CHALLENGE PROBLEM 24-4
Open the F24-4 Excel data file. Follow the step-by-step instructions in the Instructions work sheet. Modify the decimal places of the foreign currency amounts.

AUTOMATED ACCOUNTING TOOLS

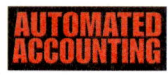

Automated Accounting has several tools available to help perform certain tasks when using the system. You have already learned about the Planning Tools which perform various savings, loan, and interest calculations. Two other useful tools are the Calculator and the Find tool.

Calculator
Click the Calc. button on the toolbar to open the on-screen Calculator. A help menu is available for the Calculator by clicking Help at the top of the calculator. The results of a calculation can be pasted into the text box in which the cursor is located.

The Find Tool
When a journal is displayed, the Find tool from the Edit menu can be used to locate any previously entered transaction. You may enter the date, reference, amount, or any other data from the transaction in the Find What text box and click OK. If a matching transaction is found, it will be displayed in the journal where it can be checked, changed, or deleted. If you select Find Next in the Edit menu, you will locate the next occurrence of the search criteria.

AUTOMATED ACCOUNTING APPLICATION PROBLEM 24-1
Open file F24-1.AA8. Display the problem instructions and complete the problem.

AUTOMATED ACCOUNTING MASTERY PROBLEM 24-3
Open file F24-3.AA8. Display the problem instructions and complete the problem.

APPENDIX A

STATEMENT OF CASH FLOWS

CASH FLOW ANALYSIS

Financial statements provide managers, investors, and other individuals with financial information about the operating efficiency and financial condition of a business. The income statement, balance sheet, and statement of stockholders' equity are prepared using accounting records of a business. On the income statement, revenues are recorded when the revenue is earned, regardless of when the cash is received. Expenses are recorded when incurred, regardless of when the cash is paid. The accounting method that records revenues when they are earned and expenses when they are incurred is called the *accrual basis of accounting*.

Accrual-based financial statements report useful information. Some individuals, however, may need more information about why cash is received and how cash is spent in a business. The cash receipts and cash payments of a company are called *cash flows*. A financial statement that reports the cash flows of a business for a fiscal period is called a *statement of cash flows*. The statement reports the source of all cash receipts and the reason for all cash payments during a fiscal period.

The statement of cash flows is divided into three sections: cash flows from operating activities, cash flows from investing activities, and cash flows from financing activities.

CASH FLOWS FROM OPERATING ACTIVITIES

The cash receipts and payments necessary to operate a business on a day-to-day basis are called *operating activities*. Cash inflows and outflows from operating activities are listed below.

Operating Activities	
Cash Inflows	**Cash Outflows**
Cash sales of merchandise	Cash paid for salaries
Cash sales of services	Cash paid for merchandise
Cash received on account	Cash paid on account
Interest income	Cash paid for supplies
	Cash paid for utilities
	Cash paid for interest

CASH FLOWS FROM INVESTING ACTIVITIES

Cash receipts and cash payments involving the sale or purchase of assets used to earn revenue over a period of time are called *investing activities*. Cash inflows and outflows from investing activities are listed below.

Investing Activities	
Cash Inflows	**Cash Outflows**
Sale of property/building	Purchase of property/building
Sale of investments	Cash paid for investment
Sale of machinery/equipment	Purchase of machinery/equipment

CASH FLOWS FROM FINANCING ACTIVITIES

Cash receipts and payments involving debt or equity transactions are called *financing activities*. Cash inflows and outflows from financing activities are listed below.

Financing Activities	
Cash Inflows	**Cash Outflows**
Issuing stock	Payment of cash dividends
Long-term loans	Repayment of loan principal
Issuing bonds	Retirement of bond principal

PREPARING THE OPERATING ACTIVITIES SECTION OF A STATEMENT OF CASH FLOWS

The first item listed in the operating activities section is the net income for the period. Since this amount is calculated using the accrual basis of accounting, several adjustments must be made to adjust the net income to actual cash flow from operating activities.

Adjusting Net Income for Depreciation

Depreciation expense is recorded on the income statement and reduces net income. However, depreciation expense is a non-cash expense, because cash is not paid out for depreciation. Therefore, even though it is an expense, it is not an outflow of cash. Since it has already been subtracted to determine net income, it has to be added back in when adjusting net income to cash flow. Sanibel Sports recorded $1,500.00 of depreciation expense for 20X2. The adjustment to add back in the amount of depreciation expense is the first adjustment listed on the statement of cash flows for Sanibel Sports on page A-5.

Adjusting Net Income for Changes in Current Assets

Increases and decreases in current assets affect cash flows and require adjustments. The balance in accounts receivable for Sanibel Sports on December 31, 20X1, was $78,550.00. On December 31, 20X2, the balance was $64,270.00. The accounts receivable account balance decreased by $14,280.00 during the year. A decrease in accounts receivable means that the sales amount reported on the income statement was less than the cash received on account. The $14,280.00 decrease in accounts receivable represents additional cash that has been received and is added to net income to determine cash flow on Sanibel Sports' statement of cash flows.

The balance in the supplies account for Sanibel Sports on December 31, 20X1, was $6,702.00. On December 31, 20X2, the balance was $7,377.00. The supplies account balance increased by $675.00 during the year. An increase in supplies means that Sanibel Sports bought more supplies than it used during the period. The amount of supplies used is listed on the income statement as an expense and reduces net income. The $675.00 increase in supplies represents additional cash that was used and is deducted from net income to determine cash flow on Sanibel Sports' statement of cash flows.

In a similar manner, all decreases in current assets will be added to net income as an adjustment. All increases in current assets will be deducted from net income as an adjustment.

Effect of Changes in Current Assets on Cash Flows

Increases in current assets ⟶ Deducted from net income
Decreases in current assets ⟶ Added to net income

Adjusting Net Income for Changes in Current Liabilities

Increases and decreases in current liabilities also affect cash flows and require adjustments. The balance in accounts payable for Sanibel Sports on December 31, 20X1, was $79,290.00. On December 31, 20X2, the balance was $63,400.00. The accounts payable account balance decreased by $15,890.00 during the year. A decrease in accounts payable means that the cash flow for purchases on account was more than the amount of purchases reported on the income statement. The $15,890.00 decrease in accounts payable represents additional cash that has been paid out and is deducted from net income to determine cash flow on Sanibel Sports' statement of cash flows.

The balance in the salaries payable account for Sanibel Sports on December 31, 20X1, was $12,500.00. On December 31, 20X2, the balance was $20,900.00. The salaries payable account balance increased by $8,400.00 during the year. An increase in salaries payable means that not all of the salaries earned during the year were paid. The amount of salaries earned is listed on the income statement and reduces net income. The $8,400.00 increase in salaries payable represents a cash savings and is added to net income to determine cash flow on Sanibel Sports' statement of cash flows.

In a similar manner, all decreases in current liabilities will be deducted from net income as an adjustment. All increases in current liabilities will be added to net income as an adjustment.

Effect of Changes in Current Liabilities on Cash Flows

Increases in current liabilities ⟶ Added to net income
Decreases in current liabilities ⟶ Deducted from net income

When all adjustments are recorded, the total adjustment to net income, $7,615.00, is calculated and entered on the statement of cash flows. Finally, net cash flows from operating activities, $69,965.00, are calculated and recorded.

PREPARING THE INVESTING ACTIVITIES SECTION OF A STATEMENT OF CASH FLOWS

The second section of the statement of cash flows reports the cash effect of investing activities. Cash flows resulting from a company's investing activities are identified by analyzing the changes in long-term asset accounts.

The balance in the equipment account for Sanibel Sports on December 31, 20X1, was $45,000.00. On December 31, 20X2, the balance was $95,000.00. The $50,000.00 increase represents the cost of new equipment purchased for cash. This amount is shown as an outflow of cash on Sanibel Sports' statement of cash flows.

The balance in the land account for Sanibel Sports on December 31, 20X1, was $35,500.00. On December 31, 20X2, the balance was $25,200.00. The $10,300.00 decrease represents land sold by Sanibel during this period.

Further investigation reveals that Sanibel sold the land for $10,300.00 during 20X2. The sale of land is an inflow of cash of $10,300.00. This amount is shown as an inflow of cash on Sanibel Sports' statement of cash flows.

When the changes in all long-term asset accounts have been analyzed and cash flows listed, the net cash flows from investing activities ($39,700.00), is calculated and recorded.

PREPARING THE FINANCING ACTIVITIES SECTION OF A STATEMENT OF CASH FLOWS

The third section of the statement of cash flows reports the cash effect of financing activities. Cash flows resulting from a company's financial activities are identified by analyzing the changes in long-term debt and stockholders' equity accounts. The balance in the loans payable account for Sanibel Sports on December 31, 20X1, was zero. On December 31, 20X2, the balance was $12,500.00. The $12,500.00 increase represents the proceeds from a loan Sanibel Sports received. This amount is shown as an inflow of cash on Sanibel Sports' statement of cash flows.

The balance in the retained earnings account for Sanibel Sports on December 31, 20X1, was $73,670.00. On December 31, 20X2, the balance was $128,020.00.

The change in this account is caused by two items. The retained earnings account increases by the amount of net income for a period and decreases by the amount of dividends paid during a period. The beginning balance of $73,670.00, plus the net income of $62,350.00, would give a balance of $136,020.00. Any difference between that amount and the actual ending balance in retained earnings is caused by dividends. Therefore, the amount of dividends declared by Sanibel Sports this period equals $8,000.00. Since this was a cash dividend, this amount is shown as an outflow of cash on Sanibel Sports' statement of cash flows.

Retained Earnings, beginning balance	$ 73,670.00
Plus net income	62,350.00
Equals	$136,020.00
Minus current balance of Retained Earnings	128,020.00
Equals dividend paid	$ 8,000.00

When all the changes in long-term debt and stockholder equity accounts have been analyzed and cash flows listed, the net cash flows from financing activities, $4,500.00, is calculated and recorded.

Sanibel Sports
Statement of Cash Flows
For Year Ended December 31, 20X2

Cash Flows from Operating Activities:			
Net Income		62,350.00	
Adjustments to Net Income:			
Depreciation Expense	1,500.00		
Changes in current assets and liabilities:			
Decrease in accounts receivable	14,280.00		
Increase in supplies	(675.00)		
Decrease in accounts payable	(15,890.00)		
Increase in salaries payable	8,400.00		
Total adjustments to net income		7,615.00	
Net cash flows from operating activities			69,965.00
Cash Flows from Investing Activities:			
Purchased equipment		(50,000.00)	
Sold land		10,300.00	
Net cash flows from investing activities			(39,700.00)
Cash Flows from Financing Activities:			
Proceeds from loan payable		12,500.00	
Dividend payment		(8,000.00)	
Net cash flows from financing activities			4,500.00
Net Change in Cash			34,765.00
Cash Balance, Beginning of Period			62,750.00
Cash Balance, End of Period			97,515.00

COMPLETING THE STATEMENT OF CASH FLOWS

The sum of the operating, investing, and financing activities sections of the statement of cash flows are added in order to calculate the net increase or decrease in cash. If all cash transactions have been accounted for, the change in cash plus the beginning cash balance should equal the ending cash balance reported on the balance sheet.

Sanibel Sports' increase in cash, $34,765.00, is added to the beginning cash balance, $62,750.00, to calculate the ending cash balance, $97,515.00. The ending cash balance equals the cash balance reported on Sanibel Sports' balance sheet. Thus, the statement of cash flows has been prepared accurately.

PRACTICE PROBLEM A-1: PREPARING A STATEMENT OF CASH FLOWS

The following information was taken from the financial records of Bonita Body Shop for the year ending December 31, 20X2:

Net Income	$15,495.00
Depreciation Expense	2,300.00

Account Title	Balance Dec. 31, 20X1	Balance Dec. 31, 20X2
Cash	$70,700.00	$51,795.00
Accounts Receivable	10,500.00	12,300.00
Prepaid Insurance	7,000.00	6,000.00
Accounts Payable	13,000.00	15,500.00
Interest Payable	1,400.00	0.00
Equipment	18,000.00	22,000.00
Loans Payable	40,000.00	10,000.00
Retained Earnings	42,000.00	54,495.00

Additional information: Equipment was purchased for $4,000.00 cash.
All dividends were paid in cash.

Statement paper is provided in the *Working Papers*.

Instructions:

1. Complete a statement of cash flows for the year ending December 31, 20X2, for Bonita Body Shop.

PRACTICE PROBLEM A-2: PREPARING A STATEMENT OF CASH FLOWS

The following information was taken from the financial records of Terrace Yard Care for the year ending December 31, 20X2:

Net Income	$3,500.00
Depreciation Expense	2,000.00

Account Title	Balance Dec. 31, 20X1	Balance Dec. 31, 20X2
Cash	$13,300.00	$15,000.00
Accounts Receivable	20,500.00	25,900.00
Supplies	700.00	400.00
Accounts Payable	18,600.00	16,600.00
Salaries Payable	0.00	800.00
Equipment	4,000.00	5,500.00
Land	8,000.00	6,000.00
Loans Payable	0.00	3,000.00
Retained Earnings	11,200.00	13,700.00

Additional information: Equipment was purchased for $1,500.00 cash.
Land was sold for $2,000.00 cash.
All dividends were paid in cash.

Statement paper is provided in the *Working Papers*.

Instructions:

1. Complete a statement of cash flows for the year ending December 31, 20X2, for Terrace Yard Care.

APPENDIX B

**BEST BUY'S FISCAL 2007
ANNUAL REPORT (selected pages)**

A WORLD OF OPPORTUNITY

Fiscal 2007 Annual Report

Source: © 2007 Best Buy

Item 6. Selected Financial Data.

The following table presents our selected financial data. The table should be read in conjunction with Item 7, *Management's Discussion and Analysis of Financial Condition and Results of Operations*, and Item 8, *Financial Statements and Supplementary Data*, of this Annual Report on Form 10-K. Certain prior-year amounts have been reclassified to conform to the current-year presentation. In fiscal 2004, we sold our interest in Musicland. All fiscal years presented reflect the classification of Musicland's financial results as discontinued operations.

Five-Year Financial Highlights

$ in millions, except per share amounts

Fiscal Year	2007[1]	2006[2]	2005[3]	2004	2003
Consolidated Statements of Earnings Data					
Revenue	$35,934	$30,848	$27,433	$24,548	$20,943
Operating income	1,999	1,644	1,442	1,304	1,010
Earnings from continuing operations	1,377	1,140	934	800	622
Loss from discontinued operations, net of tax	—	—	—	(29)	(441)
Gain (loss) on disposal of discontinued operations, net of tax	—	—	50	(66)	—
Cumulative effect of change in accounting principles, net of tax[4]	—	—	—	—	(82)
Net earnings	1,377	1,140	984	705	99
Per Share Data[5]					
Continuing operations	$ 2.79	$ 2.27	$ 1.86	$ 1.61	$ 1.27
Discontinued operations	—	—	—	(0.06)	(0.89)
Gain (loss) on disposal of discontinued operations	—	—	0.10	(0.13)	—
Cumulative effect of accounting changes	—	—	—	—	(0.16)
Net earnings	2.79	2.27	1.96	1.42	0.20
Cash dividends declared and paid	0.36	0.31	0.28	0.27	—
Common stock price:					
High	59.50	56.00	41.47	41.80	35.83
Low	43.51	31.93	29.25	17.03	11.33
Operating Statistics					
Comparable store sales gain[6]	5.0%	4.9%	4.3%	7.1%	2.4%
Gross profit rate	24.4%	25.0%	23.7%	23.9%	23.6%
Selling, general and administrative expenses rate	18.8%	19.7%	18.4%	18.6%	18.8%
Operating income rate	5.6%	5.3%	5.3%	5.3%	4.8%
Year-End Data					
Current ratio[7][8]	1.4	1.3	1.4	1.3	1.3
Total assets[7]	$13,570	$11,864	$10,294	$ 8,652	$ 7,694
Debt, including current portion[7]	650	596	600	850	834
Total shareholders' equity	6,201	5,257	4,449	3,422	2,730
Number of stores					
Domestic	868	774	694	631	567
International	304	167	144	127	112
Total	1,172	941	838	758	679
Retail square footage (000s)					
Domestic	33,959	30,826	28,465	26,640	24,432
International	7,926	3,564	3,139	2,800	2,375
Total	41,885	34,390	31,604	29,440	26,807

[1] Fiscal 2007 included 53 weeks. All other periods presented included 52 weeks.

[2] In the first quarter of fiscal 2006, we early-adopted the fair value recognition provisions of Statement of Financial Accounting Standards ("SFAS") No. 123 (revised 2004), *Share-Based Payment* ("123(R)"), requiring us to recognize expense related to the fair value of our stock-based compensation awards. We elected the modified prospective transition method as permitted by SFAS No. 123(R) and, accordingly, financial results for years prior to fiscal 2006 have not been restated. Stock-based compensation expense in fiscal 2007 and 2006 was $121 ($82 net of tax) and $132 ($87 net of tax), respectively. Stock-based compensation expense recognized in our financial results for years prior to fiscal 2006 was not significant.

Footnotes continue on next page.

$ in millions, except per share amounts

(footnotes continued)

(3) During the fourth quarter of fiscal 2005, following a review of our lease accounting practices, we recorded a cumulative charge of $36 pre-tax ($23 net of tax) to correct our accounting for certain operating lease matters. Additionally, during the same quarter, we established a sales return liability which reduced gross profit by $15 pre-tax ($10 net of tax). Further, in fiscal 2005 we recognized a $50 tax benefit related to the reversal of valuation allowances on deferred tax assets as a result of the favorable resolution of outstanding tax matters with the Internal Revenue Service regarding the disposition of our interest in Musicland. The tax benefit was classified as discontinued operations.

(4) Effective on March 3, 2002, we adopted SFAS No. 142, *Goodwill and Other Intangible Assets*. During fiscal 2003, we completed the required goodwill impairment testing and recognized an after-tax, noncash impairment charge of $40 that was reflected in our fiscal 2003 financial results as a cumulative effect of a change in accounting principle. Also effective on March 3, 2002, we changed our method of accounting for vendor allowances in accordance with Emerging Issues Task Force ("EITF") Issue No. 02-16, *Accounting by a Reseller for Cash Consideration Received from a Vendor*. The change resulted in an after-tax, noncash charge of $42 that also was reflected in our fiscal 2003 financial results as a cumulative effect of a change in accounting principle.

(5) Earnings per share is presented on a diluted basis and reflects three-for-two stock splits effected in August 2005 and May 2002.

(6) Comprised of revenue at stores and Web sites operating for at least 14 full months, as well as remodeled and expanded locations. Relocated stores are excluded from the comparable store sales calculation until at least 14 full months after reopening. Acquired stores are included in the comparable store sales calculation beginning with the first full quarter following the first anniversary of the date of acquisition. The calculation of the comparable store sales percentage gain excludes the effect of fluctuations in foreign currency exchange rates. All comparable store sales percentage calculations reflect an equal number of weeks. The method of calculating comparable store sales varies across the retail industry. As a result, our method of calculating comparable store sales may not be the same as other retailers' methods.

During fiscal 2004, we refined our methodology for calculating our comparable store sales percentage gain to reflect the impact of non-point-of-sale (non-POS) revenue transactions. We refined our comparable store sales calculation in light of changes in our business. Previously, our comparable store sales calculation was based on store POS revenue. The comparable store sales percentage gains for fiscal 2007, 2006, 2005 and 2004 have been computed using the refined methodology. The comparable store sales percentage gain for fiscal 2003 has not been computed using the refined methodology. Refining the methodology for calculating our comparable store sales percentage gain did not impact previously reported revenue, net earnings or cash flows.

(7) Includes both continuing and discontinued operations.

(8) The current ratio is calculated by dividing total current assets by total current liabilities.

Item 8. Financial Statements and Supplementary Data.

Management's Report on the Financial Statements

Our management is responsible for the preparation, integrity and objectivity of the accompanying consolidated financial statements and the related financial information. The financial statements have been prepared in conformity with accounting principles generally accepted in the United States of America and necessarily include certain amounts that are based on estimates and informed judgments. Our management also prepared the related financial information included in this Annual Report on Form 10-K and is responsible for its accuracy and consistency with the financial statements.

The consolidated financial statements have been audited by Deloitte & Touche LLP for the years ended March 3, 2007, and February 25, 2006, and by Ernst & Young LLP for the year ended February 26, 2005, independent registered public accounting firms who conducted their audits in accordance with the standards of the Public Company Accounting Oversight Board (United States). The independent registered public accounting firms' responsibility is to express an opinion as to the fairness with which such financial statements present our financial position, results of operations and cash flows in accordance with accounting principles generally accepted in the United States.

Management's Report on Internal Control Over Financial Reporting

Our management is responsible for establishing and maintaining adequate internal control over financial reporting as defined in Rule 13a-15(f) under the Securities Exchange Act of 1934. Our internal control over financial reporting is designed under the supervision of our principal executive officer and principal financial officer, and effected by our Board of Directors, management and other personnel, to provide reasonable assurance regarding the reliability of financial reporting and the preparation of financial statements for external purposes in accordance with accounting principles generally accepted in the United States and include those policies and procedures that:

(1) Pertain to the maintenance of records that in reasonable detail accurately and fairly reflect our transactions and the dispositions of our assets;

(2) Provide reasonable assurance that our transactions are recorded as necessary to permit preparation of financial statements in accordance with accounting principles generally accepted in the United States, and that our receipts and expenditures are being made only in accordance with authorizations of our management and Board of Directors; and

(3) Provide reasonable assurance regarding prevention or timely detection of unauthorized acquisition, use or disposition of our assets that could have a material effect on our financial statements.

Because of its inherent limitations, internal control over financial reporting may not prevent or detect misstatements. Therefore, even those systems determined to be effective can provide only reasonable assurance with respect to financial statement preparation and presentation.

Under the supervision and with the participation of our management, including our principal executive officer and principal financial officer, we assessed the effectiveness of our internal control over financial reporting as of March 3, 2007, using the criteria set forth by the Committee of Sponsoring Organizations of the Treadway Commission ("COSO") in *Internal Control — Integrated Framework*. Based on its assessment, management has concluded that our internal control over financial reporting was effective as of March 3, 2007. During its assessment, management did not identify any material weaknesses in our internal control over financial reporting. Management has excluded from its assessment the internal control over financial reporting at Pacific Sales Kitchen and Bath Centers, which was acquired on March 7, 2006, and whose financial statements reflect total assets and total revenues constituting 3% and 1%, respectively, of the consolidated financial statement amounts as of and for the year ended March 3, 2007. Management has also excluded from its assessment the internal control over financial reporting at Jiangsu Five Star Appliance Co., in which a 75% interest was acquired on June 8, 2006, and whose financial statements reflect total assets and total revenues constituting 5% and 2%, respectively, of the consolidated financial statement amounts as of and for the year ended March 3, 2007. Deloitte & Touche LLP, the independent registered public accounting firm that audited our consolidated financial statements for the year ended March 3, 2007, included in Item 8, *Financial Statements and Supplementary Data*, of this Annual Report on Form 10-K, has issued an unqualified attestation report on management's assessment of internal control over financial reporting.

Bradbury H. Anderson
Vice Chairman and Chief Executive Officer
(Principal Executive Officer)

Darren R. Jackson
Executive Vice President — Finance and Chief Financial Officer
(Principal Financial Officer)

Consolidated Balance Sheets

$ in millions, except per share amounts

	March 3, 2007	February 25, 2006
Assets		
Current Assets		
Cash and cash equivalents	$ 1,205	$ 748
Short-term investments	2,588	3,041
Receivables	548	449
Merchandise inventories	4,028	3,338
Other current assets	712	409
Total current assets	9,081	7,985
Property and Equipment		
Land and buildings	705	580
Leasehold improvements	1,540	1,325
Fixtures and equipment	2,627	2,898
Property under capital lease	32	33
	4,904	4,836
Less accumulated depreciation	1,966	2,124
Net property and equipment	2,938	2,712
Goodwill	919	557
Tradenames	81	44
Long-Term Investments	318	218
Other Assets	233	348
Total Assets	$ 13,570	$ 11,864
Liabilities and Shareholders' Equity		
Current Liabilities		
Accounts payable	$ 3,934	$ 3,234
Unredeemed gift card liabilities	496	469
Accrued compensation and related expenses	332	354
Accrued liabilities	990	878
Accrued income taxes	489	703
Short-term debt	41	—
Current portion of long-term debt	19	418
Total current liabilities	6,301	6,056
Long-Term Liabilities	443	373
Long-Term Debt	590	178
Minority Interests	35	—
Shareholders' Equity		
Preferred stock, $1.00 par value: Authorized — 400,000 shares; Issued and outstanding — none	—	—
Common stock, $.10 par value: Authorized — 1 billion shares; Issued and outstanding — 480,655,000 and 485,098,000 shares, respectively	48	49
Additional paid-in capital	430	643
Retained earnings	5,507	4,304
Accumulated other comprehensive income	216	261
Total shareholders' equity	6,201	5,257
Total Liabilities and Shareholders' Equity	$ 13,570	$ 11,864

See Notes to Consolidated Financial Statements.

Consolidated Statements of Earnings

$ in millions, except per share amounts

Fiscal Years Ended	March 3, 2007	February 25, 2006	February 26, 2005
Revenue	$35,934	$30,848	$27,433
Cost of goods sold	27,165	23,122	20,938
Gross profit	8,769	7,726	6,495
Selling, general and administrative expenses	6,770	6,082	5,053
Operating income	1,999	1,644	1,442
Net interest income	111	77	1
Gain on investments	20	—	—
Earnings from continuing operations before income tax expense	2,130	1,721	1,443
Income tax expense	752	581	509
Minority interest in earnings	1	—	—
Earnings from continuing operations	1,377	1,140	934
Gain on disposal of discontinued operations (Note 2), net of tax	—	—	50
Net earnings	$ 1,377	$ 1,140	$ 984
Basic earnings per share:			
Continuing operations	$ 2.86	$ 2.33	$ 1.91
Gain on disposal of discontinued operations	—	—	0.10
Basic earnings per share	$ 2.86	$ 2.33	$ 2.01
Diluted earnings per share:			
Continuing operations	$ 2.79	$ 2.27	$ 1.86
Gain on disposal of discontinued operations	—	—	0.10
Diluted earnings per share	$ 2.79	$ 2.27	$ 1.96
Basic weighted-average common shares outstanding (in millions)	482.1	490.3	488.9
Diluted weighted-average common shares outstanding (in millions)	496.2	504.8	505.0

See Notes to Consolidated Financial Statements.

Consolidated Statements of Cash Flows

$ in millions

Fiscal Years Ended	March 3, 2007	February 25, 2006	February 26, 2005
Operating Activities			
Net earnings	$ 1,377	$ 1,140	$ 984
Gain from disposal of discontinued operations, net of tax	—	—	(50)
Earnings from continuing operations	1,377	1,140	934
Adjustments to reconcile earnings from continuing operations to total cash provided by operating activities from continuing operations:			
Depreciation	509	456	459
Asset impairment charges	32	4	22
Stock-based compensation	121	132	(1)
Deferred income taxes	82	(151)	(28)
Excess tax benefits from stock-based compensation	(50)	(55)	—
Other, net	(11)	(3)	24
Changes in operating assets and liabilities, net of acquired assets and liabilities:			
Receivables	(70)	(43)	(30)
Merchandise inventories	(550)	(457)	(240)
Other assets	(47)	(11)	(50)
Accounts payable	320	385	347
Other liabilities	185	165	243
Accrued income taxes	(136)	178	301
Total cash provided by operating activities from continuing operations	1,762	1,740	1,981
Investing Activities			
Additions to property and equipment, net of $75 and $117 non-cash capital expenditures in fiscal 2006 and 2005, respectively	(733)	(648)	(502)
Purchases of available-for-sale securities	(4,541)	(4,319)	(8,517)
Sales of available-for-sale securities	4,886	4,187	7,730
Acquisitions of businesses, net of cash acquired	(421)	—	—
Proceeds from disposition of investments	24	—	—
Change in restricted assets	—	(20)	(140)
Other, net	5	46	7
Total cash used in investing activities from continuing operations	(780)	(754)	(1,422)
Financing Activities			
Repurchase of common stock	(599)	(772)	(200)
Issuance of common stock under employee stock purchase plan and for the exercise of stock options	217	292	256
Dividends paid	(174)	(151)	(137)
Repayments of debt	(84)	(69)	(371)
Proceeds from issuance of debt	96	36	—
Excess tax benefits from stock-based compensation	50	55	—
Other, net	(19)	(10)	(7)
Total cash used in financing activities from continuing operations	(513)	(619)	(459)
Effect of Exchange Rate Changes on Cash	(12)	27	9
Increase in Cash and Cash Equivalents	457	394	109
Cash and Cash Equivalents at Beginning of Year	748	354	245
Cash and Cash Equivalents at End of Year	$ 1,205	$ 748	$ 354
Supplemental Disclosure of Cash Flow Information			
Income taxes paid	$ 804	$ 547	$ 241
Interest paid	14	16	35

See Notes to Consolidated Financial Statements.

Consolidated Statements of Changes in Shareholders' Equity

$ and shares in millions

	Common Shares	Common Stock	Additional Paid-In Capital	Retained Earnings	Accumulated Other Comprehensive Income	Total
Balances at February 28, 2004	487	$49	$819	$2,468	$86	$3,422
Net earnings	—	—	—	984	—	984
Other comprehensive income, net of tax:						
Foreign currency translation adjustments	—	—	—	—	59	59
Other	—	—	—	—	4	4
Total comprehensive income						1,047
Stock options exercised	10	1	219	—	—	220
Tax benefit from stock options exercised and employee stock purchase plan	—	—	60	—	—	60
Issuance of common stock under employee stock purchase plan	2	—	36	—	—	36
Vesting of restricted stock awards	—	—	1	—	—	1
Common stock dividends, $0.28 per share	—	—	—	(137)	—	(137)
Repurchase of common stock	(6)	(1)	(199)	—	—	(200)
Balances at February 26, 2005	493	49	936	3,315	149	4,449
Net earnings	—	—	—	1,140	—	1,140
Other comprehensive income, net of tax:						
Foreign currency translation adjustments	—	—	—	—	101	101
Other	—	—	—	—	11	11
Total comprehensive income						1,252
Stock options exercised	9	1	256	—	—	257
Tax benefit from stock options exercised and employee stock purchase plan	—	—	55	—	—	55
Issuance of common stock under employee stock purchase plan	1	—	35	—	—	35
Stock-based compensation	—	—	132	—	—	132
Common stock dividends, $0.31 per share	—	—	—	(151)	—	(151)
Repurchase of common stock	(18)	(1)	(771)	—	—	(772)
Balances at February 25, 2006	485	49	643	4,304	261	5,257
Net earnings	—	—	—	1,377	—	1,377
Other comprehensive loss, net of tax:						
Foreign currency translation adjustments	—	—	—	—	(33)	(33)
Other	—	—	—	—	(12)	(12)
Total comprehensive income						1,332
Stock options exercised	7	1	167	—	—	168
Tax benefit from stock options exercised and employee stock purchase plan	—	—	47	—	—	47
Issuance of common stock under employee stock purchase plan	1	—	49	—	—	49
Stock-based compensation	—	—	121	—	—	121
Common stock dividends, $0.36 per share	—	—	—	(174)	—	(174)
Repurchase of common stock	(12)	(2)	(597)	—	—	(599)
Balances at March 3, 2007	481	$48	$430	$5,507	$216	$6,201

See Notes to Consolidated Financial Statements.

Notes to Consolidated Financial Statements

$ in millions, except per share amounts

1. Summary of Significant Accounting Policies

Description of Business

Best Buy Co., Inc. is a specialty retailer of consumer electronics, home-office products, entertainment software, appliances and related services, with fiscal 2007 revenue from continuing operations of $35.9 billion.

We operate two reportable segments: Domestic and International. The Domestic segment is comprised of all U.S. store and online operations of Best Buy, Geek Squad, Magnolia Audio Video and Pacific Sales Kitchen and Bath Centers, Inc. ("Pacific Sales"). We acquired Pacific Sales on March 7, 2006. U.S. Best Buy stores offer a wide variety of consumer electronics, home-office products, entertainment software, appliances and related services through 822 stores at the end of fiscal 2007. Geek Squad provides residential and commercial computer repair, support and installation services in all U.S. Best Buy stores and at 12 stand-alone stores at the end of fiscal 2007. Magnolia Audio Video stores offer high-end audio and video products and related services through 20 stores at the end of fiscal 2007. Pacific Sales stores offer high-end home-improvement products, appliances and related services through 14 stores at the end of fiscal 2007.

The International segment is comprised of all Canada store and online operations, including Best Buy, Future Shop and Geek Squad, as well as all China store and online operations, including Best Buy, Geek Squad and Jiangsu Five Star Appliance Co., Ltd. ("Five Star"). We acquired a 75% interest in Five Star on June 8, 2006. We opened our first China Best Buy store in Shanghai on December 28, 2006. The International segment offers products and services similar to those offered by the Domestic segment. However, Canada Best Buy stores do not carry appliances. Further, Five Star stores and our China Best Buy store do not carry entertainment software. At the end of fiscal 2007, the International segment operated 121 Future Shop stores and 47 Best Buy stores in Canada, and 135 Five Star stores and one Best Buy store in China.

In support of our retail store operations, we also maintain Web sites for each of our brands (BestBuy.com, BestBuyCanada.ca, BestBuy.com.cn, Five-Star.cn, FutureShop.ca, GeekSquad.com, GeekSquad.ca, MagnoliaAV.com and PacificSales.com).

In fiscal 2004, we sold our interest in Musicland Stores Corporation ("Musicland"). The transaction resulted in the transfer of all of Musicland's assets other than a distribution center in Franklin, Indiana, and selected nonoperating assets. In fiscal 2005, we reversed previously recorded valuation allowances on deferred tax assets related to the disposition of our interest in Musicland and recognized a tax benefit. As described in Note 2, *Discontinued Operations*, we have classified Musicland's financial results as discontinued operations for all periods presented. These Notes to Consolidated Financial Statements, except where otherwise indicated, relate to continuing operations only.

Basis of Presentation

The consolidated financial statements include the accounts of Best Buy Co., Inc. and its subsidiaries. Investments in unconsolidated entities over which we exercise significant influence but do not have control are accounted for using the equity method. Our share of the net earnings or loss was not significant for any period presented. We have eliminated all intercompany accounts and transactions.

Effective June 8, 2006, we acquired a 75% interest in Five Star. Consistent with China's statutory requirements, Five Star's fiscal year ends on December 31. Therefore, we have elected to consolidate Five Star's financial results on a two-month lag. There were no significant intervening events which would have materially affected our consolidated financial statements had they been recorded during the fiscal year. See Note 3, *Acquisitions*, for further details regarding this transaction.

Reclassifications

To maintain consistency and comparability, certain amounts from previously reported consolidated financial statements have been reclassified to conform to the current-year presentation:

- We reclassified selected balances from receivables to cash and cash equivalents in our February 25, 2006, consolidated balance sheet.

- During the third quarter of fiscal 2007, we made a one-time election to adopt the alternative transition method described in Financial Accounting Standards Board ("FASB") Staff Position ("FSP") No. FAS 123(R)-3, *Transition Election Related to*

$ in millions, except per share amounts

Accounting for the Tax Effects of Share-Based Payment Awards. This election resulted in the reclassification of excess tax benefits from operating activities to financing activities, as presented in the statement of cash flows. See *Stock-Based Compensation* below, for further details.

These reclassifications had no effect on previously reported operating income, net earnings or shareholders' equity.

Change in Accounting Principle

During the fourth quarter of fiscal 2007, we elected to change our accounting principle to recognize the purchase and sale of investments in marketable debt and equity securities on the trade date. Prior to the fourth quarter of fiscal 2007, we recognized these transactions in our consolidated financial statements on the settlement date. We concluded that use of the trade date was preferable to the settlement date as trade date reflects the risks and rewards of investment ownership on a more timely basis. In addition, this method more closely aligns with the standard methodology utilized by our new investment custodian to account for investment transactions. In accordance with Statement of Financial Accounting Standards ("SFAS") No. 154, *Accounting Changes and Error Corrections*, this change in accounting principle has been applied retrospectively to our consolidated financial statements for all prior periods. This change in accounting principle had no effect on previously reported operating income, net earnings, shareholders' equity or cash flows. The effect on the consolidated balance sheets for each applicable quarter was as follows in fiscal 2007 and 2006 (unaudited):

	2007		2006	
	3rd Quarter	2nd Quarter	4th Quarter	1st Quarter
Cash and cash equivalents				
As reported	$1,202	$1,104	$ 748	$ 458
As adjusted	1,208	1,104	748	458
Short-term investments				
As reported	1,513	1,564	3,051	2,148
As adjusted	1,802	1,534	3,041	2,101
Receivables				
As reported	1,112	483	439	350
As adjusted	1,115	513	449	413
Accrued liabilities				
As reported	1,315	958	878	741
As adjusted	1,613	958	878	757

This change in accounting principle had no effect on any quarter of fiscal 2007 or 2006 other than those in the table above.

Use of Estimates in the Preparation of Financial Statements

The preparation of financial statements in conformity with accounting principles generally accepted in the United States ("GAAP") requires us to make estimates and assumptions. These estimates and assumptions affect the reported amounts in the consolidated balance sheets and statements of earnings, as well as the disclosure of contingent liabilities. Future results could be materially affected if actual results differ from these estimates and assumptions.

Fiscal Year

Our fiscal year ends on the Saturday nearest the end of February. Fiscal 2007 included 53 weeks and fiscal 2006 and 2005 each included 52 weeks.

Cash and Cash Equivalents

Cash primarily consists of cash on hand and bank deposits. Cash equivalents primarily consist of money market accounts and other highly liquid investments with an original maturity of three months or less when purchased. We carry these investments at cost, which approximates market value. The amounts of cash equivalents at March 3, 2007, and February 25, 2006, were $695 and $350, respectively, and the weighted-average interest rates were 4.8% and 3.3%, respectively.

Outstanding checks in excess of funds on deposit ("book overdrafts") totaled $183 and $230 at March 3, 2007, and February 25, 2006, respectively, and are reflected as current liabilities in our consolidated balance sheets.

Merchandise Inventories

Merchandise inventories are recorded at the lower of average cost or market. In-bound freight-related costs from our vendors are included as part of the net cost of merchandise inventories. Also included in the cost of inventory are certain vendor allowances that are not a reimbursement of specific, incremental and identifiable costs to promote a vendor's products. Other costs associated with acquiring, storing and transporting

$ in millions, except per share amounts

merchandise inventories to our retail stores are expensed as incurred and included in cost of goods sold.

Our inventory loss reserve represents anticipated physical inventory losses (e.g., theft) that have occurred since the last physical inventory date. Independent physical inventory counts are taken on a regular basis to ensure that the inventory reported in our consolidated financial statements is properly stated. During the interim period between physical inventory counts, we reserve for anticipated physical inventory losses on a location-by-location basis.

Our markdown reserve represents the excess of the carrying value, typically average cost, over the amount we expect to realize from the ultimate sale or other disposal of the inventory. Markdowns establish a new cost basis for our inventory. Subsequent changes in facts or circumstances do not result in the reversal of previously recorded markdowns or an increase in that newly established cost basis.

Restricted Assets

Restricted cash and investments in debt securities totaled $382 and $178, at March 3, 2007, and February 25, 2006, respectively, and are included in other current assets. Such balances are pledged as collateral or restricted to use for vendor payables, general liability insurance, workers' compensation insurance and warranty programs. The increase in restricted cash and investments in debt securities compared with February 25, 2006, was due primarily to restricted cash assumed in connection with the acquisition of Five Star. Five Star's restricted cash represents bank deposits pledged as security for certain vendor payables.

Property and Equipment

Property and equipment are recorded at cost. We compute depreciation using the straight-line method over the estimated useful lives of the assets. Leasehold improvements are depreciated over the shorter of their estimated useful lives or the period from the date the assets are placed in service to the end of the initial lease term. Leasehold improvements made significantly after the initial lease term are depreciated over the shorter of their estimated useful lives or the remaining lease term, including renewal periods, if reasonably assured. Accelerated depreciation methods are generally used for income tax purposes.

When property is fully depreciated, retired or otherwise disposed of, the cost and accumulated depreciation are removed from the accounts and any resulting gain or loss is reflected in the consolidated statement of earnings.

Repairs and maintenance costs are charged directly to expense as incurred. Major renewals or replacements that substantially extend the useful life of an asset are capitalized and depreciated.

Costs associated with the acquisition or development of software for internal use are capitalized and amortized over the expected useful life of the software, from three to seven years. A subsequent addition, modification or upgrade to internal-use software is capitalized only to the extent that it enables the software to perform a task it previously did not perform. Capitalized software is included in fixtures and equipment. Software maintenance and training costs are expensed in the period incurred.

Property under capital lease is comprised of buildings and equipment used in our retail operations and corporate support functions. The related depreciation for capital lease assets is included in depreciation expense. Accumulated depreciation for property under capital lease was $6 and $5 at March 3, 2007, and February 25, 2006, respectively.

Estimated useful lives by major asset category are as follows:

Asset	Life (in years)
Buildings	30–40
Leasehold improvements	3–25
Fixtures and equipment	3–20
Property under capital lease	3–20

During the fourth quarter of fiscal 2007, we removed from our fixed asset balances $621 of fully depreciated assets that were no longer in service. This asset adjustment was based primarily on an analysis of our fixed asset records and certain other validation procedures and had no net impact to our fiscal 2007 consolidated balance sheet, statement of earnings or statement of cash flows.

Impairment of Long-Lived Assets and Costs Associated With Exit Activities

We account for the impairment or disposal of long-lived assets in accordance with SFAS No. 144, *Accounting for the Impairment or Disposal of Long-Lived Assets*, which requires long-lived assets, such as property and equipment, to be evaluated for impairment whenever events or changes in

$ in millions, except per share amounts

circumstances indicate the carrying value of an asset may not be recoverable. Factors considered important that could result in an impairment review include, but are not limited to, significant underperformance relative to historical or planned operating results, significant changes in the manner of use of the assets or significant changes in our business strategies. An impairment loss is recognized when the estimated undiscounted cash flows expected to result from the use of the asset plus net proceeds expected from disposition of the asset (if any) are less than the carrying value of the asset. When an impairment loss is recognized, the carrying amount of the asset is reduced to its estimated fair value based on quoted market prices or other valuation techniques.

The present value of costs associated with location closings, primarily future lease costs (net of expected sublease income), are charged to earnings when a location is vacated.

Pre-tax asset impairment charges recorded in selling, general and administrative expenses ("SG&A") by segment were as follows in fiscal 2007, 2006 and 2005:

	2007	2006	2005
Domestic	$26	$ 4	$22
International	6	—	—
Total	$32	$ 4	$22

The impairment charges in fiscal 2007 and 2006 related to technology and store assets that were taken out of service due to changes in our business. The impairment charges in fiscal 2005 related to technology assets that were taken out of service due to changes in our business and charges associated with the disposal of corporate facilities that had been vacated.

Leases

We conduct the majority of our retail and distribution operations from leased locations. The leases require payment of real estate taxes, insurance and common area maintenance, in addition to rent. The terms of our lease agreements generally range from 10 to 20 years. Most of the leases contain renewal options and escalation clauses, and certain store leases require contingent rents based on factors such as specified percentages of revenue or the consumer price index. Other leases contain covenants related to the maintenance of financial ratios.

For leases that contain predetermined fixed escalations of the minimum rent, we recognize the related rent expense on a straight-line basis from the date we take possession of the property to the end of the initial lease term. We record any difference between the straight-line rent amounts and amounts payable under the leases as part of deferred rent, in accrued liabilities or long-term liabilities, as appropriate.

Cash or lease incentives ("tenant allowances") received upon entering into certain store leases are recognized on a straight-line basis as a reduction to rent from the date we take possession of the property through the end of the initial lease term. We record the unamortized portion of tenant allowances as a part of deferred rent, in accrued liabilities or long-term liabilities, as appropriate.

At March 3, 2007, and February 25, 2006, deferred rent included in accrued liabilities in our consolidated balance sheets was $18 and $16, respectively, and deferred rent included in long-term liabilities in our consolidated balance sheets was $237 and $211, respectively.

Prior to fiscal 2007, we capitalized straight-line rent amounts during the major construction phase of leased properties. Beginning in the first quarter of fiscal 2007, we adopted on a prospective basis, FSP No. FAS 13-1, *Accounting for Rental Costs Incurred During a Construction Period*. FSP No. FAS 13-1 requires companies to expense rent payments for building or ground leases incurred during the construction period. The adoption of FSP No. FAS 13-1 did not have a significant effect on our operating income or net earnings. Straight-line rent is expensed as incurred subsequent to the major construction phase, including the period prior to the store opening.

Transaction costs associated with the sale and leaseback of properties and any related gain or loss are recognized on a straight-line basis over the initial period of the lease agreements. We do not have any retained or contingent interests in the properties nor do we provide any guarantees in connection with the sale and leaseback of properties, other than a corporate-level guarantee of lease payments.

We also lease certain equipment under noncancelable operating and capital leases. Assets acquired under capital leases are depreciated over the shorter of the useful life of the asset or the lease term, including renewal periods, if reasonably assured.

$ in millions, except per share amounts

Goodwill and Intangible Assets

Goodwill

Goodwill is the excess of the purchase price over the fair value of identifiable net assets acquired in business combinations accounted for under the purchase method. We do not amortize goodwill but test it for impairment annually, or when indications of potential impairment exist, utilizing a fair value approach at the reporting unit level. A reporting unit is the operating segment, or a business unit one level below that operating segment, for which discrete financial information is prepared and regularly reviewed by segment management.

Tradenames

We have an indefinite-lived intangible asset related to our Pacific Sales tradename which is included in the Domestic segment. We also have indefinite-lived intangible assets related to our Future Shop and Five Star tradenames which are included in the International segment.

We determine fair values utilizing widely accepted valuation techniques, including discounted cash flows and market multiple analyses. During the fourth quarter of fiscal 2007, we completed our annual impairment testing of our goodwill and tradenames, using the valuation techniques as described above, and determined there was no impairment.

The changes in the carrying amount of goodwill and tradenames by segment for continuing operations were as follows in fiscal 2007, 2006 and 2005:

	Goodwill			Tradenames		
	Domestic	International	Total	Domestic	International	Total
Balances at February 28, 2004	$ 3	$474	$477	$ —	$37	$ 37
Changes in foreign currency exchange rates	—	36	36	—	3	3
Balances at February 26, 2005	3	510	513	—	40	40
Changes in foreign currency exchange rates	—	40	40	—	4	4
Changes resulting from acquisitions	3	1	4	—	—	—
Balances at February 25, 2006	6	551	557	—	44	44
Changes resulting from acquisitions	369	27	396	17	21	38
Changes resulting from tax adjustment[(1)]	—	(21)	(21)	—	—	—
Changes in foreign currency exchange rates	—	(13)	(13)	—	(1)	(1)
Balances at March 3, 2007	$375	$544	$919	$17	$64	$ 81

[(1)] Adjustment related to the resolution of certain tax matters associated with our acquisition of Future Shop.

Lease Rights

Lease rights represent costs incurred to acquire the lease of a specific commercial property. Lease rights are recorded at cost and are amortized to rent expense over the remaining lease term, including renewal periods, if reasonably assured. Amortization periods range up to 16 years, beginning with the date we take possession of the property.

The gross cost and accumulated amortization of lease rights were $32 and $13 at March 3, 2007; and $29 and $10 at February 25, 2006. Lease rights amortization was $4, $3 and $4 in fiscal 2007, 2006 and 2005, respectively. Current lease rights amortization is expected to be approximately $3 for each of the next five fiscal years.

Investments

Short-term and long-term investments are comprised of municipal and United States government debt securities as well as auction-rate securities and variable rate-demand notes. In accordance with SFAS No. 115, *Accounting for Certain Investments in Debt and Equity Securities*, and based on our ability to market and sell these instruments, we classify auction-rate securities, variable-rate demand notes and other investments in debt securities as available-for-sale and carry them at amortized cost, which approximates fair value. Auction-rate securities and variable-rate demand notes are similar to short-term debt instruments because their interest rates are reset periodically. Investments in these securities can be sold for cash on the auction date. We classify auction-rate securities and variable-rate demand notes as short-term or long-term investments based on the reset dates.

$ in millions, except per share amounts

In accordance with our investment policy, we place our investments with issuers who have high-quality credit and limit the amount of investment exposure to any one issuer. We seek to preserve principal and minimize exposure to interest-rate fluctuations by limiting default risk, market risk and reinvestment risk.

We also hold investments in marketable equity securities and classify them as available-for-sale. Investments in marketable equity securities are included in other assets in our consolidated balance sheets. Investments in marketable equity securities are reported at fair value, based on quoted market prices when available. All unrealized holding gains or losses are reflected net of tax in accumulated other comprehensive income in shareholders' equity.

We review the key characteristics of our debt and marketable equity securities portfolio and their classification in accordance with GAAP on an annual basis, or when indications of potential impairment exist. If a decline in the fair value of a security is deemed by management to be other than temporary, the cost basis of the investment is written down to fair value, and the amount of the write-down is included in the determination of net earnings.

Insurance

We are self-insured for certain losses related to health, workers' compensation and general liability claims, although we obtain third-party insurance coverage to limit our exposure to these claims. A portion of these self-insured losses is managed through a wholly-owned insurance captive. We estimate our self-insured liabilities using a number of factors including historical claims experience, an estimate of incurred but not reported claims, demographic factors, severity factors and valuations provided by independent third-party actuaries. Our self-insurance liabilities included in the consolidated balance sheets were as follows:

	March 3, 2007	Feb. 25, 2006
Accrued liabilities	$51	$83
Long-term liabilities	44	—
Total	$95	$83

Inventory Financing

We have inventory financing facilities through which certain suppliers receive payments from a designated finance company on invoices we owe them. Amounts due under the facilities are collateralized by a security interest in certain merchandise inventories. The amounts extended bear interest, if we exceed certain terms, at rates specified in the agreements. We impute interest based on our borrowing rate where there is an average balance outstanding. Imputed interest is not significant. Certain agreements have provisions that entitle the lenders to a portion of the cash discounts provided by the suppliers.

At March 3, 2007, and February 25, 2006, $39 and $59, respectively, were outstanding and included in accrued liabilities on our consolidated balance sheets; and $196 and $177, respectively, were available for use under these inventory financing facilities.

Borrowings and payments on our inventory financing facilities were classified as financing activities in our consolidated statements of cash flows in other, net.

Income Taxes

We account for income taxes under the liability method. Under this method, deferred tax assets and liabilities are recognized for the estimated future tax consequences attributable to differences between the financial statement carrying amounts of existing assets and liabilities and their respective tax bases, and operating loss and tax credit carryforwards. Deferred tax assets and liabilities are measured using enacted income tax rates in effect for the year in which those temporary differences are expected to be recovered or settled. The effect on deferred tax assets and liabilities of a change in income tax rates is recognized in our consolidated statement of earnings in the period that includes the enactment date. A valuation allowance is recorded to reduce the carrying amounts of deferred tax assets if it is more likely than not that such assets will not be realized.

In determining our provision for income taxes, we use an annual effective income tax rate based on annual income, permanent differences between book and tax income, and statutory income tax rates. The effective income tax rate also reflects our assessment of the ultimate outcome of tax audits. We adjust our annual effective income tax rate as additional information on outcomes or events becomes available. Discrete events such as audit settlements or changes in tax laws are recognized in the period in which they occur.

Our income tax returns, like those of most companies, are periodically audited by domestic and foreign tax authorities. These audits include questions regarding our tax filing positions, including the timing and amount of deductions

$ in millions, except per share amounts

and the allocation of income among various tax jurisdictions. At any one time, multiple tax years are subject to audit by the various tax authorities. In evaluating the exposures associated with our various tax filing positions, we record reserves for probable exposures. A number of years may elapse before a particular matter, for which we have established a reserve, is audited and fully resolved or clarified. We adjust our tax contingencies reserve and income tax provision in the period in which actual results of a settlement with tax authorities differs from our established reserve, the statute of limitations expires for the relevant taxing authority to examine the tax position or when more information becomes available. We include our tax contingencies reserve, including accrued penalties and interest, in accrued income taxes on our consolidated balance sheets and in income tax expense in our consolidated statements of earnings.

In July 2006, the FASB issued FASB Interpretation ("FIN") No. 48, *Accounting for Uncertainty in Income Taxes, an Interpretation of FASB Statement No. 109*. In May 2007, the FASB issued FSP FIN No. 48-1, *Definition of "Settlement" in FASB Interpretation No.48*. We will adopt FIN No. 48 and FSP FIN No. 48-1 beginning in the first quarter of fiscal 2008. See *New Accounting Standards* below for further details.

Long-Term Liabilities

The major components of long-term liabilities at March 3, 2007, and February 25, 2006, included long-term rent-related liabilities, deferred compensation plan liabilities, self-insurance reserves and advances received under vendor alliance programs.

Foreign Currency

Foreign currency denominated assets and liabilities are translated into U.S. dollars using the exchange rates in effect at our consolidated balance sheet date. Results of operations and cash flows are translated using the average exchange rates throughout the period. The effect of exchange rate fluctuations on translation of assets and liabilities is included as a component of shareholders' equity in accumulated other comprehensive income. Gains and losses from foreign currency transactions, which are included in SG&A, have not been significant.

Revenue Recognition

We recognize revenue when the sales price is fixed or determinable, collectibility is reasonably assured and the customer takes possession of the merchandise, or in the case of services, at the time the service is provided. Amounts billed to customers for shipping and handling are included in revenue. Revenue is reported net of estimated sales returns and excludes sales taxes.

We estimate our sales returns reserve based on historical return rates. We initially established our sales returns reserve in the fourth quarter of fiscal 2005. Our sales returns reserve was $104 and $78, at March 3, 2007, and February 25, 2006, respectively.

We sell extended service contracts on behalf of an unrelated third party. In jurisdictions where we are not deemed to be the obligor on the contract, commissions are recognized in revenue at the time of sale. In jurisdictions where we are deemed to be the obligor on the contract, commissions are recognized in revenue ratably over the term of the service contract. Commissions represented 2.2%, 2.5% and 2.6% of revenues in fiscal 2007, 2006 and 2005, respectively.

For revenue transactions that involve multiple deliverables, we defer the revenue associated with any undelivered elements. The amount of revenue deferred in connection with the undelivered elements is determined using the relative fair value of each element, which is generally based on each element's relative retail price. See additional information regarding our customer loyalty program in *Sales Incentives* below.

Gift Cards

We sell gift cards to our customers in our retail stores, through our Web sites, and through selected third parties. We do not charge administrative fees on unused gift cards and our gift cards do not have an expiration date. We recognize income from gift cards when: (i) the gift card is redeemed by the customer; or (ii) the likelihood of the gift card being redeemed by the customer is remote ("gift card breakage") and we determine that we do not have a legal obligation to remit the value of unredeemed gift cards to the relevant jurisdictions. We determine our gift card breakage rate based upon historical redemption patterns. Based on our historical information, the likelihood of a gift card remaining unredeemed can be determined 24 months after the gift card is issued. At that time, we recognize

$ in millions, except per share amounts

breakage income for those cards for which the likelihood of redemption is deemed remote and we do not have a legal obligation to remit the value of such unredeemed gift cards to the relevant jurisdictions. Gift card breakage income is included in revenue in our consolidated statements of earnings.

We began recognizing gift card breakage income during the third quarter of fiscal 2006. Gift card breakage income was as follows in fiscal 2007, 2006 and 2005:

	2007[1]	2006[1]	2005
Gift card breakage income	$46	$43	$—

[1] Due to the resolution of certain legal matters associated with gift card liabilities, we recognized $19 and $27 of gift card breakage income in fiscal 2007 and 2006, respectively, that related to prior fiscal years.

Sales Incentives

We frequently offer sales incentives that entitle our customers to receive a reduction in the price of a product or service. Sales incentives include discounts, coupons and other offers that entitle a customer to receive a reduction in the price of a product or service by submitting a claim for a refund or rebate. For sales incentives issued to a customer in conjunction with a sale of merchandise or services, for which we are the obligor, the reduction in revenue is recognized at the time of sale, based on the retail value of the incentive expected to be redeemed.

Customer Loyalty Program

We have a customer loyalty program which allows members to earn points for each qualifying purchase. Points earned enable members to receive a certificate that may be redeemed on future purchases at U.S. Best Buy stores. There are two ways that members may participate and earn loyalty points.

First, we have a customer loyalty card where members earn points for each purchase completed at U.S. Best Buy stores or through our BestBuy.com Web site. We account for our customer loyalty program in accordance with Emerging Issues Task Force ("EITF") Issue No. 00-22, *Accounting for "Points" and Certain Other Time-Based or Volume-Based Sales Incentive Offers, and Offers for Free Products or Services to Be Delivered in the Future*. The retail value of points earned by our customer loyalty members is included in accrued liabilities and recorded as a reduction of revenue at the time the points are earned, based on the percentage of points that are projected to be redeemed. Prior to October 2006, we charged a loyalty program membership fee which was initially deferred and then recognized in revenue ratably over the membership period. Beginning in October 2006, we no longer charge a membership fee for our customer loyalty program.

Second, we have a co-branded credit card agreement with a third-party bank (the "Bank") for the issuance of a customer loyalty credit card bearing the Best Buy brand. Cardholders earn points for qualifying purchases, including purchases made at Best Buy. Points earned enable cardholders to receive certificates that may be redeemed on future purchases at U.S. Best Buy stores. The Bank is the sole owner of the accounts issued under the program and absorbs losses associated with non-payment by the cardholders and fraudulent usage of the accounts. We are responsible for redeeming the points earned by the cardholders. The Bank pays fees to us based on the number of credit card accounts activated and card usage, and reimburses us for certain costs associated with the program. In accordance with EITF No. 00-21, *Revenue Arrangements with Multiple Deliverables*, we defer revenue received from cardholder account activations and recognize revenue on a straight-line basis over the remaining term of the agreement. Card usage fees are recognized in revenue as actual credit card usage occurs.

$ in millions, except per share amounts

Cost of Goods Sold and Selling, General and Administrative Expenses

The following table illustrates the primary costs classified in each major expense category:

Cost of Goods Sold	SG&A
• Total cost of products sold including: — Freight expenses associated with moving merchandise inventories from our vendors to our distribution centers; — Vendor allowances that are not a reimbursement of specific, incremental and identifiable costs to promote a vendor's products; and — Cash discounts on payments to vendors; • Cost of services provided including; — Payroll and benefits costs for services employees; and — Cost of replacement parts and related freight expenses; • Physical inventory losses; • Markdowns; • Customer shipping and handling expenses; • Costs associated with operating our distribution network, including payroll and benefit costs, occupancy costs, and depreciation; • Freight expenses associated with moving merchandise inventories from our distribution centers to our retail stores; and • Promotional financing costs.	• Payroll and benefit costs for retail and corporate employees; • Occupancy costs of retail, services and corporate facilities; • Depreciation related to retail, services and corporate assets; • Advertising; • Vendor allowances that are a reimbursement of specific, incremental and identifiable costs to promote a vendor's products; • Charitable contributions; • Outside service fees; • Long-lived asset impairment charges; and • Other administrative costs, such as credit card service fees, supplies, and travel and lodging.

Vendor Allowances

We receive vendor allowances for various programs, primarily volume incentives and reimbursements for specific costs such as markdowns, margin protection, advertising and sales incentives. Vendor allowances provided as reimbursement of specific, incremental and identifiable costs incurred to promote a vendor's products are included as an expense reduction when the cost is incurred. All other vendor allowances, including vendor allowances received in excess of our cost to promote a vendor's product, are initially deferred and recorded as a reduction of merchandise inventories. The deferred amounts are then included as a reduction of cost of goods sold when the related product is sold.

Vendor allowances included in revenue for reimbursement of vendor-provided sales incentives and in SG&A for reimbursement of specific, incremental and identifiable SG&A costs to promote a vendor's products were as follows in fiscal 2007, 2006 and 2005:

	2007	2006	2005
Revenue	$ 29	$141	$ 85
SG&A	$158	$138	$140

Advertising Costs

Advertising costs, which are included in SG&A, are expensed the first time the advertisement runs. Advertising costs consist primarily of print and television advertisements as well as promotional events. Net advertising expenses were $692, $644 and $597 in fiscal 2007, 2006 and 2005, respectively. Allowances received from vendors for advertising of $140, $123 and $115, in fiscal 2007, 2006 and 2005, respectively, were classified as reductions of advertising expenses.

Pre-Opening Costs

Non-capital expenditures associated with opening new stores are expensed as incurred.

Stock-Based Compensation

SFAS No. 123(R)

At the beginning of fiscal 2006, we early-adopted the fair value recognition provisions of SFAS No. 123 (revised 2004), *Share-Based Payment* (123(R)), requiring us to recognize expense related to the fair value of our stock-

$ in millions, except per share amounts

based compensation awards. We elected the modified prospective transition method as permitted by SFAS No. 123(R). Under this transition method, stock-based compensation expense in fiscal 2007 and 2006 includes: (i) compensation expense for all stock-based compensation awards granted prior to, but not yet vested as of February 26, 2005, based on the grant date fair value estimated in accordance with the original provisions of SFAS No. 123, *Accounting for Stock-Based Compensation;* and (ii) compensation expense for all stock-based compensation awards granted subsequent to February 26, 2005, based on the grant-date fair value estimated in accordance with the provisions of SFAS No. 123(R). We recognize compensation expense on a straight-line basis over the requisite service period of the award (or to an employee's eligible retirement date, if earlier). Total stock-based compensation expense included in our consolidated statement of earnings in fiscal 2007 and 2006 was $121 ($82, net of tax) and $132 ($87, net of tax), respectively. In accordance with the modified prospective transition method of SFAS No. 123(R), financial results for prior periods have not been restated.

APB Opinion No. 25

Prior to fiscal 2006, we applied Accounting Principles Board ("APB") Opinion No. 25, *Accounting for Stock Issued to Employees*, and related Interpretations in accounting for stock-based compensation awards. Prior to fiscal 2006, no stock-based compensation expense was recognized in our consolidated statements of earnings for non-qualified stock options ("stock options"), as the exercise price was equal to the market price of our stock on the date of grant. In addition, we did not recognize any stock-based compensation expense for our employee stock purchase plan ("ESPP"), as it was intended to be a plan that qualifies under Section 423 of the Internal Revenue Code of 1986, as amended. However, we did recognize stock-based compensation expense for share awards.

We recognized compensation expense for time-based share awards on a straight-line basis over the vesting period (or to an employee's eligible retirement date, if earlier) based on the fair value of the award on the grant date. We recognized compensation expense for market-based share awards based on the current stock price, the number of shares expected to ultimately vest and the vesting period. Outside valuation advisors assisted us in determining the number of shares ultimately expected to vest. We recognized compensation expense for performance-based awards on a straight-line basis over the requisite service period (or to an employee's eligible retirement date, if earlier) based on management's estimate of the likelihood of achieving company or personal performance goals. If an award recipient's relationship with us is terminated, all shares still subject to restrictions are forfeited and returned to the plan.

Stock-based compensation income recognized in fiscal 2005 on a pre-tax basis was $1. The fiscal 2005 income reflects a change in vesting assumptions based on our total shareholder return relative to the performance of the Standard & Poor's 500 Index ("S&P 500") and an increase in our expected forfeiture rate.

Transition

In November 2005, the FASB issued FSP No. FAS 123(R)-3, *Transition Election Related to Accounting for Tax Effects of Share-Based Payment Awards*. During the third quarter of fiscal 2007, we elected to adopt the alternative transition method provided in FSP No. FAS 123(R)-3 to calculate the tax effects of stock-based compensation. The alternative transition method includes simplified methods to determine the beginning balance of the additional paid-in capital ("APIC") pool related to the tax effects of stock-based compensation, and to determine the subsequent impact on the APIC pool and the statement of cash flows of the tax effects of stock-based awards that were fully vested and outstanding upon the adoption of SFAS No. 123(R).

In accordance with SFAS No. 154, *Accounting Changes and Error Corrections*, this change in accounting principle has been applied retrospectively to our fiscal 2006 consolidated statement of cash flows. The effect on the consolidated statement of cash flows was a decrease in operating activities with an offsetting increase in financing activities of $22 in fiscal 2006. The adoption of FSP No. FAS 123(R)-3 did not have an impact on our operating income, net earnings or shareholders' equity.

$ in millions, except per share amounts

The table below illustrates the effect on net earnings and earnings per share as if we had applied the fair value recognition provisions of SFAS No. 123 to stock-based compensation in fiscal 2005:

Net earnings, as reported	$ 984
Add: Stock-based compensation income included in reported net earnings, net of tax[1]	(1)
Deduct: Stock-based compensation expense determined under fair value method for all awards, net of tax[2]	(60)
Net earnings, pro forma	$ 923
Earnings per share:	
Basic — as reported	$2.01
Basic — pro forma	$1.89
Diluted — as reported	$1.96
Diluted — pro forma	$1.87

[1] Amount represents the stock-based compensation costs, net of tax, recognized under APB Opinion No. 25.

[2] In the fourth quarter of fiscal 2005, we increased our expected participant stock option forfeiture rate as a result of transferring to a third-party provider certain corporate employees, and the departure of certain senior executives. This higher level of expected stock option forfeitures reduced our fiscal 2005 pro forma stock-based compensation expense. Fiscal 2005 pro forma stock-based compensation expense may not be indicative of future stock-based compensation expense.

The weighted-average fair value of stock options granted during fiscal 2005 used in computing pro forma compensation expense was $14.18 per share. The fair value of each stock option was estimated on the date of grant using the Black-Scholes option-pricing model with the following assumptions in fiscal 2005:

Risk-free interest rate[1]	3.4%
Expected dividend yield	0.9%
Expected stock price volatility[2]	40%
Expected life of stock options[3]	5.5 years

[1] Based on the five-year U.S. Treasury constant maturity interest rate whose term is consistent with the expected life of our stock options.

[2] We used an outside valuation advisor to assist us in projecting the expected stock price volatility. We considered both historical data and observable market prices of similar equity instruments.

[3] We estimated the expected life of stock options based upon historical experience.

New Accounting Standards

In July 2006, the FASB issued FIN No. 48, *Accounting for Uncertainty in Income Taxes, an Interpretation of FASB Statement No. 109*. FIN No. 48 provides guidance regarding the recognition, measurement, presentation and disclosure in the financial statements of tax positions taken or expected to be taken on a tax return, including the decision whether to file or not to file in a particular jurisdiction. FIN No. 48 is effective for fiscal years beginning after December 15, 2006. We will adopt FIN No. 48 beginning in the first quarter of fiscal 2008. The cumulative effect of applying the provisions of FIN No. 48 upon initial adoption will be reported as an adjustment to retained earnings as of the beginning of fiscal 2008. We are evaluating the impact, if any, the adoption of FIN No. 48 will have on our operating income, net earnings or retained earnings.

In May 2007, the FASB issued FSP FIN No. 48-1, *Definition of "Settlement" in FASB Interpretation No. 48*. FSP FIN No. 48-1 provides guidance on how a company should determine whether a tax position is effectively settled for the purpose of recognizing previously unrecognized tax benefits. FSP FIN No. 48-1 is effective upon initial adoption of FIN No. 48, which we will adopt in the first quarter of fiscal 2008, as indicated above.

In September 2006, the U.S. Securities and Exchange Commission ("SEC") issued Staff Accounting Bulletin ("SAB") No. 108, *Considering the Effects of Prior Year Misstatements when Quantifying Misstatements in Current Year Financial Statements*, which provides interpretive guidance on the consideration of the effects of prior-year misstatements in quantifying current-year misstatements for the purpose of a materiality assessment. SAB No. 108 is effective for fiscal years ending after November 15, 2006.

$ in millions, except per share amounts

We adopted SAB No. 108 in the fourth quarter of fiscal 2007. The cumulative effect of initially applying the provisions of SAB No. 108, may be reported as a cumulative adjustment to retained earnings at the beginning of the year of adoption. The adoption of SAB No. 108 had no impact on our net earnings or financial position.

In September 2006, the FASB issued SFAS No. 157, *Fair Value Measurements*. SFAS No. 157 defines fair value, establishes a framework for measuring fair value in generally accepted accounting principles and expands disclosures about fair value measurements. SFAS No. 157 applies under other accounting pronouncements that require or permit fair value measurements, the FASB having previously concluded in those accounting pronouncements that fair value is the relevant measurement attribute. Accordingly, SFAS No. 157 does not require any new fair value measurements. SFAS No. 157 is effective for fiscal years beginning after December 15, 2007. We plan to adopt SFAS No. 157 beginning in the first quarter of fiscal 2009. We are evaluating the impact, if any, the adoption of SFAS No. 157 will have on our operating income or net earnings.

In February 2007, the FASB issued SFAS No. 159, *The Fair Value Option for Financial Assets and Financial Liabilities*. SFAS No. 159 permits companies to choose to measure many financial instruments and certain other items at fair value. The objective is to improve financial reporting by providing companies with the opportunity to mitigate volatility in reported earnings caused by measuring related assets and liabilities differently without having to apply complex hedge accounting provisions. SFAS No. 159 is effective for fiscal years beginning after November 15, 2007. Companies are not allowed to adopt SFAS No. 159 on a retrospective basis unless they choose early adoption. We plan to adopt SFAS No. 159 at the beginning of fiscal 2009. We are evaluating the impact, if any, the adoption of SFAS No. 159 will have on our operating income or net earnings.

2. Discontinued Operations

In fiscal 2004, we sold our interest in Musicland. The buyer assumed all of Musicland's liabilities, including approximately $500 in lease obligations and paid no cash consideration, in exchange for all of the capital stock of Musicland. The transaction also resulted in the transfer of all of Musicland's assets, other than a distribution center in Franklin, Indiana, and selected nonoperating assets.

On March 25, 2005, we received notification from the Internal Revenue Service ("IRS") of a favorable resolution of outstanding tax matters regarding the disposition of our interest in Musicland. Based on the agreement with the IRS, we reversed previously recorded valuation allowances on deferred tax assets related to the disposition of our interest in Musicland and recognized a $50 tax benefit in fiscal 2005.

In accordance with SFAS No. 144, Musicland's financial results are reported separately as discontinued operations for all periods presented. No assets or liabilities of Musicland were included in our consolidated balance sheets at March 3, 2007, or February 25, 2006.

3. Acquisitions

Pacific Sales Kitchen and Bath Centers, Inc.

On March 7, 2006, we acquired all of the common stock of Pacific Sales for $411, or $408, net of cash acquired, including transaction costs. We acquired Pacific Sales, a high-end home-improvement and appliance retailer, to enhance our ability to grow with an affluent customer base and premium brands using a proven and successful showroom format. Utilizing the existing store format, we expect to expand the number of stores in order to capitalize on the expanding high-end segment of the U.S. appliance market. The acquisition was accounted for using the purchase method in accordance with SFAS No. 141, *Business Combinations*. Accordingly, we recorded the net assets at their estimated fair values, and included operating results in our Domestic segment from the date of acquisition. We allocated the purchase price on a preliminary basis using information then available. The allocation of the purchase price to the assets and liabilities acquired was finalized in the fourth quarter of fiscal 2007. There were no significant adjustments to the preliminary purchase price allocation. All goodwill is deductible for tax purposes.

APPENDIX C

USING A CALCULATOR AND COMPUTER KEYPAD

KINDS OF CALCULATORS

Many different models of calculators, both desktop and handheld, are available. All calculators have their own features and particular placement of operating keys. Therefore, it is necessary to refer to the operator's manual for specific instructions and locations of the operating keys for the calculator being used. A typical keyboard of a desktop calculator is shown in the illustration.

DESKTOP CALCULATOR SETTINGS

Several operating switches on a desktop calculator must be engaged before the calculator will produce the desired results.

The *decimal selector* sets the appropriate decimal places necessary for the numbers that will be entered. For example, if the decimal selector is set at 2, both the numbers entered and the answer will have two decimal places. If the decimal selector is set at F, the calculator automatically sets the decimal places. The F setting allows the answer to be unrounded and carried out to the maximum number of decimal places possible.

The *decimal rounding selector* rounds the answers. The down arrow position will drop any digits beyond the last digit desired. The up arrow position will drop any digits beyond the last digit desired and round the last digit up. In the 5/4 position, the calculator rounds the last desired digit up only when the following digit is 5 or greater. If the following digit is less than 5, the last desired digit remains unchanged.

The *GT* or *grand total switch* in the on position accumulates totals.

Using a Calculator and Computer Keypad

KINDS OF COMPUTER KEYBOARDS

The computer has a keypad on the right side of the keyboard, called the *numeric keypad*. Even though several styles of keyboards are found, there are two basic layouts for the numeric keypad. The standard layout and enhanced layout are shown in the illustration. On the standard keyboard, the directional arrow keys are found on the number keys. To use the numbers, press the key called *Num Lock*. (This key is found above the "7" key.) When the Num Lock is turned on, numbers are entered when the keys on the keypad are pressed. When the Num Lock is off, the arrow, Home, Page Up, Page Down, End, Insert, and Delete keys can be used.

The enhanced keyboards have the arrow keys and the other directional keys mentioned above to the left of the numeric keypad. When using the keypad on an enhanced keyboard, Num Lock can remain on.

The asterisk (*) performs a different function on the computer than the calculator. The asterisk on the calculator is used for the total while the computer uses it for multiplication.

Another difference is the division key. The computer key is the forward slash key (/). The calculator key uses the division key (÷).

Standard
Keyboard Layout

Enhanced
Keyboard Layout

TEN-KEY TOUCH SYSTEM

Striking the numbers 0 to 9 on a calculator or numeric keypad without looking at the keyboard is called the *touch system*. Using the touch system develops both speed and accuracy.

The 4, 5, and 6 keys are called the *home row*. If the right hand is used for the keyboard, the index finger is placed on the 4 key, the middle finger on the 5 key, and the ring finger on the 6 key. If the left hand is used, the ring finger is placed on the 4 key, the middle finger on the 5 key, and the index finger on the 6 key.

Place the fingers on the home row keys. Curve the fingers and keep the wrist straight. These keys may feel slightly concaved or the 5 key may have a raised dot. The differences in the home row allow the operator to recognize the home row by touch rather than by sight.

Maintain the position of the fingers on the home row. The finger used to strike the 4 key will also strike the 7 key and the 1 key. Stretch the finger up to reach the 7; then stretch the finger down to reach the 1 key. Visualize the position of these keys.

Again, place the fingers on the home row. Stretch the finger that strikes the 5 key up to reach the 8 key, then down to reach the 2 key. Likewise, stretch the finger that strikes the 6 key up to strike the 9 and down to strike the 3 key. This same finger will stretch down again to hit the decimal point.

If the right hand is used, the thumb will be used to strike the 0 and 00 keys and the little finger to strike the addition key. If the left hand is used, the little finger will be used to strike the 0 and 00 keys and the thumb to strike the addition key.

HANDHELD CALCULATORS

Handheld calculators are slightly different from desktop calculators, not only in their size and features but also in their operation. Refer to the operator's manual for specific instructions for the calculator being used.

On a handheld calculator, the numeric keys are usually very close together. In addition, the keys do not respond to touch as easily as on a desktop calculator. Therefore, the touch system is usually not used on a handheld calculator.

PERFORMING MATHEMATICAL OPERATIONS ON DESKTOP CALCULATORS

Mathematical operations can be performed on a calculator both quickly and efficiently. The basic operations of addition, subtraction, multiplication, and division are used frequently on a calculator.

Addition
Each number to be added is called an *addend*. The answer to an addition problem is called the *sum*.

Addition is performed by entering an addend and striking the addition key (+). All numbers are entered on a calculator in the exact order they are given. To enter the number 4,455.65, strike the 4, 4, 5, 5, decimal, 6, and 5 keys in that order, and then strike the addition key. Commas are not entered. Continue in this manner until all addends have been entered. To obtain the sum, strike the total key on the calculator.

Subtraction
The top number or first number of a subtraction problem is called the *minuend*. The number to be subtracted from the minuend is called the *subtrahend*. The answer to a subtraction problem is called the *difference*.

Subtraction is performed by first entering the minuend and striking the addition key (+). The subtrahend is then entered, followed by the minus key (−), followed by the total key.

Multiplication
The number to be multiplied is called the *multiplicand*. The number of times the multiplicand will be multiplied is called the *multiplier*. The answer to a multiplication problem is called the *product*.

Multiplication is performed by entering the multiplicand and striking the multiplication key (×). The multiplier is then entered, followed by the equals key (=). The calculator will automatically multiply and give the product.

Division
The number to be divided is called the *dividend*. The number the dividend will be divided by is called the *divisor*. The answer to a division problem is called the *quotient*.

Division is performed by entering the dividend and striking the division key (÷). The divisor is then entered, followed by the equals key (=). The calculator will automatically divide and give the quotient.

Correcting Errors
If an error is made while using a calculator, several methods of correction may be used. If an incorrect number has been entered and the addition key or equals key has not yet been struck, strike the clear entry (CE) key one time. This key will clear only the last number that was entered. However, if the clear entry key is depressed more than one time, the entire problem will be cleared on some calculators. If an incorrect number has been entered and the addition key has been struck, strike the minus key one time only. This will automatically subtract the last number added, thus removing it from the total.

PERFORMING MATHEMATICAL OPERATIONS ON COMPUTERS AND HANDHELD CALCULATORS

On a computer keypad or a handheld calculator, addition is performed in much the same way as on a desktop calculator. However, after the + key is depressed, the display usually shows the accumulated total. Therefore, the total key is not found. Some computer programs will not calculate the total until Enter is pressed.

Subtraction is performed differently on many computer keypads and handheld calculators. The minuend is usually entered, followed by the minus (−) key. Then the subtrahend is entered. Pressing either the + key or the = key will display the difference. Some computer programs will not calculate the difference until Enter is pressed.

Multiplication and division are performed the same way on a computer keypad and handheld calculator as on a desktop calculator. Keep in mind that computers use the * for multiplication and / for division.

SAFETY CONCERNS

Whenever electrical equipment such as a calculator or computer is being operated in a classroom or office, several safety rules apply. These rules protect the operator of the equipment, other persons in the environment, and the equipment itself.

1. Do not unplug equipment by pulling on the electrical cord. Instead, grasp the plug at the outlet and remove it.
2. Do not stretch electrical cords across an aisle where someone might trip over them.
3. Avoid food and beverages near the equipment where a spill might result in an electrical short.
4. Do not attempt to remove the cover of a calculator, computer, or keyboard for any reason while the power is turned on.
5. Do not attempt to repair equipment while it is plugged in.
6. Always turn the power off or unplug equipment when finished using it.

CALCULATION DRILLS

Instructions for Desktop Calculators
Complete each drill using the touch method. Set the decimal selector at the setting indicated in each drill. Compare the answer on the calculator to the answer in the book. If the two are the same, progress to the next problem. It is not necessary to enter 00 in the cents column if the decimal selector is set at 0-F. However, digits other than zeros in the cents column must be entered preceded by a decimal point.

Instructions for Computer Keypads
Complete each drill using the touch method. There is no decimal selector on computer keypads. Set the number of decimal places as directed in the instructions for the computer program. In spreadsheets, for example, use the formatting options to set the number of decimal places. When the drill indicates "F" for floating, leave the computer application in its default format. Compare the answer on the computer monitor to the answer in the book. If the two are the same, progress to the next problem. It is not necessary to enter 00 in the cents column. However, digits other than zeros in the cents column must be entered, preceded by a decimal point.

DRILL C-1 Performing addition using the home row keys
Decimal Selector—2

4.00	44.00	444.00	4,444.00	44,444.00
5.00	55.00	555.00	5,555.00	55,555.00
6.00	66.00	666.00	6,666.00	66,666.00
5.00	45.00	455.00	4,455.00	44,556.00
4.00	46.00	466.00	4,466.00	44,565.00
5.00	54.00	544.00	5,544.00	55,446.00
6.00	56.00	566.00	5,566.00	55,664.00
5.00	65.00	655.00	6,655.00	66,554.00
4.00	64.00	644.00	6,644.00	66,555.00
5.00	66.00	654.00	6,545.00	65,465.00
__49.00__	__561.00__	__5,649.00__	__56,540.00__	__565,470.00__

DRILL C-2 Performing addition using the 0, 1, 4, and 7 keys
Decimal Selector—2

4.00	11.00	444.00	4,440.00	44,000.00
7.00	44.00	777.00	7,770.00	77,000.00
4.00	74.00	111.00	1,110.00	11,000.00
1.00	71.00	741.00	4,400.00	41,000.00
4.00	70.00	740.00	1,100.00	71,000.00
7.00	10.00	101.00	4,007.00	10,000.00
4.00	14.00	140.00	7,001.00	10,100.00
1.00	17.00	701.00	1,007.00	40,100.00
4.00	40.00	700.00	1,004.00	70,100.00
7.00	77.00	407.00	7,700.00	74,100.00
__43.00__	__428.00__	__4,862.00__	__39,539.00__	__448,400.00__

DRILL C-3 Performing addition using the 2, 5, and 8 keys
Decimal Selector—2

5.00	58.00	588.00	8,888.00	88,855.00
8.00	52.00	522.00	5,555.00	88,822.00
5.00	85.00	888.00	2,222.00	88,852.00
2.00	52.00	222.00	8,525.00	88,222.00
5.00	25.00	258.00	2,585.00	85,258.00
8.00	58.00	852.00	8,258.00	22,255.00
5.00	82.00	225.00	8,585.00	22,288.00
2.00	28.00	885.00	5,258.00	22,258.00
5.00	88.00	882.00	2,852.00	22,888.00
8.00	22.00	228.00	2,288.00	25,852.00
__53.00__	__550.00__	__5,550.00__	__55,016.00__	__555,550.00__

Using a Calculator and Computer Keypad

DRILL C-4 Performing addition using the 3, 6, 9, and decimal point keys
Decimal Selector—2

6.00	66.66	666.66	6,666.99	66,699.33
9.00	99.99	999.99	9,999.66	99,966.66
6.00	33.33	333.33	3,333.99	33,366.33
3.00	33.66	666.99	3,366.99	36,963.36
6.36	33.99	999.66	6,699.33	69,636.36
3.36	99.66	333.66	9,966.33	33,333.66
9.36	99.33	696.36	9,636.69	66,666.99
9.63	33.36	369.63	3,696.36	99,999.33
6.33	33.69	336.69	6,963.99	96,369.63
9.93	69.63	963.36	6,699.33	36,963.36
68.97	603.30	6,366.33	67,029.66	639,965.01

DRILL C-5 Performing subtraction using all number keys
Decimal Selector—F

456.73	789.01	741.00	852.55	987.98
−123.21	−456.00	−258.10	−369.88	−102.55
333.52	333.01	482.90	482.67	885.43

DRILL C-6 Performing multiplication using all number keys
Decimal Selector—F

654.05	975.01	487.10	123.56	803.75
× 12.66	× 27.19	× 30.21	× 50.09	× 1.45
8,280.273	26,510.5219	14,715.291	6,189.1204	1,165.4375

DRILL C-7 Performing division using all number keys
Decimal Selector—F

900.56	÷	450.28	=	2.
500.25	÷	100.05	=	5.
135.66	÷	6.65	=	20.4
269.155	÷	105.55	=	2.550023685*
985.66	÷	22.66	=	43.49779346*

*Number of decimal places may vary, due to machine capacity.

APPENDIX D

RECYCLING PROBLEMS

RECYCLING PROBLEM 1-1

Determining how transactions change an accounting equation

Brian Frizza is a personal trainer and operates a business called FitnessPro. FitnessPro uses the accounts shown in the following accounting equation. Use the form given in the *Recycling Problem Working Papers* to complete this problem.

Trans. No.	Assets				=	Liabilities	+	Owner's Equity
	Cash	+ Accts. Rec.—Dean Mills	+ Supplies	+ Prepaid Insurance	=	Accts. Pay.—Topline	+	Brian Frizza, Capital
Beg. Bal.	2,200	—0—	1,100	200		200		3,300
1.	– 120							– 120 (expense)
New Bal.	2,080	—0—	1,100	200		200		3,180
2.								

Transactions:
1. Paid cash for telephone bill, $120.00.
2. Received cash from owner as an investment, $400.00.
3. Paid cash for rent, $600.00.
4. Received cash from sales, $425.00.
5. Bought supplies on account from Topline, $310.00.
6. Sold services on account to Dean Mills, $500.00.
7. Paid cash for supplies, $250.00.
8. Paid cash for advertising, $700.00.
9. Received cash on account from Dean Mills, $400.00.
10. Paid cash on account to Topline, $200.00.
11. Paid cash for insurance, $225.00.
12. Received cash from sales, $675.00.
13. Paid cash to owner for personal use, $1,000.00.

Instructions:
For each transaction, complete the following. Transaction 1 is given as an example.
1. Analyze the transaction to determine which accounts in the accounting equation are affected.
2. Write the amount in the appropriate columns, using a plus (+) if the account increases or a minus (−) if the account decreases.
3. For transactions that change owner's equity, write in parentheses a description of the transaction to the right of the amount.
4. Calculate the new balance for each account in the accounting equation.
5. Before going on to the next transaction, determine that the accounting equation is still in balance.

RECYCLING PROBLEM 2-1

Analyzing transactions into debit and credit parts

Luke Harris owns a business called Colato Copies. Colato Copies uses the following accounts.

Cash
Accounts Receivable—Flowerama
Accounts Receivable—Seaside Inn
Supplies
Prepaid Insurance
Accounts Payable—Pacific Paper
Accounts Payable—Raffi Supplies
Luke Harris, Capital

Luke Harris, Drawing
Sales
Advertising Expense
Miscellaneous Expense
Rent Expense
Repair Expense
Utilities Expense

Instructions:
Use the forms given in the *Recycling Problem Working Papers*.
1. Prepare a T account for each account.
2. Analyze each transaction into its debit and credit parts. Write the debit and credit amounts in the proper T accounts to show how each transaction changes account balances. Write the date of the transaction in parentheses before each amount.

Transactions:

July 1. Received cash from owner as an investment, $4,500.00.
    2. Paid cash for rent, $520.00.
    4. Paid cash for supplies, $300.00.
    4. Received cash from sales, $400.00.
    5. Paid cash for insurance, $200.00.
    8. Sold services on account to Flowerama, $450.00.
    9. Bought supplies on account from Raffi Supplies, $700.00.
   10. Paid cash for rent, $120.00.
   11. Received cash from owner as an investment, $2,300.00.
   11. Received cash from sales, $800.00.
   12. Bought supplies on account from Pacific Paper, $300.00.
   13. Received cash on account from Flowerama, $250.00.
   15. Paid cash for miscellaneous expense, $40.00.
   16. Paid cash on account to Raffi Supplies, $350.00.
   22. Paid cash for electric bill (utilities expense), $70.00.
   23. Paid cash for advertising, $160.00.
   25. Sold services on account to Seaside Inn, $640.00.
   26. Paid cash to owner for personal use, $1,200.00.
   30. Received cash on account from Seaside Inn, $300.00.

RECYCLING PROBLEM 3-1

Journalizing transactions in a general journal

Adeline Stein owns a service business called Stein Express, which uses the following accounts:

Cash	Accts. Pay.—Rim Supply	Sales	Repair Expense
Supplies	Accts. Pay.— Parks Co.	Advertising Expense	Utilities Expense
Prepaid Insurance	Adeline Stein, Capital	Miscellaneous Expense	
Accts. Rec.—M. Bien	Adeline Stein, Drawing	Rent Expense	

Transactions:

Aug. 1. Received cash from owner as an investment, $8,750.00. R1.
 2. Paid cash for supplies, $500.00. C1.
 3. Paid cash for rent, $300.00. C2.
 4. Bought supplies on account from Rim Supply, $1,200.00. M1.
 5. Paid cash for electric bill, $250.00. C3.
 8. Paid cash on account to Rim Supply, $700.00. C4.
 8. Received cash from sales, $425.00. T8.
 8. Sold services on account to M. Bien, $125.00. S1.
 9. Paid cash for insurance, $1,900.00. C5.
 10. Paid cash for miscellaneous expense, $27.00. C6.
 10. Received cash from sales, $297.00. T10.
 11. Paid cash for supplies, $770.00. C7.
 11. Received cash from sales, $493.00. T11.
 12. Received cash from sales, $294.00. T12.
 15. Paid cash to owner for personal use, $125.00. C8.
 15. Received cash from sales, $275.00. T15.
 16. Paid cash for repairs, $88.00. C9.
 17. Received cash on account from M. Bien, $125.00. R2.
 17. Bought supplies on account from Parks Co., $345.00. M2.
 17. Received cash from sales, $200.00. T17.
 19. Received cash from sales, $175.00. T19.
 22. Bought supplies on account from Parks Co., $80.00. M3.
 22. Received cash from sales, $450.00. T22.
 23. Paid cash for telephone bill, $50.00. C10.
 23. Sold services on account to M. Bien, $425.00. S2.
 24. Paid cash for advertising, $80.00. C11.
 24. Received cash from sales, $250.00. T24.
 25. Received cash from sales, $325.00. T25.
 26. Received cash from sales, $310.00. T26.
 29. Received cash on account from M. Bien, $425.00. R3.
 30. Paid cash to owner for personal use, $150.00. C13.
 31. Received cash from sales, $450.00. T31.

Instructions:

1. Use page 1 of the general journal given in the *Recycling Problem Working Papers*. Journalize the transactions for August 1 through August 15 of the current year. Source documents are abbreviated as follows: check, C; memorandum, M; receipt, R; sales invoice, S; calculator tape, T.
2. Use page 2 of the journal to journalize the transactions for the remainder of August.

RECYCLING PROBLEM 4-1

Journalizing transactions and posting to a general ledger

Janet Porter owns a service business called Porter's Parties. Porter's Parties' general ledger accounts are given in the *Recycling Problem Working Papers*.

Transactions:

Aug. 1. Received cash from owner as an investment, $4,500.00. R1.
    3. Paid cash for supplies, $300.00. C1.
    5. Sold services on account to Nicholas Calendo, $650.00. S1.
    6. Received cash from sales, $630.00. T6.
    9. Paid cash for electric bill, $130.00. C2.
   11. Paid cash for rent, $530.00. C3.
   13. Bought supplies on account from Jordan Supplies, $800.00. M1.
   13. Received cash from sales, $650.00. T13.
   16. Paid cash for miscellaneous expense, $55.00. C4.
   18. Paid cash on account to Jordan Supplies, $500.00. C5.
   20. Paid cash for supplies, $105.00. C6.
   20. Received cash on account from Nicholas Calendo, $350.00. R2.
   25. Paid cash for advertising, $250.00. C7.
   27. Paid cash for supplies, $75.00. C8.
   27. Received cash from sales, $1,200.00. T27.
   30. Paid cash to owner for personal use, $800.00. C9.

Instructions:

1. Open an account for Utilities Expense. Use the 3-digit numbering system described in the chapter.
2. Journalize the transactions completed during August of the current year. Use page 1 of a general journal. Source documents are abbreviated as follows: check, C; memorandum, M; receipt, R; sales invoice, S; calculator tape, T.
3. Post from the general journal to the general ledger.
4. Prove cash. The balance on the next unused check stub is $4,585.00.

RECYCLING PROBLEM 5-1

Reconciling a bank statement; journalizing a bank service charge, a dishonored check, and petty cash transactions

Tao Vang owns a business called Fast Print. Selected general ledger accounts are given below. Forms are given in the *Recycling Problem Working Papers*.

110 Cash
115 Petty Cash
120 Accts. Rec.—Corner Cafe
130 Supplies

140 Prepaid Insurance
320 Tao Vang, Drawing
520 Miscellaneous Expense
530 Rent Expense

535 Repair Expense
540 Supplies Expense
550 Utilities Expense

Instructions:

1. Journalize the following transactions completed during May of the current year. Use page 12 of a general journal. Source documents are abbreviated as follows: check, C; memorandum, M.

Transactions:

May 21. Paid cash to establish a petty cash fund, $150.00. C51.
    24. Paid cash for supplies, $72.00. C52.
    26. Paid cash for repairs, $85.00. C53.
    27. Received notice from the bank of a dishonored check from Corner Cafe, $70.00, plus $25.00 fee; total, $95.00. M22.

28. Paid cash for miscellaneous expense, $42.00. C54.
31. Paid cash to owner for personal use, $200.00. C55.
31. Paid cash to replenish the petty cash fund, $105.00: supplies, $85.00; miscellaneous expense, $20.00. C56.

2. On May 31 of the current year, Fast Print received a bank statement dated May 30. Prepare a bank statement reconciliation. Use May 31 of the current year as the date. The following information is obtained from the May 30 bank statement and from the records of the business.

Bank statement balance	$1,586.00
Bank service charge	25.00
Outstanding deposit, May 31	285.00
Outstanding checks, Nos. 55 and 56	
Checkbook balance on Check Stub No. 57	$1,591.00

3. Continue using the journal and journalize the following transaction.

Transaction:

May 31. Received bank statement showing May bank service charge, $25.00. M23.

RECYCLING PROBLEM 6-1

Completing a work sheet

On February 28 of the current year, Hibbing Hair Care has the following general ledger accounts and balances. The business uses a monthly fiscal period.

Account Balances

Account Titles	Debit	Credit
Cash	$2,609.00	
Petty Cash	300.00	
Accounts Receivable—Robert Perpich	581.00	
Supplies	895.00	
Prepaid Insurance	1,200.00	
Accounts Payable—Ely Supplies		$ 450.00
Jens Miller-Smith, Capital		4,550.00
Jens Miller-Smith, Drawing	300.00	
Income Summary		
Sales		3,100.00
Advertising Expense	425.00	
Insurance Expense		
Miscellaneous Expense	250.00	
Rent Expense	1,100.00	
Supplies Expense		
Utilities Expense	440.00	

Instructions:

1. Prepare the heading and trial balance on the work sheet given in the *Recycling Problem Working Papers*. Total and rule the Trial Balance columns.
2. Analyze the following adjustment information into debit and credit parts. Record the adjustments on the work sheet.

Adjustment Information, February 28

Supplies inventory	$ 450.00
Value of prepaid insurance	1,000.00

3. Total and rule the Adjustments columns.
4. Extend the up-to-date balances to the Balance Sheet or Income Statement columns.
5. Rule a single line across the Income Statement and Balance Sheet columns. Total each column. Calculate and record the net income or net loss. Label the amount in the Account Title column.
6. Total and rule the Income Statement and Balance Sheet columns.

RECYCLING PROBLEM 7-1

Preparing financial statements

The following information is obtained from the work sheet of SuperClean for the month ended August 31 of the current year. Forms are given in the *Recycling Problem Working Papers*.

	ACCOUNT TITLE	INCOME STATEMENT DEBIT	INCOME STATEMENT CREDIT	BALANCE SHEET DEBIT	BALANCE SHEET CREDIT	
1	Cash			5632 00		1
2	Accounts Receivable—D. Dawson			175 00		2
3	Accounts Receivable—K. Keene			315 00		3
4	Supplies			467 00		4
5	Prepaid Insurance			900 00		5
6	Accounts Payable—DV Supply				593 00	6
7	Accounts Payable—Supply Warehouse				700 00	7
8	Michelle Delist, Capital				5031 00	8
9	Michelle Delist, Drawing			1500 00		9
10	Income Summary					10
11	Sales		5881 00			11
12	Advertising Expense	625 00				12
13	Insurance Expense	150 00				13
14	Miscellaneous Expense	145 00				14
15	Supplies Expense	925 00				15
16	Utilities Expense	1371 00				16
17		3216 00	5881 00	8989 00	6324 00	17
18	Net Income	2665 00			2665 00	18
19		5881 00	5881 00	8989 00	8989 00	19
20						20

Instructions:

1. Prepare an income statement for the month ended August 31 of the current year.
2. Calculate and record the component percentages for total expenses and net income. Round percentage calculations to the nearest 0.1%.
3. Prepare a balance sheet for August 31 of the current year.

RECYCLING PROBLEM 8-1

Journalizing adjusting and closing entries

The following information is obtained from the partial work sheet of SuperClean for the month ended August 31 of the current year.

	ACCOUNT TITLE	ADJUSTMENTS DEBIT	ADJUSTMENTS CREDIT	INCOME STATEMENT DEBIT	INCOME STATEMENT CREDIT	BALANCE SHEET DEBIT	BALANCE SHEET CREDIT	
1	Cash					5632 00		1
2	Accounts Receivable—D. Dawson					175 00		2
3	Accounts Receivable—K. Keene					315 00		3
4	Supplies		(a) 925 00			467 00		4
5	Prepaid Insurance		(b) 150 00			900 00		5
6	Accounts Payable—DV Supply						593 00	6
7	Accounts Payable—Supply Warehouse						700 00	7
8	Michelle Delist, Capital						5031 00	8
9	Michelle Delist, Drawing					1500 00		9
10	Income Summary							10
11	Sales				5881 00			11
12	Advertising Expense			625 00				12
13	Insurance Expense	(b) 150 00		150 00				13
14	Miscellaneous Expense			145 00				14
15	Supplies Expense	(a) 925 00		925 00				15
16	Utilities Expense			1371 00				16
17		1075 00	1075 00	3216 00	5881 00	8989 00	6324 00	17
18	Net Income			2665 00			2665 00	18
19				5881 00	5881 00	8989 00	8989 00	19
20								20

Instructions:

1. Use page 16 of the general journal given in the *Recycling Problem Working Papers*. Journalize the adjusting entries.
2. Continue to use page 16 of the general journal. Journalize the closing entries.

RECYCLING PROBLEM 9-1

Journalizing purchases, cash payments, and other transactions

Backwoods, Inc., is a sporting goods store organized as a corporation.

Instructions:

1. Using the journals given in the *Recycling Problem Working Papers*, journalize the following transactions completed during August of the current year. Use page 9 of a purchases journal, page 15 of a cash payments journal, and page 12 of a general journal. Source documents are abbreviated as follows: check, C; memorandum, M; purchase invoice, P; debit memorandum, DM.

Transactions:

Aug. 1. Paid cash to Keller Realty for rent, $1,000.00. C772.
    2. Paid cash to LWAP Radio for advertising, $720.00. C773.
    3. Bought office supplies on account from Johnson Office Supply, $420.00. M62.
    4. Paid cash on account to Arrowhead Supply, $4,210.00, covering P436. No cash discount was offered. C774.
    6. Paid cash to City Utilities for electric bill, $420.00. C775.
    7. Paid cash on account to Johnson Office Supply covering M62, less 2% discount. C776.
    9. Paid cash to Mark's Discount Stores for store supplies, $224.00. C777.
    9. Purchased merchandise on account from Peterson Sports, $3,560.00. P445.
   11. Purchased merchandise for cash from Atlas Sports Co., $3,480.00, less a 60% trade discount. C778.
   13. Returned merchandise to Peterson Sports from P445, $233.00. DM19.
   13. Purchased merchandise for cash from Duck Crafts, $495.00. C779.
   15. Returned merchandise to Evans Sports Corporation from P438, $112.00. DM20.
   15. Paid cash on account to Peterson Sports covering P445 after a purchase return, DM19, less 2% discount. C780.
   20. Purchased merchandise for cash from Atlas Sports Co., $156.00. C781.
   21. Paid cash on account to Evans Sports Corporation, $1,950.00. No cash discount was offered. C782.
   22. Purchased merchandise on account from Camo Clothing, $8,100, less a 50% trade discount. P446.
   23. Bought store supplies on account from Mancil Marketing, $120.00. M63.
   24. Paid cash to Velmar Company for store supplies, $245.00. C783.
   29. Purchased merchandise for cash from Paintball Central, $1,154.00. C784.

2. Total the amount columns of cash payments journal page 15. Prove the equality of debits and credits and rule the cash payments journal to carry the totals forward.
3. Record the totals brought forward from cash payments journal page 15 to line 1 of page 16 of the cash payments journal.
4. Journalize the following transactions.

Transactions:

Aug. 31. Paid cash on account to Camo Clothing covering P446, less 2% cash discount. C785.
   31. Paid cash to replenish the petty cash fund, $127.80: supplies—office, $25.66; supplies—store, $48.25; miscellaneous, $54.33; and cash over, $0.44. C786.

5. Total and rule page 9 of the purchases journal.
6. Total the amount columns of cash payments journal page 16. Prove the equality of debits and credits of cash payments journal page 16.
7. Rule page 16 of the cash payments journal.

RECYCLING PROBLEM 10-1

Journalizing sales and cash receipts transactions; proving and ruling journals

Burge Supply sells lumber, brick, and other construction materials.

Sales journal page 22, cash receipts journal page 23, and general journal page 17 are given in the *Recycling Problem Working Papers*. Balances brought forward are provided on line 1 of the sales and cash receipts journals.

Instructions:

1. Journalize the following transactions completed during the remainder of November in the appropriate journal. Sales tax rate is 6%. Source documents are abbreviated as follows: receipt, R; sales invoice, S; terminal summary, TS.

Transactions:

Nov. 25. Received cash on account from Davis Construction, $1,379.84, covering S845 for $1,408.00, less 2% cash discount, $28.16. R334.
   26. Recorded cash and credit card sales, $4,844.00, plus sales tax, $290.64; total, $5,134.64. TS38.
   28. Sold merchandise on account to Margaret Sienna, $664.00, plus sales tax, $39.84; total, $703.84. S889.
   28. Received cash on account from Ventura Fencing, $2,849.00, covering S861. R335.

29. Granted credit to Davis Construction for merchandise returned, $1,820.00, plus sales tax, $109.20; total, $1,929.20. CM43.
30. Sold merchandise on account to State University, $2,118.00. State University is exempt from sales tax. S890.
30. Recorded cash and credit card sales, $839.00, plus sales tax, $50.34; total, $889.34. TS39.

2. Total and prove the equality of debits and credits for the sales journal.
3. Rule the sales journal.
4. Total and prove the equality of debits and credits for the cash receipts journal.
5. Prove cash. The November 1 cash account balance in the general ledger was $8,483.31. The November 31 cash credit total in the cash payments journal was $42,194.33. On November 31 the balance on the next unused check stub was $16,626.70.
6. Rule the cash receipts journal.

RECYCLING PROBLEM 11-1

Posting to general and subsidiary ledgers

The journals and ledgers for Custom Boots are given in the *Recycling Problem Working Papers*.

Instructions:

1. Post the separate items in the following journals to the general and subsidiary ledgers. Use the current year.
   a. Sales journal.
   b. Purchases journal.
   c. General journal.
   d. Cash receipts journal.
   e. Cash payments journal.
2. Prove and rule the sales journal. Post the totals of the special amount columns.
3. Total and rule the purchases journal. Post the total.
4. Prove and rule the cash receipts journal. Post the totals of the special amount columns.
5. Prove and rule the cash payments journal. Post the totals of the special amount columns.
6. Prepare a schedule of accounts payable and a schedule of accounts receivable. Compare the totals of the schedules with the balances of the controlling accounts, Accounts Payable and Accounts Receivable, in the general ledger. If the totals are not the same, find and correct the errors.

RECYCLING PROBLEM 12-1

Preparing a semimonthly payroll

The following information is for the semimonthly pay period July 16–31 of the current year. Forms are given in the *Recycling Problem Working Papers*.

SEMIMONTHLY PERIOD ENDED July 31, 20--

	EMPL. NO.	EMPLOYEE'S NAME	MARITAL STATUS	NO. OF ALLOWANCES	EARNINGS REGULAR	EARNINGS OVERTIME	DEDUCTIONS HEALTH INSURANCE
1	5	Abrams, Thomas	S	1	892 00		35 00
2	6	Carroll, John	M	2	880 00	90 00	60 00
3	1	Harris, Jonathan	S	1	924 00		35 00
4	4	Kennard, Mary	S	1	1056 00	72 00	35 00
5	2	Locke, Anna	M	2	994 00		60 00
6	7	Rayford, Stan	M	2	812 00		60 00
7	3	Suell, Nicole	M	3	860 00		80 00
8							
9							
10							
11							
12							

Instructions:

1. Prepare a payroll register. The date of payment is July 31. Use the income tax withholding tables shown in Chapter 12 to find the income tax withholding for each employee. Calculate social security and Medicare tax withholdings using 6.2% and 1.45% tax rates, respectively. None of the employee-accumulated earnings has exceeded the social security tax base.
2. Prepare a check for the total amount of the net pay. Make the check payable to Payroll Account 982-561-4732 and sign your name as the manager of Sanford Company. The beginning check stub balance is $11,530.50.
3. Prepare payroll checks for Thomas Abrams, Check No. 558, and Anna Locke, Check No. 562. Sign your name as the manager of Sanford Company. Record the two payroll check numbers in the payroll register.

RECYCLING PROBLEM 13-1

Journalizing payroll transactions

Wooden Cycles completed payroll transactions during the period January 1 to March 31 of the current year. Payroll tax rates are as follows: social security, 6.2%; Medicare, 1.45%; federal unemployment, 0.8%; state unemployment, 5.4%. No total earnings have exceeded the tax base for calculating unemployment taxes. Wooden Cycles is a monthly schedule depositor for payroll taxes.

Instructions:

1. Journalize the following transactions on page 14 of the cash payments journal and page 10 of the general journal given in the *Recycling Problem Working Papers*. Source documents are abbreviated as follows: check, C, and memorandum, M.

Transactions:

Jan. 31. Paid cash for monthly payroll. Gross wages, $5,920.00; withholdings: employee income tax, $360.00; calculate social security and Medicare taxes. C555.

31. Recorded employer payroll taxes expense for the January payroll. M24.

Feb. 15. Paid cash for the January liability for employee income tax, social security tax, and Medicare tax. C575.

28. Paid cash for monthly payroll. Gross wages, $6,058.00; withholdings: employee income tax, $372.00; calculate social security and Medicare taxes. C601.

28. Recorded employer payroll taxes expense for the February payroll. M28.

Mar. 15. Paid cash for the February liability for employee income tax, social security tax, and Medicare tax. C624.

31. Paid cash for monthly payroll. Gross wages, $6,120.00; withholdings: employee income tax, $394.00; calculate social security and Medicare taxes. C658.

31. Recorded employer payroll taxes expense for the March payroll. M35.

Apr. 15. Paid cash for the March liability for employee income tax, social security tax, and Medicare tax. C699.

15. Paid cash for federal unemployment tax liability for quarter ended March 31. C700.

15. Paid cash for state unemployment tax liability for quarter ended March 31. C701.

2. Prove and rule the cash payments journal.

RECYCLING PROBLEM 14-1

Preparing an 8-column work sheet for a merchandising business

The trial balance for Audio Source, Inc., as of December 31 of the current year is recorded on a work sheet in the *Recycling Problem Working Papers*. Audio Source completed the following transactions during December of the current year and January of the next year.

Transactions:

Dec. 15. The board of directors declared a dividend of $0.375 per share; capital stock issued is 20,000 shares. M114.

Jan. 15. Paid cash for dividend declared December 15. C924.

Instructions:

1. Use page 12 of a general journal. Journalize the dividend declared on December 15.
2. Use page 18 of a cash payments journal. Journalize payment of the dividend on January 15.
3. Analyze the following adjustment information collected on December 31 and record the adjustments on the work sheet. Label each adjustment using labels *(a)* through *(g)*.
   a. Uncollectible accounts are 0.4% of credit sales of $620,000.00.
   b. Merchandise inventory $270,461.36
   c. Office supplies inventory 1,081.34
   d. Store supplies inventory 1,585.90
   e. Value of prepaid insurance 160.00
   f. Estimate of office equipment depreciation 6,140.00
   g. Estimate of store equipment depreciation 5,520.00
4. Using the federal income tax table shown in Chapter 14, calculate federal income tax expense and record the income tax adjustment on the work sheet. Label the adjustment *(h)*.
5. Complete the work sheet.

RECYCLING PROBLEM 15-1

Preparing financial statements

The completed work sheet for Hawkins Parts, Inc., for the year ended December 31 of the current year and forms for completing this problem are given in the *Recycling Problem Working Papers*.

Instructions:

1. Prepare an income statement. Calculate and record the following component percentages: (a) cost of merchandise sold, (b) gross profit on sales, (c) total expenses, and (d) net income or loss before federal income tax. Round percentage calculations to the nearest 0.1%.
2. Prepare a statement of stockholders' equity. The company had 30,000 shares of $1.00 par value stock outstanding on January 1. The company issued an additional 2,000 shares during the year.
3. Prepare a balance sheet in report form.
4. Calculate the earnings per share and price-earnings ratio. The current market price of the stock is $89.00.

RECYCLING PROBLEM 16-1

Journalizing and posting adjusting and closing entries; preparing a post-closing trial balance

Use the following partial work sheet of Southern Fixtures, Inc., for the year ended December 31 of the current year. The general ledger accounts and their balances as well as forms for completing this problem are in the *Recycling Problem Working Papers*.

Southern Fixtures, Inc.
Work Sheet
For Year Ended December 31, 20--

	ACCOUNT TITLE	ADJUSTMENTS DEBIT	ADJUSTMENTS CREDIT	INCOME STATEMENT DEBIT	INCOME STATEMENT CREDIT
4	Allow. for Uncoll. Accts.		(a) 2 215 00		
5	Merchandise Inventory	(b) 4 819 00			
6	Supplies—Office		(c) 6 106 00		
7	Supplies—Store		(d) 3 154 00		
8	Prepaid Insurance		(e) 9 600 00		
9	Office Equipment				
10	Acc. Depr.—Office Equipment		(f) 4 420 00		
11	Store Equipment				
12	Acc. Depr.—Store Equipment		(g) 4 950 00		
13	Accounts Payable				
14	Federal Income Tax Payable		(h) 6 429 62		
28	Income Summary		(b) 4 819 00		4 819 00
38	Depr. Exp.—Office Equipment	(f) 4 420 00		4 420 00	
39	Depr. Exp.—Store Equipment	(g) 4 950 00		4 950 00	
40	Insurance Expense	(e) 9 600 00		9 600 00	
41	Miscellaneous Expense			13 184 80	
42	Payroll Taxes Expense			18 785 24	
43	Rent Expense			12 800 00	
44	Salary Expense			151 584 73	
45	Supplies Expense—Office	(c) 6 106 00		6 106 00	
46	Supplies Expense—Store	(d) 3 154 00		3 154 00	
47	Uncollectible Accounts Expense	(a) 2 215 00		2 215 00	
48	Utilities Expense			3 294 47	
49	Federal Income Tax Expense	(h) 6 429 62		46 429 62	
50		41 693 62	41 693 62	641 874 48	757 443 89
51	Net Income after Federal Income Tax			115 569 41	
52				757 443 89	757 443 89

Instructions:

1. Journalize the adjusting entries using page 18 of a general journal.
2. Post the adjusting entries.
3. Journalize the closing entries using page 19 of a general journal.
4. Post the closing entries.
5. Prepare a post-closing trial balance.

RECYCLING PROBLEM 17-1

Recording entries for uncollectible accounts

The accounts receivable and general ledger accounts for Fincher Industries are given in the *Recycling Problem Working Papers*. The following transactions relating to uncollectible accounts receivable occurred during the final quarter of the current fiscal year.

Instructions:

1. Journalize the following transactions completed during October using page 10 of a general journal. Post the transactions to the customer accounts and general ledger accounts.

Transactions:

Oct. 6. Wrote off Chittenden Corporation's past-due account as uncollectible, $284.75. M216.
19. Wrote off Foster Corporation's past-due account as uncollectible, $574.10. M221.

2. Journalize the following transactions completed during November using page 11 of a general journal and page 11 of a cash receipts journal. Prove the cash receipts journal. Post the transactions to the customer accounts and general ledger accounts.

Transactions:

Nov. 5. Wrote off Agnew Company's past-due account as uncollectible, $804.24. M236.
12. Received cash in full payment of Chittenden Corporation's account, previously written off as uncollectible, $284.75. M241 and R616.
17. Received cash in full payment of Dionne, Inc.'s account, previously written off as uncollectible, $468.30. M243 and R627.

3. Journalize the following transactions completed during December using page 12 of a general journal and page 12 of a cash receipts journal. Prove the cash receipts journal. Post the transactions to the customer accounts and general ledger accounts.

Transactions:

Dec. 4. Wrote off Grant Company's past-due account as uncollectible, $705.18. M257.
10. Received cash in full payment of Agnew Company's account, previously written off as uncollectible, $804.24. M259 and R702.
21. Received cash in full payment of Foster Corporation's account, previously written off as uncollectible, $574.10. M265 and R729.

4. Journalize the December 31 adjusting entry for estimated uncollectible accounts expense for the year. Use page 13 of the general journal. Uncollectible accounts expense is estimated as 1.2% of total sales on account. Total sales on account for the year were $987,660.00. Post the transaction to the general ledger accounts.

RECYCLING PROBLEM 18-1

Recording transactions for plant assets

Diamond Clothing records plant assets in two accounts: Store Equipment, Account No. 1215, and Office Equipment, Account No. 1205. Store equipment is depreciated using the straight-line method. Office equipment is depreciated using the double declining-balance method. Journals and plant asset records are given in the *Recycling Problem Working Papers*.

Instructions:

1. Record the following transactions completed during 20X1 on page 1 of a cash payments journal.

Transactions:

Jan. 3. Bought a color printer for the office: cost, $900.00; estimated salvage value, $100.00; estimated useful life, 4 years; plant asset No. 642; serial number, ZE532N34. C168.
Feb. 26. Paid property taxes on plant assets assessed at $620,000.00. The tax rate is 1.4%. C216.
Apr. 3. Purchased a store display: cost, $3,000.00; estimated salvage value, $500.00; estimated useful life, 5 years; plant asset No. 643; serial number, 754NFE. C275.

2. Complete Section 1 of a plant asset record for each new plant asset.
3. Prepare a depreciation table for each new plant asset.
4. Complete Section 3 of the plant asset records for 20X1–20X4.
5. Record the following transactions completed during 20X5. Use page 2 of a cash receipts journal and page 2 of a general journal.

Transactions:

Jan. 3. Received cash for sale of a color printer, plant asset No. 642, $60.00. R7.

June 29. Received cash for sale of a store display, plant asset No. 643, $950.00. M69 and R171.

Dec. 31. Recorded the adjusting entry for depreciation expense—store equipment. Total 20X5 depreciation expense of store equipment was $17,765.00.

6. Complete the plant asset records for each plant asset sold during 20X5.

RECYCLING PROBLEM 19-1

Determining the cost of inventory using the fifo, lifo, and weighted-average inventory costing methods

Mayfair Industries made the following purchases of a part during the fiscal year. There are 32 units in ending inventory. Forms for costing inventory are given in the *Recycling Problem Working Papers*.

Purchase Date	Quantity	Unit Price
January 1, beginning inventory	3	$12.30
January 3, purchases	20	13.00
March 29, purchases	20	13.20
August 15, purchases	15	13.25
November 13, purchases	15	13.45

Instructions:
1. Calculate the cost of ending inventory using the fifo, lifo, and weighted-average methods.
2. Which of the inventory costing methods resulted in the highest cost of merchandise sold?

RECYCLING PROBLEM 20-1

Journalizing notes payable and notes receivable transactions

The following transactions related to notes payable and notes receivable were completed by Wolverton Company during April of the current year. Journals are provided in the *Recycling Problem Working Papers*.

Transactions:

Apr. 5. Signed a 90-day, 10% note, for $30,000.00 with First National Bank. R34.

9. Accepted a 90-day, 15% note from Phillip Majure for an extension of time on his account, $650.00. NR18.

12. Received cash for the maturity value of a 60-day, 18% note for $900.00. R67.

16. Accepted a 60-day, 14% note from Avery Harris for an extension of time on her account, $2,450.00. NR19.

19. Received cash for the maturity value of a 60-day, 18% note for $500.00. R74.

20. Signed a 90-day, 15% note with Rossman Supply for an extension of time on this account payable, $2,500.00. M49.

22. Patrick Isamen dishonored his 90-day, 15% note, for $3,000.00. M53.

27. Signed a 120-day, 12% note for $20,000.00 with First Commerce Bank. R84.

29. Received cash for the maturity value of a 90-day, 18% note for $1,800.00. R89.

Instructions:

1. Journalize each transaction using page 3 of a general journal and page 6 of a cash receipts journal. Source documents are abbreviated as follows: check, C; receipt, R; memorandum, M; note receivable, NR.
2. Determine the maturity date and maturity value of each note signed by Wolverton Company.
3. Journalize the following transactions on page 10 of a cash payments journal. Use the maturity dates and maturity values calculated in Instruction 2.

Transactions:
Paid cash for the maturity value of the $30,000.00 note dated April 5. C452.
Paid cash for the maturity value of the $2,500.00 note dated April 20. C489.
Paid cash for the maturity value of the $20,000.00 note dated April 27. C672.

RECYCLING PROBLEM 21-1

Journalizing and posting entries for accrued interest revenue and expense

The accounting forms for Farrell Company are given in the *Recycling Problem Working Papers*. The balances are recorded as of December 31 of the current year before adjusting entries.

Farrell Company completed the following transactions related to notes receivable and notes payable during the current year and the following one year. The first two transactions have already been journalized and posted. One note receivable and one note payable are the only notes on hand at the end of the fiscal period. Source documents are abbreviated as follows: receipt, R; check, C; note receivable, NR.

Transactions:

20X1

Nov. 9. Accepted a 90-day, 18% note from Kayla Nelson for an extension of time on her account, $800.00. NR18.

Dec. 14. Signed a 120-day, 12% note, $4,800.00 with First National Bank. R364.

20X2

Feb. 7. Received cash for the maturity value of NR18. R132.

Apr. 13. Paid cash for the maturity value of the First National Bank note. C342.

Instructions:

1. Plan the adjustments on a work sheet. Use (a) for accrued interest income and (h) for accrued interest expense.
2. Journalize and post the adjusting entries for accrued interest income and accrued interest expense on December 31. Use page 15 of a general journal.
3. Journalize and post the closing entries for interest income and interest expense. Continue to use page 15 of a general journal.
4. Journalize and post the reversing entries for accrued interest income and accrued interest expense. Use page 16 of a general journal.
5. Journalize the receipt of cash for the maturity value of NR18. Use page 13 of a cash receipts journal. Post the amounts in the General columns of the cash receipts journal.
6. Journalize the cash payment for the maturity value of the note payable. Use page 18 of a cash payments journal. Post the amounts in the General columns of the cash payments journal.

RECYCLING PROBLEM 22-1

Preparing financial statements and end-of-fiscal-period entries for a corporation

Accounting forms are given in the *Recycling Problem Working Papers*. Applewhite Corporation completed the following transactions during December of the current year and January of the next year.

Instructions:

1. Prepare Applewhite Corporation's work sheet for the current year ended December 31. Record the adjustments on the work sheet using the following information.

    Adjustment Information, December 31

Accrued interest income	$ 64.00
Uncollectible accounts expense estimated as 0.6% of sales on account.	
Sales on account for year, $554,000.00.	
Merchandise inventory	$229,406.46
Supplies inventory	573.52
Value of prepaid insurance	1,200.00
Annual depreciation expense—office equipment	4,850.00
Annual depreciation expense—store equipment	3,480.00
Accrued interest expense	250.00

    Federal income tax is calculated using the tax table presented in Chapter 22.

2. Prepare an income statement. Calculate and record the following component percentages: (a) cost of merchandise sold; (b) gross profit on operations; (c) total operating expenses; (d) income from operations; (e) net addition or deduction resulting from other revenue and expenses; and (f) net income before federal income tax. Round percentage calculations to the nearest 0.1%.

3. Analyze the corporation's income statement by determining if component percentages are within acceptable levels. If any component percentage is not within an acceptable level, suggest steps that the company should take. The corporation considers the following component percentages acceptable.

Cost of merchandise sold	Not more than 68.0%
Gross profit on operations	Not less than 32.0%
Total operating expenses	Not more than 25.0%
Income from operations	Not less than 7.0%
Net deduction from other revenue and expenses	Not more than 0.5%
Net income before federal income tax	Not less than 6.5%

4. Prepare a statement of stockholders' equity. Use the following additional information.

January 1 balance of capital stock account (10,000 shares issued for $10.00 per share)	$100,000.00
Shares issued during the year	2,000 shares

5. Prepare a balance sheet.

6. Calculate the corporation's (a) working capital and (b) current ratio. Determine if these items are within acceptable levels. The corporation considers the following levels acceptable.

Working capital	Not less than $250,000.00
Current ratio	Between 4.0 to 1 and 6.0 to 1

7. Journalize the adjusting entries using page 15 of a general journal.
8. Journalize the closing entries using page 16 of a general journal.
9. Journalize the reversing entries using page 17 of a general journal.

RECYCLING PROBLEM 23-1

Recording partners' investments and withdrawals, preparing financial statements, and liquidating a partnership

Ashwin Akabu and Chen Wong are partners in a business called Total Toys. Journals and forms for completing this problem are given in the *Recycling Problem Working Papers*.

Total Toys completed the following transactions during June of the current year.

Transactions:

June 15. Received cash from partner, Ashwin Akabu, as an investment, $15,000.00. Receipt No. 128.
15. Received cash of $7,000 and supplies valued at $5,000.00 from partner, Chen Wong, as an investment. Receipt No. 129.
30. Ashwin Akabu, partner, withdrew merchandise for personal use, $900.00. Memorandum No. 74.
30. Chen Wong, partner, withdrew cash for personal use, $1,200. Check No. 141.

Instructions:

1. Use page 11 of a cash receipts journal. Journalize the investments on June 15.
2. Use page 17 of a cash payments journal and page 21 of a general journal. Journalize the withdrawals on June 30.

Information from Total Toys' worksheet and income statement for the month ended June 30 is given below.

Net Income for the month ended June 30	$ 7,200.00
Ashwin Akabu, Capital June 1 balance	31,770.00
Chen Wong, Capital June 1 balance	25,441.00

Instructions:

3. Prepare a distribution of net income statement for Total Toys. Net income or loss is to be distributed equally to the partners.
4. Using the balances of the general ledger capital accounts, prepare an owners' equity statement for Total Toys. The investments made on June 15 are the only additional investments made by the partners this month. The withdrawals made on June 30 are the only withdrawals made by the partners this month.

Total Toys was liquidated on June 30. On that date, after financial statements were prepared and closing entries were posted, the general ledger accounts had the following balances.

Cash	$87,061.00
Merchandise Inventory	1,000.00
Equipment	7,500.00
Accumulated Depreciation—Equipment	5,000.00
Accounts Payable	1,250.00
Ashwin Akabu, Capital	49,470.00
Chen Wong, Capital	39,841.00

The following transactions occurred on June 30 of the current year.

Transactions:

a. Received cash from the sale of merchandise inventory, $900.00. R130.
b. Received cash from the sale of equipment, $3,500.00. R131.
c. Paid cash to all creditors for amounts owed. C142.
d. Distributed balance of Loss and Gain on Realization to the partners on an equal basis. M75.
e. Distributed remaining cash to partners. C143 and C144.

Instructions:

5. Journalize the transactions. Continue on the next available line of the journals used in instructions 1 and 2.

RECYCLING PROBLEM 24-1

Recording international and Internet sales

Pacific Trade Inc. sells folk art domestically and internationally. The company has Internet sales as well. Journals and forms for completing this problem are given in the *Recycling Problem Working Papers*.

Instructions:

1. Journalize the following transactions affecting sales and cash receipts completed during November of the current year. Use page 23 of a general journal and a cash receipts journal. Source documents are abbreviated as follows: memorandum, M; receipt, R; time draft, TD; and terminal summary, TS.

Transactions:

Nov. 4. Received a 30-day time draft from Hong Kong Importers for an international sale, $2,200.00. TD72.
     7. Recorded Internet credit card sales, $8,450.00. TS330.
    12. Recorded international cash sale, $11,800.00. M65.
    14. Recorded Internet credit card sales, $5,670.00. TS331.
    15. Received cash for the value of Time Draft No. 68, $3,000.00. R103.
    18. Received cash for the value of Time Draft No. 71, $5,900.00. R110.
    21. Recorded Internet cash sale, $16,400. TS332.
    24. Recorded international cash sale, $7,500.00. M76.
    28. Recorded Internet cash sale, $3,300.00. TS333.
    30. Received a 30-day time draft from Australian Arts for international sale of merchandise, $16,040.00. TD73.

2. Prove and rule the cash receipts journal.

APPENDIX E

ANSWERS TO AUDIT YOUR UNDERSTANDING

Chapter 1, Page 9
1. Planning, recording, analyzing, and interpreting financial information.
2. Answers will vary but should involve businesses that perform activities for a fee.
3. A business owned by one person.
4. Assets = Liabilities + Owner's Equity.

Chapter 1, Page 13
1. The right side must be increased.
2. If one account is increased, another account on the same side of the equation must be decreased by the same amount.
3. Buying items or services and paying for them at a future date.

Chapter 1, Page 17
1. Increased.
2. Increased
3. Decreased.

Chapter 2, Page 31
1. ASSETS = LIABILITIES + OWNER'S EQUITY
2. (1) Account balances increase on the normal balance side of an account. (2) Account balances decrease on the side opposite the normal balance side of an account.

Chapter 2, Page 37
1. (1) Which accounts are affected? (2) How is each account classified? (3) How is each classification changed? (4) How is each amount entered in the accounts?
2. Supplies and Cash.

Chapter 2, Page 44
1. Cash and Sales.
2. Accounts Receivable and Sales.
3. Owner's drawing account and Cash.
4. Credit, because revenue increases owner's equity.
5. Debit, because expenses decrease owner's equity.

Chapter 3, Page 62
1. By date.
2. Source documents are one way to verify the accuracy of a specific journal entry.
3. Date, debit, credit, and source document.

Chapter 3, Page 67
1. Prepaid Insurance.
2. Supplies.
3. Accounts Payable.
4. Cash.

Chapter 3, Page 73
1. Cash.
2. Sales.
3. Sales.
4. C.
5. R.

Chapter 3, Page 77
1. When there is insufficient space to record any more entries.
2. Draw neat lines through all parts of the incorrect entry. Journalize the entry correctly on the next blank lines.
3. Draw neat lines through all incorrect parts of the entry. Record the correct items on the same lines as the incorrect items, directly above the canceled parts.

Chapter 4, Page 95
1. The first digit indicates in which general ledger division the account is located. The second and third digits indicate the location of the account within that division.
2. (1) Write the account title in the heading. (2) Write the account number in the heading.

Chapter 4, Page 101
1. (1) Write the date in the Date column of the account. (2) Write the journal page number in the Post. Ref. column of the account. (3) Write the amount in the Debit or Credit column. (4) Calculate and write the new account balance in the Balance Debit or Balance Credit column. (5) Write the account number in the Post. Ref. column of the journal.
2. Whenever the credits in an account exceed the debits, the balance is a credit. Whenever the debits in an account exceed the credits, the balance is a debit.

Chapter 4, Page 108
1. The cash balance as shown in the checkbook and the cash balance in the cash account.
2. A journal entry made to correct an error in the ledger.

3. To show the increase in this expense account.
4. To show the decrease in this expense account.

Chapter 5, Page 123
1. Blank endorsement, special endorsement, and restrictive endorsement.
2. (1) Write the amount of the check after the dollar sign at the top of the stub. (2) Write the date of the check on the Date line. (3) Write to whom the check is to be paid on the To line. (4) Record the purpose of the check on the For line. (5) Write the amount of the check after the words *Amt. This Check*. (6) Calculate the new checking balance and record it in the amount column on the last line of the stub.
3. (1) Write the date in the space provided. (2) Write to whom the check is to be paid following the words *Pay to the order of*. (3) Write the amount in figures following the dollar sign. (4) Write the amount in words on the line with the word *Dollars*. (5) Write the purpose of the check on the line labeled For. (6) Sign the check.

Chapter 5, Page 128
1. (1) A service charge may not have been recorded in the depositor's business records. (2) Outstanding deposits may be recorded in the depositor's records but not on a bank statement. (3) Outstanding checks may be recorded in the depositor's records but not on a bank statement. (4) A depositor may have made a math or recording error.
2. An outstanding check.

Chapter 5, Page 133
1. (1) The check appears to be altered. (2) The signature on the check does not match the signature on the signature card. (3) The amounts written in figures and in words do not agree. (4) The check is postdated. (5) The person who wrote the check has stopped payment on it. (6) The account of the person who wrote the check has insufficient funds to pay the check.
2. Cash.
3. Cash.

Chapter 5, Page 137
1. For making small cash payments.
2. The check issued to replenish petty cash is a credit to Cash and does not affect Petty Cash.

Chapter 6, Page 155
1. Name of the business, name of report, and date of report.
2. All general ledger accounts are listed in the Trial Balance columns of a work sheet, even if some accounts do not have balances.

Chapter 6, Page 161
1. An expense should be reported in the same fiscal period that it is used to produce revenue.
2. (1) What is the balance of the account? (2) What should the balance be for this account? (3) What must be done to correct the account balance? (4) What adjustment is made?

Chapter 6, Page 166
1. Asset, liability, and owner's equity accounts.
2. Revenue and expense accounts.
3. Balance Sheet Credit column.
4. Balance Sheet Debit column.

Chapter 6, Page 170
1. Subtract the smaller total from the larger total to find the difference.
2. The difference between two column totals can be divided evenly by 9.
3. A slide.

Chapter 7, Page 186
1. Heading, revenue, expenses, and net income or net loss.
2. Total Expenses *divided by* Total Sales *equals* Total Expenses Component Percentage.
3. Net Income *divided by* Total Sales *equals* Net Income Component Percentage.

Chapter 7, Page 192
1. Heading, assets, liabilities, and owner's equity.
2. Capital Account Balance *plus* Net Income *minus* Drawing Account Balance *equals* Current Capital.

Chapter 8, Page 205
1. To update general ledger accounts at the end of a fiscal period.
2. Adjustments column of the work sheet.
3. Supplies Expense and Insurance Expense.

Chapter 8, Page 212
1. Beginning balances.
2. Changes in the owner's capital for a single fiscal period.
3. (1) An entry to close income statement accounts with credit balances. (2) An entry to close income statement accounts with debit balances. (3) An entry to record net income or net loss and close the income summary account. (4) An entry to close the owner's drawing account.

Chapter 8, Page 219
1. To assure a reader that a balance has not been omitted.
2. Only those with balances (permanent accounts).
3. Because they are closed and have zero balances.

Chapter 9, Page 241
1. Purchases of merchandise on account.
2. Frequently occurring transactions.
3. Because the same two accounts are always affected by purchase on account transactions.
4. Time is saved because using special amount columns eliminates writing an account title in the Account Title column.

Chapter 9, Page 247
1. To encourage early payment.
2. Cash payment transactions that do not occur often.
3. A business purchases merchandise to sell but buys supplies for use in the business. Supplies are not intended for sale.
4. Two ten means 2% of the invoice amount may be deducted if the invoice is paid within 10 days of the invoice date. Net thirty means that the total invoice amount must be paid within 30 days.

Chapter 9, Page 253
1. The titles of the accounts for which the petty cash fund was used.
2. The balance is usually a debit because the petty cash fund is more likely to be short than over.
3. (1) Rule a single line across all amount columns. (2) Write the date in the Date column. (3) Write *Totals* in the Account Title column. (4) Write each column total below the single line. (5) Rule a double line across all amount columns.

Chapter 9, Page 258
1. General journal.
2. To note that the invoice is for store supplies and not for purchases, ensuring that no mistake is made.
3. Because the single credit amount is posted to two accounts.
4. After each general journal entry is recorded.
5. A business can track the amount of purchases returns and allowances in a fiscal period if a separate account is used.
6. A purchases return is credit allowed for the purchase price of returned merchandise. A purchases allowance is credit allowed for part of the purchase price of merchandise that is not returned.
7. When the customer wants to record the transaction immediately, without waiting for written confirmation from the vendor.

Chapter 10, Page 275
1. A merchandising business sells merchandise; a service business sells services.
2. As a percentage of sales.
3. The amount of sales tax collected is a business liability until paid to the government.
4. Accounts Receivable.

Chapter 10, Page 284
1. The POS system produces a receipt that contains detailed information about the sale, including the merchandise's description and price. The cash register receipt does not include such detailed information.
2. A batch report can be detailed, showing each credit card sale, or it can provide a summary of the number and total of sales by credit card type.
3. The funds are transferred among the banks issuing the credit cards.

Chapter 10, Page 287
1. A sales return is credit allowed a customer for the sales price of returned merchandise; a sales allowance is credit allowed a customer for part of the sales price of merchandise that is not returned.
2. Credit memorandum.
3. Sales Returns and Allowances and Sales Tax Payable are debited; Accounts Receivable is credited.
4. To provide better information to quickly identify if the amount of sales returns and allowances is greater than expected.

Chapter 11, Page 306
1. A controlling account summarizes all accounts in a subsidiary ledger. The balance of a controlling account equals the total of all account balances in its related subsidiary ledger.
2. Accounts Payable Debit column.

Chapter 11, Page 314
1. Customer accounts listed in the Accounts Receivable Debit column.
2. Accounts Receivable Credit column.
3. All customer accounts that have balances.

Chapter 11, Page 319
1. Amounts in the Debit and Credit columns.
2. (1) Write the date in the Date column of the account. (2) Write the journal page number in the Post. Ref. column of the account. (3) Write the amount in the Debit or Credit column of the account. (4) Calculate and write the new account balance in the Balance Debit or Balance Credit column of the account. (5) Write the general ledger account number in the Post. Ref. column of the journal.

Chapter 11, Page 326
1. Each special amount column.
2. (1) Sales journal, (2) purchases journal, (3) general journal, (4) cash receipts journal, (5) cash payments journal.

Chapter 11, Page 329
1. Memorandum.
2. It does not affect the general ledger accounts.
3. Only a reference to the subsidiary ledger account is entered in the Post. Ref. column of the general journal.

Chapter 12, Page 344
1. The total amount earned by all employees for a pay period.
2. 3½ hours.

3. Overtime hours × the overtime rate.
4. $506 (40 × $11.00 + 4 × $16.50).

Chapter 12, Page 350
1. Form W-4, Employee's Withholding Allowance Certificate.
2. Employee marital status and number of withholding allowances.
3. Both the employee and the employer.

Chapter 12, Page 355
1. The payroll register summarizes the payroll for one pay period and shows total earnings, payroll withholdings, and net pay of all employees.
2. By subtracting total deductions from total earnings.
3. Because a business must send a quarterly report to federal and state governments showing employee taxable earnings and taxes withheld from employee earnings.

Chapter 12, Page 358
1. To help protect and control payroll payments.
2. The payroll register.
3. Individual checks are not written and do not have to be distributed.

Chapter 13, Page 372
1. Salary Expense.
2. Employee Income Tax Payable.
3. Social Security Tax Payable.
4. Medicare Tax Payable.

Chapter 13, Page 377
1. Social security: 6.2% of earnings up to a maximum of $87,000.00 in each calendar year; Medicare: 1.45% of total employee earnings; federal unemployment: 0.8% on the first $7,000.00 earned by each employee; state unemployment: 5.4% on the first $7,000.00 earned by each employee.
2. The first $7,000.00.

Chapter 13, Page 382
1. By January 31.
2. Federal income tax, social security tax, and Medicare tax.

Chapter 13, Page 389
1. By the 15th day of the following month.
2. For paying payroll taxes and for paying federal unemployment tax.

Chapter 14, Page 408
1. Stockholders' Equity.
2. One account called Capital Stock.
3. Retained Earnings.
4. The board of directors declares a dividend.

Chapter 14, Page 414
1. Supplies—Office and Supplies Expense—Office.
2. Prepaid Insurance and Insurance Expense.

Chapter 14, Page 418
1. In the same order they appear in the general ledger.
2. Merchandise Inventory and Income Summary.
3. Debit Income Summary and credit Merchandise Inventory.
4. The Income Summary account is used to adjust the Merchandise Inventory account at the end of a fiscal period.

Chapter 14, Page 422
1. The loss is considered a regular expense of doing business. Revenue was earned when the sale was made. Failing to collect an account does not cancel the sale.
2. At the end of the fiscal period.
3. (1) Report a balance sheet amount for Accounts Receivable that reflects the amount the business expects to collect in the future. (2) Recognize the expense of uncollectible accounts in the same period in which the related revenue is recorded.
4. It reduces its related asset account, Accounts Receivable.
5. The difference between the balance of Accounts Receivable and its contra account, Allowance for Uncollectible Accounts.

Chapter 14, Page 426
1. Current assets and plant assets.
2. Original cost; estimated salvage value; estimated useful life.

Chapter 14, Page 436
1. Income Statement Debit or Credit column.
2. Balance Sheet Debit.
3. Trial balance amounts after adjustments are extended to the Adjusted Trial Balance columns, and the Adjusted Trial Balance columns are proved before extending amounts to the Income Statement and Balance Sheet columns.

Chapter 15, Page 454
1. The cost of merchandise sold section
2. Beginning merchandise inventory, *plus* purchases, *equals* total cost of merchandise available for sale, *less* ending merchandise inventory, *equals* cost of merchandise sold.
3. By comparing the amount calculated on the income statement with the amount on the work sheet.

Chapter 15, Page 460
1. (1) Cost of merchandise sold, (2) gross profit on sales, (3) total expenses, and (4) net income.
2. By making comparisons with prior fiscal periods as well as with industry standards that are published by industry organizations.
3. Net loss.

Chapter 15, Page 463

1. The changes in a corporation's ownership for a fiscal period.
2. Capital stock and retained earnings.
3. In the Capital Stock general ledger account.
4. In the Balance Sheet Credit column of a work sheet.
5. As a dividend.
6. In the Balance Sheet Debit column of a work sheet.

Chapter 15, Page 471

1. Current and plant assets.
2. (1) The balance of the asset account, (2) the balance of the asset's contra account, and (3) book value.
3. Mortgage payable.
4. From the statement of stockholders' equity.
5. Schedule of accounts payable and schedule of accounts receivable.

Chapter 16, Page 486

1. Because the heading *Adjusting Entries* is recorded in the Account Title column to explain all of the adjusting entries that follow.
2. Adjusting entry for merchandising inventory.
3. Federal Income Tax Payable.

Chapter 16, Page 493

1. Income Statement and Balance Sheet columns of the work sheet and the distribution of net income statement.
2. Income Summary.

Chapter 16, Page 498

1. General ledger accounts with balances.
2. To prove the equality of debits and credits in the general ledger.
3. In the same order as they appear in the general ledger.

Chapter 17, Page 518

1. To the contra asset account Allowance for Uncollectible Accounts and the expense account Uncollectible Accounts Expense.
2. The allowance method of recording losses from uncollectible accounts attempts to match the expense of uncollectible accounts in the same fiscal year the related sales are recorded.
3. The account is not affected.

Chapter 17, Page 524

1. The balance of the customer account is an *actual* uncollectible amount and no longer an *estimate* of an uncollectible amount.
2. The book value is the same because the same amount is deducted from the accounts receivable and the allowance accounts.
3. To show an accurate credit history.

Chapter 18, Page 537

1. Office Equipment is debited; Cash is credited.
2. Land and anything attached to the land.
3. Tax authorities referred to as assessors.

Chapter 18, Page 541

1. Matching Expenses with Revenues.
2. Original cost; estimated salvage value; estimated useful life.

Chapter 18, Page 545

1. Depreciation is credited to the contra asset account, Accumulated Depreciation, rather than crediting the asset account.
2. The balance of the asset account is not changed.

Chapter 18, Page 550

1. Disposal date, disposal method, and disposal amount.
2. Partial year's depreciation.
3. Cash received less the book value of the asset sold.
4. Other Expenses.

Chapter 18, Page 554

1. Depreciation rate.
2. Double declining-balance method.
3. It declines.
4. Its estimated salvage value.

Chapter 19, Page 568

1. Successful businesses must have merchandise available for sale that customers want. A business needs controls that assist managers in maintaining a merchandise inventory of sufficient quantity, variety, and price.
2. (1) Excess inventory requires that a business spend money for expensive store and warehouse space. (2) Excess inventory uses capital that could be invested in other assets to earn a profit for the business. (3) Excess inventory requires that a business spend money for expenses, such as taxes and insurance premiums, that increase with the cost of the merchandise inventory. (4) Excess inventory may become obsolete and unsalable.
3. At the end of a fiscal period.
4. A business frequently establishes its fiscal period to end when inventory normally is at a minimum because it takes less time to count a smaller inventory.
5. A customary practice is to take a periodic inventory at least once a fiscal period. The periodic inventory is then compared with the perpetual inventory records.

Chapter 19, Page 573

1. The most recent invoices for purchases are used in recording prices for each item on the inventory record.
2. The most recent costs of merchandise should be charged against current revenue.
3. Lifo.

4. Using the same inventory costing method for all fiscal periods provides financial statements that can be compared with other fiscal period statements. If a business changes inventory cost methods, part of the difference in gross profit and net income may be caused by the change in methods.

Chapter 19, Page 576

1. By using the gross profit method of estimating inventory.
2. Actual net sales and net purchases amounts; the beginning inventory amount; and the gross profit percentage.
3. The beginning inventory for the month is the same as the ending inventory from the previous month.

Chapter 20, Page 592

1. Sometimes a business receives more cash from sales than is needed to pay for purchases and expenses. When this occurs, a business may deposit the extra cash in a bank or other financial institution for a short period. At other times, the receipt of cash from sales does not occur at the same time and in sufficient amounts to pay for needed purchases and expenses. When this occurs, a business needs to borrow additional cash or make arrangements with its vendors to delay payment for a period of time.
2. A note can be useful in a court of law as written evidence of a debt.
3. Ten cents will be paid for the use of each dollar borrowed for a full year.
4. Multiply the principal times the interest rate times the time stated as a fraction of a year.

Chapter 20, Page 597

1. Because notes payable generally are paid within one year.
2. Accounts Payable and the vendor are debited. Notes Payable is credited.

Chapter 20, Page 602

1. A note receivable does not pay the amount the customer owes. Therefore, the amount of the asset does not change at the time the note is signed. The form of the asset does change from an account receivable to a note receivable. However, the asset will remain classified as a current asset.
2. Other Revenue.
3. Accounts Receivable and the customer account are each debited for the principal of the note and the interest. Notes Receivable is credited for the principal of the note. Interest Income is credited for the interest.
4. Because the interest has been earned.

Chapter 21, Page 621

1. Realization of Revenue.
2. To avoid the inconvenience of determining how much, if any, of each cash receipt is for interest income earned and accrued during the previous year and how much is earned in the current year.

Chapter 21, Page 627

1. So that the income statement will report all expenses for the period even though some of the expenses have not yet been paid. Also, so that the balance sheet will report all liabilities, including the accrued expenses payable.
2. Interest Payable is debited; Interest Expense is credited.

Chapter 22, Page 644

1. (1) For some accounts, the calculated estimate of the account is also the amount used in the work sheet adjustment. (2) Other accounts have a current balance when the work sheet adjustment is planned. The current balance is typically subtracted from the estimated account balance to determine the amount of the adjustment.
2. (1) Complete all adjustments other than federal income tax. (2) Extend all the accounts except Federal Income Tax Expense to the Income Statement or Balance Sheet columns. (3) Calculate temporary totals of the Income Statement accounts. (4) The difference of the Income Statement columns, excluding the estimated federal income taxes, is the net income or loss before income taxes.

Chapter 22, Page 648

1. Sales, cost of merchandise sold, and operating expenses are used to determine income from operations. Other revenue and other expenses, such as interest income, interest expense, and gains or losses on plant assets, are not normal business activities. Therefore, they are not included in calculating income from operations and are reported separately.
2. Each component percentage shows the percentage that each item is of net sales.

Chapter 22, Page 653

1. Mortgage payable.
2. The amount of total current assets less total current liabilities.
3. The current ratio permits a business to compare itself to its industry and to provide a convenient relative measure from year to year.

Chapter 22, Page 660

1. Post-closing trial balance.
2. (1) Closing entry for income statement accounts with credit balances (revenue and contra cost accounts). (2) Closing entry for income statement accounts with debit balances (cost, contra revenue, and expense accounts). (3) Closing entry to record net income or net loss in the retained earnings account and close the income summary account. (4) Closing entry for the dividends account.
3. Income Summary and Dividends.

Chapter 23, Page 679

1. Income statement and balance sheet.
2. A partnership agreement should include: the name of the business and the partners, the investments of each partner, the duties and responsibilities of each partner, how profits and losses are to be divided, what happens if a partner dies, how the partnership is to be dissolved, and the duration of the agreement.
3. The partner's drawing account increases by a debit; Cash decreases by a credit.

Chapter 23, Page 685

1. Each partner's share of net income or net loss.
2. (1) Beginning capital amount, (2) any additional investments made during the fiscal period, and (3) each partner's withdrawal of assets during the fiscal period.
3. Compute Ending Capital as follows: (1) Share of Net Income *less* Withdrawals *equals* Net Increase in Capital. (2) Beginning Capital *plus* Net Increase in Capital *equals* Ending Capital.

Chapter 23, Page 690

1. Cash received from the sale of assets during liquidation of a partnership.
2. Each partner's capital account.

Chapter 24, Page 709

1. (1) The lack of uniform commercial laws among countries makes settlement of disputes more difficult. (2) Greater distances and sometimes more complex transportation methods increase the time to complete the transaction. (3) Because it may be difficult to determine a customer's financial condition and to take legal action if a customer does not pay, the risk of uncollected amounts is increased. (4) Unstable political conditions in some countries may affect the ability to receive payments from those countries.
2. The bill of lading serves as a receipt for merchandise received and as a contract for the delivery of the merchandise.
3. A sight draft is payable when the holder presents it for payment. A time draft is payable at a fixed or determinable future time after it is accepted.
4. To assure receipt of payment for those sales.
5. A draft is generally paid by a bank and a trade acceptance is paid by the buyer. A seller generally has much more assurance of receiving payment from a bank than from a buyer.

Chapter 24, Page 712

1. To browse and compare the products offered by companies, and to do so at a convenient time and place.
2. Credit card sales information is processed in a manner similar to checks. Therefore, these sales are considered cash sales.

APPENDIX F

FINANCIAL LITERACY FOR THE 21ST CENTURY

PARTNERSHIP FOR 21ST CENTURY SKILLS

- INTEREST / INSURANCE
- CHECKING / BUDGET
- CREDIT / RISKS / IDENTITY THEFT
- BENEFITS / INVESTMENT
- SAVINGS / CASH

Did You Know?

- Thirty-three percent of high school seniors are in debt.
- Forty-five percent of college students have an average credit card debt of more than $3,000.
- Universities lose more students to credit card debt than academic failures.
- About 17.5% of Americans do not have health insurance.
- Roughly 6% of Americans earn an annual salary of over $100,000, and many Americans in this income range consider themselves broke.

Sources: http://www.dfi.wa.gov/consumers/financial_literacy_stats.htm; http://www.cdc.gov/nchs/fastats/hinsure.htm

What do these statistics mean to you? Do you know how to shop for credit? How to establish a checking account? Have you ever thought about what goes into selecting an insurance plan? Do you know how to create a budget? Do you have an idea of how long it will take to build wealth? How can you go about choosing the best investment plan? Do you know if credit cards will financially help or hurt you?

Your generation faces more financial choices than ever. You probably have some experience in making financial choices such as what to buy and the best time to buy. You may have already set financial goals for yourself such as saving for a new cell phone or a down payment for a car. You may already be learning to become financially independent.

As you proceed down life's highway, you will have many financial choices and challenges. You may receive credit card offers by the age of 18. You might need to pay for your education beyond high school, or you may want to buy a home. You will probably spend more than $2.2 million in your lifetime. Today's student needs financial literacy navigation for life's journey.

Financial Literacy for the 21st Century will guide you in exploring financial literacy topics that meet national guidelines created by the National Endowment for Financial Education (NEFE) and the Jump$tart Coalition. These two organizations are dedicated to improving financial literacy. Learning the basics of financial literacy can provide you with a foundation on which to build wealth and make sound financial decisions for a lifetime.

Real life and engaging activities allow you to apply workplace and citizenship skills such as problem solving, critical thinking, and technology. These and other skills make up the Framework for 21st Century Learning which supports the initiative to narrow the gap between what you learn in school and what you need to know to succeed beyond the classroom. The following activities are woven into financial, economic, business, and entrepreneurial themes. They will prepare you to compete in a global economy that demands creativity and innovation.

Understanding topics such as credit, savings, insurance, investments, take-home pay, taxes, and budgets will provide you with the tools you need to be financially healthy, wealthy, and wise—even when you come upon speed bumps. So, get in the driver's seat and take control of your financial future now!

WATCH YOUR MONEY GROW: THE RULE OF 72

One of the best ways to make money is to let your money work for you! When you place money in a bank, it will typically pay you a percentage of what you have deposited just for opening an account. The percentage you are paid is called interest. Interest grows money—especially compound interest. Compound interest is earning interest on interest. In other words, the money earns interest, and then the interest earns interest.

The "Rule of 72" is an important yet simple way to see the power of compound interest. This formula allows you to calculate how long it will take the original investment to double its value at a given interest rate when left alone in an interest-bearing account.

The magical number is "72." When 72 is divided by the interest rate, the answer reflects the number of years it will take to double the money. That is assuming no additional deposits are made. The Rule of 72 illustrates the advantage of saving early. For example, assume Clement earns 8% interest on his money. He would like to know how long it will take him to double his money at this rate of return. The answer would be nine years.

72 ÷ 8 (interest rate) = 9 (years to double)

However, if Clement chooses to place his money in an account that pays only 3% interest, it will take him 24 years to double his money.

72 ÷ 3 = 24

The Rule of 72 can also be used to determine how long it will take debt to double at a certain interest rate if no payments are made. Of course, payments and late charges usually apply. However, this magical number can allow one to see how quickly debt can double. Assume that Shannon borrows $5,000 from her friend at 6% interest.

72 ÷ 6 (interest rate) = 12 (years to double)

It would take 12 years for Shannon's debt to double if she did not make any payments.

Skills: Problem Solving, Creativity, Communication & Collaboration, Technology Literacy

1. Rachel dreams of starting her own business. She will need a $6,000 investment to get started; however, she has saved only $3,000. The bank pays a 4% interest rate that is compounded annually. How many years will it take for Rachel's money to double?

2. Ideally, Rachel would like to open her business in two years. What percent interest would Rachel need to receive in order to double her money in two years?

3. Apply the Rule of 72 to debt and assume that Rachel's credit card charges 18% interest. If she cannot make her payments and does not incur late fees, how long will it take for Rachel's debt to double?

4. Select a partner. Using the headline "Time Is Money," create a short, eye-catching newspaper article. Using media of your choice, explain to a younger audience how this common phrase relates to the Rule of 72.

INSURANCE

PLAYING IT SAFE WITH RENTER'S INSURANCE

Unexpected financial losses can affect your financial future. One way to manage this risk is to buy insurance.

Renter's insurance is recommended and sometimes required when renting a home or business location. The building owner may have insurance, but that may only protect the building. The renter's personal belongings may not be protected. A renter should carefully evaluate personal belongings to determine the amount of insurance coverage needed.

Renter's insurance should provide liability protection. This protects you if you are sued by someone who might be injured on your property. It covers legal fees from lawsuits. It may also cover medical payments acquired by the injured party. Find out whether your living expenses would be covered should you have to find another place to live or conduct business while damage to your home or business is being repaired. Some insurance policies compensate the policyholder for the interruption in business due to the accident or emergency.

The dollar amount reimbursed after a loss depends on the type of coverage. An actual cash value policy pays the amount of the item's current value. It does not consider what you paid for the item originally. For example, a five-year-old computer might be covered at today's value of $175 due to the wear and tear and changes in technology. It would not be covered for the original purchase price of, say, $500. A replacement cost policy pays the amount it would cost to replace the item today. The same computer today might cost $600. Most insurance policies have a deductible. A deductible is the amount that the insured pays out of pocket before the insurance coverage takes over.

Skills: Problem Solving, Critical Thinking, Technology Literacy

Lauren purchased renter's insurance with the following coverage: $100,000 liability for lawsuits and medical, $20,000 replacement cost for personal property, and a $500 deductible. One night, Lauren left a candle burning, which resulted in a fire that destroyed all of her personal belongings. The original cost of the belongings was $32,000.

1. How much will the insurance company pay for this claim?

2. How much will Lauren pay to replace her personal property?

3. If Lauren had an actual cash value policy instead of a replacement cost policy, what would be the impact?

4. Many students do not realize they will need renter's insurance while attending college.

    a. Using Excel, create a list of items you would own in an apartment and their estimated cost (as of today). Using the Auto Sum feature, determine the total value of the items.

    b. Then, call or use the Internet to research the cost of renter's insurance if you were to obtain a replacement cost policy with $0 deductible. Also, obtain the cost for the policy with a $300 deductible.

SHOP FOR A CHECKING ACCOUNT

A checking account is necessary when managing your money. A checking account is a safe and convenient way to control large sums of cash. It is also a good way to pay your bills. Your canceled checks, which are checks that have been paid, serve as a record of spending.

Not all checking accounts are the same, however, even within the same bank. You must shop around and compare features in order to find the checking account that best fits your needs. For example: Where is the nearest location? What is the required minimum deposit to open an account? Does the bank offer online banking? What is the required minimum balance in order to maintain the account? Is there unlimited check writing? Does the bank have interest-bearing accounts?

Fees should be carefully reviewed as well. Common fees include charges for ordering checks, ATM (automatic teller machine) withdrawals, monthly service fees, and a fee for insufficient funds should the amount on the check presented for payment exceed the available funds in the account.

Skills: Problem Solving, Critical Thinking, Technology Literacy

1. Compare and contrast the following two checking accounts. Based on your findings, which checking account would best fit the needs for a high school student who just started his or her first job? Explain your position.

   The Almighty Dollar Bank (ADB) Student Value Plus Checking Account requires $500 to open a checking account with no minimum balance requirement. There is a $5 monthly service charge. No ATM fees are charged unless the ATM card is used at a bank other than ADB, in which case a $3 fee is imposed by both ADB and the other bank. The first 200 checks are free. Subsequent check orders cost $17.95 for 200 checks. There is a $35 fee for insufficient funds. Online banking is free for the first three transactions each month.

   The People Friendly Bank (PFB) Free Student Checking Account has no minimum initial balance, but it charges a $5 fee if the balance falls below $50. This account pays 1% annual interest on balances over $5,000 and has no monthly service charge. There is no charge for ATM withdrawals. Checks cost $12.95 per 200, and there is a $25 fee for insufficient funds. Online banking is free.

2. Explain why a business would open a checking account instead of a savings account to manage cash.

3. Compare and contrast the costs and features of checking accounts from three different banks. Summarize your findings in an Excel spreadsheet.

Financial Literacy for the 21st Century

ROAD MAP TO YOUR FINANCIAL FUTURE

A budget is a financial road map used by individuals and companies as a guide for spending and saving so one does not spend more than they earn. Businesses and individuals must occasionally evaluate finances and adjust their budget to achieve financial goals.

One of the first steps in creating a budget is to determine the amount of income expected. The second step is to determine the expected expenses. There are two types of expenses to consider: fixed and variable.

Fixed expenses are necessary costs such as rent, transportation, insurance, and loan payments. The cost of fixed expenses does not change. A strategy called "Pay Yourself First" should be included as a fixed expense by setting aside at least 20% of your after-tax income for savings.

The costs of variable expenses change from month to month and in many cases can be controlled. Variable expenses include utilities, groceries, recreation, and clothing.

Expenses are totaled and then subtracted from your income to determine the difference. A positive number indicates that less is spent than is earned. This leaves a surplus for further investing. However, a negative number indicates that spending exceeds income. This is called a deficit.

Skills: Problem Solving, Critical Thinking

Bethany has been working full time for one year and frequently finds herself short of cash. Her total income is $39,000; however, her income after taxes is $2,500 per month. She has the following expenses: car payment, $400 per month; auto insurance, $3,000 per year; gas, $50 per week; groceries, $150 per week; clothing, $50 per week; entertainment, $25 per week; utilities, $150 per month; rent, $700 per month; and cell phone, $30 per month.

1. Using the information provided, calculate Bethany's current monthly surplus or deficit.

2. Based on the "Pay Yourself First" principle, calculate the amount that Bethany should budget for savings.

3. Classify Bethany's expenses as either fixed or variable.

4. Assume that Bethany's hours and pay are reduced. Her after-tax income is now $2,000 per month. Analyze the effect on her budget. Explain.

USING CREDIT CARDS WISELY

As students reach the legal age of 18, most will receive credit card offers. Is it good or bad to have credit? It depends on how credit is used. If a credit card is used primarily as a convenience and the account balance is paid off each month, then credit is being used wisely. Unfortunately, many credit card users only make minimum payments, which is deceptive since it often takes many months or years to pay off the balance.

Credit is not free money. It is a loan that allows the user to buy now and pay later. If not paid on time, interest is added based on an annual percentage rate (APR). The APR is often calculated monthly on credit cards. For example, Anthony's credit card has an APR of 18%. Divide 18% by 12 months, and he pays 1.5% per month. Multiply 1.5% by the $1,000 balance of the credit card, and $15 is the added cost. Anthony now owes $1,015. Because interest rates and credit terms differ among credit card issuers, it is wise to shop around. Some card companies offer a low introductory interest rate as bait, but then they increase the rate after a short period of time.

The following terms should be considered when selecting a credit card: APR (not just the introductory rate), annual fees (yearly fee just to carry the card), and, in some cases, the security deposit. Remember to read the fine print carefully before signing a credit card application. Many do not realize that a signature on the application makes it a legal contract. The Credit Card Accountability Responsibility and Disclosure Act of 2009, also known as the Credit CARD Act, was designed to protect consumers from unreasonable fees and interest rates. This law also requires the "fine print" to now have a minimum 12-point font for easier reading.

Using a credit card wisely involves evaluating each purchase according to one's needs. Purchases made with a credit card should not be impulsive. Excessive use of credit can result in long-term financial problems and a poor credit report. A credit report is much like a high school transcript. It follows a person throughout their lifetime. Credit scores enable others to evaluate a person's creditworthiness. Most people do not realize that a poor credit score can negatively affect their insurance rates and even their employability.

Skills: Critical Thinking, Problem Solving, Information Literacy, Media & Technology Literacy

1. **a.** Using the Internet, research the purpose of the Credit CARD Act. Then determine the benefits of the act for consumers.

   b. Create a brochure to inform other consumers about the Credit CARD Act. Use publishing software to explain your findings. Be sure to include at least five ways the new law benefits the consumer.

2. **a.** Go to www.bankrate.com and review credit card options. Compare the APR, annual fees, and security deposit (if applicable) for five different credit cards. Create a spreadsheet or table to report your findings.

   b. Type or write a paragraph describing the best option based on your findings. Explain why this is the best option.

3. Using moviemaker or comparable media, create an advertisement for the credit card of your choice based on your research. Be sure to explain your findings.

PHILANTHROPY

CHARITABLE CONTRIBUTIONS

Americans should be proud of their charitable giving. The average American family donates $2,000 per year. Some small businesses donate as much as 6% of their profits. American families and businesses give more than any other country. Charitable giving, also known as philanthropy, is vital to a civilized society.

Finding a charity that will use donations wisely requires research. In an effort to pressure donors, many charities create a false sense of urgency. It is never wise to give money under pressure. That can result in a poor financial choice and adversely affect one's budget.

The first step in choosing a charity is to find an issue of personal interest to you. Then, become familiar with the charities that support your cause. Study the charity's finances and see how it spends its donations. At least 75% of donations should go directly to the cause. Be cautious of organizations that spend heavily on administrative expenses, program development, or education. This may indicate much of your donation will go towards advertising, rather than the cause you want to support. Watchdog organizations monitor and report how effectively charities spend their money. The Better Business Bureau, CharityWatch.org, and Charityguide.org are examples of watchdog organizations.

Skills: Information Technology, Technology Literacy, Problem Solving, Communication, Creativity & Innovation

1. Assume you are the owner of a small business that sells children's toys.
    a. Use the Internet (search on *children's charities*) to find three charities for children that you might support. Explain why you chose these charities.
    b. Use Excel to create a chart or graph for each charity. The chart should display each charity's use of funds as a percent of expenses.
2. Explain how a small business that is not making a profit can still donate to charity.
3. List at least three ways businesses benefit from their charitable contributions.
4. Select a health-related issue. Use the Internet to search for a charity that supports this issue. Compose a persuasive letter to your school administration explaining why your school should have a fundraiser to support this charity. To support your position, be sure to include at least three reasons why your school should support this charity.

WAGE GARNISHMENT

Employers are required by law to withhold money, called deductions, from employees' wages. Examples of deductions are federal income tax, social security taxes, and Medicare taxes. State and local income taxes may also be deducted. In addition, employees may ask their employers to deduct for insurance, savings, meals, union dues, uniforms, and charitable contributions.

Some employers may be required by law to deduct wages from an employee for other reasons. Wage garnishment is a process that requires an employer to withhold a portion of an employee's paycheck to pay a court-ordered debt settlement. Common settlements include child support and damages awarded to an individual or business. Generally, the employer sends the garnished amount to the court. The court then pays the employee's creditor. All states permit wage garnishment, but limitations and types of wage garnishment vary by state.

Someone considering a loan or credit purchase that they can't afford should think twice. Garnishment may add to financial hardship. Even worse, it will result in one's employer learning that he or she is not very responsible about money.

Skills: Critical Thinking, Problem Solving, Communication & Collaboration, Information Literacy, Technology Literacy, Flexibility & Adaptability, Social & Cross-Cultural Skills

1. Explain in writing the purpose of wage garnishment.

2. Explain in writing why wage garnishment is not a voluntary deduction.

3. a. You will be placed in groups of four. Each group will research the types of wage garnishments that are permissible in a given state. Two students from the group will take on the role of the creditor (the person trying to obtain the unpaid debt). The other two students will take on the role of the employee who is having his wages garnished. Allow students time to debate and discuss the issue.

   b. At the conclusion, ask students to go to an online discussion board and discuss whether they believe that wages should be garnished.

WHAT IS A GOOD RISK?

When lenders loan money, they want to make sure the borrower can pay back the loan. While each lender is unique, most will use some variation of the five C's of credit to help determine creditworthiness of individuals and businesses before approving a loan.

1. *Character:* What is the borrower's general attitude about payment obligations? What is their educational background?

2. *Capacity:* What is their ability to repay the loan? In addition to their previous payment history, their sources of income and current debt are also considered.

3. *Capital:* What is the borrower's net worth? Usually, the greater their capital is, the greater their ability to repay.

4. *Collateral:* What assets are available as payment if the loan is not paid?

5. *Conditions:* What are current economic conditions? Is their job secure?

By determining creditworthiness, the lender may avoid the inability to collect on debt and reduce the amount of uncollectible accounts.

Skills: Creativity & Innovation, Communication & Collaboration, Social & Cross-Cultural Skills

1. Assume you are a small business owner. Use desktop publishing software to create your own credit application. Include ten questions that would help you determine creditworthiness.

2. With a partner, create an informational poster to display in your school for other students to learn about the five C's of credit.

3. If you had to pick the top three C's of credit, which three do you think are better predictors of creditworthiness? Explain why.

HOUSING

LEASE AGREEMENTS

At least once a year, every consumer should review their personal financial statements to assess income and spending. Most financial experts recommend that one spend no more than 30% of their net pay on housing. This might be a good time to review your living arrangements.

Home ownership comes with tax advantages, privacy, and fewer restrictions. Still, many find renting more appealing. The ability to relocate quickly and the benefit of maintenance-free living are advantages that many people prefer. However, luxuries like pools and clubhouses may cause many to rush into the lease agreement without properly considering their budget. This is not the time to sign quickly. A lease agreement is a legal, binding contract. The tenant is responsible for paying the rent to the property owner as agreed upon in the contract.

The lease agreement will contain the name and address of the property, the rent amount, the date rent is due, lease start and end dates, type of notice needed for termination of lease, conditions upon which landlord can enter property, and signatures. It may also contain fees for pets and parking and noise restrictions. A security deposit is typically required. The amount is usually equivalent to one month's rent. This deposit is money paid in advance to the property owner in the event of damage. The renter receives the deposit back at the end of the lease if the property is left in good condition.

Skills: Problem Solving, Creativity, Information Literacy, Communication & Collaboration

1. Read the following scenario and describe the recommended action. Be sure to explain why. Also, describe how Brandon could prevent a similar situation from occurring in the future.

   Brandon's lease just ended, and he moved to another apartment. Several months ago, Brandon allowed his friend Brady to stay with him. Now, Brandon's landlord will not return his $500 security deposit because of damage caused by his friend's dog. The property owner claims that the $500 will partially cover the cost of replacing the soiled carpet in three rooms. Brandon disagrees with the property owner. According to the lease, animals are allowed. Brandon believes that if someone should pay the charges, it should be Brady.

2. If you were the property owner, formulate a list of at least five rules and restrictions that you would place in your lease agreement using the guidelines above.

3. a. Research the Federal Fair Housing Act and Fair Housing Amendments to determine what types of housing discrimination is legal.

   b. With another student, discuss legal discrimination in housing and whether this is a fair practice.

BENEFITS

ADDING UP THE BENEFITS

Today, workers change jobs more frequently than ever before. In the past, it was common for an employee to stay with a company for an entire career spanning as much as 30 years. Frequent staff changes are costly to a company. Costs can affect the company's profit. In order to keep these costs under control, companies have become more employee-friendly. Benefits such as sick leave, paid vacation, and health insurance are becoming more flexible. These benefits may help a company keep employees longer.

Free day care, wardrobe assistance, and on-site dog parks are examples of generous benefits that companies are offering to lure and keep employees. Some companies may even offer sabbaticals. A sabbatical gives the employee time off from the job to pursue personal interests or just rest.

For the thirteenth year, software company SAS was named one of Fortune's 100 Best Companies to Work For. While some companies are reducing benefits, SAS chooses to be different. Founder and CEO, Jim Goodnight, welcomes benefits that might increase productivity or foster creativity. Offering on-site health care and free M&Ms has proven to be a winner. At a company where employees are encouraged to balance their work and personal life, SAS has one of industry's lowest turnover rates, and it is extremely profitable.

Skills: Problem Solving, Technology Literacy, Communication & Collaboration, Creativity & Innovation

1. Brainstorm with a partner and list at least ten benefits that would make you a more loyal and productive employee.

2. Research the benefits offered by two companies in your community or closest city. Use the Internet to find information or interview people who work at the two companies. Draw a Venn diagram on a poster to compare and contrast your findings.

3. If you had the option of receiving 20% additional salary or an eight-week paid sabbatical, which would you choose and why? Explain your answer in one or two paragraphs.

PURCHASES

DO NOT LOSE A CHUNK!

Many items lose their value over time. Probably the one that you can relate to the most is an automobile. While owning a car can be expensive, with costs for fuel, maintenance, repair, insurance, and interest paid on the loan, the largest cost is depreciation. Did you realize that as soon as you drive your new car off the dealer's lot, it is worth less money than you just paid?

Some vehicles depreciate faster, so there are factors to consider when buying a new car in order to minimize your monetary loss. When buying a car, try to look for one that will appeal to a lot of people rather than just your own preferences. This includes:

- *Color:* Stay away from trendy, flashy colors. It is more likely that cars with common, neutral exterior colors such as black, white, or silver will remain popular.
- *Supply and Demand:* Buy a car that is a little harder to find, and you will not have as much competition at resale time.
- *Safety:* Everyone appreciates safety features such as tire pressure warnings, pedestrian friendly bumpers, and rollover sensors.
- *Comfort:* Options such as automatic climate control, an auxiliary jack to play music devices, and navigation systems enhance the value of a vehicle.
- *Reputation:* Some brands have a reputation for having fewer maintenance issues. This should be considered when determining the overall cost of the vehicle.
- *Fuel Efficiency:* Some cars get better gas mileage. This not only helps with resale but in overall vehicle costs as well.

Once you own the vehicle, there are factors you should consider to cut down on depreciation. Maintenance records showing regularly scheduled services, low mileage, and cleanliness can help you get the highest price at resale.

Skill: Creativity & Innovation, Critical Thinking & Problem Solving, Communication & Collaboration, ICT Literacy

1. a. Shop for a car! Select a make and model. Then use the Internet to research the retail price for the car. Be sure to indicate the options you want such as power seats or a CD changer.

   b. Go to Kelley Blue Book at www.kbb.com. Research the value of the same make and model that is three years old with 36,000 miles. Then do the same for one that is five years old with 60,000 miles. Compare the two by changing the mileage to 60,000 for the three-year model and 100,000 for the five-year model. Explain your findings.

2. Use the above instructions and research three other vehicles. Create a table or spreadsheet to display your findings.

3. Assume you are a car salesperson. Your sales commission is based on selling the cars that will depreciate the fastest. Create an advertisement (print or video) highlighting the features of this car. Be sure to include factors of depreciation in your advertisement. (Example: color—bright lemon yellow)

CREDIT

WHAT IS YOUR NUMBER?—FICO SCORES

Banks and other lenders often extend services such as credit cards and loans for cars, homes, and businesses. However, lenders must consider the risk involved when extending a loan because of the chance of not being repaid on time. So, how do lenders determine if someone is creditworthy or able to repay a loan?

Banks use a credit score to help predict the likelihood that a person will repay credit obligations. The credit score is a numerical rating assigned to the consumer's credit information and credit behaviors in the past.

The most well-known type of credit score is FICO. The Fair Isaac Company developed the mathematical model for FICO in the 1950s. The model calculates a score based on a person's credit report. The credit report is a listing of all of your credit accounts and payment history. The three major credit bureaus that keep the credit history for scoring are Experian, Equifax, and TransUnion.

Many factors are considered to determine a FICO score. Among these are how much you owe each month, your history of late payments, your length of credit history, and your number of recent credit searches. Income is not a factor because ability to pay is not necessarily an indicator of willingness to pay. The score ranges from 300–850 and often determines whether a person gets the loan. The score may also determine what the interest rate will be on the loan. Prospective employers may look at your FICO score to see if you are financially responsible. In addition, property owners you want to rent an apartment from may consider your score to determine if you will be a tenant who pays rent on time. A good score can get you better insurance rates and reduce deposits required by utility companies. A credit score is often an indicator of character habits in addition to financial ones. A score over 720 is considered a very good credit risk according to many lenders. Negative information remains on your credit report for seven to ten years.

One should review his or her credit report regularly to learn what is reported and to correct any mistakes that might affect the FICO score. The Fair and Accurate Transactions Act of 2003 entitles everyone to a free report from each of the three agencies once a year. Students can begin a positive credit history by applying for a small amount of credit and paying on time and in full each month. Even your cell phone bill counts towards your credit history!

Skill: Creativity & Innovation, Critical Thinking & Problem Solving, Communication & Collaboration, ICT Literacy

1. Go to www.myfico.com and determine the categories and percentages used to calculate your FICO score. Which category is the most important in determining the FICO score?

2. Create a table or spreadsheet with headings like the one below. Based on what you have learned, read the following scenarios and determine (a) if the impact is positive or negative on the FICO score, (b) the reason for the change and (c) what needs to be done to improve the score if a negative impact was made. Note: If the impact was positive, simply write N/A.

Scenario	Impact	Reason for Change	Action to Remedy
Pay cell phone bill on time	+	*Timely Payments*	*N/A*
Overdue payment			
Obtain new car loan			
Pay off credit card			
Missed or late payment			

3. With a partner, create a one-minute public service announcement (poster, radio commercial, or video) informing other students of the FICO score and the impact it can have on their future.

SAVING

SAVING VERSUS INVESTING

The rule 70-20-10 is commonly used when planning finances. Seventy percent is the guideline for spending, twenty percent for saving, and ten percent for investing. In your budget, you will set money aside for saving and investing so you can plan for opportunities, deal with emergencies, and reach financial goals. Many think of the terms saving and investing as meaning the same, but they are quite different.

The purpose of saving is to store money in a safe place, such as a bank, so you can have easy access to the money for short-term needs while earning interest. Examples include saving for a car, a computer, or an emergency fund. Emergency funds are critical, as they provide a safety net for things such as unexpected repairs, medical expenses, or a job loss. A guideline for an emergency fund is a savings equal to six months of expenses.

There are a number of ways to save money for short-term needs. They include savings accounts, money market accounts, and certificates of deposit (CDs). These methods of saving are low risk; however, their interest rate will be low. Interest is the percentage rate paid on money saved or invested. Most all financial institutions provide similar and competitive savings plans.

The purpose of investing is to grow and build wealth for future needs—five years and beyond. Common investments include stocks, bonds, mutual funds, real estate, IRAs, and 401(k)s. An investment is a higher risk than a savings plan, but the rate of return will more likely be higher than a savings plan. Unlike individuals who choose savings, investors risk losing the entire amount invested. Due to the risk factor, most investors diversify by investing in multiple plans, not just one. Therefore, selecting the best investment to build wealth will require assessing risk and rate of return. Investing provides more opportunities to grow your money over time.

Skill: Creativity & Innovation, Critical Thinking & Problem Solving, Communication, ICT Literacy

1. a. Research methods for saving and investing. Create a model or diagram summarizing the type of savings or investment plan and its level of risk.

   b. Based on your findings, answer the following questions: Do you think buying stock in a strong company would be a wise, short-term savings vehicle? Which plan would be the best for an emergency fund? Explain your answer.

2. Interview five adults about the methods they use to save and invest. Share your findings with the class and explain why you think they selected these methods.

3. Go to www.bankrate.com. Compare and contrast the interest rates for a savings account, CD, and money market account at three different banks. Prepare your findings in a table or spreadsheet. Create a title for your results.

4. Many are unsure of the right time to buy stock. Using a website like www.finance.yahoo.com, research a common investment strategy called dollar cost averaging. Create a flyer explaining to a new investor the meaning of this concept and how it will be implemented.

TIME VALUE OF MONEY—THE POWER OF COMPOUNDING

One hundred dollars today is not necessarily $100 in the future when one invests in an interest-bearing account that grows in value over time. This is because of a very important financial concept called the time value of money. Three factors affect how much your money will grow: time, amount of money invested, and the interest rate. The interest rate is the percentage rate paid on the money saved or invested.

Save as early as you can. The sooner you begin, the more time your money has to grow. That is the power of compounding, and the best way for you to become a millionaire! Compounding interest is like earning interest on interest and is essential for understanding the time value of money. Let us look at an example.

One hundred dollars invested at 10% interest will be worth $110 in one year. Leave the $110 in the investment and get 10% interest again; you will have $121 at the end of the second year. The first year earned you $10, and the second earned you $11. You made this money while sleeping. That is better than working, so let your money work for you!

The process of leaving your initial investment plus any accumulated interest for more than one period is reinvesting the interest. This is the power of compounding interest. To determine what your investment is worth at a particular time in the future, you can use the future value formula.

$FV = PV (1 + i)^n$

FV = Future value
PV = Present value (how much you invest today)
i = Interest rate
n = Number of times interested is calculated (e.g., monthly, yearly)

Example: when you are age 17, you invest a one-time $100 gift into an account that pays 8% interest. Leave the money there until you want to retire at age 65, and the investment would be worth $4,021.06.

Solution: $\$4{,}021.06 = 100 (1 + 0.08)^{48}$

If you start an investment program when you are young, you can let the time value of money work for you. Even small investments can grow to make you a millionaire!

Skill: Creativity & Innovation, Critical Thinking & Problem Solving, Communication, Media Literacy

1. Using the future value formula, calculate the future value of an investment presently worth $10,000 with zero annual addition at a 10% interest rate. Compound interest one time per year. Calculate the future value after 1 year, 5 years, 10 years, 20 years, and 40 years. Record your answers and explain the power of time when compounding interest.

2. Using the future value formula, calculate the future value of an investment presently worth $10,000 with zero annual addition for 20 years with interest rates of 2%, 5%, 8%, and 10%. Create a line graph to show the different interest rates. Explain the importance of the interest rate in growing wealth.

3. Digital storytelling is a modern way to convey a message. Select a digital medium of your choice (e.g., slides, moviemaker) and create a story for other teens. The message you should convey is the future value of money based on the power of compounding interest. Your goal is to encourage everyone to invest at an early age. Create examples, visuals, music, text, and animations that will help tell the story without overpowering the message.

WEALTH

SO YOU WANT TO BE A MILLIONAIRE: BUILD WEALTH WITH INVESTMENTS

For most individuals, wealth is generated through long-term investments. We invest long term to obtain financial goals, such as money for a college education or retirement. We also want to stay ahead of inflation. When prices rise, we call this inflation. Therefore, long-term investments must provide returns that are greater than inflation. For investments to have returns that exceed the inflation rate, they typically involve risks. The higher the risk, the greater the return on the investment. Typical longer-term investments include bonds, stocks, mutual funds, real estate, IRAs, and 401(k)s.

A bond is a loan you provide to a corporation or government, with the promise they will pay you the original investment plus interest for the use of your money. Bondholders are repaid at maturity, which ranges from 1–30 years. Owning stock means you own part of a company. Typically, if the company does well, your stock will increase; however, stocks can be very risky. To decrease the risk of stock, many investors diversify, which means owning stock in different industries.

A good way to diversify investments is through mutual funds. Investors pool their money, and the fund is managed by a professional fund manager. Investing in real estate involves buying now and selling later for a profit, assuming the real estate will increase in value.

To take advantage of investment accounts with tax advantages, most investors will want to invest in an individual retirement account (IRA) or a 401(k). A 401(k) is an employer-sponsored plan that is an easy way to save because of automatic payroll deductions. Contributing to a 401(k) provides tax advantages and usually involves a match from your employer. This is free money! Most IRAs and 401(k)s are long-term investments; therefore, they involve penalties if contributions are withdrawn before age 59½.

A very popular investment for young people trying to build wealth is the ROTH IRA. This IRA has the unique advantage of no penalties for early withdrawals of your contribution. Therefore, many have begun using the ROTH IRA as not only a long-term investment, but also as an emergency savings fund.

Remember, the power of time is on your side! The more you invest at a higher rate at an earlier age, the greater the return on your investment.

Skill: Creativity & Innovation, Critical Thinking & Problem Solving, Communication, ICT Literacy

1. Pretend you are an investment advisor. Suggest a savings or investment plan for each scenario and explain the reason for your choice.

    a. Client A wants to begin saving to enter college in five years.

    b. Client B wants to begin saving for retirement in 40 years.

    c. Client C wants to begin saving in case of a medical emergency.

2. Go to www.money.cnn.com and select "Money 101" under the Personal Finance menu. Research investing in bonds, stocks, mutual funds, 401(k)s, and retirement accounts. Create a graphic organizer describing the features of each plan.

3. Use the Internet to search for a sample Facebook page or template. Create a sample page that will reflect you in retirement. What is your age? How will you spend your time? How do you envision your lifestyle? Be creative. Include in your status how you were able to prepare for the lifestyle described.

THE INS AND OUTS OF CASH FLOW

One of the first things you should do in managing finances is to understand the inflow and outflow of cash for a period of time. While a budget provides a plan for spending, a cash flow statement actually shows where the money came from and how it was spent. Learning to manage cash flow will prevent overspending and allow personal wealth building.

A cash flow statement contains three parts: sources of income, outflows of cash, and the net amount. Sources of income are more than just your salary. Income can be gifts, scholarships, and investment income. Anything that brings in money is considered income. Outflows of cash consist of all your expenditures, both fixed and variable. Fixed expenditures include rent, car payments, savings and investments or those costs that remain unchanged from one period to the next. Variable expenditures might include food, charitable contributions, gas, and clothing. The last component of the cash flow statement is the net cash flow. This is the cash inflow minus cash outflow. A positive number is good and means you have extra cash to invest towards financial goals and build personal wealth or even pay down debt. A negative balance is bad and means outflow is greater than inflow. A plan must be created to spend less or generate more income. One cannot become a millionaire if there is a deficit of cash.

Managing your cash flow allows you to direct the cash. Understanding money flow keeps you in control!

Skill: Critical Thinking & Problem Solving, Communication, ICT Literacy

1. Julia, a recent college graduate, just prepared a cash flow statement after her first month of employment at Hickman's Hometown Cuisine. Her cash flow statement showed the following for the month of August: Cash inflow, $3,269.27; cash outflow, $2,975.00. Julia also has student loan debt totaling $12,425. Julia would like to purchase a new computer. She does not have a savings plan or a retirement plan. Determine her net cash at the end of August. What suggestions would you make to help Julia achieve her financial goals? Explain why.

2. Elias owns Harmon's Historical Village, a living history museum. His revenue is generated through tours paid by cash or on account for large groups. His earnings were $4,971.65 for the month of May. However, his cash flow statement showed the following: Cash inflow, $9,683.75; cash outflow, $10,764.23. These numbers result in a negative cash flow. Explain how Elias could have a positive net income, yet a negative cash flow.

3. Create an Excel spreadsheet with the following headings down the side (rows): Cash Inflow, Cash Outflow, and Net Cash Flow. The following headings should be placed at the top (columns): Recent College Graduate, Newly Married, and Married with Three Kids.

    a. Assume that you are, first, a recent college graduate; second, newly married; and, lastly, married with three children. Anticipate your sources of cash inflow and a list of expenditures (cash outflow) for the different stages in your life. Record your sources and estimations. Calculate your net cash flow.

    b. Explain how the various stages of your life might affect your cash flow statement.

GLOSSARY

A

Account a record summarizing all the information pertaining to a single item in the accounting equation. (p. 10)

Account balance the amount in an account. (p. 10)

Account number the number assigned to an account. (p. 92)

Account title the name given to an account. (p. 10)

Accounting planning, recording, analyzing, and interpreting financial information. (p. 6)

Accounting cycle the series of accounting activities included in recording financial information for a fiscal period. (p. 217)

Accounting equation an equation showing the relationship among assets, liabilities, and owner's equity. (p. 8)

Accounting period see fiscal period

Accounting records organized summaries of a business's financial activities. (p. 6)

Accounting system a planned process for providing financial information that will be useful to management. (p. 6)

Accounts payable ledger a subsidiary ledger containing only accounts for vendors from whom merchandise or other items are purchased on account. (p. 298)

Accounts receivable ledger a subsidiary ledger containing only accounts for charge customers. (p. 298)

Accrued expenses expenses incurred in one fiscal period but not paid until a later fiscal period. (p. 622)

Accrued interest expense interest incurred but not yet paid. (p. 622)

Accrued interest income interest earned but not yet received. (p. 617)

Accrued revenue revenue earned in one fiscal period but not received until a later fiscal period. (p. 616)

Accumulated depreciation the total amount of depreciation expense that has been recorded since the purchase of a plant asset. (p. 424)

Adjusting entries journal entries recorded to update general ledger accounts at the end of a fiscal period. (p. 202)

Adjustments changes recorded on a work sheet to update general ledger accounts at the end of a fiscal period. (p. 157)

Allowance method of recording losses from uncollectible accounts crediting the estimated value of uncollectible accounts to a contra account. (p. 419)

Assessed value the value of an asset determined by tax authorities for the purpose of calculating taxes. (p. 536)

Asset anything of value that is owned. (p. 8)

B

Bad debts see uncollectible accounts

Balance sheet a financial statement that reports assets, liabilities, and owner's equity on a specific date. (p. 162)

Bank statement a report of deposits, withdrawals, and bank balances sent to a depositor by a bank. (p. 124)

Batch report a report of credit card sales produced by a point-of-sale terminal. (p. 278)

Batching out the process of preparing a batch report of credit card sales from a point-of-sale terminal. (p. 278)

Bill of exchange see draft

Bill of lading a receipt signed by the authorized agent of a transportation company for merchandise received that also serves as a contract for the delivery of the merchandise. (p. 704)

Blank endorsement an endorsement consisting only of the endorser's signature. (p. 120)

Board of directors a group of persons elected by the stockholders to manage a corporation. (p. 406)

Book inventory see perpetual inventory

Book value the difference between an asset's account balance and its related contra account balance. (p. 419)

Book value of a plant asset the original cost of a plant asset minus accumulated depreciation. (p. 424)

Book value of accounts receivable the difference between the balance of Accounts Receivable and its contra account, Allowance for Uncollectible Accounts. (p. 419)

Business ethics the use of ethics in making business decisions. (p. 8)

C

Capital the account used to summarize the owner's equity in a business. (p. 10)

Capital stock total shares of ownership in a corporation. (p. 234)

Cash discount a deduction from the invoice amount, allowed by a vendor to encourage early payment. (p. 242)

Cash over a petty cash on hand amount that is more than a recorded amount. (p. 248)

Cash payments journal a special journal used to record only cash payment transactions. (p. 242)

Cash receipts journal a special journal used to record only cash receipt transactions. (p. 278)

Cash sale a sale in which cash is received for the total amount of the sale at the time of the transaction. (p. 276)

Cash short a petty cash on hand amount that is less than a recorded amount. (p. 248)

Charge sale see sale on account

Chart of accounts a list of accounts used by a business. (p. 32)

Check a business form ordering a bank to pay cash from a bank account. (p. 58)

Checking account a bank account from which payments can be ordered by a depositor. (p. 119)

Closing entries journal entries used to prepare temporary accounts for a new fiscal period. (p. 206)

Code of conduct a statement that guides the ethical behavior of a company and its employees. (p. 118)

Commercial invoice a statement prepared by the seller of merchandise addressed to the buyer, showing a detailed listing and description of merchandise sold, including prices and terms. (p. 704)

Component percentage the percentage relationship between one financial statement item and the total that includes that item. (p. 184)

Contra account an account that reduces a related account on a financial statement. (p. 245)

Contract of sale a document that details all the terms agreed to by seller and buyer for a sales transaction. (p. 703)

Controlling account an account in a general ledger that summarizes all accounts in a subsidiary ledger. (p. 298)

Corporation an organization with the legal rights of a person and which may be owned by many persons. (p. 234)

Correcting entry a journal entry made to correct an error in the ledger. (p. 108)

Cost of goods sold see cost of merchandise sold.

Cost of merchandise the price a business pays for goods it purchases to sell. (p. 236)

Cost of merchandise sold the total original price of all merchandise sold during a fiscal period. (p. 450)

Credit an amount recorded on the right side of a T account. (p. 29)

Credit card sale a sale in which a credit card is used for the total amount of the sale at the time of the transaction. (p. 276)

Credit memorandum a form prepared by the vendor showing the amount deducted for returns and allowances. (p. 285)

Creditor a person or organization to whom a liability is owed. (p. 589)

Current assets cash and other assets expected to be exchanged for cash or consumed within a year. (p. 423)

Current liabilities liabilities due within a short time, usually within a year. (p. 467)

Current ratio a ratio that shows the numeric relationship of current assets to current liabilities. (p. 652)

Customer a person or business to whom merchandise or services are sold. (p. 270)

Date of a note the day a note is signed. (p. 589)

Debit an amount recorded on the left side of a T account. (p. 29)

Debit card a bank card that automatically deducts the amount of the purchase from the checking account of the cardholder. (p. 132)

Debit memorandum a form prepared by the customer showing the price deduction taken by the customer for returns and allowances. (p. 256)

Declaring a dividend action by a board of directors to distribute corporate earnings to stockholders. (p. 406)

Declining-balance method of depreciation multiplying the book value by a constant depreciation rate at the end of each fiscal period. (p. 551)

Depreciation expense the portion of a plant asset's cost that is transferred to an expense account in each fiscal period during a plant asset's useful life. (p. 423)

Dishonored check a check that a bank refuses to pay. (p. 129)

Dishonored note a note that is not paid when due. (p. 600)

Distribution of net income statement a partnership financial statement showing net income or loss distribution to partners. (p. 680)

Dividends earnings distributed to stockholders. (p. 405)

Double-entry accounting the recording of debit and credit parts of a transaction. (p. 57)

Doubtful accounts see uncollectible accounts

Draft a written, signed, and dated order from one party ordering another party, usually a bank, to pay money to a third party. (p. 704)

Earnings per share the amount of net income after federal income tax belonging to a single share of stock. (p. 459)

Electronic funds transfer a computerized cash payments system that transfers funds without the use of checks, currency, or other paper documents. (p. 131)

Employee earnings record a business form used to record details affecting payments made to an employee. (p. 353)

Endorsement a signature or stamp on the back of a check transferring ownership. (p. 120)

Endorsement in full see special endorsement

Entry information for each transaction recorded in a journal. (p. 57)

Equities financial rights to the assets of a business. (p. 8)

Estimated salvage value the amount an owner expects to receive when a plant asset is removed from use. (p. 423)

Ethics the principles of right and wrong that guide an individual in making decisions. (p. 8)

Exhibit see supporting schedule

Expense a decrease in owner's equity resulting from the operation of a business. (p. 15)

Exports goods or services shipped out of a seller's home country to a foreign country. (p. 702)

Face amount see principal of a note

Federal unemployment tax a federal tax used for state and federal administrative expenses of the unemployment program. (p. 375)

Fifo see first-in, first-out inventory costing method

File maintenance the procedure for arranging accounts in a general ledger, assigning account numbers, and keeping records current. (p. 93)

Financial ratio a comparison between two items of financial information. (p. 459)

Financial statements financial reports that summarize the financial conditions and operations of a business. (p. 6)

First-in, first-out inventory costing method using the price of merchandise purchased first to calculate the cost of merchandise sold first. (p. 569)

Fiscal period the length of time for which a business summarizes and reports financial information. (p. 152)

Gain on plant assets revenue that results when a plant asset is sold for more than book value. (p. 548)

General amount column a journal amount column that is not headed with an account title. (p. 57)

General journal a journal with two amount columns in which all kinds of entries can be recorded. (p. 57)

General ledger a ledger that contains all accounts needed to prepare financial statements. (p. 92)

Gross earnings *see* total earnings

Gross pay *see* total earnings

Gross profit method of estimating inventory estimating inventory by using the previous year's percentage of gross profit on operations. (p. 574)

Gross profit on sales the revenue remaining after cost of merchandise sold has been deducted. (p. 452)

Imports goods or services bought from a foreign country and brought into a buyer's home country. (p. 702)

Income statement a financial statement showing the revenue and expenses for a fiscal period. (p. 163)

Intellectual property any product that is protected by patents, trademarks, and copyrights. (p. 616)

Interest an amount paid for the use of money for a period of time. (p. 590)

Interest expense the interest accrued on money borrowed. (p. 594)

Interest income the interest earned on money loaned. (p. 599)

Interest rate of a note the percentage of the principal that is paid for use of the money. (p. 589)

Inventory *see* merchandise inventory

Inventory record a form used during a periodic inventory to record information about each item of merchandise on hand. (p. 566)

Invoice a form describing the goods or services sold, the quantity, and the price. (p. 58)

Journal a form for recording transactions in chronological order. (p. 56)

Journalizing recording transactions in a journal. (p. 56)

Last-in, first-out inventory costing method using the price of merchandise purchased last to calculate the cost of merchandise sold first. (p. 570)

Ledger a group of accounts. (p. 92)

Letter of credit a letter issued by a bank guaranteeing that a named individual or business will be paid a specified amount, provided stated conditions are met. (p. 703)

Liability an amount owed by a business. (p. 8)

Lifo *see* last-in, first-out inventory costing method

Limited liability partnership (LLP) a partnership that combines the advantages of the partnership and the corporation, while avoiding their disadvantages. (p. 688)

Liquidation of a partnership the process of paying a partnership's liabilities and distributing remaining assets to the partners. (p. 686)

List price the retail price listed in a catalog or on an Internet site. (p. 244)

Long-term liabilities liabilities owed for more than a year. (p. 467)

Lookback period the 12-month period that ends on June 30th of the prior year. (p. 383)

Loss on plant assets the loss that results when a plant asset is sold for less than book value. (p. 549)

Maker of a note the person or business who signs a note and thus promises to make payment. (p. 589)

Markup the amount added to the cost of merchandise to establish the selling price. (p. 236)

Maturity date of a note the date a note is due. (p. 589)

Maturity value the amount that is due on the maturity date of a note. (p. 590)

Medicare tax a federal tax paid for hospital insurance. (p. 349)

Memorandum a form on which a brief message is written describing a transaction. (p. 59)

Merchandise goods that a merchandising business purchases to sell. (p. 234)

Merchandise inventory the amount of goods on hand for sale to customers. (p. 415)

Merchandising business a business that purchases and sells goods. (p. 234)

Net income the difference between total revenue and total expenses when total revenue is greater. (p. 164)

Net loss the difference between total revenue and total expenses when total expenses are greater. (p. 165)

Net pay the total earnings paid to an employee after payroll taxes and other deductions. (p. 352)

Net sales total sales less sales discount and sales returns and allowances. (p. 449)

Nominal account *see* temporary accounts

Normal balance the side of the account that is increased. (p. 29)

Note *see* notes payable

Notes payable promissory notes signed by a business and given to a creditor. (p. 589)

Notes receivable promissory notes that a business accepts from customers. (p. 598)

Number of a note the number assigned to identify a specific note. (p. 589)

Glossary G-3

O

Opening an account writing an account title and number on the heading of an account. (p. 94)

Owner's equity the amount remaining after the value of all liabilities is subtracted from the value of all assets. (p. 8)

Owners' equity statement a financial statement that summarizes the changes in owners' equity during a fiscal period. (p. 682)

P

Par value a value assigned to a share of stock and printed on the stock certificate. (p. 461)

Partner each member of a partnership. (p. 674)

Partnership a business in which two or more persons combine their assets and skills. (p. 674)

Partnership agreement a written agreement setting forth the conditions under which a partnership is to operate. (p. 675)

Pay period the period covered by a salary payment. (p. 340)

Payee of a note the person or business to whom the amount of a note is payable. (p. 589)

Payroll the total amount earned by all employees for a pay period. (p. 340)

Payroll register a business form used to record payroll information. (p. 351)

Payroll taxes taxes based on the payroll of a business. (p. 345)

Periodic inventory a merchandise inventory determined by counting, weighing, or measuring items of merchandise on hand. (p. 565)

Permanent accounts accounts used to accumulate information from one fiscal period to the next. (p. 206)

Perpetual inventory a merchandise inventory determined by keeping a continuous record of increases, decreases, and balance on hand. (p. 565)

Personal property all property not classified as real property. (p. 536)

Petty cash an amount of cash kept on hand and used for making small payments. (p. 134)

Petty cash slip a form showing proof of a petty cash payment. (p. 135)

Physical inventory *see* periodic inventory

Plant asset record an accounting form on which a business records information about each plant asset. (p. 542)

Plant assets assets that will be used for a number of years in the operation of a business. (p. 423)

Point-of-sale (POS) terminal a computer used to collect, store, and report all the information of a sales transaction. (p. 276)

Post-closing trial balance a trial balance prepared after the closing entries are posted. (p. 216)

Postdated check a check with a future date on it. (p. 121)

Posting transferring information from a journal entry to a ledger account. (p. 96)

Price-earnings ratio the relationship between the market value per share and earnings per share of a stock. (p. 459)

Principal of a note the original amount of a note; sometimes referred to as face amount of a note. (p. 589)

Promissory note a written and signed promise to pay a sum of money at a specified time. (p. 589)

Proprietorship a business owned by one person. (p. 6)

Proving cash determining that the amount of cash agrees with the balance of the cash account in the accounting records. (p. 106)

Purchase invoice an invoice used as a source document for recording a purchase on account transaction. (p. 238)

Purchase on account a transaction in which the merchandise purchased is to be paid for later. (p. 236)

Purchases allowance credit allowed for part of the purchase price of merchandise that is not returned, resulting in a decrease in the customer's accounts payable. (p. 256)

Purchases discount a cash discount on purchases taken by a customer. (p. 242)

Purchases journal a special journal used to record only purchases of merchandise on account. (p. 237)

Purchases return credit allowed for the purchase price of returned merchandise, resulting in a decrease in the customer's accounts payable. (p. 256)

R

Real accounts *see* permanent accounts

Real estate *see* real property

Real property land and anything attached to the land. (p. 536)

Realization cash received from the sale of assets during liquidation of a partnership. (p. 686)

Receipt a business form giving written acknowledgement for cash received. (p. 59)

Residual value *see* estimated salvage value

Restrictive endorsement an endorsement restricting further transfer of a check's ownership. (p. 120)

Retail merchandising business a merchandising business that sells to those who use or consume the goods. (p. 234)

Retained earnings an amount earned by a corporation and not yet distributed to stockholders. (p. 405)

Revenue an increase in owner's equity resulting from the operation of a business. (p. 14)

Reversing entry an entry made at the beginning of one fiscal period to reverse an adjusting entry made in the previous fiscal period. (p. 619)

S

Salary the money paid for employee services. (p. 340)

Sale on account a sale for which cash will be received at a later date. (p. 14)

Sales allowance credit allowed a customer for part of the sales price of merchandise that is not returned, resulting in a decrease in the vendor's accounts receivable. (p. 285)

Sales discount a cash discount on sales. (p. 278)

Sales invoice an invoice used as a source document for recording a sale on account. (p. 58)

Sales journal a special journal used to record only sales of merchandise on account. (p. 272)

Sales return credit allowed a customer for the sales price of returned merchandise, resulting in a decrease in the vendor's accounts receivable. (p. 285)

Sales slip *see* sales invoice

Sales tax a tax on a sale of merchandise or services. (p. 270)

Salvage value *see* estimated salvage value

Schedule of accounts payable a listing of vendor accounts, account balances, and total amount due all vendors. (p. 305)

Schedule of accounts receivable a listing of customer accounts, account balances, and total amount due from all customers. (p. 313)

Scrap value *see* estimated salvage value

Service business a business that performs an activity for a fee. (p. 6)

Share of stock each unit of ownership in a corporation. (p. 234)

Sight draft a draft payable on sight when the holder presents it for payment. (p. 704)

Social security tax a federal tax paid for old-age, survivors, and disability insurance. (p. 349)

Sole proprietorship *see* proprietorship

Source document a business paper from which information is obtained for a journal entry. (p. 57)

Special amount column a journal amount column headed with an account title. (p. 57)

Special endorsement an endorsement indicating a new owner of a check. (p. 120)

Special journal a journal used to record only one kind of transaction. (p. 235)

Stakeholders any persons or groups who will be affected by an action. (p. 181)

State unemployment tax a state tax used to pay benefits to unemployed workers. (p. 375)

Statement of stockholders' equity a financial statement that shows changes in a corporation's ownership for a fiscal period. (p. 461)

Stock ledger a file of stock records for all merchandise on hand. (p. 567)

Stock record a form used to show the kind of merchandise, quantity received, quantity sold, and balance on hand. (p. 567)

Stockholder an owner of one or more shares of a corporation. (p. 234)

Straight-line method of depreciation charging an equal amount of depreciation expense for a plant asset in each year of useful life. (p. 424)

Subsidiary ledger a ledger that is summarized in a single general ledger account. (p. 298)

Supplementary report *see* supporting schedule

Supporting schedule a report prepared to give details about an item on a principal financial statement. (p. 470)

T account an accounting device used to analyze transactions. (p. 29)

Tax base the maximum amount of earnings on which a tax is calculated. (p. 349)

Temporary accounts accounts used to accumulate information until it is transferred to the owner's capital account. (p. 206)

Terminal summary the report that summarizes the cash and credit card sales of a point-of-sale terminal. (p. 276)

Terms of sale an agreement between a buyer and a seller about payment for merchandise. (p. 238)

Time draft a draft that is payable at a fixed or determinable future time after it is accepted. (p. 707)

Time of a note the days, months, or years from the date of signing until a note is to be paid. (p. 589)

Total earnings the total pay due for a pay period before deductions. (p. 343)

Trade acceptance a form signed by a buyer at the time of a sale of merchandise in which the buyer promises to pay the seller a specified sum of money, usually at a stated time in the future. (p. 708)

Trade discount a reduction in the list price granted to customers. (p. 244)

Transaction a business activity that changes assets, liabilities, or owner's equity. (p. 10)

Trial balance a proof of the equality of debits and credits in a general ledger. (p. 154)

Uncollectible accounts accounts receivable that cannot be collected. (p. 419)

Vendor a business from which merchandise is purchased or supplies or other assets are bought. (p. 236)

Weighted-average inventory costing method using the average cost of beginning inventory plus merchandise purchased during a fiscal period to calculate the cost of merchandise sold. (p. 571)

Wholesale merchandising business a business that buys and resells merchandise to retail merchandising businesses. (p. 234)

Withdrawals assets taken out of a business for the owner's personal use. (p. 16)

Withholding allowance a deduction from total earnings for each person legally supported by a taxpayer, including the employee. (p. 346)

Work sheet a columnar accounting form used to summarize the general ledger information needed to prepare financial statements. (p. 153)

Working capital the amount of total current assets less total current liabilities. (p. 652)

Writing off an account canceling the balance of a customer account because the customer does not pay. (p. 519)

INDEX

ethical issues (continued)
  morality, 28
  rading, 481
  , 270
  ual property, 616
  employees busy, 534
  of actions, 90
  learning, 514
  ng computer usage at work,
  er test, 636
  ing ethical dilemmas and
  ons, 56
  g employees' phone calls, 368
  203
  he tone at the top, 674
  ders, identifying, 181
  14
  unts
  numbers, 109
  ng software tools, 231–232
  ed accounting, 115
  2, 92
  Adventures, 147
  , 90–95
  ecorded on, 119
  f completed, 121
  ve evidence, 57
  bank service charge on, 126
  dishonored check on, 129
  ounts, 118–123
  19
  g cash in, 119
  ent of, 135
  d, 121
  8
  d, 129, 130
  ent, 120
  ve evidence, 58, 61, 63, 65,
  121, 134
  6–358
  121
  121–122
  voided checks, 122
  t pay, 356
  c., 635
  ws, 339
  in ancient, 596
  , 305
  record, 57
  sharing, 446
  ion, 345
  s with credit balance, 488,

for accounts with debit balance, 656
completed general ledger after posting, 494–495
for corporation, 492, 655
defined, 206
for dividends, 491, 657
general ledger accounts after posting, 213–215
for income statement account with credit balance, 208, 488
for income statement account with debit balance, 209, 489, 490
for income summary account, 210, 487
for net income, 210, 491, 657
for net loss, 210
for owner's drawing account, 211
recording, 206–212
recording for income statement accounts, 487–493
for service business, 200–227
COA. See Chart of accounts
Codes of conduct, 118, 153, 514
Cold Stone Creamery, 673
Collecting
  note receivable issued in previous fiscal period, 620
  payment for international sales, 704
  posting entries for collecting written-off account receivable, 523
  principal and interest on notes receivable, 599
  uncollectible accounts receivable, 519–524
Column totals
  special amount column, 320, 324–325
Columns
  adjustments, 160, 168
  amount posted to wrong, 169
  balance sheet, 168
  cents column, 107
  credit column of general journal, 97
  debit, of general journal, 96
  general amount, 242, 316
  income statement, 168
  proving adjustments, 160
  special amount, 237
  trial balance, 168
Commercial invoice, 704
Common stock, 265
Communication, misspelled words in, 61
Comparative financial statements, 193
Competencies. See Workplace competencies
Component percentages
  acceptable, 184, 455, 647
  analysis of, 456

analysis of income statement, 184, 647
cost of merchandise sold, 456
defined, 184
gross profit on sales, 456, 458
income statement analysis, 455
net income, 184, 456, 458
total expenses, 184, 456, 458
unacceptable, 455, 458
Computerized accounting. See Automated Accounting; Peachtree; Quickbooks
Computers
  monitoring usage at work, 298
  for perpetual inventory, 567
Conservation, 201
Consistent reporting, 152, 446, 572
Consolidated statement of earnings, 198
Consumer loans, 603
Continuing education, 514
Contra account, 245, 419
Contract of sale, 703
Controlling accounts
  accounts payable ledger, 299
  accounts receivable ledger, 307
  defined, 298
  general ledger, 299, 307
  ledgers, 298
Controls
  batch totals for, 78
  business forms for, 691
  cash, 139
  prenumbered documents for, 78
Corporate earnings, distributing to stockholders, 404–408
Corporations
  accounting cycle for, 398–401, 497, 610–613, 659
  accounting for, 230–669
  adjusting entries, 654
  advantages and disadvantages of, 271
  annual reports, 628
  close corporation, 345
  closing entries for, 492, 655
  defined, 234
  dissolution, 515
  end-of-fiscal-period work for, 508, 634–669, 668
  financial statements for, 444–477, 636
  formation, 234, 271
  forms of, 345
  general corporation, 345
  income statement for, 445–454, 645–648
  owner of, 470
  piercing the corporate veil, 553
  selling stock of, 626

A

Abacus, 323
Abbreviating words, 76
Accelerated depreciation method, 553
Account(s)
  analyzing how transactions affect, 32–37
  automated accounting, 115
  defined, 10, 29
  increases and decreases in, 30
  nominal, 206, 487
  opening, 94
  permanent, 206
  real, 206, 487
  temporary, 206
  uncollectible (See Uncollectible accounts)
Account balance
  after liquidation, 688
  defined, 10
  extending on work sheet, 163
  normal balance, 29
  before realization, 686
Account forms
  balance-ruled, 91
  purpose of, 90
  relationship to T account, 91
Account numbers
  assigning, 93, 109
  defined, 92
  three-digit, 92–93
Account titles
  automated accounting, 115
  defined, 10, 92
  writing, 63, 64
Accountants. See Careers in Accounting
Accounting
  in ancient civilizations, 99
  double-entry, 57
  for performing artists, 69
Accounting cycle
  accounting period cycle, 152, 162, 202, 217
  for corporation, 398–401, 497, 610–613, 659
  defined, 217
  for merchandising business, 497, 659
  for proprietorship, 147–149, 228
  for service business, 217
Accounting equation, 6–9
  analyzing, 28
  business activities and change in, 10–13
  defined, 8
  paying cash and, 11
  receiving cash and, 10
  T accounts and, 28

transactions and, 12
transactions and changes in owner's equity, 14–17
Accounting estimates, 525
Accounting period, 152
Accounting period cycle, 152, 162, 180, 202, 217, 464, 636, 646, 651
Accounting records
  accuracy of, 57, 317
  defined, 6
Accounting scandals, 8
Accounting systems
  in ancient China, 596
  defined, 6
  design of, 437
Accounts payable ledger
  controlling accounts, 299
  defined, 298
  example of completed, 304
  forms, 300
  posting credit and debit entries to, 303
  posting from cash payments journal to, 302
  posting from purchases journal to, 301
  posting to, 298–306
  proving, 305
  starting new page in, 300
Accounts payable schedule, 305
Accounts payable subsidiary ledger, 298
  See also Accounts payable ledger
Accounts receivable
  book value of, 419
  schedule of, 313
  uncollectible (See Uncollectible accounts receivable)
Accounts receivable ledger
  controlling account, 307
  defined, 298
  example of completed, 312
  forms, 308
  posting credit entry from general journal to, 311
  posting from cash receipts journal to, 310
  posting from sales journal to, 309
  posting to, 307–314
  proving, 313
Accounts receivable subsidiary ledger, 298
  See also Accounts receivable ledger
Accounts receivable turnover, 530

Accrued expenses, 622–627
  accounting software tools, 632, 633
  defined, 622
Accrued interest expense
  adjusting entry for, 623
  analyzing an adjustment for, 622
  defined, 622
  posting adjusting entry for, 623
  reversing entry for, 624
Accrued interest income
  analyzing an adjustment for, 617
  defined, 617
  posting an adjusting entry for, 618
  recording an adjustment for, 617
  reversing entry for, 619
Accrued revenue, 616–621
  accounting software tools, 632, 633
  defined, 616
Accumulated depreciation, 424, 540
Accuracy, importance of, 57, 317
Adequate disclosure, 180, 423, 446, 534, 616, 623, 646
Adjusting entries
  accounting software tools, 442
  for accrued interest expense, 623
  for accrued interest income, 618
  for allowance for uncollectible accounts, 482
  for corporation, 654
  defined, 202
  for depreciation expense, 544
  for depreciation of office equipment, 484
  for depreciation of store equipment, 485
  for federal income taxes, 485
  general ledger accounts after posting, 213–215, 494–495
  for merchandise inventory, 482
  for office supplies, 483
  planning on work sheet, 157–161
  posting for uncollectible accounts expense, 517
  for prepaid insurance, 204, 484
  recorded from work sheet, 480–481
  recording, 202, 480–486
  recording in general journal, 481
  reversing for accrued interest expense, 624

Index I-1

Adjusting entries (continued)
    reversing for accrued interest income, 619
    for service business, 200–227
    for store supplies, 483
    for supplies, 202–203
    See also Adjustments
Adjustments
    for accrued interest expense, 622
    for accrued interest income, 617
    defined, 157
    depreciation (See Depreciation adjustments)
    federal income tax expense, 427, 429, 639–640
    interest income, 638
    merchandise inventory, 415–418
    planning on work sheet, 409, 637
    prepaid insurance, 159, 413
    supplies (See Supplies adjustment)
    uncollectible accounts expense, 421, 516
    See also Adjusting entries
Adjustments columns
    errors in, 168
    proving work sheet, 160
Africa, accountancy in, 251
Africa, accounting in ancient, 99
AICPA (American Institute of Certified Public Accountants), 55, 151, 153, 270, 297
Allowance, purchases. See Purchases allowances
Allowance method of recording losses from uncollectible accounts, 419
Amazon.com, 89
American Automobile Association (AAA), 27
American Eagle Outfitters, 179
American Institute of Certified Public Accountants (AICPA), 55, 151, 153, 270, 297
Amounts, errors in, 169
Andersen, 8
Annual reports
    of corporations, 628
    to employees of taxes withheld, 378
    in Excel, 633
    of payroll taxes, 381
Apple Computer, 479
Assessed value, 536
Assets
    assessed value of, 536
    on balance sheet, 188
    categories of, 423
    current, 423, 465, 651
    defined, 8
    plant (See Plant assets)

section on balance sheet, 651
Association of Certified Fraud Examiners, 404
Audit trail, 328
Auditing, 43, 220
Auditor's Report, 628
Audits, 661
Automated Accounting
    account titles, 115
    accounts, 115
    accrued revenue and expenses, 633
    adding new accounts, 115
    adjusting entries, 177, 507
    bank statement reconciliation, 146
    Calculator tool, 718
    cash payments, 267
    changing account titles, 115
    chart of accounts, 115
    charts and graphs, 443
    closing entries, 227, 507
    deleting accounts, 115
    depreciation, 561
    end-of-fiscal-period work for corporation, 667
    error correction, 337
    financial statements, 163, 199
    Find tool, 718
    general ledger postings, 115
    Help menu, 87
    introduction to, 25
    inventory transactions, 585
    journalizing transactions, 115, 146
    manual accounting vs. Automated Accounting, 52
    Notes and Interest Planner, 609
    opening software, 53
    payroll, 365
    payroll taxes, recording, 397
    plant assets, 561
    post-closing trial balance, 227, 507
    posting amounts to general ledger, 115
    problem files, 53
    purchases, 267
    recording bank service charges, 146
    recording journal entries, 87
    sales and cash receipts, 295
    trial balance, 177
    uncollectible accounts receivable, 531

B

Babylonia, early banking system in, 99
Bad debt. See Uncollectible accounts
Balance, normal, 29
    See also Account balance; Trial balance
Balance-ruled account form, 91

Balance sheet
    analyzing, 652
    assets section, 188, 651
    current assets section, 465
    defined, 162
    example of, 469, 650
    extending account balances on work sheet, 163
    financial information on work sheet, 187–192, 464
    heading, 187
    liabilities section, 188, 467, 651
    owner's equity reported in detail on, 190
    owner's equity section, 189
    for partnership, 684
    plant assets section, 466
    preparing, 464–471, 651
    stockholders' equity section, 468, 651
    supporting schedules for, 470
Balance sheet column, errors in, 168
Bank of America, 587
Bank statements
    defined, 124
    reconciliation, 124–126, 145–146, 313
Banking
    payroll bank account, 356
    service charges, 126, 127
    services, 117
Batch reports, 277, 278
Batch totals, 78
Batching out, 278
Ben and Jerry's Ice Cream, 615
Best Buy, financial statement analysis
    accounts payable and revenues, 23
    accounts receivable, 530
    accounts receivable turnover, 530
    average total retail square footage, 113
    calculating percentages, 85, 225
    calculating revenue, 225
    cash and cash equivalents, 144
    common stock, 265
    comparable store sales, 293
    consolidated statements of earnings, 198, 225
    discount certificates, 631
    dividend yield, 441
    earnings from continuing operations, 198
    earnings per share, 505
    equity section of consolidated balance sheets, 697
    financial statements, 363
    fiscal year, 175
    graphing data, 336
    gross profit, 475
    insurance, 395

interest expense, 608
international sales, 716
inventory turnover ratio, 583
leasehold improvements, 559
long-term debt, 608
net earnings, 198
preferred stock, 265
retained earnings account, 665
sales results, increasing, 269
statement of changes in shareholders' equity, 665
total assets, 51
total equity, 51
total liabilities, 51
unredeemed discount certificates, 631
Bill of exchange, 704
Bill of lading, 704
Blank endorsement, 120
Board of directors, 406
Boise Office Solutions, 233
Book inventory, 565
Book value of accounts receivable, 419
Book value of plant assets
    calculating, 424, 540
    defined, 651
    sale of plant assets for, 546
    sale of plant assets for less than, 549
    sale of plant assets for more than, 548
Borrowing, 588
Business activities, and changes in accounting equation, 10–13
Business day, 305
Business entity, 234, 406, 674
Business ethics, defined, 8
    See also Character/ethical issues
Business forms, 691
Business owners, 66
Business plans, 50
Business transactions. See Transactions
Business year. See Fiscal year

C

Calculation errors, 167
Calculator tape, 59, 68
Calculators, early, 323
Calendar year, 207
    See also Fiscal year
Capital
    calculating, 190
    defined, 10
    partners' capital account, 682
    working capital, 652
Capital account records, 50
Capital stock
    defined, 234

section on statement of stockholders' equity, 461
Careers in accounting
    Certified Financial Planner (CFP), 218
    Certified Fraud Examiner, 404
    Certified Public Accountant (CPA), 151
    computer and information systems manager, 447
    entrepreneur/franchisee, 191
    internal auditor, 43
    law firm office manager, 601
    managing partner of accounting firm, 388
    research about, 84
    small business owner, 431
    small business owners, 66
    sole proprietor, 137
Carnival Cruise Line, 533
Carrying totals forward, 250, 251
Cash
    Best Buy analysis, 144
    business use of, 118
    depositing in checking account, 119
    paying (See Cash payments)
    as primary medium of exchange, 588
    proving, 106
    proving at end of month, 283
    receiving (See Cash receipts)
    withdrawals by partners, 677
Cash back vs. low interest, 603
Cash control systems, 116–146
Cash controls, 139
Cash discount, 242
Cash over, 248
Cash payments
    on account, 12, 36, 65, 245–246
    on account, with purchases discounts, 245–246
    on account, without purchases discounts, 246
    accounting software tools, 266–267
    for expenses, 40, 70, 243, 246
    for insurance, 11, 34, 63
    journalizing, 232–267
    for maturity value of note payable, 594
    to owner for personal use, 16, 42, 72
    for purchases, 244
    for rent, 15
    for supplies, 11, 33, 61, 243
    for telephone bill, 15
Cash payments journal, 242–247
    on account with/without purchases discounts, 245–246
    carrying totals forward, 250, 251
    defined, 242
    expenses, 243
    posting from general amount columns to general ledger, 316

stockholders' equity accounts, 405
Subchapter S, 345
work sheet for, 636–644
Correcting entries
affecting customer accounts, 327, 328
defined, 106
journal entry to record, 107
making, 106–107
memorandum for, 106
Coselli, Ray and Monica, 66
Cost, historical, 236, 244, 450, 535
Cost of goods sold. *See* Cost of merchandise sold
Cost of merchandise, 236
Cost of merchandise sold
calculating, 572
component percentage, 456
defined, 450
income statement section, 450–451
Cost of sales. *See* Cost of merchandise sold
Costing an item, 577
Costing inventory methods
first-in, first-out, 569
last-in, first-out, 570
weighted-average, 571
Cowans, Rita J., 43
CPAs (Certified Public Accountants), 151
Creative thinking, 264
Credit
analyzing transactions, 26–53
defined, 29
letter of, 703
posting to accounts receivable ledger, 311
on T account, 28–49
Credit balance
closing entry for accounts with, 488, 655
closing income statement account with, 208, 488
income statement account with, 208, 488
posting debit amount to account with, 99
Credit cards
financial literacy activities, 291
processing, 278
sales, 276, 277, 279
systems, 713
Credit checks, 515
Credit columns
posting amount from general journal, 97
Credit entries
posting for supplies bought on account, 303

posting from general journal to accounts payable ledger, 303
posting from general journal to accounts receivable ledger, 311
posting from general journal to general ledger, 318
Credit memorandum
defined, 285
as objective evidence, 285
for sales returns and allowances, 285
Creditors, 589
Cultural diversity, valuing in workplace, 540
Current assets, 423, 465, 651
Current liabilities, 467, 593, 651
Current ratio, 652
Customary system of measurement, 160
Customer accounts
correcting entries affecting, 327
posting correcting entries affecting, 328
Customers
defined, 270
notes receivable from, 598

D

Date of note, 589
Debit
analyzing transactions, 26–53
defined, 29
posting debit amount to account with balance, 98
posting debit amount to account with credit balance, 99
on T account, 28–49
Debit balance
closing entry for accounts with, 656
closing entry for income statement account with, 209, 489, 490
income statement account with, 209, 489
Debit card, 132
Debit column
of general journal, 96
posting amount from, 96
Debit entries
posting for purchases return or allowance, 303
posting from general journal to general ledger, 317
Debit memorandum
defined, 256
as objective evidence, 256
for purchases returns and allowances, 256

Declaring a dividend, 406
Declining-balance method of depreciation, 551–554
Deposits
cash into checking account, 119
federal deposit coupon, 384
recorded on check stub, 119
Depreciation, accumulated, 424, 540
Depreciation adjustments
for office equipment, 484
planning and recording, 423–426
posting for depreciation expense, 544
for store equipment, 485
Depreciation expense
accounting software tools, 560–561
calculating, 424, 538–540, 560–561
defined, 423
journalizing, 542–545
for last year, 552
for partial year, 539, 547
Depreciation methods
comparing, 553
declining-balance method of, 551–554
double declining-balance method, 551
straight-line method, 424, 538
Dictionary of Occupational Titles (DOT), 84
Discounts
cash, 242
purchases, 242, 245–246
sales, 278, 281, 282, 288
trade, 244
Discrimination, 340
Dishonored checks
defined, 129
journalizing, 130
recording on check stub, 129
Dishonored notes, 600
Dissolution, 515
Distribution
of corporate earnings and dividends, 404–408
of net income, 680, 681
to partnerships, 680–685, 689
unequal distribution of earnings, 681
Distribution of net income statement, 680
Dividend yield, 441
Dividends
closing entry for, 491, 657
declaring, 406
defined, 405
distribution of, 404–408
paying, 407
Documents, prenumbered, 78
See also Source documents

Dollar signs, writing, 76
Domestic sales vs. international sales, 703
Double declining-balance method of depreciation, 551
Double-entry accounting, 57
Drafts
    defined, 704
    sight, 704
    time, 707, 708
Drawing account
    owner's, 211
    partners', 682
DuFrene, Tim, 137

E

e-Bay, 297
e-mail, 313
Earnings
    from continuing operations, 198
    corporate, 404–408
    price-earnings ratio, 459
    retained, 405, 462, 657
    total, 343, 354
    unemployment taxable earnings, 374
    unequal distribution of, 681
Earnings per share, 459, 505
Earnings records, employee, 353–354
EDGAR, 445, 479, 513
EFT (Electronic funds transfer), 357
EFTPS (Electronic Federal Tax Payment System), 384
Electronic Federal Tax Payment System (EFTPS), 384
Electronic funds transfer (EFT), 131, 357
Electronic spreadsheets, 25, 591
    See also Excel
Employee benefits, 367, 525, 588
Employee earnings record, 353–354
Employee taxes
    annual report of taxes withheld, 378
    journalizing payment of liability for, 385
    paying liability for, 383
    See also Federal income tax; Payroll taxes
Employees
    annual report of taxes withheld, 378
    hours worked calculation, 342
    independent contractor vs., 359
    keeping busy, 534
    paying, 340
    payroll check, 357
    salaries, 340
    total earnings calculation, 343
    withholding allowance certificate, 346

End-of-fiscal-period work
    accounting software tools, 666, 667
    for corporation, 508, 634–669, 668
    for proprietorship, 228
Endorsement, 120
Endorsements in full, 120
Enron, 8
Entrepreneurs, 50, 191
Entries
    adjusting (*See* Adjusting entries)
    closing (*See* Closing entries)
    correcting, 107, 327–329
    credit, 303, 311, 318
    debit, 303, 317
    defined, 57
    errors in, 169
    to record correcting entry, 107
    reversing (*See* Reversing entries)
    writing off uncollectible accounts receivable, 520, 523
Equities, 8
    See also Owner's equity; Stockholders' equity
Errors
    in adjustments columns, 168
    in amounts, 169
    in balance sheet columns, 168
    calculation errors, 167
    correcting, 76
    correcting in Automated Accounting, 337
    in income statement column, 168
    in journal entries, 169
    posting to wrong account, 168
    preventing, 169
    in subsidiary ledger accounts, 327–329
    tracking, and source documents, 70
    in trial balance column, 168
    on work sheet, 167–170
Estimated salvage value, 423, 538
Estimated useful life, 538
Estimates
    accounting, 525
    inventory, 574–576
    uncollectible accounts expense, 420, 515
Estimating inventory, 574–576
    gross profit method, 574
    for other months, 575
Ethics, defined, 8
    See also Character/ethical issues
Ethics Resource Center, 702
Everett, C. C., 28
Excel
    annual reports, 633
    bank statement reconciliation, 145–146

    basic skill practice, 115
    calculated amounts, displaying, 267
    charts and graphs, 227, 667
    currency formats, 718
    data files, 87
    depreciation expense, 561
    downloading files into, 337
    financial information, 633
    financial statements, 199
    gridlines, formatting, 507
    inserting/deleting rows, 177
    Instructions tab, 87
    inventory, calculating, 585
    logical relationships, 443
    notes, calculating dates for, 609
    opening software, 53
    problem files, 53
    ratios, formatting display of, 531
    rounding numbers, 365
    sorting and filtering data, 295
    templates, 87
    unemployment tax, calculation, 397
    work sheet, 8-column, 177
    workbooks, 87
Exchange rate, 701, 705
Exhibit, 470
Expense
    accrued (*See* Accrued expenses)
    cash payment of, 40, 243, 246
    defined, 15
    depreciation (*See* Depreciation expense)
    interest, 594
    journalizing cash payments for, 243, 246
    matching with revenue (*See* Matching expenses with revenue)
    paid cash for expenses, 70
    section of income statement, 183
    total, component percentage, 458
    uncollectible accounts (*See* Uncollectible accounts expense)
Expense transactions, 15
Exports, 702
Extension of time
    paying note payable issued for, 596
    signing note payable for, 595
Extreme Adventures, 147

F

FASB (Financial Accounting Standards Board), 18
Fax memorandum, 112
Federal deposit coupon, 384
Federal Deposit Insurance Corporation (FDIC), 120

stockholders' equity accounts, 405
Subchapter S, 345
work sheet for, 636–644
Correcting entries
affecting customer accounts, 327, 328
defined, 106
journal entry to record, 107
making, 106–107
memorandum for, 106
Coselli, Ray and Monica, 66
Cost, historical, 236, 244, 450, 535
Cost of goods sold. *See* Cost of merchandise sold
Cost of merchandise, 236
Cost of merchandise sold
calculating, 572
component percentage, 456
defined, 450
income statement section, 450–451
Cost of sales. *See* Cost of merchandise sold
Costing an item, 577
Costing inventory methods
first-in, first-out, 569
last-in, first-out, 570
weighted-average, 571
Cowans, Rita J., 43
CPAs (Certified Public Accountants), 151
Creative thinking, 264
Credit
analyzing transactions, 26–53
defined, 29
letter of, 703
posting to accounts receivable ledger, 311
on T account, 28–49
Credit balance
closing entry for accounts with, 488, 655
closing income statement account with, 208, 488
income statement account with, 208, 488
posting debit amount to account with, 99
Credit cards
financial literacy activities, 291
processing, 278
sales, 276, 277, 279
systems, 713
Credit checks, 515
Credit columns
posting amount from general journal, 97
Credit entries
posting for supplies bought on account, 303

posting from general journal to accounts payable ledger, 303
posting from general journal to accounts receivable ledger, 311
posting from general journal to general ledger, 318
Credit memorandum
defined, 285
as objective evidence, 285
for sales returns and allowances, 285
Creditors, 589
Cultural diversity, valuing in workplace, 540
Current assets, 423, 465, 651
Current liabilities, 467, 593, 651
Current ratio, 652
Customary system of measurement, 160
Customer accounts
correcting entries affecting, 327
posting correcting entries affecting, 328
Customers
defined, 270
notes receivable from, 598

D

Date of note, 589
Debit
analyzing transactions, 26–53
defined, 29
posting debit amount to account with balance, 98
posting debit amount to account with credit balance, 99
on T account, 28–49
Debit balance
closing entry for accounts with, 656
closing entry for income statement account with, 209, 489, 490
income statement account with, 209, 489
Debit card, 132
Debit column
of general journal, 96
posting amount from, 96
Debit entries
posting for purchases return or allowance, 303
posting from general journal to general ledger, 317
Debit memorandum
defined, 256
as objective evidence, 256
for purchases returns and allowances, 256

Declaring a dividend, 406
Declining-balance method of depreciation, 551–554
Deposits
cash into checking account, 119
federal deposit coupon, 384
recorded on check stub, 119
Depreciation, accumulated, 424, 540
Depreciation adjustments
for office equipment, 484
planning and recording, 423–426
posting for depreciation expense, 544
for store equipment, 485
Depreciation expense
accounting software tools, 560–561
calculating, 424, 538–540, 560–561
defined, 423
journalizing, 542–545
for last year, 552
for partial year, 539, 547
Depreciation methods
comparing, 553
declining-balance method of, 551–554
double declining-balance method, 551
straight-line method, 424, 538
Dictionary of Occupational Titles (DOT), 84
Discounts
cash, 242
purchases, 242, 245–246
sales, 278, 281, 282, 288
trade, 244
Discrimination, 340
Dishonored checks
defined, 129
journalizing, 130
recording on check stub, 129
Dishonored notes, 600
Dissolution, 515
Distribution
of corporate earnings and dividends, 404–408
of net income, 680, 681
to partnerships, 680–685, 689
unequal distribution of earnings, 681
Distribution of net income statement, 680
Dividend yield, 441
Dividends
closing entry for, 491, 657
declaring, 406
defined, 405
distribution of, 404–408
paying, 407
Documents, prenumbered, 78
See also Source documents

Index **I-5**

Dollar signs, writing, 76
Domestic sales vs. international sales, 703
Double declining-balance method of depreciation, 551
Double-entry accounting, 57
Drafts
    defined, 704
    sight, 704
    time, 707, 708
Drawing account
    owner's, 211
    partners', 682
DuFrene, Tim, 137

E

e-Bay, 297
e-mail, 313
Earnings
    from continuing operations, 198
    corporate, 404–408
    price-earnings ratio, 459
    retained, 405, 462, 657
    total, 343, 354
    unemployment taxable earnings, 374
    unequal distribution of, 681
Earnings per share, 459, 505
Earnings records, employee, 353–354
EDGAR, 445, 479, 513
EFT (Electronic funds transfer), 357
EFTPS (Electronic Federal Tax Payment System), 384
Electronic Federal Tax Payment System (EFTPS), 384
Electronic funds transfer (EFT), 131, 357
Electronic spreadsheets, 25, 591
    See also Excel
Employee benefits, 367, 525, 588
Employee earnings record, 353–354
Employee taxes
    annual report of taxes withheld, 378
    journalizing payment of liability for, 385
    paying liability for, 383
    See also Federal income tax; Payroll taxes
Employees
    annual report of taxes withheld, 378
    hours worked calculation, 342
    independent contractor vs., 359
    keeping busy, 534
    paying, 340
    payroll check, 357
    salaries, 340
    total earnings calculation, 343
    withholding allowance certificate, 346

End-of-fiscal-period work
    accounting software tools, 666, 667
    for corporation, 508, 634–669, 668
    for proprietorship, 228
Endorsement, 120
Endorsements in full, 120
Enron, 8
Entrepreneurs, 50, 191
Entries
    adjusting (See Adjusting entries)
    closing (See Closing entries)
    correcting, 107, 327–329
    credit, 303, 311, 318
    debit, 303, 317
    defined, 57
    errors in, 169
    to record correcting entry, 107
    reversing (See Reversing entries)
    writing off uncollectible accounts receivable, 520, 523
Equities, 8
    See also Owner's equity; Stockholders' equity
Errors
    in adjustments columns, 168
    in amounts, 169
    in balance sheet columns, 168
    calculation errors, 167
    correcting, 76
    correcting in Automated Accounting, 337
    in income statement column, 168
    in journal entries, 169
    posting to wrong account, 168
    preventing, 169
    in subsidiary ledger accounts, 327–329
    tracking, and source documents, 70
    in trial balance column, 168
    on work sheet, 167–170
Estimated salvage value, 423, 538
Estimated useful life, 538
Estimates
    accounting, 525
    inventory, 574–576
    uncollectible accounts expense, 420, 515
Estimating inventory, 574–576
    gross profit method, 574
    for other months, 575
Ethics, defined, 8
    See also Character/ethical issues
Ethics Resource Center, 702
Everett, C. C., 28
Excel
    annual reports, 633
    bank statement reconciliation, 145–146

    basic skill practice, 115
    calculated amounts, displaying, 267
    charts and graphs, 227, 667
    currency formats, 718
    data files, 87
    depreciation expense, 561
    downloading files into, 337
    financial information, 633
    financial statements, 199
    gridlines, formatting, 507
    inserting/deleting rows, 177
    Instructions tab, 87
    inventory, calculating, 585
    logical relationships, 443
    notes, calculating dates for, 609
    opening software, 53
    problem files, 53
    ratios, formatting display of, 531
    rounding numbers, 365
    sorting and filtering data, 295
    templates, 87
    unemployment tax, calculation, 397
    work sheet, 8-column, 177
    workbooks, 87
Exchange rate, 701, 705
Exhibit, 470
Expense
    accrued (See Accrued expenses)
    cash payment of, 40, 243, 246
    defined, 15
    depreciation (See Depreciation expense)
    interest, 594
    journalizing cash payments for, 243, 246
    matching with revenue (See Matching expenses with revenue)
    paid cash for expenses, 70
    section of income statement, 183
    total, component percentage, 458
    uncollectible accounts (See Uncollectible accounts expense)
Expense transactions, 15
Exports, 702
Extension of time
    paying note payable issued for, 596
    signing note payable for, 595
Extreme Adventures, 147

F

FASB (Financial Accounting Standards Board), 18
Fax memorandum, 112
Federal deposit coupon, 384
Federal Deposit Insurance Corporation (FDIC), 120

INDEX

A

Abacus, 323
Abbreviating words, 76
Accelerated depreciation method, 553
Account(s)
    analyzing how transactions affect, 32–37
    automated accounting, 115
    defined, 10, 29
    increases and decreases in, 30
    nominal, 206, 487
    opening, 94
    permanent, 206
    real, 206, 487
    temporary, 206
    uncollectible (*See* Uncollectible accounts)
Account balance
    after liquidation, 688
    defined, 10
    extending on work sheet, 163
    normal balance, 29
    before realization, 686
Account forms
    balance-ruled, 91
    purpose of, 90
    relationship to T account, 91
Account numbers
    assigning, 93, 109
    defined, 92
    three-digit, 92–93
Account titles
    automated accounting, 115
    defined, 10, 92
    writing, 63, 64
Accountants. *See* Careers in Accounting
Accounting
    in ancient civilizations, 99
    double-entry, 57
    for performing artists, 69
Accounting cycle
    accounting period cycle, 152, 162, 202, 217
    for corporation, 398–401, 497, 610–613, 659
    defined, 217
    for merchandising business, 497, 659
    for proprietorship, 147–149, 228
    for service business, 217
Accounting equation, 6–9
    analyzing, 28
    business activities and change in, 10–13
    defined, 8
    paying cash and, 11
    receiving cash and, 10
    T accounts and, 28
    transactions and, 12
    transactions and changes in owner's equity, 14–17
Accounting estimates, 525
Accounting period, 152
Accounting period cycle, 152, 162, 180, 202, 217, 464, 636, 646, 651
Accounting records
    accuracy of, 57, 317
    defined, 6
Accounting scandals, 8
Accounting systems
    in ancient China, 596
    defined, 6
    design of, 437
Accounts payable ledger
    controlling accounts, 299
    defined, 298
    example of completed, 304
    forms, 300
    posting credit and debit entries to, 303
    posting from cash payments journal to, 302
    posting from purchases journal to, 301
    posting to, 298–306
    proving, 305
    starting new page in, 300
Accounts payable schedule, 305
Accounts payable subsidiary ledger, 298
    See also Accounts payable ledger
Accounts receivable
    book value of, 419
    schedule of, 313
    uncollectible (*See* Uncollectible accounts receivable)
Accounts receivable ledger
    controlling account, 307
    defined, 298
    example of completed, 312
    forms, 308
    posting credit entry from general journal to, 311
    posting from cash receipts journal to, 310
    posting from sales journal to, 309
    posting to, 307–314
    proving, 313
Accounts receivable subsidiary ledger, 298
    See also Accounts receivable ledger
Accounts receivable turnover, 530
Accrued expenses, 622–627
    accounting software tools, 632, 633
    defined, 622
Accrued interest expense
    adjusting entry for, 623
    analyzing an adjustment for, 622
    defined, 622
    posting adjusting entry for, 623
    reversing entry for, 624
Accrued interest income
    analyzing an adjustment for, 617
    defined, 617
    posting an adjusting entry for, 618
    recording an adjustment for, 617
    reversing entry for, 619
Accrued revenue, 616–621
    accounting software tools, 632, 633
    defined, 616
Accumulated depreciation, 424, 540
Accuracy, importance of, 57, 317
Adequate disclosure, 180, 423, 446, 534, 616, 623, 646
Adjusting entries
    accounting software tools, 442
    for accrued interest expense, 623
    for accrued interest income, 618
    for allowance for uncollectible accounts, 482
    for corporation, 654
    defined, 202
    for depreciation expense, 544
    for depreciation of office equipment, 484
    for depreciation of store equipment, 485
    for federal income taxes, 485
    general ledger accounts after posting, 213–215, 494–495
    for merchandise inventory, 482
    for office supplies, 483
    planning on work sheet, 157–161
    posting for uncollectible accounts expense, 517
    for prepaid insurance, 204, 484
    recorded from work sheet, 480–481
    recording, 202, 480–486
    recording in general journal, 481
    reversing for accrued interest expense, 624

Index   **I-1**

Adjusting entries *(continued)*
  reversing for accrued interest income, 619
  for service business, 200–227
  for store supplies, 483
  for supplies, 202–203
  See also Adjustments
Adjustments
  for accrued interest expense, 622
  for accrued interest income, 617
  defined, 157
  depreciation (*See* Depreciation adjustments)
  federal income tax expense, 427, 429, 639–640
  interest income, 638
  merchandise inventory, 415–418
  planning on work sheet, 409, 637
  prepaid insurance, 159, 413
  supplies (*See* Supplies adjustment)
  uncollectible accounts expense, 421, 516
  See also Adjusting entries
Adjustments columns
  errors in, 168
  proving work sheet, 160
Africa, accountancy in, 251
Africa, accounting in ancient, 99
AICPA (American Institute of Certified Public Accountants), 55, 151, 153, 270, 297
Allowance, purchases. *See* Purchases allowances
Allowance method of recording losses from uncollectible accounts, 419
Amazon.com, 89
American Automobile Association (AAA), 27
American Eagle Outfitters, 179
American Institute of Certified Public Accountants (AICPA), 55, 151, 153, 270, 297
Amounts, errors in, 169
Andersen, 8
Annual reports
  of corporations, 628
  to employees of taxes withheld, 378
  in Excel, 633
  of payroll taxes, 381
Apple Computer, 479
Assessed value, 536
Assets
  assessed value of, 536
  on balance sheet, 188
  categories of, 423
  current, 423, 465, 651
  defined, 8
  plant (*See* Plant assets)

  section on balance sheet, 651
Association of Certified Fraud Examiners, 404
Audit trail, 328
Auditing, 43, 220
Auditor's Report, 628
Audits, 661
Automated Accounting
  account titles, 115
  accounts, 115
  accrued revenue and expenses, 633
  adding new accounts, 115
  adjusting entries, 177, 507
  bank statement reconciliation, 146
  Calculator tool, 718
  cash payments, 267
  changing account titles, 115
  chart of accounts, 115
  charts and graphs, 443
  closing entries, 227, 507
  deleting accounts, 115
  depreciation, 561
  end-of-fiscal-period work for corporation, 667
  error correction, 337
  financial statements, 163, 199
  Find tool, 718
  general ledger postings, 115
  Help menu, 87
  introduction to, 25
  inventory transactions, 585
  journalizing transactions, 115, 146
  manual accounting vs. Automated Accounting, 52
  Notes and Interest Planner, 609
  opening software, 53
  payroll, 365
  payroll taxes, recording, 397
  plant assets, 561
  post-closing trial balance, 227, 507
  posting amounts to general ledger, 115
  problem files, 53
  purchases, 267
  recording bank service charges, 146
  recording journal entries, 87
  sales and cash receipts, 295
  trial balance, 177
  uncollectible accounts receivable, 531

B

Babylonia, early banking system in, 99
Bad debt. *See* Uncollectible accounts
Balance, normal, 29
  See also Account balance; Trial balance
Balance-ruled account form, 91

Balance sheet
  analyzing, 652
  assets section, 188, 651
  current assets section, 465
  defined, 162
  example of, 469, 650
  extending account balances on work sheet, 163
  financial information on work sheet, 187–192, 464
  heading, 187
  liabilities section, 188, 467, 651
  owner's equity reported in detail on, 190
  owner's equity section, 189
  for partnership, 684
  plant assets section, 466
  preparing, 464–471, 651
  stockholders' equity section, 468, 651
  supporting schedules for, 470
Balance sheet column, errors in, 168
Bank of America, 587
Bank statements
  defined, 124
  reconciliation, 124–126, 145–146, 313
Banking
  payroll bank account, 356
  service charges, 126, 127
  services, 117
Batch reports, 277, 278
Batch totals, 78
Batching out, 278
Ben and Jerry's Ice Cream, 615
Best Buy, financial statement analysis
  accounts payable and revenues, 23
  accounts receivable, 530
  accounts receivable turnover, 530
  average total retail square footage, 113
  calculating percentages, 85, 225
  calculating revenue, 225
  cash and cash equivalents, 144
  common stock, 265
  comparable store sales, 293
  consolidated statements of earnings, 198, 225
  discount certificates, 631
  dividend yield, 441
  earnings from continuing operations, 198
  earnings per share, 505
  equity section of consolidated balance sheets, 697
  financial statements, 363
  fiscal year, 175
  graphing data, 336
  gross profit, 475
  insurance, 395

interest expense, 608
international sales, 716
inventory turnover ratio, 583
leasehold improvements, 559
long-term debt, 608
net earnings, 198
preferred stock, 265
retained earnings account, 665
sales results, increasing, 269
statement of changes in shareholders' equity, 665
total assets, 51
total equity, 51
total liabilities, 51
unredeemed discount certificates, 631

Bill of exchange, 704
Bill of lading, 704
Blank endorsement, 120
Board of directors, 406
Boise Office Solutions, 233
Book inventory, 565
Book value of accounts receivable, 419
Book value of plant assets
    calculating, 424, 540
    defined, 651
    sale of plant assets for, 546
    sale of plant assets for less than, 549
    sale of plant assets for more than, 548
Borrowing, 588
Business activities, and changes in accounting equation, 10–13
Business day, 305
Business entity, 234, 406, 674
Business ethics, defined, 8
    See also Character/ethical issues
Business forms, 691
Business owners, 66
Business plans, 50
Business transactions. See Transactions
Business year. See Fiscal year

C

Calculation errors, 167
Calculator tape, 59, 68
Calculators, early, 323
Calendar year, 207
    See also Fiscal year
Capital
    calculating, 190
    defined, 10
    partners' capital account, 682
    working capital, 652
Capital account records, 50
Capital stock
    defined, 234

section on statement of stockholders' equity, 461
Careers in accounting
    Certified Financial Planner (CFP), 218
    Certified Fraud Examiner, 404
    Certified Public Accountant (CPA), 151
    computer and information systems manager, 447
    entrepreneur/franchisee, 191
    internal auditor, 43
    law firm office manager, 601
    managing partner of accounting firm, 388
    research about, 84
    small business owner, 431
    small business owners, 66
    sole proprietor, 137
Carnival Cruise Line, 533
Carrying totals forward, 250, 251
Cash
    Best Buy analysis, 144
    business use of, 118
    depositing in checking account, 119
    paying (See Cash payments)
    as primary medium of exchange, 588
    proving, 106
    proving at end of month, 283
    receiving (See Cash receipts)
    withdrawals by partners, 677
Cash back vs. low interest, 603
Cash control systems, 116–146
Cash controls, 139
Cash discount, 242
Cash over, 248
Cash payments
    on account, 12, 36, 65, 245–246
    on account, with purchases discounts, 245–246
    on account, without purchases discounts, 246
    accounting software tools, 266–267
    for expenses, 40, 70, 243, 246
    for insurance, 11, 34, 63
    journalizing, 232–267
    for maturity value of note payable, 594
    to owner for personal use, 16, 42, 72
    for purchases, 244
    for rent, 15
    for supplies, 11, 33, 61, 243
    for telephone bill, 15
Cash payments journal, 242–247
    on account with/without purchases discounts, 245–246
    carrying totals forward, 250, 251
    defined, 242
    expenses, 243
    posting from general amount columns to general ledger, 316

    posting special amount column totals to general ledger, 324–325
    posting to accounts payable ledger from, 302
    purchases, 244
    starting a new page, 251
    totaling, proving, and ruling, 250
    totaling, proving, and ruling at end of month, 252
Cash purchases, 244
Cash receipts
    on account, 16, 41, 71, 280
    accounting software tools, 294–295
    for an account previously written off, 522
    calculating cash receipts on account with sales discount, 281
    journalizing cash receipts on account, 280
    journalizing cash receipts on account with sales discounts, 282
    journalizing from time drafts, 708
    journalizing using cash receipts journal, 276–284
    journalizing using special journals, 268–295
    from owner as investment, 10, 32, 60
    recording, 50
    from sales, 14, 38, 68
Cash receipts journal, 276–284
    defined, 278
    posting special amount column totals to general ledger, 322–325
    posting to accounts receivable ledger from, 310
    totaling, proving, and ruling, 283
Cash register receipt, 276, 277
Cash sale, 276, 279
Cash short, 248
Cents column, 107
Cents signs, writing, 76
Certificate of deposit (CD), 575
Certified Financial Planner (CFP), 218
Certified Fraud Examiner (CFE), 404
Certified Public Accountant (CPA), 151
CFEs (Certified Fraud Examiners), 404
CFPs (Certified Financial Planners), 218
Character/ethical issues
    accounting scandals, 8
    business ethics, 8
    client names, disclosing, 446
    codes of conduct, 118, 153
    defined, 8
    discrimination, 340
    employee benefits, 588
    employee fraud, 404
    employee hotlines, 564
    ethics officers, 702

Character/ethical issues (continued)
    ethics vs. morality, 28
    insider trading, 481
    integrity, 270
    intellectual property, 616
    keeping employees busy, 534
    legality of actions, 90
    lifelong learning, 514
    monitoring computer usage at work, 298
    newspaper test, 636
    recognizing ethical dilemmas and actions, 56
    recording employees' phone calls, 368
    resumes, 203
    setting the tone at the top, 674
    stakeholders, identifying, 181
Charge sale, 14
Chart of accounts
    account numbers, 109
    accounting software tools, 231–232
    automated accounting, 115
    defined, 32, 92
    Extreme Adventures, 147
    preparing, 90–95
Check stubs
    deposit recorded on, 119
    example of completed, 121
    as objective evidence, 57
    recording bank service charge on, 126
    recording dishonored check on, 129
Checking accounts, 118–123
    defined, 119
    depositing cash in, 119
    management of, 135
Checks
    completed, 121
    defined, 58
    dishonored, 129, 130
    endorsement, 120
    as objective evidence, 58, 61, 63, 65, 70, 72, 121, 134
    payroll, 356–358
    postdated, 121
    preparing, 121–122
    recording voided checks, 122
    for total net pay, 356
Chico's FAS, Inc., 635
Child labor laws, 339
China
    accounting in ancient, 596
    work day in, 305
Chronological record, 57
Client names, sharing, 446
Close corporation, 345
Closing entries
    for accounts with credit balance, 488, 655
    for accounts with debit balance, 656
    completed general ledger after posting, 494–495
    for corporation, 492, 655
    defined, 206
    for dividends, 491, 657
    general ledger accounts after posting, 213–215
    for income statement account with credit balance, 208, 488
    for income statement account with debit balance, 209, 489, 490
    for income summary account, 210, 487
    for net income, 210, 491, 657
    for net loss, 210
    for owner's drawing account, 211
    recording, 206–212
    recording for income statement accounts, 487–493
    for service business, 200–227
COA. *See* Chart of accounts
Codes of conduct, 118, 153, 514
Cold Stone Creamery, 673
Collecting
    note receivable issued in previous fiscal period, 620
    payment for international sales, 704
    posting entries for collecting written-off account receivable, 523
    principal and interest on notes receivable, 599
    uncollectible accounts receivable, 519–524
Column totals
    special amount column, 320, 324–325
Columns
    adjustments, 160, 168
    amount posted to wrong, 169
    balance sheet, 168
    cents column, 107
    credit column of general journal, 97
    debit, of general journal, 96
    general amount, 242, 316
    income statement, 168
    proving adjustments, 160
    special amount, 237
    trial balance, 168
Commercial invoice, 704
Common stock, 265
Communication, misspelled words in, 61
Comparative financial statements, 193
Competencies. *See* Workplace competencies
Component percentages
    acceptable, 184, 455, 647
    analysis of, 456
    analysis of income statement, 184, 647
    cost of merchandise sold, 456
    defined, 184
    gross profit on sales, 456, 458
    income statement analysis, 455
    net income, 184, 456, 458
    total expenses, 184, 456, 458
    unacceptable, 455, 458
Computerized accounting. *See* Automated Accounting; Peachtree; Quickbooks
Computers
    monitoring usage at work, 298
    for perpetual inventory, 567
Conservation, 201
Consistent reporting, 152, 446, 572
Consolidated statement of earnings, 198
Consumer loans, 603
Continuing education, 514
Contra account, 245, 419
Contract of sale, 703
Controlling accounts
    accounts payable ledger, 299
    accounts receivable ledger, 307
    defined, 298
    general ledger, 299, 307
    ledgers, 298
Controls
    batch totals for, 78
    business forms for, 691
    cash, 139
    prenumbered documents for, 78
Corporate earnings, distributing to stockholders, 404–408
Corporations
    accounting cycle for, 398–401, 497, 610–613, 659
    accounting for, 230–669
    adjusting entries, 654
    advantages and disadvantages of, 271
    annual reports, 628
    close corporation, 345
    closing entries for, 492, 655
    defined, 234
    dissolution, 515
    end-of-fiscal-period work for, 508, 634–669, 668
    financial statements for, 444–477, 636
    formation, 234, 271
    forms of, 345
    general corporation, 345
    income statement for, 445–454, 645–648
    owner of, 470
    piercing the corporate veil, 553
    selling stock of, 626

Federal income tax
  adjusting entry for, 485
  adjustment, 639–640
  calculating, 428
  component percentage, 456, 458
  expense adjustment, 427, 429
  FICA, 349
  married persons withholding, 348
  recording adjustment, 429
  single persons withholding, 347
  withholding, 345–348, 353
  work sheet for, 430, 432–435
Federal Insurance Contributions Act (FICA), 349
Federal Reserve System, 587
Federal Tax Deposit Coupon, 384
Federal unemployment tax
  defined, 375
  journalizing payment of liability for, 387
  paying liability for, 386
Federation of Tax Administrators, 269
FedEx Corporation, 43
Fender Guitars, 563
Feng, Eric, 191
FICA (Federal Insurance Contributions Act), 349
FIFO (first-in, first-out inventory costing method), 569
File maintenance, 93
Financial Accounting Standards Board (FASB), 18
Financial information
  on balance sheet, 187–192, 464
  reporting, 180
  use of, 404
Financial literacy
  account reconciliation, 313
  checking account management, 135
  credit cards, 281
  employee benefits, 30
  personal budgets, 420
  retirement savings, 575
  taxes, 369
Financial ratios, 459
Financial statements
  accounting software tools, 198–199, 506
  in annual report, 628
  automated accounting, 163
  comparative, 193
  for corporation, 444–477, 636
  defined, 6
  extending information on work sheet, 162–166
  interim, 193
  for proprietorship, 178–199
  uses of, 446

First-in, first-out (fifo) inventory costing method, 569
Fiscal periods
  collecting a note receivable issued in previous fiscal period, 620
  defined, 152
  paying note payable signed in previous, 625
  See also End-of-fiscal-period work
Fiscal year
  alternative, 171, 472
  calendar year as, 207
  interest at end of, 616
Fiscal year end, 171
FOB (free on board), 499
Foreign currency, 701, 705
Foreign exchange rates, 701, 705
Form 941, 383
Form 8109, 384, 386
Form W-2, 378
Form W-3, 381
Form W-4, 346
Franchises, 191, 490
Freight charges, 499

GAAP (generally accepted accounting principles), 18, 220, 390
Gain on plant assets, 548
Gain on realization, 686, 687, 689
Gap, Inc., 445
GDP (Gross Domestic Product), 239
General amount column
  defined, 242
  posting from cash payments journal to general ledger, 316
General corporation, 345
General journal
  defined, 57
  posting amount from credit column, 97
  posting amount from debit column, 96
  posting credit entries from, 303
  posting credit entries to accounts receivable ledger, 311
  posting credit entries to general ledger from, 318
  posting debit entries to general ledger from, 317
  posting to general ledger from, 88–115
  purpose of, 254
  recording adjusting entries in, 481
  recording transactions using, 285–287
  recording voided checks in, 122
  starting a new page, 75

General ledger
  accounts (See General ledger accounts)
  with adjusting and closing entries posted, 213–215, 494–495
  automated accounting, 115
  controlling account, 299, 307
  defined, 92
  example of completed, 494–495
  opening accounts in, 94
  with posting completed, 102–105
  posting credit entries from general journal to, 318
  posting debit entries from general journal to, 317
  posting from cash payments journal to, 316, 324–325
  posting from cash receipts journal to, 322–323
  posting from general journal to, 88–115, 96–101
  posting from journals to, 315–319
  posting special journal totals to, 320–326
  posting to, 296–337
  posting total of purchases journal to, 321
  posting totals of sales journal to, 320
  starting new page for account in, 315
General ledger accounts
  after adjusting and closing entries posted, 213–215, 494–495
  posting total of purchases journal to two general ledger accounts, 321
Generally accepted accounting principles (GAAP), 18, 220, 390
Global issues. See International business
Going concern, 180, 235
Gold's Gym, 5
Goods. See Merchandise inventory
Google, 367
Graphs/graphing, 336, 443, 667
Greece, accounting in ancient, 99
Green Bay Packers, 339
Gross Domestic Product (GDP), 239
Gross margin, 475
Gross profit method of estimating inventory, 574
Gross profit on sales, 452–453, 456, 458, 475
Gross profit rate, 475

Hard Rock Cafe, 117
Harrison, Ken, 447

Headings
   balance sheets, 187
   income statements, 182
   work sheets, 153
Historical cost, 236, 244, 450, 535
History, and accounting, 259
Honeywell, 701
Hours of work, calculating, 342

I

Imports, 702
Imputing interest, 603
Income
   accrued interest (*See* Accrued interest income)
   interest, 599, 638
   net (*See* Net income)
   taxable, 390
Income statement
   accounts (*See* Income statement accounts)
   analyzing, 455–460, 647
   component percentage analysis of, 184, 455, 647
   for corporation, 445–454, 645–648
   cost of merchandise sold, 450–451
   defined, 163
   distribution of net income, 680, 681
   errors in, 168
   expenses section, 183
   extending account balances on work sheet, 163
   heading of, 182
   information on work sheet, 182, 448
   for merchandising business, 452–453
   net income section, 183
   net loss on, 185, 457
   preparation of, 180–186
   for proprietorship, 180–186
   revenue section, 183, 449
   with two sources of revenue and net loss, 185
   uses of, 646
Income statement accounts
   closing entry with credit balance, 208, 488
   closing entry with debit balance, 209, 489, 490
   with credit balance, 208, 488
   with debit balances, 209, 489
   extending balances on work sheet, 163
   recording closing entries for, 487–493
Income statement column, errors in, 168

Income summary accounts
   closing entry for, 210, 487
   need for, 207
Income tax. *See* Federal income tax
Independent contractor, 359
Individual Retirement Accounts (IRAs), 575
Industrial Revolution, 259
Inflation, 292
Insider trading, 481
Insurance, prepaid. *See* Prepaid insurance
Integrity, 270
Intellectual property, 616
Interest
   accounting for, 586–613
   calculating, 591
   cash back vs. low interest, 603
   collecting on notes receivable, 599
   defined, 590
   at fiscal year end, 616
   imputing, 603
   paying on notes payable, 594
   on promissory notes, 590
Interest expense, 594, 608
   See also Accrued interest expense
Interest income
   accrued (*See* Accrued interest income)
   adjustment, 638
   defined, 599
Interest rate of note, 589
Interest rates
   bank web site activity, 117
   entering on electronic spreadsheet, 591
   of promissory notes, 589
Interim financial statements, 193
Internal auditor, 43
Internal control categories, 330
Internal Revenue Service (IRS)
   Electronic Federal Tax Payment Systems, 384
   fiscal periods, 171
   Form 941, 383
   Form 8109, 384, 386
   Form W-2, 378
   Form W-3, 381
   Form W-4, 346
   independent contractor rules, 359
   online tax forms, 367
   Service Regulations, 390
International business
   business day, 305
   foreign exchange rates, 701, 705
   quality standards, 646
   See also International sales

International Chamber of Commerce, 703
International sales
   collecting payment for, 704
   compared with domestic sales, 703
   imports/exports, 702
   journalizing, 706
   processing, 703
   recording, 702–709
Internet sales
   challenges of, 710
   journalizing, 711
   recording, 710–712
Inventory
   accounting for, 562–585
   book inventory, 565
   costing methods, 569–571, 572
   estimating, 574–576
   gross profit method of estimating, 574
   most efficient quantity of, 565
   periodic, 565
   perpetual, 565, 567
   physical, 565
   turnover ratio, 583
   See also Merchandise inventory
Inventory costing methods
   comparing, 572
   first-in, first-out, 569
   last-in, first-out, 570
   weighted-average, 571
Inventory record, 566
Inventory turnover ratio, 583
Investment
   on owners' equity statement, 684
   partners' initial investments, 676
   received cash investment from owner, 10, 32, 60
Invoice amount, 244
Invoices
   commercial, 704
   defined, 58
   as objective evidence, 238
   purchase invoice, 238
   sales invoices, 58, 69, 272
IRA (Individual Retirement Accounts), 575
IRS. *See* Internal Revenue Service (IRS)

J

Johnson, Everlyn, 431
Journal(s)
   accuracy in, 57
   carrying totals forward on, 250, 251
   cash payment (*See* Cash payments journal)

cash receipts (*See* Cash receipts journal)
checking for errors in, 169
chronological record, 57
defined, 56
general (*See* General journal)
general journal, 57
posting to general ledger from, 315–319
purchases (*See* Purchases journal)
purpose of, 56
sales (*See* Sales journal)
special (*See* Special journals)
Journal entries. *See* Entries
Journal of Accountancy, 25
Journal page
example of completed, 74
with posting completed, 100
starting a new page, 74–77
Journalizing
adjustment for uncollectible accounts expense, 516
bank service charge, 127
bought supplies on account, 64
buying of plant assets, 535
buying supplies on account, 255
cash payments, 232–267
cash payments, for expenses, 40, 243, 246
cash payments, for maturity value of note payable, 594
cash payments, on account, 242–247
cash payments, on account with purchases discounts, 246
cash payments, using cash payments journal, 242–247
cash receipts, from time drafts, 708
cash receipts, on account, 280
cash receipts, on account with sales discounts, 282
cash receipts, using cash receipts journal, 276–284
cash receipts using special journals, 268–295
cash received for maturity value of note receivable, 599
cash received on account, 71
cash sales, 279
closing entries, for accounts with credit balances, 655
closing entries, for accounts with debit balances, 656
closing entries, for dividends, 657
closing entries, for net income to retained earnings, 657
correcting entries, 107
correcting entries affecting customer accounts, 327

credit card sales, 279
debit card transaction, 132
declaring a dividend, 406
defined, 56
depreciation expense, 542–545
dishonored checks, 130
dishonored notes receivable, 600
electronic funds transfer, 131
employer payroll tax, 376
entry to replenish petty cash, 136
international sales, 706
Internet sales, 711
note for extension of time on accounts receivable, 598
paid cash for expense, 70
paid cash for insurance, 63
paid cash for supplies, 61
paid cash on account, 65
paid cash to owner for personal use, 72
payment of dividends, 407
payment of liability for employee income tax, 385
payment of liability for federal unemployment tax, 387
payment of liability for Medicare tax, 385
payment of liability for social security tax, 385
payment of liability for state unemployment tax, 387
payment of payroll, 371
purchase of merchandise on account, 239
purchases, 232–267
purchases, returns and allowances, 257
purchases, using purchases journal, 234–241
receipt of cash from notes payable, 593
receipt of partners' initial investments, 676
received cash from owner as investment, 60
received cash from sales, 68
reversing entries, 658
sales and cash receipts using special journals, 268–295
sales discounts, 288
sales on account, 273
sales on account, using sales journal, 270–275
sales returns and allowances, 286
sold services on account, 69
time drafts, 707
transactions, 54–87, 147–149
transactions affecting owner's equity, 68–73

withdrawal of cash by partners, 677
withdrawals of merchandise by partners, 678
writing off uncollectible account receivable, 519

Last-in, first-out (lifo) inventory costing method, 570
Law. *See* Legal issues
Law firm office manager, 601
Leasehold improvements, 559
Leases, 555
Ledgers
accounts payable (*See* Accounts payable ledger)
accounts receivable (*See* Accounts receivable ledger)
controlling accounts and, 298
defined, 92
general (*See* General ledger)
stock, 567
subsidiary, 298
Legal issues
consultation with attorneys, 90
corporation dissolution, 515
corporation formation, 234, 271
ethics and, 90
limited liability partnerships, 688
partnership dissolution, 686–690
piercing the corporate veil, 553
proprietorship dissolution, 7
proprietorship formation, 7
training, 90
Lending, 588
Letters of credit, 703
Liabilities
on balance sheet, 188
current, 467, 593, 651
defined, 8
income tax, 383, 385
liquidating, 688
long-term, 467, 651
partnerships and, 688
section on balance sheet, 467, 651
unemployment tax, 386, 387
LIFO (last-in, first-out inventory costing method), 570
Limited liability partnerships (LLPs), 688
Liquidation of a partnership, 686, 688
List price, 244
LLPs (Limited liability partnerships), 688
Loans, Small Business Administration, 38

Lockheed Martin, 235
Long-term debt, 607
Long-term liabilities, 467, 651
Lookback period, 383
Loss
  net (*See* Net loss)
  on plant assets, 549
  on realization, 687, 689
  recording from uncollectible accounts, 419
Low interest vs. cash back, 603
Lowe's, 403

Maker of note, 589
Malpractice liability, 160-D
Management's Analysis and Discussion, 628
Manual accounting vs. Automated Accounting, 52
Markup, 236
Matching expenses with revenue, 157, 158, 159, 182, 202, 206, 390, 419, 420, 423, 481, 487, 488, 489, 494, 515, 538, 551, 570, 571, 616, 622
Maturity date of note, 589, 591
Maturity value
  defined, 590
  of notes payable, 594
  of notes receivable, 599
Measures and weights, 160
Medicare tax
  employee, 349
  employer, 373
  journalizing payment of liability for, 385
  paying liability for, 383
Memorandum
  for buying supplies on account, 254
  for correcting entries, 106
  credit, 285
  debit, 256, 257
  fax, 112
Merchandise
  cost of, 236
  cost of merchandise sold, 450–451, 456, 572
  defined, 234
  purchasing, 236
  purchasing on account, 239
  sales on account, 271
  withdrawals by partners, 678
Merchandise inventory
  accounting software tools, 584–585
  adjusting entry for, 482
  adjustment for, 415–418
  analyzing and recording adjustment for, 416–417
  defined, 415
  determining cost of, 569–573
  determining quantity of, 564–568
  importance of, 564
  methods to determine quantity of, 565
  most efficient quantity of, 565
Merchandising business
  accounting cycle for, 497, 659
  defined, 234
  income statement for, 452–453
  types of, 234
  work sheet for, 409–414
  See also specific entries
Merck & Co., Inc., 118
Metric system, 160
Microsoft Excel. *See* Excel
Mission statements, 615
Morality vs. ethics, 28

National Association of Black Accountants, Inc., 75
Net earnings, 198
Net income
  closing entries for, 210, 491, 657
  component percentage, 184, 456, 458
  defined, 164
  distribution of, 680, 681
  before federal income component percentage, 456
  before federal income tax, 458
  recording on work sheet, 164
  section of income statement, 183
  taxable income vs., 390
Net loss
  calculating and recording on work sheet, 165
  closing entries for, 210
  defined, 165
  income statement showing, 185, 457
  owners' equity statement with, 684
Net pay
  check for total net pay, 356
  defined, 352
Net sales, 449
Nominal accounts, 206, 487
Normal balance, 29
Notes payable, 593–597
  accounting software tools, 608–609
  cash payment for maturity value of, 594
  defined, 589
  issued for extension of time, 596
  maturity value of, 594
  paying principal and interest on, 594
  receipt of cash from, 593
  signed in previous fiscal period, 625
  signing, 593
  signing for extension of time, 595
Notes receivable, 598–602
  accepting from customers, 598
  accounting software tools, 608–609
  cash received for maturity value of, 599
  collecting principal and interest on, 599
  defined, 598
  dishonored, 600
  issued in previous fiscal period, 620
Notes to the Financial Statement, 628
Number of note, 589

Objective evidence
  calculator tapes, 59, 68
  cash register receipt, 276, 277
  check stub, 57
  checks, 58, 61, 63, 65, 70, 72, 121, 134
  credit memorandum, 285
  debit memorandum, 256
  defined, 57
  invoice, 238
  memorandum, 59, 64, 127, 130, 131, 132
  purchase invoice, 238
  receipts, 59, 60, 71, 280, 593
  sales invoices, 58, 69, 272
  terminal summary, 276, 279
***Occupational Outlook Handbook*,** 84
Office equipment, adjusting entry for depreciation, 484
Office manager, 601
Office supplies, 254, 483
OfficeMax, 233
On account
  cash payments, 242–247
  cash payments, with purchases discounts, 245–246
  cash payments, without purchases discounts, 246
  cash receipts, 280
  cash receipts, with sales discounts, 281, 282
  journalizing sales, 270–275
  memorandum for buying supplies, 254
  paid cash, 12, 36, 65
  purchases, 236
  purchasing merchandise, 239

I-10   Index

received cash, 16, 41, 71
sales, 14, 273
sales of merchandise, 271
sold services, 14, 39, 69
supplies, 12, 35, 64, 255, 303
transactions, 12
Opening an account, 94
Owner, cash paid for personal use, 72
Owner withdrawals, 45
Owners, cash paid for personal use, 16, 42
Owner's cash investment, 10, 32, 60
Owner's drawing account, 211
Owner's equity
accounts, 38–44
defined, 8
increases in expenses, 71
section on balance sheet, 189
journalizing transactions affecting, 68–73
reported in detail on balance sheet, 190
transactions and changes in, 14–17
Owners' equity statement, 682–685

P

P-E ratio, 459
Par value, 461
Partners
capital account, 682
cash withdrawals by, 677
defined, 674
distributing loss or gain on realization to, 689
distributing remaining cash to, 689
drawing account, 682
initial investment, 676
merchandise withdrawals by, 678
Partnership agreements, 675
Partnerships
account balances, 686, 688
accounting for, 672–699
balance sheet for, 684
defined, 674
dissolving, 686–690
distributions to, 680–685, 689
forming, 674–679
initial investments by owners, 676
liabilities and, 688
limited liability partnership, 688
liquidation of, 686, 688
owners' equity statement for, 682–685
withdrawal of cash by partner, 677
withdrawal of merchandise by partner, 678
Pay period, 340
Payee of note, 589

Paying cash. *See* Cash payments
Payroll
accounting software tools, 364–365
analyzing payment of, 370
defined, 340
different forms of information for, 368
journalizing payment of, 371
recording, 368–372
Payroll bank account, 356
Payroll checks, 356–358
Payroll records, 351–355, 395
Payroll register, 351–352, 369
Payroll taxes
accounting software tools, 396–397
calculating, 373
defined, 345
journalizing, 376
Medicare (*See* Medicare tax)
paying, 383–389
quarterly federal tax return, 379, 380
recording, 373–377
reporting, 378–382
social security (*See* Social security tax)
withholding, 345–350
Payroll time cards
analyzing, 341
preparing, 340–344
Peachtree
accrued revenue and expenses, 632
adjusting entries, 176, 442
bank statement reconciliation, 145
cash payments, 266
chart of accounts maintenance, 114
closing entries, 226
depreciation, 560
end-of-fiscal-period work for corporation, 666
financial statements, 198, 506
Help function, 86
introduction to, 24
inventory, 584
journal entry accuracy, 336
journalizing transactions, 114, 145
menus, 86
notes payable and receivable, 608
opening software, 52
payroll, 364
payroll taxes, recording, 396
plant assets, 560
post-closing trial balance, 226
problem files, 52
purchases, 266
reminders and alerts, 717
sales and cash receipts, 294
toolbar, 86
trial balance, 176
uncollectible accounts receivable, 530
vendor set up, 266

Percentages, calculating, 85
See also Component percentages
Performance Food Group, 513
Periodic inventory, 565
Permanent accounts, 206
Perpetual inventory, 565, 567
Personal property, 536
Petty cash, 134–138
defined, 134
establishing a fund, 134
journalizing entry to replenish, 136
making payments from, with petty cash slip, 135
replenishing, 136, 249
Petty cash report, 248
Petty cash slip, 135
Physical inventory, 565
Piercing the corporate veil, 553
Plant asset records, 542
Plant assets
accounting for, 532–561
accounting software tools, 560–561
book value of, 424, 540
buying, 534–535
defined, 423, 651
depreciation, 423
depreciation expense for partial year, 547
disposal of, 546–550
gain on, 548
journalizing and posting the buying of, 535
loss on, 549
property tax, 536
recording the buying of, 535
sale of for book value, 546
sale of for less than book value, 549
sale of for more than book value, 548
section on balance sheet, 466
Point-of-sale (POS) terminal, 276, 277
Post-closing trial balance
defined, 216
example of, 496
preparing, 213–219, 494–498
Post-retirement benefits, 525
Postdated checks, 121
Posting
to accounts payable ledger, 298–306
to accounts receivable ledger, 307–314
adjusting entry, for accrued interest expense, 623
adjusting entry, for accrued interest income, 618
adjusting entry, for depreciation expense, 544
adjusting entry, for uncollectible accounts expense, 517

Posting *(continued)*
- amount from credit column of general ledger, 97
- amount from debit column of general journal, 96
- buying of a plant assets, 535
- from cash payments journal to general ledger, 316
- from cash receipts journal to accounts receivable ledger, 302, 310
- correcting entries affecting customer accounts, 328
- credit entry, for supplies bought on account, 303
- credit entry, from general journal to accounts receivable ledger, 311
- credit entry, from general journal to general ledger, 318
- credit entry, to accounts payable ledger, 303
- debit amount to account with balance, 98
- debit amount to account with credit balance, 99
- debit entry, for purchases return or allowance, 303
- debit entry, from general journal to general ledger, 317
- defined, 96
- entry for collecting written-off account receivable, 523
- entry to write off uncollectible account receivable, 520
- from general journal to general ledger, 88–115, 96–101
- to general ledger, 296–337
- general ledger with completed, 102–105
- journal page with completed, 100
- from journals to general ledger, 315–319
- from purchases journal to accounts payable ledger, 301
- from sales journal to accounts receivable ledger, 309
- special amount column totals, of cash payments journal to general ledger, 324–325
- special amount column totals, of cash receipts journal to general ledger, 322–323
- special amount column totals, of sales journal, 320
- special journal totals to general ledger, 320–326
- to subsidiary ledger, 296–337
- total of purchases journal to general ledger, 321
- total of purchases journal to two general ledger accounts, 321
- totals of sales journal to general ledger, 320
- to wrong account, 168

Preferred stock, 265
Prenumbered documents, 78
Prepaid insurance
- adjustment, 159, 204, 413, 484
- analyzing and recording on work sheet, 413
- paid cash for, 11, 34

Price, Anna McNeese, 218
Price, list, 244
Price-earnings ratio, 459
Price table, 292
Primary markets, 626
Principal
- collecting on notes receivable, 599
- paying on notes payable, 594
- of promissory notes, 589

Principal of note, 589
Prioritization, 50
Professional organizations, 75
Promissory notes, 588–592
- date of, 589
- defined, 589
- interest on, 590
- interest rate of, 589
- maker of, 589
- maturity date, 589, 591
- number of, 589
- payee of, 589
- principal of, 589
- time of, 589
- uses of, 589
- *See also* Notes payable; Notes receivable

Property tax, 536
Proprietorship, 137
- accounting cycle for, 147–149, 228
- advantages and disadvantages of, 7
- defined, 6
- end-of-fiscal-period work, 228
- financial statements for, 178–199
- forming and dissolving, 7
- income statement for, 180–186
- owner withdrawals and, 45

Proving
- accounts payable ledger, 305
- accounts receivable ledger, 313
- adjustments columns of work sheet, 160
- cash, 106
- cash at end of month, 283
- cash payments journal, 250, 252
- cash receipts journal, 283
- sales journal, 274
- totals, 250

Public accounting firms, 220
Purchase invoice, 238
Purchase on account, 236
Purchases
- on account, 236, 239
- cash payments for, 244
- journalizing, 232–267
- of merchandise, 236
- of merchandise on account, 239

Purchases allowances
- debit memorandum for, 256
- defined, 256
- journalizing, 257
- posting debit entry for, 303

Purchases discount, 242, 245–246
Purchases journal, 234–241
- defined, 237
- posting to accounts payable ledger from, 301
- posting total to general ledger, 321
- posting total to two general ledger accounts, 321
- totaling and ruling, 240

Purchases returns
- debit memorandum for, 256
- defined, 256
- journalizing, 257
- posting debit entry for, 303

Q

Quality standards, 646
Quarterly federal tax return, 379, 380
QuickBooks
- accrued revenue and expenses, 632
- adjusting entries, 176, 442–443
- bank statement reconciliation, 145–146
- cash payments, 266
- chart of accounts maintenance, 114
- closing entries, 226
- depreciation, 560–561
- end-of-fiscal-period work for corporation, 666
- financial statements, 198, 506–507
- Help function, 86
- introduction to, 24
- inventory, 584–585
- journal entry accuracy, 336–337
- journalizing transactions, 114, 145–146
- menus, 86
- notes payable and receivable, 608–609
- opening software, 52

payroll, 364–35
payroll taxes, recording, 396–397
plant assets, 560–561
portable files, 717
post-closing trial balance, 226
problem files, 52
purchases, 266
sales and cash receipts, 294–295
toolbar, 86
trial balance, 176
uncollectible accounts receivable, 530–531
vendor set up, 266

R

Ranking activities, 50
Ratios
   current, 652
   Excel formatting, 531
   financial, 459
   inventory turnover ratio, 583
   price-earnings, 459
Reading skills, 292
Real accounts, 206, 487
Real estate, 536
Real property, 536
Realization
   defined, 686
   gain on, 686, 687, 689
   recognizing loss on, 687, 689
   of revenue, 14, 271, 273, 616
Receipts
   cash (*See* Cash receipts)
   cash register, 276, 277
   defined, 59
   as objective evidence, 59
Receiving cash
   on account, 71
   from sales, 68
Reconciliation, bank, 124–128, 135
Records, accounting
   accuracy of, 317
   defined, 6
Rent, paid cash for, 15
Responsibility, 143
Restrictive endorsement, 120
Resumes, 22, 203
Retail merchandising business, 234
   See also Merchandising business
Retained earnings, 405, 462, 657
Retirement savings, 575
Revenue
   accrued (*See* Accrued revenue)
   defined, 14
   income statement with two sources of, 185
   matching expenses with (*See* Matching expenses with revenue)
   realization of, 14, 271, 273, 616
   section of income statement, 183, 449
   transactions, 14
Reversing entries
   for accrued interest expense, 624
   for accrued interest income, 619
   defined, 619
   effect of not using, 626
   journalizing, 658
Roth IRAs, 575
Ruled accounting paper, writing amounts on, 60
Ruling
   cash payments journal, 250, 252
   cash receipts journal, 283
   purchases journal, 240
   sales journal, 274
   standard practices, 76
   work sheet, 164
Russia, business culture and accountancy in, 681

S

Salary, 340
Sales
   on account, 14, 270–275
   cash, 276, 279
   credit card, 276, 277, 279
   gross profit on, 452–453, 456, 458
   international, 702–709
   of merchandise on account, 271
   net, 449
   of plant asset for book value, 546
   of plant asset for less than book value, 549
   of plant asset for more than book value, 548
   received cash from, 14, 38, 68
   terms of, 238
Sales allowances
   credit memorandum for, 285
   defined, 285
   journalizing, 286
   posting credit entry from general journal to accounts receivable ledger, 311
Sales discount
   calculating cash receipts on account with, 281
   defined, 278
   journalizing cash receipts on account with, 282
Sales invoices, 58, 69, 272
Sales journal
   Automated Accounting, 294–295
   defined, 272
   journalizing sales on account using, 270–275
   posting each special amount column total of, 320
   posting to accounts receivable ledger from, 309
   posting totals to general ledger, 320
   totaling, proving, and ruling, 274
Sales on account
   defined, 14
   journalizing, 270–275
Sales receipts, 294–295
Sales return
   credit memorandum for, 285
   defined, 285
   journalizing, 286
   posting credit entry from general journal to accounts receivable ledger, 311
Sales slip, 58
Sales tax, 269, 270
Sales ticket, 58
Sales transactions, 276–277
Salvage value, estimated, 423, 538
Sarbanes-Oxley Act, 564
SBA (Small Business Administration), 5, 38, 56
SBDC (Small Business Development Centers), 564
Schedule of accounts payable, 305
Schedule of accounts receivable, 313
SEC (Securities and Exchange Commission), 18, 193, 445
Securities and Exchange Commission (SEC), 18, 89, 193, 445
Service business
   accounting cycle for, 217
   adjusting and closing entries for, 200–227
   defined, 6
   work sheet for, 150–177
Service fees, bank, 126, 127
Services, sold on account, 14, 39, 69
Share of stock, 234, 405, 470
   See also Stock
Sight draft, 704
Skype, 297
Small business
   characteristics of owners, 74
   franchises, 490
   motivations of owners, 127
   statistics, 409
   top ways of starting, 318
Small Business Administration (SBA), 5, 38, 56

Index **I-13**

Small Business Development Centers (SBDC), 564
Sociability, 581
Social security number, 346
Social security tax
   defined, 349
   employer, 373
   journalizing payment of liability for, 385
   paying liability for, 383
Software tools. *See* Automated Accounting; Peachtree; Quickbooks
Sold services on account, 14, 39, 69
Sole proprietorship. *See* Proprietorship
Source documents
   calculator tapes, 59, 68
   defined, 57
   memorandum, 59
   tracking errors and, 70
   See also Objective evidence
Spain, business day, 305
Special amount column
   defined, 237
   posting each column total of sales journal, 320
   posting totals of cash payments journal to general ledger, 324–325
   posting totals of cash receipts journal to general ledger, 322–323
Special endorsement, 120
Special journals
   defined, 235
   journalizing sales and cash receipts using, 268–295
   order of posting from, 325
   posting totals to general ledger, 320–326
Spreadsheets, 25, 591
   See also Excel
Stakeholders, 181
Standard accounting practices, 76
State sales tax rates, 269
State unemployment tax
   defined, 375
   journalizing payment of liability for, 387
Statement of stockholders' equity
   capital stock section, 461
   defined, 461
   preparing, 649
   retained earnings section, 462
Stock
   capital, 234, 461
   common, 265
   income vs. growth, 441
   preferred, 265
   purchase, 470
   selling, 626

Stock ledger, 567
Stock record, 567
Stockholders
   defined, 234
   distributing dividends to, 404–408
Stockholders' equity
   accounts used by corporations, 405
   section of balance sheet, 468, 651
   statement of, 461–463, 649
Store equipment, adjusting entry for depreciation, 485
Straight-line method of depreciation, 424, 538
Strategic plan, 490
Subchapter S corporation, 345
Subsidiary ledger
   defined, 298
   posting to, 296–337
Subsidiary ledger accounts, correcting errors in, 327–329
Supplementary report, 470
Supplies
   on account, 12, 35, 64, 255, 303
   analyzing and recording on work sheet, 411–412
   credit entry for supplies bought on account, 303
   memorandum for buying on account, 254
   paid cash for, 11, 33, 61, 243
   recording, 158, 411, 412
   on work sheet, 158, 638
Supplies adjustment
   entries for, 202–203
   entry for office supplies, 483
   entry for store supplies, 483
Supporting schedule, 470

T

T accounts
   accounting equation and, 28
   analyzing transactions into debit and credit parts, 28–49
   defined, 29
   drawing, 42, 61
   relationship to account form, 91
Talbot, Missie T., 601
Tax base, 349
Tax forms
   Form 941, 383
   Form 8109, 384, 386
   Form W-2, 378
   Form W-3, 381
   Form W-4, 346
   online, 384

Taxes
   employee (*See* Employee taxes)
   income (*See* Federal income tax)
   payroll (*See* Payroll taxes)
   property, 536
   purpose of, 369
   sales, 269, 270
   unemployment (*See* Unemployment tax)
   value added, 704, 706, 707
Telephone bill, paid cash for, 15
Temporary accounts, 206
Terminal summary, 276, 277
Terms of sale, 238
Time cards, preparing, 340–344
Time drafts, 707, 708
Time of note, 589
Total assets, 51
Total earnings, 343, 354
Total equity, 51
Total expenses, 184, 456, 458
Total liabilities, 51
Totals
   batch totals, 78
   carrying forward, 250, 251
   work sheet, 164
   See also Column totals
Trade acceptances, 708
Trade discount, 244
Transactions
   on account, 12
   accounting equation and, 12
   analyzing effects on accounts, 32–37
   analyzing effects on owner's equity accounts, 38–44
   analyzing into debit and credit parts, 26–53
   changes in owner's equity and, 14–17
   controls for cash, 139
   debit card, 132
   defined, 10
   expense transactions, 15
   journalizing, 54–87, 147–149
   journalizing transactions affecting owner's equity, 68–73
   recording in general journal, 285–287
   revenue transactions, 14
   sales transactions, 276–277
Travelocity, 55
Trial balance
   defined, 154
   entering on work sheet, 409, 637
   errors in column, 168
   post-closing, 213–219, 494–498
   recording on work sheet, 410
   on work sheet, 154

Turnover
of accounts receivable, 530
of inventory, 583

U

Uncollectible accounts, 514–518
adjusting entry for allowance for, 482
allowance method of recording losses from, 419
defined, 419
Uncollectible accounts expense
analyzing and journalizing adjustment for, 516
analyzing and recording adjustment for, 421
estimating, 420, 515
posting adjusting entry for, 517
recording, 515
Uncollectible accounts receivable, 512–531
accounting software tools, 530–531
journalizing writing off, 519
posting entries for collecting written-off account receivable, 523
posting entries to write off, 520
recording cash received for account previously written off, 522
reopening account previously written off, 521
writing off and collecting, 519–524
Unemployment tax
calculation with Excel, 397
federal, 375, 386, 387
liabilities, 386, 387
state, 375, 387
Unemployment taxable earnings, 374
Unit of measurement, 10, 160, 588, 705
Universal Product Code (UPC), 276, 567
USA Today, 615
Useful life, estimated, 538
Utilitarian theory, 181

V

Value
assessed, 536
book (*See* Book value of plant assets)
estimated salvage, 423, 538
maturity value, 590, 594, 599
par, 461
Value added tax (VAT), 704, 706, 707
Vendor
defined, 236
starting new page in accounts payable ledger for, 300
Visualizing, 224
Voided checks, 122

W

Wages, 340
Walt Disney Company, 201
Weighted-average inventory costing method, 571
Weights and measures, 160
Wholesale merchandising business, 234
Withdrawals
cash withdrawal by partner, 677
defined, 16
merchandise withdrawal by partner, 678
owner withdrawals, 45
Withholding
employee taxes, 347, 348
federal income tax, 347–348, 353
paying, 383–389
payroll taxes, 345–350
reporting, 378–382
Withholding allowance, 346
Wood, Wally, 388
Work sheets
adjusting entries recorded from, 480–481
balance sheet information on, 187–192, 464
completing for income tax, 430, 432–435
for corporation, 636–644
creating, 152–156
defined, 153, 409
8-column, 409–414, 432–433
errors on, 167–170
example of, 642–643
extending balance sheet account, 163
extending financial statement information on, 162–166
extending income statement account balances on, 163
federal income tax adjustment, 639–640
heading of, 153
income statement information on, 182, 448
for merchandising business, 409–414
net income on, 164
net loss on, 165
planning adjusting entries on, 157–161
planning adjustments on, 409, 637
prepaid insurance adjustment on, 159, 413
proving adjustments columns, 160
ruling, 164
for service business, 150–177
supplies adjustments on, 158, 411–412, 638
10-column, 434–435
totaling, 164
trial balance on, 154, 409, 410, 637
use of, 637
Working capital, 652
Workplace competencies
creative thinking, 264
knowing how to learn, 505
monitoring and correcting performance, 696
organizing and maintaining information, 113
ranking activities, 50
reading, 292
responsibility, 143
sociability, 581
visualization, 224
visualizing skills, 224
writing, 84
WorldCom, 8
Writing off an account, 519–524
Writing skills, 84

Y

Year
calendar, 207
fiscal (*See* Fiscal year)